CONNECT FEATURES

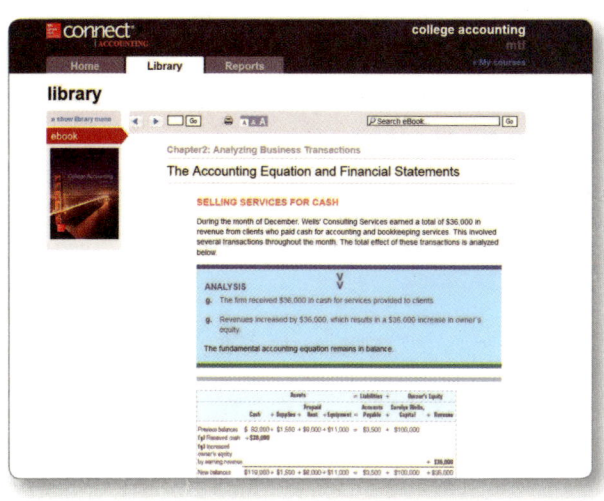

Intelligent Response Technology

Intelligent Response Technology (IRT) is a redesigned student interface for our end-of-chapter assessment content. In addition to a streamlined interface, IRT provides improved answer acceptance to reduce students' frustration with formatting issues (such as rounding), and, for select questions, provides an expanded table that guides students through the process of solving the problem. Many questions have been redesigned to more fully test students' mastery of the content.

Guided Examples

Guided Examples provide narrated and animated step-by-step walkthroughs of algorithmic versions of assigned exercises. This allows students to identify, review, or reinforce the concepts and activities covered in class. Guided Examples provide immediate feedback and focus on the areas where students need the most guidance.

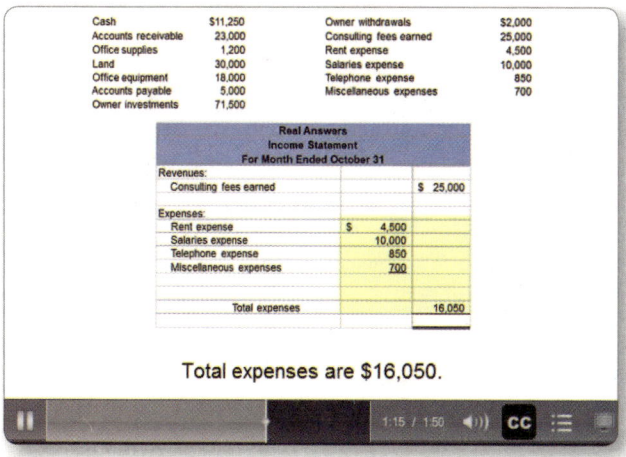

eBook

Connect Plus includes a media-rich eBook that allows you to share your notes with your students. Your students can insert and review their own notes, highlight the text, search for specific information, and interact with media resources. Using an eBook with Connect Plus gives your students a complete digital solution that allows them to access their materials from any computer.

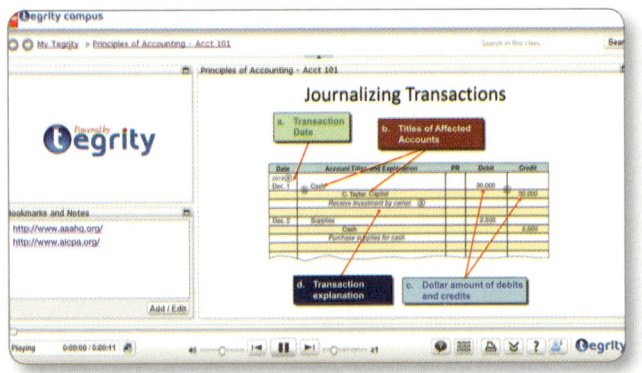

Tegrity

Make your classes available anytime, anywhere. With simple, one-click recording, students can search for a word or phrase and be taken to the exact place in your lecture that they need to review.

EASY TO USE

Learning Management System Integration

McGraw-Hill Campus is a one-stop teaching and learning experience available to use with any learning management system. McGraw-Hill Campus provides single sign-on to faculty and students for all McGraw-Hill material and technology from within the school website. McGraw-Hill Campus also allows instructors instant access to all supplements and teaching materials for all McGraw-Hill products.

Blackboard users also benefit from McGraw-Hill's industry-leading integration, providing single sign-on to access all Connect assignments and automatic feeding of assignment results to the Blackboard grade book.

The **Best** of **Both Worlds**

POWERFUL REPORTING

Connect generates comprehensive reports and graphs that provide instructors with an instant view of the performance of individual students, a specific section, or multiple sections. Since all content is mapped to learning objectives, Connect reporting is ideal for accreditation or other administrative documentation.

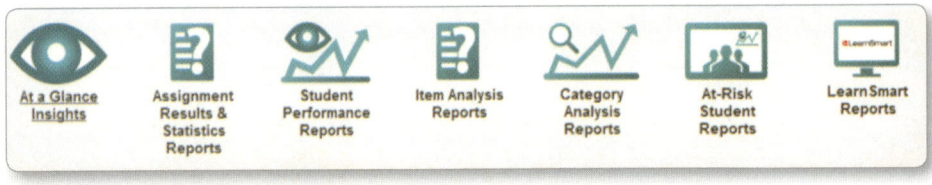

fourteenth edition

College Accounting

Chapters 1–24

fourteenth edition

College Accounting

Chapters 1–24

JOHN ELLIS PRICE, Ph.D., CPA
Professor of Accounting
University of North Texas
Denton, Texas

M. DAVID HADDOCK, JR., Ed.D., CPA
Professor of Accounting (Retired)
Chattanooga State Community College
Director of Training
Lattimore Black Morgan & Cain, PC
Brentwood, Tennessee

MICHAEL J. FARINA, MBA, CPA, CGMA
Professor of Accounting
Cerritos College
Norwalk, California

COLLEGE ACCOUNTING, FOURTEENTH EDITION

Chapters 1-24

Published by McGraw-Hill Education, 2 Penn Plaza, New York, NY 10121. Copyright © 2015 by McGraw-Hill Education. All rights reserved. Printed in the United States of America. Previous editions © 2012, 2009, and 2007. No part of this publication may be reproduced or distributed in any form or by any means, or stored in a database or retrieval system, without the prior written consent of McGraw-Hill Education, including, but not limited to, in any network or other electronic storage or transmission, or broadcast for distance learning.

Some ancillaries, including electronic and print components, may not be available to customers outside the United States.

This book is printed on acid-free paper.

1 2 3 4 5 6 7 8 9 0 DOW/DOW 1 0 9 8 7 6 5 4

ISBN 978-0-07-786239-8 (chapters 1–30)
MHID 0-07-786239-2 (chapters 1–30)
ISBN 978-0-07-763992-1 (chapters 1–24)
MHID 0-07-763992-8 (chapters 1–24)
ISBN 978-0-07-763991-4 (chapters 1–13)
MHID 0-07-763991-X (chapters 1–13)

Senior Vice President, Products & Markets: *Kurt L. Strand*
Vice President, Content Production & Technology Services: *Kimberly Meriwether David*
Director: *Tim Vertovec*
Executive Brand Manager: *Steve Schuetz*
Executive Director of Development: *Ann Torbert*
Managing Development Editor: *Christina A. Sanders*
Director of Digital Content: *Patricia Plumb*
Digital Development Editor: *Julie Hankins*
Senior Marketing Manager: *Michelle Nolte*
Director, Content Production: *Terri Schiesl*
Content Project Manager: *Bruce Gin*
Senior Buyer: *Michael R. McCormick*
Design: *Matthew Baldwin*
Cover Image: *Adam Jones/Getty Images*
Content Licensing Specialist: *Joanne Mennemeier*
Typeface: *10.5/12 Times Roman*
Compositor: *Laserwords Private Limited*
Printer: *R. R. Donnelley*

All credits appearing on page or at the end of the book are considered to be an extension of the copyright page.

The Library of Congress has cataloged the single volume edition of this work as follows

Price, John Ellis.
  College accounting / John Ellis Price, Ph.D., CPA, Professor of Accounting, University of North Texas, Denton, Texas, M. David Haddock, JR., Ed.D., CPA, Professor of Accounting Emeritus, Chattanooga State Community College, Director of Training, Lattimore Black Morgan & Cain, PC, Brentwood, Tennessee, Michael J. Farina, MBA, CPA, Professor of Accounting, Cerritos College, Norwalk, California. — 14th Edition.
    pages cm
  Includes index.
  ISBN 978-0-07-786239-8 (chapters 1–30 : alk. paper) — ISBN 0-07-786239-2 (chapters 1–30 : alk. paper) — ISBN 978-0-07-763992-1 (chapters 1–24 : alk. paper) — ISBN 0-07-763992-8 (chapters 1–24 : alk. paper) — ISBN 978-0-07-763991-4 (chapters 1–13 : alk. paper) — ISBN 0-07-763991-X (chapters 1–13 : alk. paper)
  1. Accounting. I. Haddock, M. David. II. Title.
  HF5636.P747 2015
  657'.044—dc23

                                                    2013034693

The Internet addresses listed in the text were accurate at the time of publication. The inclusion of a website does not indicate an endorsement by the authors or McGraw-Hill Education, and McGraw-Hill Education does not guarantee the accuracy of the information presented at these sites.

www.mhhe.com

About the Authors

JOHN ELLIS PRICE is professor of accounting at the University of North Texas. Dr. Price has previously held positions of professor and assistant professor, as well as chair and dean, at the University of North Texas, Jackson State University, and the University of Southern Mississippi. Dr. Price has also been active in the Internal Revenue Service as a member of the Commissioner's Advisory Group for two terms and as an Internal Revenue agent.

Professor Price is a certified public accountant who has twice received the UNT College of Business Administration's Outstanding Teaching Award and the university's President's Council Award. Majoring in accounting, he received his BBA and MS degrees from the University of Southern Mississippi and his PhD in accounting from the University of North Texas.

Dr. Price is a member of the Mississippi Society of Certified Public Accountants, the American Accounting Association, and the American Taxation Association (serving as past chair of the Subcommittee on Relations with the IRS and Treasury). Dr. Price has also served as chair of the American Institute of Certified Public Accountants Minority Initiatives Committee and as a member of the Foundation Trustees.

M. DAVID HADDOCK, JR., is currently director of training for Lattimore, Black, Morgan, & Cain, PC, one of the top 50 CPA firms in the US. He is located in the Brentwood, Tennessee, office. He recently retired from a 35-year career in higher education, having served in faculty and administrative roles at Auburn University at Montgomery, the University of Alabama in Birmingham, the University of West Georgia, and Chattanooga State Community College. He retired as professor of accounting at Chattanooga State Community College in Tennessee. In addition to his teaching, he maintained a sole proprietorship tax practice for 20 years prior to taking his current position.

He received his BS in accounting and MS in adult education from the University of Tennessee, and the EdD degree in administration of higher education from Auburn University. He is a licensed CPA in Tennessee.

Dr. Haddock served as chair of the Tennessee Society of CPAs and the Educational & Memorial Foundation of the TSCPAs for 2012–2013 and a member of AICPA Council. He is a frequent speaker for Continuing Professional Education programs.

MICHAEL J. FARINA is professor of accounting and finance at Cerritos College in California. Prior to joining Cerritos College, Professor Farina was a manager in the audit department at a large multinational firm of certified public accountants and held management positions with other companies in private industry.

He received an AA in business administration from Cerritos College, a BA in business administration from California State University, Fullerton, and an MBA from the University of California, Irvine. Professor Farina is a member of Beta Gamma Sigma, an honorary fraternity for graduate business students. He is a licensed certified public accountant in California, and a member of the American Institute of Certified Public Accountants and the California Society of Certified Public Accountants. Professor Farina is also a Chartered Global Management Accountant, a designation bestowed by a joint venture of the American Institute of Certified Public Accountants and the Chartered Institute of Management Accountants.

Professor Farina is currently the cochair of the Accounting and Finance Department at Cerritos College. Professor Farina has received an Outstanding Faculty award from Cerritos College.

Price/Haddock/Farina

For students just embarking on a college career, an accounting course can seem daunting, like a rushing river with no clear path to the other side. As the most trusted and readable text on the market, *College Accounting*, 14e, by Price, Haddock, and Farina presents material in a way that will help students understand the content better and more quickly. Through proven pedagogy, time-tested and accurate problem material, and a straightforward approach to the basics of accounting, Price/Haddock/Farina **bridges the rushing river,** offering first-time accounting students a path to understanding and mastery.

Whether a student is taking the course in preparation for a four-year degree or as the first step to a career in business, Price/Haddock/Farina guides them over the bridge to success. The authors represent the breadth of educational environments—a community college, a career school, and a four-year university—ensuring that the text is appropriate for all student populations. Throughout, they have adhered to a common philosophy about textbooks: they should be readable, contain many opportunities for practice, and be able to make accounting relevant for all.

Bridges College to Career

- **Encourages Reading** The authors' writing style and clear step-by-step examples make key concepts easy to grasp. *College Accounting*'s concise chapters are broken into manageable sections to avoid overwhelming students who might be seeing the material for the first time. Features like the Business Transaction Analysis Model make it easy for students to see how to analyze business transactions. The Important and Recall margin elements briefly highlight important concepts and remind students of key term definitions as the topics begin to build on each other.

- **Emphasizes Practice** Self reviews at the end of each section give students the opportunity to practice what they've just learned before moving on to the next topic. The author-created end-of-chapter material includes A and B problem sets, exercises, critical thinking problems, and Business Connection problems that utilize real-world companies and scenarios and address important topics like ethics. Mini-practice sets included within the text itself allow students to put theory into practice without paying additional money for a separate practice set. Select end-of-chapter content is tied to templates in **Sage 50 Complete Accounting** and **Quickbooks,** allowing students to practice using software they are likely to encounter in the real world.

- **Answers the Question "Why Is Accounting Important?"** The "Why It's Important" explanation that accompanies each learning objective explains to students why the topics they're studying matter. Well-known companies like Google, Southwest, and Urban Outfitters are used in vignettes and examples throughout the text, making a clear bridge for students between the concepts they're learning and how those concepts are applied in the real world.

> The Price College Accounting text is thoughtfully planned and well laid out. It goes into detail incorporating real-world examples and context for the accounting student, making it easier for students to understand the content and its application.
>
> —Lora Miller,
> Centura College

How Does Price/Haddock/Farina Bridge the Gap from Learning to Mastery?

College Accounting is designed to help students learn and master the material.

Chapter Opener

Brief features about **real-world companies**—like **Google, Kellogg's, Whole Foods, and Carnival Cruise Lines**—allow students to see how the chapter's information and insights apply to the world outside the classroom. Thinking Critically questions stimulate thought on the topics to be explored in the chapter.

Closing Entries and the Postclosing Trial Balance — Chapter 6

Carnival
FUN FOR ALL. ALL FOR FUN.
www.carnival.com

The folks at Carnival Cruise Lines have made it their business to help people enjoy their leisure time. For nearly 40 years, Carnival has made luxurious ocean cruising a reasonable vacation option for many individuals. Often, for under $100 per person per day passengers can enjoy a seven-day Caribbean cruise on a ship with soaring atriums, expansive spas, children's facilities, and double promenades offering a myriad of

Learning Objectives

Appearing in the chapter opener and within the margins of the text, learning objectives alert students to what they should expect as they progress through the chapter. Many students question the relevance of what they're learning, which is why we explain **"Why It's Important."**

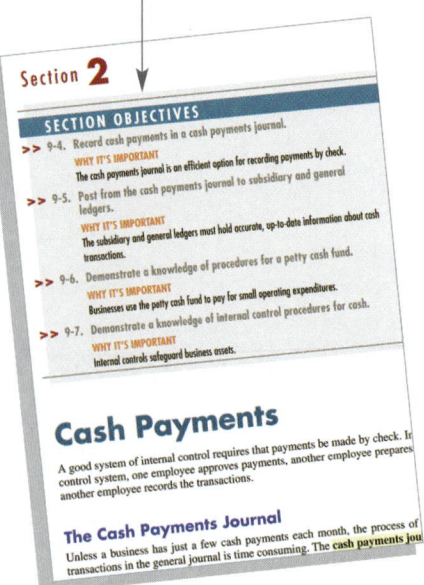

Section **2**

SECTION OBJECTIVES

>> 9-4. Record cash payments in a cash payments journal.
   WHY IT'S IMPORTANT
   The cash payments journal is an efficient option for recording payments by check.

>> 9-5. Post from the cash payments journal to subsidiary and general ledgers.
   WHY IT'S IMPORTANT
   The subsidiary and general ledgers must hold accurate, up-to-date information about cash transactions.

>> 9-6. Demonstrate a knowledge of procedures for a petty cash fund.
   WHY IT'S IMPORTANT
   Businesses use the petty cash fund to pay for small operating expenditures.

>> 9-7. Demonstrate a knowledge of internal control procedures for cash.
   WHY IT'S IMPORTANT
   Internal controls safeguard business assets.

Cash Payments

A good system of internal control requires that payments be made by check. In control system, one employee approves payments, another employee prepares another employee records the transactions.

The Cash Payments Journal

Unless a business has just a few cash payments each month, the process of transactions in the general journal is time consuming. The **cash payments jou**

> The Price/Haddock/Farina College Accounting text is designed to introduce a nonaccounting student to a succinct study of accounting concepts. Each chapter is concise using effective visual aids to motivate the student to read actively, while the additional learning resources encourage practice to improve a student's retention.
>
> —Gisela Dicklin,
> Edmonds Community College

Recall and Important!

Recall is a series of brief reinforcements that serve as reminders of material covered in *previous* chapters that are relevant to the new information being presented. **Important!** draws students' attention to critical materials introduced in the *current* chapter.

important!

For liability T accounts
- right side shows increases,
- left side shows decreases.

Business Transaction Analysis Models

Instructors say mastering the ability to properly analyze transactions is critical to success in this course. Price's step-by-step transaction analysis illustrations show how to identify the appropriate general ledger accounts affected, determine debit or credit activity, present the transaction in T-account form, and record the entry in the general journal.

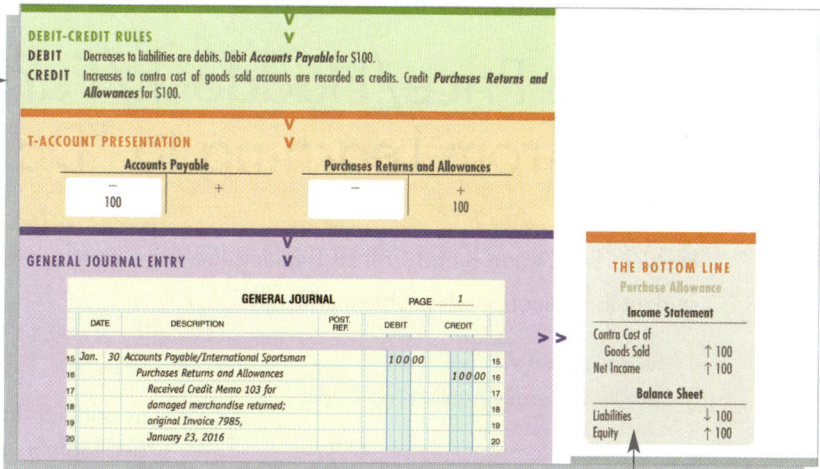

The Bottom Line

Appears in the margins alongside select transactions and concepts in the text. These visuals offer a summary of the effects of these transactions—the end result—on the financial statements of a business.

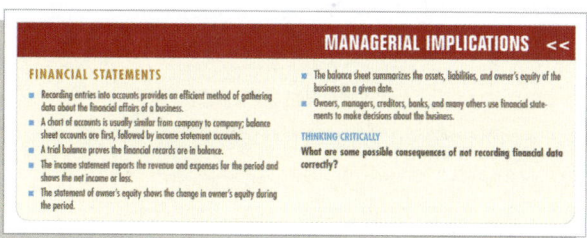

I love the business transaction illustrations that show students the analysis of a transaction, applies debit/credit rules, T-account presentation, and journal entry.

—Morgan Rocket
Moberly Area Community College

Managerial Implications

Puts your students in the role of managers and asks them to apply the concepts learned in the chapter.

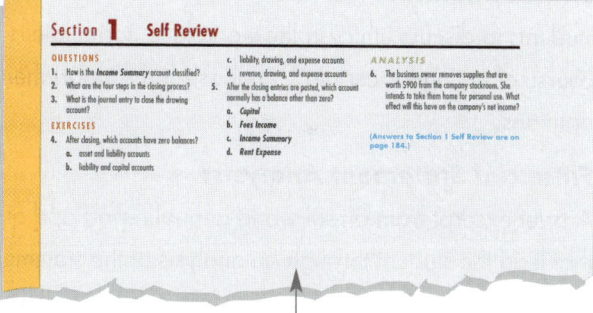

About Accounting

These marginal notes contain interesting examples of how accounting is used in the real world, providing relevance to students who might not be going on to a career in accounting.

Self Review

Each section concludes with a Self Review that includes questions, multiple-choice exercises, and an analysis assignment. A Comprehensive Self Review appears at the end of each chapter. Answers are provided at the end of the chapter.

How Can Price/Haddock/Farina Bridge the Gap from Learning to "Doing"?

Problem Sets A and B and Critical Thinking Problems conclude with an **Analyze** question asking the student to evaluate each problem critically.

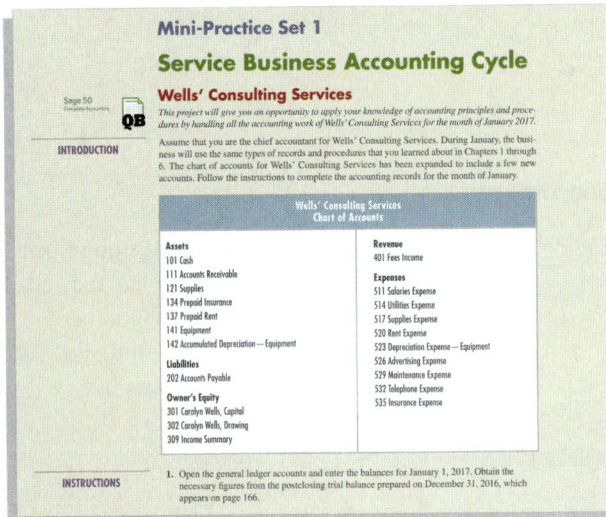

Mini-Practice Sets

In addition to two full-length practice sets that are available to your students for purchase with the textbook, Price/Haddock/Farina offers a number of mini-practice sets right in the book. This means additional practice, but less cost, for your students.

Business Connections

Reinforces chapter materials from practical and real-world perspectives:

Managerial Focus: Applies accounting concepts to business situations.

Ethical Dilemma: Provides the opportunity for students to discuss ethics in the workplace, formulate a course of action for certain scenarios, and support their opinions.

Financial Statement Analysis:
A brief excerpt from a real-world annual report and questions that lead the student through an analysis of the statement, concluding with an Analyze Online activity where students research the company's most recent financial reports on the Internet.

TeamWork: Each chapter contains a collaborative learning activity to prepare students for team-oriented projects and work environments.

Internet Connection: These activities give students the opportunity to conduct online research about major companies, accounting trends, organizations, and government agencies.

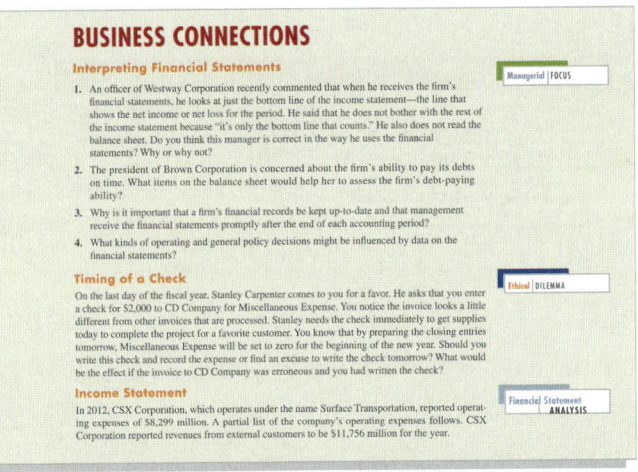

College Accounting is an excellent textbook to introduce students to the world of accounting. The way Haddock/Price/Farina break down the steps in the Accounting Cycle, then move on to other topics, makes it very easy for students to grasp the accounting concepts. The wide variety of student and instructor resources is very helpful.

—Kathy Bowen,
Murray State College

New to the Fourteenth Edition

- Chapter Openers have been revised featuring companies such as: AT&T, Kellogg's, Marek Brothers, Williams-Sonoma, Urban Outfitters, Green Mountain Coffee Roasters, Best Buy, HJ Heinz, Teva Pharmaceuticals, Ford, and Avon

- Real-world examples throughout text have been updated

- End-of-chapter exercises, problems, and critical thinking problems have been revised and updated throughout the text

- Business Connections section of end-of-chapter Financial Statement Analysis questions have been updated to include the latest financial data

- **NEW** section on the perpetual inventory system has been added to Chapters 8 and 9

- Examples in Chapter 10 reflect the latest earnings base for the Social Security tax and minimum hourly rate of pay

- Section on Reporting and Paying State unemployment taxes has been completely revised in Chapter 11

- **NEW** section on Accounts Receivable turnover has been added in Chapter 13

- Updated section on International Accounting Standards Board has been added in Chapter 14

- Revised section on Qualitative Characteristics of Financial Reports has been added in Chapter 14

- **NEW** McGraw-Hill *Connect Accounting* Intelligent Response Technology is an online assignment and assessment solution that connects students with the tools and resources needed to achieve success through faster learning, more efficient studying, and higher retention of knowledge

NEW McGraw-Hill LearnSmart™ is an adaptive learning program that identifies what an individual student knows and doesn't know. LearnSmart's adaptive learning path helps students learn faster, study more efficiently, and retain more knowledge.

Also, NEW with this edition is McGraw-Hill SmartBook, part of McGraw-Hill's LearnSmart suite of products.

Learn with Adaptive

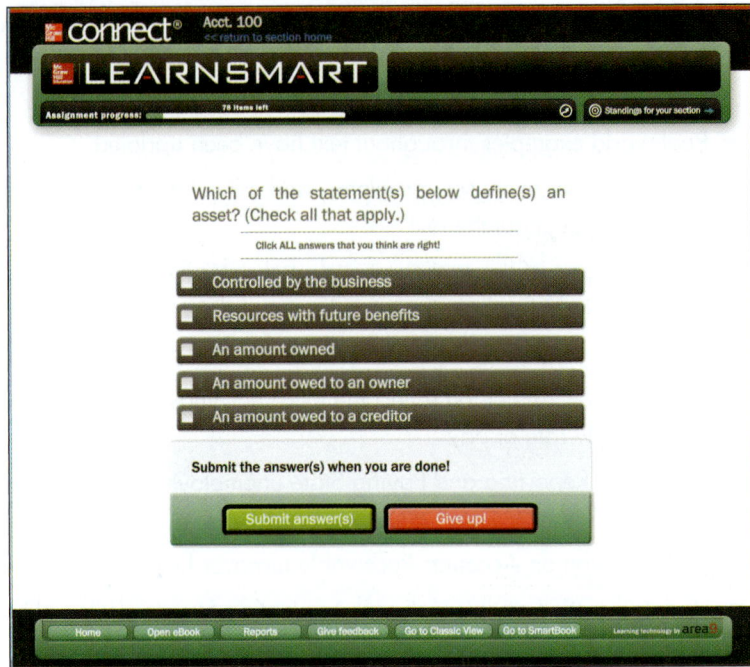

LEARNSMART®

LearnSmart is one of the most effective and successful adaptive learning resources available on the market today. More than 2 million students have answered more than 1.3 billion questions in LearnSmart since 2009, making it the most widely used and intelligent adaptive study tool that's proven to strengthen memory recall, keep students in class, and boost grades. Students using LearnSmart are 13% more likely to pass their classes and 35% less likely to drop out.

Distinguishing what students know from what they don't, and honing in on concepts they are most likely to forget, LearnSmart continuously adapts to each student's needs by building an individual learning path so students study smarter and retain more knowledge. Turnkey reports provide valuable insight to instructors, so precious class time can be spent on higher-level concepts and discussion.

This revolutionary learning resource is available only from McGraw-Hill Education, and because LearnSmart is available for most course areas, instructors can recommend it to students in almost every class they teach.

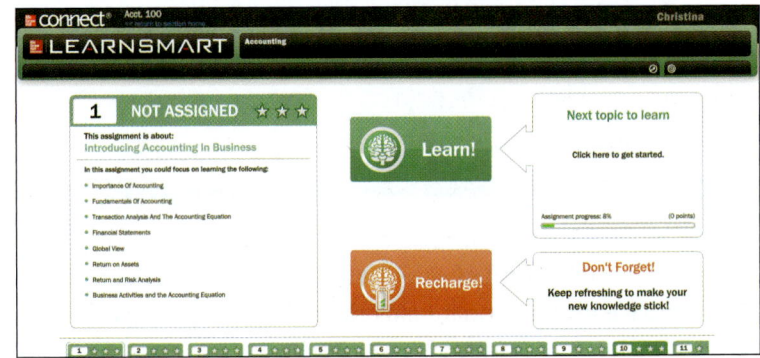

Technology

||SMARTBOOK™

Fueled by LearnSmart—the most widely used and intelligent adaptive learning resource—SmartBook is the first and only adaptive reading experience available today.

Distinguishing what a student knows from what they don't, and honing in on concepts they are most likely to forget, SmartBook personalizes content for each student in a continuously adapting reading experience. Reading is no longer a passive and linear experience, but an engaging and dynamic one where students are more likely

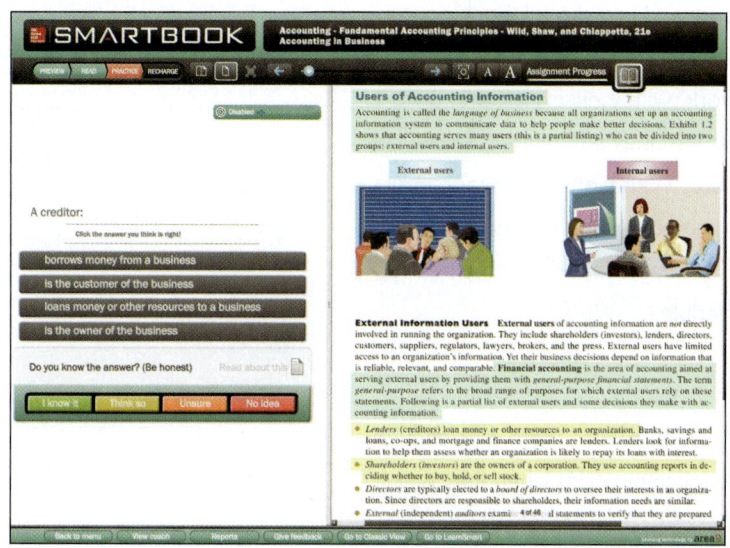

to master and retain important concepts, coming to class better prepared. Valuable reports provide instructors insight as to how students are progressing through textbook content, and are useful for shaping inclass time or assessment. As a result of the adaptive reading experience found in SmartBook, students are more likely to retain knowledge, stay in class, and get better grades.

This revolutionary technology is available only from McGraw-Hill Education and for hundreds of course areas as part of the LearnSmart Advantage series.

How Does SmartBook Work?

Each SmartBook contains four components: Preview, Read, Practice, and Recharge. Starting with an initial preview of each chapter and key learning objectives, students read the material and are guided to topics that need the most practice based on their responses to a continuously adapting diagnostic. Read and practice continue until SmartBook directs students to recharge important material they are most likely to forget to ensure concept mastery and retention.

Leading Technology Extends Learning

McGraw-Hill *Connect Accounting*

Get *Connect Accounting.* Get Results.

McGraw-Hill *Connect Accounting* is a digital teaching and learning environment that gives students the means to better connect with their coursework, with their instructors, and with the important concepts that they will need to know for success now and in the future. With *Connect Accounting,* instructors can deliver assignments, quizzes, and tests easily online. Students can practice important skills at their own pace and on their own schedule.

Online Assignments

Connect Accounting helps students learn more efficiently by providing feedback and practice material when they need it, where they need it. *Connect Accounting* grades home-work automatically and gives immediate feedback on any questions students may have missed.

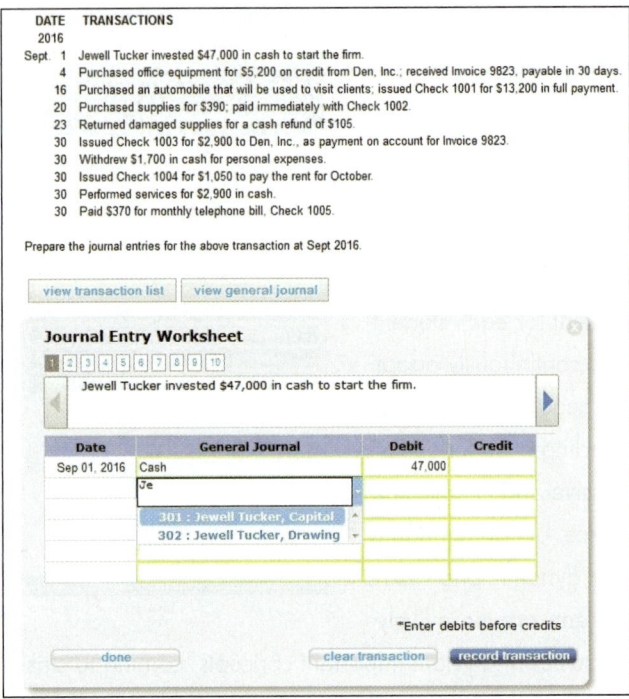

Intelligent Response Technology (IRT)

IRT is a redesigned student interface for our end-of-chapter assessment content. The benefits include improved answer acceptance to reduce students' frus-tration with formatting issues (such as rounding). Also, select questions have been redesigned to test students' knowledge more fully. They now include tables for students to work through rather than requiring that all calculations be done offline.

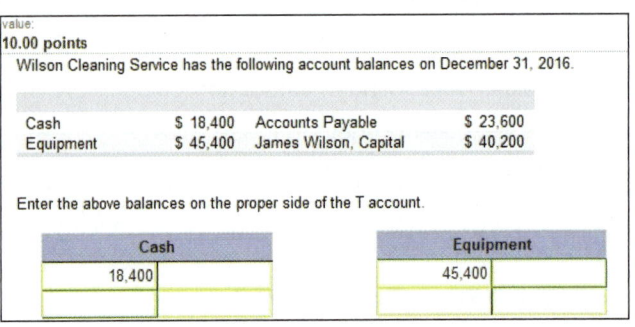

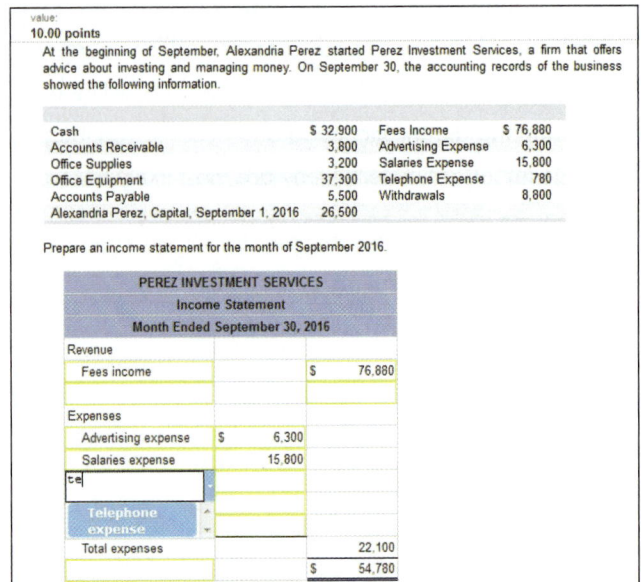

Beyond the Classroom

Guided Examples

The Guided Examples in *Connect Accounting* provide a narrated, animated, step-by-step walk-through of select exercises similar to those assigned. These short presentations provide reinforcement when students need it most.

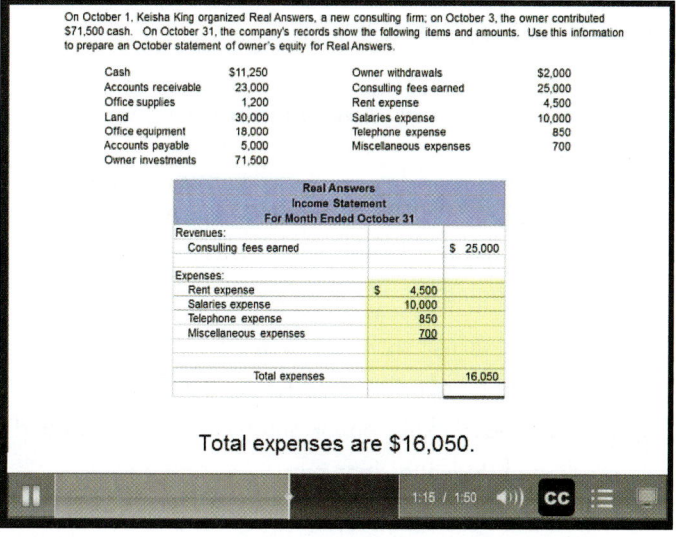

Student Library

The *Connect Accounting* Student Library gives students access to additional resources such as recorded lectures, online practice materials, an eBook, and more.

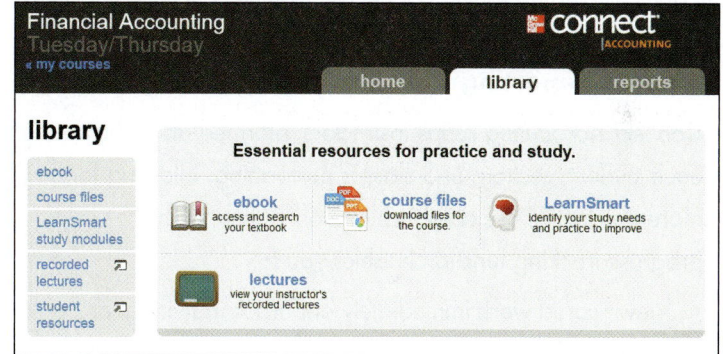

The online *Connect* component has changed the way I teach accounting! It is a central location for everything that I need to teach my course.

—Laura Bantz,
McHenry Community College

McGraw-Hill *Connect Accounting* Features

Connect Accounting offers a number of powerful tools and features to make managing assignments easier, so faculty can spend more time teaching.

Simple Assignment Management and Smart Grading

With *Connect Accounting,* creating assignments is easier than ever, so instructors can spend more time teaching and less time managing.

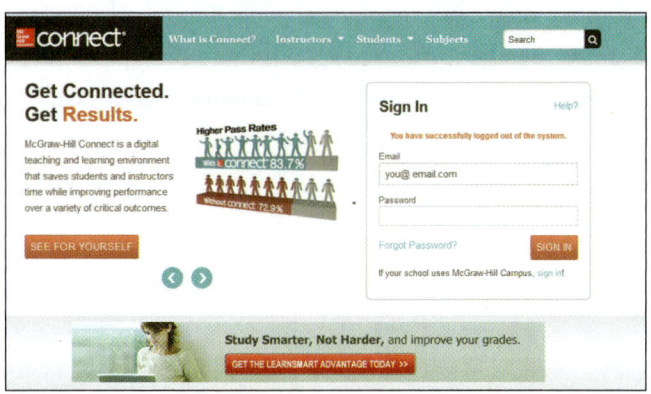

- Create and deliver assignments easily with selectable end-of-chapter questions and Test Bank items.
- Go paperless with the eBook and online submission and grading of student assignments.
- Have assignments scored automatically, giving students immediate feedback on their work and side-by-side comparisons with correct answers.
- Access and review each response; manually change grades or leave comments for students to review.
- Reinforce classroom concepts with practice tests and instant quizzes.

Student Reporting

Connect Accounting keeps instructors informed about how each student, section, and class is performing, allowing for more productive use of lecture and office hours. The progress-tracking function enables you to:

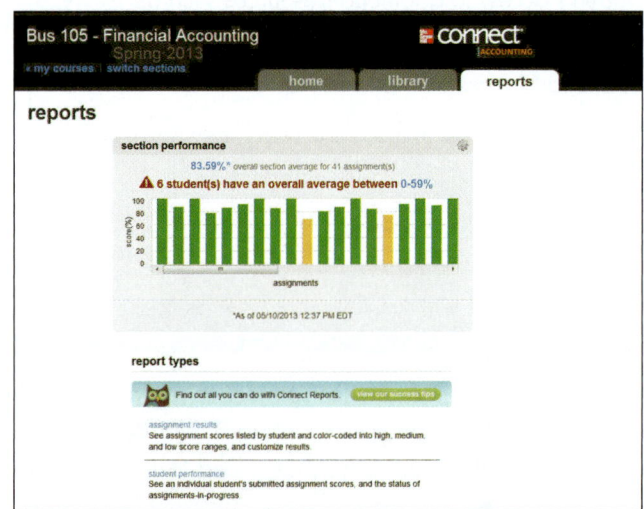

- View scored work immediately and track individual or group performance with assignment and grade reports.
- Access an instant view of student or class performance relative to learning objectives.
- Collect data and generate reports required by many accreditation organizations, such as AACSB and AICPA.

Instructor Library

The *Connect Accounting* Instructor Library is a repository for additional resources to improve student engagement in and out of class. You can select and use any asset that enhances your lecture. The *Connect Accounting* Instructor Library includes access to the eBook version of the text, videos, slide presentations, Solutions Manual, Instructor's Manual, and Test Bank. The *Connect Accounting* Instructor Library also allows you to upload your own files.

McGraw-Hill *Connect Plus Accounting*

 McGraw-Hill reinvents the textbook learning experience for the modern student with *Connect Plus Accounting.*

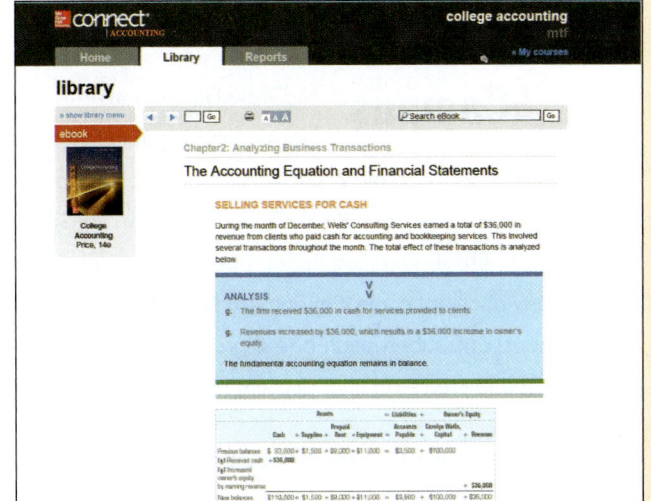

A seamless integration of an eBook and *Connect Accounting,* *Connect Plus Accounting* provides all of the Connect Accounting features plus the following:

- An integrated, media-rich eBook, allowing for anytime, anywhere access to the textbook.
- Media-rich capabilities like embedded audio/visual presentations, highlighting, and sharing notes.
- Dynamic links between the problems or questions you assign to your students and the location in the eBook where that concept is covered.
- A powerful search function to pinpoint key concepts for review.

In short, *Connect Plus Accounting* offers students powerful tools and features that optimize their time and energy, enabling them to focus on learning.

For more information about *Connect Plus Accounting,* go to www.mcgrawhillconnect.com, or contact your local McGraw-Hill sales representative.

Tegrity Campus: Lectures 24/7

 Tegrity Campus is a service that makes class time available 24/7 by automatically capturing every lecture. With a simple one-click start-and-stop process, you capture all computer screens and corresponding audio in a format that is easily searchable, frame by frame. Students can replay any part of any class with easy-to-use browser-based viewing on a PC, Mac, iPod, or other mobile device.

Educators know that the more students can see, hear, and experience class resources, the better they learn. In fact, studies prove it. Tegrity Campus's unique search feature helps students efficiently find what they need, when they need it, across an entire semester of class recordings. Help turn your students' study time into learning moments immediately supported by your lecture. With Tegrity Campus, you also increase intent listening and class participation by easing students' concerns about note-taking. Tegrity Campus will make it more likely you will see students' faces, not the tops of their heads.

To learn more about Tegrity, watch a 2-minute Flash demo at http://tegritycampus.mhhe.com.

McGraw-Hill Campus

 **Campus** McGraw-Hill Campus™ is a new one-stop teaching and learning experience available to users of any learning management system. This institutional service allows faculty and students to enjoy single sign-on (SSO) access to all McGraw-Hill Higher Education materials, including the award-winning McGraw-Hill *Connect* platform, directly from within the institution's website. McGraw-Hill Campus provides faculty with instant access to teaching materials (e.g., eTextbooks, Test Banks, PowerPoint slides, animations, and learning objects), allowing them to browse, search, and use any ancillary content in our vast library. Students enjoy SSO access to a variety of free products (e.g., quizzes, and presentations) and subscription-based products (e.g., McGraw-Hill *Connect*). With McGraw-Hill Campus, faculty and students will never need to create another account to access McGraw-Hill products and services.

Custom Publishing through Create

McGraw-Hill Create™ is a new, self-service website that allows instructors to create custom course materials by drawing upon McGraw-Hill's comprehensive, cross-disciplinary content. Instructors can add their own content quickly and easily and tap into other rights-secured third party sources as well, then arrange the content in a way that makes the most sense for their course. Instructors can even personalize their book with the course name and information and choose the best format for their students—color print, black-and-white print, or an eBook.

Through Create, instructors can

- Select and arrange the content in a way that makes the most sense for their course.
- Combine material from different sources and even upload their own content.
- Choose the best format for their students—print or eBook.
- Edit and update their course materials as often as they'd like.

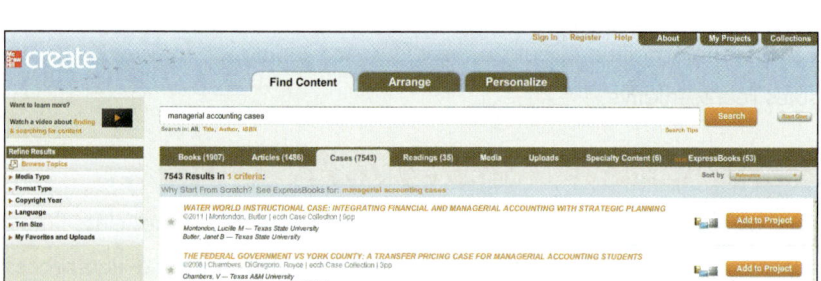

Begin creating now at www.mcgrawhillcreate.com.

CourseSmart

Learn Smart. Choose Smart.

CourseSmart is a way for faculty to find and review eTextbooks. It's also a great option for students who are interested in accessing their course materials digitally and saving money.

CourseSmart offers thousands of the most commonly adopted textbooks across hundreds of courses from a wide variety of higher education publishers. It is the only place for faculty to review and compare the full text of a textbook online, providing immediate access without the environmental impact of requesting a print exam copy.

With the CourseSmart eTextbook, students can save up to 45 percent off the cost of a print book, reduce their impact on the environment, and access powerful web tools for learning. CourseSmart is an online eTextbook, which means users access and view their textbook online when connected to the Internet. Students can also print sections of the book for maximum portability. CourseSmart eTextbooks are available in one standard online reader with full text search, notes and highlighting, and e-mail tools for sharing notes between classmates. For more information on CourseSmart, go to www.coursesmart.com.

Instructor Supplements

Instructor CD-ROM

ISBN: 9780077639808 (MHID: 0077639804)

This all-in-one resource incorporates the Test Bank, PowerPoint® Slides, Instructor's Resource Guide, and Solutions Manual.

• Instructor's Resource Guide

This supplement contains extensive chapter-by-chapter lecture notes, along with useful suggestions for presenting key concepts and ideas, to help with classroom presentation. The lecture notes coordinate closely with the PowerPoint® Slides, making lesson planning even easier.

• Solutions Manual

This supplement contains completed step-by-step calculations to all assignment and Study Guide material, as well as a general discussion of the Thinking Critically questions that appear throughout the text.

• Test Bank

This comprehensive Test Bank includes more than 2,000 true/false, multiple-choice, and completion questions and problems.

Online Learning Center (OLC)

www.mhhe.com/price14e

The Online Learning Center (OLC) that accompanies *College Accounting* provides a wealth of extra material for both instructors and students. With content specific to each chapter of the book, the Price OLC doesn't require any building or maintenance on your part.

A secure **Instructor Edition** stores your essential course materials to save you prep time before class. The **Instructor's Resource Guide, Solutions Manual, PowerPoint® Slides, Test Bank,** and **EZ Test Online Test Bank** are now just a couple of clicks away.

• EZ Test

McGraw-Hill's EZ Test Online is a flexible and easy-to-use electronic testing program that allows instructors to create tests from book-specific items. EZ Test accommodates a wide range of question types and allows instructors to add their own questions. Multiple versions of the test can be created and any test can be exported for use with course management systems such as BlackBoard/WebCT.

The OLC website also serves as a doorway to McGraw-Hill's other technology solutions.

Assurance of Learning Ready

Many educational institutions today are focused on the notion of assurance of learning, an important element of some accreditation standards. *College Accounting*, 14e, is designed specifically to support your assurance of learning initiatives with a simple, yet powerful, solution.

Each test bank question for *College Accounting*, 14e, maps to a specific chapter learning objective listed in the text. You can use our test bank software, *EZ Test, EZ Test Online,* or *Connect Accounting* to easily query for learning objectives that directly relate to the learning objectives for your course. You can then use the reporting features of *EZ Test* to aggregate student results in similar fashion, making the collection and presentation of assurance of learning data simple and easy.

AACSB Statement

McGraw-Hill Companies is a proud corporate member of AACSB International. Understanding the importance and value of AACSB accreditation, *College Accounting* recognizes the curricula guidelines detailed in AACSB standards for business accreditation by connecting selected questions in the test bank to the general knowledge and skill guidelines found in the AACSB standards.

The statements contained in *College Accounting*, 14e, are provided only as a guide for the users of this text. The AACSB leaves content coverage and assessment clearly within the realm and control of individual schools, the mission of the school, and the faculty. While *College Accounting*, 14e, and the teaching package make no claim of any specific AACSB qualification or evaluation, we have, within *College Accounting*, 14e, labeled selected questions according to the six general knowledge and skills areas.

Student Supplements

Study Guide/Working Papers

Chapters 1–13—ISBN: 9780077639884
(MHID: 007763988X)
Chapters 14–24—ISBN: 9780077639907
(MHID: 0077639901)
Chapters 1–30—ISBN: 9780077639891
(MHID: 0077639898)

This study aid summarizes essential points in each chapter, tests students' knowledge using self-test questions, and contains forms that help students organize their solutions to homework problems.

Action Video Practice Set

Available through Create

Action Video Productions is a sole proprietorship service business that uses source documents, a general journal, a general ledger, worksheets, and a filing system to provide students with a usable practice set. The strength of this set is the use of source documents in conjunction with the daily business activities. This set can be completed after Chapter 6 of *College Accounting*.

Home Team Advantage Practice Set

Available through Create

Home Team Advantage is a sole proprietorship merchandising business that uses source documents, special journals, a general ledger, a subsidiary ledger, a worksheet, accounting forms, and a filing system for student use. This very realistic retail business will give a student accounting practice where merchandise inventory and the cost of goods sold become an integral part of the income statement. This set can be completed after Chapter 13.

Student Guide for QuickBooks Accountant with QuickBooks Accountant Templates

ISBN: 9780077639877 (MHID: 0077639871)

To better prepare students for accounting in the real world, end-of-chapter material in Price is tied to QuickBooks Accountant 2014 software. The accompanying study guide provides a step-by-step walkthrough for students on how to complete the problem in the software.

Sage 50 Complete Accounting Templates

Available on the Online Learning Center. Selected problems in the text are tied to templates created in Sage 50 Complete Accounting. Students use the accompanying guide to complete the problem in the software.

Online Learning Center (OLC)

www.mhhe.com/price14e

The Online Learning Center (OLC) is full of resources for students, including: Online Quizzing, PowerPoint Presentations, and Sage 50 Templates.

> Excellent textbook for our community college students and dual credit accounting. Has all the bells and whistles we need to keep students interested in the topics and help them improve their grades.
>
> —Marina Grau,
> Houston Community College
> –Southwest College

Acknowledgments

The authors are deeply grateful to the following accounting educators for their input during development of *College Accounting, 14e*. The feedback from these knowledgeable instructors provided the authors with valuable assistance in meeting the changing needs of the college accounting classroom.

Cornelia Alsheimer,
Santa Barbara City College

Julia Angel,
North Arkansas College

James R. Armbrester,
Lawson State Community College – Bessemer Campus

Laura Bantz,
McHenry County College

Victoria Bentz,
Yavapai College

Anne Bikofsky,
College of Westchester

David Bland,
Cape Fear Community College

Patrick Borja,
Citrus College

Kathy Bowen,
Murray State College

Gerald Caton,
Yavapai College

Steven L. Christian,
Jackson Community College

Marilyn Ciolino,
Delgado Community College

Jean Condon,
Mid-Plains Community College Area (Nebraska)

Joan Cook,
Milwaukee Area Technical College

Gisela Dicklin,
Edmonds Community College

Michael Discello,
Pittsburgh Technical Institute

Sid Downey,
Cochise College

Steven Ernest,
Baton Rouge Community College

Ann Esarco,
McHenry County College

Paul Fisher,
Rogue Community College

Allen Ford,
Institute for the Deaf, Rochester Institute of Tech

Jeff Forrest,
Saint Louis Community College

David Forsyth,
Palomar College

Mark Fronke,
Cerritos College

Nancy Goehring,
Monterey Peninsula College

Renee Goffinet,
Spokane Community College

Jane Goforth,
North Seattle Community College

David Grooms,
Maui Community College

Lori Grady,
Buck County Community College

Gretchen Graham,
Community College of Allegheny County

Marina Grau,
Houston Community College

Chad Grooms,
Gateway Community and Technical College

Sue Gudmunson,
Lewis-Clark State College

Becky Hancock,
El Paso Community College

Christina Hata,
Miracosta College

Scott Hays,
Central Oregon Community College

Mary Jane Hollars,
Vincennes University

R. Stephen Holman,
Elizabethtown Community and Technical College

Ray Ingram,
Southwest Georgia Technical College

Dennis Jirkovsky,
Indiana Business College

Stacy Johnson,
Iowa Central Community College

Jane Jones,
Mountain Empire Community College

Dmitriy Kalyagin,
Chabot College

Norm Katz,
National College–Stow

Sandra Kemper,
Front Range Community College

Patty Kolarik,
Hutchinson Community College

Elida Kraja,
Saint Louis Community College–Flors Valley

Greg Lauer,
North Iowa Area Community College

David Laurel,
South Texas College

Thomas E Lynch,
Hocking College

Josephine Mathias,
Mercer County Community College

Roger McMillian,
Mineral Area College

Jim Meir
Cleveland State Community College

Michelle Meyer,
Joliet Junior College

John Miller,
Metropolitan Community College

Lora Miller,
Centura College

Peter Neshwat,
Brookline College

Marc Newman,
Hocking Technical College

Anthony Newton,
Highline Community College

Anthony Newton,
Highline Community College

Kenneth Newton,
Cleveland State Community College

Jon Nitschke,
Montana State University

Joel Peralto,
University of Hawaii–Hawaii Community College

Shirley Powell,
Arkansas State University

Carol Reinke,
Empire College

Barbara Rice,
Gateway Community and Technical College

Reynold Robles,
Texas State Technical College–Harlingen

Morgan Rockett,
Moberly Area Community College

Joan Ryan,
Clackamas Community College

Patricia Scales,
Brookstone College

Michael Schaub,
Shasta College

Tom Snavely,
Yavapai College

Rick Street,
Spokane Community College

Domenico Tavella,
Pittsburgh Technical Institute

Judy Toland,
Bucks County Community College

Donald Townsend,
Forsyth Technical Community College

Patricia Walczak,
Lansing Community College

Linda Whitten,
Skyline College

Thank You . . .

WE ARE GRATEFUL for the outstanding support from McGraw-Hill/Irwin. In particular, we would like to thank Tim Vertovec Director; Steve Schuetz, Executive Brand Manager; Christina Sanders, Managing Development Editor; Bruce Gin, Senior Project Manager; Michael McCormick, Senior Buyer; Matt Baldwin, Senior Designer; Joanne Mennemeier, Photo Research Coordinator; and Ron Nelms, Media Project Manager.

Finally, we would like to thank our supplement authors and accuracy checkers: David Krug, Johnson County Community College; Mark McCarthy, East Carolina University: Debra Schmidt, Cerritos College; Anna Boulware, St. Charles Community College; Linda Muren, Cuyahoga Community College; Jeanine Metzler, Northampton Community College; Dominique Svarc, William Rainey Harper College; Jeannie Folk, College of DuPage; Kathleen O'Donnell, Onongada Community College; Jason Bess, Stautzenberger College; Beth Woods; Carol Yacht; Linda Flowers, Houston Community College; Matt Lowenkron; Renee Goffinet, Spokane Community College; and Teresa Alenikov, Cerritos College.

John Price • David Haddock • Michael Farina

The Price College Accounting textbook is a well written and planned out approach to a college accounting approach. It goes into more detail and coverage of topics than most college accounting textbooks that I have seen. Each chapter includes great examples and transactional analysis as the topics progress.

—Roger McMillian
Mineral Area College

To the Student

Welcome to *College Accounting*. This book and the accompanying study materials will help you bridge the gap from your first course in accounting to your next business course . . . and beyond, to your career.

Marginal Icons are used throughout the text to link content to support materials on the web or via other media, or to highlight consistent elements throughout the text:

This icon indicates that the content being discussed is related to internal control.

Continuing problems build on one another from chapter to chapter, allowing you to use the concepts you've just been introduced to in a chapter to revisit and further reinforce material you've learned in previous chapters.

The Quickbooks software grew out of the success of the personal finance software Quicken. Problems are pulled into Quickbooks, giving you another way to practice using software that you are likely to run into in the business world. There is also a Student Guide for Quickbooks Pro available to you as a printed supplement that will assist you in working with Quickbooks.

Sage 50 Complete Accounting (formerly known as Peachtree) is an accounting tool that you are likely to encounter if you decide to make accounting your career. This icon indicates that you can work the problem in Sage 50, gaining experience that will be invaluable once you graduate. The Sage 50 templates are available on the Online Learning Center.

McGraw-Hill's *Connect Accounting* system allows you to submit homework online if your professor chooses to utilize it in the classroom. Your professor will request that you obtain this software when you purchase your book if he/she plans to ask you to submit your homework online.

Self Reviews are a great way to double-check that you've understood what you've just read in your book or what your professor has just covered in lecture. There is a Self Review at the end of every section. Answers to the self reviews can be found at the end of each chapter so you can check your work and make sure you understand a topic before moving on to the next section.

Learning Objectives can be found at the beginning of each chapter as well as at the beginning of each section. The section opener objectives also contain a brief explanation for "Why It's Important" to study the concept presented.

Online Learning Center (www.mhhe.com/price14e) The website that accompanies Price/Haddock/Farina's *College Accounting*, 14e, is a great resource for you. Don't be afraid to use it! On the Online Learning Center (OLC), there are a lot of great materials that will help you not only get through your course, but also get a good grade and remember what you learned. You will find things like Practice Quizzes and PowerPoint® Slides.

To access the OLC, just go to the link above and look to the left. You'll see a link to the "Student Edition"—click on this and you will find a variety of Course-Wide Content in the top left corner, including accounting videos. Under this, you will see a drop-down menu from which you can choose whatever chapter you want and find additional resources.

Practice Sets *College Accounting*, 14e, comes with two different full-length practice sets (in addition to the Mini-Practice Sets included inside the textbook) that you can purchase to get additional practice applying the concepts you've learned in class. Your instructor can provide you with the answers so you can check your work.

Study Guide and Working Papers In addition to giving you a hard copy place to enter the answers to the questions, exercises, and problems your instructor assigns you in class, the Study Guide and Working Papers also include additional activities, exercises, true/false questions, and a demonstration problem that you can work—all of which give you more chances to practice what you're going to see on the test!

Our two main goals are to help you understand and apply accounting and prepare you for the future, whether that includes additional study or a new workplace. We hope the aids we've provided for you as listed above will help enhance your study and ultimately give you a greater understanding of accounting and how it applies in the real world.

Good luck with your studies. We think it will be well worth your efforts.

Brief Contents

Contents

Chapter 21

College Accounting

Accounting:
The Language of Business

Chapter 1

Google

www.google.com

There are so many careers out there for students to be curious about. How do you find out about them? Most of us turn to the Internet—We get directions, check the local weather, and research news using *Google*.

Google's features and performance have grown over the years and attracted new users at an astounding rate. By 2000, *Google* officially became the world's largest search engine with its introduction of a billion-page index. As a publicly owned global Internet communications, commerce, and media company, *Google* hires a lot of accountants to record its business transactions.

You might be curious about a career in accounting. Maybe you're wondering what accountants do every day at companies like *Google* and who looks at the reports generated by their efforts. This information is not only essential to *Google*'s management team, but many other groups rely on it as well. A final question, you may want to *Google*, is why can users trust the information that accountants have prepared?

thinking critically

Can you think of any of the organizations that would be interested in how *Google* is performing?

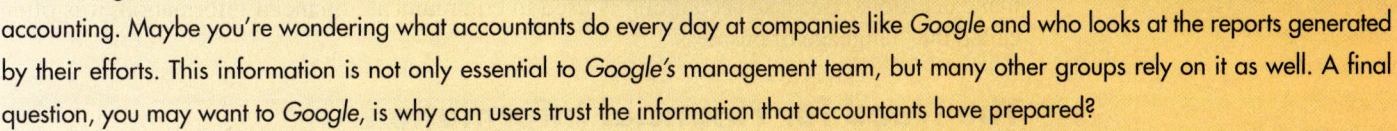

LEARNING OBJECTIVES	NEW TERMS	
1-1. Define accounting.	accounting	generally accepted
1-2. Identify and discuss career opportunities in accounting.	Accounting Standards Codification	accounting principles (GAAP) governmental accounting
1-3. Identify the users of financial information.	Accounting Standards Update	international accounting management advisory
1-4. Compare and contrast the three types of business entities.	accounting system auditing	services managerial accounting
1-5. Describe the process used to develop generally accepted accounting principles.	auditor's report certified public accountant (CPA)	partnership public accountants separate entity assumption
1-6. Define the accounting terms new to this chapter.	corporation creditor	social entity sole proprietorship
	discussion memorandum economic entity	Statements of Financial Accounting Standards
	entity exposure draft	stock stockholders
	financial statements	tax accounting

SECTION OBJECTIVES	TERMS TO LEARN
>> 1-1. Define accounting. **WHY IT'S IMPORTANT** Business transactions affect many aspects of our lives.	accounting accounting system auditing certified public accountant (CPA) financial statements governmental accounting management advisory services managerial accounting public accountants tax accounting
>> 1-2. Identify and discuss career opportunities in accounting. **WHY IT'S IMPORTANT** There's something for everyone in the field of accounting. Accounting professionals are found in every workplace from public accounting firms to government agencies, from corporations to nonprofit organizations.	
>> 1-3. Identify the users of financial information. **WHY IT'S IMPORTANT** A wide variety of individuals and businesses depend on financial information to make decisions.	

What Is Accounting?

Accounting provides financial information about a business or a nonprofit organization. Owners, managers, investors, and other interested parties need financial information in order to make decisions. Because accounting is used to communicate financial information, it is often called the "language of business."

The Need for Financial Information

Suppose a relative leaves you a substantial sum of money and you decide to carry out your life-long dream of opening a small sportswear shop. You rent space in a local shopping center, purchase fixtures and equipment, purchase goods to sell, hire salespeople, and open the store to customers. Before long you realize that, to run your business successfully, you need financial information about the business. You probably need information that provides answers to the following questions:

- How much cash does the business have?
- How much money do customers owe the business?
- What is the cost of the merchandise sold?
- What is the change in sales volume?
- How much money is owed to suppliers?
- What is the profit or loss?

As your business grows, you will need even more financial information to evaluate the firm's performance and make decisions about the future. An efficient accounting system allows owners and managers to quickly obtain a wide range of useful information. The need for timely information is one reason that businesses have an accounting system directed by a professional staff.

>>1-1. OBJECTIVE

Define accounting.

Accounting Defined

Accounting is the process by which financial information about a business is recorded, classified, summarized, interpreted, and communicated to owners, managers, and other interested parties. An **accounting system** is designed to accumulate data about a firm's financial affairs, classify the data in a meaningful way, and summarize it in periodic reports called **financial statements.** Owners and managers obtain a lot of information from financial statements. The accountant:

■ establishes the records and procedures that make up the accounting system,

■ supervises the operations of the system,

■ interprets the resulting financial information.

Most owners and managers rely heavily on the accountant's judgment and knowledge when making financial decisions.

Accounting Careers

Many jobs are available in the accounting profession, and they require varying amounts of education and experience. Bookkeepers and accountants are responsible for keeping records and providing financial information about the business. Generally, bookkeepers are responsible for recording business transactions. In large firms, bookkeepers may also supervise the work of accounting clerks. Accounting clerks are responsible for recordkeeping for a part of the accounting system—perhaps payroll, accounts receivable, or accounts payable. Accountants usually supervise bookkeepers and prepare the financial statements and reports of the business.

Newspapers and websites often have job listings for accounting clerks, bookkeepers, and accountants:

■ Accounting clerk positions usually require one to two accounting courses and little or no experience.

■ Bookkeeper positions usually require one to two years of accounting education plus experience as an accounting clerk.

■ Accountant positions usually require a bachelor's degree but are sometimes filled by experienced bookkeepers or individuals with a two-year college degree. Most entry-level accountant positions do not have an experience requirement. Both the education and experience requirements for accountant positions vary according to the size of the firm.

Accountants usually choose to practice in one of three areas:

■ public accounting

■ managerial accounting

■ governmental accounting

Table 1.1 on page 6 shows a list of occupations with job duties that are similar to those of accountants and auditors.

PUBLIC ACCOUNTING

Public accountants work for public accounting firms. Public accounting firms provide accounting services for other companies. Usually they offer three services:

■ auditing

■ tax accounting

■ management advisory services

The largest public accounting firms in the United States are called the "Big Four." The "Big Four" are Deloitte & Touche, Ernst & Young, KPMG, and PricewaterhouseCoopers.

Many public accountants are **certified public accountants (CPAs).** To become a CPA, an individual must have a certain number of college credits in accounting courses, demonstrate good personal character, pass the Uniform CPA Examination, and fulfill the experience requirements of the state of practice. CPAs must follow the professional code of ethics.

Auditing is the review of financial statements to assess their fairness and adherence to generally accepted accounting principles. Accountants who are CPAs perform financial audits.

>>**1-2. OBJECTIVE**
Identify and discuss career opportunities in accounting.

ABOUT
ACCOUNTING

Accounting Services
The role of the CPA is expanding. In the past, accounting firms handled audits and taxes. Today accountants provide a wide range of services, including financial planning, investment advice, accounting and tax software advice, and profitability consulting. Accountants provide clients with information and advice on electronic business, health care performance measurement, risk assessment, business performance measurement, and information system reliability.

TABLE 1.1   Occupations with Similar Job Duties to Accountants and Auditors

Occupation	Job Duties	Entry-Level Education
Bookkeeping, Accounting, and Auditing Clerks	Bookkeeping, accounting, and auditing clerks produce financial records for organizations. They record financial transactions, update statements, and check financial records for accuracy.	High school diploma or equivalent
Budget Analysts	Budget analysts help public and private institutions organize their finances. They prepare budget reports and monitor institutional spending.	Bachelor's degree
Cost Estimators	Cost estimators collect and analyze data to estimate the time, money, resources, and labor required for product manufacturing, construction projects, or services. Some specialize in a particular industry or product type.	Bachelor's degree
Financial Analysts	Financial analysts provide guidance to businesses and individuals making investment decisions. They assess the performance of stocks, bonds, and other types of investments.	Bachelor's degree
Financial Examiners	Financial examiners ensure compliance with laws governing financial institutions and transactions. They review balance sheets, evaluate the risk level of loans, and assess bank management.	Bachelor's degree
Financial Managers	Financial managers are responsible for the financial health of an organization. They produce financial reports, direct investment activities, and develop strategies and plans for the long-term financial goals of their organization.	Bachelor's degree
Management Analysts	Management analysts, often called management consultants, propose ways to improve an organization's efficiency. They advise managers on how to make organizations more profitable through reduced costs and increased revenues.	Bachelor's degree
Personal Financial Advisors	Personal financial advisors give financial advice to people. They help with investments, taxes, and insurance decisions.	Bachelor's degree
Postsecondary Teachers	Postsecondary teachers instruct students in a wide variety of academic and vocational subjects beyond the high school level. They also conduct research and publish scholarly papers and books.	Doctoral or professional degree
Tax Examiners and Collectors, and Revenue Agents	Tax examiners and collectors, and revenue agents ensure that governments get their tax money from businesses and citizens. They review tax returns, conduct audits, identify taxes owed, and collect overdue tax payments.	Bachelor's degree
Top Executives	Top executives devise strategies and policies to ensure that an organization meets its goals. They plan, direct, and coordinate operational activities of companies and public or private-sector organizations.	Bachelor's degree

Source: Bureau of Labor Statistics, U.S. Department of Labor, Occupational Outlook Handbook, 2012–13 Edition, Accountants and Auditors, on the Internet at http://www.bls.gov/ooh/business-and-financial/accountants-and-auditors.htm (visited March 25, 2013).

Tax accounting involves tax compliance and tax planning. *Tax compliance* deals with the preparation of tax returns and the audit of those returns. *Tax planning* involves giving advice to clients on how to structure their financial affairs in order to reduce their tax liability.

Management advisory services involve helping clients improve their information systems or their business performance.

MANAGERIAL ACCOUNTING

Managerial accounting, also referred to as *private accounting,* involves working for a single business in industry. Managerial accountants perform a wide range of activities, including:

- establishing accounting policies,
- managing the accounting system,
- preparing financial statements,
- interpreting financial information,
- providing financial advice to management,
- preparing tax forms,
- performing tax planning services,
- preparing internal reports for management.

GOVERNMENTAL ACCOUNTING

Governmental accounting involves keeping financial records and preparing financial reports as part of the staff of federal, state, or local governmental units. Governmental units do not earn profits. However, governmental units receive and pay out huge amounts of money and need procedures for recording and managing this money.

Some governmental agencies hire accountants to audit the financial statements and records of the businesses under their jurisdiction and to uncover possible violations of the law. The Securities and Exchange Commission, the Internal Revenue Service, the Federal Bureau of Investigation, and Homeland Security employ a large number of accountants.

Users of Financial Information

The results of the accounting process are communicated to many individuals and organizations. Who are these individuals and organizations, and why do they want financial information about a particular firm?

>>1-3. OBJECTIVE
Identify the users of financial information.

OWNERS AND MANAGERS

Assume your sportswear shop is in full operation. One user of financial information about the business is you, the owner. You need information that will help you evaluate the results of your operations and plan and make decisions for the future. Questions such as the following are difficult to answer without financial information:

- Should you drop the long-sleeved pullover that is not selling well from the product line, or should you just reduce the price?
- How much should you charge for the denim jacket that you are adding to the product line?
- How much should you spend on advertising?
- How does this month's profit compare with last month's profit?
- Should you open a new store?

SUPPLIERS

A number of other people are interested in the financial information about your business. For example, businesses that supply you with sportswear need to assess the ability of your firm to pay its bills. They also need to set a credit limit for your firm.

BANKS

What if you decide to ask your bank for a loan so that you can open a new store? The bank needs to be sure that your firm will repay the loan on time. The bank will ask for financial information prepared by your accountant. Based on this information, the bank will decide whether to make the loan and the terms of the loan.

TAX AUTHORITIES

The Internal Revenue Service (IRS) and other state and local tax authorities are interested in financial information about your firm. This information is used to determine the tax base:

- Income taxes are based on taxable income.
- Sales taxes are based on sales income.
- Property taxes are based on the assessed value of buildings, equipment, and inventory (the goods available for sale).

The accounting process provides all of this information.

REGULATORY AGENCIES AND INVESTORS

If an industry is regulated by a governmental agency, businesses in that industry have to supply financial information to the regulating agency. For example, the Federal Communications Commission receives financial information from radio and television stations. The Securities and Exchange Commission (SEC) oversees the financial information provided by publicly owned corporations to their investors and potential investors. Publicly owned corporations trade their shares on stock exchanges and in over-the-counter markets. Congress passed the Securities Act of 1933 and the Securities Exchange Act of 1934 in order to protect those who invest in publicly owned corporations.

The SEC is responsible for reviewing the accounting methods used by publicly owned corporations. The SEC has delegated this review to the accounting profession but still has the final say on any financial accounting issue faced by publicly owned corporations. If the SEC does not agree with the reporting that results from an accounting method, the SEC can suspend trading of a company's shares on the stock exchanges.

> Major changes were made to the regulatory environment in the accounting profession with the passage of the Public Company Accounting Reform and Investor Protection Act of 2002 (also known as the Sarbanes-Oxley Act) that was signed into law by President Bush on August 2, 2002. The Act was the most far-reaching regulatory crackdown on corporate fraud and corruption since the creation of the Securities and Exchange Commission in 1934.

The Sarbanes-Oxley Act was passed in response to the wave of corporate accounting scandals starting with the demise of Enron Corporation in 2001, the arrest of top executives at WorldCom and Adelphia Communications Corporation, and ultimately the demise of Arthur Andersen, an international public accounting firm formerly a member of the "Big Five." Arthur Andersen was found guilty of an obstruction of justice charge after admitting that the firm destroyed thousands of documents and electronic files related to the Enron audit engagement. Although on May 31, 2008, the Supreme Court of the United States reversed the Andersen guilty verdict, Arthur Andersen has not returned as a viable business. As a result of the demise of Arthur Andersen, the "Big Five" are now the "Big Four."

The Act significantly tightens regulation of financial reporting by publicly held companies and their accountants and auditors. The Sarbanes-Oxley Act creates a five-member Public Company Accounting Oversight Board. The Board will have investigative and enforcement powers to oversee the accounting profession and to discipline corrupt accountants and auditors. The Securities and Exchange Commission will oversee the Board. Two members of the Board will be certified public accountants, to regulate the accountants who audit public companies, and the remaining three must not be and cannot have been CPAs. The chair of the Board may be held by one of the CPA members, provided that the individual has not been engaged as a practicing CPA for five years.

Major provisions of the bill include rules on consulting services, auditor rotation, criminal penalties, corporate governance, and securities regulation. The Act prohibits accountants from offering a broad range of consulting services to publicly traded companies that they audit and requires accounting firms to change the lead audit or coordinating partner and the reviewing partner for a company every five years. Additionally, it is a felony to "knowingly" destroy or create documents to "impede, obstruct or influence" any existing or contemplated federal investigation. Auditors are also required to maintain all audit or review work papers for seven years. Criminal penalties, up to 20 years in prison, are imposed for obstruction of justice and the Act raises the maximum sentence for defrauding pension funds to 10 years.

Chief executives and chief financial officers of publicly traded corporations are now required to certify their financial statements and these executives will face up to 20 years in prison if they "knowingly or willfully" allow materially misleading information into their financial statements. Companies must also disclose, as quickly as possible, material changes in their financial position. Wall Street investment firms are prohibited from retaliating against analysts who criticize investment-banking clients of the firm. The Act contains a provision with broad new protection for whistle-blowers and lengthens the time that investors have to file lawsuits against corporations for securities fraud.

By narrowing the type of consulting services that accountants can provide to companies that they audit, requiring auditor rotation, and imposing stiff criminal penalties for violation of the Act, it appears that this new legislation will significantly help to restore public confidence in financial statements and markets and change the regulatory environment in which accountants operate.

CUSTOMERS

Customers pay special attention to financial information about the firms with which they do business. For example, before a business spends a lot of money on a new computer system, the business wants to know that the computer manufacturer will be around for the

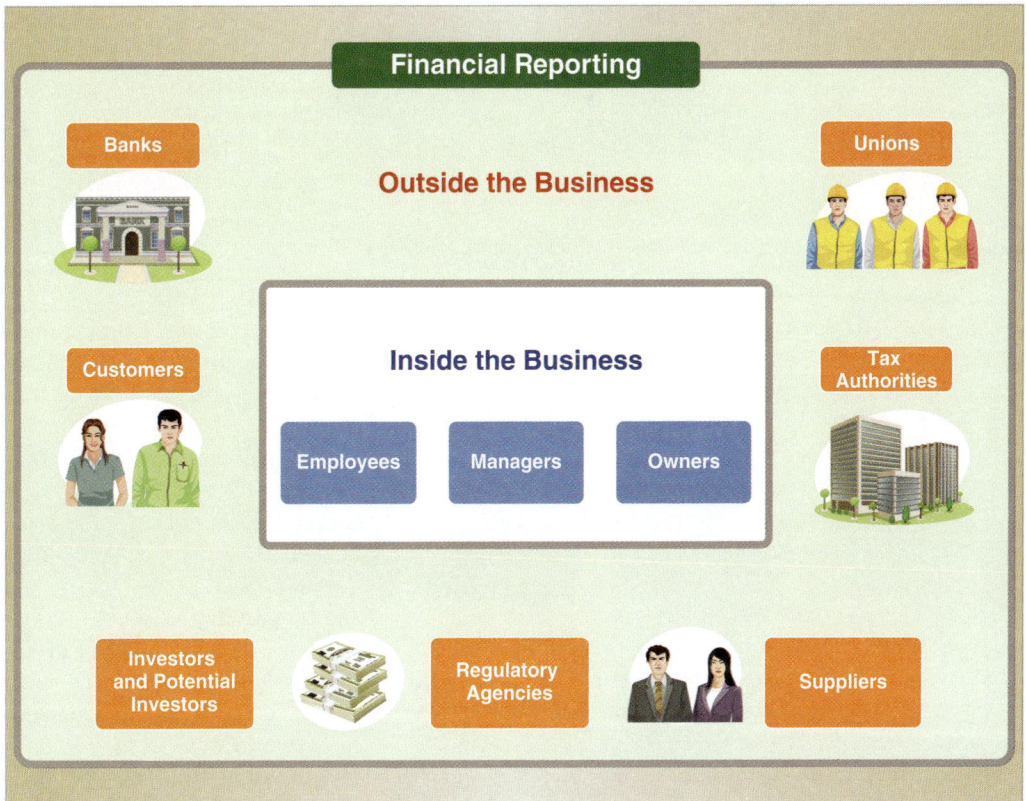

FIGURE 1.1

Users of Financial Information

next several years in order to service the computer, replace parts, and provide additional components. The business analyzes the financial information about the computer manufacturer in order to determine its economic health and the likelihood that it will remain in business.

EMPLOYEES AND UNIONS

Often employees are interested in the financial information of the business that employs them. Employees who are members of a profit-sharing plan pay close attention to the financial results because they affect employee income. Employees who are members of a labor union use financial information about the firm to negotiate wages and benefits.

Figure 1.1 on page 9 illustrates different financial information users. As you learn about the accounting process, you will appreciate why financial information is so important to these individuals and organizations. You will learn how financial information meets users' needs.

Section 1   Self Review

QUESTIONS

1. Why is accounting called the "language of business"?

2. What are financial statements?

3. What are the names of three accounting job positions?

EXERCISES

4. One requirement for becoming a CPA is to pass the:

    a. Final CPA Examination

    b. SEC Accounting Examination

    c. Uniform CPA Examination

    d. State Board Examination

5. Which organization has the final say on financial accounting issues faced by publicly owned corporations?

    a. Securities and Exchange Commission

    b. Federal Trade Commission

    c. U.S. Treasury Department

    d. Internal Revenue Service

ANALYSIS

6. The owner of the sporting goods store where you work has decided to expand the store. She has decided to apply for a loan. What type of information will she need to give to the bank?

(Answers to Section 1 Self Review are on page 20.)

Business and Accounting

The accounting process involves recording, classifying, summarizing, interpreting, and communicating financial information about an economic or social entity. An **entity** is recognized as having its own separate identity. An entity may be an individual, a town, a university, or a business. The term **economic entity** usually refers to a business or organization whose major purpose is to produce a profit for its owners. **Social entities** are nonprofit organizations, such as cities, public schools, and public hospitals. This book focuses on the accounting process for businesses, but keep in mind that nonprofit organizations also need financial information.

Types of Business Entities

The three major legal forms of business entity are the sole proprietorship, the partnership, and the corporation. In general, the accounting process is the same for all three forms of business. Later in the book you will study the different ways certain transactions are handled depending on the type of business entity. For now, however, you will learn about the different types of business entities.

>>1-4. OBJECTIVE
Compare and contrast the three types of business entities.

SOLE PROPRIETORSHIPS

A **sole proprietorship** is a business entity owned by one person. The life of the business ends when the owner is no longer willing or able to keep the business going. Many small businesses are operated as sole proprietorships.

The owner of a sole proprietorship is legally responsible for the debts and taxes of the business. If the business is unable to pay its debts, the **creditors** (those people, companies, or government agencies to whom the business owes money) can turn to the owner for payment. The owner may have to pay the debts of the business from personal resources, including personal savings. When the time comes to pay income taxes, the owner's income and the income of the business are combined to compute the total tax responsibility of the owner.

It is important that the business transactions be kept separate from the owner's personal transactions. If the owner's personal transactions are mixed with those of the business, it will be difficult to measure the performance of the business. The term **separate entity assumption** describes the concept of keeping the firm's financial records separate from the owner's personal financial records.

PARTNERSHIPS

A **partnership** is a business entity owned by two or more people. The partnership structure is common in businesses that offer professional services, such as law firms, accounting firms, architectural firms, medical practices, and dental practices. At the beginning of the partnership, two or more individuals enter into a contract that details the rights, obligations, and limitations of each partner, including:

- the amount each partner will contribute to the business,
- each partner's percentage of ownership,
- each partner's share of the profits,
- the duties each partner will perform,
- the responsibility each partner has for the amounts owed by the business to creditors and tax authorities.

The partners choose how to share the ownership and profits of the business. They may share equally or in any proportion agreed upon in the contract. When a partner leaves, the partnership is dissolved and a new partnership may be formed with the remaining partners.

Partners are individually, and as a group, responsible for the debts and taxes of the partnership. If the partnership is unable to pay its debts or taxes, the partners' personal property, including personal bank accounts, may be used to provide payment. It is important that partnership transactions be kept separate from the personal financial transactions of the partners.

> Under the Limited Liability Partnership Act of most states, a Limited Liability Partnership (LLP) may be formed. An LLP is a general partnership that provides some limited liability for all partners. LLP partners are responsible and have liability for their own actions and the actions of those under their control or supervision. They are not liable for the actions or malfeasance of another partner. Except for the limited liability aspect, LLPs generally have the same characteristics, advantages, and disadvantages as any other partnership.

CORPORATIONS

A **corporation** is a business entity that is separate from its owners. A corporation has a legal right to own property and do business in its own name. Corporations are very different from sole proprietorships and partnerships.

Stock, issued in the form of stock certificates, represents the ownership of the corporation. Corporations may be *privately* or *publicly* owned. Privately owned corporations are also called *closely held* corporations. The ownership of privately owned corporations is limited to specific individuals, usually family members. Stock of closely held corporations is not traded on an exchange. In contrast, stock of publicly owned corporations is bought and sold on stock exchanges and in over-the-counter markets. Most large corporations have issued (sold) thousands of shares of stock.

important!

Separate Entity Assumption
For *accounting* purposes, all forms of business are considered separate entities from their owners. However, the corporation is the only form of business that is a separate *legal* entity.

An owner's share of the corporation is determined by the number of shares of stock held by the owner compared to the total number of shares issued by the corporation. Assume that Hector Flores owns 600 shares of Sample Corporation. If Sample Corporation has issued 2,000 shares of stock, Flores owns 30 percent of the corporation (600 shares ÷ 2,000 shares = 0.30 or 30%). Some corporate decisions require a vote by the owners. For Sample Corporation, Flores has 600 votes, one for each share of stock that he owns. The other owners have 1,400 votes.

> Subchapter S Corporations, also known as S corporations, are entities formed as corporations which meet the requirements of Subchapter S of the Internal Revenue Code to be treated essentially as a partnership so the corporation pays no income tax. Instead, shareholders include their share of corporate profits, and any items that require special tax treatment, on their individual income tax returns. Otherwise, S corporations have all of the characteristics of regular corporations. The advantage of the S corporation is that the owners have limited liability and avoid double taxation.

One of the advantages of the corporate form of business is the indefinite life of the corporation. A sole proprietorship ends when the owner dies or discontinues the business. A partnership ends on the death or withdrawal of a partner. In contrast, a corporation does not end when ownership changes. Some corporations have new owners daily because their shares are actively traded (sold) on stock exchanges.

Corporate owners, called **stockholders** or *shareholders,* are not personally responsible for the debts or taxes of the corporation. If the corporation is unable to pay its bills, the most stockholders can lose is their investment in the corporation. In other words, the stockholders will not lose more than the cost of the shares of stock.

The accounting process for the corporate entity, like that of the sole proprietorship and the partnership, is separate from the financial affairs of its owners. Usually this separation is easy to maintain. Most stockholders do not participate in the day-to-day operations of the business.

Table 1.2 summarizes the business characteristics for sole proprietorships, partnerships, and corporations.

Generally Accepted Accounting Principles

The Securities and Exchange Commission has the final say on matters of financial reporting by publicly owned corporations. The SEC has delegated the job of determining proper accounting standards to the accounting profession. However, the SEC sometimes overrides decisions the

TABLE 1.2

Major Characteristics of Business Entities

Characteristic	Type of Business Entity		
	Sole Proprietorship	Partnership	Corporation
Ownership	One owner	Two or more owners	One or more owners, even thousands
Life of the business	Ends when the owner dies, is unable to carry on operations, or decides to close the firm	Ends when one or more partners withdraw, when a partner dies, or when the partners decide to close the firm	Can continue indefinitely; ends only when the business goes bankrupt or when the stockholders vote to liquidate
Responsibility for debts of the business	Owner is responsible for firm's debt when the firm is unable to pay	Partners are responsible individually and jointly for firm's debts when the firm is unable to pay	Stockholders are not responsible for firm's debts; they can lose only the amount they invested

accounting profession makes. To fulfill its responsibility, the accounting profession has developed, and continues to develop, **generally accepted accounting principles (GAAP).** Generally accepted accounting principles must be followed by publicly owned companies unless they can show that doing so would produce information which is misleading.

THE DEVELOPMENT OF GENERALLY ACCEPTED ACCOUNTING PRINCIPLES

Generally accepted accounting principles are developed by the Financial Accounting Standards Board (FASB), which is composed of five full-time members. Prior to 2009, the FASB issued 168 **Statements of Financial Accounting Standards.** The FASB developed these statements and, before issuing them, obtained feedback from interested people and organizations.

First, the FASB wrote a **discussion memorandum** to explain the topic being considered. Then public hearings were held where interested parties could express their opinions, either orally or in writing. The groups that consistently expressed opinions about proposed FASB statements were the SEC, the American Institute of Certified Public Accountants (AICPA), public accounting firms, the American Accounting Association (AAA), and businesses with a direct interest in a particular statement.

The AICPA is a national association for certified public accountants. The AAA is a group of accounting educators. AAA members research possible effects of a proposed FASB statement and offer their opinions to the FASB.

After public hearings, the FASB released an **exposure draft,** which described the proposed statement. Then the FASB received and evaluated public comment about the exposure draft. Finally, FASB members voted on the statement. If at least four members approved, the statement was issued.

The above process was used until 2009. Effective July 1, 2009, the source of authoritative U.S. GAAP is the FASB **Accounting Standards Codification,** which are communicated through an **Accounting Standards Update** (Update). The Codification reorganizes U.S. GAAP pronouncements into approximately 90 accounting topics. It also includes relevant U.S. Securities and Exchange Commission (SEC) guidance that follows the same topical structure in separate sections in the Codification.

Updates are now published on these accounting topics for all authoritative U.S. GAAP promulgated by the FASB, regardless of the form in which such guidance may have been issued prior to the release of the FASB Codification. An Update summarizes the key provisions of the project that led to the Update, details the specific amendments to the FASB Codification, and explains the basis for the Board's decision.

Accounting principles vary from country to country. **International accounting** is the study of the accounting principles used by different countries. In 1973, the International Accounting Standards Committee (IASC) was formed. Recently, the IASC's name was changed to the International Accounting Standards Board (IASB). The ISAB deals with issues caused by the lack of uniform accounting principles. The IASB also makes recommendations to enhance comparability of reporting practices.

THE USE OF GENERALLY ACCEPTED ACCOUNTING PRINCIPLES

Every year, publicly traded companies submit financial statements to the SEC. The financial statements are audited by independent certified public accountants (CPAs). The CPAs are called *independent* because they are not employees of the company being audited and they do not have a financial interest in the company. The financial statements include the auditor's report. The **auditor's report** contains the auditor's opinion about the fair presentation of the operating results and financial position of the business. The auditor's report also confirms that the financial information is prepared in conformity with generally accepted accounting principles. The financial statements and the auditor's report are made available to the public, including existing and potential stockholders.

MANAGERIAL IMPLICATIONS   <<

FINANCIAL INFORMATION

- Managers of a business make sure that the firm's accounting system produces financial information that is timely, accurate, and fair.
- Financial statements should be based on generally accepted accounting principles.
- Each year a publicly traded company must submit financial statements, including an independent auditor's report, to the SEC.
- Internal reports for management need not follow generally accepted accounting principles but should provide useful information that will aid in monitoring and controlling operations.

- Financial information can help managers to control present operations, make decisions, and plan for the future.
- The sound use of financial information is essential to good management.

THINKING CRITICALLY

If you were a manager, how would you use financial information to make decisions?

Businesses and the environment in which they operate are constantly changing. The economy, technology, and laws change. Generally accepted accounting principles are changed and refined as accountants respond to the changing environment.

Section 2   Self Review

QUESTIONS

1. What are generally accepted accounting principles?
2. Why are generally accepted accounting principles needed?
3. How are generally accepted accounting principles developed?

EXERCISES

4. An organization that has two or more owners who are legally responsible for the debts and taxes of the business is a:
   a. social entity
   b. partnership
   c. sole proprietorship
   d. corporation

5. A nonprofit organization such as a public school is a(n):
   a. social unit
   b. economic unit
   c. social entity
   d. economic entity

6. You plan to open a business with two of your friends. You would like to form a corporation, but your friends prefer the partnership form of business. What are some of the advantages of the corporate form of business?

(Answers to Section 2 Self Review are on page 20.)

1 Chapter REVIEW Chapter Summary

Accounting is often called the "language of business." The financial information about a business is communicated to interested parties in financial statements.

Learning Objectives

1-1   Define accounting.

Accounting is the process by which financial information about a business is recorded, classified, summarized, interpreted, and communicated to owners, managers, and other interested parties. Accurate accounting information is essential for making business decisions.

1-2   Identify and discuss career opportunities in accounting.

- There are many job opportunities in accounting.
- Accounting clerk positions, such as accounts receivable clerk, accounts payable clerk, and payroll clerk, require the least education and experience.
- Bookkeepers usually have experience as accounting clerks and a minimum of one to two years of accounting education.
- Most entry-level accounting positions require a college degree or significant experience as a bookkeeper.
- Accountants usually specialize in one of three major areas: public, managerial, or governmental accounting.
  - Some accountants work for public accounting firms and perform auditing, tax accounting, or management advisory functions.
  - Other accountants work in private industry where they set up and supervise accounting systems, prepare financial reports, prepare internal reports, or assist in determining the prices to charge for the firm's products.
  - Still other accountants work for government agencies. They keep track of public funds and expenditures, or they audit the financial records of businesses and individuals to determine whether the records are in compliance with regulatory laws, tax laws, and other laws. The Securities and Exchange Commission, the Internal Revenue Service, the Federal Bureau of Investigation, and Homeland Security employ many accountants.

1-3   Identify the users of financial information.

All types of businesses need and use financial information. Users of financial information include owners and managers, employees, suppliers, banks, tax authorities, regulatory agencies, and investors. Nonprofit organizations need similar financial information.

1-4   Compare and contrast the three types of business entities.

- A sole proprietorship is owned by one person. The owner is legally responsible for the debts and taxes of the business.
- A partnership is owned by two or more people. The owners are legally responsible for the debts and taxes of the business.
- A corporation is a separate legal entity from its owners.
- Note that all three types of business entities are considered separate entities for accounting purposes.

1-5   Describe the process used to develop generally accepted accounting principles.

- The SEC has delegated the authority to develop generally accepted accounting principles to the accounting profession. The Financial Accounting Standards Board handles this task. A series of steps used by the FASB includes issuing a discussion memorandum, an exposure draft, and a statement of principle.
- The SEC oversees the Public Company Accounting Oversight Board that was created by the Sarbanes-Oxley Act. The Board regulates financial reporting by accountants and auditors of publicly held companies.
- Each year, firms that sell stock on stock exchanges or in over-the-counter markets must publish audited financial reports that follow generally accepted accounting principles. They must submit their reports to the Securities and Exchange Commission. They must also make the reports available to stockholders.

1-6   Define the accounting terms new to this chapter.

Glossary

Accounting (p. 4) The process by which financial information about a business is recorded, classified, summarized, interpreted, and communicated to owners, managers, and other interested parties

Accounting Standards Codification (p. 14) The source of authoritative U.S. GAAP

Accounting Standards Update (p. 14) Changes to Accounting Standards Codification are communicated through Accounting Standards Update covering approximately 90 topics

Accounting system (p. 4) A process designed to accumulate, classify, and summarize financial data

Auditing (p. 5) The review of financial statements to assess their fairness and adherence to generally accepted accounting principles

Auditor's report (p. 14) An independent accountant's review of a firm's financial statements

Certified public accountant (CPA) (p. 5) An independent accountant who provides accounting services to the public for a fee

Corporation (p. 12) A publicly or privately owned business entity that is separate from its owners and has a legal right to own property and do business in its own name; stockholders are not responsible for the debts or taxes of the business

Creditor (p. 12) One to whom money is owed

Discussion memorandum (p. 14) An explanation of a topic under consideration by the Financial Accounting Standards Board

Economic entity (p. 11) A business or organization whose major purpose is to produce a profit for its owners

Entity (p. 11) Anything having its own separate identity, such as an individual, a town, a university, or a business

Exposure draft (p. 14) A proposed solution to a problem being considered by the Financial Accounting Standards Board

Financial statements (p. 5) Periodic reports of a firm's financial position or operating results

Generally accepted accounting principles (GAAP) (p. 14) Accounting standards developed and applied by professional accountants

Governmental accounting (p. 7) Accounting work performed for a federal, state, or local governmental unit

International accounting (p. 14) The study of accounting principles used by different countries

Management advisory services (p. 7) Services designed to help clients improve their information systems or their business performance

Managerial accounting (p. 7) Accounting work carried on by an accountant employed by a single business in industry

Partnership (p. 12) A business entity owned by two or more people who are legally responsible for the debts and taxes of the business

Public accountants (p. 5) Members of firms that perform accounting services for other companies

Separate entity assumption (p. 12) The concept of keeping a firm's financial records separate from the owner's personal financial records

Social entity (p. 11) A nonprofit organization, such as a city, public school, or public hospital

Sole proprietorship (p. 11) A business entity owned by one person who is legally responsible for the debts and taxes of the business

Statements of Financial Accounting Standards (p. 14) Accounting principles established by the Financial Accounting Standards Board

Stock (p. 12) Certificates that represent ownership of a corporation

Stockholders (p. 13) The owners of a corporation; also called shareholders

Tax accounting (p. 7) A service that involves tax compliance and tax planning

Comprehensive **Self Review**

1. What are the three types of business entities?
2. How is the ownership of a corporation different from that of a sole proprietorship?
3. What is the purpose of accounting?
4. What does the accounting process involve?
5. What is the purpose of the auditor's report?

(Answers to Comprehensive Self Review are on page 20.)

Discussion Questions

1. What are the three major areas of accounting?
2. What types of services do public accountants provide?
3. What is tax planning?
4. What are the major functions or activities performed by accountants in private industry?
5. What are the three types of business entities, and how do they differ?
6. Why is it important for business records to be separate from the records of the business's owner or owners? What is the term accountants use to describe this separation of personal and business records?
7. What types of people or organizations are interested in financial information about a firm, and why are they interested in this information?
8. What is the purpose of the Financial Accounting Standards Board?
9. What groups consistently offer opinions about proposed FASB statements?
10. What is the function of the Securities and Exchange Commission?
11. What led to the passage of the Public Company Accounting Reform and Investor Protection Act of 2002?
12. What is the purpose of the Public Company Accounting Oversight Board?

PROBLEM

Critical Thinking Problem

Which Type of Business Entity?

Since graduating from college six years ago, Heidi Cantu has worked for a national chain of shoe stores. She has held several positions within the company and is currently manager of a local branch store.

Over the past six years, Heidi has observed a pattern in women's shoe purchases. She informs you that a large majority of the shoes sold are white, black, blue, or gray and that almost every woman owns at least three pairs of each of these colors. Since she has always wanted to be in business for herself, Heidi's idea is to open a women's shoe store that sells only white, black, blue, or gray shoes. She has discussed her plan with a number of people in the industry, and they have encouraged her to pursue her dream of becoming an entrepreneur.

A new upscale shopping mall is opening nearby, and Heidi has decided that now is the time to take the plunge and go into business for herself. She plans to open a shop in the new mall called WBBG Shoes that will only sell white, black, blue, and gray shoes.

One of the things Heidi must decide in the process of transforming her idea into reality is the form of ownership for her new business. Should it be organized as a sole proprietorship, a partnership, or a corporation?

What advice would you give Heidi? What advantages or disadvantages are there to each choice? What do you think of the proposed name for the business, WBBG Shoes?

Business Entity	Advantages	Disadvantages
Sole Proprietorship		
Partnership		
Corporation		

BUSINESS CONNECTIONS

Know Accounting

1. As an owner or manager of a business, what questions would you ask to judge the firm's performance, control operations, make decisions, and plan for the future?

2. Why is financial information important?

3. Besides earning a profit, what other objectives might a business have? Can financial information play an important role in these objectives?

4. What kind of problems can you foresee if a business owner and/or manager does not have a basic knowledge of accounting?

5. What would you tell a small business owner who says he does not see a need for an accounting system in his business because he closely supervises the day-to-day operations and knows exactly what is happening with the business?

6. What is the role of the manager versus the accountant?

7. Does a business owner/manager need to worry about the separate entity assumption? Why or why not?

8. Why are international accounting standards important to management?

To Tell or Not to Tell

You are employed as an accountant for Innovative Computing. Your company is in the process of signing a large contract with an electronics components supplier. You have a personal friend that works for the electronics components supplier, and you have personal knowledge that they have trouble paying their bills. Should you report this to your employer before the purchase?

Notes to Financial Statements

Within a company's annual report, a section called "Notes to Consolidated Financial Statements" offers general information about the company along with detailed notes related to its financial statements.

Analyze Online: On the American Eagle Outfitters, Inc., website (www.ae.com), click on About AE located at the bottom of the page. Then click on AE Investment Information.

Analyze:

1. What types of merchandise does this company sell?

2. Who are the potential users of the information presented? Why would this information be helpful to these users?

3. What age consumer does the company target?

4. Would American Eagle Outfitters, Inc. be considered an economic entity or a social entity? Why?

Determining Information

Restful Sleep Mattress Company is planning to expand into selling bedroom furniture. This expansion will require a loan from the bank. The bank has requested financial information. Discuss, in a group, the information the bank would require. What information, if any, would you not provide the bank?

FASB—What is it?

Go to the FASB website at www.FASB.org. How many Accounting Standards Updates were issued in the current year? How are they cited?

Answers to **Self Reviews**

Answers to Section 1 Self Review

1. The results of the accounting process—financial statements—communicate essential information about a business to concerned individuals and organizations.
2. Periodic reports that summarize the financial affairs of a business.
3. Clerk, bookkeeper, and accountant.
4. **c.** Uniform CPA Examination
5. **a.** Securities and Exchange Commission
6. Current sales and expenses figures, anticipated sales and expenses, and the cost of the expansion.

Answers to Section 2 Self Review

1. Accounting standards that are changed and refined in response to changes in the environment in which businesses operate.
2. GAAP help to ensure that financial information fairly presents a firm's operating results and financial position.
3. The FASB develops proposed statements and solicits feedback from interested individuals, groups, and companies. The FASB evaluates the opinions received and votes on the statement.
4. **b.** partnership
5. **c.** social entity
6. The shareholders are not responsible for the debts and taxes of the corporation. Corporations can continue in existence indefinitely.

Answers to Comprehensive Self Review

1. Sole proprietorship, partnership, and corporation.
2. A sole proprietorship is a business entity owned by one person. A corporation is a separate legal entity that has a legal right to own property and do business in its own name.
3. To gather and communicate financial information about a business.
4. Recording, classifying, summarizing, interpreting, and communicating financial information about a business.
5. To obtain the objective opinion of a professional accountant from outside the company that the statements fairly present the operating results and financial position of the business and that the information was prepared according to GAAP.

Analyzing Business Transactions

SOUTHWEST.COM®
www.southwest.com

Rollin King and Herb Kelleher had a simple notion when they got into the airline business: "If you get your passengers to their destinations when they want to get there, on time, at the lowest possible fares, and make darn sure they have a good time doing it, people will fly your airline."

Today, Southwest has become one of the most profitable airlines—posting a profit for the 40th consecutive year in a row! However, running an airline is no easy task. Think of all of the financial transactions that take place on a

daily basis. The airline has to buy planes, equipment, and supplies—like those peanuts we are so fond of. It also has to pay employees, pay for repairs on their equipment, and buy insurance, just to name a few expenses. Then, it has to sell enough tickets in order to be able to generate money to pay for all of these things. Yikes. That is a lot of cash coming in and going out. With an emphasis on customer service, Southwest has a reputation of being fun, quirky, and having a sense of humor. You never know what might happen when you board a Southwest flight but you know you'll have a good time.

thinking critically

How does Southwest keep track of all of these transactions so that it can continue to run its airlines profitably?

LEARNING OBJECTIVES	NEW TERMS	
2-1. Record in equation form the financial effects of a business transaction.	accounts payable	equation
	accounts receivable	income statement
2-2. Define, identify, and understand the relationship between asset, liability, and owner's equity accounts.	assets	liabilities
	balance sheet	net income
	break even	net loss
2-3. Analyze the effects of business transactions on a firm's assets, liabilities, and owner's equity and record these effects in accounting equation form.	business transaction	on account
	capital	owner's equity
	equity	revenue
2-4. Prepare an income statement.	expense	statement of owner's
2-5. Prepare a statement of owner's equity and a balance sheet.	fair market value	equity
	fundamental accounting	withdrawals
2-6. Define the accounting terms new to this chapter.		

SECTION OBJECTIVES	TERMS TO LEARN
>> 2-1. Record in equation form the financial effects of a business transaction.	accounts payable
WHY IT'S IMPORTANT	assets
Learning the fundamental accounting equation is a basis for understanding business transactions.	balance sheet
	business transaction
>> 2-2. Define, identify, and understand the relationship between asset, liability, and owner's equity accounts.	capital
	equity
WHY IT'S IMPORTANT	liabilities
The relationship between assets, liabilities, and owner's equity is the basis for the entire accounting system.	on account
	owner's equity

Property and Financial Interest

The accounting process starts with the analysis of business transactions. A **business transaction** is any financial event that changes the resources of a firm. For example, purchases, sales, payments, and receipts of cash are all business transactions. The accountant analyzes each business transaction to decide what information to record and where to record it.

>>2-1. OBJECTIVE

Record in equation form the financial effects of a business transaction.

Beginning with Analysis

Let's analyze the transactions of Wells' Consulting Services, a firm that provides a wide range of accounting and consulting services. Carolyn Wells, CPA, has a master's degree in accounting. She is the sole proprietor of Wells' Consulting Services. Carlos Valdez, the office manager, has an associate's degree in business and has taken 12 semester hours of accounting. The firm is located in a large office complex.

Every month, Wells' Consulting Services bills clients for the accounting and consulting services provided that month. Customers can also pay in cash when the services are rendered.

STARTING A BUSINESS

Let's start from the beginning. Carolyn Wells obtained the funds to start the business by withdrawing $100,000 from her personal savings account. The first transaction of the new business was opening a checking account in the name of Wells' Consulting Services. The separate bank account helps Wells keep her financial interest in the business separate from her personal funds.

When a business transaction occurs, it is analyzed to identify how it affects the equation *property equals financial interest.* This equation reflects the fact that in a free enterprise system, all property is owned by someone. In this case, Wells owns the business because she supplied the property (cash).

Use these steps to analyze the effect of a business transaction:

1. Describe the financial event.
   - Identify the property.
   - Identify who owns the property.
   - Determine the amount of increase or decrease.

2. Make sure the equation is in balance.

Property	=	Financial Interest

BUSINESS TRANSACTION

Carolyn Wells withdrew $100,000 from personal savings and deposited it in a new checking account in the name of Wells' Consulting Services.

ANALYSIS

a. The business received $100,000 of *property* in the form of cash.

a. Wells had a $100,000 *financial interest* in the business.

Note that the equation *property equals financial interest* remains in balance. The total of one side of the equation must always equal the total of the other side.

Property		=	Financial Interest
	Cash	=	**Carolyn Wells, Capital**
(a) Invested cash	+$100,000		
(a) Increased equity			+$100,000
New balances	$100,000	=	$100,000

An owner's financial interest in the business is called **equity,** or **capital.** Carolyn Wells has $100,000 equity in Wells' Consulting Services.

PURCHASING EQUIPMENT FOR CASH

The first priority for office manager Carlos Valdez was to get the business ready for opening day on December 1.

BUSINESS TRANSACTION

Wells' Consulting Services issued a $5,000 check to purchase a computer and other equipment.

ANALYSIS

b. The firm purchased new property (equipment) for $5,000.

b. The firm paid out $5,000 in cash.

The equation remains in balance.

Property				=	Financial Interest
	Cash	+	Equipment	=	Carolyn Wells, Capital
Previous balances	$100,000			=	$100,000
(b) Purchased equipment		+	$5,000		
(b) Paid cash	−5,000				
New balances	$95,000	+	$5,000	=	$100,000

Notice that there is a change in the composition of the firm's property. Now the firm has cash and equipment. The equation shows that the total value of the property remains the same, $100,000. Carolyn Wells' financial interest, or equity, is also unchanged. Note that property (Cash and Equipment) is equal to financial interest (Carolyn Wells, Capital).

These activities are recorded for the business entity Wells' Consulting Services. Carolyn Wells' personal assets, such as her personal bank account, house, furniture, and automobile, are kept separate from the property of the firm. Nonbusiness property is not included in the accounting records of the business entity.

PURCHASING EQUIPMENT ON CREDIT

Valdez purchased additional office equipment. Office Plus, the store selling the equipment, allows Wells' Consulting Services 60 days to pay the bill. This arrangement is called buying **on account.** The business has a *charge account,* or *open-account credit,* with its suppliers. Amounts that a business must pay in the future are known as **accounts payable.** The companies or individuals to whom the amounts are owed are called *creditors.*

BUSINESS TRANSACTION

Wells' Consulting Services purchased office equipment on account from Office Plus for $6,000.

ANALYSIS

c.   The firm purchased new property (equipment) that cost $6,000.
c.   The firm owes $6,000 to Office Plus.
The equation remains in balance.

	Property			=	Financial Interest		
	Cash	+	Equipment	=	Accounts Payable	+	Carolyn Wells, Capital
Previous balances	$95,000	+	$ 5,000	=			$100,000
(c) Purchased equip.		+	6,000	=			
(c) Incurred debt					+$6,000		
New balances	$95,000	+	$11,000	=	$6,000	+	$100,000

Office Plus is willing to accept a claim against Wells' Consulting Services until the bill is paid. Now there are two different financial interests or claims against the firm's property—the creditor's claim (Accounts Payable) and the owner's claim (Carolyn Wells, Capital). Notice that the total property increases to $106,000. Cash is $95,000 and equipment is $11,000. Carolyn Wells, Capital stays the same; but the creditor's claim increases to $6,000. After this transaction is recorded, the left side of the equation still equals the right side.

When Ben Cohen and Jerry Greenfield founded Ben & Jerry's Homemade Ice Cream, Inc., in 1978, they invested $8,000 of their own funds and borrowed funds of $4,000. The equation *property equals financial interest* is expressed as

Property	=	Financial Interest
cash	=	creditors' claims
		+ owners' claims
$12,000	=	$ 4,000
		+8,000
		$12,000

PURCHASING SUPPLIES

Valdez purchased supplies so that Wells' Consulting Services could start operations. The company that sold the items requires cash payments from companies that have been in business less than six months.

BUSINESS TRANSACTION

Wells' Consulting Services issued a check for $1,500 to Office Delux, Inc., to purchase office supplies.

ANALYSIS
d. The firm purchased office supplies that cost $1,500.
d. The firm paid $1,500 in cash.
The equation remains in balance.

	Property					=	Financial Interest		
	Cash	+	Supplies	+	Equipment	=	Accounts Payable	+	Carolyn Wells, Capital
Previous balances	$95,000			+	$11,000	=	$6,000	+	$100,000
(d) Purchased supplies		+	$ 1,500						
(d) Paid cash	−$1,500								
New balances	$93,500	+	$1,500	+	$11,000	=	$6,000	+	$100,000

Notice that total property remains the same, even though the form of the property has changed. Also note that all of the property (left side) equals all of the financial interests (right side).

PAYING A CREDITOR

Valdez decided to reduce the firm's debt to Office Plus by $2,500.

BUSINESS TRANSACTION

Wells' Consulting Services issued a check for $2,500 to Office Plus.

ANALYSIS

e.   The firm paid $2,500 in cash.
e.   The claim of Office Plus against the firm decreased by $2,500.
The equation remains in balance.

	Property					=	Financial Interest		
	Cash	+	Supplies	+	Equipment	=	Accounts Payable	+	Carolyn Wells, Capital
Previous balances	$93,500	+	$1,500	+	$11,000	=	$6,000	+	$100,000
(e) Paid cash	−$2,500								
(e) Decreased debt							−$2,500		
New balances	$91,000	+	$1,500	+	$11,000	=	$3,500	+	$100,000

RENTING FACILITIES

In November, Valdez arranged to rent facilities for $4,000 per month, beginning in December. The landlord required that rent for the first two months—December and January—be paid in advance. The firm prepaid (paid in advance) the rent for two months. As a result, the firm obtained the right to occupy facilities for a two-month period. In accounting, this right is considered a form of property.

BUSINESS TRANSACTION

Wells' Consulting Services issued a check for $8,000 to pay for rent for the months of December and January.

ANALYSIS

f.   The firm prepaid the rent for the next two months in the amount of $8,000.
f.   The firm decreased its cash balance by $8,000.
The equation remains in balance.

	Property							=	Financial Interest		
	Cash	+	Supplies	+	Prepaid Rent	+	Equipment	=	Accounts Payable	+	Carolyn Wells, Capital
Previous balances	$91,000	+	$1,500			+	$11,000	=	$3,500	+	$100,000
(f) Paid cash	−$8,000										
(f) Prepaid rent					+$8,000						
New balances	$83,000	+	$1,500	+	$8,000	+	$11,000	=	$3,500	+	$100,000

Notice that when property values and financial interests increase or decrease, the total of the items on one side of the equation still equals the total on the other side.

Property		=	Financial Interest	
Cash	$ 83,000		Accounts Payable	$ 3,500
Supplies	1,500		Carolyn Wells, Capital	100,000
Prepaid Rent	8,000			
Equipment	11,000			
Total	$103,500		Total	$103,500

> The balance sheet is also called the *statement of financial position.* Caterpillar Inc. reported assets of $89.4 billion, liabilities of $71.8 billion, and owners' equity of $17.6 billion on its statement of financial position at December 31, 2012.

Assets, Liabilities, and Owner's Equity

Accountants use special accounting terms when they refer to property and financial interests. For example, they refer to the property that a business owns as **assets** and to the debts or obligations of the business as **liabilities.** The owner's financial interest is called **owner's equity.** (Sometimes owner's equity is called *proprietorship* or *net worth.* Owner's equity is the preferred term and is used throughout this book.) At regular intervals, Wells reviews the status of the firm's assets, liabilities, and owner's equity in a financial statement called a **balance sheet.** The balance sheet shows the firm's financial position on a given date. Figure 2.1 shows the firm's balance sheet on November 30, the day before the company opened for business.

The assets are listed on the left side of the balance sheet and the liabilities and owner's equity are on the right side. This arrangement is similar to the equation *property equals financial interest.* Property is shown on the left side of the equation, and financial interest appears on the right side.

The balance sheet in Figure 2.1 shows:

- the amount and types of property the business owns,
- the amount owed to creditors,
- the owner's interest.

This statement gives Carolyn Wells a complete picture of the financial position of her business on November 30.

>>2-2. OBJECTIVE
Define, identify, and understand the relationship between asset, liability, and owner's equity accounts.

FIGURE 2.1   Balance Sheet for Wells' Consulting Services

Wells' Consulting Services						
Balance Sheet						
November 30, 2016						
Assets			Liabilities			
Cash	83 000 00		Accounts Payable	3 500 00		
Supplies	1 500 00					
Prepaid Rent	8 000 00		Owner's Equity			
Equipment	11 000 00		Carolyn Wells, Capital	100 000 00		
Total Assets	103 500 00		Total Liabilities and Owner's Equity	103 500 00		

Section 1   Self Review

QUESTIONS

1. Describe a transaction that increases an asset and the owner's equity.

2. What does the term "accounts payable" mean?

3. What is a business transaction?

EXERCISES

4. John Ellis began a new business by depositing $150,000 in the business bank account. He wrote two checks from the business account: $24,000 for office furniture and $8,000 for office supplies. What is his financial interest in the company?

   a. $122,000

   b. $118,000

   c. $126,000

   d. $150,000

5. Teresa Wells purchased a computer for $2,950 on account for her business. What is the effect of this transaction?

   a. Equipment increase of $2,950 and accounts payable increase of $2,950.

   b. Equipment decrease of $2,950 and accounts payable increase of $2,950.

   c. Equipment increase of $2,950 and cash increase of $2,950.

   d. Cash decrease of $2,950 and owner's equity increase of $2,950.

ANALYSIS

6. China Import Co. has no liabilities. The asset and owner's equity balances are as follows. What is the balance of "Supplies"?

Cash	$ 50,000
Office Equipment	$ 30,000
Supplies	????
John Wong, Capital	$100,000

(Answers to Section 1 Self Review are on page 50.)

The Accounting Equation and Financial Statements

The word *balance* in the title "balance sheet" has a special meaning. It emphasizes that the total on the left side of the report must equal, or balance, the total on the right side.

The Fundamental Accounting Equation

In accounting terms, the firm's assets must equal the total of its liabilities and owner's equity. This equality can be expressed in equation form, as illustrated here. The amounts are for Wells' Consulting Services on November 30.

>> **2-3. OBJECTIVE**

Analyze the effects of business transactions on a firm's assets, liabilities, and owner's equity and record these effects in accounting equation form.

Assets	=	Liabilities	+	Owner's Equity
$103,500	=	$3,500	+	$100,000

The relationship between assets and liabilities plus owner's equity is called the **fundamental accounting equation.** The entire accounting process of analyzing, recording, and reporting business transactions is based on the fundamental accounting equation.

If any two parts of the equation are known, the third part can be determined. For example, consider the basic accounting equation for Wells' Consulting Services on November 30, with some information missing.

	Assets	=	Liabilities	+	Owner's Equity
1.	?	=	$3,500	+	$100,000
2.	$103,500	=	?	+	$100,000
3.	$103,000	=	$3,500	+	?

In the first case, we can solve for assets by adding liabilities to owner's equity ($3,500 + $100,000) to determine that assets are $103,500. In the second case, we can solve for liabilities by subtracting owner's equity from assets ($103,500 − $100,000) to determine that liabilities are $3,500. In the third case, we can solve for owner's equity by subtracting liabilities from assets ($103,500 − $3,500) to determine that owner's equity is $100,000.

important!

Revenues increase owner's equity.
Expenses decrease owner's equity.

EARNING REVENUE AND INCURRING EXPENSES

Wells' Consulting Services opened for business on December 1. Some of the other businesses in the office complex became the firm's first clients. Wells also used her contacts in the community to identify other clients. Providing services to clients started a stream of revenue for the business. **Revenue,** or *income,* is the inflow of money or other assets that results from the sales of goods or services or from the use of money or property. A sale on account does not increase money, but it does create a claim to money. When a sale occurs, the revenue increases assets and also increases owner's equity.

An **expense,** on the other hand, involves the outflow of money, the use of other assets, or the incurring of a liability. Expenses include the costs of any materials, labor, supplies, and services used to produce revenue. Expenses cause a decrease in owner's equity.

A firm's accounting records show increases and decreases in assets, liabilities, and owner's equity as well as details of all transactions involving revenue and expenses. Let's use the fundamental accounting equation to show how revenue and expenses affect the business.

SELLING SERVICES FOR CASH

During the month of December, Wells' Consulting Services earned a total of $36,000 in revenue from clients who paid cash for accounting and bookkeeping services. This involved several transactions throughout the month. The total effect of these transactions is analyzed below.

ANALYSIS

g. The firm received $36,000 in cash for services provided to clients.

g. Revenues increased by $36,000, which results in a $36,000 increase in owner's equity.

The fundamental accounting equation remains in balance.

	Assets							=	Liabilities	+	Owner's Equity		
	Cash	+	Supplies	+	Prepaid Rent	+	Equipment	=	Accounts Payable	+	Carolyn Wells, Capital	+	Revenue
Previous balances	$ 83,000	+	$1,500	+	$8,000	+	$11,000	=	$3,500	+	$100,000		
(g) Received cash	+$36,000												
(g) Increased owner's equity by earning revenue												+	$36,000
New balances	$119,000	+	$1,500	+	$8,000	+	$11,000	=	$3,500	+	$100,000	+	$ 36,000
			$139,500								$139,500		

Notice that revenue amounts are recorded in a separate column under owner's equity. Keeping revenue separate from the owner's equity will help the firm compute total revenue more easily when the financial statements are prepared.

SELLING SERVICES ON CREDIT

Wells' Consulting Services has some charge account clients. These clients are allowed 30 days to pay. Amounts owed by these clients are known as **accounts receivable.** This is a new form of asset for the firm—claims for future collection from customers. During December, Wells' Consulting Services earned $11,000 of revenue from charge account clients. The effect of these transactions is analyzed as follows:

ANALYSIS

h. The firm acquired a new asset, accounts receivable, of $11,000.

h. Revenues increased by $11,000, which results in an $11,000 increase in owner's equity.

The fundamental accounting equation remains in balance.

	Cash	+	Accts. Rec.	+	Supp.	+	Prepaid Rent	+	Equip.	=	Accts. Pay.	+	Carolyn Wells, Capital	+	Rev.
Previous balances	$119,000			+	$1,500	+	$8,000	+	$11,000	=	$3,500	+	$100,000	+	$36,000
(h) Received new asset—accts. rec.			+$11,000												
(h) Increased owner's equity by earning revenue														+	$11,000
New balances	$119,000	+	$11,000	+	$1,500	+	$8,000	+	$11,000	=	$3,500	+	$100,000	+	$47,000

$150,500　　　　　　　　　$150,500

COLLECTING RECEIVABLES

During December, Wells' Consulting Services received $6,000 on account from clients who owed money for services previously billed. The effect of these transactions is analyzed below.

ANALYSIS

i. The firm received $6,000 in cash.

i. Accounts receivable decreased by $6,000.

The fundamental accounting equation remains in balance.

	Cash	+	Accts. Rec.	+	Supp.	+	Prepaid Rent	+	Equip.	=	Accts. Pay.	+	Carolyn Wells, Capital	+	Rev.
Previous balances	$119,000	+	$11,000	+	$1,500	+	$8,000	+	$11,000	=	$3,500	+	$100,000	+	$47,000
(i) Received cash	+$6,000														
(i) Decreased accounts receivable			−$6,000												
New balances	$125,000	+	$5,000	+	$1,500	+	$8,000	+	$11,000	=	$3,500	+	$100,000	+	$47,000

$150,500　　　　　　　　　$150,500

In this type of transaction, one asset is changed for another asset (accounts receivable for cash). Notice that revenue is not increased when cash is collected from charge account clients. The revenue was recorded when the sale on account took place (see entry (**h**)). Notice that the fundamental accounting equation, *assets equal liabilities plus owner's equity,* stays in balance regardless of the changes arising from individual transactions.

PAYING EMPLOYEES' SALARIES

So far Wells has done very well. Her equity has increased by the revenues earned. However, running a business costs money, and these expenses reduce owner's equity.

During the first month of operations, Wells' Consulting Services hired an accounting clerk. The salaries for the new accounting clerk and the office manager are considered an expense to the firm.

BUSINESS TRANSACTION

In December, Wells' Consulting Services paid $8,000 in salaries for the accounting clerk and Carlos Valdez.

ANALYSIS

j. The firm decreased its cash balance by $8,000.

j. The firm paid salaries expense in the amount of $8,000, which decreased owner's equity.

The fundamental accounting equation remains in balance.

		Assets				=	Liab. +		Owner's Equity		
	Cash +	Accts. Rec. +	Supp. +	Prepaid Rent +	Equip. =		Accts. Pay. +	Carolyn Wells, Capital	+ Rev.	− Exp.	
Previous balances	$125,000 +	$5,000 +	$1,500 +	$8,000 +	$11,000 =		$3,500 +	$100,000	+ $47,000		
(j) Paid cash	−$8,000										
(j) Decreased owner's equity by incurring salaries exp.										+ $8,000	
New balances	$117,000 +	$5,000 +	$1,500 +	$8,000 +	$11,000 =		$3,500 +	$100,000	+ $47,000	− $8,000	
	$142,500						$142,500				

Notice that expenses are recorded in a separate column under owner's equity. The separate record of expenses is kept for the same reason that the separate record of revenue is kept—to analyze operations for the period.

PAYING UTILITIES EXPENSE

At the end of December, the firm received a $650 utilities bill.

BUSINESS TRANSACTION

Wells' Consulting Services issued a check for $650 to pay the utilities bill.

ANALYSIS

k. The firm decreased its cash balance by $650.

k. The firm paid utilities expense of $650, which decreased owner's equity.

The fundamental accounting equation remains in balance.

	Assets									=	Liab.	+		Owner's Equity			
	Cash	+	Accts. Rec.	+	Supp.	+	Prepaid Rent	+	Equip.	=	Accts. Pay.	+	C. Wells, Capital	+	Rev.	−	Exp.
Previous balances	$117,000	+	$5,000	+	$1,500	+	$8,000	+	$11,000	=	$3,500	+	$100,000	+	$47,000	−	$8,000
(k) Paid cash	−$650																
(k) Decreased owner's equity by utilities exp.																+	$650
New balances	$116,350	+	$5,000	+	$1,500	+	$8,000	+	$11,000	=	$3,500	+	$100,000	+	$47,000	−	$8,650

$141,850 $141,850

EFFECT OF OWNER'S WITHDRAWALS

On December 30, Wells withdrew $5,000 in cash for personal expenses. **Withdrawals** are funds taken from the business by the owner for personal use. Withdrawals are not a business expense but a decrease in the owner's equity.

BUSINESS TRANSACTION

Carolyn Wells wrote a check to withdraw $5,000 cash for personal use.

ANALYSIS
1. The firm decreased its cash balance by $5,000.
1. Owner's equity decreased by $5,000.
The fundamental accounting equation remains in balance.

	Assets									=	Liab.	+		Owner's Equity			
	Cash	+	Accts. Rec.	+	Supp.	+	Prepaid Rent	+	Equip.	=	Accts. Pay.	+	Carolyn Wells, Capital	+	Rev.	−	Exp.
Previous balances	$116,350	+	$5,000	+	$1,500	+	$8,000	+	$11,000	=	$3,500	+	$100,000	+	$47,000	−	$8,650
(l) Withdrew cash	−$5,000																
(l) Decreased owner's equity													−	$5,000			
New balances	$111,350	+	$5,000	+	$1,500	+	$8,000	+	$11,000	=	$3,500	+	$95,000	+	$47,000	−	$8,650

$136,850 $136,850

SUMMARY OF TRANSACTIONS

Figure 2.2 on page 34 summarizes the transactions of Wells' Consulting Services through December 31. Notice that after each transaction, the fundamental accounting equation is in balance. Test your understanding by describing the nature of each transaction. Then check your results by referring to the discussion of each transaction.

FIGURE 2.2   Transactions of Wells' Consulting Services Through December 31, 2016

	Cash	+	Accts. Rec.	+	Supp.	+	Prepaid Rent	+	Equip.	=	Accts. Pay.	+	C. Wells, Capital	+	Rev.	−	Exp.
(a)	+$100,000											+	$100,000				
Balances	100,000									=			100,000				
(b)	−5,000						+$5,000										
Balances	95,000						+5,000			=			100,000				
(c)								+	6,000	+	$6,000						
Balances	95,000							+	11,000	=	6,000	+	100,000				
(d)	−1,500		+$1,500														
Balances	93,500		+1,500					+	11,000	=	6,000	+	100,000				
(e)	−2,500										−2,500						
Balances	91,000		+1,500					+	11,000	=	3,500	+	100,000				
(f)	−8,000				+$8,000												
Balances	83,000		+1,500	+	8,000	+			11,000	=	3,500	+	100,000				
(g)	+36,000													+	$36,000		
Balances	119,000		+1,500	+	8,000	+			11,000	=	3,500	+	100,000	+	36,000		
(h)		+	$11,000											+	11,000		
Balances	119,000	+	11,000	+	1,500	+			8,000	+	11,000	=	3,500	+	100,000	+	47,000
(i)	+6,000	−	6,000														
Balances	125,000	+	5,000	+	1,500	+	8,000	+	11,000	=	3,500	+	100,000	+	47,000		
(j)	−8,000															+	$8,000
Balances	117,000	+	5,000	+	1,500	+	8,000	+	11,000	=	3,500	+	100,000	+	47,000	−	8,000
(k)	−650															+	650
Balances	116,350	+	5,000	+	1,500	+	8,000	+	11,000	=	3,500	+	100,000	+	47,000	−	8,650
(l)	−5,000											−	5,000				
Balances	$111,350	+	$5,000	+	$1,500	+	$8,000	+	$11,000	=	$3,500	+	$95,000	+	$47,000	−	$8,650

$136,850

$136,850

The Income Statement

>>2-4. OBJECTIVE

Prepare an income statement.

Financial Statements

Financial statements are reports that summarize a firm's financial affairs.

To be meaningful to owners, managers, and other interested parties, financial statements should provide information about revenue and expenses, assets and claims on the assets, and owner's equity.

The **income statement** shows the results of business operations for a specific period of time such as a month, a quarter, or a year. The income statement shows the revenue earned and the expenses of doing business. (The income statement is sometimes called a *profit and loss statement* or a *statement of income and expenses.* The most common term, income statement, is used throughout this text.) Figure 2.3 shows the income statement for Wells' Consulting Services for its first month of operation.

The income statement shows the difference between revenue from services provided or goods sold and the amount spent to operate the business. **Net income** results when revenue is greater than the expenses for the period. When expenses are greater than revenue, the result is a **net loss.** In the rare case when revenue and expenses are equal, the firm is said to **break even.** The income statement in Figure 2.3 shows a net income; revenue is greater than expenses.

The three-line heading of the income statement shows *who*, *what,* and *when.*

FIGURE 2.3

Income Statement for Wells' Consulting Services

Wells' Consulting Services						
Income Statement						
Month Ended December 31, 2016						
Revenue						
Fees Income				4 7 0 0 0	00	
Expenses						
Salaries Expense	8 0 0 0	00				
Utilities Expense	6 5 0	00				
Total Expenses				8 6 5 0	00	
Net Income				3 8 3 5 0	00	

- Who—the business name appears on the first line.
- What—the report title appears on the second line.
- When—the period covered appears on the third line.

The third line of the income statement heading in Figure 2.3 indicates that the report covers operations for the "Month Ended December 31, 2016." Review how other time periods are reported on the third line of the income statement heading.

Period Covered	Third Line of Heading
Jan., Feb., Mar.	Three-Month Period Ended March 31, 2016
Jan. to Dec.	Year Ended December 31, 2016
July 1 to June 30	Fiscal Year Ended June 30, 2016

Note the use of single and double rules in amount columns. A single line is used to show that the amounts above it are being added or subtracted. Double lines are used under the final amount in a column or section of a report to show that the amount is complete. Nothing is added to or subtracted from an amount with a double line.

> Some companies refer to the income statement as the *statement of operations*. American Eagle Outfitters, Inc., reported $3.16 billion in sales on consolidated statements of operations for the fiscal year ended January 2012.

The income statement for Wells' Consulting Services does not have dollar signs because it was prepared on accounting paper with ruled columns. However, dollar signs are used on income statements that are prepared on plain paper, that is, not on a ruled form.

The Statement of Owner's Equity and the Balance Sheet

>>2-5. OBJECTIVE

Prepare a statement of owner's equity and a balance sheet.

The **statement of owner's equity** reports the changes that occurred in the owner's financial interest during the reporting period. This statement is prepared before the balance sheet so that the amount of the ending capital balance is available for presentation on the balance sheet. Figure 2.4 on page 36 shows the statement of owner's equity for Wells' Consulting Services. Note that the statement of owner's equity has a three-line heading: *who, what,* and *when.*

- The first line of the statement of owner's equity is the capital balance at the beginning of the period.
- Net income is an increase to owner's equity; net loss is a decrease to owner's equity.
- Withdrawals by the owner are a decrease to owner's equity.

FIGURE 2.4

Statement of Owner's Equity for Wells' Consulting Services

Wells' Consulting Services							
Statement of Owner's Equity							
Month Ended December 31, 2016							
Carolyn Wells, Capital, December 1, 2016					1 0 0 0 0 0	00
Net Income for December	3 8 3 5 0	00				
Less Withdrawals for December	5 0 0 0	00				
Increase in Capital					3 3 3 5 0	00
Carolyn Wells, Capital, December 31, 2016					1 3 3 3 5 0	00

- Additional investments by the owners are an increase to owner's equity.
- The total of changes in equity is reported on the line "Increase in Capital" (or "Decrease in Capital").
- The last line of the statement of owner's equity is the capital balance at the end of the period.

If Carolyn Wells had made any additional investments during December, this would appear as a separate line on Figure 2.4. Additional investments can be cash or other assets such as equipment. If an investment is made in a form other than cash, the investment is recorded at its fair market value. **Fair market value** is the current worth of an asset or the price the asset would bring if sold on the open market.

The ending balances in the asset and liability accounts are used to prepare the balance sheet.

	Assets							=	Liab.	+	Owner's Equity					
	Cash	+	Accts. Rec.	+	Supp.	+	Prepaid Rent	+	Equip.	=	Accts. Pay.	+	C. Wells, Capital	+	Rev.	−	Exp.
New balances	$111,350	+	$5,000	+	$1,500	+	$8,000	+	$11,000	=	$3,500	+	$95,000	+	$47,000	−	$8,650
	$136,850										$136,850					

important!

Financial Statements

The balance sheet is a snapshot of the firm's financial position on a specific date. The income statement, like a movie or video, shows the results of business operations over a period of time.

The ending capital balance from the statement of owner's equity is also used to prepare the balance sheet. Figure 2.5 shows the balance sheet for Wells' Consulting Services on December 31, 2016.

The balance sheet shows:

- Assets—the types and amounts of property that the business owns,
- Liabilities—the amounts owed to creditors,
- Owner's Equity—the owner's equity on the reporting date.

In preparing a balance sheet, remember the following:

- The three-line heading gives the firm's name (who), the title of the report (what), and the date of the report (when).
- Balance sheets prepared using the account form (as in Figure 2.5) show total assets on the same horizontal line as the total liabilities and owner's equity.
- Dollar signs are omitted when financial statements are prepared on paper with ruled columns. Statements that are prepared on plain paper, not ruled forms, show dollar signs with the first amount in each column and with each total.
- A single line shows that the amounts above it are being added or subtracted. Double lines indicate that the amount is the final amount in a column or section of a report.

Figure 2.6 shows the connections among the financial statements. Financial statements are prepared in a specific order:

- income statement
- statement of owner's equity
- balance sheet

FIGURE 2.5   Balance Sheet for Wells' Consulting Services

Wells' Consulting Services
Balance Sheet
December 31, 2016

Assets			Liabilities		
Cash	1 1 1 3 5 0	00	Accounts Payable	3 5 0 0	00
Accounts Receivable	5 0 0 0	00			
Supplies	1 5 0 0	00			
Prepaid Rent	8 0 0 0	00	Owner's Equity		
Equipment	1 1 0 0 0	00	Carolyn Wells, Capital	1 3 3 3 5 0	00
Total Assets	1 3 6 8 5 0	00	Total Liabilities and Owner's Equity	1 3 6 8 5 0	00

Step 1: Prepare the Income Statement

Wells' Consulting Services
Income Statement
Month Ended December 31, 2016

Revenue					
Fees Income			4 7 0 0 0	00	
Expenses					
Salaries Expense	8 0 0 0	00			
Utilities Expense	6 5 0	00			
Total Expenses			8 6 5 0	00	
Net Income			3 8 3 5 0	00	

Step 2: Prepare the Statement of Owner's Equity

Wells' Consulting Services
Statement of Owner's Equity
Month Ended December 31, 2016

Carolyn Wells, Capital, December 1, 2016			1 0 0 0 0 0	00	
Net Income for December	3 8 3 5 0	00			
Less Withdrawals for December	5 0 0 0	00			
Increase in Capital			3 3 3 5 0	00	
Carolyn Wells, Capital, December 31, 2016			1 3 3 3 5 0	00	

Step 3: Prepare the Balance Sheet

Wells' Consulting Services
Balance Sheet
December 31, 2016

Assets			Liabilities		
Cash	1 1 1 3 5 0	00	Accounts Payable	3 5 0 0	00
Accounts Receivable	5 0 0 0	00			
Supplies	1 5 0 0	00			
Prepaid Rent	8 0 0 0	00	Owner's Equity		
Equipment	1 1 0 0 0	00	Carolyn Wells, Capital	1 3 3 3 5 0	00
Total Assets	1 3 6 8 5 0	00	Total Liabilities and Owner's Equity	1 3 6 8 5 0	00

FIGURE 2.6

Process for Preparing Financial Statements

Net income (or loss) is transferred to the statement of owner's equity.

The ending capital balance is transferred to the balance sheet.

MANAGERIAL IMPLICATIONS   <<

ACCOUNTING SYSTEMS

- Sound financial records and statements are necessary so that businesspeople can make good decisions.
- Financial statements show:
  - the amount of profit or loss,
  - the assets on hand,
  - the amount owed to creditors,
  - the amount of owner's equity.

- Well-run and efficiently managed businesses have good accounting systems that provide timely and useful information.
- Transactions involving revenue and expenses are recorded separately from owner's equity in order to analyze operations for the period.

THINKING CRITICALLY

If you were buying a business, what would you look for in the company's financial statements?

Net income from the income statement is used to prepare the statement of owner's equity. The ending capital balance from the statement of owner's equity is used to prepare the balance sheet.

The Importance of Financial Statements

Preparing financial statements is one of the accountant's most important jobs. Each day millions of business decisions are made based on the information in financial statements.

Business managers and owners use the balance sheet and the income statement to control current operations and plan for the future. Creditors, prospective investors, governmental agencies, and others are interested in the profits of the business and in the asset and equity structure.

Section 2   Self Review

QUESTIONS

1. If an owner gives personal tools to the business, how is the transaction recorded?

2. What information is included in the financial statement headings?

3. What are withdrawals and how do they affect the basic accounting equation?

EXERCISES

4. Design Interiors has assets of $180,000 and liabilities of $70,000. What is the owner's equity?

   a. $50,000
   b. $30,000
   c. $160,000
   d. $110,000

5. Haden Hardware had revenues of $110,000 and expenses of $52,000. How does this affect owner's equity?

ANALYSIS

6. What information is contained in the income statement?

   a. assets, liabilities, and owner's equity on a specific date
   b. assets, liabilities, and owner's equity for a period of time
   c. revenue and expenses on a specific date
   d. revenues and expenses for a period of time

(Answers to Section 2 Self Review are on page 50.)

REVIEW   Chapter Summary

Accounting begins with the analysis of business transactions. Each transaction changes the financial position of a business. In this chapter, you have learned how to analyze business transactions and how they affect assets, liabilities, and owner's equity. After transactions are analyzed and recorded, financial statements reflect the summarized changes to and results of business operations.

Learning Objectives

2-1 **Record in equation form the financial effects of a business transaction.**

The equation *property equals financial interest* reflects the fact that in a free enterprise system all property is owned by someone. This equation remains in balance after each business transaction.

2-2 **Define, identify, and understand the relationship between asset, liability, and owner's equity accounts.**

The term *assets* refers to property. The terms *liabilities* and *owner's equity* refer to financial interest. The relationship between assets, liabilities, and owner's equity is shown in equation form.

Assets   = Liabilities + Owner's Equity

Owner's Equity = Assets   − Liabilities

Liabilities   = Assets   − Owner's Equity

2-3 **Analyze the effects of business transactions on a firm's assets, liabilities, and owner's equity and record these effects in accounting equation form.**

1. Describe the financial event.
   - Identify the property.
   - Identify who owns the property.
   - Determine the amount of the increase or decrease.
2. Make sure the equation is in balance.

2-4 **Prepare an income statement.**

The income statement summarizes changes in owner's equity that result from revenue and expenses. The difference between revenue and expenses is the net income or net loss of the business for the period.

An income statement has a three-line heading:
- who
- what
- when

For the income statement, "when" refers to a period of time.

2-5 **Prepare a statement of owner's equity and a balance sheet.**

Changes in owner's equity for the period are summarized on the statement of owner's equity.
- Net income increases owner's equity.
- Added investments increase owner's equity.
- A net loss for the period decreases owner's equity.
- Withdrawals by the owner decrease owner's equity.

A statement of owner's equity has a three-line heading:
- who
- what
- when

For the statement of owner's equity, "when" refers to a period of time.

The balance sheet shows the assets, liabilities, and owner's equity on a given date.

A balance sheet has a three-line heading:
- who
- what
- when

For the balance sheet, "when" refers to a single date.

The financial statements are prepared in the following order.
1. Income Statement
2. Statement of Owner's Equity
3. Balance Sheet

2-6 **Define the accounting terms new to this chapter.**

Glossary

Accounts payable (p. 24) Amounts a business must pay in the future

Accounts receivable (p. 30) Claims for future collection from customers

Assets (p. 27) Property owned by a business

Balance sheet (p. 27) A formal report of a business's financial condition on a certain date; reports the assets, liabilities, and owner's equity of the business

Break even (p. 34) A point at which revenue equals expenses

Business transaction (p. 22) A financial event that changes the resources of a firm

Capital (p. 23) Financial investment in a business; equity

Equity (p. 23) An owner's financial interest in a business

Expense (p. 30) An outflow of cash, use of other assets, or incurring of a liability

Fair market value (p. 36) The current worth of an asset or the price the asset would bring if sold on the open market

Fundamental accounting equation (p. 29) The relationship between assets and liabilities plus owner's equity

Income statement (p. 34) A formal report of business operations covering a specific period of time; also called a profit and loss statement or a statement of income and expenses

Liabilities (p. 27) Debts or obligations of a business

Net income (p. 34) The result of an excess of revenue over expenses

Net loss (p. 34) The result of an excess of expenses over revenue

On account (p. 24) An arrangement to allow payment at a later date; also called a charge account or open-account credit

Owner's equity (p. 27) The financial interest of the owner of a business; also called proprietorship or net worth

Revenue (p. 30) An inflow of money or other assets that results from the sales of goods or services or from the use of money or property; also called income

Statement of owner's equity (p. 35) A formal report of changes that occurred in the owner's financial interest during a reporting period

Withdrawals (p. 33) Funds taken from the business by the owner for personal use

Comprehensive **Self Review**

1. In what order are the financial statements prepared? Why?
2. What effect do revenue and expenses have on owner's equity?
3. What is the difference between buying for cash and buying on account?
4. If one side of the fundamental accounting equation is decreased, what will happen to the other side? Why?
5. Describe a transaction that will cause Accounts Payable and Cash to decrease by $1,200.

(Answers to Comprehensive Self Review are on page 51.)

Discussion Questions

1. What is the fundamental accounting equation?
2. What are assets, liabilities, and owner's equity?
3. What information does the balance sheet contain?

4. What information does the income statement contain?

5. What information does the statement of owner's equity contain?

6. What information is shown in the heading of a financial statement?

7. Why does the third line of the headings differ on the balance sheet and the income statement?

8. What is revenue?

9. What are expenses?

10. How is net income determined?

11. How does net income affect owner's equity?

12. Describe the effects of each of the following business transactions on assets, liabilities, and owner's equity.

   a. Bought equipment on credit.

   b. Paid salaries to employees.

   c. Sold services for cash.

   d. Paid cash to a creditor.

   e. Bought furniture for cash.

   f. Sold services on credit.

APPLICATIONS

Exercises

Determining accounting equation amounts.

◀ **Exercise 2.1**
Objectives 2-1, 2-2

Just before Walker Laboratories opened for business, James Walker, the owner, had the following assets and liabilities. Determine the totals that would appear in the firm's fundamental accounting equation (Assets = Liabilities + Owner's Equity).

Cash	$41,500
Laboratory Equipment	76,600
Laboratory Supplies	7,800
Loan Payable	16,100
Accounts Payable	10,125

Completing the accounting equation.

◀ **Exercise 2.2**
Objectives 2-1, 2-2

The fundamental accounting equation for several businesses follows. Supply the missing amounts.

	Assets	=	Liabilities	+	Owner's Equity
1.	$27,800	=	$5,560	+	$?
2.	$24,200	=	$5,180	+	$?
3.	$16,075	=	$?	+	$10,400
4.	$?	=	$4,400	+	$32,325
5.	$34,000	=	$?	+	$25,125

Exercise 2.3

Objectives 2-1,
2-2, 2-3

▶ **Determining the effects of transactions on the accounting equation.**

Indicate the impact of each of the transactions below on the fundamental accounting equation (Assets = Liabilities + Owner's Equity) by placing a "+" to indicate an increase and a "−" to indicate a decrease. The first transaction is entered as an example.

	Assets	=	Liabilities	+	Owner's Equity
Transaction 1	+				+

TRANSACTIONS

1. Owner invested $90,000 in the business.
2. Purchased $26,700 supplies on account.
3. Purchased equipment for $21,000 cash.
4. Paid $6,000 for rent (in advance).
5. Performed services for $7,800 cash.
6. Paid $2,160 for utilities.
7. Performed services for $10,500 on account.
8. Received $6,600 from charge account customers.
9. Paid salaries of $4,500 to employees.
10. Paid $6,000 to a creditor on account.

Exercise 2.4

Objectives 2-1,
2-2, 2-3

▶ **Determining balance sheet amounts.**

The following financial data are for the dental practice of Dr. David Malone when he began operations in July. Determine the amounts that would appear in Dr. Malone's balance sheet.

1. Owes $19,000 to the Davis Equipment Company.
2. Has cash balance of $13,500.
3. Has dental supplies of $3,650.
4. Owes $4,180 to 21st Century Furniture Supply.
5. Has dental equipment of $26,550.
6. Has office furniture of $8,000.

Exercise 2.5

Objectives 2-1,
2-2, 2-3

▶ **Determining the effects of transactions on the accounting equation.**

EZ Copy had the transactions listed below during the month of June. Show how each transaction would be recorded in the accounting equation. Compute the totals at the end of the month. The headings to be used in the equation follow.

Assets			=	Liabilities	+	Owner's Equity			
Cash	+	Accounts Receivable	+	Equipment	=	Accounts Payable	+	John Amos, Capital	+	Revenue	−	Expenses

TRANSACTIONS

1. John Amos started the business with a cash investment of $60,000.
2. Purchased equipment for $22,000 on credit.
3. Performed services for $3,100 in cash.

4. Purchased additional equipment for $4,600 in cash.
5. Performed services for $5,050 on credit.
6. Paid salaries of $4,450 to employees.
7. Received $3,200 cash from charge account customers.
8. Paid $13,000 to a creditor on account.

Computing net income or net loss.

◀ **Exercise 2.6**
Objective 2-4

Computer Maintenance and Repair Shop had the following revenue and expenses during the month ended July 31. Did the firm earn a net income or incur a net loss for the period? What was the amount?

Fees for computer repairs	$44,600
Advertising expense	6,300
Salaries expense	19,100
Telephone expense	1,150
Fees for printer repairs	6,550
Utilities expense	1,600

Identifying transactions.

◀ **Exercise 2.7**
Objectives 2-1, 2-2, 2-3

The following equation shows the effects of a number of transactions that took place at Beck Auto Repair Company during the month of July. Describe each transaction.

	Assets			=	Liabilities	+	Owner's Equity				
	Cash +	Accounts Receivable +	Equipment =		Accounts Payable +		Peter Beck, Capital +		Revenue	−	Expenses
Bal.	$80,000 +	$6,000 +	$64,000 =		$38,000 +		$112,000 +		0	−	0
1.	+10,000								+$10,000		
2.	−7,600		+7,600								
3.	−3,800				−3,800						
4.	−6,700										+$6,700
5.	+1,500	− 1,500									
6.		+12,000							+12,000		
7.	−4,100										+4,100

Preparing an income statement.

◀ **Exercise 2.8**
Objective 2-4

At the beginning of September, Alexandria Perez started Perez Investment Services, a firm that offers advice about investing and managing money. On September 30, the accounting records of the business showed the following information. Prepare an income statement for the month of September 2016.

Cash	$33,100	Fees Income	$77,900
Accounts Receivable	4,000	Advertising Expense	6,500
Office Supplies	3,400	Salaries Expense	16,000
Office Equipment	37,500	Telephone Expense	800
Accounts Payable	5,700	Withdrawals	9,000
Alexandria Perez, Capital, September 1, 2016	26,700		

Computing net income or net loss.

◀ **Exercise 2.9**
Objective 2-4

On December 1, Kate Holmes opened a speech and hearing clinic. During December, her firm had the following transactions involving revenue and expenses. Did the firm earn a net income or incur a net loss for the period? What was the amount?

Paid $3,100 for advertising.

Provided services for $2,800 in cash.

Paid $800 for telephone service.

Paid salaries of $2,600 to employees.

Provided services for $3,000 on credit.

Paid $450 for office cleaning service.

Exercise 2.10
Objective 2-5

▶ ## Preparing a statement of owner's equity and a balance sheet.

Using the information provided in Exercise 2.8, prepare a statement of owner's equity for the month of September and a balance sheet for Perez Investment Services as of September 30, 2016.

PROBLEMS

Problem Set A

Problem 2.1A
Objectives 2-1, 2-2, 2-3

▶ ## Analyzing the effects of transactions on the accounting equation.

On July 1, Guy Fernandez established Fernandez Home Appraisal Services, a firm that provides expert residential appraisals and represents clients in home appraisal hearings.

INSTRUCTIONS

Analyze the following transactions. Record in equation form the changes that occur in assets, liabilities, and owner's equity. (Use plus, minus, and equals signs.)

TRANSACTIONS

1. The owner invested $97,000 in cash to begin the business.
2. Paid $19,750 in cash for the purchase of equipment.
3. Purchased additional equipment for $14,400 on credit.
4. Paid $11,800 in cash to creditors.
5. The owner made an additional investment of $30,000 in cash.
6. Performed services for $8,200 in cash.
7. Performed services for $6,300 on account.
8. Paid $4,000 for rent expense.
9. Received $3,500 in cash from credit clients.
10. Paid $6,460 in cash for office supplies.
11. The owner withdrew $9,000 in cash for personal expenses.

Analyze: What is the ending balance of cash after all transactions have been recorded?

Problem 2.2A
Objectives 2-1, 2-2, 2-3

▶ ## Analyzing the effects of transactions on the accounting equation.

Maurice Dickey is a painting contractor who specializes in painting commercial buildings. At the beginning of June, his firm's financial records showed the following assets, liabilities, and owner's equity.

Cash	$61,000	Accounts Payable	$11,200
Accounts Receivable	16,600	Maurice Dickey, Capital	91,500
Office Furniture	35,800	Revenue	58,600
Auto	23,500	Expenses	24,400

INSTRUCTIONS

Set up an accounting equation using the balances given above. Record the effects of the following transactions in the equation. (Use plus, minus, and equals signs.) Record new balances after each transaction has been entered. Prove the equality of the two sides of the final equation on a separate sheet of paper.

TRANSACTIONS

1. Performed services for $6,680 on credit.
2. Paid $1,700 in cash for new office chairs.
3. Received $11,200 in cash from credit clients.
4. Paid $880 in cash for telephone service.
5. Sent a check for $4,500 in partial payment of the amount due creditors.
6. Paid salaries of $9,700 in cash.
7. Sent a check for $1,120 to pay electric bill.
8. Performed services for $10,500 in cash.
9. Paid $2,350 in cash for auto repairs.
10. Performed services for $12,500 on account.

Analyze: What is the amount of total assets after all transactions have been recorded?

Preparing a balance sheet.

◀ **Problem 2.3A**
Objective 2-5

Brown Equipment Repair Service is owned by James Brown.

INSTRUCTIONS

Use the following figures to prepare a balance sheet dated February 29, 2016. (You will need to compute the owner's equity.)

Cash	$34,300	Equipment	$78,000
Supplies	6,380	Accounts Payable	24,000
Accounts Receivable	13,200		

Analyze: What is the net worth, or owner's equity, at February 29, 2016 for Brown Equipment Repair Service?

Preparing an income statement, a statement of owner's equity, and a balance sheet.

◀ **Problem 2.4A**
Objectives 2-4, 2-5

The following equation shows the transactions of Cotton Cleaning Service during May. The business is owned by Taylor Cotton.

	Assets				=	Liab. +	Owner's Equity		
		Accts.				Accts.	T. Cotton,		
	Cash +	Rec. +	Supp. +	Equip.	=	Pay. +	Capital +	Rev. −	Exp.
Balances, May 1	15,000 +	3,000 +	5,800 +	33,800	=	7,000 +	50,600 +	0 −	0
Paid for utilities	−980								+980
New balances	14,020 +	3,000 +	5,800 +	33,800	=	7,000 +	50,600 +	0 −	980
Sold services for cash	+4,980							+4,980	
New balances	19,000 +	3,000 +	5,800 +	33,800	=	7,000 +	50,600 +	4,980 −	980
Paid a creditor	−2,100					−2,100			
New balances	16,900 +	3,000 +	5,800 +	33,800	=	4,900 +	50,600 +	4,980 −	980
Sold services on credit		+2,900						+2,900	
New balances	16,900 +	5,900 +	5,800 +	33,800	=	4,900 +	50,600 +	7,880 −	980
Paid salaries	−8,900								+8,900
New balances	8,000 +	5,900 +	5,800 +	33,800	=	4,900 +	50,600 +	7,880 −	9,880
Paid telephone bill	−314								+314
New balances	7,686 +	5,900 +	5,800 +	33,800	=	4,900 +	50,600 +	7,880 −	10,194
Withdrew cash for personal expenses	−3,000						−3,000		
New balances	4,686 +	5,900 +	5,800 +	33,800	=	4,900 +	47,600 +	7,880 −	10,194

INSTRUCTIONS

Analyze each transaction carefully. Prepare an income statement and a statement of owner's equity for the month. Prepare a balance sheet for May 31, 2016. List the expenses in detail on the income statement.

Analyze: In order to complete the balance sheet, which amount was transferred from the statement of owner's equity?

Problem Set B

Problem 2.1B

Objectives 2-1, 2-2, 2-3

▶ ## Analyzing the effects of transactions on the accounting equation.

On September 1, Rosa Escobedo opened Self Confidence Tutoring Service.

INSTRUCTIONS

Analyze the following transactions. Use the fundamental accounting equation form to record the changes in property, claims of creditors, and owner's equity. (Use plus, minus, and equals signs.)

TRANSACTIONS

1. The owner invested $72,000 in cash to begin the business.
2. Purchased equipment for $32,000 in cash.
3. Purchased $12,000 of additional equipment on credit.
4. Paid $6,000 in cash to creditors.
5. The owner made an additional investment of $12,000 in cash.
6. Performed services for $8,400 in cash.
7. Performed services for $7,300 on account.
8. Paid $5,200 for rent expense.
9. Received $5,000 in cash from credit clients.
10. Paid $6,300 in cash for office supplies.
11. The owner withdrew $10,000 in cash for personal expenses.

Analyze: Which transactions increased the company's debt? By what amount?

Problem 2.2B

Objectives 2-1, 2-2, 2-3

▶ ## Analyzing the effects of transactions on the accounting equation.

Sherrye Cravens owns Cravens's Consulting Service. At the beginning of September, her firm's financial records showed the following assets, liabilities, and owner's equity.

Cash	$38,000	Accounts Payable	$10,000
Accounts Receivable	12,000	Sherrye Cravens, Capital	49,800
Supplies	12,800	Revenue	52,000
Office Furniture	24,000	Expenses	25,000

INSTRUCTIONS

Set up an equation using the balances given above. Record the effects of the following transactions in the equation. (Use plus, minus, and equals signs.) Record new balances after each transaction has been entered. Prove the equality of the two sides of the final equation on a separate sheet of paper.

TRANSACTIONS

1. Performed services for $8,000 on credit.
2. Paid $2,880 in cash for utilities.
3. Performed services for $10,000 in cash.
4. Paid $1,600 in cash for office cleaning service.
5. Sent a check for $4,800 to a creditor.
6. Paid $1,920 in cash for the telephone bill.

7. Issued checks for $14,000 to pay salaries.

8. Performed services for $11,200 in cash.

9. Purchased additional supplies for $2,000 on credit.

10. Received $6,000 in cash from credit clients.

Analyze: What is the ending balance for owner's equity after all transactions have been recorded?

Preparing a balance sheet.

◀ **Problem 2.3B**
Objective 2-5

Douglas Smith is opening a tax preparation service on December 1, which will be called Smith's Tax Service. Douglas plans to open the business by depositing $50,000 cash into a business checking account. The following assets will also be owned by the business: furniture (fair market value of $10,000) and computers and printers (fair market value of $12,000). There are no outstanding debts of the business as it is formed.

INSTRUCTIONS

Prepare a balance sheet for December 1, 2016, for Smith's Tax Service by entering the correct balances in the appropriate accounts. (You will need to use the accounting equation to compute owner's equity.)

Analyze: If Smith's Tax Service had an outstanding debt of $16,000 when the business was formed, what amount should be reported on the balance sheet for owner's equity?

Preparing an income statement, a statement of owner's equity, and a balance sheet.

◀ **Problem 2.4B**
Objectives 2-4, 2-5

The equation below shows the transactions of Kathryn Proctor, Attorney and Counselor of Law, during August. This law firm is owned by Kathryn Proctor.

	Assets				=	Liab. +		Owner's Equity		
	Cash +	Accts. Rec. +	Supp. +	Equip. =		Accts. Pay. +	K. Proctor, Capital +	Rev.	−	Exp.
Balances, Aug. 1	7,200	1,800 +	5,400 +	10,000 =		1,200 +	23,200 +	0	−	0
Paid for utilities	−600									+600
New balances	6,600 +	1,800 +	5,400 +	10,000 =		1,200 +	23,200 +	0	−	600
Performed services for cash	+6,000							+6,000		
New balances	12,600 +	1,800 +	5,400 +	10,000 =		1,200 +	23,200 +	6,000	−	600
Paid a creditor	−600					−600				
New balances	12,000 +	1,800 +	5,400 +	10,000 =		600 +	23,200 +	6,000	−	600
Performed services on credit		+4,800						+4,800		
New balances	12,000 +	6,600 +	5,400 +	10,000 =		600 +	23,200 +	10,800	−	600
Paid salaries	−5,400									+5,400
New balances	6,600 +	6,600 +	5,400 +	10,000 =		600 +	23,200 +	10,800	−	6,000
Paid telephone bill	−600									+600
New balances	6,000 +	6,600 +	5,400 +	10,000 =		600 +	23,200 +	10,800	−	6,600
Withdrew cash for personal expenses	−1,200						−1,200			
New balances	4,800 +	6,600 +	5,400 +	10,000 =		600 +	22,000 +	10,800	−	6,600

INSTRUCTIONS

Analyze each transaction carefully. Prepare an income statement and a statement of owner's equity for the month. Prepare a balance sheet for August 31, 2016. List the expenses in detail on the income statement.

Analyze: In order to complete the statement of owner's equity, which amount was transferred from the income statement?

Critical Thinking Problem 2.1

Financial Statements

The following account balances are for Carl Nicholson, Certified Public Accountant, as of April 30, 2016.

Cash	$30,000
Accounts Receivable	12,000
Maintenance Expense	4,600
Advertising Expense	3,890
Fees Earned	26,800
Carl Nicholson, Capital, April 1	?
Salaries Expense	13,000
Machinery	21,000
Accounts Payable	13,200
Carl Nicholson, Drawing	6,800

INSTRUCTIONS

Using the accounting equation form, determine the balance for Carl Nicholson, Capital, April 1, 2016. Prepare an income statement for the month of April, a statement of owner's equity, and a balance sheet as of April 30, 2016. List the expenses on the income statement in alphabetical order.

Analyze: What net change in owner's equity occurred during the month of April?

Critical Thinking Problem 2.2

Accounting for a New Company

James Mitchell opened a gym and fitness studio called Body Builders Fitness Center at the beginning of November of the current year. It is now the end of December, and James is trying to determine whether he made a profit during his first two months of operations. You offer to help him and ask to see his accounting records. He shows you a shoe box and tells you that every piece of paper pertaining to the business is in that box.

As you go through the material in the shoe box, you discover the following:

a. A receipt from Clayton Properties for $8,000 for November's rent on the exercise studio.

b. Bank deposit slips totaling $7,360 for money collected from customers who attended exercise classes.

c. An invoice for $50,000 for exercise equipment. The first payment is not due until December 31.

d. A bill for $2,100 from the maintenance service that cleans the studio. James has not yet paid this bill.

e. A December 19 parking ticket for $200. James says he was in a hurry that morning to get to the Fitness Center on time and forgot to put money in the parking meter.

f. A handwritten list of customers and fees for the classes they have taken. As the customers attend the classes, James writes their names and the amount of each customer's fee on the list. As customers pay, James crosses their names off the list. Fees not crossed off the list amount to $2,400.

g. A credit card receipt for $800 for printing flyers advertising the grand opening of the studio. For convenience, James used his personal credit card.

h. A credit card receipt for $800 for four warm-up suits James bought to wear at the studio. He also put this purchase on his personal credit card.

Use the concepts you have learned in this chapter to help James.

1. Prepare an income statement for the first two months of operation of Body Builders Fitness Center.

2. How would you evaluate the results of the first two months of operation?

3. What advice would you give James concerning his system of accounting?

BUSINESS CONNECTIONS

Interpreting Results

1. After examining financial data for a monthly period, the owner of a small business expressed surprise that the firm's cash balance had decreased during the month even though there was substantial net income. Do you think this owner is right to expect cash to increase because of a substantial net income? Why or why not?

2. Is it reasonable to expect that all new businesses will have a net income from the first month's operations? From the first year's operations?

3. Why should managers be concerned with changes in the amount of creditors' claims against the business?

4. How does an accounting system help managers control operations and make sound decisions?

Managerial | FOCUS

To Record or Not to Record

You are Julia, a new Accounts Receivable Clerk for Nixon Paper and Office Supply. Toward the end of the month, Carol Reed, a very personable sales associate, tells you that the previous A/R clerk always recorded a Sales Invoice when she got a verbal agreement from a customer to buy paper or office supplies. She has a verbal order from her favorite customer for $10,000 of paper and wants you to create a Sales Invoice today. You know that in order to create a Sales Invoice you need a purchase order from the customer. You also know that Ms. Reed receives a monthly bonus based on the monthly sales. If her sales are above $20,000, she gets a 10 percent bonus. Would you agree to record the sales of products before receiving the purchase order from the customer? What effect would it have on the customer, on the Sales Associate, on the company, and on the job?

Ethical DILEMMA

Income Statement

Review the following excerpt from the 2012 consolidated statement of income for Southwest Airlines Co. Answer the questions that follow.

Financial Statement
ANALYSIS

Southwest Airlines Co.			
Consolidated Statement of Income			
Years Ended December 31, 2010, 2011, and 2012			
	2012	*2011*	*2010*
Operating Revenues (in millions):			
Passenger	$16,093	$14,735	$11,489
Freight	160	139	125
Other	835	784	490
Total operating revenues	17,088	15,658	12,104
Net Income	$421	$178	$459

SOUTHWEST.COM

Analyze:

1. Although the format for the heading of an income statement can vary from company to company, the heading should contain the answers to who, what, and when. List the answers to each question for the statement presented above.

2. What three types of revenue are reflected on this statement?

3. The net income of $421,000,000 reflected on Southwest Airlines Co.'s consolidated statement of income for 2012 will be transferred to the next financial statement to be prepared. Net income is needed to complete which statement?

Analyze Online: Find the *Investor Relations* section of the Southwest Airlines Co. website (www.southwest.com) and answer the following questions.

4. What total operating revenues did Southwest Airlines Co. report for the most recent quarter?

5. Find the most recent press release posted on the website. Read the press release, and summarize the topic discussed. What effect, if any, do you think this will have on company earnings? Why?

Selling on Internet

Internet | CONNECTION

Go to the Federated Corporation website at www.federated-fds.com. What companies are included in this corporation? Can you see a link to purchase items on line? What transaction, if any, would you record when an item is ordered from the Internet? Does the website include job offerings? What jobs would be available in Finance (go to Support operations, finance to find the requirements for a job)?

Working to Provide Accurate Data

TEAMWORK

Gloria's Fabrics is a large fabric provider to the general public. The accounting office has three employees: accounts receivable clerk, accounts payable clerk, and full charge bookkeeper. The accounts receivable clerk creates the sales invoices and records the cash receipts, the accounts payable clerk creates and pays the purchase orders, and the full charge bookkeeper reconciles the checking account. Assign each group member one of the three jobs. Identify the accounts and describe the transactions that would be recorded by that assigned job. What effect would each transaction have on each account? How would each member of the accounting department work together to present accurate information for the decision makers?

Answers to **Self Reviews**

Answers to Section 1 Self Review

1. An example is the initial investment of cash in a business by the owner.

2. Amounts that a company must pay to creditors in the future.

3. A financial event that changes the resources of the firm.

4. **d.** $150,000

5. **a.** Equipment is increased by $2,950 and accounts payable is increased by $2,950.

6. $20,000

Answers to Section 2 Self Review

1. As an additional investment by the owner recorded on the basis of fair market value.

2. The firm's name (who), the title of the statement (what), and the time period covered by the report (when).

3. Funds taken from the business to pay for personal expenses. They decrease the owner's equity in the business.

4. **d.** $110,000

5. $58,000 increase

6. **d.** revenue and expenses for a period of time

Answers to Comprehensive Self Review

1. The income statement is prepared first because the net income or loss is needed to complete the statement of owner's equity. The statement of owner's equity is prepared next to update the change in owner's equity. The balance sheet is prepared last.

2. Revenue increases owner's equity. Expenses decrease owner's equity.

3. Buying for cash results in an immediate decrease in cash; buying on account results in a liability recorded as accounts payable.

4. The opposite side of the accounting equation will decrease because a decrease in assets results in a corresponding decrease in either a liability or the owner's equity.

5. The payment of $1,200 to a creditor on account.

Analyzing Business Transactions Using T Accounts

at&t
www.att.com

When Alexander Graham Bell invented the telephone in 1876, and gave birth to the company that would become *AT&T*, he had no idea that a century and a half later, millions of people worldwide would be relying on his "namesake" to call, text, and e-mail the people in their lives. Since being formed in 1877, *AT&T* has broadened its offerings through new-product development and diversification. Recognized as one of the leading worldwide providers of IP-based communications services to business, *AT&T* also offers the greatest number of phones that work in most countries; the largest Wi-Fi network in the United States; and the largest number of high-speed Internet access subscribers in the United States.

Keeping track of the multitude of transactions initiated by these services has been the job of the accountant. However, because the accounting equation-table is just too clumsy to be used in a company that has thousands upon thousands of transactions every month, accountants use a more streamlined recordkeeping approach. Accountants, throughout the world, rely instead, on a double-entry system of debits and credits.

thinking critically

How might accountants in 1877 have recorded *The Bell Telephone Company*'s first telephone service revenue transaction? How did this transaction affect the fundamental accounting equation?

LEARNING OBJECTIVES	NEW TERMS	
3-1. Set up T accounts for assets, liabilities, and owner's equity.	account balance	footing
3-2. Analyze business transactions and enter them in the accounts.	accounts	normal balance
	chart of accounts	permanent account
3-3. Determine the balance of an account.	classification	slide
3-4. Set up T accounts for revenue and expenses.	credit	T account
3-5. Prepare a trial balance from T accounts.	debit	temporary account
	double-entry system	transposition
3-6. Prepare an income statement, a statement of owner's equity, and a balance sheet.	drawing account	trial balance
3-7. Develop a chart of accounts.		
3-8. Define the accounting terms new to this chapter.		

>> **3-1.** Set up T accounts for assets, liabilities, and owner's equity.

WHY IT'S IMPORTANT

The T account is an important visual tool used as an alternative to the fundamental accounting equation.

>> **3-2.** Analyze business transactions and enter them in the accounts.

WHY IT'S IMPORTANT

Accountants often use T accounts to help analyze and classify business transactions.

>> **3-3.** Determine the balance of an account.

WHY IT'S IMPORTANT

Accurate account balances contribute to a reliable accounting system.

TERMS TO LEARN

account balance
accounts
classification
footing
normal balance
T account

Transactions That Affect Assets, Liabilities, and Owner's Equity

In this chapter, you will learn how to record the changes caused by business transactions. This recordkeeping is a basic part of accounting systems.

Asset, Liability, and Owner's Equity Accounts

The accounting equation is one tool for analyzing the effects of business transactions. However, businesses do not record transactions in equation form. Instead, businesses establish separate records, called **accounts,** for assets, liabilities, and owner's equity. Use of accounts helps owners and staff analyze, record, classify, summarize, and report financial information. Accounts are recognized by their **classification** as assets, liabilities, or owner's equity. Asset accounts show the property a business owns. Liability accounts show the debts of the business. Owner's equity accounts show the owner's financial interest in the business. Each account has a name that describes the type of property, the debt, or the financial interest.

Accountants use T accounts to analyze transactions. A **T account** consists of a vertical line and a horizontal line that resemble the letter **T.** The name of the account is written on the horizontal (top) line. Increases and decreases in the account are entered on either side of the vertical line.

The following are T accounts for assets, liabilities, and owner's equity:

ASSETS		=	LIABILITIES		+	OWNER'S EQUITY	
+	−		−	+		−	+
Record increases	Record decreases		Record decreases	Record increases		Record decreases	Record increases

RECORDING A CASH INVESTMENT

>> 3-1. OBJECTIVE
Set up T accounts for assets, liabilities, and owner's equity.

Asset accounts show items of value owned by a business. Carolyn Wells invested $100,000 in the business. Carlos Valdez, the office manager for Wells' Consulting Services, set up a *Cash* account. Cash is an asset. Assets appear on the left side of the accounting equation. Cash increases appear on the left side of the *Cash* T account. Decreases are shown on the right side. Valdez entered the cash investment of $100,000 **(a)** on the left side of the *Cash* account.

T accounts normally do not have plus and minus signs. We show them to help you identify increases (+) and decreases (−) in accounts.

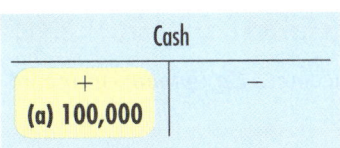

recall

The Accounting Equation
Assets = Liabilities + Owner's
Equity

Carlos Valdez set up an account for owner's equity called *Carolyn Wells, Capital.* Owner's equity appears on the right side of the accounting equation (Assets = Liabilities + Owner's Equity). Increases in owner's equity appear on the right side of the T account. Decreases in owner's equity appear on the left side. Valdez entered the investment of $100,000 **(a)** on the right side of the *Carolyn Wells, Capital* account.

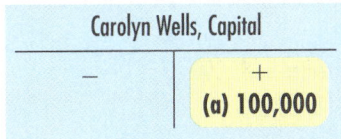

Use these steps to analyze the effects of the business transactions:

>> 3-2. OBJECTIVE
Analyze business transactions and enter them in the accounts.

1. Analyze the financial event.
   • Identify the accounts affected.
   • Classify the accounts affected.
   • Determine the amount of increase or decrease for each account.
2. Apply the left-right rules for each account affected.
3. Make the entry in T-account form.

BUSINESS TRANSACTION

Carolyn Wells withdrew $100,000 from personal savings and deposited it in the new business checking account for Wells' Consulting Services.

ANALYSIS
a. The asset account, *Cash,* is increased by $100,000.
a. The owner's equity account, *Carolyn Wells, Capital,* is increased by $100,000.

LEFT-RIGHT RULES
LEFT   Increases to asset accounts are recorded on the left side of the T account. Record $100,000 on the left side of the *Cash* T account.
RIGHT   Increases to owner's equity accounts are recorded on the right side of the T account. Record $100,000 on the right side of the *Carolyn Wells, Capital* T account.

T-ACCOUNT PRESENTATION

Cash			Carolyn Wells, Capital	
+	−		−	+
(a) 100,000				(a) 100,000

RECORDING A CASH PURCHASE OF EQUIPMENT

Carlos Valdez set up an asset account, *Equipment,* to record the purchase of a computer and other equipment.

BUSINESS TRANSACTION

Wells' Consulting Services issued a $5,000 check to purchase a computer and other equipment.

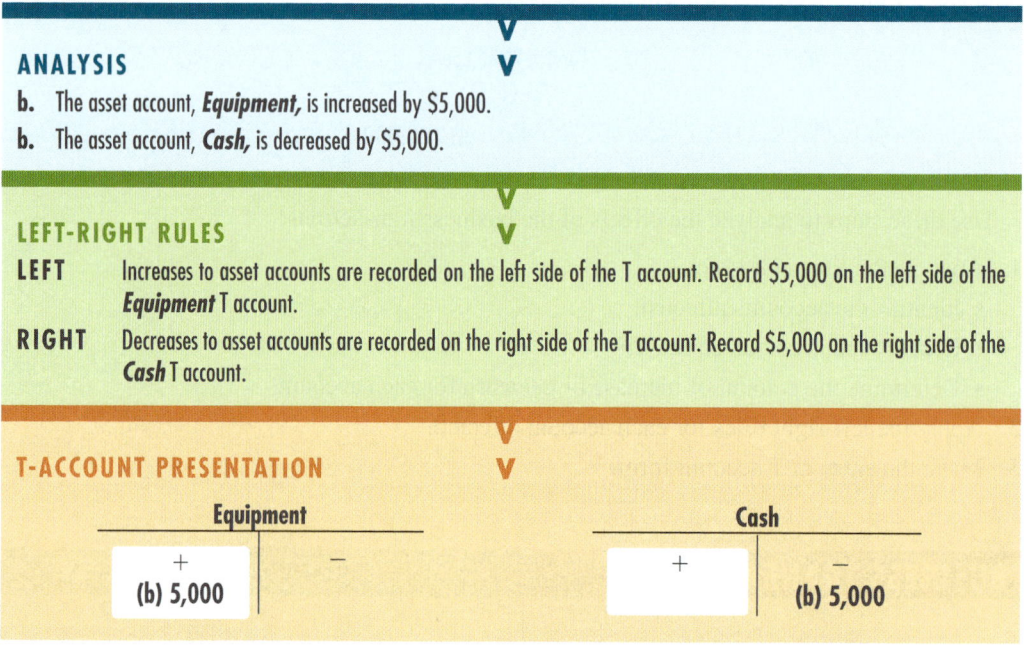

ANALYSIS

b. The asset account, *Equipment,* is increased by $5,000.
b. The asset account, *Cash,* is decreased by $5,000.

LEFT-RIGHT RULES

LEFT   Increases to asset accounts are recorded on the left side of the T account. Record $5,000 on the left side of the *Equipment* T account.

RIGHT   Decreases to asset accounts are recorded on the right side of the T account. Record $5,000 on the right side of the *Cash* T account.

T-ACCOUNT PRESENTATION

Equipment			Cash	
+	−		+	−
(b) 5,000				(b) 5,000

Let's look at the T accounts to review the effects of the transactions. Valdez entered $5,000 **(b)** on the left (increase) side of the *Equipment* account. He entered $5,000 **(b)** on the right (decrease) side of the *Cash* account. Notice that the *Cash* account shows the effects of two transactions.

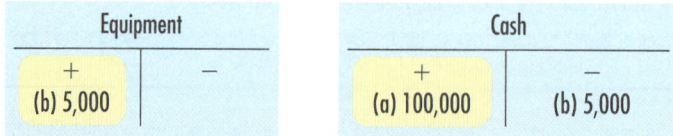

Equipment			Cash	
+	−		+	−
(b) 5,000			(a) 100,000	(b) 5,000

RECORDING A CREDIT PURCHASE OF EQUIPMENT

Liabilities are amounts a business owes its creditors. Liabilities appear on the right side of the accounting equation (Assets = Liabilities + Owner's Equity). Increases in liabilities are on the right side of liability T accounts. Decreases in liabilities are on the left side of liability T accounts.

BUSINESS TRANSACTION

The firm bought office equipment for $6,000 on account from Office Plus.

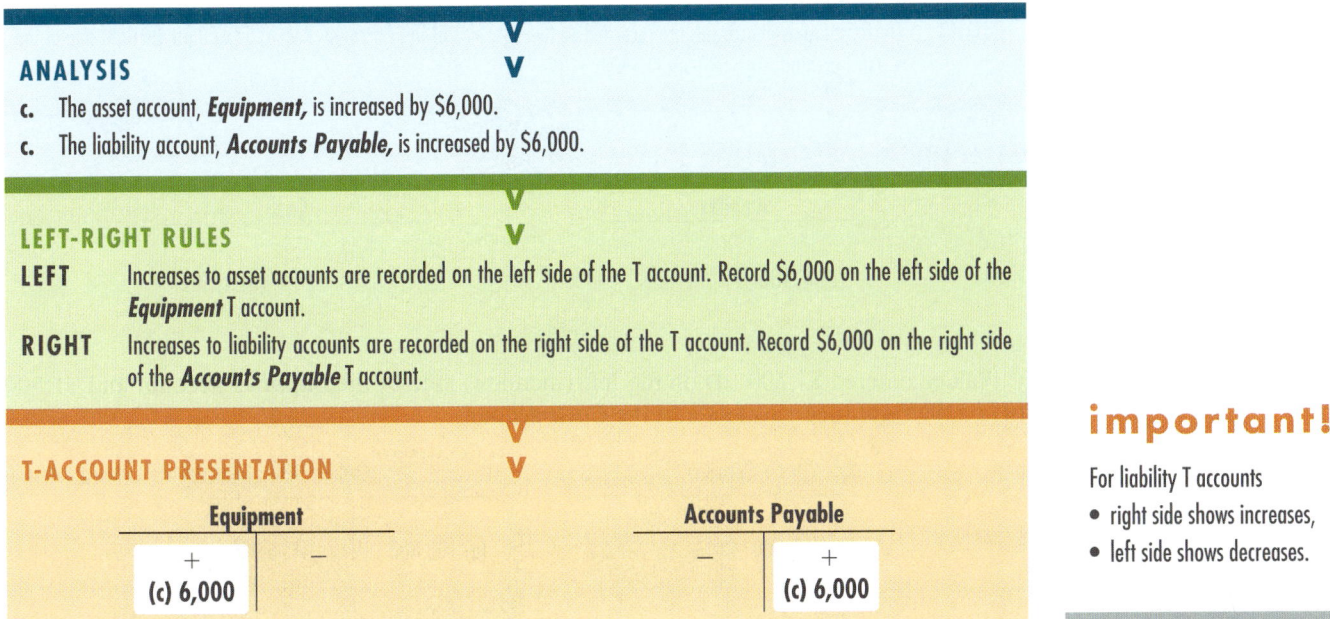

ANALYSIS

c.   The asset account, *Equipment,* is increased by $6,000.

c.   The liability account, *Accounts Payable,* is increased by $6,000.

LEFT-RIGHT RULES

LEFT   Increases to asset accounts are recorded on the left side of the T account. Record $6,000 on the left side of the *Equipment* T account.

RIGHT   Increases to liability accounts are recorded on the right side of the T account. Record $6,000 on the right side of the *Accounts Payable* T account.

T-ACCOUNT PRESENTATION

Equipment	
+	−
(c) 6,000	

Accounts Payable	
−	+
	(c) 6,000

important!

For liability T accounts
- right side shows increases,
- left side shows decreases.

   Let's look at the T accounts to review the effects of the transactions. Valdez entered $6,000 **(c)** on the left (increase) side of the *Equipment* account. It now shows two transactions. He entered $6,000 **(c)** on the right (increase) side of the *Accounts Payable* account.

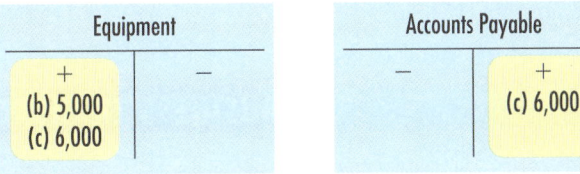

Equipment	
+	−
(b) 5,000	
(c) 6,000	

Accounts Payable	
−	+
	(c) 6,000

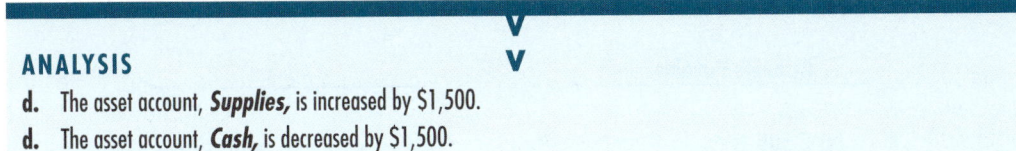

The balance sheet of Avery Dennison Corporation at January 1, 2012, showed net property, plant, and equipment of $1.015 billion.

RECORDING A CASH PURCHASE OF SUPPLIES

Carlos Valdez set up an asset account called *Supplies.*

BUSINESS TRANSACTION

Wells' Consulting Services issued a check for $1,500 to Office Delux Inc. to purchase office supplies.

ANALYSIS

d.   The asset account, *Supplies,* is increased by $1,500.

d.   The asset account, *Cash,* is decreased by $1,500.

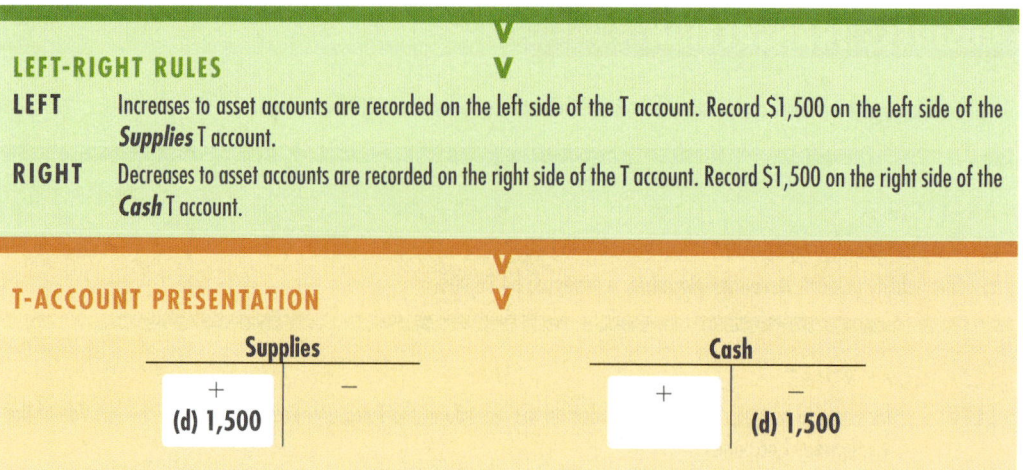

Valdez entered $1,500 **(d)** on the left (increase) side of the ***Supplies*** account and $1,500 **(d)** on the right (decrease) side of the ***Cash*** account.

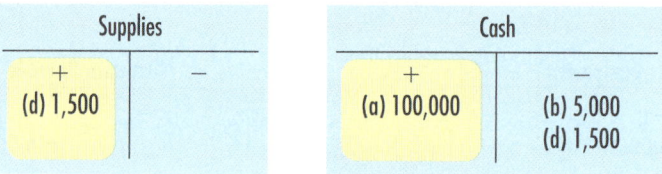

Notice that the ***Cash*** account now shows three transactions: the initial investment by the owner (**a**), the cash purchase of equipment (**b**), and the cash purchase of supplies (**d**).

RECORDING A PAYMENT TO A CREDITOR

On November 30, the business paid $2,500 to Office Plus to apply against the debt of $6,000 shown in ***Accounts Payable.***

BUSINESS TRANSACTION

Wells' Consulting Services issued a check in the amount of $2,500 to Office Plus.

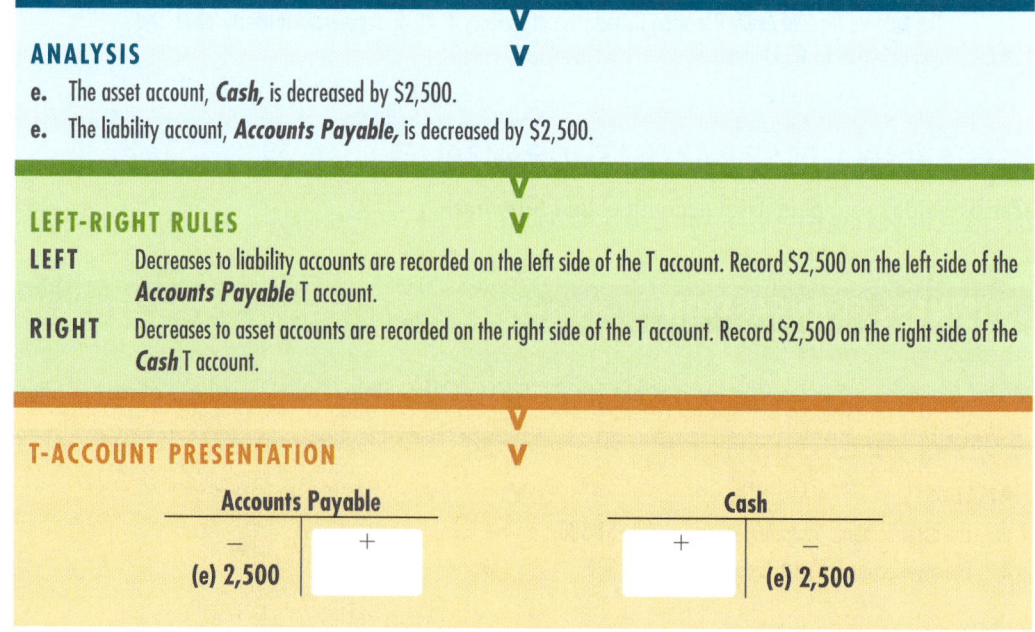

Let's look at the T accounts to review the effects of the transactions. Valdez entered $2,500 (**e**) on the right (decrease) side of the **Cash** account. He entered $2,500 (**e**) on the left (decrease) side of the **Accounts Payable** account. Notice that both accounts show the effects of several transactions.

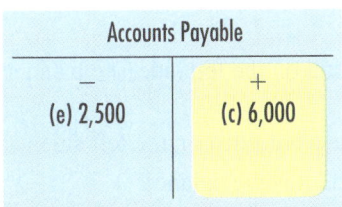

Accounts Payable	
−	+
(e) 2,500	(c) 6,000

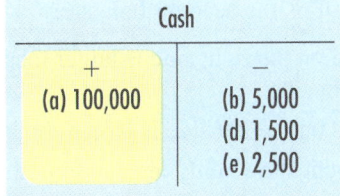

Cash	
+	−
(a) 100,000	(b) 5,000
	(d) 1,500
	(e) 2,500

RECORDING PREPAID RENT

In November, Wells' Consulting Services was required to pay the December and January rent in advance. Valdez set up an asset account called **Prepaid Rent.**

BUSINESS TRANSACTION

Wells' Consulting Services issued a check for $8,000 to pay rent for the months of December and January.

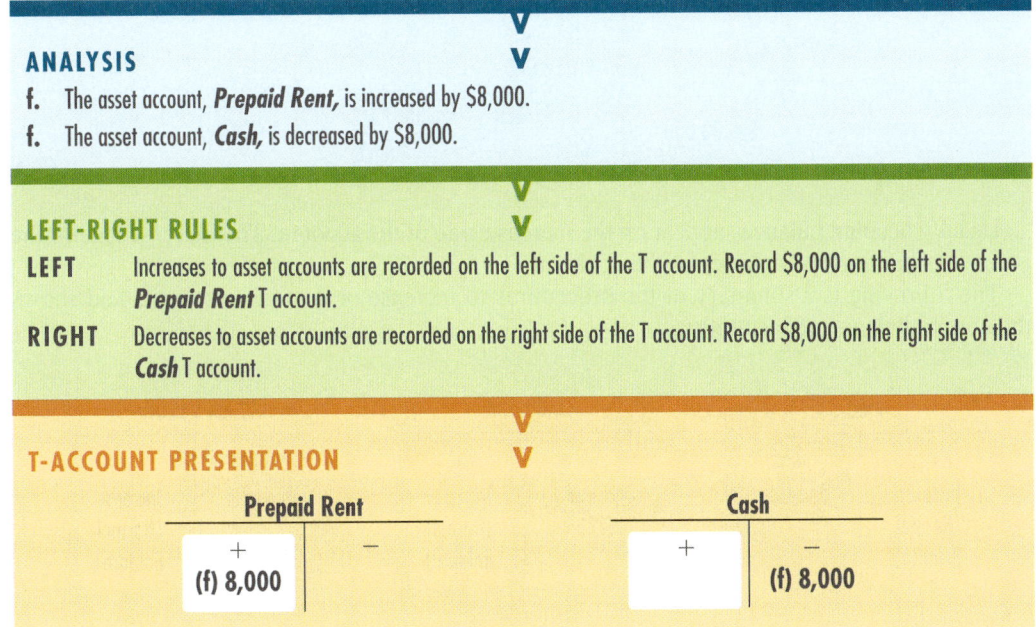

ANALYSIS

f.   The asset account, **Prepaid Rent,** is increased by $8,000.

f.   The asset account, **Cash,** is decreased by $8,000.

LEFT-RIGHT RULES

LEFT   Increases to asset accounts are recorded on the left side of the T account. Record $8,000 on the left side of the **Prepaid Rent** T account.

RIGHT   Decreases to asset accounts are recorded on the right side of the T account. Record $8,000 on the right side of the **Cash** T account.

T-ACCOUNT PRESENTATION

Prepaid Rent	
+	−
(f) 8,000	

Cash	
+	−
	(f) 8,000

Let's review the T accounts to see the effects of the transactions. Valdez entered $8,000 (**f**) on the left (increase) side of the **Prepaid Rent** account. He entered $8,000 (**f**) on the right (decrease) side of the **Cash** account.

Notice that the **Cash** account shows the effects of numerous transactions. It shows initial investment (**a**), equipment purchase (**b**), supplies purchase (**d**), payment on account (**e**), and advance rent payment (**f**).

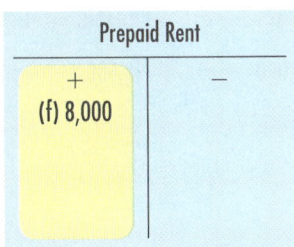

Prepaid Rent	
+	−
(f) 8,000	

Cash	
+	−
(a) 100,000	(b) 5,000
	(d) 1,500
	(e) 2,500
	(f) 8,000

>> **3-3. OBJECTIVE**

Determine the balance of an account.

Account Balances

An **account balance** is the difference between the amounts on the two sides of the account. First add the figures on each side of the account. If the column has more than one figure, enter the total in small pencil figures called a **footing.** Then subtract the smaller total from the larger total. The result is the account balance.

- If the total on the right side is larger than the total on the left side, the balance is recorded on the right side.
- If the total on the left side is larger, the balance is recorded on the left side.
- If an account shows only one amount, that amount is the balance.
- If an account contains entries on only one side, the total of those entries is the account balance.

Let's look at the *Cash* account for Wells' Consulting Services. The left side shows $100,000. The total of the right side is $17,000. Subtract the footing of $17,000 from $100,000. The result is the account balance of $83,000. The account balance is shown on the left side of the account.

	Cash	
+	–	
(a) 100,000	(b) 5,000	
	(d) 1,500	
	(e) 2,500	
	(f) 8,000	
	17,000 ← Footing	
Bal. 83,000		

Usually account balances appear on the increase side of the account. The increase side of the account is the **normal balance** of the account.

The following is a summary of the procedures to increase or decrease accounts and shows the normal balance of accounts.

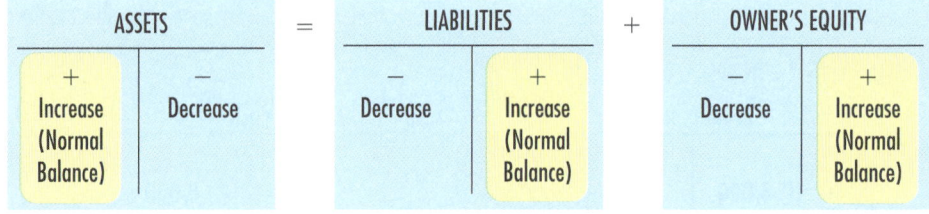

Figure 3.1 shows a summary of the account balances for Wells' Consulting Services.
Figure 3.2 shows a balance sheet prepared for November 30, 2016.
In equation form, the firm's position after these transactions is:

Assets							=	Liabilities	+	Owner's Equity
Cash	+	Supp.	+	Prepaid Rent	+	Equip.	=	Accounts Payable	+	Carolyn Wells, Capital
$83,000	+	$1,500	+	$8,000	+	$11,000	=	$3,500	+	$100,000

FIGURE 3.1

T-Account Balances for Wells'
Consulting Services

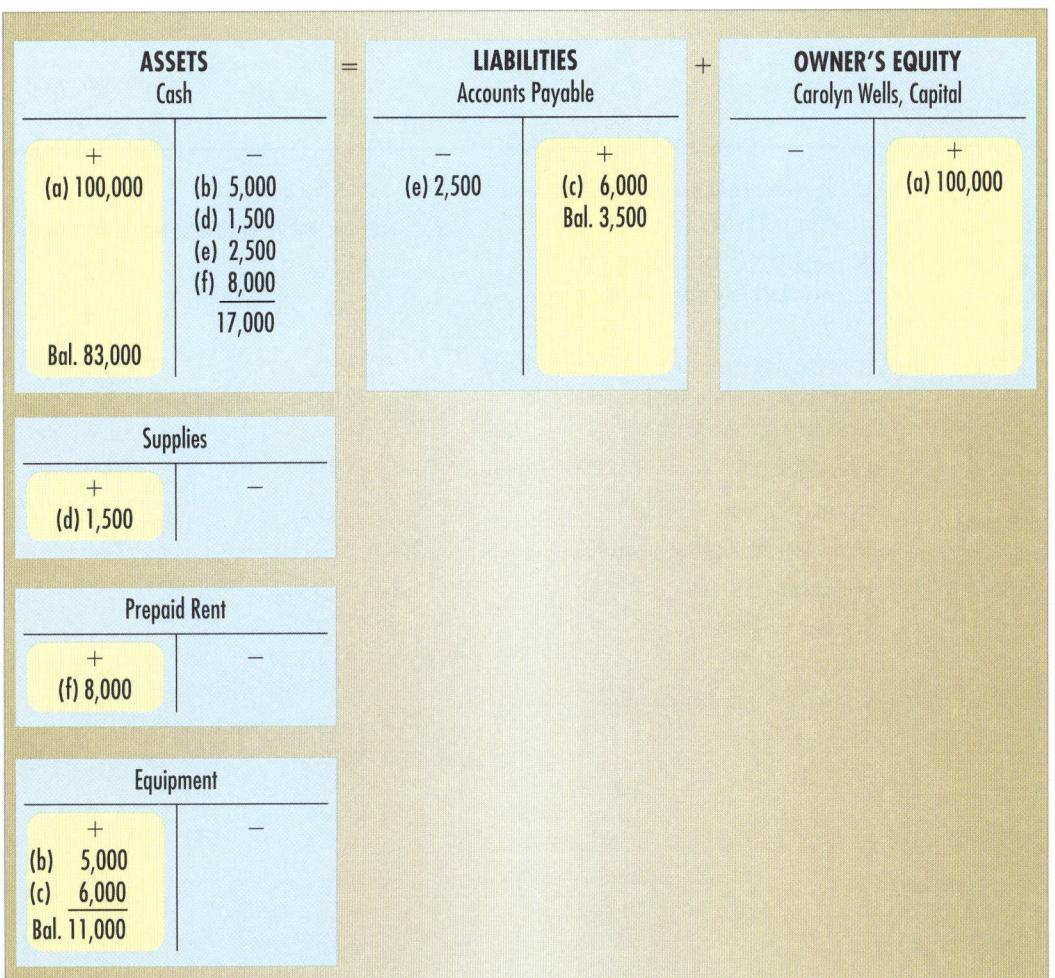

FIGURE 3.2   Balance Sheet for Wells' Consulting Services

Assets				Liabilities			
				Wells' Consulting Services			
				Balance Sheet			
				November 30, 2016			
Cash	83 0 0 0	00		Accounts Payable	3 5 0 0	00	
Supplies	1 5 0 0	00					
Prepaid Rent	8 0 0 0	00		Owner's Equity			
Equipment	1 1 0 0 0	00		Carolyn Wells, Capital	100 0 0 0	00	
Total Assets	1 0 3 5 0 0	00		Total Liabilities and Owner's Equity	103 5 0 0	00	

Notice how the balance sheet reflects the fundamental accounting equation.

Section 1   Self Review

QUESTIONS

1. What is a footing?

2. What is meant by the "normal balance" of an account? What is the normal balance side for asset, liability, and owner's equity accounts?

3. Increases are recorded on which side of asset, liability, and owner's equity accounts?

EXERCISES

4. The Wilson Company purchased new computers for $20,200 from Office Supplies, Inc., to be paid in 30 days. Which of the following is correct?

   a. *Equipment* is increased by $20,200. *Accounts Payable* is increased by $20,200.

   b. *Equipment* is decreased by $20,200. *Accounts Payable* is increased by $20,200.

   c. *Equipment* is increased by $20,200. *Cash* is decreased by $20,200.

   d. *Equipment* is increased by $20,200. *Accounts Payable* is decreased by $20,200.

5. From the following accounts, show that the fundamental accounting equation is in balance. All accounts have normal balances.

   Cash—$30,800

   Accounts Payable—$40,000

   David Jenkins, Capital—$60,000

   Equipment—$20,000

   Supplies—$9,200

ANALYSIS

6. Foot and find the balance of the *Cash* account.

Cash	
+	−
36,000	12,000
22,000	5,000
	5,200
	2,350

    a.   58,000

    b.   32,000

    c.   33,450

    d.   24,100

(Answers to Section 1 Self Review are on pages 86–87.)

Transactions That Affect Revenue, Expenses, and Withdrawals

Let's examine the revenue and expense transactions of Wells' Consulting Services for December to see how they are recorded.

Revenue and Expense Accounts

Some owner's equity accounts are classified as revenue or expense accounts. Separate accounts are used to record revenue and expense transactions.

RECORDING REVENUE FROM SERVICES SOLD FOR CASH

During December, the business earned $36,000 in revenue from clients who paid cash for bookkeeping, accounting, and consulting services. This involved several transactions. Carlos Valdez entered $36,000 **(g)** on the left (increase) side of the asset account ***Cash.***

Cash	
+	**−**
Bal. 83,000	
(g) 36,000	

How is the increase in owner's equity recorded? One way would be to record the $36,000 on the right side of the **Carolyn Wells, Capital** account. However, the preferred way is to keep revenue separate from the owner's investment until the end of the accounting period. Therefore, Valdez opened a revenue account for **Fees Income.**

Valdez entered $36,000 (**g**) on the right side of the **Fees Income** account. Revenues increase owner's equity. Increases in owner's equity appear on the right side of the T account. Therefore, increases in revenue appear on the right side of revenue T accounts.

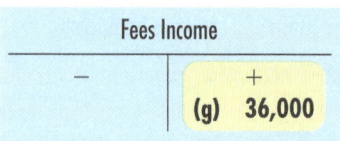

The right side of the revenue account shows increases and the left side shows decreases. Decreases in revenue accounts are rare but might occur because of corrections or transfers.

Let's review the effects of the transactions. Valdez entered $36,000 (**g**) on the left (increase) side of the **Cash** account and $36,000 (**g**) on the right (increase) side of the **Fees Income** account.

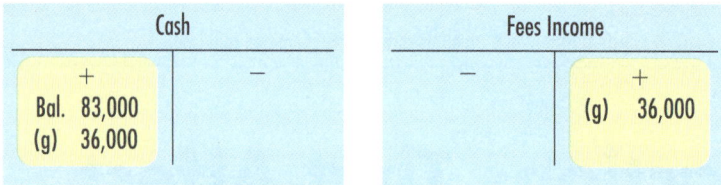

At this point, the firm needs just one revenue account. Most businesses have separate accounts for different types of revenue. For example, sales of goods such as clothes are recorded in the revenue account **Sales.**

RECORDING REVENUE FROM SERVICES SOLD ON CREDIT

In December, Wells' Consulting Services earned $11,000 from various charge account clients. Valdez set up an asset account, **Accounts Receivable.**

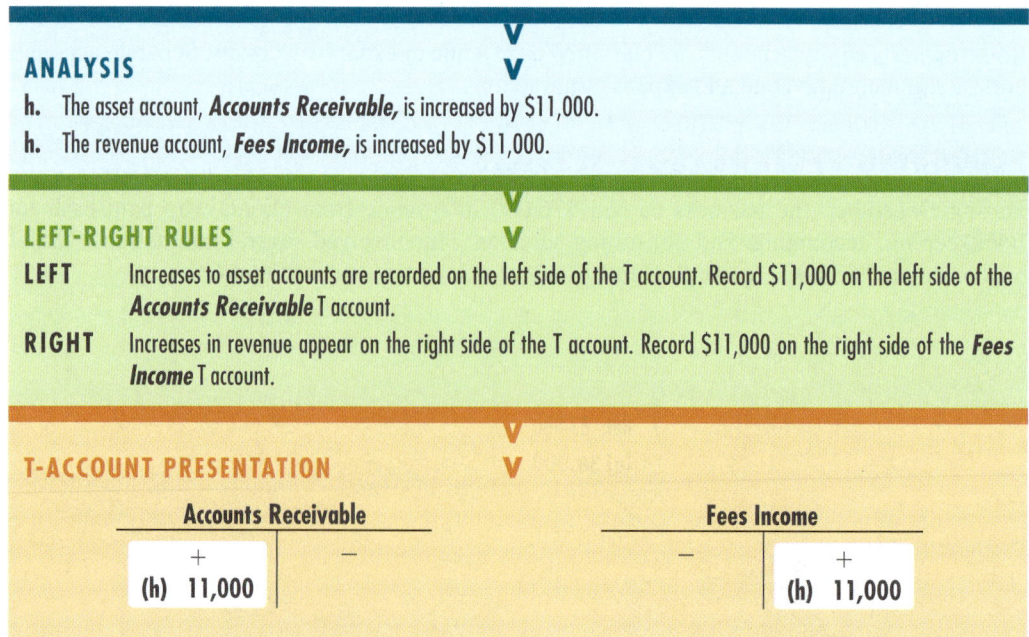

ANALYSIS

h. The asset account, **Accounts Receivable,** is increased by $11,000.
h. The revenue account, **Fees Income,** is increased by $11,000.

LEFT-RIGHT RULES

LEFT   Increases to asset accounts are recorded on the left side of the T account. Record $11,000 on the left side of the **Accounts Receivable** T account.

RIGHT   Increases in revenue appear on the right side of the T account. Record $11,000 on the right side of the **Fees Income** T account.

T-ACCOUNT PRESENTATION

Let's review the effects of the transactions. Valdez entered $11,000 (**h**) on the left (increase) side of the *Accounts Receivable* account and $11,000 (**h**) on the right (increase) side of the *Fees Income* account.

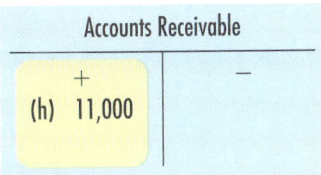

RECORDING COLLECTIONS FROM ACCOUNTS RECEIVABLE

Charge account clients paid $6,000, reducing the amount owed to Wells' Consulting Services.

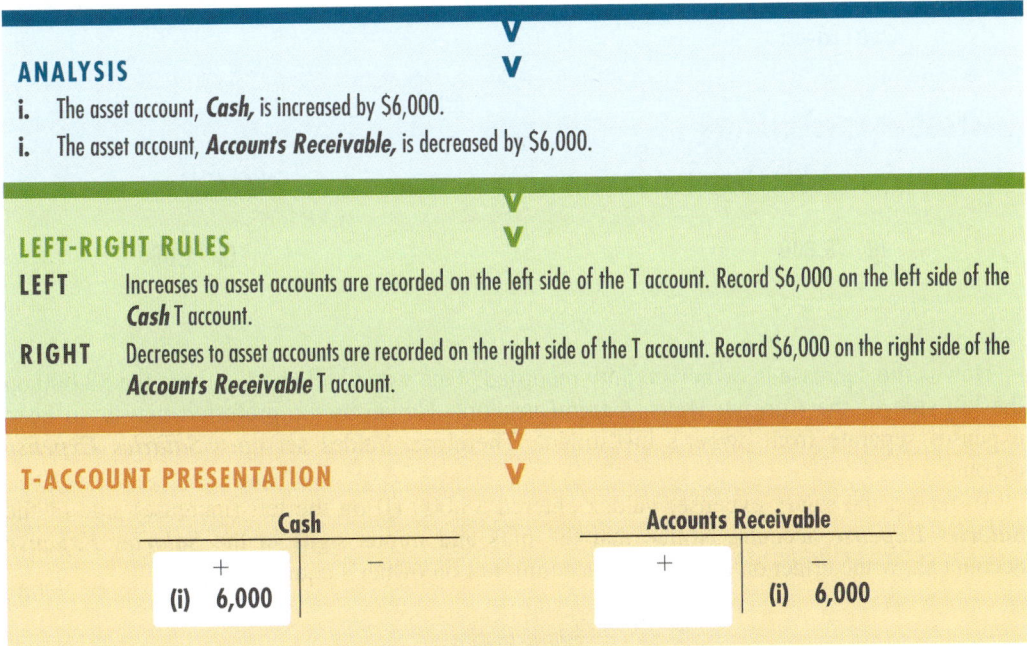

Let's review the effects of the transactions. Valdez entered $6,000 (**i**) on the left (increase) side of the *Cash* account and $6,000 (**i**) on the right (decrease) side of the *Accounts Receivable* account. Notice that revenue is not recorded when cash is collected from charge account clients. The revenue was recorded when the sales on credit were recorded (**h**).

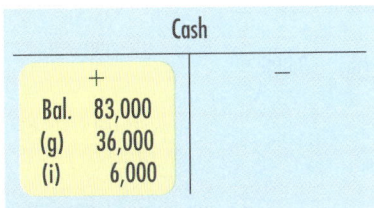

RECORDING AN EXPENSE FOR SALARIES

Expenses decrease owner's equity. Decreases in owner's equity appear on the left side of the T account. Therefore, increases in expenses (which are decreases in owner's equity) are recorded on the left side of expense T accounts. Decreases in expenses are recorded on the right side of the T accounts. Decreases in expenses are rare but may result from corrections or transfers.

Expense

An expense is an outflow of cash, the use of other assets, or the incurring of a liability.

BUSINESS TRANSACTION

In December, Wells' Consulting Services paid $8,000 in salaries.

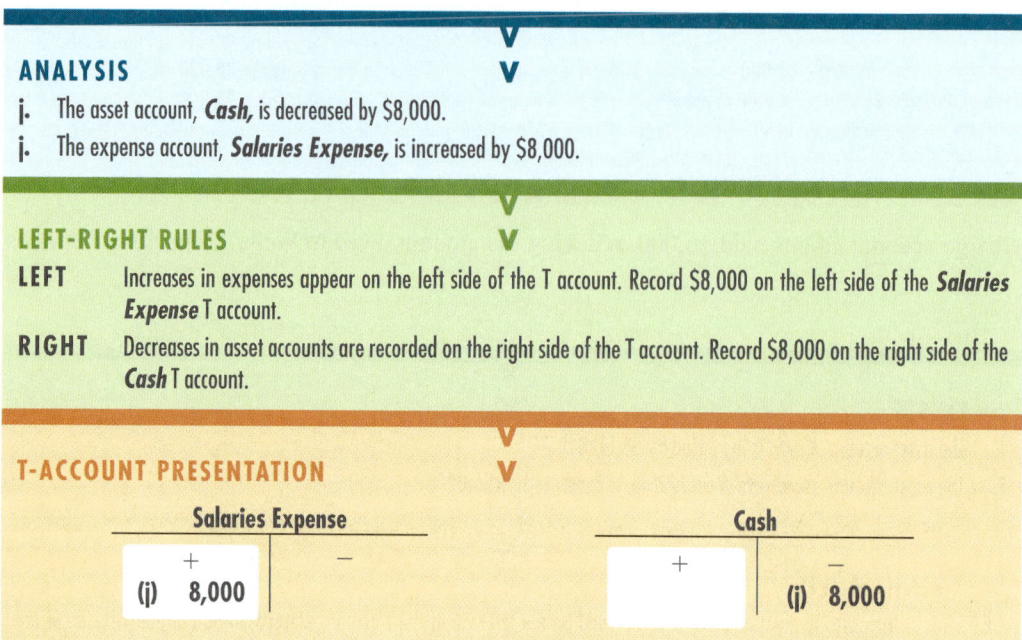

ANALYSIS

j. The asset account, *Cash,* is decreased by $8,000.

j. The expense account, *Salaries Expense,* is increased by $8,000.

LEFT-RIGHT RULES

LEFT   Increases in expenses appear on the left side of the T account. Record $8,000 on the left side of the *Salaries Expense* T account.

RIGHT   Decreases in asset accounts are recorded on the right side of the T account. Record $8,000 on the right side of the *Cash* T account.

T-ACCOUNT PRESENTATION

Salaries Expense				Cash	
+	−			+	−
(j) 8,000					(j) 8,000

How is the decrease in owner's equity recorded? One way would be to record the $8,000 on the left side of the ***Carolyn Wells, Capital*** account. However, the preferred way is to keep expenses separate from owner's investment. Therefore, Valdez set up a ***Salaries Expense*** account.

To record the salary expense, Valdez entered $8,000 **(j)** on the left (increase) side of the ***Salaries Expense*** account. Notice that the plus and minus signs in the ***Salaries Expense*** account show the effect on the expense account, not on owner's equity.

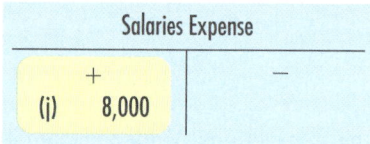

Salaries Expense	
+	−
(j) 8,000	

Valdez entered $8,000 **(j)** on the right (decrease) side of the ***Cash*** T account.

Cash	
+	−
Bal. 83,000	(j) 8,000
(g) 36,000	
(i) 6,000	

Most companies have numerous expense accounts. The various expense accounts appear in the Expenses section of the income statement.

RECORDING AN EXPENSE FOR UTILITIES

At the end of December, Wells' Consulting Services received a $650 bill for utilities. Valdez set up an account for ***Utilities Expense.***

BUSINESS TRANSACTION

Wells' Consulting Services issued a check for $650 to pay the utilities bill.

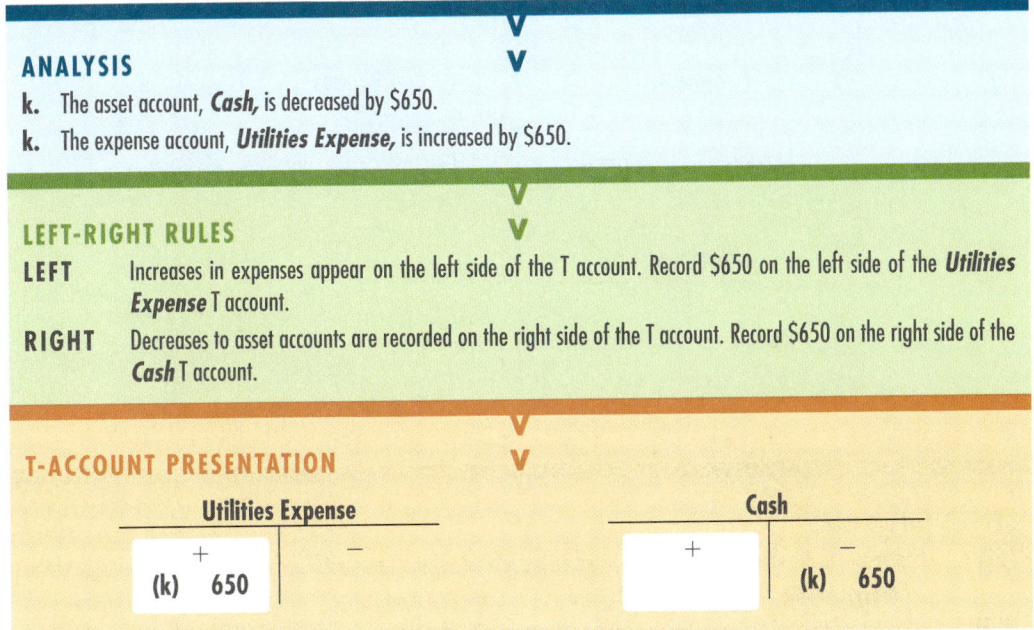

ANALYSIS
k. The asset account, *Cash,* is decreased by $650.
k. The expense account, *Utilities Expense,* is increased by $650.

LEFT-RIGHT RULES
LEFT   Increases in expenses appear on the left side of the T account. Record $650 on the left side of the *Utilities Expense* T account.
RIGHT   Decreases to asset accounts are recorded on the right side of the T account. Record $650 on the right side of the *Cash* T account.

T-ACCOUNT PRESENTATION

Utilities Expense				Cash	
+	−			+	−
(k) 650					(k) 650

Let's review the effects of the transactions.

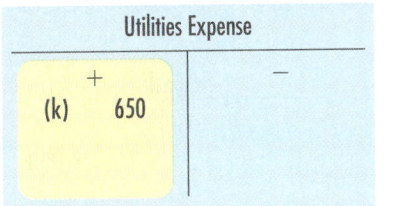

Utilities Expense			Cash	
+	−		+	−
(k) 650			Bal. 83,000	(j) 8,000
			(g) 36,000	(k) 650
			(i) 6,000	

The Drawing Account

In sole proprietorships and partnerships, the owners generally do not pay themselves salaries. To obtain funds for personal living expenses, owners make withdrawals of cash. The withdrawals are against previously earned profits that have become part of capital or against profits that are expected in the future.

Since withdrawals decrease owner's equity, withdrawals could be recorded on the left side of the capital account. However, the preferred way is to keep withdrawals separate from the owner's capital account until the end of the accounting period. An owner's equity account called a **drawing account** is set up to record withdrawals. Increases in the drawing account (which are decreases in owner's equity) are recorded on the left side of the drawing T accounts.

BUSINESS TRANSACTION

Carolyn Wells wrote a check to withdraw $5,000 cash for personal use.

ANALYSIS
l. The asset account, *Cash,* is decreased by $5,000.
l. The owner's equity account, *Carolyn Wells, Drawing,* is increased by $5,000.

FIGURE 3.3

The Relationship between Owner's Equity and Revenue, Expenses, and Withdrawals

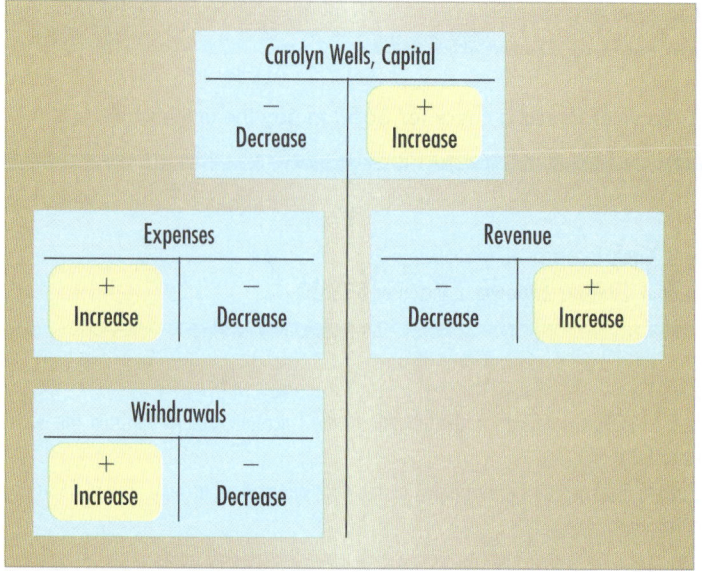

LEFT-RIGHT RULES

LEFT   Increases to drawing accounts are recorded on the left side of the T account. Record $5,000 on the left side of the ***Carolyn Wells, Drawing*** T account.

RIGHT   Decreases to asset accounts are recorded on the right side of the T account. Record $5,000 on the right side of the ***Cash*** T account.

T-ACCOUNT PRESENTATION

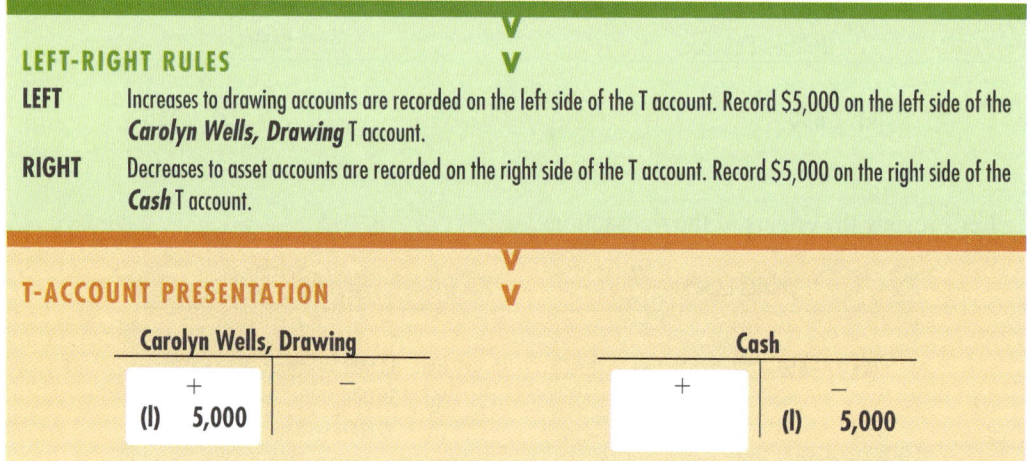

Let's review the transactions. Valdez entered $5,000 **(l)** on the right (decrease) side of the asset account, ***Cash,*** and $5,000 **(l)** on the left (increase) side of ***Carolyn Wells, Drawing.*** Note that the plus and minus signs show the effect on the drawing account, not on owner's equity.

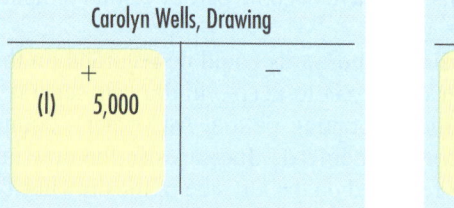

Carolyn Wells, Drawing		Cash	
+	−	+	−
(l) 5,000		Bal. 83,000	(j) 8,000
		(g) 36,000	(k) 650
		(i) 6,000	(l) 5,000

Figure 3.3 shows a summary of the relationship between the capital account and the revenue, expense, and drawing accounts.

The Rules of Debit and Credit

Accountants do not use the terms *left side* and *right side* when they talk about making entries in accounts. Instead, they use the term **debit** for an entry on the left side and **credit** for an entry on the right side. Figure 3.4 summarizes the rules for debits and credits. The accounting system is called the **double-entry system.** This is because each transaction has at least two entries—a debit and a credit.

important!

Normal Balances

Debit:	Credit:
Asset	Liability
Expense	Revenue
Drawing	Capital

FIGURE 3.4   Rules for Debits and Credits

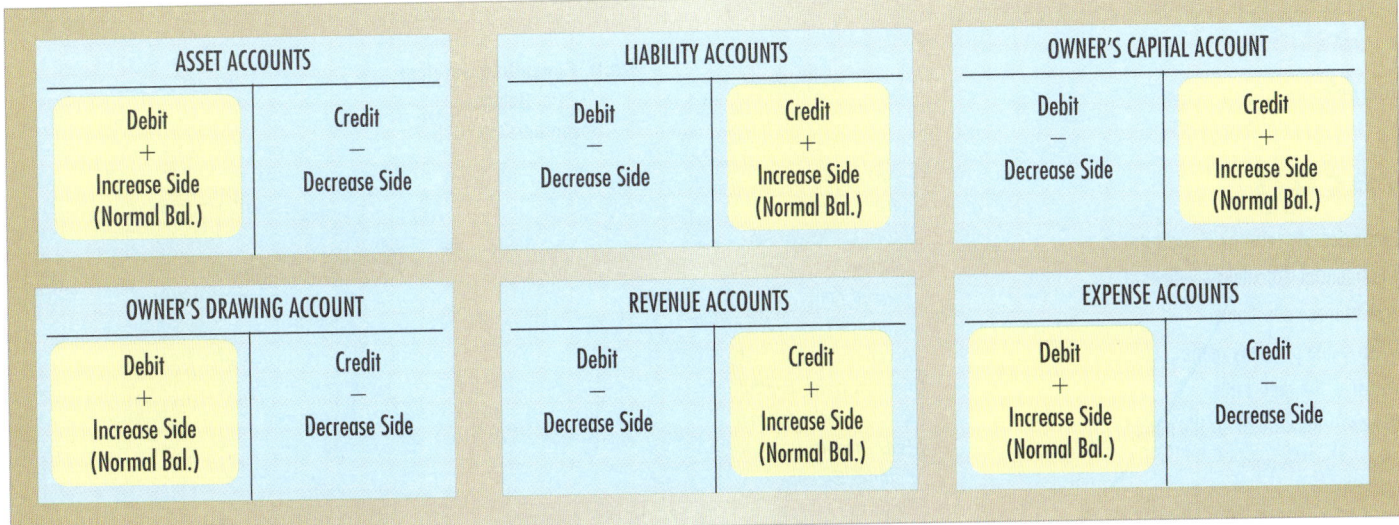

After the December transactions for Wells' Consulting Services are recorded, the account balances are calculated. Figure 3.5 below shows the account balances at the end of December. Notice that the fundamental accounting equation remains in balance (Assets = Liabilities + Owner's Equity).

The Trial Balance

Once the account balances are computed, a trial balance is prepared. The **trial balance** is a statement that tests the accuracy of total debits and credits after transactions have been

FIGURE 3.5

End-of-December 2016 Account Balances

ASSETS				=	LIABILITIES			+	OWNER'S EQUITY		
Cash					**Accounts Payable**				**Carolyn Wells, Capital**		
Bal.	83,000	(j)	8,000				Bal.	3,500		Bal.	100,000
(g)	36,000	(k)	650								
(i)	6,000	(l)	5,000								
	125,000		13,650								
Bal.	111,350										

Accounts Receivable					**Carolyn Wells, Drawing**	
(h)	11,000	(i)	6,000		(l)	5,000
Bal.	5,000					

Supplies			**Fees Income**		
Bal.	1,500			(g)	36,000
				(h)	11,000
				Bal.	47,000

Prepaid Rent			**Salaries Expense**	
Bal.	8,000		(j)	8,000

Equipment			**Utilities Expense**	
Bal.	11,000		(k)	650

FIGURE 3.6

Trial Balance

recall

recall

Financial Statement Headings

The financial statement headings answer three questions:

Who — the company name

What — the report title

When — the date of, or the period covered by, the report

ACCOUNT NAME	DEBIT	CREDIT
	Wells' Consulting Services	
	Trial Balance	
	December 31, 2016	
Cash	111 3 5 0 00	
Accounts Receivable	5 0 0 0 00	
Supplies	1 5 0 0 00	
Prepaid Rent	8 0 0 0 00	
Equipment	11 0 0 0 00	
Accounts Payable		3 5 0 0 00
Carolyn Wells, Capital		100 0 0 0 00
Carolyn Wells, Drawing	5 0 0 0 00	
Fees Income		47 0 0 0 00
Salaries Expense	8 0 0 0 00	
Utilities Expense	6 5 0 00	
Totals	150 5 0 0 00	150 5 0 0 00

recorded. If total debits do not equal total credits, there is an error. Figure 3.6 above shows the trial balance for Wells' Consulting Services. To prepare a trial balance, perform the following steps:

1. Enter the trial balance heading showing the company name, report title, and closing date for the accounting period.

2. List the account names in the same order as they appear on the financial statements.
   - Assets
   - Liabilities
   - Owner's Equity
   - Revenue
   - Expenses

3. Enter the ending balance of each account in the appropriate Debit or Credit column.

4. Total the Debit column.

5. Total the Credit column.

6. Compare the total debits with the total credits.

MANAGERIAL IMPLICATIONS <<

FINANCIAL STATEMENTS

- Recording entries into accounts provides an efficient method of gathering data about the financial affairs of a business.

- A chart of accounts is usually similar from company to company; balance sheet accounts are first, followed by income statement accounts.

- A trial balance proves the financial records are in balance.

- The income statement reports the revenue and expenses for the period and shows the net income or loss.

- The statement of owner's equity shows the change in owner's equity during the period.

- The balance sheet summarizes the assets, liabilities, and owner's equity of the business on a given date.

- Owners, managers, creditors, banks, and many others use financial statements to make decisions about the business.

THINKING CRITICALLY

What are some possible consequences of not recording financial data correctly?

UNDERSTANDING TRIAL BALANCE ERRORS

>> 3-5. OBJECTIVE
Prepare a trial balance from T accounts.

If the totals of the Debit and Credit columns are equal, the financial records are in balance. If the totals of the Debit and Credit columns are not equal, there is an error. The error may be in the trial balance, or it may be in the financial records. Some common errors are:

- adding trial balance columns incorrectly;
- recording only half a transaction—for example, recording a debit but not recording a credit, or vice versa;
- recording both halves of a transaction as debits or credits rather than recording one debit and one credit;
- recording an amount incorrectly from a transaction;
- recording a debit for one amount and a credit for a different amount;
- making an error when calculating the account balances.

FINDING TRIAL BALANCE ERRORS

If the trial balance does not balance, try the following procedures:

1. Check the arithmetic. If the columns were originally added from top to bottom, verify the total by adding from bottom to top.
2. Check that the correct account balances were transferred to the correct trial balance columns.
3. Check the arithmetic used to compute the account balances.
4. Check that each transaction was recorded correctly in the accounts by tracing the amounts to the analysis of the transaction.

Sometimes you can determine the type of the error by the amount of the difference. Compute the difference between the debit total and the credit total. If the difference is divisible by 2, a debit might be recorded as a credit, or a credit recorded as a debit.

If the difference is divisible by 9, there might be a transposition. A **transposition** occurs when the digits of a number are switched (357 for 375). The test for a transposition is:

$$375$$
$$\underline{-357}$$
$$18$$
$$18/9 = 2$$

Also check for slides. A **slide** occurs when the decimal point is misplaced (375 for 37.50). We can test for a slide in the following manner:

$$375.00$$
$$\underline{37.50}$$
$$337.50$$
$$337.50/9 = 37.50$$

Financial Statements

>>3-6. OBJECTIVE
Prepare an income statement, a statement of owner's equity, and a balance sheet.

After the trial balance is prepared, the financial statements are prepared. Figure 3.7 shows the financial statements for Wells' Consulting Services. The amounts are taken from the trial balance. As you study the financial statements, note that net income from the income statement is used on the statement of owner's equity. Also note that the ending balance of the *Carolyn Wells, Capital* account, computed on the statement of owner's equity, is used on the balance sheet.

Chart of Accounts

>>3-7. OBJECTIVE
Develop a chart of accounts.

A **chart of accounts** is a list of all the accounts used by a business. Figure 3.8 shows the chart of accounts for Wells' Consulting Services. Each account has a number and a name. The balance sheet accounts are listed first, followed by the income statement accounts. The account number is assigned based on the type of account.

FIGURE 3.7

Financial Statements for Wells'
Consulting Services

Wells' Consulting Services
Income Statement
Month Ended December 31, 2016

Revenue		
Fees Income		47 000 00
Expenses		
Salaries Expense	8 000 00	
Utilities Expense	6 50 00	
Total Expenses		8 650 00
Net Income		38 350 00

Wells' Consulting Services
Statement of Owner's Equity
Month Ended December 31, 2016

Carolyn Wells, Capital, December 1, 2016		100 000 00
Net Income for December	38 350 00	
Less Withdrawals for December	5 000 00	
Increase in Capital		33 350 00
Carolyn Wells, Capital, December 31, 2016		133 350 00

Wells' Consulting Services
Balance Sheet
December 31, 2016

Assets		*Liabilities*	
Cash	111 350 00	Accounts Payable	3 500 00
Accounts Receivable	5 000 00		
Supplies	1 500 00		
Prepaid Rent	8 000 00	*Owner's Equity*	
Equipment	11 000 00	Carolyn Wells, Capital	133 350 00
Total Assets	136 850 00	Total Liabilities and Owner's Equity	136 850 00

Asset Accounts	100–199	Revenue Accounts	400–499
Liability Accounts	200–299	Expense Accounts	500–599
Owner's Equity Accounts	300–399		

Notice that the accounts are not numbered consecutively. For example, asset account numbers jump from 101 to 111 and then to 121, 137, and 141. In each block of numbers, gaps are left so that additional accounts can be added when needed.

Permanent and Temporary Accounts

The asset, liability, and owner's equity accounts appear on the balance sheet at the end of an accounting period. The balances of these accounts are then carried forward to start the new period. Because they continue from one accounting period to the next, these accounts are called **permanent accounts** or *real accounts*.

Revenue and expense accounts appear on the income statement. The drawing account appears on the statement of owner's equity. These accounts classify and summarize changes in owner's equity during the period. They are called **temporary accounts** or *nominal accounts* because the balances in these accounts are transferred to the capital account at the end of the accounting period. In the next period, these accounts start with zero balances.

Wells' Consulting Services
Chart of Accounts

Account Number	Account Name
Balance Sheet Accounts	
100–199	**ASSETS**
101	Cash
111	Accounts Receivable
121	Supplies
137	Prepaid Rent
141	Equipment
200–299	**LIABILITIES**
202	Accounts Payable
300–399	**OWNER'S EQUITY**
301	Carolyn Wells, Capital
Statement of Owner's Equity Account	
302	Carolyn Wells, Drawing
Income Statement Accounts	
400–499	**REVENUE**
401	Fees Income
500–599	**EXPENSES**
511	Salaries Expense
514	Utilities Expense

FIGURE 3.8

Chart of Accounts

important!

Balance Sheet Accounts
The amounts on the balance sheet are carried forward to the next accounting period.

important!

Income Statement Accounts
The amounts on the income statement are transferred to the capital account at the end of the accounting period.

Section 2   Self Review

QUESTIONS

1. What is a trial balance and what is its purpose?
2. What is a transposition? A slide?
3. What is the increase side for *Cash; Accounts Payable;* and *Carolyn Wells, Capital?*

EXERCISES

4. Which account has a normal debit balance?
   a. Accounts Payable
   b. J. P., Capital
   c. J. P., Drawing
   d. Fees Income

5. The company owner took $4,000 cash for personal use. What is the entry for this transaction?
   a. Debit *Cash* and credit *Caleb Parker, Drawing.*
   b. Debit *Caleb Parker, Drawing* and credit *Cash.*
   c. Debit *Caleb Parker, Capital* and credit *Cash.*
   d. Debit *Cash* and credit *Caleb Parker, Capital.*

ANALYSIS

6. Describe the errors in the Parker Interiors trial balance.

Parker Interiors
Trial Balance
December 31, 2016

	DEBIT	CREDIT
Cash	15 0 0 0 00	
Accts. Rec.	10 0 0 0 00	
Equip.	7 0 0 0 00	
Accts. Pay.		15 0 0 0 00
C. Parker, Capital		22 0 0 0 00
C. Parker, Drawing		10 0 0 0 00
Fees Income	14 0 0 0 00	
Rent Exp.	2 0 0 0 00	
Supplies Exp.	2 0 0 0 00	
Telephone Exp.	5 0 0 0 00	
Totals	55 0 0 0 00	47 0 0 0 00

(Answers to Section 2 Self Review are on page 87.)

3 Chapter   **REVIEW**   **Chapter Summary**

In this chapter, you have learned how to use T accounts to help analyze and record business transactions. A chart of accounts can be developed to easily identify all the accounts used by a business. After determining the balance for all accounts, the trial balance is prepared to test the accuracy of total debits and credits after transactions have been recorded.

Learning Objectives

3-1 Set up T accounts for assets, liabilities, and owner's equity.

T accounts consist of two lines, one vertical and one horizontal, that resemble the letter T. The account name is written on the top line. Increases and decreases to the account are entered on either the left side or the right side of the vertical line.

3-2 Analyze business transactions and enter them in the accounts.

Each business transaction is analyzed for its effects on the fundamental accounting equation, Assets = Liabilities + Owner's Equity. Then these effects are recorded in the proper accounts. Accounts are classified as assets, liabilities, or owner's equity.

- Increases in an asset account appear on the debit, or left, side because assets are on the left side of the accounting equation. The credit, or right, side records decreases.

- An increase in a liability account is recorded on the credit, or right, side. The left, or debit, side of a liability account is used for recording decreases.

- Increases in owner's equity are shown on the credit (right) side of an account. Decreases appear on the debit (left) side.

- The drawing account is used to record the withdrawal of cash from the business by the owner. The drawing account decreases owner's equity.

3-3 Determine the balance of an account.

The difference between the amounts recorded on the two sides of an account is known as the balance of the account.

3-4 Set up T accounts for revenue and expenses.

- Revenue accounts increase owner's equity; therefore, increases are recorded on the credit side of revenue accounts.

- Expenses are recorded on the debit side of the expense accounts because expenses decrease owner's equity.

3-5 Prepare a trial balance from T accounts.

The trial balance is a statement to test the accuracy of the financial records. Total debits should equal total credits.

3-6 Prepare an income statement, a statement of owner's equity, and a balance sheet.

The income statement is prepared to report the revenue and expenses for the period. The statement of owner's equity is prepared to analyze the change in owner's equity during the period. Then the balance sheet is prepared to summarize the assets, liabilities, and owner's equity of the business at the end of the period.

3-7 Develop a chart of accounts.

A firm's list of accounts is called its chart of accounts. Accounts are arranged in a predetermined order and are numbered for handy reference and quick identification. Typically, accounts are numbered in the order in which they appear on the financial statements. Balance sheet accounts come first, followed by income statement accounts.

3-8 Define the accounting terms new to this chapter.

Glossary

Account balance (p. 60) The difference between the amounts recorded on the two sides of an account

Accounts (p. 54) Written records of the assets, liabilities, and owner's equity of a business

Chart of accounts (p. 71) A list of the accounts used by a business to record its financial transactions

Classification (p. 54) A means of identifying each account as an asset, liability, or owner's equity

Credit (p. 68) An entry on the right side of an account

Debit (p. 68) An entry on the left side of an account

Double-entry system (p. 68) An accounting system that involves recording the effects of each transaction as debits and credits

Drawing account (p. 67) A special type of owner's equity account set up to record the owner's withdrawal of cash from the business

Footing (p. 60) A small pencil figure written at the base of an amount column showing the sum of the entries in the column

Normal balance (p. 60) The increase side of an account

Permanent account (p. 72) An account that is kept open from one accounting period to the next

Slide (p. 71) An accounting error involving a misplaced decimal point

T account (p. 54) A type of account, resembling a T, used to analyze the effects of a business transaction

Temporary account (p. 72) An account whose balance is transferred to another account at the end of an accounting period

Transposition (p. 71) An accounting error involving misplaced digits in a number

Trial balance (p. 69) A statement to test the accuracy of total debits and credits after transactions have been recorded

Comprehensive **Self Review**

1. What is a chart of accounts?
2. What are withdrawals and how are they recorded?
3. What type of accounts are found on the balance sheet?
4. On which side of asset, liability, and owner's equity accounts are decreases recorded?
5. Your friend has prepared financial statements for her business. She has asked you to review the statements for accuracy. The trial balance debit column totals $91,000 and the credit column totals $104,000. What steps would you take to find the error?

(Answers to Comprehensive Self Review are on page 87.)

Discussion Questions

1. What are accounts?
2. How is the balance of an account determined?
3. Indicate whether each of the following types of accounts would normally have a debit balance or a credit balance:
    a. An asset account
    b. A liability account
    c. The owner's capital account
    d. A revenue account
    e. An expense account
4. What is the purpose of a chart of accounts?
5. In what order do accounts appear in the chart of accounts?
6. When a chart of accounts is created, number gaps are left within groups of accounts. Why are these number gaps necessary?
7. Accounts are classified as permanent or temporary accounts. What do these classifications mean?

8. Are the following accounts permanent or temporary accounts?

   a. Fees Income

   b. Johnny Jones, Drawing

   c. Accounts Payable

   d. Accounts Receivable

   e. Johnny Jones, Capital

   f. Prepaid Rent

   g. Cash

   h. Advertising Expense

   i. Utilities Expense

   j. Equipment

   k. Salaries Expense

   l. Prepaid Insurance

9. The terms *debit* and *credit* are often used in describing the effects of transactions on different accounts. What do these terms mean?

10. Why is **Prepaid Rent** considered an asset account?

11. Why is the modern system of accounting usually called the double-entry system?

APPLICATIONS

Exercises

Exercise 3.1

Objective 3-1

▶ **Setting up T accounts.**

Wilson Cleaning Service has the following account balances on December 31, 2016. Set up a T account for each account and enter the balance on the proper side of the account.

Cash	$19,000	Accounts Payable	$24,200
Equipment	$46,000	James Wilson, Capital	$40,800

Exercise 3.2

Objective 3-2

▶ **Using T accounts to analyze transactions.**

Denise Carswell decided to start a dental practice. The first five transactions for the business follow. For each transaction, (1) determine which two accounts are affected, (2) set up T accounts for the affected accounts, and (3) enter the debit and credit amounts in the T accounts.

1. Denise invested $90,000 cash in the business.

2. Paid $30,000 in cash for equipment.

3. Performed services for cash amounting to $9,000.

4. Paid $3,800 in cash for advertising expense.

5. Paid $3,000 in cash for supplies.

Exercise 3.3

Objective 3-3

▶ **Determining debit and credit balances.**

Indicate whether each of the following accounts normally has a debit balance or a credit balance:

1. Ned Cruz, Capital

2. Cash

3. Fees Income
4. Accounts Payable
5. Supplies
6. Salaries Expense
7. Accounts Receivable
8. Equipment

Identifying debits and credits.

◀ **Exercise 3.4**

Objective 3-3

In each of the following sentences, fill in the blanks with the word *debit* or *credit:*

1. The owner's capital account normally has a ___?___ balance. This account increases on the ___?___ side and decreases on the ___?___ side.
2. Expense accounts normally have ___?___ balances. These accounts increase on the ___?___ side and decrease on the ___?___ side.
3. Asset accounts normally have ___?___ balances. These accounts increase on the ___?___ side and decrease on the ___?___ side.
4. Liability accounts normally have ___?___ balances. These accounts increase on the ___?___ side and decrease on the ___?___ side.
5. Revenue accounts normally have ___?___ balances. These accounts increase on the ___?___ side and decrease on the ___?___ side.

Determining account balances.

◀ **Exercise 3.5**

Objective 3-3

The following T accounts show transactions that were recorded by Housing Locators, a firm that specializes in local housing renting. The entries for the first transaction are labeled with the letter (a), the entries for the second transaction with the letter (b), and so on. Determine the balance of each account.

Cash				
(a)	190,000	(b)	46,000	
(d)	30,000	(e)	700	
(g)	3,000	(h)	11,000	
		(i)	5,000	

Equipment		
(c)	80,000	

Accounts Receivable		
(f)	10,000	(g)	3,000

Accounts Payable		
		(c)	80,000

Supplies	
(b)	46,000

Wade Wilson, Capital		
		(a)	190,000

Fees Income		
		(d)	30,000
		(f)	10,000

Telephone Expense	
(e)	700

Wade Wilson, Drawing	
(i)	5,000

Salaries Expense	
(h)	11,000

Preparing a trial balance and an income statement.

◀ **Exercise 3.6**

Objectives 3-5, 3-6

CONTINUING >>>
Problem

Using the account balances from Exercise 3.5, prepare a trial balance and an income statement for Housing Locators. The trial balance is for December 31, 2016, and the income statement is for the month ended December 31, 2016.

Exercise 3.7
Objective 3-6

Problem

▶ **Preparing a statement of owner's equity and a balance sheet.**

From the trial balance and the net income or net loss determined in Exercise 3.6, prepare a statement of owner's equity and a balance sheet for Housing Locators as of December 31, 2016.

Exercise 3.8
Objective 3-7

▶ **Preparing a chart of accounts.**

The accounts that will be used by Three Brothers Moving Company follow. Prepare a chart of accounts for the firm. Classify the accounts by type, arrange them in an appropriate order, and assign suitable account numbers.

Trey Calhoun, Capital	Salaries Expense
Office Supplies	Prepaid Rent
Accounts Payable	Fees Income
Cash	Accounts Receivable
Utilities Expense	Telephone Expense
Office Equipment	Trey Calhoun, Drawing

PROBLEMS

Problem Set A

Problem 3.1A
Objective 3-1

▶ **Using T accounts to record transactions involving assets, liabilities, and owner's equity.**

The following transactions occurred at several different businesses and are not related.

INSTRUCTIONS

Analyze each of the transactions. For each, decide what accounts are affected and set up T accounts. Record the effects of the transaction in the T accounts. Use plus and minus signs before the amounts to show the increases and decreases.

TRANSACTIONS

1. Hunter Thompson, an owner, made an additional investment of $21,000 in cash.
2. A firm purchased equipment for $10,000 in cash.
3. A firm sold some surplus office furniture for $1,700 in cash.
4. A firm purchased a computer for $3,700, to be paid in 60 days.
5. A firm purchased office equipment for $11,200 on credit. The amount is due in 60 days.
6. Nancy Fowler, owner of Fowler Travel Agency, withdrew $6,000 of her original cash investment.
7. A firm bought a delivery truck for $37,000 on credit; payment is due in 90 days.
8. A firm issued a check for $3,500 to a supplier in partial payment of an open account balance.

Analyze: List the transactions that directly affected an owner's equity account.

Using T accounts to record transactions involving assets, liabilities, and owner's equity.

◀   **Problem 3.2A**
Objectives 3-1, 3-2

The following transactions took place at Confidential Counseling Services, a business established by Gloria Williams.

INSTRUCTIONS

For each transaction, set up T accounts from this list: *Cash; Office Furniture; Office Equipment; Automobile; Accounts Payable; Gloria Williams, Capital;* and *Gloria Williams, Drawing.* Analyze each transaction. Record the amounts in the T accounts affected by that transaction. Use plus and minus signs to show increases and decreases in each account.

TRANSACTIONS

1. Gloria Williams invested $70,000 cash in the business.
2. Purchased office furniture for $17,000 in cash.
3. Bought a fax machine for $1,050; payment is due in 30 days.
4. Purchased a used car for the firm for $17,000 in cash.
5. Williams invested an additional $11,000 cash in the business.
6. Bought a new computer for $4,000; payment is due in 60 days.
7. Paid $1,050 to settle the amount owed on the fax machine.
8. Williams withdrew $5,000 in cash for personal expenses.

Analyze: Which transactions affected asset accounts?

Using T accounts to record transactions involving revenues and expenses.

◀   **Problem 3.3A**
Objectives 3-2, 3-4

The following occurred during June at Young's Professional Counseling.

INSTRUCTIONS

Analyze each transaction. Use T accounts to record these transactions and be sure to put the name of the account on the top of each account. Record the effects of the transaction in the T accounts. Use plus and minus signs before the amounts to show the increases and decreases.

TRANSACTIONS

1. Purchased office supplies for $3,000 in cash.
2. Delivered monthly statements, collected fee income of $26,000.
3. Paid the current month's office rent of $5,000.
4. Completed professional counseling, billed client for $4,000.
5. Client paid fee of $2,000 for weekly counseling, previously billed.
6. Paid office salary of $4,600.
7. Paid telephone bill of $580.
8. Billed client for $3,000 fee for preparing a counseling memorandum.

9. Purchased office supplies of $1,100 on account.

10. Paid office salary of $4,600.

11. Collected $3,000 from client who was billed.

12. Clients paid a total of $9,100 cash in fees.

Analyze: How much cash did the business spend during the month?

Problem 3.4A

Objectives 3-1, 3-2, 3-4

▶ **Using T accounts to record all business transactions.**

The following accounts and transactions are for Horace Brock, Landscape Consultant.

INSTRUCTIONS

Analyze the transactions. Record each in the appropriate T accounts. Use plus and minus signs in front of the amounts to show the increases and decreases. Identify each entry in the T accounts by writing the letter of the transaction next to the entry.

ASSETS
Cash
Accounts Receivable
Office Furniture
Office Equipment
LIABILITIES
Accounts Payable
OWNER'S EQUITY
Horace Brock, Capital
Horace Brock, Drawing
REVENUE
Fees Income
EXPENSES
Rent Expense
Utilities Expense
Salaries Expense
Telephone Expense
Miscellaneous Expense

TRANSACTIONS

a. Brock invested $160,000 in cash to start the business.

b. Paid $6,000 for the current month's rent.

c. Bought office furniture for $16,720 in cash.

d. Performed services for $8,200 in cash.

e. Paid $1,250 for the monthly telephone bill.

f. Performed services for $14,000 on credit.

g. Purchased a computer and copier for $38,000, paid $13,000 in cash immediately with the balance due in 30 days.

h. Received $7,000 from credit clients.

i. Paid $4,000 in cash for office cleaning services for the month.

j. Purchased additional office chairs for $5,800; received credit terms of 30 days.

k. Purchased office equipment for $40,000 and paid half of this amount in cash immediately; the balance is due in 30 days.

l. Issued a check for $9,400 to pay salaries.

m. Performed services for $14,500 in cash.

n. Performed services for $16,000 on credit.

o. Collected $8,000 on accounts receivable from charge customers.

p. Issued a check for $2,900 in partial payment of the amount owed for office chairs.

q. Paid $700 to a duplicating company for photocopy work performed during the month.

r. Paid $1,220 for the monthly electric bill.

s. Brock withdrew $9,000 in cash for personal expenses.

Analyze: What liabilities does the business have after all transactions have been recorded?

Preparing financial statements from T accounts.

The accountant for the firm owned by Horace Brock prepares financial statements at the end of each month.

INSTRUCTIONS

Use the figures in the T accounts for Problem 3.4A to prepare a trial balance, an income statement, a statement of owner's equity, and a balance sheet. (The first line of the statement headings should read "Horace Brock, Landscape Consultant.") Assume that the transactions took place during the month ended June 30, 2016. Determine the account balances before you start work on the financial statements.

Analyze: What is the change in owner's equity for the month of June?

◀　　**Problem 3.5A**
**Objectives 3-3,
3-5, 3-6**

Problem Set B

Using T accounts to record transactions involving assets, liabilities, and owner's equity.

The following transactions occurred at several different businesses and are not related.

INSTRUCTIONS

Analyze each of the transactions. For each transaction, set up T accounts. Record the effects of the transaction in the T accounts. Use plus and minus signs to show the increases and decreases.

TRANSACTIONS

1. A firm purchased equipment for $32,000 in cash.

2. The owner, Gloria Bahamon, withdrew $8,000 cash.

3. A firm sold a piece of surplus equipment for $6,000 in cash.

4. A firm purchased a used delivery truck for $24,000 in cash.

5. A firm paid $7,200 in cash to apply against an account owed.

6. A firm purchased office equipment for $10,000. The amount is to be paid in 60 days.

7. Kevin Fralicks, owner of the company, made an additional investment of $40,000 in cash.

8. A firm paid $3,000 by check for office equipment that it had previously purchased on credit.

Analyze: Which transactions affect liability accounts?

◀　　**Problem 3.1B**
Objectives 3-1, 3-2

Problem 3.2B
Objectives 3-1, 3-2

▶ **Using T accounts to record transactions involving assets, liabilities, and owner's equity.**

The following transactions took place at Windmill Equipment Service.

INSTRUCTIONS

For each transaction, set up T accounts from the following list: *Cash*; *Shop Equipment; Store Equipment; Truck; Accounts Payable; Royce West, Capital;* and *Royce West, Drawing*. Analyze each transaction. Record the effects of the transactions in the T accounts. Use plus and minus signs before the amounts to show the increases and decreases.

TRANSACTIONS

1. Royce West invested $40,000 cash in the business.
2. Purchased shop equipment for $3,600 in cash.
3. Bought store fixtures for $2,400; payment is due in 30 days.
4. Purchased a used truck for $20,000 in cash.
5. West gave the firm his personal tools that have a fair market value of $6,000.
6. Bought a used cash register for $5,000; payment is due in 30 days.
7. Paid $800 in cash to apply to the amount owed for store fixtures.
8. West withdrew $3,200 in cash for personal expenses.

Analyze: Which transactions affect the *Cash* account?

Problem 3.3B
Objectives 3-2, 3-4

▶ **Using T accounts to record transactions involving revenue and expenses.**

The following transactions took place at Quick Perfection Laundry and Cleaners.

INSTRUCTIONS

Analyze each of the transactions. For each transaction, decide what accounts are affected and set up T accounts. Record the effects of the transaction in the T accounts. Use plus and minus signs before the amounts to show the increases and decreases.

TRANSACTIONS

1. Paid $7,500 for the current month's rent.
2. Performed services for $9,000 in cash.
3. Paid salaries of $6,800.
4. Performed additional services for $12,200 on credit.
5. Paid $1,580 for the monthly telephone bill.
6. Collected $8,000 from accounts receivable.
7. Received a $380 refund for an overcharge on the telephone bill.

8. Performed services for $8,560 on credit.

9. Paid $950 in cash for the monthly electric bill.

10. Paid $1,590 in cash for gasoline purchased for the firm's van during the month.

11. Received $6,250 from charge account customers.

12. Performed services for $9,400 in cash.

Analyze: What total cash was collected for Accounts Receivable during the month?

Using T accounts to record all business transactions.

◀ **Problem 3.4B**
Objectives 3-1,
3-2, 3-4

The accounts and transactions of Conner McAllister, Counselor and Attorney at Law, follow.

INSTRUCTIONS

Analyze the transactions. Record each in the appropriate T accounts. Use plus and minus signs in front of the amounts to show the increases and decreases. Identify each entry in the T accounts by writing the letter of the transaction next to the entry.

ASSETS
Cash
Accounts Receivable
Office Furniture
Office Equipment
Automobile

LIABILITIES
Accounts Payable

OWNER'S EQUITY
Conner McAllister, Capital
Conner McAllister, Drawing

REVENUE
Fees Income

EXPENSES
Automobile Expense
Rent Expense
Utilities Expense
Salaries Expense
Telephone Expense

TRANSACTIONS

a. Conner McAllister invested $140,000 in cash to start the business.

b. Paid $7,800 for the current month's rent.

c. Bought a used automobile for the firm for $38,500 in cash.

d. Performed services for $10,500 in cash.

e. Paid $1,850 for automobile repairs.

f. Performed services for $11,280 on credit.

g. Purchased office chairs for $6,500 on credit.

h. Received $5,400 from credit clients.

i. Paid $3,800 to reduce the amount owed for the office chairs.

j. Issued a check for $1,590 to pay the monthly utility bill.

k. Purchased office equipment for $22,800 and paid half of this amount in cash immediately; the balance is due in 30 days.

l. Issued a check for $18,900 to pay salaries.

    m. Performed services for $7,450 in cash.

    n. Performed services for $6,500 on credit.

    o. Paid $967 for the monthly telephone bill.

    p. Collected $4,200 on accounts receivable from charge customers.

    q. Purchased additional office equipment and received a bill for $6,880 due in 30 days.

    r. Paid $900 in cash for gasoline purchased for the automobile during the month.

    s. Conner McAllister withdrew $8,000 in cash for personal expenses.

Analyze: What outstanding amount is owed to the company from its credit customers?

Problem 3.5B

Objectives 3-3, 3-5, 3-6

CONTINUING >>> Problem

▶ **Preparing financial statements from T accounts.**

The accountant for the firm owned by Conner McAllister prepares financial statements at the end of each month.

INSTRUCTIONS

Use the figures in the T accounts for Problem 3.4B to prepare a trial balance, an income statement, a statement of owner's equity, and a balance sheet. (The first line of the statement headings should read "Conner McAllister, Counselor and Attorney at Law.") Assume that the transactions took place during the month ended April 30, 2016. Determine the account balances before you start work on the financial statements.

Analyze: What net change in owner's equity occurred during the month of April?

Critical Thinking Problem 3.1

Financial Condition

At the beginning of the summer, Jack Wells was looking for a way to earn money to pay for his college tuition in the fall. He decided to start a lawn service business in his neighborhood. To get the business started, Jack used $6,000 from his savings account to open a checking account for his new business, Elegant Lawn Care. He purchased two used power mowers and various lawn care tools for $2,000, and paid $3,600 for a second-hand truck to transport the mowers.

    Several of his neighbors hired him to cut their grass on a weekly basis. He sent these customers monthly bills. By the end of the summer, they had paid him $1,200 in cash and owed him another $2,300. Jack also cut grass on an as-needed basis for other neighbors who paid him $1,000.

    During the summer, Jack spent $400 for gasoline for the truck and mowers. He paid $1,000 to a friend who helped him on several occasions. An advertisement in the local paper cost $200. Now, at the end of the summer, Jack is concerned because he has only $1,000 left in his checking account. He says, "I worked hard all summer and have only $1,000 to show for it. It would have been better to leave the money in the bank."

    Prepare an income statement, a statement of owner's equity, and a balance sheet for Elegant Lawn Care. Explain to Jack whether or not he is "better off" than he was at the beginning of the summer. (Hint: T accounts might be helpful in organizing the data.)

Critical Thinking Problem 3.2

Sole Proprietorship

John Arrow is an architect who operates his own business. The accounts and transactions for the business follow.

INSTRUCTIONS

(1) Analyze the transactions for January 2016. Record each in the appropriate T accounts. Use plus and minus signs in front of the amounts to show the increases and decreases. Identify each entry in the T account by writing the letter of the transaction next to the entry.

(2) Determine the account balances. Prepare a trial balance, an income statement, a statement of owner's equity, and a balance sheet.

ASSETS

Cash

Accounts Receivable

Office Furniture

Office Equipment

LIABILITIES

Accounts Payable

OWNER'S EQUITY

John Arrow, Capital

John Arrow, Drawing

REVENUE

Fees Income

EXPENSES

Advertising Expense

Utilities Expense

Salaries Expense

Telephone Expense

Miscellaneous Expense

TRANSACTIONS

a. John Arrow invested $40,000 in cash to start the business.

b. Paid $4,000 for advertisements in a design magazine.

c. Purchased office furniture for $4,600 in cash.

d. Performed services for $9,100 in cash.

e. Paid $420 for the monthly telephone bill.

f. Performed services for $3,120 on credit.

g. Purchased a fax machine for $650; paid $150 in cash with the balance due in 30 days.

h. Paid a bill for $1,100 from the office cleaning service.

i. Received $4,260 from clients on account.

j. Purchased additional office chairs for $1,090; received credit terms of 30 days.

k. Paid $8,000 for salaries.

l. Issued a check for $550 in partial payment of the amount owed for office chairs.

m. Received $4,600 in cash for services performed.

n. Issued a check for $920 for utilities expense.

o. Performed services for $4,300 on credit.

p. Collected $1,800 from clients on account.

q. John Arrow withdrew $5,000 in cash for personal expenses.

r. Paid $1,200 to Quick Copy Service for photocopy work performed during the month.

Analyze: Using the basic accounting equation, what is the financial condition of John Arrow's business at month-end?

BUSINESS CONNECTIONS

Informed Decisions

Managerial FOCUS

1. In discussing a firm's latest financial statements, a manager says that it is the "results on the bottom line" that really count. What does the manager mean?

2. If a firm's expenses equal or exceed its revenue, what actions might management take?

3. How can management find out, at any time, whether a firm can pay its bills as they become due?

4. How do the income statement and the balance sheet help management make sound decisions?

To Open or Not to Open

As the bookkeeper of a new start-up company, you are responsible for keeping the chart of accounts up to date. At the end of each year, you analyze the accounts to verify that each account should be active for accumulation of costs, revenues, and expenses. In July, the accounts payable clerk has asked you to open an account named New Expenses. You know that an account name should be specific and well defined. You feel that the A/P clerk might want to charge some expenses to that account that would not be appropriate. Why do you think the A/P clerk needs this New Expenses account? Who needs to know this information and what action should you consider?

Management Letter and Annual Report

Annual reports released by publicly held companies include a letter to the stockholders written by the chief executive officer, chairman of the board, or president.

Analyze Online: Locate the Adobe Systems Incorporated website (www.adobe.com). Within *Investor Relations* in the *About Adobe* link, find the annual report for the current year. Read the letter to the stockholders within the annual report.

Analyze:

1. What types of information can a company's management deliver using the letter to stockholders?

2. What annual revenue did Adobe Systems Incorporated report for fiscal 2012?

3. What amount of cash, cash equivalents, and short term investments did Adobe have on hand at the end of 2012?

4. Are the financial results presented in the current year more or less favorable than those presented for fiscal 2011?

5. What is Adobe's targeted revenue for the first quarter of 2013?

Specific Chart of Accounts

A chart of accounts varies with each type of business as well as each company. In a group, compare and contrast the accounts that would appear in Cole's Real Estate Office, Sarah's Clothing Emporium, Neal's Grocery Store, and Tanner Plumbing Service. What accounts would appear in all companies? What accounts would be specific to each business?

10K Reports

Financial statements can reveal a great deal about a company. Corporations are required to produce a 10K report that includes the income statement and balance sheet. Go to the companies' websites listed below, select investor relations, annual report, and 10K report. From the income statement, decide the most profitable company. From the balance sheet, decide the company with the largest amount of cash available and the one with the most assets. (www.jcpenny.com) (www.honeywell.com)

Answers to **Self Reviews**

Answers to Section 1 Self Review

1. The sum of several entries on either side of an account that is entered in small pencil figures.

2. The increase side of an account. The normal balance of an asset account is on the left side. The normal balance of liability and owner's equity accounts is on the right side.

3. Increases in asset accounts are recorded on the left side. Increases in liability and owner's equity accounts are recorded on the right side.

4. a. *Equipment* is increased by $20,200. *Accounts Payable* is increased by $20,200.

5.

Cash	+	Equipment	+	Supplies	=	Accounts Payable	+	David Jenkins, Capital
$30,800	+	$40,000	+	$9,200	=	$20,000	+	$60,000
				$80,000	=	$80,000		

6. c. 33,450

Answers to Section 2 Self Review

1. The trial balance is a list of all the accounts and their balances. Its purpose is to prove the equality of the total debits and credits.

2. A transposition is an error in which the digits of a number are switched, for example, when 517 is recorded as 571. A slide is an error in which the decimal point is misplaced, for example, when 317 is written as 3.17.

3. The increase side of *Cash* is the left, or debit, side. The increase side of *Accounts Payable* is the right, or credit, side. The increase side of *Carolyn Wells, Capital* is the right, or credit, side.

4. c. *J. P., Drawing*

5. b. *Caleb Parker, Drawing* would be debited and *Cash* would be credited.

6. *C. Parker, Drawing*—10,000 should be in the Debit column.

Fees Income—14,000 should be in the Credit column.

The new column totals will be 51,000.

Answers to Comprehensive Self Review

1. A list of the numbers and names of the accounts of a business. It provides a system by which the accounts of the business can be easily identified and located.

2. Cash taken from the business by the owner to obtain funds for personal living expenses. Withdrawals are recorded in a special type of owner's equity account called a drawing account.

3. The asset, liability, and owner's equity accounts.

4. Decreases in asset accounts are recorded on the credit side. Decreases in liability and owner's equity accounts are recorded on the debit side.

5.
- Check the math by adding the columns again.
- Determine whether the account balances are in the correct columns.
- Check the accounts to see whether the balances in the accounts were computed correctly.
- Check the accuracy of transactions recorded during the period.

The General Journal and the General Ledger

Boeing
www.boeing.com

The International Space Station (ISS) is a truly global project; involving the scientific and technological resources of 16 countries and the efforts of more than 100,000 people throughout the world. As the prime contractor, Boeing has been responsible for design, development, construction, and integration of the ISS, as well as assistance to NASA with the operation of this orbital outpost.

The ISS is the largest, most complex international scientific project in history and our largest adventure into space to date. It cost roughly 150 billion dollars to build! To keep track of the expenditures involved, it was important for Boeing to maintain not only a chronological record of the costs and expenses incurred in developing and constructing the station, but it was equally important to update individual cost accounts so that accurate and timely cost data were available at any given time. If they were not able to carefully track their spending, the Space Station's construction bill might have cost U.S. taxpayers a heck of a lot more than $150 billion!

In 2010, Boeing officially turned over the U.S. on-orbit segment of the ISS to NASA. Often referred to as "handing over the keys," the DD-250 is equivalent to a final bill of sale that formally transfers ownership. Through the review board, NASA and Boeing verified the delivery, assembly, integration, and activation of all hardware and software required by contract. The success of the ISS has validated Boeing's position as a leader in the defense industry and has contributed to the company's overall revenue growth.

thinking critically

How do you think Boeing would record the purchase of a robotic arm that could handle large payloads, move equipment and supplies around the station, and support astronauts working outside the space station?

LEARNING OBJECTIVES

4-1. Record transactions in the general journal.

4-2. Prepare compound journal entries.

4-3. Post journal entries to general ledger accounts.

4-4. Correct errors made in the journal or ledger.

4-5. Define the accounting terms new to this chapter.

NEW TERMS

accounting cycle
audit trail
balance ledger form
chronological order
compound entry
correcting entry

general journal
general ledger
journal
journalizing
ledger
posting

| SECTION OBJECTIVES | TERMS TO LEARN |

SECTION OBJECTIVES

>> **4-1.** Record transactions in the general journal.

WHY IT'S IMPORTANT

Written records for all business transactions are necessary. The general journal acts as the "diary" of the business.

>> **4-2.** Prepare compound journal entries.

WHY IT'S IMPORTANT

Compound entries contain several debits or credits for a single business transaction, creating efficiencies in journalizing.

TERMS TO LEARN

accounting cycle
audit trail
chronological order
compound entry
general journal
journal
journalizing

The General Journal

The **accounting cycle** is a series of steps performed during each accounting period to classify, record, and summarize data for a business and to produce needed financial information. The first step in the accounting cycle is to analyze business transactions. You learned this skill in Chapter 3. The second step in the accounting cycle is to prepare a record of business transactions.

Journals

Business transactions are recorded in a **journal,** which is a diary of business activities. The journal lists transactions in **chronological order,** that is, in the order in which they occur. The journal is sometimes called the *record of original entry* because it is where transactions are first entered in the accounting records. There are different types of journals. This chapter will examine the general journal. You will become familiar with other journals in later chapters.

> Most corporations use accounting software to record business transactions. Industry-specific software is available for accounting firms, oil and gas companies, construction firms, medical firms, and any other industry-specific business enterprise.

>> **4-1. OBJECTIVE**

Record transactions in the general journal.

important!

The Diary of a Business
The general journal is similar to a diary. The general journal details, in chronological order, the economic events of the business.

The General Journal

The **general journal** is a financial record for entering all types of business transactions. **Journalizing** is the process of recording transactions in the general journal.

Figure 4.1 shows the general journal for Wells' Consulting Services. Notice that the general journal has a page number. To record a transaction, enter the year at the top of the Date column. In the Date column, write the month and day on the first line of the first entry. After the first entry, enter the year and month only when a new page is started or when the year or the month changes. In the Date column, write the day of each transaction on the first line of each transaction.

In the Description column, enter the account to be debited. Write the account name close to the left margin of the Description column, and enter the amount on the same line in the Debit column.

Enter the account to be credited on the line beneath the debit. Indent the account name about one-half inch from the left margin. Enter the amount on the same line in the Credit column.

Then enter a complete but concise description of the transaction in the Description column. Begin the description on the line following the credit. The description is indented about one inch from the left margin.

Write account names exactly as they appear in the chart of accounts. This will minimize errors when amounts are transferred from the general journal to the accounts.

FIGURE 4.1

General Journal Entry

	DATE		DESCRIPTION	POST. REF.	DEBIT	CREDIT	
1	2016						1
2	Nov.	6	Cash		100 00 0 00		2
3			Carolyn Wells, Capital			100 00 0 00	3
4			Investment by owner				4
5							5

GENERAL JOURNAL   PAGE ___1___

— Record the year first, then the month and day.
— Record the debit first.
— Indent about one-half inch and record the credit.
— Indent again and write the description.

Leave a blank line between general journal entries. Some accountants use this blank line to number each general journal entry.

When possible, the journal entry description should refer to the source of the information. For example, the journal entry to record a payment should include the check number in the description. Document numbers are part of the audit trail. The **audit trail** is a chain of references that makes it possible to trace information, locate errors, and prevent fraud. The audit trail provides a means of checking the journal entry against the original data on the documents.

important!

Audit Trail
To maintain the audit trail, descriptions should refer to document numbers whenever possible.

RECORDING NOVEMBER TRANSACTIONS IN THE GENERAL JOURNAL

In Chapters 2 and 3, you learned a step-by-step method for analyzing business transactions. In this chapter, you will learn how to complete the journal entry for a business transaction in the same manner. Review the following steps before you continue:

1. Analyze the financial event:
   - Identify the accounts affected.
   - Classify the accounts affected.
   - Determine the amount of increase or decrease for each account affected.
2. Apply the rules of debit and credit:
   a. Which account is debited? For what amount?
   b. Which account is credited? For what amount?
3. Make the entry in T-account form.
4. Record the complete entry in general journal form.

BUSINESS TRANSACTION

On November 6, Carolyn Wells withdrew $100,000 from personal savings and deposited it in a new business checking account for Wells' Consulting Services.

MEMORANDUM 01

WELLS' CONSULTING SERVICES

TO: Carlos Valdez
FROM: Carolyn Wells
DATE: November 6, 2016
SUBJECT: Contributed personal funds to the business

I contributed $100,000 from my personal savings to Wells' Consulting Services.

ANALYSIS
a. The asset account, *Cash,* is increased by $100,000.
a. The owner's equity account, *Carolyn Wells, Capital,* is increased by $100,000.

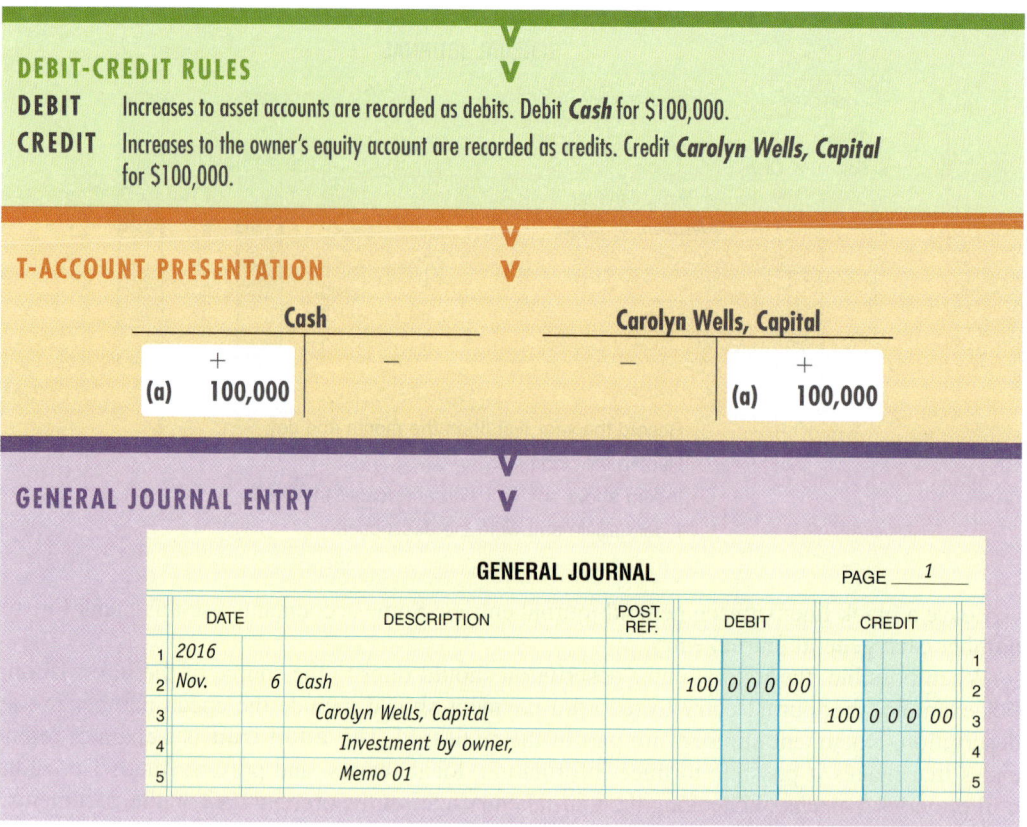

DEBIT-CREDIT RULES

DEBIT   Increases to asset accounts are recorded as debits. Debit *Cash* for $100,000.

CREDIT   Increases to the owner's equity account are recorded as credits. Credit *Carolyn Wells, Capital* for $100,000.

T-ACCOUNT PRESENTATION

Cash		Carolyn Wells, Capital	
+	–	–	+
(a) 100,000			(a) 100,000

GENERAL JOURNAL ENTRY

GENERAL JOURNAL   PAGE ___1___

	DATE		DESCRIPTION	POST. REF.	DEBIT	CREDIT	
1	2016						1
2	Nov.	6	Cash		100 0 0 0 00		2
3			Carolyn Wells, Capital			100 0 0 0 00	3
4			Investment by owner,				4
5			Memo 01				5

BUSINESS TRANSACTION

On November 7, Wells' Consulting Services issued Check 1001 for $5,000 to purchase a computer and other equipment.

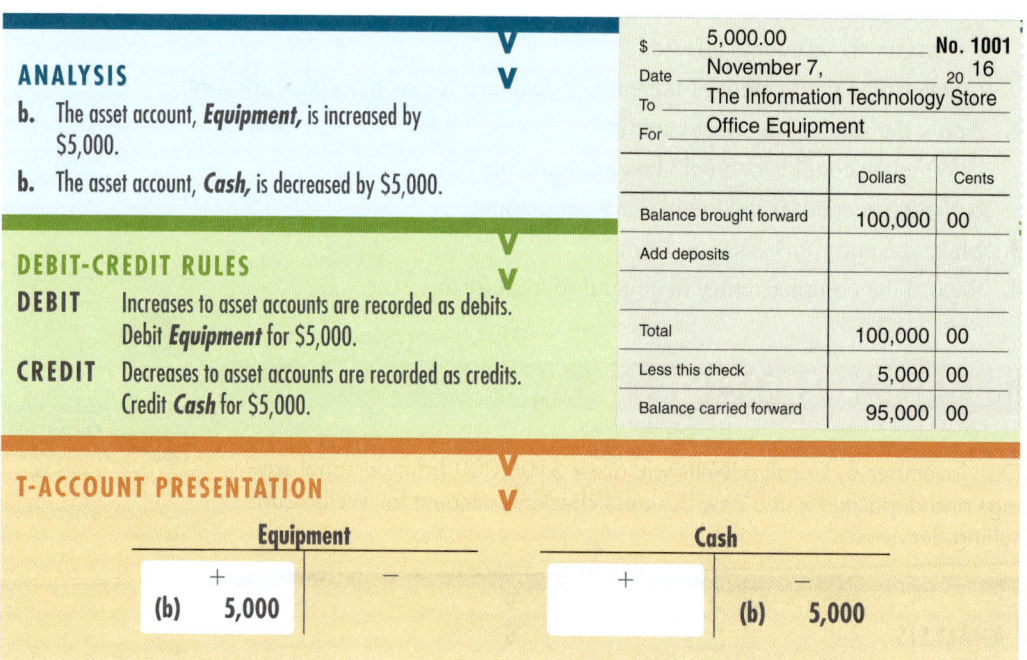

ANALYSIS

b. The asset account, *Equipment,* is increased by $5,000.

b. The asset account, *Cash,* is decreased by $5,000.

DEBIT-CREDIT RULES

DEBIT   Increases to asset accounts are recorded as debits. Debit *Equipment* for $5,000.

CREDIT   Decreases to asset accounts are recorded as credits. Credit *Cash* for $5,000.

$	5,000.00		No. 1001
Date	November 7,		20 16
To	The Information Technology Store		
For	Office Equipment		

	Dollars	Cents
Balance brought forward	100,000	00
Add deposits		
Total	100,000	00
Less this check	5,000	00
Balance carried forward	95,000	00

T-ACCOUNT PRESENTATION

Equipment		Cash	
+	–	+	–
(b) 5,000			(b) 5,000

GENERAL JOURNAL ENTRY

	DATE	DESCRIPTION	POST. REF.	DEBIT	CREDIT	
		GENERAL JOURNAL			PAGE ___1___	
6	Nov. 7	Equipment		5 0 0 0 00		6
7		Cash			5 0 0 0 00	7
8		Purchased equip., Check 1001				8

The check number appears in the description and forms part of the audit trail for the transaction.

BUSINESS TRANSACTION

On November 10, Wells' Consulting Services purchased office equipment on account for $6,000.

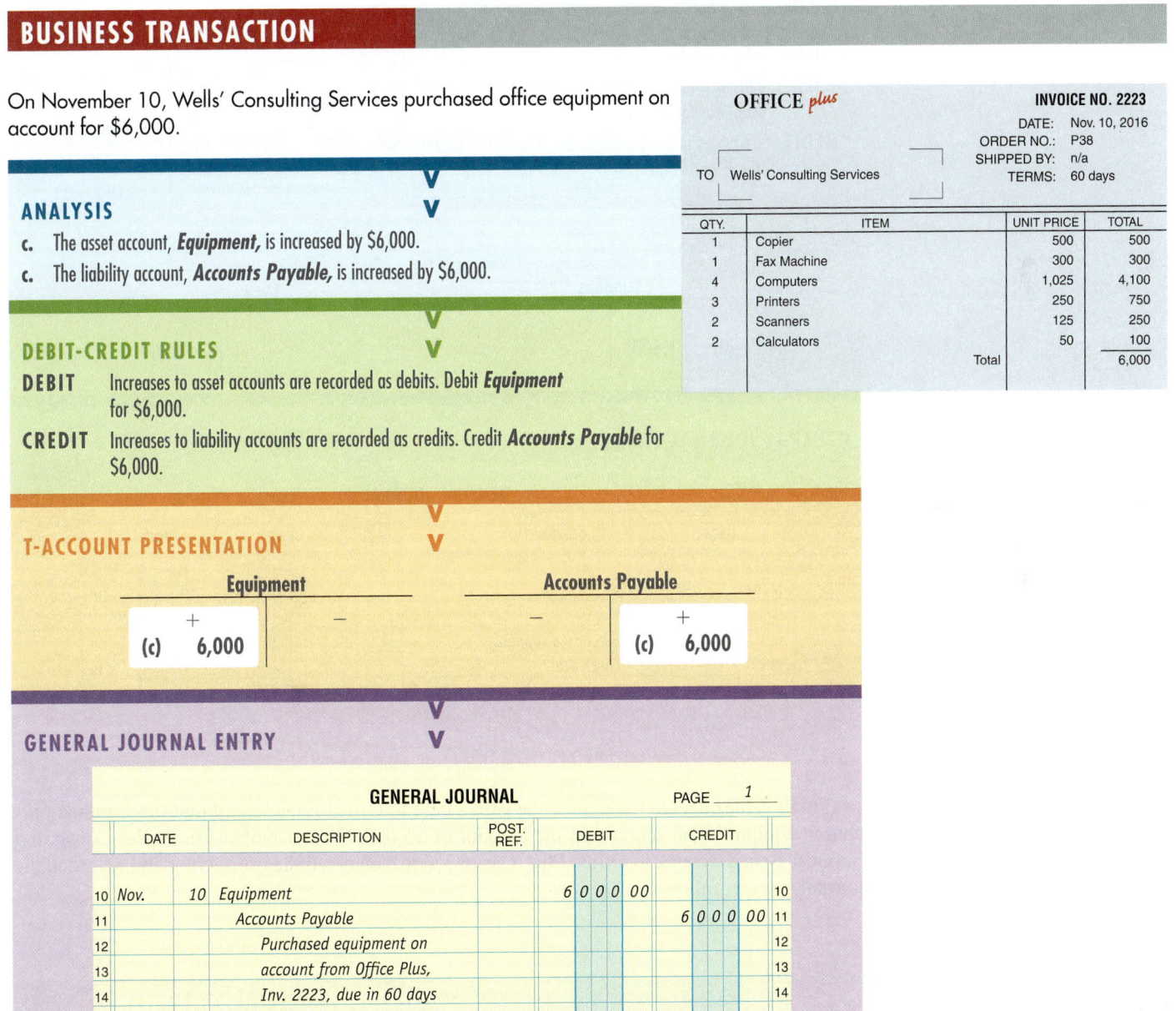

	OFFICE *plus*		INVOICE NO. 2223
			DATE: Nov. 10, 2016
			ORDER NO.: P38
			SHIPPED BY: n/a
TO Wells' Consulting Services			TERMS: 60 days

QTY.	ITEM	UNIT PRICE	TOTAL
1	Copier	500	500
1	Fax Machine	300	300
4	Computers	1,025	4,100
3	Printers	250	750
2	Scanners	125	250
2	Calculators	50	100
		Total	6,000

ANALYSIS
c. The asset account, *Equipment,* is increased by $6,000.
c. The liability account, *Accounts Payable,* is increased by $6,000.

DEBIT-CREDIT RULES
DEBIT Increases to asset accounts are recorded as debits. Debit *Equipment* for $6,000.

CREDIT Increases to liability accounts are recorded as credits. Credit *Accounts Payable* for $6,000.

T-ACCOUNT PRESENTATION

Equipment		Accounts Payable	
+	–	–	+
(c) 6,000			(c) 6,000

GENERAL JOURNAL ENTRY

	DATE	DESCRIPTION	POST. REF.	DEBIT	CREDIT	
		GENERAL JOURNAL			PAGE ___1___	
10	Nov. 10	Equipment		6 0 0 0 00		10
11		Accounts Payable			6 0 0 0 00	11
12		Purchased equipment on				12
13		account from Office Plus,				13
14		Inv. 2223, due in 60 days				14

The supplier's name (Office Plus) and invoice number (2223) appear in the journal entry description and form part of the audit trail for the transaction. The journal entry can be checked against the data on the original document, Invoice 2223.

On November 28, Wells' Consulting Services purchased supplies for $1,500, Check 1002.

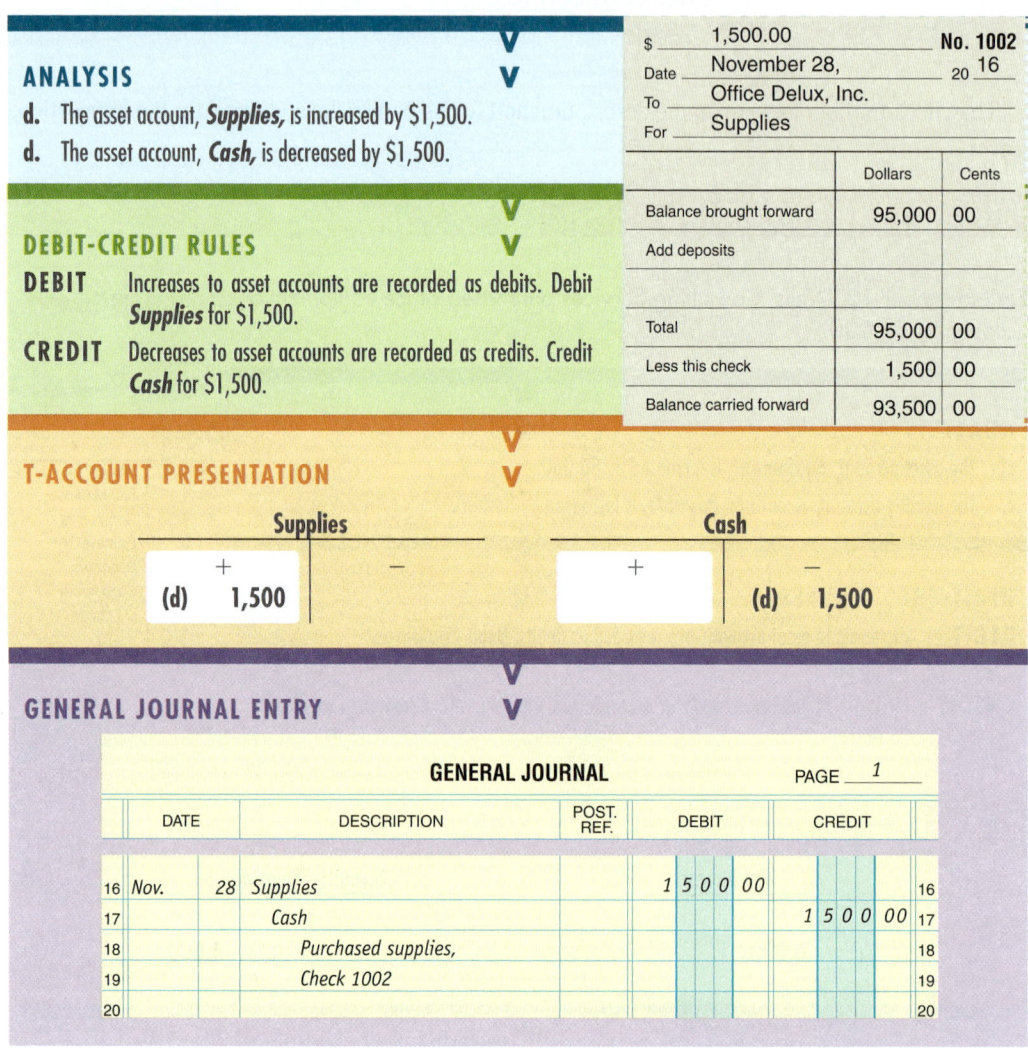

Carlos Valdez decided to reduce the firm's debt to Office Plus. Recall that the firm had purchased equipment on account in the amount of $6,000. On November 30, Wells' Consulting Services issued a check to Office Plus. Carlos Valdez analyzed the transaction and recorded the journal entry as follows.

On November 30, Wells' Consulting Services paid Office Plus $2,500 in partial payment of Invoice 2223, Check 1003.

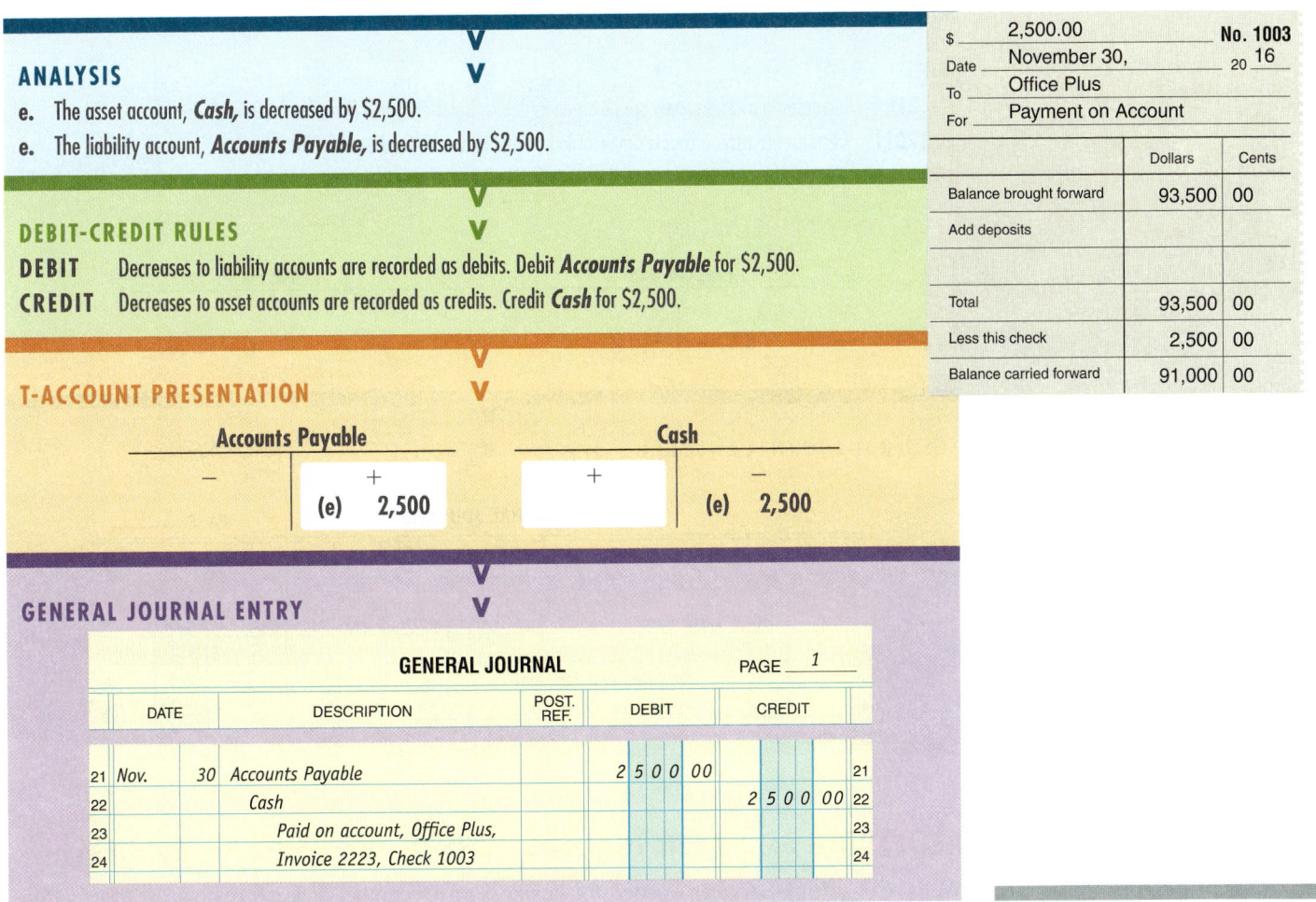

$ 2,500.00		No. 1003
Date November 30,		20 16
To Office Plus		
For Payment on Account		

	Dollars	Cents
Balance brought forward	93,500	00
Add deposits		
Total	93,500	00
Less this check	2,500	00
Balance carried forward	91,000	00

ANALYSIS
e. The asset account, *Cash,* is decreased by $2,500.
e. The liability account, *Accounts Payable,* is decreased by $2,500.

DEBIT-CREDIT RULES
DEBIT   Decreases to liability accounts are recorded as debits. Debit *Accounts Payable* for $2,500.
CREDIT   Decreases to asset accounts are recorded as credits. Credit *Cash* for $2,500.

T-ACCOUNT PRESENTATION

Accounts Payable
− | + (e) 2,500

Cash
+ | − (e) 2,500

GENERAL JOURNAL ENTRY

GENERAL JOURNAL   PAGE 1

	DATE	DESCRIPTION	POST. REF.	DEBIT	CREDIT	
21	Nov. 30	Accounts Payable		2 5 0 0 00		21
22		Cash			2 5 0 0 00	22
23		Paid on account, Office Plus,				23
24		Invoice 2223, Check 1003				24

Notice that the general journal Description column includes three important items for the audit trail:

- the supplier name,
- the invoice number,
- the check number.

In the general journal, always enter debits before credits. This is the case even if the credit item is considered first when mentally analyzing the transaction.

Wells' Consulting Services issued a check in November to pay December and January rent in advance. Recall that the right to occupy facilities is considered a form of property. Carlos Valdez analyzed the transaction and recorded the journal entry as follows.

BUSINESS TRANSACTION

On November 30, Wells' Consulting Services wrote Check 1004 for $8,000 to prepay rent for December and January.

$ 8,000.00		No. 1004
Date November 30,		20 16
To Davidson Properties		
For Prepaid Rent		

	Dollars	Cents
Balance brought forward	91,000	00
Add deposits		
Total	91,000	00
Less this check	8,000	00
Balance carried forward	83,000	00

ANALYSIS
f. The asset account, *Prepaid Rent,* is increased by $8,000.
f. The asset account, *Cash,* is decreased by $8,000.

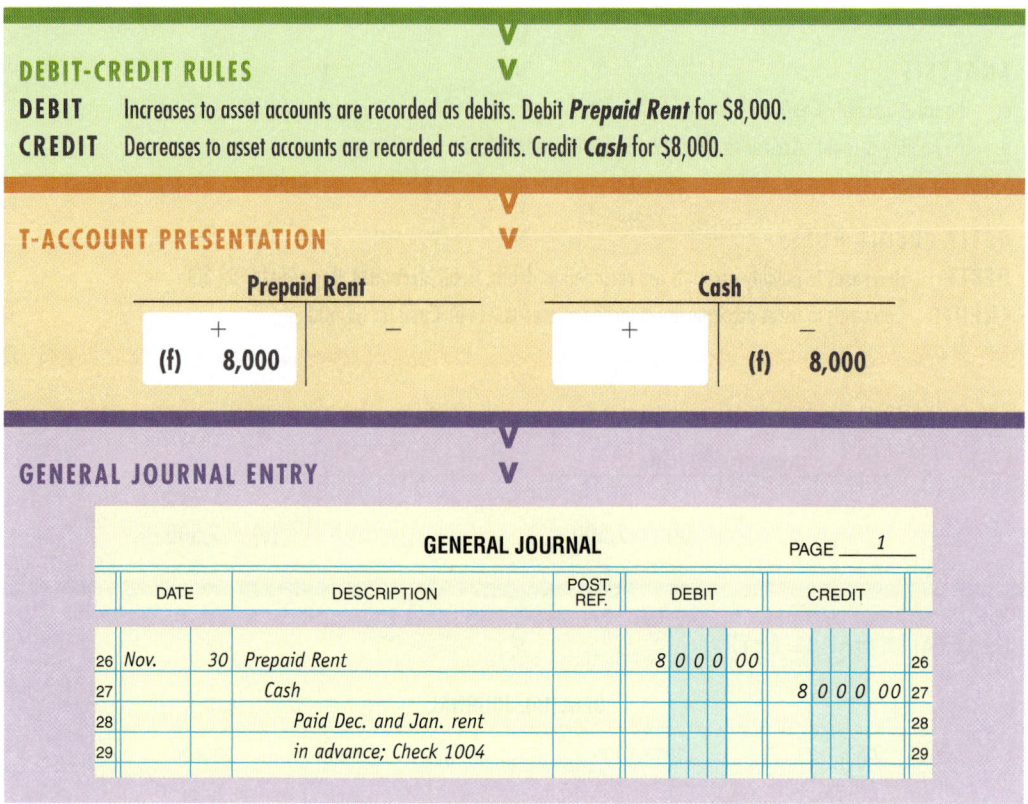

DEBIT-CREDIT RULES

DEBIT   Increases to asset accounts are recorded as debits. Debit *Prepaid Rent* for $8,000.

CREDIT   Decreases to asset accounts are recorded as credits. Credit *Cash* for $8,000.

T-ACCOUNT PRESENTATION

Prepaid Rent		Cash	
+	−	+	−
(f) 8,000			(f) 8,000

GENERAL JOURNAL ENTRY

		GENERAL JOURNAL			PAGE _1_	
	DATE	DESCRIPTION	POST. REF.	DEBIT	CREDIT	
26	Nov. 30	Prepaid Rent		8 0 0 0 00		26
27		Cash			8 0 0 0 00	27
28		Paid Dec. and Jan. rent				28
29		in advance; Check 1004				29

RECORDING DECEMBER TRANSACTIONS IN THE GENERAL JOURNAL

Wells' Consulting Services opened for business on December 1. Let's review the transactions that occurred in December. Refer to items **g** through **l** in Chapter 3 for the analysis of each transaction.

1. Performed services for $36,000 in cash.
2. Performed services for $11,000 on credit.
3. Received $6,000 in cash from credit clients on their accounts.
4. Paid $8,000 for salaries.
5. Paid $650 for a utility bill.
6. The owner withdrew $5,000 for personal expenses.

Figure 4.2 shows the entries in the general journal. In an actual business, transactions involving fees income and accounts receivable occur throughout the month and are recorded when they take place. For the sake of simplicity, these transactions are summarized and recorded as of December 31 for Wells' Consulting Services.

>> **4-2. OBJECTIVE**

Prepare compound journal entries.

PREPARING COMPOUND ENTRIES

So far, each journal entry consists of one debit and one credit. Some transactions require a **compound entry**—a journal entry that contains more than one debit or credit. In a compound entry, record all debits first followed by the credits.

When Allstate purchased an insurance division of CNA Financial Corporation, Allstate paid cash and issued a 10-year note payable (a promise to pay). Detailed accounting records are not available to the public, but a compound journal entry was probably used to record this transaction.

FIGURE 4.2

General Journal Entries
for December

	DATE		DESCRIPTION	POST. REF.	DEBIT	CREDIT	
1	2016						1
2	Dec.	31	Cash		36 000 00		2
3			Fees Income			36 000 00	3
4			Performed services for cash				4
5							5
6		31	Accounts Receivable		11 000 00		6
7			Fees Income			11 000 00	7
8			Performed services on credit				8
9							9
10		31	Cash		6 000 00		10
11			Accounts Receivable			6 000 00	11
12			Received cash from credit				12
13			clients on account				13
14							14
15		31	Salaries Expense		8 000 00		15
16			Cash			8 000 00	16
17			Paid monthly salaries to				17
18			employees, Checks				18
19			1005–1006				19
20							20
21		31	Utilities Expense		6 50 00		21
22			Cash			6 50 00	22
23			Paid monthly bill for utilities,				23
24			Check 1007				24
25							25
26		31	Carolyn Wells, Drawing		5 000 00		26
27			Cash			5 000 00	27
28			Owner withdrew cash for				28
29			personal expenses,				29
30			Check 1008				30
31							31
32							32
33							33
34							34
35							35

GENERAL JOURNAL PAGE ___2___

Suppose that on November 7, when Wells' Consulting Services purchased the equipment for $5,000, Carolyn Wells paid $2,500 in cash and agreed to pay the balance in 30 days. This transaction is analyzed below and on the next page.

BUSINESS TRANSACTION

On November 7, the firm purchased equipment for $5,000, issued Check 1001 for $2,500, and agreed to pay the balance in 30 days.

ANALYSIS

The asset account, **Equipment,** is increased by $5,000. The asset account, **Cash,** is decreased by $2,500.
The liability account, **Accounts Payable,** is increased by $2,500.

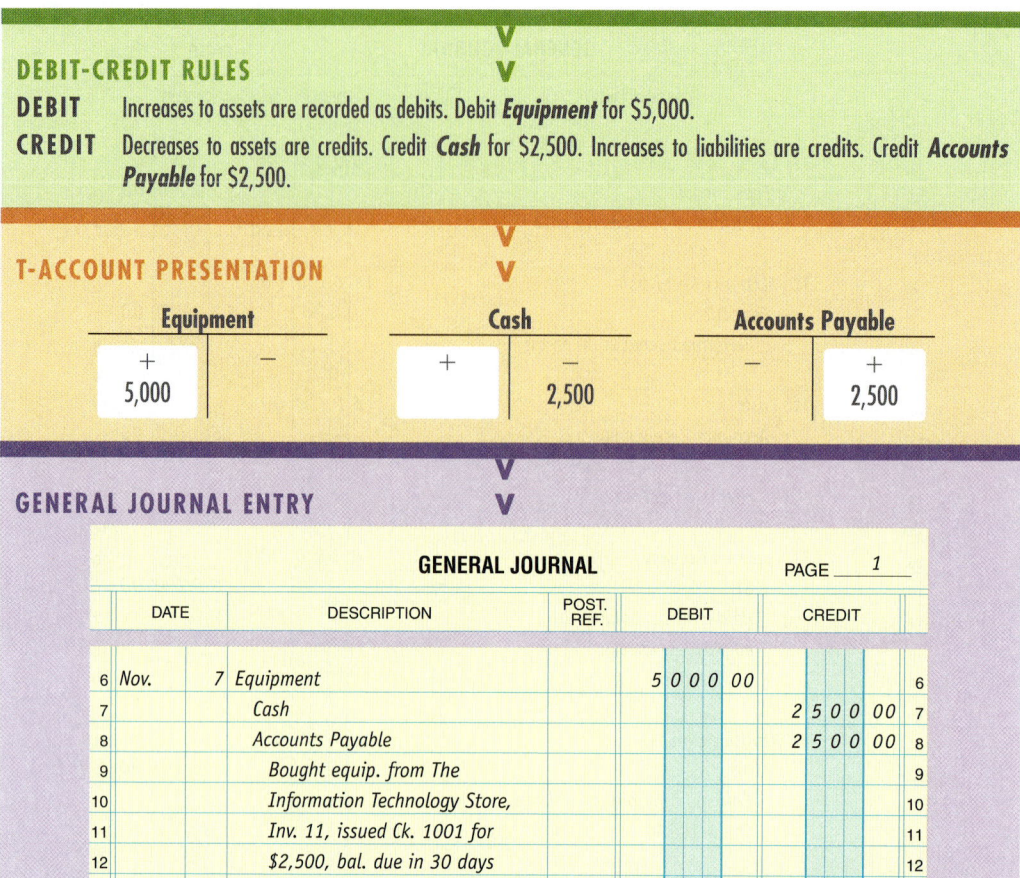

DEBIT-CREDIT RULES

DEBIT   Increases to assets are recorded as debits. Debit **Equipment** for $5,000.

CREDIT   Decreases to assets are credits. Credit **Cash** for $2,500. Increases to liabilities are credits. Credit **Accounts Payable** for $2,500.

T-ACCOUNT PRESENTATION

Equipment		Cash		Accounts Payable	
+	−	+	−	−	+
5,000			2,500		2,500

GENERAL JOURNAL ENTRY

GENERAL JOURNAL PAGE ___1___

	DATE	DESCRIPTION	POST. REF.	DEBIT	CREDIT	
6	Nov. 7	Equipment		5 0 0 0 00		6
7		Cash			2 5 0 0 00	7
8		Accounts Payable			2 5 0 0 00	8
9		Bought equip. from The				9
10		Information Technology Store,				10
11		Inv. 11, issued Ck. 1001 for				11
12		$2,500, bal. due in 30 days				12

recall

Debits = Credits

No matter how many accounts are affected by a transaction, total debits must equal total credits.

Section 1   Self Review

EXERCISES

1. A general journal is like a(n):
   a. address book.
   b. appointment calendar.
   c. diary.
   d. to-do list.

2. The part of the journal entry to be recorded first is the:
   a. asset.
   b. credit.
   c. debit.
   d. liability.

QUESTIONS

3. Why is the journal referred to as the "record of original entry"?

4. In a compound journal entry, if two accounts are debited, must two accounts be credited?

5. Why are check and invoice numbers included in the journal entry description?

ANALYSIS

6. The accountant for Elegant Lawncare never includes descriptions when making journal entries. What effect will this have on the accounting system?

(Answers to Section 1 Self Review are on page 120.)

SECTION OBJECTIVES	TERMS TO LEARN
>> 4-3. Post journal entries to general ledger accounts.	balance ledger form
WHY IT'S IMPORTANT	correcting entry
The general ledger provides a permanent, classified record for a company's accounts.	general ledger
>> 4-4. Correct errors made in the journal or ledger.	ledger
WHY IT'S IMPORTANT	posting
Errors must be corrected to ensure a proper audit trail and to provide good information.	

The General Ledger

You learned that a journal contains a chronological (day-by-day) record of a firm's transactions. Each journal entry shows the accounts and the amounts involved. Using the journal as a guide, you can enter transaction data in the accounts.

Ledgers

T accounts are used to analyze transactions quickly but are not used to maintain financial records. Instead, businesses keep account records on a special form that makes it possible to record all data efficiently. There is a separate form for each account. The account forms are kept in a book or binder called a **ledger.** The ledger is called the *record of final entry* because the ledger is the last place that accounting transactions are recorded.

The process of transferring data from the journal to the ledger is known as **posting.** Posting takes place after transactions are journalized. Posting is the third step of the accounting cycle.

THE GENERAL LEDGER

Every business has a general ledger. The **general ledger** is the master reference file for the accounting system. It provides a permanent, classified record of all accounts used in a firm's operations.

LEDGER ACCOUNT FORMS

There are different types of general ledger account forms. Carlos Valdez decided to use a balance ledger form. A **balance ledger form** shows the balance of the account after each entry is posted. Look at Figure 4.3 on page 100. It shows the first general journal entry, the investment by the owner. It also shows the general ledger forms for *Cash* and *Carolyn Wells, Capital.* On the ledger form, notice the:

- account name and number;
- columns for date, description, and posting reference (post. ref.);
- columns for debit, credit, balance debit, and balance credit.

important!

General Journal and General Ledger
The general journal is the record of *original* entry. The general ledger is the record of *final* entry.

GENERAL JOURNAL   PAGE __1__

	DATE		DESCRIPTION	POST. REF.	DEBIT	CREDIT	
1	2016						1
2	Nov.	6	Cash	101	100 000 00		2
3			Carolyn Wells, Capital	301		100 000 00	3
4			Investment by owner				4
5							5
6							6
7							7

ACCOUNT _Cash_   ACCOUNT NO. __101__

DATE		DESCRIPTION	POST. REF.	DEBIT	CREDIT	BALANCE DEBIT	BALANCE CREDIT
2016							
Nov.	6		J1	100 000 00		100 000 00	

ACCOUNT _Carolyn Wells, Capital_   ACCOUNT NO. __301__

DATE		DESCRIPTION	POST. REF.	DEBIT	CREDIT	BALANCE DEBIT	BALANCE CREDIT
2016							
Nov.	6		J1		100 000 00		100 000 00

> > 4-3. OBJECTIVE

Post journal entries to general ledger
accounts.

recall

Normal Balance

The normal balance of an account is its
increase side.

POSTING TO THE GENERAL LEDGER

Examine Figure 4.4. On November 7, Carlos Valdez made a general journal entry to record the purchase of equipment. To post the data from the journal to the general ledger, Valdez entered the debit amount in the Debit column in the *Equipment* account and the credit amount in the Credit column in the *Cash* account.

In the general journal, identify the first account listed. In Figure 4.4, *Equipment* is the first account. In the general ledger, find the ledger form for the first account listed. In Figure 4.4, this is the *Equipment* ledger form.

The steps to post from the general journal to the general ledger follow:

1. On the ledger form, enter the date of the transaction. Enter a description of the entry, if necessary. Usually routine entries do not require descriptions.

2. On the ledger form, enter the general journal page in the Posting Reference column. On the *Equipment* ledger form, the **J1** in the Posting Reference column indicates that the journal entry is recorded on page 1 of the general journal. The letter **J** refers to the general journal.

3. On the ledger form, enter the debit amount in the Debit column or the credit amount in the Credit column. In Figure 4.4 on the *Equipment* ledger form, $5,000 is entered in the Debit column.

4. On the ledger form, compute the balance and enter it in the Debit Balance column or the Credit Balance column. In Figure 4.4, the balance in the *Equipment* account is a $5,000 debit.

5. On the general journal, enter the ledger account number in the Posting Reference column. In Figure 4.4, the account number 141 is entered in the Posting Reference column next to "Equipment."

Repeat the process for the next account in the general journal. In Figure 4.4, Valdez posted the credit amount from the general journal to the *Cash* ledger account. Notice on the *Cash* ledger form that he entered the credit of $5,000 and then computed the account balance. After the transaction is posted, the balance of the *Cash* account is $95,000.

Be sure to enter the numbers in the Posting Reference columns. This indicates that the entry was posted and ensures against posting the same entry twice. Posting references are part of the audit trail. They allow a transaction to be traced from the ledger to the journal entry, and then to the source document.

FIGURE 4.4

Posting to the General Ledger

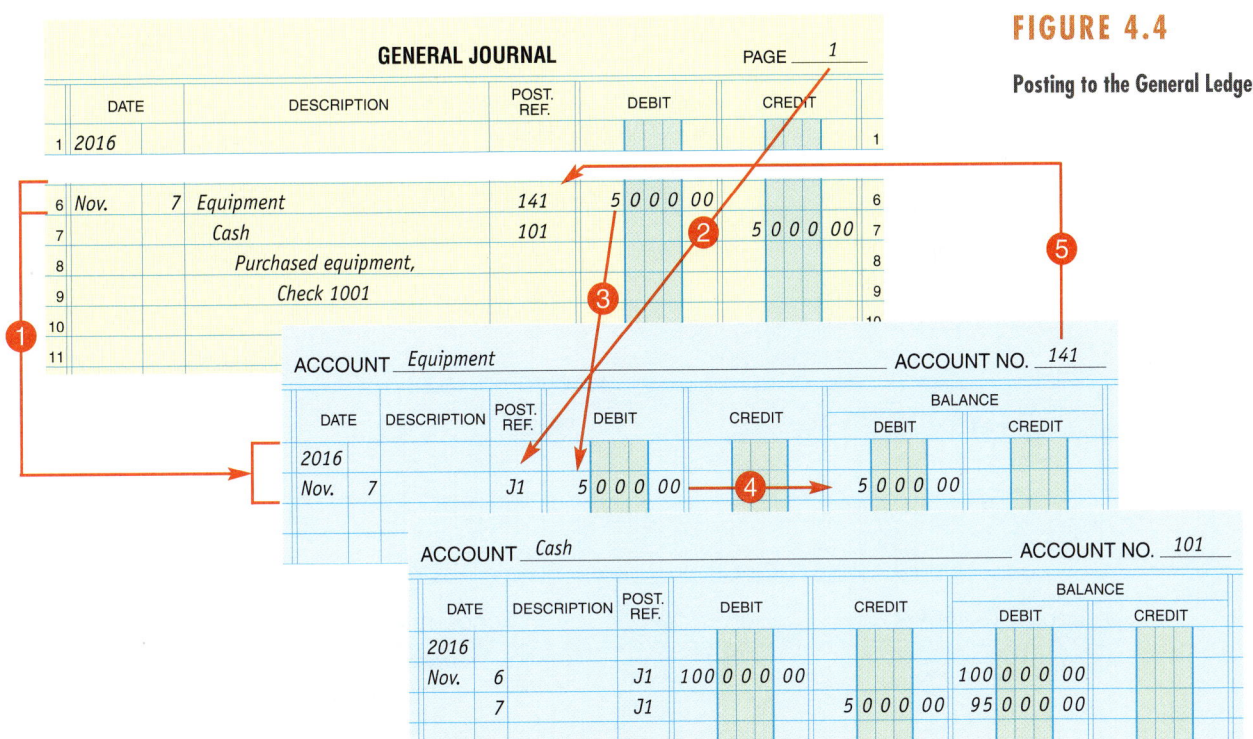

Figure 4.5 shows the general ledger after all the entries for November and December are posted.

Each ledger account provides a complete record of the increases and decreases to that account. The balance ledger form also shows the current balance for the account.

In the general ledger accounts, the balance sheet accounts appear first and are followed by the income statement accounts. The order is:

- assets
- liabilities
- owner's equity
- revenue
- expenses

This arrangement speeds the preparation of the trial balance and the financial statements.

FIGURE 4.5

Posted General Ledger Accounts

ACCOUNT Cash   ACCOUNT NO. 101

DATE		DESCRIPTION	POST. REF.	DEBIT	CREDIT	BALANCE DEBIT	BALANCE CREDIT
2016							
Nov.	6		J1	100 000 00		100 000 00	
	7		J1		5 000 00	95 000 00	
	28		J1		1 500 00	93 500 00	
	30		J1		2 500 00	91 000 00	
	30		J1		8 000 00	83 000 00	
Dec.	31		J2	36 000 00		119 000 00	
	31		J2	6 000 00		125 000 00	
	31		J2		8 000 00	117 000 00	
	31		J2		650 00	116 350 00	
	31		J2		5 000 00	111 350 00	

(continued)

FIGURE 4.5 (continued)

ACCOUNT Accounts Receivable   **ACCOUNT NO.** 111

DATE	DESCRIPTION	POST. REF.	DEBIT	CREDIT	BALANCE DEBIT	BALANCE CREDIT
2016						
Dec. 31		J2	11 000 00		11 000 00	
31		J2		6 000 00	5 000 00	

ACCOUNT Supplies   **ACCOUNT NO.** 121

DATE	DESCRIPTION	POST. REF.	DEBIT	CREDIT	BALANCE DEBIT	BALANCE CREDIT
2016						
Nov. 28		J1	1 500 00		1 500 00	

ACCOUNT Prepaid Rent   **ACCOUNT NO.** 137

DATE	DESCRIPTION	POST. REF.	DEBIT	CREDIT	BALANCE DEBIT	BALANCE CREDIT
2016						
Nov. 30		J1	8 000 00		8 000 00	

ACCOUNT Equipment   **ACCOUNT NO.** 141

DATE	DESCRIPTION	POST. REF.	DEBIT	CREDIT	BALANCE DEBIT	BALANCE CREDIT
2016						
Nov. 7		J1	5 000 00		5 000 00	
10		J1	6 000 00		11 000 00	

ACCOUNT Accounts Payable   **ACCOUNT NO.** 202

DATE	DESCRIPTION	POST. REF.	DEBIT	CREDIT	BALANCE DEBIT	BALANCE CREDIT
2016						
Nov. 10		J1		6 000 00		6 000 00
30		J1	2 500 00			3 500 00

ACCOUNT Carolyn Wells, Capital   **ACCOUNT NO.** 301

DATE	DESCRIPTION	POST. REF.	DEBIT	CREDIT	BALANCE DEBIT	BALANCE CREDIT
2016						
Nov. 6		J1		100 000 00		100 000 00

ACCOUNT Carolyn Wells, Drawing   **ACCOUNT NO.** 302

DATE	DESCRIPTION	POST. REF.	DEBIT	CREDIT	BALANCE DEBIT	BALANCE CREDIT
2016						
Dec. 31		J2	5 000 00		5 000 00	

(continued)

FIGURE 4.5 (continued)

ACCOUNT	Fees Income						ACCOUNT NO.	401	

DATE		DESCRIPTION	POST. REF.	DEBIT	CREDIT	BALANCE DEBIT	BALANCE CREDIT
2016							
Dec.	31		J2		36 000 00		36 000 00
	31		J2		11 000 00		47 000 00

ACCOUNT	Salaries Expense						ACCOUNT NO.	511	

DATE		DESCRIPTION	POST. REF.	DEBIT	CREDIT	BALANCE DEBIT	BALANCE CREDIT
2016							
Dec.	31		J2	8 000 00		8 000 00	

ACCOUNT	Utilities Expense						ACCOUNT NO.	514	

DATE		DESCRIPTION	POST. REF.	DEBIT	CREDIT	BALANCE DEBIT	BALANCE CREDIT
2016							
Dec.	31		J2	650 00		650 00	

Correcting Journal and Ledger Errors

Sometimes errors are made when recording transactions in the journal. For example, a journal entry may show the wrong account name or amount. The method used to correct an error depends on whether or not the journal entry has been posted to the ledger:

■ If the error is discovered *before* the entry is posted, neatly cross out the incorrect item and write the correct data above it. Do not erase the error. To ensure honesty and provide a clear audit trail, erasures are not made in the journal.

■ If the error is discovered *after* posting, a **correcting entry**—a journal entry made to correct the erroneous entry—is journalized and posted. Do not erase or change the journal entry or the postings in the ledger accounts.

Note that erasures are never permitted in the journal or ledger.

>> 4-4. OBJECTIVE
Correct errors made in the journal or ledger.

recall

Order of Accounts

The general ledger lists accounts in the same order as they appear on the trial balance: assets, liabilities, owner's equity, revenue, and expenses.

MANAGERIAL IMPLICATIONS <<

ACCOUNTING SYSTEMS

■ Business managers should be sure that their firms have efficient procedures for recording transactions.

■ A well-designed accounting system allows timely and accurate posting of data to the ledger accounts.

■ The information that appears in the financial statements is taken from the general ledger.

■ Since management uses financial information for decision making, it is essential that the financial statements be prepared quickly at the end of each period and that they contain the correct amounts.

■ The promptness and accuracy of the statements depend on the efficiency of the recording process.

■ A well-designed accounting system has a strong audit trail.

■ Every business should be able to trace amounts through the accounting records and back to the documents where the transactions were first recorded.

THINKING CRITICALLY

What are the consequences of not having a good audit trail?

Let's look at an example. On September 1, an automobile repair shop purchased some shop equipment for $18,000 in cash. By mistake, the journal entry debited the **Office Equipment** account rather than the **Shop Equipment** account, as follows.

	DATE	DESCRIPTION	POST. REF.	DEBIT	CREDIT	
		GENERAL JOURNAL PAGE 16				
1	2016					1
2	Sept.	1 Office Equipment	141	18 0 0 0 00		2
3		Cash	101		18 0 0 0 00	3
4		Purchased equipment,				4
5		Check 1104				5
6						6
7						7

The error was discovered after the entry was posted to the ledger. To correct the error, a correcting journal entry was prepared and posted. The correcting entry debits **Shop Equipment** and credits **Office Equipment** for $18,000. This entry transfers $18,000 out of the **Office Equipment** account and into the **Shop Equipment** account.

	DATE	DESCRIPTION	POST. REF.	DEBIT	CREDIT	
		GENERAL JOURNAL PAGE 28				
1	2016					1
2	Oct.	1 Shop Equipment	151	18 0 0 0 00		2
3		Office Equipment	141		18 0 0 0 00	3
4		To correct error made on				4
5		Sept. 1 when a purchase				5
6		of shop equipment was				6
7		recorded as office				7
8		equipment				8
9						9

Suppose that the error was discovered before the journal entry was posted to the ledger. In that case, the accountant would neatly cross out "Office Equipment" and write "Shop Equipment" above it. The correct account (**Shop Equipment**) would be posted to the ledger in the usual manner.

Section 2   Self Review

QUESTIONS

1. Are the following statements true or false? Why?

   a. "If a journal entry that contains an error has been posted, erase the entry and change the posting in the ledger accounts."

   b. "Once an incorrect journal entry has been posted, the incorrect amounts remain in the general ledger accounts."

2. What is entered in the Posting Reference column of the general journal?

3. Why are posting references made in ledger accounts and in the journal?

EXERCISES

4. The general ledger organizes accounting information in:

   a. account order.

   b. alphabetical order.

   c. date order.

5. The general journal organizes accounting information in:

   a. account order.

   b. alphabetical order.

   c. date order.

ANALYSIS

6. Draw a diagram of the first three steps of the accounting cycle.

(Answers to Section 2 Self Review are on page 120.)

REVIEW   Chapter Summary

In this chapter, you have studied the method for journalizing business transactions in the records of a company. The details of each transaction are then posted to the general ledger. A well-designed accounting system provides for prompt and accurate journalizing and posting of all transactions.

Learning Objectives

4-1   Record transactions in the general journal.

- Recording transactions in a journal is called journalizing, the second step in the accounting cycle.
  - A journal is a daily record of transactions.
  - A written analysis of each transaction is contained in a journal.
- The general journal is widely used in business. It can accommodate all kinds of business transactions. Use the following steps to record a transaction in the general journal:
  - Number each page in the general journal. The page number will be used as a posting reference.
  - Enter the year at the top of the Date column. After that, enter the year only when a new page is started or when the year changes.
  - Enter the month and day in the Date column of the first line of the first entry. After that, enter the month only when a new page is started or when the month changes. Always enter the day on the first line of a new entry.
  - Enter the name of the account to be debited in the Description column.
  - Enter the amount to be debited in the Debit column.
  - Enter the name of the account to be credited on the next line. Indent the account name about one-half inch.
  - Enter the amount to be credited in the Credit column.
  - Enter a complete but concise description on the next line. Indent the description about one inch.
- Note that the debit portion is always recorded first.
- If possible, include source document numbers in descriptions in order to create an audit trail.

4-2   Prepare compound journal entries.

A transaction might require a journal entry that contains several debits or credits. All debits are recorded first, followed by the credits.

4-3   Post journal entries to general ledger accounts.

- Posting to the general ledger is the third step in the accounting cycle. Posting is the transfer of data from journal entries to ledger accounts.
- The individual accounts together form a ledger. All the accounts needed to prepare financial statements are found in the general ledger.
- Use the following steps to post a transaction.
  - On the ledger form:
    1. Enter the date of the transaction. Enter the description, if necessary.
    2. Enter the posting reference in the Posting Reference column. When posting from the general journal, use the letter **J** followed by the general journal page number.
    3. Enter the amount in either the Debit column or the Credit column.
    4. Compute the new balance and enter it in either the Debit Balance column or the Credit Balance column.
  - On the general journal:
    5. Enter the ledger account number in the Posting Reference column.
- To summarize the steps of the accounting cycle discussed so far:
  1. Analyze transactions.
  2. Journalize transactions.
  3. Post transactions.

4-4   Correct errors made in the journal or ledger.

To ensure honesty and to provide a clear audit trail, erasures are not permitted in a journal. A correcting entry is journalized and posted to correct a previous mistake. Posting references in the journal and the ledger accounts cross reference the entries and form another part of the audit trail. They make it possible to trace or recheck any transaction.

4-5   Define the accounting terms new to this chapter.

Glossary

Accounting cycle (p. 90) A series of steps performed during each accounting period to classify, record, and summarize data for a business and to produce needed financial information

Audit trail (p. 91) A chain of references that makes it possible to trace information, locate errors, and prevent fraud

Balance ledger form (p. 99) A ledger account form that shows the balance of the account after each entry is posted

Chronological order (p. 90) Organized in the order in which the events occur

Compound entry (p. 96) A journal entry with more than one debit or credit

Correcting entry (p. 103) A journal entry made to correct an erroneous entry

General journal (p. 90) A financial record for entering all types of business transactions; a record of original entry

General ledger (p. 99) A permanent, classified record of all accounts used in a firm's operation; a record of final entry

Journal (p. 90 The record of original entry

Journalizing (p. 90) Recording transactions in a journal

Ledger (p. 99) The record of final entry

Posting (p. 99) Transferring data from a journal to a ledger

Comprehensive **Self Review**

1. Give examples of items that might appear in an audit trail.
2. Which of the following shows both the debits and credits of the entire transaction?
   a. An entry in the general journal
   b. A posting to a general ledger account
3. What is recorded in the Posting Reference column of a general journal?
4. Why is the ledger called the "record of final entry"?
5. How do you correct an incorrect journal entry that has not been posted?

(Answers to Comprehensive Self Review are on pages 120–121.)

Discussion Questions

1. What is posting?
2. What is a ledger?
3. In what order are accounts arranged in the general ledger? Why?
4. What are posting references? Why are they used?
5. What is the purpose of a journal?
6. What is the value of having a description for each general journal entry?
7. What procedure is used to record an entry in the general journal?
8. What is a compound journal entry?
9. How should corrections be made in the general journal?
10. What is an audit trail? Why is it desirable to have an audit trail?
11. What is the accounting cycle?

APPLICATIONS

Exercises

Analyzing transactions.

◄ **Exercise 4.1**
Objective 4-1

Selected accounts from the general ledger of the Zantex Shipping Service follow. Analyze the following transactions and indicate by number what accounts should be debited and credited for each transaction.

101 Cash
111 Accounts Receivable
121 Supplies
131 Equipment
202 Accounts Payable
301 Sam Taylor, Capital
401 Fees Income
511 Rent Expense
514 Salaries Expense
517 Utilities Expense

TRANSACTIONS

1. Gave a cash refund of $1,500 to a customer because of a lost package. (The customer had previously paid in cash.)
2. Sent a check for $2,100 to the utility company to pay the monthly bill.
3. Provided services for $15,600 on credit.
4. Purchased new equipment for $9,200 and paid for it immediately by check.
5. Issued a check for $7,000 to pay a creditor on account.
6. Performed services for $10,500 in cash.
7. Collected $12,500 from credit customers.
8. The owner made an additional investment of $50,000 in cash.
9. Purchased supplies for $6,500 on credit.
10. Issued a check for $7,500 to pay the monthly rent.

Recording transactions in the general journal.

◄ **Exercise 4.2**
Objective 4-1

Selected accounts from the general ledger of Tucker Consulting Services follow. Record the general journal entries that would be made to record the following transactions. Be sure to include dates and descriptions in these entries.

101 Cash
111 Accounts Receivable
121 Supplies
131 Equipment
141 Automobile
202 Accounts Payable
301 Jewell Tucker, Capital
302 Jewell Tucker, Drawing
401 Fees Income
511 Rent Expense
514 Salaries Expense
517 Telephone Expense

DATE	TRANSACTIONS
2016	
Sept. 1	Jewell Tucker invested $60,000 in cash to start the firm.
4	Purchased office equipment for $6,500 on credit from Den, Inc.; received Invoice 9823, payable in 30 days.
16	Purchased an automobile that will be used to visit clients; issued Check 1001 for $14,500 in full payment.
20	Purchased supplies for $520; paid immediately with Check 1002.
23	Returned damaged supplies for a cash refund of $170.
30	Issued Check 1003 for $4,200 to Den, Inc., as payment on account for Invoice 9823.
30	Withdrew $3,000 in cash for personal expenses.
30	Issued Check 1004 for $1,700 to pay the rent for October.
30	Performed services for $2,750 in cash.
30	Paid $435 for monthly telephone bill, Check 1005.

Exercise 4.3

Objectives 4-1, 4-3

CONTINUING >>> Problem

▶ **Posting to the general ledger.**

Post the journal entries that you prepared for Exercise 4.2 to the general ledger. Use the account names shown in Exercise 4.2.

Exercise 4.4

Objective 4-2

▶ **Compound journal entries.**

The following transactions took place at the Apollo Employment Agency during November 2016. Record the general journal entries that would be made for these transactions. Use a compound entry for each transaction.

DATE	TRANSACTIONS
Nov. 5	Performed services for Job Search, Inc., for $40,000; received $19,000 in cash and the client promised to pay the balance in 60 days.
18	Purchased a graphing calculator for $425 and some supplies for $575 from Office Supply; issued Check 1008 for the total.
23	Received Invoice 1602 for $2,100 from Automotive Technicians Repair for repairs to the firm's automobile; issued Check 1009 for half the amount and arranged to pay the other half in 30 days.

Exercise 4.5

Objective 4-4

▶ **Recording a correcting entry.**

On July 9, 2016, an employee of Capital Corporation mistakenly debited *Utilities Expense* rather than *Telephone Expense* when recording a bill of $1,000 for the May telephone service. The error was discovered on July 30. Prepare a general journal entry to correct the error.

Exercise 4.6

Objective 4-4

▶ **Recording a correcting entry.**

On September 16, 2016, an employee of Cannon Company mistakenly debited the *Truck* account rather than the *Repair Expense* account when recording a bill of $800 for repairs. The error was discovered on October 1. Prepare a general journal entry to correct the error.

PROBLEMS

Problem Set A

Recording transactions in the general journal.

The transactions that follow took place at the Cedar Hill Sports Arena during September 2016. This firm has indoor courts where customers can play tennis for a fee. It also rents equipment and offers tennis lessons.

◀ **Problem 4.1A**
Objective 4-1

INSTRUCTIONS

Record each transaction in the general journal, using the following chart of accounts. Be sure to number the journal page 1 and to write the year at the top of the Date column. Include a description for each entry.

ASSETS
101 Cash
111 Accounts Receivable
121 Supplies
141 Equipment

LIABILITIES
202 Accounts Payable

OWNER'S EQUITY
301 Selena Cantu, Capital
302 Selena Cantu, Drawing

REVENUE
401 Fees Income

EXPENSES
511 Equipment Repair Expense
512 Rent Expense
513 Salaries Expense
514 Telephone Expense
517 Utilities Expense

DATE		TRANSACTIONS
Sept.	1	Issued Check 1169 for $1,900 to pay the September rent.
	5	Performed services for $3,000 in cash.
	6	Performed services for $1,850 on credit.
	10	Paid $700 for monthly telephone bill; issued Check 1170.
	11	Paid for equipment repairs of $940 with Check 1171.
	12	Received $3,700 on account from credit clients.
	15	Issued Checks 1172–1177 for $4,700 for salaries.
	18	Issued Check 1178 for $2,500 to purchase supplies.
	19	Purchased new tennis rackets for $2,750 on credit from The Tennis Supply Shop; received Invoice 3108, payable in 30 days.
	20	Issued Check 1179 for $2,860 to purchase new nets. (Equip.)
	21	Received $1,050 on account from credit clients.
	21	Returned a damaged net and received a cash refund of $550.
	22	Performed services for $3,360 in cash.
	23	Performed services for $4,950 on credit.
	26	Issued Check 1180 for $560 to purchase supplies.
	28	Paid the monthly electric bill of $2,350 with Check 1181.
	30	Issued Checks 1182–1187 for $4,700 for salaries.
	30	Issued Check 1188 for $4,700 cash to Selena Cantu for personal expenses.

Analyze: If the company paid a bill for supplies on October 1, what check number would be included in the journal entry description?

Problem 4.2A

**Objectives 4-1,
4-2, 4-3**

Sage 50
Complete Accounting

▶ Journalizing and posting transactions.

On October 1, 2016, Satillo Richey opened an advertising agency. He plans to use the chart of accounts listed below.

INSTRUCTIONS

1. Journalize the transactions. Number the journal page 1, write the year at the top of the Date column, and include a description for each entry.
2. Post to the ledger accounts. Before you start the posting process, open accounts by entering account names and numbers in the headings. Follow the order of the accounts in the chart of accounts.

ASSETS
101 Cash
111 Accounts Receivable
121 Supplies
141 Office Equipment
151 Art Equipment

LIABILITIES
202 Accounts Payable

OWNER'S EQUITY
301 Satillo Richey, Capital
302 Satillo Richey, Drawing

REVENUE
401 Fees Income

EXPENSES
511 Office Cleaning Expense
514 Rent Expense
517 Salaries Expense
520 Telephone Expense
523 Utilities Expense

DATE		TRANSACTIONS
Oct.	1	Satillo Richey invested $60,000 cash in the business.
	2	Paid October office rent of $3,000; issued Check 1001.
	5	Purchased desks and other office furniture for $15,000 from Office Furniture Mart, Inc.; received Invoice 6704 payable in 60 days.
	6	Issued Check 1002 for $3,200 to purchase art equipment.
	7	Purchased supplies for $1,550; paid with Check 1003.
	10	Issued Check 1004 for $600 for office cleaning service.
	12	Performed services for $4,100 in cash and $1,900 on credit. (Use a compound entry.)
	15	Returned damaged supplies for a cash refund of $400.
	18	Purchased a computer for $3,000 from Office Furniture Mart, Inc., Invoice 7108; issued Check 1005 for a $1,750 down payment, with the balance payable in 30 days. (Use one compound entry.)
	20	Issued Check 1006 for $7,500 to Office Furniture Mart, Inc., as payment on account for Invoice 6704.
	26	Performed services for $4,400 on credit.
	27	Paid $325 for monthly telephone bill; issued Check 1007.
	30	Received $3,700 in cash from credit customers.
	30	Mailed Check 1008 to pay the monthly utility bill of $400.
	30	Issued Checks 1009–1011 for $8,000 for salaries.

Analyze: What is the balance of account 202 in the general ledger?

Recording correcting entries.

◄ **Problem 4.3A**
Objective 4-4

The following journal entries were prepared by an employee of Global Marketing Company who does not have an adequate knowledge of accounting.

INSTRUCTIONS

Examine the journal entries carefully to locate the errors. Provide a brief written description of each error. Assume that *Office Equipment* and *Office Supplies* were recorded at the correct values.

	DATE		DESCRIPTION	POST. REF.	DEBIT	CREDIT	
1	2016						1
2	April	1	Accounts Payable		12 400 00		2
3			Fees Income			12 400 00	3
4			Performed services on credit				4
5							5
6		2	Cash		5 0 0 00		6
7			Telephone Expense			5 0 0 00	7
8			Paid for March telephone				8
9			service, Check 1917				9
10							10
11		3	Office Equipment		7 2 0 0 00		11
12			Office Supplies		8 0 0 00		12
13			Cash			8 4 0 0 00	13
14			Purchased file cabinet and				14
15			office supplies, Check 1918				15

GENERAL JOURNAL   PAGE 3

Analyze: After the correcting journal entries have been posted, what effect do the corrections have on the company's reported assets?

Problem 4.4A

Objectives 4-1,
4-2, 4-3

Sage 50
Complete Accounting

QB

Journalizing and posting transactions

Four transactions for Farmers Market and Repair Shop that took place in November 2016 appear below, along with the general ledger accounts used by the company.

INSTRUCTIONS

Record the transactions in the general journal and post them to the appropriate ledger accounts. Be sure to number the journal page 1 and to write the year at the top of the Date column.

Cash	101	Equipment	151
Accounts Receivable	111	Accounts Payable	202
Office Supplies	121	Dennis Ortiz, Capital	301
Tools	131	Fees Income	401
Machinery	141		

DATE	TRANSACTIONS
Nov. 1	Dennis Ortiz invested $55,000 in cash plus tools with a fair market value of $2,000 to start the business.
2	Purchased equipment for $2,050 and supplies for $550 from Office Depot, Invoice 501; issued Check 100 for $700 as a down payment with the balance due in 30 days.
10	Performed services for Hazel Sneed for $2,900, who paid $1,000 in cash with the balance due in 30 days.
20	Purchased machinery for $4,000 from Craft Machinery, Inc., Invoice 709; issued Check 101 for $1,500 in cash as a down payment with the balance due in 30 days.

Analyze: What liabilities does the business owe as of November 30?

Problem Set B

Recording transactions in the general journal.

◀　**Problem 4.1B**
Objective 4-1

The transactions listed below took place at Brown Building Cleaning Service during September 2016. This firm cleans commercial buildings for a fee.

INSTRUCTIONS

Analyze and record each transaction in the general journal. Choose the account names from the chart of accounts shown below. Be sure to number the journal page 1 and to write the year at the top of the Date column.

ASSETS
101 Cash
111 Accounts Receivable
141 Equipment

LIABILITIES
202 Accounts Payable

OWNER'S EQUITY
301 Charles Brown, Capital
302 Charles Brown, Drawing

REVENUE
401 Fees Income

EXPENSES
501 Cleaning Supplies Expense
502 Equipment Repair Expense
503 Office Supplies Expense
511 Rent Expense
514 Salaries Expense
521 Telephone Expense
524 Utilities Expense

DATE		TRANSACTIONS
Sept.	1	Charles Brown invested $50,000 in cash to start the business.
	5	Performed services for $6,000 in cash.
	6	Issued Check 1000 for $2,500 to pay the September rent.
	7	Performed services for $6,300 on credit.
	9	Paid $640 for monthly telephone bill; issued Check 1001.
	10	Issued Check 1002 for $675 for equipment repairs.
	12	Received $1,090 from credit clients.
	14	Issued Checks 1003–1004 for $12,500 to pay salaries.
	18	Issued Check 1005 for $800 for cleaning supplies.
	19	Issued Check 1006 for $950 for office supplies.
	20	Purchased equipment for $10,000 from Razor Equipment, Inc., Invoice 1012; issued Check 1007 for $2,000 with the balance due in 30 days.
	22	Performed services for $4,800 in cash.
	24	Issued Check 1008 for $950 for the monthly electric bill.
	26	Performed services for $7,200 on account.
	30	Issued Checks 1009–1010 for $12,500 to pay salaries.
	30	Issued Check 1011 for $6,000 to Charles Brown to pay for personal expenses.

Analyze: How many transactions affected expense accounts?

Problem 4.2B

Objectives 4-1, 4-2, 4-3

▶ ## Journalizing and posting transactions.

In June 2016, Carolyn Davis opened a photography studio that provides services to public and private schools. Her firm's financial activities for the first month of operations and the chart of accounts appear below.

INSTRUCTIONS

1. Journalize the transactions. Number the journal page 1 and write the year at the top of the Date column. Describe each entry.

2. Post to the ledger accounts. Before you start the posting process, open the accounts by entering the names and numbers in the headings. Follow the order of the accounts in the chart of accounts.

ASSETS	REVENUE
101 Cash	401 Fees Income
111 Accounts Receivable	
121 Supplies	EXPENSES
141 Office Equipment	511 Office Cleaning Expense
151 Photographic Equipment	514 Rent Expense
	517 Salaries Expense
LIABILITIES	520 Telephone Expense
202 Accounts Payable	523 Utilities Expense
OWNER'S EQUITY	
301 Carolyn Davis, Capital	
302 Carolyn Davis, Drawing	

DATE		TRANSACTIONS
June	1	Carolyn Davis invested $18,000 cash in the business.
	2	Issued Check 1001 for $1,250 to pay the June rent.
	5	Purchased desks and other office furniture for $7,500 from Desoto, Inc., received Invoice 5312, payable in 60 days.
	6	Issued Check 1002 for $1,900 to purchase photographic equipment.
	7	Purchased supplies for $538; paid with Check 1003.
	10	Issued Check 1004 for $400 for office cleaning service.
	12	Performed services for $1,300 in cash and $1,300 on credit. (Use one compound entry.)
	15	Returned damaged supplies; received a $150 cash refund.
	18	Purchased a computer for $1,850 from Denison Office Supply, Invoice 304; issued Check 1005 for a $500 down payment. The balance is payable in 30 days. (Use one compound entry.)
	20	Issued Check 1006 for $2,500 to Desoto, Inc., as payment on account for office furniture, Invoice 5312.
	26	Performed services for $2,000 on credit.
	27	Paid $580 for monthly telephone bill; issued Check 1007.
	30	Received $2,100 in cash from credit clients on account.
	30	Issued Check 1008 to pay the monthly utility bill of $575.
	30	Issued Checks 1009–1011 for $5,600 for salaries.

Analyze: What was the *Cash* account balance after the transaction of June 27 was recorded?

Recording correcting entries.

◄   **Problem 4.3B**
Objective 4-4

All the journal entries shown below contain errors. The entries were prepared by an employee of New Zealand Corporation who does not have an adequate knowledge of accounting.

INSTRUCTIONS

Examine the journal entries carefully to locate the errors. Provide a brief written description of each error. Assume that *Office Equipment* and *Office Supplies* were recorded at the correct values.

	DATE		DESCRIPTION	POST. REF.	DEBIT	CREDIT	
1	2016						1
2	Jan.	1	Accounts Payable		1 0 0 00		2
3			Fees Income			1 0 0 00	3
4			Performed services on credit				4
5							5
6		2	Cash		7 5 00		6
7			Telephone Expense			7 5 00	7
8			Paid for January telephone				8
9			service, Check 1601				9
10							10
11		3	Office Equipment		4 7 5 00		11
12			Office Supplies		1 0 5 00		12
13			Cash			5 5 0 00	13
14			Purchased file cabinet and				14
15			office supplies, Check 1602				15
16							16

GENERAL JOURNAL   PAGE __1__

Analyze: After the correcting journal entries have been posted, what effect do the corrections have on the reported assets of the company?

Problem 4.4B

Objectives 4-1, 4-2, 4-3

▶ **Journalizing and posting transactions.**

Several transactions that occurred during December 2016, the first month of operation for Boynton's Accounting Services, follow. The company uses the general ledger accounts listed below.

INSTRUCTIONS

Record the transactions in the general journal (page 1) and post to the appropriate accounts.

Cash	101	Furniture & Fixtures	151
Accounts Receivable	111	Accounts Payable	202
Office Supplies	121	James Boynton, Capital	301
Computers	131	Fees Income	401
Office Equipment	141		

DATE	TRANSACTIONS
Dec. 3	James Boynton began business by depositing $20,000 cash into a business checking account.
4	Purchased a computer for $2,400 cash.
5	Purchased furniture and fixtures on account for $6,500.
6	Purchased office equipment for $2,150 cash.
10	Rendered services to client and sent bill for $2,600.
11	Purchased office supplies for $950 in cash.
15	Received invoice for furniture purchased on December 5 and paid it.

Analyze: Describe the activity for account 202 during the month.

Critical Thinking Problem 4.1

Financial Statements

Ned Turner is a new staff accountant for Sarah's Beauty Supply. He has asked you to review the financial statements prepared for April to find and correct any errors. Review the income statement and balance sheet that follow and identify the errors Turner made (he did not prepare a statement of owner's equity). Prepare a corrected income statement and balance sheet, as well as a statement of owner's equity, for Sarah's Beauty Supply.

Sarah's Beauty Supply
Income Statement
April 30, 2016

Revenue		
Fees Income		36 600 00
Expenses		
Salaries Expense	9 000 00	
Rent Expense	1 800 00	
Repair Expense	300 00	
Utilities Expense	1 700 00	
Drawing	4 000 00	
Total Expenses		17 700 00
Net Income		21 400 00

Sarah's Beauty Supply
Balance Sheet
Month Ended April 30, 2016

Assets		Liabilities	
Land	12 000 00	Accounts Receivable	7 000 00
Building	40 000 00		
Cash	15 000 00	Owner's Equity	
Accounts Payable	5 000 00	Sarah Davis, Capital, April 1, 2016	49 200 00
Total Assets	56 200 00	Total Liabilities and Owner's Equity	56 200 00

Critical Thinking Problem 4.2

Start-Up Business

On June 1, 2016, Ashley Jackson opened the Leadership Talent Agency. He plans to use the chart of accounts given below.

INSTRUCTIONS

1. Journalize the transactions. Be sure to number the journal pages and write the year at the top of the Date column. Include a description for each entry.

2. Post to the ledger accounts. Before you start the posting process, open the accounts by entering the account names and numbers in the headings. Using the list of accounts below, assign appropriate account numbers and place them in the correct order in the ledger.

3. Prepare a trial balance.

4. Prepare the income statement.

5. Prepare a statement of owner's equity.

6. Prepare the balance sheet.

ACCOUNTS

Accounts Payable	Ashley Jackson, Drawing
Office Furniture	Recording Equipment
Accounts Receivable	Rent Expense
Advertising Expense	Salaries Expense
Cash	Supplies
Fees Income	Telephone Expense
Ashley Jackson, Capital	Utilities Expense

DATE		TRANSACTIONS
June	1	Ashley Jackson invested $30,000 cash to start the business.
	2	Issued Check 201 for $1,800 to pay the June rent for the office.
	3	Purchased desk and other office furniture for $12,000 from Lowe's Office Supply, Invoice 5103; issued Check 202 for a $2,000 down payment with the balance due in 30 days.
	4	Issued Check 203 for $1,500 for supplies.
	6	Performed services for $6,000 in cash.
	7	Issued Check 204 for $2,000 to pay for advertising expense.
	8	Purchased recording equipment for $15,000 from Special Moves, Inc., Invoice 2122; issued Check 205 for a down payment of $5,000 with the balance due in 30 days.
	10	Performed services for $4,500 on account.
	11	Issued Check 206 for $3,000 to Lowe's Office Supply as payment on account.
	12	Performed services for $9,000 in cash.
	15	Issued Check 207 for $5,000 to pay an employee's salary.
	18	Received payments of $4,000 from credit clients on account.
	20	Issued Check 208 for $6,000 to Special Moves, Inc. as payment on account.
	25	Issued Check 209 in the amount of $350 for the monthly telephone bill.
	27	Issued Check 210 in the amount of $800 for the monthly electric bill.
	28	Issued Check 211 to Ashley Jackson for $4,000 for personal living expenses.
	30	Issued Check 212 for $5,000 to pay salary of an employee.

Analyze: How many postings were made to the **Cash** account?

BUSINESS CONNECTIONS

Business Records

Managerial FOCUS

1. How might a poor set of recording procedures affect the flow of information to management?

2. Why should management be concerned about the efficiency of a firm's procedures for journalizing and posting transactions?

3. Why should management insist that a firm's accounting system have a strong audit trail?

4. The owner of a new business recently questioned the accountant about the value of having both a journal and a ledger. The owner believes that it is a waste of effort to enter data about transactions in two different records. How would you explain the value of having both records?

Correcting Entries

Ethical DILEMMA

As the full-time bookkeeper, your job is to make any corrections to the general ledger accounts. Each correction needs the reason for the change and the effect on each account, whether it is an increase or decrease.

Mesia has come to you for help. For the third time this month, she has recorded a cash receipt twice. She wants you to record a correcting entry that will reverse her mistakes. The correcting entry she wants you to make will record a credit to the Cash account and a debit to Sales. What should you investigate before making a decision about the correcting entry? What is happening to the cash account? Is this a continual problem for Mesia? Would you accept a dinner offer from Mesia if you fix her mistake?

Balance Sheet

Financial Statement ANALYSIS

Review the following excerpt taken from the Walmart consolidated balance sheet as of January 31, 2013.

Analyze:

Walmart Stores, Inc. Consolidated Balance Sheet January 31, 2013	
(Amounts in millions)	
Property and Equipment:	
Property and Equipment	$165,825
Property under Capital Leases:	
Property under Capital Leases	$ 5,899

1. When the accountant for Walmart records a purchase of property and equipment, what type of account is debited? If Walmart purchases equipment on credit, what account might be credited?

2. What type of source document might be reflected in the journal entry to record the purchase of equipment?

3. If the accounting manager reviewed the *Equipment* account in the general ledger, what types of information might be listed there?

Analyze Online: Locate the website for Walmart (www.walmartstores.com), which provides an online store for consumers as well as corporate information. Within the website, locate the consolidated balance sheet for the current year.

4. What is the balance reported for cash and cash equivalents at January 31 of the current year?

5. What is the balance reported for inventories at January 31 of the current year?

Audit Trail

An audit trail allows an individual to track a transaction from the journal entry to the general ledger through to the financial statements. The audit trail can also find all the transactions that comprise the dollar amount for each account listed on the income statement and balance sheet. Your team has been assigned the duty to diagram the audit trail for your company. In your diagram, show several transactions and how they would be tracked from the journal entry to the financial statement and back to the journal entry.

Accounting Careers

Enter "Accounting Careers" in a search tool like Google. Select a site that will provide the skills and talents required for an accountant. Also find the salaries for accountants in your local area. Note the amount of experience and education needed to receive the salary you want to be earning in the next five years.

Answers to **Self Reviews**

Answers to Section 1 Self Review

1. **c.** diary.
2. **c.** debit.
3. It is the first accounting record where transactions are entered.
4. No. The only requirement is that the total debits must equal the total credits.
5. To provide an audit trail to trace information through the accounting system.
6. The audit trail will be very difficult to follow.

Answers to Section 2 Self Review

1. Both statements are false. If an incorrect journal entry was posted, a correcting entry should be journalized and posted. To ensure honesty and provide a clear audit trail, erasures are not permitted in the journal.
2. The ledger account number.
3. They indicate that the entry has been posted and ensure against posting the same entry twice.
4. **a.** account order.
5. **c.** date order.
6.

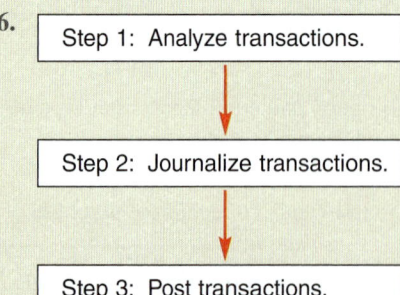

Answers to Comprehensive Self Review

1. Check number.

   Invoice number for goods purchased on credit from a vendor.

   Invoice number for services billed to a charge account customer.

   Memorandum number.

2. **a.** An entry in the general journal.

3. The general ledger account number.

4. It is the last accounting record in which a transaction is recorded.

5. Neatly cross out the incorrect item and write the correct data above it.

Adjustments and the Worksheet

Chapter 5

WILLAMETTE VALLEY
VINEYARDS
www.willamettevalleyvinyards.com

The Willamette Valley is the heart of Oregon's agriculture country. The valley is one of Oregon's major wine-growing regions and boasts over 200 wineries that produce a variety of vintages. *Willamette Valley Vineyards* is regarded as one of Oregon's top wineries. Started in 1983 with a small 50-acre vineyard, the company has carefully nurtured its growth, producing top-quality wines that have been served at the White House and consistently earn high marks from *Wine Spectator* and *Wine Enthusiast*. In any given year, Willamette incurs expenses like wages and advertising as well as the expenses associated with harvesting its grapes. When it sells its wine, the

company records the revenue on the sale. The company must make sure that the expenses associated with the making of the wine are recorded in the same year as the sale of the wine so that the company has an accurate annual view of how the business is doing.

The importance of matching these revenues and expenses within the same year was hammered home in 2006 by the Alcohol and Tobacco Tax Trade Board. Willamette pays alcohol excise taxes based on product sales to both the Oregon Liquor Control Commission and to the U.S. Department of the Treasury, Alcohol and Tobacco Tax and Trade Bureau. An audit by the Alcohol and Tobacco Tax Trade Board uncovered some reporting issues and though Willamette Valley disputed the findings, it eventually acknowledged that an expense of $80,000 claimed should have been recognized as a liability across three years rather than recognizing it all in one year. The company had to restate its financial statements for three previous years to reflect the correct excise tax for each of those periods and to record the estimated interest and penalties with respect to the related estimated excise tax liability.

thinking critically
Careful recordkeeping is critical to all businesses, large and small. Why does matching these revenues and expenses within the same year matter so much?

LEARNING OBJECTIVES

5-1. Complete a trial balance on a worksheet.

5-2. Prepare adjustments for unrecorded business transactions.

5-3. Complete the worksheet.

5-4. Prepare an income statement, statement of owner's equity, and balance sheet from the completed worksheet.

5-5. Journalize and post the adjusting entries.

5-6. Define the accounting terms new to this chapter.

NEW TERMS

account form balance sheet
adjusting entries
adjustments
book value
contra account
contra asset account
depreciation
prepaid expenses
report form balance sheet
salvage value
straight-line depreciation
worksheet

The Worksheet

Financial statements are completed as soon as possible in order to be useful. One way to speed the preparation of financial statements is to use a worksheet. A **worksheet** is a form used to gather all data needed at the end of an accounting period to prepare the financial statements. Preparation of the worksheet is the fourth step in the accounting cycle.

Figure 5.1 shows a common type of worksheet. The heading shows the company name, report title, and period covered. In addition to the Account Name column, this worksheet contains five sections: Trial Balance, Adjustments, Adjusted Trial Balance, Income Statement, and Balance Sheet. Each section includes a Debit column and a Credit column. The worksheet has 10 columns in which to enter dollar amounts.

>> **5-1. OBJECTIVE**

Complete a trial balance on a worksheet.

recall

Trial Balance

If total debits do not equal total credits, there is an error in the financial records. The error must be found and corrected.

The Trial Balance Section

Refer to Figure 5.2 as you read about how to prepare the Trial Balance section of the worksheet.

1. Enter the general ledger account names.
2. Transfer the general ledger account balances to the Debit and Credit columns of the Trial Balance section.
3. Total the Debit and Credit columns to prove that the trial balance is in balance.
4. Place a double rule under each Trial Balance column to show that the work in that column is complete.

FIGURE 5.1

Ten-Column Worksheet

Wells' Consulting Services
Worksheet
Month Ended December 31, 2016

ACCOUNT NAME	TRIAL BALANCE		ADJUSTMENTS	
	DEBIT	CREDIT	DEBIT	CREDIT
1				
2				
3				
4				
5				

FIGURE 5.2   A Partial Worksheet

Wells' Consulting Services
Worksheet
Month Ended December 31, 2016

	ACCOUNT NAME	TRIAL BALANCE		ADJUSTMENTS	
		DEBIT	CREDIT	DEBIT	CREDIT
1	Cash	111 3 5 0 00			
2	Accounts Receivable	5 0 0 0 00			
3	Supplies	1 5 0 0 00			(a) 5 0 0 00
4	Prepaid Rent	8 0 0 0 00			(b) 4 0 0 0 00
5	Equipment	11 0 0 0 00			
6	Accumulated Depreciation—Equipment				(c) 1 8 3 00
7	Accounts Payable		3 5 0 0 00		
8	Carolyn Wells, Capital		100 0 0 0 00		
9	Carolyn Wells, Drawing	5 0 0 0 00			
10	Fees Income		47 0 0 0 00		
11	Salaries Expense	8 0 0 0 00			
12	Utilities Expense	6 5 0 00			
13	Supplies Expense			(a) 5 0 0 00	
14	Rent Expense			(b) 4 0 0 0 00	
15	Depreciation Expense—Equipment			(c) 1 8 3 00	
16	Totals	150 5 0 0 00	150 5 0 0 00	4 6 8 3 00	4 6 8 3 00
17					
18					
19					

Notice that the trial balance has four new accounts: ***Accumulated Depreciation—Equipment, Supplies Expense, Rent Expense,*** and ***Depreciation Expense—Equipment.*** These accounts have zero balances now, but they will be needed later as the worksheet is completed.

The Adjustments Section

Usually, account balances change because of transactions with other businesses or individuals. For Wells' Consulting Services, the account changes recorded in Chapter 4 were caused by transactions with the firm's suppliers, customers, the landlord, and employees. It is easy to recognize, journalize, and post these transactions as they occur.

Some changes are not caused by transactions with other businesses or individuals. They arise from the internal operations of the firm during the accounting period. Journal entries made to update accounts for previously unrecorded items are called **adjustments** or **adjusting entries.** These changes are first entered on the worksheet at the end of each accounting period. The worksheet provides a convenient form for gathering the information and determining the effects of the changes. Let's look at the adjustments made by Wells' Consulting Services on December 31, 2016.

>> 5-2. OBJECTIVE

Prepare adjustments for unrecorded business transactions.

ADJUSTED TRIAL BALANCE		INCOME STATEMENT		BALANCE SHEET		
DEBIT	CREDIT	DEBIT	CREDIT	DEBIT	CREDIT	
						1
						2
						3
						4
						5

ADJUSTING FOR SUPPLIES USED

On November 28, 2016, Wells' Consulting Services purchased $1,500 of supplies. On December 31, the trial balance shows a $1,500 balance in the *Supplies* account. This amount is too high because some of the supplies were used during December.

An adjustment must be made for the supplies used. Otherwise, the asset account, *Supplies,* is overstated because fewer supplies are actually on hand. The expense account, *Supplies Expense,* is understated. The cost of the supplies used represents an operating expense that has not been recorded.

On December 31, Carlos Valdez counted the supplies. Remaining supplies totaled $1,000. This meant that supplies amounting to $500 were used during December ($1,500 − $1,000 = $500). At the end of December, an adjustment must be made to reflect the supplies used. The adjustment reduces the *Supplies* account to $1,000, the amount of supplies remaining. It increases the *Supplies Expense* account by $500 for the amount of supplies used. Notice that the adjustment for supplies is based on actual usage.

Refer to Figure 5.2 on page 125 to review the adjustment on the worksheet: a debit of $500 to *Supplies Expense* and a credit of $500 to *Supplies.* Both the debit and credit are labeled **(a)** to identify the two parts of the adjustment.

Supplies is a type of prepaid expense. **Prepaid expenses** are items that are acquired and paid for in advance of their use. Other common prepaid expenses are prepaid rent, prepaid insurance, and prepaid advertising. When cash is paid for these items, amounts are debited to *Prepaid Rent, Prepaid Insurance,* and *Prepaid Advertising;* all are asset accounts. As prepaid expenses are used, an adjustment is made to reduce the asset accounts and to increase the related expense accounts.

ADJUSTMENT

Record the adjustment for supplies.

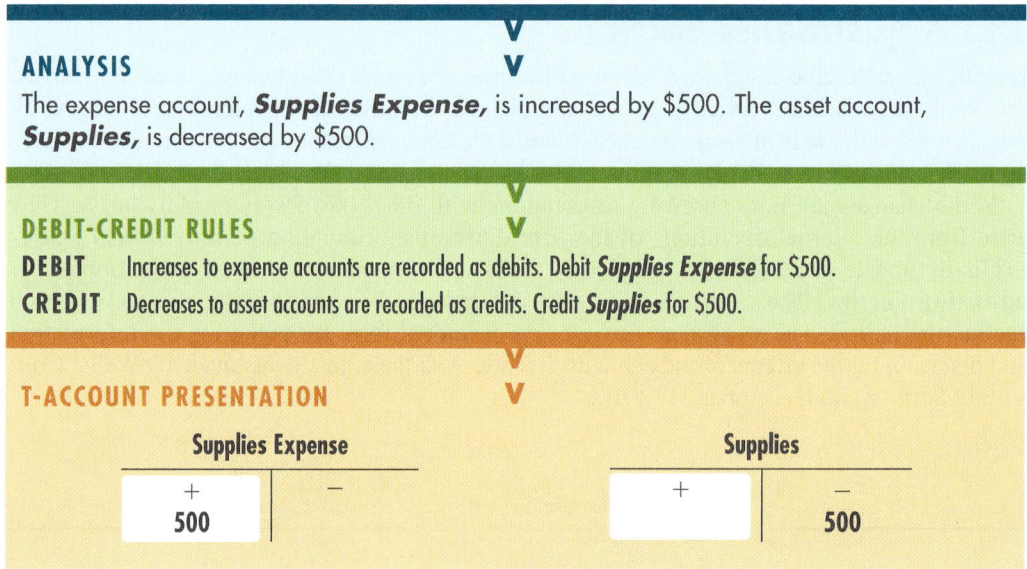

ANALYSIS
The expense account, **Supplies Expense,** is increased by $500. The asset account, **Supplies,** is decreased by $500.

DEBIT-CREDIT RULES
DEBIT Increases to expense accounts are recorded as debits. Debit *Supplies Expense* for $500.
CREDIT Decreases to asset accounts are recorded as credits. Credit *Supplies* for $500.

T-ACCOUNT PRESENTATION

Supplies Expense		Supplies	
+	−	+	−
500			500

Let's review the effect of the adjustment on the asset account, *Supplies.* Recall that the *Supplies* account already had a balance of $1,500. If no adjustment is made, the balance would remain at $1,500, even though only $1,000 of supplies are left.

Supplies				
	+		−	
Bal.	1,500	Adj.		500
Bal.	1,000			

ADJUSTING FOR EXPIRED RENT

On November 30, 2016, Wells' Consulting Services paid $8,000 rent for December and January. The right to occupy facilities for the specified period is an asset. The $8,000 was debited to *Prepaid Rent,* an asset account. On December 31, 2016, the *Prepaid Rent* balance is $8,000. This is too high because one month of rent has been used. The expired rent is $4,000 ($8,000 ÷ 2 months). At the end of December, an adjustment is made to reflect the expired rent.

ADJUSTMENT

Record the adjustment for expired rent.

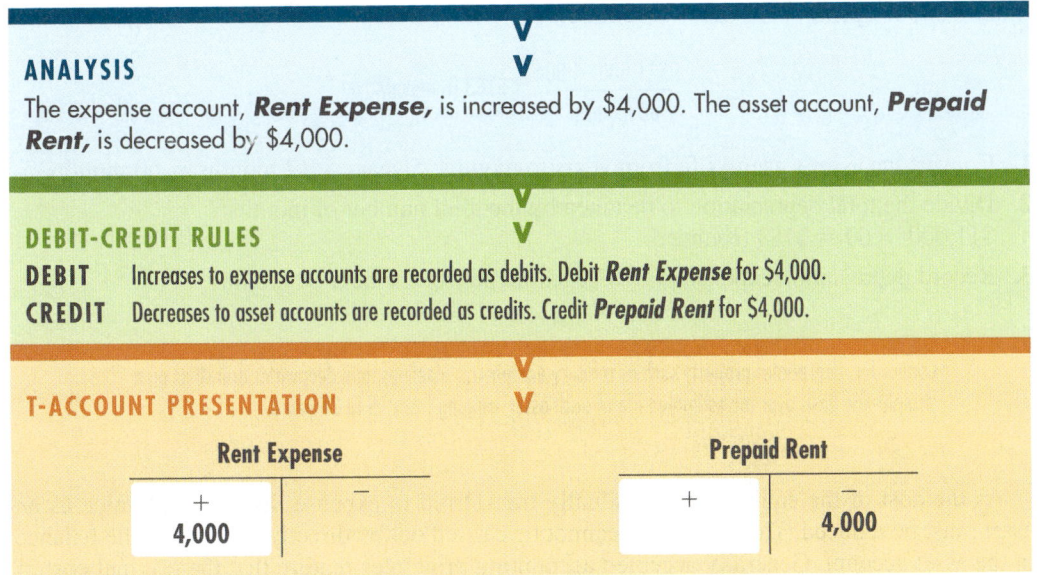

ANALYSIS

The expense account, **Rent Expense,** is increased by $4,000. The asset account, **Prepaid Rent,** is decreased by $4,000.

DEBIT-CREDIT RULES

DEBIT   Increases to expense accounts are recorded as debits. Debit **Rent Expense** for $4,000.

CREDIT   Decreases to asset accounts are recorded as credits. Credit **Prepaid Rent** for $4,000.

T-ACCOUNT PRESENTATION

Rent Expense			Prepaid Rent	
+	−		+	−
4,000				4,000

Let's review the effect of the adjustment on the asset account, *Prepaid Rent.* The beginning balance of $8,000 represents prepaid rent for the months of December and January. By December 31, the prepaid rent for the month of December is "used up." The adjustment reducing *Prepaid Rent* recognizes the expense of occupying the facilities in December. The $4,000 ending balance represents prepaid rent for the month of January.

important!

Prepaid Expense
Prepaid rent is recorded as an asset at the time it is paid. As time elapses, the asset is used up. An adjustment is made to reduce the asset and to recognize rent expense.

Prepaid Rent				
	+		−	
Bal.	8,000	Adj.		4,000
Bal.	4,000			

Refer again to Figure 5.2 to review the adjustment on the worksheet: a debit of $4,000 to **Rent Expense** and a credit of $4,000 to **Prepaid Rent.** Both parts of the adjustment are labeled (**b**).

ADJUSTING FOR DEPRECIATION

There is one more adjustment to make at the end of December. It involves the equipment purchased in November. The cost of long-term assets such as equipment is not recorded as an expense when purchased. Instead, the cost is recorded as an asset and spread over the time the assets are used for the business. **Depreciation** is the process of allocating the cost of long-term assets over their expected useful lives. There are many ways to calculate depreciation. Wells' Consulting Services uses the **straight-line depreciation** method. This method results in an equal amount of depreciation being charged to each accounting period during the asset's useful life. The formula for straight-line depreciation is

$$\text{Depreciation} = \frac{\text{Cost} - \text{Salvage value}}{\text{Estimated useful life}}$$

Salvage value is an estimate of the amount that may be received by selling or disposing of an asset at the end of its useful life.

Wells' Consulting Services purchased $11,000 worth of equipment. The equipment has an estimated useful life of five years and no salvage value. The depreciation for December, the first month of operations, is $183 (rounded).

$$\frac{\$11,000 - \$0}{60 \text{ months}} = \$183 \text{ (rounded)}$$

1. Convert the asset's useful life from years to months: 5 years × 12 months = 60 months.

2. Divide the total depreciation to be taken by the total number of months: $11,000 ÷ 60 = $183 (rounded).

3. Record depreciation expense of $183 each month for the next 60 months.

> Conoco Inc. depreciates property such as refinery equipment, pipelines, and deepwater drill ships on a straight-line basis over the estimated life of each asset, ranging from 15 to 25 years.

As the cost of the equipment is gradually transferred to expense, its recorded value as an asset must be reduced. This procedure cannot be carried out by directly decreasing the balance in the asset account. Generally accepted accounting principles require that the original cost of a long-term asset continue to appear in the asset account until the firm has used up or disposed of the asset.

The adjustment for depreciation is recorded in a contra account entitled ***Accumulated Depreciation—Equipment.*** A **contra account** has a normal balance that is opposite that of a related account. For example, the *Equipment* account is an asset and has a normal debit balance. *Accumulated Depreciation—Equipment* is a **contra asset account** with a normal credit balance, which is opposite the normal balance of an asset account. The adjustment to reflect depreciation for December is a $183 debit to ***Depreciation Expense—Equipment*** and a $183 credit to ***Accumulated Depreciation—Equipment.***

The ***Accumulated Depreciation—Equipment*** account is a record of all depreciation taken on the equipment. The financial records show the original cost of the equipment (***Equipment,***

important!

Contra Accounts

The normal balance for a contra account is the opposite of the related account.

Accumulated Depreciation is a contra asset account. The normal balance of an asset account is a *debit*. The normal balance of a contra asset account is a *credit*.

$11,000) and all depreciation taken (***Accumulated Depreciation—Equipment,*** $183). The difference between the two accounts is called book value. <mark>**Book value**</mark> is that portion of an asset's original cost that has not yet been depreciated. Three amounts are reported on the financial statements for equipment:

Equipment	$11,000
Less accumulated depreciation	−183
Equipment at book value	$10,817

ADJUSTMENT

Record the adjustment for depreciation.

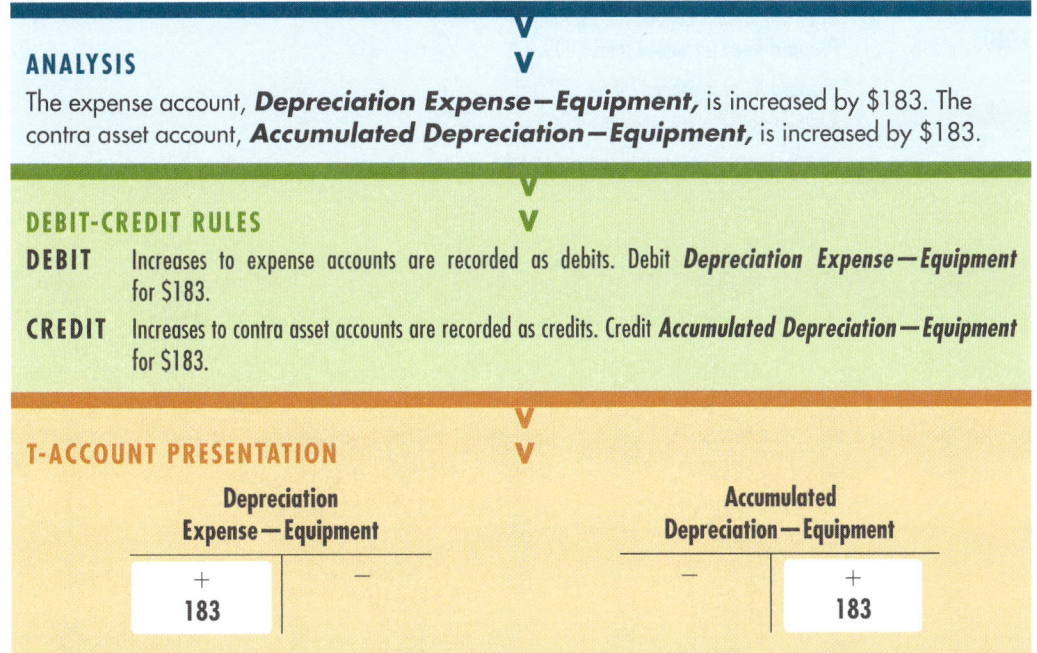

ANALYSIS

The expense account, **Depreciation Expense—Equipment,** is increased by $183. The contra asset account, **Accumulated Depreciation—Equipment,** is increased by $183.

DEBIT-CREDIT RULES

DEBIT   Increases to expense accounts are recorded as debits. Debit **Depreciation Expense—Equipment** for $183.

CREDIT   Increases to contra asset accounts are recorded as credits. Credit **Accumulated Depreciation—Equipment** for $183.

T-ACCOUNT PRESENTATION

Depreciation Expense—Equipment		Accumulated Depreciation—Equipment	
+	−	−	+
183			183

Refer to Figure 5.2 on page 125 to review the depreciation adjustment on the worksheet. The two parts of the adjustment are labeled **(c)**.

If Wells' Consulting Services had other kinds of long-term tangible assets, an adjustment for depreciation would be made for each one. Long-term tangible assets include land, buildings, equipment, trucks, automobiles, furniture, and fixtures. Depreciation is calculated on all long-term tangible assets except land. Land is not depreciated.

Notice that each adjustment involved a balance sheet account (an asset or a contra asset) and an income statement account (an expense). When all adjustments have been entered, total and rule the Adjustments columns. Be sure that the totals of the Debit and Credit columns are equal. If they are not, locate and correct the error or errors before continuing. Figure 5.2 shows the completed Adjustments section.

Section 1   Self Review

QUESTIONS

1. Why is the worksheet prepared?
2. Why are prepaid expenses adjusted at the end of an accounting period?
3. What are adjustments?

EXERCISES

4. A firm paid $2,400 for supplies during the accounting period. At the end of the accounting period, the firm had $500 of supplies on hand. What adjustment is entered on the worksheet?

   a. *Supplies Expense* is debited for $1,900 and *Supplies* is credited for $1,900.

   b. *Supplies* is debited for $500 and *Supplies Expense* is credited for $500.

   c. *Supplies Expense* is debited for $500 and *Supplies* is credited for $500.

   d. *Supplies* is debited for $1,900 and *Supplies Expense* is credited for $1,900.

5. On January 1, a firm paid $24,000 for six months' rent, January through June. What is the adjustment for rent expense at the end of January?

   a. *Rent Expense* is debited for $24,000 and *Prepaid Rent* is credited for $24,000.

   b. *Rent Expense* is debited for $4,000 and *Prepaid Rent* is credited for $4,000.

   c. *Prepaid Rent* is debited for $4,000 and *Rent Expense* is credited for $4,000.

   d. No adjustment is made until the end of June.

ANALYSIS

6. Three years ago, KB Delivery bought a delivery truck for $90,000. The truck has no salvage value and a five-year useful life. What is the book value of the truck at the end of three years?

(Answers to Section 1 Self Review are on page 153.)

SECTION OBJECTIVES	TERMS TO LEARN
>> 5-3. Complete the worksheet. **WHY IT'S IMPORTANT** The worksheet summarizes both internal and external financial events of a period. **>> 5-4. Prepare an income statement, statement of owner's equity, and balance sheet from the completed worksheet.** **WHY IT'S IMPORTANT** Using a worksheet saves time in preparing the financial statements. **>> 5-5. Journalize and post the adjusting entries.** **WHY IT'S IMPORTANT** Adjusting entries update the financial records of the business.	account form balance sheet report form balance sheet

Financial Statements

The worksheet is used to prepare the financial statements. Preparing financial statements is the fifth step in the accounting cycle.

The Adjusted Trial Balance Section

>> **5-3. OBJECTIVE**
Complete the worksheet.

The next task is to prepare the Adjusted Trial Balance section.

1. Combine the figures from the Trial Balance section and the Adjustments section of the worksheet. Record the computed results in the Adjusted Trial Balance columns.
2. Total the Debit and Credit columns in the Adjusted Trial Balance section. Confirm that debits equal credits.

Figure 5.3 on pages 132–133 shows the completed Adjusted Trial Balance section of the worksheet. The accounts that do not have adjustments are simply extended from the Trial Balance section to the Adjusted Trial Balance section. For example, the **Cash** account balance of $111,350 is recorded in the Debit column of the Adjusted Trial Balance section without change.

The balances of accounts that are affected by adjustments are recomputed. Look at the **Supplies** account. It has a $1,500 debit balance in the Trial Balance section and shows a $500 credit in the Adjustments section. The new balance is $1,000 ($1,500 − $500). It is recorded in the Debit column of the Adjusted Trial Balance section.

Use the following guidelines to compute the amounts for the Adjusted Trial Balance section.

■ If the account has a debit balance in the Trial Balance section and a debit entry in the Adjustments section, add the two amounts.

If the Trial Balance section has a:	AND if the entry in the Adjustments section is a:	Then:
Debit balance	Debit	Add the amounts.
Debit balance	Credit	Subtract the credit amount.
Credit balance	Credit	Add the amounts.
Credit balance	Debit	Subtract the debit amount.

FIGURE 5.3 A Partial Worksheet

Wells' Consulting Services
Worksheet
Month Ended December 31, 2016

	ACCOUNT NAME	TRIAL BALANCE DEBIT	TRIAL BALANCE CREDIT	ADJUSTMENTS DEBIT	ADJUSTMENTS CREDIT
1	Cash	111 350 00			
2	Accounts Receivable	5 000 00			
3	Supplies	1 500 00			(a) 500 00
4	Prepaid Rent	8 000 00			(b) 4 000 00
5	Equipment	11 000 00			
6	Accumulated Depreciation—Equipment				(c) 183 00
7	Accounts Payable		3 500 00		
8	Carolyn Wells, Capital		100 000 00		
9	Carolyn Wells, Drawing	5 000 00			
10	Fees Income		47 000 00		
11	Salaries Expense	8 000 00			
12	Utilities Expense	650 00			
13	Supplies Expense			(a) 500 00	
14	Rent Expense			(b) 4 000 00	
15	Depreciation Expense—Equipment			(c) 183 00	
16	Totals	150 500 00	150 500 00	4 683 00	4 683 00
17	Net Income				

- If the account has a debit balance in the Trial Balance section and a credit entry in the Adjustments section, subtract the credit amount.
- If the account has a credit balance in the Trial Balance section and a credit entry in the Adjustments section, add the two amounts.
- If the account has a credit balance in the Trial Balance section and a debit entry in the Adjustments section, subtract the debit amount.

Prepaid Rent has a Trial Balance debit of \$8,000 and an Adjustments credit of \$4,000. Enter \$4,000 (\$8,000 − \$4,000) in the Adjusted Trial Balance Debit column.

Four accounts that started with zero balances in the Trial Balance section are affected by adjustments. They are ***Accumulated Depreciation—Equipment, Supplies Expense, Rent Expense,*** and ***Depreciation Expense—Equipment.*** The figures in the Adjustments section are simply extended to the Adjusted Trial Balance section. For example, ***Accumulated Depreciation—Equipment*** has a zero balance in the Trial Balance section and a \$183 credit in the Adjustments section. Extend the \$183 to the Adjusted Trial Balance Credit column.

Once all account balances are recorded in the Adjusted Trial Balance section, total and rule the Debit and Credit columns. Be sure that total debits equal total credits. If they are not equal, find and correct the error or errors.

The Income Statement and Balance Sheet Sections

The Income Statement and Balance Sheet sections of the worksheet are used to separate the amounts needed for the balance sheet and the income statement. For example, to prepare an income statement, all revenue and expense account balances must be in one place.

Starting at the top of the Adjusted Trial Balance section, examine each general ledger account. For accounts that appear on the balance sheet, enter the amount in the appropriate column of the Balance Sheet section. For accounts that appear on the income statement, enter the amount in the appropriate column of the Income Statement section. Take care to enter debit amounts in the Debit column and credit amounts in the Credit column.

| ADJUSTED TRIAL BALANCE | | INCOME STATEMENT | | BALANCE SHEET | | |
DEBIT	CREDIT	DEBIT	CREDIT	DEBIT	CREDIT	
111 350 00						1
5 000 00						2
1 000 00						3
4 000 00						4
11 000 00						5
	183 00					6
	3 500 00					7
	100 000 00					8
5 000 00						9
	47 000 00					10
8 000 00						11
650 00						12
500 00						13
4 000 00						14
183 00						15
150 683 00	150 683 00					16
						17

PREPARING THE BALANCE SHEET SECTION

Refer to Figure 5.4 on pages 134–135 as you learn how to complete the worksheet. Asset, liability, and owner's equity accounts appear on the balance sheet. The first five accounts that appear on the worksheet are assets. Extend the asset accounts to the Debit column of the Balance Sheet section. The next account, *Accumulated Depreciation—Equipment,* is a contra asset account. Extend it to the Credit column of the Balance Sheet section. Extend *Accounts Payable* and *Carolyn Wells, Capital* to the Credit column of the Balance Sheet section. Extend *Carolyn Wells, Drawing* to the Debit column of the Balance Sheet section.

PREPARING THE INCOME STATEMENT SECTION

Revenue and expense accounts appear on the income statement. Extend the *Fees Income* account to the Credit column of the Income Statement section. The last five accounts on the worksheet are expense accounts. Extend these accounts to the Debit column of the Income Statement section.

After all account balances are transferred from the Adjusted Trial Balance section of the worksheet to the financial statement sections, total the Debit and Credit columns in the Income Statement section. For Wells' Consulting Services, the debits (expenses) total $13,333 and the credits (revenue) total $47,000.

Next, total the columns in the Balance Sheet section. For Wells' Consulting Services, the debits (assets and drawing account) total $137,350 and the credits (contra asset, liabilities, and owner's equity) total $103,683.

Return to the Income Statement section. The totals of these columns are used to determine the net income or net loss. Subtract the smaller column total from the larger one. Enter the difference on the line below the smaller total. In the Account Name column, enter "Net Income" or "Net Loss."

In this case, the total of the Credit column, $47,000, exceeds the total of the Debit column, $13,333. The Credit column total represents revenue. The Debit column total represents expenses. The difference between the two amounts is a net income of $33,667. Enter $33,667 in the Debit column of the Income Statement section.

recall

Locating Errors
If total debits do not equal total credits, find the difference between total debits and total credits. If the difference is divisible by 9, there could be a transposition error. If the difference is divisible by 2, an amount could be entered in the wrong (Debit or Credit) column.

FIGURE 5.4   **A Completed Worksheet**

		TRIAL BALANCE		ADJUSTMENTS	
	ACCOUNT NAME	DEBIT	CREDIT	DEBIT	CREDIT
1	Cash	111 3 5 0 00			
2	Accounts Receivable	5 0 0 0 00			
3	Supplies	1 5 0 0 00			(a) 5 0 0 00
4	Prepaid Rent	8 0 0 0 00			(b) 4 0 0 0 00
5	Equipment	11 0 0 0 00			
6	Accumulated Depreciation—Equipment				(c) 1 8 3 00
7	Accounts Payable		3 5 0 0 00		
8	Carolyn Wells, Capital		100 0 0 0 00		
9	Carolyn Wells, Drawing	5 0 0 0 00			
10	Fees Income		47 0 0 0 00		
11	Salaries Expense	8 0 0 0 00			
12	Utilities Expense	6 5 0 00			
13	Supplies Expense			(a) 5 0 0 00	
14	Rent Expense			(b) 4 0 0 0 00	
15	Depreciation Expense—Equipment			(c) 1 8 3 00	
16	Totals	150 5 0 0 00	150 5 0 0 00	4 6 8 3 00	4 6 8 3 00
17	Net Income				
18					

Wells' Consulting Services
Worksheet
Month Ended December 31, 2016

important!

Net Income

The difference between the Debit and Credit columns of the Income Statement section represents net income. The difference between the Debit and Credit columns of the Balance Sheet section should equal the net income amount.

Net income causes a net increase in owner's equity. As a check on accuracy, the amount in the Balance Sheet Debit column is subtracted from the amount in the Credit column and compared to net income. In the Balance Sheet section, subtract the smaller column total from the larger one. The difference should equal the net income or net loss computed in the Income Statement section. Enter the difference on the line below the smaller total. For Wells' Consulting Services, enter $33,667 in the Credit column of the Balance Sheet section.

Total the Income Statement and Balance Sheet columns. Make sure that total debits equal total credits for each section.

Wells' Consulting Services had a net income. If it had a loss, the loss would be entered in the Credit column of the Income Statement section and the Debit column of the Balance Sheet section. "Net Loss" would be entered in the Account Name column on the worksheet.

Preparing Financial Statements

When the worksheet is complete, the next step is to prepare the financial statements, starting with the income statement. Preparation of the financial statements is the fifth step in the accounting cycle.

>> **5-4. OBJECTIVE**

Prepare an income statement, statement of owner's equity, and balance sheet from the completed worksheet.

PREPARING THE INCOME STATEMENT

Use the Income Statement section of the worksheet to prepare the income statement. Figure 5.5 on page 136 shows the income statement for Wells' Consulting Services. Compare it to the worksheet in Figure 5.4.

If the firm had incurred a net loss, the final amount on the income statement would be labeled "Net Loss for the Month."

	ADJUSTED TRIAL BALANCE		INCOME STATEMENT		BALANCE SHEET		
	DEBIT	CREDIT	DEBIT	CREDIT	DEBIT	CREDIT	
	111 3 5 0 00				111 3 5 0 00		1
	5 0 0 0 00				5 0 0 0 00		2
	1 0 0 0 00				1 0 0 0 00		3
	4 0 0 0 00				4 0 0 0 00		4
	11 0 0 0 00				11 0 0 0 00		5
		1 8 3 00				1 8 3 00	6
		3 5 0 0 00				3 5 0 0 00	7
		100 0 0 0 00				100 0 0 0 00	8
	5 0 0 0 00				5 0 0 0 00		9
		47 0 0 0 00		47 0 0 0 00			10
	8 0 0 0 00		8 0 0 0 00				11
	6 5 0 00		6 5 0 00				12
	5 0 0 00		5 0 0 00				13
	4 0 0 0 00		4 0 0 0 00				14
	1 8 3 00		1 8 3 00				15
	150 6 8 3 00	150 6 8 3 00	13 3 3 3 00	47 0 0 0 00	137 3 5 0 00	103 6 8 3 00	16
			33 6 6 7 00			33 6 6 7 00	17
			47 0 0 0 00	47 0 0 0 00	137 3 5 0 00	137 3 5 0 00	18

PREPARING THE STATEMENT OF OWNER'S EQUITY

The statement of owner's equity reports the changes that have occurred in the owner's financial interest during the reporting period. Use the data in the Balance Sheet section of the worksheet, as well as the net income or net loss figure, to prepare the statement of owner's equity.

- From the Balance Sheet section of the worksheet, use the amounts for owner's capital; owner's withdrawals, if any; and owner's investments, if any.

- From the Income Statement section of the worksheet, use the amount calculated for net income or net loss.

The statement of owner's equity is prepared before the balance sheet because the ending capital balance is needed to prepare the balance sheet. The statement of owner's equity reports the change in owner's capital during the period ($28,667) as well as the ending capital ($128,667). Figure 5.6 on page 136 shows the statement of owner's equity for Wells' Consulting Services.

PREPARING THE BALANCE SHEET

The accounts listed on the balance sheet are taken directly from the Balance Sheet section of the worksheet. Figure 5.7 on page 136 shows the balance sheet for Wells' Consulting Services.

Note that the equipment's book value is reported on the balance sheet ($10,817). Do not confuse book value with market value. Book value is the portion of the original cost that has not been depreciated. *Market value* is what a willing buyer will pay a willing seller for the asset. Market value may be higher or lower than book value.

Notice that the amount for *Carolyn Wells, Capital,* $128,667, comes from the statement of owner's equity.

The balance sheet in Figure 5.7 is prepared using the report form. The **report form balance sheet** lists the asset accounts first, followed by liabilities and owner's equity. Chapters 2 and 3 illustrated the **account form balance sheet,** with assets on the left and liabilities

FIGURE 5.5

Income Statement

Wells' Consulting Services
Income Statement
Month Ended December 31, 2016

Revenue			
Fees Income			47 0 0 0 00
Expenses			
Salaries Expense	8 0 0 0 00		
Utilities Expense	6 5 0 00		
Supplies Expense	5 0 0 00		
Rent Expense	4 0 0 0 00		
Depreciation Expense—Equipment	1 8 3 00		
Total Expenses			13 3 3 3 00
Net Income for the Month			33 6 6 7 00

FIGURE 5.6

Statement of Owner's Equity

Wells' Consulting Services
Statement of Owner's Equity
Month Ended December 31, 2016

Carolyn Wells, Capital, December 1, 2016			100 0 0 0 00
Net Income for December	33 6 6 7 00		
Less Withdrawals for December	5 0 0 0 00		
Increase in Capital			28 6 6 7 00
Carolyn Wells, Capital, December 31, 2016			128 6 6 7 00

FIGURE 5.7

Balance Sheet

Wells' Consulting Services
Balance Sheet
December 31, 2016

Assets			
Cash			111 3 5 0 00
Accounts Receivable			5 0 0 0 00
Supplies			1 0 0 0 00
Prepaid Rent			4 0 0 0 00
Equipment	11 0 0 0 00		
Less Accumulated Depreciation	1 8 3 00		10 8 1 7 00
Total Assets			132 1 6 7 00
Liabilities and Owner's Equity			
Liabilities			
Accounts Payable			3 5 0 0 00
Owner's Equity			
Carolyn Wells, Capital			128 6 6 7 00
Total Liabilities and Owner's Equity			132 1 6 7 00

FIGURE 5.8A   Worksheet Summary

The worksheet is used to gather all the data needed at the end of an accounting period to prepare the financial statements. The worksheet heading contains the name of the company (WHO), the title of the statement being prepared (WHAT), and the period covered (WHEN). The worksheet contains 10 money columns that are arranged in five sections labeled Trial Balance, Adjustments, Adjusted Trial Balance, Income Statement, and Balance Sheet. Each section includes a Debit column and a Credit column.

The information reflected in the worksheet below is for Wells' Consulting Services for the period ending December 31, 2016. The illustrations that follow will highlight the preparation of each part of the worksheet.

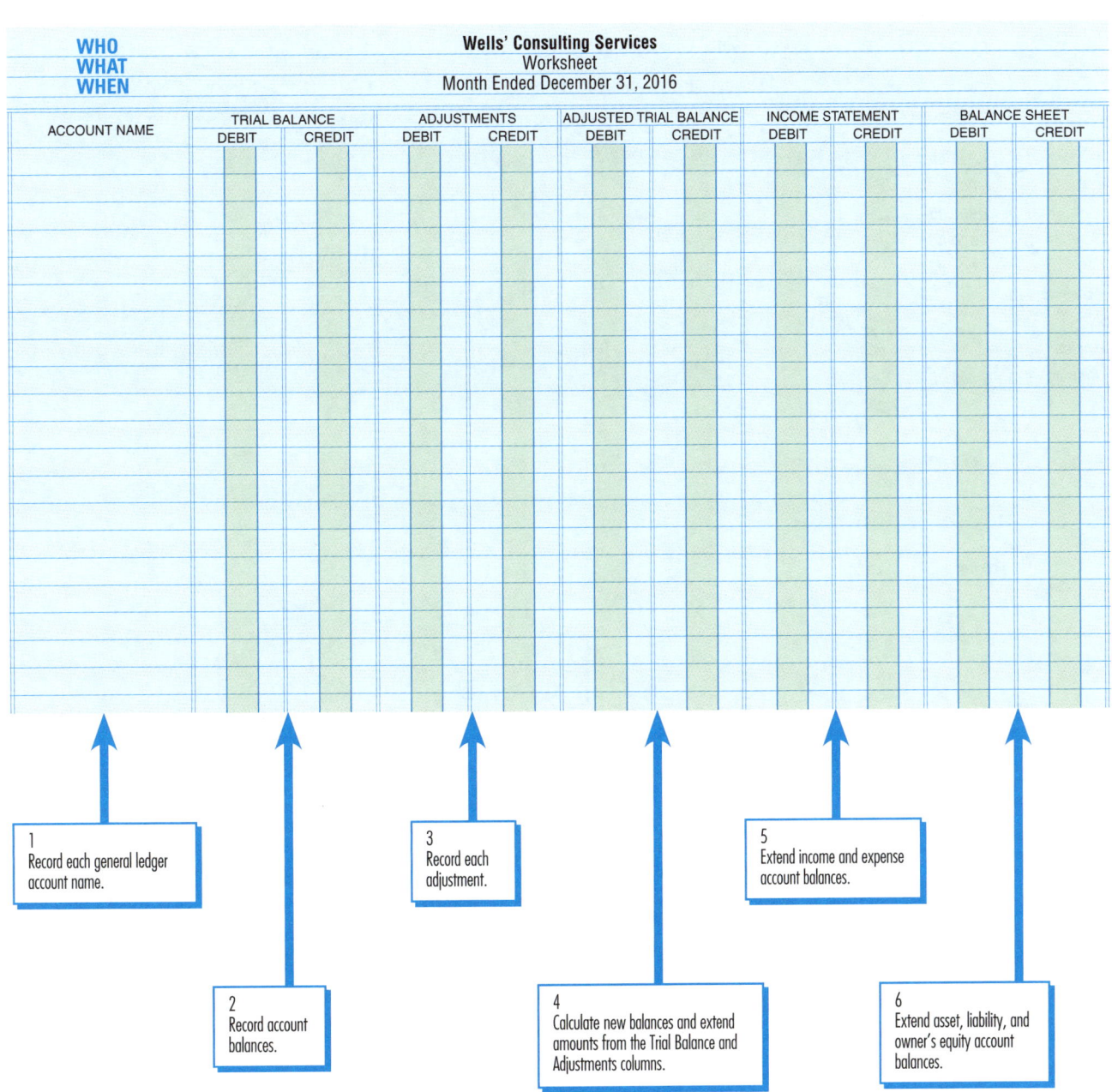

WHO
WHAT
WHEN

Wells' Consulting Services
Worksheet
Month Ended December 31, 2016

ACCOUNT NAME	TRIAL BALANCE		ADJUSTMENTS		ADJUSTED TRIAL BALANCE		INCOME STATEMENT		BALANCE SHEET	
	DEBIT	CREDIT	DEBIT	CREDIT	DEBIT	CREDIT	DEBIT	CREDIT	DEBIT	CREDIT

1 Record each general ledger account name.

2 Record account balances.

3 Record each adjustment.

4 Calculate new balances and extend amounts from the Trial Balance and Adjustments columns.

5 Extend income and expense account balances.

6 Extend asset, liability, and owner's equity account balances.

FIGURE 5.8B The Trial Balance Columns

The first step in preparing the worksheet for Wells' Consulting Services is to list the general ledger accounts and their balances in the Account Name and Trial Balance sections of the worksheet. The equality of total debits and credits is proved by totaling the Debit and Credit columns.

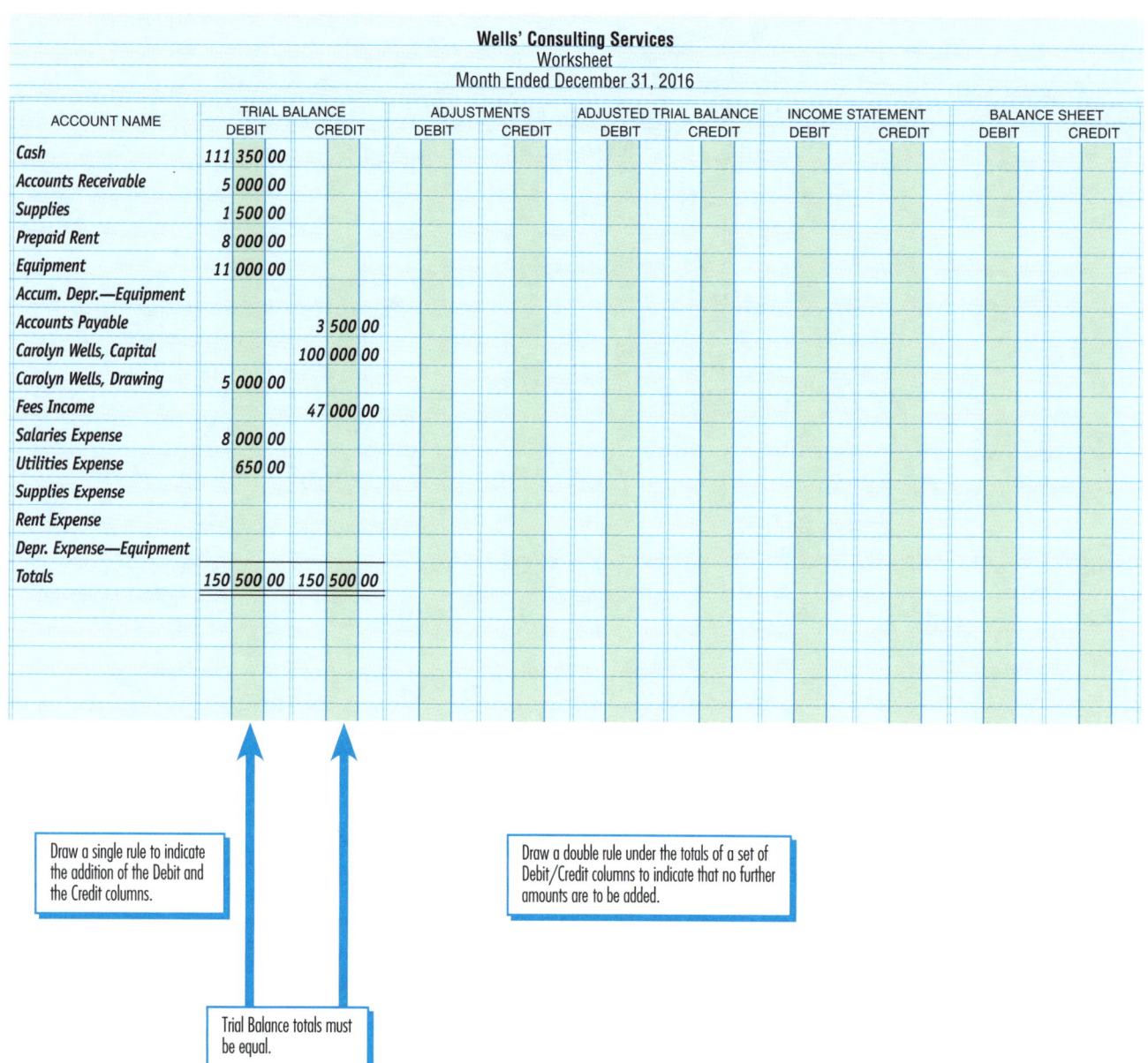

Wells' Consulting Services
Worksheet
Month Ended December 31, 2016

ACCOUNT NAME	TRIAL BALANCE		ADJUSTMENTS		ADJUSTED TRIAL BALANCE		INCOME STATEMENT		BALANCE SHEET	
	DEBIT	CREDIT	DEBIT	CREDIT	DEBIT	CREDIT	DEBIT	CREDIT	DEBIT	CREDIT
Cash	111 350 00									
Accounts Receivable	5 000 00									
Supplies	1 500 00									
Prepaid Rent	8 000 00									
Equipment	11 000 00									
Accum. Depr.—Equipment										
Accounts Payable		3 500 00								
Carolyn Wells, Capital		100 000 00								
Carolyn Wells, Drawing	5 000 00									
Fees Income		47 000 00								
Salaries Expense	8 000 00									
Utilities Expense	650 00									
Supplies Expense										
Rent Expense										
Depr. Expense—Equipment										
Totals	150 500 00	150 500 00								

Draw a single rule to indicate the addition of the Debit and the Credit columns.

Draw a double rule under the totals of a set of Debit/Credit columns to indicate that no further amounts are to be added.

Trial Balance totals must be equal.

FIGURE 5.8G   Preparing the Financial Statements

The information needed to prepare the financial statements is obtained from the worksheet.

Wells' Consulting Services
Income Statement
Month Ended December 31, 2016

Revenue		
Fees Income		47 000 00
Expenses		
Salaries Expense	8 000 00	
Utilities Expense	650 00	
Supplies Expense	500 00	
Rent Expense	4 000 00	
Depreciation Expense—Equipment	183 00	
Total Expenses		13 333 00
Net Income for the Month		33 667 00

> When expenses for the period are less than revenue, a net income results. The net income is transferred to the statement of owner's equity.

Wells' Consulting Services
Statement of Owner's Equity
Month Ended December 31, 2016

Carolyn Wells, Capital, December 1, 2016		100 000 00
Net Income for December	33 667 00	
Less Withdrawals for December	5 000 00	
Increase in Capital		28 667 00
Carolyn Wells, Capital, December 31, 2016		128 667 00

> The withdrawals are subtracted from the net income for the period to determine the change in owner's equity.

Wells' Consulting Services
Balance Sheet
December 31, 2016

Assets		
Cash		111 350 00
Accounts Receivable		5 000 00
Supplies		1 000 00
Prepaid Rent		4 000 00
Equipment	11 000 00	
Less Accumulated Depreciation	183 00	10 817 00
Total Assets		132 167 00
Liabilities and Owner's Equity		
Liabilities		
Accounts Payable		3 500 00
Owner's Equity		
Carolyn Wells, Capital		128 667 00
Total Liabilities and Owner's Equity		132 167 00

> The ending capital balance is transferred from the statement of owner's equity to the balance sheet.

SUMMARY OF FINANCIAL STATEMENTS

THE INCOME STATEMENT

The income statement is prepared directly from the data in the Income Statement section of the worksheet. The heading of the income statement contains the name of the firm (WHO), the name of the statement (WHAT), and the period covered by the statement (WHEN). The revenue section of the statement is prepared first. The revenue account name is obtained from the Account Name column of the worksheet. The balance of the revenue account is obtained from the Credit column of the Income Statement section of the worksheet. The expenses section of the income statement is prepared next. The expense account titles are obtained from the Account Name column of the worksheet. The balance of each expense account is obtained from the Debit column of the Income Statement section of the worksheet.

Determining the net income or net loss for the period is the last step in preparing the income statement. If the firm has more revenue than expenses, a net income is reported for the period. If the firm has more expenses than revenue, a net loss is reported. The net income or net loss reported must agree with the amount calculated on the worksheet.

THE STATEMENT OF OWNER'S EQUITY

The statement of owner's equity is prepared from the data in the Balance Sheet section of the worksheet and the general ledger capital account. The statement of owner's equity is prepared before the balance sheet so that the amount of the ending capital balance is available for presentation on the balance sheet. The heading of the statement contains the name of the firm (WHO), the name of the statement (WHAT), and the date of the statement (WHEN).

The statement begins with the capital account balance at the beginning of the period. Next, the increase or decrease in the owner's capital account is determined. The increase or decrease is computed by adding the net income (or subtracting the net loss) for the period to any additional investments made by the owner during the period and subtracting withdrawals for the period. The increase or decrease is added to the beginning capital balance to obtain the ending capital balance.

THE BALANCE SHEET

The balance sheet is prepared from the data in the Balance Sheet section of the worksheet and the statement of owner's equity. The balance sheet reflects the assets, liabilities, and owner's equity of the firm on the balance sheet date. The heading of the statement contains the name of the firm (WHO), the name of the statement (WHAT), and the date of the statement (WHEN).

The assets section of the statement is prepared first. The asset account titles are obtained from the Account Name column of the worksheet. The balance of each asset account is obtained from the Debit column of the Balance Sheet section of the worksheet. The liability and owner's equity section is prepared next. The liability and owner's equity account titles are obtained from the Account Name column of the worksheet. The balance of each liability account is obtained from the Credit column of the Balance Sheet section of the worksheet. The ending balance for the owner's capital account is obtained from the statement of owner's equity. Total liabilities and owner's equity must equal total assets.

and owner's equity on the right. The report form is widely used because it provides more space for entering account names and its format is easier to prepare.

> Some companies show long-term assets at a net amount. "Net" means that accumulated depreciation has been subtracted from the original cost. For example, The Boeing Company's consolidated statement of financial position as of December 31, 2011, states:
>   Property, plant, and equipment, net: $9,313 million
> The accumulated depreciation amount does not appear on the balance sheet.

Figure 5.8A through 5.8G on the preceding pages provides a step-by-step demonstration of how to complete the worksheet and financial statements for Wells' Consulting Services.

Journalizing and Posting Adjusting Entries

The worksheet is a tool. It is used to determine the effects of adjustments on account balances. It is also used to prepare the financial statements. However, the worksheet is not part of the permanent accounting record.

After the financial statements are prepared, the adjustments shown on the worksheet must become part of the permanent accounting record. Each adjustment is journalized and posted to the general ledger accounts. Journalizing and posting adjusting entries is the sixth step in the accounting cycle.

>> **5-5. OBJECTIVE**
Journalize and post the adjusting entries.

For Wells' Consulting Services, three adjustments are needed to provide a complete picture of the firm's operating results and its financial position. Adjustments are needed for supplies expense, rent expense, and depreciation expense.

Refer to Figure 5.4 on pages 134–135 for data needed to record the adjustments. Enter the words "Adjusting Entries" in the Description column of the general journal. Some accountants prefer to start a new page when they record the adjusting entries. Then journalize the adjustments in the order in which they appear on the worksheet.

After journalizing the adjusting entries, post them to the general ledger accounts. Figure 5.9 on page 138 shows how the adjusting entries for Wells' Consulting Services on December 31, 2016, were journalized and posted. Account numbers appear in the general journal Posting Reference column because all entries have been posted. In each general ledger account, the word "Adjusting" appears in the Description column.

Remember that the worksheet is not part of the accounting records. Adjustments that are on the worksheet must be recorded in the general journal and posted to the general ledger in order to become part of the permanent accounting records.

FIGURE 5.9

Journalized and Posted
Adjusting Entries

	DATE		DESCRIPTION	POST. REF.	DEBIT	CREDIT	
1	2016		*Adjusting Entries*				1
2	Dec.	31	Supplies Expense	517	5 0 0 00		2
3			Supplies	121		5 0 0 00	3
4							4
5		31	Rent Expense	520	4 0 0 0 00		5
6			Prepaid Rent	137		4 0 0 0 00	6
7							7
8		31	Depr. Expense—Equipment	523	1 8 3 00		8
9			Accum. Depr.—Equipment	142		1 8 3 00	9
10							10
11							11

GENERAL JOURNAL   PAGE _3_

ACCOUNT _Supplies_   ACCOUNT NO. _121_

DATE		DESCRIPTION	POST. REF.	DEBIT	CREDIT	BALANCE DEBIT	BALANCE CREDIT
2016							
Nov.	28		J1	1 5 0 0 00		1 5 0 0 00	
Dec.	31	Adjusting	J3		5 0 0 00	1 0 0 0 00	

ACCOUNT _Prepaid Rent_   ACCOUNT NO. _137_

DATE		DESCRIPTION	POST. REF.	DEBIT	CREDIT	BALANCE DEBIT	BALANCE CREDIT
2016							
Nov.	30		J2	8 0 0 0 00		8 0 0 0 00	
Dec.	31	Adjusting	J3		4 0 0 0 00	4 0 0 0 00	

ACCOUNT _Accumulated Depreciation—Equipment_   ACCOUNT NO. _142_

DATE		DESCRIPTION	POST. REF.	DEBIT	CREDIT	BALANCE DEBIT	BALANCE CREDIT
2016							
Dec.	31	Adjusting	J3		1 8 3 00		1 8 3 00

ACCOUNT _Supplies Expense_   ACCOUNT NO. _517_

DATE		DESCRIPTION	POST. REF.	DEBIT	CREDIT	BALANCE DEBIT	BALANCE CREDIT
2016							
Dec.	31	Adjusting	J3	5 0 0 00		5 0 0 00	

ACCOUNT _Rent Expense_   ACCOUNT NO. _520_

DATE		DESCRIPTION	POST. REF.	DEBIT	CREDIT	BALANCE DEBIT	BALANCE CREDIT
2016							
Dec.	31	Adjusting	J3	4 0 0 0 00		4 0 0 0 00	

ACCOUNT _Depreciation Expense—Equipment_   ACCOUNT NO. _523_

DATE		DESCRIPTION	POST. REF.	DEBIT	CREDIT	BALANCE DEBIT	BALANCE CREDIT
2016							
Dec.	31	Adjusting	J3	1 8 3 00		1 8 3 00	

MANAGERIAL IMPLICATIONS   <<

WORKSHEETS

- The worksheet permits quick preparation of the financial statements. Quick preparation of financial statements allows management to obtain timely information.
- Timely information allows management to:
  - evaluate the results of operations,
  - evaluate the financial position of the business,
  - make decisions.
- The worksheet provides a convenient form for gathering information and determining the effects of internal changes, such as:
  - recording an expense for the use of a long-term asset like equipment,
  - recording the actual use of prepaid items.

- The more accounts that a firm has in its general ledger, the more useful the worksheet is in speeding the preparation of the financial statements.
- It is important to management that the appropriate adjustments are recorded in order to present a complete and accurate picture of the firm's financial affairs.

THINKING CRITICALLY

Why is it necessary to record an adjustment for depreciation?

Section 2   Self Review

QUESTIONS

1. What amounts appear on the statement of owner's equity?

2. What is the difference between a report form balance sheet and an account form balance sheet?

3. Why is it necessary to journalize and post adjusting entries even though the data are already recorded on the worksheet?

EXERCISES

4. On a worksheet, the adjusted balance of the *Supplies* account is extended to the:
   a. Balance Sheet Credit column.
   b. Income Statement Credit column.
   c. Income Statement Debit column.
   d. Balance Sheet Debit column.

5. *Accumulated Depreciation—Equipment* is a(n):
   a. contra liability account.
   b. liability account.

   c. contra asset account.
   d. asset account.

ANALYSIS

6. Exes Repair Shop purchased equipment for $32,000. *Depreciation Expense* for the month is $800. What is the balance of the *Equipment* account after posting the depreciation entry? Why?

(Answers to Section 2 Self Review are on page 153.)

5 Chapter   REVIEW   Chapter Summary

At the end of the operating period, adjustments for internal events are recorded to update the accounting records. In this chapter, you have learned how the accountant uses the worksheet and adjusting entries to accomplish this task.

Learning Objectives

5-1   **Complete a trial balance on a worksheet.**

A worksheet is normally used to save time in preparing the financial statements. Preparation of the worksheet is the fourth step in the accounting cycle. The trial balance is the first section of the worksheet to be prepared.

5-2   **Prepare adjustments for unrecorded business transactions.**

Some changes arise from the internal operations of the firm itself. Adjusting entries are made to record these changes. Any adjustments to account balances should be entered in the Adjustments section of the worksheet.

■ Prepaid expenses are expense items that are acquired and paid for in advance of their use. At the time of their acquisition, these items represent assets and are recorded in asset accounts. As they are used, their cost is transferred to expense by means of adjusting entries at the end of each accounting period.

Examples of general ledger asset accounts and the related expense accounts follow:

Asset Accounts	Expense Accounts
Supplies	Supplies Expense
Prepaid Rent	Rent Expense
Prepaid Insurance	Insurance Expense

■ Depreciation is the process of allocating the cost of a long-term tangible asset to operations over its expected useful life. Part of the asset's cost is charged off as an expense at the end of each accounting period during the asset's useful life. The straight-line method of depreciation is widely used. The formula for straight-line depreciation is:

$$\text{Depreciation} = \frac{\text{Cost} - \text{Salvage value}}{\text{Estimated useful life}}$$

5-3   **Complete the worksheet.**

An adjusted trial balance is prepared to prove the equality of the debits and credits after adjustments have been entered on the worksheet. Once the Debit and Credit columns have been totaled and ruled, the Income Statement and Balance Sheet columns of the worksheet are completed. The net income or net loss for the period is determined, and the worksheet is completed.

5-4   **Prepare an income statement, statement of owner's equity, and balance sheet from the completed worksheet.**

All figures needed to prepare the financial statements are properly reflected on the completed worksheet. The accounts are arranged in the order in which they must appear on the income statement and balance sheet. Preparation of the financial statements is the fifth step of the accounting cycle.

5-5   **Journalize and post the adjusting entries.**

After the financial statements have been prepared, the accountant must make permanent entries in the accounting records for the adjustments shown on the worksheet. The adjusting entries are then posted to the general ledger. Journalizing and posting the adjusting entries is the sixth step in the accounting cycle.

To summarize the steps of the accounting cycle discussed so far:

1. Analyze transactions.
2. Journalize transactions.
3. Post the journal entries.
4. Prepare a worksheet.
5. Prepare financial statements.
6. Record adjusting entries.

5-6   **Define the accounting terms new to this chapter.**

Glossary

Account form balance sheet (p. 135) A balance sheet that lists assets on the left and liabilities and owner's equity on the right (see Report form balance sheet)

Adjusting entries (p. 125) Journal entries made to update accounts for items that were not recorded during the accounting period

Adjustments (p. 125) See Adjusting entries

Book value (p. 129) That portion of an asset's original cost that has not yet been depreciated

Contra account (p. 128) An account with a normal balance that is opposite that of a related account

Contra asset account (p. 128) An asset account with a credit balance, which is contrary to the normal balance of an asset account

Depreciation (p. 128) Allocation of the cost of a long-term asset to operations during its expected useful life

Prepaid expenses (p. 126) Expense items acquired, recorded, and paid for in advance of their use

Report form balance sheet (p. 135) A balance sheet that lists the asset accounts first, followed by liabilities and owner's equity

Salvage value (p. 128) An estimate of the amount that could be received by selling or disposing of an asset at the end of its useful life

Straight-line depreciation (p. 128) Allocation of an asset's cost in equal amounts to each accounting period of the asset's useful life

Worksheet (p. 124) A form used to gather all data needed at the end of an accounting period to prepare financial statements

Comprehensive **Self Review**

1. Why are assets depreciated?
2. The *Supplies* account has a debit balance of $8,000 in the Trial Balance column. The Credit column in the Adjustments section is $2,400. What is the new balance? The new balance will be extended to which column of the worksheet?
3. Is the normal balance for *Accumulated Depreciation* a debit or credit balance?
4. Why is the net income for a period recorded in the Balance Sheet section of the worksheet as well as the Income Statement section?
5. The *Drawing* account is extended to which column of the worksheet?

(Answers to Comprehensive Self Review are on page 153.)

Discussion Questions

1. Why is it necessary to make an adjustment for supplies used?
2. What are prepaid expenses? Give four examples.
3. What adjustment would be recorded for expired insurance?
4. A firm purchases machinery, which has an estimated useful life of 10 years and no salvage value, for $48,000 at the beginning of the accounting period. What is the adjusting entry for depreciation at the end of one month if the firm uses the straight-line method of depreciation?

5.   What effect does each of the following items have on net income?

    a.   The owner withdrew cash from the business.

    b.   Credit customers paid $1,000 on outstanding balances that were past due.

    c.   The business bought equipment on account that cost $10,000.

    d.   The business journalized and posted an adjustment for depreciation of equipment.

6.   What effect does each item in Question 5 have on owner's equity?

7.   Why is it necessary to journalize and post adjusting entries?

8.   What three amounts are reported on the balance sheet for a long-term asset such as equipment?

9.   What is book value?

10.   How does a contra asset account differ from a regular asset account?

11.   Why is an accumulated depreciation account used in making the adjustment for depreciation?

12.   Are the following assets depreciated? Why or why not?

    a.   Prepaid Insurance

    b.   Delivery Truck

    c.   Land

    d.   Manufacturing Equipment

    e.   Prepaid Rent

    f.   Furniture

    g.   Store Equipment

    h.   Prepaid Advertising

    i.   Computers

13.   How does the straight-line method of depreciation work?

14.   Give three examples of assets that are subject to depreciation.

APPLICATIONS

Exercises

Exercise 5.1

Objective 5-2

▶ **Calculating adjustments.**

Determine the necessary end-of-June adjustments for Brown Company.

1.   On June 1, 2016, Brown Company, a new firm, paid $7,000 rent in advance for a seven-month period. The $7,000 was debited to the *Prepaid Rent* account.

2.   On June 1, 2016, the firm bought supplies for $7,950. The $7,950 was debited to the *Supplies* account. An inventory of supplies at the end of June showed that items costing $3,300 were on hand.

3.   On June 1, 2016, the firm bought equipment costing $64,800. The equipment has an expected useful life of 9 years and no salvage value. The firm will use the straight-line method of depreciation.

Exercise 5.2

Objective 5-2

▶ **Calculating adjustments.**

For each of the following situations, determine the necessary adjustments.

1.   A firm purchased a three-year insurance policy for $12,600 on July 1, 2016. The $12,600 was debited to the *Prepaid Insurance* account. What adjustment should be made to record expired insurance on the firm's July 31, 2016, worksheet?

2. On December 1, 2016, a firm signed a contract with a local radio station for advertising that will extend over a two-year period. The firm paid $32,400 in advance and debited the amount to **Prepaid Advertising.** What adjustment should be made to record expired advertising on the firm's December 31, 2016, worksheet?

Worksheet through Adjusted Trial Balance.

◄ **Exercise 5.3**
Objectives 5-1, 5-2

On January 31, 2016, the general ledger of Meeks Company showed the following account balances. Prepare the worksheet through the Adjusted Trial Balance section. Assume that every account has the normal debit or credit balance. The worksheet covers the month of January.

ACCOUNTS	
Cash	63,000
Accounts Receivable	22,500
Supplies	9,000
Prepaid Insurance	8,200
Equipment	91,500
Accum. Depr. — Equip.	0
Accounts Payable	16,700
Lorraine Meeks, Capital	81,950
Fees Income	117,000
Depreciation Exp. — Equip.	0
Insurance Expense	0
Rent Expense	10,600
Salaries Expense	10,850
Supplies Expense	0

Additional information:

a. Supplies used during January totaled $5,700.

b. Expired insurance totaled $2,050.

c. Depreciation expense for the month was $1,825.

Correcting net income.

◄ **Exercise 5.4**
Objectives 5-2, 5-3

Assume that a firm reports net income of $90,000 prior to making adjusting entries for the following items: expired rent, $7,000; depreciation expense, $8,200; and supplies used, $3,600.
   Assume that the required adjusting entries have not been made. What effect do these errors have on the reported net income?

Journalizing and posting adjustments.

◄ **Exercise 5.5**
Objective 5-5

Zavier Company must make three adjusting entries on December 31, 2016.

a. Supplies used, $11,000; (supplies totaling $18,000 were purchased on December 1, 2016, and debited to the **Supplies** account).

b. Expired insurance, $8,200; on December 1, 2016, the firm paid $49,200 for six months' insurance coverage in advance and debited **Prepaid Insurance** for this amount.

c. Depreciation expense for equipment, $5,800.

Make the journal entries for these adjustments and post the entries to the general ledger accounts: Use page 3 of the general journal for the adjusting entries. Use the following accounts and numbers.

Supplies	121
Prepaid Insurance	131
Accum. Depr. — Equip.	142
Depreciation Exp. — Equip.	517
Insurance Expense	521
Supplies Expense	523

PROBLEMS

Problem Set A

Problem 5.1A
Objectives 5-1, 5-2, 5-3

▶ **Completing the worksheet.**

The trial balance of Nixon Company as of January 31, 2016, after the company completed the first month of operations, is shown in the partial worksheet below.

INSTRUCTIONS

1. Record the trial balance in the Trial Balance section of the worksheet.
2. Complete the worksheet by making the following adjustments: supplies on hand at the end of the month, $4,200; expired insurance, $5,500; depreciation expense for the period, $1,600.

Analyze: How does the insurance adjustment affect *Prepaid Insurance?*

		Nixon Company			
		Worksheet (Partial)			
		Month Ended January 31, 2016			

ACCOUNT NAME	TRIAL BALANCE		ADJUSTMENTS	
	DEBIT	CREDIT	DEBIT	CREDIT
1 Cash	105 0 0 0 00			
2 Accounts Receivable	21 8 0 0 00			
3 Supplies	39 4 0 0 00			
4 Prepaid Insurance	66 0 0 0 00			
5 Equipment	109 0 0 0 00			
6 Accumulated Depreciation—Equipment				
7 Accounts Payable		25 8 0 0 00		
8 Robert Nixon, Capital		253 0 0 0 00		
9 Robert Nixon, Drawing	15 4 0 0 00			
10 Fees Income		114 2 0 0 00		
11 Depreciation Expense—Equipment				
12 Insurance Expense				
13 Salaries Expense	32 2 0 0 00			
14 Supplies Expense				
15 Utilities Expense	4 2 0 0 00			
16 Totals	393 0 0 0 00	393 0 0 0 00		

Problem 5.2A
Objectives 5-1, 5-2, 5-3

▶ **Reconstructing a partial worksheet.**

The adjusted trial balance of College Book Store as of November 30, 2016, after the firm's first month of operations, appears on the next page.
    Appropriate adjustments have been made for the following items:

a. Supplies used during the month, $5,800.

b. Expired rent for the month, $7,000.

c. Depreciation expense for the month, $1,900.

INSTRUCTIONS

1. Record the Adjusted Trial Balance in the Adjusted Trial Balance columns of the worksheet.
2. Prepare the adjusting entries in the Adjustments columns.
3. Complete the Trial Balance columns of the worksheet prior to making the adjusting entries.

Analyze: What was the balance of *Prepaid Rent* prior to the adjusting entry for expired rent?

College Book Store Adjusted Trial Balance November 30, 2016		
Account Name	**Debit**	**Credit**
Cash	$ 46,150	
Accounts Receivable	7,624	
Supplies	9,200	
Prepaid Rent	42,000	
Equipment	55,000	
Accumulated Depreciation — Equipment		$ 1,900
Accounts Payable		18,000
Randy Moss, Capital		83,674
Randy Moss, Drawing	8,000	
Fees Income		97,100
Depreciation Expense — Equipment	1,900	
Rent Expense	7,000	
Salaries Expense	17,000	
Supplies Expense	5,800	
Utilities Expense	1,000	
Totals	$200,674	$200,674

Preparing financial statements from the worksheet.

◀ **Problem 5.3A**
Objective 5-4

The completed worksheet for Vasquez Corporation as of December 31, 2016, after the company had completed the first month of operation, appears across the tops of pages 146–147.

INSTRUCTIONS

1. Prepare an income statement.

2. Prepare a statement of owner's equity. The owner made no additional investments during the month.

3. Prepare a balance sheet (use the report form).

Analyze: If the adjustment to *Prepaid Advertising* had been $6,800 instead of $3,400, what net income would have resulted?

Preparing a worksheet and financial statements, journalizing adjusting entries, and posting to ledger accounts.

◀ **Problem 5.4A**
Objectives
5-1, 5-2, 5-3, 5-4, 5-5

Paula Judge owns Judge Creative Designs. The trial balance of the firm for January 31, 2016, the first month of operations, is shown on the bottom of page 146.

Sage 50
Complete Accounting

INSTRUCTIONS

1. Complete the worksheet for the month.

2. Prepare an income statement, statement of owner's equity, and balance sheet. No additional investments were made by the owner during the month.

3. Journalize and post the adjusting entries. Use 3 for the journal page number. Use the following account numbers: Supplies, 121; Prepaid Advertising, 130; Prepaid Rent, 131; Accumulated Depreciation—Equipment, 142; Supplies Expense, 517; Advertising Expense, 519; Rent Expense, 520; Depreciation Expense, 523.

End-of-the-month adjustments must account for the following items:

a. Supplies were purchased on January 1, 2016; inventory of supplies on January 31, 2016, is $1,600.

b. The prepaid advertising contract was signed on January 1, 2016, and covers a four-month period.

Vasquez Corporation
Worksheet
Month Ended December 31, 2016

	ACCOUNT NAME	TRIAL BALANCE DEBIT	TRIAL BALANCE CREDIT	ADJUSTMENTS DEBIT	ADJUSTMENTS CREDIT
1	Cash	78 2 0 0 00			
2	Accounts Receivable	13 0 0 0 00			
3	Supplies	12 1 0 0 00			(a) 7 0 0 0 00
4	Prepaid Advertising	20 4 0 0 00			(b) 3 4 0 0 00
5	Equipment	85 0 0 0 00			
6	Accumulated Depreciation—Equipment				(c) 1 7 0 0 00
7	Accounts Payable		13 0 0 0 00		
8	Rosa Vasquez, Capital		109 0 0 0 00		
9	Rosa Vasquez, Drawing	8 2 0 0 00			
10	Fees Income		115 5 0 0 00		
11	Advertising Expense			(b) 3 4 0 0 00	
12	Depreciation Expense—Equipment			(c) 1 7 0 0 00	
13	Salaries Expense	17 8 0 0 00			
14	Supplies Expense			(a) 7 0 0 0 00	
15	Utilities Expense	2 8 0 0 00			
16	Totals	237 5 0 0 00	237 5 0 0 00	12 1 0 0 00	12 1 0 0 00
17	Net Income				
18					
19					

c. Rent of $2,100 expired during the month.

d. Depreciation is computed using the straight-line method. The equipment has an estimated useful life of 10 years with no salvage value.

Analyze: If the adjusting entries had not been made for the month, would net income be overstated or understated?

Judge Creative Designs
Worksheet (Partial)
Month Ended January 31, 2016

	ACCOUNT NAME	TRIAL BALANCE DEBIT	TRIAL BALANCE CREDIT
1	Cash	36 5 0 0 00	
2	Accounts Receivable	13 6 0 0 00	
3	Supplies	9 7 5 0 00	
4	Prepaid Advertising	12 4 0 0 00	
5	Prepaid Rent	25 2 0 0 00	
6	Equipment	33 6 0 0 00	
7	Accumulated Depreciation—Equipment		
8	Accounts Payable		16 5 5 0 00
9	Paula Judge, Capital		61 0 0 0 00
10	Paula Judge, Drawing	8 0 0 0 00	
11	Fees Income		74 1 0 0 00
12	Advertising Expense		
13	Depreciation Expense—Equipment		
14	Rent Expense		
15	Salaries Expense	10 7 0 0 00	
16	Supplies Expense		
17	Utilities Expense	1 9 0 0 00	
18	Totals	151 6 5 0 00	151 6 5 0 00
19			

	ADJUSTED TRIAL BALANCE		INCOME STATEMENT		BALANCE SHEET		
	DEBIT	CREDIT	DEBIT	CREDIT	DEBIT	CREDIT	
	78 2 0 0 00				78 2 0 0 00		1
	13 0 0 0 00				13 0 0 0 00		2
	5 1 0 0 00				5 1 0 0 00		3
	17 0 0 0 00				17 0 0 0 00		4
	85 0 0 0 00				85 0 0 0 00		5
		1 7 0 0 00				1 7 0 0 00	6
		13 0 0 0 00				13 0 0 0 00	7
		109 0 0 0 00				109 0 0 0 00	8
	8 2 0 0 00				8 2 0 0 00		9
		115 5 0 0 00		115 5 0 0 00			10
	3 4 0 0 00		3 4 0 0 00				11
	1 7 0 0 00		1 7 0 0 00				12
	17 8 0 0 00		17 8 0 0 00				13
	7 0 0 0 00		7 0 0 0 00				14
	2 8 0 0 00		2 8 0 0 00				15
	239 2 0 0 00	239 2 0 0 00	32 7 0 0 00	115 5 0 0 00	206 5 0 0 00	123 7 0 0 00	16
			82 8 0 0 00			82 8 0 0 00	17
			115 5 0 0 00	115 5 0 0 00	206 5 0 0 00	206 5 0 0 00	18
							19

Problem Set B

Completing the worksheet.

The trial balance of Sanchez Company as of February 29, 2016, appears below.

◀   **Problem 5.1B**
Objectives 5-1, 5-2, 5-3

Sanchez Company
Worksheet (Partial)
Month Ended February 29, 2016

	ACCOUNT NAME	TRIAL BALANCE		ADJUSTMENTS	
		DEBIT	CREDIT	DEBIT	CREDIT
1	Cash	73 0 0 0 00			
2	Accounts Receivable	6 4 0 0 00			
3	Supplies	4 2 0 0 00			
4	Prepaid Rent	24 0 0 0 00			
5	Equipment	46 0 0 0 00			
6	Accumulated Depreciation—Equipment				
7	Accounts Payable		12 0 0 0 00		
8	Maria Sanchez, Capital		98 5 0 0 00		
9	Maria Sanchez, Drawing	3 0 0 0 00			
10	Fees Income		54 0 0 0 00		
11	Depreciation Expense—Equipment				
12	Rent Expense				
13	Salaries Expense	6 3 0 0 00			
14	Supplies Expense				
15	Utilities Expense	1 6 0 0 00			
16	Totals	164 5 0 0 00	164 5 0 0 00		
17					

INSTRUCTIONS

1. Record the trial balance in the Trial Balance section of the worksheet.

2. Complete the worksheet by making the following adjustments: supplies on hand at the end of the month, $2,200; expired rent, $2,000; depreciation expense for the period, $1,000.

Analyze: Why do you think the account *Accumulated Depreciation—Equipment* has a zero balance on the trial balance shown?

Problem 5.2B ▶ **Reconstructing a partial worksheet.**

Objectives 5-1, 5-2, 5-3

The adjusted trial balance of Lisa Morgan, Attorney-at-Law, as of November 30, 2016, after the company had completed the first month of operations, appears below.
    Appropriate adjustments have been made for the following items:

a. Supplies used during the month, $14,400.

b. Expired rent for the month, $13,600.

c. Depreciation expense for the month, $2,200.

Lisa Morgan, Attorney-at-Law Adjusted Trial Balance Month Ended November 30, 2016		
Account Name	**Debit**	**Credit**
Cash	$140,200	
Accounts Receivable	34,000	
Supplies	27,200	
Prepaid Rent	163,200	
Equipment	264,000	
Accumulated Depreciation — Equipment		$ 2,200
Accounts Payable		68,000
Lisa Morgan, Capital		320,000
Lisa Morgan, Drawing	24,000	
Fees Income		342,800
Depreciation Expense — Equipment	2,200	
Rent Expense	13,600	
Salaries Expense	43,200	
Supplies Expense	14,400	
Utilities Expense	7,000	
Totals	$733,000	$733,000

INSTRUCTIONS

1. Record the adjusted trial balance in the Adjusted Trial Balance columns of the worksheet.
2. Prepare the adjusting entries in the Adjustments columns.
3. Complete the Trial Balance columns of the worksheet prior to making the adjusting entries.

Analyze: Which contra asset account is on the adjusted trial balance?

Problem 5.3B ▶ **Preparing financial statements from the worksheet.**

Objective 5-4

The completed worksheet for CJ's Accounting Services for the month ended December 31, 2016, appears on pages 150–151.

INSTRUCTIONS

1. Prepare an income statement.

2. Prepare a statement of owner's equity. The owner made no additional investments during the month.

3. Prepare a balance sheet.

Analyze: By what total amount did the value of assets reported on the balance sheet decrease due to the adjusting entries?

Preparing a worksheet and financial statements, journalizing adjusting entries, and posting to ledger accounts.

◄ **Problem 5.4B**

Objectives
5-1, 5-2, 5-3, 5-4, 5-5

Sam Nix owns Nix Estate Planning and Investments. The trial balance of the firm for June 30, 2016, the first month of operations, is shown below.

Nix Estate Planning and Investments
Worksheet (Partial)
Month Ended June 30, 2016

	ACCOUNT NAME	TRIAL BALANCE DEBIT	TRIAL BALANCE CREDIT	ADJUSTMENTS DEBIT	ADJUSTMENTS CREDIT
1	Cash	39 4 0 0 00			
2	Accounts Receivable	12 2 0 0 00			
3	Supplies	15 2 0 0 00			
4	Prepaid Advertising	28 8 0 0 00			
5	Prepaid Rent	72 0 0 0 00			
6	Equipment	96 0 0 0 00			
7	Accumulated Depreciation—Equipment				
8	Accounts Payable		21 6 0 0 00		
9	Sam Nix, Capital		120 2 0 0 00		
10	Sam Nix, Drawing	8 0 0 0 00			
11	Fees Income		147 6 0 0 00		
12	Advertising Expense				
13	Depreciation Expense—Equipment				
14	Rent Expense				
15	Salaries Expense	15 2 0 0 00			
16	Supplies Expense				
17	Utilities Expense	2 6 0 0 00			
18	Totals	289 4 0 0 00	289 4 0 0 00		
19					

INSTRUCTIONS

1. Complete the worksheet for the month.

2. Prepare an income statement, statement of owner's equity, and balance sheet. No additional investments were made by the owner during the month.

3. Journalize and post the adjusting entries. Use 3 for the journal page number. Use the account numbers provided in Problem 5.4A.

End-of-month adjustments must account for the following:

a. The supplies were purchased on June 1, 2016; inventory of supplies on June 30, 2016, showed a value of $6,000.

b. The prepaid advertising contract was signed on June 1, 2016, and covers a four-month period.

c. Rent of $6,000 expired during the month.

d. Depreciation is computed using the straight-line method. The equipment has an estimated useful life of five years with no salvage value.

Analyze: Why are the costs that reduce the value of equipment not directly posted to the asset account Equipment?

CJ's Accounting Services
Worksheet
Month Ended December 31, 2016

	ACCOUNT NAME	TRIAL BALANCE		ADJUSTMENTS		
		DEBIT	CREDIT	DEBIT		CREDIT
1	Cash	16 9 5 0 00				
2	Accounts Receivable	2 2 0 0 00				
3	Supplies	1 5 0 0 00			(a)	6 0 0 00
4	Prepaid Advertising	4 0 0 0 00			(b)	8 0 0 00
5	Fixtures	18 0 0 0 00				
6	Accumulated Depreciation—Fixtures				(c)	3 0 0 00
7	Accounts Payable		7 5 0 0 00			
8	Charlene Jordan, Capital		30 0 0 0 00			
9	Charlene Jordan, Drawing	3 0 0 0 00				
10	Fees Income		31 3 3 0 00			
11	Advertising Expense			(b)	8 0 0 00	
12	Depreciation Expense—Fixtures			(c)	3 0 0 00	
13	Rent Expense	3 5 0 0 00				
14	Salaries Expense	18 6 0 0 00				
15	Supplies Expense			(a)	6 0 0 00	
16	Utilities Expense	1 0 8 0 00				
17	Totals	68 8 3 0 00	68 8 3 0 00	1 7 0 0 00		1 7 0 0 00
18	Net Income					
19						
20						

Critical Thinking Problem 5.1

The Effect of Adjustments

Assume you are the accountant for Parkland Industries. James Parkland, the owner of the company, is in a hurry to receive the financial statements for the year ended December 31, 2016, and asks you how soon they will be ready. You tell him you have just completed the trial balance and are getting ready to prepare the adjusting entries. Mr. Parkland tells you not to waste time preparing adjusting entries but to complete the worksheet without them and prepare the financial statements based on the data in the trial balance. According to him, the adjusting entries will not make that much difference. The trial balance shows the following account balances:

Prepaid Rent	$ 21,000
Supplies	9,000
Building	210,000
Accumulated Depreciation—Building	16,800

If the income statement were prepared using trial balance amounts, the net income would be $82,750.

A review of the company's records reveals the following information:

1. Rent of $21,000 was paid on July 1, 2016, for 12 months.

2. Purchases of supplies during the year totaled $9,000. An inventory of supplies taken at year-end showed supplies on hand of $1,750.

3. The building was purchased three years ago and has an estimated life of 25 years.

4. No adjustments have been made to any of the accounts during the year.

Write a memo to Mr. Parkland explaining the effect on the financial statements of omitting the adjustments. Indicate the change to net income that results from the adjusting entries.

	ADJUSTED TRIAL BALANCE		INCOME STATEMENT		BALANCE SHEET		
	DEBIT	CREDIT	DEBIT	CREDIT	DEBIT	CREDIT	
	16 9 5 0 00				16 9 5 0 00		1
	2 2 0 0 00				2 2 0 0 00		2
	9 0 0 00				9 0 0 00		3
	3 2 0 0 00				3 2 0 0 00		4
	18 0 0 0 00				18 0 0 0 00		5
		3 0 0 00				3 0 0 00	6
		7 5 0 0 00				7 5 0 0 00	7
		30 0 0 0 00				30 0 0 0 00	8
	3 0 0 0 00				3 0 0 0 00		9
		31 3 3 0 00		31 3 3 0 00			10
	8 0 0 00		8 0 0 00				11
	3 0 0 00		3 0 0 00				12
	3 5 0 0 00		3 5 0 0 00				13
	18 6 0 0 00		18 6 0 0 00				14
	6 0 0 00		6 0 0 00				15
	1 0 8 0 00		1 0 8 0 00				16
	69 1 3 0 00	69 1 3 0 00	24 8 8 0 00	31 3 3 0 00	44 2 5 0 00	37 8 0 0 00	17
			6 4 5 0 00			6 4 5 0 00	18
			31 3 3 0 00	31 3 3 0 00	44 2 5 0 00	42 2 5 0 00	19
							20

Critical Thinking Problem 5.2

Worksheet and Financial Statements

The account balances for the Rogers International Company on January 31, 2016, follow. The balances shown are after the first month of operations.

101	Cash	$18,475	401	Fees Income	$30,925
111	Accounts Receivable	3,400	511	Advertising Expense	1,500
121	Supplies	2,150	514	Depr. Expense — Equip.	0
131	Prepaid Insurance	15,000	517	Insurance Expense	0
141	Equipment	24,000	518	Rent Expense	2,500
142	Accum. Depr. — Equip.	0	519	Salaries Expense	6,700
202	Accounts Payable	6,000	520	Supplies Expense	0
301	Maxine Rogers, Capital	40,000	523	Telephone Expense	350
302	Maxine Rogers, Drawing	2,000	524	Utilities Expense	850

INSTRUCTIONS

1. Prepare the Trial Balance section of the worksheet.
2. Record the following adjustments in the Adjustments section of the worksheet:
   a. Supplies used during the month amounted to $1,050.
   b. The amount in the **Prepaid Insurance** account represents a payment made on January 1, 2016, for six months of insurance coverage.
   c. The equipment, purchased on January 1, 2016, has an estimated useful life of 10 years with no salvage value. The firm uses the straight-line method of depreciation.

3. Complete the worksheet.

4. Prepare an income statement, statement of owner's equity, and balance sheet (use the report form).

5. Record the balances in the general ledger accounts, then journalize and post the adjusting entries. Use 3 for the journal page number.

Analyze: If the useful life of the equipment had been 12 years instead of 10 years, how would net income have been affected?

BUSINESS CONNECTIONS

Understanding Adjustments

1. A building owned by Hopewell Company was recently valued at $850,000 by a real estate expert. The president of the company is questioning the accuracy of the firm's latest balance sheet because it shows a book value of $550,000 for the building. How would you explain this situation to the president?

2. At the beginning of the year, Mandela Company purchased a new building and some expensive new machinery. An officer of the firm has asked you whether this purchase will affect the firm's year-end income statement. What answer would you give?

3. Suppose the president of a company where you work as an accountant questions whether it is worthwhile for you to spend time making adjustments at the end of each accounting period. How would you explain the value of the adjustments?

4. How does the worksheet help provide vital information to management?

Adjustments

The supplies adjustment records the supplies used for the month from a cupboard that is filled at various times of the month. Molly asks you to record a larger supplies adjustment than is indicated from the ending balance in the supplies cupboard. Molly wants to use these supplies at the nonprofit organization she attends. Would you record a higher supplies expense so Molly could take these extra supplies to her charitable organization?

Depreciation

DuPont reported depreciation expense of $1,319 million on its consolidated financial statements for the period ended December 31, 2012. The following excerpt is taken from the company's consolidated balance sheet for the same year:

(Dollars in millions, except per share) December 31, 2012

Property, Plant and Equipment	$31,826
Less: Accumulated depreciation	19,085
Net property, plant, and equipment	12,741

Analyze:

1. What percentage of the original cost of property, plant, and equipment was depreciated *during* 2012?

2. What percentage of property, plant, and equipment cost was depreciated *as of* December 31, 2012?

3. If the company continued to record depreciation expense at this level each year, how many years remain until all assets would be fully depreciated? (Assume no salvage values.)

Analyze Online: Connect to the DuPont website (www.dupont.com). Click on the *Investor Center* link to find information on quarterly earnings.

4. What is the most recent quarterly earnings statement presented? What period does the statement cover?

5. For the most recent quarter, what depreciation expense was reported?

Matching Expenses with Revenues

Edward Foster is a building contractor. He and his customer have agreed that he will submit a bill to them when he is 25 percent complete, 50 percent complete, 75 percent complete, and 100 percent complete. For example, he has a $200,000 room addition. When he has completed 25 percent, he will bill his customer $50,000. The problem occurs when he is 40 percent complete, has incurred expenses but cannot yet bill his customer. How can his revenue and expenses match? Discuss in a group several ways that Edward's accountant could solve this problem. What accounts would be used?

Prepaid Insurance

Prepaid insurance is the most common adjusting entry for a company. Use google.com to do a search of the various insurance companies that provide a variety of insurances to business. Try business insurance companies. Which type of insurances do they offer a business?

Answers to **Self Reviews**

Answers to Section 1 Self Review

1. So that the financial statements can be prepared more efficiently.
2. To properly reflect the remaining cost to be used by the business (asset) and the amount already used by the business (expense).
3. Entries made to update accounts at the end of an accounting period to include previously unrecorded items that belong to the period.
4. **a.** *Supplies Expense* is debited for $1,900. *Supplies* is credited for $1,900.
5. **b.** *Rent Expense* is debited for $4,000. *Prepaid Rent* is credited for $4,000.
6. $36,000 ($90,000/5 = $18,000 × 3 = $54,000 − $90,000).

Answers to Section 2 Self Review

1. **(a)** Beginning owner's equity.
   (b) Net income or net loss for the period.
   (c) Additional investments by the owner for the period.
   (d) Withdrawals by the owner for the period.
   (e) Ending balance of owner's equity.
2. On a report form balance sheet, the liabilities and owner's equity are listed under the assets. On the account form, they are listed to the right of the assets.
3. The worksheet is only a tool that aids in the preparation of financial statements. Any changes in account balances recorded on the worksheet are not shown in the general journal and the general ledger until the adjusting entries have been journalized and posted.
4. **d.** Balance Sheet Debit column.
5. **d.** contra asset account.
6. $32,000. The adjustment for equipment depreciation is a debit to *Depreciation Expense* and a credit to *Accumulated Depreciation—Equipment.* The *Equipment* account is not changed.

Answers to Comprehensive Self Review

1. To allocate the cost of the asset to operations during its expected useful life.
2. $5,600. Debit column of the Balance Sheet section.
3. Credit balance.
4. Net income causes a net increase in owner's equity.
5. Debit column of the Balance Sheet section.

Closing Entries and the Postclosing Trial Balance

www.carnival.com

The folks at Carnival Cruise Lines have made it their business to help people enjoy their leisure time. For nearly 40 years, Carnival has made luxurious ocean cruising a reasonable vacation option for many individuals. Often, for under $100 per person per day passengers can enjoy a seven-day Caribbean cruise on a ship with soaring atriums, expansive spas, children's facilities, and double promenades offering a myriad of entertainment venues.

Since the TSS *Mardi Gras* made its first voyage in 1972, Carnival

Corporation has grown to become the most popular cruise line in the world, attracting four million guests annually. Carnival Cruise Lines is the flagship company of Carnival Corporation & plc, the largest cruise vacation group in the world, with a portfolio of cruise brands in North America, Europe, Australia, and Asia. Headquartered in Miami, Florida, and London, England, Carnival Corporation & plc generated $15.4 billion in revenues in 2012 and realized a total net income of over $1.3 billion.

When a company has been around as long as Carnival much of their success is dependent on being able to compare their revenues and expenses from one year to the next. In order to do this, Carnival needs to separate revenues and expenses into separate accounting periods so that they can "start fresh" each year. This separation enables the company to evaluate how they are performing from one year to the next. It can help the company pinpoint problem areas—for example, higher ship-to-shore excursion costs—but it can also spotlight improvements—for example, increased revenues in the onboard casinos.

thinking critically

How do Carnival's managers use financial statements to evaluate performance? How might these evaluations affect business policies or strategies?

LEARNING OBJECTIVES

6-1. Journalize and post closing entries.

6-2. Prepare a postclosing trial balance.

6-3. Interpret financial statements.

6-4. Review the steps in the accounting cycle.

6-5. Define the accounting terms new to this chapter.

NEW TERMS

closing entries
Income Summary account

interpret
postclosing trial balance

SECTION OBJECTIVE

>> 6-1. Journalize and post closing entries.

WHY IT'S IMPORTANT

A business ends its accounting cycle at a given point in time. The closing process prepares the accounting records for the beginning of a new accounting cycle.

TERMS TO LEARN

closing entries
Income Summary account

Closing Entries

In Chapter 5, we discussed the worksheet and the adjusting entries. In this chapter, you will learn about closing entries.

The Closing Process

The seventh step in the accounting cycle is to journalize and post closing entries. **Closing entries** are journal entries that:

- transfer the results of operations (net income or net loss) to owner's equity,
- reduce revenue, expense, and drawing account balances to zero.

THE INCOME SUMMARY ACCOUNT

The *Income Summary* **account** is a special owner's equity account that is used only in the closing process to summarize results of operations. *Income Summary* has a zero balance after the closing process, and it remains with a zero balance until after the closing procedure for the next period.

FIGURE 6.1   Worksheet for Wells' Consulting Services

Wells' Consulting Services
Worksheet
Month Ended December 31, 2016

	ACCOUNT NAME	TRIAL BALANCE DEBIT	TRIAL BALANCE CREDIT	ADJUSTMENTS DEBIT	ADJUSTMENTS CREDIT
1	Cash	111 350 00			
2	Accounts Receivable	5 000 00			
3	Supplies	1 500 00			(a) 500 00
4	Prepaid Rent	8 000 00			(b) 4 000 00
5	Equipment	11 000 00			
6	Accum. Dep.—Equipment				(c) 183 00
7	Accounts Payable		3 500 00		
8	Carolyn Wells, Capital		100 000 00		
9	Carolyn Wells, Drawing	5 000 00			
10	Fees Income		47 000 00		
11	Salaries Expense	8 000 00			
12	Utilities Expense	650 00			
13	Supplies Expense			(a) 500 00	
14	Rent Expense			(b) 4 000 00	
15	Dep. Expense—Equipment			(c) 183 00	
16					
17	Totals	150 500 00	150 500 00	4 683 00	4 683 00
18	Net Income				
19					

Income Summary is classified as a temporary owner's equity account. Other names for this account are *Revenue and Expense Summary* and *Income and Expense Summary*.

STEPS IN THE CLOSING PROCESS

>> 6-1. OBJECTIVE

Journalize and post closing entries.

There are four steps in the closing process:

1. Transfer the balance of the revenue account to the *Income Summary* account.

2. Transfer the expense account balances to the *Income Summary* account.

3. Transfer the balance of the *Income Summary* account to the owner's capital account.

4. Transfer the balance of the drawing account to the owner's capital account.

The worksheet contains the data necessary to make the closing entries. Refer to Figure 6.1 as you study each closing entry.

STEP 1: TRANSFER REVENUE ACCOUNT BALANCES

On December 31, the worksheet for Wells' Consulting Services shows one revenue account, *Fees Income.* It has a credit balance of $47,000. To *close* an account means to reduce its balance to zero. In the general journal, enter a debit of $47,000 to close the *Fees Income* account. To balance the journal entry, enter a credit of $47,000 to the *Income Summary* account. This closing entry transfers the total revenue for the period to the *Income Summary* account and reduces the balance of the revenue account to zero.

The analysis of this closing entry is shown on the next page. In this chapter, the visual analyses will show the beginning balances in all T accounts in order to illustrate closing entries.

ADJUSTED TRIAL BALANCE		INCOME STATEMENT		BALANCE SHEET		
DEBIT	CREDIT	DEBIT	CREDIT	DEBIT	CREDIT	
111 3 5 0 00				111 3 5 0 00		1
5 0 0 0 00				5 0 0 0 00		2
1 0 0 0 00				1 0 0 0 00		3
4 0 0 0 00				4 0 0 0 00		4
11 0 0 0 00				11 0 0 0 00		5
	1 8 3 00				1 8 3 00	6
	3 5 0 0 00				3 5 0 0 00	7
	100 0 0 0 00				100 0 0 0 00	8
5 0 0 0 00				5 0 0 0 00		9
	47 0 0 0 00		47 0 0 0 00			10
8 0 0 0 00		8 0 0 0 00				11
6 5 0 00		6 5 0 00				12
5 0 0 00		5 0 0 00				13
4 0 0 0 00		4 0 0 0 00				14
1 8 3 00		1 8 3 00				15
						16
150 6 8 3 00	150 6 8 3 00	13 3 3 3 00	47 0 0 0 00	137 3 5 0 00	103 6 8 3 00	17
		33 6 6 7 00			33 6 6 7 00	18
		47 0 0 0 00	47 0 0 0 00	137 3 5 0 00	137 3 5 0 00	19

CLOSING ENTRY

First Closing Entry—Close Revenue to Income Summary

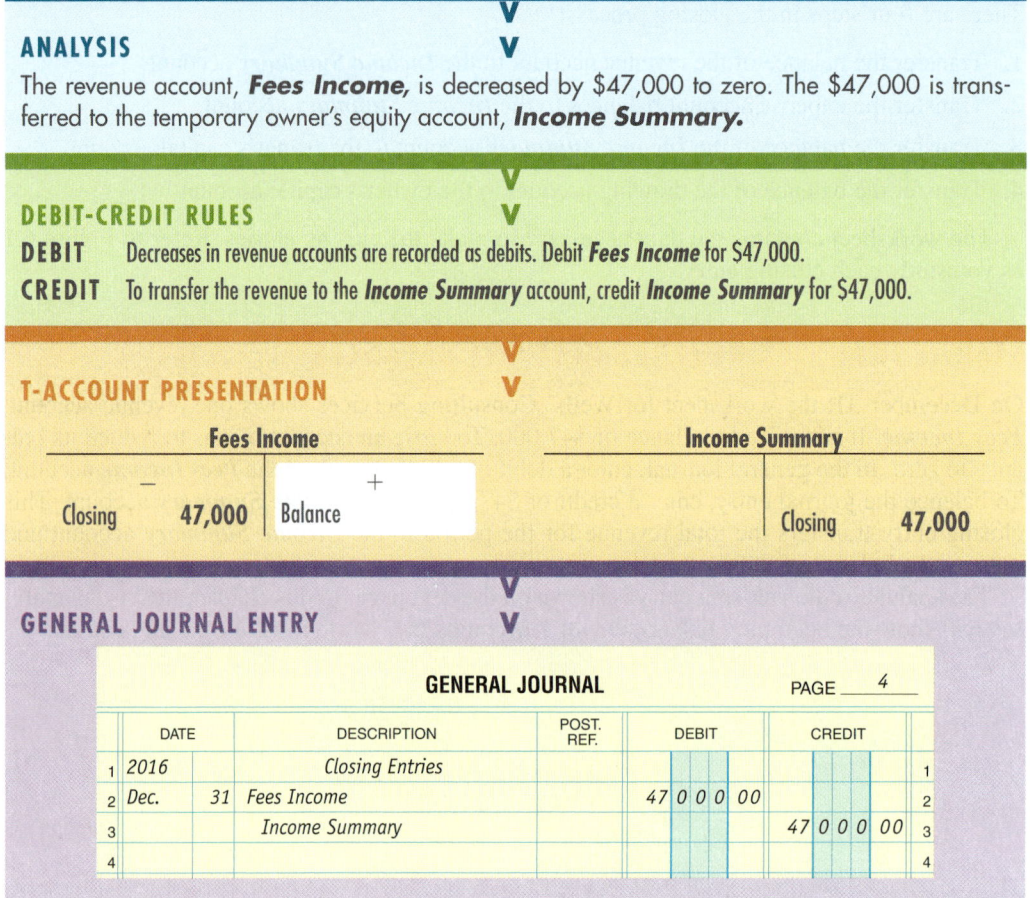

ANALYSIS

The revenue account, *Fees Income,* is decreased by $47,000 to zero. The $47,000 is transferred to the temporary owner's equity account, *Income Summary.*

DEBIT-CREDIT RULES

DEBIT   Decreases in revenue accounts are recorded as debits. Debit *Fees Income* for $47,000.

CREDIT   To transfer the revenue to the *Income Summary* account, credit *Income Summary* for $47,000.

T-ACCOUNT PRESENTATION

Fees Income		Income Summary	
−	+		
Closing 47,000	Balance		Closing 47,000

GENERAL JOURNAL ENTRY

GENERAL JOURNAL   PAGE ___4___

	DATE		DESCRIPTION	POST. REF.	DEBIT	CREDIT	
1	2016		*Closing Entries*				1
2	Dec.	31	Fees Income		47 0 0 0 00		2
3			Income Summary			47 0 0 0 00	3
4							4

    Write "Closing Entries" in the Description column of the general journal on the line above the first closing entry.

> Safeway Inc. reported sales of $44.2 billion for the fiscal year ended December 31, 2012. To close the revenue, the company would debit the *Sales* account and credit the *Income Summary* account.

STEP 2: TRANSFER EXPENSE ACCOUNT BALANCES

The Income Statement section of the worksheet for Wells' Consulting Services lists five expense accounts. Since expense accounts have debit balances, enter a credit in each account to reduce its balance to zero. Debit the total of the expenses, $13,333, to the *Income Summary* account. This closing entry transfers total expenses to the *Income Summary* account and reduces the balances of the expense accounts to zero. This is a compound journal entry; it has more than one credit.

CLOSING ENTRY

Second Closing Entry—Close Expenses to Income Summary

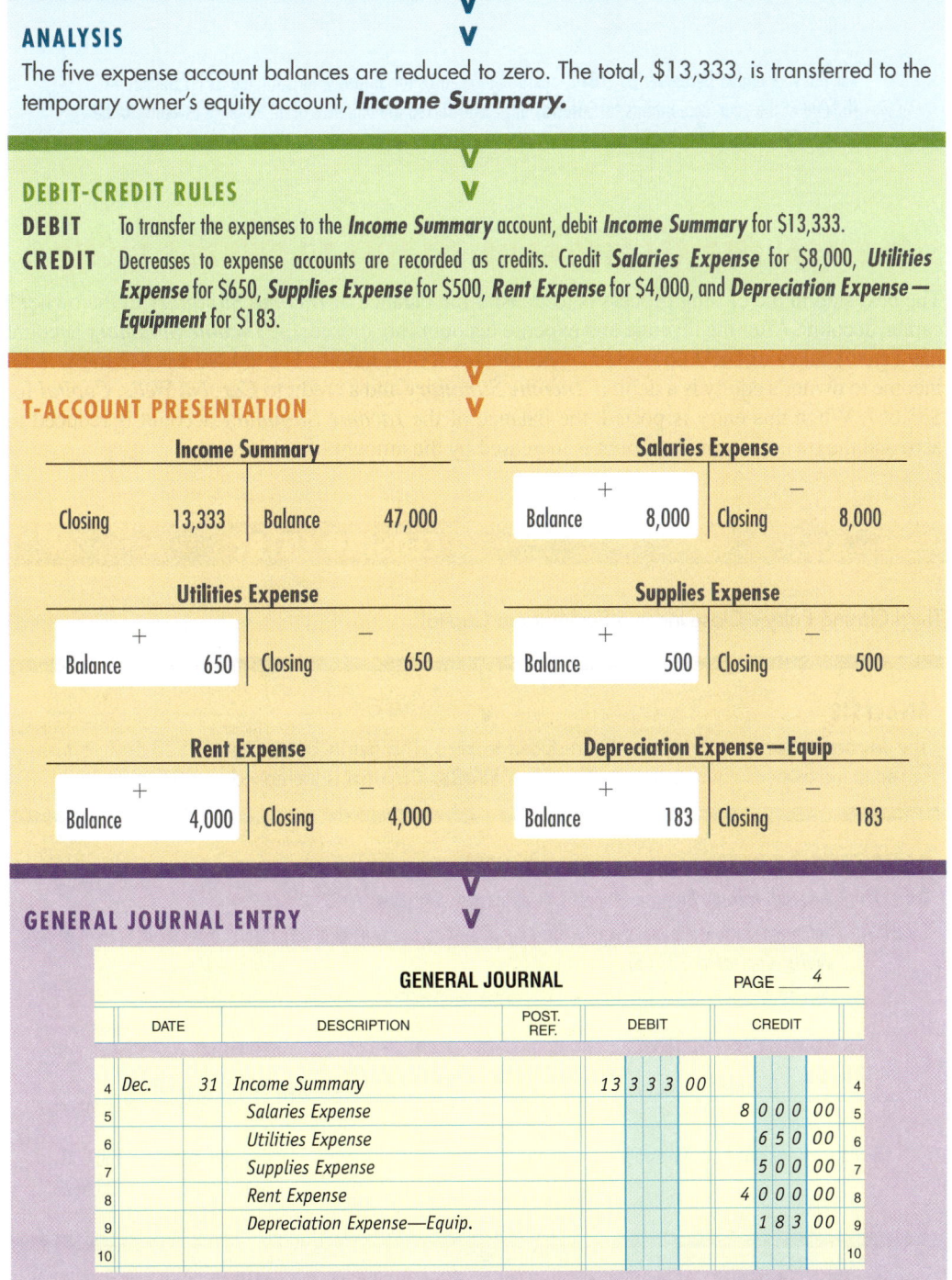

ANALYSIS

The five expense account balances are reduced to zero. The total, $13,333, is transferred to the temporary owner's equity account, *Income Summary.*

DEBIT-CREDIT RULES

DEBIT To transfer the expenses to the *Income Summary* account, debit *Income Summary* for $13,333.

CREDIT Decreases to expense accounts are recorded as credits. Credit *Salaries Expense* for $8,000, *Utilities Expense* for $650, *Supplies Expense* for $500, *Rent Expense* for $4,000, and *Depreciation Expense— Equipment* for $183.

T-ACCOUNT PRESENTATION

Income Summary			
Closing	13,333	Balance	47,000

Salaries Expense			
+		−	
Balance	8,000	Closing	8,000

Utilities Expense			
+		−	
Balance	650	Closing	650

Supplies Expense			
+		−	
Balance	500	Closing	500

Rent Expense			
+		−	
Balance	4,000	Closing	4,000

Depreciation Expense—Equip			
+		−	
Balance	183	Closing	183

GENERAL JOURNAL ENTRY

GENERAL JOURNAL

PAGE _____ 4 _____

	DATE		DESCRIPTION	POST. REF.	DEBIT	CREDIT	
4	Dec.	31	Income Summary		13 3 3 3 00		4
5			Salaries Expense			8 0 0 0 00	5
6			Utilities Expense			6 5 0 00	6
7			Supplies Expense			5 0 0 00	7
8			Rent Expense			4 0 0 0 00	8
9			Depreciation Expense—Equip.			1 8 3 00	9
10							10

recall

Revenue
Revenue increases owner's equity.

recall

Expenses
Expenses decrease owner's equity.

After the second closing entry, the *Income Summary* account reflects all of the entries in the Income Statement columns of the worksheet.

Income Summary			
	Dr.		Cr.
Closing	13,333	Closing	47,000
		Balance	33,667

For the year ended December 31, 2012, operating expenses for Safeway, Inc., totaled $11.1 million. At the end of the year, accountants for Safeway, Inc., transferred the balances of all expense accounts to the *Income Summary* account.

STEP 3: TRANSFER NET INCOME OR NET LOSS TO OWNER'S EQUITY

The next step in the closing process is to transfer the balance of *Income Summary* to the owner's capital account. After the revenue and expense accounts are closed, the *Income Summary* account has a credit balance of $33,667, which is net income for the month. The journal entry to transfer net income to owner's equity is a debit to *Income Summary* and a credit to *Carolyn Wells, Capital* for $33,667. When this entry is posted, the balance of the *Income Summary* account is reduced to zero and the owner's capital account is increased by the amount of net income.

CLOSING ENTRY

Third Closing Entry—Close Income Summary to Capital

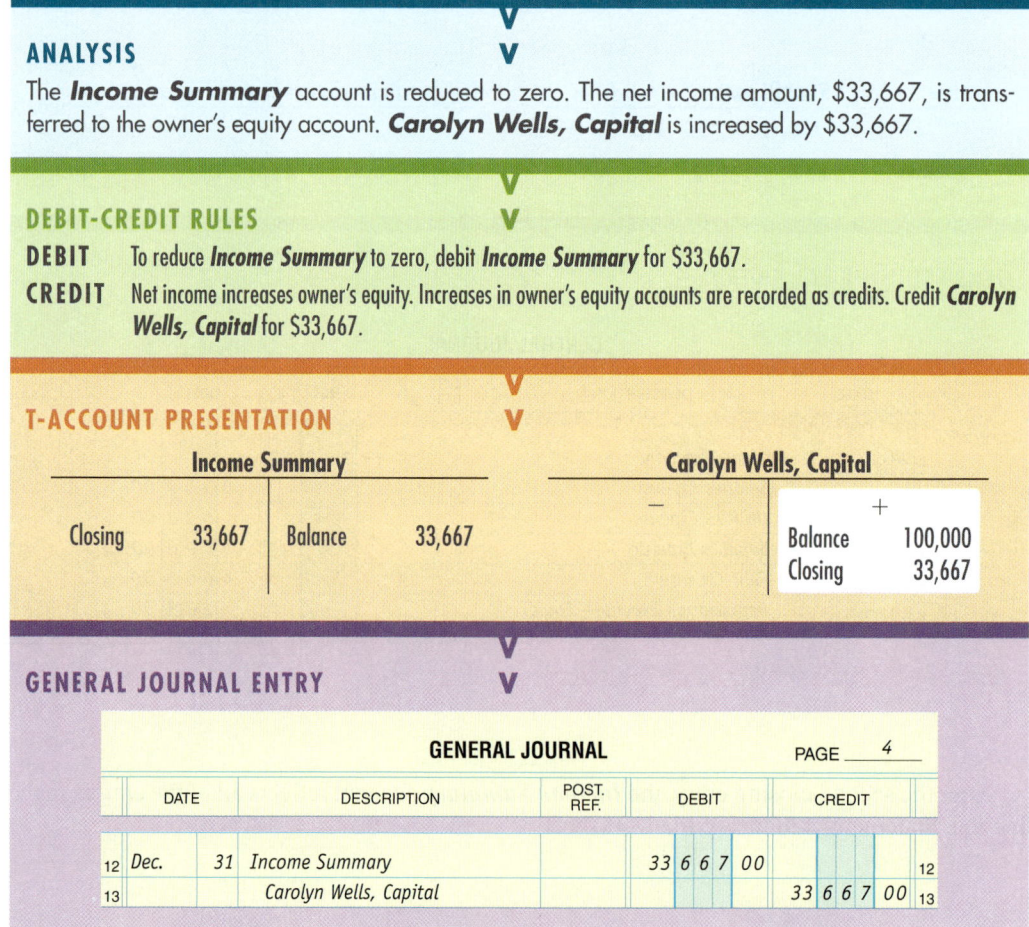

ANALYSIS

The *Income Summary* account is reduced to zero. The net income amount, $33,667, is transferred to the owner's equity account. *Carolyn Wells, Capital* is increased by $33,667.

DEBIT-CREDIT RULES

DEBIT To reduce *Income Summary* to zero, debit *Income Summary* for $33,667.

CREDIT Net income increases owner's equity. Increases in owner's equity accounts are recorded as credits. Credit *Carolyn Wells, Capital* for $33,667.

T-ACCOUNT PRESENTATION

Income Summary			
Closing	33,667	Balance	33,667

Carolyn Wells, Capital	
−	+
	Balance 100,000
	Closing 33,667

GENERAL JOURNAL ENTRY

	GENERAL JOURNAL			PAGE ___4___
DATE	DESCRIPTION	POST. REF.	DEBIT	CREDIT
Dec. 31	Income Summary		33 6 6 7 00	
	Carolyn Wells, Capital			33 6 6 7 00

After the third closing entry, the *Income Summary* account has a zero balance. The summarized expenses ($13,333) and revenue ($47,000) have been transferred to the owner's equity account ($33,667 net income).

Income Summary			
Dr.		**Cr.**	
Expenses	13,333	Revenue	47,000
Closing	33,667		
Balance	0		

Carolyn Wells, Capital			
Dr.		**Cr.**	
−		+	
		Balance	100,000
		Net Inc.	33,667
		Balance	133,667

STEP 4: TRANSFER THE DRAWING ACCOUNT BALANCE TO CAPITAL

You will recall that withdrawals are funds taken from the business by the owner for personal use. Withdrawals are recorded in the drawing account. Withdrawals are not expenses of the business. They do not affect net income or net loss.

Withdrawals appear in the statement of owner's equity as a deduction from capital. Therefore, the drawing account is closed directly to the capital account.

When this entry is posted, the balance of the drawing account is reduced to zero and the owner's capital account is decreased by the amount of the withdrawals.

recall

Withdrawals
Withdrawals decrease owner's equity.

CLOSING ENTRY

Fourth Closing Entry—Close Withdrawals to Capital

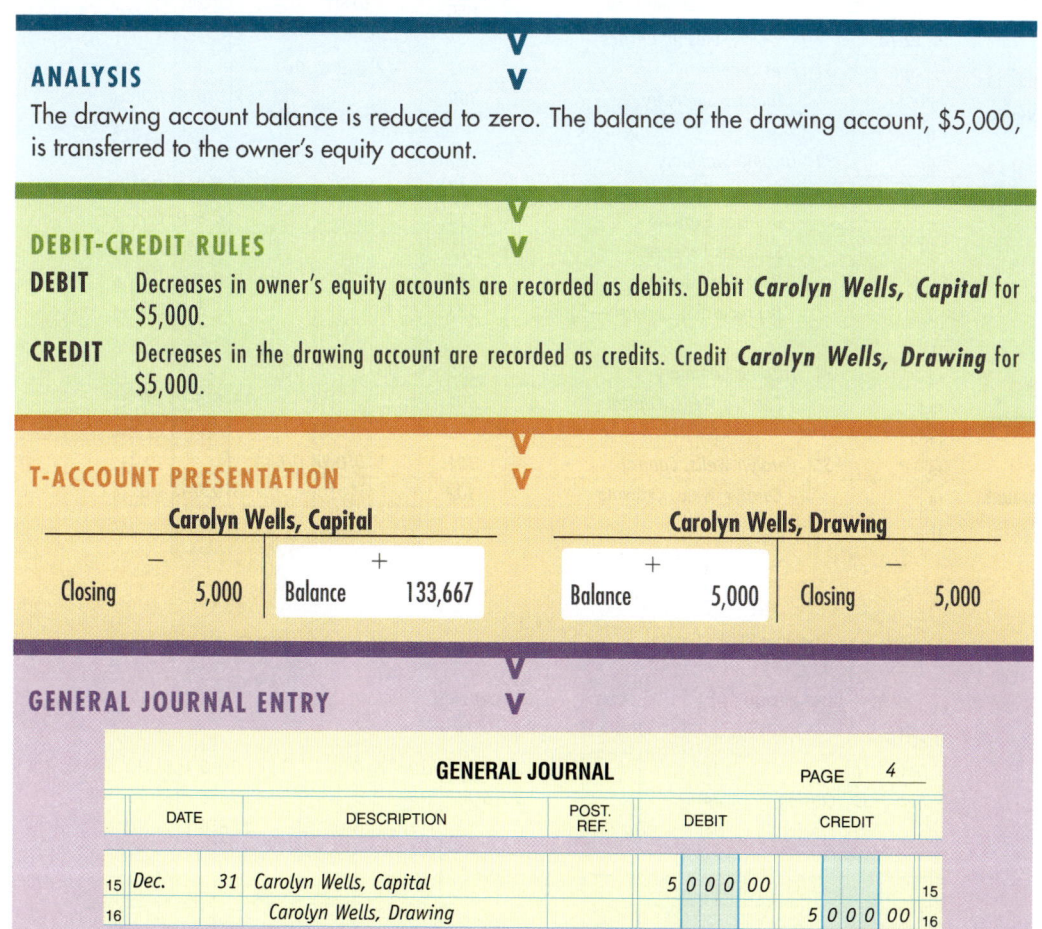

ANALYSIS
The drawing account balance is reduced to zero. The balance of the drawing account, $5,000, is transferred to the owner's equity account.

DEBIT-CREDIT RULES
DEBIT Decreases in owner's equity accounts are recorded as debits. Debit *Carolyn Wells, Capital* for $5,000.
CREDIT Decreases in the drawing account are recorded as credits. Credit *Carolyn Wells, Drawing* for $5,000.

T-ACCOUNT PRESENTATION

Carolyn Wells, Capital			
−		+	
Closing	5,000	Balance	133,667

Carolyn Wells, Drawing			
+		−	
Balance	5,000	Closing	5,000

GENERAL JOURNAL ENTRY

	GENERAL JOURNAL			PAGE __4__

	DATE		DESCRIPTION	POST. REF.	DEBIT	CREDIT	
15	Dec.	31	Carolyn Wells, Capital		5 0 0 0 00		15
16			Carolyn Wells, Drawing			5 0 0 0 00	16

The new balance of the *Carolyn Wells, Capital* account agrees with the amount listed in the Owner's Equity section of the balance sheet.

Carolyn Wells, Drawing				Carolyn Wells, Capital			
Dr.		**Cr.**		**Dr.**		**Cr.**	
+		–		–		+	
						Balance	100,000
						Net Inc.	33,667
Balance	5,000	Closing	5,000	Drawing	5,000	Balance	128,667
Balance	0						

Figure 6.2 shows the general journal and general ledger for Wells' Consulting Services after the closing entries are recorded and posted. Note that:

- "Closing" is entered in the Description column of the ledger accounts;
- the balance of *Carolyn Wells, Capital* agrees with the amount shown on the balance sheet for December 31;
- the ending balances of the drawing, revenue, and expense accounts are zero.

This example shows the closing process at the end of one month. Usually businesses make closing entries at the end of the fiscal year only.

FIGURE 6.2

Closing Process Completed:
General Journal and General Ledger

Step 1
Close revenue.

Step 2
Close expense accounts.

Step 3
Close Income Summary.

Step 4
Close Drawing account.

GENERAL JOURNAL   PAGE 4

	DATE		DESCRIPTION	POST. REF.	DEBIT	CREDIT	
1	2016		Closing Entries				1
2	Dec.	31	Fees Income	401	47 000 00		2
3			Income Summary	309		47 000 00	3
4							4
5		31	Income Summary	309	13 333 00		5
6			Salaries Expense	511		8 000 00	6
7			Utilities Expense	514		6 50 00	7
8			Supplies Expense	517		5 00 00	8
9			Rent Expense	520		4 000 00	9
10			Depreciation Expense—Equip.	523		1 83 00	10
11							11
12		31	Income Summary	309	33 667 00		12
13			Carolyn Wells, Capital	301		33 667 00	13
14							14
15		31	Carolyn Wells, Capital	301	5 000 00		15
16			Carolyn Wells, Drawing	302		5 000 00	16
17							17

ACCOUNT _Carolyn Wells, Capital_   ACCOUNT NO. _301_

DATE		DESCRIPTION	POST. REF.	DEBIT	CREDIT	BALANCE DEBIT	BALANCE CREDIT
2016							
Nov.	6		J1		100 000 00		100 000 00
Dec.	31	Closing	J4		33 667 00		133 667 00
	31	Closing	J4	5 000 00			128 667 00

ACCOUNT _Carolyn Wells, Drawing_   ACCOUNT NO. _302_

DATE		DESCRIPTION	POST. REF.	DEBIT	CREDIT	BALANCE DEBIT	BALANCE CREDIT
2016							
Dec.	31		J2	5 0 0 0 00		5 0 0 0 00	
	31	Closing	J4		5 0 0 0 00	– 0 –	

ACCOUNT _Income Summary_   ACCOUNT NO. _309_

DATE		DESCRIPTION	POST. REF.	DEBIT	CREDIT	BALANCE DEBIT	BALANCE CREDIT
2016							
Dec.	31	Closing	J4		47 0 0 0 00		47 0 0 0 00
	31	Closing	J4	13 3 3 3 00			33 6 6 7 00
	31	Closing	J4	33 6 6 7 00			– 0 –

ACCOUNT _Fees Income_   ACCOUNT NO. _401_

DATE		DESCRIPTION	POST. REF.	DEBIT	CREDIT	BALANCE DEBIT	BALANCE CREDIT
2016							
Dec.	31		J2		36 0 0 0 00		36 0 0 0 00
	31		J2		11 0 0 0 00		47 0 0 0 00
	31	Closing	J4	47 0 0 0 00			– 0 –

ACCOUNT _Salaries Expense_   ACCOUNT NO. _511_

DATE		DESCRIPTION	POST. REF.	DEBIT	CREDIT	BALANCE DEBIT	BALANCE CREDIT
2016							
Dec.	31		J2	8 0 0 0 00		8 0 0 0 00	
	31	Closing	J4		8 0 0 0 00	– 0 –	

ACCOUNT _Utilities Expense_   ACCOUNT NO. _514_

DATE		DESCRIPTION	POST. REF.	DEBIT	CREDIT	BALANCE DEBIT	BALANCE CREDIT
2016							
Dec.	31		J2	6 5 0 00		6 5 0 00	
	31	Closing	J4		6 5 0 00	– 0 –	

ACCOUNT _Supplies Expense_   ACCOUNT NO. _517_

DATE		DESCRIPTION	POST. REF.	DEBIT	CREDIT	BALANCE DEBIT	BALANCE CREDIT
2016							
Dec.	31	Adjusting	J3	5 0 0 00		5 0 0 00	
	31	Closing	J4		5 0 0 00	– 0 –	

(continued)

FIGURE 6.2 (continued)

ACCOUNT _Rent Expense_ ACCOUNT NO. _520_

DATE		DESCRIPTION	POST. REF.	DEBIT	CREDIT	BALANCE	
						DEBIT	CREDIT
2016							
Dec.	31	Adjusting	J3	4 0 0 0 00		4 0 0 0 00	
	31	Closing	J4		4 0 0 0 00	– 0 –	

ACCOUNT _Depreciation Expense—Equipment_ ACCOUNT NO. _523_

DATE		DESCRIPTION	POST. REF.	DEBIT	CREDIT	BALANCE	
						DEBIT	CREDIT
2016							
Dec.	31	Adjusting	J3	1 8 3 00		1 8 3 00	
	31	Closing	J4		1 8 3 00	– 0 –	

You have now seen seven steps of the accounting cycle. The steps we have discussed are (1) analyze transactions, (2) journalize the transactions, (3) post the transactions, (4) prepare a worksheet, (5) prepare financial statements, (6) record adjusting entries, and (7) record closing entries. Two steps remain. They are (8) prepare a postclosing trial balance, and (9) interpret the financial information.

Section 1 Self Review

QUESTIONS

1. How is the **Income Summary** account classified?
2. What are the four steps in the closing process?
3. What is the journal entry to close the drawing account?

EXERCISES

4. After closing, which accounts have zero balances?
   a. asset and liability accounts
   b. liability and capital accounts
   c. liability, drawing, and expense accounts
   d. revenue, drawing, and expense accounts

5. After the closing entries are posted, which account normally has a balance other than zero?
   a. **Capital**
   b. **Fees Income**
   c. **Income Summary**
   d. **Rent Expense**

ANALYSIS

6. The business owner removes supplies that are worth $900 from the company stockroom. She intends to take them home for personal use. What effect will this have on the company's net income?

(Answers to Section 1 Self Review are on page 184.)

>> 6-2. **Prepare a postclosing trial balance.**

WHY IT'S IMPORTANT

The postclosing trial balance helps the accountant identify any errors in the closing process.

>> 6-3. **Interpret financial statements.**

WHY IT'S IMPORTANT

Financial statements contain information that can impact and drive operating decisions and plans for the future of the company.

>> 6-4. **Review the steps in the accounting cycle.**

WHY IT'S IMPORTANT

Proper treatment of data as it flows through the accounting system ensures reliable financial reports.

TERMS TO LEARN

interpret
postclosing trial balance

Using Accounting Information

In this section, we will complete the accounting cycle for Wells' Consulting Services.

Preparing the Postclosing Trial Balance

>> **6-2. OBJECTIVE**

Prepare a postclosing trial balance.

The eighth step in the accounting cycle is to prepare the postclosing trial balance, or *after-closing trial balance*. The **postclosing trial balance** is a statement that is prepared to prove the equality of total debits and credits. It is the last step in the end-of-period routine. The postclosing trial balance verifies that:

- total debits equal total credits;
- revenue, expense, and drawing accounts have zero balances.

On the postclosing trial balance, the only accounts with balances are the permanent accounts:

- assets
- liabilities
- owner's equity

Figure 6.3 shows the postclosing trial balance for Wells' Consulting Services.

FIGURE 6.3

Postclosing Trial Balance

Wells' Consulting Services
Postclosing Trial Balance
December 31, 2016

ACCOUNT NAME	DEBIT	CREDIT
Cash	111 3 5 0 00	
Accounts Receivable	5 0 0 0 00	
Supplies	1 0 0 0 00	
Prepaid Rent	4 0 0 0 00	
Equipment	11 0 0 0 00	
Accumulated Depreciation—Equipment		1 8 3 00
Accounts Payable		3 5 0 0 00
Carolyn Wells, Capital		128 6 6 7 00
Totals	132 3 5 0 00	132 3 5 0 00

FINDING AND CORRECTING ERRORS

If the postclosing trial balance does not balance, there are errors in the accounting records. Find and correct the errors before continuing. Refer to Chapter 3 for tips on how to find common errors. Also use the audit trail to trace data through the accounting records to find errors.

>> 6-3. OBJECTIVE

Interpret financial statements.

Interpreting the Financial Statements

The ninth and last step in the accounting cycle is interpreting the financial statements. Management needs timely and accurate financial information to operate the business successfully. To **interpret** the financial statements means to understand and explain the meaning and importance of information in accounting reports. Information in the financial statements provides answers to many questions:

- What is the cash balance?
- How much do customers owe the business?
- How much does the business owe suppliers?
- What is the profit or loss?

> Managers of The Home Depot, Inc., use the corporation's financial statements to answer questions about the business. How much cash does our business have? What net earnings did our company report this year? For the fiscal year ended February 3, 2013, The Home Depot, Inc., reported an ending cash balance of $2.5 billion and net earnings of $4.5 billion.

Figure 6.4 shows the financial statements for Wells' Consulting Services at the end of its first accounting period. By interpreting these statements, management learns that:

- the cash balance is $111,350,
- customers owe $5,000 to the business,
- the business owes $3,500 to its suppliers,
- the profit was $33,667.

FIGURE 6.4

End-of-Month Financial Statements

Wells' Consulting Services
Income Statement
Month Ended December 31, 2016

Revenue			
Fees Income			47 0 0 0 00
Expenses			
Salaries Expense	8 0 0 0 00		
Utilities Expense	6 5 0 00		
Supplies Expense	5 0 0 00		
Rent Expense	4 0 0 0 00		
Depreciation Expense—Equipment	1 8 3 00		
Total Expenses		13 3 3 3 00	
Net Income for the Month		33 6 6 7 00	

Wells' Consulting Services
Statement of Owner's Equity
Month Ended December 31, 2016

Carolyn Wells, Capital, December 1, 2016		100 0 0 0 00	
Net Income for December	33 6 6 7 00		
Less Withdrawals for December	5 0 0 0 00		
Increase in Capital		28 6 6 7 00	
Carolyn Wells, Capital, December 31, 2016		128 6 6 7 00	

Wells' Consulting Services
Balance Sheet
December 31, 2016

Assets			
Cash		111 3 5 0 00	
Accounts Receivable		5 0 0 0 00	
Supplies		1 0 0 0 00	
Prepaid Rent		4 0 0 0 00	
Equipment	11 0 0 0 00		
Less Accumulated Depreciation	1 8 3 00	10 8 1 7 00	
Total Assets		132 1 6 7 00	
Liabilities and Owner's Equity			
Liabilities			
Accounts Payable		3 5 0 0 00	
Owner's Equity			
Carolyn Wells, Capital		128 6 6 7 00	
Total Liabilities and Owner's Equity		132 1 6 7 00	

The Accounting Cycle

You have learned about the entire accounting cycle as you studied the financial affairs of Wells' Consulting Services during its first month of operations. Figure 6.5 summarizes the steps in the accounting cycle.

Step 1.   **Analyze transactions.** Analyze source documents to determine their effects on the basic accounting equation. The data about transactions appears on a variety of source documents such as:

- sales slips,
- purchase invoices,
- credit memorandums,
- check stubs.

Step 2.   **Journalize the transactions.** Record the effects of the transactions in a journal.

Step 3.   **Post the journal entries.** Transfer data from the journal to the general ledger accounts.

Step 4.   **Prepare a worksheet.** At the end of each period, prepare a worksheet.

- Use the Trial Balance section to prove the equality of debits and credits in the general ledger.
- Use the Adjustments section to enter changes in account balances that are needed to present an accurate and complete picture of the financial affairs of the business.
- Use the Adjusted Trial Balance section to verify the equality of debits and credits after the adjustments. Extend the amounts from the Adjusted Trial Balance section to the Income Statement and Balance Sheet sections.
- Use the Income Statement and Balance Sheet sections to prepare the financial statements.

Step 5.   **Prepare financial statements.** Prepare financial statements to report information to owners, managers, and other interested parties.

- The income statement shows the results of operations for the period.
- The statement of owner's equity reports the changes in the owner's financial interest during the period.
- The balance sheet shows the financial position of the business at the end of the period.

recall

The Accounting Cycle

The accounting cycle is a series of steps performed during each period to classify, record, and summarize data to produce needed financial information.

FIGURE 6.5

The Accounting Cycle

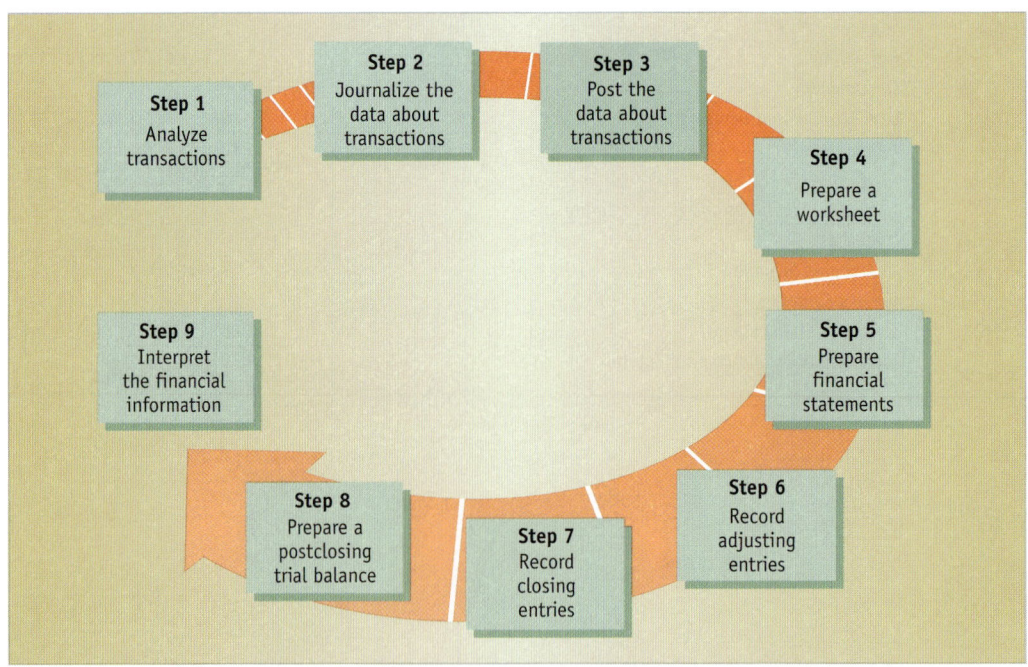

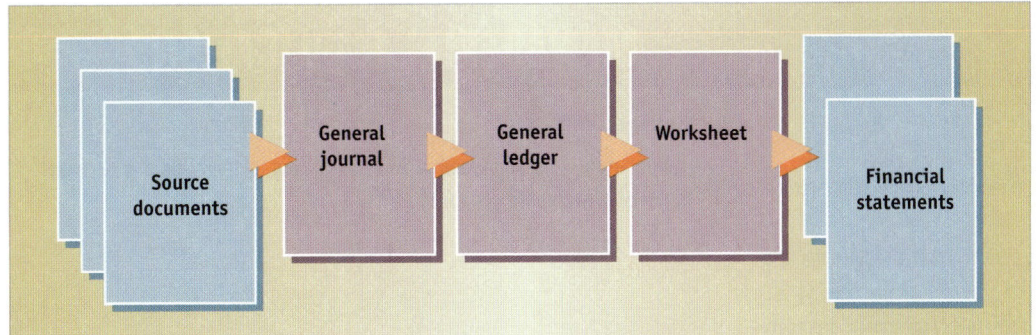

FIGURE 6.6

Flow of Data through a Simple Accounting System

Step 6. **Record adjusting entries.** Use the worksheet to journalize and post adjusting entries. The adjusting entries are a permanent record of the changes in account balances shown on the worksheet.

Step 7. **Record closing entries.** Journalize and post the closing entries to:
- transfer net income or net loss to owner's equity;
- reduce the balances of the revenue, expense, and drawing accounts to zero.

Step 8. **Prepare a postclosing trial balance.** The postclosing trial balance shows that the general ledger is in balance after the closing entries are posted. It is also used to verify that there are zero balances in revenue, expense, and drawing accounts.

Step 9. **Interpret the financial information.** Use financial statements to understand and communicate financial information and to make decisions. Accountants, owners, managers, and other interested parties interpret financial statements by comparing such things as profit, revenue, and expenses from one accounting period to the next.

> In addition to financial statements, Adobe Systems Incorporated prepares a Financial Highlights report. This report lists total assets, revenue, net income, and the number of worldwide employees for the past five years.

After studying the accounting cycle of Wells' Consulting Services, you have an understanding of how data flows through a simple accounting system for a small business:

- Source documents are analyzed.
- Transactions are recorded in the general journal.
- Transactions are posted from the general journal to the general ledger.
- Financial information is proved, adjusted, and summarized on the worksheet.
- Financial information is reported on financial statements.

Figure 6.6 illustrates this data flow.

As you will learn in later chapters, some accounting systems have more complex records, procedures, and financial statements. However, the steps of the accounting cycle and the underlying accounting principles remain the same.

MANAGERIAL IMPLICATIONS <<

FINANCIAL INFORMATION

- Management needs timely and accurate financial information to control operations and make decisions.
- A well-designed and well-run accounting system provides reliable financial statements to management.
- Although management is not involved in day-to-day accounting procedures and end-of-period processes, the efficiency of the procedures affects the quality and promptness of the financial information that management receives.

THINKING CRITICALLY

If you owned or managed a business, how often would you want financial statements prepared? Why?

Section 2   Self Review

QUESTIONS

1. Why is a postclosing trial balance prepared?
2. What accounts appear on the postclosing trial balance?
3. What are the last three steps in the accounting cycle?

EXERCISES

4. Which of the following accounts will not appear on the postclosing trial balance?
   a. **H.D. Hill, Drawing**
   b. **Cash**
   c. **H.D. Hill, Capital**
   d. **Accounts Payable**

5. After the revenue and expense accounts are closed, **Income Summary** has a debit balance of $30,000. What does this figure represent?
   a. net profit of $30,000
   b. net loss of $30,000
   c. owner's withdrawals of $30,000
   d. increase in owner's equity of $30,000

ANALYSIS

6. On which financial statement would you find the answer to each question?
   - What were the total fees earned this month?
   - How much money is owed to suppliers?
   - Did the business make a profit?
   - Is there enough cash to purchase new equipment?
   - What were the expenses?
   - Do customers owe money to the business?

(Answers to Section 2 Self Review are on page 185.)

REVIEW   Chapter Summary

After the worksheet and financial statements have been completed and adjusting entries have been journalized and posted, the closing entries are recorded and a postclosing trial balance is prepared.

Learning Objectives

6-1   **Journalize and post closing entries.**

Journalizing and posting the closing entries is the seventh step in the accounting cycle. Closing entries transfer the results of operations to owner's equity and reduce the balances of the revenue and expense accounts to zero. The worksheet provides the data necessary for the closing entries. A temporary owner's equity account, *Income Summary,* is used. There are four steps in the closing process:

1. The balance of the revenue account is transferred to the *Income Summary* account.

    Debit *Revenue*

    Credit *Income Summary*

2. The balances of the expense accounts are transferred to the *Income Summary* account.

    Debit *Income Summary*

    Credit *Expenses*

3. The balance of the *Income Summary* account—net income or net loss—is transferred to the owner's capital account.

    If *Income Summary* has a credit balance:

      Debit *Income Summary*

      Credit *Owner's Capital*

    If *Income Summary* has a debit balance:

      Debit *Owner's Capital*

      Credit *Income Summary*

4. The drawing account is closed to the owner's capital account.

    Debit *Owner's Capital*

    Credit *Drawing*

After the closing entries have been posted, the capital account reflects the results of operations for the period. The revenue and expense accounts, with zero balances, are ready to accumulate data for the next period.

6-2   **Prepare a postclosing trial balance.**

Preparing the postclosing trial balance is the eighth step in the accounting cycle. A postclosing trial balance is prepared to test the equality of total debit and credit balances in the general ledger after the adjusting and closing entries have been recorded. This report lists only permanent accounts open at the end of the period—asset, liability, and the owner's capital accounts. The temporary accounts—revenue, expenses, drawing, and *Income Summary*—apply only to one accounting period and do not appear on the postclosing trial balance.

6-3   **Interpret financial statements.**

The ninth step in the accounting cycle is interpreting the financial statements. Business decisions must be based on accurate and timely financial information.

6-4   **Review the steps in the accounting cycle.**

The accounting cycle consists of a series of steps that are repeated in each fiscal period. These steps are designed to classify, record, and summarize the data needed to produce financial information.

The steps of the accounting cycle are:

1. Analyze transactions.
2. Journalize the transactions.
3. Post the journal entries.
4. Prepare a worksheet.
5. Prepare financial statements.
6. Record adjusting entries.
7. Record closing entries.
8. Prepare a postclosing trial balance.
9. Interpret the financial information.

6-5   **Define the accounting terms new to this chapter.**

Glossary

Closing entries (p. 156) Journal entries that transfer the results of operations (net income or net loss) to owner's equity and reduce the revenue, expense, and drawing account balances to zero

Income Summary **account** (p. 156) A special owner's equity account that is used only in the closing process to summarize the results of operations

Interpret (p. 166) To understand and explain the meaning and importance of something (such as financial statements)

Postclosing trial balance (p. 165) A statement that is prepared to prove the equality of total debits and credits after the closing process is completed

---

Comprehensive **Self Review**

1. What is the last step in the accounting cycle?
2. Is the following statement true or false? Why? "All owner's equity accounts appear on the postclosing trial balance."
3. What three financial statements are prepared during the accounting cycle?
4. A firm has the following expenses: *Rent Expense,* $7,200; *Salaries Expense,* $14,000; *Supplies Expense,* $3,000. Give the entry to close the expense accounts.
5. A firm has $60,000 in revenue for the period. Give the entry to close the *Fees Income* account.

(Answers to Comprehensive Self Review are on page 185.)

Discussion Questions

1. Where does the accountant obtain the data needed for the adjusting entries?
2. Why does the accountant record closing entries at the end of a period?
3. Where does the accountant obtain the data needed for the closing entries?
4. How is the *Income Summary* account used in the closing procedure?
5. Briefly describe the flow of data through a simple accounting system.
6. What three procedures are performed at the end of each accounting period before the financial information is interpreted?
7. Name the steps of the accounting cycle.
8. What is the accounting cycle?
9. What accounts appear on a postclosing trial balance?
10. Why is a postclosing trial balance prepared?

APPLICATIONS

Exercises

Exercise 6.1
Objective 6-1

▶ **Journalize closing entries.**

On December 31, 2016, the ledger of Hernandez Company contained the following account balances:

Cash	$33,000	Maria Hernandez, Drawing	$26,000
Accounts Receivable	2,900	Fees Income	53,750
Supplies	2,100	Depreciation Expense	2,750

Equipment	26,000	Salaries Expense	17,000
Accumulated Depreciation	2,500	Supplies Expense	3,000
Accounts Payable	3,000	Telephone Expense	2,600
Maria Hernandez, Capital	48,250	Utilities Expense	4,650

All the accounts have normal balances. Journalize the closing entries. Use 4 as the general journal page number.

Accounting cycle.

Following are the steps in the accounting cycle. Arrange the steps in the proper sequence.

◀ **Exercise 6.2**
Objective 6-4

1. Record closing entries.
2. Interpret the financial information.
3. Prepare a postclosing trial balance.
4. Prepare financial statements.
5. Prepare a worksheet.
6. Record adjusting entries.
7. Analyze transactions.
8. Journalize the transactions.
9. Post the journal entries.

Postclosing trial balance.

From the following list, identify the accounts that will appear on the postclosing trial balance.

◀ **Exercise 6.3**
Objective 6-2

ACCOUNTS

1. Cash
2. Accounts Receivable
3. Supplies
4. Equipment
5. Accumulated Depreciation
6. Accounts Payable
7. John Martin, Capital
8. John Martin, Drawing
9. Fees Income
10. Depreciation Expense
11. Salaries Expense
12. Supplies Expense
13. Utilities Expense

Financial statements.

Managers often consult financial statements for specific types of information. Indicate whether each of the following items would appear on the income statement, statement of owner's equity, or the balance sheet. Use *I* for the income statement, *E* for the statement of owner's equity, and *B* for the balance sheet. If an item appears on more than one statement, use all letters that apply to that item.

◀ **Exercise 6.4**
Objective 6-3

1. Accumulated depreciation on the firm's equipment
2. Amount of depreciation charged off on the firm's equipment during the period
3. Original cost of the firm's equipment
4. Book value of the firm's equipment
5. Total expenses for the period
6. Accounts payable of the business
7. Owner's withdrawals for the period
8. Cash on hand

9. Revenue earned during the period
10. Total assets of the business
11. Net income for the period
12. Owner's capital at the end of the period
13. Supplies on hand
14. Cost of supplies used during the period
15. Accounts receivable of the business

Exercise 6.5
Objective 6-1

▶ **Closing entries.**

The *Income Summary* and *Levi Simmons, Capital* accounts for Simmons Production Company at the end of its accounting period follow.

ACCOUNT *Income Summary*   ACCOUNT NO. _399_

DATE		DESCRIPTION	POST. REF.	DEBIT	CREDIT	BALANCE DEBIT	BALANCE CREDIT
2016							
Dec.	31	Closing	J4		67 0 0 0 00		67 0 0 0 00
	31	Closing	J4	35 9 0 0 00			31 1 0 0 00
	31	Closing	J4	31 1 0 0 00			– 0 –

ACCOUNT *Levi Simmons, Capital*   ACCOUNT NO. _301_

DATE		DESCRIPTION	POST. REF.	DEBIT	CREDIT	BALANCE DEBIT	BALANCE CREDIT
2016							
Dec.	1		J1		120 0 0 0 00		120 0 0 0 00
	31	Closing	J4		31 1 0 0 00		151 1 0 0 00
	31	Closing	J4	11 0 0 0 00			140 1 0 0 00

Complete the following statements:

1. Total revenue for the period is _____.
2. Total expenses for the period are _____.
3. Net income for the period is _____.
4. Owner's withdrawals for the period are _____.

Exercise 6.6
Objective 6-1

▶ **Closing entries.**

The ledger accounts of I-Cloud Internet Company appear as follows on March 31, 2016:

ACCOUNT NO.	ACCOUNT	BALANCE
101	Cash	$80,000
111	Accounts Receivable	58,820
121	Supplies	10,600
131	Prepaid Insurance	25,000
141	Equipment	118,000
142	Accumulated Depreciation — Equipment	41,320
202	Accounts Payable	13,000
301	Lee Retha Hale, Capital	130,000
302	Lee Retha Hale, Drawing	13,000
401	Fees Income	374,460
510	Depreciation Expense — Equipment	21,160

511	Insurance Expense	11,400
514	Rent Expense	33,000
517	Salaries Expense	166,000
518	Supplies Expense	5,600
519	Telephone Expense	6,800
523	Utilities Expense	9,400

All accounts have normal balances. Journalize and post the closing entries. Use 4 as the page number for the general journal in journalizing the closing entries. Use account number 399 for the Income Summary Account.

Closing entries.

On December 31, the *Income Summary* account of Davison Company has a debit balance of $37,000 after revenue of $39,000 and expenses of $76,000 were closed to the account. *Michelle Davison, Drawing* has a debit balance of $4,000 and *Michelle Davison, Capital* has a credit balance of $58,000. Record the journal entries necessary to complete closing the accounts. What is the new balance of *Michelle Davison, Capital?*

◀ **Exercise 6.7**
Objective 6-1

Accounting cycle.

Complete a chart of the accounting cycle by writing the steps of the cycle in their proper sequence.

◀ **Exercise 6.8**
Objective 6-4

PROBLEMS

Problem Set A

Adjusting and closing entries.

Consumer Research Associates, owned by Sam Hill, is retained by large companies to test consumer reaction to new products. On January 31, 2016, the firm's worksheet showed the following adjustments data: (a) supplies used, $2,340; (b) expired rent, $13,000; and (c) depreciation on office equipment, $4,580. The balances of the revenue and expense accounts listed in the Income Statement section of the worksheet and the drawing account listed in the Balance Sheet section of the worksheet are given below:

◀ **Problem 6.1A**
Objective 6-1

 Sage 50
Complete Accounting

REVENUE AND EXPENSE ACCOUNTS

401 Fees Income	$100,000 Cr.
511 Depr. Expense—Office Equipment	4,580 Dr.
514 Rent Expense	13,000 Dr.
517 Salaries Expense	49,500 Dr.
520 Supplies Expense	2,340 Dr.
523 Telephone Expense	1,350 Dr.
526 Travel Expense	10,390 Dr.
529 Utilities Expense	1,250 Dr.

DRAWING ACCOUNT

| 302 Sam Hill, Drawing | 11,000 Dr. |

INSTRUCTIONS

1. Record the adjusting entries in the general journal, page 3.
2. Record the closing entries in the general journal, page 4.

Analyze: What closing entry is required to close a drawing account?

Problem 6.2A

Objectives 6-1, 6-2

Sage 50
Complete Accounting

QB

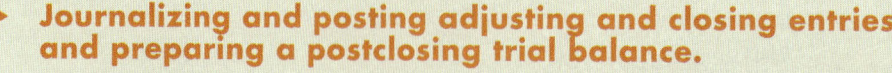

▶ **Journalizing and posting adjusting and closing entries and preparing a postclosing trial balance.**

A completed worksheet for The King Group is shown on the bottom of these two pages.

INSTRUCTIONS

1. Record balances as of December 31, 2016, in the ledger accounts.
2. Journalize (use 3 as the page number) and post the adjusting entries. Use account number 131 for Prepaid Advertising and the same account numbers for all other accounts shown on page 186 for Wells' Consulting Services chart of accounts.
3. Journalize (use 4 as the page number) and post the closing entries.
4. Prepare a postclosing trial balance.

Analyze: How many accounts are listed in the Adjusted Trial Balance section? How many accounts are listed on the postclosing trial balance?

Problem 6.3A

Objective 6-1

▶ **Journalizing and posting closing entries.**

On December 31, after adjustments, Gomez Company's ledger contains the following account balances:

101 Cash	$47,200 Dr.
111 Accounts Receivable	17,800 Dr.
121 Supplies	4,000 Dr.
131 Prepaid Rent	40,600 Dr.
141 Equipment	64,000 Dr.
142 Accumulated Depreciation—Equip.	2,000 Cr.
202 Accounts Payable	8,500 Cr.
301 Andrea Gomez, Capital (12/1/2016)	65,620 Cr.
302 Andrea Gomez, Drawing	8,200 Dr.

The King Group
Worksheet
Month Ended December 31, 2016

	ACCOUNT NAME	TRIAL BALANCE DEBIT	TRIAL BALANCE CREDIT	ADJUSTMENTS DEBIT	ADJUSTMENTS CREDIT	
1	Cash	93 4 0 0 00				
2	Accounts Receivable	13 0 0 0 00				
3	Supplies	8 0 0 0 00			(a) 3 4 0 0 00	
4	Prepaid Advertising	32 0 0 0 00			(b) 4 0 0 0 00	
5	Equipment	85 0 0 0 00				
6	Accumulated Depreciation—Equipment				(c) 3 4 0 0 00	
7	Accounts Payable		13 0 0 0 00			
8	Delva King, Capital		142 0 0 0 00			
9	Delva King, Drawing	9 4 0 0 00				
10	Fees Income		103 5 0 0 00			
11	Supplies Expense			(a) 3 4 0 0 00		
12	Advertising Expense			(b) 4 0 0 0 00		
13	Depreciation Expense—Equipment			(c) 3 4 0 0 00		
14	Salaries Expense	15 4 0 0 00				
15	Utilities Expense	2 3 0 0 00				
16	Totals	258 5 0 0 00	258 5 0 0 00	10 8 0 0 00	10 8 0 0 00	
17	Net Income					
18						
19						

401 Fees Income	163,600 Cr.
511 Advertising Expense	5,800 Dr.
514 Depreciation Expense—Equip.	1,000 Dr.
517 Rent Expense	4,600 Dr.
519 Salaries Expense	38,800 Dr.
523 Utilities Expense	7,720 Dr.

INSTRUCTIONS

1. Record the balances in the ledger accounts as of December 31.
2. Journalize the closing entries in the general journal, page 4. Use account number 399 for the Income Summary Account.
3. Post the closing entries to the general ledger accounts.

Analyze: What is the balance of the *Salaries Expense* account after closing entries are posted?

Worksheet, journalizing and posting adjusting and closing entries, and the postclosing trial balance.

◄   **Problem 6.4A**
Objectives 6-1, 6-2

A partially completed worksheet for Home Auto Detailing Service, a firm that details cars and vans, follows on page 178.

INSTRUCTIONS

1. Record balances as of December 31 in the ledger accounts.
2. Prepare the worksheet.
3. Journalize (use 3 as the journal page number) and post the adjusting entries. Use account number 131 for Prepaid Advertising and the same account numbers for all other accounts shown on page 186 for Wells' Consulting Services chart of accounts.
4. Journalize (use 4 as the journal page number) and post the closing entries.
5. Prepare a postclosing trial balance.

	ADJUSTED TRIAL BALANCE			INCOME STATEMENT			BALANCE SHEET		
	DEBIT	CREDIT		DEBIT	CREDIT		DEBIT	CREDIT	
	93 4 0 0 00						93 4 0 0 00		1
	13 0 0 0 00						13 0 0 0 00		2
	4 6 0 0 00						4 6 0 0 00		3
	28 0 0 0 00						28 0 0 0 00		4
	85 0 0 0 00						85 0 0 0 00		5
		3 4 0 0 00						3 4 0 0 00	6
		13 0 0 0 00						13 0 0 0 00	7
		142 0 0 0 00						142 0 0 0 00	8
	9 4 0 0 00						9 4 0 0 00		9
		103 5 0 0 00			103 5 0 0 00				10
	3 4 0 0 00			3 4 0 0 00					11
	4 0 0 0 00			4 0 0 0 00					12
	3 4 0 0 00			3 4 0 0 00					13
	15 4 0 0 00			15 4 0 0 00					14
	2 3 0 0 00			2 3 0 0 00					15
	261 9 0 0 00	261 9 0 0 00		28 5 0 0 00	103 5 0 0 00		233 4 0 0 00	158 4 0 0 00	16
				75 0 0 0 00				75 0 0 0 00	17
				103 5 0 0 00	103 5 0 0 00		233 4 0 0 00	233 4 0 0 00	18
									19

Home Auto Detailing Service
Worksheet
Month Ended December 31, 2016

	ACCOUNT NAME	TRIAL BALANCE		ADJUSTMENTS	
		DEBIT	CREDIT	DEBIT	CREDIT
1	Cash	32 0 5 0 00			
2	Accounts Receivable	5 4 5 0 00			
3	Supplies	6 0 0 0 00			(a) 2 1 0 0 00
4	Prepaid Advertising	4 0 0 0 00			(b) 1 9 0 0 00
5	Equipment	21 0 0 0 00			
6	Accumulated Depreciation—Equipment				(c) 5 8 0 00
7	Accounts Payable		6 0 0 0 00		
8	Clifton Davis, Capital		45 5 0 0 00		
9	Clifton Davis, Drawing	3 0 0 0 00			
10	Fees Income		26 6 0 0 00		
11	Salaries Expense	5 8 0 0 00			
12	Utilities Expense	8 0 0 00			
13	Supplies Expense			(a) 2 1 0 0 00	
14	Advertising Expense			(b) 1 9 0 0 00	
15	Depreciation Expense—Equipment			(c) 5 8 0 00	
16	Totals	78 1 0 0 00	78 1 0 0 00	4 5 8 0 00	4 5 8 0 00
17					
18					
19					

Analyze: What total debits were posted to the general ledger to complete all closing entries for the month of December?

Problem Set B

Problem 6.1B

Objective 6-1

▶ **Adjusting and closing entries.**

Sanford Cleaning and Maintenance, owned by Fred Sanford, provides cleaning services to hotels, motels, and hospitals. On January 31, 2016, the firm's worksheet showed the following adjustment data. The balances of the revenue and expense accounts listed in the Income Statement section of the worksheet and the drawing account listed in the Balance Sheet section of the worksheet are also given.

ADJUSTMENTS

a. Supplies used, $4,290

b. Expired insurance, $2,220

c. Depreciation on machinery, $1,680

REVENUE AND EXPENSE ACCOUNTS

401 Fees Income	$49,200 Cr.
511 Depreciation Expense—Machinery	1,680 Dr.
514 Insurance Expense	2,220 Dr.
517 Rent Expense	4,500 Dr.
520 Salaries Expense	24,000 Dr.
523 Supplies Expense	4,290 Dr.
526 Telephone Expense	315 Dr.

529 Utilities Expense	960 Dr.
DRAWING ACCOUNT	
302 Fred Sanford, Drawing	3,600 Dr.

INSTRUCTIONS

1. Record the adjusting entries in the general journal, page 3.

2. Record the closing entries in the general journal, page 4. Use account numbers provided on page 186 for any account number not given.

Analyze: What effect did the adjusting entry for expired insurance have on the *Insurance Expense* account?

Journalizing and posting adjusting and closing entries and preparing a postclosing trial balance.

◀ **Problem 6.2B**
Objectives 6-1, 6-2

A completed worksheet for Cedar Valley Nursery and Landscape is shown on pages 180–181.

INSTRUCTIONS

1. Record the balances as of December 31 in the ledger accounts.

2. Journalize (use 3 as the page number) and post the adjusting entries. Use account number 131 for Prepaid Advertising and the same account numbers for all other accounts as shown on page 186 for Wells' Consulting Services chart of accounts.

3. Journalize (use 4 as the page number) and post the closing entries.

4. Prepare a postclosing trial balance.

Analyze: What total credits were posted to the general ledger to complete the closing entries?

Journalizing and posting closing entries.

◀ **Problem 6.3B**
Objective 6-1

On December 31, after adjustments, The Jackson Family Farm's ledger contains the following account balances.

101 Cash	$85,500 Dr.
111 Accounts Receivable	21,600 Dr.
121 Supplies	9,000 Dr.
131 Prepaid Rent	69,300 Dr.
141 Equipment	108,000 Dr.
142 Accumulated Depreciation—Equip.	2,700 Cr.
202 Accounts Payable	29,250 Cr.
301 Taylor Jackson, Capital (12/1/2016)	172,350 Cr.
302 Taylor Jackson, Drawing	10,800 Dr.
401 Fees Income	162,000 Cr.
511 Advertising Expense	9,900 Dr.
514 Depreciation Expense—Equip.	2,700 Dr.
517 Rent Expense	6,300 Dr.
519 Salaries Expense	32,400 Dr.
523 Utilities Expense	10,800 Dr.

INSTRUCTIONS

1. Record the balances in the ledger accounts as of December 31.

2. Journalize the closing entries in the general journal, page 4. Use account number 399 for the Income Summary Account

3. Post the closing entries to the general ledger accounts.

Analyze: List the accounts affected by closing entries for the month of December.

Cedar Valley Nursery and Landscape
Worksheet
Month Ended December 31, 2016

	ACCOUNT NAME	TRIAL BALANCE DEBIT	TRIAL BALANCE CREDIT	ADJUSTMENTS DEBIT	ADJUSTMENTS CREDIT
1	Cash	32 4 0 0 00			
2	Accounts Receivable	6 0 0 0 00			
3	Supplies	6 0 0 0 00			(a) 3 0 0 0 00
4	Prepaid Advertising	9 0 0 0 00			(b) 1 2 0 0 00
5	Equipment	60 0 0 0 00			
6	Accumulated Depreciation—Equipment				(c) 1 5 0 0 00
7	Accounts Payable		9 0 0 0 00		
8	Scott Jeremy, Capital		82 2 0 0 00		
9	Scott Jeremy, Drawing	8 4 0 0 00			
10	Fees Income		46 8 0 0 00		
11	Supplies Expense			(a) 3 0 0 0 00	
12	Advertising Expense			(b) 1 2 0 0 00	
13	Depreciation Expense—Equipment			(c) 1 5 0 0 00	
14	Salaries Expense	14 4 0 0 00			
15	Utilities Expense	1 8 0 0 00			
16	Totals	138 0 0 0 00	138 0 0 0 00	5 7 0 0 00	5 7 0 0 00
17	Net Income				
18					
19					
20					

Problem 6.4B

Objectives 6-1, 6-2, 6-4

▶ **Worksheet, journalizing and posting adjusting and closing entries, and the postclosing trial balance.**

A partially completed worksheet for Christopher Cobb, CPA, for the month ending June 30, 2016, is shown below.

Christopher Cobb, CPA
Worksheet
Month Ended June 30, 2016

	ACCOUNT NAME	TRIAL BALANCE DEBIT	TRIAL BALANCE CREDIT	ADJUSTMENTS DEBIT	ADJUSTMENTS CREDIT
1	Cash	63 9 0 0 00			
2	Accounts Receivable	22 6 8 0 00			
3	Supplies	31 5 0 0 00			(a) 5 4 0 0 00
4	Computers	57 6 0 0 00			
5	Accumulated Depreciation—Computers		5 7 6 0 00		(b) 4 8 0 00
6	Accounts Payable		25 2 0 0 00		
7	Christopher Cobb, Capital		124 4 7 0 00		
8	Christopher Cobb, Drawing	24 0 0 0 00			
9	Fees Income		135 9 0 0 00		
10	Salaries Expense	75 4 5 0 00			
11	Supplies Expense			(a) 5 4 0 0 00	
12	Depreciation Expense—Computers			(b) 4 8 0 00	
13	Travel Expense	10 8 0 0 00			
14	Utilities Expense	5 4 0 0 00			
15	Totals	291 3 3 0 00	291 3 3 0 00	5 8 8 0 00	5 8 8 0 00
16					
17					

ADJUSTED TRIAL BALANCE		INCOME STATEMENT		BALANCE SHEET		
DEBIT	CREDIT	DEBIT	CREDIT	DEBIT	CREDIT	
32 4 0 0 00				32 4 0 0 00		1
6 0 0 0 00				6 0 0 0 00		2
3 0 0 0 00				3 0 0 0 00		3
7 8 0 0 00				7 8 0 0 00		4
60 0 0 0 00				60 0 0 0 00		5
	1 5 0 0 00				1 5 0 0 00	6
	9 0 0 00				9 0 0 00	7
	82 2 0 0 00				82 2 0 0 00	8
8 4 0 0 00				8 4 0 0 00		9
	46 8 0 0 00		46 8 0 0 00			10
3 0 0 0 00		3 0 0 0 00				11
1 2 0 0 00		1 2 0 0 00				12
1 5 0 0 00		1 5 0 0 00				13
14 4 0 0 00		14 4 0 0 00				14
1 8 0 0 00		1 8 0 0 00				15
139 5 0 0 00	139 5 0 0 00	21 9 0 0 00	46 8 0 0 00	117 6 0 0 00	92 7 0 0 00	16
		24 9 0 0 00			24 9 0 0 00	17
		46 8 0 0 00	46 8 0 0 00	117 6 0 0 00	117 6 0 0 00	18
						19
						20

INSTRUCTIONS

1. Record the balances as of June 30 in the ledger accounts.

2. Prepare the worksheet.

3. Journalize (use 3 as the journal page number) and post the adjusting entries. Use account number 121 for Supplies; 131 for Computers; 142 for the Accumulated Depreciation account; 309 for Income Summary; 517 for Supplies Expense; 519 for Travel Expense; and 523 for Depreciation Expense.

4. Journalize (use 4 as the journal page number) and post the closing entries.

5. Prepare a postclosing trial balance.

Analyze: What is the reported net income for the month of June for Christopher Cobb, CPA?

Critical Thinking Problem 6.1

The Closing Process

The Trial Balance section of the worksheet for 21st Century Fashions for the period ended December 31, 2016, appears on the next page. Adjustments data are also given.

ADJUSTMENTS
a. Supplies used, $7,200
b. Expired insurance, $4,800
c. Depreciation expense for machinery, $2,400

INSTRUCTIONS

1. Complete the worksheet.

2. Prepare an income statement.

3. Prepare a statement of owner's equity.

21st Century Fashions
Worksheet
Month Ended December 31, 2016

| | ACCOUNT NAME | TRIAL BALANCE | | ADJUSTMENTS | |
		DEBIT	CREDIT	DEBIT	CREDIT
1	Cash	81 6 0 0 00			
2	Accounts Receivable	18 0 0 0 00			
3	Supplies	14 4 0 0 00			(a) 7 2 0 0 00
4	Prepaid Insurance	21 6 0 0 00			(b) 4 8 0 0 00
5	Machinery	168 0 0 0 00			
6	Accumulated Depreciation—Machinery				(c) 2 4 0 0 00
7	Accounts Payable		27 0 0 0 00		
8	Carolyn Davis, Capital		149 1 6 0 00		
9	Carolyn Davis, Drawing	12 0 0 0 00			
10	Fees Income		165 0 0 0 00		
11	Supplies Expense			(a) 7 2 0 0 00	
12	Insurance Expense			(b) 4 8 0 0 00	
13	Salaries Expense	22 2 0 0 00			
14	Depreciation Expense—Machinery			(c) 2 4 0 0 00	
15	Utilities Expense	3 3 6 0 00			
16	Totals	341 1 6 0 00	341 1 6 0 00	14 4 0 0 00	14 4 0 0 00
17					
18					
19					

4. Prepare a balance sheet.

5. Journalize the adjusting entries in the general journal, page 3.

6. Journalize the closing entries in the general journal, page 4.

7. Prepare a postclosing trial balance.

Analyze: If the adjusting entry for expired insurance had been recorded in error as a credit to *Insurance Expense* and a debit to *Prepaid Insurance* for $4,800, what reported net income would have resulted?

Critical Thinking Problem 6.2

Owner's Equity

Demetria Davis, the bookkeeper for Home Interiors and Designs Company, has just finished posting the closing entries for the year to the ledger. She is concerned about the following balances:

Capital account balance in the general ledger:	$97,100
Ending capital balance on the statement of owner's equity:	55,600

Davis knows that these amounts should agree and asks for your assistance in reviewing her work.

Your review of the general ledger of Home Interiors and Designs Company reveals a beginning capital balance of $50,000. You also review the general journal for the accounting period and find the closing entries shown on the next page.

1. What errors did Ms. Davis make in preparing the closing entries for the period?

2. Prepare a general journal entry to correct the errors made.

3. Explain why the balance of the capital account in the ledger after closing entries have been posted will be the same as the ending capital balance on the statement of owner's equity.

	DATE		DESCRIPTION	POST. REF.	DEBIT	CREDIT	
			GENERAL JOURNAL			PAGE ___15___	
1	2016		*Closing Entries*				1
2	Dec.	31	Fees Income		98 0 0 0 00		2
3			Accumulated Depreciation		8 5 0 0 00		3
4			Accounts Payable		33 0 0 0 00		4
5			Income Summary			139 5 0 0 00	5
6							6
7		31	Income Summary		92 4 0 0 00		7
8			Salaries Expense			78 0 0 0 00	8
9			Supplies Expense			5 0 0 0 00	9
10			Depreciation Expense			2 4 0 0 00	10
11			Thomas Richey, Drawing			7 0 0 0 00	11
12							12
13							13
14							14

BUSINESS CONNECTIONS

Interpreting Financial Statements

Managerial FOCUS

1. An officer of Westway Corporation recently commented that when he receives the firm's financial statements, he looks at just the bottom line of the income statement—the line that shows the net income or net loss for the period. He said that he does not bother with the rest of the income statement because "it's only the bottom line that counts." He also does not read the balance sheet. Do you think this manager is correct in the way he uses the financial statements? Why or why not?

2. The president of Brown Corporation is concerned about the firm's ability to pay its debts on time. What items on the balance sheet would help her to assess the firm's debt-paying ability?

3. Why is it important that a firm's financial records be kept up-to-date and that management receive the financial statements promptly after the end of each accounting period?

4. What kinds of operating and general policy decisions might be influenced by data on the financial statements?

Timing of a Check

Ethical DILEMMA

On the last day of the fiscal year, Stanley Carpenter comes to you for a favor. He asks that you enter a check for $2,000 to CD Company for Miscellaneous Expense. You notice the invoice looks a little different from other invoices that are processed. Stanley needs the check immediately to get supplies today to complete the project for a favorite customer. You know that by preparing the closing entries tomorrow, Miscellaneous Expense will be set to zero for the beginning of the new year. Should you write this check and record the expense or find an excuse to write the check tomorrow? What would be the effect if the invoice to CD Company was erroneous and you had written the check?

Income Statement

Financial Statement ANALYSIS

In 2012, CSX Corporation, which operates under the name Surface Transportation, reported operating expenses of $8,299 million. A partial list of the company's operating expenses follows. CSX Corporation reported revenues from external customers to be $11,756 million for the year.

Consolidated Income Statement

(Dollars in millions)

Revenue	$11,756

Operating Expenses

(Dollars in millions)

Labor and Fringe Benefits	$3,020
Materials, Supplies, and Other	2,156
Fuel	1,672
Depreciation	1,059
Equipment and Other Rents	392

Analyze:

1. If the given categories represent the related general ledger accounts, what journal entry would be made to close the expense accounts at year-end?

2. What journal entry would be made to close the revenue accounts?

Analyze Online: Locate the website for CSX Corporation (www.csx.com). Click on *CSX Corporation* and then click on *Investor Relations*. Within the *Financial Information* link, find the most recent annual report.

3. On the consolidated statement of earnings, what was the amount reported for operating expenses?

4. What percentage increase or decrease does this figure represent from the operating expenses reported in 2012 of $8,299 million?

Accounting Cycle

Understanding the steps in the accounting cycle is important to get accurate information about the condition of your company. In teams, make strips of paper with the nine steps of the accounting cycle. Give two or three strips to each member of the group. Each team member needs to put his or her strips in the proper order of the nine steps.

Certified Bookkeeper

Certification in your field indicates you have a certain level of education and training. Go to the American Institute of Professional Bookkeepers website at www.aipb.com. From the certification program icon, determine the three requirements to become a certified bookkeeper.

Answers to **Self Reviews**

Answers to Section 1 Self Review

1. A temporary owner's equity account.

2. Close the revenue account to *Income Summary.*

   Close the expense accounts to *Income Summary.*

   Close the *Income Summary* account to the capital account.

   Close the drawing account to the capital account.

3. Debit *Capital* and credit *Drawing.*

4. **d.** revenue, drawing, and expense accounts

5. **a.** *Capital*

6. No effect on net income.

Answers to Section 2 Self Review

1. To make sure the general ledger is in balance after the adjusting and closing entries are posted.
2. Asset, liability, and the owner's capital accounts.
3. (7) Record closing entries, (8) prepare a postclosing trial balance, (9) interpret the financial statements.
4. a. *H.D. Hill, Drawing*
5. b. net loss of $30,000
6. The income statement will answer questions about fees earned, expenses incurred, and profit. The balance sheet will answer questions about the cash balance, the amount owed by customers, and the amount owed to suppliers.

Answers to Comprehensive Self Review

1. Interpret the financial statements.
2. False. The *temporary* owner's equity accounts do not appear on the postclosing trial balance. The temporary owner's equity accounts are the drawing account and *Income Summary.*
3. Income statement, statement of owner's equity, and balance sheet.
4.

Income Summary	24,200	
Rent Expense		7,200
Salaries Expense		14,000
Supplies Expense		3,000

5.

| Fees Income | 60,000 | |
| Income Summary | | 60,000 |

Mini-Practice Set 1

Service Business Accounting Cycle

Sage 50
Complete Accounting

Wells' Consulting Services

This project will give you an opportunity to apply your knowledge of accounting principles and procedures by handling all the accounting work of Wells' Consulting Services for the month of January 2017.

INTRODUCTION

Assume that you are the chief accountant for Wells' Consulting Services. During January, the business will use the same types of records and procedures that you learned about in Chapters 1 through 6. The chart of accounts for Wells' Consulting Services has been expanded to include a few new accounts. Follow the instructions to complete the accounting records for the month of January.

Wells' Consulting Services Chart of Accounts	
Assets	**Revenue**
101 Cash	401 Fees Income
111 Accounts Receivable	
121 Supplies	**Expenses**
134 Prepaid Insurance	511 Salaries Expense
137 Prepaid Rent	514 Utilities Expense
141 Equipment	517 Supplies Expense
142 Accumulated Depreciation — Equipment	520 Rent Expense
	523 Depreciation Expense — Equipment
Liabilities	526 Advertising Expense
202 Accounts Payable	529 Maintenance Expense
	532 Telephone Expense
Owner's Equity	535 Insurance Expense
301 Carolyn Wells, Capital	
302 Carolyn Wells, Drawing	
309 Income Summary	

INSTRUCTIONS

1. Open the general ledger accounts and enter the balances for January 1, 2017. Obtain the necessary figures from the postclosing trial balance prepared on December 31, 2016, which appears on page 166.

2. Analyze each transaction and record it in the general journal. Use page 3 to begin January's transactions.

3. Post the transactions to the general ledger accounts.

4. Prepare the Trial Balance section of the worksheet.

5. Prepare the Adjustments section of the worksheet.

   a. Compute and record the adjustment for supplies used during the month. An inventory taken on January 31 showed supplies of $4,200 on hand.

   b. Compute and record the adjustment for expired insurance for the month.

   c. Record the adjustment for one month of expired rent of $4,000.

   d. Record the adjustment for depreciation of $183 on the old equipment for the month. The first adjustment for depreciation for the new equipment will be recorded in February.

6. Complete the worksheet.

7. Prepare an income statement for the month.

8. Prepare a statement of owner's equity.

9. Prepare a balance sheet using the report form.

10. Journalize and post the adjusting entries.

11. Journalize and post the closing entries.

12. Prepare a postclosing trial balance.

Analyze: Compare the January 31 balance sheet you prepared with the December 31 balance sheet shown on page 167.

a. What changes occurred in total assets, liabilities, and the owner's ending capital?

b. What changes occurred in *Cash* and *Accounts Receivable* accounts?

c. Has there been an improvement in the firm's financial position? Why or why not?

DATE		TRANSACTIONS
Jan.	2	Purchased supplies for $6,000; issued Check 1015.
	2	Purchased a one-year insurance policy for $7,200; issued Check 1016.
	7	Sold services for $20,000 in cash and $4,000 on credit during the first week of January.
	12	Collected a total of $4,000 on account from credit customers during the first week of January.
	12	Issued Check 1017 for $3,200 to pay for special promotional advertising to new businesses on the local radio station during the month.
	13	Collected a total of $3,500 on account from credit customers during the second week of January.
	14	Returned supplies that were damaged for a cash refund of $650.
	15	Sold services for $20,700 in cash and $2,300 on credit during the second week of January.
	20	Purchased supplies for $4,600 from White's, Inc.; received Invoice 2384 payable in 30 days.
	20	Sold services for $12,500 in cash and $3,350 on credit during the third week of January.
	20	Collected a total of $4,500 on account from credit customers during the third week of January.
	21	Issued Check 1018 for $6,075 to pay for maintenance work on the office equipment.
	22	Issued Check 1019 for $3,200 to pay for special promotional advertising to new businesses in the local newspaper.
	23	Received the monthly telephone bill for $925 and paid it with Check 1020.
	26	Collected a total of $1,600 on account from credit customers during the fourth week of January.
	27	Issued Check 1021 for $3,000 to Office Plus, as payment on account for Invoice 2223.
	28	Sent Check 1022 for $2,350 in payment of the monthly bill for utilities.
	29	Sold services for $19,000 in cash and $2,750 on credit during the fourth week of January.
	31	Issued Checks 1023–1027 for $25,750 to pay the monthly salaries of the regular employees and three part-time workers.
	31	Issued Check 1028 for $15,000 for personal use.
	31	Issued Check 1029 for $4,150 to pay for maintenance services for the month.
	31	Purchased additional equipment for $15,000 from Contemporary Equipment Company; issued Check 1030 for $10,000 and bought the rest on credit. The equipment has a five-year life and no salvage value.
	31	Sold services for $5,600 in cash and $1,580 on credit on January 31.

Accounting for Sales and Accounts Receivable

Chapter 7

Kellogg's Company
www.kelloggcompany.com

More than 100 years ago, W.K. Kellogg created the first-ever breakfast cereal, the single corn flake, and then went on to shape an entire industry. Motivated by a passion for people, quality, and innovation, Kellogg soon became a household name. Today, W.K. Kellogg's legacy continues to inspire the company.

As a leading food producer, the company serves the world a delicious choice of cereals, snacks, meals, drinks, and more. And every day they look for ways to create even better experiences for all of their consumers. The company produces not only cereal. Its other brands include: *Pringles, Keebler, Cheez-Its,* and *Townhouse* and they continue to strive to provide even more.

Thousands of stores all over the world stock Kellogg's food products. In their first quarter of 2013, the company reported net sales of $3.9 billion. It also reported a net Accounts Receivable balance of nearly $1.6 billion. Keeping track of these product sales as well as store accounts receivable balances can be a daunting task for any accountant, but careful recordkeeping is a must if Kellogg wants to maintain its strong relationships with customers. The company strives to ensure that sales and accounts receivable data are accurate and that individual records of their customers' accounts receivable are updated daily.

If asked his opinion about the company, their mascot, Tony the Tiger, would say, "They're Grrrrreat!"

thinking critically
Do you think that Kellogg Company varies the discounts that it offers to its various store customers?

LEARNING OBJECTIVES

7-1. Record credit sales in a sales journal.

7-2. Post from the sales journal to the general ledger accounts.

7-3. Post from the sales journal to the customers' accounts in the accounts receivable subsidiary ledger.

7-4. Record sales returns and allowances in the general journal.

7-5. Post sales returns and allowances.

7-6. Prepare a schedule of accounts receivable.

7-7. Compute trade discounts.

7-8. Record credit card sales in appropriate journals.

7-9. Prepare the state sales tax return.

7-10. Define the accounting terms new to this chapter.

NEW TERMS

accounts receivable ledger
charge-account sales
contra revenue account
control account
credit memorandum
invoice
list price
manufacturing business
merchandise inventory
merchandising business
net price
net sales
open-account credit
retail business
sales allowance
sales journal
sales return
Sales Returns and Allowances
schedule of accounts receivable
service business
special journal
subsidiary ledger
trade discount
wholesale business

Merchandise Sales

When an accounting system is developed for a firm, one important consideration is the nature of the firm's operations. The three basic types of businesses are a **service business,** which sells services; a **merchandising business,** which sells goods that it purchases for resale; and a **manufacturing business,** which sells goods that it produces.

Wells' Consulting Services, the firm that was described in Chapters 2 through 6, is a service business. The firm that we will examine next, Maxx-Out Sporting Goods, is a merchandising business that sells the latest sporting goods and sportswear for men, women, and children. It is a **retail business,** which sells goods and services directly to individual consumers. Maxx-Out Sporting Goods is a sole proprietorship owned and operated by Max Ferraro, who was formerly a sales manager for a major retail clothing store.

Maxx-Out Sporting Goods must account for purchases and sales of goods, and for **merchandise inventory**—the stock of goods that is kept on hand. Refer to the chart of accounts for Maxx-Out Sporting Goods on the next page. You will learn about the accounts in this and following chapters.

To allow for efficient recording of financial data, the accounting systems of most merchandising businesses include special journals and subsidiary ledgers.

Special Journals and Subsidiary Ledgers

A **special journal** is a journal that is used to record only one type of transaction. A **subsidiary ledger** is a ledger that contains accounts of a single type. Table 7.1 lists the journals and ledgers that merchandising businesses generally use in their accounting systems. In this chapter, we will discuss the sales journal and the accounts receivable subsidiary ledger.

The Sales Journal

The **sales journal** is used to record only sales of merchandise on credit. To understand the need for a sales journal, consider how credit sales made at Maxx-Out Sporting Goods would be entered and posted using a general journal and general ledger. Refer to Figure 7.1 on pages 192–193.

Note the word "Balance" in the ledger accounts. To record beginning balances, enter the date in the Date column, the word "Balance" in the Description column, a check mark in the Posting Reference column, and the amount in the Debit or Credit Balance column.

Most state and many local governments impose a sales tax on retail sales of certain goods and services. Businesses are required to collect this tax from their customers and send it to the proper tax agency at regular intervals. When goods or services are sold on credit, the sales tax is usually recorded at the time of the sale even though it will not be collected immediately. A liability account called **Sales Tax Payable** is credited for the sales tax charged.

JOURNALS	
Type of Journal	**Purpose**
Sales	To record sales of merchandise on credit
Purchases	To record purchases of merchandise on credit
Cash receipts	To record cash received from all sources
Cash payments	To record all disbursements of cash
General	To record all transactions that are not recorded in another special journal and all adjusting and closing entries

LEDGERS	
Type of Ledger	**Content**
General	Assets, liabilities, owner's equity, revenue, and expense accounts
Accounts receivable	Accounts for credit customers
Accounts payable	Accounts for creditors

TABLE 7.1

Journals and Ledgers Used by Merchandising Businesses

Maxx-Out Sporting Goods — Chart of Accounts

Assets

101	Cash
105	Petty Cash Fund
109	Notes Receivable
111	Accounts Receivable
112	Allowance for Doubtful Accounts
116	Interest Receivable
121	Merchandise Inventory
126	Prepaid Insurance
127	Prepaid Interest
129	Supplies
131	Store Equipment
132	Accumulated Depreciation—Store Equipment
141	Office Equipment
142	Accumulated Depreciation—Office Equipment

Liabilities

201	Notes Payable—Trade
202	Notes Payable—Bank
205	Accounts Payable
216	Interest Payable
221	Social Security Tax Payable
222	Medicare Tax Payable
223	Employee Income Tax Payable
225	Federal Unemployment Tax Payable
227	State Unemployment Tax Payable
229	Salaries Payable
231	Sales Tax Payable

Owner's Equity

301	Max Ferraro, Capital
302	Max Ferraro, Drawing
399	Income Summary

Revenue

401	Sales
451	Sales Returns and Allowances
491	Interest Income
493	Miscellaneous Income

Cost of Goods Sold

501	Purchases
502	Freight In
503	Purchases Returns and Allowances
504	Purchases Discounts

Expenses

611	Salaries Expense—Sales
612	Supplies Expense
614	Advertising Expense
617	Cash Short or Over
626	Depreciation Expense—Store Equipment
634	Rent Expense
637	Salaries Expense—Office
639	Insurance Expense
641	Payroll Taxes Expense
643	Utilities Expense
649	Telephone Expense
651	Uncollectible Accounts Expense
657	Bank Fees Expense
658	Delivery Expense
659	Depreciation Expense—Office Equipment
691	Interest Expense
693	Miscellaneous Expense

FIGURE 7.1

Journalizing and Posting Credit Sales

		GENERAL JOURNAL			PAGE ___2___	
	DATE	DESCRIPTION	POST. REF.	DEBIT	CREDIT	
1	2016					1
2	Jan. 3	Accounts Receivable	111	7 0 2 00		2
3		Sales Tax Payable	231		5 2 00	3
4		Sales	401		6 5 0 00	4
5		Sold merchandise on				5
6		credit to Ann Anh,				6
7		Sales Slip 1101				7
8						8
9	8	Accounts Receivable	111	6 4 8 00		9
10		Sales Tax Payable	231		4 8 00	10
11		Sales	401		6 0 0 00	11
12		Sold merchandise on				12
13		credit to Cathy Ball,				13
14		Sales Slip 1102				14
15						15
16	11	Accounts Receivable	111	7 5 6 00		16
17		Sales Tax Payable	231		5 6 00	17
18		Sales	401		7 0 0 00	18
19		Sold merchandise on				19
20		credit to Barbara Coe, Sales				20
21		Slip 1103				21
22						22
23	15	Accounts Receivable	111	3 2 4 00		23
24		Sales Tax Payable	231		2 4 00	24
25		Sales	401		3 0 0 00	25
26		Sold merchandise on				26
27		credit to Amalia Rodriguez,				27
28		Sales Slip 1104				28
29						29
30						30
31						31
32						32

ACCOUNT _Accounts Receivable_   ACCOUNT NO. _111_

DATE		DESCRIPTION	POST. REF.	DEBIT	CREDIT	BALANCE	
						DEBIT	CREDIT
2016							
Jan.	1	Balance	✓			3 2 4 0 00	
	3		J2	7 0 2 00		3 9 4 2 00	
	8		J2	6 4 8 00		4 5 9 0 00	
	11		J2	7 5 6 00		5 3 4 6 00	
	15		J2	3 2 4 00		5 6 7 0 00	

(continued)

As you can see, a great amount of repetition is involved in both journalizing and posting these sales. The four credit sales made on January 3, 8, 11, and 15 required four separate entries in the general journal and involved four debits to *Accounts Receivable,* four credits to *Sales Tax Payable,* four credits to *Sales* (the firm's revenue account), and four descriptions. The posting of 12 items to the three general ledger accounts represents still further duplication of effort. This recording procedure is not efficient for a business that has a substantial number of credit sales each month.

FIGURE 7.1 (continued)

ACCOUNT	Sales Tax Payable						ACCOUNT NO. 231	
DATE	DESCRIPTION	POST. REF.	DEBIT	CREDIT	BALANCE DEBIT		BALANCE CREDIT	
2016								
Jan. 1	Balance	✓					7 5 6 00	
3		J2		5 2 00			8 0 8 00	
8		J2		4 8 00			8 5 6 00	
11		J2		5 6 00			9 1 2 00	
15		J2		2 4 00			9 3 6 00	

ACCOUNT	Sales						ACCOUNT NO. 401	
DATE	DESCRIPTION	POST. REF.	DEBIT	CREDIT	BALANCE DEBIT		BALANCE CREDIT	
2016								
Jan. 3		J2		6 5 0 00			6 5 0 00	
8		J2		6 0 0 00			1 2 5 0 00	
11		J2		7 0 0 00			1 9 5 0 00	
15		J2		3 0 0 00			2 2 5 0 00	

RECORDING TRANSACTIONS IN A SALES JOURNAL

A special journal intended only for credit sales provides a more efficient method of recording these transactions. Figure 7.2 shows the January credit sales of Maxx-Out Sporting Goods recorded in a sales journal. Since Maxx-Out Sporting Goods is located in a state that has an 8 percent sales tax on retail transactions, its sales journal includes a Sales Tax Payable Credit column. For the sake of simplicity, the sales journal shown here includes a limited number of transactions. The firm actually has many more credit sales each month.

Notice that the headings and columns in the sales journal speed up the recording process. No general ledger account names are entered. Only one line is needed to record all information for each transaction—date, sales slip number, customer's name, debit to *Accounts Receivable,* credit to *Sales Tax Payable,* and credit to *Sales.* Since the sales journal is used for a single purpose, there is no need to enter any descriptions. Thus, a great deal of repetition is avoided.

Entries in the sales journal are usually made daily. In a retail business such as Maxx-Out Sporting Goods, the data needed for each entry is taken from a copy of the customer's sales slip, as shown in Figure 7.3.

>> **7-1. OBJECTIVE**

Record credit sales in a sales journal.

Journals

A journal is a day-to-day record of a firm's transactions.

FIGURE 7.2

A Sales Journal

		SALES JOURNAL					PAGE 1		
	DATE	SALES SLIP NO.	CUSTOMER'S ACCOUNT DEBITED	POST. REF.	ACCOUNTS RECEIVABLE DEBIT	SALES TAX PAYABLE CREDIT	SALES CREDIT		
1	2016								1
2	Jan. 3	1101	Ann Anh		7 0 2 00	5 2 00	6 5 0 00		2
3	8	1102	Cathy Ball		6 4 8 00	4 8 00	6 0 0 00		3
4	11	1103	Barbara Coe		7 5 6 00	5 6 00	7 0 0 00		4
5	15	1104	Amalia Rodriguez		3 2 4 00	2 4 00	3 0 0 00		5
6	18	1105	Fred Wu		8 1 0 00	6 0 00	7 5 0 00		6
7	21	1106	Linda Carter		4 8 6 00	3 6 00	4 5 0 00		7
8	28	1107	Kim Ramirez		1 0 8 00	8 00	1 0 0 00		8
9	29	1108	Mesia Davis		1 0 8 0 00	8 0 00	1 0 0 0 00		9
10	31	1109	Alma Sanchez		9 7 2 00	7 2 00	9 0 0 00		10
11	31	1110	Ann Anh		2 7 0 00	2 0 00	2 5 0 00		11
12									12

FIGURE 7.3

Customer's Sales Slip

Maxx-Out Sporting Goods				
	Qty.	Description	Unit Price	Amount
2007 Trendsetter Lane Dallas, Texas 75268-0967	1	Olympic weight set	350 00	350 00
	1	Mountain Bike	300 00	300 00

DATE 1/3/16 SALESPERSON S.Harris AUTH.

Goods Taken [X] To Be Delivered [ ]

Send to

Special Instructions:

I authorize this purchase to be charged on my account.

Sales Tax 52 00

Amount 702 00

NAME: Ann Anh
ADDRESS: 8913 South Hampton Road
Dallas, TX 75232-6002

Signature

SALES SLIP 1101

Many small retail firms use a sales journal similar to the one shown in Figure 7.2. However, keep in mind that special journals vary in format according to the needs of individual businesses.

>> 7-2. OBJECTIVE

Post from the sales journal to the general ledger accounts.

POSTING FROM A SALES JOURNAL

A sales journal not only simplifies the initial recording of credit sales, it also eliminates a great deal of repetition in posting these transactions. With a sales journal, it is not necessary to post each credit sale individually to general ledger accounts. Instead, summary postings are made at the end of the month after the amount columns of the sales journal are totaled. See Figure 7.4 for an illustration of posting from the sales journal to the general ledger.

In actual practice, before any posting takes place, the equality of the debits and credits recorded in the sales journal is proved by comparing the column totals. The proof for the sales journal in Figure 7.4 is given below. All multicolumn special journals should be proved in a similar manner before their totals are posted.

Proof of Sales Journal	
	Debits
Accounts Receivable Debit column	$6,156.00
	Credits
Sales Tax Payable Credit column	$ 456.00
Sales Credit column	5,700.00
	$6,156.00

After the equality of the debits and credits has been verified, the sales journal is ruled and the column totals are posted to the general ledger accounts involved. To indicate that the postings have been made, the general ledger account numbers are entered in parentheses under the column totals in the sales journal. The abbreviation S1 is written in the Posting Reference column of the accounts, showing that the data was posted from page 1 of the sales journal.

The check marks in the sales journal in Figure 7.4 indicate that the amounts have been posted to the individual customer accounts. Posting from the sales journal to the customer accounts in the subsidiary ledger is illustrated later in this chapter.

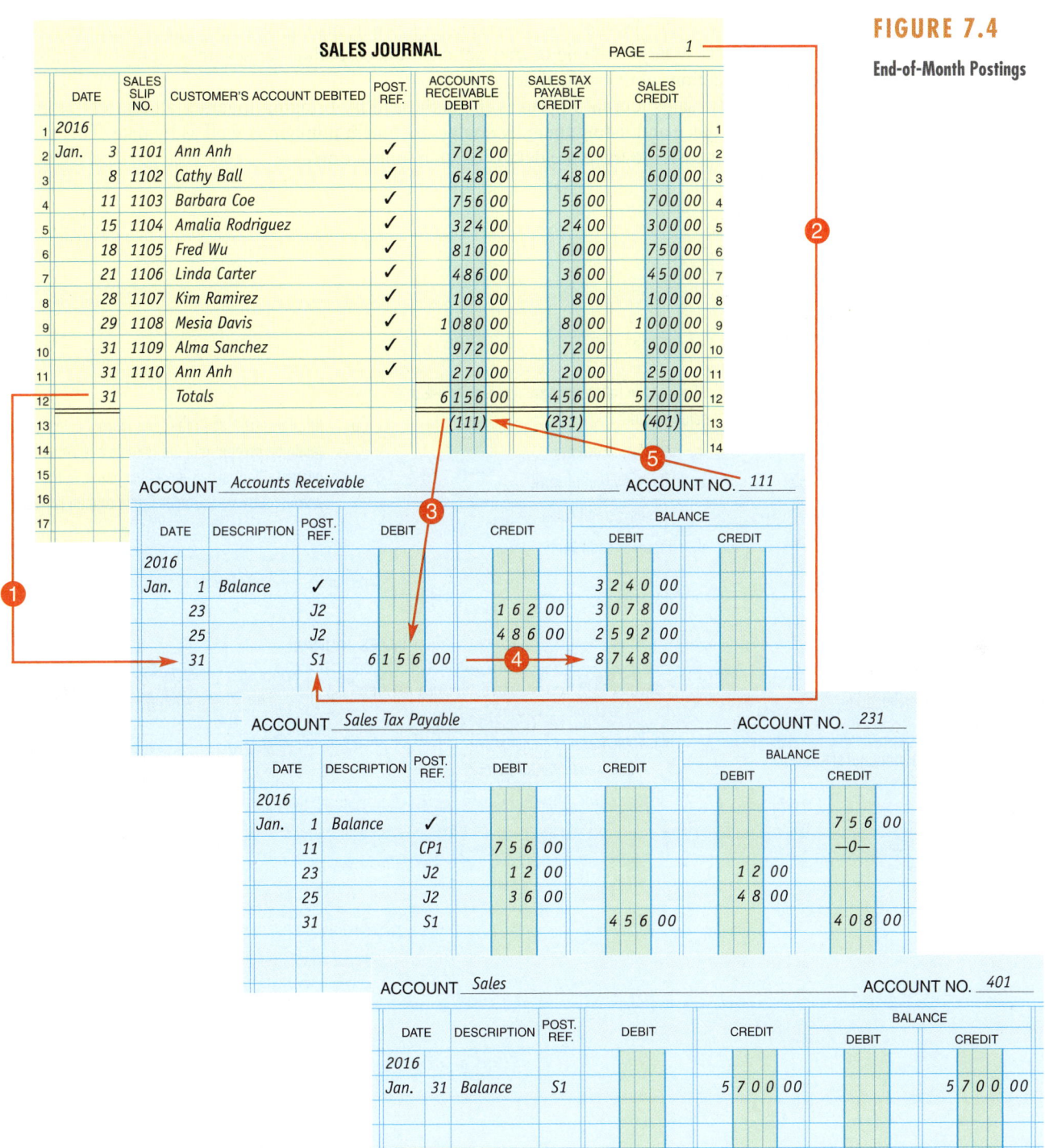

FIGURE 7.4

End-of-Month Postings

ADVANTAGES OF A SALES JOURNAL

Using a special journal for credit sales saves time, effort, and recording space. Both the journalizing process and the posting process become more efficient, but the advantage in the posting process is especially significant. If a business used the general journal to record 300 credit sales a month, the firm would have to make 900 postings to the general ledger—300 to **Accounts Receivable,** 300 to **Sales Tax Payable,** and 300 to **Sales.** With a sales journal, the firm makes only three summary postings to the general ledger at the end of each month no matter how many credit sales were entered.

important!

Posting

When posting from the sales journal, post information moving from left to right across the ledger form.

The use of a sales journal and other special journals also allows division of work. In a business with a fairly large volume of transactions, it is essential that several employees be able to record transactions at the same time.

Finally, the sales journal improves the audit trail by bringing together all entries for credit sales in one place and listing them by source document number as well as by date. This procedure makes it easier to trace the details of such transactions.

Section 1　Self Review

QUESTIONS

1. What is a special journal? Give four examples of special journals.

2. What type of transaction is recorded in the sales journal?

3. What is a subsidiary ledger? Give two examples of subsidiary ledgers.

EXERCISES

4. Types of business operations are:
   a. service, merchandising, corporation.
   b. sole proprietorship, merchandising, manufacturing.
   c. service, merchandising, manufacturing.

5. Which of the following is not a reason to use a sales journal?
   a. increases efficiency
   b. allows division of work
   c. increases credit sales
   d. improves audit trail

ANALYSIS

6. All sales recorded in the sales journal below were made on account and are taxable at a rate of 8 percent. What errors have been made in the entries? Assume the Sales Credit column is correct.

(Answers to Section 1 Self Review are on pages 232–233.)

			SALES JOURNAL				PAGE _____ 1
DATE	SALES SLIP NO.	CUSTOMER'S ACCOUNT DEBITED	POST. REF.	ACCOUNTS RECEIVABLE DEBIT	SALES TAX PAYABLE CREDIT	SALES CREDIT	
12	Apr. 25	4100	Carolyn Harris		6 4 2 00	42 00	6 0 0 00	12
13	25	4101	Teresa Wells		8 7 2 00	72 00	9 0 0 00	13

Accounts Receivable

A business that extends credit to customers must manage its accounts receivable carefully. Accounts receivable represents a substantial asset for many businesses, and this asset must be converted into cash in a timely manner. Otherwise, a firm may not be able to pay its bills even though it has a large volume of sales and earns a satisfactory profit.

The Accounts Receivable Ledger

The accountant needs detailed information about the transactions with credit customers and the balances owed by such customers at all times. This information is provided by an **accounts receivable ledger** with individual accounts for all credit customers. The accounts receivable ledger is referred to as a subsidiary ledger because it is separate from and subordinate to the general ledger.

Using an accounts receivable ledger makes it possible to verify that customers are paying their balances on time and that they are within their credit limits. The accounts receivable ledger also provides a convenient way to answer questions from credit customers. Customers may ask about their current balances or about a possible billing error.

The accounts for credit customers are maintained in a balance ledger form with three money columns, as shown in Figure 7.5 on the next page. Notice that this form does not contain a column for indicating the type of account balance. The balances in the customer accounts are presumed to be debit balances since asset accounts normally have debit balances. However, occasionally there is a credit balance because a customer has overpaid an amount owed or has returned goods that were already paid for. One common procedure for dealing with this situation is to circle the balance in order to show that it is a credit amount.

For a small business such as Maxx-Out Sporting Goods, customer accounts are alphabetized in the accounts receivable ledger. Larger firms and firms that use computers assign an account number to each credit customer and arrange the customer accounts in numeric order. Postings to the accounts receivable ledger are usually made daily so that the customer accounts can be kept up to date at all times.

>> 7-3. OBJECTIVE

Post from the sales journal to the customers' accounts in the accounts receivable subsidiary ledger.

POSTING A CREDIT SALE

Each credit sale recorded in the sales journal is posted to the appropriate customer's account in the accounts receivable ledger, as shown in Figure 7.5. The date, the sales slip number, and the amount that the customer owes as a result of the sale are transferred from the sales journal to the customer's account. The amount is taken from the Accounts Receivable Debit column of the journal and is entered in the Debit column of the account. Next, the new balance is determined and recorded.

To show that the posting has been completed, a check mark (✓) is entered in the sales journal and the abbreviation S1 is entered in the Posting Reference column of the customer's account. As noted before, this abbreviation identifies page 1 of the sales journal.

POSTING CASH RECEIVED ON ACCOUNT

When the transaction involves cash received on account from a credit customer, the cash collected is first recorded in a cash receipts journal. (The necessary entry in the cash receipts journal is discussed in Chapter 9.) The cash is then posted to the individual customer account in the accounts receivable ledger. Figure 7.6 shows a posting for cash received on January 7 from Ann Anh, a credit customer of Maxx-Out Sporting Goods.

>> 7-4. OBJECTIVE

Record sales returns and allowances in the general journal.

Sales Returns and Allowances

A sale is entered in the accounting records when the goods are sold or the service is provided. If something is wrong with the goods or service, the firm may take back the goods, resulting in a **sales return,** or give the customer a reduction in price, resulting in a **sales allowance.**

When a return or allowance is related to a credit sale, the normal practice is to issue a document called a **credit memorandum** to the customer rather than giving a cash refund. The

FIGURE 7.5

Posting from the Sales Journal to the Accounts Receivable Ledger

FIGURE 7.6

Posting for Cash Received on Account

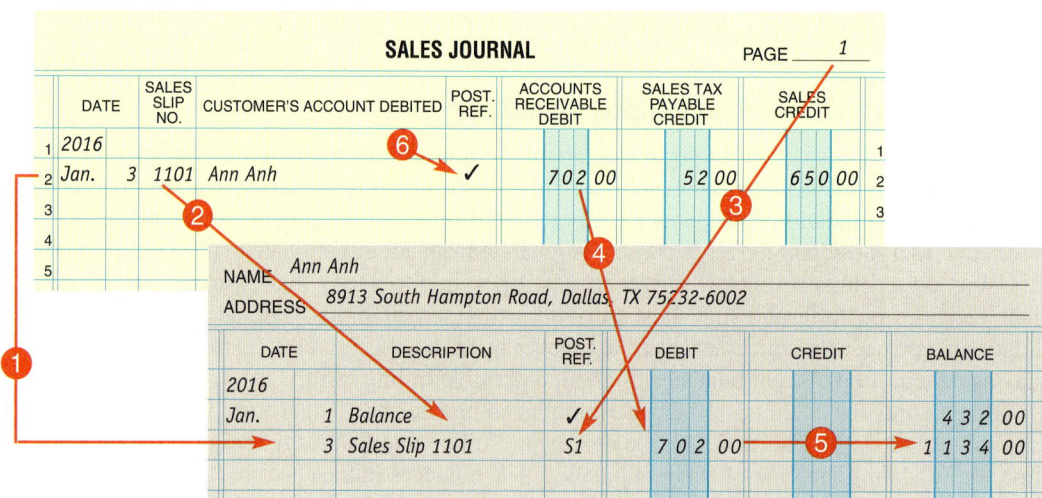

credit memorandum states that the customer's account is being reduced by the amount of the return or allowance plus any sales tax. A copy of the credit memorandum provides the data needed to enter the transaction in the firm's accounting records.

A debit to the **Sales Returns and Allowances** account is preferred to making a direct debit to **Sales.** This procedure gives a complete record of sales returns and allowances for each accounting period. Business managers use this record as a measure of operating efficiency. The **Sales Returns and Allowances** account is a **contra revenue account** because it has a debit balance, which is contrary, or opposite, to the normal credit balance for a revenue account.

BUSINESS TRANSACTION

On January 23, Maxx-Out Sporting Goods issued Credit Memorandum 101 for a sales allowance to Fred Wu for merchandise purchased on account. The merchandise was damaged but still usable.

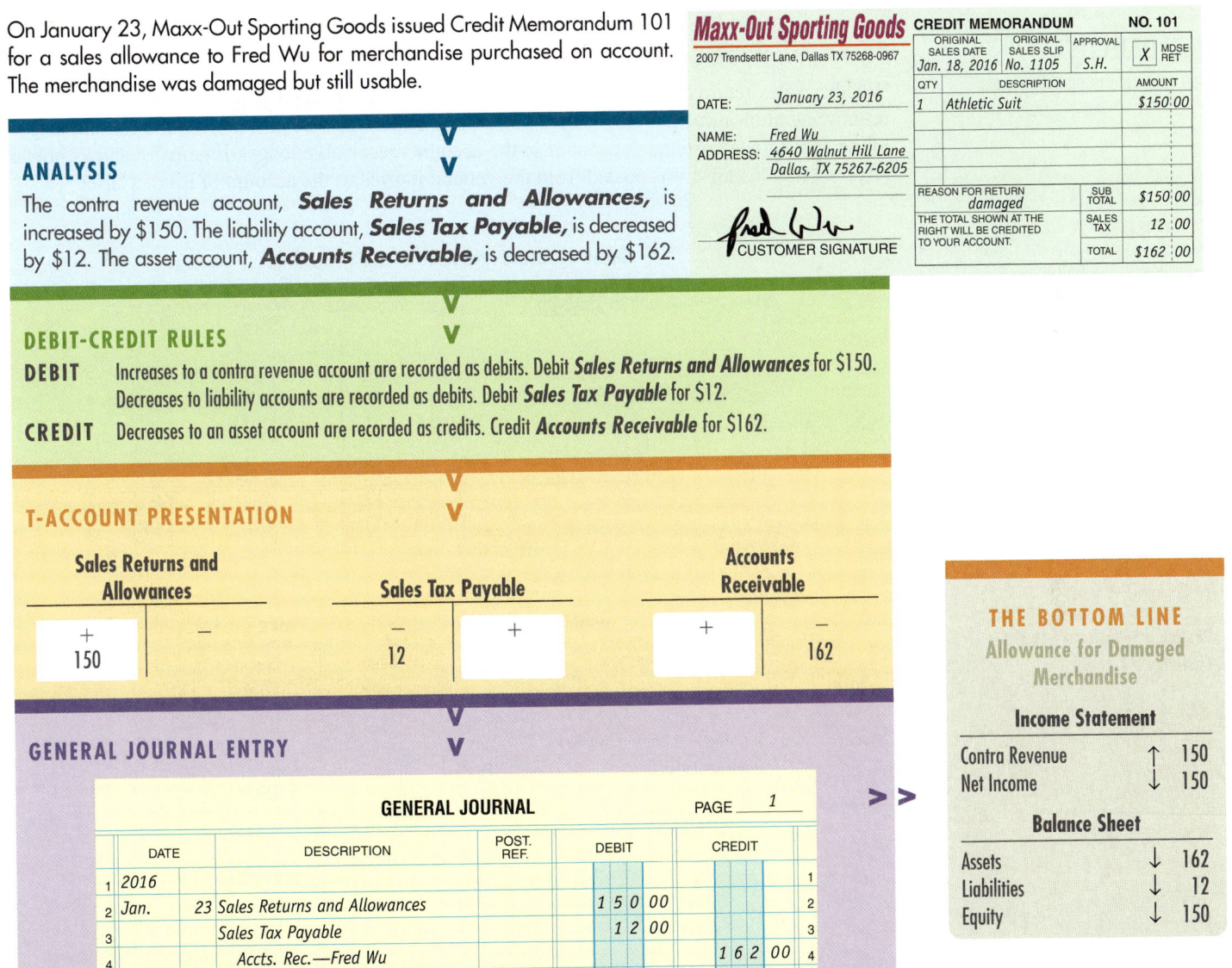

ANALYSIS

The contra revenue account, **Sales Returns and Allowances,** is increased by $150. The liability account, **Sales Tax Payable,** is decreased by $12. The asset account, **Accounts Receivable,** is decreased by $162.

DEBIT-CREDIT RULES

DEBIT   Increases to a contra revenue account are recorded as debits. Debit **Sales Returns and Allowances** for $150. Decreases to liability accounts are recorded as debits. Debit **Sales Tax Payable** for $12.

CREDIT   Decreases to an asset account are recorded as credits. Credit **Accounts Receivable** for $162.

T-ACCOUNT PRESENTATION

Sales Returns and Allowances		Sales Tax Payable		Accounts Receivable	
+	−	−	+	+	−
150		12			162

GENERAL JOURNAL ENTRY

GENERAL JOURNAL   PAGE ___1___

	DATE	DESCRIPTION	POST. REF.	DEBIT	CREDIT	
1	2016					1
2	Jan. 23	Sales Returns and Allowances		1 5 0 00		2
3		Sales Tax Payable		1 2 00		3
4		Accts. Rec.—Fred Wu			1 6 2 00	4

THE BOTTOM LINE
Allowance for Damaged Merchandise

Income Statement

Contra Revenue	↑	150
Net Income	↓	150

Balance Sheet

Assets	↓	162
Liabilities	↓	12
Equity	↓	150

What is the ultimate effect of this transaction on the financial statements? An increase in contra revenue causes a decrease in net income. Note that the $150 decrease in net income causes a $150 decrease in owner's equity. The asset **Accounts Receivable** is decreased, and the liability **Sales Tax Payable** is also decreased. The eventual effect of this transaction on the income statement and the balance sheet is summarized in the box titled *The Bottom Line.*

RECORDING SALES RETURNS AND ALLOWANCES

Depending on the volume of sales returns and allowances, a business may use a general journal to record these transactions, or it may use a special sales returns and allowances journal.

Using the General Journal for Sales Returns and Allowances A small firm that has a limited number of sales returns and allowances each month has no need to establish a special journal for such transactions. Instead, the required entries are made in the general journal.

Using a Sales Returns and Allowances Journal In a business having many sales returns and allowances, it is efficient to use a special journal for these transactions. An example of a *sales returns and allowances journal* is shown in Figure 7.7.

>> **7-5. OBJECTIVE**

Post sales returns and allowances.

POSTING A SALES RETURN OR ALLOWANCE

Whether sales returns and allowances are recorded in the general journal or in a special sales returns and allowances journal, each of these transactions must be posted from the general ledger to the appropriate customer's account in the accounts receivable ledger. Figure 7.8 shows how a return of merchandise was posted from the general journal to the account of Linda Carter.

FIGURE 7.7

Sales Returns and Allowances Journal

SALES RETURNS AND ALLOWANCES JOURNAL   PAGE ___8___

	DATE	SALES SLIP NO.	CUSTOMER'S ACCOUNT CREDITED	POST. REF.	ACCOUNTS RECEIVABLE CREDIT	SALES TAX PAYABLE DEBIT	SALES RET. & ALLOW. DEBIT	
1	2016							1
2	Jan. 23	1105	Fred Wu	✓	162 00	12 00	150 00	2
3	25	1106	Linda Carter	✓	486 00	36 00	450 00	3
4								4
17	31		Totals		3 240 00	240 00	3 000 00	17
18					(111)	(231)	(451)	18
19								19

FIGURE 7.8

Posting a Sales Return to the Customer's Account

GENERAL JOURNAL   PAGE ___1___

	DATE	DESCRIPTION	POST. REF.	DEBIT	CREDIT	
1	2016					1
6	Jan. 25	Sales Returns and Allowances	451	4 5 0 00		6
7		Sales Tax Payable	231	3 6 00		7
8		Accounts Rec./Linda Carter	111 ✓		4 8 6 00	8
9		Accepted a return of				9
10		defective merchandise,				10
11		Credit Memorandum 102;				11
12		original sale made on Sales				12
13		Slip 1106 of January 21.				13
14						14
15						15

NAME   Linda Carter
ADDRESS   1819 Belt Line Road, Dallas, Texas 75267-6318

DATE	DESCRIPTION	POST. REF.	DEBIT	CREDIT	BALANCE
2016					
Jan. 1	Balance	✓			5 4 00
21	Sales Slip 1106	S1	4 8 6 00		5 4 0 00
25	CM 102	J1		4 8 6 00	5 4 00

Because the credit amount in the general journal entry for this transaction requires two postings, the account number 111 and a check mark are entered in the Posting Reference column of the journal. The 111 indicates that the amount was posted to the **Accounts Receivable** account in the general ledger, and the check mark indicates that the amount was posted to the customer's account in the accounts receivable ledger. Notice that a diagonal line was used to separate the two posting references.

Refer to Figure 7.7, which shows a special sales returns and allowances journal instead of a general journal. The account numbers at the bottom of each column are the posting references for the three general ledger accounts: **Accounts Receivable, Sales Tax Payable,** and **Sales Returns and Allowances.** The check marks in the Posting Reference column show that the credits were posted to individual customer accounts in the accounts receivable subsidiary ledger.

Remember that a business can use the general journal or special journals for transactions related to credit sales. A special journal is an efficient option for recording and posting large numbers of transactions.

Figure 7.9 shows the accounts receivable ledger after posting is completed.

REPORTING NET SALES

At the end of each accounting period, the balance of the **Sales Returns and Allowances** account is subtracted from the balance of the **Sales** account in the Revenue section of the income statement. The resulting figure is the **net sales** for the period.

For example, assume the **Sales Returns and Allowances** account contains a balance of $600 at the end of January. Also assume the **Sales** account has a balance of $25,700 at the end of January. The Revenue section of the firm's income statement will appear as follows.

Maxx-Out Sporting Goods
Income Statement (Partial)
Month Ended January 31, 2016

Revenue	
Sales	$25,700
Less Sales Returns and Allowances	600
Net Sales	$25,100

FIGURE 7.9

Accounts Receivable Ledger

NAME Ann Anh
ADDRESS 8913 South Hampton Road, Dallas, Texas 75232-6002

DATE		DESCRIPTION	POST. REF.	DEBIT	CREDIT	BALANCE
2016						
Jan.	1	Balance	✓			432 00
	3	Sales Slip 1101	S1	702 00		1134 00
	7		CR1		432 00	702 00
	31	Sales Slip 1110	S1	270 00		972 00

NAME Cathy Ball
ADDRESS 7517 Woodrow Wilson Lane, Dallas, Texas 75267-6205

DATE		DESCRIPTION	POST. REF.	DEBIT	CREDIT	BALANCE
2016						
Jan.	8	Sales Slip 1102	S1	648 00		648 00

(continued)

FIGURE 7.9

(continued)

NAME _Vickie Bowman_

ADDRESS _1712 Red Bird Lane, Dallas, Texas 75267-6502_

DATE		DESCRIPTION	POST. REF.	DEBIT	CREDIT	BALANCE
2016						
Jan.	1	Balance	✓			270 00
	11		CR1		270 00	—0—

NAME _Linda Carter_

ADDRESS _1819 Belt Line Road, Dallas, Texas 75267-6318_

DATE		DESCRIPTION	POST. REF.	DEBIT	CREDIT	BALANCE
2016						
Jan.	1	Balance	✓			54 00
	21	Sales Slip 1106	S1	486 00		540 00
	25	CM 102	J1		486 00	54 00

NAME _Barbara Coe_

ADDRESS _1864 Elm Street, Dallas, Texas 75267-6205_

DATE		DESCRIPTION	POST. REF.	DEBIT	CREDIT	BALANCE
2016						
Jan.	1	Balance	✓			1080 00
	11	Sales Slip 1103	S1	756 00		1836 00
	13		CR1		540 00	1296 00

NAME _Mesia Davis_

ADDRESS _1008 University Boulevard, Dallas, Texas 75267-6318_

DATE		DESCRIPTION	POST. REF.	DEBIT	CREDIT	BALANCE
2016						
Jan.	1	Balance	✓			216 00
	29	Sales Slip 1108	S1	1080 00		1296 00
	31		CR1		275 00	1021 00

NAME _Kim Ramirez_

ADDRESS _5787 Valley View Lane, Dallas, Texas 75267-6318_

DATE		DESCRIPTION	POST. REF.	DEBIT	CREDIT	BALANCE
2016						
Jan.	1	Balance	✓			216 00
	28	Sales Slip 1107	S1	108 00		324 00
	31		CR1		108 00	216 00

FIGURE 7.9

(concluded)

NAME Amalia Rodriguez

ADDRESS 8108 Sherman Drive, Dallas, Texas 75267-6205

DATE		DESCRIPTION	POST. REF.	DEBIT	CREDIT	BALANCE
2016						
Jan.	1	Balance	✓			6 4 8 00
	15	Sales Slip 1104	S1	3 2 4 00		9 7 2 00

NAME Alma Sanchez

ADDRESS 1382 Clark Road, Dallas, Texas 75267-6205

DATE		DESCRIPTION	POST. REF.	DEBIT	CREDIT	BALANCE
2016						
Jan.	1	Balance	✓			1 0 8 00
	16		CR1		1 0 8 00	—0—
	31	Sales Slip 1109	S1	9 7 2 00		9 7 2 00

NAME Fred Wu

ADDRESS 4640 Walnut Hill Lane, Dallas, Texas 75267-6205

DATE		DESCRIPTION	POST. REF.	DEBIT	CREDIT	BALANCE
2016						
Jan.	1	Balance	✓			2 1 6 00
	18	Sales Slip 1105	S1	8 1 0 00		1 0 2 6 00
	22		CR1		4 0 0 00	6 2 6 00
	23	CM 101	J1		1 6 2 00	4 6 4 00

Schedule of Accounts Receivable

The use of an accounts receivable ledger does not eliminate the need for the *Accounts Receivable* account in the general ledger. This account remains in the general ledger and continues to appear on the balance sheet at the end of each fiscal period. However, the *Accounts Receivable* account is now considered a control account. A control account serves as a link between a subsidiary ledger and the general ledger. Its balance summarizes the balances of its related accounts in the subsidiary ledger.

At the end of each month, after all the postings have been made from the sales journal, the cash receipts journal, and the general journal to the accounts receivable ledger, the balances in the accounts receivable ledger must be proved against the balance of the *Accounts Receivable* general ledger account. First a schedule of accounts receivable, which lists the subsidiary ledger account balances, is prepared. The total of the schedule is compared with the balance of the *Accounts Receivable* account. If the two figures are not equal, errors must be located and corrected.

On January 31, the accounts receivable ledger at Maxx-Out Sporting Goods contains the accounts shown in Figure 7.9. To prepare a schedule of accounts receivable, the names of all customers with account balances are listed with the amount of their unpaid balances. Next the figures are added to find the total owed to the business by its credit customers.

>> 7-6. OBJECTIVE

Prepare a schedule of accounts receivable.

Best Buy Co., Inc., reported accounts receivable of approximately $2.3 billion at March 3, 2012.

FIGURE 7.10

Schedule of Accounts Receivable
and the Accounts Receivable Account

Maxx-Out Sporting Goods
Schedule of Accounts Receivable
January 31, 2016

Ann Anh	9 7 2 00
Cathy Ball	6 4 8 00
Linda Carter	5 4 00
Barbara Coe	1 2 9 6 00
Mesia Davis	1 0 2 1 00
Kim Ramirez	2 1 6 00
Amalia Rodriguez	9 7 2 00
Alma Sanchez	9 7 2 00
Fred Wu	4 6 4 00
Total	6 6 1 5 00

ACCOUNT Accounts Receivable   ACCOUNT NO. 111

DATE		DESCRIPTION	POST. REF.	DEBIT	CREDIT	BALANCE DEBIT	BALANCE CREDIT
2016							
Jan.	1	Balance	✓			3 2 4 0 00	
	23		J1		1 6 2 00	3 0 7 8 00	
	25		J1		4 8 6 00	2 5 9 2 00	
	31		S1	6 1 5 6 00		8 7 4 8 00	
	31		CR1		2 1 3 3 00	6 6 1 5 00	

A comparison of the total of the schedule of accounts receivable prepared at Maxx-Out Sporting Goods on January 31 and the balance of the *Accounts Receivable* account in the general ledger shows that the two figures are the same, as shown in Figure 7.10. The posting reference CR1 refers to the cash receipts journal, which is discussed in Chapter 9.

In addition to providing a proof of the subsidiary ledger, the schedule of accounts receivable serves another function. It reports information about the firm's accounts receivable at the end of the month. Management can review the schedule to see exactly how much each customer owes.

Section 2   Self Review

QUESTIONS

1. What are net sales?

2. What is a sales return? What is a sales allowance?

3. Which accounts are kept in the accounts receivable ledger?

EXERCISES

4. Where would you report net sales?

   a. sales general ledger account

   b. general journal

   c. income statement

   d. sales journal

5. Which of the following general ledger accounts would appear in a sales returns and allowances journal?

   a. *Sales Returns and Allowances, Sales Tax Payable, Accounts Receivable*

   b. *Sales Returns and Allowances, Sales, Accounts Receivable*

   c. *Sales Returns, Sales Allowances, Sales*

ANALYSIS

6. Draw a diagram showing the relationship between the accounts receivable ledger, the schedule of accounts receivable, and the general ledger.

(Answers to Section 2 Self Review are on page 233.)

| SECTION OBJECTIVES | TERMS TO LEARN |

SECTION OBJECTIVES

>> 7-7. Compute trade discounts.

WHY IT'S IMPORTANT

Trade discounts allow for flexible pricing structures.

>> 7-8. Record credit card sales in appropriate journals.

WHY IT'S IMPORTANT

Credit cards are widely used in merchandising transactions.

>> 7-9. Prepare the state sales tax return.

WHY IT'S IMPORTANT

Businesses are legally responsible for accurately reporting and remitting sales taxes.

TERMS TO LEARN

charge-account sales
invoice
list price
net price
open-account credit
trade discount
wholesale business

Special Topics in Merchandising

Merchandisers have many accounting concerns. These include pricing, credit, and sales taxes.

Credit Sales for a Wholesale Business

The operations of Maxx-Out Sporting Goods are typical of those of many retail businesses—businesses that sell goods and services directly to individual consumers. In contrast, a **wholesale business** is a manufacturer or distributor of goods that sells to retailers or large consumers such as hotels and hospitals. The basic procedures used by wholesalers to handle sales and accounts receivable are the same as those used by retailers. However, many wholesalers offer cash discounts and trade discounts, which are not commonly found in retail operations.

The procedures used in connection with cash discounts are examined in Chapter 9. The handling of trade discounts is described here.

COMPUTING TRADE DISCOUNTS

A wholesale business offers goods to trade customers at less than retail prices. This price adjustment is based on the volume purchased by trade customers and takes the form of a **trade discount,** which is a reduction from the **list price**—the established retail price. There may be a single trade discount or a series of discounts for each type of goods. The **net price** (list price less all trade discounts) is the amount the wholesaler records in its sales journal.

The same goods may be offered to different customers at different trade discounts, depending on the size of the order and the costs of selling to the various types of customers.

Single Trade Discount Suppose the list price of goods is $1,500 and the trade discount is 40 percent. The amount of the discount is $600, and the net price to be shown on the invoice and recorded in the sales journal is $900.

List price	$1,500
Less 40% discount ($1,500 × 0.40)	600
Invoice price	$ 900

>> 7-7. OBJECTIVE
Compute trade discounts.

important!

Trade Discounts
The amount of sales revenue recorded is the list price minus the trade discount.

important!

Special Journal Format
Special journals such as the sales journal can vary in format from company to company.

Series of Trade Discounts If the list price of goods is $1,500 and the trade discount is quoted in a series such as 25 and 15 percent, a different net price will result.

List price	$1,500.00
Less first discount ($1,500 × 0.25)	375.00
Difference	$1,125.00
Less second discount ($1,125 × 0.15)	168.75
Invoice price	$ 956.25

USING A SALES JOURNAL FOR A WHOLESALE BUSINESS

Since sales taxes apply only to retail transactions, a wholesale business does not need to account for such taxes. Its sales journal may therefore be as simple as the one illustrated in Figure 7.11. This sales journal has a single amount column. The total of this column is posted to the general ledger at the end of the month as a debit to the *Accounts Receivable* account and a credit to the *Sales* account (Figure 7.12). During the month, the individual entries in the sales journal are posted to the customer accounts in the accounts receivable ledger.

Wholesale businesses issue invoices. An **invoice** is a customer billing for merchandise bought on credit. Copies of the invoices are used to enter the transactions in the sales journal.

The next merchandising topic, credit policies, applies to both wholesalers and retailers. The discussion in this textbook focuses on credit policies and accounting for retail firms.

FIGURE 7.11

Wholesaler's Sales Journal

FIGURE 7.12

General Ledger Accounts

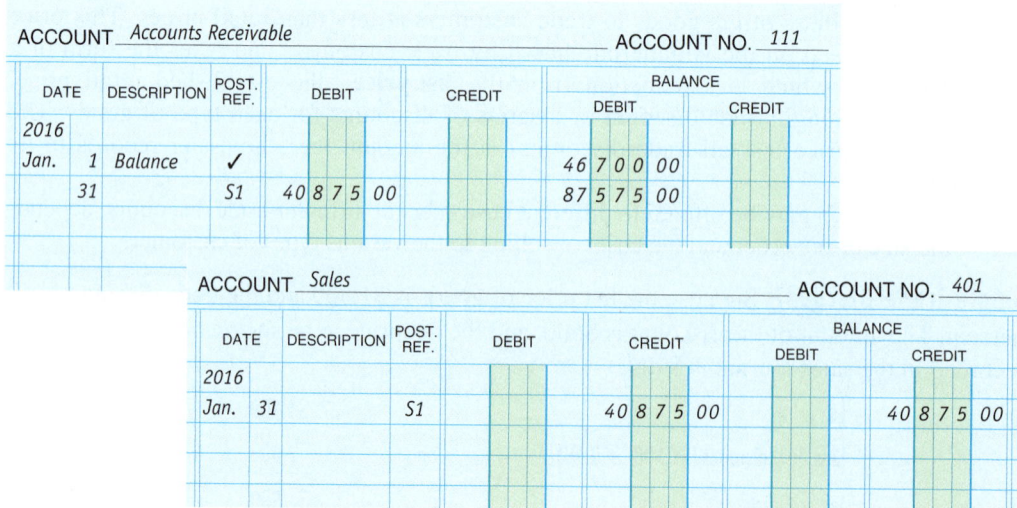

Credit Policies

The use of credit is considered to be one of the most important factors in the rapid growth of modern economic systems. Sales on credit are made by large numbers of wholesalers and retailers of goods and by many professional people and service businesses. The assumption is that the volume of both sales and profits will increase if buyers are given a period of a month or more to pay for the goods or services they purchase.

However, the increase in profits a business expects when it grants credit will be realized only if each customer completes the transaction by paying for the goods or services purchased. If payment is not received, the expected profits become actual losses and the purpose for granting the credit is defeated. Business firms try to protect against the possibility of such losses by investigating a customer's credit record and ability to pay for purchases before allowing any credit to the customer.

Professional people such as doctors, lawyers, architects, and owners of small businesses like Maxx-Out Sporting Goods usually make their own decisions about granting credit. Such decisions may be based on personal judgment or on reports available from credit bureaus, information supplied by other creditors, and credit ratings supplied by national firms such as Dun & Bradstreet.

> Dun & Bradstreet is a leader in providing credit information. For the year ended December 31, 2012, the company reported revenues of $1.6 billion.

Larger businesses maintain a credit department to determine the amounts and types of credit that should be granted to customers. In addition to using credit data supplied by institutions, the credit department may obtain financial statements and related reports from customers who have applied for credit. This information is analyzed to help determine the maximum amount of credit that may be granted and suitable credit terms for the customer. Financial statements that have been audited by certified public accountants are used extensively by credit departments.

Even though the credit investigation is thorough, some accounts receivable become uncollectible. Unexpected business developments, errors of judgment, incorrect financial data, and many other causes may lead to defaults in payments by customers. Experienced managers know that some uncollectible accounts are to be expected in normal business operations and that limited losses indicate that a firm's credit policies are sound. Provisions for such limited losses from uncollectible accounts are usually made in budgets and other financial projections.

Each business must develop credit policies that achieve maximum sales with minimum losses from uncollectible accounts:

■ A credit policy that is too tight results in a low level of losses at the expense of increases in sales volume.

■ A credit policy that is too lenient may result in increased sales volume accompanied by a high level of losses.

Good judgment based on knowledge and experience must be used to achieve a well-balanced credit policy.

Different types of credit have evolved with the growing economy and changing technology. The different types of credit require different accounting treatments.

ACCOUNTING FOR DIFFERENT TYPES OF CREDIT SALES

The most common types of credit sales are:

■ open-account credit,

■ business credit cards,

■ bank credit cards,

■ cards issued by credit card companies.

Open-Account Credit The form of credit most commonly offered by professional people and small businesses permits the sale of services or goods to the customer with the understanding that the amount is to be paid at a later date. This type of arrangement is called **open-account credit.** It is usually granted on the basis of personal acquaintance or knowledge of the customer. However, formal credit checks may also be used. The amount involved in each transaction is usually small, and payment is expected within 30 days or on receipt of a monthly statement. Open-account sales are also referred to as **charge-account sales.**

Maxx-Out Sporting Goods uses the open-account credit arrangement. Sales transactions are recorded as debits to the *Accounts Receivable* account and credits to the *Sales* account. Collections on account are recorded as debits to the *Cash* account and credits to the *Accounts Receivable* account.

Business Credit Cards Many retail businesses, especially large ones such as department store chains and gasoline companies, provide their own credit cards (sometimes called charge cards) to customers who have established credit. Whenever a sale is completed using a business credit card, a sales slip is prepared in the usual manner. Then the sales slip and the credit card are placed in a mechanical device that prints the customer's name, account number, and other data on all copies of the sales slip. Many companies use computerized card readers and sales registers that print out a sales slip with the customer information and a line for the customer's signature. Some businesses require that the salesclerk contact the credit department by telephone or computer terminal to verify the customer's credit status before completing the transaction.

Business credit card sales are similar to open-account credit sales. A business credit card sale is recorded as:

- a debit to *Accounts Receivable,*
- a credit to a revenue account such as *Sales.*

A customer payment is recorded as:

- a debit to *Cash,*
- a credit to *Accounts Receivable.*

Bank Credit Cards Retailers can provide credit while minimizing or avoiding the risk of losses from uncollectible accounts by accepting bank credit cards. The most widely accepted bank credit cards are MasterCard and Visa. Many banks participate in one or both of these credit card programs, and other banks have their own credit cards. Bank credit cards are issued to consumers directly by banks.

A business may participate in these credit card programs by meeting conditions set by the bank. Banks review such factors as:

- The business's financial history.
- The industry in which the business operates.
- The type of business, online, physical store, or both.
- Any past merchant account history.

When a sale is made to a cardholder, the sale is processed using a magnetic swipe machine (see Figure 7.13). Most businesses use an online credit card processing terminal. This type of terminal transmits information to the bank using an Internet connection.

When a business makes a sale to a customer using a bank credit card, it acquires an asset that can be converted into cash immediately without responsibility for later collection from the customer. In most cases, the bank deposits the cash from the sale into the business's bank account the same day.

Banks charge the business a fee, called a *discount,* for processing the sale. The discount is usually between 1.5 and 4 percent of the amount charged. Depending on the arrangements that have been made, the bank will deduct the discount and immediately credit the depositor's checking account with the net amount of the sale, or it will credit the depositor's checking account for the full amount of the sale and deduct the discount at the end of the month. If the second procedure is used, the total discount for the month's sales will appear on the bank statement.

The bank is responsible for collecting from the cardholder. If any amounts are uncollectible, the bank sustains the loss. For the retailer, bank credit card sales are like cash sales. The accounting procedures for such sales are therefore quite similar to the accounting procedures

FIGURE 7.13

Credit Card Reader

```
                MAXX-OUT SPORTING GOODS
                       DALLAS, TX
        ******************************

        SWEATSUIT              $125.00
        SALES TAX              $10.00
        TOTAL                  $135.00
        NAME :
        CONNORS/JAMES
        TYPE :
        PURCHASED             SWIPED
        VISTA
        **********222
        INVOICE #          08789798234
        AUTH CODE :              12345
        DATE :                01/28/16
        TIME                     17:02


        James Connors
        Signature :
```

FIGURE 7.14

Credit Card Receipt

for cash sales, which will be discussed in Chapter 9. If the business is billed once each month for the bank's discount, the total amount involved in the daily deposit of the credit card sales slips is debited to **Cash** and credited to **Sales.**

Credit Card Companies Credit cards such as American Express and Diners Club are issued by business firms or subsidiaries of business firms that are operated for the special purpose of handling credit card transactions. The potential cardholder must submit an application and pay an annual fee to the credit card company. If the credit references are satisfactory, the credit card is issued. It is normally reissued at one-year intervals so long as the company's credit experience with the cardholder remains satisfactory.

Hotels, restaurants, airline companies, many types of retail stores, and a wide variety of other businesses accept these credit cards. When making sales to cardholders, sellers usually prepare their own sales slip or bill and then complete a special sales slip required by the credit card company (see Figure 7.14). As with the sales slips for bank credit cards, the forms must be imprinted with the identifying data on the customer's card and signed by the customer. Such sales slips are sometimes referred to as *sales invoices, sales drafts,* or *sales vouchers.* The term used varies from one credit card company to another.

The seller acquires an account receivable from the credit card company rather than from the customer. At approximately one-month intervals, the credit card company bills the cardholders for all sales slips it has acquired during the period. It is the responsibility of the credit card company to collect from the cardholders.

>> **7-8. OBJECTIVE**

Record credit card sales in appropriate journals.

ACCOUNTING FOR CREDIT CARD SALES

The procedure used to account for credit card sales is similar to the procedure for recording open-account credit sales. However, the account receivable is with the credit card company, not with the cardholders who buy the goods or services.

There are two basic methods of recording these sales. Businesses that have few transactions with credit card companies normally debit the amounts of such sales to the usual **Accounts Receivable** account in the general ledger and credit them to the same **Sales** account that is used for cash sales and other types of credit sales. An individual account for each credit card company is set up in the accounts receivable subsidiary ledger. This method of recording sales is shown in Figure 7.15.

Payment from a credit card company is recorded in the cash receipts journal, a procedure discussed in Chapter 9. Fees charged by the credit card companies for processing these sales are debited to an account called **Discount Expense on Credit Card Sales.** For example, assume that American Express charges a 7 percent discount fee on the sale charged by Wilson Davis on January 3 and remits the balance to the firm. This transaction would be recorded in the cash receipts journal by debiting **Cash** for $502.20, debiting **Discount Expense on Credit Card Sales** for $37.80, and crediting **Accounts Receivable** for $540.00.

Firms that do a large volume of business with credit card companies may debit all such sales to a special **Accounts Receivable from Credit Card Companies** account in the general ledger, thus separating this type of receivable from the accounts receivable resulting from open-account credit sales. A special account called **Sales—Credit Card Companies** is credited for the revenue from these transactions. Figure 7.16 shows how the necessary entries are made in the sales journal.

FIGURE 7.15

Recording Credit Card Company Sales

SALES JOURNAL   PAGE 17

	DATE	SALES SLIP NO.	CUSTOMER'S ACCOUNT DEBITED	POST. REF.	ACCOUNTS RECEIVABLE DEBIT	SALES TAX PAYABLE CREDIT	SALES CREDIT	
1	2016							1
2	Jan. 3	533	American Express		540 00	40 00	500 00	2
3			(Wilson Davis)					3
26	11	651	MasterCard		216 00	16 00	200 00	26
27			(Teresa Logan)					27
28								28

FIGURE 7.16   Recording Sales for Accounts Receivable from Credit Card Companies

SALES JOURNAL   PAGE 7

	DATE	SALES SLIP NO.	CUSTOMER'S ACCOUNT DEBITED	POST. REF.	ACCOUNTS RECEIVABLE DEBIT	ACCT. REC.—CREDIT CARD COMPANIES DEBIT	SALES TAX PAYABLE CREDIT	SALES CREDIT	SALES—CREDIT CARD COMPANIES CREDIT	
1	2016									1
2	Jan. 3		Summary of credit card sales/			9 720 00	720 00		9 000 00	2
3			American Express							3
5										5
16	11		Summary of credit card sales/			5 400 00	400 00		5 000 00	16
17			MasterCard							17
29	31		Totals			48 600 00	3 600 00		45 000 00	29
30						(114)	(231)		(404)	30
31										31

Sales Taxes

Many cities and states impose a tax on retail sales. Sales taxes imposed by city and state governments vary. However, the procedures used to account for these taxes are similar.

A sales tax may be levied on all retail sales, but often certain items are exempt. In most cases, the amount of the sales tax is stated separately and then added to the retail price of the merchandise.

> In November 2012, California voters approved an initiative to raise the state sales tax by .25%.

The retailer is required to collect sales tax from customers, make periodic (usually monthly) reports to the taxing authority, and pay the taxes due when the reports are filed. The government may allow the retailer to retain part of the tax as compensation for collecting it.

PREPARING THE STATE SALES TAX RETURN

>> 7-9. OBJECTIVE
Prepare the state sales tax return.

At the end of each month, after the accounts have all been posted, Maxx-Out Sporting Goods prepares the sales tax return. The information required for the monthly return comes from the accounting data of the current month. Three accounts are involved: *Sales Tax Payable, Sales,* and *Sales Returns and Allowances.* In some states, the sales tax return is filed quarterly rather than monthly.

The procedures to file a sales tax return are similar to those used by Maxx-Out Sporting Goods on February 7 when it filed the monthly sales tax return for January with the state tax commissioner. The firm's sales are subject to an 8 percent state sales tax. To highlight the data needed, the January postings are shown in the ledger accounts in Figure 7.17.

FIGURE 7.17

Ledger Account Postings for Sales Tax

ACCOUNT Sales Tax Payable   ACCOUNT NO. 231

DATE	DESCRIPTION	POST. REF.	DEBIT	CREDIT	BALANCE DEBIT	BALANCE CREDIT
2016						
Jan. 1	Balance	✓				756 00
11		CP1	756 00			—0—
23		J1	12 00		12 00	
25		J1	36 00		48 00	
31		S1		456 00		408 00
31		CR1		1800 00		2208 00

ACCOUNT Sales   ACCOUNT NO. 401

DATE	DESCRIPTION	POST. REF.	DEBIT	CREDIT	BALANCE DEBIT	BALANCE CREDIT
2016						
Jan. 31		S1		5700 00		5700 00
31		CR1		22500 00		28200 00

ACCOUNT Sales Returns and Allowances   ACCOUNT NO. 451

DATE	DESCRIPTION	POST. REF.	DEBIT	CREDIT	BALANCE DEBIT	BALANCE CREDIT
2016						
Jan. 23		J1	150 00		150 00	
25		J1	450 00		600 00	

Using these figures as a basis, the amount of the firm's taxable gross sales for January is determined as follows:

Cash Sales	$22,500
Credit Sales	5,700
Total Sales	$28,200
Less Sales Returns and Allowances	600
Taxable Gross Sales for January	$27,600

> THE BOTTOM LINE
> **Retail Sales**
>
> **Income Statement**
>
> | | | |
> |---|---|---:|
> | Revenue | ↑ | 27,600 |
> | Net Income | ↑ | 27,600 |
>
> **Balance Sheet**
>
> | | | |
> |---|---|---:|
> | Assets | ↑ | 29,808.00 |
> | Liabilities | ↑ | 2,208.00 |
> | Equity | ↑ | 27,600.00 |

> > The 8 percent sales tax on the gross sales of $27,600 amounts to $2,208.00. Note that the firm's increase in assets (**Cash** and **Accounts Receivable**) is equal to sales revenue plus the sales tax liability on that revenue.

In the state where Maxx-Out Sporting Goods is located, a retailer who files the sales tax return (see Figure 7.19 on the next page) on time and who pays the tax when it is due is entitled to a discount. The discount is intended to compensate the retailer, at least in part, for acting as a collection agent for the government. The discount rate depends on the amount of tax to be paid. For amounts over $1,000, the rate is 1 percent of the total tax due. For Maxx-Out Sporting Goods, the discount for January is determined as follows:

Taxable Gross Sales for January	$27,600.00
8% Sales Tax Rate	× 0.08
Sales Tax Due	$ 2,208.00
1% Discount Rate	× 0.01
Discount	$22.08
Sales Tax Due	$ 2,208.00
Discount	(22.08)
Net Sales Tax Due	$ 2,185.92

The firm sends a check for the net sales tax due with the sales tax return. The accounting entry made to record this payment includes a debit to **Sales Tax Payable** and a credit to **Cash** (for $2,185.92 in this case). After the amount of the payment is posted, the balance in the **Sales Tax Payable** account should be equal to the discount, as shown in Figure 7.18. Slight differences can arise because the tax collected at the time of the sale is determined by a tax bracket method that can give results slightly more or less than the final computations on the tax return.

FIGURE 7.18

Effect of Paying Sales Tax

ACCOUNT _Sales Tax Payable_ ACCOUNT NO. _231_

DATE		DESCRIPTION	POST. REF.	DEBIT	CREDIT	BALANCE DEBIT	BALANCE CREDIT
2016							
Jan.	1	Balance	✓				7 5 6 00
	11		CP1	7 5 6 00			—0—
	23		J1	1 2 00		1 2 00	
	25		J1	3 6 00		4 8 00	
	31		S1		4 5 6 00		4 0 8 00
	31		CR1		1 8 0 0 00		2 2 0 8 00
Feb.	6		CP1	2 1 8 5 92			2 2 08

Tax payment ⟶

Amount of discount ⟶

FIGURE 7.19

State Sales Tax Return

SALES TAX RETURN

	LICENSE NUMBER
ALWAYS REFER TO THIS NUMBER WHEN WRITING THE DIVISION →	217539

—IMPORTANT—
ANY CHANGE IN OWNERSHIP REQUIRES A NEW LICENSE: NOTIFY THIS DIVISION IMMEDIATELY.

This return DUE on the 1st day of month following period covered by the return, and becomes DELINQUENT on the 21st day.

37-9462315
FED. E.I. NO. OR S.S NO.

STATE TAX COMMISSION
SALES AND USE TAX DIVISION
DRAWER 20
CAPITAL CITY, STATE 78711
RETURN REQUESTED

January 31, 2016
—Sales for period ending—

MAKE ALL REMITTANCES PAYABLE TO
STATE TAX COMMISSIOIN
DO NOT SEND CASH
STAMPS NOT ACCEPTED

OWNER'S NAME AND LOCATION

Maxx-Out Sporting Goods
2007 Trendsetter Lane
Dallas, Texas 75268-0967

COMPUTATION OF SALES TAX	For Taxpayer's Use	Do Not Use This Column
1. TOTAL Gross proceeds of sales or Gross Receipts (to include rentals)	27,600.00	
2. Add cost of personal property purchased on a RETAIL LICENSE FOR RESALE but USED BY YOU or YOUR EMPLOYEES, including GIFTS and PREMIUMS	–0–	
3. USE TAX—Add cost of personal property purchased outside of STATE for your use, storage, or consumption	–0–	
4. Total (Lines 1, 2, and 3)	27,600.00	
5. LESS ALLOWABLE DEDUCTIONS (Must be itemized on reverse side)	–0–	
6. Net taxable total (Line 4 minus Line 5)	27,600.00	
7. Sales and Use Tax Due (8% of Line 6)	2,208.00	
8. LESS TAXPAYER'S DISCOUNT—(Deductible only when amount of TAX due is not delinquent at time of payment)	22.08	
IF LINE 7 IS LESS THAN $100.00 —DEDUCT 3% IF LINE 7 IS $100 BUT LESS THAN $1,000.00 —DEDUCT 2% IF LINE 7 IS $1,000.00 OR MORE —DEDUCT 1%		
9. NET AMOUNT OF TAX PAYABLE (Line 7 minus Line 8)	2,185.92	
Add the following penalty and interest if return or remittance is late. 10. Specific Penalty: 25% of tax _____ $_____ 11. Interest: 1/2 of 1% per month from due date until paid. $_____ TOTAL PENALTY AND INTEREST		
12. TOTAL TAX, PENALTY AND INTEREST	2,185.92	
13. Subtract credit memo No.		
14. TOTAL AMOUNT DUE (IF NO SALES MADE SO STATE)	2,185.92	

I certify that this return, including the accompanying schedules or statements, has been examined by me and to the best of my knowledge and belief, a true and complete return, made in good faith, for the period stated, pursuant to the provisions of the Code of Laws, 20–, and Acts Amendatory Thereto.

URGENT—SEE THAT LICENSE NUMBER IS ON RETURN

Max Ferraro
SIGNATURE

Division Use Only

Owner   February 7, 2016
Owner, partner or title   Date

Return must be signed by owner or if corporation, authorized person.

If there is a balance in the **Sales Tax Payable** account after the sales tax liability is satisfied, the balance is transferred to an account called **Miscellaneous Income** by a general journal entry. This entry consists of a debit to **Sales Tax Payable** and a credit to **Miscellaneous Income**.

RECORDING SALES TAX IN THE SALES ACCOUNT

In some states, retailers can credit the entire sales price plus tax to the **Sales** account. At the end of each month or quarter, they must remove from the **Sales** account the amount of tax included and transfer that amount to the **Sales Tax Payable** account. Assume that during January a retailer whose sales are all taxable sells merchandise for a total price of $20,250, which includes an 8 percent tax. The entry to record these sales is summarized in general journal form shown here.

		GENERAL JOURNAL				PAGE ___4___
	DATE	DESCRIPTION	POST. REF.	DEBIT	CREDIT	
1	2016					1
2	Jan. 31	Accounts Receivable	111	20 2 5 0 00		2
3		Sales	401		20 2 5 0 00	3
4		To record total sales and				4
5		sales tax collected during				5
6		the month				6
7						7

At the end of the month, the retailer must transfer the sales tax from the **Sales** account to the **Sales Tax Payable** account. The first step in the transfer process is to determine the amount of tax involved. The sales tax payable is computed as follows on the next page.

MANAGERIAL IMPLICATIONS <<

CREDIT SALES

- Credit sales are a major source of revenue in many businesses, and accounts receivable represent a major asset.
- Management needs up-to-date and correct information about both sales and accounts receivable in order to monitor the financial health of the firm.
- Special journals save time and effort and reduce the cost of accounting work.
- In a retail firm that must handle sales tax, the sales journal and the cash receipts journal provide a convenient method of recording the amounts owed for sales tax.
  - When the data is posted to the Sales Tax Payable account in the general ledger, the firm has a complete and systematic record that speeds the completion of the periodic sales tax return.
  - The firm has detailed proof of its sales tax figures in the case of a tax audit.
- An accounts receivable subsidiary ledger provides management and the credit department with up-to-date information about the balances owed by all customers.
  - This information is useful in controlling credit and collections.

- Detailed information helps in evaluating the effectiveness of credit policies.
- Management must keep a close watch on the promptness of customer payments because much of the cash needed for day-to-day operations usually comes from payments on accounts receivable.
- A well-balanced credit policy helps increase sales volume but also keeps losses from uncollectible accounts at an acceptable level.
- Retailers are liable for any undercollection of sales taxes. This situation can be avoided with an efficient control system.

THINKING CRITICALLY

What are some possible consequences of out-of-date accounts receivable records?

Sales + tax	= $20,250
100% of sales + 8% of sales	= $20,250
108% of sales	= $20,250
Sales	= $20,250/1.08
Sales	= $18,750
Tax	= $18,750 × 0.08 = $1,500

The firm then makes the following entry to transfer the liability from the *Sales* account.

	GENERAL JOURNAL					PAGE ___4___		
	DATE	DESCRIPTION	POST. REF.	DEBIT		CREDIT		
1	2016							1
8	Jan. 31	Sales	401	1 5 0 0 00				8
9		Sales Tax Payable	231			1 5 0 0 00		9
10		To transfer sales tax						10
11		payable from the Sales						11
12		account to the liability						12
13		account						13
14								14
15								15

The retailer in this example originally recorded the entire sales price plus tax in the *Sales* account. The sales tax was transferred to the *Sales Tax Payable* account at the end of the month.

Section 3   Self Review

QUESTIONS

1. What are four types of credit sales?

2. What is the difference between list price and net price?

3. What account is used to record sales tax owed by a business to a city or state?

EXERCISES

4. A company that buys $4,000 of goods from a wholesaler offering trade discounts of 20 and 10 percent will pay what amount for the goods?

   a. $1,760
   b. $2,800
   c. $2,880
   d. $2,780

5. If a wholesale business offers a trade discount of 35 percent on a sale of $7,200, what is the amount of the discount?

   a. $240
   b. $252
   c. $2,400
   d. $2,520

ANALYSIS

6. What factors would you consider in deciding whether or not to extend credit to a customer?

(Answers to Section 3 Self Review are on page 233.)

7 Chapter REVIEW Chapter Summary

The nature of the operations of a business, the volume of its transactions, and other factors influence the design of an accounting system. In this chapter, you have learned about the use of special journals and subsidiary ledgers suitable for a merchandising business. These additional journals and ledgers increase the efficiency of recording credit transactions and permit the division of labor.

Learning Objectives

7-1 Record credit sales in a sales journal.

The sales journal is used to record credit sales transactions, usually on a daily basis. For sales transactions that include sales tax, the sales tax liability is recorded at the time of the sale to ensure that company records reflect the appropriate amount of sales tax liability.

7-2 Post from the sales journal to the general ledger accounts.

At the end of each month, the sales journal is totaled, proved, and ruled. Column totals are then posted to the general ledger. Using a sales journal rather than a general journal to record sales saves the time and effort of posting individual entries to the general ledger during the month.

7-3 Post from the sales journal to the customers' accounts in the accounts receivable subsidiary ledger.

The accounts of individual credit customers are kept in a subsidiary ledger called the accounts receivable ledger. Daily postings are made to this ledger from the sales journal, the cash receipts journal, and the general journal or the sales returns and allowances journal. The current balance of a customer's account is computed after each posting so that the amount owed is known at all times.

7-4 Record sales returns and allowances in the general journal.

Sales returns and allowances are usually debited to a contra revenue account. A firm with relatively few sales returns and allowances could use the general journal to record these transactions.

7-5 Post sales returns and allowances.

Sales returns and allowances transactions must be posted to the general ledger and to the appropriate accounts receivable subsidiary ledgers. The balance of the *Sales Returns and Allowances* account is subtracted from the balance of the *Sales* account to show net sales on the income statement.

7-6 Prepare a schedule of accounts receivable.

Each month a schedule of accounts receivable is prepared. It is used to prove the subsidiary ledger against the *Accounts Receivable* account. It also reports the amounts due from credit customers.

7-7 Compute trade discounts.

Wholesale businesses often offer goods to trade customers at less than retail prices. Trade discounts are expressed as a percentage off the list price. Multiply the list price by the percentage trade discount offered to compute the dollar amount.

7-8 Record credit card sales in appropriate journals.

Credit sales are common, and different credit arrangements are used. Businesses that have few transactions with credit card companies normally record these transactions in the sales journal by debiting the usual *Accounts Receivable* account in the general ledger and crediting the same *Sales* account that is used for cash sales.

7-9 Prepare the state sales tax return.

In states and cities that have a sales tax, the retailer must prepare a sales tax return and send the total tax collected to the taxing authority.

7-10 Define the accounting terms new to this chapter.

Glossary

Accounts receivable ledger (p. 197) A subsidiary ledger that contains credit customer accounts

Charge-account sales (p. 208) Sales made through the use of open-account credit or one of various types of credit cards

Contra revenue account (p. 199) An account with a debit balance, which is contrary to the normal balance for a revenue account

Control account (p. 203) An account that links a subsidiary ledger and the general ledger since its balance summarizes the balances of the accounts in the subsidiary ledger

Credit memorandum (p. 198) A note verifying that a customer's account is being reduced by the amount of a sales return or sales allowance plus any sales tax that may have been involved

Invoice (p. 206) A customer billing for merchandise bought on credit

List price (p. 205) An established retail price

Manufacturing business (p. 190) A business that sells goods that it has produced

Merchandise inventory (p. 190) The stock of goods a merchandising business keeps on hand

Merchandising business (p. 190) A business that sells goods purchased for resale

Net price (p. 205) The list price less all trade discounts

Net sales (p. 201) The difference between the balance in the *Sales* account and the balance in the *Sales Returns and Allowances* account

Open-account credit (p. 208) A system that allows the sale of services or goods with the understanding that payment will be made at a later date

Retail business (p. 190) A business that sells directly to individual consumers

Sales allowance (p. 198) A reduction in the price originally charged to customers for goods or services

Sales journal (p. 190) A special journal used to record sales of merchandise on credit

Sales return (p. 198) A firm's acceptance of a return of goods from a customer

Sales Returns and Allowances (p. 199) A contra revenue account where sales returns and sales allowances are recorded; sales returns and allowances are subtracted from sales to determine net sales

Schedule of accounts receivable (p. 203) A listing of all balances of the accounts in the accounts receivable subsidiary ledger

Service business (p. 190) A business that sells services

Special journal (p. 190) A journal used to record only one type of transaction

Subsidiary ledger (p. 190) A ledger dedicated to accounts of a single type and showing details to support a general ledger account

Trade discount (p. 205) A reduction from list price

Wholesale business (p. 205) A business that manufactures or distributes goods to retail businesses or large consumers such as hotels and hospitals

Comprehensive **Self Review**

1. Name the two different time periods usually covered in sales tax returns.
2. What is a control account?
3. Why does a small merchandising business usually need a more complex set of financial records and statements than a small service business?
4. Why is it useful for a firm to have an accounts receivable ledger?
5. Explain how service, merchandising, and manufacturing businesses differ from each other.

(Answers to Comprehensive Self Review are on page 234.)

Discussion **Questions**

1. How are the net sales for an accounting period determined?
2. What purposes does the schedule of accounts receivable serve?
3. How do retail and wholesale businesses differ?

4. Why is a sales return or allowance usually recorded in a special *Sales Returns and Allowances* account rather than being debited to the *Sales* account?

5. How is a multicolumn special journal proved at the end of each month?

6. What kind of account is *Sales Returns and Allowances?*

7. The sales tax on a credit sale is not collected from the customer immediately. When is this tax usually entered in a firm's accounting records? What account is used to record this tax?

8. In a particular state, the sales tax rate is 5 percent of sales. The retailer is allowed to record both the selling price and the tax in the same account. Explain how to compute the sales tax due when this method is used.

9. What two methods are commonly used to record sales involving credit cards issued by credit card companies?

10. What procedure does a business use to collect amounts owed to it for sales on credit cards issued by credit card companies?

11. When a firm makes a sale involving a credit card issued by a credit card company, does the firm have an account receivable with the cardholder or with the credit card company?

12. What is the discount on credit card sales? What type of account is used to record this item?

13. Why are bank credit card sales similar to cash sales for a business?

14. What is open-account credit?

15. What is a trade discount? Why do some firms offer trade discounts to their customers?

APPLICATIONS

Exercises

Exercise 7.1	▶	**Identifying the journal to record transactions.**
Objective 7-1		The accounting system of Healthy Focus Natural Foods includes the journals listed below. Indicate the specific journal in which each of the transactions listed below would be recorded.

JOURNALS

Cash receipts journal	Sales journal	Purchases journal
Cash payments journal	General journal	

DATE		TRANSACTIONS
May	1	Sold merchandise on credit.
	2	Accepted a return of merchandise from a credit customer.
	3	Sold merchandise for cash.
	4	Purchased merchandise on credit.
	5	Gave a $400 allowance for damaged merchandise.
	6	Collected sums on account from credit customers.
	7	Received an additional cash investment from the owner.
	8	Issued a check to pay a creditor on account.

Identifying the accounts used to record sales and related transactions.

◄ **Exercise 7.2**
Objective 7-1

The transactions below took place at Outdoor Adventures, a retail business that sells outdoor clothing and camping equipment. Indicate the numbers of the general ledger accounts that would be debited and credited to record each transaction.

GENERAL LEDGER ACCOUNTS

101 Cash	401 Sales
111 Accounts Receivable	451 Sales Returns and Allowances
231 Sales Tax Payable	

DATE	TRANSACTIONS
May 1	Sold merchandise on credit; the transaction involved sales tax.
2	Received checks from credit customers on account.
3	Accepted a return of merchandise from a credit customer; the original sale involved sales tax.
4	Sold merchandise for cash; the transaction involved sales tax.
5	Gave an allowance to a credit customer for damaged merchandise; the original sale involved sales tax.
6	Provided a cash refund to a customer who returned merchandise; the original sale was made for cash and involved sales tax.

Recording credit sales.

◄ **Exercise 7.3**
Objective 7-2
CONTINUING >>>
Problem

The following transactions took place at Outdoor Adventures during May. Enter these transactions in a sales journal like the one shown in Figure 7.2. Use 18 as the page number for the sales journal.

DATE	TRANSACTIONS
May 1	Sold a tent and other items on credit to Justin Williams; issued Sales Slip 1101 for $550 plus sales tax of $44.
2	Sold a backpack, an air mattress, and other items to Diane Le; issued Sales Slip 1102 for $500 plus sales tax of $40.
3	Sold a lantern, cooking utensils, and other items to Richard Rodriguez; issued Sales Slip 1103 for $575 plus sales tax of $46.

Recording sales returns and allowances.

◄ **Exercise 7.4**
Objective 7-2

Record the general journal entries for the following transactions of Luxurious Linens that occurred in June. Use 15 as the page number for the general journal.

DATE	TRANSACTIONS
June 5	Accepted a return of damaged merchandise from Tiffany Monroe, a credit customer; issued Credit Memorandum 301 for $918, which includes sales tax of $68; the original sale was made on Sales Slip 1610 of May 31.
25	Gave an allowance to Brian Barnes, a credit customer, for merchandise that was slightly damaged but usable; issued Credit Memorandum 302 for $1,242, which includes sales tax of $92; the original sale was made on Sales Slip 1663 of June 17.

Exercise 7.5
Objective 7-2

▶ **Posting from the sales journal.**

The sales journal for Charleston Company is shown below. Describe how the amounts would be posted to the general ledger accounts.

	DATE		SALES SLIP NO.	CUSTOMER'S ACCOUNT DEBITED	POST. REF.	ACCOUNTS RECEIVABLE DEBIT	SALES TAX PAYABLE CREDIT	SALES CREDIT	
				SALES JOURNAL			PAGE ___ 1 ___		
1	2016								1
2	July	2	1101	Scott Cohen		540 00	40 00	500 00	2
3		7	1102	Julia Hoang		864 00	64 00	800 00	3
11		31	1110	Barbara Baxter		324 00	24 00	300 00	11
12		31		Totals		6 480 00	480 00	6 000 00	12
13						(111)	(231)	(401)	13
14									14

Exercise 7.6
Objective 7-7

▶ **Computing a trade discount.**

The Alpha Wholesale Company made sales using the following list prices and trade discounts. What amount will be recorded for each sale in the sales journal?

1. List price of $600 and trade discount of 10 percent
2. List price of $750 and trade discount of 20 percent
3. List price of $250 and trade discount of 30 percent

Exercise 7.7
Objective 7-7

▶ **Computing a series of trade discounts.**

Patio Dudes, a wholesale firm, made sales using the following list prices and trade discounts. What amount will be recorded for each sale in the sales journal?

1. List price of $6,250 and trade discounts of 20 and 12 percent
2. List price of $4,000 and trade discounts of 30 and 10 percent
3. List price of $2,500 and trade discounts of 20 and 5 percent

Exercise 7.8
Objective 7-9

▶ **Computing the sales tax due and recording its payment.**

The balances of certain accounts of Vanessa Corporation on April 30, 2016, were as follows:

Sales	$230,000
Sales Returns and Allowances	$ 4,000

The firm's net sales are subject to a 6 percent sales tax. Prepare the general journal entry to record payment of the sales tax payable on April 30, 2016.

Exercise 7.9
Objective 7-6

▶ **Preparing a schedule of accounts receivable.**

The accounts receivable ledger for The Old Country Barn follows on the next page.

1. Prepare a schedule of accounts receivable as of January 31, 2016.
2. What should the balance in the *Accounts Receivable* (control) account be?

Exercise 7.10
Objective 7-5

▶ **Posting sales returns and allowances.**

Post the journal entries on page 222 to the appropriate ledger accounts. Assume the following account balances as of March 1, 2016:

Accounts Receivable (control account)	$1,688
Accounts Receivable—Cara Fountain	940
Accounts Receivable—Sadie Palmer	748

NAME _Cheryl Amos_

ADDRESS _917 Broadway, New York, NY 10018_

DATE		DESCRIPTION	POST. REF.	DEBIT	CREDIT	BALANCE
2016						
Jan.	1	Balance	✓			1 5 7 5 00
	2	Sales Slip 1801	S1	5 4 0 00		2 1 1 5 00

NAME _Edward Cooke_

ADDRESS _2022 5th Avenue, New York, NY 10018_

DATE		DESCRIPTION	POST. REF.	DEBIT	CREDIT	BALANCE
2016						
Jan.	1	Balance	✓			3 7 8 00
	27	Sales Slip 1824	S1	1 8 9 00		5 6 7 00
	31		CR1		2 8 4 00	2 8 3 00

NAME _Neal Fitzgerald_

ADDRESS _98 Houston Street, New York, NY 10018_

DATE		DESCRIPTION	POST. REF.	DEBIT	CREDIT	BALANCE
2016						
Jan.	1	Balance	✓			3 2 4 00
	15	Sales Slip 1812	CR1		3 2 4 00	—0—
	31		S1	7 5 6 00		7 5 6 00

NAME _David Pifer_

ADDRESS _5063 Park Avenue, New York, NY 10019_

DATE		DESCRIPTION	POST. REF.	DEBIT	CREDIT	BALANCE
2016						
Jan.	1	Balance	✓			6 4 8 00
	20	Sales Slip 1819	S1	2 1 6 00		8 6 4 00
	21		CR1		4 5 0 00	4 1 4 00
	22	Sales Slip 1822	S1	8 1 0 00		1 2 2 4 00

NAME _Lisa Stanton_

ADDRESS _2111 West 32nd Street, New York, NY 10019_

DATE		DESCRIPTION	POST. REF.	DEBIT	CREDIT	BALANCE
2016						
Jan.	1	Balance	✓			4 8 6 00
	31	Sales Slip 1840	S1	2 2 1 4 00		2 7 0 0 00

NAME _Nikki Whitaker_

ADDRESS _721 Lexington Avenue, New York, NY 10027_

DATE		DESCRIPTION	POST. REF.	DEBIT	CREDIT	BALANCE
2016						
Jan.	1	Balance	✓			2 3 7 6 00
	12		CR1		1 1 8 8 00	1 1 8 8 00
	17	Sales Slip 1817	S1	8 6 4 00		2 0 5 2 00

			GENERAL JOURNAL								PAGE ___42___			
	DATE		DESCRIPTION	POST. REF.	DEBIT			CREDIT						
1	2016													1
2	Mar.	14	Sales Returns and Allowances		3 0 0	00							2
3			Sales Tax Payable		2 4	00							3
4			Accounts Rec.—Cara Fountain					3 2 4	00				4
5			Accepted return on defective										5
6			merchandise, Credit Memo										6
7			101; original sale of Feb. 23,										7
8			Sales Slip 1101										8
9													9
10		22	Sales Returns and Allowances		1 0 0	00							10
11			Sales Tax Payable		8	00							11
12			Accounts Rec.—Sadie Palmer					1 0 8	00				12
13			Gave allowance for damaged										13
14			merchandise, Credit Memo										14
15			102; original sale Mar. 15,										15
16			Sales Slip 1150										16

PROBLEMS

Problem Set A

Problem 7.1A

Objectives 7-1, 7-2

Sage 50
Complete Accounting

► Recording credit sales and posting from the sales journal.

Best Appliances is a retail store that sells household appliances. Merchandise sales are subject to an 8 percent sales tax. The firm's credit sales for July are listed below, along with the general ledger accounts used to record these sales. The balance shown for **Accounts Receivable** is for the beginning of the month.

DATE		TRANSACTIONS
July	1	Sold a dishwasher to Perry Martin; issued Sales Slip 501 for $1,150 plus sales tax of $92.
	6	Sold a washer to Cindy Han; issued Sales Slip 502 for $2,425 plus sales tax of $194.
	11	Sold a high-definition television set to Richard Slocomb; issued Sales Slip 503 for $2,600 plus sales tax of $208.
	17	Sold an electric dryer to Mary Schneider; issued Sales Slip 504 for $1,275 plus sales tax of $102.
	23	Sold a trash compactor to Veronica Velazquez; issued Sales Slip 505 for $900 plus sales tax of $72.
	27	Sold a color television set to Jeff Budd; issued Sales Slip 506 for $1,725 plus sales tax of $138.
	29	Sold an electric range to Michelle Ly; issued Sales Slip 507 for $1,450 plus sales tax of $116.
	31	Sold a double oven to Phil Long; issued Sales Slip 508 for $625 plus sales tax of $50.

INSTRUCTIONS

1. Open the general ledger accounts and enter the balance of **Accounts Receivable** for July 1, 2016.
2. Record the transactions in a sales journal like the one shown in Figure 7.4. Use 8 as the journal page number.

3. Total, prove, and rule the sales journal as of July 31.

4. Post the column totals from the sales journal to the proper general ledger accounts.

GENERAL LEDGER ACCOUNTS

111   Accounts Receivable, $34,500 Dr.

231   Sales Tax Payable

401   Sales

Analyze: What percentage of credit sales were for entertainment items?

Journalizing, posting, and reporting sales transactions.

◄ **Problem 7.2A**
Objectives 7-1,
7-2, 7-4

Sage 50
Complete Accounting

Towncenter Furniture specializes in modern living room and dining room furniture. Merchandise sales are subject to an 8 percent sales tax. The firm's credit sales and sales returns and allowances for February 2016 are reflected below, along with the general ledger accounts used to record these transactions. The balances shown are for the beginning of the month.

DATE		TRANSACTIONS
Feb.	1	Sold a living room sofa to Sun Yoo; issued Sales Slip 1615 for $4,790 plus sales tax of $383.20.
	5	Sold three recliners to Jacqueline Moore; issued Sales Slip 1616 for $2,350 plus sales tax of $188.
	9	Sold a dining room set to Hazel Tran; issued Sales Slip 1617 for $6,550 plus sales tax of $524.
	11	Accepted a return of one damaged recliner from Jacqueline Moore that was originally sold on Sales Slip 1616 of February 5; issued Credit Memorandum 702 for $1,026, which includes sales tax of $76.00.
	17	Sold living room tables and bookcases to Ann Brown; issued Sales Slip 1618 for $9,550 plus sales tax of $764.
	23	Sold eight dining room chairs to Domingo Salas; issued Sales Slip 1619 for $3,650 plus sales tax of $292.
	25	Gave Ann Brown an allowance for scratches on her bookcases; issued Credit Memorandum 703 for $702, which includes sales taxes of $52; the bookcases were originally sold on Sales Slip 1618 of February 17.
	27	Sold a living room sofa and four chairs to Jose Saucedo; issued Sales Slip 1620 for $4,225 plus sales tax of $338.
	28	Sold a dining room table to Mimi Yuki; issued Sales Slip 1621 for $2,050 plus sales tax of $164.
	28	Sold a living room modular wall unit to Alan Baker; issued Sales Slip 1622 for $3,900 plus sales tax of $312.

INSTRUCTIONS

1. Open the general ledger accounts and enter the balances for February 1.

2. Record the transactions in a sales journal and in a general journal. Use 8 as the page number for the sales journal and 24 as the page number for the general journal.

3. Post the entries from the general journal to the general ledger.

4. Total, prove, and rule the sales journal as of February 28.

5. Post the column totals from the sales journal.

6. Prepare the heading and the Revenue section of the firm's income statement for the month ended February 28, 2016.

GENERAL LEDGER ACCOUNTS

111 Accounts Receivable, $16,636 Dr.

231 Sales Tax Payable, $7,270 Cr.

401 Sales

451 Sales Returns and Allowances

Analyze: Based on the beginning balance of the *Sales Tax Payable* account, what was the amount of net sales for January? (Hint: Sales tax returns are filed and paid to the state quarterly.)

Problem 7.3A

Objectives 7-1, 7-2, 7-3, 7-4, 7-6

▶ **Recording sales transactions, posting to the accounts receivable ledger, and preparing a schedule of accounts receivable.**

The Elegant Table sells china, glassware, and other gift items that are subject to an 8 percent sales tax. The shop uses a general journal and a sales journal similar to those illustrated in this chapter.

DATE		TRANSACTIONS
Nov.	1	Sold china to Pauline Judge; issued Sales Slip 1001 for $1,750 plus $140 sales tax.
	5	Sold a brass serving tray to Janet Hutchison; issued Sales Slip 1002 for $2,350 plus $188 sales tax.
	6	Sold a vase to Charles Brown; issued Sales Slip 1003 for $950 plus $76 sales tax.
	10	Sold a punch bowl and glasses to Lisa Morgan; issued Sales Slip 1004 for $1,950 plus $156 sales tax.
	14	Sold a set of serving bowls to Dorothy Watts; issued Sales Slip 1005 for $800 plus $64 sales tax.
	17	Gave Lisa Morgan an allowance because of a broken glass discovered when unpacking the punch bowl and glasses sold on November 10, Sales Slip 1004; issued Credit Memorandum 102 for $162.00, which includes sales tax of $12.
	21	Sold a coffee table to Teresa Yu; issued Sales Slip 1006 for $3,450 plus $276 sales tax.
	24	Sold sterling silver teaspoons to Henry Okafor; issued Sales Slip 1007 for $850 plus $68 sales tax.
	25	Gave Teresa Yu an allowance for scratches on her coffee table sold on November 21, Sales Slip 1006; issued Credit Memorandum 103 for $378, which includes $28 in sales tax.
	30	Sold a clock to Elaine Brock; issued Sales Slip 1008 for $4,050 plus $324 sales tax.

INSTRUCTIONS

1. Record the transactions for November in the proper journal. Use 6 as the page number for the sales journal and 16 as the page number for the general journal.

2. Immediately after recording each transaction, post to the accounts receivable ledger.

3. Post the amounts from the general journal daily. Post the sales journal amount as a total at the end of the month.

4. Prepare a schedule of accounts receivable. Compare the balance of the *Accounts Receivable* control account with the total of the schedule.

Analyze: Which customer has the highest balance owed at November 30, 2016?

Recording sales transactions, posting to the accounts receivable ledger, and preparing a schedule of accounts receivable.

◀ **Problem 7.4A**
Objectives 7-1, 7-2, 7-3, 7-4, 7-6

Sage 50
Complete Accounting

Bella Floral Designs is a wholesale shop that sells flowers, plants, and plant supplies. The transactions shown below took place during January.

DATE	TRANSACTIONS
Jan. 3	Sold a floral arrangement to Thomas Florist; issued Invoice 1081 for $600.
8	Sold potted plants to Carter Garden Supply; issued Invoice 1082 for $825.
9	Sold floral arrangements to Thomasville Flower Shop; issued Invoice 1083 for $482.
10	Sold corsages to Moore's Flower Shop; issued Invoice 1084 for $630.
15	Gave Thomasville Flower Shop an allowance because of withered blossoms discovered in one of the floral arrangements sold on Invoice 1083 on January 9; issued Credit Memorandum 101 for $60.
20	Sold table arrangements to Cedar Hill Floral Shop; issued Invoice 1085 for $580.
22	Sold plants to Applegate Nursery; issued Invoice 1086 for $780.
25	Sold roses to Moore's Flower Shop; issued Invoice 1087 for $437.
27	Sold several floral arrangements to Thomas Florist; issued Invoice 1088 for $975.
31	Gave Thomas Florist an allowance because of withered blossoms discovered in one of the floral arrangements sold on Invoice 1088 on January 27; issued Credit Memorandum 102 for $200.

INSTRUCTIONS

1. Record the transactions in the proper journal. Use 7 as the page number for the sales journal and 11 as the page number for the general journal.

2. Immediately after recording each transaction, post to the accounts receivable ledger.

3. Post the amounts from the general journal daily. Post the sales journal amount as a total at the end of the month.

4. Prepare a schedule of accounts receivable. Compare the balance of the *Accounts Receivable* control account with the total of the schedule.

Analyze: Damaged goods decreased sales by what dollar amount? By what percentage amount?

Problem Set B

Recording credit sales and posting from the sales journal.

◀ **Problem 7.1B**
Objectives 7-1, 7-2

J&J Appliances is a retail store that sells household appliances. Merchandise sales are subject to an 8 percent sales tax. The firm's credit sales for June are listed below Instruction 4, along with the general ledger accounts used to record these sales. The balance shown for Accounts Receivable is for the beginning of the month.

INSTRUCTIONS

1. Open the general ledger accounts and enter the balance of *Accounts Receivable* for June 1.

2. Record the transactions in a sales journal like the one shown in Figure 7.4. Use 8 as the journal page number.

3. Total, prove, and rule the sales journal as of June 30.

4. Post the column totals from the sales journal to the proper general ledger accounts.

DATE		TRANSACTIONS
June	1	Sold a dishwasher to Omar Aslam; issued Sales Slip 201 for $2,100 plus sales tax of $168.
	6	Sold a washer to Gilbert Gomez; issued Sales Slip 202 for $925 plus sales tax of $74.
	11	Sold a high-definition television set to Tyrone Jones; issued Sales Slip 203 for $3,000 plus sales tax of $240.
	17	Sold an electric dryer to Betty Odom; issued Sales Slip 204 for $850 plus sales tax of $68.
	23	Sold a trash compactor to Evie Young; issued Sales Slip 205 for $500 plus sales tax of $40.
	27	Sold a portable color television set to Joon Yi; issued Sales Slip 206 for $1,200 plus sales tax of $96.
	29	Sold an electric range to Ty Long; issued Sales Slip 207 for $1,325 plus sales tax of $106.
	30	Sold a microwave oven to Sophia Castro; issued Sales Slip 208 for $250 plus sales tax of $20.

GENERAL LEDGER ACCOUNTS

111   Accounts Receivable, $83,000 Dr.

231   Sales Tax Payable

401   Sales

Analyze: What percentage of sales were for entertainment items?

Problem 7.2B

Objectives 7-1, 7-2, 7-4

▶ Journalizing, posting, and reporting sales transactions.

The Furniture Lot is a retail store that specializes in modern living room and dining room furniture. Merchandise sales are subject to an 8 percent sales tax. The firm's credit sales and sales returns and allowances for June are reflected below, along with the general ledger accounts used to record these transactions. The balances shown are for the beginning of the month.

INSTRUCTIONS

1. Open the general ledger accounts and enter the balances for June 1.

2. Record the transactions in a sales journal and a general journal. Use 9 as the page number for the sales journal and 26 as the page number for the general journal.

3. Post the entries from the general journal to the general ledger.

4. Total, prove, and rule the sales journal as of June 30.

5. Post the column totals from the sales journal.

6. Prepare the heading and the Revenue section of the firm's income statement for the month ended June 30, 2016.

GENERAL LEDGER ACCOUNTS

111   Accounts Receivable, $24,150 Dr.

231   Sales Tax Payable, $4,515 Cr.

401   Sales

451   Sales Returns and Allowances

DATE		TRANSACTIONS
June	1	Sold a living room sofa to Kenya Jackson; issued Sales Slip 1601 for $2,525 plus sales tax of $202.
	5	Sold three recliners to Carmen Cruz; issued Sales Slip 1602 for $1,500 plus sales tax of $120.
	9	Sold a dining room set to Lu Chang; issued Sales Slip 1603 for $6,025 plus sales tax of $482.
	11	Accepted a return of a damaged chair from Carmen Cruz; the chair was originally sold on Sales Slip 1602 of June 5; issued Credit Memorandum 215 for $540, which includes sales tax of $40.
	17	Sold living room tables and bookcases to Rick Jones; issued Sales Slip 1604 for $4,000 plus sales tax of $320.
	23	Sold eight dining room chairs to Demitri Brown; issued Sales Slip 1605 for $2,400 plus sales tax of $192.
	25	Gave Rick Jones an allowance for scratches on his bookcases; issued Credit Memorandum 216 for $270, which includes sales taxes of $20; the bookcases were originally sold on Sales Slip 1604 of June 17.
	27	Sold a living room sofa and four chairs to Paul Rivera; issued Sales Slip 1606 for $2,575 plus sales tax of $206.
	29	Sold a dining room table to Rosie Seltz; issued Sales Slip 1607 for $1,150 plus sales tax of $92.
	30	Sold a living room modular wall unit to Jim Mayor; issued Sales Slip 1608 for $3,100 plus sales tax of $248.

Analyze: Based on the beginning balance of the *Sales Tax Payable* account, what was the amount of total net sales for April and May? (Hint: Sales tax returns are filed and paid to the state quarterly.)

Recording sales transactions, posting to the accounts receivable ledger, and preparing a schedule of accounts receivable.

◄   **Problem 7.3B**
Objectives 7-1, 7-2,
7-3, 7-4, 7-6

Wine Country Gift Shop sells cards, supplies, and various holiday gift items. All sales are subject to a sales tax of 8 percent. The shop uses a sales journal and general journal.

DATE		TRANSACTIONS
Feb.	3	Sold Joel Bennett a box of holiday greeting cards for $75 plus sales tax of $6 on Sales Slip 201.
	4	Sold Ken Hamlett a Valentine's Day party pack for $200 plus sales tax of $16 on Sales Slip 202.
	5	Vickie Neal bought 10 boxes of Valentine's Day gift packs for her office. Sales Slip 203 was issued for $300 plus sales tax of $24.
	8	Sold Amy Peloza a set of crystal glasses for $400 plus sales tax of $32 on Sales Slip 204.
	9	Larry Edwards purchased two statues for $300 plus $24 sales tax on Sales Slip 205.
	9	Gave Vickie Neal an allowance because of incomplete items in two gift packs; issued Credit Memorandum 101 for $54, which includes sales tax of $4.
	10	Sold Gordon Dunn a Valentine Birthday package for $150 plus $12 sales tax on Sales Slip 206.

DATE	7.3B (cont.) TRANSACTIONS
Feb. 13	Gave Amy Peloza an allowance of $50 because of two broken glasses in the set she purchased on February 8. Credit Memorandum 102 was issued for the allowance plus sales tax of $4.
14	Sold Joel Bennett 12 boxes of gift candy for $200 plus sales tax of $16 on Sales Slip 207.
15	Sold a punch serving set with glasses for $300 to Kerry Goree. Sales tax of $24 was included on Sales Slip 208.
20	Sold Ned Jones a box of holiday greeting cards for $100 plus sales tax of $8 on Sales Slip 209.
22	Sold Stacie Andrews a set of crystal glasses for $400 plus sales tax of $32 on Sales Slip 210.
28	Melissa Thomas purchased three statues for $600 plus $48 sales tax on Sales Slip 211.

INSTRUCTIONS

1. Record the credit sale transactions for February in the proper journal. Use 6 as the page number for the sales journal and 16 as the page number for the general journal.

2. Immediately after recording each transaction, post to the accounts receivable ledger.

3. Post the entries to the appropriate accounts.

4. Prepare a schedule of accounts receivable and compare the balance due with the amount shown in the *Accounts Receivable* control account.

Analyze: How many postings were made to the general ledger?

Problem 7.4B
Objectives 7-1, 7-2, 7-3, 7-4, 7-6

▶ **Recording sales transactions, posting to the accounts receivable ledger, and preparing a schedule of accounts receivable.**

The Vintage Nursery is a wholesale shop that sells flowers, plants, and plant supplies. The transactions shown below took place during February.

DATE	TRANSACTIONS
Feb. 3	Sold a floral arrangement to Thompson Funerals; issued Invoice 2201 for $400.
8	Sold potted plants to Meadows Nursery; issued Invoice 2202 for $800.
9	Sold floral arrangements to DeSoto Flower Shop; issued Invoice 2203 for $1,050.
10	Sold corsages to Lovelace Nursery; issued Invoice 2204 for $700.
15	Gave DeSoto Flower Shop an allowance because of withered blossoms discovered in one of the floral arrangements sold on Invoice 2203 on February 9; issued Credit Memorandum 105 for $100.
20	Sold table arrangements to Lovelace Nursery; issued Invoice 2205 for $650.
22	Sold plants to Southwest Nursery; issued Invoice 2206 for $850.
25	Sold roses to Denton Flower Shop; issued Invoice 2207 for $450.
27	Sold several floral arrangements to Thompson Funerals; issued Invoice 2208 for $750.
28	Gave Thompson Funerals an allowance because of withered blossoms discovered in one of the floral arrangements sold on Invoice 2208 on February 27; issued Credit Memorandum 106 for $75.

INSTRUCTIONS

1. Record the transactions in the proper journal. Use 5 as the page number for the sales journal and 10 as the page number for the general journal.

2. Immediately after recording each transaction, post to the accounts receivable ledger.

3. Post the amounts from the general journal daily. Post the sales journal amount as a total at the end of the month.

4. Prepare a schedule of accounts receivable. Compare the balance of the *Accounts Receivable* control account with the total of the schedule.

Analyze: Damaged goods decreased sales by what dollar amount? By what percentage amount?

Critical Thinking Problem 7.1
Wholesaler Transactions

Matrix Toy Company sells toys and games to retail stores. The firm offers a trade discount of 40 percent on toys and 30 percent on games. Its credit sales and sales returns and allowances transactions for August are shown on the next page. The general ledger accounts used to record these transactions are listed below. The balance shown for *Accounts Receivable* is as of the beginning of August.

INSTRUCTIONS

1. Open the general ledger accounts and enter the balance of *Accounts Receivable* for August 1.

2. Set up an accounts receivable subsidiary ledger. Open an account for each of the credit customers listed below and enter the balances as of August 1. Enter n/45 in the blank space after "Terms." This means each customer has 45 days to pay for the merchandise they purchased.

Bombay's Department Store	$28,900
Little Annie's Toy Store	30,500
Reader's Bookstores	
Pinkerton Toy Center	
Super Game Center	19,010
The Game Store	

3. Record the transactions in a sales journal and in a general journal. Use 9 as the page number for the sales journal and 25 as the page number for the general journal. Be sure to enter each sale at its net price.

4. Post the individual entries from the sales journal and the general journal.

5. Total and rule the sales journal as of August 31.

6. Post the column total from the sales journal to the proper general ledger accounts.

7. Prepare the heading and the Revenue section of the firm's income statement for the month ended August 31.

8. Prepare a schedule of accounts receivable for August 31.

9. Check the total of the schedule of accounts receivable against the balance of the *Accounts Receivable* account in the general ledger. The two amounts should be equal.

GENERAL LEDGER ACCOUNTS

111   Accounts Receivable, $78,410 Dr.
401   Sales
451   Sales Returns and Allowances

DATE	TRANSACTIONS
August 1	Sold toys to Bombay's Department Store; issued Invoice 1001, which shows a list price of $19,500 and a trade discount of 40 percent.
5	Sold games to the Reader's Bookstores; issued Invoice 1002, which shows a list price of $21,250 and a trade discount of 30 percent.
9	Sold games to the Super Game Center; issued Invoice 1003, which shows a list price of $7,500 and a trade discount of 30 percent.
14	Sold toys to the Little Annie's Toy Store; issued Invoice 1004, which shows a list price of $26,400 and a trade discount of 40 percent.
18	Accepted a return of all the games shipped to the Super Game Center because they were damaged in transit; issued Credit Memo 151 for the original sale made on Invoice 1003 on August 9.
22	Sold toys to The Game Store; issued Invoice 1005, which shows a list price of $16,200 and a trade discount of 40 percent.
26	Sold games to the Bombay's Department Store; issued Invoice 1006, which shows a list price of $20,600 and a trade discount of 30 percent.
30	Sold toys to the Pinkerton Toy Center; issued Invoice 1007, which shows a list price of $22,800 and a trade discount of 40 percent.

Analyze: What is the effect on net sales if the company offers a series of trade discounts on toys (25 percent, 15 percent) instead of a single 40 percent discount?

Critical Thinking Problem 7.2
Retail Store

Tony Zendejas is the owner of Housewares Galore, a housewares store that sells a wide variety of items for the kitchen, bathroom, and home. Housewares Galore offers a company credit card to customers.

The company has experienced an increase in sales since the credit card was introduced. Tony is considering replacing his manual system of recording sales with electronic point-of-sale cash registers that are linked to a computer.

Cash sales are now rung up by the salesclerks on a cash register that generates a tape listing total cash sales at the end of the day. For credit sales, salesclerks prepare handwritten sales slips that are forwarded to the accountant for manual entry into the sales journal and accounts receivable ledger.

The electronic register system Tony is considering would use an optical scanner to read coded labels attached to the merchandise. As the merchandise is passed over the scanner, the code is sent to the computer. The computer is programmed to read the code and identify the item being sold, record the amount of the sale, maintain a record of total sales, update the inventory record, and keep a record of cash received.

If the sale is a credit transaction, the customer's company credit card number is swiped through a card reader connected with the register. The computer updates the customer's account in the accounts receivable ledger stored in computer memory.

If this system is used, many of the accounting functions are done automatically as sales are entered into the register. At the end of the day, the computer prints a complete sales journal, along with up-to-date balances for the general ledger and the accounts receivable ledger accounts related to sales transactions.

Listed below are four situations that Tony is eager to eliminate. Would use of an electronic point-of-sale system as described above reduce or prevent these problems? Why or why not?

1. The accountant did not post a sale to the customer's subsidiary ledger account.
2. The salesclerk did not charge a customer for an item.
3. The customer purchased merchandise using a stolen credit card.
4. The salesclerk was not aware that the item purchased was on sale and did not give the customer the sale price.

BUSINESS CONNECTIONS

Retail Sales

Managerial FOCUS

1. How does the *Sales Returns and Allowances* account provide management with a measure of operating efficiency? What problems might be indicated by a high level of returns and allowances?
2. Suppose you are the accountant for a small chain of clothing stores. Up to now, the firm has offered open-account credit to qualified customers but has not allowed the use of bank credit cards. The president of the chain has asked your advice about changing the firm's credit policy. What advantages might there be in eliminating the open-account credit and accepting bank credit cards instead? Do you see any disadvantages?
3. Suppose a manager in your company has suggested that the firm not hire an accountant to advise it on tax matters and to file tax returns. He states that tax matters are merely procedural in nature and that anyone who can read the tax form instructions can do the necessary work. Comment on this idea.
4. During the past year, Cravens Company has had a substantial increase in its losses from uncollectible accounts. Assume that you are the newly hired controller of this firm and that you have been asked to find the reason for the increase. What policies and procedures would you investigate?
5. Why is it usually worthwhile for a business to sell on credit even though it will have some losses from uncollectible accounts?
6. How can a firm's credit policy affect its profitability?
7. How can efficient accounting records help management maintain sound credit and collection policies?
8. Why should management insist that all sales on credit and other transactions affecting the firm's accounts receivable be journalized and posted promptly?

Sales Return and Allowances

Ethical DILEMMA

Credit memos are created when a product is returned. A debit to Sales Returns and Allowances and a credit to A/R is recorded when a credit memo is created. A credit memo will reduce A/R and write off the invoice. You have noticed that the A/R clerk, Wes, has created an abnormally high number of credit memos. You notice the inventory does not reflect the additional inventory resulting from the Sales Returns and Allowances. What would you do and how would you document this decision?

Income Statement

An excerpt from the Consolidated Statements of Earnings for The Home Depot, Inc., is presented below. Review the financial data and answer the following analysis questions:

(Amounts in millions except per share data) Fiscal Year	2013	2012	2011
Revenues:			
Net Sales	$74,754	$70,395	$67,997

Analyze:

1. The Home Depot, Inc.'s statement reports one figure for net sales. Name one account whose balance may have been deducted from the *Sales* account balance to determine a net sales amount.

2. The data presented demonstrate a steady increase in net sales over the three-year period. By what percentage have net sales of 2013 increased from sales of 2011?

Analyze Online: Find the most recent consolidated statements of income on The Home Depot, Inc., website (www.homedepot.com). Click on *Investor Relations* then *Financial Reports* then *Annual Reports,* then select the link for the most recent annual report.

3. What dollar amount is reported for net sales for the most recent year?
4. What is the trend in net sales over the last three years?
5. What are some possible reasons for this trend?

Customer to Vendor

Divide into groups of four individuals. Your company is named Cole's Cooking Supplies. Assign one person as Cole's sales associate; one as the company's A/R clerk; one as the customer, Louisa's Cooking School; and one as Louisa's A/P clerk. Record the transaction each individual would record from a sale of $50,000 for cooking supplies.

Accounting General Ledger Packages

Go to the QuickBooks and Sage websites at quickbooks.com and na.sage.com. Compare products at each site. What are some activities that each program can facilitate?

Answers to **Self Reviews**

Answers to Section 1 Self Review

1. A journal that is used to record only one type of transaction. Examples are the sales journal, the purchases journal, the cash receipts journal, and the cash payments journal.
2. Sales of merchandise on credit.
3. A ledger that contains accounts of a single type. Examples are the accounts receivable ledger and the accounts payable ledger.
4. **c.** service, merchandising, manufacturing.
5. **c.** increases credit sales

6. The sale to Harris was recorded at a taxable rate of 7 percent instead of 8 percent. Therefore, the Sales Tax Payable column should have an entry of $48, not $42. The Accounts Receivable Debit column should have an entry of $648, not $642.
   The sale to Wells should have an entry in the Accounts Receivable Debit column of $972, not $872.

Answers to Section 2 Self Review

1. Sales minus sales returns.
2. A sales return results when a customer returns goods and the firm takes them back. A sales allowance results when the firm gives a customer a reduction in the price of the good or service.
3. Individual accounts for all credit customers.
4. **c.** income statement
5. **a.** *Sales Returns and Allowances, Sales Tax Payable, Accounts Receivable*
6.

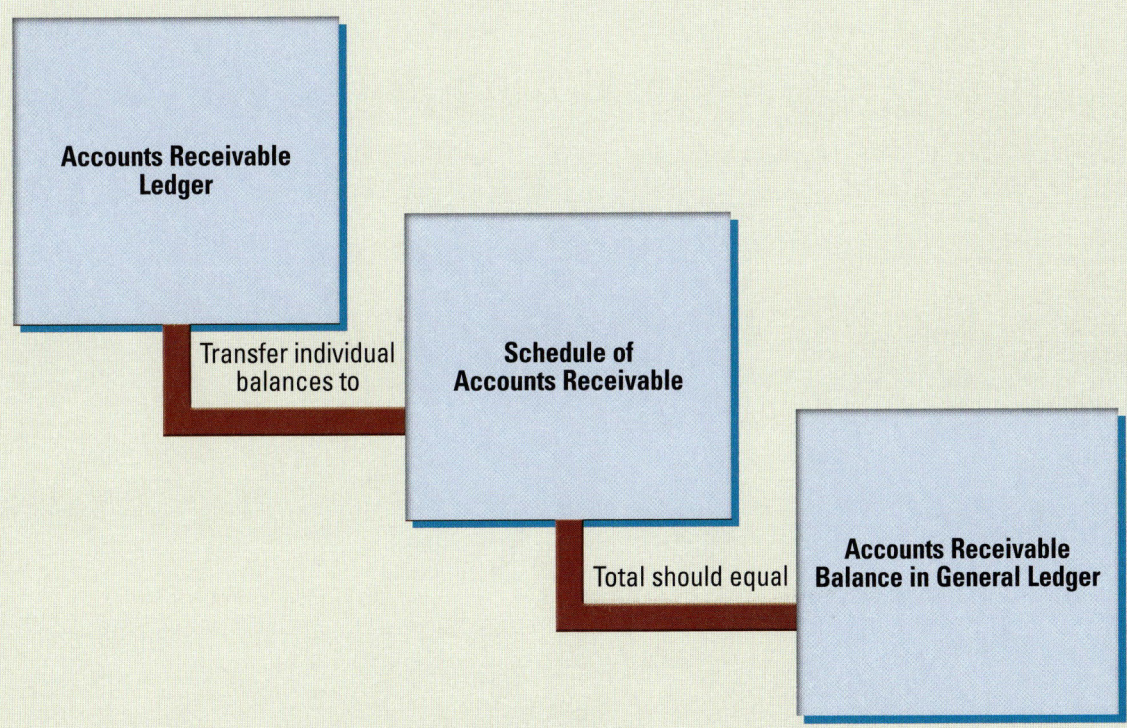

Answers to Section 3 Self Review

1. Four types of credit sales are open-account credit, business credit card sales, bank credit card sales, and credit card company sales.
2. List price is the established retail price of an item; net price is the amount left after all trade discounts are subtracted from the list price.
3. *Sales Tax Payable* is the account used to record the liability for sales taxes to be paid in the future.
4. **c.** $2,880
5. **d.** $2,520
6. Possible factors are payment history, amount of current debt, amount of potential debt (available credit cards), employment history, salary, references from other creditors.

Answers to Comprehensive Self Review

1. The month and the quarter.

2. A control account is an account that serves as a link between a subsidiary ledger and the general ledger because its balance summarizes the balances of the accounts in the subsidiary ledger.

3. A merchandising business must account for the purchase and sale of goods and for its merchandise inventory.

4. It contains detailed information about the transactions with credit customers and shows the balances owed by credit customers at all times.

5. A service business sells services; a merchandising business sells goods that it has purchased for resale; and a manufacturing business sells goods that it has produced.

Accounting for Purchases and Accounts Payable

Chapter 8

Williams-Sonoma
www.williams-sonoma.com

Williams-Sonoma began in 1956, when Chuck Williams opened a small specialty cookware shop in Sonoma, California. By offering French kitchen equipment most Americans had never seen before, the store gained popularity among home cooks and professional chefs from across the country. Since its humble beginnings in the late 1950s, Williams-Sonoma has evolved into a multibillion-dollar corporation.

Part of this success has been keeping track of the items that customers want most and making sure that those items are in stock. To combat challenging economic conditions, not only has it lowered prices on some of its high-ticket items, but has also ramped up its e-mail marketing efforts and increased focus on new product lines and exclusive merchandise to gain new customers.

Since the company buys its products from so many different suppliers, it records all of its purchases made on account, in a special journal. By keeping detailed records of who it owes and how soon payment is due, the company is better able to monitor its cash payment needs.

These strategies seem to be paying off—the company recently reported that net earnings increased by 15 percent in the year ended January 29, 2012, compared to the prior year.

thinking critically
Do you think that companies such as Williams-Sonoma pay their bills at the last possible minute? Why or why not?

LEARNING OBJECTIVES

8-1. Record purchases of merchandise on credit in a three-column purchases journal.

8-2. Post from the three-column purchases journal to the general ledger accounts.

8-3. Post credit purchases from the purchases journal to the accounts payable subsidiary ledger.

8-4. Record purchases returns and allowances in the general journal and post them to the accounts payable subsidiary ledger.

8-5. Prepare a schedule of accounts payable.

8-6. Compute the net delivered cost of purchases.

8-7. Demonstrate a knowledge of the procedures for effective internal control of purchases.

8-8. Record purchases, sales, and returns using the perpetual inventory system.

8-9. Define the accounting terms new to this chapter.

NEW TERMS

accounts payable ledger
cash discount
cost of goods sold
Freight In account
periodic inventory system
perpetual inventory system
purchase allowance
purchase invoice
purchase order
purchase requisition
purchase return
Purchases account
purchases discount
purchases journal
receiving report
sales discount
sales invoice
schedule of accounts payable
Transportation In account

Merchandise Purchases

In this chapter, you will learn how Maxx-Out Sporting Goods manages its purchases of goods for resale and its accounts payable.

Accounting for Purchases

Most merchandising businesses purchase goods on credit under open-account arrangements. A large firm usually has a centralized purchasing department that is responsible for locating suppliers, obtaining price quotations, negotiating credit terms, and placing orders. In small firms, purchasing activities are handled by a single individual, usually the owner or manager.

PURCHASING PROCEDURES

When a sales department needs goods, it sends the purchasing department a purchase requisition (Figure 8.1). A **purchase requisition** lists the items to be ordered. It is signed by someone with the authority to approve requests for merchandise, usually the manager of the sales department. The purchasing department selects a supplier who can furnish the goods at a competitive price and then issues a purchase order (Figure 8.2). The **purchase order** specifies the exact items, quantity, price, and credit terms. It is signed by someone with authority to approve purchases, usually the purchasing agent.

When the goods arrive at the business, they are inspected. A **receiving report** is prepared to show the quantity and condition of the goods received. The purchasing department receives a copy of the receiving report and compares it to the purchase order. If defective goods or the wrong quantity of goods are received, the purchasing department contacts the supplier and settles the problem.

Figure 8.3 shows the invoice, or *bill,* for items ordered and shipped. The customer, Maxx-Out Sporting Goods, calls it a **purchase invoice.** The supplier, International Sportsman, calls it a **sales invoice.** The customer's accounting department compares the invoice to copies of the purchase order and receiving report. The accounting department checks the quantities, prices, and math on the invoice and then records the purchase. It is important to record purchases in the accounting records as soon as the invoice is verified. Shortly before the due date of the invoice, the accounting department issues a check to the supplier and records the payment.

> The purchasing department for The Home Depot, Inc., purchases 30,000 to 40,000 different kinds of home improvement supplies, building materials, and lawn and garden products.

Maxx-Out Sporting Goods
2007 Trendsetter Lane
Dallas, TX 75268-0967

PURCHASE REQUISITION
No. 325

DEPARTMENT Men's
DATE OF REQUEST January 2, 2016
ADVISE ON DELIVERY Max Ferraro
DATE REQUIRED January 25, 2016

QUANTITY	DESCRIPTION
10	Assorted colors men's sweatsuits

APPROVED BY
REQUESTED BY

FOR PURCHASING DEPARTMENT USE ONLY

PURCHASE ORDER 9001
DATE January 5, 2016
ISSUED TO: International Sportsman
1718 Sherry Lane
Denton, TX 75267-6205

FIGURE 8.1

Purchase Requisition

Maxx-Out Sporting Goods
2007 Trendsetter Lane
Dallas, TX 75268-0967

PURCHASE ORDER

To International Sportsman
1718 Sherry Lane
Denton, TX 75267-6205

Date: January 5, 2016
Order No: 9001
Terms: n/30
FOB: Denton

QUANTITY	ITEM	UNIT PRICE	TOTAL
10	Assorted colors men's sweatsuits	55.00	550.00

APPROVED BY *Max Ferraro*

FIGURE 8.2

Purchase Order

International Sportsman
1718 Sherry Lane
Denton, TX 75267-6205

INVOICE NO. 7985

SOLD TO: Maxx-Out Sporting Goods
2007 Trendsetter Lane
Dallas, TX 75268-0967

DATE: January 23, 2016
ORDER NO.: 9001
SHIPPED BY: Metroplex Express
TERMS: n/30

YOUR ORDER NO.	SALESPERSON	TERMS
9001		n/30
DATE SHIPPED	SHIPPED BY	FOB
January 23, 2016	Metroplex Express	Denton

QUANTITY	DESCRIPTION	UNIT PRICE	TOTAL
10	Assorted colors men's sweatsuits	55 00	550 00
	Freight		50 00
	Total		600 00

FIGURE 8.3

Invoice

THE PURCHASES ACCOUNT

The purchase of merchandise for resale is a cost of doing business. The purchase of merchandise is debited to the *Purchases* **account.** *Purchases* is a temporary account classified as a cost of goods sold account. The **cost of goods sold** is the actual cost to the business of the merchandise sold to customers.

Cost of goods sold accounts follow the debit and credit rules of expense accounts. The *Purchases* account is increased by debits and decreased by credits. Its normal balance is a debit. In the chart of accounts, the cost of goods sold accounts appear just before the expense accounts.

> Walmart purchases private-label products from suppliers and markets these as Walmart brands. Products such as Ol'Roy™ dog food and EverStart® batteries are purchased at lower costs than nationally known brands. Thus, Walmart can sell these items at a lower price to its customers.

FREIGHT CHARGES FOR PURCHASES

Sometimes the buyer pays the freight charge—the cost of shipping the goods from the seller's warehouse to the buyer's location. There are two ways to handle the freight charges paid by the buyer:

- The buyer is billed directly by the transportation company for the freight charge. The buyer issues a check directly to the freight company.
- The seller pays the freight charge and includes it on the invoice. The invoice includes the price of the goods and the freight charge.

The freight charge is debited to the *Freight In* or *Transportation In* **account.** This is a cost of goods sold account showing transportation charges for merchandise purchased. The buyer enters three elements in the accounting records:

Price of goods (debit *Purchases*)	$550.00
Freight charge (debit *Freight In*)	50.00
Total invoice (credit *Accounts Payable*)	$600.00

Purchases			Freight In			Accounts Payable	
Dr.	Cr.		Dr.	Cr.		Dr.	Cr.
+	−		+	−		−	+
550			50				600

THE PURCHASES JOURNAL

For most merchandising businesses, it is not efficient to enter purchases of goods in the general journal. Instead, credit purchases of merchandise are recorded in a special journal called the **purchases journal.**

The following illustrates how credit purchases appear in a general journal. Each entry involves a debit to *Purchases* and *Freight In* and a credit to *Accounts Payable* plus a detailed explanation.

These 4 general journal entries require 12 separate postings to general ledger accounts: 4 to *Purchases,* 4 to *Freight In,* and 4 to *Accounts Payable.* As you can see from the ledger accounts that follow, it takes a great deal of time and effort to post these entries.

important!

Credit Purchases

The purchases journal is used to record only credit purchases of merchandise for resale. Credit purchases of other items used in the business are recorded in the general journal.

GENERAL JOURNAL   PAGE ___1___

	DATE		DESCRIPTION	POST. REF.	DEBIT	CREDIT	
1	2016						1
2	Jan.	3	Purchases	501	2 675 00		2
3			Freight In	502	190 00		3
4			Accounts Payable	205		2 865 00	4
5			Purchased merchandise from				5
6			Active Designs, Invoice 5879,				6
7			dated January 2, 2016,				7
8			terms 2/10, n/30				8
9							9
10		5	Purchases	501	3 880 00		10
11			Freight In	502	175 00		11
12			Accounts Payable	205		4 055 00	12
13			Purchased merchandise from				13
14			The Sports Warehouse, Invoice 633,				14
15			dated January 3, 2016,				15
16			terms n/30				16
17							17
18		6	Purchases	501	2 900 00		18
19			Freight In	502	240 00		19
20			Accounts Payable	205		3 140 00	20
21			Purchased merchandise from				21
22			The Modern Sportsman,				22
23			Invoice 8011, dated				23
24			January 4, 2016, terms n/30				24
25							25
26		7	Purchases	501	3 675 00		26
27			Freight In	502	260 00		27
28			Accounts Payable	205		3 935 00	28
29			Purchased merchandise from				29
30			World of Sports, Invoice 4321,				30
31			dated January 4, 2016,				31
			terms 2/10, n/30				

ACCOUNT Accounts Payable   **ACCOUNT NO.** 205

DATE		DESCRIPTION	POST. REF.	DEBIT	CREDIT	BALANCE DEBIT	BALANCE CREDIT
2016							
Jan.	1	Balance	✓				10 800 00
	3		J1		2 865 00		13 665 00
	5		J1		4 055 00		17 720 00
	6		J1		3 140 00		20 860 00
	7		J1		3 935 00		24 795 00

ACCOUNT Purchases   **ACCOUNT NO.** 501

DATE		DESCRIPTION	POST. REF.	DEBIT	CREDIT	BALANCE DEBIT	BALANCE CREDIT
2016							
Jan.	3		J1	2 675 00		2 675 00	
	5		J1	3 880 00		6 555 00	
	6		J1	2 900 00		9 455 00	
	7		J1	3 675 00		13 130 00	

>> 8-1. OBJECTIVE

Record purchases of merchandise on credit in a three-column purchases journal.

ACCOUNT Freight In						ACCOUNT NO. 502	
DATE	DESCRIPTION	POST. REF.	DEBIT	CREDIT	BALANCE		
					DEBIT	CREDIT	
2016							
Jan. 3		J1	1 9 0 00		1 9 0 00		
5		J1	1 7 5 00		3 6 5 00		
6		J1	2 4 0 00		6 0 5 00		
7		J1	2 6 0 00		8 6 5 00		

Figure 8.4 shows the purchases journal for Maxx-Out Sporting Goods. Remember that the purchases journal is only for credit purchases of merchandise for resale to customers. Notice how the columns efficiently organize the data about the credit purchases. The purchases journal makes it possible to record each purchase on a single line. In addition, there is no need to enter account names and descriptions.

RECORDING TRANSACTIONS IN A PURCHASES JOURNAL

Use the information on the purchase invoice to make the entry in the purchases journal:

1. Enter the date, supplier name, invoice number, invoice date, and credit terms.
2. In the Accounts Payable Credit column, enter the total owed to the supplier.
3. In the Purchases Debit column, enter the price of the goods purchased.
4. In the Freight In Debit column, enter the freight amount.

The total of the Purchases Debit and Freight In Debit columns must equal the amount entered in the Accounts Payable Credit column.

The invoice date and credit terms determine when payment is due. The following credit terms often appear on invoices:

- *Net 30 days* or *n/30* means that payment in full is due 30 days after the date of the invoice.
- *Net 10 days EOM,* or *n/10 EOM,* means that payment in full is due 10 days after the end of the month in which the invoice was issued.
- *2% 10 days, net 30 days,* or *2/10, n/30* means that if payment is made within 10 days of the invoice date, the customer can take a 2 percent discount. Otherwise, payment in full is due in 30 days.

The 2 percent discount is a **cash discount;** it is a discount offered by suppliers to encourage quick payment by customers. To the customer it is known as a **purchases discount.** To the supplier it is known as a **sales discount.**

FIGURE 8.4 Purchases Journal

	PURCHASES JOURNAL								PAGE 1
DATE	PURCHASED FROM	INVOICE NUMBER	INVOICE DATE	TERMS	POST. REF.	ACCOUNTS PAYABLE CREDIT	PURCHASES DEBIT	FREIGHT IN DEBIT	
2016									
Jan. 3	Active Designs	5879	01/02/16	2/10, n/30		2 8 6 5 00	2 6 7 5 00	1 9 0 00	
5	The Sports Warehouse	633	01/03/16	n/30		4 0 5 5 00	3 8 8 0 00	1 7 5 00	
6	The Modern Sportsman	8011	01/04/16	n/30		3 1 4 0 00	2 9 0 0 00	2 4 0 00	
7	World of Sports	4321	01/04/16	2/10, n/30		3 9 3 5 00	3 6 7 5 00	2 6 0 00	
19	Athletic Equipment, Inc.	8997	01/15/16	2/10, n/30		4 2 0 0 00	3 8 6 0 00	3 4 0 00	
23	International Sportsman	7985	01/22/16	n/30		6 0 0 00	5 5 0 00	5 0 00	
31						18 7 9 5 00	17 5 4 0 00	1 2 5 5 00	

FIGURE 8.5   Posting to the General Ledger

PURCHASES JOURNAL   PAGE ___1___

DATE		CUSTOMER'S NAME	INVOICE NUMBER	INVOICE DATE	TERMS	POST. REF.	ACCOUNTS PAYABLE CREDIT	PURCHASES DEBIT	FREIGHT IN DEBIT
2016									
Jan.	3	Active Designs	5879	01/02/16	2/10, n/30	✓	2 865 00	2 675 00	190 00
	5	The Sports Warehouse	633	01/03/16	n/30	✓	4 055 00	3 880 00	175 00
	6	The Modern Sportsman	8011	01/04/16	n/30	✓	3 140 00	2 900 00	240 00
	7	World of Sports	4321	01/04/16	2/10, n/30	✓	3 935 00	3 675 00	260 00
	19	Athletic Equipment, Inc.	8997	01/15/16	2/10, n/30	✓	4 200 00	3 860 00	340 00
	23	International Sportsman	7985	01/22/16	n/30	✓	600 00	550 00	50 00
	31						18 795 00	17 540 00	1 255 00
							(205)	(501)	(502)

ACCOUNT _Accounts Payable_   ACCOUNT NO. _205_

DATE		DESCRIPTION	POST. REF.	DEBIT	CREDIT	BALANCE DEBIT	BALANCE CREDIT
2016							
Jan.	1	Balance	✓				10 800 00
	31		P1		18 795 00		29 595 00

ACCOUNT _Purchases_   ACCOUNT NO. _501_

DATE	DESCRIPTION	POST. REF.	DEBIT	CREDIT	BALANCE DEBIT	BALANCE CREDIT
2016						
Jan. 31		P1	17 540 00		17 540 00	

ACCOUNT _Freight In_   ACCOUNT NO. _502_

DATE	DESCRIPTION	POST. REF.	DEBIT	CREDIT	BALANCE DEBIT	BALANCE CREDIT
2016						
Jan. 31		P1	1 255 00		1 255 00	

POSTING TO THE GENERAL LEDGER

The purchases journal simplifies the posting process. Summary amounts are posted at the end of the month. Refer to Figure 8.5 as you learn how to post from the purchases journal to the general ledger accounts.

Total the Accounts Payable Credit, the Purchases Debit, and the Freight In Debit columns. Before posting, prove the equality of the debits and credits recorded in the purchases journal.

>> **8-2. OBJECTIVE**

Post from the three-column purchases journal to the general ledger accounts.

Proof of Purchases Journal	
	Debits
Purchases Debit column	$17,540.00
Freight In Debit column	1,255.00
	$18,795.00
	Credits
Accounts Payable Credit column	$18,795.00

important!

Cash Discounts

In the purchases journal, record the amount shown on the invoice. The cash discount is recorded when the payment is made.

After the equality of debits and credits is verified, rule the purchases journal. The steps to post the column totals to the general ledger follow:

1. Locate the *Accounts Payable* ledger account.
2. Enter the date.
3. Enter the posting reference, P1. The **P** is for purchases journal. The **1** is the purchases journal page number.
4. Enter the amount from the Accounts Payable Credit column in the purchases journal in the Credit column of the *Accounts Payable* ledger account.
5. Compute the new balance and enter it in the Balance Credit column.
6. In the purchases journal, enter the *Accounts Payable* ledger account number (205) under the column total.
7. Repeat the steps for the *Purchases* Debit and *Freight In* Debit columns.

During the month, the individual entries in the purchases journal are posted to the creditor accounts in the accounts payable ledger. The check marks in the purchases journal in Figure 8.5 indicate that these postings have been completed. This procedure is discussed later in this chapter.

ADVANTAGES OF A PURCHASES JOURNAL

Every business has certain types of transactions that occur over and over again. A well-designed accounting system includes journals that permit efficient recording of such transactions. In most merchandising firms, purchases of goods on credit take place often enough to make it worthwhile to use a purchases journal.

A special journal for credit purchases of merchandise saves time and effort when recording and posting purchases. The use of a purchases journal and other special journals allows for the division of accounting work among different employees. The purchases journal strengthens the audit trail. All credit purchases are recorded in one place, and each entry refers to the number and date of the invoice.

Section 1 — Self Review

QUESTIONS

1. What activities does a purchasing department perform?
2. What type of transaction is recorded in the purchases journal?
3. What are the advantages of using a purchases journal?

EXERCISES

4. When the sales department needs goods, what document is sent to the purchasing department?
   a. Purchase invoice
   b. Purchase order
   c. Purchase requisition
   d. Sales requisition
5. What form is sent to the supplier to order goods?
   a. Purchase invoice
   b. Purchase order
   c. Purchase requisition
   d. Sales invoice

ANALYSIS

6. An invoice dated March 15 for $4,000 shows credit terms 2/10, n/30. What do the credit terms mean?

(Answers to Section 1 Self Review are on page 268.)

>> 8-3. Post credit purchases from the purchases journal to the accounts payable subsidiary ledger.

WHY IT'S IMPORTANT

Up-to-date records allow prompt payment of invoices.

>> 8-4. Record purchases returns and allowances in the general journal and post them to the accounts payable subsidiary ledger.

WHY IT'S IMPORTANT

For unsatisfactory goods received, an allowance or return is reflected in the accounting records.

>> 8-5. Prepare a schedule of accounts payable.

WHY IT'S IMPORTANT

This schedule provides a snapshot of amounts owed to suppliers.

>> 8-6. Compute the net delivered cost of purchases.

WHY IT'S IMPORTANT

This is an important component in measuring operational results.

>> 8-7. Demonstrate a knowledge of the procedures for effective internal control of purchases.

WHY IT'S IMPORTANT

Businesses try to prevent fraud, errors, and holding excess inventory.

>> 8-8. Record purchases, sales, and returns using the perpetual inventory system.

WHY IT'S IMPORTANT

Larger businesses require up-to-date information about inventories on hand and use the perpetual system.

TERMS TO LEARN

accounts payable ledger
periodic inventory system
perpetual inventory system
purchase allowance
purchase return
schedule of accounts payable

Accounts Payable

Businesses that buy merchandise on credit can conduct more extensive operations and use financial resources more effectively than if they paid cash for all purchases. It is important to pay invoices on time so that the business maintains a good credit reputation with its suppliers.

The Accounts Payable Ledger

Businesses need detailed records in order to pay invoices promptly. The **accounts payable ledger** provides information about the individual accounts for all creditors. The accounts payable ledger is a subsidiary ledger; it is separate from and subordinate to the general ledger. The accounts payable ledger contains a separate account for each creditor. Each account shows purchases, payments, and returns and allowances. The balance of the account shows the amount owed to the creditor.

Figure 8.6 on the next page shows the accounts payable ledger account for International Sportsman. Notice that the Balance column does not indicate whether the balance is a debit or a credit. The form assumes that the balance will be a credit because the normal balance of liability accounts is a credit. A debit balance may exist if more than the amount owed was paid to the creditor or if returned goods were already paid for. If the balance is a debit, circle the amount to show that the account does not have the normal balance.

Small businesses like Maxx-Out Sporting Goods arrange the accounts payable ledger in alphabetical order. Large businesses and businesses that use computerized accounting systems assign an account number to each creditor and arrange the accounts payable ledger in numeric order.

>> 8-3. OBJECTIVE

Post credit purchases from the purchases journal to the accounts payable subsidiary ledger.

POSTING A CREDIT PURCHASE

To keep the accounting records up to date, invoices are posted to the accounts payable subsidiary ledger every day. Refer to Figure 8.6 as you learn how to post to the accounts payable ledger.

1. Locate the accounts payable ledger account for the creditor International Sportsman.
2. Enter the date.
3. In the Description column, enter the invoice number and date.
4. In the Posting Reference column, enter the purchases journal page number.
5. Enter the amount from the *Accounts Payable* Credit column in the purchases journal in the Credit column of the accounts payable subsidiary ledger.
6. Compute and enter the new balance in the Balance column.
7. In the purchases journal (Figure 8.5 on page 241), enter a check mark (✓) in the Posting Reference column. This indicates that the transaction is posted in the accounts payable subsidiary ledger.

POSTING CASH PAID ON ACCOUNT

When the transaction involves cash paid on account to a supplier, the payment is first recorded in a cash payments journal. (The cash payments journal is discussed in Chapter 9.) The cash payment is then posted to the individual creditor's account in the accounts payable ledger. Figure 8.7 shows a posting for cash paid to a creditor on January 27.

>> 8-4. OBJECTIVE

Record purchases returns and allowances in the general journal and post them to the accounts payable subsidiary ledger.

Purchases Returns and Allowances

When merchandise arrives, it is examined to confirm that it is satisfactory. Occasionally, the wrong goods are shipped, or items are damaged or defective. A **purchase return** is when the business returns the goods. A **purchase allowance** is when the purchaser keeps the goods but receives a reduction in the price of the goods. The supplier issues a credit memorandum for the return or allowance. The credit memorandum reduces the amount that the purchaser owes.

Purchases returns and allowances are entered in the *Purchases Returns and Allowances* account, not in the *Purchases* account. The *Purchases Returns and Allowances* account is a complete record of returns and allowances. Business managers analyze this account to identify problem suppliers.

Purchases Returns and Allowances is a contra cost of goods sold account. The normal balance of cost of goods sold accounts is a debit. The normal balance of *Purchases Returns and Allowances,* a contra cost of goods sold account, is a credit.

RECORDING PURCHASES RETURNS AND ALLOWANCES

Maxx-Out Sporting Goods received merchandise from International Sportsman on January 23. Some goods were damaged, and the supplier granted a $100 purchase allowance. Maxx-Out Sporting Goods recorded the full amount of the invoice, $600, in the purchases journal. The purchase allowance was recorded separately in the general journal.

recall

Subsidiary Ledger

The total of the accounts in the subsidiary ledger must equal the control account balance.

FIGURE 8.6

Accounts Payable Ledger Account

NAME	International Sportsman				TERMS	n/30		
ADDRESS	1718 Sherry Lane, Dallas, Texas 75267-6205							

DATE		DESCRIPTION	POST. REF.	DEBIT	CREDIT	BALANCE
2016						
Jan.	1	Balance	✓			1 6 0 0 00
	23	Invoice 7985, 01/23/16	P1		6 0 0 00	2 2 0 0 00

FIGURE 8.7

Posting a Payment Made on Account

NAME	International Sportsman				TERMS	n/30			
ADDRESS	1718 Sherry Lane, Dallas, Texas 75267-6205								

DATE		DESCRIPTION	POST. REF.	DEBIT	CREDIT	BALANCE
2016						
Jan.	1	Balance	✓			1 6 0 0 00
	23	Invoice 7985, 01/23/16	P1		6 0 0 00	2 2 0 0 00
	27		CP1	1 0 0 0 00		1 2 0 0 00

BUSINESS TRANSACTION

On January 30, Maxx-Out Sporting Goods received a credit memorandum for $100 from International Sportsman as an allowance for damaged merchandise.

International Sportsman
1718 Sherry Lane
Dallas, TX 75267-6205

TO: Maxx-Out Sporting Goods
2007 Trendsetter Lane
Dallas, TX 75268-0967

CREDIT MEMORANDUM
NUMBER: 103
DATE: January 30, 2016

ORIGINAL INVOICE: 7985
INVOICE DATE: January 23, 2016
DESCRIPTION: Credit for damaged merchandise: $100.00

ANALYSIS

The liability account, **Accounts Payable,** is decreased by $100. The contra cost of goods sold account, **Purchases Returns and Allowances,** is increased by $100.

DEBIT-CREDIT RULES

DEBIT   Decreases to liabilities are debits. Debit **Accounts Payable** for $100.

CREDIT Increases to contra cost of goods sold accounts are recorded as credits. Credit **Purchases Returns and Allowances** for $100.

T-ACCOUNT PRESENTATION

Accounts Payable		Purchases Returns and Allowances	
−	+	−	+
100			100

GENERAL JOURNAL ENTRY

	GENERAL JOURNAL		PAGE	1	

	DATE	DESCRIPTION	POST. REF.	DEBIT	CREDIT	
15	Jan. 30	Accounts Payable/International Sportsman		1 0 0 00		15
16		Purchases Returns and Allowances			1 0 0 00	16
17		Received Credit Memo 103 for				17
18		damaged merchandise returned;				18
19		original Invoice 7985,				19
20		January 23, 2016				20

THE BOTTOM LINE
Purchase Allowance

Income Statement

Contra Cost of Goods Sold	↑ 100
Net Income	↑ 100

Balance Sheet

Liabilities	↓ 100
Equity	↑ 100

FIGURE 8.8

Posting to a Creditor's Account

GENERAL JOURNAL   PAGE _____1_____

	DATE	DESCRIPTION	POST. REF.	DEBIT	CREDIT	
1	2016					1
15	Jan. 30	Accounts Payable/International Sportsman	205 ✓	1 0 0 00		16
16		Purchases Returns and Allowances	503		1 0 0 00	17
17		Received Credit Memo 103 for				18
18		damaged merchandise				19
19		returned; original				20
20		Invoice 7985, January 23, 2016				21
21						22
22						

NAME   International Sportsman   TERMS   n/30

ADDRESS   1718 Sherry Lane, Dallas, Texas 75267-6205

DATE		DESCRIPTION	POST. REF.	DEBIT	CREDIT	BALANCE
2016						
Jan.	1	Balance	✓			1 6 0 0 00
	23	Invoice 7985, 01/23/16	P1		6 0 0 00	2 2 0 0 00
	27		CP1	1 0 0 0 00		1 2 0 0 00
	30	CM 103	J1	1 0 0 00		1 1 0 0 00

recall

Contra Accounts

The *Purchases Returns and Allowances* account is a contra account. Contra accounts have normal balances that are the opposite of related accounts.

Notice that this entry includes a debit to *Accounts Payable* and a credit to *Purchases Returns and Allowances.* In addition, there is a debit to the creditor's account in the accounts payable subsidiary ledger. Businesses that have few returns and allowances use the general journal to record these transactions. Businesses with many returns and allowances use a special journal for purchases returns and allowances.

POSTING A PURCHASES RETURN OR ALLOWANCE

Whether recorded in the general journal or in a special journal, it is important to promptly post returns and allowances to the creditor's account in the accounts payable ledger. Refer to Figure 8.8 to learn how to post purchases returns and allowances to the supplier's account.

1. Enter the date.
2. In the Description column, enter the credit memorandum number.
3. In the Posting Reference column, enter the general journal page number.
4. Enter the amount of the return or allowance in the Debit column.
5. Compute the new balance and enter it in the Balance column.
6. In the general journal, enter a check mark (✓) to show that the transaction was posted to the creditor's account in the accounts payable subsidiary ledger.

After the transaction is posted to the general ledger, enter the *Purchases Returns and Allowances* ledger account number in the Posting Reference column.

>> **8-5. OBJECTIVE**

Prepare a schedule of accounts payable.

Schedule of Accounts Payable

The total of the individual creditor accounts in the subsidiary ledger must equal the balance of the *Accounts Payable* control account. To prove that the control account and the subsidiary ledger are equal, businesses prepare a **schedule of accounts payable**—a list of all balances owed to creditors. Figure 8.9 shows the accounts payable subsidiary ledger for Maxx-Out Sporting Goods on January 31.

Figure 8.10 on page 248 shows the schedule of accounts payable for Maxx-Out Sporting Goods. Notice that the accounts payable control account balance is $20,245. This equals the total on the schedule of accounts payable. If the amounts are not equal, it is essential to locate and correct the errors.

FIGURE 8.9

The Accounts Payable Ledger

NAME Active Designs   TERMS 2/10, n/30
ADDRESS 2313 Belt Line Road, Dallas, Texas 75267-6205

DATE		DESCRIPTION	POST. REF.	DEBIT	CREDIT	BALANCE
2016						
Jan.	1	Balance	✓			2 2 0 0 00
	3	Invoice 5879, 01/02/16	P1		2 8 6 5 00	5 0 6 5 00
	13		CP1	3 2 0 0 00		1 8 6 5 00
	30		CP1	8 0 0 00		1 0 6 5 00

NAME Athletic Equipment, Inc.   TERMS 2/10, n/30
ADDRESS 1027 St James Avenue, Dallas, Texas 75267-6205

DATE		DESCRIPTION	POST. REF.	DEBIT	CREDIT	BALANCE
2016						
Jan.	19	Invoice 8997, 01/15/16	P1		4 2 0 0 00	4 2 0 0 00

NAME International Sportsman   TERMS n/30
ADDRESS 1718 Sherry Lane, Dallas, Texas 75267-6205

DATE		DESCRIPTION	POST. REF.	DEBIT	CREDIT	BALANCE
2016						
Jan.	1	Balance	✓			1 6 0 0 00
	23	Invoice 7985, 01/23/16	P1		6 0 0 00	2 2 0 0 00
	27		CP1	1 0 0 0 00		1 2 0 0 00
	30	CM 103	J1	1 0 0 00		1 1 0 0 00

NAME The Modern Sportsman   TERMS n/30
ADDRESS 2860 Jackson Drive, Dallas, Texas 75267-6205

DATE		DESCRIPTION	POST. REF.	DEBIT	CREDIT	BALANCE
2016						
Jan.	1	Balance	✓			1 6 0 0 00
	6	Invoice 8011, 01/04/16	P1		3 1 4 0 00	4 7 4 0 00

NAME The Sports Warehouse   TERMS n/30
ADDRESS 1313 Sunset Drive, Dallas, Texas 75267-6205

DATE		DESCRIPTION	POST. REF.	DEBIT	CREDIT	BALANCE
2016						
Jan.	1	Balance	✓			2 4 0 0 00
	5	Invoice 633, 01/03/16	P1		4 0 5 5 00	6 4 5 5 00
	17		CP1	4 2 5 0 00		2 2 0 5 00

NAME World of Sports   TERMS 2/10, n/30
ADDRESS 1729 Parker Road, Dallas, Texas 75267-6205

DATE		DESCRIPTION	POST. REF.	DEBIT	CREDIT	BALANCE
2016						
Jan.	1	Balance	✓			3 0 0 0 00
	7	Invoice 4321, 01/04/16	P1		3 9 3 5 00	6 9 3 5 00

FIGURE 8.10

Schedule of Accounts Payable and the Accounts Payable Account

Maxx-Out Sporting Goods
Schedule of Accounts Payable
January 31, 2016

Active Designs	1 0 6 5 00
Athletic Equipment, Inc.	4 2 0 0 00
International Sportsman	1 1 0 0 00
The Modern Sportsman	4 7 4 0 00
The Sports Warehouse	2 2 0 5 00
World of Sports	6 9 3 5 00
Total	2 0 2 4 5 00

ACCOUNT _Accounts Payable_   ACCOUNT NO. _205_

DATE		DESCRIPTION	POST. REF.	DEBIT	CREDIT	BALANCE DEBIT	BALANCE CREDIT
2016							
Jan.	1	Balance					10 8 0 0 00
	30		J1	1 0 0 00			10 7 0 0 00
	31		P1		18 7 9 5 00		29 4 9 5 00
	31		CP1	9 2 5 0 00			20 2 4 5 00

>> 8-6. OBJECTIVE

Compute the net delivered cost of purchases.

Determining the Cost of Purchases

The **Purchases** account accumulates the cost of merchandise bought for resale. The income statement of a merchandising business contains a section showing the total cost of purchases. This section combines information about the cost of the purchases, freight in, and purchases returns and allowances for the period. Maxx-Out Sporting Goods has the following general ledger account balances at January 31:

Purchases	$17,540
Freight In	1,255
Purchases Returns and Allowances	100

The net delivered cost of purchases for Maxx-Out Sporting Goods for January is calculated as follows:

Purchases	$17,540
Freight In	1,255
Delivered Cost of Purchases	$18,795
Less Purchases Returns and Allowances	100
Net Delivered Cost of Purchases	$18,695

For firms that do not have freight charges, the amount of net purchases is calculated as follows:

Purchases	$17,540
Less Purchases Returns and Allowances	100
Net Purchases	$17,440

In Chapter 13, you will see how the complete income statement for a merchandising business is prepared. You will learn about the Cost of Goods Sold section and how the net delivered cost of purchases is used in calculating the results of operations.

Internal Control of Purchases

Internal controls are the company's policies and procedures in place to safeguard assets, ensure reliability of accounting data, and promote compliance with management policies and applicable laws. Because of the large amount of money spent to purchase goods, businesses should develop careful procedures to control purchases and payments. A business should ensure its control process includes sufficient safeguards to:

- create written proof that purchases and payments are authorized;
- ensure that different people are involved in the process of buying goods, receiving goods, and making payments.

Separating duties among employees provides a system of checks and balances. In a small business with just a few employees, it might be very difficult to separate duties. This means the owner must be involved in daily operations. Even a small business, however, should design a set of control procedures as effective as resources allow. Effective systems for small businesses should have the following controls in place:

1. All purchases should be made only after proper authorization has been given in writing.
2. Goods should be carefully checked when received. They should then be compared with the purchase order and with the invoice received from the supplier.
3. The purchase order, receiving report, and invoice should be checked to confirm that the information on the documents is in agreement.
4. The computations on the invoice should be checked for accuracy.
5. Authorization for payment should be made by someone other than the person who ordered the goods.
6. Another person should write the check for payment.
7. Prenumbered forms should be used for purchase requisitions, purchase orders, and checks. The numbers on the documents issued should be verified periodically to make sure all forms can be accounted for.

Medium- and large-sized businesses often use the voucher system. As a business grows, the owner finds it increasingly difficult to be involved in all the firm's transactions. The owner cannot personally approve or sign all checks. That's when the internal controls provided by the voucher system become increasingly important.

Controls built into a voucher system include the following:

- All liabilities are authorized. For example, a properly approved purchase order is required for each purchase of merchandise on account.
- All payments are made by check.
- All checks are issued based on a properly approved voucher.
- Vouchers are used to cover bills and invoices received from outside parties.
- All bills and invoices are verified before they are approved for payment.
- Only experienced and responsible employees are allowed to approve bills and invoices for payment.
- Invoices are attached to the vouchers to provide supporting documentation.
- Different employees approve the vouchers, record the vouchers and payments, and sign and mail the checks.
- All paid vouchers, including supporting documentation, are kept on file for a specified period of time.

>> **8-7. OBJECTIVE**

Demonstrate a knowledge of the procedures for effective internal control of purchases.

ABOUT ACCOUNTING

Employee Fraud
According to the U.S. Chamber of Commerce, businesses lose billions of dollars each year to employee fraud. The best defense against fraud is to use good internal controls: Have multiple employees in contact with suppliers and screen employees and vendors to reduce fraud opportunities.

>> 8-8. OBJECTIVE

Record purchases, sales, and returns using the perpetual inventory system.

The Perpetual Inventory System

The accounting for sales and purchases discussed in Chapter 7 and so far in Chapter 8 has assumed use of the **periodic inventory system.** When the periodic system is used, the inventory records are only updated when a physical inventory is taken. A physical inventory is an actual count of units on hand. This system is adequate for smaller businesses.

Larger businesses require up-to-date information of inventories on hand, and use the **perpetual inventory system.** The perpetual inventory system updates both the general ledger merchandise inventory account and inventory items in the inventory ledger with each purchase, sale, and return. Using a perpetual inventory system requires a substantial investment in point-of-sale cash registers, scanning devices, and computer software.

Perpetual inventory management systems give management more control over the company's inventory. Management can use computers to access inventory records to know exactly how much of each item in inventory is on hand. This assists management in inventory control and purchasing activities. The perpetual inventory system also allows for cycle counts of inventory. A cycle count is an inventory management procedure in which only certain inventory items are counted and compared with the perpetual inventory records. Shortages of inventory on hand can be investigated and corrective actions taken.

When the perpetual inventory system is used, an account called *Merchandise Inventory* replaces the *Purchases, Purchases Returns,* and *Freight In* accounts used in the periodic inventory system. Merchandise Inventory is an asset account whose balance represents the cost of merchandise inventory on hand.

Additionally, perpetual inventory accounting requires a second entry when sales are made. This entry debits the *Cost of Goods Sold* account and credits the *Merchandise Inventory* account. The *Cost of Goods Sold* account shows the actual cost of the merchandise sold to customers, and is classified as an expense in a perpetual inventory system. If a sales return is processed, an additional entry to debit *Merchandise Inventory* and credit *Cost of Goods Sold* is made.

Figure 8.11 presents the general journal entries for the purchase, sales, and return transactions in Chapters 7 and 8 using both the periodic system and the perpetual system.

FIGURE 8.11

Journal Entries Using Both the Periodic and Perpetual Inventory Systems

Journal Entry to Record Transaction, Using the:		
Transaction	**Periodic System**	**Perpetual System**

June 20: Purchased merchandise inventory for $2,050 plus freight of $120 from Holtz Industries, Invoice 5027; the terms are 2/10, n/30.	Purchases 2,050
	Freight In 120
	  Accounts Payable/Holtz Industries 2,170
		Merchandise Inventory 2,170
		  Accounts Payable/Holtz Industries 2,170

June 22: Received Credit Memorandum 110 for $150 from Holtz Industries for defective product returned; they were originally purchased on Invoice 5027, dated June 20.	Accounts Payable/Holtz Industries 150
	  Purchases Returns and Allowances 150
		Accounts Payable/Holtz Industries 150
		  Merchandise Inventory 150

July 1: Sold merchandise on credit to Cervantes Company; issued Invoice 109 for $1,250, terms 2/10, n/30. The cost of the merchandise sold was $800.	Accounts Receivable/Cervantes Company 1,250
	  Sales 1,250
		Accounts Receivable/Cervantes Company 1,250
		  Sales 1,250
		Cost of Goods Sold 800
		  Merchandise Inventory 800

July 3: Issued Credit Memorandum 138 for $50 to Cervantes Company for defective product returned; they were originally purchased Invoice 109, dated July 1. The cost of the merchandise returned was $32.	Sales Returns and Allowances 50
	  Accounts Receivable/Cervantes Company 50
		Sales Returns and Allowances 50
		  Accounts Receivable/Cervantes Company 50
		Merchandise Inventory 32
		  Cost of Goods Sold 32

MANAGERIAL IMPLICATIONS   <<

ACCOUNTING FOR PURCHASES

- Management and the accounting staff need to work together to make sure that there are good internal controls over purchasing.

- A carefully designed system of checks and balances protects the business against fraud, errors, and excessive investment in merchandise.

- The accounting staff needs to record transactions efficiently so that up-to-date information about creditors is available.

- Using the purchases journal and the accounts payable subsidiary ledger improves efficiency.

- To maintain a good credit reputation with suppliers, it is important to have an accounting system that ensures prompt payment of invoices.

- A well-run accounting system provides management with information about cash: cash required to pay suppliers, short-term loans needed to cover temporary cash shortages, and cash available for short-term investments.

- Separate accounts for recording purchases, freight charges, and purchases returns and allowances make it easy to analyze the elements in the cost of purchases.

THINKING CRITICALLY

As a manager, what internal controls would you put in your accounting system?

Section 2   Self Review

QUESTIONS

1. What is the purpose of the schedule of accounts payable?

2. A firm has a debit balance of $62,450 in its *Purchases* account and a credit balance of $2,875 in its *Purchases Returns and Allowances* account. Calculate net purchases for the period.

3. A firm receives an invoice that reflects the price of goods as $1,375 and the freight charge as $92. How is this transaction recorded?

EXERCISES

4. The net delivered cost of purchases for the period appears on the:

   a. balance sheet

   b. income statement

   c. schedule of accounts payable

   d. statement of owner's equity

5. In the accounts payable ledger, a supplier's account has a beginning balance of $4,800. A transaction of $1,600 is posted from the purchases journal. What is the balance of the supplier's account?

   a. $3,200 debit

   b. $3,200 credit

   c. $6,400 debit

   d. $6,400 credit

ANALYSIS

6. In the general ledger, the *Accounts Payable* account has a balance of $15,500. The schedule of accounts payable lists accounts totaling $20,500. What could cause this error?

(Answers to Section 2 Self Review are on page 268.)

8 Chapter   REVIEW   Chapter Summary

In this chapter, you have learned about the accounting journals and ledgers required for the efficient processing of purchases for a business. Businesses with strong internal controls establish and follow procedures for approving requests for new merchandise, choosing suppliers, placing orders with suppliers, checking goods after they arrive, identifying invoices, and approving payments.

Learning Objectives

8-1   Record purchases of merchandise on credit in a three-column purchases journal.

Purchases and payments on account must be entered in the firm's accounting records promptly and accurately. Most merchandising businesses normally purchase goods on credit. The most efficient system for recording purchases on credit is the use of a special purchases journal. With this type of journal, only one line is needed to enter all the data.

The purchases journal is used only to record the credit purchase of goods for resale. General business expenses are not recorded in the purchases journal.

8-2   Post from the three-column purchases journal to the general ledger accounts.

The use of the three-column purchases journal simplifies the posting process because nothing is posted to the general ledger until the month's end. Then, summary postings are made to the *Purchases, Freight In,* and *Accounts Payable* accounts.

8-3   Post credit purchases from the purchases journal to the accounts payable subsidiary ledger.

An accounts payable subsidiary ledger helps a firm keep track of the amounts it owes to creditors. Postings are made to this ledger on a daily basis.

- Each credit purchase is posted from the purchases journal to the accounts payable subsidiary ledger.

- Each payment on account is posted from the cash payments journal to the accounts payable subsidiary ledger.

8-4   Record purchases returns and allowances in the general journal and post them to the accounts payable subsidiary ledger.

Returns and allowances on purchases of goods are credited to an account called *Purchases Returns and*

Allowances. These transactions may be recorded in the general journal or in a special purchases returns and allowances journal. Each return or allowance on a credit purchase is posted to the accounts payable subsidiary ledger.

8-5   Prepare a schedule of accounts payable.

At the month's end, a schedule of accounts payable is prepared. The schedule lists the balances owed to the firm's creditors and proves the accuracy of the subsidiary ledger. The total of the schedule of accounts payable is compared with the balance of the *Accounts Payable* account in the general ledger, which acts as a control account. The two amounts should be equal.

8-6   Compute the net delivered cost of purchases.

The net delivered cost of purchases is computed by adding the cost of purchases and freight in, then subtracting any purchases returns and allowances. Net delivered cost of purchases is reported in the Cost of Goods Sold section of the income statement.

8-7   Demonstrate a knowledge of the procedures for effective internal control of purchases.

Purchases and payments should be properly authorized and processed with appropriate documentation to provide a system of checks and balances. A division of responsibilities within the purchases process ensures strong internal controls.

8-8   Record purchases, sales, and returns using the perpetual inventory system.

Perpetual inventory systems give management more control over the company's inventory, and assist management in inventory control and purchasing activities.

8-9   Define the accounting terms new to this chapter.

Glossary

Accounts payable ledger (p. 243) A subsidiary ledger that contains a separate account for each creditor

Cash discount (p. 240) A discount offered by suppliers for payment received within a specified period of time

Cost of goods sold (p. 238) The actual cost to the business of the merchandise sold to customers

Freight In **account** (p. 238) An account showing transportation charges for items purchased

Periodic inventory system (p. 250) An inventory system in which the merchandise inventory balance is only updated when a physical inventory is taken

Perpetual inventory system (p. 250) An inventory system in which merchandise inventory is updated for each purchase, sale, and return

Purchase allowance (p. 244) A price reduction from the amount originally billed

Purchase invoice (p. 236) A bill received for goods purchased

Purchase order (p. 236) An order to the supplier of goods specifying items needed, quantity, price, and credit terms

Purchase requisition (p. 236) A list sent to the purchasing department showing the items to be ordered

Purchase return (p. 244) Return of unsatisfactory goods

Purchases **account** (p. 238) An account used to record cost of goods bought for resale during a period

Purchases discount (p. 240) A cash discount offered to the customer for payment within a specified period

Purchases journal (p. 238) A special journal used to record the purchase of goods on credit

Receiving report (p. 236) A form showing quantity and condition of goods received

Sales discount (p. 240) A cash discount offered by the supplier for payment within a specified period

Sales invoice (p. 236) A supplier's billing document

Schedule of accounts payable (p. 246) A list of all balances owed to creditors

Transportation In **account** (p. 238) See Freight In account

---

Comprehensive **Self Review**

1. What type of account is *Purchases Returns and Allowances?*
2. What is a cash discount and why is it offered?
3. What is the purpose of the *Freight In* account?
4. What is the purpose of a purchase requisition? A purchase order?
5. What is the difference between a receiving report and an invoice?

(Answers to Comprehensive Self Review are on page 268.)

Discussion Questions

1. Why are the invoice date and terms recorded in the purchases journal?
2. What major safeguards should be built into a system of internal control for purchases of goods?
3. What is the purpose of a credit memorandum?
4. What is a purchase allowance?
5. What is a purchase return?
6. What is a schedule of accounts payable? Why is it prepared?
7. What is the relationship of the *Accounts Payable* account in the general ledger to the accounts payable subsidiary ledger?
8. What type of accounts are kept in the accounts payable ledger?
9. Why is it useful for a business to have an accounts payable ledger?
10. How is the net delivered cost of purchases computed?
11. What journals can be used to enter various merchandise purchase transactions?
12. What is the difference between a purchase invoice and a sales invoice?
13. What is the normal balance of the *Purchases* account?

14. On what financial statement do the accounts related to purchases of merchandise appear? In which section of this statement are they reported?

15. Why is the use of a *Purchases Returns and Allowances* account preferred to crediting these transactions to *Purchases?*

16. What do the following credit terms mean?

   a. n/30

   b. 2/10, n/30

   c. n/10 EOM

   d. n/20

   e. 1/10, n/20

   f. 3/5, n/30

   g. n/15 EOM

17. A business has purchased some new equipment for use in its operations, not for resale to customers. The terms of the invoice are n/30. Should this transaction be entered in the purchases journal? If not, where should it be recorded?

18. What account is debited for the purchase of merchandise inventory when (a) the periodic system is used and (b) the perpetual inventory system is used?

19. What account is credited for the return of merchandise inventory when (a) the periodic system is used and (b) the perpetual inventory system is used?

20. What account is debited for freight charges on merchandise inventory purchases when (a) the periodic system is used and (b) the perpetual inventory system is used?

APPLICATIONS

Exercises

Exercise 8.1
Objective 8-1

▶ **Identifying the journals used to record purchases and related transactions.**

The accounting system of Shoe City includes the following journals. Indicate which journal is used to record each transaction.

JOURNALS

Cash receipts journal
Cash payments journal
Purchases journal
Sales journal
General journal

TRANSACTIONS

1. Purchased merchandise for $3,000; the terms are 2/10, n/30.

2. Returned damaged merchandise to a supplier and received a credit memorandum for $800.

3. Issued a check for $3,600 to a supplier as a payment on account.

4. Purchased merchandise for $2,000 plus a freight charge of $140; the supplier's invoice is payable in 30 days.

5. Received an allowance for merchandise that was damaged but can be sold at a reduced price; the supplier's credit memorandum is for $475.

6. Purchased merchandise for $3,500 in cash.

◀ **Exercise 8.2**
Objective 8-1

Identifying journals used to record purchases and related transactions.

The following transactions took place at Extreme Bikers. Indicate the general ledger account numbers that would be debited and credited to record each transaction.

GENERAL LEDGER ACCOUNTS

101   Cash
205   Accounts Payable
501   Purchases
502   Freight In
503   Purchases Returns and Allowances

TRANSACTIONS

1. Purchased merchandise for $1,500; the terms are 2/10, n/30.
2. Returned damaged merchandise to a supplier and received a credit memorandum for $300.
3. Issued a check for $800 to a supplier as a payment on account.
4. Purchased merchandise for $2,400 plus a freight charge of $260; the supplier's invoice is payable in 30 days.
5. Received an allowance for merchandise that was damaged but can be sold at a reduced price; the supplier's credit memorandum is for $400.
6. Purchased merchandise for $4,200 in cash.

◀ **Exercise 8.3**
Objective 8-1

Recording credit purchases.

The following transactions took place at Cerritos Auto Parts and Custom Shop during the first week of July. Indicate how these transactions would be entered in a purchases journal like the one shown in this chapter.

DATE	TRANSACTIONS
July 1	Purchased batteries for $2,060 plus a freight charge of $132 from Auto Parts Corporation; received Invoice 6812, dated June 27, which has terms of n/30.
3	Purchased mufflers for $3,250 plus a freight charge of $89 from Aplex Company; received Invoice 441, dated June 30, which has terms of 1/10, n/60.
5	Purchased car radios for $2,470 plus freight of $127 from The Custom Sounds Shop, Inc.; received Invoice 5601, dated July 1, which has terms of 2/10, n/30.
10	Purchased truck tires for $4,270 from Specialty Tire Company; received Invoice 1102, dated July 8, which has terms of 2/10, n/30.

◀ **Exercise 8.4**
Objective 8-4

Recording a purchase return.

On February 9, Sophisticated Kitchens, a retail store, received Credit Memorandum 244 for $4,320 from M & J Appliance Corporation. The credit memorandum covered a return of damaged trash compactors originally purchased on Invoice 4101 dated January 3. Prepare the general journal entry that Sophisticated Kitchens would make for this transaction.

◀ **Exercise 8.5**
Objective 8-4

Recording a purchase allowance.

On March 17, All-Star Appliances was given an allowance of $1,175 by Uptown Kitchens, which issued Credit Memorandum 112. The allowance was for scratches on stoves that were originally purchased on Invoice 911 dated February 20. Prepare the general journal entry that All-Star Appliances would make for this transaction.

Exercise 8.6

Objective 8-4

▶ **Determining the cost of purchases.**

On June 30 the general ledger of Bentleys New York, a clothing store, showed a balance of $53,495 in the *Purchases* account, a balance of $2,875 in the *Freight In* account, and a balance of $5,220 in the *Purchases Returns and Allowances* account. What was the delivered cost of the purchases made during June? What was the net delivered cost of these purchases?

Exercise 8.7

Objectives
8-1, 8-4

▶ **Errors in recording purchase transactions.**

The following errors were made in recording transactions in posting from the purchases journal. How will these errors be detected?

a. A credit of $2,000 to Thomastown Furniture Company account in the accounts payable ledger was posted as $200.

b. The Accounts Payable column total of the purchases journal was understated by $200.

c. An invoice of $1,680 for merchandise from Johnson Company was recorded as having been received from Baxton Company, another supplier.

d. A $500 payment to Baxton Company was debited to Johnson Company.

Exercise 8.8

Objective 8-4

▶ **Determining the cost of purchases.**

Complete the following schedule by supplying the missing information.

Net Delivered Cost of Purchases	Case A	Case B
Purchases	(a)	95,570
Freight In	4,275	(c)
Delivered Cost of Purchases	97,750	(d)
Less Purchases Returns and Allowances	(b)	3,930
Net Delivered Cost of Purchases	93,825	97,920

Exercise 8.9

Objective 8-8

▶ **Recording transactions using the perpetual inventory system.**

The following transactions took place at Fine Fashions Outlet during July 2016. Fine Fashions Outlet uses a perpetual inventory system. Record the transactions in a general journal. Use 8 as the page number for the general journal. Omit descriptions.

DATE	TRANSACTIONS
July 3	Purchased dresses for $3,500 plus a freight charge of $120 from Fashion Expo, Invoice 101, dated July 1; the terms are net 30 days.
5	Sold two dresses on account to Alice Chu, terms net 30 days; issued Sales Slip 788 for $600. The cost of the dresses sold was $400.
7	Received Credit Memorandum 210 for $550 from Fashion Expo for damaged dresses returned; the goods were purchased on Invoice 101 dated July 1.
9	Accepted a return of a dress from Alice Chu; the dress was originally sold on Sales Slip 788 of July 5; issued Credit Memorandum 89 for $200. The cost of the returned dress was $135.

PROBLEMS

Problem Set A

Journalizing credit purchases and purchases returns and allowances and posting to the general ledger.

Digital World is a retail store that sells cameras and photography supplies. The firm's credit purchases and purchases returns and allowances transactions for June 2016 appear below, along with the general ledger accounts used to record these transactions. The balance shown in *Accounts Payable* is for the beginning of June.

◀   **Problem 8.1A**
Objectives 8-1,
8-2, 8-3

Sage 50
Complete Accounting

INSTRUCTIONS

1. Open the general ledger accounts and enter the balance of **Accounts Payable** for June 1, 2016.
2. Record the transactions in a three-column purchases journal and in a general journal. Use 14 as the page number for the purchases journal and 38 as the page number for the general journal.
3. Post entries from the general journal to the general ledger accounts.
4. Total and rule the purchases journal as of June 30.
5. Post the column totals from the purchases journal to the proper general ledger accounts.
6. Compute the net purchases of the firm for the month of June.

GENERAL LEDGER ACCOUNTS

205   Accounts Payable, $14,404 Cr.
501   Purchases
502   Freight In
503   Purchases Returns and Allowances

DATE		TRANSACTIONS
June	1	Purchased instant cameras for $2,050 plus a freight charge of $230 from Pro Photo Equipment, Invoice 4241, dated May 27; the terms are 60 days net.
	8	Purchased film for $1,394 from Photo Supplies, Invoice 1102, dated June 3, net payable in 45 days.
	12	Purchased lenses for $916 from Nano Glass, Invoice 7282, dated June 9; the terms are 1/10, n/60.
	18	Received Credit Memorandum 110 for $400 from Pro Photo Equipment for defective cameras that were returned; they were originally purchased on Invoice 4241, dated May 27.
	20	Purchased color film for $1,200 plus freight of $75 from Photo Supplies, Invoice 1148, dated June 15, net payable in 45 days.
	23	Purchased camera cases for $1,956 from Hi-Qual Case, Invoice 3108, dated June 18, net due and payable in 45 days.
	28	Purchased lens filters for $2,470 plus freight of $120 from Holtz Spectrum, Invoice 5027, dated June 24; the terms are 2/10, n/30.
	30	Received Credit Memorandum 1108 for $310 from Hi-Qual Case; the amount is an allowance for damaged but usable goods purchased on Invoice 3108, dated June 18.

(**Note:** Save your working papers for use in Problem 8.2A.)

Analyze: What total purchases were posted to the **Purchases** general ledger account for June?

Problem 8.2A

Objectives 8-4, 8-6

CONTINUING >>>
        Problem

Posting to the accounts payable ledger and preparing a schedule of accounts payable.

This problem is a continuation of Problem 8.1A.

INSTRUCTIONS

1. Set up an accounts payable subsidiary ledger for Digital World. Open an account for each of the creditors listed below and enter the balances as of June 1, 2016. Arrange the accounts payable ledger in alphabetical order.
2. Post the individual entries from the purchases journal and the general journal prepared in Problem 8.1A.
3. Prepare a schedule of accounts payable for June 30.
4. Check the total of the schedule of accounts payable against the balance of the *Accounts Payable* account in the general ledger. The two amounts should be equal.

Creditors		
Name	**Terms**	**Balance**
Photo Supplies	n/45	$10,580
Hi-Qual Case	n/45	1,300
Pro Photo Equipment	n/60	
Nano Glass	1/10, n/60	2,524
Holtz Spectrum	2/10, n/30	

Analyze: What amount is owed to Nano Glass on June 30?

Problem 8.3A

Objectives 8-1, 8-2, 8-3, 8-4, 8-5, 8-6

Sage 50
Complete Accounting
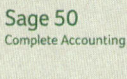

Journalizing credit purchases and purchases returns and allowances, computing the net delivered cost of goods, posting to the general ledger, posting to the accounts payable ledger, and preparing a schedule of accounts payable.

The English Garden Shop is a retail store that sells garden equipment, furniture, and supplies. Its credit purchases and purchases returns and allowances for July are listed on the next page. The general ledger accounts used to record these transactions are also provided. The balance shown is for the beginning of July 2016.

INSTRUCTIONS

PART I

1. Open the general ledger accounts and enter the balance of *Accounts Payable* for July 1.
2. Record the transactions in a three-column purchases journal and in a general journal. Use 8 as the page number for the purchases journal and 20 as the page number for the general journal.
3. Post the entries from the general journal to the proper general ledger accounts.
4. Total, prove, and rule the purchases journal as of July 31.
5. Post the column totals from the purchases journal to the proper general ledger accounts.
6. Compute the net delivered cost of the firm's purchases for the month of July.

GENERAL LEDGER ACCOUNTS

205	Accounts Payable, $35,980 Cr.	502	Freight In
501	Purchases	503	Purchases Returns and Allowances

DATE		TRANSACTIONS
July	1	Purchased lawn mowers for $9,310 plus a freight charge of $259 from Brown Corporation, Invoice 1011, dated June 26, net due and payable in 60 days.
	5	Purchased outdoor chairs and tables for $4,470 plus a freight charge of $562 from Brooks Garden Furniture Company, Invoice 639, dated July 2, net due and payable in 45 days.
	9	Purchased grass seed for $1,590 from Lawn and Gardens Supply, Invoice 8164, dated July 5; the terms are 30 days net.
	16	Received Credit Memorandum 110 for $700 from Brooks Garden Furniture Company; the amount is an allowance for scratches on some of the chairs and tables originally purchased on Invoice 639, dated July 2.
	19	Purchased fertilizer for $1,300 plus a freight charge of $266 from Lawn and Gardens Supply, Invoice 9050, dated July 15; the terms are 30 days net.
	21	Purchased hoses from Cameron Rubber Company for $3,780 plus a freight charge of $234, Invoice 1785, dated July 17; terms are 1/15, n/60.
	28	Received Credit Memorandum 223 for $530 from Cameron Rubber Company for damaged hoses that were returned; the goods were purchased on Invoice 1785, dated July 17.
	31	Purchased lawn sprinkler systems for $10,410 plus a freight charge of $288 from Wilson Industrial Products, Invoice 8985, dated July 26; the terms are 2/10, n/30.

INSTRUCTIONS

PART II

1. Set up an accounts payable subsidiary ledger for The English Garden Shop. Open an account for each of the creditors listed below and enter the balances as of July 1.

2. Post the individual entries from the purchases journal and the general journal prepared in Part I.

3. Prepare a schedule of accounts payable for July 31, 2016.

4. Check the total of the schedule of accounts payable against the balance of the *Accounts Payable* account in the general ledger. The two amounts should be equal.

Creditors		
Name	**Terms**	**Balance**
Brooks Garden Furniture Company	n/45	$11,220
Brown Corporation	n/60	18,220
Cameron Rubber Company	1/15, n/60	
Lawn and Gardens Supply	n/30	6,540
Wilson Industrial Products	2/10, n/30	

Analyze: What total freight charges were posted to the general ledger for the month of July?

Journalizing credit purchases and purchases returns and allowances, posting to the general ledger, posting to the accounts payable ledger, and preparing a schedule of accounts payable.

◀   **Problem 8.4A**
Objectives 8-1, 8-2, 8-3, 8-4, 8-5, 8-6

Sage 50
Complete Accounting

Office Plus is a retail business that sells office equipment, furniture, and supplies. Its credit purchases and purchases returns and allowances for September are shown on the next page. The general ledger accounts and the creditors' accounts in the accounts payable subsidiary ledger used to record these transactions are also provided. All balances shown are for the beginning of September.

INSTRUCTIONS

1. Open the general ledger accounts and enter the balance of *Accounts Payable* for September 1, 2016.

2. Open the creditors' accounts in the accounts payable subsidiary ledger and enter the balances for September 1.

3. Record the transactions in a three-column purchases journal and in a general journal. Use 5 as the page number for the purchases journal and 14 as the page number for the general journal.

4. Post to the accounts payable subsidiary ledger daily.

5. Post the entries from the general journal to the proper general ledger accounts at the end of the month.

6. Total and rule the purchases journal as of September 30.

7. Post the column totals from the purchases journal to the proper general ledger accounts.

8. Prepare a schedule of accounts payable and compare the balance of the *Accounts Payable* control account with the schedule of accounts payable.

GENERAL LEDGER ACCOUNTS

205	Accounts Payable, $28,356 Cr.	502	Freight In
501	Purchases	503	Purchases Returns and Allowances

Creditors		
Name	**Terms**	**Balance**
Apex Office Machines, Inc.	n/60	$11,060
Brown Paper Company	1/10, n/30	2,220
Dalton Office Furniture Company	n/30	9,676
Davis Corporation	n/30	
Zenn Furniture, Inc.	2/10, n/30	5,400

DATE	TRANSACTIONS
Sept. 3	Purchased desks for $8,020 plus a freight charge of $222 from Dalton Office Furniture Company, Invoice 4213, dated August 29; the terms are 30 days net.
7	Purchased computers for $12,300 from Apex Office Machines, Inc., Invoice 9217, dated September 2, net due and payable in 60 days.
10	Received Credit Memorandum 511 for $700 from Dalton Office Furniture Company; the amount is an allowance for damaged but usable desks purchased on Invoice 4213, dated August 29.
16	Purchased file cabinets for $2,656 plus a freight charge of $134 from Davis Corporation, Invoice 8066, dated September 11; the terms are 30 days net.
20	Purchased electronic desk calculators for $1,100 from Apex Office Machines, Inc., Invoice 11011, dated September 15, net due and payable in 60 days.
23	Purchased bond paper and copy machine paper for $8,500 plus a freight charge of $100 from Brown Paper Company, Invoice 6498, dated September 18; the terms are 1/10, n/30.
28	Received Credit Memorandum 312 for $980 from Apex Office Machines, Inc., for defective calculators that were returned; the calculators were originally purchased on Invoice 11011, dated September 15.
30	Purchased office chairs for $3,940 plus a freight charge of $170 from Zenn Furniture, Inc., Invoice 696, dated September 25, the terms are 2/10, n/30.

Analyze: What total amount was recorded for purchases returns and allowances in the month of September? What percentage of total purchases does this represent?

Problem Set B

Journalizing credit purchases and purchases returns and allowances and posting to the general ledger.

◄   **Problem 8.1B**
Objectives 8-1, 8-2, 8-3

Mountain Ski Shop is a retail store that sells ski equipment and clothing. The firm's credit purchases and purchases returns and allowances during May 2016 follow, along with the general ledger accounts used to record these transactions. The balance shown in *Accounts Payable* is for the beginning of May.

INSTRUCTIONS

1. Open the general ledger accounts and enter the balance of *Accounts Payable* for May 1, 2016.
2. Record the transactions in a three-column purchases journal and in a general journal. Use 15 as the page number for the purchases journal and 38 as the page number for the general journal.
3. Post the entries from the general journal to the proper general ledger accounts.
4. Total and rule the purchases journal as of May 31.
5. Post the column totals from the purchases journal to the proper general ledger accounts.
6. Compute the net purchases of the firm for the month of May.

GENERAL LEDGER ACCOUNTS

205   Accounts Payable, $21,608 Cr.
501   Purchases
502   Freight In
503   Purchases Returns and Allowances

DATE	TRANSACTIONS
May 1	Purchased ski boots for $6,600 plus a freight charge of $120 from East Coast Snow Shop, Invoice 6572, dated April 28; the terms are 45 days net.
8	Purchased skis for $12,500 from May-Day Ski Shop, Invoice 4916, dated May 2; the terms are net payable in 30 days.
9	Received Credit Memorandum 155 for $1,050 from East Coast Snow Shop for damaged ski boots that were returned; the boots were originally purchased on Invoice 6572, dated April 28.
12	Purchased ski jackets for $5,200 from Fashion Ski Wear, Invoice 986, dated May 11, net due and payable in 60 days.
16	Purchased ski poles for $2,650 from May-Day Ski Shop, Invoice 5011, dated May 15; the terms are n/30.
22	Purchased ski pants for $3,160 from Winter Sports Clothing, Invoice 4019, dated May 16; the terms are 1/10, n/60.
28	Received Credit Memorandum 38 for $480 from May-Day Ski Shop for defective ski poles that were returned; the items were originally purchased on Invoice 5011, dated May 15.
31	Purchased sweaters for $3,630 plus a freight charge of $220 from Golden Skis & Clothing, Invoice 8354, dated May 27; the terms are 2/10, n/30.

(**Note:** Save your working papers for use in Problem 8.2B.)
Analyze: What total accounts payable were posted from the purchases journal to the general ledger for the month?

Problem 8.2B

Objectives 8-4, 8-6

CONTINUING >>> Problem

▶ **Posting to the accounts payable ledger and preparing a schedule of accounts payable.**

This problem is a continuation of Problem 8.1B.

INSTRUCTIONS

1. Set up an accounts payable subsidiary ledger for Mountain Ski Shop. Open an account for each of the creditors listed below and enter the balances as of May 1, 2016. Arrange the accounts payable ledger in alphabetical order.

2. Post the individual entries from the purchases journal and the general journal prepared in Problem 8.1B.

3. Prepare a schedule of accounts payable for May 31.

4. Check the total of the schedule of accounts payable against the balance of the *Accounts Payable* account in the general ledger. The two amounts should be equal.

Creditors		
Name	**Terms**	**Balance**
May-Day Ski Shop	n/30	$1,700
Fashion Ski Wear	n/60	8,720
Winter Sports Clothing	1/10, n/60	5,000
East Coast Snow Shop	n/45	6,188
Golden Skis & Clothing	2/10, n/30	

Analyze: What amount did Mountain Ski Shop owe to its supplier, East Coast Snow Shop, on May 31?

Problem 8.3B

Objectives 8-1, 8-2, 8-3, 8-4, 8-5, 8-6

▶ **Journalizing credit purchases and purchases returns and allowances, computing the net delivered cost of goods, posting to the general ledger, posting to the accounts payable ledger, and preparing a schedule of accounts payable.**

The Landscape Supply Center is a retail store that sells garden equipment, furniture, and supplies. Its credit purchases and purchases returns and allowances for December are shown below. The general ledger accounts used to record these transactions are also provided. The balance shown is for the beginning of December 2016.

INSTRUCTIONS

PART I

1. Open the general ledger accounts and enter the balance of *Accounts Payable* for December 1.

2. Record the transactions in a three-column purchases journal and in a general journal. Use 8 as the page number for the purchases journal and 20 as the page number for the general journal.

3. Post the entries from the general journal to the proper general ledger accounts.

4. Total, prove, and rule the purchases journal as of December 31.

5. Post the column totals from the purchases journal to the proper general ledger accounts.

6. Compute the net delivered cost of the firm's purchases for the month of December.

GENERAL LEDGER ACCOUNTS

205	Accounts Payable, $13,490 Cr.
501	Purchases
502	Freight In
503	Purchases Returns and Allowances

DATE	TRANSACTIONS
Dec. 1	Purchased lawn mowers for $5,780 plus a freight charge of $156 from Selby Corporation, Invoice 2110, dated November 26, net due and payable in 45 days.
5	Purchased outdoor chairs and tables for $5,700 plus a freight charge of $100 from Patio Furniture Shop, Invoice 633, dated December 2; the terms are 1/15, n/60.
9	Purchased grass seed for $1,148 from Spring Lawn Center, Invoice 1127, dated December 4; the terms are 30 days net.
16	Received Credit Memorandum 101 for $400 from Patio Furniture Shop; the amount is an allowance for scratches on some of the chairs and tables originally purchased on Invoice 633, dated December 2.
19	Purchased fertilizer for $1,600 plus a freight charge of $156 from Spring Lawn Center, Invoice 1131, dated December 15; the terms are 30 days net.
21	Purchased garden hoses for $760 plus a freight charge of $76 from Delta Rubber Company, Invoice 8517, dated December 17; the terms are n/60.
28	Received Credit Memorandum 210 for $150 from Delta Rubber Company for damaged hoses that were returned; the goods were purchased on Invoice 8517, dated December 17.
31	Purchased lawn sprinkler systems for $3,700 plus a freight charge of $80 from Cason Industries, Invoice 8819, dated December 26; the terms are 2/10, n/30.

INSTRUCTIONS

PART II

1. Set up an accounts payable subsidiary ledger for The Landscape Supply Center. Open an account for each of the following creditors and enter the balances as of December 1.
2. Post the individual entries from the purchases journal and the general journal prepared in Part I.
3. Prepare a schedule of accounts payable for December 31.
4. Check the total of the schedule of accounts payable against the balance of the *Accounts Payable* account in the general ledger. The two amounts should be equal.

Creditors		
Name	**Terms**	**Balance**
Cason Industries	2/10, n/30	$2,150
Delta Rubber Company	n/60	3,850
Patio Furniture Shop	1/15, n/60	
Selby Corporation	n/45	4,842
Spring Lawn Center	n/30	2,648

Analyze: By what amount did Accounts Payable increase during the month of December?

Journalizing credit purchases and purchases returns and allowances, posting to the general ledger, posting to the accounts payable ledger, and preparing a schedule of accounts payable.

◀   **Problem 8.4B**
Objectives 8-1, 8-2, 8-3, 8-4, 8-5, 8-6

Simpson's Card and Novelty Shop is a retail card, novelty, and business supply store. Its credit purchases and purchases returns and allowances for February 2016 appear on the next page. The general ledger accounts and the creditors' accounts in the accounts payable subsidiary ledger used to record these transactions are also provided. The balance shown is for the beginning of February.

INSTRUCTIONS

1. Open the general ledger accounts and enter the balance of *Accounts Payable* for February.

2. Open the creditors' accounts in the accounts payable subsidiary ledger and enter the balances for February 1, 2016.

3. Record each transaction in the appropriate journal, purchases or general. Use page 4 in the purchases journal and page 12 in the general journal.

4. Post entries to the accounts payable subsidiary ledger daily.

5. Post entries in the general journal to the proper general ledger accounts at the end of the month.

6. Total and rule the purchases journal as of February 29.

7. Post the totals to the appropriate general ledger accounts.

8. Calculate the net delivered cost of purchases.

9. Prepare a schedule of accounts payable and compare the balance of the *Accounts Payable* control account with the schedule of accounts payable.

GENERAL LEDGER ACCOUNTS

203   Accounts Payable, $15,200 credit balance
501   Purchases
502   Freight In
503   Purchases Returns and Allowances

Creditors		
Name	**Terms**	**Balance**
Business Forms, Inc.	n/30	$8,000
Gifts and Holiday Cards	2/10, n/30	4,000
Packing and Mailing Supply Center	2/10, n/30	3,200
Specialty Business Cards	1/10, n/45	

DATE	TRANSACTIONS
Feb. 5	Purchased copy paper from Packing and Mailing Supply Center for $2,000 plus $100 shipping charges on Invoice 502, dated February 2.
8	Purchased assorted holiday cards from Gifts and Holiday Cards on Invoice 2808, $1,900, dated February 5.
12	Purchased five boxes of novelty items from Gifts and Holiday Cards for a total cost of $1,200, Invoice 2904, dated February 8.
13	Purchased tray of cards from Specialty Business Cards on Invoice 2013 for $1,100, dated February 9.
19	Purchased supply of forms from Business Forms, Inc., for $1,980 plus shipping charges of $60 on Invoice 2019, dated February 16.
20	One box of cards purchased on February 8 from Gifts and Holiday Cards was water damaged. Received Credit Memorandum 102 for $200.
21	Toner supplies are purchased from Specialty Business Cards for $3,600 plus shipping charges of $110, Invoice 1376, dated February 19.
27	Received Credit Memorandum 118 for $240 from Gifts and Holiday Cards as an allowance for damaged novelty items purchased on February 12.

Analyze: What total amount did Simpson's Card and Novelty Shop pay in freight charges during the month of February? What percentage of delivered cost of purchases does this represent?

Critical Thinking Problem 8.1

Merchandising: Sales and Purchases

Fashion Standards is a retail clothing store. Sales of merchandise and purchases of goods on account for January 2016, the first month of operations, appear below.

INSTRUCTIONS

1. Record the purchases of goods on account on page 6 of a three-column purchases journal.
2. Record the sales of merchandise on account on page 1 of a sales journal.
3. Post the entries from the purchases journal and the sales journal to the individual accounts in the accounts payable and accounts receivable subsidiary ledgers. Use the following account numbers:

   Accounts Receivable 111
   Accounts Payable 205
   Sales Tax Payable 231
   Sales 401
   Purchases 501
   Freight In 502
   All customers have n/30 credit terms.

4. Total, prove, and rule the journals as of January 31.
5. Post the column totals from the special journals to the proper general ledger accounts.
6. Prepare a schedule of accounts payable for January 31.
7. Prepare a schedule of accounts receivable for January 31.

		PURCHASES OF GOODS ON ACCOUNT
Jan.	3	Purchased dresses for $4,500 plus a freight charge of $120 from Fashion Expo, Invoice 101, dated December 26; the terms are net 30 days.
	5	Purchased handbags for $3,480 plus a freight charge of $89 from Tru Totes & Co., Invoice 223, dated December 28; the terms are 2/10, n/30.
	7	Purchased blouses for $3,000 plus a freight charge of $75 from Extreme Fashions, Invoice 556, dated January 3; the terms are 2/10, n/30.
	9	Purchased casual pants for $2,360 from Comfy Casuals, Invoice 110, dated January 5; terms are n/30.
	12	Purchased business suits for $6,400 plus a freight charge of $150 from Professional Wears, Invoice 104, dated January 9; the terms are 2/10, n/30.
	18	Purchased shoes for $3,120 plus freight of $80 from City Walks, Invoice 118, dated January 14; the terms are n/60.
	25	Purchased hosiery for $1,025 from Silky Legs Express, Invoice 1012, dated January 20; the terms are 2/10, n/30.
	29	Purchased scarves and gloves for $1,600 from Comfy Casuals, Invoice 315, dated January 26; the terms are n/30.
	31	Purchased party dresses for $7,500 plus a freight charge of $250 from Special Occasions Dress Shop, Invoice 1044, dated January 27; the terms are 2/10, n/30.

SALES OF MERCHANDISE ON ACCOUNT	
Jan. 4	Sold two dresses to Vivian Cho; issued Sales Slip 101 for $600 plus $48 sales tax.
5	Sold a handbag to Dina Bates; issued Sales Slip 102 for $525 plus $42 sales tax.
6	Sold four blouses to Julia Adams; issued Sales Slip 103 for $400 plus $32 sales tax.
10	Sold casual pants and a blouse to Cheryl Scott; issued Sales Slip 104 for $350 plus $28 sales tax.
14	Sold a business suit to Alleen De Revere; issued Sales Slip 105 for $500 plus $40 sales tax.
17	Sold hosiery, shoes, and gloves to Sasha Ramirez; issued Sales Slip 106 for $625 plus $50 sales tax.
21	Sold dresses and scarves to Elaine Patterson; issued Sales Slip 107 for $1,500 plus $120 sales tax.
24	Sold a business suit to Andrea Aguilar; issued Sales Slip 108 for $500 plus $40 sales tax.
25	Sold shoes to Tracy Mai; issued Sales Slip 109 for $300 plus $24 sales tax.
29	Sold a casual pants set to Toni Garcia; issued Sales Slip 110 for $600 plus $48 sales tax.
31	Sold a dress and handbag to Linda Martin; issued Sales Slip 111 for $950 plus $76 sales tax.

Analyze: What is the net delivered cost of purchases for the month of January?

Critical Thinking Problem 8.2

Internal Control

Celeste Renard, owner of Sensual Linens Shop, was preparing checks for payment of the current month's purchase invoices when she realized that there were two invoices from Passionate Linens Company, each for the purchase of 100 red, heart-imprinted king size linen sets. Alexander thinks that Passionate Linens Company must have billed Sensual Linens Shop twice for the same shipment because she knows the shop would not have needed two orders for 100 red linen sets within a month.

1. How can Renard determine whether Passionate Linens Company billed Sensual Linens Shop in error or whether Sensual Linens Shop placed two identical orders for red, heart-imprinted linen sets?

2. If two orders were placed, how can Renard prevent duplicate purchases from happening in the future?

BUSINESS CONNECTIONS

Managerial | FOCUS

Cash Management

1. Why should management be concerned about paying its invoices on a timely basis?

2. Why is it important for a firm to maintain a satisfactory credit rating?

3. Suppose you are the new controller of a small but growing company and you find that the firm has a policy of paying cash for all purchases of goods even though it could obtain credit. The president of the company does not like the idea of having debts, but the vice president thinks this is a poor business policy that will hurt the firm in the future. The president has asked your opinion. Would you agree with the president or the vice president? Why?

4. How would excessive investment in merchandise harm a business?

5. How can good internal controls over purchases protect a firm from fraud and errors and from excessive investment in merchandise?

6. Why should management be concerned about internal controls over purchases?

Adding New Vendors

Anna Abraham is the accounts payable clerk for Jiffy Delivery Service. This company runs 10 branches in the San Diego area. The company pays for a variety of expenses. Anna writes the checks for each of the vendors and the controller signs the checks. Anna has decided she needs a raise and the controller has told her to wait for six months. Anna has devised a plan to get a raise on her own. She creates a new vendor for her friend's business with the name John's Car Detailing. She also creates two purchase orders for car detailing service from John's for $75 and $70. She writes checks to John's Car Detailing to pay these invoices. She knows the controller will sign all checks only looking at the checks over $100. She delivers the checks to John who will deposit the checks in his bank account. John then writes a check to her for $145. Is this a good way for Anna to obtain a raise? Is it an ethical practice? Eventually what will be the effect of her actions? What can the company do to prevent this type of behavior?

Income Statement

The following financial statement excerpt is taken from the *2012 Annual Report (for the fiscal year ended February 3, 2013)* for The Home Depot, Inc.

Consolidated Statements of Earnings		
	For the fiscal year ended	
	February 3, 2013	January 29, 2012
(In millions)		
Net Sales	$ 74,754	$ 70,395
Cost of Sales	48,912	46,133
Gross Profit	$ 25,842	$ 24,262

1. The Cost of Sales amount on The Home Depot, Inc., consolidated statements of earnings represents the net cost of the goods that were sold for the period. For 2013, what percentage of net sales was the cost of sales? For fiscal 2012?

2. What factors might affect a merchandising company's cost of sales from one period to another?

Analyze Online: On The Home Depot, Inc., website (www.homedepot.com), locate the Investor Relations' section.

3. Review the consolidated statements of operations found in the current year's annual report.

4. What amount is reported for cost of sales?

5. What amount is reported for net sales?

Payment Terms

A company needs to develop an objective for paying bills. Do they want to stretch their cash flow as far as they can? Do they want to have a good reputation of always paying bills on time? Do they want to be sure to get paid by their customers before they pay their vendors? In a group, discuss what would be the best payment terms to use for each objective and its impact on the company.

Computer Check Format

Go to the QuickBooks and Sage websites at quickbooks.com and na.sage.com. Select product overview and more information. You want to be sure to see a copy of a check and purchase order. Compare and contrast the information contained on each check and purchase order. How many copies can you get of the check and purchase order? How is the form different? How is it the same? What information should be included on a company's check and purchase invoice?

Answers to **Self Reviews**

Answers to Section 1 Self Review

1. Locating suitable suppliers, obtaining price quotations and credit terms, and placing orders.
2. Merchandise purchased on credit for resale.
3. It saves time and effort, and it strengthens the audit trail.
4. **c.** Purchase requisition
5. **b.** Purchase order
6. The business will receive a 2 percent discount if the invoice is paid within 10 days. If the invoice is not paid within 10 days, the total amount is due within 30 days.

Answers to Section 2 Self Review

1. It lists all of the creditors to whom money is owed.
2. $59,575 ($62,450 – $2,875)
3. Purchases   1,375.00

   Freight In   92.00

      Accounts Payable   1,467.00
4. **b.** income statement
5. **d.** $6,400 credit ($4,800 + $1,600)
6. A payment was made and recorded in the general ledger account, but was not recorded in the creditor's subsidiary ledger account.

Answers to Comprehensive Self Review

1. A contra cost of goods sold account.
2. A price reduction offered to encourage quick payment of invoices by customers.
3. To accumulate freight charges paid for purchases.
4. The purchase requisition is used by a sales department to notify the purchasing department of the items wanted. The purchase order is prepared by the purchasing department to order the necessary goods at an appropriate price from the selected supplier.
5. The receiving report shows the quantity of goods received and the condition of the goods. The invoice shows quantities and prices; it is the document from which checks are prepared in payment of purchases.

Cash Receipts, Cash Payments, and Banking Procedures

Chapter **9**

www.clifbar.com

Gary Erickson, an avid cyclist, was inspired to create a better-tasting energy bar while forcing down a less-than-delicious snack on a 175-mile bike ride. With help from his mom, Gary concocted the CLIF® Bar. The LUNA® Bar, the CLIF® Builder's Bar, and the CLIF® Crunch have joined the original CLIF® Bar, and Gary's idea for a better energy bar evolved into a $200 million business.

All of the ingredients in CLIF Bars, from the peanut butter to the chocolate chips, need to be purchased by the company. Just like Gary's mom wrote checks to buy ingredients CLIF Bar writes checks and has to ensure that there is enough money in the bank to cover those checks. When it sells its bars to retailers, CLIF Bar needs to keep track of who owes them money and be able to account for the receivables that are due to them. The company is dedicated to the health and welfare of its employees but is also a company that credits some of its success to effective management of its customer receivables and its cash flow.

thinking critically

Does CLIF Bar write checks for everything?

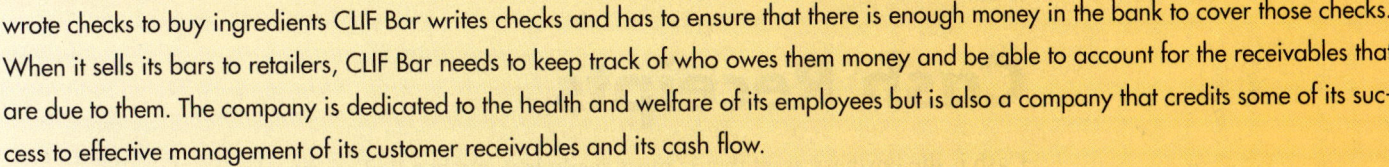

LEARNING OBJECTIVES

9-1. Record cash receipts in a cash receipts journal.

9-2. Account for cash short or over.

9-3. Post from the cash receipts journal to subsidiary and general ledgers.

9-4. Record cash payments in a cash payments journal.

9-5. Post from the cash payments journal to subsidiary and general ledgers.

9-6. Demonstrate a knowledge of procedures for a petty cash fund.

9-7. Demonstrate a knowledge of internal control procedures for cash.

9-8. Write a check, endorse checks, prepare a bank deposit slip, and maintain a checkbook balance.

9-9. Reconcile the monthly bank statement.

9-10. Record any adjusting entries required from the bank reconciliation.

9-11. Understand how businesses use online banking to manage cash activities.

9-12. Record cash payments and cash receipts using the perpetual inventory system.

9-13. Define the accounting terms new to this chapter.

NEW TERMS

bank reconciliation statement
blank endorsement
bonding
canceled check
cash
cash payments journal
cash receipts journal
cash register proof
Cash Short or Over account
check
credit memorandum
debit memorandum
deposit in transit
deposit slip
dishonored (NSF) check

drawee
drawer
electronic funds transfer (EFT)
endorsement
full endorsement
negotiable
outstanding checks
payee
petty cash analysis sheet
petty cash fund
petty cash voucher
postdated check
promissory note
restrictive endorsement
service charge
statement of account

SECTION OBJECTIVES	TERMS TO LEARN
>> 9-1. **Record cash receipts in a cash receipts journal.** **WHY IT'S IMPORTANT** The cash receipts journal is an efficient option for recording incoming cash.	cash cash receipts journal cash register proof *Cash Short or Over* account petty cash fund promissory note statement of account
>> 9-2. **Account for cash short or over.** **WHY IT'S IMPORTANT** Discrepancies in cash are a possible indication that cash is mismanaged.	
>> 9-3. **Post from the cash receipts journal to subsidiary and general ledgers.** **WHY IT'S IMPORTANT** The subsidiary and general ledgers must hold accurate, up-to-date information about cash transactions.	

Cash Receipts

Cash is the business asset that is most easily lost, mishandled, or even stolen. A well-managed business has careful procedures for controlling cash and recording cash transactions.

Cash Transactions

In accounting, the term **cash** is used for currency, coins, checks, money orders, and funds on deposit in a bank. Most cash transactions involve checks.

CASH RECEIPTS

The type of cash receipts depends on the nature of the business. Supermarkets receive checks as well as currency and coins. Department stores receive checks in the mail from charge account customers. Cash received by wholesalers is usually in the form of checks.

CASH PAYMENTS

For safety and convenience, most businesses make payments by check. Sometimes a limited number of transactions are paid with currency and coins. The **petty cash fund** is used to handle payments involving small amounts of money, such as postage stamps, delivery charges, and minor purchases of office supplies. Some businesses maintain a fund to provide cash for business-related travel and entertainment expenses.

The Cash Receipts Journal

To improve the recordkeeping of cash receipts, many businesses use a special **cash receipts journal.** The cash receipts journal simplifies the recording of transactions and eliminates repetition in posting.

RECORDING TRANSACTIONS IN THE CASH RECEIPTS JOURNAL

>> **9-1. OBJECTIVE**

Record cash receipts in a cash receipts journal.

The format of the cash receipts journal varies according to the needs of each business. Figure 9.1 shows the cash receipts journal for Maxx-Out Sporting Goods, which has two major

FIGURE 9.1 Cash Receipts Journal

CASH RECEIPTS JOURNAL   PAGE ___1___

DATE		DESCRIPTION	POST. REF.	ACCOUNTS RECEIVABLE CREDIT	SALES TAX PAYABLE CREDIT	SALES CREDIT	OTHER ACCOUNTS CREDIT			CASH DEBIT
							ACCOUNT NAME	POST. REF.	AMOUNT	
2016										
Jan.	7	Ann Anh		702 00						702 00
	8	Cash Sales			360 00	4 500 00				4 860 00
	11	Vickie Bowman		270 00						270 00
	12	Investment					M. Ferraro, Capital		15 000 00	15 000 00
	13	Barbara Coe		540 00						540 00
	15	Cash Sales			384 00	4 800 00	Cash Short/Over		18 00	5 166 00
	16	Alma Sanchez		108 00						108 00
	17	Cash Refund					Supplies		75 00	75 00
	22	Fred Wu		400 00						400 00
	22	Cash Sales			400 00	5 000 00				5 400 00
	29	Cash Sales			216 00	2 700 00	Cash Short/Over		16 00	2 932 00
	31	Kim Ramirez		108 00						108 00
	31	Mesia Davis		275 00						275 00
	31	Cash Sales			440 00	5 550 00				5 940 00
	31	Note Collection/					Notes Receivable		800 00	
		Stacee Fairley					Interest Income		36 00	836 00

sources of cash receipts: checks from credit customers who are making payments on account, and currency and coins from cash sales.

The cash receipts journal has separate columns for the accounts frequently used when recording cash receipts. There are columns for:

- debits to *Cash,*
- credits to *Accounts Receivable* for payments received on account,
- credits to *Sales* and *Sales Tax Payable* for cash sales.

At the end of the month, the totals of these columns are posted to the general ledger.

Notice the Other Accounts Credit section, which is for entries that do not fit into one of the special columns. Entries in the Other Accounts Credit section are individually posted to the general ledger.

Cash Sales and Sales Taxes Maxx-Out Sporting Goods uses a cash register to record cash sales and to store currency and coins. As each transaction is entered, the cash register prints a receipt for the customer. It also records the sale and the sales tax on an audit tape locked inside the machine. At the end of the day, when the machine is cleared, the cash register prints the transaction totals on the audit tape. The manager of the store removes the audit tape, and a cash register proof is prepared. The **cash register proof** is a verification that the amount in the cash register agrees with the amount shown on the audit tape. The cash register proof is used to record cash sales and sales tax in the cash receipts journal. The currency and coins are deposited in the firm's bank.

Refer to Figure 9.1, the cash receipts journal for Maxx-Out Sporting Goods. To keep it simple, it shows weekly, rather than daily, cash sales entries. Look at the January 8 entry. The steps to record the January 8 sales follow:

1. Enter the sales tax collected, $360.00, in the Sales Tax Payable Credit column.
2. Enter the sales, $4,500.00, in the Sales Credit column.
3. Enter the cash received, $4,860.00, in the Cash Debit column.
4. Confirm that total credits equal total debits ($360.00 + $4,500.00 = $4,860.00).

Cash Short or Over Occasionally, errors occur when making change. When errors happen, the cash in the cash register is either more than or less than the cash listed on the audit tape.

>> **9-2. OBJECTIVE**
Account for cash short or over.

When cash in the register is more than the audit tape, cash is over. When cash in the register is less than the audit tape, cash is *short*. Cash tends to be short more often than over because customers are more likely to notice and complain if they receive too little change.

Record short or over amounts in the **Cash Short or Over account.** If the account has a credit balance, there is an overage, which is treated as revenue. If the account has a debit balance, there is a shortage, which is treated as an expense.

Figure 9.1 shows how cash overages and shortages appear in the cash receipts journal. Look at the January 29 entry. Cash sales were $2,700. Sales tax collected was $216. The cash drawer was over $16. Overages are recorded as credits. Notice that the account name and the overage are entered in the Other Accounts Credit section.

Now look at the January 15 entry. This time the cash register was short. Shortages are recorded as debits. Debits are not the normal balance of the Other Accounts Credit column, so the debit entry is circled.

Businesses that have frequent entries for cash shortages and overages add a Cash Short or Over column to the cash receipts journal.

Cash Received on Account

Maxx-Out Sporting Goods makes sales on account and bills customers once a month. It sends a **statement of account** that shows the transactions during the month and the balance owed. Customers are asked to pay within 30 days of receiving the statement. Checks from credit customers are entered in the cash receipts journal, and then the checks are deposited in the bank.

Figure 9.1 shows how cash received on account is recorded. Look at the January 7 entry for Ann Anh. The check amount is entered in the Accounts Receivable Credit and the Cash Debit columns.

Cash Discounts on Sales

Maxx-Out Sporting Goods, like most retail businesses, does not offer cash discounts. However, many wholesale businesses offer cash discounts to customers who pay within a certain time period. For example, a wholesaler may offer a 1 percent discount if the customer pays within 10 days. To the wholesaler this is a *sales discount.* Sales discounts are recorded when the payment is received. Sales discounts are recorded in a contra revenue account, **Sales Discounts.** Businesses with many sales discounts add a Sales Discounts Debit column to the cash receipts journal.

Additional Investment by the Owner

Figure 9.1 shows that on January 12, the owner Max Ferraro invested an additional $15,000 in Maxx-Out Sporting Goods. He intends to use the money to expand the product line. The account name and amount are entered in the Other Accounts Credit section. The debit is entered in the Cash Debit column.

Receipt of a Cash Refund

Sometimes a business receives a cash refund for supplies, equipment, or other assets that are returned to the supplier. Figure 9.1 shows that on January 17, Maxx-Out Sporting Goods received a $75 cash refund for supplies that were returned to the seller. The account name and amount are entered in the Other Accounts Credit section. The debit is entered in the Cash Debit column.

Collection of a Promissory Note and Interest

A **promissory note** is a written promise to pay a specified amount of money on a certain date. Most notes require that interest is paid at a specified rate. Businesses use promissory notes to extend credit for some sales transactions.

FIGURE 9.2

A Promissory Note

$ 800.00   July 31, 2015

___Six Months___   AFTER DATE _I_   PROMISE TO PAY

TO THE ORDER OF   _Maxx-Out Sporting Goods_

___Eight Hundred and no/100_____ DOLLARS

PAYABLE AT _First Texas Bank_

VALUE RECEIVED *with interest at 9%*

NO. _30_   DUE _January 31, 2016_   _Stacee Fairley_

Sometimes promissory notes are used to replace an accounts receivable balance when the account is overdue. For example, on July 31 Maxx-Out Sporting Goods accepted a six-month promissory note from Stacee Fairley, who owed $800 on account (see Figure 9.2). Fairley had asked for more time to pay his balance. Maxx-Out Sporting Goods agreed to grant more time if Fairley signed a promissory note with 9 percent annual interest. The note provides more legal protection than an account receivable. The interest is compensation for the delay in receiving payment.

On the date of the transaction, July 31, Maxx-Out Sporting Goods recorded a general journal entry to increase notes receivable and to decrease accounts receivable for $800. The asset account, *Notes Receivable,* was debited and *Accounts Receivable* was credited.

	GENERAL JOURNAL				PAGE 16	
	DATE	DESCRIPTION	POST. REF.	DEBIT	CREDIT	
1	2015					1
2	July 31	Notes Receivable	109	800 00		2
3		Accounts Receivable/Stacee Fairley	111 ✓		800 00	3
4		Received a 6-month, 9% note from				4
5		Stacee Fairley to replace open account				5

On January 31, the due date of the note, Maxx-Out Sporting Goods received a check for $836 from Fairley. This sum covered the amount of the note ($800) and the interest owed for the six-month period ($36). Figure 9.1 shows the entry in the cash receipts journal. The account names, *Notes Receivable* and *Interest Income,* and the amounts are entered on two lines in the Other Accounts Credit section. The debit is in the Cash Debit column.

POSTING FROM THE CASH RECEIPTS JOURNAL

During the month, the amounts recorded in the Accounts Receivable Credit column are posted to individual accounts in the accounts receivable subsidiary ledger. Similarly, the amounts that appear in the Other Accounts Credit column are posted individually to the general ledger accounts during the month. The "CR1" posting references in the *Cash Short or Over* general ledger account below show that the entries appear on the first page of the cash receipts journal.

>> **9-3. OBJECTIVE**
Post from the cash receipts journal to subsidiary and general ledgers.

ACCOUNT Cash Short or Over							ACCOUNT NO. 617	
DATE	DESCRIPTION	POST. REF.	DEBIT	CREDIT	BALANCE			
					DEBIT	CREDIT		
2016								
Jan. 15		CR1	18 00		18 00			
29		CR1		16 00	2 00			

Posting the Column Totals   At the end of the month, the cash receipts journal is totaled and the equality of debits and credits is proved.

Proof of Cash Receipts Journal	
	Debits
Cash Debit column	$42,612.00
	Credits
Accounts Receivable Credit column	$ 2,403.00
Sales Tax Payable Credit column	1,800.00
Sales Credit column	22,500.00
Other Accounts Credit column	15,909.00
Total Credits	$42,612.00

FIGURE 9.3 Posted Cash Receipts Journal

CASH RECEIPTS JOURNAL   PAGE ____1____

DATE	DESCRIPTION	POST. REF.	ACCOUNTS RECEIVABLE CREDIT	SALES TAX PAYABLE CREDIT	SALES CREDIT	OTHER ACCOUNTS CREDIT ACCOUNT NAME	POST. REF.	AMOUNT	CASH DEBIT
2016									
Jan. 7	Ann Anh	✓	702 00						702 00
8	Cash Sales			360 00	4500 00				4860 00
11	Vickie Bowman	✓	270 00						270 00
12	Investment					M. Ferraro, Capital	301	15000 00	15000 00
13	Barbara Coe	✓	540 00						540 00
15	Cash Sales			384 00	4800 00	Cash Short/Over	617	⟨18 00⟩	5166 00
16	Alma Sanchez	✓	108 00						108 00
17	Cash Refund					Supplies	129	75 00	75 00
22	Fred Wu	✓	400 00						400 00
22	Cash Sales			400 00	5000 00				5400 00
29	Cash Sales			216 00	2700 00	Cash Short/Over	617	16 00	2932 00
31	Kim Ramirez	✓	108 00						108 00
31	Mesia Davis	✓	275 00						275 00
31	Cash Sales			440 00	5500 00				5940 00
31	Note Collection/					Notes Receivable	109	800 00	
	Stacee Fairley					Interest Income	491	36 00	836 00
	Totals		2403 00	1800 00	22500 00			15909 00	42612 00
			(111)	(231)	(401)			(X)	(101)

Figure 9.3 shows the cash receipts journal after all posting is completed.

When the cash receipts journal has been proved, rule the columns and post the totals to the general ledger. Figure 9.4 shows how to post from the cash receipts journal to the general ledger accounts.

To post a column total to a general ledger account, enter "CR1" in the Posting Reference column to show that the entry is from the first page of the cash receipts journal. Enter the column total in the general ledger account Debit or Credit column. Figure 9.4 shows the entries to *Accounts Receivable* (1), *Sales Tax Payable* (2), *Sales* (3), and *Cash* (4). Compute the new balance for each account and enter it in the Balance Debit or Balance Credit column.

Enter the general ledger account numbers under the column totals on the cash receipts journal. The (X) in the Other Accounts Credit Amount column indicates that the individual amounts were posted, not the total.

Posting to the Accounts Receivable Ledger To keep customer balances current, accountants post entries from the Accounts Receivable Credit column to the customers' accounts in the accounts receivable subsidiary ledger daily. For example, on January 7, $702 was posted to Ann Anh's account in the subsidiary ledger. The "CR1" in the Posting Reference column indicates that the transaction appears on page 1 of the cash receipts journal. The check mark (✓) in the Posting Reference column in the cash receipts journal (Figure 9.4) shows that the amount was posted to Ann Anh's account in the accounts receivable subsidiary ledger.

NAME   Ann Anh

ADDRESS   8913 South Hampton Road, Dallas, Texas 75232-6002

DATE	DESCRIPTION	POST. REF.	DEBIT	CREDIT	BALANCE
2016					
Jan. 1	Balance	✓			432 00
3	Sales Slip 1101	S1	702 00		1134 00
7		CR1		702 00	432 00
31	Sales Slip 1110	S1	267 50		699 50

FIGURE 9.4   **Posting from the Cash Receipts Journal**

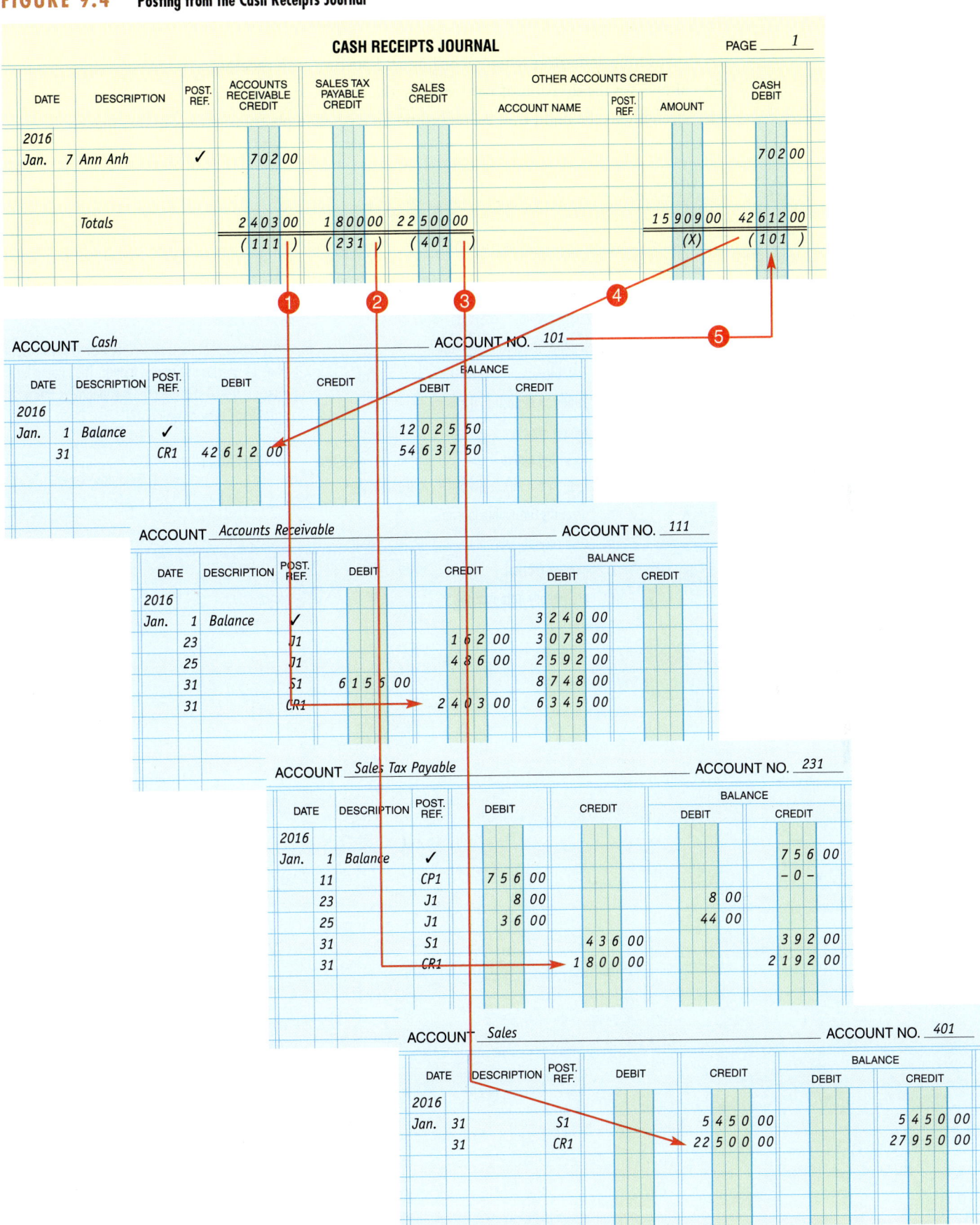

ADVANTAGES OF THE CASH RECEIPTS JOURNAL

The cash receipts journal:

- saves time and effort when recording and posting cash receipts,
- allows for the division of work among the accounting staff,
- strengthens the audit trail by recording all cash receipts transactions in one place.

Section 1   Self Review

QUESTIONS

1. How and when are the amounts in the Accounts Receivable Credit column of the cash receipts journal posted?

2. What is a promissory note? In what situation would a business accept a promissory note?

3. What is a cash shortage? A cash overage? How are they recorded?

EXERCISES

4. Which items are considered cash?
   a. Currency
   b. Funds on deposit in the bank
   c. Money orders
   d. All of the above

5. Collection of a note receivable is recorded in the:
   a. accounts receivable journal.
   b. cash receipts journal.
   c. general journal.
   d. promissory note journal.

ANALYSIS

6. You notice that the *Cash Short or Over* account has 15 entries during the month. The ending balance is a $10 shortage for the month. Is this a problem? Why or why not?

(Answers to Section 1 Self Review are on pages 324–325.)

SECTION OBJECTIVES	TERMS TO LEARN
>> **9-4.** Record cash payments in a cash payments journal.	bonding
WHY IT'S IMPORTANT	cash payments journal
The cash payments journal is an efficient option for recording payments by check.	petty cash analysis sheet
>> **9-5.** Post from the cash payments journal to subsidiary and general ledgers.	petty cash voucher
WHY IT'S IMPORTANT	
The subsidiary and general ledgers must hold accurate, up-to-date information about cash transactions.	
>> **9-6.** Demonstrate a knowledge of procedures for a petty cash fund.	
WHY IT'S IMPORTANT	
Businesses use the petty cash fund to pay for small operating expenditures.	
>> **9-7.** Demonstrate a knowledge of internal control procedures for cash.	
WHY IT'S IMPORTANT	
Internal controls safeguard business assets.	

Cash Payments

A good system of internal control requires that payments be made by check. In a good internal control system, one employee approves payments, another employee prepares the checks, and another employee records the transactions.

The Cash Payments Journal

Unless a business has just a few cash payments each month, the process of recording these transactions in the general journal is time consuming. The **cash payments journal** is a special journal used to record transactions involving the payment of cash.

RECORDING TRANSACTIONS IN THE CASH PAYMENTS JOURNAL

>> **9-4. OBJECTIVE**

Record cash payments in a cash payments journal.

Refer to Figure 9.5 on page 279 for Maxx-Out Sporting Goods' cash payments journal. Notice that there are separate columns for the accounts frequently used when recording cash payments—*Cash, Accounts Payable,* and *Purchases Discounts.* At the end of the month, the totals of these columns are posted to the general ledger.

The Other Accounts Debit section is for entries that do not fit into one of the special columns. Entries in the Other Accounts Debit section are individually posted to the general ledger.

Payments for Expenses Businesses write checks for a variety of expenses each month. In January, Maxx-Out Sporting Goods issued checks for rent, electricity, telephone service, advertising, and salaries. Refer to the January 3 entry for rent expense in Figure 9.5. Notice that the account name and amount are entered in the Other Accounts Debit section. The credit is in the Cash Credit column.

Payments on Account Merchandising businesses usually make numerous payments on account for goods that were purchased on credit. If there is no cash discount, the entry in the cash payments journal is a debit to *Accounts Payable* and a credit to *Cash.* For an example of a payment without a discount, refer to the January 27 entry for International Sportsman in Figure 9.5.

Purchases Discounts is a contra cost of goods sold account that appears in the Cost of Goods Sold section of the income statement. Purchases discounts are subtracted from purchases to obtain net purchases.

For an example of a payment with a discount, refer to the January 13 entry for Active Designs in Figure 9.5. Maxx-Out Sporting Goods takes a 2 percent discount for paying within the discount period ($2,865 \times 0.02 = 57.30). When there is a cash discount, three elements must be recorded:

- Debit *Accounts Payable* for the invoice amount, $2,865.
- Credit *Purchases Discounts* for the amount of the discount, $57.30.
- Credit *Cash* for the amount of cash paid, $2,807.70.

> Debit cards (also called check cards) look like credit cards or ATM (automated teller machine) cards, but operate like cash or a personal check. In this context, debit means "subtract" so when you use your debit card, you are subtracting your money from your bank account. Funds on deposit with a bank represent a liability from the bank's perspective. By debiting accounts when depositors use their debit cards, the bank reduces the depositors' account balances, thus reducing the bank's liabilities to depositors. Debit cards are accepted almost everywhere including grocery stores, retail stores, gasoline stations, and restaurants. Debit cards are popular because they offer an alternative to carrying checks or cash. Transactions that are completed with the debit card will appear on your bank statement.

Cash Purchases of Equipment and Supplies Businesses use cash to purchase equipment, supplies, and other assets. These transactions are recorded in the cash payments journal. In January, Maxx-Out Sporting Goods issued checks for store fixtures and store supplies. Refer to the entries on January 10 and 14 in Figure 9.5. Notice that the account names and amounts appear in the Other Accounts Debit section. The credits are recorded in the Cash Credit column.

Payment of Taxes Retail businesses collect sales tax from their customers. Periodically, the sales tax is remitted to the taxing authority. Refer to the entry on January 11 in Figure 9.5. Maxx-Out Sporting Goods issued a check for $756 to pay the December sales tax. Notice that the account name and amount appear in the Other Accounts Debit section. The credit is in the Cash Credit column.

Cash Purchases of Merchandise Most merchandising businesses buy their goods on credit. Occasionally, purchases are made for cash. These purchases are recorded in the cash payments journal. Refer to the January 31 entry for the purchase of goods in Figure 9.5.

Payment of Freight Charges Freight charges on purchases of goods are handled in two ways. In some cases, the seller pays the freight charge and then includes it on the invoice. This method was covered in Chapter 8. The other method is for the buyer to pay the transportation company when the goods arrive. The buyer issues a check for the freight charge and records it in the cash payments journal. Refer to the entry on January 31 in Figure 9.5. The account name and amount appear in the Other Accounts Debit section. The credit is in the Cash Credit column.

Payment of a Cash Refund When a customer purchases goods for cash and later returns them or receives an allowance, the customer is usually given a cash refund. Refer to the January 31 entry in Figure 9.5. Maxx-Out Sporting Goods issued a check for $172.80 to a customer who returned a defective item. When there is a cash refund, three elements are recorded:

FIGURE 9.5   **Cash Payments Journal**

CASH PAYMENTS JOURNAL   PAGE ___1___

DATE		CK. NO.	DESCRIPTION	POST. REF.	ACCOUNTS PAYABLE DEBIT	OTHER ACCOUNTS DEBIT			PURCHASES DISCOUNTS CREDIT	CASH CREDIT
						ACCOUNT TITLE	POST. REF.	AMOUNT		
2016										
Jan.	3	111	January rent			Rent Expense		1 500 00		1 500 00
	10	112	Store fixtures			Store Equipment		2 400 00		2 400 00
	11	113	Tax remittance			Sales Tax Payable		756 00		756 00
	11	114	World of Sports		3 935 00				78 70	3 856 30
	13	115	Active Designs		2 865 00				57 30	2 807 70
	14	116	Store Supplies			Supplies		900 00		900 00
	15	117	Withdrawal			M. Ferraro, Drawing		3 000 00		3 000 00
	17	118	Electric bill			Utilities Expense		318 00		318 00
	17	119	The Sports Warehouse		4 250 00					4 250 00
	21	120	Telephone bill			Telephone Expense		276 00		276 00
	25	121	Newspaper ad			Advertising Expense		840 00		840 00
	27	122	International Sportsman		1 000 00					1 000 00
	30	123	Active Designs		1 135 00					1 135 00
	31	124	World of Sports		565 00					565 00
	31	125	January payroll			Salaries Expense		4 950 00		4 950 00
	31	126	Purchase of goods			Purchases		3 200 00		3 200 00
	31	127	Freight charge			Freight In		175 00		175 00
	31	128	Cash refund			Sales Returns & Allow.		160 00		
						Sales Tax Payable		12 80		172 80
	31	129	Note Paid to			Notes Payable		6 000 00		
			Metroplex Equip. Co.			Interest Expense		300 00		6 300 00
	31	130	Establish Petty Cash fund			Petty Cash Fund		175 00		175 00
			TOTALS		13 750 00			24 962 80	136 00	38 576 80

- Debit *Sales Returns and Allowances* for the amount of the purchase, $160.00.
- Debit *Sales Tax Payable* for the sales tax, $12.80.
- Credit *Cash* for the amount of cash paid, $172.80.

Notice that the debits in the Other Accounts Debit section appear on two lines because two general ledger accounts are debited.

Payment of a Promissory Note and Interest   A promissory note can be issued to settle an overdue account or to obtain goods, equipment, or other property. For example, on August 2 Maxx-Out Sporting Goods issued a six-month promissory note for $6,000 to purchase store fixtures from Metroplex Equipment Company. The note had an interest rate of 10 percent. Maxx-Out Sporting Goods recorded this transaction in the general journal by debiting *Store Equipment* and crediting *Notes Payable,* a liability account.

GENERAL JOURNAL   PAGE ___16___

	DATE		DESCRIPTION	POST. REF.	DEBIT	CREDIT	
1	2015						1
2	Aug.	2	Store Equipment	131	6 000 00		2
3			Notes Payable	201		6 000 00	3
4			Issued a 6-month, 10% note to				4
5			Metroplex Equipment Company for				5
6			purchase of new store fixtures				6
7							7

On January 31, Maxx-Out Sporting Goods issued a check for $6,300 in payment of the note, $6,000, and the interest, $300. This transaction was recorded in the cash payments journal in Figure 9.5.

- Debit *Notes Payable,* $6,000.
- Debit *Interest Expense,* $300.
- Credit *Cash,* $6,300.

Notice that the debits in the Other Accounts Debit section appear on two lines.

>> **9-5. OBJECTIVE**

Post from the cash payments journal to subsidiary and general ledgers.

POSTING FROM THE CASH PAYMENTS JOURNAL

During the month, the amounts recorded in the Accounts Payable Debit column are posted to individual accounts in the accounts payable subsidiary ledger. The amounts in the Other Accounts Debit column are also posted individually to the general ledger accounts during the month. For example, the January 3 entry in the cash payments journal was posted to the *Rent Expense* account. The "CP1" indicates that the entry is recorded on page 1 of the cash payments journal.

ACCOUNT _Rent Expense_					ACCOUNT NO. _634_	
					BALANCE	
DATE	DESCRIPTION	POST. REF.	DEBIT	CREDIT	DEBIT	CREDIT
2016						
Jan. 3		CP1	1 5 0 0 00		1 5 0 0 00	

Posting the Column Totals   At the end of the month, the cash payments journal is totaled and proved. The total debits must equal total credits.

Proof of Cash Payments Journal	
	Debits
Accounts Payable Debit column	$13,750.00
Other Accounts Debit column	24,962.80
Total Debits	$38,712.80
	Credits
Purchases Discount Credit column	$ 136.00
Cash Credit column	38,576.80
Total Credits	$38,712.80

Figure 9.6 shows the January cash payments journal after posting for Maxx-Out Sporting Goods. Notice that the account numbers appear in the Posting Reference column of the Other Accounts Debit section to show that the amounts were posted.

When the cash payments journal has been proved, rule the columns and post the totals to the general ledger. Figure 9.7 on page 282 shows how to post from the cash payments journal to the general ledger accounts.

To post a column total to a general ledger account, enter "CP1" in the Posting Reference column to show that the entry is from page 1 of the cash payments journal.

Enter the column total in the general ledger account Debit or Credit column. Figure 9.7 shows the entries to *Accounts Payable* (1), *Purchases Discounts* (2), and *Cash* (3). Compute the new balance and enter it in the Balance Debit or Balance Credit column.

FIGURE 9.6   Posted Cash Payments Journal

					OTHER ACCOUNTS DEBIT				
DATE	CK. NO.	DESCRIPTION	POST. REF.	ACCOUNTS PAYABLE DEBIT	ACCOUNT TITLE	POST. REF.	AMOUNT	PURCHASES DISCOUNTS CREDIT	CASH CREDIT
2016									
Jan. 3	111	January rent			Rent Expense	634	1 500 00		1 500 00
10	112	Store fixtures			Store Equipment	131	2 400 00		2 400 00
11	113	Tax remittance			Sales Tax Payable	231	7 56 00		7 56 00
11	114	World of Sports	✓	3 935 00				78 70	3 856 30
13	115	Active Designs	✓	2 865 00				57 30	2 807 70
14	116	Store Supplies			Supplies	129	9 00 00		9 00 00
15	117	Withdrawal			M. Ferraro, Drawing	302	3 000 00		3 000 00
17	118	Electric bill			Utilities Expense	643	3 18 00		3 18 00
17	119	The Sports Warehouse	✓	4 250 00					4 250 00
21	120	Telephone bill			Telephone Expense	649	2 76 00		2 76 00
25	121	Newspaper ad			Advertising Expense	614	8 40 00		8 40 00
27	122	International Sportsman	✓	1 000 00					1 000 00
30	123	Active Designs	✓	1 135 00					1 135 00
31	124	World of Sports	✓	5 65 00					5 65 00
31	125	January payroll			Salaries Expense	637	4 950 00		4 950 00
31	126	Purchase of goods			Purchases	501	3 200 00		3 200 00
31	127	Freight charge			Freight In	502	1 75 00		1 75 00
31	128	Cash refund			Sales Returns & Allow.	451	1 60 00		
					Sales Tax Payable	231	12 80		1 72 80
31	129	Note Paid to Metroplex			Notes Payable	201	6 000 00		
		Equipment Company			Interest Expense	691	3 00 00		6 300 00
31	130	Establish Petty Cash fund			Petty Cash Fund	105	1 75 00		1 75 00
31		Totals		13 750 00			24 962 80	1 36 00	38 576 80
				(205)			(X)	(504)	(101)

CASH PAYMENTS JOURNAL   PAGE ___1___

Enter the general ledger account numbers under the column totals on the cash payments journal. The (X) in the Other Accounts Debit column indicates that the individual accounts were posted, not the total.

Posting to the Accounts Payable Ledger   To keep balances current, accountants post entries from the Accounts Payable Debit column of the cash payments journal to the vendor accounts in the accounts payable subsidiary ledger daily. For example, on January 13, $2,865 was posted to Active Designs account in the subsidiary ledger. The "CP1" in the Posting Reference column indicates that the entry is recorded on page 1 of the cash payments journal. The check mark (✓) in the Posting Reference column of the cash payments journal (Figure 9.7 on page 282) shows that the amount was posted to the supplier's account in the accounts payable subsidiary ledger.

NAME   Active Designs   TERMS   2/10, n/30
ADDRESS   2313 Belt Line Road, Dallas, Texas 75267-6205

DATE	DESCRIPTION	POST. REF.	DEBIT	CREDIT	BALANCE
2016					
Jan. 1	Balance	✓			2 200 00
3	Invoice 5879, 01/02/13	P1		2 865 00	5 065 00
13		CP1	2 865 00		2 200 00
30		CP1	1 135 00		1 065 00

ADVANTAGES OF THE CASH PAYMENTS JOURNAL

The cash payments journal:

- saves time and effort when recording and posting cash payments,
- allows for a division of labor among the accounting staff,
- improves the audit trail because all cash payments are recorded in one place and listed by check number.

FIGURE 9.7   Posted General Ledger Accounts

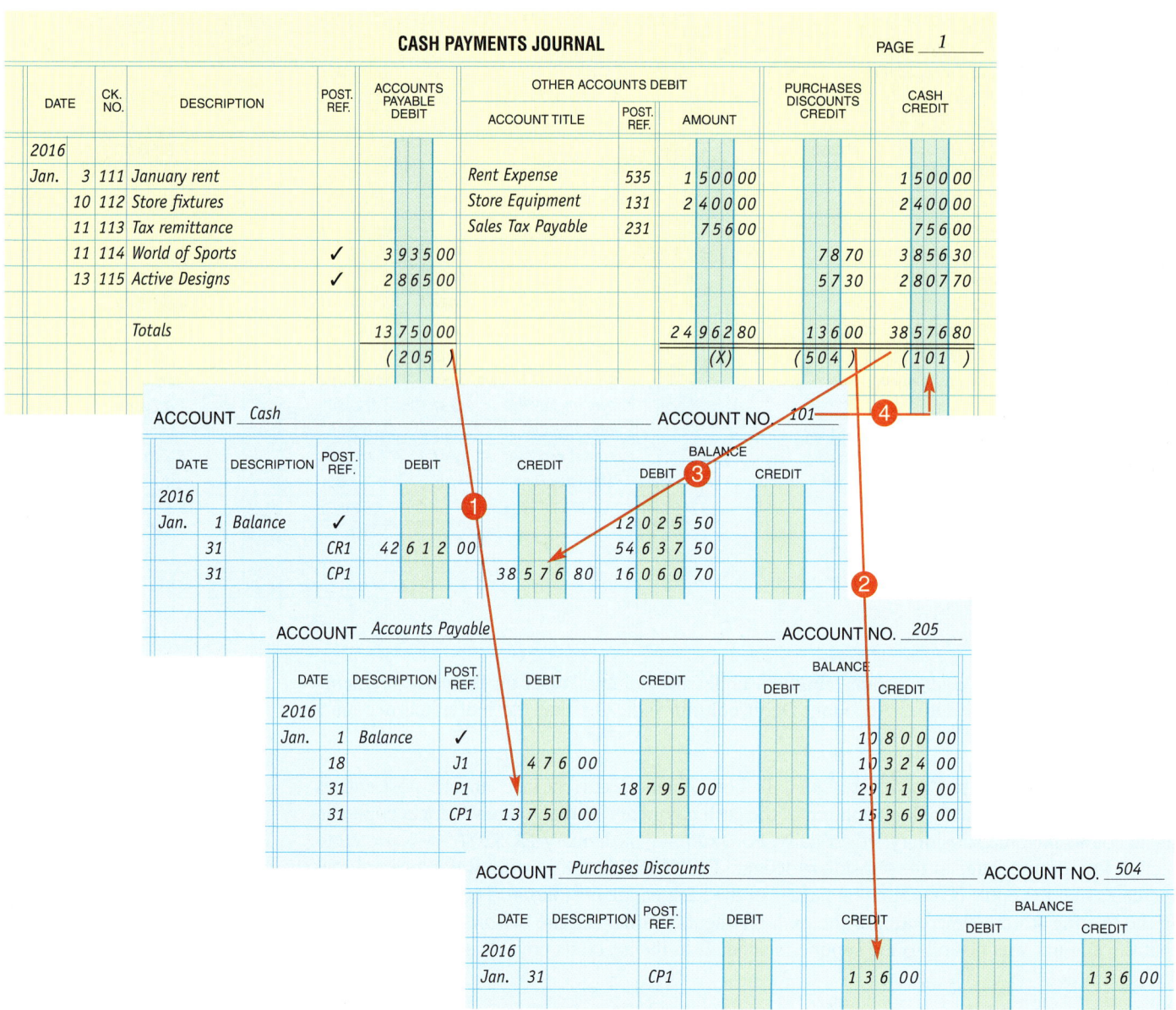

>> 9-6. OBJECTIVE

Demonstrate a knowledge of procedures for a petty cash fund.

The Petty Cash Fund

In a well-managed business, most bills are paid by check. However, there are times when small expenditures are made with currency and coins. Most businesses use a petty cash fund to pay for small expenditures. Suppose that in the next two hours the office manager needs a $4 folder for a customer. It is not practical to obtain an approval and write a check for $4 in the time available. Instead, the office manager takes $4 from the petty cash fund to purchase the folder.

ESTABLISHING THE FUND

The amount of the petty cash fund depends on the needs of the business. Usually the office manager, cashier, or assistant is in charge of the petty cash fund. The cashier is responsible for petty cash. To set up the petty cash fund, Maxx-Out Sporting Goods wrote a $175 check to the cashier. She cashed the check and put the currency in a locked cash box.

The establishment of the petty cash fund should be recorded in the cash payments journal. Debit *Petty Cash Fund* in the Other Accounts Debit section of the journal, and enter the credit in the Cash Credit column.

MAKING PAYMENTS FROM THE FUND

Petty cash fund payments are limited to small amounts. A **petty cash voucher** is used to record the payments made from the petty cash fund. The petty cash voucher shows the voucher number, amount, purpose of the expenditure, and account to debit. The person receiving the funds signs the voucher, and the person who controls the petty cash fund initials the voucher. Figure 9.8 shows a petty cash voucher for $16.25 for office supplies.

THE PETTY CASH ANALYSIS SHEET

Most businesses use a **petty cash analysis sheet** to record transactions involving petty cash. The Receipts column shows cash put in the fund, and the Payments column shows the cash paid out. There are special columns for accounts that are used frequently, such as *Supplies, Freight In,* and *Miscellaneous Expense.* There is an Other Accounts Debit column for entries that do not fit in a special column. Figure 9.9 on the next page shows the petty cash analysis sheet for Maxx-Out Sporting Goods for February.

Replenishing the Fund   The total vouchers plus the cash on hand should always equal the amount of the fund—$175 for Maxx-Out Sporting Goods. Replenish the petty cash fund at the end of each month or sooner if the fund is low. Refer to Figures 9.9 and 9.10 as you learn how to replenish the petty cash fund.

1. Total the columns on the petty cash analysis sheet.
2. Prove the petty cash fund by adding cash on hand and total payments. This should equal the petty cash fund balance ($15.25 + $159.75 = $175.00).
3. Write a check to restore the petty cash fund to its original balance.
4. Record the check in the cash payments journal. Refer to the petty cash analysis sheet for the accounts and amounts to debit. Notice that the debits appear on four lines of the Other Accounts Debit section. The credit appears in the Cash Credit column.

INTERNAL CONTROL OF THE PETTY CASH FUND

Whenever there is valuable property or cash to protect, appropriate safeguards must be established. Petty cash is no exception. The following internal control procedures apply to petty cash:

1. Use the petty cash fund only for small payments that cannot conveniently be made by check.

important!

Petty Cash
Only one person controls the petty cash fund. That person should keep receipts for all expenditures.

FIGURE 9.8

Petty Cash Voucher

PETTY CASH VOUCHER 1
NOTE: This form must be computer processed or filled out in black ink.

DESCRIPTION OF EXPENDITURE	ACCOUNTS TO BE CHARGED	AMOUNT
Office supplies	Supplies 129	16 25
	Total	16 25

RECEIVED
THE SUM OF __Sixteen__ --- DOLLARS AND __25/100__ CENTS
SIGNED __L.T. Green__ DATE __2/3/16__ APPROVED BY __M.F.__ DATE __2/3/16__
Metroplex Office Supply Co.

FIGURE 9.9   Petty Cash Analysis Sheet

PETTY CASH ANALYSIS   PAGE ____1____

DATE	VOU. NO.	DESCRIPTION	RECEIPTS	PAYMENTS	SUPPLIES DEBIT	DELIVERY EXPENSE DEBIT	MISC. EXPENSE DEBIT	OTHER ACCOUNTS DEBIT	
								ACCOUNT TITLE	AMOUNT
2016									
Feb. 1		Establish fund	175 00						
3	1	Office supplies		16 25	16 25				
6	2	Delivery service		24 00		24 00			
11	3	Withdrawal		25 00				M. Ferraro, Drawing	25 00
15	4	Postage stamps		37 00			37 00		
20	5	Delivery service		17 50		17 50			
26	6	Window washing		26 00			26 00		
28	7	Store supplies		14 00	14 00				
28		Totals	175 00	159 75	30 25	41 50	63 00		25 00
28		Balance on hand		15 25					
			175 00	175 00					
28		Balance on hand	15 25						
28		Replenish fund	159 75						
28		Carried forward	175 00						

FIGURE 9.10   Reimbursing the Petty Cash Fund

CASH PAYMENTS JOURNAL   PAGE ____1____

DATE	CK. NO.	DESCRIPTION	POST. REF.	ACCOUNTS PAYABLE DEBIT	OTHER ACCOUNTS DEBIT			PURCHASES DISCOUNTS CREDIT	CASH CREDIT
					ACCOUNT TITLE	POST. REF.	AMOUNT		
2016									
Feb. 28	191	Replenish Petty Cash fund			Supplies	129	30 25		
					M. Ferraro, Drawing	302	25 00		
					Delivery Expense	523	41 50		
					Miscellaneous Expense	593	63 00		159 75

2. Limit the amount set aside for petty cash to the approximate amount needed to cover one month's payments from the fund.

3. Write petty cash fund checks to the person in charge of the fund, not to the order of "Cash."

4. Assign one person to control the petty cash fund. This person has sole control of the money and is the only one authorized to make payments from the fund.

5. Keep petty cash in a safe, a locked cash box, or a locked drawer.

6. Prepare a petty cash voucher for each payment. The voucher should be signed by the person who receives the money and should show the payment details. This provides an audit trail for the fund. Additionally, obtain a vendor's invoice or other receipt as documentation for each petty cash voucher.

>> 9-7. OBJECTIVE

Demonstrate a knowledge of internal control procedures for cash.

Internal Control over Cash

In a well-managed business, there are internal control procedures for handling and recording cash receipts and cash payments. The internal control over cash should be tailored to the needs of the business. Accountants play a vital role in designing, establishing, and monitoring the cash control system. In developing internal control procedures for cash, certain basic principles must be followed.

CONTROL OF CASH RECEIPTS

As noted already, cash is the asset that is most easily stolen, lost, or mishandled. Yet cash is essential to carrying on business operations. It is important to protect all cash receipts to make sure that funds are available to pay expenses and take care of other business obligations. The following are essential cash receipt controls:

1. Have only designated employees receive and handle cash whether it consists of checks and money orders, or currency and coins. These employees should be carefully chosen for reliability and accuracy and should be carefully trained. In some businesses, employees who handle cash are bonded. **Bonding** is the process by which employees are investigated by an insurance company. Employees who pass the background check can be bonded; that is, the employer can purchase insurance on the employees. If the bonded employees steal or mishandle cash, the business is insured against the loss.

2. Keep cash receipts in a cash register, a locked cash drawer, or a safe while they are on the premises.

3. Make a record of all cash receipts as the funds come into the business. For checks, endorse each check when received. For currency and coins, this record is the audit tape in a cash register or duplicate copies of numbered sales slips. The use of a cash register provides an especially effective means of control because the machine automatically produces a tape showing the amounts entered. This tape is locked inside the cash register until it is removed by a supervisor.

4. Before a bank deposit is made, check the funds to be deposited against the record made when the cash was received. The employee who checks the deposit is someone other than the one who receives or records the cash.

5. Deposit cash receipts in the bank promptly—every day or several times a day. Deposit the funds intact—do not make payments directly from the cash receipts. The person who makes the bank deposit is someone other than the one who receives and records the funds.

6. Enter cash receipts transactions in the accounting records promptly. The person who records cash receipts is not the one who receives or deposits the funds.

7. Have the monthly bank statement sent to and reconciled by someone other than the employees who handle, record, and deposit the funds.

One of the advantages of efficient procedures for handling and recording cash receipts is that the funds reach the bank sooner. Cash receipts are not kept on the premises for more than a short time, which means that the funds are safer and are readily available for paying bills owed by the firm.

CONTROL OF CASH PAYMENTS

It is important to control cash payments so that the payments are made only for authorized business purposes. The following are essential cash payment controls:

1. Make all payments by check except for payments from special-purpose cash funds such as a petty cash fund or a travel and entertainment fund.

2. Issue checks only with an approved bill, invoice, or other document that describes the reason for the payment.

3. Have only designated personnel, who are experienced and reliable, approve bills and invoices.

4. Have checks prepared and recorded in the checkbook or check register by someone other than the person who approves the payments.

5. Have still another person sign and mail the checks to creditors. Consider requiring that two people sign all checks greater than a predesignated amount.

6. Use prenumbered check forms. Periodically the numbers of the checks that were issued and the numbers of the blank check forms remaining should be verified to make sure that all check numbers are accounted for.

7. During the bank reconciliation process, compare the canceled checks to the checkbook or check register. The person who does the bank reconciliation should be someone other than the person who prepares or records the checks.

8. Enter promptly in the accounting records all cash payment transactions. The person who records cash payments should not be the one who approves payments or the one who writes the checks.

Small businesses usually cannot achieve the division of responsibility recommended for cash receipts and cash payments. However, no matter what size the firm, efforts should be made to set up effective control procedures for cash.

Section 2   Self Review

QUESTIONS

1. How and when are amounts in the Other Accounts Debit column of the cash payments journal posted?

2. What cash payments journal entry records a cash withdrawal by the owner of a sole proprietorship?

3. Why does a business use a petty cash fund?

EXERCISES

4. To take the discount, what is the payment date for an invoice dated January 20 with terms 3/15, n/30?

  a. February 3
  b. February 4
  c. February 5
  d. February 6

5. Cash purchases of merchandise are recorded in the:
  a. cash receipts journal.
  b. general journal.
  c. cash payments journal.
  d. purchases journal.

ANALYSIS

6. Your employer keeps a $200 petty cash fund. She asked you to replenish the fund. She is missing a receipt for $7.40, which she says she spent on postage. How should you handle this?

(Answers to Section 2 Self Review are on page 325.)

SECTION OBJECTIVES	TERMS TO LEARN

SECTION OBJECTIVES

>> **9-8.** Write a check, endorse checks, prepare a bank deposit slip, and maintain a checkbook balance.

   WHY IT'S IMPORTANT
   Banking tasks are basic practices in every business.

>> **9-9.** Reconcile the monthly bank statement.

   WHY IT'S IMPORTANT
   Reconciliation of the bank statement provides a good control of cash.

>> **9-10.** Record any adjusting entries required from the bank reconciliation.

   WHY IT'S IMPORTANT
   Certain items are not recorded in the accounting records during the month.

>> **9-11.** Understand how businesses use online banking to manage cash activities.

   WHY IT'S IMPORTANT
   Many businesses use online banking to manage a significant portion of cash activities.

>> **9-12.** Record cash payments and cash receipts using the perpetual inventory system.

   WHY IT'S IMPORTANT
   Many large companies use the perpetual inventory system as it provides updated information concerning inventories on hand.

TERMS TO LEARN

bank reconciliation statement
blank endorsement
canceled check
check
credit memorandum
debit memorandum
deposit in transit
deposit slip
dishonored (NSF) check
drawee
drawer
electronic funds transfer (EFT)
endorsement
full endorsement
negotiable
outstanding checks
payee
postdated check
restrictive endorsement
service charge

Banking Procedures

Businesses with good internal control systems safeguard cash. Many businesses make a daily bank deposit, and some make two or three deposits a day. Keeping excess cash is a dangerous practice. Also, frequent bank deposits provide a steady flow of funds for the payment of expenses.

Writing Checks

A **check** is a written order signed by an authorized person, the **drawer,** instructing a bank, the **drawee,** to pay a specific sum of money to a designated person or business, the **payee.** The checks in Figure 9.11 on the next page are **negotiable,** which means that ownership of the checks can be transferred to another person or business.

Before writing the check, complete the check stub. In Figure 9.11, the check stub for Check 111 shows:

- Balance brought forward: $12,025.50
- Check amount: $1,500.00
- Balance: $10,525.50
- Date: January 3, 2016
- Payee: Carter Real Estate Group
- Purpose: January rent

Once the stub has been completed, fill in the check. Carefully enter the date, the payee, and the amount in figures and words. Draw a line to fill any empty space after the payee's name and after the amount in words. To be valid, checks need an authorized signature. For Maxx-Out Sporting Goods only Max Ferraro, the owner, is authorized to sign checks.

Figure 9.11 shows the check stub for Check 112, a cash purchase from The Retail Equipment Center for $2,400. After Check 112, the account balance is $8,125.50 ($10,525.50 − $2,400.00).

Endorsing Checks

Each check needs an endorsement to be deposited. The **endorsement** is a written authorization that transfers ownership of a check. After the payee transfers ownership to the bank by an endorsement, the bank has a legal right to collect payment from the drawer, the person or business that issued the check. If the check cannot be collected, the payee guarantees payment to all subsequent holders.

Several forms of endorsement are shown in Figure 9.12. Endorsements are placed on the back of the check, on the left, near the perforated edge where the check was separated from the stub.

A **blank endorsement** is the signature of the payee that transfers ownership of the check without specifying to whom or for what purpose. Checks with a blank endorsement can be further endorsed by anyone who has the check, even if the check is lost or stolen.

A **full endorsement** is a signature transferring a check to a specific person, business, or bank. Only the person, business, or bank named in the full endorsement can transfer it to someone else.

The safest endorsement is the **restrictive endorsement.** A restrictive endorsement is a signature that transfers the check to a specific party for a specific purpose, usually for deposit to a bank account. Most businesses restrictively endorse the checks they receive using a rubber stamp.

>> 9-8. OBJECTIVE

Write a check, endorse checks, prepare a bank deposit slip, and maintain a checkbook balance.

Preparing the Deposit Slip

Businesses prepare a **deposit slip** to record each deposit of cash or checks to a bank account. Usually the bank provides deposit slips preprinted with the account name and number. Figure 9.13, above, shows the deposit slip for the January 8 deposit for Maxx-Out Sporting Goods.

FIGURE 9.11   Checks and Check Stubs

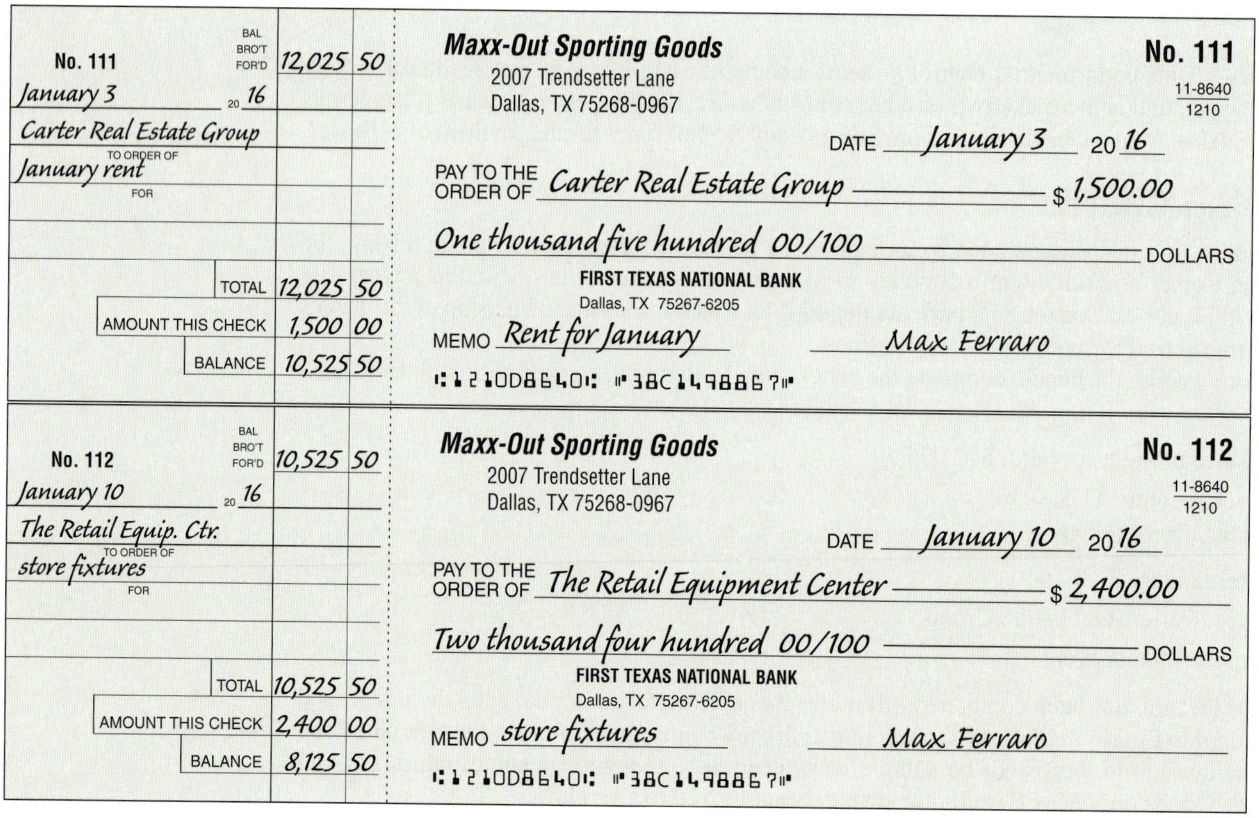

FIGURE 9.12

Types of Check Endorsement

Full Endorsement

PAY TO THE ORDER OF
FIRST TEXAS NATIONAL BANK
Maxx-Out Sporting Goods
38-14-98867

Blank Endorsement

Max Ferraro
38-14-98867

Restrictive Endorsement

PAY TO THE ORDER OF
FIRST TEXAS NATIONAL BANK
FOR DEPOSIT ONLY
Maxx-Out Sporting Goods
38-14-98867

FIGURE 9.13

Deposit Slip

CHECKING ACCOUNT DEPOSIT

DATE _January 8, 2016_

MAXX-OUT SPORTING GOODS
2007 Trendsetter Lane
Dallas, TX 75268-0967

FIRST TEXAS NATIONAL BANK
Dallas, TX 75267-6205

Checks and other items are received for deposit subject to the terms and conditions of this bank's collection agreement.

CURRENCY	DOLLARS	CENTS
	1810	00
COIN	219	80
1 11-2818	260	75
2 11-2818	290	18
3 11-1652	180	65
4 11-1652	598	32
5 11-5074	800	30
6 11-5074	700	00
7		
8		
9		
10		
11		
12		
TOTAL FROM OTHER SIDE OR ATTACHED LIST		
TOTAL	4,860.00	

ENTER ADDITIONAL CHECKS ON OTHER SIDE

⑆1210⑈8640⑉ ⑈38⑉149886 7⑈

Notice the printed numbers on the lower edge of the deposit slip. These are the same numbers on the bottom of the checks, Figure 9.11. The numbers are printed using a special *magnetic ink character recognition (MICR)* type that can be "read" by machine. Deposit slips and checks encoded with MICR are rapidly and efficiently processed by machine.

- The 12 indicates that the bank is in the 12th Federal Reserve District.
- The 10 is the routing number used in processing the document.
- The 8640 identifies First Texas National Bank.
- The 38 14 98867 is the account number.

The deposit slip for Maxx-Out Sporting Goods shows the date, January 8. *Currency* is the paper money, $1,810.00. *Coin* is the amount in coins, $219.80. The checks and money orders are individually listed. Some banks ask that the *American Bankers Association (ABA) transit number* for each check be entered on the deposit slip. The transit number appears on the top part of the fraction that appears in the upper right corner of the check. In Figure 9.11, the transit number is 11-8640.

Many banks now allow businesses to deposit checks to an automated teller machine (ATM) without using deposit slips. The ATM receipt provides the depositor with images of the checks deposited as well as the total amount of the deposit.

Handling Postdated Checks

Occasionally, a business will receive a postdated check. A **postdated check** is dated some time in the future. If the business receives a postdated check, it should not deposit it before the date on the check. Otherwise, the check could be refused by the drawer's bank. Postdated checks are written by drawers who do not have sufficient funds to cover the check. The drawer expects to have adequate funds in the bank by the date on the check. Issuing or accepting post-dated checks is not a proper business practice.

>> 9-9. OBJECTIVE

Reconcile the monthly bank statement.

Reconciling the Bank Statement

Once a month, the bank sends a statement of the deposits received and the checks paid for each account. Figure 9.14, below, shows the bank statement for Maxx-Out Sporting Goods. It shows a day-to-day listing of all transactions during the month. A code, explained at the

FIGURE 9.14

Bank Statement

FIRST TEXAS NATIONAL BANK

MAXX-OUT SPORTING GOODS   1-877-TEXBANK
2007 Trendsetter Lane
Dallas, TX 75268-0967

Account Number: 38-14-98867   January 1–January 31, 2016
Activity Summary:

Balance, January 1	$ 12,025.50
Deposits and credits	36,672.00
Withdrawals and debits	(25,189.00)
Balance, January 31	$ 23,508.50

DATE	DESCRIPTION	DEPOSITS/ CREDITS	WITHDRAWALS/ DEBITS	BALANCE
1/1/16	Opening balance			$ 12,025.50
1/7/16	Deposit	702.00		12,727.50
1/7/16	Check No. 111		1,500.00	11,227.50
1/8/16	Check No. 112		2,400.00	8,827.50
1/8/16	Deposit	4,860.00		13,687.50
1/11/16	Deposit	270.00		13,957.50
1/11/16	Check No. 113		756.00	13,201.50
1/12/16	Check No. 114		3,856.30	9,345.20
1/12/16	Deposit	15,000.00		24,345.20
1/13/16	Check No. 115		2,807.70	21,537.50
1/13/16	Deposit	540.00		22,077.50
1/15/16	Deposit	5,166.00		27,243.50
1/15/16	Check No. 116		900.00	26,343.50
1/17/16	Deposit	108.00		26,451.50
1/17/16	Check No. 117		3,000.00	23,451.50
1/17/16	Check No. 118		318.00	23,133.50
1/18/16	Deposit	75.00		23,208.50
1/18/16	Check No. 119		4,250.00	18,958.50
1/18/16	Check No. 120		276.00	18,682.50
1/22/16	Deposit	400.00		19,082.50
1/22/16	Deposit	5,400.00		24,482.50
1/22/16	Check No. 121		840.00	23,642.50
1/22/16	Check No. 122		1,000.00	22,642.50
1/22/16	Check No. 10087		1,600.00	21,042.50
1/29/16	Deposit	2,932.00		23,974.50
1/29/16	Debit for NSF Check		525.00	23,449.50
1/31/16	Deposit	108.00		23,557.50
1/31/16	Deposit	275.00		23,832.50
1/31/16	Credit for funds collected	836.00		24,668.50
1/31/16	Service fee for NSF check		25.00	24,643.50
1/31/16	Check No. 123		1,135.00	23,508.50
	Totals	36,672.00	25,189.00	

bottom, identifies transactions that do not involve checks or deposits. For example, SC indicates a service charge. The last column of the bank statement shows the account balance at the beginning of the period, after each day's transactions, and at the end of the period.

Often the bank encloses canceled checks with the bank statement. **Canceled checks** are checks paid by the bank during the month. Canceled checks are proof of payment. They are filed after the bank reconciliation is complete.

Usually there is a difference between the ending balance shown on the bank statement and the balance shown in the checkbook. A bank reconciliation determines why the difference exists and brings the records into agreement.

CHANGES IN THE CHECKING ACCOUNT BALANCE

A **credit memorandum** explains any addition, other than a deposit, to the checking account. For example, when a note receivable is due, the bank may collect the note from the maker and place the proceeds in the checking account. The amount collected appears on the bank statement, and the credit memorandum showing the details of the transaction is enclosed with the bank statement.

A **debit memorandum** explains any deduction, other than a check, to the checking account. Service charges and dishonored checks appear as debit memorandums.

Bank **service charges** are fees charged by banks to cover the costs of maintaining accounts and providing services, such as the use of the night deposit box and the collection of promissory notes. The debit memorandum shows the type and amount of each service charge.

Figure 9.15 shows a debit memorandum for a $525.00 dishonored check. A **dishonored check** is one that is returned to the depositor unpaid. Normally, checks are dishonored because there are insufficient funds in the drawer's account to cover the check. The bank usually stamps the letters *NSF* for *Not Sufficient Funds* on the check. The business records a journal entry to debit Accounts Receivable and credit Cash for the amount of the dishonored check.

When a check is dishonored, the business contacts the drawer to arrange for collection. The drawer can ask the business to redeposit the check because the funds are now in the account. If so, the business records the check deposit again. Sometimes, the business requests a cash payment.

THE BANK RECONCILIATION PROCESS: AN ILLUSTRATION

When the bank statement is received, it is reconciled with the financial records of the business. On February 5, Maxx-Out Sporting Goods received the bank statement shown in Figure 9.14. The ending cash balance according to the bank is $23,508.50. On January 31, the *Cash* account, called the *book balance of cash,* is $16,060.70. The same amount appears on the check stub at the end of January.

Sometimes the difference between the bank balance and the book balance is due to errors. The bank might make an arithmetic error, give credit to the wrong depositor, or charge a check against the wrong account. Some banks require that errors in the bank statement be reported within a short period of time. The errors made by businesses include not recording a check or deposit, or recording a check or deposit for the wrong amount.

FIGURE 9.15

Debit Memorandum

FIGURE 9.16

Bank Reconciliation Statement

Maxx-Out Sporting Goods Bank Reconciliation Statement January 31, 2016			
Balance on Bank Statement			23 5 0 8 50
Additions:			
Deposit of January 31 in transit	5 9 4 0 00		
Check incorrectly charged to account	1 6 0 0 00	7 5 4 0 00	
		31 0 4 8 50	
Deductions for outstanding checks:			
Check 124 of January 31	5 6 5 00		
Check 125 of January 31	4 9 5 0 00		
Check 126 of January 31	3 2 0 0 00		
Check 127 of January 31	1 7 5 00		
Check 128 of January 31	1 7 2 80		
Check 129 of January 31	6 3 0 0 00		
Check 130 of January 31	1 7 5 00		
Total Checks Outstanding		15 5 3 7 80	
Adjusted Bank Balance		15 5 1 0 70	
Balance in Books		16 0 6 0 70	
Deductions:			
NSF Check from David Newhouse	5 2 5 00		
Bank Service Charge	2 5 00	5 5 0 00	
Adjusted Book Balance		15 5 1 0 70	

Other than errors, there are four reasons why the book balance of cash may not agree with the balance on the bank statement.

1. **Outstanding checks** are checks that are recorded in the cash payments journal but have not been paid by the bank.
2. **Deposit in transit** is a deposit that is recorded in the cash receipts journal but that reaches the bank too late to be shown on the monthly bank statement.
3. Service charges and other deductions are not recorded in the business records.
4. Deposits, such as the collection of promissory notes, are not recorded in the business records.

Figure 9.16 shows a **bank reconciliation statement** that accounts for the differences between the balance on the bank statement and the book balance of cash. The bank reconciliation statement format is:

First Section		Second Section	
	Bank statement balance		Book balance
+	deposits in transit	+	deposits not recorded
−	outstanding checks	−	deductions
+ or −	bank errors	+ or −	errors in the books
	Adjusted bank balance		Adjusted book balance

When the bank reconciliation statement is complete, the adjusted bank balance must equal the adjusted book balance.

Use the following steps to prepare the bank reconciliation statement:

First Section

1. Enter the balance on the bank statement, $23,508.50.
2. Compare the deposits in the checkbook with the deposits on the bank statement. Maxx-Out Sporting Goods had one deposit in transit. On January 31, receipts of $5,940.00 were

placed in the bank's night deposit box. The bank recorded the deposit on February 1. The deposit will appear on the February bank statement.

3. List the outstanding checks.
   • Put the canceled checks in numeric order.
   • Compare the canceled checks to the check stubs, verifying the check numbers and amounts.
   • Examine the endorsements to make sure that they agree with the names of the payees.
   • List the checks that have not cleared the bank.
   • Maxx-Out Sporting Goods has seven outstanding checks totaling $15,537.80.

4. While reviewing the canceled checks for Maxx-Out Sporting Goods, Max Ferraro found a $1,600 check issued by The Dress Barn. The $1,600 was deducted from Maxx-Out Sporting Goods' account; it should have been deducted from the account for The Dress Barn. This is a bank error. Max Ferraro contacted the bank about the error. The correction will appear on the next bank statement. The bank error amount is added to the bank statement balance on the bank reconciliation statement.

5. The adjusted bank balance is $15,510.70.

Second Section

1. Enter the balance in books from the *Cash* account, $16,060.70.

2. Record any deposits made by the bank that have not been recorded in the accounting records. Maxx-Out Sporting Goods did not have any.

3. Record deductions made by the bank. There are two items:
   • the NSF check for $525,
   • the bank service charge for $25.

4. Record any errors in the accounting records that were discovered during the reconciliation process. Maxx-Out Sporting Goods did not have any errors in January.

5. The adjusted book balance is $15,510.70.

Notice that the adjusted bank balance and the adjusted book balance agree.

Adjusting the Financial Records

Items in the second section of the bank reconciliation statement include additions and deductions made by the bank that do not appear in the accounting records. Businesses prepare journal entries to record these items in the books.

For Maxx-Out Sporting Goods, two entries must be made. The first entry is for the NSF check from David Newhouse, a credit customer. The second entry is for the bank service charge. The effect of the two items is a decrease in the *Cash* account balance.

important!

Adjusted Book Balance
Make journal entries to record additions and deductions that appear on the bank statement but that have not been recorded in the general ledger.

>> **9-10. OBJECTIVE**
Record any adjusting entries required from the bank reconciliation.

MANAGERIAL IMPLICATIONS <<

CASH

■ It is important to safeguard cash against loss and theft.

■ Management and the accountant need to work together:
   ■ to make sure that there are effective controls for cash receipts and cash payments,
   ■ to monitor the internal control system to make sure that it functions properly,
   ■ to develop procedures that ensure the quick and efficient recording of cash transactions.

■ To make decisions, management needs up-to-date information about the cash position so that it can anticipate cash shortages and arrange loans or arrange for the temporary investment of excess funds.

■ Management and the accountant need to establish controls over the banking activities — depositing funds, issuing checks, recording checking account transactions, and reconciling the monthly bank statement.

THINKING CRITICALLY

How would you determine how much cash to keep in the business checking account, as opposed to in a short-term investment?

BUSINESS TRANSACTION

The January bank reconciliation statement (Figure 9.16 on page 292) shows an NSF check of $525 and a bank service charge of $25.

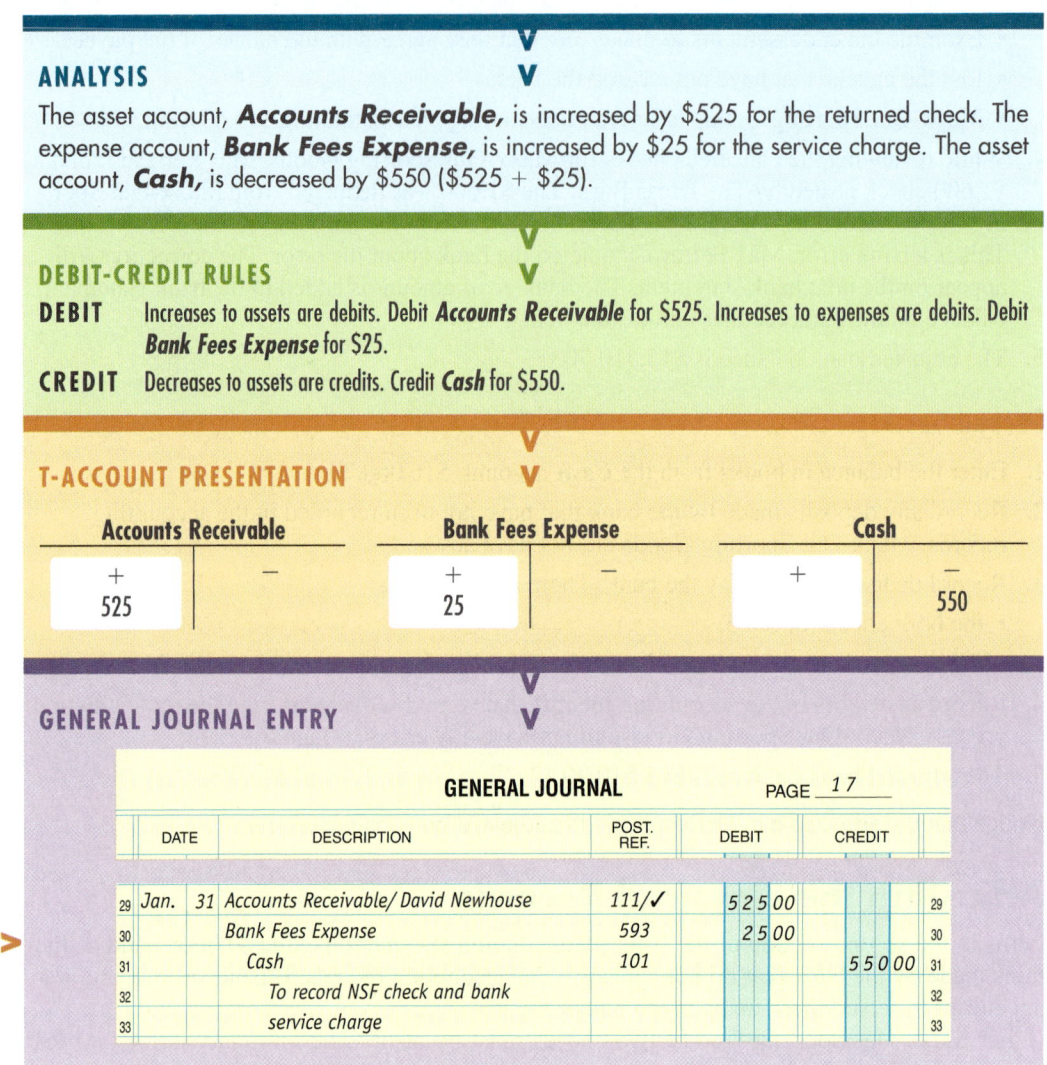

ANALYSIS

The asset account, **Accounts Receivable,** is increased by $525 for the returned check. The expense account, **Bank Fees Expense,** is increased by $25 for the service charge. The asset account, **Cash,** is decreased by $550 ($525 + $25).

DEBIT-CREDIT RULES

DEBIT   Increases to assets are debits. Debit **Accounts Receivable** for $525. Increases to expenses are debits. Debit **Bank Fees Expense** for $25.

CREDIT   Decreases to assets are credits. Credit **Cash** for $550.

T-ACCOUNT PRESENTATION

Accounts Receivable		Bank Fees Expense		Cash	
+	−	+	−	+	−
525		25			550

GENERAL JOURNAL ENTRY

THE BOTTOM LINE
Adjusting Entries

Income Statement

Expenses	↑	25
Net Income	↓	25

Balance Sheet

Assets	↓	25
Equity	↓	25

GENERAL JOURNAL   PAGE _17_

	DATE		DESCRIPTION	POST. REF.	DEBIT	CREDIT	
29	Jan.	31	Accounts Receivable/ David Newhouse	111/✓	525 00		29
30			Bank Fees Expense	593	25 00		30
31			Cash	101		550 00	31
32			To record NSF check and bank				32
33			service charge				33

After posting, the **Cash** account appears as follows.

ACCOUNT _Cash_   ACCOUNT NO. _101_

DATE		DESCRIPTION	POST. REF.	DEBIT	CREDIT	BALANCE DEBIT	BALANCE CREDIT
2016							
Jan.	1	Balance	✓			12 025 50	
	31		CR1	42 612 00		54 637 50	
	31		CP1		38 576 80	16 060 70	
	31		J17		550 00	15 510 70	

Notice that $15,510.70 is the adjusted bank balance, the adjusted book balance, and the general ledger **Cash** balance. A notation is made on the latest check stub to deduct the amounts ($525 and $25). The notation includes the reasons for the deductions.

Sometimes the bank reconciliation reveals an error in the firm's financial records. For example, the February bank reconciliation for Maxx-Out Sporting Goods found that Check 151 was written for $465. The amount on the bank statement is $465. However, the check was recorded in the accounting records as $445. The business made a $20 error when recording the check. Maxx-Out Sporting Goods prepared the following journal entry to correct the error. The $20 is also deducted on the check stub.

	GENERAL JOURNAL			PAGE __18__	
DATE	DESCRIPTION	POST. REF.	DEBIT	CREDIT	
1	2016				1
2					2
29	Feb. 28 Advertising Expense	514	20 00		29
30	Cash	101		20 00	30
31	To correct error for check				31
32	151 of February 22				32

Internal Control of Banking Activities

Well-run businesses put the following internal controls in place:

1. Limit access to the checkbook to designated employees. When the checkbook is not in use, keep it in a locked drawer or cabinet.

2. Use prenumbered check forms. Periodically, verify and account for all checks. Examine checks before signing them. Match each check to an approved invoice or other payment authorization.

3. Separate duties.
   - The person who writes the check should not sign or mail the check.
   - The person who performs the bank reconciliation should not handle or deposit cash receipts or write, record, sign, or mail checks.

4. File all deposit receipts, canceled checks, voided checks, and bank statements for future reference. These documents provide a strong audit trail for the checking account.

5. Require employees working with cash receipts or cash payments to take mandatory annual vacations.

> In November 2012, Rita Crundwell, former comptroller for a small Illinois town, pleaded guilty to stealing $53 million from city funds. These funds were used to support a lavish lifestyle, including purchase of a $2 million custom RV, a Florida vacation home, and a horse-breeding farm. Crundwell was the sole person responsible for managing the town's finances. The crime was uncovered by another employee while Crundwell was on vacation.

Using Online Banking

>> 9-11. OBJECTIVE
Understand how businesses use online banking to manage cash activities.

Many businesses now manage a significant portion of their cash activities using online banking. Online banking offers many features to make businesses more efficient. These features include:

- Businesses can initiate **electronic funds transfers (EFT)** to vendors from a computer instead of writing checks.

- Payments to government agencies for taxes can be submitted online, using the government agency website, to avoid late payment penalties.

- Businesses can receive EFT from customers, rather than receiving checks in the mail. This is especially important in transacting cash receipts from foreign customers. Routine payments, such as those for utilities expenses and loan payments can be automatically deducted from the company's bank account.

- Many banks offer security alerts for such instances as changes in mailing addresses and ATM and automatic payment withdrawals that exceed specified limits. Such alerts are often sent to the responsible company official via email or phone text messages. When an alert is received, the company should view account activity online to ensure cash transactions are legitimate.

FIGURE 9.17   Online Account Activity

Business Checking				Account #987-654321		
Date	**Type**	**Description**	**Additions**	**Payments**	**Balance**
7/31/2016	ATM	ATM withdrawal		$200.00	$27,819.91
7/31/2016	Check	Check #1421 (view)		$1,225.95	$28,019.91
7/30/2016	Bill payment	Online payment		$248.52	$29,245.86
7/30/2016	Check	Check #1420 (view)		$428.20	$29,494.38
7/30/2016	ACH credit	Baden Holding	$10,200.00		$29,922.58
7/30/2016	Deposit	Deposit ID #8989	$5,400.00		$19,722.58
7/30/2016	Loan payment	Online transfer to WC XXX		$3,900.00	$14,322.58
7/29/2016	Check	Check #1422 (view)		$850.00	$18,222.58

There are usually no source documents for the transactions listed above. The accountant should check bank activity online frequently to ensure all EFT and other transactions initiated electronically are recorded in the accounting records.

For example, the online account activity of Western Imports and Exports for July 29, 30, and 31, 2016, is shown in Figure 9.17. The company's accountant was out of town during that period.

In matching these transactions to the company's Cash account in the general ledger, the accountant identified the following unrecorded transactions:

1. The loan payment on 7/30/2016 was an automatic debit by Western Equipment for the company's monthly payment on an equipment loan. The loan does not bear interest.
2. The ACH credit on 7/30/2016 was an EFT payment sent by Baden Holding, a German customer, on account.
3. The bill payment of 7/30/2016 was an automatic debit by West Communications (telephone).
4. The ATM withdrawal of 7/31/2016 was for personal use by the owner, Susan De Angelis.

The accountant recorded these transactions in the general journal, as follows:

GENERAL JOURNAL   PAGE _10_

	DATE		DESCRIPTION	POST. REF.	DEBIT	CREDIT	
1	2016						1
2	July	30	Notes Payable		3 9 0 0 00		2
3			Cash			3 9 0 0 00	3
4			To record loan payment to Western				4
5			Equipment				5
6							6
7		30	Cash		10 2 0 0 00		7
8			Accounts Receivable/Baden Holding			10 2 0 0 00	8
9			To record EFT received on account				9
10			from Baden Holding				10
11							11
12		30	Telephone Expense		2 4 8 52		12
13			Cash			2 4 8 52	13
14			To record online payment to				14
15			West Communications				15
16							16
17		31	Susan De Angelis, Drawing		2 0 0 00		17
18			Cash			2 0 0 00	18
19			To record ATM withdrawal by				19
20			Susan De Angelis for personal use				20

In addition to the internal controls over banking activities discussed on page 295, companies using online banking should allow only authorized check signors access to the company's online account. Additionally, log-in information, such as user identification and passwords, should be changed frequently.

The Perpetual Inventory System, Continued

The perpetual inventory system was introduced in Chapter 8. Figure 8.11 on page 250 demonstrated the general journal entries to record purchases, sales, and return transactions using both the periodic system and the perpetual system.

We will now discuss how cash receipts and cash payments are recorded when a perpetual inventory system is used.

When the perpetual inventory system is used, the purchasing company credits the Merchandise Inventory account when a cash discount is taken. The Purchases Discounts account is credited for a cash discount on the purchasing company's books when the periodic system is used.

The journal entry to record the receipt of cash on account is identical under both the perpetual and periodic inventory systems.

Figure 9.18 continues the examples illustrated in Figure 8.11 on page 250. The payment due to Holtz Industries is $1,982, calculated as follows:

Purchase	$2,050
Less return	150
Subtotal	1,900
Less discount (2% × $1,900)	(38)
Net purchase	1,862
Add freight	120
Payment due to Holtz Industries	$1,982

The payment due from Cervantes Company is $1,176. Calculations follow.

Sale	$1,250
Less return	50
Subtotal	1,200
Less discount (2% × $1,200)	(24)
Payment due from Cervantes Company	$1,176

Figure 9.18 illustrates the journal entries to record the payment to Holtz Industries and the cash received from Cervantes Company, using both the periodic system and the perpetual system.

> **> 9-12. OBJECTIVE**
>
> Record cash payments and cash receipts using the perpetual inventory system.

FIGURE 9.18

Journal Entries for Cash Receipts and Cash Payments Using Both the Periodic and Perpetual Inventory Systems

Journal Entry to Record Transaction, Using the:		
Transaction	**Periodic System**	**Perpetual System**

July 1: Issued Check 3820 for $1,982 to Holtz Industries for invoice of June 20, less return of June 22 and less a cash discount of $38.	Accounts Payable/Holtz Industries 2,020
	  Purchases Discounts 38
	  Cash 1,982
		Accounts Payable/Holtz Industries 2,020
		  Merchandise Inventory 38
		  Cash 1,982

July 9: Received a check for $1,176 from Cervantes Company for invoice of July 1, less return of July 3 and less a cash discount of $24.	Cash 1,176
	Sales Discounts 24
	  Accounts Receivable/
	  Cervantes Company 1,200
		Cash 1,176
		Sales Discounts 24
		  Accounts Receivable/
		  Cervantes Company 1,200

Section 3   Self Review

QUESTIONS

1. What is a postdated check? When should post-dated checks be deposited?

2. Why does a payee endorse a check before depositing it?

3. Which bank reconciliation items require journal entries?

EXERCISES

4. Which of the following does not require an adjustment to the financial records?

   a. Deposits in transit

   b. Bank service charge

   c. Check that was incorrectly recorded at $115, but was written and paid by the bank as $151

   d. NSF check from a customer

5. On the bank reconciliation statement, you would not find a list of:

   a. deposits in transit.

   b. canceled checks.

   c. outstanding checks.

   d. NSF checks.

ANALYSIS

6. James is one of several accounting clerks at Uptown Beverage Company. His job duties include recording invoices as they are received, filing the invoices, and writing the checks for accounts payable. He is a fast and efficient clerk and usually has some time available each day to help other clerks. It has been suggested that reconciling the bank statement should be added to his job duties. Do you agree or disagree? Why or why not?

(Answers to Section 3 Self Review are on page 325.)

REVIEW   Chapter Summary

In this chapter, you have learned the basic principles of accounting for cash payments and cash receipts.

Learning Objectives

9-1 Record cash receipts in a cash receipts journal.

Use of special journals leads to an efficient recording process for cash transactions. The cash receipts journal has separate columns for the accounts used most often for cash receipt transactions.

9-2 Account for cash short or over.

Errors can occur when making change. Cash register discrepancies should be recorded using the expense account *Cash Short or Over.*

9-3 Post from the cash receipts journal to subsidiary and general ledgers.

Individual accounts receivable amounts are posted to the subsidiary ledger daily. Figures in the Other Accounts Credit column are posted individually to the general ledger during the month. All other postings are done on a summary basis at month-end.

9-4 Record cash payments in a cash payments journal.

The cash payments journal has separate columns for the accounts used most often, eliminating the need to record the same account names repeatedly.

9-5 Post from the cash payments journal to subsidiary and general ledgers.

Individual accounts payable amounts are posted daily to the accounts payable subsidiary ledger. Amounts listed in the Other Accounts Debit column are posted individually to the general ledger during the month. All other postings are completed on a summary basis at the end of the month.

9-6 Demonstrate a knowledge of procedures for a petty cash fund.

Although most payments are made by check, small payments are often made through a petty cash fund. A petty cash voucher is prepared for each payment and signed by the person receiving the money. The person in charge of the fund records expenditures on a petty cash analysis sheet. The fund is replenished with a check for the sum spent. An entry is made in the cash payments journal to debit the accounts involved.

9-7 Demonstrate a knowledge of internal control procedures for cash.

All businesses need a system of internal controls to protect cash from theft and mishandling and to ensure accurate records of cash transactions. A checking account is essential to store cash safely and to make cash payments efficiently. For maximum control over outgoing cash, all payments should be made by check except those from carefully controlled special-purpose cash funds such as a petty cash fund.

9-8 Write a check, endorse checks, prepare a bank deposit slip, and maintain a checkbook balance.

Check writing requires careful attention to details. If a standard checkbook is used, the stub should be completed before the check so that it will not be forgotten. The stub gives the data needed to journalize the payment.

9-9 Reconcile the monthly bank statement.

A bank statement should be immediately reconciled with the cash balance in the firm's financial records. Usually, differences are due to deposits in transit, outstanding checks, and bank service charges, but many factors can cause lack of agreement between the bank balance and the book balance.

9-10 Record any adjusting entries required from the bank reconciliation.

Some differences between the bank balance and the book balance may require that the firm's records be adjusted after the bank statement is reconciled. Journal entries are recorded and then posted to correct the *Cash* account balance and the checkbook balance.

9-11 Understand how businesses use online banking to manage cash activities.

Many businesses now use online banking to receive cash payments from customers and to initiate cash payments.

9-12 Record cash payments and cash receipts using the perpetual inventory system.

Perpetual inventory systems give management more control over the company's inventory, and assist management in inventory control and purchasing activities.

9-13 Define the accounting terms new to this chapter.

Glossary

Bank reconciliation statement (p. 292) A statement that accounts for all differences between the balance on the bank statement and the book balance of cash

Blank endorsement (p. 288) A signature of the payee written on the back of the check that transfers ownership of the check without specifying to whom or for what purpose

Bonding (p. 285) The process by which employees are investigated by an insurance company that will insure the business against losses through employee theft or mishandling of funds

Canceled check (p. 291) A check paid by the bank on which it was drawn

Cash (p. 270) In accounting, currency, coins, checks, money orders, and funds on deposit in a bank

Cash payments journal (p. 277) A special journal used to record transactions involving the payment of cash

Cash receipts journal (p. 270) A special journal used to record and post transactions involving the receipt of cash

Cash register proof (p. 271) A verification that the amount of currency and coins in a cash register agrees with the amount shown on the cash register audit tape

Cash Short or Over **account** (p. 272) An account used to record any discrepancies between the amount of currency and coins in the cash register and the amount shown on the audit tape

Check (p. 287) A written order signed by an authorized person instructing a bank to pay a specific sum of money to a designated person or business

Credit memorandum (p. 290) A form that explains any addition, other than a deposit, to a checking account

Debit memorandum (p. 290) A form that explains any deduction, other than a check, from a checking account

Deposit in transit (p. 292) A deposit that is recorded in the cash receipts journal but that reaches the bank too late to be shown on the monthly bank statement

Deposit slip (p. 288) A form prepared to record the deposit of cash or checks to a bank account

Dishonored (NSF) check (p. 290) A check returned to the depositor unpaid because of insufficient funds in the drawer's account; also called an NSF check

Drawee (p. 287) The bank on which a check is written

Drawer (p. 287) The person or firm issuing a check

Electronic funds transfer (EFT) (p. 295) An electronic transfer of money from one account to another

Endorsement (p. 288) A written authorization that transfers ownership of a check

Full endorsement (p. 288) A signature transferring a check to a specific person, firm, or bank

Negotiable (p. 287) A financial instrument whose ownership can be transferred to another person or business

Outstanding checks (p. 292) Checks that have been recorded in the cash payments journal but have not yet been paid by the bank

Payee (p. 287) The person or firm to whom a check is payable

Petty cash analysis sheet (p. 283) A form used to record transactions involving petty cash

Petty cash fund (p. 270) A special-purpose fund used to handle payments involving small amounts of money

Petty cash voucher (p. 283) A form used to record the payments made from a petty cash fund

Postdated check (p. 289) A check dated some time in the future

Promissory note (p. 272) A written promise to pay a specified amount of money on a specific date

Restrictive endorsement (p. 288) A signature that transfers a check to a specific party for a stated purpose

Service charge (p. 290) A fee charged by a bank to cover the costs of maintaining accounts and providing services

Statement of account (p. 272) A form sent to a firm's customers showing transactions during the month and the balance owed

Comprehensive **Self Review**

1. Describe a full endorsement.
2. What is a petty cash voucher?
3. When is the petty cash fund replenished?
4. What are the advantages of using special journals for cash receipts and cash payments?
5. What does the term *cash* mean in business?

(Answers to Comprehensive Self Review are on page 325.)

Discussion Questions

1. Why is a bank reconciliation prepared?
2. Why are journal entries sometimes needed after the bank reconciliation statement is prepared?
3. Give some reasons why the bank balance and the book balance of cash might differ.
4. What is the book balance of cash?
5. What procedures are used to achieve internal control over banking activities?
6. What information is shown on the bank statement?
7. What is a check?
8. What type of information is entered on a check stub? Why should a check stub be prepared before the check is written?
9. Why are MICR numbers printed on deposit slips and checks?
10. Which type of endorsement is most appropriate for a business to use?
11. How are cash shortages and overages recorded?
12. When are petty cash expenditures entered in a firm's accounting records?
13. Describe the major controls for petty cash.
14. What type of account is **Purchases Discounts?** How is this account presented on the income statement?
15. How does a firm record a payment on account to a creditor when a cash discount is involved? Which journal is used?
16. How does a wholesale business record a check received on account from a customer when a cash discount is involved? Which journal is used?
17. Why do some wholesale businesses offer cash discounts to their customers?
18. What is a promissory note? What entry is made to record the collection of a promissory note and interest? Which journal is used?
19. Describe the major controls for cash payments.
20. Explain what *bonding* means. How does bonding relate to safeguarding cash?
21. Describe the major controls for cash receipts.
22. Explain the meaning of the following terms:
    a. Canceled check
    b. Outstanding check
    c. Deposit in transit
    d. Debit memorandum
    e. Credit memorandum
    f. Dishonored check
    g. Blank endorsement
    h. Deposit slip
    i. Drawee

     j. Restrictive endorsement

     k. Payee

     l. Drawer

     m. Service charge

23. What account is credited for a cash discount taken by the purchaser when (a) the periodic system is used and (b) the perpetual inventory system is used?

APPLICATIONS

Exercises

Exercise 9.1

Objective 9-1

> ### Recording cash receipts.

The following transactions took place at Eddie's Sports Gear during the first week of October 2016. Indicate how these transactions would be entered in a cash receipts journal.

DATE		TRANSACTIONS
Oct.	1	Had cash sales of $6,600 plus sales tax of $528; there was a cash overage of $12.
	2	Collected $890 on account from Jerry Lin, a credit customer.
	3	Had cash sales of $5,500 plus sales tax of $440.
	4	Eddie Reynolds, the owner, made an additional cash investment of $24,000.
	6	Had cash sales of $7,400 plus sales tax of $592; there was a cash shortage of $20.

Exercise 9.2

Objective 9-4

> ### Recording cash payments.

The following transactions took place at Eddie's Sports Gear during the first week of October 2016. Indicate how these transactions would be entered in a cash payments journal.

DATE		TRANSACTIONS
Oct.	1	Issued Check 3850 for $3,600 to pay the monthly rent.
	1	Issued Check 3851 for $3,200 to Fisher Company, a creditor, on account.
	2	Issued Check 3852 for $13,100 to purchase new equipment.
	2	Issued Check 3853 for $1,520 to remit sales tax to the state sales tax authority.
	3	Issued Check 3854 for $1,960 to Sports Emporium, a creditor, on account for invoice of $2,000 less cash discount of $40.
	4	Issued Check 3855 for $3,925 to purchase merchandise.
	6	Issued Check 3856 for $4,906 as a cash withdrawal for personal use by Eddie Reynolds, the owner.

Exercise 9.3

Objective 9-6

> ### Recording the establishment of a petty cash fund.

On January 2, Santa Ana Legal Clinic issued Check 2108 for $450 to establish a petty cash fund. Indicate how this transaction would be recorded in a cash payments journal.

Exercise 9.4

Objective 9-6

> ### Recording the replenishment of a petty cash fund.

On January 31, Vanessa's Floral Supplies Inc. issued Check 3159 to replenish its petty cash fund. An analysis of payments from the fund showed these totals: *Supplies,* $58; *Delivery Expense,* $99; and *Miscellaneous Expense,* $34. Indicate how this transaction would be recorded in a cash payments journal.

Preparing a bank reconciliation statement.

◀ **Exercise 9.5**
Objectives 9-9, 9-10

Chan Corporation received a bank statement showing a balance of $15,200 as of October 31, 2016. The firm's records showed a book balance of $14,672 on October 31. The difference between the two balances was caused by the following items. Prepare the adjusted bank balance section and the adjusted book balance section of the bank reconciliation statement. Also prepare the necessary journal entry.

1. A debit memorandum for an NSF check from James Dear for $434.
2. Three outstanding checks: Check 7017 for $134, Check 7098 for $65, and Check 7107 for $1,660.
3. A bank service charge of $30.
4. A deposit in transit of $867.

Analyzing bank reconciliation items.

◀ **Exercise 9.6**
Objective 9-9

At Livermore Delivery and Courier Service, the following items were found to cause a difference between the bank statement and the firm's records. Indicate whether each item will affect the bank balance or the book balance when the bank reconciliation statement is prepared. Also indicate which items will require an accounting entry after the bank reconciliation is completed.

1. A deposit in transit.
2. A debit memorandum for a dishonored check.
3. A credit memorandum for a promissory note that the bank collected for Livermore.
4. An error found in Livermore's records, which involves the amount of a check. The firm's checkbook and cash payments journal indicate $808 as the amount, but the canceled check itself and the listing on the bank statement show that $880 was the actual sum.
5. An outstanding check.
6. A bank service charge.
7. A check issued by another firm that was charged to Livermore's account by mistake.

Preparing a bank reconciliation statement.

◀ **Exercise 9.7**
Objective 9-9

Di Sisto Office Supply Company received a bank statement showing a balance of $68,505 as of March 31, 2016. The firm's records showed a book balance of $69,547 on March 31. The difference between the two balances was caused by the following items. Prepare a bank reconciliation statement for the firm as of March 31 and the necessary journal entries from the statement.

1. A debit memorandum for $60, which covers the bank's collection fee for the note.
2. A deposit in transit of $4,200.
3. A check for $258 issued by another firm that was mistakenly charged to Di Sisto's account.
4. A debit memorandum for an NSF check of $6,185 issued by Wilson Construction Company, a credit customer.
5. Outstanding checks: Check 3782 for $2,700; Check 3840 for $161.
6. A credit memorandum for a $6,800 noninterest-bearing note receivable that the bank collected for the firm.

Determining the adjusted bank balance.

◀ **Exercise 9.8**
Objective 9-9

Fierro Company received a bank statement showing a balance of $13,800 on November 30, 2016. During the bank reconciliation process, Fierro's accountant noted the following bank errors:

1. A check for $161 issued by Ferro, Inc., was mistakenly charged to Fierro Company's account.
2. Check 2782 was written for $300 but was paid by the bank as $1,300.
3. Check 2920 for $95 was paid by the bank twice.
4. A deposit for $690 on November 22 was credited by the bank for $960.

Assuming outstanding checks total $2,250, prepare the adjusted bank balance section of the November 30, 2016, bank reconciliation.

Exercise 9.9
Objective 9-11

▶ **Journalizing electronic transactions**

After returning from a three-day business trip, the accountant for Southeast Sales, Johanna Estrada, checked bank activity in the company's checking account online. The activity for the last three days follows.

Business Checking		Account #123456-987			
Date	**Type**	**Description**	**Additions**	**Payments**	**Balance**
09/24/2016	Loan Payment	Online Transfer to HMG XXXX		$3,500.00	$15,675.06
09/24/2016	Deposit	DEPOSIT ID NUMBER 8888	$2,269.60		$19,175.06
09/23/2016	Check	CHECK #1554 (view)		$3,500.00	$16,905.46
09/23/2016	Bill Payment	Online Payment		$36.05	$20,405.46
09/22/2016	Check	CHECK #1553 (view)		$240.00	$20,441.51
09/22/2016	Check	CHECK #1551 (view)		$1,750.00	$20,681.51
09/22/2016	ACH Credit	Edwards UK AP PAYMENT	$8,900.00		$22,431.51
09/22/2016	ATM	ATM WITHDRAWAL		$240.00	$13,531.51

After matching these transactions to the company's *Cash* account in the general ledger, Johanna noted the following unrecorded transactions:

1. The ATM withdrawal on 9/22/2016 was for personal use by the owner, Robert Savage.
2. The ACH credit on 9/22/2016 was an electronic funds payment received on account from Edwards UK, a credit customer located in Great Britain.
3. The bill payment made 9/23/2016 to Waste Control Trash Services (utilities).
4. The loan payment on 9/24/2016 was an automatic debit by Central Motors for the company's monthly payment on a loan for its automobiles. The loan does not bear interest.

Prepare the journal entries in a general journal to record the four transactions above. Use 21 as the page number.

Exercise 9.10
Objective 9-12

▶ **Recording a payment on account using the perpetual inventory system.**

On July 3, Fine Fashions Outlet purchased dresses for $3,500, plus a freight charge of $120, from Fashion Expo, Invoice 101, dated July 1; the terms are 2/10, net 30 days. On July 7, Fine Fashions Outlet received Credit Memorandum 210 for $550 from Fashion Expo for damaged dresses returned; the goods were purchased on Invoice 101 dated July 1. On July 10, Fine Fashions Outlet issued Check 1255 to pay the amount due to Fashion Expo for Invoice 101, dated July 1, less the return of July 7 and less the cash discount.

1. Determine the amount to be paid by Fine Fashions Outlet on July 10.
2. Record the payment on July 10 in a general journal. Use 10 as the journal page number. Fine Fashions Outlet uses the perpetual inventory system.

PROBLEMS

Problem 9.1A
Objectives 9-1, 9-2, 9-3

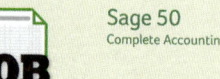

Problem Set A

Journalizing cash receipts and posting to the general ledger.

Entertainment Inc. is a retail store that rents movies and sells music CDs over the Internet. The firm's cash receipts for February are listed below. The general ledger accounts used to record these transactions appear on the next page.

INSTRUCTIONS

1. Open the general ledger accounts and enter the balances as of February 1, 2016.
2. Record the transactions in a cash receipts journal. Use 4 as the page number.
3. Post the individual entries from the Other Accounts Credit section of the cash receipts journal to the proper general ledger accounts.
4. Total, prove, and rule the cash receipts journal as of February 29, 2016.
5. Post the column totals from the cash receipts journal to the proper general ledger accounts.

GENERAL LEDGER ACCOUNTS

101	Cash	$ 5,060 Dr.	401	Sales	
109	Notes Receivable	900 Dr.	491	Interest Income	
111	Accounts Receivable	4,125 Dr.	620	Cash Short or Over	
129	Supplies	710 Dr.			
231	Sales Tax Payable	345 Cr.			
301	Jason Wilson, Capital	35,000 Cr.			

DATE		TRANSACTIONS
Feb.	3	Received $600 from Danielle Pelzel, a credit customer, on account.
	5	Received a cash refund of $130 for damaged supplies.
	7	Had cash sales of $5,800 plus sales tax of $464 during the first week of February; there was a cash shortage of $70.
	9	Jason Wilson, the owner, invested an additional $16,000 cash in the business.
	12	Received $480 from Kyela Jones, a credit customer, in payment of her account.
	14	Had cash sales of $4,550 plus sales tax of $364 during the second week of February; there was an overage of $38.
	16	Received $550 from Sadie Nelson, a credit customer, to apply toward her account.
	19	Received a check from Ketura Pittman to pay her $900 promissory note plus interest of $36.
	21	Had cash sales of $5,050 plus sales tax of $404 during the third week of February.
	25	Alfred Herron, a credit customer, sent a check for $680 to pay the balance he owes.
	28	Had cash sales of $5,100 plus sales tax of $408 during the fourth week of February; there was a cash shortage of $46.

Analyze: What total accounts receivable were collected in February?

Journalizing cash payments, recording petty cash, and posting to the general ledger.

◄ **Problem 9.2A**
Objectives 9-4, 9-5, 9-6

The cash payments of The Aristocrat's Jewels, a retail business, for June are listed below. The general ledger accounts used to record these transactions appear below.

INSTRUCTIONS

1. Open the general ledger accounts and enter the balances as of June 1.
2. Record all payments by check in a cash payments journal; use 8 as the page number.
3. Record all payments from the petty cash fund on a petty cash analysis sheet; use 8 as the sheet number.
4. Post the individual entries from the Other Accounts Debit section of the cash payments journal to the proper general ledger accounts.
5. Total, prove, and rule the petty cash analysis sheet as of June 30. Record the replenishment of the fund and the final balance on the sheet.
6. Total, prove, and rule the cash payments journal as of June 30.
7. Post the column totals from the cash payments journal to the proper general ledger accounts.

GENERAL LEDGER ACCOUNTS

101	Cash	$46,740 Dr.
105	Petty Cash Fund	
129	Supplies	1,160 Dr.
201	Notes Payable	4,200 Cr.
205	Accounts Payable	19,880 Cr.
231	Sales Tax Payable	5,200 Cr.
302	Larry Jennings, Drawing	
451	Sales Returns and Allowances	
504	Purchases Discounts	
611	Delivery Expense	
620	Rent Expense	
623	Salaries Expense	
626	Telephone Expense	
634	Interest Expense	
635	Miscellaneous Expense	

DATE		TRANSACTIONS
June	1	Issued Check 4121 for $3,500 to pay the monthly rent.
	2	Issued Check 4122 for $5,200 to remit the state sales tax.
	3	Issued Check 4123 for $2,880 to Perfect Timing Watch Company, a creditor, in payment of Invoice 6808, dated May 5.
	4	Issued Check 4124 for $250 to establish a petty cash fund. (After journalizing this transaction, be sure to enter it on the first line of the petty cash analysis sheet.)
	5	Paid $40 from the petty cash fund for office supplies, Petty Cash Voucher 1.
	7	Issued Check 4125 for $4,368 to Perry Corporation in payment of a $4,200 promissory note and interest of $168.
	8	Paid $30 from the petty cash fund for postage stamps, Petty Cash Voucher 2.
	10	Issued Check 4126 for $604 to a customer as a cash refund for a defective watch that was returned; the original sale was made for cash.
	12	Issued Check 4127 for $286 to pay the telephone bill.
	14	Issued Check 4128 for $5,831 to International Jewelry Company, a creditor, in payment of Invoice 8629, dated May 6 ($5,950), less a cash discount ($119).
	15	Paid $19 from the petty cash fund for delivery service, Petty Cash Voucher 3.
	17	Issued Check 4129 for $960 to purchase store supplies.
	20	Issued Check 4130 for $3,920 to Nelson's Jewelry and Accessories, a creditor, in payment of Invoice 1513, dated June 12 ($4,000), less a cash discount ($80).
	22	Paid $34 from the petty cash fund for a personal withdrawal by Larry Jennings, the owner, Petty Cash Voucher 4.
	25	Paid $40 from the petty cash fund to have the store windows washed and repaired, Petty Cash Voucher 5.
	27	Issued Check 4131 for $3,750 to Classy Creations, a creditor, in payment of Invoice 667, dated May 30.
	30	Paid $34 from the petty cash fund for delivery service, Petty Cash Voucher 6.
	30	Issued Check 4132 for $7,925 to pay the monthly salaries.
	30	Issued Check 4133 for $6,000 to Larry Jennings, the owner, as a withdrawal for personal use.
	30	Issued Check 4134 for $197 to replenish the petty cash fund. (Foot the columns of the petty cash analysis sheet in order to determine the accounts that should be debited and the amounts involved.)

Analyze: What total payments were made from the petty cash fund for the month?

Journalizing sales and cash receipts and posting to the general ledger.

◀ **Problem 9.3A**
Objectives 9-1, 9-2, 9-3

Sage 50
Complete Accounting

Awesome Sounds is a wholesale business that sells musical instruments. Transactions involving sales and cash receipts for the firm during April 2016 follow, along with the general ledger accounts used to record these transactions.

INSTRUCTIONS

1. Open the general ledger accounts and enter the balances as of April 1, 2016.
2. Record the transactions in a sales journal, a cash receipts journal, and a general journal. Use 7 as the page number for each of the special journals and 17 as the page number for the general journal.
3. Post the entries from the general journal to the general ledger.
4. Total, prove, and rule the special journals as of April 30, 2016.
5. Post the column totals from the special journals to the proper general ledger accounts.
6. Prepare the heading and the Revenue section of the firm's income statement for the month ended April 30.

GENERAL LEDGER ACCOUNTS

101	Cash	$17,400 Dr.
109	Notes Receivable	
111	Accounts Receivable	22,000 Dr.
401	Sales	
451	Sales Returns and Allowances	
452	Sales Discounts	

DATE	TRANSACTIONS
April 1	Sold merchandise for $4,900 to Soprano Music Center; issued Invoice 9312 with terms of 2/10, n/30.
3	Received a check for $1,960 from Music Supply Store in payment of Invoice 6718 of March 25 ($2,000), less a cash discount ($40).
5	Sold merchandise for $1,825 in cash to a new customer who has not yet established credit.
8	Sold merchandise for $5,500 to Music Warehouse, issued Invoice 9313 with terms of 2/10, n/30.
10	Soprano Music Center sent a check for $4,802 in payment of Invoice 9312 of April 1 ($4,900), less a cash discount ($98).
15	Accepted a return of damaged merchandise from Music Warehouse; issued Credit Memorandum 105 for $900; the original sale was made on Invoice 9313 of April 8.
19	Sold merchandise for $11,500 to Eagleton Music Center; issued Invoice 9314 with terms of 2/10, n/30.
23	Collected $3,225 from Sounds From Yesterday for Invoice 6725 of March 25.
26	Accepted a two-month promissory note for $6,500 from Country Music Store in settlement of its overdue account; the note has an interest rate of 12 percent.
28	Received a check for $11,270 from Eagleton Music Center in payment of Invoice 9314, dated April 19 ($11,500), less a cash discount ($230).
30	Sold merchandise for $10,800 to Contemporary Sounds, Inc.; issued Invoice 9315 with terms of 2/10, n/30.

Analyze: What total sales on account were made in the month of April, prior to any returns or allowances?

Problem 9.4A
Objectives 9-4, 9-5

▶ **Journalizing purchases, cash payments, and purchases discounts; posting to the general ledger.**

Sage 50
Complete Accounting

QB

The Bike and Hike Outlet is a retail store. Transactions involving purchases and cash payments for the firm during June 2016 are listed below as are the general ledger accounts used to record these transactions.

INSTRUCTIONS

1. Open the general ledger accounts and enter the balances as of June 1, 2016.

2. Record the transactions in a purchases journal, a cash payments journal, and a general journal. Use 8 as the page number for each of the special journals and 20 as the page number for the general journal.

3. Post the entries from the general journal and from the Other Accounts Debit section of the cash payments journal to the proper general ledger accounts.

4. Total, prove, and rule the special journals as of June 30.

5. Post the column totals from the special journals to the general ledger.

6. Show how the firm's net cost of purchases would be reported on its income statement for the month ended June 30.

GENERAL LEDGER ACCOUNTS

101	Cash	$21,900 Dr.
131	Equipment	66,000 Dr.
201	Notes Payable	
205	Accounts Payable	4,980 Cr.
501	Purchases	
503	Purchases Ret. and Allow.	
504	Purchases Discounts	
611	Rent Expense	
614	Salaries Expense	
617	Telephone Expense	

DATE	TRANSACTIONS
June 1	Issued Check 1101 for $3,400 to pay the monthly rent.
3	Purchased merchandise for $3,100 from Perfect Fit Shoe Shop, Invoice 746, dated June 1; the terms are 2/10, n/30.
5	Purchased new store equipment for $5,500 from Middleton Company, Invoice 9067 dated June 4, net payable in 30 days.
7	Issued Check 1102 for $1,570 to Leisure Wear Clothing Company, a creditor, in payment of Invoice 3342 of May 9.
8	Issued Check 1103 for $3,038 to Perfect Fit Shoe Shop, a creditor, in payment of Invoice 746 dated June 1 ($3,100), less a cash discount ($62).
12	Purchased merchandise for $2,300 from Juanda's Coat Shop, Invoice 9922, dated June 9, net due and payable in 30 days.
15	Issued Check 1104 for $238 to pay the monthly telephone bill.
18	Received Credit Memorandum 203 for $800 from Juanda's Coat Shop for defective goods that were returned; the original purchase was made on Invoice 9922 dated June 9.
21	Purchased new store equipment for $10,500 from Warren Company; issued a three-month promissory note with interest at 12 percent.
23	Purchased merchandise for $6,400 from The Motor Speedway, Invoice 1927, dated June 20; terms of 2/10, n/30.

DATE	9.4A (cont.) TRANSACTIONS
25	Issued Check 1105 for $1,500 to Juanda's Coat Shop, a creditor, in payment of Invoice 7416 dated May 28.
28	Issued Check 1106 for $6,272 to The Motor Speedway, a creditor, in payment of Invoice 1927 of June 20 ($6,400), less a cash discount ($128).
30	Purchased merchandise for $2,080 from Jogging Shoes Store, Invoice 4713, dated June 26; the terms are 1/10, n/30.
30	Issued Check 1107 for $5,800 to pay the monthly salaries of the employees.

Analyze: Assuming that all relevant information is included in this problem, what total liabilities does the company have at month-end?

Preparing a bank reconciliation statement and journalizing entries to adjust the cash balance.

◄ **Problem 9.5A**
Objectives 9-9,
9-10

On May 2, 2016, PHF Vacations received its April bank statement from First City Bank and Trust. Enclosed with the bank statement, which appears below, was a debit memorandum for $210 that covered an NSF check issued by Doris Fisher, a credit customer. The firm's checkbook contained the following information about deposits made and checks issued during April. The balance of the *Cash* account and the checkbook on April 30, 2016, was $3,012.

DATE		TRANSACTIONS	
April	1	Balance	$6,099
	1	Check 1207	110
	3	Check 1208	400
	5	Deposit	450
	5	Check 1209	325
	10	Check 1210	3,000
	17	Check 1211	60
	19	Deposit	200
	22	Check 1212	8
	23	Deposit	200
	26	Check 1213	250
	28	Check 1214	18
	30	Check 1215	16
	30	Deposit	250

FIRST CITY BANK AND TRUST

PHF Vacations   1-877-123-9876
1718 Jade Lane
San Diego, CA 92111-4998

Account Number: 23-11070-08   April 1–30, 2016
Activity Summary:

Balance, April 1	$ 6,099.00
Deposits and credits	850.00
Withdrawals and debits	(4,370.00)
Balance, April 30	$ 2,579.00

DATE	DESCRIPTION	DEPOSITS/CREDITS	WITHDRAWALS/DEBITS	BALANCE
4/1/16	Opening balance			$6,099.00
4/6/16	Deposit	450.00		6,549.00
4/6/16	Check No. 1207		110.00	6,439.00
4/10/16	Check No. 1208		400.00	6,039.00
4/10/16	Check No. 1209		325.00	5,714.00
4/13/16	Check No. 1210		3,000.00	2,714.00
4/14/16	Service fee		7.00	2,707.00
4/20/16	Deposit	200.00		2,907.00
4/22/16	Check No. 1211		60.00	2,847.00
4/25/16	Deposit	200.00		3,047.00
4/26/16	Check No. 1212		8.00	3,039.00
4/29/16	Debit for NSF Check		210.00	2,829.00
4/29/16	Check No. 1213		250.00	2,579.00
	Totals	850.00	4,370.00	

INSTRUCTIONS

1. Prepare a bank reconciliation statement for the firm as of April 30, 2016.
2. Record general journal entries for any items on the bank reconciliation statement that must be journalized. Date the entries April 30, 2016.

Analyze: What checks remain outstanding after the bank statement has been reconciled?

Problem 9.6A
Objectives 9-9, 9-10

▶ **Preparing a bank reconciliation statement and journalizing entries to adjust the cash balance.**

On August 31, 2016, the balance in the checkbook and the *Cash* account of the Sonoma Inn was $12,370. The balance shown on the bank statement on the same date was $13,247.

Notes

a. The firm's records indicate that a $1,550 deposit dated August 30 and a $711 deposit dated August 31 do not appear on the bank statement.

b. A service charge of $7 and a debit memorandum of $370 covering an NSF check have not yet been entered in the firm's records. (The check was issued by Art Corts, a credit customer.)

c. The following checks were issued but have not yet been paid by the bank:

Check 712, $120
Check 713, $135
Check 716, $248
Check 736, $587
Check 739, $88
Check 741, $130

d. A credit memorandum shows that the bank collected a $2,134 note receivable and interest of $73 for the firm. These amounts have not yet been entered in the firm's records.

INSTRUCTIONS

1. Prepare a bank reconciliation statement for the firm as of August 31.
2. Record general journal entries for items on the bank reconciliation statement that must be journalized. Date the entries August 31, 2016.

Analyze: What effect did the journal entries recorded as a result of the bank reconciliation have on the fundamental accounting equation?

Correcting errors revealed by a bank reconciliation.

◀ **Problem 9.7A**
Objectives 9-9, 9-10

During the bank reconciliation process at A. Fontes Consultancy on May 2, 2016, the following two errors were discovered in the firm's records.

a. The checkbook and the cash payments journal indicated that Check 2206 dated April 17 was issued for $715 to make a cash purchase of supplies. However, examination of the canceled check and the listing on the bank statement showed that the actual amount of the check was $24.

b. The checkbook and the cash payments journal indicated that Check 2247 dated April 20 was issued for $130 to pay a utility bill. However, examination of the canceled check and the listing on the bank statement showed that the actual amount of the check was $184.

INSTRUCTIONS

1. Prepare the adjusted book balance section of the firm's bank reconciliation statement. The book balance as of April 30 was $20,325. The errors listed above are the only two items that affect the book balance.
2. Prepare general journal entries to correct the errors. Use page 11 and date the entries April 30, 2016. Check 2206 was correctly debited to *Supplies* on April 17, and Check 2247 was debited to *Utilities Expense* on April 20.

Analyze: If the errors described had not been corrected, would net income for the period be overstated or understated? By what amount?

Preparing a bank reconciliation statement and journalizing entries to adjust the cash balance.

◀ **Problem 9.8A**
Objectives 9-9, 9-10, 9-11

On August 1, 2016, the accountant for Western Imports downloaded the company's July 31, 2016, bank statement from the bank's website. The balance shown on the bank statement was $28,760. The July 31, 2016, balance in the Cash account in the general ledger was $14,242.

Jenny Irvine, the accountant for Western Imports, noted the following differences between the bank's records and the company's *Cash* account in the general ledger.

a. An electronic funds transfer for $14,400 from Foncier Ricard, a customer located in France, was received by the bank on July 31.
b. Check 1422 was correctly written and recorded for $1,200. The bank mistakenly paid the check for $1,280.
c. The accounting records indicate that Check 1425 was issued for $60 to make a purchase of supplies. However, examination of the check online showed that the actual amount of the check was for $90.
d. A deposit of $900 made after banking hours on July 31 did not appear on the July 31 bank statement.
e. The following checks were outstanding: Check 1429 for $1,249, and Check 1430 for $141.
f. An automatic debit of $262 on July 31 from CentralComm for telephone service appeared on the bank statement but had not been recorded in the company's accounting records.

INSTRUCTIONS

1. Prepare a bank reconciliation for the firm as of July 31.

2. Record general journal entries for the items on the bank reconciliation that must be journalized. Date the entries July 31, 2016. Use 19 as the page number.

Analyze: What effect on total expenses occurred as a result of the general journal entries recorded?

Problem Set B

Problem 9.1B

Objectives 9-1, 9-2, 9-3

▶ ## Journalizing cash receipts and posting to the general ledger.

The Book Peddler is a retail store that sells books, cards, business supplies, and novelties. The firm's cash receipts during June 2016 are shown below. The general ledger accounts used to record these transactions appear below.

INSTRUCTIONS

1. Open the general ledger accounts and enter the balances as of June 1.

2. Record the transactions in a cash receipts journal. (Use page 14.)

3. Post the individual entries from the Other Accounts Credit section of the cash receipts journal to the proper general ledger accounts.

4. Total, prove, and rule the cash receipts journal as of June 30.

5. From the cash receipts journal, post the totals to the general ledger.

GENERAL LEDGER ACCOUNTS

102	Cash	$1,200
111	Accounts Receivable	8,400
115	Notes Receivable	1,700
129	Office Supplies	1,000
231	Sales Tax Payable	400
302	Tina Kapoor, Capital	7,600
401	Sales	
791	Interest Income	

DATE		TRANSACTIONS
June	3	Received $500 from Do It Yourself Copy Center, a credit customer.
	4	Received a check for $1,802 from Amanda Whitehead to pay her note receivable; the total included $102 of interest.
	5	Received a $310 refund for damaged supplies purchased from Books-R-Us.
	7	Recorded cash sales of $1,700 plus sales tax payable of $136.
	10	Received $1,200 from Linda Park, a credit customer.
	13	Tina Kapoor, the owner, contributed additional capital of $13,000 to the business.
	14	Recorded cash sales of $1,600 plus sales tax of $128.
	18	Received $1,760 from Karen Cho, a credit customer.
	19	Received $1,300 from Nancy Matthews, a credit customer.
	21	Recorded cash sales of $1,800 plus sales tax of $144.
	27	Received $850 from Alex Holloway, a credit customer.

Analyze: Assuming that all relevant information is included in this problem, what are total assets for The Book Peddler at June 30, 2016?

Journalizing cash payments and recording petty cash; posting to the general ledger. ◀

Problem 9.2B
Objectives 9-4,
9-5, 9-6

The cash payments of European Gift Shop, a retail business, for September are listed on the next page. The general ledger accounts used to record these transactions appear below.

INSTRUCTIONS

1. Open the general ledger accounts and enter the balances as of September 1, 2016.
2. Record all payments by check in a cash payments journal. Use 12 as the page number.
3. Record all payments from the petty cash fund on a petty cash analysis sheet with special columns for *Delivery Expense* and *Miscellaneous Expense.* Use 12 as the sheet number.
4. Post the individual entries from the Other Accounts Debit section of the cash payments journal to the proper general ledger accounts.
5. Total, prove, and rule the petty cash analysis sheet as of September 30, then record the replenishment of the fund and the final balance on the sheet.
6. Total, prove, and rule the cash payments journal as of September 30.
7. Post the column totals from the cash payments journal to the proper general ledger accounts.

GENERAL LEDGER ACCOUNTS

101	Cash	$21,530 Dr.	504	Purchases Discounts
105	Petty Cash Fund		511	Delivery Expense
141	Equipment	43,000 Dr.	611	Interest Expense
201	Notes Payable	1,000 Cr.	614	Miscellaneous Expense
205	Accounts Payable	9,800 Cr.	620	Rent Expense
231	Sales Tax Payable	1,344 Cr.	623	Salaries Expense
302	Fred Lynn, Drawing		626	Telephone Expense
451	Sales Ret. and Allow.			

DATE		TRANSACTIONS
Sept.	1	Issued Check 401 for $1,344 to remit sales tax to the state tax commission.
	2	Issued Check 402 for $1,700 to pay the monthly rent.
	4	Issued Check 403 for $100 to establish a petty cash fund. (After journalizing this transaction, be sure to enter it on the first line of the petty cash analysis sheet.)
	5	Issued Check 404 for $1,470 to Elegant Glassware, a creditor, in payment of Invoice 6793, dated August 28 ($1,500), less a cash discount ($30).
	6	Paid $12.00 from the petty cash fund for delivery service, Petty Cash Voucher 1.
	9	Purchased store equipment for $1,000; issued Check 405.
	11	Paid $16 from the petty cash fund for office supplies, Petty Cash Voucher 2 (charge to *Miscellaneous Expense*).
	13	Issued Check 406 for $970 to Taylor Company, a creditor, in payment of Invoice 7925, dated August 15.
		(continued)

DATE	9.2B (cont.) TRANSACTIONS
Sept. 14	Issued Check 407 for $425 to a customer as a cash refund for a defective watch that was returned; the original sale was made for cash.
16	Paid $10 from the petty cash fund for a personal withdrawal by Fred Lynn, the owner, Petty Cash Voucher 3.
18	Issued Check 408 for $187 to pay the monthly telephone bill.
21	Issued Check 409 for $833 to African Imports, a creditor, in payment of Invoice 1822, dated September 13 ($850), less a cash discount ($17).
23	Paid $13 from the petty cash fund for postage stamps, Petty Cash Voucher 4 (charge to Miscellaneous Expense).
24	Issued Check 410 for $1,040 to Zachary Corporation in payment of a $1,000 promissory note and interest of $40.
26	Issued Check 411 for $1,240 to Atlantic Ceramics, a creditor, in payment of Invoice 3510, dated August 29.
27	Paid $10 from the petty cash fund for delivery service, Petty Cash Voucher 5.
28	Issued Check 412 for $1,500 to Fred Lynn, the owner, as a withdrawal for personal use.
30	Issued Check 413 for $2,500 to pay the monthly salaries of the employees.
30	Issued Check 414 for $61 to replenish the petty cash fund. (Foot the columns of the petty cash analysis sheet in order to determine the accounts that should be debited and the amounts involved.)

Analyze: What was the amount of total debits to general ledger liability accounts during the month of September?

Problem 9.3B
Objectives 9-1, 9-2, 9-3

► **Journalizing sales and cash receipts and posting to the general ledger.**

Royal Construction Company is a wholesale business. The transactions involving sales and cash receipts for the firm during August 2016 are listed below. The general ledger accounts used to record these transactions are listed below.

INSTRUCTIONS

1. Open the general ledger accounts and enter the balances as of August 1, 2016.

2. Record the transactions in a sales journal, a cash receipts journal, and a general journal. Use 10 as the page number for each of the special journals and 24 as the page number for the general journal.

3. Post the entries from the general journal to the proper general ledger accounts.

4. Total, prove, and rule the special journals as of August 31, 2016.

5. Post the column totals from the special journals to the proper general ledger accounts.

6. Prepare the heading and the Revenue section of the firm's income statement for the month ended August 31, 2016.

GENERAL LEDGER ACCOUNTS

101	Cash	$15,070 Dr.	401	Sales	
109	Notes Receivable		451	Sales Returns and Allowances	
111	Accounts Receivable	22,507 Dr.	452	Sales Discounts	

DATE		TRANSACTIONS
Aug.	1	Received a check for $6,468 from Construction Supply Company in payment of Invoice 8277 dated July 21 ($6,600), less a cash discount ($132).
	2	Sold merchandise for $19,450 to Jamison Builders; issued Invoice 2978 with terms of 2/10, n/30.
	4	Accepted a three-month promissory note for $12,000 from Davis Custom Homes to settle its overdue account; the note has an interest rate of 12 percent.
	7	Sold merchandise for $18,550 to Branch Construction Company; issued Invoice 2979 with terms of 2/10, n/30.
	11	Collected $19,061 from Jamison Builders for Invoice 2978 dated August 2 ($19,450), less a cash discount ($389.00).
	14	Sold merchandise for $7,050 in cash to a new customer who has not yet established credit.
	16	Branch Construction Company sent a check for $18,179 in payment of Invoice 2979 dated August 7 ($18,550), less a cash discount ($371.00).
	22	Sold merchandise for $6,850 to Contemporary Homes; issued Invoice 2980 with terms of 2/10, n/30.
	24	Received a check for $6,000 from Garcia Homes Center to pay Invoice 2877, dated July 23.
	26	Accepted a return of damaged merchandise from Contemporary Homes; issued Credit Memorandum 101 for $550; the original sale was made on Invoice 2980, dated August 22.
	31	Sold merchandise for $17,440 to Denton County Builders; issued Invoice 2981 with terms of 2/10, n/30.

Analyze: What total sales on account were made in August? Include sales returns and allowances in your computation.

Journalizing purchases, cash payments, and purchases discounts; posting to the general ledger.

◀ **Problem 9.4B**
Objectives 9-4, 9-5

Contemporary Appliance Center is a retail store that sells a variety of household appliances. Transactions involving purchases and cash payments for the firm during December 2016 are listed below and on the next page. The general ledger accounts used to record these transactions appear below.

INSTRUCTIONS

1. Open the general ledger accounts and enter the balances in these accounts as of December 1, 2016.

2. Record the transactions in a purchases journal, a cash payments journal, and a general journal. Use 12 as the page number for each of the special journals and 30 as the page number for the general journal.

3. Post the entries from the general journal and from the Other Accounts Debit section of the cash payments journal to the proper accounts in the general ledger.

4. Total, prove, and rule the special journals as of December 31, 2016.

5. Post the column totals from the special journals to the general ledger accounts.

6. Show how the firm's cost of purchases would be reported on its income statement for the month ended December 31, 2016.

GENERAL LEDGER ACCOUNTS

101	Cash	$60,700 Dr.
131	Equipment	68,000 Dr.
201	Notes Payable	
205	Accounts Payable	7,600 Cr.

GENERAL LEDGER ACCOUNTS (CONT.)

501 Purchases

503 Purchases Returns and Allowances

504 Purchases Discounts

611 Rent Expense

614 Salaries Expense

617 Telephone Expense

DATE		TRANSACTIONS
Dec.	1	Purchased merchandise for $6,600 from Alexis Products for Homes, Invoice 6559, dated November 28; the terms are 2/10, n/30.
	2	Issued Check 1801 for $3,000 to pay the monthly rent.
	4	Purchased new store equipment for $14,000 from Kesterson Company; issued a two-month promissory note with interest at 10 percent.
	6	Issued Check 1802 for $6,468 to Alexis Products for Homes, a creditor, in payment of Invoice 6559, dated November 28 ($6,600), less a cash discount ($132).
	10	Purchased merchandise for $9,200 from the Baxter Corporation, Invoice 5119, dated December 7; terms of 2/10, n/30.
	13	Issued Check 1803 for $265 to pay the monthly telephone bill.
	15	Issued Check 1804 for $9,016 to Baxter Corporation, a creditor, in payment of Invoice 5119, dated December 7 ($9,200), less a cash discount ($184).
	18	Purchased merchandise for $12,400 from Household Appliance Center, Invoice 7238, dated December 16; terms of 3/10, n/30.
	20	Purchased new store equipment for $6,000 from Safety Security Systems Inc., Invoice 536, dated December 17, net payable in 45 days.
	21	Issued Check 1805 for $4,200 to Chain Lighting and Appliances, a creditor, in payment of Invoice 7813, dated November 23.
	22	Purchased merchandise for $5,800 from Zale Corporation, Invoice 3161, dated December 19, net due in 30 days.
	24	Issued Check 1806 for $12,028 to Household Appliance Center, a creditor, in payment of Invoice 7238, dated December 16 ($12,400), less a cash discount ($372).
	28	Received Credit Memorandum 201 for $1,050 from Zale Corporation for damaged goods that were returned; the original purchase was made on Invoice 3161, dated December 19.
	31	Issued Check 1807 for $6,500 to pay the monthly salaries of the employees.

Analyze: List the dates for transactions in December that would be categorized as expenses of the business.

Problem 9.5B

Objectives 9-9, 9-10

▶ **Preparing a bank reconciliation statement and journalizing entries to adjust the cash balance.**

On October 7, 2016, Peter Chen, Attorney-at-Law, received his September bank statement from First Texas National Bank. Enclosed with the bank statement was a debit memorandum for $118 that covered an NSF check issued by Annette Cole, a credit customer. The firm's checkbook contained the following information about deposits made and checks issued during September. The balance of the *Cash* account and the checkbook on September 30 was $8,134.

INSTRUCTIONS

1. Prepare a bank reconciliation statement for the firm as of September 30, 2016.

2. Record general journal entries for any items on the bank reconciliation statement that must be journalized. Date the entries September 30, 2016.

DATE		TRANSACTIONS	
Sept.	1	Balance	$6,500
	1	Check 104	100
	3	Check 105	10
	3	Deposit	500
	6	Check 106	225
	10	Deposit	410
	11	Check 107	200
	15	Check 108	75
	21	Check 109	60
	22	Deposit	730
	25	Check 110	16
	25	Check 111	80
	27	Check 112	140
	28	Deposit	900

FIRST TEXAS NATIONAL BANK

Peter Chen, Attorney-at-Law
3510 North Central Expressway
Dallas, TX 75232-2709

1-877-987-6543

Account Number: 22-5654-30
September 1–30, 2016
Activity Summary:

Balance, September 1	$ 6,500.00
Deposits and credits	1,640.00
Withdrawals and debits	(816.50)
Balance, September 30	$ 7,323.50

DATE	DESCRIPTION	DEPOSITS/CREDITS	WITHDRAWALS/DEBITS	BALANCE
9/1/16	Opening balance			$6,500.00
9/3/16	Deposit	500.00		7,000.00
9/6/16	Check No. 104		100.00	6,900.00
9/11/16	Deposit	410.00		7,310.00
9/11/16	Check No. 105		10.00	7,300.00
9/11/16	Check No. 107		200.00	7,100.00
9/15/16	Check No. 106		225.00	6,875.00
9/19/16	Check No. 109		60.00	6,815.00
9/23/16	Deposit	730.00		7,545.00
9/25/16	Check No. 110		16.00	7,529.00
9/25/16	Check No. 111		80.00	7,449.00
9/28/16	Debit for NSF Check		118.00	7,331.00
9/28/16	Service charge		7.50	7,323.50
	Totals	1,640.00	816.50	

Analyze: How many checks were paid (cleared the bank) according to the September 30 bank statement?

Problem 9.6B

Objectives 9-9, 9-10

▶ **Preparing a bank reconciliation statement and journalizing entries to adjust the cash balance.**

On July 31, 2016, the balance in Gourmet Kitchen Appliances' checkbook and *Cash* account was $7,318.59. The balance shown on the bank statement on the same date was $8,442.03.

Notes

a. The following checks were issued but have not yet been paid by the bank: Check 533 for $148.95, Check 535 for $122.50, and Check 537 for $625.40.

b. A credit memorandum shows that the bank has collected a $1,450 note receivable and interest of $30 for the firm. These amounts have not yet been entered in the firm's records.

c. The firm's records indicate that a deposit of $1,094.07 made on July 31 does not appear on the bank statement.

d. A service charge of $14.34 and a debit memorandum of $145 covering an NSF check have not yet been entered in the firm's records. (The check was issued by Robert Briggs, a credit customer.)

INSTRUCTIONS

1. Prepare a bank reconciliation statement for the firm as of July 31, 2016.

2. Record general journal entries for any items on the bank reconciliation statement that must be journalized. Date the entries July 31, 2016.

Analyze: After all journal entries have been recorded and posted, what is the balance in the *Cash* account at July 31, 2016?

Problem 9.7B

Objectives 9-9, 9-10

▶ **Correcting errors revealed by a bank reconciliation.**

During the bank reconciliation process at Big Dudes Moving Corporation on March 3, 2016, the following errors were discovered in the firm's records.

a. The checkbook and the cash payments journal indicated that Check 1301 dated February 18 was issued for $316 to pay for hauling expenses. However, examination of the canceled check and the listing on the bank statement showed that the actual amount of the check was $308.

b. The checkbook and the cash payments journal indicated that Check 1322 dated February 24 was issued for $404 to pay a telephone bill. However, examination of the canceled check and the listing on the bank statement showed that the actual amount of the check was $440.

INSTRUCTIONS

1. Prepare the adjusted book balance section of the firm's bank reconciliation statement. The book balance as of February 29, 2016, was $19,851. The errors listed are the only two items that affect the book balance.

2. Prepare general journal entries to correct the errors. Date the entries February 29, 2016. Check 1301 was debited to *Hauling Expense* on February 18, and Check 1322 was debited to *Telephone Expense* on February 24.

Analyze: What net change to the *Cash* account occurred as a result of the correcting journal entries?

Problem 9.8B

Objectives 9-9, 9-10, 9-11

▶ **Preparing a bank reconciliation statement and journalizing entries to adjust the cash balance.**

On December 1, 2016, the accountant for Euro Specialty Products downloaded the company's November 30, 2016, bank statement from the bank's website. The balance shown on the bank statement was $29,734. The November 30, 2016, balance in the *Cash* account in the general ledger was $16,630.

Robert Kang, the accountant for Euro Specialty Products, noted the following differences between the bank's records and the company's *Cash* account in the general ledger.

a. The following checks were outstanding: Check 4129 for $1,322, and Check 4130 for $239.

b. A deposit of $1,224 made after banking hours on November 30 did not appear on the November 30 bank statement.

c. An automatic debit of $323 on November 30 from ClearComm for telephone service appeared on the bank statement but had not been recorded in the company's accounting records.

d. An electronic funds transfer for $12,800 from Cantori Cucine, a customer located in Italy, was received by the bank on November 30.

e. Check 4122 was correctly written and recorded for $1,200. The bank mistakenly paid the check for $1,000.

f. The accounting records indicate that Check 4125 was issued for $980 to make a purchase of equipment. However, examination of the check online showed that the actual amount of the check was for $890.

INSTRUCTIONS

1. Prepare a bank reconciliation for the firm as of November 30.

2. Record general journal entries for the items on the bank reconciliation that must be journalized. Date the entries November 30, 2016. Use 44 as the page number.

Analyze: What effect did the journal entries recorded as a result of the bank reconciliation have on total assets?

Critical Thinking Problem 9.1

Special Journals

During September 2016, Interior Designs Specialty Shop, a retail store, had the transactions listed on pages 320–321. The general ledger accounts used to record these transactions are provided on page 320.

INSTRUCTIONS

1. Open the general ledger accounts and enter the balances as of September 1, 2016.

2. Record the transactions in a sales journal, a cash receipts journal, a purchases journal, a cash payments journal, and a general journal. Use page 12 as the page number for each of the special journals and page 32 as the page number for the general journal.

3. Post the entries from the general journal to the proper general ledger accounts.

4. Post the entries from the Other Accounts Credit section of the cash receipts journal to the proper general ledger accounts.

5. Post the entries from the Other Accounts Debit section of the cash payments journal to the proper general ledger accounts.

6. Total, prove, and rule the special journals as of September 30.

7. Post the column totals from the special journals to the proper general ledger accounts.

8. Set up an accounts receivable ledger for Interior Designs Specialty Shop. Open an account for each of the customers listed below, and enter the balances as of September 1. All of these customers have terms of n/30.

Credit Customers	
Name	**Balance 9/01/16**
Rachel Carter	
Mesia Davis	$1,260.00
Robert Kent	1,730.00
Pam Lawrence	
David Prater	1,050.00
Henry Tolliver	
Jason Williams	2,100.00

9. Post the individual entries from the sales journal, cash receipts journal, and the general journal to the accounts receivable subsidiary ledger.

10. Prepare a schedule of accounts receivable for September 30, 2016.

11. Check the total of the schedule of accounts receivable against the balance of the *Accounts Receivable* account in the general ledger. The two amounts should be the same.

Creditors		
Name	**Balance 9/01/16**	**Terms**
Booker, Inc.		n/45
McKnight Corporation	$5,500	1/10, n/30
Nelson Craft Products		2/10, n/30
Rocker Company		n/30
Reed Millings Company		2/10, n/30
Sadler Floor Coverings	1,940	n/30
Wells Products	2,120	n/30

12. Set up an accounts payable subsidiary ledger for Interior Designs Specialty Shop. Open an account for each of the creditors listed above, and enter the balances as of September 1, 2016.

13. Post the individual entries from the purchases journal, the cash payments journal, and the general journal to the accounts payable subsidiary ledger.

14. Prepare a schedule of accounts payable for September 1, 2016.

15. Check the total of the schedule of accounts payable against the balance of the *Accounts Payable* account in the general ledger. The two amounts should be the same.

GENERAL LEDGER ACCOUNTS

101	Cash	$18,945 Dr.	451	Sales Returns and Allowances
109	Notes Receivable		501	Purchases
111	Accounts Receivable	6,140 Dr.	502	Freight In
121	Supplies	710 Dr.	503	Purchases Returns and Allowances
131	Inventory	29,365 Dr.	504	Purchases Discounts
201	Notes Payable		611	Cash Short or Over
205	Accounts Payable	9,560 Cr.	614	Rent Expense
231	Sales Tax Payable		617	Salaries Expense
301	Sergio Cortez, Capital	45,600 Cr.	619	Utilities Expense
401	Sales			

DATE	TRANSACTIONS
Sept. 1	Received a check for $1,050 from David Prater to pay his account.
1	Issued Check 1401 for $1,940 to Sadler Floor Coverings, a creditor, in payment of Invoice 6325 dated August 3.
2	Issued Check 1402 for $2,500 to pay the monthly rent.
3	Sold a table on credit for $650 plus sales tax of $52.00 to Pam Lawrence, Sales Slip 1850.
5	Sergio Cortez, the owner, invested an additional $15,000 cash in the business in order to expand operations.
6	Had cash sales of $3,900 plus sales tax of $312 during the period September 1–6; there was a cash shortage of $20.

(continued)

DATE	SPECIAL JOURNALS (cont.) TRANSACTIONS
6	Purchased carpeting for $4,450 from Reed Millings Company, Invoice 827, dated September 3; terms of 2/10, n/30.
6	Issued Check 1403 for $158 to Tri-City Trucking Company to pay the freight charge on goods received from Reed Millings Company.
8	Purchased store supplies for $370 from Rocker Company, Invoice 4204, dated September 6, net amount due in 30 days.
8	Sold chairs on credit for $950 plus sales tax of $76.00 to Henry Tolliver, Sales Slip 1851.
11	Accepted a two-month promissory note for $2,100 from Jason Williams to settle his overdue account; the note has an interest rate of 10 percent.
11	Issued Check 1404 for $4,361 to Reed Millings Company, a creditor, in payment of Invoice 827 dated September 3 ($4,450) less a cash discount ($89).
13	Had cash sales of $3,850 plus sales tax of $308 during the period September 8–13.
14	Purchased carpeting for $3,700 plus a freight charge of $84 from Wells Products, Invoice 9453, dated September 11, net due and payable in 30 days.
15	Collected $1,260 on account from Mesia Davis.
17	Gave a two-month promissory note for $5,500 to McKnight Corporation, a creditor, to settle an overdue balance; the note bears interest at 12 percent.
19	Sold a lamp on credit to Rachel Carter for $250 plus sales tax of $20, Sales Slip 1852.
20	Had cash sales of $4,100 plus sales tax of $328 during the period September 15–20; there was a cash shortage of $9.00.
21	Purchased area rugs for $2,800 from Nelson Craft Products, Invoice 677, dated September 18; the terms are 2/10, n/30.
22	Issued Check 1405 for $306 to pay the monthly utility bill.
23	Granted an allowance to Rachel Carter for scratches on the lamp that she bought on Sales Slip 1852 of September 19; issued Credit Memorandum 151 for $54, which includes a price reduction of $50 and sales tax of $4.
24	Received Credit Memorandum 110 for $300 from Nelson Craft Products for a damaged rug that was returned; the original purchase was made on Invoice 677 dated September 18.
24	Robert Kent sent a check for $1,730 to pay the balance he owes.
25	Issued Check 1406 for $3,600 to make a cash purchase of merchandise.
26	Issued Check 1407 for $2,450 to Nelson Craft Products, a creditor, in payment of Invoice 677 of September 18 ($2,800), less a return ($300) and a cash discount ($50).
27	Purchased hooked rugs for $4,200 plus a freight charge of $128 from Booker, Inc., Invoice 1368, dated September 23, net payable in 45 days.
27	Had cash sales of $4,800 plus sales tax of $384 during the period September 22–27.
28	Issued Check 1408 for $2,120 to Wells Products, a creditor, in payment of Invoice 8984 dated August 30.
29	Sold a cabinet on credit to Mesia Davis for $1,200 plus sales tax of $96, Sales Slip 1853.
30	Had cash sales of $1,500 plus sales tax of $120 for September 29–30; there was a cash overage of $10.
30	Issued Check 1409 for $6,800 to pay the monthly salaries of the employees.

Analyze: What were the total cash payments for September?

Critical Thinking Problem 9.2

Cash Controls

Mike Lucci is the owner of Lucci Contractors, a successful small construction company. He spends most of his time out of the office supervising work at various construction sites, leaving the operation of the office to the company's cashier/bookkeeper, Gloria Harris. Gloria makes bank deposits, pays the company's bills, maintains the accounting records, and prepares monthly bank reconciliations.

Recently a friend told Mike that while he was at a party he overheard Gloria bragging that she paid for her new clothes with money from the company's cash receipts. She said her boss would never know because he never checks the cash records.

Mike admits that he does not check on Gloria's work. He now wants to know if Gloria is stealing from him. He asks you to examine the company's cash records to determine whether Gloria has stolen cash from the business and, if so, how much.

Your examination of the company's cash records reveals the following information:

1. Gloria prepared the following August 31, 2016, bank reconciliation.

Balance in books, August 31, 2016			$18,786
Additions:			
Outstanding checks			
Check 1780		$ 792	
Check 1784		1,819	
Check 1806		384	2,695
			$21,481
Deductions:			
Deposit in transit, August 28, 2016		$4,882	
Bank service charge		10	4,892
Balance on bank statement, August 31, 2016			$16,589

2. An examination of the general ledger shows the *Cash* account with a balance of $18,786 on August 31, 2016.

3. The August 31 bank statement shows a balance of $16,589.

4. The August 28 deposit of $4,882 does not appear on the August 31 bank statement.

5. A comparison of canceled checks returned with the August 31 bank statement with the cash payments journal reveals the following checks as outstanding:

Check 1590	$ 263
Check 1680	1,218
Check 1724	486
Check 1780	792
Check 1784	1,819
Check 1806	384

Prepare a bank statement using the format presented in this chapter for the month of August. Assume there were no bank or bookkeeping errors in August. Did Gloria take cash from the company? If so, how much and how did she try to conceal the theft? How can Mike improve his company's internal controls over cash?

BUSINESS CONNECTIONS

Cash Management

1. The new accountant for Asheville Hardware Center, a large retail store, found the following weaknesses in the firm's cash-handling procedures. How would you explain to management why each of these procedures should be changed?

   a. No cash register proof is prepared at the end of each day. The amount of money in the register is considered the amount of cash sales for the day.

   b. Small payments are sometimes made from the currency and coins in the cash register. (The store has no petty cash fund.)

   c. During busy periods for the firm, cash receipts are sometimes kept on the premises for several days before a bank deposit is made.

   d. When funds are removed from the cash register at the end of each day, they are placed in an unlocked office cabinet until they are deposited.

   e. The person who makes the bank deposits also records them in the checkbook, journalizes cash receipts, and reconciles the bank statement.

2. Why should management be concerned about having accurate information about the firm's cash position available at all times?

3. Many banks now offer a variety of computer services to clients. Why is it not advisable for a firm to pay its bank to complete the reconciliation procedure at the end of each month?

4. Assume that you are the newly hired controller at Norton Company and that you have observed the following banking procedures in use at the firm. Would you change any of these procedures? Why or why not?

   a. A blank endorsement is made on all checks to be deposited.

   b. The checkbook is kept on the top of a desk so that it will be handy.

   c. The same person prepares bank deposits, issues checks, and reconciles the bank statement.

   d. The reconciliation process usually takes place two or three weeks after the bank statement is received.

   e. The bank statement and the canceled checks are thrown away after the reconciliation process is completed.

   f. As a shortcut in the reconciliation process, there is no attempt to compare the endorsements on the back of the canceled checks with the names of the payees shown on the face of these checks.

5. Why should management be concerned about achieving effective internal control over cash receipts and cash payments?

6. How does management benefit when cash transactions are recorded quickly and efficiently?

7. Why do some companies require that all employees who handle cash be bonded?

8. Why is it a good practice for a business to make all payments by check except for minor payments from a petty cash fund?

Borrowing from Petty Cash

Daniel Brown is in charge of the $250 petty cash fund for Metro Auto Repair Service. When an employee needs a special part that is not in inventory, Daniel takes money from petty cash to buy the part. One day Daniel was short of cash and needed some lunch money. He decides to borrow $10 that he will pay back on payday in three days. Daniel continues this practice for three days for a total of $30. He does not have enough to pay the petty cash back. When he reconciles the petty cash, he records this $30 as Cash short/over expense. This is the first time he has done it. Is this an ethical action? What should Daniel do to fix this problem if there is one?

Balance Sheet

The following excerpt was taken from The Home Depot, Inc. *2012 Annual Report (for the fiscal year ended February 3, 2013).*

The Home Depot, Inc.		
Consolidated Balance Sheets		
	As of	
amounts in millions	February 3, 2013	January 29, 2012
ASSETS		
Current Assets:		
Cash and cash equivalents*	$ 2,494	$ 1,987
Total assets	$41,084	$40,518
* Cash and Cash Equivalents: Short-term investments that have		
maturities of three months or less when purchased are considered		
to be cash equivalents.		

Analyze:

1. What percentage of total assets is made up of cash and cash equivalents at February 3, 2013?

2. Cash receipt and cash payment transactions affect the total value of a company's assets. By what amount did the category "Cash and cash equivalents" change from January 29, 2012 to February 3, 2013?

3. If accountants at The Home Depot, Inc. failed to record cash receipts of $125,000 on February 3, 2013, what impact would this error have on the balance sheet category "Cash and cash equivalents"?

Internal Controls of Cash

You and four friends have decided to create a new service company called Unpacking for You. Your company unpacks for families once they have moved into a new house. Your business is primarily a cash business. Each family will pay you $100 for each room that is unpacked on the same day you finish the service. How will your business make sure that the payment from the customer is valid? How will you ensure that you will receive the cash when the customer pays the employee in cash?

Bank Charges

Many times a negative cash flow is a potential problem in a business. Go to the website for the local banks in your community. Check the requirements for a line of credit or mortgage in case your company needs cash quickly to buy a product you know you will sell for a large profit. Some bank websites could be: www.bankofamerica.com   www.wellsfargo.com   www.chasebank.com

Answers to **Self Reviews**

Answers to Section 1 Self Review

1. Amounts from the Accounts Receivable Credit column are posted as credits to the individual customers' accounts in the accounts receivable subsidiary ledger daily. The total of the Accounts Receivable Credit column is posted as a credit to the **Accounts Receivable** control account in the general ledger at the end of the accounting period.

2. A written promise to pay a specified amount of money on a specified date. To grant credit in certain sales transactions or to replace open-account credit when a customer has an overdue balance.

3. A cash shortage occurs when cash in the register is less than the audit tape; an overage occurs when cash is more than the audit tape. Debit shortages and credit overages in the *Cash Short or Over* account.

4. **d.** all of the above

5. **b.** cash receipts journal

6. The frequency of cash discrepancies indicates that a problem may exist in the handling of the cash. However, depending on the size of the business and the number of registers, 15 entries may not be unusual.

Answers to Section 2 Self Review

1. Amounts in the Other Accounts Debit section are posted individually to the general ledger accounts daily. The total of the Other Accounts Debit column is not posted because the individual amounts were previously posted to the general ledger.

2. Record the name of the owner's drawing account and the amount in the Other Accounts Debit section of the cash payments journal, and record the amount in the Cash Credit column.

3. To make small expenditures that require currency and coins.

4. **b.** February 4

5. **c.** cash payments journal

6. You should explain to your employer that she must keep all receipts regardless of the amount. Ask your employer to complete a voucher for that amount, then record the entry in the proper account.

Answers to Section 3 Self Review

1. A check that is dated in the future. It should not be deposited before its date because the drawer of the check may not have sufficient funds in the bank to cover the check at the current time.

2. Endorsement is the legal process by which the payee transfers ownership of the check to the bank.

3. Items in the second section of the bank reconciliation statement require entries in the firm's financial records to correct the *Cash* account balance and make it equal to the checkbook balance. These may include bank fees, debit memorandums, NSF checks, and interest income.

4. **a.** Deposits in transit

5. **b.** canceled checks

6. Disagree. Good internal control requires separation of duties.

Answers to Comprehensive Self Review

1. A full endorsement contains the name of the payee plus the name of the firm or bank to whom the check is payable.

2. A record of when a payment is made from petty cash, the amount and purpose of the expenditure, and the account to be charged.

3. Petty cash can be replenished at any time if the fund runs low, but it should be replenished at the end of each month so that all expenses for the month are recorded.

4. They eliminate repetition in postings; the initial recording of transactions is faster.

5. Checks, money orders, and funds on deposit in a bank as well as currency and coins.

Payroll Computations, Records, and Payment

Chapter 10

H&R BLOCK®

www.hrblock.com

In the 1940s Henry, Leon, and Richard Bloch borrowed $5,000 from a relative and founded United Business Company, an accounting services firm. By the mid-1950s they had 12 employees and were keeping books for various small local businesses in the Kansas City area. Things would change quickly, however. In 1954, based on the recommendation from a client, the Blochs ran an ad for their tax preparation services, and the small office was flooded with calls. It seems just as the IRS was phasing out its free tax preparation services and turning taxpayers away, the Bloch brothers were advertising their services.

United Business Company changed its name to H&R Block and shifted its focus from general accounting services to tax preparation. Today, H&R Block employs quite a few more employees than they did in 1950 and with those added employees, the company's payroll responsibilities have also grown. Not only does it file tax returns for its clients, it also, as an employer, must deduct appropriate taxes from its employees' paychecks.

H&R Block is currently the largest consumer tax services company in the United States and has filed over 500 million tax returns since 1955. It earned $4.1 billion in revenues in 2012 with in-person and digital tax solutions.

thinking critically

What kinds of taxes and other deductions come out of an H&R Block's employee paycheck? What deductions come out of yours?

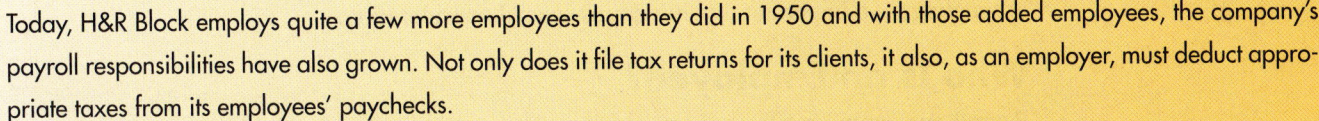

LEARNING OBJECTIVES

10-1. Explain the major federal laws relating to employee earnings and withholding.

10-2. Compute gross earnings of employees.

10-3. Determine employee deductions for social security tax.

10-4. Determine employee deductions for Medicare tax.

10-5. Determine employee deductions for income tax.

10-6. Enter gross earnings, deductions, and net pay in the payroll register.

10-7. Journalize payroll transactions in the general journal.

10-8. Maintain an earnings record for each employee.

10-9. Define the accounting terms new to this chapter.

NEW TERMS

commission basis
compensation record
employee
Employee's Withholding Allowance Certificate (Form W-4)
exempt employees
federal unemployment taxes (FUTA)
hourly rate basis
independent contractor
individual earnings record
Medicare tax
payroll register
piece-rate basis
salary basis
Social Security Act
social security (OASDI) tax
state unemployment taxes (SUTA)
tax-exempt wages
time and a half
wage-bracket table method
workers' compensation insurance

SECTION OBJECTIVE	TERMS TO LEARN
>> 10-1. **Explain the major federal laws relating to employee earnings and withholding.** **WHY IT'S IMPORTANT** Tax and labor laws protect the rights of both the employee and the employer. Income tax withholding laws ensure continued funding of certain federal and state programs.	**employee** **federal unemployment taxes (FUTA)** **independent contractor** **Medicare tax** **Social Security Act** **social security (OASDI) tax** **state unemployment taxes (SUTA)** **time and a half** **workers' compensation insurance**

Payroll Laws and Taxes

A large component of the activity of any business is concerned with payroll work. Payroll accounting is so important that it requires special consideration.

Who Is an Employee?

Payroll accounting relates only to earnings of those individuals classified as employees. An **employee** is hired by and works under the control and direction of the employer. Usually the employer provides the tools or equipment used by the employee, sets the employee's working hours, and determines how the employee completes the job. Examples of employees are the company president, the bookkeeper, the sales clerk, and the warehouse worker.

In contrast to an employee, an **independent contractor** is paid by the company to carry out a specific task or job, but is not under the direct supervision or control of the company. The independent contractor is told what needs to be done, but the means of doing the job are left to the independent contractor. The IRS has a set of guidelines to determine if a vendor meets the definition of independent contractor. Examples of independent contractors are the accountant who performs the independent audit, the outside attorney who renders legal advice, and the consultant who installs a new accounting system.

This text addresses issues related to employees but not to independent contractors. When dealing with independent contractors, businesses do not have to follow federal labor laws regulating minimum rates of pay and maximum hours of employment. The business is not required to withhold or match payroll taxes on amounts paid to independent contractors. The independent contractor is responsible for paying all payroll taxes related to income.

Federal Employee Earnings and Withholding Laws

>> **10-1. OBJECTIVE**

Explain the major federal laws relating to employee earnings and withholding.

Since the 1930s, many federal and state laws have affected the relationship between employers and employees. Some of these laws deal with working conditions, including hours and earnings. Others relate to income tax withholding. Some concern taxes that are levied against the employer to provide specific employee benefits.

THE FAIR LABOR STANDARDS ACT

The *Fair Labor Standards Act* of 1938, often referred to as the Wage and Hour Law, applies only to firms engaged directly or indirectly in interstate commerce. It sets a minimum hourly rate of pay and maximum hours of work per week to be performed at the regular rate of pay.

When this book was printed, the minimum hourly rate of pay was $7.25, and the maximum number of hours at the regular pay rate was 40 hours per week. When an employee works more than 40 hours in a week, the employee earns at least one and one-half times the regular hourly rate of pay for the extra hours. This overtime rate is called **time and a half.** Even if the federal law does not apply to them, many employers pay time and a half for overtime because of union contracts or simply as good business practice.

SOCIAL SECURITY TAX

The *Federal Insurance Contributions Act (FICA)* is commonly referred to as the **Social Security Act.** The act, first passed in the 1930s, has been amended frequently. Social Security's Old-Age, Survivors, and Disability Insurance (OASDI) program provides the following benefits:

- Retirement benefits when a worker reaches the eligible retirement age.
- Benefits for the dependents of the retired worker.
- Benefits for the worker and the worker's dependents when the worker is disabled.

These retirement and disability benefits are paid by the **social security tax,** sometimes called the **FICA** or **OASDI tax.** Both the employer and the employee pay an equal amount of social security tax. The employer is required to withhold social security tax from the employee's pay. Periodically the employer sends the social security tax withheld to the federal government.

The rate of the social security tax and the calendar year earnings base to which it applies are frequently changed by Congress. In recent years, the social security tax rate has remained constant at 6.2 percent. The earnings base to which the tax applies has increased yearly. In 2013, the social security tax rate was 6.2 percent of the first $113,700 of salary or wages paid to each employee. In examples and problems, this text uses a social security tax rate of 6.2 percent of the first $113,700 of salary or wages.

MEDICARE TAX

The Medicare tax is closely related to the social security tax. Prior to 1992, it was a part of the social security tax. The **Medicare tax** is a tax levied equally on employees and employers to provide medical care for the employee and the employee's spouse after each has reached age 65.

In recent years, the Medicare tax rate has remained constant at 1.45 percent. The Medicare tax applies to all salaries and wages paid during the year. The employer is required to withhold the Medicare tax from the employee's pay and periodically send it to the federal government.

Note that the social security tax has an earnings base limit. The Medicare tax does not have an earnings base limit. Therefore, the Medicare tax applies to *all* earnings paid during the year.

FEDERAL INCOME TAX

Employers are required to withhold from employees' earnings an estimated amount of income tax that will be payable by the employee on the earnings. The amount depends on several factors. Later in this chapter you will learn how to determine the amount to withhold from an employee's paycheck.

State and Local Taxes

Most states, and many local governments, require employers to withhold income taxes from employees' earnings to prepay the employees' state and local income taxes. These rules are generally almost identical to those governing federal income tax withholding, but they require separate general ledger accounts in the firm's accounting system.

Employer's Payroll Taxes and Insurance Costs

Remember that employers withhold social security and Medicare taxes from employees' earnings. In addition, employers pay social security and Medicare taxes on their employees'

important!

Wage Base Limit
The social security tax has a wage base limit. There is no wage base limit for the Medicare tax. All salaries and wages are subject to the Medicare tax.

earnings. Employers are also required to pay federal and state taxes for unemployment benefits and to carry workers' compensation insurance.

SOCIAL SECURITY TAX

The employer's share of the social security tax is 6.2 percent up to the earnings base. (In this text, the social security tax is 6.2 percent of the first $113,700 of earnings.) Periodically the employer pays to the federal government the social security tax withheld plus the employer's share of the social security tax.

	Social Security
Employee (withheld)	6.2%
Employer (match)	6.2
Total	12.4%

MEDICARE TAX

The employer's share of Medicare tax is 1.45 percent of earnings. Periodically the employer pays to the federal government the Medicare tax withheld plus the employer's share of the Medicare tax.

The Medicare tax rates the employer remits to the federal government are shown below:

	Medicare
Employee (withheld)	1.45%
Employer (match)	1.45
Total	2.90%

FEDERAL UNEMPLOYMENT TAX

The *Federal Unemployment Tax Act (FUTA)* provides benefits for employees who become unemployed. Taxes levied by the federal government against employers to benefit unemployed workers are called **federal unemployment taxes (FUTA).** Employers pay the entire amount of these taxes. In this text, we assume that the taxable earnings base is $7,000. That is, the tax applies to the first $7,000 of each employee's earnings for the year. In 2013, the FUTA tax rate was 6.0 percent, but can be reduced by the state unemployment tax rate. In examples and problems, this text uses a FUTA tax rate of 6.0%.

STATE UNEMPLOYMENT TAX

The federal and state unemployment programs work together to provide benefits for employees who become unemployed. Employers pay all of the **state unemployment taxes (SUTA).** Usually the earnings base for the federal and state unemployment taxes are the same, the first $7,000 of each employee's earnings for the year. For many states the SUTA tax rate is 5.4 percent.

The federal unemployment tax rate (6.0 percent) can be reduced by the rate charged by the state (5.4 percent in this example), so the FUTA rate can be as low as 0.6 percent (6.0% − 5.4%).

SUTA tax		5.4%
FUTA tax rate	6.0%	
Less SUTA tax	(5.4)	
Net FUTA tax		0.6
Total federal and state unemployment tax		6.0%

TABLE 10.1

Summary of Payroll Tax Liabilities

Federal Income Tax	Social Security Tax	Medicare Tax	Unemployment Tax
Employee	Employee Employer	Employee Employer	Employer
The employee pays these taxes by the withholding of the tax from the periodic wage payment.			
The employer pays these taxes through the deposits/filing and reporting on the appropriate forms.			

WORKERS' COMPENSATION INSURANCE

Workers' compensation insurance is not a tax, but insurance that protects employees against losses from job-related injuries or illnesses, or compensates their families if death occurs in the course of the employment. Workers' compensation requirements are defined by each state, not the federal government. Most states mandate workers' compensation insurance.

Employee Records Required by Law

> Many companies outsource payroll duties to professional payroll companies. ADP, Inc., is the world's largest provider of payroll services and employee information systems.

Federal laws require that certain payroll records be maintained. For each employee the employer must keep a record of:

- the employee's name, address, social security number, and date of birth;
- hours worked each day and week, and wages paid at the regular and overtime rates (certain exceptions exist for employees who earn salaries);
- cumulative wages paid throughout the year;
- amount of income tax, social security tax, and Medicare tax withheld for each pay period;
- proof that the employee is a United States citizen or has a valid work permit.

Section 1   Self Review

QUESTIONS

1. What is "time and a half"?
2. How are unemployment insurance benefits financed?
3. How are social security benefits financed?

EXERCISES

4. The purpose of FUTA is to provide benefits for:
   a. employees who become unemployed.
   b. employees who become injured while on the job.
   c. retired workers.
   d. disabled employees.
5. Who pays the social security tax?
   a. Employee only.
   b. Employer only.
   c. Both employee and employer.
   d. None of the above.

ANALYSIS

6. Henri Harvey was hired by Harvey Architects to create three oil paintings for the president's office. Is Kennedy an employee? Why or why not?

(Answers to Section 1 Self Review are on page 361.)

SECTION OBJECTIVES	TERMS TO LEARN
>> 10-2. **Compute gross earnings of employees.**	commission basis
WHY IT'S IMPORTANT	Employee's Withholding
Payroll is a large part of business activity.	Allowance Certificate
	(Form W-4)
>> 10-3. **Determine employee deductions for social security tax.**	exempt employees
WHY IT'S IMPORTANT	hourly rate basis
Employers are legally responsible for collecting and remitting this tax.	payroll register
	piece-rate basis
>> 10-4. **Determine employee deductions for Medicare tax.**	salary basis
WHY IT'S IMPORTANT	tax-exempt wages
Employers have legal responsibility.	wage-bracket table method
>> 10-5. **Determine employee deductions for income tax.**	
WHY IT'S IMPORTANT	
Employers are legally responsible.	
>> 10-6. **Enter gross earnings, deductions, and net pay in the payroll register.**	
WHY IT'S IMPORTANT	
The payroll register provides information needed to prepare paychecks.	

Calculating Earnings and Taxes

Tomlin Furniture Company is a sole proprietorship owned and managed by Sarah Tomlin. Tomlin Furniture Company imports furniture and novelty items to sell over the Internet. It has five employees. The three shipping clerks and the shipping supervisor are paid on an hourly basis. The office clerk is paid a weekly salary. Payday is each Monday; it covers the wages and salaries earned the previous week. The employees are subject to withholding of social security, Medicare, and federal income taxes. The business pays social security and Medicare taxes, and federal and state unemployment insurance taxes. The business is required by state law to carry workers' compensation insurance. Since it is involved in interstate commerce, Tomlin Furniture Company is subject to the Fair Labor Standards Act.

From time to time, Sarah Tomlin, the owner, makes cash withdrawals to cover her personal expenses. The withdrawals of the owner of a sole proprietorship are not treated as salaries or wages.

Computing Total Earnings of Employees

The first step in preparing payroll is to compute the gross wages or salary for each employee. There are several ways to compute earnings:

Hourly rate basis workers earn a stated rate per hour. Gross pay depends on the number of hours worked.

Salary basis workers earn an agreed-upon amount for each week, month, or other period.

Commission basis workers, usually salespeople, earn a percentage of net sales.

Piece-rate basis manufacturing workers are paid based on the number of units produced.

> Walmart has approximately 2 million employees in its worldwide operations, which include Walmart discount stores, Sam's Clubs, the distribution centers, and the home office. Fifty-one percent of its stores are in the United States. It is the number 1 retailer in Canada and Mexico. It also has operations in Asia, the United Kingdom, Central America, and South America.

Determining Pay for Hourly Employees

>> 10-2. OBJECTIVE
Compute gross earnings of employees.

Two pieces of data are needed to compute gross pay for hourly rate basis employees: the number of hours worked during the payroll period, and the rate of pay.

HOURS WORKED

At Tomlin Furniture Company, the shipping supervisor keeps a weekly time sheet. Each day she enters the hours worked by each shipping clerk. At the end of the week, the office clerk uses the time sheet to compute the total hours worked and to prepare the payroll.

Many businesses use time clocks for hourly employees. Each employee has a time card and inserts it in the time clock to record the times of arrival and departure. The payroll clerk collects the cards at the end of the week, determines the hours worked by each employee, and multiplies the number of hours by the pay rate to compute the *gross pay*. Some time cards are machine readable. A computer determines the hours worked and makes the earnings calculations.

recall

Owner Withdrawals

Withdrawals by the owner of a sole proprietorship are debited to a temporary owner's equity account (in this case, **Sarah Tomlin, Drawing**). Withdrawals are not treated as salary or wages, but serve to reduce the owner's equity or capital.

GROSS PAY

Alicia Martinez, Jorge Rodriguez, and George Dunlap are shipping clerks at Tomlin Furniture Company. They are hourly employees. Their gross pay for the week ended January 6 is determined as follows:

- Martinez worked 40 hours. She earns $10 an hour. Her gross pay is $400 (40 hours × $10).

- Rodriguez worked 40 hours. He earns $9.50 an hour. His gross pay is $380 (40 × $9.50).

- Dunlap earns $9 per hour. He worked 45 hours. He is paid 40 hours at regular pay and 5 hours at time and a half. There are two ways to compute Dunlap's gross pay:

    1. The Wage and Hour Law method identifies the *overtime premium*, the amount the firm could have saved if all the hours were paid at the regular rate. The overtime premium rate is $4.50, one-half of the regular rate ($9 × 1/2 = $4.50).

Total hours × regular rate:	
45 hours × $9	$405.00
Overtime premium:	
5 hours × $4.50	22.50
Gross pay	$427.50

2. The second method identifies how much the employee earned by working overtime.

Regular earnings:	
40 hours × $9	$360.00
Overtime earnings:	
5 hours × $13.50 ($9 × 1 1/2)	67.50
Gross pay	$427.50

Cecilia Wu is the shipping supervisor at Tomlin Furniture Company. She is an hourly employee. She earns $14 an hour, and she worked 40 hours. Her gross pay is $560 (40 × $14).

WITHHOLDINGS FOR HOURLY EMPLOYEES REQUIRED BY LAW

Recall that three deductions from employees' gross pay are required by federal law. They are social security tax, Medicare tax, and federal income tax withholding.

>> **10-3. OBJECTIVE**
Determine employee deductions for social security tax.

Social Security Tax   The social security tax is levied on both the employer and the employee. This text calculates social security tax using a 6.2 percent tax rate on the first $113,700 of wages paid during the calendar year. **Tax-exempt wages** are earnings in excess of the base amount set by the Social Security Act ($113,700). Tax-exempt wages are not subject to social security withholding.

If an employee works for more than one employer during the year, the social security tax is deducted and matched by each employer. When the employee files a federal income tax return, any excess social security tax withheld from the employee's earnings is refunded by the government or applied to payment of the employee's federal income taxes.

To determine the amount of social security tax to withhold from an employee's pay, multiply the taxable wages by the social security tax rate. Round the result to the nearest cent.

The following shows the social security tax deductions for Tomlin Furniture Company's hourly employees.

Employee	Gross Pay	Tax Rate	Tax
Alicia Martinez	$400.00	6.2%	$ 24.80
Jorge Rodriguez	380.00	6.2	23.56
George Dunlap	427.50	6.2	26.51
Cecilia Wu	560.00	6.2	34.72
Total social security tax			$109.59

>> **10-4. OBJECTIVE**
Determine employee deductions for Medicare tax.

Medicare Tax   The Medicare tax is levied on both the employee and the employer. To compute the Medicare tax to withhold from the employee's paycheck, multiply the wages by the Medicare tax rate, 1.45 percent. The following shows the Medicare tax deduction for hourly employees.

Employee	Gross Pay	Tax Rate	Tax
Alicia Martinez	$400.00	1.45%	$ 5.80
Jorge Rodriguez	380.00	1.45	5.51
George Dunlap	427.50	1.45	6.20
Cecilia Wu	560.00	1.45	8.12
Total Medicare tax			$25.63

Federal Income Tax A substantial portion of the federal government's revenue comes from the income tax on individuals. Employers are required to withhold federal income tax from employees' pay. Periodically the employer pays the federal income tax withheld to the federal government. After the end of the year, the employee files an income tax return. If the amount of federal income tax withheld does not cover the amount of income tax due, the employee pays the balance. If too much federal income tax has been withheld, the employee receives a refund.

>> 10-5. OBJECTIVE
Determine employee deductions for income tax.

> The federal income tax is a pay-as-you-go tax. There are two ways to pay. If you are an employee, your employer will withhold income tax from your pay based on your instructions in Form W-4. If you do not pay tax through withholdings, or do not pay enough taxes through withholdings because of income from other sources, you might have to pay estimated taxes. Individuals who are in business for themselves generally have to pay taxes through the estimated tax system. The Electronic Federal Tax Payment System (EFTPS) is a free service from the IRS through which taxpayers can use the Internet or telephone to pay their federal taxes, especially 1040 estimated taxes.

Withholding Allowances The amount of federal income tax to withhold from an employee's earnings depends on the:

- earnings during the pay period,
- length of the pay period,
- marital status,
- number of withholding allowances.

Determining the number of withholding allowances for some taxpayers is complex. In the simplest circumstances, a taxpayer claims a withholding allowance for:

- the taxpayer,
- a spouse who does not also claim an allowance,
- each dependent for whom the taxpayer provides more than half the support during the year.

As the number of withholding allowances increases, the amount of federal income tax withheld decreases. The goal is to claim the number of withholding allowances so that the federal income tax withheld is about the same as the employee's tax liability.

To claim withholding allowances, employees complete **Employee's Withholding Allowance Certificate, Form W-4.** The employee gives the completed Form W-4 to the employer. If the number of exemption allowances decreases, the employee must file a new Form W-4 within 10 days. If the number of exemption allowances increases, the employee may, but is not required to, file another Form W-4. If an employee does not file a Form W-4, the employer withholds federal income tax based on zero withholding allowances.

Figure 10.1 shows Form W-4 for Alicia Martinez. Notice that on Line 5, Martinez claims one withholding allowance.

Computing Federal Income Tax Withholding Although there are several ways to compute the federal income tax to withhold from an employee's earnings, the **wage-bracket table method** is almost universally used. The wage-bracket tables are in *Publication 15, Circular E*. This publication contains withholding tables for weekly, biweekly, semimonthly, monthly, and daily or miscellaneous payroll periods for single and married persons. Figure 10.2 on pages 337–338 shows partial tables for single and married persons who are paid weekly.

Use the following steps to determine the amount to withhold:

1. Choose the table for the pay period and the employee's marital status.
2. Find the row in the table that matches the wages earned. Find the column that matches the number of withholding allowances claimed on Form W-4. The income tax to withhold is the intersection of the row and the column.

important!

Pay-As-You-Go
Employee income tax withholding is designed to place employees on a pay-as-you-go basis in paying their federal income tax.

important!

Get It in Writing
Employers need a signed Form W-4 in order to change the employee's federal income tax withholding.

Employee	Gross Pay	Marital Status	Withholding Allowances	Income Tax Withholding
Alicia Martinez	$400.00	Married	1	$ 19.00
Jorge Rodriguez	380.00	Single	1	34.00
George Dunlap	427.50	Single	3	23.00
Cecilia Wu	560.00	Married	2	30.00
				$106.00

As an example, let's determine the amount to withhold from Cecilia Wu's gross pay. Wu is married, claims two withholding allowances, and earned $560 for the week:

1. Go to the table for married persons paid weekly, Figure 10.2B.
2. Find the line covering wages between $560 and $570. Find the column for two withholding allowances. The tax to withhold is $30; this is where the row and the column intersect.

Using the wage-bracket tables, can you find the federal income tax amounts to withhold for Martinez, Rodriguez, and Dunlap?

Other Deductions Required by Law Most states and some local governments require employers to withhold state and local income taxes from earnings. In some states, employers are also required to withhold disability or other taxes. The procedures are similar to those for federal income tax withholding. Apply the tax rate to the earnings, or use withholding tables.

FIGURE 10.1 Form W-4 (Partial)

Cut here and give Form W-4 to your employer. Keep the top part for your records.

Form **W-4**

Department of the Treasury
Internal Revenue Service

Employee's Withholding Allowance Certificate

► Whether you are entitled to claim a certain number of allowances or exemption from withholding is subject to review by the IRS. Your employer may be required to send a copy of this form to the IRS.

OMB No. 1545-0010

2016

1 Type or print your first name and middle initial	Last name	2 Your social security number
Alicia	**Martinez**	**123 45 6789**

Home address (number and street or rural route)
1712 Windmill Hill Lane

City or town, state, and ZIP code
Dallas, TX 75232-6002

3 ☐ Single ☑ Married ☐ Married, but withhold at higher Single rate.
Note. If married, but legally separated, or spouse is a nonresident alien, check the "Single" box.

4 If your last name differs from that shown on your social security card, check here. You must call 1-800-772-1213 for a new card. ► ☐

5 Total number of allowances you are claiming (from line **H** above **or** from the applicable worksheet on page 2) — **5** | **1**

6 Additional amount, if any, you want withheld from each paycheck — **6** $

7 I claim exemption from withholding for 2016, and I certify that I meet **both** of the following conditions for exemption.
• Last year I had a right to a refund of **all** federal income tax withheld because I had **no** tax liability **and**
• This year I expect a refund of **all** federal income tax withheld because I expect to have **no** tax liability.
If you meet both conditions, write "Exempt" here ► **7**

Under penalties of perjury, I declare that I have examined this certificate and to the best of my knowledge and belief, it is true, correct, and complete.

Employee's signature
(Form is not valid unless you sign it.) ► *Alicia Martinez*

Date ► *November 5, 2016*

8 Employer's name and address (Employer: Complete lines 8 and 10 only if sending to the IRS.)
Tomlin Furniture Co. 5910 Lake June Road, Dallas, TX 75232-6017

9 Office code (optional)

10 Employer identification number (EIN)
75 1234567

For Privacy Act and Paperwork Reduction Act Notice, see page 2.   Cat. No. 220Q   Form **W-4**

SINGLE Persons—WEEKLY Payroll Period   (For Wages Paid Through December 2016)

If the wages are —		And the number of withholding allowances claimed is —										
At least	But less than	0	1	2	3	4	5	6	7	8	9	10
		The amount of income tax to be withheld is —										
$0	$55	$0	$0	$0	$0	$0	$0	$0	$0	$0	$0	$0
55	60	1	0	0	0	0	0	0	0	0	0	0
60	65	1	0	0	0	0	0	0	0	0	0	0
65	70	2	0	0	0	0	0	0	0	0	0	0
70	75	2	0	0	0	0	0	0	0	0	0	0
75	80	3	0	0	0	0	0	0	0	0	0	0
80	85	3	0	0	0	0	0	0	0	0	0	0
85	90	4	0	0	0	0	0	0	0	0	0	0
90	95	4	0	0	0	0	0	0	0	0	0	0
95	100	5	0	0	0	0	0	0	0	0	0	0
100	105	5	0	0	0	0	0	0	0	0	0	0
105	110	6	0	0	0	0	0	0	0	0	0	0
110	115	6	0	0	0	0	0	0	0	0	0	0
115	120	7	1	0	0	0	0	0	0	0	0	0
120	125	7	1	0	0	0	0	0	0	0	0	0
125	130	8	2	0	0	0	0	0	0	0	0	0
130	135	8	2	0	0	0	0	0	0	0	0	0
135	140	9	3	0	0	0	0	0	0	0	0	0
140	145	9	3	0	0	0	0	0	0	0	0	0
145	150	10	4	0	0	0	0	0	0	0	0	0
150	155	10	4	0	0	0	0	0	0	0	0	0
155	160	11	5	0	0	0	0	0	0	0	0	0
160	165	11	5	0	0	0	0	0	0	0	0	0
165	170	12	6	0	0	0	0	0	0	0	0	0
170	175	12	6	0	0	0	0	0	0	0	0	0
175	180	13	7	1	0	0	0	0	0	0	0	0
180	185	13	7	1	0	0	0	0	0	0	0	0
185	190	14	8	2	0	0	0	0	0	0	0	0
190	195	14	8	2	0	0	0	0	0	0	0	0
195	200	15	9	3	0	0	0	0	0	0	0	0
200	210	16	9	3	0	0	0	0	0	0	0	0
210	220	18	10	4	0	0	0	0	0	0	0	0
220	230	19	11	5	0	0	0	0	0	0	0	0
230	240	21	12	6	1	0	0	0	0	0	0	0
240	250	22	13	7	2	0	0	0	0	0	0	0
250	260	24	15	8	3	0	0	0	0	0	0	0
260	270	25	16	9	4	0	0	0	0	0	0	0
270	280	27	18	10	5	0	0	0	0	0	0	0
280	290	28	19	11	6	0	0	0	0	0	0	0
290	300	30	21	12	7	1	0	0	0	0	0	0
300	310	31	22	13	8	2	0	0	0	0	0	0
310	320	33	24	15	9	3	0	0	0	0	0	0
320	330	34	25	16	10	4	0	0	0	0	0	0
330	340	36	27	18	11	5	0	0	0	0	0	0
340	350	37	28	19	12	6	0	0	0	0	0	0
350	360	39	30	21	13	7	1	0	0	0	0	0
360	370	40	31	22	14	8	2	0	0	0	0	0
370	380	42	33	24	15	9	3	0	0	0	0	0
380	390	43	34	25	17	10	4	0	0	0	0	0
390	400	45	36	27	18	11	5	0	0	0	0	0
400	410	46	37	28	20	12	6	0	0	0	0	0
410	420	48	39	30	21	13	7	1	0	0	0	0
420	430	49	40	31	23	14	8	2	0	0	0	0
430	440	51	42	33	24	15	9	3	0	0	0	0
440	450	52	43	34	26	17	10	4	0	0	0	0
450	460	54	45	36	27	18	11	5	0	0	0	0
460	470	55	46	37	29	20	12	6	0	0	0	0
470	480	57	48	39	30	21	13	7	1	0	0	0
480	490	58	49	40	32	23	14	8	2	0	0	0
490	500	60	51	42	33	24	15	9	3	0	0	0
500	510	61	52	43	35	26	17	10	4	0	0	0
510	520	63	54	45	36	27	18	11	5	0	0	0
520	530	64	55	46	38	29	20	12	6	0	0	0
530	540	66	57	48	39	30	21	13	7	1	0	0
540	550	67	58	49	41	32	23	14	8	2	0	0
550	560	69	60	51	42	33	24	15	9	3	0	0
560	570	70	61	52	44	35	26	17	10	4	0	0
570	580	72	63	54	45	36	27	18	11	5	0	0
580	590	73	64	55	47	38	29	20	12	6	0	0
590	600	75	66	57	48	39	30	21	13	7	1	0

FIGURE 10.2A

Sample Federal Withholding Tax Tables (Partial) Single Persons— Weekly Payroll Period

This table does not contain actual withholding amounts for the year 2016, and should not be used to determine payroll withholdings for 2016.

FIGURE 10.2B

Sample Federal Withholding Tax Tables (Partial) Married Persons— Weekly Payroll Period

MARRIED Persons—WEEKLY Payroll Period											(For Wages Paid Through December 2016)
If the wages are –		And the number of withholding allowances claimed is –									
At least	But less than	0	1	2	3	4	5	6	7	8	9	10
		The amount of income tax to be withheld is –									
$0	$125	$0	$0	$0	$0	$0	$0	$0	$0	$0	$0	$0
125	130	0	0	0	0	0	0	0	0	0	0	0
130	135	0	0	0	0	0	0	0	0	0	0	0
135	140	0	0	0	0	0	0	0	0	0	0	0
140	145	0	0	0	0	0	0	0	0	0	0	0
145	150	0	0	0	0	0	0	0	0	0	0	0
150	155	0	0	0	0	0	0	0	0	0	0	0
155	160	0	0	0	0	0	0	0	0	0	0	0
160	165	1	0	0	0	0	0	0	0	0	0	0
165	170	1	0	0	0	0	0	0	0	0	0	0
170	175	2	0	0	0	0	0	0	0	0	0	0
175	180	2	0	0	0	0	0	0	0	0	0	0
180	185	3	0	0	0	0	0	0	0	0	0	0
185	190	3	0	0	0	0	0	0	0	0	0	0
190	195	4	0	0	0	0	0	0	0	0	0	0
195	200	4	0	0	0	0	0	0	0	0	0	0
200	210	5	0	0	0	0	0	0	0	0	0	0
210	220	6	0	0	0	0	0	0	0	0	0	0
220	230	7	1	0	0	0	0	0	0	0	0	0
230	240	8	2	0	0	0	0	0	0	0	0	0
240	250	9	3	0	0	0	0	0	0	0	0	0
250	260	10	4	0	0	0	0	0	0	0	0	0
260	270	11	5	0	0	0	0	0	0	0	0	0
270	280	12	6	0	0	0	0	0	0	0	0	0
280	290	13	7	1	0	0	0	0	0	0	0	0
290	300	14	8	2	0	0	0	0	0	0	0	0
300	310	15	9	3	0	0	0	0	0	0	0	0
310	320	16	10	4	0	0	0	0	0	0	0	0
320	330	17	11	5	0	0	0	0	0	0	0	0
330	340	18	12	6	0	0	0	0	0	0	0	0
340	350	19	13	7	1	0	0	0	0	0	0	0
350	360	20	14	8	2	0	0	0	0	0	0	0
360	370	21	15	9	3	0	0	0	0	0	0	0
370	380	22	16	10	4	0	0	0	0	0	0	0
380	390	23	17	11	5	0	0	0	0	0	0	0
390	400	24	18	12	6	0	0	0	0	0	0	0
400	410	25	19	13	7	1	0	0	0	0	0	0
410	420	26	20	14	8	2	0	0	0	0	0	0
420	430	27	21	15	9	3	0	0	0	0	0	0
430	440	28	22	16	10	4	0	0	0	0	0	0
440	450	30	23	17	11	5	0	0	0	0	0	0
450	460	31	24	18	12	6	0	0	0	0	0	0
460	470	33	25	19	13	7	1	0	0	0	0	0
470	480	34	26	20	14	8	2	0	0	0	0	0
480	490	36	27	21	15	9	3	0	0	0	0	0
490	500	37	28	22	16	10	4	0	0	0	0	0
500	510	39	30	23	17	11	5	0	0	0	0	0
510	520	40	31	24	18	12	6	0	0	0	0	0
520	530	42	33	25	19	13	7	1	0	0	0	0
530	540	43	34	26	20	14	8	2	0	0	0	0
540	550	45	36	27	21	15	9	3	0	0	0	0
550	560	46	37	29	22	16	10	4	0	0	0	0
560	570	48	39	30	23	17	11	5	0	0	0	0
570	580	49	40	32	24	18	12	6	0	0	0	0
580	590	51	42	33	25	19	13	7	1	0	0	0
590	600	52	43	35	26	20	14	8	2	0	0	0
600	610	54	45	36	27	21	15	9	3	0	0	0
610	620	55	46	38	29	22	16	10	4	0	0	0
620	630	57	48	39	30	23	17	11	5	0	0	0
630	640	58	49	41	32	24	18	12	6	0	0	0
640	650	60	51	42	33	25	19	13	7	1	0	0
650	660	61	52	44	35	26	20	14	8	2	0	0
660	670	63	54	45	36	27	21	15	9	3	0	0
670	680	64	55	47	38	29	22	16	10	4	0	0
680	690	66	57	48	39	30	23	17	11	5	0	0
690	700	67	58	50	41	32	24	18	12	6	0	0
700	710	69	60	51	42	33	25	19	13	7	1	0
710	720	70	61	53	44	35	26	20	14	8	2	0
720	730	72	63	54	45	36	27	21	15	9	3	0
730	740	73	64	56	47	38	29	22	16	10	4	0

This table does not contain actual withholding amounts for the year 2016, and should not be used to determine payroll withholdings for 2016.

WITHHOLDINGS NOT REQUIRED BY LAW

There are many payroll deductions not required by law but made by agreement between the employee and the employer. Some examples are:

■ group life insurance,

■ group medical insurance,

- company retirement plans,
- bank or credit union savings plans or loan repayments,
- United States saving bonds purchase plans,
- stocks and other investment purchase plans,
- employer loan repayments,
- union dues.

These and other payroll deductions increase the payroll recordkeeping work but do not involve any new principles or procedures. They are handled in the same way as the deductions for social security, Medicare, and federal income taxes. The amounts withheld from the employee's pay are recorded as liabilities on payday.

Tomlin Furniture Company pays all medical insurance premiums for each employee. If the employee chooses to have medical coverage for a spouse or dependent, Tomlin Furniture Company deducts $40 per week for coverage for the spouse and each dependent. Dunlap and Wu each have $40 per week deducted to obtain the medical coverage.

Determining Pay for Salaried Employees

A salaried employee earns a specific sum of money for each payroll period. The office clerk at Tomlin Furniture Company earns a weekly salary.

HOURS WORKED

Salaried workers who do not hold supervisory jobs are covered by the provisions of the Wage and Hour Law that deal with maximum hours and overtime premium pay. Employers keep time records for all nonsupervisory salaried workers to make sure that their hourly earnings meet the legal requirements.

Salaried employees who hold supervisory or managerial positions are called **exempt employees.** They are not subject to the maximum hour and overtime premium pay provisions of the Wage and Hour Law.

GROSS EARNINGS

Cynthia Booker is the office clerk at Tomlin Furniture Company. During the first week of January, she worked 40 hours, her regular schedule. There are no overtime earnings because she did not work more than 40 hours during the week. Her salary of $480 is her gross pay for the week.

WITHHOLDINGS FOR SALARIED EMPLOYEES REQUIRED BY LAW

The procedures for withholding taxes for salaried employees is the same as withholding for hourly rate employees. Apply the tax rate to the earnings, or use withholding tables.

Recording Payroll Information for Employees

A payroll register is prepared for each pay period. The **payroll register** shows all the payroll information for the pay period.

THE PAYROLL REGISTER

>> **10-6. OBJECTIVE**

Enter gross earnings, deductions, and net pay in the payroll register.

Figure 10.3 on pages 340–341 shows the payroll register for Tomlin Furniture Company for the week ended January 6. Note that all employees were paid for eight hours on January 1, a holiday. To learn how to complete the payroll register, refer to Figure 10.3 and follow these steps:

1. *Columns A, B, and E.* Enter the employee's name (Column A), number of withholding allowances and marital status (Column B), and rate of pay (Column E). In a computerized payroll system, this information is entered once and is automatically retrieved each time payroll is prepared.

2. *Column C.* The Cumulative Earnings column (Column C) shows the total earnings for the calendar year before the current pay period. This figure is needed to determine

FIGURE 10.3   Payroll Register

NAME	NO. OF ALLOW.	MARITAL STATUS	CUMULATIVE EARNINGS	NO. OF HRS.	RATE/ SALARY	EARNINGS			CUMULATIVE EARNINGS
						REGULAR	OVERTIME	GROSS AMOUNT	
Martinez, Alicia	1	M		40	10.00	400 00		400 00	400 00
Rodriguez, Jorge	1	S		40	9.50	380 00		380 00	380 00
Dunlap, George	3	S		45	9.00	360 00	67 50	427 50	427 50
Wu, Cecilia	2	M		40	14.00	560 00		560 00	560 00
Booker, Cynthia	1	S		40	480.00	480 00		480 00	480 00
			0 00			2 180 00	67 50	2 247 50	2 247 50
(A)	(B)		(C)	(D)	(E)	(F)	(G)	(H)	(I)

PAYROLL REGISTER   WEEK BEGINNING *January 1, 2016*

whether the employee has exceeded the earnings limit for the social security and FUTA taxes. Since this is the first payroll period of the year, there are no cumulative earnings prior to the current pay period.

3. *Column D.* In Column D, enter the total number of hours worked in the current period. This data comes from the weekly time sheet.

4. *Columns F, G, and H.* Using the hours worked and the pay rate, calculate regular pay (Column F), the overtime earnings (Column G), and gross pay (Column H).

5. *Column I.* Calculate the cumulative earnings after this pay period (Column I) by adding the beginning cumulative earnings (Column C) and the current period's gross pay (Column H).

6. *Columns J, K, and L.* The Taxable Wages columns show the earnings subject to taxes for social security (Column J), Medicare (Column K), and FUTA (Column L). Only the earnings at or under the earnings limit are included in these columns.

7. *Columns M, N, O, and P.* The Deductions columns show the withholding for social security tax (Column M), Medicare tax (Column N), federal income tax (Column O), and medical insurance (Column P).

8. *Column Q.* Subtract the deductions (Columns M, N, O, and P) from the gross earnings (Column H). Enter the results in the Net Amount column (Column Q). This is the amount paid to each employee.

9. *Column R.* Enter the check number in Column R.

10. *Columns S and T.* The payroll register's last two columns classify employee earnings as office salaries (Column S) or shipping wages (Column T).

When the payroll data for all employees has been entered in the payroll register, total the columns. Check the balances of the following columns:

■ Total regular earnings plus total overtime earnings must equal the gross amount (Columns F + G = Column H).

■ The total gross amount less total deductions must equal the total net amount.

Gross amount		$2,247.50
Less deductions:		
Social security tax	$139.35	
Medicare tax	32.59	
Income tax	155.00	
Health insurance	80.00	
Total deductions		406.94
Net amount		$1,840.56

AND ENDING _January 6, 2016_   **PAID** _January 8, 2016_

| TAXABLE WAGES | | | DEDUCTIONS | | | | DISTRIBUTION | | | |
SOCIAL SECURITY	MEDICARE	FUTA	SOCIAL SECURITY	MEDICARE	INCOME TAX	HEALTH INSURANCE	NET AMOUNT	CHECK NO.	OFFICE SALARIES	SHIPPING WAGES
400 00	400 00	400 00	24 80	5 80	19 00		350 40	1601		400 00
380 00	380 00	380 00	23 56	5 51	34 00		316 93	1602		380 00
427 50	427 50	427 50	26 51	6 20	23 00	40 00	331 79	1603		427 50
560 00	560 00	560 00	34 72	8 12	30 00	40 00	447 16	1604		560 00
480 00	480 00	480 00	29 76	6 96	49 00		394 28	1605	480 00	
2 247 50	2 247 50	2 247 50	139 35	32 59	155 00	80 00	1 840 56		480 00	1 767 50
(J)	(K)	(L)	(M)	(N)	(O)	(P)	(Q)	(R)	(S)	(T)

■ The office salaries and the shipping wages must equal gross earnings (Columns S + T = Column H).

     The payroll register supplies all the information to make the journal entry to record the payroll. Journalizing the payroll is discussed in Section 3.

Section 2   Self Review

QUESTIONS

1. What three payroll deductions does federal law require?

2. What factors determine the amount of federal income tax to be withheld from an employee's earnings?

3. List four payroll deductions that are not required by law but can be made by agreement between the employee and the employer.

EXERCISES

4. Which of the following affects the amount of Medicare tax to be withheld from an hourly rate employee's pay?

   a. medical insurance premium

   b. marital status

   c. withholding allowances claimed on Form W-4

   d. hours worked

5. Stacy Anderson worked 48 hours during the week ending November 17. Her regular rate is $9 per hour. Calculate her gross earnings for the week.

   a. $432

   b. $492

   c. $468

   d. $444

ANALYSIS

6. Rosie Peper left a voice mail asking you to withhold an additional $40 of federal income tax from her wages each pay period, starting June 1. When should you begin withholding the extra amount?

(Answers to Section 2 Self Review are on page 361.)

Section **3**

SECTION OBJECTIVES	TERMS TO LEARN

>> **10-7.** Journalize payroll transactions in the general journal.

WHY IT'S IMPORTANT
Payroll cost is an operating expense.

>> **10-8.** Maintain an earnings record for each employee.

WHY IT'S IMPORTANT
Federal law requires that employers maintain records.

TERMS TO LEARN
compensation record
individual earnings record

Recording Payroll Information

In this section you will learn how to prepare paychecks and journalize and post payroll transactions by following the January payroll activity for Tomlin Furniture Company.

>> **10-7. OBJECTIVE**

Journalize payroll transactions in the general journal.

Recording Payroll

Recording payroll involves two separate entries: one to record the payroll expense and another to pay the employees. The general journal entry to record the payroll expense is based on the payroll register. The gross pay is debited to *Shipping Wages Expense* for the shipping clerks and supervisor and to *Office Salaries Expense* for the office clerk. Each type of deduction is credited to a separate liability account (*Social Security Tax Payable, Medicare Tax Payable, Employee Income Tax Payable, Health Insurance Premiums Payable*). Net pay is credited to the liability account, *Salaries and Wages Payable.*

Refer to Figure 10.3 on pages 340–341 to see how the data on the payroll register is used to prepare the January 8 payroll journal entry for Tomlin Furniture Company. Following is an analysis of the entry.

BUSINESS TRANSACTION

The information in the payroll register (Figure 10.3) is used to record the payroll expense.

ANALYSIS
The expense account, **Office Salaries Expense,** is increased by $480.00. The expense account, **Shipping Wages Expense,** is increased by $1,767.50. The liability account for each deduction is increased: **Social Security Tax Payable,** $139.35; **Medicare Tax Payable,** $32.59; **Employee Income Tax Payable,** $155.00; **Health Insurance Premiums Payable,** $80.00. The liability account, **Salaries and Wages Payable,** is increased by the net amount of the payroll, $1,840.56.

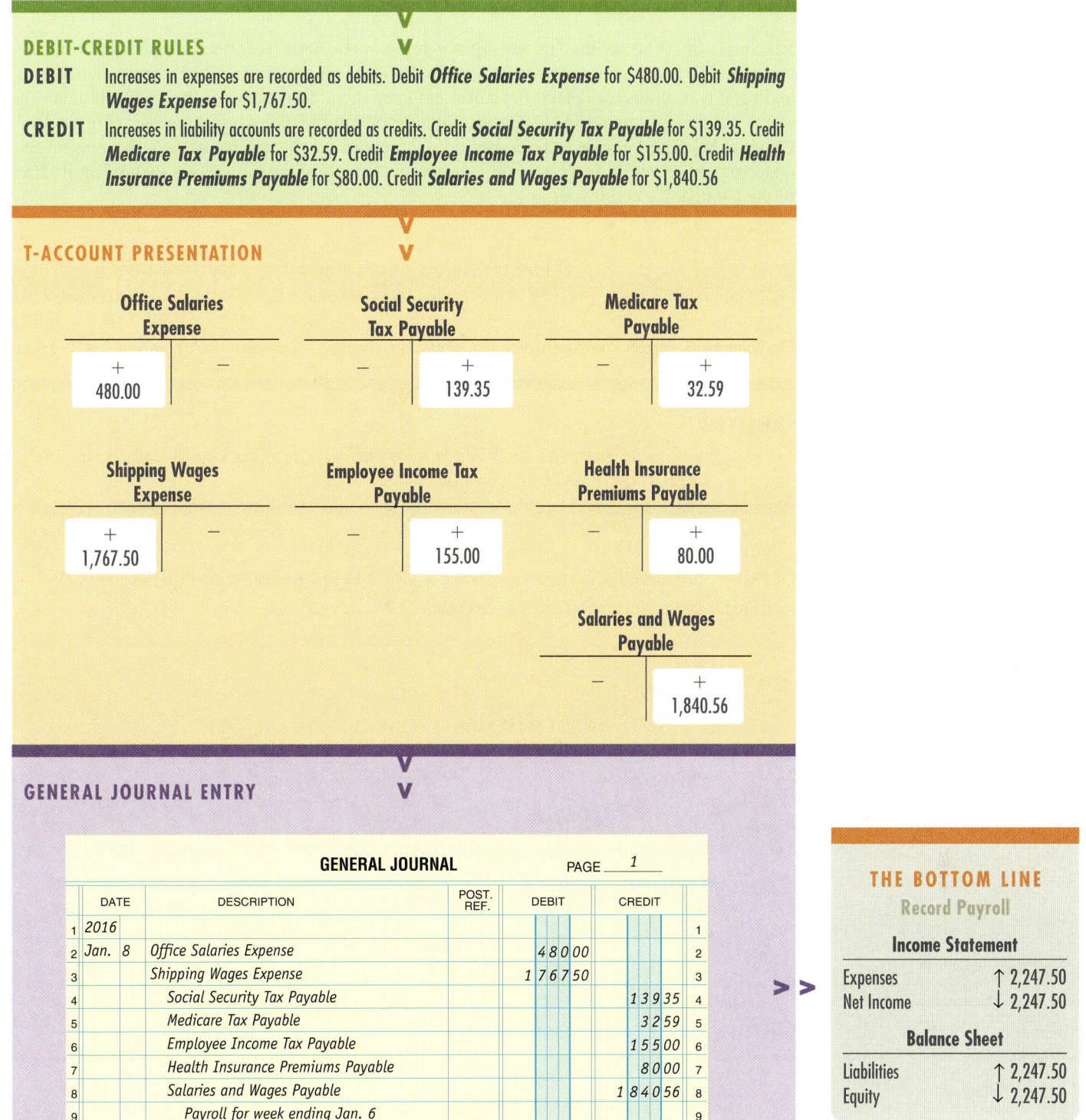

DEBIT-CREDIT RULES

DEBIT Increases in expenses are recorded as debits. Debit *Office Salaries Expense* for $480.00. Debit *Shipping Wages Expense* for $1,767.50.

CREDIT Increases in liability accounts are recorded as credits. Credit *Social Security Tax Payable* for $139.35. Credit *Medicare Tax Payable* for $32.59. Credit *Employee Income Tax Payable* for $155.00. Credit *Health Insurance Premiums Payable* for $80.00. Credit *Salaries and Wages Payable* for $1,840.56

T-ACCOUNT PRESENTATION

Office Salaries Expense		Social Security Tax Payable		Medicare Tax Payable	
+	−	−	+	−	+
480.00			139.35		32.59

Shipping Wages Expense		Employee Income Tax Payable		Health Insurance Premiums Payable	
+	−	−	+	−	+
1,767.50			155.00		80.00

Salaries and Wages Payable	
−	+
	1,840.56

GENERAL JOURNAL ENTRY

	DATE	DESCRIPTION	POST. REF.	DEBIT	CREDIT	
1	2016					1
2	Jan. 8	Office Salaries Expense		480 00		2
3		Shipping Wages Expense		1 767 50		3
4		Social Security Tax Payable			139 35	4
5		Medicare Tax Payable			32 59	5
6		Employee Income Tax Payable			155 00	6
7		Health Insurance Premiums Payable			80 00	7
8		Salaries and Wages Payable			1 840 56	8
9		Payroll for week ending Jan. 6				9

GENERAL JOURNAL   PAGE ___1___

>>

THE BOTTOM LINE

Record Payroll

Income Statement

Expenses	↑ 2,247.50
Net Income	↓ 2,247.50

Balance Sheet

Liabilities	↑ 2,247.50
Equity	↓ 2,247.50

Southwest Airlines Co. recorded salaries, wages, and benefits of more than $4.75 billion for the year ended December 31, 2012.

Paying Employees

Most businesses pay their employees by check or by direct deposit. By using these methods, the business avoids the inconvenience and risk involved in dealing with currency.

important!

Payroll Liabilities
Deductions from employee paychecks are liabilities for the employer.

PAYING BY CHECK

Paychecks may be written on the firm's regular checking account or on a payroll bank account. The check stub shows information about the employee's gross earnings, deductions, and net pay. Employees detach the stubs and keep them as a record of their payroll data. The check number is entered in the Check Number column of the payroll register (Figure 10.3, Column R). The canceled check provides a record of the payment, and the employee's endorsement serves as a receipt. Following is an analysis of the transaction to pay Tomlin Furniture Company's employees.

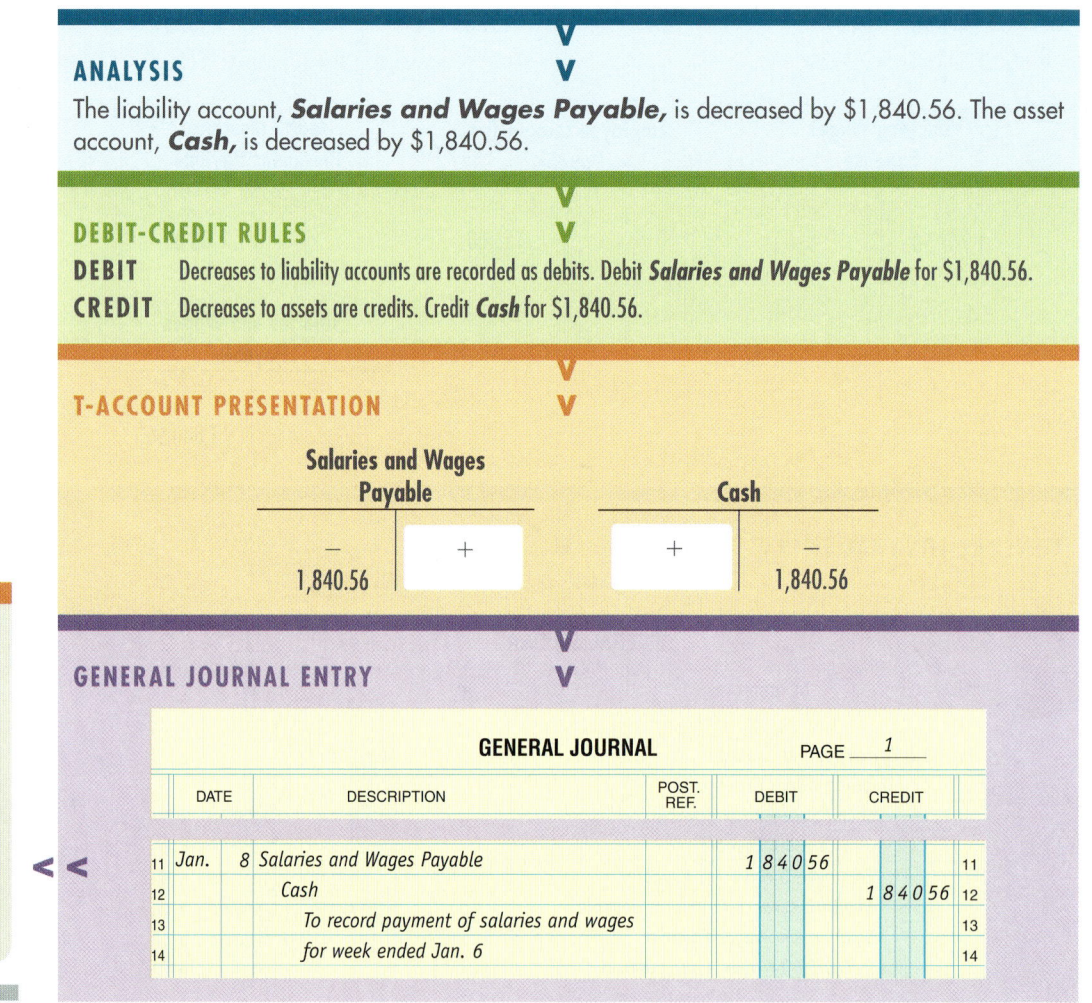

BUSINESS TRANSACTION

On January 8, Tomlin Furniture Company wrote five checks for payroll, check numbers 1601–1605.

ANALYSIS
The liability account, **Salaries and Wages Payable,** is decreased by $1,840.56. The asset account, **Cash,** is decreased by $1,840.56.

DEBIT-CREDIT RULES
DEBIT Decreases to liability accounts are recorded as debits. Debit *Salaries and Wages Payable* for $1,840.56.
CREDIT Decreases to assets are credits. Credit *Cash* for $1,840.56.

T-ACCOUNT PRESENTATION

Salaries and Wages Payable		Cash	
−	+	+	−
1,840.56			1,840.56

GENERAL JOURNAL ENTRY

	GENERAL JOURNAL		PAGE ___1___		
DATE	DESCRIPTION	POST. REF.	DEBIT	CREDIT	
11 Jan. 8	Salaries and Wages Payable		1 840 56		11
12	Cash			1 840 56	12
13	To record payment of salaries and wages				13
14	for week ended Jan. 6				14

THE BOTTOM LINE
Issue Paychecks

Income Statement
No effect on net income

Balance Sheet

Assets	↓	1,840.56
Liabilities	↓	1,840.56

No effect on equity

important!

Separate Payroll Account
Using a separate payroll account facilitates the bank reconciliation and provides better internal control.

Checks Written on a Separate Payroll Account Many businesses write payroll checks from a separate payroll bank account. This is a two-step process:

1. A check is drawn on the regular bank account for the total amount of net pay and deposited in the payroll bank account.
2. Individual payroll checks are issued from the payroll bank account.

MANAGERIAL IMPLICATIONS <<

LAWS AND CONTROLS

- It is management's responsibility to ensure that the payroll procedures and records comply with federal, state, and local laws.

- For most businesses, wages and salaries are a large part of operating expenses. Payroll records help management to keep track of and control expenses.

- Management should investigate large or frequent overtime expenditures.

- To prevent errors and fraud, management periodically should have the payroll records audited and payroll procedures evaluated.

- Two common payroll frauds are the overstatement of hours worked and the issuance of checks to nonexistent employees.

THINKING CRITICALLY
What controls would you put in place to prevent payroll fraud?

Using a separate payroll account simplifies the bank reconciliation of the regular checking account and makes it easier to identify outstanding payroll checks.

PAYING BY DIRECT DEPOSIT

The most popular method of paying employees is the direct deposit method. The bank electronically transfers net pay from the employer's account to the personal account of the employee. On payday, the employee receives a statement showing gross earnings, deductions, and net pay.

Individual Earnings Records

An **individual earnings record,** also called a **compensation record,** is created for each employee. This record contains the employee's name, address, social security number, date of birth, number of withholding allowances claimed, rate of pay, and any other information needed to compute earnings and complete tax reports.

The payroll register provides the details that are entered on the employee's individual earnings record for each pay period. Figure 10.4 shows the earnings record for Alicia Martinez.

The earnings record shows the payroll period, the date paid, the regular and overtime hours, the regular and overtime earnings, the deductions, and the net pay. The cumulative earnings on the earnings record agrees with Column I of the payroll register (Figure 10.3). The earnings records are totaled monthly and at the end of each calendar quarter. This provides information needed to make tax payments and file tax returns.

>> **10-8. OBJECTIVE**

Maintain an earnings record for each employee.

FIGURE 10.4   An Individual Earnings Record

EARNINGS RECORD FOR ___2016___

NAME _Alicia Martinez_   RATE _$10 per hour_   SOCIAL SECURITY NO. _123-45-6789_

ADDRESS ___1712 Windmill Hill Lane, Dallas, TX 75232-6002___   DATE OF BIRTH _November 23, 1979_

WITHHOLDING ALLOWANCES ___1___   MARITAL STATUS _M_

PAYROLL NO.	DATE WK. END.	PAID	HOURS RG	OT	EARNINGS REGULAR	OVERTIME	TOTAL	CUMULATIVE	DEDUCTIONS SOCIAL SECURITY	MEDICARE	INCOME TAX	OTHER	NET PAY
1	1/06	1/08	40		4 0 0 00		4 0 0 00	4 0 0 00	2 4 80	5 80	1 9 00		3 5 0 40
2	1/13	1/15	40		4 0 0 00		4 0 0 00	8 0 0 00	2 4 80	5 80	1 9 00		3 5 0 40
3	1/20	1/22	40		4 0 0 00		4 0 0 00	1 2 0 0 00	2 4 80	5 80	1 9 00		3 5 0 40
4	1/27	1/29	40		4 0 0 00		4 0 0 00	1 6 0 0 00	2 4 80	5 80	1 9 00		3 5 0 40
	January				1 6 0 0 00		1 6 0 0 00		9 9 20	2 3 20	7 6 00		1 4 0 1 60

Completing January Payrolls

Figure 10.5 shows the entire cycle of computing, paying, journalizing, and posting payroll data. In order to complete the January payroll for Tomlin Furniture Company, assume that all employees worked the same number of hours each week of the month as they did the first week. Thus, they had the same earnings, deductions, and net pay each week.

ENTRY TO RECORD PAYROLL

As illustrated earlier in this section, one general journal entry is made to record the weekly payroll for all employees of Tomlin Furniture Company. This general journal entry records the payroll expense and liability, but not the payments to employees. Since we are assuming an identical payroll for each week of the month, each of the four weekly payrolls requires general journal entries identical to the one shown in Figure 10.5. Notice how the payroll register column totals are recorded in the general journal.

ENTRY TO RECORD PAYMENT OF PAYROLL

The weekly entries in the general journal to record payments to employees debit *Salaries and Wages Payable* and credit *Cash.*

POSTINGS TO LEDGER ACCOUNTS

The entries to record the weekly payroll expense and liability amounts are posted from the general journal to the accounts in the general ledger. The total of the Salaries and Wages Payable Debit column in the cash payments journal is posted to the *Salaries and Wages Payable* general ledger account.

FIGURE 10.5 Journalizing and Posting Payroll Data

TAXABLE WAGES			DEDUCTIONS				DISTRIBUTION			
SOCIAL SECURITY	MEDICARE	FUTA	SOCIAL SECURITY	MEDICARE	INCOME TAX	HEALTH INSURANCE	NET AMOUNT	CHECK NO.	OFFICE SALARIES	SHIPPING WAGES
400 00	400 00	400 00	24 80	5 80	19 00		350 40	1601		400 00
380 00	380 00	380 00	23 56	5 51	34 00		316 93	1602		380 00
427 50	427 50	427 50	26 51	6 20	23 00	40 00	331 79	1603		427 50
560 00	560 00	560 00	34 72	8 12	30 00	40 00	447 16	1604		560 00
480 00	480 00	480 00	29 76	6 96	49 00		394 28	1605	480 00	
2 247 50	2 247 50	2 247 50	139 35	32 59	155 00	80 00	1 840 56		480 00	1 767 50
(J)	(K)	(L)	(M)	(N)	(O)	(P)	(Q)	(R)	(S)	(T)

AND ENDING January 6, 2016   **PAID** January 8, 2016

1	2016					
2	Jan.	8	Office Salaries Expense	541	4 8 0 00	
3			Shipping Wages Expense	542	1 7 6 7 50	
4			Social Security Tax Payable	221		1 3 9 35
5			Medicare Tax Payable	222		3 2 59
6			Employee Income Tax Payable	223		1 5 5 00
7			Health Insurance Premiums Payable	224		8 0 00
8			Salaries and Wages Payable	229		1 8 4 0 56
9			Payroll for week ending Jan. 6			

FIGURE 10.5 (continued)

	2016					
	Jan. 8	Office Salaries Expense	541	480 00		
		Shipping Wages Expense	542	1 767 50		
		Social Security Tax Payable	221		1 39 35	
		Medicare Tax Payable	222		32 59	
		Employee Income Tax Payable	223		1 55 00	
		Health Insurance Premiums Payable	224		80 00	
		Salaries and Wages Payable	229		1 840 56	
		Payroll for week ending Jan. 6				

Office Salaries Expense

1/08	480.00	
1/15	480.00	
1/22	480.00	
1/29	480.00	

Medicare Tax Payable

	1/08	32.59
	1/15	32.59
	1/22	32.59
	1/29	32.59

Shipping Wages Expense

1/08	1,767.50	
1/15	1,767.50	
1/22	1,767.50	
1/29	1,767.50	

Employee Income Tax Payable

	1/08	155.00
	1/15	155.00
	1/22	155.00
	1/29	155.00

Health Ins. Premiums Payable

	1/08	80.00
	1/15	80.00
	1/22	80.00
	1/29	80.00

Social Security Tax Payable

	1/08	139.35
	1/15	139.35
	1/22	139.35
	1/29	139.35

Salaries and Wages Payable

1/08	1,840.56	1/08	1,840.56
1/15	1,840.56	1/15	1,840.56
1/22	1,840.56	1/22	1,840.56
1/29	1,840.56	1/29	1,840.56

GENERAL JOURNAL   PAGE __1__

	DATE	DESCRIPTION	POST. REF.	DEBIT	CREDIT	
1	2016					1
2	Jan. 8	Salaries and Wages Payable		1 840 56		2
3		Cash			1 840 56	3
4		To record payment of				4
5		salaries and wages				5
6		for week				6
7		ended Jan. 6				7

Section 3   Self Review

QUESTIONS

1. What is the purpose of a payroll bank account?

2. What accounts are debited and credited when individual payroll checks are written on the regular checking account?

3. What appears on an individual earnings record?

EXERCISES

4. Details related to all employees' gross earnings, deductions, and net pay for a period are found in the:

   a. payroll register.

   b. individual earnings record.

   c. general journal.

   d. cash payments journal.

5. Payroll deductions are recorded in a separate:

   a. asset account.

   b. expense account.

   c. liability account.

   d. revenue account.

ANALYSIS

6. This general journal entry was made to record the payroll liability.

Ofc. Salaries Exp.	600.00	
Shipping Wages Exp.	2,586.00	
Health Ins. Prem. Exp.	40.00	
Soc. Sec. Taxes Exp.	197.41	
Medicare Taxes Pay.	48.17	
Employee Income Tax Payable	266.00	
Cash	2,634.42	

What corrections should be made to this journal entry?

(Answers to Section 3 Self Review are on page 361.)

REVIEW   Chapter Summary   Chapter **10**

The main goal of payroll work is to compute the gross wages or salaries earned by each employee, the amounts to be deducted for various taxes and other purposes, and the net amount payable.

Learning Objectives

10-1 **Explain the major federal laws relating to employee earnings and withholding.**

Several federal laws affect payroll.

- The federal Wage and Hour Law limits to 40 the number of hours per week an employee can work at the regular rate of pay. For more than 40 hours of work a week, an employer involved in interstate commerce must pay one and one-half times the regular rate.

- Federal laws require that the employer withhold at least three taxes from the employee's pay: the employee's share of social security tax, the employee's share of Medicare tax, and federal income tax. Instructions for computing these taxes are provided by the government.

- If required, state disability and other income taxes can also be deducted.

- Voluntary deductions can also be made.

10-2 **Compute gross earnings of employees.**

To compute gross earnings for an employee, it is necessary to know whether the employee is paid using an hourly rate basis, a salary basis, a commission basis, or a piece-rate basis.

10-3 **Determine employee deductions for social security tax.**

The social security tax is levied in an equal amount on both the employer and the employee. The tax is a percentage of the employee's gross wages during a calendar year up to a wage base limit.

10-4 **Determine employee deductions for Medicare tax.**

The Medicare tax is levied in an equal amount on both the employer and the employee. There is no wage base limit for Medicare taxes.

10-5 **Determine employee deductions for income tax.**

Income taxes are deducted from an employee's paycheck by the employer and then are paid to the government periodically. Although several methods can be used to compute the amount of federal income tax to be withheld from employee earnings, the wage-bracket table method is most often used. The wage-bracket tables are in *Publication 15, Circular E, Employer's Tax Guide.* Withholding tables for various pay periods for single and married persons are contained in *Circular E.*

10-6 **Enter gross earnings, deductions, and net pay in the payroll register.**

Daily records of the hours worked by each nonsupervisory employee are kept. Using these hourly time sheets, the payroll clerk computes the employees' earnings, deductions, and net pay for each payroll period and records the data in a payroll register.

10-7 **Journalize payroll transactions in the general journal.**

The payroll register is used to prepare a general journal entry to record payroll expense and liability amounts. A separate journal entry is made to record payments to employees.

10-8 **Maintain an earnings record for each employee.**

At the beginning of each year, the employer sets up an individual earnings record for each employee. The amounts in the payroll register are posted to the individual earnings records throughout the year so that the firm has detailed payroll information for each employee. At the end of the year, employers provide reports that show gross earnings and total deductions to each employee.

10-9 **Define the accounting terms new to this chapter.**

Glossary

Commission basis (p. 333) A method of paying employees according to a percentage of net sales

Compensation record (p. 345) See Individual earnings record

Employee (p. 328) A person who is hired by and works under the control and direction of the employer

Employee's Withholding Allowance Certificate, Form W-4 (p. 335) A form used to claim exemption (withholding) allowances

Exempt employees (p. 339) Salaried employees who hold supervisory or managerial positions who are not subject to the maximum hour and overtime pay provisions of the Wage and Hour Law

Federal unemployment taxes (FUTA) (p. 330) Taxes levied by the federal government against employers to benefit unemployed workers

Hourly rate basis (p. 332) A method of paying employees according to a stated rate per hour

Independent contractor (p. 328) One who is paid by a company to carry out a specific task or job but is not under the direct supervision or control of the company

Individual earnings record (p. 345) An employee record that contains information needed to compute earnings and complete tax reports

Medicare tax (p. 329) A tax levied on employees and employers to provide medical care for the employee and the employee's spouse after each has reached age 65

Payroll register (p. 339) A record of payroll information for each employee for the pay period

Piece-rate basis (p. 333) A method of paying employees according to the number of units produced

Salary basis (p. 333) A method of paying employees according to an agreed-upon amount for each week or month

Social Security Act (p. 329) A federal act providing certain benefits for employees and their families; officially the Federal Insurance Contributions Act

Social security (FICA or **OASDI) tax** (p. 329) A tax imposed by the Federal Insurance Contributions Act and collected on employee earnings to provide retirement and disability benefits

State unemployment taxes (SUTA) (p. 330) Taxes levied by a state government against employers to benefit unemployed workers

Tax-exempt wages (p. 334) Earnings in excess of the base amount set by the Social Security Act

Time and a half (p. 329) Rate of pay for an employee's work in excess of 40 hours a week

Wage-bracket table method (p. 335) A simple method to determine the amount of federal income tax to be withheld using a table provided by the government

Workers' compensation insurance (p. 331) Insurance that protects employees against losses from job-related injuries or illnesses, or compensates their families if death occurs in the course of the employment

---

Comprehensive **Self Review**

1. What is the purpose of the payroll register?
2. How does an independent contractor differ from an employee?
3. From an accounting and internal control viewpoint, would it be preferable to pay employees by check or cash? Explain.
4. How is the amount of social security tax to be withheld from an employee's earnings determined?
5. What is the purpose of workers' compensation insurance?

(Answers to Comprehensive Self Review are on page 361.)

Discussion Questions

1. How does the Fair Labor Standards Act affect the wages paid by many firms? What types of firms are regulated by the act?
2. What factors affect how much federal income tax must be withheld from an employee's earnings?

3. What aspects of employment are regulated by the Fair Labor Standards Act? What is another commonly used name for this act?

4. What is an exempt employee?

5. How are the federal and state unemployment taxes related?

6. Does the employee bear any part of the SUTA tax? Explain.

7. Give two examples of common payroll fraud.

8. How are earnings determined when employees are paid on the hourly rate basis?

9. What is the purpose of the Medicare tax?

10. What is the purpose of the social security tax?

11. How does the direct deposit method of paying employees operate?

12. What are the four bases for determining employee gross earnings?

13. What is the simplest method for finding the amount of federal income tax to be deducted from an employee's gross pay?

14. What publication of the Internal Revenue Service provides information about the current federal income tax rates and the procedures that employers should use to withhold federal income tax from an employee's earnings?

15. How does the salary basis differ from the hourly rate basis of paying employees?

APPLICATIONS

Exercises

Computing gross earnings.

◀ **Exercise 10.1**
Objective 10-2

The hourly rates of four employees of Ernesto's Enterprises follow, along with the hours that these employees worked during one week. Determine the gross earnings of each employee.

Employee No.	Hourly Rate	Hours Worked
1	$9.71	38
2	9.25	30
3	9.92	33
4	9.13	32

Computing regular earnings, overtime earnings, and gross pay.

◀ **Exercise 10.2**
Objective 10-2

During one week, four production employees of Martinez Manufacturing Company worked the hours shown below. All these employees receive overtime pay at one and one-half times their regular hourly rate for any hours worked beyond 40 in a week. Determine the regular earnings, overtime earnings, and gross earnings for each employee.

Employee No.	Hourly Rate	Hours Worked
1	$11.00	46
2	10.62	47
3	10.46	38
4	10.80	48

Exercise 10.3

Objective 10-3

▶ **Determining social security withholding.**

The monthly salaries for December and the year-to-date earnings of the employees of Canzano Consulting Company as of November 30 follow.

Employee No.	December Salary	Year-to-Date Earnings through November 30
1	$ 9,900	$ 98,900
2	10,000	73,000
3	10,709	106,800
4	10,000	100,000

Determine the amount of social security tax to be withheld from each employee's gross pay for December. Assume a 6.2 percent social security tax rate and an earnings base of $113,700 for the calendar year.

Exercise 10.4

Objective 10-4

CONTINUING >>>
Problem

▶ **Determining deduction for Medicare tax.**

Using the earnings data given in Exercise 10.3, determine the amount of Medicare tax to be withheld from each employee's gross pay for December. Assume a 1.45 percent Medicare tax rate and that all salaries and wages are subject to the tax.

Exercise 10.5

Objective 10-5

▶ **Determining federal income tax withholding.**

Data about the marital status, withholding allowances, and weekly salaries of the four office workers at Amos Publishing Company follow. Use the tax tables in Figure 10.2 on pages 337–338 to find the amount of federal income tax to be deducted from each employee's gross pay.

Employee No.	Marital Status	Withholding Allowances	Weekly Salary
1	M	2	$675
2	S	1	565
3	M	2	665
4	S	1	495

Exercise 10.6

Objective 10-7

▶ **Recording payroll transactions in the general journal.**

Private Publishing has two office employees. A summary of their earnings and the related taxes withheld from their pay for the week ending August 7, 2016, follows.

	Ann Chen	David Kendrick
Gross earnings	$1,420.00	$1,290.00
Social security deduction	(88.04)	(79.98)
Medicare deduction	(20.59)	(18.71)
Income tax withholding	(380.16)	(232.32)
Net pay for week	$ 931.21	$ 958.99

1. Prepare the general journal entry to record the company's payroll for the week. Use the account names given in this chapter. Use 16 as the page number for the general journal.

2. Prepare the general journal entry to summarize the checks to pay the weekly payroll.

Journalizing payroll transactions.

On July 31, 2016, the payroll register of Reed Wholesale Company showed the following totals for the month: gross earnings, $39,600; social security tax, $2,455.20; Medicare tax, $574.20; income tax, $3,135.16; and net amount due, $33,435.44. Of the total earnings, $31,258.46 was for sales salaries and $8,341.54 was for office salaries. Prepare a general journal entry to record the monthly payroll of the firm on July 31, 2016. Use 20 as the page number for the general journal.

◄ **Exercise 10.7**
Objective 10-7

PROBLEMS

Problem Set A

Computing gross earnings, determining deductions, journalizing payroll transactions.

Kathy Burnett works for Triumph Industries. Her pay rate is $13.44 per hour and she receives overtime pay at one and one-half times her regular hourly rate for any hours worked beyond 40 in a week. During the pay period that ended December 31, 2016, Kathy worked 42 hours. Kathy is married and claims three withholding allowances on her W-4 form. Kathy's cumulative earnings prior to this pay period total $29,000. Kathy's wages are subject to the following deductions:

◄ **Problem 10.1A**
**Objectives 10-2,
10-3, 10-4,
10-5, 10-7**

1. Social Security tax at 6.2 percent

2. Medicare tax at 1.45 percent

3. Federal income tax (use the withholding table shown in Figure 10.2B on page 338)

4. Health and disability insurance premiums, $161

5. Charitable contribution, $18

6. United States Savings Bond, $100

INSTRUCTIONS

1. Compute Kathy's regular, overtime, gross, and net pay.

2. Assuming the weekly payroll has been recorded, journalize the payment of her wages for the week ended December 31, 2016. Use 54 as the page number for the general journal.

Analyze: Based on Kathy's cumulative earnings through December 31, how much overtime pay did she earn this year?

Computing gross earnings, determining deductions, preparing payroll register, journalizing payroll transactions.

City Place Movie Theaters has four employees and pays them on an hourly basis. During the week beginning June 24 and ending June 30, 2016, these employees worked the hours shown below. Information about hourly rates, marital status, withholding allowances, and cumulative earnings prior to the current pay period also appears below.

◄ **Problem 10.2A**
**Objectives 10-2,
10-3, 10-4,
10-5**

Employee	Regular Hours Worked	Hourly Rate	Marital Status	Withholding Allowances	Cumulative Earnings
Nelda Anderson	48	$12.70	M	1	$17,640
Earl Benson	48	11.50	M	4	16,975
Frank Cortez	40	11.20	M	1	16,080
Winnie Wu	50	10.70	S	2	14,660

INSTRUCTIONS

1. Enter the basic payroll information for each employee in a payroll register. Record the employee's name, number of withholding allowances, marital status, total and overtime hours, and regular hourly rate. Consider any hours worked beyond 40 in the week as overtime hours.

2. Compute the regular, overtime, and gross earnings for each employee. Enter the figures in the payroll register.

3. Compute the amount of social security tax to be withheld from each employee's earnings. Assume a 6.2 percent social security rate on the first $113,700 earned by the employee during the year. Enter the figures in the payroll register.

4. Compute the amount of Medicare tax to be withheld from each employee's earnings. Assume a 1.45 percent Medicare tax rate on all salaries and wages earned by the employee during the year. Enter the figures in the payroll register.

5. Determine the amount of federal income tax to be withheld from each employee's total earnings. Use the tax tables in Figure 10.2 on pages 337–338. Enter the figures in the payroll register.

6. Compute the net pay of each employee and enter the figures in the payroll register.

7. Total and prove the payroll register.

8. Prepare a general journal entry to record the payroll for the week ended June 30, 2016. Use 15 as the page number for the general journal.

9. Record the general journal entry to summarize payment of the payroll on July 3, 2016.

Analyze: What are Nelda Anderson's cumulative earnings on June 30, 2016?

Problem 10.3A
Objectives 10-2, 10-3, 10-4, 10-5

▶ **Computing gross earnings, determining deductions, preparing payroll register, journalizing payroll transactions.**

Alexander Wilson operates Metroplex Courier and Delivery Service. He has four employees who are paid on an hourly basis. During the work week beginning December 15 and ending December 21, 2016, his employees worked the number of hours shown below. Information about their hourly rates, marital status, and withholding allowances also appears below, along with their cumulative earnings for the year prior to the December 15–21 payroll period.

Employee	Hours Worked	Regular Hourly Rate	Marital Status	Withholding Allowances	Cumulative Earnings
Gloria Bahamon	47	$16.70	M	4	$32,860
Alex Garcia	43	28.50	S	1	57,300
Ron Price	49	26.90	M	3	53,972
Sara Russell	40	13.70	S	0	26,620

INSTRUCTIONS

1. Enter the basic payroll information for each employee in a payroll register. Record the employee's name, number of withholding allowances, marital status, total and overtime hours, and regular hourly rate. Consider any hours worked beyond 40 in the week as overtime hours.

2. Compute the regular, overtime, and gross earnings for each employee. Enter the figures in the payroll register.

3. Compute the amount of social security tax to be withheld from each employee's gross earnings. Assume a 6.2 percent social security rate on the first $113,700 earned by the employee during the year. Enter the figures in the payroll register.

4. Compute the amount of Medicare tax to be withheld from each employee's gross earnings. Assume a 1.45 percent Medicare tax rate on all salaries and wages earned by the employee during the year. Enter the figures in the payroll register.

5. Determine the amount of federal income tax to be withheld from each employee's total earnings. Use the tax tables in Figure 10.2 on pages 337–338 to determine the withholding for Russell. Withholdings for Bahamon is $112.00, $323.00 for Garcia, and $258 for Price. Enter the figures in the payroll register.

6. Compute the net amount due each employee and enter the figures in the payroll register.

7. Total and prove the payroll register. Bahamon and Russell are office workers. Garcia and Price are delivery workers.

8. Prepare a general journal entry to record the payroll for the week ended December 21, 2016. Use 32 as the page number for the general journal.

9. Prepare a general journal entry on December 23 to summarize payment of wages for the week.

Analyze: What percentage of total taxable wages was delivery wages?

Computing gross earnings, determining deduction and net amount due, journalizing payroll transactions.

◀ **Problem 10.4A**
Objectives 10-2, 10-3, 10-4, 10-5, 10-6, 10- 7

Nature's Best Publishing Company pays its employees monthly. Payments made by the company on October 31, 2016, follow. Cumulative amounts paid to the persons named prior to October 31 are also given.

1. Sara Parker, president, gross monthly salary of $20,400; gross earnings prior to October 31, $171,700.

2. Carolyn Wells, vice president, gross monthly salary of $16,600; gross earnings paid prior to October 31, $152,700.

3. Michelle Clark, independent accountant who audits the company's accounts and performs consulting services, $16,500; gross amounts paid prior to October 31, $44,900.

4. James Wu, treasurer, gross monthly salary of $6,000; gross earnings prior to October 31, $52,800.

5. Payment to Editorial Publishing Services for monthly services of Betty Jo Bradley, an editorial expert, $6,000; amount paid to Editorial Publishing Services prior to October 31, 2016, $34,100.

INSTRUCTIONS

1. Use an earnings ceiling of $113,700 for social security taxes and a tax rate of 6.2 percent and a tax rate of 1.45 percent on all earnings for Medicare taxes. Prepare a schedule showing the following information:
   a. Each employee's cumulative earnings prior to October 31.
   b. Each employee's gross earnings for October.
   c. The amounts to be withheld for each payroll tax from each employee's earnings; the employee's income tax withholdings are Sara Parker, $5,348; Carolyn Wells, $4,668; James Wu, $1,377.
   d. The net amount due each employee.
   e. The total gross earnings, the total of each payroll tax deduction, and the total net amount payable to employees.

2. Prepare the general journal entry to record the company's payroll on October 31. Use journal page 22. Omit explanations.

3. Prepare the general journal entry to record payments to employees on October 31.

Analyze: What distinguishes an employee from an independent contractor?

Problem Set B

Computing gross earnings, determining deductions, journalizing payroll transactions.

◀ **Problem 10.1B**
Objectives 10-2, 10-3, 10-4, 10-5, 10-7

Juan Padronas works for H&C Commercial Builders, Inc. His pay rate is $13.00 per hour and he receives overtime pay at one and one-half times his regular hourly rate for any hours worked beyond

40 in a week. During the pay period ended December 31, 2016, Juan worked 48 hours. Juan is married and claims three withholding allowances on his W-4 form. Juan's cumulative earnings prior to this pay period total $28,000. Juan's wages are subject to the following deductions:

1. Social security tax at 6.2 percent
2. Medicare tax at 1.45 percent
3. Federal income tax (use the withholding table shown in Figure 10.2B on page 338)
4. Health insurance premiums, $150
5. Charitable contribution, $20
6. Credit Union Savings, $25

INSTRUCTIONS

1. Compute Juan's regular, overtime, gross, and net pay.
2. Assuming the weekly payroll has been recorded, journalize the payment of his wages for the week ended December 31, 2016. Use journal page 18.

Analyze: Based on Juan's cumulative earnings through December 31, how much overtime pay did he earn this year?

Problem 10.2B
Objectives 10-2, 10-3, 10-4, 10-5

▶ **Computing earnings, determining deductions and net amount due, preparing payroll register, journalizing payroll transactions.**

The four employees for JackWorks are paid on an hourly basis. During the week of December 25–31, 2016, these employees worked the hours indicated. Information about their hourly rates, marital status, withholding allowances, and cumulative earnings prior to the current pay period also appears below.

Employee	Hours Worked	Regular Hourly Rate	Marital Status	Withholding Allowances	Cumulative Earnings
Betty Brooks	45	$12.80	M	3	$ 44,179.00
Cynthia Carter	48	13.40	M	2	53,015.00
Mary Easley	44	29.50	M	4	82,748.00
James Periot	30	37.00	S	2	104,486.00

INSTRUCTIONS

1. Enter the basic payroll information for each employee in a payroll register. Record the employee's name, number of withholding allowances, marital status, total hours, overtime hours, and regular hourly rate. Consider any hours worked beyond 40 in the week as overtime hours.
2. Compute the regular earnings, overtime premium, and gross earnings for each employee. Enter the figures in the payroll register.
3. Compute the amount of social security tax to be withheld from each employee's gross earnings. Assume a 6.2 percent social security tax rate on the first $113,700 earned by each employee during the year. Enter the figures in the payroll register.
4. Compute the amount of Medicare tax to be withheld from each employee's gross earnings. Assume a 1.45 percent Medicare tax rate on all earnings for each employee during the year. Enter the figure on the payroll register.
5. Determine the amount of federal income tax to be withheld from each employee's gross earnings. Income tax withholdings for Easley is $235 and $238 for Periot. Enter these figures in the payroll register.
6. Compute the net amount due each employee and enter the figures in the payroll register.
7. Complete the payroll register for the store employees.

8. Prepare a general journal entry to record the payroll for the week ended December 31, 2016. Use page 18 for the journal.

9. Record the general journal entry to summarize the payment on December 31, 2016, of the net amount due employees.

Analyze: What is the difference between the amount credited to the *Cash* account on December 31, 2016, for the payroll week ended December 31 and the amount debited to *Wages Expense* for the same payroll period? What causes the difference between the two figures?

Computing earnings, determining deductions and net amount due, preparing payroll register, journalizing payroll transactions.

◀ **Problem 10.3B**
Objectives 10-2, 10-3, 10-4, 10-5

Barbara Merino operates Merino Consulting Services. She has four employees and pays them on an hourly basis. During the week ended November 12, 2016, her employees worked the number of hours shown below. Information about their hourly rates, marital status, withholding allowances, and cumulative earnings for the year prior to the current pay period also appears below.

Employee	Hours Worked	Regular Hourly Rate	Marital Status	Withholding Allowances	Cumulative Earnings
Kathryn Allen	43	$10.50	M	3	$26,565
Calvin Cooke	36	10.25	S	2	25,933
Maria Vasquez	45	29.75	M	4	75,268
Hollie Visage	41	32.75	S	2	82,858

INSTRUCTIONS

1. Enter the basic payroll information for each employee in a payroll register. Record the employee's name, number of withholding allowances, marital status, total hours, overtime hours, and regular hourly rate. Consider any hours worked beyond 40 in the week as overtime hours.

2. Compute the regular earnings, overtime premium, and gross earnings for each employee. Enter the figures in the payroll register.

3. Compute the amount of social security tax to be withheld from each employee's gross earnings. Assume a 6.2 percent social security rate on the first $113,700 earned by the employee during the year. Enter the figures in the payroll register.

4. Compute the amount of Medicare tax to be withheld from each employee's gross earnings. Assume a 1.45 percent Medicare tax rate on all earning paid during the year. Enter the figures in the payroll register.

5. Use the tax tables in Figure 10.2 on pages 337–338 to determine the federal income tax to be withheld. Federal income tax to be withheld from Vasquez's pay is $192 and from Visage's pay is $267. Enter the figures in the payroll register.

6. Compute the net amount due each employee and enter the figures in the payroll register.

7. Complete the payroll register. Allen and Cooke are office workers. Earnings for Vasquez and Visage are charged to consulting wages.

8. Prepare a general journal entry to record the payroll for the week ended November 12, 2016. Use the account titles given in this chapter. Use journal page 32.

9. Prepare the general journal entry to summarize payment of amounts due employees on November 15, 2016.

Analyze: What total deductions were taken from employee paychecks for the pay period ended November 12?

Computing gross earnings, determining deduction and net amount due, journalizing payroll transactions.

◀ **Problem 10.4B**
Objectives 10-2, 10-3, 10-4, 10-5, 10-7

Constantino Public Relations pays its employees monthly. Payments made by the company on November 30, 2016, follow. Cumulative amounts paid to the persons named prior to November 30 are also given.

1. Tony Constantino, president, gross monthly salary of $18,000; gross earnings prior to November 30, $180,000.

2. Chris Stamos, vice president, gross monthly salary of $15,000; gross earnings paid prior to November 30, $150,000.

3. Brenda Cates, independent media buyer who purchases media contracts for companies and performs other public relations consulting services, $15,650; gross amounts paid prior to November 30, $52,850.

4. Elaine Hayakawa, treasurer, gross monthly salary of $6,400; gross earnings prior to November 30, $64,000.

5. Payment to the Queen Marketing Group for monthly services of Cheryl Queen, a marketing and public relations expert, $15,500; amount paid to the Queen Marketing Group prior to November 30, $46,500.

INSTRUCTIONS

1. Use an earnings ceiling of $113,700 and a tax rate of 6.2 percent for social security taxes and a tax rate of 1.45 percent on all earnings for Medicare taxes. Prepare a schedule showing the following information:

   a. Each employee's cumulative earnings prior to November 30.

   b. Each employee's gross earnings for November.

   c. The amounts to be withheld for each payroll tax from each employee's earnings; the employee's income tax withholdings are Tony Constantino, $5,110; Chris Stamos, $3,700; Elaine Hayakawa, $1,200.

   d. The net amount due each employee.

   e. The total gross earnings, the total of each payroll tax deduction, and the total net amount payable to employees.

2. Give the general journal entry to record the company's payroll on November 30. Use journal page 24. Omit explanations.

3. Give the general journal entry to record payments to employees on November 30.

Analyze: What month in 2016 did Chris Stamos reach the withholding limit for social security?

Critical Thinking Problem 10.1

Payroll Accounting

Anthony Company pays salaries and wages on the last day of each month. Payments made on December 31, 2016, for amounts incurred during December are shown below. Cumulative amounts paid prior to December 31 to the persons named are also shown.

a. Mark Anthony, president, gross monthly salary $12,000; gross earnings paid prior to December 31, $132,000.

b. Carol Swartz, vice president, gross monthly salary $10,000; gross earnings paid prior to December 31, $100,000.

c. Jenny Rios, independent accountant who audits the company's accounts and performs certain consulting services, $13,000; gross amount paid prior to December 31, $25,000.

d. Henry House, treasurer, gross monthly salary $6,500; gross earnings paid prior to December 31, $71,500.

e. Payment to Wright Security Services for Eddie Wright, a security guard who is on duty on Saturdays and Sundays, $1,000; amount paid to Wright Security Services prior to December 31, $11,000.

INSTRUCTIONS

1. Using the tax rates and earnings ceilings given in this chapter, prepare a schedule showing the following information:

   a. Each employee's cumulative earnings prior to December 31.

   b. Each employee's gross earnings for December.

    c. The amounts to be withheld for each payroll tax from each employee's earnings (employee income tax withholdings for Anthony are $3,216; for Swartz, $2,646; and for House, $1,244).

    d. The net amount due each employee.

    e. The total gross earnings, the total of each payroll tax deduction, and the total net amount payable to employees.

2. Record the general journal entry for the company's payroll on December 31. Use journal page 32.

3. Record the general journal entry for payments to employees on December 31.

Analyze: What is the balance of the *Salaries Payable* account after all payroll entries have been posted for the month?

Critical Thinking Problem 10.2

Payroll Internal Controls

Several years ago, Paul Rivera opened Tito's Tacos, a restaurant specializing in homemade tacos. The restaurant was so successful that Rivera was able to expand, and his company now operates eight restaurants in the local area.

    Rivera tells you that when he first started, he handled all aspects of the business himself. Now that there are eight Tito's Tacos, he depends on the managers of each restaurant to make decisions and oversee day-to-day operations. Paul oversees operations at the company's headquarters, which is located at the first Tito's Tacos.

    Each manager interviews and hires new employees for a restaurant. The new employee is required to complete a W-4, which is sent by the manager to the headquarters office. Each restaurant has a time clock and employees are required to clock in as they arrive or depart. Blank time cards are kept in a box under the time clock. At the beginning of each week, employees complete the top of the card they will use during the week. The manager collects the cards at the end of the week and sends them to headquarters.

    Paul hired his cousin Anna to prepare the payroll instead of assigning this task to the accounting staff. Because she is a relative, Paul trusts her and has confidence that confidential payroll information will not be divulged to other employees.

    When Anna receives a W-4 for a new employee, she sets up an individual earnings record for the employee. Each week, using the time cards sent by each restaurant's manager, she computes the gross pay, deductions, and net pay for all the employees. She then posts details to the employees' earnings records and prepares and signs the payroll checks. The checks are sent to the managers, who distribute them to the employees.

    As long as Anna receives a time card for an employee, she prepares a paycheck. If she fails to get a time card for an employee, she checks with the manager to see if the employee was terminated or has quit. At the end of the month, Anna reconciles the payroll bank account and prepares quarterly and annual payroll tax returns.

1. Identify any weaknesses in Tito's Tacos's payroll system.

2. Identify one way a manager could defraud Tito's Tacos under the present payroll system.

3. What internal control procedures would you recommend to Paul to protect against the fraud you identified above?

BUSINESS CONNECTIONS

Cash Management

Managerial FOCUS

1. Why should managers check the amount spent for overtime?

2. The new controller for TAG Company, a manufacturing firm, has suggested to management that the business change from paying the factory employees in cash to paying them by check. What reasons would you offer to support this suggestion?

3. Why should management make sure that a firm has an adequate set of payroll records?

4. How can detailed payroll records help managers control expenses?

Salary vs. Hourly

Susie's Sweater Factory employs two managers for the factory. These managers work 12 hours per day at $16 per hour. After eight hours, they receive overtime pay. Management is trying to cut costs. They have decided to promote the managers to a salary position. The managers will be offered a daily salary of $200. Since they would be promoted to a salary position they will not receive overtime. The company has required they accept the promotion or find employment elsewhere. Is it ethical for the company to offer the managers a salary position? Is it ethical to require the employee to accept the promotion? Should the managers accept the promotion?

Balance Sheet

The Home Depot, Inc. reported the following data in its *2012 Annual Report (for the fiscal year ended February 3, 2013)*:

The Home Depot, Inc. and Subsidiaries		
Consolidated Balance Sheets		
(in millions except per share amounts)	Feb. 3, 2013	Jan. 29, 2012
Current liabilities:		
Accrued salaries and related expenses	1,414	1,372
Total current liabilities	11,462	9,376

Analyze:

1. What percentage of total current liabilities is made up of accrued salaries and related expenses at February 3, 2013?

2. By what amount did accrued salaries and related expenses change from fiscal 2012 to fiscal 2013?

Cycle to Pay Employee

There are many approvals needed to create a paycheck for an employee. Divide into groups of five to identify the jobs necessary to create a paycheck for an employee. Describe the function and, if necessary, the journal entry for each job.

Certified Payroll Professional

Log onto the Certified Payroll Professional (CPP) website at www.americanpayroll.org. Find the requirements to become a CPP. How many years of experience are required? What is the fee to take the exam? Describe the testing procedure.

Answers to **Self Reviews**

Answers to Section 1 Self Review

1. The federal requirement that covered employees be paid at a rate equal to one and one-half times their normal hourly rate for each hour worked in excess of 40 hours per week.
2. By state and federal taxes levied on the employer.
3. By a tax levied equally on both employers and employees. The tax amount is based on the earnings.
4. **a.** employees who become unemployed
5. **c.** Both employee and employer.
6. He is not an employee. He is an independent contractor because he has been hired to complete a specific job and is not under the control of the employer.

Answers to Section 2 Self Review

1. Social security tax, Medicare tax, and federal income tax.
2. Amount of earnings, period covered by the payment, employee's marital status, and the number of withholding allowances.
3. Health insurance premiums, life insurance premiums, union dues, retirement plans.
4. **d.** hours worked
5. **c.** $468
6. When you receive a signed Form W-4 for the change in withholding.

Answers to Section 3 Self Review

1. Using a separate payroll account simplifies the bank reconciliation procedure and makes it easier to identify outstanding payroll checks.
2. Debit *Salaries and Wages Payable* and credit *Cash.*
3. Employee's name, address, social security number, date of birth, number of withholding allowances claimed, marital status, rate of pay, and any other information needed to compute earnings and complete tax reports.
4. **a.** payroll register
5. **c.** liability account
6. *Health Insurance Premiums Expense* Dr. 40.00 should be *Health Insurance Premiums Payable* Cr. 40.00; *Social Security Taxes Expense* Cr. 197.41 should be *Social Security Tax Payable* Cr. 197.41; *Cash* Cr. 2,634.42 should be *Salaries and Wages Payable* Cr. 2,634.42

Answers to Comprehensive Self Review

1. To record in one place all information about an employee's earnings and withholdings for the period.
2. An employee is one who is hired by the employer and who is under the control and direction of the employer. An independent contractor is paid by the company to carry out a specific task or job and is not under the direct supervision and control of the employer.
3. By check because there is far less possibility of mistake, lost money, or fraud. The check serves as a receipt and permanent record of the transaction.
4. Social security taxes are determined by multiplying the amount of taxable earnings by the social security tax rate.
5. To compensate workers for losses suffered from job-related injuries or to compensate their families if the employee's death occurs in the course of employment.

Payroll Taxes, Deposits, and Reports

Chapter 11

Marek Brothers Systems, Inc.
www.marekbros.com

"In sports, true champions are measured by their ability to prevail despite the circumstances. The business world is no different."

At the *Marek Family of Companies,* one of the largest commercial interior contractors in Texas, they have always regarded themselves as champions, with more than 75 years of not only existence but success, growth, and leadership in the construction industry. The company prides itself on its strong values and principles that have always been a part of the *Marek* difference.

They pay employees well and also pay the employer's portion of social security, Medicare, and unemployment taxes—everything they're supposed to—just like a company in other industries. They also pride themselves in supporting their community. This value was underscored with the participation of 29 Marek employees that provided day and night help from start to finish building an *Extreme Makeover* home for the Johnson family in Houston, Texas. The home, which would normally have taken about four months to complete, was built in seven days!

Marek has been in business 75 years and even though competition within the Texas construction industry is fierce, the company is committed to their people and the community they serve.

thinking critically

What types of benefits do you think are important to people working in industries such as construction? What would be important to you?

LEARNING OBJECTIVES

11-1. Explain how and when payroll taxes are paid to the government.

11-2. Compute and record the employer's social security and Medicare taxes.

11-3. Record deposit of social security, Medicare, and employee income taxes.

11-4. Prepare an Employer's Quarterly Federal Tax Return, Form 941.

11-5. Prepare Wage and Tax Statement (Form W-2) and Annual Transmittal of Wage and Tax Statements (Form W-3).

11-6. Compute and record liability for federal and state unemployment taxes and record payment of the taxes.

11-7. Prepare an Employer's Federal Unemployment Tax Return, Form 940.

11-8. Compute and record workers' compensation insurance premiums.

11-9. Define the accounting terms new to this chapter.

NEW TERMS

Employer's Annual Federal Unemployment Tax Return, Form 940
Employer's Quarterly Federal Tax Return, Form 941
experience rating system
merit rating system

Transmittal of Wage and Tax Statements, Form W-3
unemployment insurance program
Wage and Tax Statement, Form W-2
withholding statement

Social Security, Medicare, and Employee Income Tax

In Chapter 10, you learned that the law requires employers to act as collection agents for certain taxes due from employees. In this chapter, you will learn how to compute the employer's taxes, make tax payments, and file the required tax returns and reports.

>> **11-1. OBJECTIVE**

Explain how and when payroll taxes are paid to the government.

Payment of Payroll Taxes

The payroll register provides information about wages subject to payroll taxes. Figure 11.1 shows a portion of the payroll register for Tomlin Furniture Company for the week ending January 6.

Employers make tax deposits for federal income tax withheld from employee earnings, the employees' share of social security and Medicare taxes withheld from earnings, and the employer's share of social security and Medicare taxes. The deposits are made in a Federal Reserve Bank or other authorized financial institution. Businesses usually make payroll tax deposits at their own bank. There are two ways to deposit payroll taxes: by electronic deposit or with a tax deposit coupon.

The *Electronic Federal Tax Payment System (EFTPS)* is a system for electronically depositing employment taxes using a telephone or a computer. Electronic filing of taxes due is now required in most instances. An employer *must* use EFTPS if the annual federal tax deposits are more than $200,000. Employers who are required to make electronic deposits and do not do so can be subject to a 10 percent penalty.

The frequency of deposits depends on the amount of tax liability. The amount currently owed is compared to the tax liability threshold. For simplicity, this textbook uses $2,500 as the tax liability threshold.

FIGURE 11.1   Portion of a Payroll Register

AND ENDING _____ January 6, 2016 _____   PAID _____ January 8, 2016 _____

TAXABLE WAGES			DEDUCTIONS				DISTRIBUTION			
SOCIAL SECURITY	MEDICARE	FUTA	SOCIAL SECURITY	MEDICARE	INCOME TAX	HEALTH INSURANCE	NET AMOUNT	CHECK NO.	OFFICE SALARIES	SHIPPING WAGES
400 00	400 00	400 00	24 80	5 80	19 00		350 40	1601		400 00
380 00	380 00	380 00	23 56	5 51	34 00		316 93	1602		380 00
427 50	427 50	427 50	26 51	6 20	23 00	40 00	331 79	1603		427 50
560 00	560 00	560 00	34 72	8 12	30 00	40 00	447 16	1604		560 00
480 00	480 00	480 00	29 76	6 96	49 00		394 28	1605	480 00	
2 247 50	2 247 50	2 247 50	139 35	32 59	155 00	80 00	1 840 56		480 00	1 767 50

The deposit schedules are not related to how often employees are paid. The deposit schedules are based on the amount currently owed and the amount reported in the lookback period. The *lookback period* is a four-quarter period ending on June 30 of the preceding year.

1. If the amount owed is less than $2,500, payment is due quarterly with the payroll tax return (Form 941).

   Example. An employer's tax liability is as follows:

January	$580
February	640
March	620
	$1,840

   Since at no time during the quarter is the accumulated tax liability $2,500 or more, no deposit is required during the quarter. The employer may pay the amount with the payroll tax returns.

2. If the amount owed is $2,500 or more, the schedule is determined from the total taxes reported on Form 941 during the lookback period.

   a. If the amount reported in the lookback period was $50,000 or less, the employer is subject to the *Monthly Deposit Schedule Rule.* Monthly payments are due on the 15th day of the following month. For example, the January payment is due by February 15.

   b. If the amount reported in the lookback period was more than $50,000, the employer is subject to the *Semiweekly Deposit Schedule Rule.* "Semiweekly" refers to the fact that deposits are due on either Wednesdays or Fridays, depending on the employer's payday.

      • If payday is a Wednesday, Thursday, or Friday, the deposit is due on the following Wednesday.

      • If payday is a Saturday, Sunday, Monday, or Tuesday, the deposit is due on the following Friday.

   c. For new employers with no lookback period, if the amount owed is $2,500 or more, payments are due under the Monthly Deposit Schedule Rule.

3. If the total accumulated tax liability reaches $100,000 or more on any day, a deposit is due on the next banking day. This applies even if the employer is on a monthly or a semiweekly deposit schedule.

EMPLOYER'S SOCIAL SECURITY AND MEDICARE TAX EXPENSES

Remember that both employers and employees pay social security and Medicare taxes. Figure 11.1 shows the *employee's* share of these payroll taxes. The *employer* pays the same amount of payroll taxes. At the assumed rate of 6.2 percent for social security and 1.45 percent for Medicare tax, the employer's tax liability is $343.88.

important!

As this text is being prepared, the Affordable Healthcare Act provisions are beginning to be implemented. Many of these requirements (and taxes) will be tracked and reported through the summary earnings report and other federal filings.

>> **11-2. OBJECTIVE**

Compute and record the employer's social security and Medicare taxes.

	Employee (Withheld)	Employer (Matched)
Social security	$139.35	$139.35
Medicare	32.59	32.59
	$171.94	$171.94
Total	$343.88	

important!

Tax Liability

The employer's tax liability is the amount owed for:

- employee withholdings (income tax, social security tax, Medicare tax);
- employer's share of social security and Medicare taxes.

In Chapter 10, you learned how to record employee payroll deductions. The entry to record the employer's share (commonly called "matching") of social security and Medicare taxes is made at the end of each payroll period. The debit is to the **Payroll Taxes Expense** account. The credits are to the same liability accounts used to record the employee's share of payroll taxes.

BUSINESS TRANSACTION

On January 8, Tomlin Furniture Company recorded the employer's share of social security and Medicare taxes. The information on the payroll register (Figure 11.1) is used to record the payroll taxes expense.

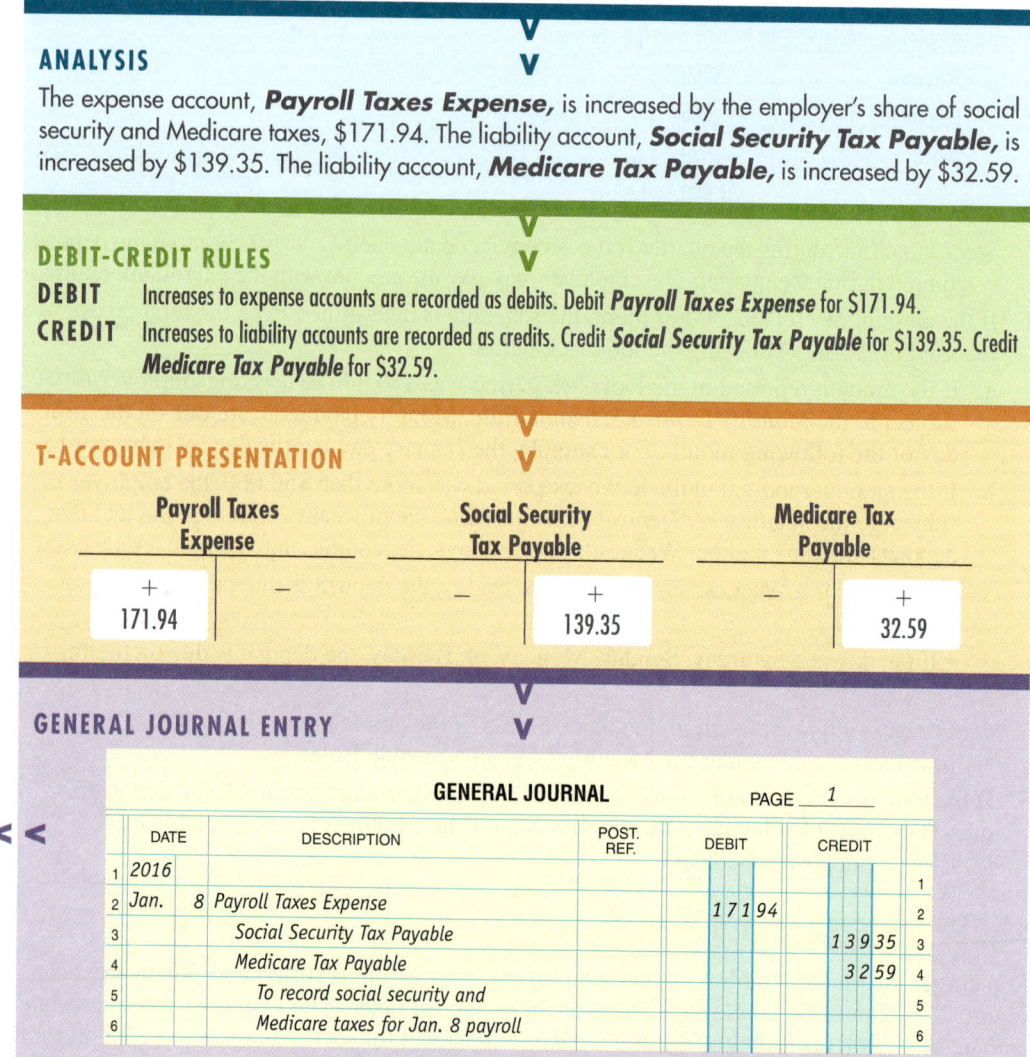

ANALYSIS

The expense account, **Payroll Taxes Expense,** is increased by the employer's share of social security and Medicare taxes, $171.94. The liability account, **Social Security Tax Payable,** is increased by $139.35. The liability account, **Medicare Tax Payable,** is increased by $32.59.

DEBIT-CREDIT RULES

DEBIT   Increases to expense accounts are recorded as debits. Debit **Payroll Taxes Expense** for $171.94.

CREDIT   Increases to liability accounts are recorded as credits. Credit **Social Security Tax Payable** for $139.35. Credit **Medicare Tax Payable** for $32.59.

T-ACCOUNT PRESENTATION

Payroll Taxes Expense		Social Security Tax Payable		Medicare Tax Payable	
+	−	−	+	−	+
171.94			139.35		32.59

GENERAL JOURNAL ENTRY

GENERAL JOURNAL   PAGE 1

	DATE		DESCRIPTION	POST. REF.	DEBIT	CREDIT	
1	2016						1
2	Jan.	8	Payroll Taxes Expense		171 94		2
3			Social Security Tax Payable			139 35	3
4			Medicare Tax Payable			32 59	4
5			To record social security and				5
6			Medicare taxes for Jan. 8 payroll				6

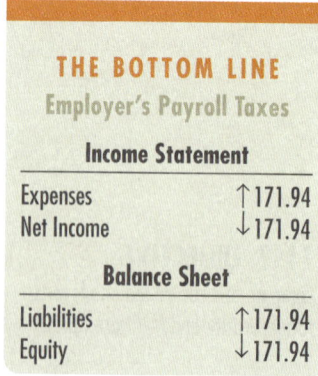

THE BOTTOM LINE

Employer's Payroll Taxes

Income Statement

Expenses	↑171.94
Net Income	↓171.94

Balance Sheet

Liabilities	↑171.94
Equity	↓171.94

According to the Social Security Administration benefits were being paid to approximately 62 million men, women, and children in 2013. It is essential that earnings are correctly reported so that future benefits can be calculated accurately.

RECORDING THE PAYMENT OF TAXES WITHHELD

>> 11-3. OBJECTIVE
Record deposit of social security, Medicare, and employee income taxes.

At the end of January, the accounting records for Tomlin Furniture Company contained the following information:

	Employee (Withheld)	Employer (Matched)	Total
Social security	$ 557.40	$557.40	$1,114.80
Medicare	130.36	130.36	260.72
Federal income tax	620.00	—	620.00
Total	$1,307.76	$687.76	$1,995.52

Tomlin Furniture Company is on a monthly payment schedule. The amount reported in the lookback period is less than $50,000. The payroll tax liability for the quarter ending March 31, 2016, is more than $2,500. (Recall that this textbook uses $2,500 as the tax liability threshold.) A tax payment is due on the 15th day of the following month, February 15.

The tax liability for the first quarter is deposited electronically.

The entry to record the tax deposit is shown below. The entry is shown in general journal form for illustration purposes only. (Tomlin Furniture Company actually uses a cash payments journal.)

	DATE	DESCRIPTION	POST. REF.	DEBIT	CREDIT	
		GENERAL JOURNAL			PAGE 2	
1	2016					1
21						21
22	Feb. 15	Social Security Tax Payable		1 1 1 4 80		22
23		Medicare Tax Payable		2 6 0 72		23
24		Employee Income Tax Payable		6 2 0 00		24
25		Cash			1 9 9 5 52	25
26		Deposit of payroll taxes withholding				26
27		at First State Bank				27
28						28

FEBRUARY PAYROLL RECORDS

There were four weekly payroll periods in February. Each hourly employee worked the same number of hours each week and had the same gross pay and deductions as in January. The office clerk earned her regular salary and had the same deductions as in January. At the end of the month:

■ the individual earnings records were updated;

■ the taxes were deposited before March 15;

■ the tax deposit was recorded in the cash payments journal.

MARCH PAYROLL RECORDS

There were five weekly payroll periods in March. Assume that the payroll period ended on March 31, and the payday was on March 31. Also assume that the earnings and deductions of the employees were the same for each week as in January and February. At the end of the month, the individual earnings records were updated, the taxes were deposited, and the tax deposit was recorded in the cash payments journal.

QUARTERLY SUMMARY OF EARNINGS RECORDS

At the end of each quarter, the individual earnings records are totaled. This involves adding the columns in the Earnings, Deductions, and Net Pay sections. Figure 11.2 shows the earnings record, posted and summarized, for Alicia Martinez for the first quarter.

Table 11.1 shows the quarterly totals for each employee of Tomlin Furniture Company. This information is taken from the individual earnings records. Through the end of the first quarter, no employee has exceeded the social security earnings limit ($113,700) and the FUTA/SUTA limit ($7,000) has only been exceeded by Cecilia Wu.

>> **11-4. OBJECTIVE**

Prepare an Employer's Quarterly Federal Tax Return, Form 941.

EMPLOYER'S QUARTERLY FEDERAL TAX RETURN

Each quarter an employer files an **Employer's Quarterly Federal Tax Return, Form 941** with the Internal Revenue Service. Form 941 must be filed by all employers subject to federal income tax withholding, social security tax, or Medicare tax, with certain exceptions as specified in *Publication 15, Circular E.* This tax return provides information about employee earnings, the tax liability for each month in the quarter, and the deposits made.

FIGURE 11.2   Individual Earnings Record

PAYROLL NO.	DATE WK. END.	DATE PAID	HOURS RG	HOURS OT	EARNINGS REGULAR	EARNINGS OVERTIME	EARNINGS TOTAL	EARNINGS CUMULATIVE	DEDUCTIONS SOCIAL SECURITY	DEDUCTIONS MEDICARE	DEDUCTIONS INCOME TAX	DEDUCTIONS OTHER	NET PAY
1	1/06	1/08	40		400 00		400 00	400 00	24 80	5 80	19 00		350 40
2	1/13	1/15	40		400 00		400 00	400 00	24 80	5 80	19 00		350 40
3	1/20	1/22	40		400 00		400 00	400 00	24 80	5 80	19 00		350 40
4	1/27	1/29	40		400 00		400 00	400 00	24 80	5 80	19 00		350 40
	January				1600 00		1600 00	1600 00	99 20	23 20	76 00		1401 60
1	2/03	2/05	40		400 00		400 00	400 00	24 80	5 80	19 00		350 40
2	2/10	2/12	40		400 00		400 00	400 00	24 80	5 80	19 00		350 40
3	2/17	2/19	40		400 00		400 00	400 00	24 80	5 80	19 00		350 40
4	2/24	2/25	40		400 00		400 00	400 00	24 80	5 80	19 00		350 40
	February				1600 00		1600 00	1600 00	99 20	23 20	76 00		1401 60
1	3/03	3/05	40		400 00		400 00	400 00	24 80	5 80	19 00		350 40
2	3/10	3/12	40		400 00		400 00	400 00	24 80	5 80	19 00		350 40
3	3/17	3/19	40		400 00		400 00	400 00	24 80	5 80	19 00		350 40
4	3/24	3/26	40		400 00		400 00	400 00	24 80	5 80	19 00		350 40
5	3/31	3/31	40		400 00		400 00	400 00	24 80	5 80	19 00		350 40
	March				2000 00		2000 00	2000 00	124 00	29 00	95 00		1752 00
	First Quarter				5200 00		5200 00	5200 00	322 40	75 40	247 00		4555 20

EARNINGS RECORD FOR _2016_

NAME _Alicia Martinez_
ADDRESS _1712 Windmill Hill Lane, Dallas TX 75232-6002_
WITHHOLDING ALLOWANCES _1_

RATE _$10 per hour_

SOCIAL SECURITY NO. _123-45-6789_
DATE OF BIRTH _October 31, 1979_
MARITAL STATUS _M_

| Employee | Taxable Earnings | | | | Deductions | | |
	Total Earnings	Social Security	Medicare	SUTA & FUTA	Social Security	Medicare Tax	Income Tax
Alicia Martinez	5,200.00	5,200.00	5,200.00	5,200.00	322.40	75.40	247.00
Jorge Rodriguez	4,940.00	4,940.00	4,940.00	4,940.00	306.28	71.63	442.00
George Dunlap	5,557.50	5,557.50	5,557.50	5,557.50	344.57	80.58	299.00
Cecilia Wu	7,280.00	7,280.00	7,280.00	7,000.00	451.36	105.56	390.00
Cynthia Booker	6,240.00	6,240.00	6,240.00	6,240.00	386.88	90.48	637.00
Totals	29,217.50	29,217.50	29,217.50	28,937.50	1,811.49	423.65	2,015.00

TABLE 11.1

Summary of Earnings, Quarter Ended March 31, 2016

The Social Security Administration administers the Old Age and Survivors, Disability Insurance, and Supplemental Security Income Programs. These programs are funded by the social security taxes collected from employees and matched by employers. The system currently takes in more in revenue from the 12.4 percent payroll taxes than it pays out in benefits. The trust fund is expected to begin paying out more in benefits than it collects in 2032.

When to File Form 941 The due date for Form 941 is the last day of the month following the end of each calendar quarter. If the taxes for the quarter were deposited when due, the due date is extended by 10 days.

Completing Form 941 Figure 11.3 on pages 370 and 371 shows Form 941 for Tomlin Furniture Company. Form 941 is prepared using the data on the quarterly summary of earnings records shown in Table 11.1. Let's examine Form 941.

- Use the preprinted form if it is available. Otherwise, enter the employer's name, address, and identification number at the top of Form 941. Check the applicable quarter.
- *Line 1* is completed for each quarter. Enter the number of employees for the pay periods indicated.
- *Line 2* shows total wages and tips subject to withholding. For Tomlin Furniture Company the total subject to withholdings is $29,217.50.
- *Line 3* shows the total employee income tax withheld during the quarter, $2,015.00.
- *Line 4* is checked if no wages or tips are subject to social security or Medicare tax.
- *Line 5a* shows the total amount of wages that are subject to social security taxes, $29,217.50. The amount is multiplied by the combined social security rate, 12.4 percent.

Social Security Tax:	
Employee's share	6.2%
Employer's share	6.2
Total	12.4%

The amount of taxes is $3,622.97 ($29,217.50 × 12.4%).

- *Line 5b* is left blank since no employees at Tomlin Furniture Company had taxable social security tips.

important!

Quarters

A quarter is a three-month period. There are four quarters in a year:

- 1st quarter: January, February, March
- 2nd quarter: April, May, June
- 3rd quarter: July, August, September
- 4th quarter: October, November, December

FIGURE 11.3   Employer's Quarterly Federal Tax Return, Form 941

Form **941 for 2016:** **Employer's Quarterly Federal Tax Return**   9901

Department of the Treasury — Internal Revenue Service

OMB No. 1545-0029

Employer identification number   7 5 – 1 2 3 4 5 6 7

Name *(not your trade name)*   Sarah Tomlin

Trade name *(if any)*   Tomlin Furniture Company

Address   5910 Lake June Road

Number	Street		Suite or room number
Dallas		TX	75232-6017
City		State	ZIP code

Report for this Quarter ...
(Check one.)

- ☑ **1:** January, February, March
- ☐ **2:** April, May, June
- ☐ **3:** July, August, September
- ☐ **4:** October, November, December

Read the separate instructions before you fill out this form. Please type or print within the boxes.

Part 1: Answer these questions for this quarter.

1 Number of employees who received wages, tips, or other compensation for the pay period including: *Mar. 16* (Quarter 1), *June 16* (Quarter 2), *Sept. 16* (Quarter 3), *Dec. 16* (Quarter 4)   **1**   5

2 Wages, tips, and other compensation . . . .   **2**   29,217 . 50

3 Total income tax withheld from wages, tips, and other compensation . . . .   **3**   2,015 . 00

4 If no wages, tips, and other compensation are subject to social security or Medicare tax . .   ☐ Check and go to line 6.

5 Taxable social security and Medicare wages and tips:

	Column 1		Column 2
5a Taxable social security wages	29,217 . 50	× .124 =	3,622 . 97
5b Taxable social security tips	.	× .124 =	.
5c Taxable Medicare wages & tips	29,217 . 50	× .029 =	847 . 31

5d Total social security and Medicare taxes (*Column 2*, lines 5a + 5b + 5c = line 5d) . . **5d**   4,470 . 28

6 Total taxes before adjustments (lines 3 + 5d = line 6) . . . .   **6**   6,485 . 28

7 Tax adjustments (If your answer is a negative number, write it in brackets.):

7a Current quarter's fractions of cents . . . .

7b Current quarter's sick pay . . . .

7c Current quarter's adjustments for tips and group-term life insurance   .

7d Current year's income tax withholding (Attach Form 941c) . . .   .

7e Prior quarters' social security and Medicare taxes (Attach Form 941c)   .

7f Special additions to federal income tax (reserved use) . . . . .   .

7g Special additions to social security and Medicare (reserved use)   .

7h Total adjustments (Combine all amounts: lines 7a through 7g.) . . . . **7h**   .

8 Total taxes after adjustments (Combine lines 6 and 7h.) . . . .   **8**   6,485 . 28

9 Advance earned income credit (EIC) payments made to employees . . . . . .   **9**   .

10 Total taxes after adjustment for advance EIC (lines 8 – 9 = line 10) . . . . .   **10**   6,485 . 28

11 Total deposits for this quarter, including overpayment applied from a prior quarter . .   **11**   6,485 . 28

12 Balance due (lines 10 – 11 = line 12) Make checks payable to the *United States Treasury* . .   **12**   0 .

13 Overpayment (If line 11 is more than line 10, write the difference here.)   .   Check one ☐ Apply to next return.
☐ Send a refund.

Next ➡

For Privacy Act and Paperwork Reduction Act Notice, see the back of the Payment Voucher.   Cat. No. 17001Z   Form **941**

FIGURE 11.3 (concluded)

9902

Name *(not your trade name)*	Employer identification number
Sarah Tomlin	**75-1234567**

Part 2: Tell us about your deposit schedule for this quarter.

If you are unsure about whether you are a monthly schedule depositor or a semiweekly schedule depositor, see *Pub. 15 (Circular E)*, section 11.

14 **T X** Write the state abbreviation for the state where you made your deposits OR write "MU" if you made your deposits in *multiple* states.

15 Check one: ☐ Line 10 is less than $2,500. Go to Part 3.

☑ **You were a monthly schedule depositor for the entire quarter. Fill out your tax liability for each month.** Then go to Part 3.

Tax liability:	Month 1	1,995 . 52
	Month 2	1,995 . 52
	Month 3	2,494 . 24
	Total	6,485 . 28	Total must equal line 10.

☐ **You were a semiweekly schedule depositor for any part of this quarter.** Fill out *Schedule B (Form 941): Report of Tax Liability for Semiweekly Schedule Depositors*, and attach it to this form.

Part 3: Tell us about your business. If a question does NOT apply to your business, leave it blank.

16 If your business has closed and you do not have to file returns in the future . . . . ☐ Check here, and

enter the final date you paid wages [/   /   ] .

17 If you are a seasonal employer and you do not have to file a return for every quarter of the year . . ☐ Check here.

Part 4: May we contact your third-party designee?

Do you want to allow an employee, a paid tax preparer, or another person to discuss this return with the IRS? See the instructions for details.

☐ Yes. Designee's name

Phone (   )   –   Personal Identification Number (PIN) ☐ ☐ ☐ ☐ ☐

☑ No.

Part 5: Sign here

Under penalties of perjury, I declare that I have examined this return, including accompanying schedules and statements, and to the best of my knowledge and belief, it is true, correct, and complete.

X

Sign your name here *Sarah Tomlin*

Print name and title **Sarah Tomlin, Owner**

Date 04 / 30 / 16   Phone (972) 709 – 4567

Part 6: For paid preparers only *(optional)*

Preparer's signature		
Firm's name		
Address		EIN
		ZIP code
Date / / Phone ( ) –		SSN/PTIN

☐ Check if you are self-employed.

■ *Line 5c* shows the total amount of wages that are subject to Medicare taxes, $29,217.50. The amount is multiplied by the combined Medicare tax rate, 2.9 percent.

Medicare Tax:	
Employee's share	1.45%
Employer's share	1.45
Total	2.90%

The amount of taxes is $847.31 ($29,217.50 × 2.90%).

■ *Line 5d* shows the total social security and Medicare taxes, $4,470.28.

■ *Line 6* shows the total tax liability for withheld income taxes, social security, and Medicare Taxes, $6,485.28.

■ *Lines 7a* through *7h* are for adjustments. Tomlin Furniture Company had no adjustments this quarter. If there is a difference due to rounding that difference can be adjusted on line 7a.

■ *Line 8* shows total taxes after adjustments, $6,485.28.

■ *Line 9* is for deducting the amount of any advance earned income credit payments to employees. Tomlin Furniture Company had no advance payments for earned income credit payments to employees.

■ *Line 10* shows total taxes after adjustments, $6,485.28.

■ *Line 11* shows total deposits made during the quarter including overpayments applied from a prior quarter, $6,485.28.

■ Any balance due is entered on *Line 12* or overpayment is entered on *Line 13*.

■ The state where deposits were made is entered on *Line 14*.

■ *Line 15* shows the monthly deposits made by Tomlin Furniture Company.

recall

Tax Calculations
Social security and Medicare taxes are calculated by multiplying the taxable wages by the tax rate.

Notice that on Line 15 if the amount of taxes is less than $2,500, the amount may be paid with the return or with a financial depositor. There is no need to complete the record of monthly deposits. Since the amount of taxes due for Tomlin Furniture Company is greater than $2,500, and Tomlin is a monthly depositor, the record of monthly tax deposits must be completed on Line 15. The total deposits shown on Line 15 must equal the taxes shown on Line 10.

If the employer did not deduct enough taxes from an employee's earnings, the business pays the difference. The deficiency is debited to ***Payroll Taxes Expense.***

Wage and Tax Statement, Form W-2

Employers provide a **Wage and Tax Statement, Form W-2,** to each employee by January 31 for the previous calendar year's earnings. Form W-2 is sometimes called a **withholding statement.** Form W-2 contains information about the employee's earnings and tax withholdings for the year. The information for Form W-2 comes from the employee's earnings record.

Employees who stop working for the business during the year may ask that a Form W-2 be issued early. The Form W-2 must be issued within 30 days after the request or after the final wage payment, whichever is later.

Figure 11.4 on page 373 shows Form W-2 for Alicia Martinez. This is the standard form provided by the Internal Revenue Service (IRS). Some employers use a "substitute" Form W-2 that is approved by the IRS. The substitute form permits the employer to list total deductions and to reconcile the gross earnings, the deductions, and the net pay. If the firm issues 250 or more Forms W-2, the returns must be filed electronically.

At least four copies of each of Form W-2 are prepared:

>> **11-5. OBJECTIVE**
Prepare Wage and Tax Statement (Form W-2) and Annual Transmittal of Wage and Tax Statements (Form W-3).

1. One copy for the employer to send to the Social Security Administration, which shares the information with the IRS.

FIGURE 11.4   Wage and Tax Statement, Form W-2

a Control number З З З З З Void ☐	For Official Use Only ▶ OMB No. 1545-0008		
b Employer identification number 75-1234567	**1** Wages, tips, other compensation 20,800.00	**2** Federal income tax withheld 988.00	
c Employer's name, address, and ZIP code Tomlin Furniture Co. 5910 Lake June Road Dallas, TX 75232-6017	**3** Social security wages 20,800.00	**4** Social security tax withheld 1,289.60	
	5 Medicare wages and tips 20,800.00	**6** Medicare tax withheld 301.60	
	7 Social security tips	**8** Allocated tips	
d Employee's social security number 123-45-6789	**9** Advance EIC payment	**10** Dependent care benefits	
e Employee's first name and initial Alicia Last name Martinez	**11** Nonqualified plans	**12a** See instructions for box 12	
1712 Windmill Hill Lane Dallas, Texas 75232-6002	**13** Statutory employee ☐ Retirement plan ☐ Third-party sick pay ☐	**12b**	
	14 Other	**12c**	
		12d	
f Employee's address and ZIP code			

15 State Employer's state I.D. no. TX | 12-9876500	**16** State wages, tips, etc. 20,800.00	**17** State income tax	**18** Local wages, tips, etc.	**19** Local income tax	**20** Locality name

Form **W-2** Wage and Tax Statement   20 16

Copy A For Social Security Administration—Send this entire page with Form W-3 to the Social Security Administration; photocopies are **not** acceptable.   Cat. No. 10134D

Department of the Treasury—Internal Revenue Service **For Privacy Act and Paperwork Reduction Act Notice, see back of Copy D.**

Do NOT Cut, Fold, or Staple Forms on This Page—Do NOT Cut, Fold, or Staple Forms on This Page

2. One copy for the employee to attach to the federal income tax return.

3. One copy for the employee's records.

4. One copy for the employer's records.

   If there is a state income tax, two more copies of Form W-2 are prepared:

5. One copy for the employer to send to the state tax department.

6. One copy for the employee to attach to the state income tax return.

   Additional copies are prepared if there is a city or county income tax.

Annual Transmittal of Wage and Tax Statements, Form W-3

The **Transmittal of Wage and Tax Statements, Form W-3,** is submitted with Forms W-2 to the Social Security Administration. Form W-3 reports the total social security wages; total Medicare wages; total social security tax withheld; total Medicare tax withheld; total wages, tips, and other compensation; total federal income tax withheld; and other information.

A copy of Form W-2 for each employee is attached to Form W-3. Form W-3 is due by the last day of February following the end of the calendar year. The Social Security Administration shares the tax information on Forms W-2 with the Internal Revenue Service. Figure 11.5 on page 374 shows the completed Form W-3 for Tomlin Furniture Company.

important!

Form W-2

The employer must provide each employee with a Wage and Tax Statement, Form W-2, by January 31 of the following year. All payroll forms are revised each year. Those used in the text are illustrative of current forms at the time of publication.

FIGURE 11.5

Transmittal of Wage and Tax Statements, Form W-3

a Control number	33333	For Official Use Only ▶ OMB No. 1545-0008		

| b | Kind of Payer ▶ | 941 ☒ CT-1 ☐ | Military ☐ Hshld. emp. ☐ | 943 ☐ Medicare govt. emp. ☐ | Third-party sick pay ☐ | 1 Wages, tips, other compensation 116,870.00 | 2 Federal income tax withheld 8,060.00 |

3 Social security wages 116,870.00	4 Social security tax withheld 7,245.96

| c Total number of Forms W-2 5 | d Establishment number | 5 Medicare wages and tips 116,870.00 | 6 Medicare tax withheld 1,694.60 |

| e Employer identification number 75-1234567 | 7 Social security tips | 8 Allocated tips |

| f Employer's name Tomlin Furniture Co. | 9 Advance EIC payments | 10 Dependent care benefits |

| 11 Nonqualified plans | 12 Deferred compensation |

5910 Lake June Road
Dallas, TX 75232-6017

| 13 For third-party sick pay use only |

| 14 Income tax withheld by third-party sick pay |

g Employer's address and ZIP code
h Other EIN used this year

15 State TX	Employer's state I.D. no. 12-9876500	16 State wages, tips, etc.	17 State income tax
		18 Local wages, tips, etc.	19 Local income tax

Contact person Sarah Tomlin	Telephone number (972) 709-4567	For Official Use Only
E-mail address	Fax number ( )	

Under penalties of perjury, I declare that I have examined this return and accompanying documents, and, to the best of my knowledge and belief, they are true, correct, and complete.

Signature ▶ *Sarah Tamlin*   Title ▶ *Owner*   Date ▶ *February 10, 2017*

Form **W-3** Transmittal of Wage and Tax Statements   **2016**   Department of the Treasury
Internal Revenue Service

The amounts on Form W-3 must equal the sums of the amounts on the attached Forms W-2. For example, the amount entered in Box 1 of Form W-3 must equal the sum of the amounts entered in Box 1 of all the Forms W-2.

The amounts on Form W-3 also must equal the sums of the amounts reported on the Forms 941 during the year. For example, the social security wages reported on the Form W-3 must equal the sum of the social security wages reported on the four Forms 941.

The filing of Form W-3 marks the end of the routine procedures needed to account for payrolls and for payroll tax withholdings.

Section 1   Self Review

QUESTIONS

1. What is the purpose of Form W-2?
2. How does a business deposit federal payroll taxes?
3. What is the purpose of Form 941?

EXERCISES

4. Which tax is paid equally by the employee and employer?
   a. Federal income tax
   b. State income tax
   c. Social security tax
   d. Federal unemployment tax

5. Employers usually record social security taxes in the accounting records at the end of:
   a. each payroll period.
   b. each month.
   c. each quarter.
   d. the year.

ANALYSIS

6. Your business currently owes $2,910 in payroll taxes. During the lookback period, your business paid $10,000 in payroll taxes. How often does your business need to make payroll tax deposits?

(Answers to Section 1 Self Review are on page 396.)

Section 2

SECTION OBJECTIVES	TERMS TO LEARN
>> 11-6. Compute and record liability for federal and state unemployment taxes and record payment of the taxes. **WHY IT'S IMPORTANT** Businesses need to record all payroll tax liabilities. **>> 11-7.** Prepare an Employer's Federal Unemployment Tax Return, Form 940. **WHY IT'S IMPORTANT** The unemployment insurance programs provide support to individuals during temporary periods of unemployment. **>> 11-8.** Compute and record workers' compensation insurance premiums. **WHY IT'S IMPORTANT** Businesses need insurance to cover workplace injury claims.	Employer's Annual Federal Unemployment Tax Return, Form 940 experience rating system merit rating system unemployment insurance program

Unemployment Tax and Workers' Compensation

In Section 1, we discussed taxes that are withheld from employees' earnings and, in some cases, matched by the employer. In this section, we will discuss payroll related expenses that are paid solely by the employer.

Unemployment Compensation Insurance Taxes

The unemployment compensation tax program, often called the **unemployment insurance program,** provides unemployment compensation through a tax levied on employers.

COORDINATION OF FEDERAL AND STATE UNEMPLOYMENT RATES

The unemployment insurance program is a federal program that encourages states to provide unemployment insurance for employees working in the state. The federal government allows a credit—or reduction—in the federal unemployment tax for amounts charged by the state for unemployment taxes.

This text assumes that the federal unemployment tax rate is 6.0 percent less a state unemployment tax credit of 5.4 percent; thus, the federal tax rate is reduced to 0.6 percent (6.0% − 5.4%). The earnings limits for the federal and the state unemployment tax are usually the same, $7,000.

A few states levy an unemployment tax on the employee. The tax is withheld from employee pay and remitted by the employer to the state.

For businesses that provide steady employment, the state unemployment tax rate may be lowered based on an **experience rating system,** or a **merit rating system.** Under the experience rating system, the state tax rate may be reduced to less than 1 percent for businesses that provide steady employment. In contrast, some states levy penalty rates as high as 10 percent for employers with poor records of providing steady employment.

The reduction of state unemployment taxes because of favorable experience ratings does not affect the credit allowable against the federal tax. An employer may take a credit against the federal unemployment tax as though it were paid at the normal state rate even though the employer actually pays the state a lower rate.

Because of its experience rating, Tomlin Furniture Company pays state unemployment tax of 4.0 percent, which is less than the standard rate of 5.4 percent. Note that the business may take the credit for the full amount of the state rate (5.4%) against the federal rate, even though the business actually pays a state rate of 4.0%.

>> 11-6. OBJECTIVE

Compute and record liability for federal and state unemployment taxes and record payment of the taxes.

COMPUTING AND RECORDING UNEMPLOYMENT TAXES

Tomlin Furniture Company records its state and federal unemployment tax expense at the end of each payroll period. The unemployment taxes for the payroll period ending January 6 are as follows:

Federal unemployment tax	($2,247.50 × 0.006)	=	$ 13.49
State unemployment tax	($2,247.50 × 0.040)	=	89.90
Total unemployment taxes		=	$103.39

The entry to record the employer's unemployment payroll taxes follows.

	DATE		DESCRIPTION	POST. REF.	DEBIT	CREDIT	
	GENERAL JOURNAL					PAGE 1	
1	2016						1
8	Jan.	8	Payroll Taxes Expense		103 39		8
9			Federal Unemployment Tax Payable			13 49	9
10			State Unemployment Tax Payable			89 90	10
11			Unemployment taxes on				11
12			weekly payroll				12

REPORTING AND PAYING STATE UNEMPLOYMENT TAXES

In most states, the due date for the unemployment tax return is the last day of the month following the end of the quarter. Generally, the tax is paid, electronically, with the return.

Employer's Quarterly Report Each state requires reporting of wages for unemployment tax purposes. Since Tomlin Furniture Company is located in Texas, it will complete the Texas state unemployment tax form and submit the tax due. Generally, each state requires quarterly reporting of wages and depositing of state unemployment taxes due. Amounts of wages subject to tax and the state tax rate are determined by each state.

Tomlin Furniture Company submits the report and issues a check payable to the state tax authority for the amount due. The entry is recorded in the cash payments journal. The transaction is shown here in general journal form for purposes of illustration:

	DATE		DESCRIPTION	POST. REF.	DEBIT	CREDIT	
	GENERAL JOURNAL					PAGE	
1	2016						1
2	Apr.	29	State Unemployment Tax Payable		1 157 50		2
3			Cash			1 157 50	3
4			Paid SUTA taxes for quarter				4
5			ending March 31				5
6							6

Earnings in Excess of Base Amount State unemployment tax is paid on the first $7,000 of annual earnings for each employee. Earnings over $7,000 are not subject to state unemployment tax.

For example, Cecilia Wu earns $560 every week of the year. Table 11.1 on page 369 shows that she earned $7,280 at the end of the first quarter. In the four weeks of January, February, and March, she earned $2,240 ($560 × 4).

	Earnings	Cumulative Earnings
January	$2,240	$2,240
February	2,240	4,480
March	2,240	6,720
March, week 5	560	7,280

In the fifth week of March, Wu earned $560, but only $280 of it is subject to state unemployment tax ($7,000 earnings limit − $6,720 cumulative earnings = $280). For the rest of the calendar year, Wu's earnings are not subject to state unemployment tax.

REPORTING AND PAYING FEDERAL UNEMPLOYMENT TAXES

The rules for reporting and depositing federal unemployment taxes differ from those used for social security and Medicare taxes.

Depositing Federal Unemployment Taxes Generally, federal unemployment tax payments are electronically deposited through EFTPS. Deposits are made quarterly and are due on the last day of the month following the end of the quarter.

The federal unemployment tax is calculated at the end of each quarter. It is computed by multiplying the first $7,000 of each employee's wages by 0.006. A deposit is required when more than $500 of federal unemployment tax is owed. If $500 or less is owed, no deposit is due. Any deposit due of $500 or more should be electronically deposited.

For example, suppose that a business calculates its federal unemployment tax to be $325 at the end of the first quarter. Since it is not more than $500, no deposit is due. At the end of the second quarter, it calculates its federal unemployment taxes on second quarter wages to be $200. The total undeposited unemployment tax now is more than $500, so a deposit is required.

First quarter undeposited tax	$325
Second quarter undeposited tax	200
Total deposit due	$525

In the case of Tomlin Furniture Company, the company owed $173.63 in federal unemployment tax at the end of March. Since this is less than $500, no deposit is due.

Month	Taxable Earnings Paid	Rate	Tax Due	Deposit Due Date
January	$ 8,990.00	0.006	$ 53.94	April 30
February	8,990.00	0.006	53.94	April 30
March	10,957.50	0.006	65.75	April 30
Total	$28,937.50		$173.63	

The payment of federal unemployment tax is recorded by debiting the *Federal Unemployment Tax Payable* account and crediting the *Cash* account.

Reporting Federal Unemployment Tax, Form 940 Tax returns are not due quarterly for the federal unemployment tax. The employer submits an annual return. The **Employer's Annual Federal Unemployment Tax Return, Form 940,** is a preprinted government form used to

>> **11-7. OBJECTIVE**

Prepare an Employer's Federal Unemployment Tax Return, Form 940.

report unemployment taxes for the calendar year. It is due by January 31 of the following year. The due date is extended to February 10 if all tax deposits were made on time.

The information needed to complete Form 940 comes from the annual summary of individual earnings records and from the state unemployment tax returns filed during the year.

Figure 11.6 shows Form 940 prepared for Tomlin Furniture Company. Refer to it as you learn how to complete Form 940.

PART 1: Asks the filer if he or she was required to pay SUTA tax in more than one state.

PART 2: Determine your FUTA tax before adjustments

- *Line 3* shows the total compensation paid to employees, $116,870.00.
- *Line 4* is blank because there were no exempt payments for Tomlin Furniture Company.
- *Line 5* shows the compensation that exceeds the $7,000 earnings limit, $81,870 ($116,870 − $35,000).
- *Line 6* shows the wages not subject to federal unemployment tax, $81,870.
- *Line 7* shows the taxable wages for the year, $35,000. This amount must agree with the total taxable FUTA wages shown on the individual employee earnings records for the year.
- *Line 8* shows the FUTA tax, $210 ($35,000 × 0.006).

PART 3: Determine your adjustments.

- *Lines 9, 10, and 11* are blank because Tomlin Furniture Company had no adjustments.

PART 4: Determine your FUTA tax and balance due or over payment.

- *Line 12* shows the total FUTA tax, after adjustments, $210.
- *Line 13* shows the FUTA tax deposited during the year, $0.
- *Line 14* shows the balance due.
- *Line 15* is blank because there is no overpayment.

PART 5: Report your FUTA tax liability by quarter. This section is not applicable to Tomlin Furniture Company, because its total FUTA liability is less than $500.

>> 11-8. OBJECTIVE

Compute and record workers' compensation insurance premiums.

WORKERS' COMPENSATION INSURANCE

Workers' compensation provides benefits for employees who are injured on the job. The insurance premium, which is paid by the employer, depends on the risk involved with the work performed. It is important to classify earnings according to the type of work the employees perform and to summarize labor costs according to the insurance premium classifications.

For instance, workers' compensation insurance will cost much more for workers in a coal mine or on an oil rig than it will for workers in an office setting. Insurance companies will have different rates for each category of risk of a company's workers.

There are two ways to handle workers' compensation insurance. The method a business uses depends on the number of its employees.

Estimated Annual Premium in Advance. Employers who have few employees pay an estimated premium in advance. At the end of the year, the employer calculates the actual premium. If the actual premium is more than the estimated premium paid, the employer pays the balance due. If the actual premium is less than the estimated premium paid, the employer receives a refund.

Tomlin Furniture Company has two work classifications: office work and shipping work. The workers' compensation premium rates are:

Office workers	$0.45 per $100 of labor costs
Shipping workers	1.25 per $100 of labor costs

FIGURE 11.6 Employer's Annual Federal Unemployment Tax Return, Form 940

Form **940 for 2016:** **Employer's Annual Federal Unemployment (FUTA) Tax Return**

850109

Department of the Treasury — Internal Revenue Service

OMB No. 1545-0028

(EIN) Employer identification number: 75 – 1 2 3 4 5 6 7

Name (not your trade name): Sarah Tomlin

Trade name (if any): Tomlin Furniture Company

Address: 5910 June Lake Road

Dallas TX 75322-6017

Type of Return (Check all that apply.)

- a. Amended
- b. Successor employer
- c. No payments to employees in 2016
- d. Final: Business closed or stopped paying wages

Read the separate instructions before you fill out this form. Please type or print within the boxes.

Part 1: Tell us about your return. If any line does NOT apply, leave it blank.

1 If you were required to pay your state unemployment tax in ...

1a One state only, write the state abbreviation . . . . 1a **T X**

- OR -

1b More than one state (You are a multi-state employer) . . . . 1b Check here. Fill out Schedule A.

2 If you paid wages in a state that is subject to CREDIT REDUCTION . . . . . 2 Check here. Fill out Schedule A (Form 940), Part 2.

Part 2: Determine your FUTA tax before adjustments for 2016. If any line does NOT apply, leave it blank.

3 Total payments to all employees 3 116870.00

4 Payments exempt from FUTA tax 4

Check all that apply: 4a Fringe benefits 4c Retirement/Pension 4e Other 4b Group-term life insurance 4d Dependent care

5 Total of payments made to each employee in excess of $7,000 5 81870.00

6 Subtotal (line 4 + line 5 = line 6) 6 81870.00

7 Total taxable FUTA wages (line 3 – line 6 = line 7) . . 7 35000.00

8 FUTA tax before adjustments (line 7 × .006 = line 8) 8 210.00

Part 3: Determine your adjustments. If any line does NOT apply, leave it blank.

9 If ALL of the taxable FUTA wages you paid were excluded from state unemployment tax, multiply line 7 by .054 (line 7 × .054 = line 9). Then go to line 12 . . . 9

10 If SOME of the taxable FUTA wages you paid were excluded from state unemployment tax, OR you paid ANY state unemployment tax late (after the due date for filing Form 940), fill out the worksheet in the instructions. Enter the amount from line 7 of the worksheet 10

11 If credit reduction applies, enter the amount from line 3 of Schedule A (Form 940) 11

Part 4: Determine your FUTA tax and balance due or overpayment for 2016. If any line does NOT apply, leave it blank.

12 Total FUTA tax after adjustments (lines 8 + 9 + 10 + 11 = line 12) 12 210.00

13 FUTA tax deposited for the year, including any overpayment applied from a prior year . . 13 0.00

14 Balance due (If line 12 is more than line 13, enter the difference on line 14.)
- If line 14 is more than $500, you must deposit your tax.
- If line 14 is $500 or less, you may pay with this return. For more information on how to pay, see the separate instructions 14 210.00

15 Overpayment (If line 13 is more than line 12, enter the difference on line 15 and check a box below.) . . 15

Check one: Apply to next return. Send a refund.

▶ You **MUST** fill out both pages of this form and **SIGN** it.

Next ➡

For Privacy Act and Paperwork Reduction Act Notice, see the back of Form 940-V, Payment Voucher. Cat. No. 11234O Form **940**

FIGURE 11.6   (concluded)

850209

Name (not your trade name)	Employer identification number (EIN)
Sarah Tomlin	75-123456

Part 5: Report your FUTA tax liability by quarter only if line 12 is more than $500. If not, go to Part 6.

16 Report the amount of your FUTA tax liability for each quarter; do NOT enter the amount you deposited. If you had no liability for a quarter, leave the line blank.

16a **1st quarter** (January 1 – March 31) . . . . 16a [.   ]

16b **2nd quarter** (April 1 – June 30) . . . . 16b [.   ]

16c **3rd quarter** (July 1 – September 30) . . . . 16c [.   ]

16d **4th quarter** (October 1 – December 31) . . . . . 16d [.   ]

17 **Total tax liability for the year** (lines 16a + 16b + 16c + 16d = line 17) **17** [.   ] Total must equal line 12.

Part 6: May we speak with your third-party designee?

Do you want to allow an employee, a paid tax preparer, or another person to discuss this return with the IRS? See the instructions for details.

☐ **Yes.**   Designee's name and phone number [   ]   (   )   –

Select a 5-digit Personal Identification Number (PIN) to use when talking to IRS [ ][ ][ ][ ][ ]

☑ **No.**

Part 7: Sign here. You MUST fill out both pages of this form and SIGN it.

Under penalties of perjury, I declare that I have examined this return, including accompanying schedules and statements, and to the best of my knowledge and belief, it is true, correct, and complete, and that no part of any payment made to a state unemployment fund claimed as a credit was, or is to be, deducted from the payments made to employees. Declaration of preparer (other than taxpayer) is based on all information of which preparer has any knowledge.

X Sign your name here	*Sarah Tomlin*	Print your name here	Sarah Tomlin
		Print your title here	Owner
Date	01 / 31 / 2017	Best daytime phone	(972) 123 – 8766

Paid preparer's use only   Check if you are self-employed . . . ☐

Preparer's name	[ ]	Preparer's SSN/PTIN	[ ]
Preparer's signature	[ ]	Date	/ /
Firm's name (or yours if self-employed)	[ ]	EIN	[ ]
Address	[ ]	Phone	( ) –
City	[ ] State [ ]	ZIP code	[ ]

The insurance premium rates recognize that injuries are more likely to occur to shipping workers than to office workers. Based on employee earnings for the previous year, Tomlin Furniture Company paid an estimated premium of $1,000 for the new year. The payment was made on January 15.

	DATE		DESCRIPTION	POST. REF.	DEBIT	CREDIT	
	GENERAL JOURNAL					PAGE _____	
1	2016						1
14	Jan.	15	Prepaid Workers' Compensation Insurance Expense		1 000 00		14
15			Cash			1 000 00	15
16			Estimated workers' compensation				16
17			insurance for 2016				17
18							18

At the end of the year, the actual premium was computed, $1,261.20. The actual premium was computed by applying the proper rates to the payroll data for the year:

- The office wages were $24,960.

  ($24,960 ÷ $100) × $0.45 =

  249.60 × $0.45 = $ 112.32

- The shipping wages were $91,910.

  ($91,910 ÷ $100) × $1.25 =

  919.1 × $1.25 = $1,148.88

- Total premium for year   = $1,261.20

Classification	Payroll	Rate	Premium
Office work	$24,960	$0.45 per $100	$ 112.32
Shipping work	91,910	1.25 per $100	1,148.88
Total premium for year			$1,261.20
Less estimated premium paid			1,000.00
Balance of premium due			$ 261.20

MANAGERIAL IMPLICATIONS

PAYROLL TAXES

- Management must ensure that payroll taxes are computed properly and paid on time.
- In order to avoid penalties, it is essential that a business prepares its payroll tax returns accurately and files the returns and required forms promptly.
- The payroll system should ensure that payroll reports are prepared in an efficient manner.
- Managers need to be familiar with all payroll taxes and how they impact operating expenses.

- Managers must be knowledgeable about unemployment tax regulations in their state because favorable experience ratings can reduce unemployment tax expense.
- Management is responsible for developing effective internal control procedures over payroll operations and ensuring that they are followed.

THINKING CRITICALLY

What accounting records are used to prepare Form 941?

On December 31, the balance due to the insurance company is recorded as a liability by an adjusting entry. Tomlin Furniture Company owes $261.20 ($1,261.20 − $1,000.00) for the workers' compensation insurance.

	DATE		DESCRIPTION	POST. REF.	DEBIT	CREDIT	
1	2016						1
2	Dec.	31	Workers' Compensation Insurance Expense		2 6 1 20		2
3			Workers' Compensation Insurance Payable			2 6 1 20	3
4							4

GENERAL JOURNAL   PAGE _____

Additionally, an adjusting journal would be recorded on December 31, 2016, for prepaid workers' compensation insurance expired.

Suppose that on January 15, Tomlin Furniture Company had paid an estimated premium of $1,400 instead of $1,000. The actual premium at the end of the year was $1,261.20. Tomlin Furniture Company would be due a refund from the insurance company for the amount overpaid, $138.80 ($1,400.00 − $1,261.20).

Deposit and Monthly Premium Payments Employers with many employees use a different method to handle workers' compensation insurance. At the beginning of the year, they make large deposits, often 25 percent of the estimated annual premium. From January through November, they pay the actual premium due based on an audit of the month's wages. The premium for the last month is deducted from the deposit. Any balance is refunded or applied toward the following year's deposit.

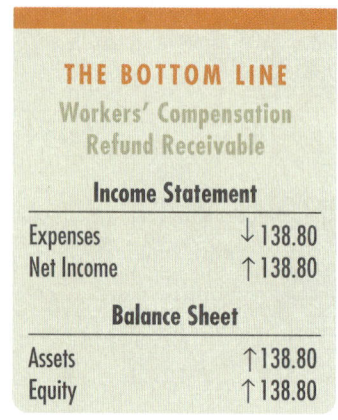

THE BOTTOM LINE

Workers' Compensation
Refund Receivable

Income Statement

Expenses	↓ 138.80
Net Income	↑ 138.80

Balance Sheet

Assets	↑ 138.80
Equity	↑ 138.80

Internal Control over Payroll Operations

Now that we have examined the basic accounting procedures used for payrolls and payroll taxes, let's look at some internal control procedures that are recommended to protect payroll operations.

1. Assign only highly responsible, well-trained employees to work in payroll operations.
2. Keep payroll records in locked files. Train payroll employees to maintain confidentiality about pay rates and other information in the payroll records.
3. Add new employees to the payroll system and make all changes in employee pay rates only with proper written authorization from management.
4. Make changes to an employee's withholding allowances based only on a Form W-4 properly completed and signed by the employee.
5. Make voluntary deductions from employee earnings based only on a signed authorization from the employee.
6. Have the payroll checks examined by someone other than the person who prepares them. Compare each check to the entry for the employee in the payroll register.
7. Have payroll checks distributed to the employees by someone other than the person who prepares them.
8. Have the monthly payroll bank account statement received and reconciled by someone other than the person who prepares the payroll checks.
9. Use prenumbered forms for the payroll checks. Periodically the numbers of the checks issued and the numbers of the unused checks should be verified to make sure that all checks can be accounted for.
10. Maintain files of all authorization forms for adding new employees, changing pay rates, and making voluntary deductions. Also retain all Forms W-4.

Section 2   Self Review

QUESTIONS

1. Why is it important for workers' compensation wages to be classified according to the type of work performed?

2. Who pays the federal unemployment tax? The state unemployment tax?

3. How does a favorable experience rating affect the state unemployment tax rate?

EXERCISES

4. State unemployment taxes are filed:
   a. monthly.
   b. quarterly.
   c. yearly.
   d. at the end of each pay period.

5. The federal unemployment taxes are reported on:
   a. Form 941.
   b. Form 8109.
   c. Form W-3.
   d. Form 940.

ANALYSIS

6. At the end of the year, the business has a balance due for workers' compensation insurance. If no adjusting entry is made, will the amount of net income reported be correct? If not, how will it be wrong?

(Answers to Section 2 Self Review are on page 396.)

11 Chapter   REVIEW   Chapter Summary

Employers must pay social security, SUTA, FUTA, and Medicare taxes. They must also collect federal and state taxes from their employees and then remit those taxes to the appropriate taxing authorities. In this chapter, you have learned how to compute the employer's taxes and how to file the required tax returns and reports.

Learning Objectives

11-1 Explain how and when payroll taxes are paid to the government.

Employers act as collection agents for social security, Medicare, and federal income taxes withheld from employee earnings. Employers must remit these sums, with their own share of social security and Medicare taxes, to the government. The taxes must be deposited in an authorized depository, usually a commercial bank. The methods and schedules for deposits vary according to the sums involved.

11-2 Compute and record the employer's social security and Medicare taxes.

Employers should multiply the social security and Medicare tax rates by taxable wages to compute the employer's portion of taxes due.

11-3 Record deposit of social security, Medicare, and employee income taxes.

As taxes are paid to the government, the accounting records should be updated to reflect the payment, thereby reducing tax liability accounts.

11-4 Prepare an Employer's Quarterly Federal Tax Return, Form 941.

The Form 941 reports wages paid, federal employee income tax withheld, and applicable social security and Medicare taxes.

11-5 Prepare Wage and Tax Statement (Form W-2) and Annual Transmittal of Wage and Tax Statements (Form W-3).

By the end of January, each employee must be given a Wage and Tax Statement, Form W-2, showing the previous year's earnings and withholdings for social security, Medicare, and employee income tax. The employer files a Transmittal of Wage and Tax Statements, Form W-3, with copies of employees' Forms W-2.

Form W-3 is due by the last day of February following the end of the calendar year.

11-6 Compute and record liability for federal and state unemployment taxes and record payment of the taxes.

Unemployment insurance taxes are paid by the employer to both state and federal governments. State unemployment tax returns differ from state to state but usually require a list of employees, their social security numbers, and taxable wages paid. The rate of state unemployment tax depends on the employer's experience rating. The net federal unemployment tax rate can be as low as 0.8 percent.

11-7 Prepare an Employer's Federal Unemployment Tax Return, Form 940.

An Employer's Annual Federal Unemployment Tax Return, Form 940, must be filed in January for the preceding calendar year. The form shows the total wages paid, the amount of wages subject to unemployment tax, and the federal unemployment tax owed for the year. A credit is allowed against gross federal tax for unemployment tax charged under state plans, up to 5.4 percent of wages subject to the federal tax.

11-8 Compute and record workers' compensation insurance premiums.

By state law, employers might be required to carry workers' compensation insurance. For companies with a few employees, an estimated premium is paid at the start of the year. A final settlement is made with the insurance company on the basis of an audit of the payroll after the end of the year. Premiums vary according to the type of work performed by each employee. Other premium payment plans can be used for larger employers.

11-9 Define the accounting terms new to this chapter.

Glossary

Employer's Annual Federal Unemployment Tax Return, Form 940 (p. 377) Preprinted government form used by the employer to report unemployment taxes for the calendar year

Employer's Quarterly Federal Tax Return, Form 941 (p. 368) Preprinted government form used by the employer to report payroll tax information relating to social security, Medicare, and employee income tax withholding to the Internal Revenue Service

Date Wages Paid		Total Earnings	Social Security Tax Withheld	Medicare Tax Withheld	Federal Income Tax Withheld
July	7	$2,000.00	$ 124.00	$ 29.00	$ 175.00
	14	2,000.00	124.00	29.00	175.00
	21	2,100.00	130.20	30.45	190.00
	28	1,980.00	122.76	28.71	160.00
		$8,080.00	$ 500.96	$117.16	$ 700.00
Aug.	4	$2,100.00	$ 130.20	$ 30.45	190.00
	11	2,400.00	148.80	34.80	210.00
	18	2,400.00	148.80	34.80	210.00
	25	2,600.00	161.20	37.70	230.00
		$9,500.00	$ 589.00	$137.75	$ 840.00
Sept.	2	$2,000.00	$ 124.00	$ 29.00	$ 175.00
	9	2,100.00	130.20	30.45	190.00
	16	2,100.00	130.20	30.45	190.00
	23	2,200.00	136.40	31.90	200.00
	30	1,900.00	117.80	27.55	160.00
		$10,300.00	$ 638.60	$149.35	$ 915.00
Totals		$27,880.00	$1,728.56	$404.26	$2,455.00

INSTRUCTIONS

1. Prepare the general journal entry on July 7, 2016, to record the employer's payroll tax expense on the payroll ending that date. Use journal page 31. All earnings are subject to the following taxes:

Social security	6.2 percent
Medicare	1.45
FUTA	0.6
SUTA	2.2

2. Make the entries in general journal form to record deposit of the employee income tax withheld and the social security and Medicare taxes (both employees' withholding and employer's matching portion) on August 15 for July taxes and on September 15 for the August taxes.

Analyze: How much would a SUTA rate of 1.5 percent reduce the tax for the payroll of July 7?

This is a continuation of Problem 11.2B for Today's Teen; recording payment of taxes and preparing employer's quarterly federal tax return.

◀ **Problem 11.3B**
Objectives 11-4, 11-6

CONTINUING >>> Problem

1. On October 15, the firm made a deposit through EFTPS for the federal income tax withheld and the FICA tax (both employees' withholding and employer's matching portion). Based on your computations in Problem 11.2B, record the issuance of the check in general journal form. Use journal page 31.

2. Complete Form 941 in accordance with the discussions in this chapter and the instructions on the form. Use a 12.4 percent social security rate and a 2.9 percent Medicare rate in computations. Use the following address for the company: 12001 Pioneer Blvd., Artesia, CA 90650. The firm's phone number is 562-860-5451. Use 75-5555555 as the employer identification number. Date the return October 31, 2016.

Analyze: What total taxes were deposited with the IRS for the quarter ended September 30, 2016?

Problem 11.4B

Objectives 11-6, 11-7

▶ ### Computing and recording unemployment taxes; completing Form 940.

Certain transactions and procedures relating to federal and state unemployment taxes are given below for The Game Wizard, a retail store owned by Helen Kim. The firm's address is 4560 LBJ Freeway, Dallas, TX 75232-6002. The firm's phone number is 972-456-1201. The employer's federal and state identification numbers are 75-9999999 and 37-6789015, respectively. Carry out the procedures as instructed in each step.

INSTRUCTIONS

1. Compute the state unemployment insurance tax owed for the quarter ended March 31, 2016. This information will be shown on the employer's quarterly report to the state agency that collects SUTA tax. The employer has recorded the tax expense and liability on each payroll date. Although the state charges a 5.4 percent unemployment tax rate, The Game Wizard has received a favorable experience rating and therefore pays only a 2.3 percent state tax rate. The employee earnings for the first quarter are given below. All earnings are subject to SUTA tax.

Name of Employee	Total Earnings
Brian Morris	$ 3,880
Stan Cantu	3,650
Alicia Chiu	3,225
Yvonne Martinez	3,780
Patricia Jones	2,890
John Phan	2,910
Total	$20,335

2. On April 30, 2016, the firm issued a check for the amount computed above. Record the transaction in general journal form. Use journal page 21.

Analyze: If Brian Morris made the same amount for the quarter ended June 30, 2016, how much of his earnings would be subject to the federal unemployment tax?

Problem 11.5B

Objectives 11-6, 11-7

CONTINUING >>> Problem

▶ ### This is a continuation of Problem 11.4B for The Game Wizard; computing and recording unemployment taxes; completing Form 940.

1. Complete Form 940, the Employer's Annual Federal Unemployment Tax Return. Assume that all wages have been paid and that all quarterly payments have been submitted to the state as required. The payroll information for 2016 appears below. The firm's FUTA tax liability by quarter follows. 1st quarter, $122.01; 2nd quarter, $127.50; third quarter, $76.50; and fourth quarter, $87.30. The firm made no FUTA deposits in 2016. Date the unemployment tax return January 27, 2017. A check for the balance due will be sent with Form 940.

Quarter Ended	Total Wages Paid	Wages Paid in Excess of $7,000	State Unemployment Tax Paid
Mar. 31	$20,335.00	–0–	$ 467.71
June 30	21,250.00	–0–	488.75
Sept. 30	22,050.00	$ 9,300.00	293.25
Dec. 31	34,800.00	20,250.00	334.65
Totals	$98,435.00	$29,550.00	$1,584.36

2. On January 27, 2017, the firm paid the amount shown on line 14, Part 4 of form 940. In general journal form, record the payment. Use journal page 48.

Analyze: What is the balance of the *Federal Unemployment Tax Payable* account on January 27, 2017?

Computing and recording premiums on workers' compensation insurance.

◀ **Problem 11.6B**
Objective 11-8

The following information is for Union Express Delivery Service workers' compensation insurance premiums. On January 15, 2016, the company estimated its premium for workers' compensation insurance for the year on the basis of the following data:

Work Classification	Amount of Estimated Wages	Insurance Rates
Office work	$ 50,000	$0.50/$100
Delivery work	308,000	$6.00/$100

INSTRUCTIONS

1. Use the information to compute the estimated premium for the year.

2. A check was issued to pay the estimated premium on January 17, 2016. Record the transaction in general journal form. Use 7 as the page number.

3. On January 19, 2017, an audit of the firm's payroll records showed that it had actually paid wages of $52,970 to its office employees and wages of $316,240 to its delivery employees. Compute the actual premium for the year and the balance due the insurance company or the credit due the firm.

4. Give the general journal entry to adjust the *Workers' Compensation Insurance Expense* account. Date the entry December 31, 2016. Use 88 as the page number.

Analyze: What is the balance of the *Workers' Compensation Insurance Expense* account at December 31, 2016, after all journal entries have been posted?

Critical Thinking Problem 11.1

Comparing Employees and Independent Contractors

The *Mound Gazette* is a local newspaper that is published Monday through Friday. It sells 90,000 copies daily. The paper is currently in a profit squeeze, and the publisher, Harley Hews, is looking for ways to reduce expenses.

A review of current distribution procedures reveals that the *Mound Gazette* employs 100 truck drivers to drop off bundles of newspapers to 1,300 teenagers who deliver papers to individual homes. The drivers are paid an hourly wage while the teenagers receive 4 cents for each paper they deliver.

Hews is considering an alternative method of distributing the papers, which he says has worked in other cities the size of Flower Mound (where the *Mound Gazette* is published). Under the new system, the newspaper would retain 20 truck drivers to transport papers to five distribution centers around the city. The distribution centers are operated by independent contractors who would be responsible for making their own arrangements to deliver papers to subscribers' homes. The 20 drivers retained by the *Mound Gazette* would receive the same hourly rate as they currently earn, and the independent contractors would receive 20 cents for each paper delivered.

1. What payroll information does Hews need in order to make a decision about adopting the alternative distribution method?

2. Assume the following information:

   a. The average driver earns $42,000 per year.

   b. Average employee income tax withholding is 15 percent.

   c. The social security tax is 6.2 percent of the first $113,700 of earnings.

d. The Medicare tax is 1.45 percent of all earnings.

e. The state unemployment tax is 5 percent, and the federal unemployment tax is 0.6 percent of the first $7,000 of earnings.

f. Workers' compensation insurance is 70 cents per $100 of wages.

g. The paper pays $300 per month for health insurance for each driver and contributes $250 per month to each driver's pension plan.

h. The paper has liability insurance coverage for all teenage carriers that costs $100,000 per year.

Prepare a schedule showing the costs of distributing the newspapers under the current system and the proposed new system. Based on your analysis, which system would you recommend to Hews?

3. What other factors, monetary and nonmonetary, might influence your decision?

Critical Thinking Problem 11.2
Determining Employee Status

In each of the following independent situations, decide whether the business organization should treat the person being paid as an employee and should withhold social security, Medicare, and employee income taxes from the payment made.

1. Tony Jacobs owns and operates a crafts shop, as a sole proprietor. Jacobs withdraws $2,000 a week from the crafts shop.

2. Guy Gagliardi is a court reporter. He has an office at the Metroplex Court Reporting Center but pays no rent. The manager of the center receives requests from attorneys for court reporters to take depositions at legal hearings. The manager then chooses a court reporter who best meets the needs of the client and contacts the court reporter chosen. The court reporter has the right to refuse to take on the job, and the court reporter controls his or her working hours and days. Clients make payments to the center, which deducts a 30 percent fee for providing facilities and rendering services to support the court reporter. The balance is paid to the court reporter. During the current month, the center collected fees of $30,000 for Guy, deducted $9,000 for the center's fee, and remitted the remainder to Guy.

3. Ken, a registered nurse, has retired from full-time work. However, because of his experience and special skills, on each Monday, Wednesday, and Thursday afternoon he assists Dr. Grace Liu, a dermatologist. Ken is paid an hourly fee by Dr. Liu. During the current week, his hourly fees totaled $800.

4. After working several years as an editor for a magazine publisher, Lisa quit her job to stay at home with her two small children. Later, the publisher asked her to work in her home performing editorial work as needed. Lisa is paid an hourly fee for the work she performs. In some cases, she goes to the publishing company's offices to pick up or return a manuscript. In other cases the firm sends a manuscript to her, or she returns one by mail. During the current month, Lisa's hourly earnings totaled $2,500.

5. Investor Corporation carries on very little business activity. It merely holds land and certain assets. The board of directors has concluded that they need no employees. They have decided instead to pay Ron Christie, one of the shareholders, a consulting fee of $20,000 per year to serve as president, secretary, and treasurer and to manage all the affairs of the company. Christie spends an average of one hour per week on the corporation's business affairs. However, his fee is fixed regardless of how few or how many hours he works.

Analyze: What characteristics do the persons you identified as "employees" have in common?

BUSINESS CONNECTIONS

Payroll

1. Carolina Company recently discovered that a payroll clerk had issued checks to nonexistent employees for several years and cashed the checks himself. The firm does not have any internal control procedures for its payroll operations. What specific controls might have led to the discovery of this fraud more quickly or discouraged the payroll clerk from even attempting the fraud?

2. Johnson Company has 20 employees. Some employees work in the office, others in the warehouse, and still others in the retail store. In the company's records, all employees are simply referred to as "general employees." Explain to management why this is not an acceptable practice.

3. Why should management be concerned about the accuracy and promptness of payroll tax deposits and payroll tax returns?

4. What is the significance to management of the experience rating system used to determine the employer's tax under the state unemployment insurance laws?

Ghost Employee

Johan Jordan owns a dress shop that has been very successful. He employs 3 sales associates who get paid $10 per hour for a 40-hour week. He decides to open up another dress shop on the other side of town. He hires three more sales associates with the same pay arrangements. After three months, Johan notices he is not making the same profit he did. His sales have doubled and his expenses are the same proportion except for wages. He knows that each sales associate should receive $1,720 each month yet his total wages expense for the month is $12,040. He worries that he is not paying close enough attention to the old store. What is his problem? Should he discuss this problem with all the sales associates?

Employee Data

The Home Depot, Inc. reported the following data in its *2012 Annual Report (for the fiscal year ended February 3, 2013)*:

Number of employees at February 3, 2013	340,000
Contributions to employees' retirement plans during the year ended February 3, 2013	$182 million

Analyze:

1. Assume all employees receive contributions to their retirement plan. What was the average retirement plan contribution made by The Home Depot for full-time employees?

Determining Information

Wages and payroll tax expense are the largest cost that a company incurs. At times, a company has a problem paying wages and cash deposits for payroll taxes. Your company has a cash flow problem. In a group of 4 employees, brainstorm ways to cut the costs of wages and payroll taxes.

Internal Revenue Service

Go to the Internal Revenue website at www.irs.gov. Does the website contain the necessary federal forms? Can you use these forms to submit your report? What reports must be obtained from the IRS in an original, not downloaded, form?

Answers to **Self Reviews**

Answers to Section 1 Self Review

1. Form W-2 provides information to enable the employees to complete their federal income tax return. Copies are given to the employee and to the federal government (and to other governmental units that levy an income tax).
2. Federal Reserve Bank or a commercial bank that is designated as a federal depository.
3. Form 941 shows income taxes withheld, social security and Medicare taxes due for the quarter, and tax deposits. The form is due on the last day of the month following the end of the quarter.
4. **c.** Social security tax
5. **a.** each payroll period
6. Monthly

Answers to Section 2 Self Review

1. The amount of the premium depends on the type of work the employee performs.
2. The employer pays FUTA. Usually the employer pays SUTA, although a few states also levy SUTA on employees.
3. It reduces the rate of SUTA tax that must actually be paid.
4. **b.** quarterly
5. **d.** Form 940
6. Expenses will be understated. Net income will be overstated.

Answers to Comprehensive Self Review

1. Form W-3 is sent to the Social Security Administration. It reports the total social security wages; total Medicare wages; total social security and Medicare taxes withheld; total wages, tips, and other compensation; total employee income tax withheld; and other information.
2. Smaller
3. A credit, with limits, is allowed against the federal tax for unemployment tax charged by the state.
4. By the 15th day of the following month.
5. **b.** Amount of taxes reported in the lookback period
   d. Amount of taxes currently owed

Accruals, Deferrals, and the Worksheet

Urban Outfitters, Inc.
www.urbanoutfittersinc.com

Urban Outfitters, Inc., is an innovative specialty retail company that targets highly defined customer niches. The brands—Urban Outfitters, Anthropologie, Free People, BHLDN, and Terrain—are all distinct. The company designs innovative stores that resonate with the target audience. Stores offer an eclectic mix of merchandise and unique product displays that incorporate found objects into creative selling vignettes.

The strategy is working. While many retailers struggled through tough economic times in the past few years, net sales at Anthropologie, Free People, and Urban Outfitters have been strong. Total company net sales for the first quarter of fiscal 2014 increased to a record $648 million, or 14 percent over the same quarter last year. "Our brands delivered solid growth across all channels in the first quarter, especially in our direct-to-consumer channel," said Chief Executive Officer Richard A. Hayne.

Given the context of an uncertain economic environment, the company recognizes that they need to be able to adapt to the ever-changing fashion trends. Because all of their stores are leased, typically for a term of 10 years, the company needs to recognize rental expenses every year for each of their Urban Outfitters, Anthropologie, Free People, Terrain, and BHLDN stores. By leasing their stores, it gives the company more freedom to relocate a store if conditions change or if they need to expand.

Seasonal fluctuations also affect their inventory levels, as they usually order merchandise in advance of peak selling periods and sometimes are forced to carry a significant amount of inventory, especially before the back-to-school and holiday selling periods. Nevertheless, the company monitors their store inventory closely and at year-end, prices their products to move in order to make room for new inventory to be stocked. They believe that their mix of products, together with their stores' inviting atmosphere, will continue to entice their core customers to shop frequently.

thinking critically

What types of inventory issues do you think Urban Outfitters reflects upon at the end of each year?

LEARNING OBJECTIVES

12-1. Determine the adjustment for merchandise inventory, and enter the adjustment on the worksheet.

12-2. Compute adjustments for accrued and prepaid expense items, and enter the adjustments on the worksheet.

12-3. Compute adjustments for accrued and deferred income items, and enter the adjustments on the worksheet.

12-4. Complete a 10-column worksheet.

12-5. Define the accounting terms new to this chapter.

NEW TERMS

accrual basis
accrued expenses
accrued income
deferred expenses
deferred income
inventory sheet

net income line
property, plant, and equipment
unearned income
updated account balances

Calculating and Recording Adjustments

In Chapter 5, you learned how to make adjustments so that all revenue and expenses that apply to a fiscal period appear on the income statement for that period. In this chapter, you will learn more about adjustments and how they affect Whiteside Antiques, a retail merchandising business owned by Bill Whiteside.

The Accrual Basis of Accounting

Financial statements usually are prepared using the **accrual basis** of accounting because it most nearly attains the goal of matching expenses and revenue in an accounting period.

- *Revenue is recognized when earned, not necessarily when the cash is received.* Revenue is recognized when the sale is complete. A sale is complete when title to the goods passes to the customer or when the service is provided. For sales on account, revenue is recognized when the sale occurs even though the cash is not collected immediately.

- *Expenses are recognized when incurred or used, not necessarily when cash is paid.* Each expense is assigned to the accounting period in which it helped to earn revenue for the business, even if cash is not paid at that time. This is often referred to as *matching revenues and expenses.*

Sometimes cash changes hands before the revenue or expense is recognized. For example, insurance premiums are normally paid in advance, and the coverage extends over several accounting periods. In other cases, cash changes hands after the revenue or expense has been recognized. For example, employees might work during December but be paid in January of the following year. Because of these timing differences, adjustments are made to ensure that revenue and expenses are recognized in the appropriate period.

Using the Worksheet to Record Adjustments

The worksheet is used to assemble data about adjustments and to organize the information for the financial statements. Figure 12.1 on pages 400–401 shows the first two sections of the worksheet for Whiteside Antiques. Let's review how to prepare the worksheet:

- Enter the trial balance in the Trial Balance section. Total the columns. Be sure that total debits equal total credits.

- Enter the adjustments in the Adjustments section. Use the same letter to identify the debit part and the credit part of each adjustment. Total the columns. Be sure that total debits equal total credits.

- For each account, combine the amounts in the Trial Balance section and the Adjustments section. Enter the results in the Adjusted Trial Balance section, total the columns, and make sure that total debits equal total credits.

- Extend account balances to the Income Statement and Balance Sheet sections and complete the worksheet.

ADJUSTMENT FOR MERCHANDISE INVENTORY

Merchandise inventory consists of the goods that a business has on hand for sale to customers. An asset account for merchandise inventory is maintained in the general ledger. During the accounting period, all purchases of merchandise are debited to the **Purchases** account. All sales of merchandise are credited to the revenue account **Sales.**

Notice that no entries are made directly to the **Merchandise Inventory** account during the accounting period. Consequently, when the trial balance is prepared at the end of the period, the **Merchandise Inventory** account still shows the *beginning* inventory for the period. At the end of each period, a business determines the *ending* balance of the **Merchandise Inventory** account. The first step in determining the ending inventory is to count the number of units of each type of item on hand. As the merchandise is counted, the quantity on hand is entered on an inventory sheet. The **inventory sheet** lists the quantity of each type of goods a firm has in stock. This process is called a physical inventory. For each item, the quantity is multiplied by the unit cost to find the totals per item. The totals for all items are added to compute the total cost of merchandise inventory.

The trial balance for Whiteside Antiques shows **Merchandise Inventory** of $52,000. Based on a count taken on December 31, merchandise inventory at the end of the year actually totaled $47,000. Whiteside Antiques needs to adjust the **Merchandise Inventory** account to reflect the balance at the end of the year.

The adjustment is made in two steps, using the accounts **Merchandise Inventory** and **Income Summary.**

1. The beginning inventory ($52,000) is taken off the books by transferring the account balance to the **Income Summary** account. This entry is labeled **(a)** on the worksheet in Figure 12.1 and is illustrated in T-account form below.

Merchandise Inventory		Income Summary	
Bal. 52,000	Adj. 52,000	Adj. 52,000	

——— (a) ———

2. The ending inventory ($47,000) is placed on the books by debiting **Merchandise Inventory** and crediting **Income Summary.** This entry is labeled **(b)** on the worksheet in Figure 12.1.

Merchandise Inventory		Income Summary	
Bal. 52,000	Adj. 52,000	Adj. 52,000	Adj. 47,000
Adj. 47,000			

——— (a) ———
——— (b) ———

important!

Recognize
The word "recognize" means to record in the accounting records.

>> **12-1. OBJECTIVE**
Determine the adjustment for merchandise inventory, and enter the adjustment on the worksheet.

recall

Income Summary
The **Income Summary** account is a temporary owner's equity account used in the closing process.

FIGURE 12.1   10-Column Worksheet—Partial

Whiteside Antiques
Worksheet
Year Ended December 31, 2016

	ACCOUNT NAME	TRIAL BALANCE DEBIT	TRIAL BALANCE CREDIT	ADJUSTMENTS DEBIT	ADJUSTMENTS CREDIT
1	Cash	13 136 00			
2	Petty Cash Fund	100 00			
3	Notes Receivable	1 200 00			
4	Accounts Receivable	32 000 00			
5	Allowance for Doubtful Accounts		250 00		(c) 800 00
6	Interest Receivable			(m) 30 00	
7	Merchandise Inventory	52 000 00		(b) 47 000 00	(a) 52 000 00
8	Prepaid Insurance	7 350 00			(k) 2 450 00
9	Prepaid Interest	225 00			(l) 150 00
10	Supplies	6 300 00			(j) 4 975 00
11	Store Equipment	30 000 00			
12	Accumulated Depreciation—Store Equipment				(d) 2 400 00
13	Office Equipment	5 000 00			
14	Accumulated Depreciation—Office Equipment				(e) 700 00
15	Notes Payable—Trade		2 000 00		
16	Notes Payable—Bank		9 000 00		
17	Accounts Payable		24 129 00		
18	Interest Payable				(i) 20 00
19	Social Security Tax Payable		1 084 00		(g) 74 40
20	Medicare Tax Payable		250 00		(g) 17 40
21	Employee Income Taxes Payable		990 00		
22	Federal Unemployment Tax Payable				(h) 7 20
23	State Unemployment Tax Payable				(h) 64 80
24	Salaries Payable				(f) 1 200 00
25	Sales Tax Payable		720 00		
26	Bill Whiteside, Capital		61 221 00		
27	Bill Whiteside, Drawing	27 600 00			
28	Income Summary			(a) 52 000 00	(b) 47 000 00
29	Sales		561 650 00		
30	Sales Returns and Allowances	12 500 00			
31	Interest Income		136 00		
32	Miscellaneous Income		366 00		(m) 30 00
33	Purchases	321 500 00			
34	Freight In	9 800 00			
35	Purchases Returns and Allowances		3 050 00		
36	Purchases Discounts		3 130 00		
37	Salaries Expense—Sales	78 490 00		(f) 1 200 00	
38	Advertising Expense	7 425 00			
39	Cash Short or Over	125 00			
40	Supplies Expense			(j) 4 975 00	

FIGURE 12.1 10-Column Worksheet—Partial (concluded)

	ACCOUNT NAME	TRIAL BALANCE		ADJUSTMENTS	
		DEBIT	CREDIT	DEBIT	CREDIT
41	Depreciation Expense—Store Equipment			(d) 2 4 0 0 00	
42	Rent Expense	27 6 0 0 00			
43	Salaries Expense—Office	26 5 0 0 00			
44	Insurance Expense			(k) 2 4 5 0 00	
45	Payroll Taxes Expense	7 2 0 5 00		(g) 9 1 80	
				(h) 7 2 00	
46					
47	Telephone Expense	1 8 7 5 00			
48	Uncollectible Accounts Expense			(c) 8 0 0 00	
49	Utilities Expense	5 9 2 5 00			
50	Depreciation Expense—Office Equipment			(e) 7 0 0 00	
51	Interest Expense	6 0 0 00		(i) 2 0 00	
52				(l) 1 5 0 00	
53	Totals	674 4 5 6 00	674 4 5 6 00	111 8 8 8 80	111 8 8 8 80

The effect of this adjustment is to remove the beginning merchandise inventory balance and replace it with the ending merchandise inventory balance. Merchandise inventory is adjusted in two steps on the worksheet because both the beginning and the ending inventory figures appear on the income statement, which is prepared directly from the worksheet.

The merchandise inventory adjustment is not necessary if the perpetual inventory system is used.

ADJUSTMENT FOR LOSS FROM UNCOLLECTIBLE ACCOUNTS

Credit sales are made with the expectation that the customers will pay the amount due later. Sometimes the account receivable is never collected. Losses from uncollectible accounts are classified as operating expenses.

Under accrual accounting, the expense for uncollectible accounts is recorded in the same period as the related sale. The expense is estimated because the actual amount of uncollectible accounts is not known until later periods. To match the expense for uncollectible accounts with the sales revenue for the same period, the estimated expense is debited to an account named *Uncollectible Accounts Expense.*

Several methods exist for estimating the expense for uncollectible accounts. Whiteside Antiques uses the *percentage of net credit sales* method. The rate used is based on the company's past experience with uncollectible accounts and management's assessment of current business conditions. Whiteside Antiques estimates that four-fifths of 1 percent (0.80 percent) of net credit sales will be uncollectible. Net credit sales for the year were $100,000. The estimated expense for uncollectible accounts is $800 ($100,000 × 0.0080).

The entry to record the expense for uncollectible accounts includes a credit to a contra asset account, *Allowance for Doubtful Accounts.* This account appears on the balance sheet as follows:

Accounts Receivable	$32,000
Allowance for Doubtful Accounts ($800 + $250)	1,050
Net Accounts Receivable	$30,950

Adjustment **(c)** appears on the worksheet in Figure 12.1 for the expense for uncollectible accounts.

>> **12-2. OBJECTIVE**
Compute adjustments for accrued and prepaid expense items, and enter the adjustments on the worksheet.

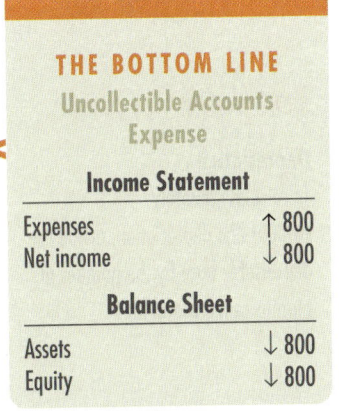

THE BOTTOM LINE

Uncollectible Accounts Expense

Income Statement

Expenses	↑ 800
Net income	↓ 800

Balance Sheet

Assets	↓ 800
Equity	↓ 800

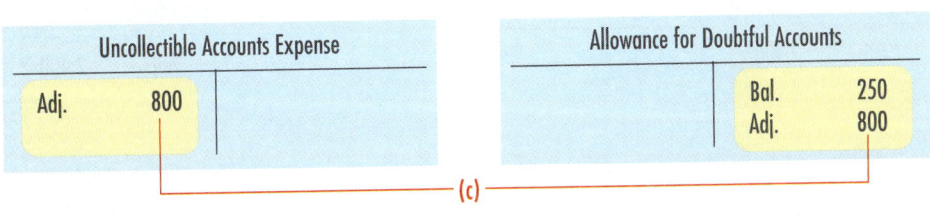

When a specific account becomes uncollectible, it is written off:

- The entry is a debit to *Allowance for Doubtful Accounts* and a credit to *Accounts Receivable.*
- The customer's account in the accounts receivable subsidiary ledger is also reduced.

Uncollectible Accounts Expense is not affected by the write-off of individual accounts identified as uncollectible. It is used only when the end-of-period adjustment is recorded.

Notice that net income is decreased at the end of the period when the adjustment for *estimated* expense for uncollectible accounts is made. When a specific customer account is written off, net income is *not* affected. The write-off of a specific account affects only the balance sheet accounts *Accounts Receivable* (asset) and *Allowance for Doubtful Accounts* (contra asset).

The balance of *Allowance for Doubtful Accounts* is reduced throughout the year as customer accounts are written off. Notice that *Allowance for Doubtful Accounts* already has a credit balance of $250 in the Trial Balance section of the worksheet. When the estimate of uncollectible accounts expense is based on sales, any remaining balance from previous periods is not considered when recording the adjustment.

ADJUSTMENTS FOR DEPRECIATION

Most businesses have long-term assets that are used in the operation of the business. These are often referred to as **property, plant, and equipment.** Property, plant, and equipment includes buildings, trucks, automobiles, machinery, furniture, fixtures, office equipment, and land.

Property, plant, and equipment costs are not charged to expense accounts when purchased. Instead, the cost of a long-term asset is allocated over the asset's expected useful life by depreciation. This process involves the gradual transfer of acquisition cost to expense. This concept was first introduced in Chapter 5. There is one exception. Land is not depreciated.

There are many ways to calculate depreciation. Whiteside Antiques uses the straight-line method, so an equal amount of depreciation is taken in each year of the asset's useful life. The formula for straight-line depreciation is:

$$\frac{\text{Cost} - \text{Salvage value}}{\text{Estimated useful life}} = \text{Depreciation}$$

Salvage value is an estimate of the amount that could be obtained from the sale or disposition of an asset at the end of its useful life. Cost minus salvage value is called the *depreciable base.*

Depreciation of Store Equipment The trial balance shows that Whiteside Antiques has $30,000 of store equipment. Estimated salvage value is $6,000. What is the amount of annual depreciation expense using the straight-line method?

Cost of store equipment	$30,000
Salvage value	(6,000)
Depreciable base	$24,000
Estimated useful life	10 years

$$\frac{\$30,000 - \$6,000}{10 \text{ years}} = \$2,400 \text{ per year}$$

The annual depreciation expense is $2,400. Adjustment **(d)** appears on the worksheet in Figure 12.1 for the depreciation expense for store equipment.

important!

Depreciation
To calculate monthly straight-line depreciation, divide the depreciable base by the number of months in the useful life.

Depr. Expense—Store Equipment			Accum. Depr.—Store Equipment	
Adj. 2,400				Adj. 2,400

(d)

Depreciation of Office Equipment Whiteside Antiques reports $5,000 of office equipment on the trial balance. What is the amount of annual depreciation expense using the straight-line method if estimated salvage value is $800 and estimated life is 6 years?

Cost of office equipment	$5,000
Salvage value	(800)
Depreciable base	$4,200
Estimated useful life	6 years

$$\frac{\$5,000 - \$800}{6\ \text{Years}} = \$700 \text{ per year}$$

Annual depreciation expense is $700. Adjustment (**e**) appears on the worksheet in Figure 12.1 for depreciation expense for office equipment.

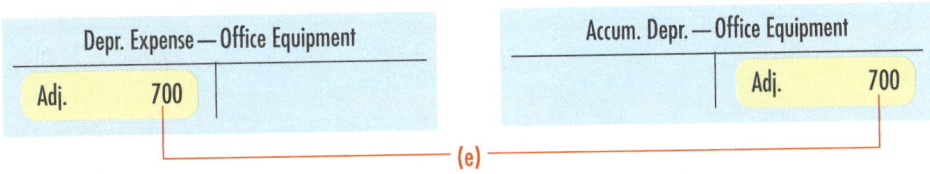

As discussed in Chapter 5, *Accumulated Depreciation* is a contra asset account. It has a normal credit balance, which is opposite the normal balance of an asset account.

ADJUSTMENTS FOR ACCRUED EXPENSES

Many expense items are paid for, recorded, and used in the same accounting period. However, some expense items are paid for and recorded in one period but used in a later period. Other expense items are used in one period and paid for in a later period. In these situations, adjustments are made so that the financial statements show all expenses in the appropriate period.

Accrued expenses are expenses that relate to (are used in) the current period but have not yet been paid and do not yet appear in the accounting records. Whiteside Antiques makes adjustments for three types of accrued expenses:

- accrued salaries
- accrued payroll taxes
- accrued interest on notes payable

Because accrued expenses involve amounts that must be paid in the future, the adjustment for each item is a debit to an expense account and a credit to a liability account.

Accrued Salaries At Whiteside Antiques, all full-time sales and office employees are paid semimonthly—on the 15th and the last day of the month. The trial balance in Figure 12.1 shows the correct salaries expense for the full-time employees for the year. From December 28 to January 3, the firm hired several part-time sales clerks for the year-end sale. Through December 31, 2016, these employees earned $1,200. The part-time salaries expense has not yet been recorded because the employees will not be paid until January 3, 2017. An adjustment is made to record the amount owed, but not yet paid, as of the end of December.

Adjustment (**f**) appears on the worksheet in Figure 12.1 for accrued salaries.

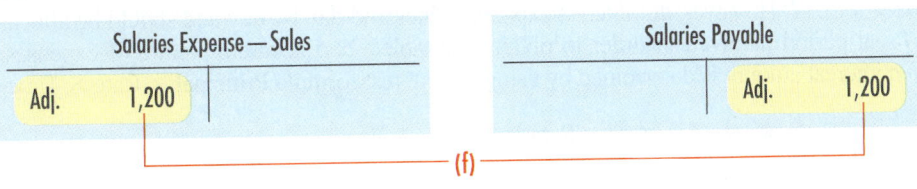

Accrued Payroll Taxes Payroll taxes are not legally owed until the salaries are paid. Businesses that want to match revenue and expenses in the appropriate period make adjustments to accrue the employer's payroll taxes even though the taxes are technically not yet due. Whiteside Antiques makes adjustments for accrued employer's payroll taxes.

The payroll taxes related to the full-time employees of Whiteside Antiques have been recorded and appear on the trial balance. However, the payroll taxes for the part-time sales clerks have not been recorded. None of the part-time clerks have reached the social security wage base limit. The entire $1,200 of accrued salaries is subject to the employer's share of social security and Medicare taxes. The accrued employer's payroll taxes are:

Social security tax	$1,200	×	0.0620	=	$74.40
Medicare tax	$1,200	×	0.0145	=	17.40
Total accrued payroll taxes					$91.80

Adjustment (**g**) appears on the worksheet in Figure 12.1 for accrued payroll taxes.

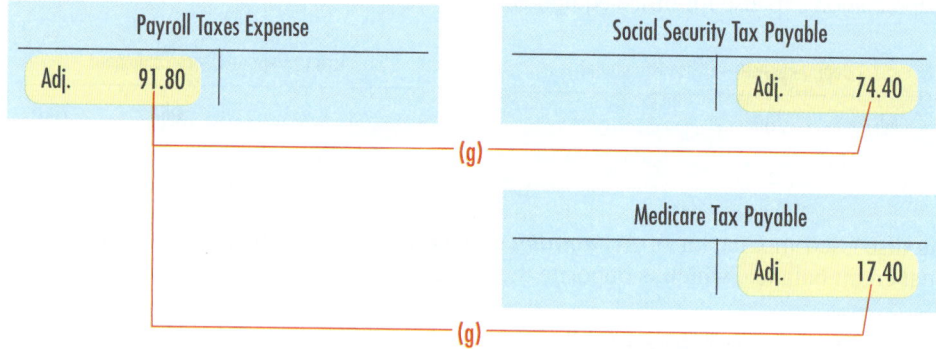

The entire $1,200 of accrued salaries is also subject to unemployment taxes. The unemployment tax rates for Whiteside Antiques are 0.6 percent for federal and 5.4 percent for state.

Federal unemployment tax	$1,200	×	0.006	=	$ 7.20
State unemployment tax	$1,200	×	0.054	=	64.80
Total accrued taxes					$72.00

Adjustment (**h**) appears on the worksheet in Figure 12.1 for accrued unemployment taxes.

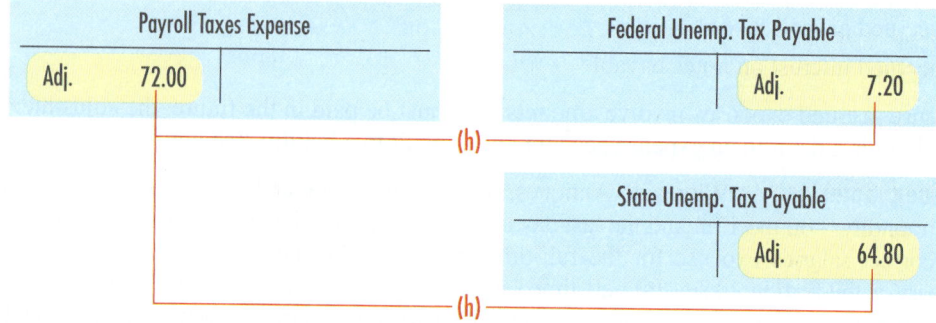

Accrued Interest on Notes Payable   On December 1, 2016, Whiteside Antiques issued a two-month note for $2,000, with annual interest of 12 percent. The note was recorded in the *Notes Payable—Trade* account. Whiteside Antiques will pay the interest when the note matures on February 1, 2017. However, the interest expense is incurred day by day and should be allocated to each fiscal period involved in order to obtain a complete and accurate picture of expenses. The accrued interest amount is determined by using the interest formula Principal × Rate × Time.

Principal	×	**Rate**	×	**Time**		
$2,000	×	0.12	×	1/12	=	$20

The fraction ¹⁄₁₂ represents one month, which is 1/12 of a year.

Adjustment **(i)** appears on the worksheet in Figure 12.1 for the accrued interest expense.

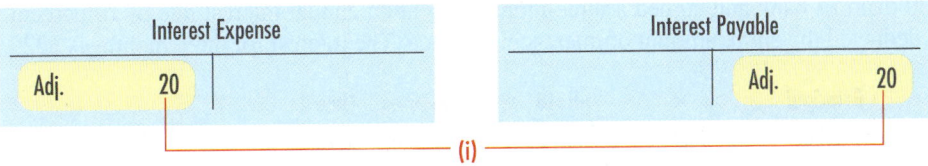

Other Accrued Expenses

Most businesses pay property taxes to state and local governments. They accrue these taxes at the end of the accounting period. Adjustments might also be necessary for commissions, professional services, and many other accrued expenses.

> In its December 31, 2011, balance sheet, JetBlue Airways Corporation reported the following current liabilities (all in millions of dollars): Accounts payable, $148; Air traffic liability, $627; Accrued salaries, wages, and benefits, $152; Other accrued liabilities, $199; Short-term borrowings, $88; and Current maturities of long-term debt and capital leases, $198.

ADJUSTMENTS FOR PREPAID EXPENSES

Prepaid expenses, or **deferred expenses,** are expenses that are paid for and recorded before they are used. Often a portion of a prepaid item remains unused at the end of the period; it is applicable to future periods. When paid for, these items are recorded as assets. At the end of the period, an adjustment is made to recognize as an expense the portion used during the period. Whiteside Antiques makes adjustments for three types of prepaid expenses:

- prepaid supplies
- prepaid insurance
- prepaid interest on notes payable

The adjusting entries for supplies used and insurance expired were introduced in Chapter 5. The adjusting entry for prepaid interest on notes payable is new to this chapter.

Supplies Used When supplies are purchased, they are debited to the asset account *Supplies.* On the trial balance in Figure 12.1, *Supplies* has a balance of $6,300. A physical count on December 31 showed $1,325 of supplies on hand. This means that $4,975 ($6,300 − $1,325) of supplies were used during the year. An adjustment is made to charge the cost of supplies used to the current year's operations and to reflect the value of the supplies on hand.

Adjustment **(j)** appears on the worksheet in Figure 12.1 for supplies expense.

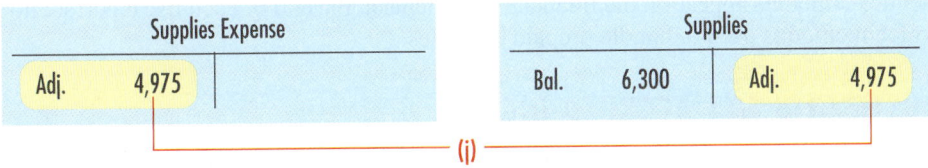

Expired Insurance On January 2, 2016, Whiteside Antiques wrote a check for $7,350 for a three-year insurance policy. The asset account *Prepaid Insurance* was debited for $7,350. On December 31, 2016, one year of insurance had expired. An adjustment for $2,450 ($7,350 × 1/3) was made to charge the cost of the expired insurance to operations and to decrease *Prepaid Insurance* to reflect the prepaid insurance premium that remains.

Adjustment **(k)** appears on the worksheet in Figure 12.1 for the insurance.

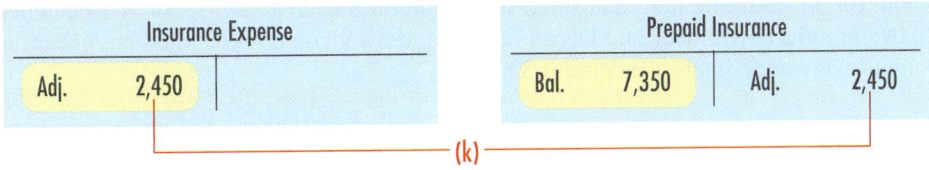

Prepaid Interest on Notes Payable   On November 1, 2016, Whiteside Antiques borrowed $9,000 from its bank and signed a three-month note at an annual interest rate of 10 percent. The bank deducted the entire amount of interest in advance. The interest for three months is $225.

Principal	×	Rate	×	Time		
$9,000	×	0.10	×	3/12	=	$225

Whiteside Antiques received $8,775 ($9,000 − $225). The transaction was recorded as a debit to *Cash* for $8,775, a debit to *Prepaid Interest* for $225, and a credit to *Notes Payable—Bank* for $9,000.

On December 31, two months of prepaid interest ($225 × 2/3 = $150) had been incurred and needed to be recorded as an expense. The adjustment consists of a debit to *Interest Expense* and a credit to *Prepaid Interest.*

Adjustment **(l)** appears on the worksheet in Figure 12.1 for the interest expense.

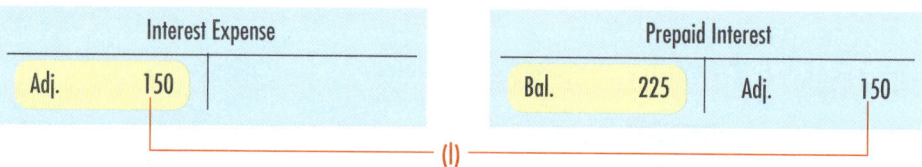

Other Prepaid Expenses   Other common prepaid expenses are prepaid rent, prepaid advertising, and prepaid taxes. When paid, the amounts are debited to the asset accounts *Prepaid Rent, Prepaid Advertising,* and *Prepaid Taxes.* At the end of each period, an adjustment is made to transfer the portion used from the asset account to an expense account. For example, the adjustment for expired rent would be a debit to *Rent Expense* and a credit to *Prepaid Rent.*

Alternative Method   Some businesses use a different method for prepaid expenses. At the time cash is paid, they debit an expense account (not an asset account). At the end of each period, they make an adjustment to transfer the portion that is not used from the expense account to an asset account.

Suppose that Whiteside used this alternative method when purchasing the two-year insurance policy. On January 1, 2016, the transaction would have been recorded as a debit to *Insurance Expense* for $7,350 and a credit to *Cash* for $7,350. On December 31, 2016, after the insurance coverage for one year had expired, coverage for two years remained. The adjustment would be recorded as a debit to *Prepaid Insurance* for $4,900 ($7,350 × 2/3) and a credit to *Insurance Expense* for $4,900.

Identical amounts appear on the financial statements at the end of each fiscal period, no matter which method is used to handle prepaid expenses.

ADJUSTMENTS FOR ACCRUED INCOME

Accrued income is income that has been earned but not yet received and recorded. On December 31, 2013, Whiteside Antiques had accrued interest on notes receivable.

Accrued Interest on Notes Receivable   Interest-bearing notes receivable are recorded at face value and are carried in the accounting records at this value until they are collected. The interest income is recorded when it is received, which is normally when the note matures. However, interest income is earned day by day. At the end of the period, an adjustment is made to recognize interest income earned but not yet received or recorded.

On November 1, 2016, Whiteside Antiques accepted from a customer a four-month, 15 percent note for $1,200. The note and interest are due on March 1, 2017. As of December 31, 2016, two months (November and December) of interest income was earned but not received. The amount of earned interest income is $30.

important!

Some assets and liabilities always require adjustments
Although prepaid expenses are usually charged to an asset account when they are paid, some businesses charge most prepayments to expense. In either case, at the time financial statements are prepared the accounts must be adjusted to show the correct expense and prepayment.

>> 12-3. OBJECTIVE
Compute adjustments for accrued and deferred income items, and enter the adjustments on the worksheet.

Principal	×	Rate	×	Time		
$1,200	×	0.15	×	2/12	=	$30

Adjustment (**m**) appears on the worksheet in Figure 12.1 for the interest income. To record the interest income of $30 earned, but not yet received, an adjustment debiting the asset account *Interest Receivable* and crediting a revenue account called *Interest Income* is made.

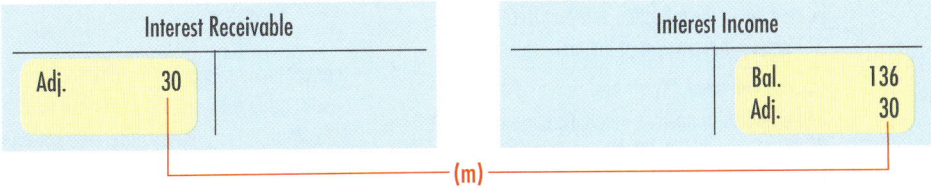

ADJUSTMENTS FOR UNEARNED INCOME

Unearned income, or **deferred income,** exists when cash is received before income is earned. Under the accrual basis of accounting, only income that has been earned appears on the income statement. Whiteside Antiques has no unearned income. The following is an example of unearned income for another business.

Unearned Subscription Income for a Publisher Magazine publishers receive cash in advance for subscriptions. When the publisher receives the cash, it is unearned income and is a liability. It is a liability because the publisher has an obligation to provide magazines during the subscription period. As the magazines are sent to the subscribers, income is earned and the liability decreases.

Tech Publishing Corporation publishes *Consumer Technology Today*. When subscriptions are received, *Cash* is debited and *Unearned Subscription Income,* a liability account, is credited. At the end of the year, *Unearned Subscription Income* had a balance of $450,000. During the year, $184,000 of magazines were delivered; income was earned in the amount of $184,000. The adjustment to recognize income is a debit to *Unearned Subscription Income* for $184,000 and a credit to *Subscription Income* for $184,000.

After the adjustment, the *Unearned Subscription Income* account has a balance of $266,000, which represents subscriptions for future periods.

	Unearned Subscription Income		
12/31 Adj. 184,000	12/31 Bal.	450,000
	12/31 Bal.	266,000

Other Unearned Income Items Other types of unearned income include management fees, rental income, legal fees, architectural fees, construction fees, and advertising income. The cash received in advance is recorded as unearned income. As the income is earned, the amount is transferred from the liability account to a revenue account.

Alternative Method Some businesses use a different method to handle unearned income. At the time the cash is received, a credit is made to a revenue account (not a liability account). At the end of each period, the adjustment transfers the portion that is not earned to a liability account. For example, suppose Tech Publishing Corporation uses this method. When cash for subscriptions is received, it is credited to *Subscription Income.* At the end of the period, an adjustment is made to transfer the unearned income to a liability account. The entry is a debit to *Subscription Income* and a credit to *Unearned Subscription Income.*

Identical amounts appear on the financial statements at the end of each fiscal period no matter which method is used to handle unearned income.

recall

Two Ways to Record Transactions

Earlier in this chapter you learned that prepaid expenses are usually charged to an asset account when paid, but may be charged to an expense account at that time. Likewise, unearned income is usually credited to a liability account when received, but may be credited to an income account. Be sure to understand how the transaction was originally entered before you begin making the adjusting entry.

Section 1   Self Review

QUESTIONS

1. Why is a 10-column worksheet used as part of the procedures for adjusting and closing accounts and preparing financial statements?

2. Why are there two amounts (a debit and a credit) in the adjustments column on the line for Merchandise Inventory in the 10-column worksheet?

3. Why are adjusting entries necessary?

EXERCISES

4. In Caymus Company's December 31 trial balance, a credit balance of $31,500 appears in Unearned Fee Income. This amount represents cash received from a customer on November 1 covering work to be performed by Caymus in November through January. At December 31, Caymus had earned $10,500 of the amount received on November 1. What account will be debited and what account will be credited in the adjusting entry on December 31? What is the amount of the adjustment?

5. Caymus Company adjusts and closes its accounts and prepares financial statements each month. In the December 31 Trial Balance column for debit balances, a balance of $9,000 is found in the Prepaid Rent account. A payment of $18,000 for prepayment of six months' rent was made on September 1.

   a. What is the amount of the adjusting entry for this item?

   b. What account would be debited and what account would be credited in the December 31 adjustments?

ANALYSIS

6. Your company prepares financial statements each month, using a 10-column worksheet to assemble data. What is the primary difference between the adjustments made on a monthly basis and those made on an annual basis?

(Answers to Section 1 Self Review are on page 434.)

SECTION OBJECTIVE	TERMS TO LEARN
>> 12-4. Complete a 10-column worksheet. **WHY IT'S IMPORTANT** Using the worksheet is a convenient way to gather the information needed for the financial statements.	net income line updated account balances

Completing the Worksheet

After all adjustments have been entered on the worksheet, total the Adjustments Debit and Credit columns and verify that debits and credits are equal. The next step in the process is to prepare the Adjusted Trial Balance section.

Preparing the Adjusted Trial Balance Section

>> 12-4. OBJECTIVE
Complete a 10-column worksheet.

Figure 12.2 on pages 410–413 shows the completed worksheet for Whiteside Antiques. The Adjusted Trial Balance section of the worksheet is completed as follows:

1. Combine the amount in the Trial Balance section and the Adjustments section for each account.
2. Enter the results in the Adjusted Trial Balance section. The accounts that do not have adjustments are simply extended from the Trial Balance section to the Adjusted Trial Balance section. For example, the balance of the **Cash** account is recorded in the Debit column of the Adjusted Trial Balance section without change.
3. The accounts that are affected by adjustments are recomputed. Follow these rules to combine amounts on the worksheet:

Trial Balance Section	Adjustments Section	Action
Debit	Debit	Add
Debit	Credit	Subtract
Credit	Credit	Add
Credit	Debit	Subtract

- If the account has a debit balance in the Trial Balance section and a debit entry in the Adjustments section, add the two amounts. Look at the **Salaries Expense—Sales** account. It has a $78,490 debit balance in the Trial Balance section and a $1,200 debit entry in the Adjustments section. The new balance is $79,690 ($78,490 + $1,200). It is entered in the Debit column of the Adjusted Trial Balance section.

- If the account has a debit balance in the Trial Balance section and a credit entry in the Adjustments section, subtract the credit amount. Look at the **Supplies** account. It has a $6,300 debit balance in the Trial Balance section and a $4,975 credit entry in the Adjustments section. The new balance is $1,325 ($6,300 − $4,975). It is entered in the Debit column of the Adjusted Trial Balance section.

FIGURE 12.2 Ten-Column Worksheet—Complete

Whiteside Antiques

Worksheet

Year Ended December 31, 2016

	ACCOUNT NAME	TRIAL BALANCE DEBIT	TRIAL BALANCE CREDIT	ADJUSTMENTS DEBIT	ADJUSTMENTS CREDIT
1	Cash	13 136 00			
2	Petty Cash Fund	100 00			
3	Notes Receivable	1 200 00			
4	Accounts Receivable	32 000 00			
5	Allowance for Doubtful Accounts		250 00		(c) 800 00
6	Interest Receivable			(m) 30 00	
7	Merchandise Inventory	52 000 00		(b) 47 000 00	(a) 52 000 00
8	Prepaid Insurance	7 350 00			(k) 2 450 00
9	Prepaid Interest	225 00			(l) 150 00
10	Supplies	6 300 00			(j) 4 975 00
11	Store Equipment	30 000 00			
12	Accumulated Depreciation—Store Equipment				(d) 2 400 00
13	Office Equipment	5 000 00			
14	Accumulated Depreciation—Office Equipment				(e) 700 00
15	Notes Payable—Trade		2 000 00		
16	Notes Payable—Bank		9 000 00		
17	Accounts Payable		24 129 00		
18	Interest Payable				(i) 20 00
19	Social Security Tax Payable		1 084 00		(g) 74 40
20	Medicare Tax Payable		250 00		(g) 17 40
21	Employee Income Taxes Payable		990 00		
22	Federal Unemployment Tax Payable				(h) 7 20
23	State Unemployment Tax Payable				(h) 64 80
24	Salaries Payable				(f) 1 200 00
25	Sales Tax Payable		720 00		
26	Bill Whiteside, Capital		61 221 00		
27	Bill Whiteside, Drawing	27 600 00			
28	Income Summary			(a) 52 000 00	(b) 47 000 00
29	Sales		561 650 00		
30	Sales Returns and Allowances	12 500 00			
31	Interest Income		136 00		(m) 30 00
32	Miscellaneous Income		366 00		
33	Purchases	321 500 00			
34	Freight In	9 800 00			
35	Purchases Returns and Allowances		3 050 00		
36	Purchases Discounts		3 130 00		
37	Salaries Expense—Sales	78 490 00		(f) 1 200 00	
38	Advertising Expense	7 425 00			
39	Cash Short or Over	125 00			
40	Supplies Expense			(j) 4 975 00	

	ADJUSTED TRIAL BALANCE		INCOME STATEMENT		BALANCE SHEET		
	DEBIT	CREDIT	DEBIT	CREDIT	DEBIT	CREDIT	
1	13 136 00				13 136 00		1
2	100 00				100 00		2
3	1 200 00				1 200 00		3
4	32 000 00				32 000 00		4
5		1 050 00				1 050 00	5
6		30 00				30 00	6
7	47 000 00				47 000 00		7
8	4 900 00				4 900 00		8
9		75 00				75 00	9
10	1 325 00				1 325 00		10
11	30 000 00				30 000 00		11
12		2 400 00				2 400 00	12
13	5 000 00				5 000 00		13
14		700 00				700 00	14
15		2 000 00				2 000 00	15
16		9 000 00				9 000 00	16
17		24 129 00				24 129 00	17
18		2 00				2 00	18
19		1 158 40				1 158 40	19
20		267 40				267 40	20
21		990 00				990 00	21
22		7 20				7 20	22
23		64 80				64 80	23
24		1 200 00				1 200 00	24
25		7 200 00				7 200 00	25
26		61 221 00				61 221 00	26
27	27 600 00				27 600 00		27
28	52 000 00	47 000 00	52 000 00	47 000 00			28
29		561 650 00		561 650 00			29
30	12 500 00		12 500 00				30
31		166 00		166 00			31
32		366 00		366 00			32
33	321 500 00		321 500 00				33
34	9 800 00		9 800 00				34
35		3 050 00		3 050 00			35
36		3 130 00		3 130 00			36
37	79 690 00		79 690 00				37
38	7 425 00		7 425 00				38
39	125 00		125 00				39
40	4 975 00		4 975 00				40

FIGURE 12.2   Ten-Column Worksheet—Complete (concluded)

	ACCOUNT NAME	TRIAL BALANCE		ADJUSTMENTS		
		DEBIT	CREDIT		DEBIT	CREDIT
41	Depreciation Expense—Store Equipment			(d)	2 4 0 0 00	
42	Rent Expense	27 6 0 0 00				
43	Salaries Expense—Office	26 5 0 0 00				
44	Insurance Expense			(k)	2 4 5 0 00	
45	Payroll Taxes Expense	7 2 0 5 00		(g)	9 1 80	
46				(h)	7 2 00	
47	Telephone Expense	1 8 7 5 00				
48	Uncollectible Accounts Expense			(c)	8 0 0 00	
49	Utilities Expense	5 9 2 5 00				
50	Depreciation Expense—Office Equipment			(e)	7 0 0 00	
51	Interest Expense	6 0 0 00		(i)	2 0 00	
52				(l)	1 5 0 00	
53	Totals	674 4 5 6 00	674 4 5 6 00		111 8 8 8 80	111 8 8 8 80
54	Net Income					

- If the account has a credit balance in the Trial Balance section and a credit entry in the Adjustments section, add the two amounts. Look at **Allowance for Doubtful Accounts.** It has a $250 credit balance in the Trial Balance section and an $800 credit entry in the Adjustments section. The new balance is $1,050 ($250 + $800). It is entered in the Credit column of the Adjusted Trial Balance section.

- If the account has a credit balance in the Trial Balance section and a debit entry in the Adjustments section, subtract the debit amount. Whiteside Antiques had no such adjustments.

The Adjusted Trial Balance section now contains the <mark>updated account balances</mark> that will be used in preparing the financial statements.

Look at the **Income Summary** account. Recall that the debit entry in this account removed the *beginning* balance from **Merchandise Inventory** and the credit entry added the *ending* balance to **Merchandise Inventory.** Notice that the debit and credit amounts in **Income Summary** are not combined in the Adjusted Trial Balance section.

Once all the updated account balances have been entered in the Adjusted Trial Balance section, total and rule the columns. Confirm that total debits equal total credits.

Preparing the Balance Sheet and Income Statement Sections

To complete the Income Statement and Balance Sheet sections of the worksheet, identify the accounts that appear on the balance sheet. On Figure 12.2, the accounts from **Cash** through **Bill Whiteside, Drawing** appear on the balance sheet. For each account enter the amount in the appropriate Debit or Credit column of the Balance Sheet section of the worksheet.

For accounts that appear on the income statement, **Sales** through **Interest Expense,** enter the amounts in the appropriate Debit or Credit column of the Income Statement section. The **Income Summary** debit and credit amounts are also entered in the Income Statement section of the worksheet. Notice that the debit and credit amounts in **Income Summary** are not combined in the Income Statement section.

Calculating Net Income or Net Loss

Once all account balances have been entered in the financial statement sections of the worksheet, the net income or net loss for the period is determined.

| ADJUSTED TRIAL BALANCE | | INCOME STATEMENT | | BALANCE SHEET | | |
DEBIT	CREDIT	DEBIT	CREDIT	DEBIT	CREDIT	
2 4 0 0 00		2 4 0 0 00				41
27 6 0 0 00		27 6 0 0 00				42
26 5 0 0 00		26 5 0 0 00				43
2 4 5 0 00		2 4 5 0 00				44
7 3 6 8 80		7 3 6 8 80				45
						46
1 8 7 5 00		1 8 7 5 00				47
8 0 0 00		8 0 0 00				48
5 9 2 5 00		5 9 2 5 00				49
7 0 0 00		7 0 0 00				50
7 7 0 00		7 7 0 00				51
						52
726 7 6 9 80	726 7 6 9 80	564 4 0 3 80	615 3 6 2 00	162 3 6 6 00	111 4 0 7 80	53
		50 9 5 8 20			50 9 5 8 20	54
		615 3 6 2 00	615 3 6 2 00	162 3 6 6 00	162 3 6 6 00	55
						56

1. Total the Debit and Credit columns in the Income Statement section. For Whiteside Antiques, the debits total $564,403.80 and the credits total $615,362.00. Since the credits exceed the debits, the difference represents net income of $50,958.20.

2. To balance the Debit and the Credit columns in the Income Statement section, enter $50,958.20 in the Debit column of the Income Statement section. Total each column again and record the final total of each column ($615,362.00) on the worksheet.

3. Total the columns in the Balance Sheet section. Total debits are $162,366.00 and total credits are $111,407.80. The difference must equal the net income for the year, $50,958.20.

4. Enter $50,958.20 in the Credit column of the Balance Sheet section. Total each column again and record the final total in each column ($162,366.00).

5. Rule the Debit and Credit columns in all sections to show that the worksheet is complete.

MANAGERIAL IMPLICATIONS <<

EFFECT OF ADJUSTMENTS ON FINANCIAL STATEMENTS

- If managers are to know the true revenue, expenses, and net income or net loss for a period, the matching process is necessary.

- If accounts are not adjusted, the financial statements will be incomplete, misleading, and of little help in evaluating operations.

- Managers need to be familiar with the procedures and underlying assumptions used by the accountant to make adjustments because adjustments increase or decrease net income.

- Managers need information about uncollectible accounts expense in order to review the firm's credit policy. If losses are too high, management might tighten the requirements for obtaining credit. If losses are very low,

management might investigate whether easing credit requirements would increase net income.

- The worksheet is a useful device for gathering data about adjustments and for preparing the financial statements.

- Managers are keenly interested in receiving timely financial statements, especially the income statement, which shows the results of operations.

- Managers are also interested in the prompt preparation of the balance sheet because it shows the financial position of the business at the end of the period.

THINKING CRITICALLY
What are some possible consequences of not making adjusting entries?

Notice that the net income is recorded in two places on the **net income line** of the worksheet. It is recorded in the Credit column of the Balance Sheet section because net income *increases* owner's equity. It is recorded in the Debit column of the Income Statement section to balance the two columns in that section.

Section 2   Self Review

QUESTIONS

1. In the adjusting entry for depreciation, is the *Depreciation Expense* account increased or decreased? Is the book value of the asset being depreciated increased or is it decreased?

2. In its December 31, 2016, financial reports, St. Claire Company's accountant made two errors: (1) failed to record interest of $600 accrued on a note payable; and (2) failed to record interest of $1,600 accrued on a note receivable. What is the net effect of these two errors on assets, on liabilities, on expenses, on income, and on owner's equity?

3. The trial balance in the first two columns of the worksheet balances and the adjustments in the next two columns balance. However, the adjusted trial balance does not balance. What is the likely source of the trouble?

EXERCISES

4. What account is debited and what account is credited to accrue interest on notes payable?

5. The amount of net income appears on the worksheet in the:

   a. Credit column of the adjusted trial balance section.

   b. Debit column of the balance sheet section.

   c. Credit column of the income statement section.

   d. Debit column of the income statement section.

ANALYZE

6. Explain why an error in the amount of an adjusting entry usually affects at least two accounting periods.

(Answers to Section 2 Self Review are on page 435.)

REVIEW   Chapter Summary

Accrual basis accounting requires that all revenue and expenses for a fiscal period be matched and reported on the income statement to determine net income or net loss for the period. In this chapter, you have learned the techniques used to adjust accounts so that they accurately reflect the operations of the period.

Learning Objectives

12-1 **Determine the adjustment for merchandise inventory, and enter the adjustment on the worksheet.**

Merchandise inventory consists of goods that a business has on hand for sale to customers. When the trial balance is prepared at the end of the period, the *Merchandise Inventory* account still reflects the beginning inventory. Before the financial statements can be prepared, *Merchandise Inventory* must be updated to reflect the ending inventory for the period. The actual quantity of the goods on hand at the end of the period must be counted. Then the adjustment is completed in two steps:

1. Remove the beginning inventory balance from the *Merchandise Inventory* account. Debit *Income Summary;* credit *Merchandise Inventory.*

2. Add the ending inventory to the *Merchandise Inventory* account. Debit *Merchandise Inventory;* credit *Income Summary.*

12-2 **Compute adjustments for accrued and prepaid expense items, and enter the adjustments on the worksheet.**

Expense accounts are adjusted at the end of the period so that they correctly reflect the current period. Examples of adjustments include provision for uncollectible accounts and depreciation. Other typical adjustments of expense accounts involve accrued expenses and prepaid expenses.

■ Accrued expenses are expense items that have been incurred or used but not yet paid or recorded. They include salaries, payroll taxes, interest on notes payable, and property taxes.

■ Prepaid expenses are expense items that a business pays for and records before it

actually uses the items. Rent, insurance, and advertising paid in advance are examples.

12-3 **Compute adjustments for accrued and deferred income items, and enter the adjustments on the worksheet.**

Revenue accounts are adjusted at the end of the period so that they correctly reflect the current period.

■ Adjustments can affect either accrued income or deferred income.

■ Accrued income is income that has been earned but not yet received and recorded.

■ Deferred, or unearned, income is income that has not yet been earned but has been received.

12-4 **Complete a 10-column worksheet.**

When all adjustments have been entered on the worksheet, the worksheet is completed so that the financial statements can be prepared easily.

1. Figures in the Trial Balance section are combined with the adjustments to obtain an adjusted trial balance.

2. Each item in the Adjusted Trial Balance section is extended to the Income Statement or the Balance Sheet sections of the worksheet.

3. The Income Statement columns are totaled and the net income or net loss is determined and entered in the net income line.

4. The amount of net income or net loss is entered in the net income line in the Balance Sheet section. After net income or net loss is added, the total debits must equal the total credits in the Balance Sheet section columns.

12-5 **Define the accounting terms new to this chapter.**

Glossary

Accrual basis (p. 398) A system of accounting by which all revenues and expenses are matched and reported on financial statements for the applicable period, regardless of when the cash related to the transaction is received or paid

Accrued expenses (p. 403) Expense items that relate to the current period but have not yet been paid and do not yet appear in the accounting records

Accrued income (p. 406) Income that has been earned but not yet received and recorded

Deferred expenses (p. 405) See Prepaid expenses

Deferred income (p. 407) See Unearned income

Inventory sheet (p. 399) A form used to list the volume and type of goods a firm has in stock

Net income line (p. 414) The worksheet line immediately following the column totals on which net income (or net loss) is recorded in two places: the Income Statement section and the Balance Sheet section

Property, plant, and equipment (p. 402) Long-term assets that are used in the operation of a business and that are subject to depreciation (except for land, which is not depreciated)

Unearned income (p. 407) Income received before it is earned

Updated account balances (p. 412) The amounts entered in the Adjusted Trial Balance section of the worksheet

---

Comprehensive **Self Review**

1. Why is the accrual basis of accounting favored?

2. What is meant by the term "accrued income"?

3. How, if at all, does "accrued income" differ from "unearned income"?

4. A completed worksheet for Holiday Company on December 31, 2016, showed a total of $930,000 in the debit column of the Income Statement section and a total credit of $902,000 in the credit column. Does this represent a profit or a loss for the year? How much?

5. On July 1, 2016, a landlord received $36,000 cash from a tenant, covering rent from July 1, 2016, through June 30, 2017. The payment was credited to *Unearned Rent Income.* Assuming no entry has been made in the *Unearned Rent Income* account since the payment was received, what would be the adjusting entry on December 31, 2016?

6. On July 1, 2016, a landlord received $36,000 cash from a tenant, covering rent from that date through June 30, 2017. The payment was credited to *Rent Income.* Assuming no entry has been made in the income account since receipt of the payment, what would be the adjusting entry on December 31, 2016?

(Answers to Comprehensive Self Review are on page 435.)

Discussion Questions

1. What adjustment is made to record the estimated expense for uncollectible accounts?

2. When a specific account receivable is deemed uncollectible it is written off by debiting _____ and crediting _____ .

3. Income Summary amounts are extended to which statement columns on the worksheet?

4. Why is depreciation recorded?

5. What types of assets are subject to depreciation? Give three examples of such assets.

6. Explain the meaning of the following terms that relate to depreciation:
   a. Salvage value
   b. Depreciable base
   c. Useful life
   d. Straight-line method

7. What adjustment is made for depreciation on office equipment?

8. What is an accrued expense? Give three examples of items that often become accrued expenses.

9. What adjustment is made to record accrued salaries?

10. What is a prepaid expense? Give three examples of prepaid expense items.

11. How is the cost of an insurance policy recorded when the policy is purchased?

12. What adjustment is made to record expired insurance?

13. What is the alternative method of handling prepaid expenses?

14. What is accrued income? Give an example of an item that might produce accrued income.

15. What adjustment is made for accrued interest on a note receivable?

16. What is unearned income? Give two examples of items that would be classified as unearned income.

17. How is unearned income recorded when it is received?

18. What adjustment is made to record income earned during a period?

19. What is the alternative method of handling unearned income?

20. *Unearned Fees Income* is classified as which type of account?

21. How does the worksheet help the accountant to prepare financial statements more efficiently?

APPLICATIONS

Exercises

Determining the adjustments for inventory.   ◄   Exercise 12.1
                                                        Objective 12-1

The beginning inventory of a merchandising business was $131,000, and the ending inventory is $111,519. What entries are needed at the end of the fiscal period to adjust *Merchandise Inventory?*

Determining the adjustments for inventory.   ◄   Exercise 12.2
                                                        Objective 12-1

The Income Statement section of the worksheet of Sampson Company for the year ended December 31, has $189,000 recorded in the Debit column and $212,344 in the Credit column on the line for the *Income Summary* account. What were the beginning and ending balances for *Merchandise Inventory?*

Computing adjustments for accrued and prepaid expense items.   ◄   Exercise 12.3
                                                                       Objective 12-2

For each of the following independent situations, indicate the adjusting entry that must be made on the December 31, 2016, worksheet. Omit descriptions.

a. During the year 2016, Johnson Company had net credit sales of $990,000. Past experience shows that 0.5 percent of the firm's net credit sales result in uncollectible accounts.

b. Equipment purchased by Chu Consultancy for $28,220 on January 2, 2016, has an estimated useful life of eight years and an estimated salvage value of $2,700. What adjustment for depreciation should be recorded on the firm's worksheet for the year ended December 31, 2016?

c. On December 31, 2016, Parrish Plumbing Supply owed wages of $5,700 to its factory employees, who are paid weekly.

d. On December 31, 2016, Parrish Plumbing Supply owed the employer's social security (6.2%) and Medicare (1.45%) taxes on the entire $5,700 of accrued wages for its factory employees.

e. On December 31, 2016, Parrish Plumbing Supply owed federal (0.6%) and state (5.4%) unemployment taxes on the entire $5,700 of accrued wages for its factory employees.

Computing adjustments for accrued and prepaid expense items.   ◄   Exercise 12.4
                                                                       Objective 12-2

For each of the following independent situations, indicate the adjusting entry that must be made on the December 31, 2016, worksheet. Omit descriptions.

a. On December 31, 2016, the *Notes Payable* account at Queens Manufacturing Company had a balance of $19,000. This balance represented a three-month, 9 percent note issued on November 1.

b. On January 2, 2016, Campbell Computer Consultants purchased flash drives, paper, and other supplies for $6,230 in cash. On December 31, 2016, an inventory of supplies showed that items costing $1,610 were on hand. The *Supplies* account has a balance of $6,230.

c. On August 1, 2016, North Texas Manufacturing paid a premium of $13,440 in cash for a one-year insurance policy. On December 31, 2016, an examination of the insurance records showed that coverage for a period of five months had expired.

d. On April 1, 2016, Cathy's Crafts signed a one-year advertising contract with a local radio station and issued a check for $14,160 to pay the total amount owed. On December 31, 2016, the *Prepaid Advertising* account has a balance of $14,160.

Exercise 12.5
Objective 12-2

▶ **Recording adjustments for accrued and prepaid expense items.**

On December 1, 2016, Jim's Java Joint borrowed $50,000 from its bank in order to expand its operations. The firm issued a four-month, 6 percent note for $50,000 to the bank and received $49,000 in cash because the bank deducted the interest for the entire period in advance. In general journal form, show the entry that would be made to record this transaction and the adjustment for prepaid interest that should be recorded on the firm's worksheet for the year ended December 31, 2016. Omit descriptions. Round your answers to the nearest dollar.

Exercise 12.6
Objective 12-2

▶ **Recording adjustments for accrued and prepaid expense items.**

On December 31, 2016, the *Notes Payable* account at Beth's Boutique Shop had a balance of $64,000. This amount represented funds borrowed on a six-month, 12 percent note from the firm's bank on December 1. Record the journal entry for interest expense on this note that should be recorded on the firm's worksheet for the year ended December 31, 2016. Omit descriptions.

Exercise 12.7
Objective 12-3

▶ **Recording adjustments for accrued and deferred income items.**

For each of the following independent situations, indicate the adjusting entry that must be made on the December 31, 2016, worksheet. Omit descriptions.

a. On December 31, 2016, the *Notes Receivable* account at Manton Materials had a balance of $21,000, which represented a six-month, 10 percent note received from a customer on September 1.

b. During the week ended June 7, 2016, Parker Media received $50,000 from customers for subscriptions to its magazine *Modern Business.* On December 31, 2016, an analysis of the *Unearned Subscription Revenue* account showed that half of the subscriptions were earned in 2016.

c. On November 1, 2016, Prentice Realty Company rented a commercial building to a new tenant and received $54,000 in advance to cover the rent for six months. Upon receipt, the $54,000 was recorded in the *Unearned Rent* account.

d. On November 1, 2016, the Mighty Bucks Hockey Club sold season tickets for 50 home games, receiving $8,500,000. Upon receipt, the $8,500,000 was recorded in the *Unearned Season Tickets Income* account. At December 31, 2016, the Mighty Bucks Hockey Club had played 4 home games.

PROBLEMS

Problem Set A

Problem 12.1A
Objectives 12-2, 12-3, 12-5

▶ **Recording adjustments for accrued and prepaid items and unearned income.**

Based on the information below, record the adjusting journal entries that must be made for Garibaldi Consulting on June 30, 2016. The company has a June 30 fiscal year-end. Use 18 as the page number for the general journal.

a.–b. *Merchandise Inventory,* before adjustment, has a balance of $8,500. The newly counted inventory balance is $9,000.

c. *Unearned Seminar Fees* has a balance of $7,000, representing prepayment by customers for five seminars to be conducted in June, July, and August 2016. Two seminars had been conducted by June 30, 2016.

d. *Prepaid Insurance* has a balance of $18,000 for six months insurance paid in advance on May 1, 2016.

e. Store equipment costing $8,760 was purchased on March 31, 2016 It has a salvage value of $600, and a useful life of four years.

f. Employees have earned $350 that has not been paid at June 30, 2016.

g. The employer owes the following taxes on wages not paid at June 30, 2016: SUTA, $10.50; FUTA, $2.10; Medicare, $5.08; and social security, $21.70.

h. Management estimates uncollectible accounts expense at 1% of sales. This year's sales were $3,000,000.

i. *Prepaid Rent* has a balance of $8,100 for six months' rent paid in advance on March 1, 2016.

j. The *Supplies* account in the general ledger has a balance of $500. A count of supplies on hand at June 30, 2016 indicated $200 of supplies remain.

k. The company borrowed $10,100 from First Bank on June 1, 2016 and issued a four-month note. The note bears interest at 12%.

Analyze: After all adjusting entries have been journalized and posted, what is the balance of the *Prepaid Rent* account?

Recording adjustments for accrued and prepaid expense items and unearned income.

◀   **Problem 12.2A**

Objectives 12-2, 12-3, 12-6

Sage 50
Complete Accounting

On July 1, 2016, Sean McConnell established his own accounting practice. Selected transactions for the first few days of July follow.

INSTRUCTIONS

1. Record the transactions on page 1 of the general journal. Omit descriptions. Assume that the firm initially records prepaid expenses as assets and unearned income as a liability.

2. Record the adjusting journal entries that must be made on July 31, 2016, on page 2 of the general journal. Omit descriptions.

DATE		TRANSACTIONS
July	1	Signed a lease for an office and issued Check 101 for $14,700 to pay the rent in advance for six months.
	1	Borrowed money from First National Bank by issuing a four-month, 9 percent note for $40,000; received $38,800 because the bank deducted the interest in advance.
	1	Signed an agreement with Young Corp. to provide accounting and tax services for one year at $7,000 per month; received the entire fee of $84,000 in advance.
	1	Purchased office equipment for $15,900 from Office Outfitters; issued a two-month, 12 percent note in payment. The equipment is estimated to have a useful life of five years and a $1,500 salvage value. The equipment will be depreciated using the straight-line method.
	1	Purchased a one-year insurance policy and issued Check 102 for $1,740 to pay the entire premium.
	3	Purchased office furniture for $16,080 from Office Warehouse; issued Check 103 for $8,480 and agreed to pay the balance in 60 days. The equipment has an estimated useful life of four years and a $1,200 salvage value. The office furniture will be depreciated using the straight-line method.
	5	Purchased office supplies for $2,010 with Check 104. Assume $900 of supplies are on hand July 31, 2016.

Analyze: What balance should be reflected in *Unearned Accounting Fees* at July 31, 2016?

Problem 12.3A

Objectives 12-2,
12-3

▶ **Recording adjustments for accrued and prepaid expense items and earned income.**

On July 31, 2016, after one month of operation, the general ledger of Michael Domenici, Consultant, contained the accounts and balances given below.

INSTRUCTIONS

1. Prepare a partial worksheet with the following sections: Trial Balance, Adjustments, and Adjusted Trial Balance. Use the data about the firm's accounts and balances to complete the Trial Balance section.
2. Enter the adjustments described below in the Adjustments section. Identify each adjustment with the appropriate letter.
3. Complete the Adjusted Trial Balance section.

ACCOUNTS AND BALANCES

Cash	$25,510	Dr.
Accounts Receivable	1,440	Dr.
Supplies	960	Dr.
Prepaid Rent	10,500	Dr.
Prepaid Insurance	2,220	Dr.
Prepaid Interest	400	Dr.
Furniture	14,760	Dr.
Accumulated Depreciation—Furniture		
Equipment	7,250	Dr.
Accumulated Depreciation—Equipment		
Notes Payable	17,700	Cr.
Accounts Payable	5,500	Cr.
Interest Payable		
Unearned Consulting Fees	6,000	Cr.
Michael Domenici, Capital	32,520	Cr.
Michael Domenici, Drawing	3,000	Dr.
Consulting Fees	9,000	Cr.
Salaries Expense	4,200	Dr.
Utilities Expense	270	Dr.
Telephone Expense	210	Dr.
Supplies Expense		
Rent Expense		
Insurance Expense		
Depreciation Expense—Furniture		
Depreciation Expense—Equipment		
Interest Expense		

ADJUSTMENTS

a. On July 31, an inventory of the supplies showed that items costing $630 were on hand.
b. On July 1, the firm paid $10,500 in advance for six months of rent.
c. On July 1, the firm purchased a one-year insurance policy for $2,220.
d. On July 1, the firm paid $400 interest in advance on a four-month note that it issued to the bank.
e. On July 1, the firm purchased office furniture for $14,760. The furniture is expected to have a useful life of eight years and a salvage value of $1,800.

f. On July 1, the firm purchased office equipment for $7,250. The equipment is expected to have a useful life of five years and a salvage value of $1,850

g. On July 1, the firm issued a three-month, 6 percent note for $9,800.

h. On July 1, the firm received a consulting fee of $6,000 in advance for a one-year period.

Analyze: By what total amount were the expense accounts of the business adjusted?

Recording adjustments and completing the worksheet.

◀ **Problem 12.4A**
Objectives 12-1, 12-2, 12-3, 12-4

The Green Thumb Gardener is a retail store that sells plants, soil, and decorative pots. On December 31, 2016, the firm's general ledger contained the accounts and balances that appear below.

INSTRUCTIONS

1. Prepare the Trial Balance section of a 10-column worksheet. The worksheet covers the year ended December 31, 2016.

2. Enter the adjustments below in the Adjustments section of the worksheet. Identify each adjustment with the appropriate letter.

3. Complete the worksheet.

ACCOUNTS AND BALANCES

Cash	$ 6,700	Dr.
Accounts Receivable	3,600	Dr.
Allowance for Doubtful Accounts	62	Cr.
Merchandise Inventory	12,300	Dr.
Supplies	1,300	Dr.
Prepaid Advertising	1,080	Dr.
Store Equipment	8,700	Dr.
Accumulated Depreciation—Store Equipment	1,600	Cr.
Office Equipment	2,200	Dr.
Accumulated Depreciation—Office Equipment	380	Cr.
Accounts Payable	2,725	Cr.
Social Security Tax Payable	530	Cr.
Medicare Tax Payable	88	Cr.
Federal Unemployment Tax Payable		
State Unemployment Tax Payable		
Salaries Payable		
Beth Argo, Capital	30,677	Cr.
Beth Argo, Drawing	21,000	Dr.
Sales	95,048	Cr.
Sales Returns and Allowances	1,200	Dr.
Purchases	49,400	Dr.
Purchases Returns and Allowances	530	Cr.
Rent Expense	7,000	Dr.
Telephone Expense	690	Dr.
Salaries Expense	15,100	Dr.
Payroll Taxes Expense	1,370	Dr.
Income Summary		
Supplies Expense		
Advertising Expense		
Depreciation Expense—Store Equipment		
Depreciation Expense—Office Equipment		
Uncollectible Accounts Expense		

ADJUSTMENTS

a.–b. Merchandise inventory on December 31, 2016, is $13,321.

c. During 2016, the firm had net credit sales of $45,000; the firm estimates that 0.5 percent of these sales will result in uncollectible accounts.

d. On December 31, 2016, an inventory of the supplies showed that items costing $325 were on hand.

e. On October 1, 2016, the firm signed a six-month advertising contract for $1,080 with a local newspaper and paid the full amount in advance.

f. On January 2, 2015, the firm purchased store equipment for $8,700. At that time, the equipment was estimated to have a useful life of five years and a salvage value of $700.

g. On January 2, 2015, the firm purchased office equipment for $2,200. At that time, the equipment was estimated to have a useful life of five years and a salvage value of $300.

h. On December 31, 2016, the firm owed salaries of $1,930 that will not be paid until 2017.

i. On December 31, 2016, the firm owed the employer's social security tax (assume 6.2 percent) and Medicare tax (assume 1.45 percent) on the entire $1,930 of accrued wages.

j. On December 31, 2016, the firm owed federal unemployment tax (assume 0.6 percent) and state unemployment tax (assume 5.4 percent) on the entire $1,930 of accrued wages.

Analyze: By what amount were the assets of the business affected by adjustments?

Problem 12.5A ▶

Objectives 12-1, 12-2, 12-3, 12-4

CONTINUING >>> Problem

Recording adjustments and completing the worksheet.

Healthy Eating Foods Company is a distributor of nutritious snack foods such as granola bars. On December 31, 2016, the firm's general ledger contained the accounts and balances that follow.

INSTRUCTIONS

1. Prepare the Trial Balance section of a 10-column worksheet. The worksheet covers the year ended December 31, 2016.

2. Enter the adjustments in the Adjustments section of the worksheet. Identify each adjustment with the appropriate letter.

3. Complete the worksheet.

Note: This problem will be required to complete Problem 13.4A in Chapter 13.

ACCOUNTS AND BALANCES

Cash	$ 30,100	Dr.
Accounts Receivable	35,200	Dr.
Allowance for Doubtful Accounts	420	Cr.
Merchandise Inventory	86,000	Dr.
Supplies	10,400	Dr.
Prepaid Insurance	5,400	Dr.
Office Equipment	8,300	Dr.
Accum. Depreciation—Office Equipment	2,650	Cr.
Warehouse Equipment	28,000	Dr.
Accum. Depreciation—Warehouse Equipment	9,600	Cr.
Notes Payable—Bank	32,000	Cr.
Accounts Payable	12,200	Cr.
Interest Payable		
Social Security Tax Payable	1,680	Cr.
Medicare Tax Payable	388	Cr.
Federal Unemployment Tax Payable		
State Unemployment Tax Payable		
Salaries Payable		
Phillip Tucker, Capital	108,684	Cr.

ACCOUNTS AND BALANCES (CONT.)

Phillip Tucker, Drawing	56,000	Dr.
Sales	653,778	Cr.
Sales Returns and Allowances	10,000	Dr.
Purchases	350,000	Dr.
Purchases Returns and Allowances	9,200	Cr.
Income Summary		
Rent Expense	36,000	Dr.
Telephone Expense	2,200	Dr.
Salaries Expense	160,000	Dr.
Payroll Taxes Expense	13,000	Dr.
Supplies Expense		
Insurance Expense		
Depreciation Expense—Office Equip.		
Depreciation Expense—Warehouse Equip.		
Uncollectible Accounts Expense		
Interest Expense		

ADJUSTMENTS

a.–b. Merchandise inventory on December 31, 2016, is $78,000.

c. During 2016, the firm had net credit sales of $560,000; past experience indicates that 0.5 percent of these sales should result in uncollectible accounts.

d. On December 31, 2016, an inventory of supplies showed that items costing $1,180 were on hand.

e. On May 1, 2016, the firm purchased a one-year insurance policy for $5,400.

f. On January 2, 2014, the firm purchased office equipment for $8,300. At that time, the equipment was estimated to have a useful life of six years and a salvage value of $350.

g. On January 2, 2014, the firm purchased warehouse equipment for $28,000. At that time, the equipment was estimated to have a useful life of five years and a salvage value of $4,000.

h. On November 1, 2016, the firm issued a four-month, 12 percent note for $32,000.

i. On December 31, 2016, the firm owed salaries of $5,000 that will not be paid until 2017.

j. On December 31, 2016, the firm owed the employer's social security tax (assume 6.2 percent) and Medicare tax (assume 1.45 percent) on the entire $5,000 of accrued wages.

k. On December 31, 2016, the firm owed the federal unemployment tax (assume 0.6 percent) and the state unemployment tax (assume 5.4 percent) on the entire $5,000 of accrued wages.

Analyze: When the financial statements for Healthy Eating Foods Company are prepared, what net income will be reported for the period ended December 31, 2016?

Recording adjustments and completing the worksheet.

◄ **Problem 12.6A**

Objectives 12-1, 12-2, 12-3, 12-4

The Artisan Wines is a retail store selling vintage wines. On December 31, 2016, the firm's general ledger contained the accounts and balances below. All account balances are normal.

Cash	28,386
Accounts Receivable	500
Prepaid Advertising	480
Supplies	300
Merchandise Inventory	15,000
Store Equipment	25,000
Accumulated Depreciation—Store Equipment	3,000
Office Equipment	5,000

Accumulated Depreciation—Office Equipment	1,500
Notes Payable, due 2017	20,000
Accounts Payable	2,705
Wages Payable	
Social Security Tax Payable	
Medicare Tax Payable	
Unearned Seminar Fees	6,000
Interest Payable	
Vincent Arroyo, Capital	32,700
Vincent Arroyo, Drawing	14,110
Income Summary	
Sales	153,970
Sales Discounts	200
Seminar Fee Income	
Purchases	91,000
Purchases Returns and Allowances	1,000
Freight In	225
Rent Expense	13,200
Wages Expense	24,000
Payroll Taxes Expense	3,324
Depreciation Expense—Store Equipment	
Depreciation Expense—Office Equipment	
Advertising Expense	
Supplies Expense	
Interest Expense	150

INSTRUCTIONS:

1. Prepare the Trial Balance section of a 10-column worksheet. The worksheet covers the year ended December 31, 2016.

2. Enter the adjustments below in the Adjustments section of the worksheet. Identify each adjustment with the appropriate letter.

3. Complete the worksheet.

ADJUSTMENTS:

a.–b. Merchandise inventory at December 31, 2016, was counted, and determined to be $13,000.

c. The amount recorded as prepaid advertising represents $480 paid on September 1, 2016, for 12 months of advertising.

d. The amount of supplies on hand at December 31 was $160.

e. Depreciation on store equipment was $3,000 for 2016.

f. Depreciation on office equipment was $1,125 for 2016.

g. Unearned Seminar Fees represents $6,000 received on November 1, 2016, for six seminars. At December 31, four of these seminars had been conducted.

h. Wages owed but not paid at December 31 were $500.

i. On December 31, 2016, the firm owed the employer's social security tax ($31.00) and Medicare tax ($7.25).

j. The note payable bears interest at 6% per annum. One month interest is owed at December 31, 2016.

Analyze: What was the amount of revenue earned by conducting seminars during the year ended December 31, 2016?

Problem Set B

Recording adjustments for accrued and prepaid items and unearned income.

◄ **Problem 12.1B**
Objectives 12-2,
12-3, 12-6

Based on the information below, record the adjusting journal entries that must be made for June Kang Consulting Services on December 31, 2016. The company has a December 31 fiscal year-end. Use 18 as the page number for the general journal.

a.–b. *Merchandise Inventory,* before adjustment, has a balance of $9,500. The newly counted inventory balance is $10,500.

c. *Unearned Seminar Fee*s has a balance of $16,000, representing prepayment by customers for four seminars to be conducted in December 2016 and January 2017. Three seminars had been conducted by December 31, 2016.

d. *Prepaid Insurance* has a balance of $15,000 for six months insurance paid in advance on October 1, 2016.

e. Store equipment costing $6,000 was purchased on September 1, 2016. It has a salvage value of $600, and a useful life of five years.

f. Employees have earned $500 of wages not paid at December 31, 2016.

g. The employer owes the following taxes on wages not paid at December 31, 2016: SUTA, $15.00; FUTA, $3.00; Medicare, $7.25; and social security, $31.00.

h. Management estimates uncollectible accounts expense at 1.5% (0.015) of sales. This year's sales were $4,000,000.

i. *Prepaid Rent* has a balance of $18,000 for nine months' rent paid in advance on October 1, 2016.

j. The *Supplies* account in the general ledger has a balance of $500. A count of supplies on hand at December 31, 2016, indicated $125 of supplies remain.

k. The company borrowed $12,000 on a two-month note payable dated December 1, 2016. The note bears interest at 6%.

Analyze: After all adjusting entries have been journalized and posted, what is the balance of the *Unearned Seminar Fees* account?

Recording adjustments for accrued and prepaid expense items and unearned income.

◄ **Problem 12.2B**
Objectives 12-2,
12-3

On June 1, 2016, Penelope Bermudez established her own advertising firm. Selected transactions for the first few days of June follow.

1. Record the transactions on page 1 of the general journal. Omit descriptions. Assume that the firm initially records prepaid expenses as assets and unearned income as a liability.

2. Record the adjusting journal entries that must be made on June 30, 2016, on page 2 of the general journal. Omit descriptions.

DATE	TRANSACTIONS
2016	
June 1	Signed a lease for an office and issued Check 101 for $18,000 to pay the rent in advance for six months.
1	Borrowed money from National Trust Bank by issuing a three-month, 10 percent note for $18,000; received $17,550 because the bank deducted interest in advance.
1	Signed an agreement with Glass Decorations Inc. to provide advertising consulting for one year at $4,550 per month; received the entire fee of $54,600 in advance.
1	Purchased office equipment for $15,400 from The Equipment Depot; issued a three-month, 12 percent note in payment. The equipment is estimated to have a useful life of five years and a $1,000 salvage value and will be depreciated using the straight-line method.
1	Purchased a one-year insurance policy and issued Check 102 for $1,944 to pay the entire premium.
3	Purchased office furniture for $17,400 from Office Gallery; issued Check 103 for $8,400 and agreed to pay the balance in 60 days. The furniture is estimated to have a useful life of five years and a $1,200 salvage value and will be depreciated using the straight-line method.
5	Purchased office supplies for $2,810 with Check 104; assume $1,150 of supplies are on hand June 30, 2016.

Analyze: At the end of the year, 2016, how much of the rent paid on June 1 will have been charged to expense?

Problem 12.3B
Objectives 12-2, 12-3

▶ ### Recording adjustments for accrued and prepaid expense items and unearned income.

On September 30, 2016, after one month of operation, the general ledger of Cross Timbers Company contained the accounts and balances shown below.

INSTRUCTIONS

1. Prepare a partial worksheet with the following sections: Trial Balance, Adjustments, and Adjusted Trial Balance. Use the data about the firm's accounts and balances to complete the Trial Balance section.

2. Enter the adjustments described below in the Adjustments section. Identify each adjustment with the appropriate letter. (Some items may not require adjustments.)

3. Complete the Adjusted Trial Balance section.

ACCOUNTS AND BALANCES

Cash	$26,460	Dr.
Supplies	740	Dr.
Prepaid Rent	4,200	Dr.
Prepaid Advertising	3,750	Dr.
Prepaid Interest	450	Dr.
Furniture	4,840	Dr.
Accumulated Depreciation—Furniture		
Equipment	9,000	Dr.
Accumulated Depreciation—Equipment		
Notes Payable	20,250	Cr.
Accounts Payable	4,400	Cr.
Interest Payable		

ACCOUNTS AND BALANCES (CONT.)

Unearned Course Fees	22,000	Cr.
Scott Nelson, Capital	6,730	Cr.
Scott Nelson, Drawing	2,000	Dr.
Course Fees		
Salaries Expense	1,600	Dr.
Telephone Expense	120	Dr.
Entertainment Expense	220	Dr.
Supplies Expense		
Rent Expense		
Advertising Expense		
Depreciation Expense—Furniture		
Depreciation Expense—Equipment		
Interest Expense		

ADJUSTMENTS

a. On September 30, an inventory of the supplies showed that items costing $705 were on hand.

b. On September 1, the firm paid $4,200 in advance for six months of rent.

c. On September 1, the firm signed a six-month advertising contract for $3,750 and paid the full amount in advance.

d. On September 1, the firm paid $450 interest in advance on a three-month note that it issued to the bank.

e. On September 1, the firm purchased office furniture for $4,840. The furniture is expected to have a useful life of five years and a salvage value of $340.

f. On September 3, the firm purchased equipment for $9,000. The equipment is expected to have a useful life of five years and a salvage value of $1,200.

g. On September 1, the firm issued a two-month, 8 percent note for $5,250.

h. During September, the firm received $22,000 fees in advance. An analysis of the firm's records shows that $7,000 applies to services provided in September and the rest pertains to future months.

Analyze: What was the net dollar effect on income of the adjustments to the accounting records of the business?

Recording adjustments and completing the worksheet.

◄ **Problem 12.4B**
**Objectives 12-1,
12-2, 12-3, 12-4**

Fun Depot is a retail store that sells toys, games, and bicycles. On December 31, 2016, the firm's general ledger contained the following accounts and balances.

INSTRUCTIONS

1. Prepare the Trial Balance section of a 10-column worksheet. The worksheet covers the year ended December 31, 2016.

2. Enter the adjustments below in the Adjustments section of the worksheet. Identify each adjustment with the appropriate letter.

3. Complete the worksheet.

ACCOUNTS AND BALANCES

Cash	$ 26,400	Dr.
Accounts Receivable	22,700	Dr.
Allowance for Doubtful Accounts	320	Cr.
Merchandise Inventory	138,000	Dr.
Supplies	11,600	Dr.

ACCOUNTS AND BALANCES (CONT.)

Prepaid Advertising	5,280	Dr.
Store Equipment	32,500	Dr.
Accumulated Depreciation—Store Equipment	5,760	Cr.
Office Equipment	8,400	Dr.
Accumulated Depreciation—Office Equipment	1,440	Cr.
Accounts Payable	8,600	Cr.
Social Security Tax Payable	5,920	Cr.
Medicare Tax Payable	1,368	Cr.
Federal Unemployment Tax Payable		
State Unemployment Tax Payable		
Salaries Payable		
Janie Fielder, Capital	112,250	Cr.
Janie Fielder, Drawing	100,000	Dr.
Sales	1,043,662	Cr.
Sales Returns and Allowances	17,200	Dr.
Purchases	507,600	Dr.
Purchases Returns and Allowances	5,040	Cr.
Rent Expense	125,000	Dr.
Telephone Expense	4,280	Dr.
Salaries Expense	164,200	Dr.
Payroll Taxes Expense	15,200	Dr.
Income Summary		
Supplies Expense		
Advertising Expense	6,000	Dr.
Depreciation Expense—Store Equipment		
Depreciation Expense—Office Equipment		
Uncollectible Accounts Expense		

ADJUSTMENTS

a.–b. Merchandise inventory on December 31, 2016, is $148,000.

c. During 2016, the firm had net credit sales of $440,000. The firm estimates that 0.7 percent of these sales will result in uncollectible accounts.

d. On December 31, 2016, an inventory of the supplies showed that items costing $2,960 were on hand.

e. On September 1, 2016, the firm signed a six-month advertising contract for $5,280 with a local newspaper and paid the full amount in advance.

f. On January 2, 2015, the firm purchased store equipment for $32,500. At that time, the equipment was estimated to have a useful life of five years and a salvage value of $3,700.

g. On January 2, 2015, the firm purchased office equipment for $8,400. At that time, the equipment was estimated to have a useful life of five years and a salvage value of $1,200.

h. On December 31, 2016, the firm owed salaries of $8,000 that will not be paid until 2014.

i. On December 31, 2016, the firm owed the employer's social security tax (assume 6.2 percent) and Medicare tax (assume 1.45 percent) on the entire $8,000 of accrued wages.

j. On December 31, 2016, the firm owed federal unemployment tax (assume 0.6 percent) and state unemployment tax (assume 5.4 percent) on the entire $8,000 of accrued wages.

Analyze: If the adjustment for advertising had not been recorded, what would the reported net income have been?

Recording adjustments and completing the worksheet.

Whatnots is a retail seller of cards, novelty items, and business products. On December 31, 2016, the firm's general ledger contained the following accounts and balances.

◄   **Problem 12.5B**
Objectives 12-1,
12-2, 12-3, 12-4

Problem

INSTRUCTIONS

1. Prepare the Trial Balance section of a 10-column worksheet. The worksheet covers the year ended December 31, 2016.

2. Enter the adjustments in the Adjustments section of the worksheet. Identify each adjustment with the appropriate letter.

3. Complete the worksheet.

Note: This problem will be required to complete Problem 13.4B in Chapter 13.

ACCOUNTS AND BALANCES

Cash	$ 3,235	Dr.
Accounts Receivable	6,910	Dr.
Allowance for Doubtful Accounts	600	Cr.
Merchandise Inventory	16,985	Dr.
Supplies	750	Dr.
Prepaid Insurance	2,400	Dr.
Store Equipment	6,000	Dr.
Accumulated Depreciation—Store Equip.	2,000	Cr.
Store Fixtures	15,760	Dr.
Accumulated Depreciation—Store Fixtures	4,100	Cr.
Notes Payable	4,000	Cr.
Accounts Payable	600	Cr.
Interest Payable		
Social Security Tax Payable		
Medicare Tax Payable		
Federal Unemployment Tax Payable		
State Unemployment Tax Payable		
Salaries Payable		
Preston Allen, Capital	39,780	Cr.
Preston Allen, Drawing	8,000	Dr.
Sales	236,560	Cr.
Sales Returns and Allowances	6,000	Dr.
Purchases	160,000	Dr.
Purchases Returns and Allowances	2,000	Cr.
Income Summary		
Rent Expense	18,000	Dr.
Telephone Expense	2,400	Dr.
Salaries Expense	40,000	Dr.
Payroll Tax Expense	3,200	Dr.
Supplies Expense		
Insurance Expense		
Depreciation Expense—Store Equipment		
Depreciation Expense—Store Fixtures		
Uncollectible Accounts Expense		
Interest Expense		

ADJUSTMENTS

a.–b. Merchandise inventory on hand on December 31, 2016, is $15,840.

c. During 2016, the firm had net credit sales of $160,000. Past experience indicates that 0.8 percent of these sales should result in uncollectible accounts.

d. On December 31, 2016, an inventory of supplies showed that items costing $245 were on hand.

e. On July 1, 2016, the firm purchased a one-year insurance policy for $2,400.

f. On January 2, 2014, the firm purchased store equipment for $6,000. The equipment was estimated to have a five-year useful life and a salvage value of $1,000.

g. On January 4, 2014, the firm purchased store fixtures for $15,760. At the time of the purchase, the fixtures were assumed to have a useful life of seven years and a salvage value of $1,410.

h. On October 1, 2016, the firm issued a six-month, $4,000 note payable at 9 percent interest with a local bank.

i. At year-end (December 31, 2016), the firm owed salaries of $1,450 that will not be paid until January 2017.

j. On December 31, 2016, the firm owed the employer's social security tax (assume 6.2 percent) and Medicare tax (assume 1.45 percent) on the entire $1,450 of accrued wages.

k. On December 31, 2016, the firm owed federal unemployment tax (assume 0.6 percent) and state unemployment tax (assume 5.0 percent) on the entire $1,450 of accrued wages.

Analyze: After all adjustments have been recorded, what is the net book value of the company's assets?

Problem 12.6B

Objectives 12-1, 12-2, 12-3, 12-4

▶ ## Recording adjustments and completing the worksheet.

The Game Place is a retail store that sells computer games, owned by Matt Huffman. On December 31, 2016, the firm's general ledger contained the accounts and balances below. All account balances are normal.

Cash	34,465
Accounts Receivable	1,669
Prepaid Advertising	480
Supplies	425
Merchandise Inventory	18,500
Store Equipment	30,000
Accumulated Depreciation—Store Equipment	3,000
Office Equipment	4,800
Accumulated Depreciation—Office Equipment	1,500
Notes Payable, due 2017	22,500
Accounts Payable	5,725
Wages Payable	
Social Security Tax Payable	
Medicare Tax Payable	
Unearned Seminar Fees	7,500
Interest Payable	
Matt Huffman, Capital	43,000
Matt Huffman, Drawing	18,000
Income Summary	
Sales	163,660
Sales Discounts	180
Seminar Fee Income	
Purchases	92,500
Purchases Returns and Allowances	770
Freight In	275
Rent Expense	26,400
Wages Expense	18,000

ACCOUNTS AND BALANCES (CONT.)

Payroll Taxes Expense	1,811
Depreciation Expense — Store Equipment	
Depreciation Expense — Office Equipment	
Advertising Expense	
Supplies Expense	
Interest Expense	150

INSTRUCTIONS

1. Prepare the Trial Balance section of a 10-column worksheet. The worksheet covers the year ended December 31, 2016.
2. Enter the adjustments below in the Adjustments section of the worksheet. Identify each adjustment with the appropriate letter.
3. Complete the worksheet.

ADJUSTMENTS

a.–b. Merchandise inventory at December 31, 2016, was counted, and determined to be $21,200.

c. The amount recorded as prepaid advertising represents $480 paid on September 1, 2016, for six months of advertising.

d. The amount of supplies on hand at December 31 was $125.

e. Depreciation on store equipment was $4,500 for 2016.

f. Depreciation on office equipment was $1,500 for 2016.

g. Unearned seminar fees represents $7,500 received on November 1, 2016, for five seminars. At December 31, three of these seminars had been conducted.

h. Wages owed but not paid at December 31 were $800.

i. On December 31, 2016, the firm owed the employer's social security tax ($49.60) and Medicare tax ($11.60).

j. The note payable bears interest at 8% per annum. One month interest is owed at December 31, 2016.

Analyze: How did the balance of merchandise inventory change during the year ended December 31, 2016?

Critical Thinking Problem 12.1

Completing the Worksheet

The unadjusted trial balance of Ben's Jewelers on December 31, 2016, the end of its fiscal year, appears on page 432.

INSTRUCTIONS

1. Copy the unadjusted trial balance onto a worksheet and complete the worksheet using the following information:

  a.–b. Ending merchandise inventory, $98,700.

  c. Uncollectible accounts expense, $1,000.

  d. Store supplies on hand December 31, 2016, $625.

  e. Office supplies on hand December 31, 2016, $305.

  f. Depreciation on store equipment, $11,360.

  g. Depreciation on office equipment, $3,300.

  h. Accrued sales salaries, $4,000, and accrued office salaries, $1,000.

  i. Social security tax on accrued salaries, $326; Medicare tax on accrued salaries, $76. (Assumes that tax rates have increased.)

  j. Federal unemployment tax on accrued salaries, $56; state unemployment tax on accrued salaries, $270.

2. Journalize the adjusting entries on page 30 of the general journal. Omit descriptions.

3. Journalize the closing entries on page 32 of the general journal. Omit descriptions.

4. Compute the following:

    a. net sales

    b. net delivered cost of purchases

    c. cost of goods sold

    d. net income or net loss

    e. balance of *Ben Waites, Capital* on December 31, 2016.

Analyze: What change(s) to *Ben Waites, Capital* will be reported on the statement of owner's equity?

BEN'S JEWELERS Trial Balance December 31, 2016		
Cash	$ 13,050	Dr
Accounts Receivable	49,900	Dr.
Allowance for Doubtful Accounts	2,000	Cr.
Merchandise Inventory	105,900	Dr.
Store Supplies	4,230	Dr.
Office Supplies	2,950	Dr.
Store Equipment	113,590	Dr.
Accumulated Depreciation — Store Equipment	13,010	Cr.
Office Equipment	27,640	Dr.
Accumulated Depreciation — Office Equipment	4,930	Cr.
Accounts Payable	4,390	Cr.
Salaries Payable		
Social Security Tax Payable		
Medicare Tax Payable		
Federal Unemployment Tax Payable		
State Unemployment Tax Payable		
Ben Waites, Capital	166,310	Cr.
Ben Waites, Drawing	30,000	Dr.
Income Summary		
Sales	862,230	Cr.
Sales Returns and Allowances	7,580	Dr.
Purchases	504,810	Dr.
Purchases Returns and Allowances	4,240	Cr.
Purchases Discounts	10,770	Cr.
Freight In	7,000	Dr.
Salaries Expense — Sales	75,950	Dr.
Rent Expense	35,500	Dr.
Advertising Expense	12,300	Dr.
Store Supplies Expense		
Depreciation Expense — Store Equipment		
Salaries Expense — Office	77,480	Dr.
Payroll Taxes Expense		
Uncollectible Accounts Expense		
Office Supplies Expense		
Depreciation Expense — Office Equipment		

Critical Thinking Problem 12.2

Net Profit

When Sara Yu's father died suddenly, Sara had just completed the semester in college, so she stepped in to run the family business, AAA Couriers, until it could be sold. Under her father's direction, the company was a successful operation and provided ample money to meet the family's needs.

Sara was majoring in biology in college and knew little about business or accounting, but she was eager to do a good job of running the business so it would command a good selling price. Since all of the services performed were paid in cash, Sara figured that she would do all right as long as the *Cash* account increased. Thus, she was delighted to watch the cash balance increase from $24,800 at the beginning of the first month to $63,028 at the end of the second month—an increase of $38,228 during the two months she had been in charge. When she was presented an income statement for the two months by the company's bookkeeper, she could not understand why it did not show that amount as income but instead reported only $21,100 as net income.

Knowing that you are taking an accounting class, Sara brings the income statement, shown below, to you and asks if you can help her understand the difference.

AAA COURIERS		
Income Statement		
Months of June and July, 2016		
Operating Revenues		
Delivery Fees		$205,018
Operating Expenses		
Salaries and Related Taxes	$128,224	
Gasoline and Oil	31,000	
Repairs Expense	6,570	
Supplies Expense	2,268	
Insurance Expense	2,856	
Depreciation Expense	13,000	
Total Operating Expense		183,918
Net Income		$ 21,100

In addition, Sara permits you to examine the accounting records, which show that the balance of *Salaries Payable* was $2,680 at the beginning of the first month but had increased to $4,240 at the end of the second month. Most of the balance in the *Insurance Expense* account reflects monthly insurance payments covering only one month each. However, the *Prepaid Insurance* account had decreased $300 during the two months, and all supplies had been purchased before Sara took over. The balances of the company's other asset and liability accounts showed no changes.

1. Explain the cause of the difference between the increase in the *Cash* account balance and the net income for the two months.

2. Prepare a schedule that accounts for this difference.

BUSINESS CONNECTIONS

Out of Balance

Ethical DILEMMA

The president of Murray Stainless Steel Corporation has told you to go out to the factory and count merchandise inventory. He said the stockholders were coming for a meeting and he wanted to put on a good show. He asked you to make the inventory a bit heavy by counting one row twice. The higher ending inventory will show a higher net income. What should you do?

Balance Sheet

McCormick and Company, Incorporated reported the following in its *2012 Annual Report:*

Consolidated Balance Sheet		
at November 30 (millions)	*2012*	*2011*
Assets		
Cash and cash equivalents	$ 79.0	$ 53.9
Trade accounts receivable, less allowances	465.9	427.0
Inventories	615.0	613.7
Prepaid expenses and other current assets	125.5	128.3
Total current assets	1,285.4	1,222.9
Property, plant, and equipment, net	547.3	523.1

Analyze:

1. Based on the information presented above, which categories might require adjusting entries at the end of an operating period?

2. List the potential adjusting entries. Disregard dollar amounts.

3. By what percentage did McCormick's cash and cash equivalents increase from 2011 to 2012?

TEAMWORK

Both Sellers and Servers Adjust

Accruals and deferrals can vary for each company. The adjusting entries for a service company will differ from those of a merchandising company. Brainstorm the adjusting entries similarities and differences for a service company and a merchandising company.

Internet | CONNECTION

There Is Help for Preparing a Trial Balance

The trial balance worksheet is an organizational tool to view the accruals and deferrals on one piece of paper. Use your search engine to search for *Trial Balance Worksheet Templates.* Download several different forms of worksheets and notice the number of helpful Excel templates available to download.

Answers to **Self Reviews**

Answers to Section 1 Self Review

1. The worksheet facilitates the end-of-period activities by assembling all data needed in one document. The worksheet provides a place for the trial balance, for entering the necessary adjusting entries, an adjusted trial balance to greatly reduce the chance for mathematical errors, and all the information necessary for closing entries and preparing the income statement, statement of owner's equity, and balance sheet.

2. Both the beginning and ending inventory are presented in the income statement, so both should ultimately appear in the Income Statement columns. In the adjusting entries, the beginning balance is closed and transferred to the Income Summary. The ending inventory is entered in the *Inventory* account by a debit in the Adjustments column and a credit to *Income Summary* because it reduces the cost of goods sold.

3. Adjusting entries are necessary because the amounts shown for many accounts in the trial balance reflect old data that ignore the fact that assets shown have been partially consumed, that expenses and incomes have not been entered in the accounts even though they have been incurred or earned, and that some liabilities and assets are not reflected in the accounts.

4. *Unearned Fee Income* will be debited for $10,500 and *Fee Income* will be credited for that amount.

5. **a.** The amount of adjustments is $3,000 ($18,000 ÷ 6).

   b. *Rent Expense* will be debited and *Prepaid Rent* will be credited.

6. There is no difference except that the amounts will be different because in one case they reflect only one month's activities and in the other case they reflect 12 months' activities.

Answers to Section 2 Self Review

1. The *Depreciation Expense* account is increased. The book value of the asset is decreased.

2. The net effects are:

   a. Assets are understated by $1,600.

   b. Liabilities are understated by $600.

   c. Expenses are understated by $600.

   d. Income is understated by $1,600.

   e. Owner's equity is understated by $1,000.

3. It appears that there is an error in adding the adjustment amount, or subtracting that amount from, some trial balance amount(s).

4. *Interest Expense* is debited and *Interest Payable* is credited.

5. **d.** "debit" income statement column

6. Adjusting entries almost invariably involve the assignment of revenues or expenses to a specific accounting period. If the revenue or expense is not assigned to the correct period, it is assigned to an incorrect period. Thus, both periods are incorrectly stated.

Answers to Comprehensive Self Review

1. The accrual method properly matches expenses with revenues in each accounting period so that statement users can rely on the financial statements prepared for each period.

2. Accrued income is income that has been earned but which has not yet been received in cash or other assets.

3. Accrued income is income earned but not yet received. Unearned income is the reverse of accrued income: It is an amount that has been received, but which has not yet been earned.

4. This represents a loss because expenses are greater than income. The loss is $28,000.

5. *Unearned Rent Income* will be debited for $18,000 and *Rent Income* will be credited for $18,000.

6. *Rent Income* will be debited for $18,000 and *Unearned Rent Income* will be credited for that amount.

Financial Statements and Closing Procedures

Chapter 13

Whole Foods
www.wholefoodsmarket.com

Founded in 1980 in Austin, Texas, Whole Foods Market is the world's leading retailer of natural and organic foods. In 2012, the company reported sales of nearly $12 billion. The company operates approximately 340 stores in the United States, Canada, and the United Kingdom.

2012 was the best year in the company's 32-year history. They delivered their strongest financial performance, breaking records on many levels. They opened 25 new stores, expanded into eight new markets, and reported their eleventh consecutive quarter of comparable store sales growth of 7.8 percent or better. Their stellar results substantially exceeded their own expectations.

They are successfully utilizing social media as a powerful way to gain positive exposure and connect with their Internet-savvy customers on a global and local level. At year-end, the company had over one million "likes" on *Facebook,* and they were the top retail brand on *Twitter* with over three million followers.

Whole Foods Market outlook for fiscal year 2013 reflects another year of healthy comparable store sales growth and incremental operating margin improvement. Before the company can begin tracking this improvement, they will close the books, so to speak, on 2012 so that a clear comparison can be made against financial results of the exciting year to come.

thinking critically
What kinds of revenues and expenses do you think Whole Foods Market would include on their income statement that would be typical for a grocery store?

LEARNING OBJECTIVES

13-1. Prepare a classified income statement from the worksheet.

13-2. Prepare a statement of owner's equity from the worksheet.

13-3. Prepare a classified balance sheet from the worksheet.

13-4. Journalize and post the adjusting entries.

13-5. Journalize and post the closing entries.

13-6. Prepare a postclosing trial balance.

13-7. Journalize and post reversing entries.

13-8. Define the accounting terms new to this chapter.

NEW TERMS

accounts receivable turnover
classified financial statement
current assets
current liabilities
current ratio
gross profit
gross profit percentage
inventory turnover
liquidity
long-term liabilities
multiple-step income statement
plant and equipment
reversing entries
single-step income statement
working capital

Preparing the Financial Statements

The information needed to prepare the financial statements is on the worksheet in the Income Statement and Balance Sheet sections. At the end of the period, Whiteside Antiques prepares three financial statements: income statement, statement of owner's equity, and balance sheet, based on the worksheet you studied in Chapter 12. The income statement and the balance sheet are arranged in a classified format. On **classified financial statements,** revenues, expenses, assets, and liabilities are divided into groups of similar accounts and a subtotal is given for each group. This makes the financial statements more useful to the readers.

> The annual report of the Coca-Cola Company includes Consolidated Balance Sheets, Consolidated Statements of Income, and Consolidated Statements of Shareowners' Equity. The annual report also contains a table of Selected Financial Data that reports five consecutive years of summarized financial information.

The Classified Income Statement

A classified income statement is sometimes called a **multiple-step income statement** because several subtotals are computed before net income is calculated. The simpler income statement you learned about in previous chapters is called a **single-step income statement.** It lists all revenues in one section and all expenses in another section. Only one computation is necessary to determine the net income (Total Revenue − Total Expenses = Net Income).

Figure 13.1 shows the classified income statement for Whiteside Antiques. Refer to it as you learn how to prepare a multiple-step income statement.

>> 13-1. OBJECTIVE

Prepare a classified income statement from the worksheet.

OPERATING REVENUE

The first section of the classified income statement contains the revenue from operations. This is the revenue earned from normal business activities. Other income is presented separately near the bottom of the statement. For Whiteside Antiques, all operating revenue comes from sales of merchandise.

FIGURE 13.1 Classified Income Statement

Whiteside Antiques
Income Statement
Year Ended December 31, 2016

Operating Revenue				
Sales				561 650 00
Less Sales Returns and Allowances				12 500 00
Net Sales				549 150 00
Cost of Goods Sold				
Merchandise Inventory, Jan. 1, 2016			52 000 00	
Purchases		321 500 00		
Freight In		9 800 00		
Delivered Cost of Purchases		331 300 00		
Less Purchases Returns and Allowances	3 050 00			
Purchases Discounts	3 130 00	6 180 00		
Net Delivered Cost of Purchases			325 120 00	
Total Merchandise Available for Sale			377 120 00	
Less Merchandise Inventory, Dec. 31, 2016			47 000 00	
Cost of Goods Sold				330 120 00
Gross Profit on Sales				219 030 00
Operating Expenses				
Selling Expenses				
Salaries Expense—Sales		79 690 00		
Advertising Expense		7 425 00		
Cash Short or Over		125 00		
Supplies Expense		4 975 00		
Depreciation Expense—Store Equipment		2 400 00		
Total Selling Expenses			94 615 00	
General and Administrative Expenses				
Rent Expense		27 600 00		
Salaries Expense—Office		26 500 00		
Insurance Expense		2 450 00		
Payroll Taxes Expense		7 368 80		
Telephone Expense		1 875 00		
Uncollectible Accounts Expense		800 00		
Utilities Expense		5 925 00		
Depreciation Expense—Office Equipment		700 00		
Total General and Administrative Expenses			73 218 80	
Total Operating Expenses				167 833 80
Net Income from Operations				51 196 20
Other Income				
Interest Income		166 00		
Miscellaneous Income		366 00		
Total Other Income			532 00	
Other Expenses				
Interest Expense		770 00		
Net Nonoperating Expense				238 00
Net Income for Year				50 958 20

Because Whiteside Antiques is a retail firm, it does not offer sales discounts to its customers. If it did, the sales discounts would be deducted from total sales in order to compute net sales. The net sales amount is computed as follows:

> Sales
> (Sales Returns and Allowances)
> (Sales Discounts)
> ─────────────────────
> Net Sales

The parentheses indicate that the amount is subtracted. Net sales for Whiteside Antiques are $549,150 for 2016.

COST OF GOODS SOLD

The Cost of Goods Sold section contains information about the cost of the merchandise that was sold during the period. Three elements are needed to compute the cost of goods sold: beginning inventory, net delivered cost of purchases, and ending inventory. The format is:

>   Purchases
> + Freight In
>   (Purchases Returns and Allowances)
>   (Purchases Discounts)
> ─────────────────────
>   Net Delivered Cost of Purchases
>
>   Beginning Merchandise Inventory
> + Net Delivered Cost of Purchases
> ─────────────────────
>   Total Merchandise Available for Sale
>   (Ending Merchandise Inventory)
> ─────────────────────
>   Cost of Goods Sold

For Whiteside Antiques, the net delivered cost of purchases is $325,120 and the cost of goods sold is $330,120. ***Merchandise Inventory*** is the one account that appears on both the income statement and the balance sheet. Beginning and ending merchandise inventory balances appear on the income statement. Ending merchandise inventory also appears on the balance sheet in the Assets section.

GROSS PROFIT ON SALES

The **gross profit** on sales is the difference between the net sales and the cost of goods sold. For Whiteside, net sales is the revenue earned from selling antique items. Cost of goods sold is what Whiteside paid for the antiques that were sold during the fiscal period. Gross profit is what is left to cover operating expenses and provide a profit. The format is:

> Net Sales
> (Cost of Goods Sold)
> ─────────────────────
> Gross Profit on Sales

The gross profit on sales is $219,030.

OPERATING EXPENSES

Operating expenses are expenses that arise from normal business activities. Whiteside Antiques separates operating expenses into two categories: *Selling Expenses* and *General and Administrative Expenses.* The selling expenses relate directly to the marketing, sale, and delivery of goods. The general and administrative expenses are necessary for business operations but are not directly connected with the sales function. Rent, utilities, and salaries for office employees are examples of general and administrative expenses.

Merchandising firms usually use warehouses to store inventory. These firms would have an additional operating expense category: *Warehouse Expenses.*

FIGURE 13.2

Statement of Owner's Equity

Whiteside Antiques Statement of Owner's Equity Year Ended December 31, 2016			
Bill Whiteside, Capital, January 1, 2016			61 2 2 1 00
Net Income for Year	50 9 5 8 20		
Less Withdrawals for the Year	27 6 0 0 00		
Increase in Capital			23 3 5 8 20
Bill Whiteside, Capital, December 31, 2016			84 5 7 9 20

NET INCOME OR NET LOSS FROM OPERATIONS

Keeping operating and nonoperating income separate helps financial statement users learn about the operating efficiency of the firm. The format for determining net income (or net loss) from operations is:

> Gross Profit on Sales
> (Total Operating Expenses)
> _____
> Net Income (or Net Loss) from Operations

For Whiteside Antiques, net income from operations is $51,196.20.

OTHER INCOME AND OTHER EXPENSES

Income that is earned from sources other than normal business activities appears in the Other Income section. For Whiteside Antiques, other income includes interest on notes receivable and one miscellaneous income item.

Expenses that are not directly connected with business operations appear in the Other Expenses section. The only other expense for Whiteside Antiques is interest expense.

NET INCOME OR NET LOSS

Net income is all the revenue minus all the expenses. For Whiteside Antiques, net income is $50,958.20. If there is a net loss, it appears in parentheses. Net income or net loss is used to prepare the statement of owner's equity.

Many companies provide condensed financial statements to vendors and creditors. A condensed income statement summarizes much of the detail into a few lines of information. An income statement for Whiteside Antiques is prepared below, in whole dollars.

Whiteside Antiques Income Statement Year Ended December 31, 2016		
Net Sales		549,150
Cost of Goods Sold		330,120
Gross Profit		219,030
Operating Expenses:		
Selling Expenses	94,615	
General and Administrative Expenses	73,219	
Total Operating Expenses		167,834
Net Income from Operations		51,196
Other Expense, Net		238
Net Income for Year		50,958

The Statement of Owner's Equity

The statement of owner's equity reports the changes that occurred in the owner's financial interest during the period. Figure 13.2 on page 441 shows the statement of owner's equity for Whiteside Antiques. The ending capital balance for Bill Whiteside, $84,576.80, is used to prepare the balance sheet.

The Classified Balance Sheet

The classified balance sheet divides the various assets and liabilities into groups. Figure 13.3 below shows the balance sheet for Whiteside Antiques. Refer to it as you learn how to prepare a classified balance sheet.

FIGURE 13.3

Classified Balance Sheet

Whiteside Antiques
Balance Sheet
December 31, 2016

Assets			
Current Assets			
Cash			13 1 3 6 00
Petty Cash Fund			1 0 0 00
Notes Receivable			1 2 0 0 00
Accounts Receivable	32 0 0 0 00		
Less Allowance for Doubtful Accounts	1 0 5 0 00	30 9 5 0 00	
Interest Receivable			3 0 00
Merchandise Inventory			47 0 0 0 00
Prepaid Expenses			
Supplies	1 3 2 5 00		
Prepaid Insurance	4 9 0 0 00		
Prepaid Interest	7 5 00	6 3 0 0 00	
Total Current Assets			98 7 1 6 00
Plant and Equipment			
Store Equipment	30 0 0 0 00		
Less Accumulated Depreciation	2 4 0 0 00	27 6 0 0 00	
Office Equipment	5 0 0 0 00		
Less Accumulated Depreciation	7 0 0 00	4 3 0 0 00	
Total Plant and Equipment			31 9 0 0 00
Total Assets			130 6 1 6 00
Liabilities and Owner's Equity			
Current Liabilities			
Notes Payable—Trade	2 0 0 0 00		
Notes Payable—Bank	9 0 0 0 00		
Accounts Payable	24 1 2 9 00		
Interest Payable	2 0 00		
Social Security Tax Payable	1 1 5 8 40		
Medicare Tax Payable	2 6 7 40		
Employee Income Tax Payable	9 9 0 00		
Federal Unemployment Tax Payable	7 20		
State Unemployment Tax Payable	6 4 80		
Salaries Payable	1 2 0 0 00		
Sales Tax Payable	7 2 0 0 00		
Total Current Liabilities			46 0 3 6 80
Owner's Equity			
Bill Whiteside, Capital			84 5 7 9 20
Total Liabilities and Owner's Equity			130 6 1 6 00

CURRENT ASSETS

Current assets consist of cash, items that will normally be converted into cash within one year, and items that will be used up within one year. Current assets are usually listed in order of liquidity. **Liquidity** is the ease with which an item can be converted into cash. Current assets are vital to the survival of a business because they provide the funds needed to pay bills and meet expenses. The current assets for Whiteside Antiques total $98,716.

PLANT AND EQUIPMENT

Noncurrent assets are called *long-term assets*. An important category of long-term assets is plant and equipment. **Plant and equipment** consists of property that will be used in the business for longer than one year. For many businesses, plant and equipment represents a sizable investment. The balance sheet shows three amounts for each category of plant and equipment:

> Asset
> (Accumulated depreciation)
> ───────────────────
> Book value

For Whiteside Antiques, total plant and equipment is $31,900.

CURRENT LIABILITIES

Current liabilities are the debts that must be paid within one year. They are usually listed in order of priority of payment. Management must ensure that funds are available to pay current liabilities when they become due in order to maintain the firm's good credit reputation. For Whiteside Antiques, total current liabilities are $46,036.80.

LONG-TERM LIABILITIES

Long-term liabilities are debts of the business that are due more than one year in the future. Although repayment of long-term liabilities might not be due for several years, management must make sure that periodic interest is paid promptly. Long-term liabilities include mortgages, notes payable, and loans payable. Whiteside Antiques had no long-term liabilities on December 31, 2016.

OWNER'S EQUITY

Whiteside Antiques prepares a separate statement of owner's equity that reports all information about changes that occurred in Bill Whiteside's financial interest during the period. The ending balance from that statement is transferred to the Owner's Equity section of the balance sheet.

recall

Book Value
Book value is the portion of the original cost that has not been depreciated. Usually, book value bears no relation to the market value of the asset.

Section 1 Self Review

QUESTIONS

1. Why are financial statements prepared in classified form?

2. What is the distinction between current liabilities and long-term liabilities?

3. What is gross profit on sales?

EXERCISES

4. Which of the following is not a current asset?

   a. Merchandise inventory

   b. A note receivable due in 11 months

   c. Prepaid insurance covering the next eight months

   d. A note receivable due in 13 months

5. How should purchases returns and allowances be shown on the income statement?

   a. As Other Income

   b. As an addition to the delivered cost of purchases

   c. As a deduction from the delivered cost of purchases

   d. As Other Expenses

ANALYSIS

6. Assume that a business listed the **Freight In** account in the Operating Expense section of the income statement. What is the effect on net purchases? On total operating expenses? On net income from operations?

(Answers to Section 1 Self Review are on page 477.)

>> 13-4. Journalize and post the adjusting entries.

WHY IT'S IMPORTANT

Adjusting entries match revenue and expenses to the proper periods.

>> 13-5. Journalize and post the closing entries.

WHY IT'S IMPORTANT

The temporary accounts are closed in order to prepare for the next accounting period.

>> 13-6. Prepare a postclosing trial balance.

WHY IT'S IMPORTANT

The general ledger must remain in balance.

>> 13-7. Journalize and post reversing entries.

WHY IT'S IMPORTANT

Reversing entries are made so that transactions can be recorded in the usual way in the next accounting period.

accounts receivable turnover
current ratio
gross profit percentage
inventory turnover
reversing entries
working capital

Completing the Accounting Cycle

The complete accounting cycle was presented in Chapter 6 (pages 168–169). In this section, we will complete the accounting cycle for Whiteside Antiques.

>> 13-4. OBJECTIVE

Journalize and post the adjusting entries.

Journalizing and Posting the Adjusting Entries

All adjustments are shown on the worksheet. After the financial statements have been prepared, the adjustments are made a permanent part of the accounting records. They are recorded in the general journal as adjusting journal entries and are posted to the general ledger.

JOURNALIZING THE ADJUSTING ENTRIES

Figure 13.4 shows the adjusting journal entries for Whiteside Antiques. Each adjusting entry shows how the adjustment was calculated. Supervisors and auditors need to understand, without additional explanation, why the adjustment was made.

Let's review the types of adjusting entries made by Whiteside Antiques:

Type of Adjustment	Worksheet Reference	Purpose
Inventory	(a–b)	Removes beginning inventory and adds ending inventory to the accounting records.
Expense	(c–e)	Matches expense to revenue for the period; the credit is to a contra asset account.
Accrued Expense	(f–i)	Matches expense to revenue for the period; the credit is to a liability account.
Prepaid Expense	(j–l)	Matches expense to revenue for the period; the credit is to an asset account.
Accrued Income	(m)	Recognizes income earned in the period. The debit is to an asset account **(Interest Receivable)**.

FIGURE 13.4

Adjusting Entries in the
General Journal

	DATE		DESCRIPTION	POST. REF.	DEBIT	CREDIT	
1			Adjusting Entries				1
2	2016		(Adjustment a)				2
3	Dec.	31	Income Summary	399	52 000 00		3
4			Merchandise Inventory	121		52 000 00	4
5			To transfer beginning inventory				5
6			to Income Summary				6
7							7
8			(Adjustment b)				8
9		31	Merchandise Inventory	121	47 000 00		9
10			Income Summary	399		47 000 00	10
11			To record ending inventory				11
12							12
13			(Adjustment c)				13
14		31	Uncollectible Accounts Expense	685	800 00		14
15			Allowance For Doubtful Accounts	112		800 00	15
16			To record estimated loss				16
17			from uncollectible accounts				17
18			based on 0.80% of net				18
19			credit sales of $100,000				19
20							20
21			(Adjustment d)				21
22		31	Depreciation Expense—Store Equip.	620	2 400 00		22
23			Accum. Depreciation—Store Equip.	132		2 400 00	23
24			To record depreciation				24
25			for 2016 as shown by				25
26			schedule on file				26
27							27
28			(Adjustment e)				28
29		31	Depreciation Expense—Office Equip.	689	700 00		29
30			Accum. Depreciation—Office Equip.	142		700 00	30
31			To record depreciation				31
32			for 2016 as shown by				32
33			schedule on file				33
34							34
35			(Adjustment f)				35
36		31	Salaries Expense—Sales	602	1 200 00		36
37			Salaries Payable	229		1 200 00	37
38			To record accrued salaries				38
39			of part-time sales clerks				39
40			for Dec. 28–31				40

GENERAL JOURNAL   PAGE 25

(continued)

FIGURE 13.4

Adjusting Entries in the General Journal (continued)

GENERAL JOURNAL   PAGE _____26_____

	DATE		DESCRIPTION	POST. REF.	DEBIT	CREDIT	
1			*Adjusting Entries*				1
2	*2016*		*(Adjustment g)*				2
3	*Dec.*	*31*	*Payroll Taxes Expense*	665	9 1 80		3
4			*Social Security Tax Payable*	221		7 4 40	4
5			*Medicare Tax Payable*	223		1 7 40	5
6			*To record accrued payroll*				6
7			*taxes on accrued salaries*				7
8			*for Dec. 28–31*				8
9							9
10			*(Adjustment h)*				10
11		*31*	*Payroll Taxes Expense*	665	7 2 00		11
12			*Fed. Unemployment Tax Payable*	225		7 20	12
13			*State Unemployment Tax Payable*	227		6 4 80	13
14			*To record accrued payroll*				14
15			*taxes on accrued salaries*				15
16			*for Dec. 28–31*				16
17							17
18			*(Adjustment i)*				18
19		*31*	*Interest Expense*	695	2 0 00		19
20			*Interest Payable*	216		2 0 00	20
21			*To record interest on a*				21
22			*2-month, $2,000, 12%*				22
23			*note payable dated*				23
24			*Dec. 1, 2016*				24
25							25
26			*(Adjustment j)*				26
27		*31*	*Supplies Expense*	615	4 9 7 5 00		27
28			*Supplies*	129		4 9 7 5 00	28
29			*To record supplies used*				29
30							30
31			*(Adjustment k)*				31
32		*31*	*Insurance Expense*	660	2 4 5 0 00		32
33			*Prepaid Insurance*	126		2 4 5 0 00	33
34			*To record expired*				34
35			*insurance on 3-year*				35
36			*policy purchased for*				36
37			*$7,350 on Jan. 2, 2016*				37
38							38
39							39
40							40

FIGURE 13.4

Adjusting Entries in the General
Journal (concluded)

	DATE		DESCRIPTION	POST. REF.	DEBIT	CREDIT	
1	2016		(Adjustment l)				1
2	Dec.	31	Interest Expense	695	1 5 0 00		2
3			Prepaid Interest	127		1 5 0 00	3
4			To record transfer of 2/3				4
5			of prepaid interest of				5
6			$225 for a 3-month,				6
7			10% note payable issued				7
8			to bank on Nov. 1, 2016				8
9							9
10			(Adjustment m)				10
11		31	Interest Receivable	116	3 0 00		11
12			Interest Income	491		3 0 00	12
13			To record accrued interest				13
14			earned on a 4-month,				14
15			15% note receivable				15
16			dated Nov. 1, 2016				16
17			($1,200 x 0.15 x 2/12)				17
18							18

GENERAL JOURNAL   PAGE 27

POSTING THE ADJUSTING ENTRIES

After the adjustments have been recorded in the general journal, they are promptly posted to the general ledger. The word *Adjusting* is entered in the Description column of the general ledger account. This distinguishes it from entries for transactions that occurred during that period. After the adjusting entries have been posted, the general ledger account balances match the amounts shown in the Adjusted Trial Balance section of the worksheet in Figure 12.2.

Journalizing and Posting the Closing Entries

At the end of the period, the temporary accounts are closed. The temporary accounts are the revenue, cost of goods sold, expense, and drawing accounts.

JOURNALIZING THE CLOSING ENTRIES

>> **13-5. OBJECTIVE**

Journalize and post the closing entries.

The Income Statement section of the worksheet in Figure 12.2 on pages 410–413 provides the data needed to prepare closing entries. There are four steps in the closing process:

1. Close revenue accounts and cost of goods sold accounts with credit balances to *Income Summary.*
2. Close expense accounts and cost of goods sold accounts with debit balances to *Income Summary.*
3. Close *Income Summary,* which now reflects the net income or loss for the period, to owner's capital.
4. Close the drawing account to owner's capital.

Step 1: Closing the Revenue Accounts and the Cost of Goods Sold Accounts with Credit Balances. The first entry closes the revenue accounts and other temporary income statement accounts with credit balances. Look at the Income Statement section of the worksheet in Figure 12.2. There are five items listed in the Credit column, not including *Income Summary*. Debit each account, except *Income Summary*, for its balance. Credit *Income Summary* for the total, $568,362.

	DATE		DESCRIPTION	POST. REF.	DEBIT	CREDIT	
			GENERAL JOURNAL			PAGE _28_	
1	2016		Closing Entries				1
2	Dec.	31	Sales	401	561 650 00		2
3			Interest Income	491	166 00		3
4			Miscellaneous Income	493	366 00		4
5			Purchases Returns and Allowances	503	3 050 00		5
6			Purchases Discounts	504	3 130 00		6
7			Income Summary			568 362 00	7

Step 2: **Closing the Expense Accounts and the Cost of Goods Sold Accounts with Debit Balances.** The Debit column of the Income Statement section of the worksheet in Figure 12.2 shows the expense accounts and the cost of goods sold accounts with debit balances. Credit each account, *except Income Summary,* for its balance. Debit *Income Summary* for the total, $512,403.80.

	DATE		DESCRIPTION	POST. REF.	DEBIT	CREDIT	
			GENERAL JOURNAL			PAGE _28_	
1	2016						1
9	Dec.	31	Income Summary	399	512 403 80		9
10			Sales Returns and Allowances	451		12 500 00	10
11			Purchases	501		321 500 00	11
12			Freight In	502		9 800 00	12
13			Salaries Expense—Sales	602		79 690 00	13
14			Advertising Expense	605		7 425 00	14
15			Cash Short or Over	610		125 00	15
16			Supplies Expense	615		4 975 00	16
17			Depreciation Expense—Store Equip.	620		2 400 00	17
18			Rent Expense	640		27 600 00	18
19			Salaries Expense—Office	645		26 500 00	19
20			Insurance Expense	660		2 450 00	20
21			Payroll Taxes Expense	665		7 368 80	21
22			Telephone Expense	680		1 875 00	22
23			Uncollectible Accounts Expense	685		800 00	23
24			Utilities Expense	687		5 925 00	24
25			Depreciation Expense—Office Equip.	689		700 00	25
26			Interest Expense	695		770 00	26

Step 3: **Closing the Income Summary Account.** After the first two closing entries have been posted, the balance of the *Income Summary* account is equal to the net income or net loss for the period. The third closing entry transfers the *Income Summary* balance to the owner's capital account. *Income Summary* after the second closing entry has a balance of $50,958.20.

	Income Summary		
Adjusting Entries (a–b)	12/31	52,000.00	12/31	47,000.00
Closing Entries	12/31	512,403.80	12/31	568,362.00
		564,403.80		615,362.00
			Bal.	50,958.20

For Whiteside Antiques, the third closing entry is as follows. This closes the **Income Summary** account, which remains closed until it is used in the end-of-period process for the next year.

	GENERAL JOURNAL		PAGE __28__		
DATE	DESCRIPTION	POST. REF.	DEBIT	CREDIT	
28	Dec. 31 Income Summary	399	50 9 5 8 20		28
29	Bill Whiteside, Capital	301		50 9 5 8 20	29

Step 4: Closing the Drawing Account. This entry closes the drawing account and updates the capital account so that its balance agrees with the ending capital reported on the statement of owner's equity and on the balance sheet.

	GENERAL JOURNAL		PAGE __28__		
DATE	DESCRIPTION	POST. REF.	DEBIT	CREDIT	
31	Dec. 31 Bill Whiteside, Capital	301	27 6 0 0 00		31
32	Bill Whiteside, Drawing	302		27 6 0 0 00	32

POSTING THE CLOSING ENTRIES

The closing entries are posted from the general journal to the general ledger. The word *Closing* is entered in the Description column of each account that is closed. After the closing entry is posted, each temporary account balance is zero.

Preparing a Postclosing Trial Balance

>> 13-6. OBJECTIVE
Prepare a postclosing trial balance.

After the closing entries have been posted, prepare a postclosing trial balance to confirm that the general ledger is in balance. Only the accounts that have balances—the asset, liability and owner's capital accounts—appear on the postclosing trial balance. The postclosing trial balance matches the amounts reported on the balance sheet. To verify this, compare the postclosing trial balance, Figure 13.5 on the next page, with the balance sheet, Figure 13.3 on page 442.

If the postclosing trial balance shows that the general ledger is out of balance, find and correct the error or errors immediately. Any necessary correcting entries must be journalized and posted so that the general ledger is in balance before any transactions can be recorded for the new period.

FIGURE 13.5

Postclosing Trial Balance

Whiteside Antiques
Postclosing Trial Balance
December 31, 2016

ACCOUNT NAME	DEBIT	CREDIT
Cash	13 136 00	
Petty Cash Fund	100 00	
Notes Receivable	1 200 00	
Accounts Receivable	32 000 00	
Allowance for Doubtful Accounts		1 050 00
Interest Receivable	30 00	
Merchandise Inventory	47 000 00	
Supplies	1 325 00	
Prepaid Insurance	4 900 00	
Prepaid Interest	75 00	
Store Equipment	30 000 00	
Accumulated Depreciation—Store Equipment		2 400 00
Office Equipment	5 000 00	
Accumulated Depreciation—Office Equipment		700 00
Notes Payable—Trade		2 000 00
Notes Payable—Bank		9 000 00
Accounts Payable		24 129 00
Interest Payable		20 00
Social Security Tax Payable		1 158 40
Medicare Tax Payable		267 40
Employee Income Taxes Payable		990 00
Federal Unemployment Tax Payable		7 20
State Unemployment Tax Payable		64 80
Salaries Payable		1 200 00
Sales Tax Payable		7 200 00
Bill Whiteside, Capital		84 579 20
Totals	134 766 00	134 766 00

Interpreting the Financial Statements

Interested parties analyze the financial statements to evaluate the results of operations and to make decisions. Interpreting financial statements requires an understanding of the business and the environment in which it operates as well as the nature and limitations of accounting information. Ratios and other measurements are used to analyze and interpret financial statements. Four such measurements are used by Whiteside Antiques.

The **gross profit percentage** reveals the amount of gross profit from each sales dollar. The gross profit percentage is calculated by dividing gross profit by net sales. For Whiteside, for every dollar of net sales, gross profit was almost 40 cents.

$$\frac{\text{Gross profit}}{\text{Net sales}} = \frac{\$219,030}{\$549,150} = 0.3988 = 39.9\%$$

Working capital is the difference between total current assets and total current liabilities. It is a measure of the firm's ability to pay its current obligations. Whiteside Antiques' working capital is $52,676.80, calculated as follows:

$$\text{Current assets} - \text{Current liabilities} = \$98,716.00 - \$46,036.80 = \$52,679.20$$

The **current ratio** is a relationship between current assets and current liabilities that provides a measure of a firm's ability to pay its current debts. Whiteside has $2.14 in current assets for every dollar of current liabilities. The current ratio may also be compared to other firms in the same business. The current ratio is calculated in the following manner:

$$\frac{\text{Current assets}}{\text{Current liabilities}} = \frac{\$98,716.00}{\$46,036.80} = 2.14 \text{ to } 1$$

important!

Current Ratio
Banks and other lenders look closely at the current ratio of each loan applicant.
```
```

Caterpillar Inc. reported current assets of $42.5 billion and current liabilities of $29.8 billion on December 31, 2012. The current ratio shows that the business has $1.43 of current assets for each dollar of current liabilities.

Inventory turnover shows the number of times inventory is replaced during the accounting period. Inventory turnover is calculated in the following manner:

$$\text{Inventory turnover} = \frac{\text{Cost of goods sold}}{\text{Average inventory}}$$

$$\text{Average inventory} = \frac{\text{Beginning inventory} + \text{Ending inventory}}{2}$$

$$\text{Average inventory} = \frac{\$52,000 + \$47,000}{2} = \$49,500$$

$$\text{Inventory turnover} = \frac{\$330,120}{\$49,500} = 6.67 \text{ times}$$

For Whiteside Antiques, the average inventory for the year was $49,500. The inventory turnover was 6.67; that is, inventory was replaced about seven times during the year.

A company needs to collect accounts receivable promptly. This minimizes the amount of working capital tied up in receivables and improves cash flow. The **accounts receivable turnover** measures the reasonableness of accounts receivable outstanding, and can be used to estimate the average collection period of accounts receivable.

The accounts receivable turnover is computed as follows:

$$\text{Accounts receivable turnover} = \frac{\text{Net credit sales}}{\text{Average accounts receivable}}$$

Assume the net credit sales for Whiteside Antiques were $326,975 in 2016 and that the balance of accounts receivable at December 31, 2015, was $28,500. The average accounts receivable are $29,725, calculated as:

$$\text{Average accounts receivable} = \frac{\$28,500 + \$30,950}{2} = \$29,725$$

The accounts receivable turnover is 11. The calculation follows.

$$\text{Accounts receivable turnover} = \frac{\$326,975}{\$29,725} = 11.0 \text{ times}$$

We can use the accounts receivable turnover to estimate the average collection period. The average collection period is computed by dividing 365 days by the accounts receivable turnover. For Whiteside Antiques, their average collection period in 2016 was 33.2 days, calculated as:

$$\text{Average collection period} = \frac{365 \text{ days}}{11.0} = 33.2 \text{ days.}$$

If Whiteside Antiques grants credit terms of n/30 days, their average collection period would be considered satisfactory.

Journalizing and Posting Reversing Entries

>> **13-7. OBJECTIVE**

Journalize and post reversing entries.

Some adjustments made at the end of one period can cause problems in the next period. **Reversing entries** are made to reverse the effect of certain adjustments. This helps prevent errors in recording payments or cash receipts in the new accounting period.

Let's use adjustment **(f)** as an illustration of how reversing entries are helpful. On December 31, Whiteside Antiques owed $1,200 of salaries to its part-time sales clerks. The salaries will

Accrual Basis

Revenues are recognized when earned, and expenses are recognized when incurred or used, regardless of when cash is received or paid.

be paid in January. To recognize the salaries expense in December, adjustment **(f)** was made to debit *Salaries Expense—Sales* for $1,200 and credit *Salaries Payable* for $1,200. The adjustment was recorded and posted in the accounting records.

By payday on January 3, the part-time sales clerks have earned $1,700:

$1,200   earned in December
$ 500   earned in January

The entry to record the January 3 payment of the salaries is a debit to *Salaries Expense—Sales* for $500, a debit to *Salaries Payable* for $1,200, and a credit to *Cash* for $1,700. This entry recognizes the salary expense for January and reduces the *Salaries Payable* account to zero.

Salaries Expense — Sales		
1/3	500	

Cash				
12/31	13,136	1/3	1,700
Bal.	11,436		

Salaries Payable			
1/3	1,200	12/31	1,200
		Bal.	0

To record this transaction, the accountant had to review the adjustment in the end-of-period records and divide the amount paid between the expense and liability accounts. This review is time consuming, can cause errors, and is sometimes forgotten.

Reversing entries provide a way to guard against oversights, eliminate the review of accounting records, and simplify the entry made in the new period. As an example of a reversing entry, we will analyze the same transaction (January 3 payroll of $1,700) if reversing entries are made.

First, record the adjustment on December 31. Then record the reversing entry on January 1. Note that the reversing entry is the exact opposite (the reverse) of the adjustment. After the reversing entry is posted, the *Salaries Payable* account shows a zero balance and the *Salaries Expense—Sales* account has a credit balance. This is unusual because the normal balance of an expense account is a debit.

GENERAL JOURNAL   PAGE   25

	DATE	DESCRIPTION	POST. REF.	DEBIT	CREDIT	
1	2016	*Adjusting Entries*				1
35		(Adjustment f)				35
36	Dec. 31	Salaries Expense—Sales	602	1 2 0 0 00		36
37		Salaries Payable	229		1 2 0 0 00	37

GENERAL JOURNAL   PAGE   29

	DATE	DESCRIPTION	POST. REF.	DEBIT	CREDIT	
1	2017	*Reversing Entries*				1
2	Jan. 1	Salaries Payable	229	1 2 0 0 00		2
3		Salaries Expense—Sales	602		1 2 0 0 00	3

ACCOUNT _Salaries Payable_   ACCOUNT NO. _229_

DATE		DESCRIPTION	POST. REF.	DEBIT	CREDIT	BALANCE DEBIT	BALANCE CREDIT
2016							
Dec.	31	Adjusting	J25		1 2 0 0 00		1 2 0 0 00
2017							
Jan.	1	Reversing	J29	1 2 0 0 00			—0—

ACCOUNT _Salaries Expense—Sales_   ACCOUNT NO. _602_

DATE		DESCRIPTION	POST. REF.	DEBIT	CREDIT	BALANCE DEBIT	BALANCE CREDIT
2016							
Dec.	31	Balance				78 4 9 0 00	
	31	Adjusting	J25	1 2 0 0 00		79 6 9 0 00	
	31	Closing	J28		79 6 9 0 00	—0—	
2017							
Jan.	1	Reversing	J29		1 2 0 0 00		1 2 0 0 00

On January 3, the payment of $1,700 of salaries is recorded in the normal manner. Notice that this entry reduces cash and increases the expense account for the entire $1,700. It does not allocate the $1,700 between the expense and liability accounts.

GENERAL JOURNAL   PAGE _30_

	DATE		DESCRIPTION	POST. REF.	DEBIT	CREDIT	
1	2017						1
2	Jan.	3	Salaries Expense—Sales	602	1 7 0 0 00		2
3			Cash	101		1 7 0 0 00	3

After this entry is posted, the expenses are properly divided between the two periods: $1,200 in December and $500 in January. The **Salaries Payable** account has a zero balance. The accountant did not have to review the previous records or allocate the payment between two accounts when the salaries were paid.

ACCOUNT _Salaries Expense—Sales_   ACCOUNT NO. _602_

DATE		DESCRIPTION	POST. REF.	DEBIT	CREDIT	BALANCE DEBIT	BALANCE CREDIT
2016							
Dec.	31	Balance				78 4 9 0 00	
	31	Adjusting	J25	1 2 0 0 00		79 6 9 0 00	
	31	Closing	J28		79 6 9 0 00	—0—	
2017							
Jan.	1	Reversing	J29		1 2 0 0 00		1 2 0 0 00
	3		J30	1 7 0 0 00		5 0 0 00	

IDENTIFYING ITEMS FOR REVERSAL

Not all adjustments need to be reversed. Normally, reversing entries are made for accrued items that involve future payments or receipts of cash. Reversing entries are not made for uncollectible accounts, depreciation, and prepaid expenses—if they are initially recorded as assets. However, when prepaid expenses are initially recorded as expenses (the alternative method), the end-of-period adjustment needs to be reversed.

Whiteside Antiques makes reversing entries for:

■ accrued salaries—adjustment **(f)**,

■ accrued payroll taxes—adjustments **(g)** and **(h)**,

■ interest payable—adjustment **(i)**,

■ interest receivable—adjustment **(m)**.

JOURNALIZING REVERSING ENTRIES

We just analyzed the reversing entry for accrued salaries, adjustment **(f).** The next two reversing entries are for accrued payroll taxes. Making these reversing entries means that the accountant does not have to review the year-end adjustments before recording the payment of payroll taxes in the next year.

GENERAL JOURNAL   PAGE 29

	DATE		DESCRIPTION	POST. REF.	DEBIT	CREDIT	
1	2017						1
6	Jan.	1	Social Security Tax Payable	221	7 4 40		6
7			Medicare Tax Payable	223	1 7 40		7
8			Payroll Taxes Expense	665		9 1 80	8
9			To reverse adjusting entry				9
10			(g) made Dec. 31, 2016				10
11							11
12		1	Federal Unemployment Tax Payable	225	7 20		12
13			State Unemployment Tax Payable	227	6 4 80		13
14			Payroll Taxes Expense	665		7 2 00	14
15			To reverse adjusting entry				15
16			(h) made Dec. 31, 2016				16

The next reversing entry is for accrued interest expense. The reversing entry that follows prevents recording difficulties when the note is paid on February 1.

GENERAL JOURNAL   PAGE 29

	DATE		DESCRIPTION	POST. REF.	DEBIT	CREDIT	
18	Jan.	1	Interest Payable	216	2 0 00		18
19			Interest Expense	695		2 0 00	19
20			To reverse adjusting entry				20
21			(i) made Dec. 31, 2016				21

In addition to adjustments for accrued expenses, Whiteside Antiques made two adjustments for accrued income items. The next reversing entry is for accrued interest income on the note receivable. Whiteside will receive cash for the note and the interest on March 1. The reversing entry eliminates any difficulties in recording the interest income when the note is paid on March 1.

GENERAL JOURNAL   PAGE 29

	DATE		DESCRIPTION	POST. REF.	DEBIT	CREDIT	
23	Jan.	1	Interest Income	491	3 0 00		23
24			Interest Receivable	116		3 0 00	24
25			To reverse adjusting entry				25
26			(m) made Dec. 31, 2016				26

After the reversing entry has been posted, the *Interest Receivable* account has a zero balance and the *Interest Income* account has a debit balance of $30. This is unusual because the normal balance of *Interest Income* is a credit.

On March 1, Whiteside Antiques received a check for $1,260 in payment of the note ($1,200) and the interest ($60). The transaction is recorded in the normal manner as a debit to *Cash* for $1,260, a credit to *Notes Receivable* for $1,200, and a credit to *Interest Income* for $60.

Refer to the *Interest Income* general ledger account below. After this entry has been posted, interest income is properly divided between the two periods, $30 in the previous year and $30 in the current year. The balance of *Interest Receivable* is zero. The accountant does not have to review the year-end adjustments before recording the receipt of the principal and interest relating to the note receivable on March 1.

ACCOUNT _Interest Receivable_   ACCOUNT NO. _116_

DATE		DESCRIPTION	POST. REF.	DEBIT	CREDIT	BALANCE DEBIT	BALANCE CREDIT
2016							
Dec.	31	Adjusting	J27	3 0 00		3 0 00	
2017							
Jan.	1	Reversing	J29		3 0 00	—0—	

ACCOUNT _Interest Income_   ACCOUNT NO. _491_

DATE		DESCRIPTION	POST. REF.	DEBIT	CREDIT	BALANCE DEBIT	BALANCE CREDIT
2016							
Dec.	31	Balance					1 3 6 00
	31	Adjusting	J27		3 0 00		1 6 6 00
	31	Closing	J28	1 6 6 00			—0—
2017							
Jan.	1	Reversing	J29	3 0 00		3 0 00	
Mar.	1		CR3		6 0 00		3 0 00

Review of the Accounting Cycle

In Chapters 7, 8, and 9, Maxx-Out Sporting Goods was used to introduce accounting procedures, records, and statements for merchandising businesses. In Chapters 12 and 13, Whiteside Antiques was used to illustrate the end-of-period activities for merchandising businesses. Underlying the various procedures described were the steps in the accounting cycle. Let's review the accounting cycle.

1. *Analyze transactions.* Transaction data comes into an accounting system from a variety of source documents—sales slips, purchase invoices, credit memorandums, check stubs, and so on. Each document is analyzed to determine the accounts and amounts affected.

2. *Journalize the data about transactions.* Each transaction is recorded in either a special journal or the general journal.

3. *Post the data about transactions.* Each transaction is transferred from the journal to the ledger accounts. Merchandising businesses typically maintain several subsidiary ledgers in addition to the general ledger.

4. *Prepare a worksheet.* At the end of each period, a worksheet is prepared. The Trial Balance section of the worksheet is used to prove the equality of the debits and credits in the general ledger. Adjustments are entered in the Adjustments section so that the financial statements will be prepared using the accrual basis of accounting. The Adjusted Trial Balance section is used to prove the equality of the debits and credits of the updated account balances. The Income Statement and Balance Sheet sections are used to arrange data in an orderly manner.

5. *Prepare financial statements.* A formal set of financial statements is prepared to report information to interested parties.

6. *Journalize and post adjusting entries.* Adjusting entries are journalized and posted in the accounting records. This creates a permanent record of the changes shown on the worksheet.

7. *Journalize and post closing entries.* Closing entries are journalized and posted in order to transfer the results of operations to owner's equity and to prepare the temporary accounts for the next period. The closing entries reduce the temporary account balances to zero.

8. *Prepare a postclosing trial balance.* The postclosing trial balance confirms that the general ledger is still in balance and that the temporary accounts have zero balances.

9. *Interpret the financial information.* The accountant, owners, managers, and other interested parties interpret the information shown in the financial statements and other less formal financial reports that might be prepared. This information is used to evaluate the results of operations and the financial position of the business and to make decisions.

In addition to the nine steps listed here, some firms record reversing entries. Reversing entries simplify the recording of cash payments for accrued expenses and cash receipts for accrued income.

Figure 13.6 shows the flow of data through an accounting system that uses special journals and subsidiary ledgers. The system is composed of subsystems that perform specialized functions.

The accounts receivable area records transactions involving sales and cash receipts and maintains the individual accounts for credit customers. This area also handles billing for credit customers.

The accounts payable area records transactions involving purchases and cash payments and maintains the individual accounts for creditors.

The general ledger and financial reporting area records transactions in the general journal, maintains the general ledger accounts, performs the end-of-period procedures, and prepares financial statements. This area is the focal point for the accounting system because all transactions eventually flow into the general ledger. In turn, the general ledger provides the data that appear in the financial statements.

MANAGERIAL IMPLICATIONS <<

FINANCIAL STATEMENTS

■ Managers carefully study the financial statements to evaluate the operating efficiency and financial strength of the business.

■ A common analysis technique is to compare the data on current statements with the data from previous statements. This can reveal developing trends.

■ In large businesses, financial statements are compared with the published financial reports of other companies in the same industry.

■ In order to evaluate information on classified financial statements, managers need to understand the nature and significance of the groupings.

■ Management ensures that closing entries are promptly made so that transactions for the new period can be recorded. Any significant delay means that valuable information, such as the firm's cash position, will not be available or up to date.

■ The efficiency and effectiveness of the adjusting and closing procedures can have a positive effect on the annual independent audit. For example, detailed descriptions in the general journal make it easy for the auditor to understand the adjusting entries.

THINKING CRITICALLY

How can managers use the financial statements to learn about a company's operating efficiency?

FIGURE 13.6　Flow of Financial Data through an Accounting System

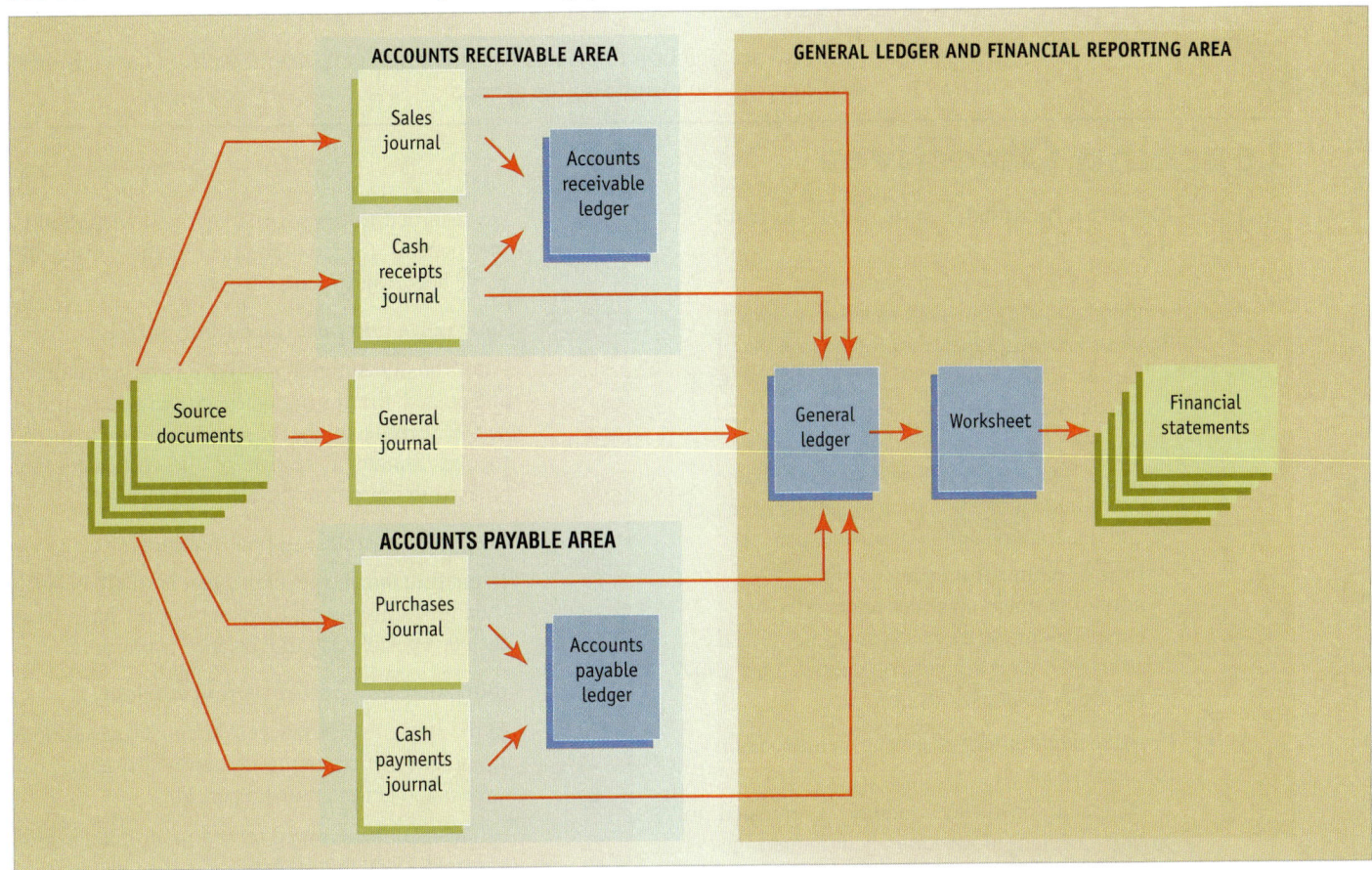

Section 2　Self Review

QUESTIONS

1. Why do adjusting entries need detailed explanations in the general journal?

2. Which adjusting entries should be reversed?

3. What do the four steps in the closing process accomplish?

EXERCISES

4. A reversing entry is made for an end-of-period adjustment that recorded:

   a. estimated bad debts for the period.

   b. an accrued expense that involves future cash payments.

   c. a transfer of an amount from a prepaid expense account to an expense account.

   d. the change in merchandise inventory.

5. The current ratio is:

   a. current liabilities divided by current assets,

   b. the sum of cash, accounts receivable and notes receivable, divided by current liabilities.

   c. current assets divided by current liabilities.

   d. current assets divided by total liabilities.

ANALYSIS

6. At the end of the previous accounting period, an adjusting entry to record accrued employer's payroll taxes was made. Reversing entries were not made for the current accounting period. What effect will this have on the current period's financial statements?

(Answers to Section 2 Self Review are on page 477.)

13 Chapter   REVIEW   Chapter Summary

In this chapter, you have learned how to prepare classified financial statements from the worksheet and how to close the accounting records for the period.

Learning Objectives

13-1 Prepare a classified income statement from the worksheet.

■ A classified income statement for a merchandising business usually includes these sections: Operating Revenue, Cost of Goods Sold, Gross Profit on Sales, Operating Expenses, and Net Income.

■ To make the income statement even more useful, operating expenses may be broken down into categories, such as selling expenses and general and administrative expenses.

■ Income earned from sources other than normal business activities appears in the Other Income section. Expenses not directly connected with business operations appear in the Other Expenses section.

13-2 Prepare a statement of owner's equity from the worksheet.

A statement of owner's equity is prepared to provide detailed information about the changes in the owner's financial interest during the period. The ending owner's capital balance is used to prepare the balance sheet.

13-3 Prepare a classified balance sheet from the worksheet.

■ Assets are usually presented in two groups— current assets, and plant and equipment. Current assets consist of cash, items to be converted into cash within one year, and items to be used up within one year. Plant and equipment consists of property that will be used for a long time in the operations of the business.

■ Liabilities are also divided into two groups— current liabilities and long-term liabilities. Current liabilities will normally be paid within one year. Long-term liabilities are due in more than one year.

13-4 Journalize and post the adjusting entries.

When the year-end worksheet and financial statements have been completed, adjusting entries

are recorded in the general journal and posted to the general ledger. The data comes from the worksheet Adjustments section.

13-5 Journalize and post the closing entries.

After the adjusting entries have been journalized and posted, the closing entries should be recorded in the records of the business. The data in the Income Statement section of the worksheet can be used to journalize the closing entries.

13-6 Prepare a postclosing trial balance.

To confirm that the general ledger is still in balance after the adjusting and closing entries have been posted, a postclosing trial balance is prepared.

13-7 Journalize and post reversing entries.

At the start of each new period, most firms follow the practice of reversing certain adjustments that were made in the previous period.

■ This is done to avoid recording problems with transactions that will occur in the new period.

■ Usually, only adjusting entries for accrued expenses and accrued income need be considered for reversing. Of these, usually only accrued expense and income items involving future payments and receipts of cash can cause difficulties later and should therefore be reversed.

■ The use of reversing entries is optional. Reversing entries save time, promote efficiency, and help to achieve a proper matching of revenue and expenses in each period.

■ With reversing entries, there is no need to examine each transaction to see whether a portion applies to the past period and then divide the amount of the transaction between the two periods.

13-8 Define the accounting terms new to this chapter.

Glossary

Accounts receivable turnover (p. 451) A measure of the speed with which sales on account are collected; the ratio of net credit sales to average receivables

Classified financial statement (p. 438) A format by which revenues and expenses on the income statement, and assets and liabilities on the balance sheet, are divided into groups of similar accounts and a subtotal is given for each group

Current assets (p. 443) Assets consisting of cash, items that normally will be converted into cash within one year, or items that will be used up within one year

Current liabilities (p. 443) Debts that must be paid within one year

Current ratio (p. 450) A relationship between current assets and current liabilities that provides a measure of a firm's ability to pay its current debts (current ratio = current assets ÷ current liabilities)

Gross profit (p. 440) The difference between net sales and the cost of goods sold (gross profit = net sales − cost of goods sold)

Gross profit percentage (p. 450) The amount of gross profit from each dollar of sales (gross profit percentage = gross profit ÷ net sales)

Inventory turnover (p. 451) The number of times inventory is purchased and sold during the accounting period (inventory turnover = cost of goods sold ÷ average inventory)

Liquidity (p. 443) The ease with which an item can be converted into cash

Long-term liabilities (p. 443) Debts of a business that are due more than one year in the future

Multiple-step income statement (p. 438) A type of income statement on which several subtotals are computed before the net income is calculated

Plant and equipment (p. 443) Property that will be used in the business for longer than one year

Reversing entries (p. 451) Journal entries made to reverse the effect of certain adjusting entries involving accrued income or accrued expenses to avoid problems in recording future payments or receipts of cash in a new accounting period

Single-step income statement (p. 438) A type of income statement where only one computation is needed to determine the net income (total revenue − total expenses = net income)

Working capital (p. 450) The difference between current assets and current liabilities. It is a measure of the firm's ability to pay current obligations.

Comprehensive **Self Review**

1. Explain the difference between a single-step income statement and a multiple-step income statement. Which is normally favored?

2. What journal entry(ies) is (are) made in the adjustment column for beginning and ending inventories?

3. Why would a fax machine used in the office not be considered a current asset?

4. Immediately after closing entries are posted, which of the following types of accounts will have zero balances?

   a. asset accounts

   b. expense accounts

   c. liability accounts

   d. owner's drawing account

   e. *Income Summary* account

   f. owner's capital account

   g. revenue accounts

5. Which of the following should have a debit balance in the adjusted trial balance?

   a. *Sales Returns and Allowances*

   b. *Purchases Discounts*

   c. *Salaries Payable*

   d. *Unearned Rental Income*

6. Describe the entry that would be made to close the *Income Summary* account in each of the following cases. The owner of the firm is Jan Hanson.

   a. There is net income of $58,000.

   b. There is a net loss of $8,000.

7. Give the sequence in which the following journal entries are posted to the accounts.

   a. adjusting entries

   b. entries to close expense accounts

    c. entries to close revenue accounts

    d. reversing entries

(Answers to Comprehensive Self Review are on pages 477–478.)

Discussion Questions

1. What is the difference, if any, between the classification Other Revenue and Expense and the classification Extraordinary Gains and Losses?
2. Which section of the income statement contains information about the purchases made during the period and the beginning and ending inventories?
3. What are operating expenses?
4. What is the purpose of the balance sheet?
5. What are current assets that usually are classified as Current Assets on the balance sheet?
6. How do current liabilities and long-term liabilities differ?
7. What information is provided by the statement of owner's equity?
8. What account balances or other amount are included on two different financial statements for the period? Which statements are involved?
9. What is the purpose of the postclosing trial balance?
10. What accounts appear on the postclosing trial balance?
11. If the totals of the adjusted trial balance Debit and Credit columns are equal, but the postclosing trial balance does not balance, what is the likely cause of the problem?
12. What types of adjustments are reversed?
13. On December 31, Klien Company made an adjusting entry debiting *Interest Receivable* and crediting *Interest Income* for $300 of accrued interest. What reversing entry, if any, should be recorded for this item on January 1?
14. Various adjustments made at Acres Company are listed below. Which of the adjustments would normally be reversed?

    a. Adjustment for accrued payroll taxes expense

    b. Adjustment for supplies used

    c. Adjustment for depreciation on the building

    d. Adjustment for estimated uncollectible accounts

    e. Adjustment for accrued interest income

    f. Adjustment for beginning inventory

    g. Adjustment for ending inventory

    h. Adjustment to record portion of insurance premiums that have expired

15. If the owner invests additional capital in the business during the month, how would that new investment be shown in the financial statements?
16. What are the steps in the accounting cycle?
17. Kagan Company's inventory turnover ratio was 9 times in 2015 and 8 times in 2016. Did Kagan Company sell its inventory more quickly, or more slowly, in 2016 compared to 2015?

APPLICATIONS

Exercises

Exercise 13.1

Objective 13-1

▶ **Classifying income statement items.**

The accounts listed on the next page appear on the worksheet of Santo's Craft Store. Indicate the section of the classified income statement in which each account will be reported.

SECTIONS OF CLASSIFIED INCOME STATEMENT

a. Operating Revenue

b. Cost of Goods Sold

c. Operating Expenses

d. Other Income

e. Other Expenses

ACCOUNTS

1. Purchases Returns and Allowances

2. Telephone Expense

3. Sales Returns and Allowances

4. Purchases

5. Interest Income

6. Merchandise Inventory

7. Interest Expense

8. Sales

9. Depreciation Expense—Store Equipment

10. Rent Expense

Classifying balance sheet items.

◄ **Exercise 13.2**
Objective 13-3

The following accounts appear on the worksheet of Santo's Craft Store at December 31, 2016. Indicate the section of the classified balance sheet in which each account will be reported.

SECTIONS OF CLASSIFIED BALANCE SHEET

a. Current Assets

b. Plant and Equipment

c. Current Liabilities

d. Long-Term Liabilities

e. Owner's Equity

ACCOUNTS

1. Accounts Receivable

2. Delivery Van

3. Prepaid Insurance

4. Notes Payable, due 2017

5. Store Supplies

6. Accounts Payable

7. Merchandise Inventory

8. Ray Lynch, Capital

9. Cash

10. Unearned Subscriptions Income

Preparing a classified income statement.

◄ **Exercise 13.3**
Objective 13-1

The worksheet of Bridget's Office Supplies contains the following revenue, cost, and expense accounts. Prepare a classified income statement for this firm for the year ended December 31, 2016. The merchandise inventory amounted to $59,775 on January 1, 2016, and $52,725 on December 31, 2016. The expense accounts numbered 611 through 617 represent selling expenses, and those numbered 631 through 646 represent general and administrative expenses.

ACCOUNTS

401	Sales	$248,900	Cr.
451	Sales Returns and Allowances	4,350	Dr.
491	Miscellaneous Income	400	Cr.
501	Purchases	103,600	Dr.
502	Freight In	1,975	Dr.
503	Purchases Returns and Allowances	3,600	Cr.
504	Purchases Discounts	1,800	Cr.
611	Salaries Expense—Sales	45,300	Dr.
614	Store Supplies Expense	2,310	Dr.
617	Depreciation Expense—Store Equipment	1,510	Dr.
631	Rent Expense	13,500	Dr.
634	Utilities Expense	3,000	Dr.
637	Salaries Expense—Office	21,100	Dr.
640	Payroll Taxes Expense	6,000	Dr.
643	Depreciation Expense—Office Equipment	570	Dr.
646	Uncollectible Accounts Expense	720	Dr.
691	Interest Expense	740	Dr.

Exercise 13.4
Objective 13-2

▶ **Preparing a statement of owner's equity.**

The worksheet of Bridget's Office Supplies contains the following owner's equity accounts. Use this data and the net income determined in Exercise 13.3 to prepare a statement of owner's equity for the year ended December 31, 2016. No additional investments were made during the period.

ACCOUNTS

301	Bridget Swanson, Capital	$63,760	Cr.
302	Bridget Swanson, Drawing	40,700	Dr.

Exercise 13.5
Objective 13-3

▶ **Preparing a classified balance sheet.**

The worksheet of Bridget's Office Supplies contains the following asset and liability accounts. The balance of the **Notes Payable** account consists of notes that are due within a year. Prepare a balance sheet dated December 31, 2016. Obtain the ending capital for the period from the statement of owner's equity completed in Exercise 13.4.

ACCOUNTS

101	Cash	$5,605	Dr.
107	Change Fund	500	Dr.
111	Accounts Receivable	5,140	Dr.
112	Allowance for Doubtful Accounts	860	Cr.
121	Merchandise Inventory	52,725	Dr.
131	Store Supplies	1,100	Dr.
133	Prepaid Interest	130	Dr.
141	Store Equipment	11,200	Dr.
142	Accum. Depreciation—Store Equipment	1,180	Cr.
151	Office Equipment	3,400	Dr.
152	Accum. Depreciation—Office Equipment	500	Cr.
201	Notes Payable	5,500	Cr.
203	Accounts Payable	3,725	Cr.
216	Interest Payable	110	Cr.
231	Sales Tax Payable	1,890	Cr.

Recording closing entries.

◀ **Exercise 13.6**
Objective 13-5

On December 31, 2016, the Income Statement section of the worksheet for Soto Company contained the following information. Give the entries that should be made in the general journal to close the revenue, cost of goods sold, expense, and other temporary accounts. Use journal page 16.

INCOME STATEMENT SECTION

	Debit	Credit
Income Summary	$ 39,600	$ 42,900
Sales		259,500
Sales Returns and Allowances	4,400	
Sales Discounts	3,400	
Interest Income		220
Purchases	135,400	
Freight In	2,700	
Purchases Returns and Allowances		2,500
Purchases Discounts		1,630
Rent Expense	9,000	
Utilities Expense	3,030	
Telephone Expense	1,640	
Salaries Expense	67,100	
Payroll Taxes Expense	5,370	
Supplies Expense	1,800	
Depreciation Expense	3,000	
Interest Expense	440	
Totals	$276,880	$306,750

Assume further that the owner of the firm is Armando Soto and that the *Armando Soto, Drawing* account had a balance of $26,700 on December 31, 2016.

Journalizing reversing entries.

◀ **Exercise 13.7**
Objective 13-7

Examine the following adjusting entries and determine which ones should be reversed. Show the reversing entries that should be recorded in the general journal as of January 1, 2017. Include appropriate descriptions.

2016	(Adjustment a)		
Dec. 31	Uncollectible Accounts Expense	2,940.00	
	Allowance for Doubtful Accounts		2,940.00
	To record estimated loss from uncollectible accounts based on 0.4% of net credit sales, $735,000		
	(Adjustment b)		
Dec. 31	Supplies Expense	5,700.00	
	Supplies		5,700.00
	To record supplies used during the year		
	(Adjustment c)		
31	Insurance Expense	1,650.00	
	Prepaid Insurance		1,650.00
	To record expired insurance on 1-year $6,600 policy purchased on Oct. 1		
	(Adjustment d)		
31	Depreciation. Exp. — Store Equipment	15,300.00	
	Accum. Depreciation — Store Equip.		15,300.00
	To record depreciation		

(Adjustment e)

31	Salaries Expense — Office	3,800.00	
	Salaries Payable		3,800.00
	To record accrued salaries for Dec. 29–31		

(Adjustment f)

31	Payroll Taxes Expense	290.70	
	Social Security Tax Payable		235.60
	Medicare Tax Payable		55.10
	To record accrued payroll taxes on accrued salaries: social security, 6.2% × 3,800 = $235.60; Medicare, 1.45% × 3,800 = $55.10		

(Adjustment g)

31	Interest Expense	300.00	
	Interest Payable		300.00
	To record accrued interest on a 4-month, 6% trade note payable dated Nov. 1: $30,000 × 0.06 × $^2/_{12}$ = $300		

(Adjustment h)

31	Interest Receivable	188.00	
	Interest Income		188.00
	To record interest earned on 6-month, 8% note receivable dated Oct. 1: $9,400 × 0.08 × $^3/_{12}$ = $188		

Exercise 13.8
Objective 13-6

▶ Preparing a postclosing trial balance.

The Adjusted Trial Balance section of the worksheet for Vandermeer Farm Supply follows. The owner made no additional investments during the year. Prepare a postclosing trial balance for the firm on December 31, 2016.

ACCOUNTS

	Debit	Credit
Cash	$ 19,600	
Accounts Receivable	60,800	
Allowance for Doubtful Accounts		$ 220
Merchandise Inventory	187,200	
Supplies	7,240	
Prepaid Insurance	3,160	
Equipment	52,000	
Accumulated Depreciation — Equipment		18,800
Notes Payable		10,500
Accounts Payable		9,700
Social Security Tax Payable		1,490
Medicare Tax Payable		410
Ken Vandermeer, Capital		271,140
Ken Vandermeer, Drawing	75,000	
Income Summary	181,000	187,200
Sales		778,000
Sales Returns and Allowances	15,400	
Purchases	487,900	
Freight In	6,400	

ACCOUNTS (CONT.)

	Debit	Credit
Purchases Returns and Allowances		9,500
Purchases Discounts		6,300
Rent Expense	34,800	
Telephone Expense	6,340	
Salaries Expense	124,140	
Payroll Taxes Expense	12,700	
Supplies Expense	7,600	
Insurance Expense	1,660	
Depreciation Expense—Equipment	9,100	
Uncollectible Accounts Expense	1,220	
Totals	$1,293,260	$1,293,260

Calculating ratios.

The following selected accounts were taken from the financial records of Santa Rosa Distributors at December 31, 2016. All accounts have normal balances.

Cash	$ 26,760
Accounts receivable	47,700
Note receivable, due 2017	9,500
Merchandise inventory	35,700
Prepaid insurance	2,350
Supplies	1,410
Equipment	43,500
Accumulated depreciation, equipment	23,500
Note payable to bank, due 2017	35,000
Accounts payable	13,050
Interest payable	350
Sales	530,000
Sales discounts	3,200
Cost of goods sold	348,540

◀ **Exercise 13.9**
Objective 13-6

Merchandise inventory at December 31, 2015 was $58,500. Based on the account balances above, calculate the following:

a. The gross profit percentage
b. Working capital
c. The current ratio
d. The inventory turnover

Calculating the accounts receivable turnover and the inventory turnover.

◀ **Exercise 13.10**
Objective 13-6

Namala Company reports the following in its most recent year of operations:

- Sales, $1,000,000 (all on account)
- Cost of goods sold, $570,000
- Gross profit, $430,000
- Accounts receivable, beginning of year, $90,000
- Accounts receivable, end of year, $110,000
- Merchandise inventory, beginning of year, $55,000
- Merchandise inventory, end of year, $65,000.

Based on these balances, compute:

a. the accounts receivable turnover

b. the inventory turnover

PROBLEMS

Problem Set A

Problem 13.1A

Objectives 13-1, 13-2, 13-3

QB Sage 50
Complete Accounting

▶ **Preparing classified financial statements.**

Quality Hardwoods Company distributes hardwood products to small furniture manufacturers. The adjusted trial balance data given below is from the firm's worksheet for the year ended December 31, 2016.

INSTRUCTIONS

1. Prepare a classified income statement for the year ended December 31, 2016. The expense accounts represent warehouse expenses, selling expenses, and general and administrative expenses.

2. Prepare a statement of owner's equity for the year ended December 31, 2016. No additional investments were made during the period.

3. Prepare a classified balance sheet as of December 31, 2016. The mortgage and the loans extend for more than a year.

ACCOUNTS

	Debit	Credit
Cash	$ 24,100	
Petty Cash Fund	500	
Notes Receivable	11,800	
Accounts Receivable	96,000	
Allowance for Doubtful Accounts		$ 6,000
Merchandise Inventory	234,000	
Warehouse Supplies	2,860	
Office Supplies	1,420	
Prepaid Insurance	10,200	
Land	46,000	
Building	178,000	
Accumulated Depreciation—Building		54,000
Warehouse Equipment	37,000	
Accumulated Depreciation—Warehouse Equipment		17,400
Delivery Equipment	51,000	
Accumulated Depreciation—Delivery Equipment		19,600
Office Equipment	25,000	
Accumulated Depreciation—Office Equipment		12,000
Notes Payable		20,200
Accounts Payable		39,000
Interest Payable		580
Mortgage Payable		61,000

ACCOUNTS (CONT.)

	Debit	Credit
Loans Payable, Long-term		17,000
Chuck Kirby, Capital (Jan. 1)		462,460
Chuck Kirby, Drawing	127,000	
Income Summary	244,000	234,000
Sales		1,685,000
Sales Returns and Allowances	18,200	
Interest Income		1,580
Purchases	767,000	
Freight In	13,800	
Purchases Returns and Allowances		8,440
Purchases Discounts		11,160
Warehouse Wages Expense	199,600	
Warehouse Supplies Expense	7,100	
Depreciation Expense—Warehouse Equipment	5,800	
Salaries Expense—Sales	269,200	
Travel and Entertainment Expense	21,500	
Delivery Wages Expense	60,330	
Depreciation Expense—Delivery Equipment	9,800	
Salaries Expense—Office	70,600	
Office Supplies Expense	4,000	
Insurance Expense	6,200	
Utilities Expense	9,290	
Telephone Expense	6,520	
Payroll Taxes Expense	59,000	
Property Taxes Expense	5,600	
Uncollectible Accounts Expense	5,800	
Depreciation Expense—Building	9,000	
Depreciation Expense—Office Equipment	4,000	
Interest Expense	8,200	
Totals	$2,649,420	$2,649,420

Analyze: What is the current ratio for this business?

Preparing classified financial statements.

◀ **Problem 13.2A**
Objectives 13-1, 13-2, 13-3

Good to Go Auto Products distributes automobile parts to service stations and repair shops. The adjusted trial balance data that follows is from the firm's worksheet for the year ended December 31, 2016.

INSTRUCTIONS

1. Prepare a classified income statement for the year ended December 31, 2016. The expense accounts represent warehouse expenses, selling expenses, and general and administrative expenses.

2. Prepare a statement of owner's equity for the year ended December 31, 2016. No additional investments were made during the period.

3. Prepare a classified balance sheet as of December 31, 2016. The mortgage and the long-term notes extend for more than one year.

ACCOUNTS

	Debit	Credit
Cash	$ 99,000	
Petty Cash Fund	600	
Notes Receivable	15,000	
Accounts Receivable	140,200	
Allowance for Doubtful Accounts		$ 3,800
Interest Receivable	150	
Merchandise Inventory	128,500	
Warehouse Supplies	3,300	
Office Supplies	700	
Prepaid Insurance	4,640	
Land	16,000	
Building	107,000	
Accumulated Depreciation — Building		16,700
Warehouse Equipment	19,800	
Accumulated Depreciation — Warehouse Equipment		9,500
Office Equipment	9,400	
Accumulated Depreciation — Office Equipment		3,900
Notes Payable — Short-Term		15,000
Accounts Payable		56,900
Interest Payable		400
Notes Payable — Long-Term		17,000
Mortgage Payable		20,000
Colin O'Brien, Capital (Jan. 1)		326,870
Colin O'Brien, Drawing	70,650	
Income Summary	131,400	128,500
Sales		1,110,300
Sales Returns and Allowances	8,400	
Interest Income		580
Purchases	463,000	
Freight In	9,800	
Purchases Returns and Allowances		13,650
Purchases Discounts		9,240
Warehouse Wages Expense	108,600	
Warehouse Supplies Expense	5,800	
Depreciation Expense — Warehouse Equipment	3,400	
Salaries Expense — Sales	151,700	
Travel Expense	24,000	
Delivery Expense	37,425	
Salaries Expense — Office	85,000	
Office Supplies Expense	1,220	
Insurance Expense	9,875	
Utilities Expense	8,000	
Telephone Expense	3,280	
Payroll Taxes Expense	31,600	
Building Repairs Expense	3,700	

ACCOUNTS (CONT.)

	Debit	Credit
Property Taxes Expense	16,400	
Uncollectible Accounts Expense	3,580	
Depreciation Expense—Building	5,600	
Depreciation Expense—Office Equipment	1,620	
Interest Expense	4,000	
Totals	$1,732,340	$1,732,340

Analyze: What percentage of total operating expenses is attributable to warehouse expenses?

Preparing classified financial statements.

Obtain all data necessary from the worksheet prepared for Artisan Wines in Problem 12.6A at the end of Chapter 12. Then follow the instructions to complete this problem.

◀ Problem 13.3A
Objectives 13-1,
13-2, 13-3

INSTRUCTIONS

1. Prepare a classified income statement for the year ended December 31, 2016. The company does not classify its operating expenses as selling expenses and general and administrative expenses.

2. Prepare a statement of owner's equity for the year ended December 31, 2016. No additional investments were made during the year.

3. Prepare a classified balance sheet as of December 31, 2016.

Analyze: What is the inventory turnover for Artisan Wines?

Journalizing adjusting, closing, and reversing entries.

Obtain all data that is necessary from the worksheet prepared for Healthy Eating Foods Company in Problem 12.5A at the end of Chapter 12. Then follow the instructions to complete this problem.

◀ Problem 13.4A
Objectives 13-4,
13-5, 13-7

CONTINUING >>>
Problem

INSTRUCTIONS

1. Record adjusting entries in the general journal as of December 31, 2016. Use 25 as the first journal page number. Include descriptions for the entries.

2. Record closing entries in the general journal as of December 31, 2016. Include descriptions.

3. Record reversing entries in the general journal as of January 1, 2017. Include descriptions.

Analyze: Assuming that the firm did not record a reversing entry for salaries payable, what entry is required when salaries of $6,000 are paid on January 3?

Journalizing adjusting and reversing entries.

The data below concerns adjustments to be made at Victoria Company.

◀ Problem 13.5A
Objectives 13-4,
13-7

Sage 50
Complete Accounting

INSTRUCTIONS

1. Record the adjusting entries in the general journal as of December 31, 2016. Use 25 as the first journal page number. Include descriptions.

2. Record reversing entries in the general journal as of January 1, 2017. Include descriptions.

ADJUSTMENTS

a. On October 1, 2016, the firm signed a lease for a warehouse and paid rent of $20,700 in advance for a six-month period.

b. On December 31, 2016, an inventory of supplies showed that items costing $1,940 were on hand. The balance of the *Supplies* account was $11,620.

c. A depreciation schedule for the firm's equipment shows that a total of $9,200 should be charged off as depreciation for 2016.

d. On December 31, 2016, the firm owed salaries of $5,400 that will not be paid until January 2017.

e. On December 31, 2016, the firm owed the employer's social security (6.2 percent) and Medicare (1.45 percent) taxes on all accrued salaries.

f. On September 1, 2016, the firm received a five-month, 6 percent note for $5,500 from a customer with an overdue balance.

Analyze: After the adjusting entries have been posted, what is the balance of the *Prepaid Rent* account on January 1, 2017?

Problem Set B

Problem 13.1B

Objectives 13-1, 13-2, 13-3

▶ **Preparing classified financial statements.**

Lite Speed Electronics is a retail store that sells computers and computer supplies. The adjusted trial balance data given below is from the firm's worksheet for the year ended December 31, 2016.

INSTRUCTIONS

1. Prepare a classified income statement for the year ended December 31, 2016. The expense accounts represent warehouse expenses, selling expenses, and general and administrative expenses.

2. Prepare a statement of owner's equity for the year ended December 31, 2016. No additional investments were made during the period.

3. Prepare a classified balance sheet as of December 31, 2016. The mortgage and the loans extend for more than one year.

ACCOUNTS

	Debit	Credit
Cash	$ 10,200	
Petty Cash Fund	100	
Notes Receivable	3,200	
Accounts Receivable	21,250	
Allowance for Doubtful Accounts		$ 2,250
Merchandise Inventory	35,400	
Warehouse Supplies	775	
Office Supplies	780	
Prepaid Insurance	2,200	
Land	7,642	
Building	48,500	
Accum. Depr. — Building		13,000
Warehouse Equipment	8,000	
Accumulated Depreciation — Warehouse Equipment		2,300
Delivery Equipment	16,400	
Accumulated Depreciation — Delivery Equipment		3,600
Office Equipment	6,000	
Accumulated Depreciation — Office Equipment		2,500
Notes Payable		5,000
Accounts Payable		13,140
Interest Payable		240
Mortgage Payable		15,950
Loans Payable		4,000
Toshi Takahashi, Capital (Jan. 1)		60,940
Toshi Takahashi, Drawing	24,000	

ACCOUNTS (CONT.)

	Debit	Credit
Income Summary	33,125	35,400
Sales		429,800
Sales Returns and Allowances	3,150	
Interest Income		462
Purchases	179,600	
Freight In	2,200	
Purchases Returns and Allowances		2,520
Purchases Discounts		2,350
Warehouse Wages Expense	38,900	
Warehouse Supplies Expense	1,790	
Depreciation Expense—Warehouse Equipment	1,400	
Salaries Expense—Sales	67,200	
Travel and Entertainment Expense	6,300	
Delivery Wages Expense	26,900	
Depreciation Expense—Delivery Equipment	2,440	
Salaries Expense—Office	15,900	
Office Supplies Expense	1,150	
Insurance Expense	1,500	
Utilities Expense	2,400	
Telephone Expense	1,380	
Payroll Taxes Expense	15,250	
Property Taxes Expense	1,750	
Uncollectible Accounts Expense	1,050	
Depreciation Expense—Building	3,000	
Depreciation Expense—Office Equipment	1,020	
Interest Expense	1,600	
Totals	$593,452	$593,452

Analyze: What is the gross profit percentage for the period ended December 31, 2016?

Preparing classified financial statements.

◀ **Problem 13.2B**
Objectives 13-1, 13-2, 13-3

Hog Wild is a retail firm that sells motorcycles, parts, and accessories. The adjusted trial balance data given below is from the firm's worksheet for the year ended December 31, 2016.

INSTRUCTIONS

1. Prepare a classified income statement for the year ended December 31, 2016. The expense accounts represent warehouse expenses, selling expenses, and general and administrative expenses.

2. Prepare a statement of owner's equity for the year ended December 31, 2016. No additional investments were made during the period.

3. Prepare a classified balance sheet as of December 31, 2016. The mortgage and the long-term notes extend for more than one year.

ACCOUNTS

	Debit	Credit
Cash	$14,350	
Petty Cash Fund	200	
Notes Receivable	6,000	
Accounts Receivable	54,600	

ACCOUNTS (CONT.)

	Debit	Credit
Allowance for Doubtful Accounts		$ 5,000
Interest Receivable	200	
Merchandise Inventory	87,915	
Warehouse Supplies	3,700	
Office Supplies	1,800	
Prepaid Insurance	6,900	
Land	20,400	
Building	53,100	
Accumulated Depreciation — Building		8,400
Warehouse Equipment	24,000	
Accumulated Depreciation — Warehouse Equipment		4,000
Office Equipment	12,800	
Accumulated Depreciation — Office Equipment		1,800
Notes Payable — Short-Term		8,000
Accounts Payable		32,500
Interest Payable		1,800
Notes Payable — Long-Term		6,000
Mortgage Payable		35,875
Nick Henry, Capital (Jan. 1)		198,710
Nick Henry, Drawing	56,000	
Income Summary	88,980	87,915
Sales		608,417
Sales Returns and Allowances	9,400	
Interest Income		720
Purchases	230,050	
Freight In	9,600	
Purchases Returns and Allowances		6,420
Purchases Discounts		5,760
Warehouse Wages Expense	64,300	
Warehouse Supplies Expense	4,300	
Depreciation Expense — Warehouse Equipment	2,400	
Salaries Expense — Sales	78,900	
Travel Expense — Sales	21,000	
Delivery Expense	35,400	
Salaries Expense — Office	57,500	
Office Supplies Expense	1,360	
Insurance Expense	9,500	
Utilities Expense	6,912	
Telephone Expense	4,370	
Payroll Taxes Expense	19,200	
Building Repairs Expense	3,100	
Property Taxes Expense	11,700	
Uncollectible Accounts Expense	2,900	
Depreciation Expense — Building	3,200	
Depreciation Expense — Office Equipment	1,680	
Interest Expense	3,600	
Totals	$1,011,317	$1,011,317

Analyze: What is the inventory turnover for Hog Wild?

Preparing classified financial statements.

◄ **Problem 13.3B**
**Objectives 13-1,
13-2, 13-3**

Obtain all data necessary from the worksheet prepared for The Game Place in Problem 12.6B at the end of Chapter 12. Then follow the instructions to complete this problem.

INSTRUCTIONS

1. Prepare a classified income statement for the year ended December 31, 2016. The company does not classify its operating expenses as selling expenses and general and administrative expenses.

2. Prepare a statement of owner's equity for the year ended December 31, 2016. No additional investments were made during the year.

3. Prepare a classified balance sheet as of December 31, 2016.

Analyze: What is the amount of working capital for The Game Place?

Journalizing adjusting, closing, and reversing entries.

◄ **Problem 13.4B**
**Objectives 13-4,
13-5, 13-7**
CONTINUING >>>
Problem

Obtain all data that is necessary from the worksheet prepared for Whatnots in Problem 12.5B at the end of Chapter 12. Then follow the instructions to complete this problem.

INSTRUCTIONS

1. Record adjusting entries in the general journal as of December 31, 2016. Use 29 as the first journal page number. Include descriptions for the entries.

2. Record closing entries in the general journal as of December 31, 2016. Include descriptions.

3. Record reversing entries in the general journal as of January 1, 2017. Include descriptions.

Analyze: Assuming that the company did not record a reversing entry for salaries payable, what entry is required when salaries of $2,600 are paid on January 4? (Ignore payroll taxes withheld.)

Journalizing adjusting and reversing entries.

◄ **Problem 13.5B**
**Objectives 13-4,
13-7**

The data below concerns adjustments to be made at Ramos Company.

INSTRUCTIONS

1. Record the adjusting entries in the general journal as of December 31, 2016. Use 25 as the first journal page number. Include descriptions.

2. Record reversing entries in the general journal as of January 1, 2017. Include descriptions.

ADJUSTMENTS

a. On August 1, 2016, the firm signed a six-month advertising contract with a trade magazine and paid the entire amount, $17,700, in advance. *Prepaid Advertising* had a balance of $17,700 on December 31, 2016.

b. On December 31, 2016, an inventory of supplies showed that items costing $3,040 were on hand. The balance of the *Supplies* account was $11,120.

c. A depreciation schedule for the firm's store equipment shows that a total of $9,800 should be charged off as depreciation for 2016.

d. On December 31, 2016, the firm owed salaries of $4,400 that will not be paid until January 2017.

e. On December 31, 2016, the firm owed the employer's social security (6.2 percent) and Medicare (1.45 percent) taxes on all accrued salaries.

f. On December 1, 2016, the firm received a five-month, 6 percent note for $5,500 from a customer with an overdue balance.

Analyze: After the adjusting entries have been posted, what is the balance of the Prepaid Advertising account on December 31?

Critical Thinking Problem 13.1

Year-End Processing

Programs Plus is a retail firm that sells computer programs for home and business use. On December 31, 2016, its general ledger contained the accounts and balances shown below:

ACCOUNTS	BALANCES	
Cash	$ 15,280	Dr.
Accounts Receivable	26,600	Dr.
Allowance for Doubtful Accounts	95	Cr.
Merchandise Inventory	62,375	Dr.
Supplies	6,740	Dr.
Prepaid Insurance	2,380	Dr.
Equipment	34,000	Dr.
Accumulated Depreciation — Equipment	10,100	Cr.
Notes Payable	7,264	Cr.
Accounts Payable	6,500	Cr.
Social Security Tax Payable	560	Cr.
Medicare Tax Payable	130	Cr.
Yasser Tousson, Capital	93,620	Cr.
Yasser Tousson, Drawing	50,000	Dr.
Sales	514,980	Cr.
Sales Returns and Allowances	9,600	Dr.
Purchases	319,430	Dr.
Freight In	3,600	Dr.
Purchases Returns and Allowances	7,145	Cr.
Purchases Discounts	5,760	Cr.
Rent Expense	14,500	Dr.
Telephone Expense	2,164	Dr.
Salaries Expense	92,000	Dr.
Payroll Taxes Expense	7,300	Dr.
Interest Expense	185	Dr.

The following accounts had zero balances:

Interest Payable
Salaries Payable
Income Summary
Supplies Expense
Insurance Expense
Depreciation Expense — Equipment
Uncollectible Accounts Expense

The data needed for the adjustments on December 31 are as follows:

a.–b. Ending merchandise inventory, $67,850.

c. Uncollectible accounts, 0.5 percent of net credit sales of $245,000.

d. Supplies on hand December 31, $1,020.

e. Expired insurance, $1,190.

f. *Depreciation Expense—Equipment,* $5,600.

g. Accrued interest expense on notes payable, $325.

h. Accrued salaries, $2,100.

i. *Social Security Tax Payable* (6.2 percent) and *Medicare Tax Payable* (1.45 percent) of accrued salaries.

INSTRUCTIONS

1. Prepare a worksheet for the year ended December 31, 2016.
2. Prepare a classified income statement. The firm does not divide its operating expenses into selling and administrative expenses.
3. Prepare a statement of owner's equity. No additional investments were made during the period.
4. Prepare a classified balance sheet. All notes payable are due within one year.
5. Journalize the adjusting entries. Use 25 as the first journal page number.
6. Journalize the closing entries.
7. Journalize the reversing entries.

Analyze: By what percentage did the owner's capital account change in the period from January 1, 2016, to December 31, 2016?

Critical Thinking Problem 13.2

Classified Balance Sheet

Teagan Fitzgerald is the owner of Newport Jewelry, a store specializing in gold, platinum, and special stones. During the past year, in response to increased demand, Teagan doubled her selling space by expanding into the vacant building space next door to her store. This expansion has been expensive because of the need to increase inventory and to purchase new store fixtures and equipment, including carpeting and state-of-the-art built-in fixtures. Teagan notes that the company's cash position has gone down and she is worried about future demands on cash to finance the growth.

Teagan presents you with a statement showing the assets, liabilities, and her equity for year-end 2015 and 2016, and asks your opinion on the company's ability to pay for the recent expansion. She did not have income and expense data available at the time. She commented that she had not made any new investment in the business in the past two years and was not financially able to do so presently. The information presented is shown below:

	December 31, 2015		December 31, 2016	
Assets				
Cash	$150,000		$ 30,000	
Accounts Receivable	45,000		91,500	
Inventory	105,000		234,000	
Prepaid Expenses	6,000		9,000	
Store Fixtures and Equipment	180,000		390,000	
Total Assets		$486,000		$754,500
Liabilities and Owner's Equity				
Liabilities				
Notes Payable (due in 4 years)	$ 90,000		$240,000	
Accounts Payable	132,000		171,000	
Salaries Payable	18,000		19,500	
Total Liabilities		$240,000		$430,500
Owner's Equity				
Teagan Fitzgerald, Capital		246,000		324,000
Total Liabilities and Owner's Equity		$486,000		$754,500

INSTRUCTIONS

1. Prepare classified balance sheets for Newport Jewelry for December 31, 2015, and December 31, 2016. (Ignore depreciation.)

2. Based on the information presented in the classified balance sheets, what is your opinion of Newport Jewelry's ability to pay its current bills in a timely manner?

3. What is the advantage of a classified balance sheet over a balance sheet that is not classified?

BUSINESS CONNECTIONS

Understanding Financial Statements

Managerial FOCUS

1. Why should management be concerned about the efficiency of the end-of-period procedures?

2. Spector Company had an increase in sales and net income during its last fiscal year, but cash decreased and the firm was having difficulty paying its bills by the end of the year. What factors might cause a shortage of cash even though a firm is profitable?

3. For the last three years, the balance sheet of Desai Hardware Center, a large retail store, has shown a substantial increase in merchandise inventory. Why might management be concerned about this development?

4. Why is it important to compare the financial statements of the current year with those of prior years?

5. Should a manager be concerned if the balance sheet shows a large increase in current liabilities and a large decrease in current assets? Explain your answer.

6. The latest income statement prepared at Wilkes Company shows that net sales increased by 10 percent over the previous year and selling expenses increased by 25 percent. Do you think that management should investigate the reasons for the increase in selling expenses? Why or why not?

7. Why is it useful for management to compare a firm's financial statements with financial information from other companies in the same industry?

Helping Your Boss May Be Wrong

Ethical DILEMMA

It is standard accounting procedures, or GAAP, to make a journal entry to remove the current year's principle from the long-term liabilities. This entry reduces the long-term liabilities and increases the current liabilities. You are the bookkeeper for Biker's Business. Biker's Business has a bank loan that requires a current ratio of 1.5 times. The owner has asked that you do not make the adjusting entry to take the current portion from the long-term liabilities. You know if you make the adjusting entry Biker's Business's loan will need to be repaid immediately (or the loan called). What should you do?

Balance Sheet

Financial Statement ANALYSIS

McCormick & Company, Incorporated, is a global leader in the manufacture, marketing, and distribution of spices, seasoning mixes, condiments, and other products to the food industry. McCormick and Company, Incorporated, reported the following in its *2012 Annual Report:*

Consolidated Balance Sheet		
	November 30	
(in millions)	*2012*	*2011*
Total Current Assets	$1,285.4	$1,222.9
Total Assets	$4,165.4	$4,087.8
Total Current Liabilities	$1,187.6	$ 993.3
Total Liabilities	$2,465.2	$2,469.3

Analyze:

1. What is the current ratio for both 2012 and 2011?

2. Did the current ratio improve from 2011 to 2012?

3. The company reported net sales of $4,014.2 million and gross profit of $1,617.8 million for its fiscal year ended November 30, 2012. What is the gross profit percentage for this period?

Analyzing Home Depot

Ratios are an important part of financial analysis. Divide into groups of two or three. Each person should choose one year from the Home Depot *Annual Report* in Appendix A. Calculate the current ratio, gross profit percentage, and inventory turnover. Is Home Depot doing better or worse than the previous year? What account is causing this change?

TEAMWORK

Using Financial Statements from the Internet

Choose the website of a corporation. You can find most corporate websites by typing the corporation's name after www., then .com. Find the 10K or annual report. Locate the income statement, balance sheet, and cash flow statements for the corporation. Notice the current assets and current liabilities. Calculate the current ratio, gross profit percentage, and inventory turnover.

Internet CONNECTION

Answers to **Self Reviews**

Answers to Section 1 Self Review

1. Classified statements permit users to better interpret the statements and analyze operations and financial conditions.

2. Current liabilities are those that fall due within one year. Long-term liabilities are those that will be due in more than one year.

3. Gross profit is the difference between net sales and the cost of goods sold.

4. **d.** A note receivable due in 13 months

5. **c.** As a deduction from the delivered cost of purchases

6. Net delivered cost of purchases is understated. Operating expenses are overstated. The net income from operations is unchanged.

Answers to Section 2 Self Review

1. So that anyone who needs to examine the entries at a later date will understand how and why the adjustments were made.

2. Adjustments that include entries in asset and liability accounts that have not been used during the period.

3. They provide a systematic and uniform method for closing all accounts that affect profit or loss for the period and transferring that profit or loss, adjusted for owner's withdrawals, to the owner's capital account.

4. **b.** an accrued expense that involves future cash payments.

5. **c.** current assets divided by current liabilities.

6. If the accountant correctly allocates the entire future payment to the payroll taxes expense account and the accrued liability account, there will be no effects on the proper allocation of expense between periods. If the accountant debits the payment in the subsequent month to the payroll taxes expense account, payroll tax expense will be correctly stated in the earlier period and overstated in the current period. *Payroll Taxes Payable* will be overstated during the later period.

Answers to Comprehensive Self Review

1. Single-step: all revenues listed in one section and all related costs and expenses in another section. Multiple-step: various sections in which subtotals and totals are computed in arriving at net income. Multi-step statements are generally preferred.

2. An entry in the debit column on the *Income Summary* line and a credit to *Merchandise Inventory* for the amount of beginning inventory closes the beginning inventory. A debit on the *Merchandise Inventory* line and a credit to *Income Summary* for the amount of ending inventory sets up the ending inventory.

3. It generally has a life of more than one year and is used in business operations.

4. **b.** expense accounts   **e.** *Income Summary* account

   d. owner's drawing account   **g.** revenue accounts

5. **a.** *Sales Returns and Allowances*

6. **a.** Debit *Income Summary* and credit *Jan Hanson, Capital* for $58,000.

   b. Debit *Jan Hanson, Capital* and credit **Income Summary** for $8,000.

7. **a.** adjusting entries; **c.** entries to close revenue accounts; **b.** entries to close expense accounts; **d.** reversing entries

Mini-Practice Set 2

Merchandising Business Accounting Cycle

The Fashion Rack

The Fashion Rack is a retail merchandising business that sells brand-name clothing at discount prices. The firm is owned and managed by Teresa Lojay, who started the business on April 1, 2016. This project will give you an opportunity to put your knowledge of accounting into practice as you handle the accounting work of The Fashion Rack during the month of October 2016.

Sage 50
Complete Accounting

INTRODUCTION

The Fashion Rack has a monthly accounting period. The firm's chart of accounts is shown below and on the next page. The journals used to record transactions are the sales journal, purchases journal, cash receipts journal, cash payments journal, and general journal. Postings are made from the journals to the accounts receivable ledger, accounts payable ledger, and general ledger. The employees are paid at the end of the month. A computerized payroll service prepares all payroll records and checks.

INSTRUCTIONS

1. Open the general ledger accounts and enter the balances for October 1, 2016. Obtain the necessary figures from the postclosing trial balance prepared on September 30, 2016, which is shown on page 482. (If you are using the *Study Guide & Working Papers,* you will find that the general ledger accounts are already open.)

2. Open the subsidiary ledger accounts and enter the balances for October 1, 2016. Obtain the necessary figures from the schedule of accounts payable and schedule of accounts receivable prepared on September 30, 2016, which appear on page 483. (If you are using the *Study Guide & Working Papers,* you will find that the subsidiary ledger accounts are already open.)

3. Analyze the transactions for October and record each transaction in the proper journal. (Use 10 as the number for the first page of each special journal and 16 as the number for the first page of the general journal.)

4. Post the individual entries that involve customer and creditor accounts from the journals to the subsidiary ledgers on a daily basis. Post the individual entries that appear in the general journal and in the Other Accounts sections of the cash receipts and cash payments journals to the general ledger on a daily basis.

5. Total, prove, and rule the special journals as of October 31, 2016.

6. Post the column totals from the special journals to the general ledger accounts.

The Fashion Rack Chart of Accounts		
Assets	**Liabilities**	
101 Cash	203	Accounts Payable
111 Accounts Receivable	221	Social Security Tax Payable
112 Allowance for Doubtful Accounts	222	Medicare Tax Payable
121 Merchandise Inventory	223	Employee Income Tax Payable
131 Supplies	225	Federal Unemployment Tax Payable
133 Prepaid Insurance	227	State Unemployment Tax Payable
135 Prepaid Advertising	229	Salaries Payable
141 Equipment	231	Sales Tax Payable
142 Accumulated Depreciation—Equipment		

The Fashion Rack
Chart of Accounts (continued)

Owner's Equity

301	Teresa Lojay, Capital
302	Teresa Lojay, Drawing
399	Income Summary

Revenues

401	Sales
402	Sales Returns and Allowances

Cost of Goods Sold

501	Purchases
502	Freight In
503	Purchases Returns and Allowances
504	Purchases Discounts

Expenses

611	Advertising Expense
614	Depreciation Expense — Equipment
617	Insurance Expense
620	Uncollectible Accounts Expense
623	Janitorial Services Expense
626	Payroll Taxes Expense
629	Rent Expense
632	Salaries Expense
635	Supplies Expense
638	Telephone Expense
644	Utilities Expense

7. Check the accuracy of the subsidiary ledgers by preparing a schedule of accounts receivable and a schedule of accounts payable as of October 31, 2016. Compare the totals with the balances of the *Accounts Receivable* account and the *Accounts Payable* account in the general ledger.

8. Check the accuracy of the general ledger by preparing a trial balance in the first two columns of a 10-column worksheet. Make sure that the total debits and the total credits are equal.

9. Complete the Adjustments section of the worksheet. Use the following data. Identify each adjustment with the appropriate letter.

   a. During October, the firm had net credit sales of $9,810. From experience with similar businesses, the previous accountant had estimated that 1.0 percent of the firm's net credit sales would result in uncollectible accounts. Record an adjustment for the expected loss from uncollectible accounts for the month of October.

   b. On October 31, an inventory of the supplies showed that items costing $3,240 were on hand. Record an adjustment for the supplies used in October.

   c. On September 30, 2016, the firm purchased a six-month insurance policy for $8,400. Record an adjustment for the expired insurance for October.

   d. On October 1, the firm signed a three-month advertising contract for $4,800 with a local cable television station and paid the full amount in advance. Record an adjustment for the expired advertising for October.

   e. On April 1, 2016, the firm purchased equipment for $83,000. The equipment was estimated to have a useful life of five years and a salvage value of $12,500. Record an adjustment for depreciation on the equipment for October.

   f.–g. Based on a physical count, ending merchandise inventory was determined to be $81,260.

10. Complete the Adjusted Trial Balance section of the worksheet.

11. Determine the net income or net loss for October and complete the worksheet.

12. Prepare a classified income statement for the month ended October 31, 2016. (The firm does not divide its operating expenses into selling and administrative expenses.)

13. Prepare a statement of owner's equity for the month ended October 31, 2016.

14. Prepare a classified balance sheet as of October 31, 2016.

15. Journalize and post the adjusting entries using general journal page 17.

16. Prepare and post the closing entries using general journal page 18.

17. Prepare a postclosing trial balance.

DATE	TRANSACTIONS
Oct. 1	Issued Check 601 for $4,200 to pay City Properties the monthly rent.
1	Signed a three-month radio advertising contract with Cable Station KOTU for $4,800; issued Check 602 to pay the full amount in advance.
2	Received $520 from Megan Greening, a credit customer, in payment of her account.
2	Issued Check 603 for $17,820 to remit the sales tax owed for July through September to the State Tax Commission.
2	Issued Check 604 for $7,673.40 to A Fashion Statement, a creditor, in payment of Invoice 9387 ($7,830), less a cash discount ($156.60).
3	Sold merchandise on credit for $2,480 plus sales tax of $124 to Dimitri Sayegh, Sales Slip 241.
4	Issued Check 605 for $1,050 to BMX Supply Co. for supplies.
4	Issued Check 606 for $8,594.60 to Today's Woman, a creditor, in payment of Invoice 5671 ($8,770), less a cash discount ($175.40).
5	Collected $1,700.00 on account from Emily Tran, a credit customer.
5	Accepted a return of merchandise from Dimitri Sayegh. The merchandise was originally sold on Sales Slip 241, dated October 3; issued Credit Memorandum 18 for $630, which includes sales tax of $30.
5	Issued Check 607 for $1,666 to Classy Threads, a creditor, in payment of Invoice 3292 ($1,700), less a cash discount ($34).
6	Had cash sales of $18,600 plus sales tax of $930 during October 1–6.
8	Received a check from James Helmer, a credit customer, for $832 to pay the balance he owes.
8	Issued Check 608 for $1,884 to deposit social security tax ($702), Medicare tax ($162), and federal income tax withholding ($1,020) from the September payroll. Record this check in the cash payments journal.
9	Sold merchandise on credit for $2,050 plus sales tax of $102.50 to Emma Maldonado, Sales Slip 242.
10	Issued Check 609 for $1,445 to pay *The City Daily* for a newspaper advertisement that appeared in October.
11	Purchased merchandise for $4,820 from A Fashion Statement, Invoice 9422, dated October 8; the terms are 2/10, n/30.
12	Issued Check 610 for $375 to pay freight charges to Ace Freight Company, the trucking company that delivered merchandise from A Fashion Statement on September 27 and October 11.
13	Had cash sales of $12,300 plus sales tax of $615 during October 8–13.
15	Sold merchandise on credit for $1,940 plus sales tax of $97 to James Helmer, Sales Slip 243.
16	Purchased discontinued merchandise from Acme Jobbers; paid for it immediately with Check 611 for $6,420.
16	Received $510 on account from Dimitri Sayegh, a credit customer.
16	Issued Check 612 for $4,723.60 to A Fashion Statement, a creditor, in payment of Invoice 9422 ($4,820.00), less cash discount ($96.40).
18	Issued Check 613 for $7,200 to Teresa Lojay as a withdrawal for personal use.
20	Had cash sales of $13,500 plus sales tax of $675 during October 15–20.
22	Issued Check 614 to City Utilities for $1,112 to pay the monthly electric bill.
24	Sold merchandise on credit for $820 plus sales tax of $41 to Megan Greening, Sales Slip 244.
25	Purchased merchandise for $3,380 from Classy Threads, Invoice 3418, dated October 23; the terms are 2/10, n/30.
26	Issued Check 615 to Regional Telephone for $780 to pay the monthly telephone bill.
27	Had cash sales of $14,240 plus sales tax of $712 during October 22–27.
29	Received Credit Memorandum 175 for $430 from Classy Threads Inc. for defective goods that were returned. The original purchase was recorded on October 25.

(continued)

DATE		TRANSACTIONS (CONT.)
Oct.	29	Sold merchandise on credit for $3,120 plus sales tax of $156 to Emily Tran, Sales Slip 245.
	29	Recorded the October payroll. The records prepared by the payroll service show the following totals: earnings, $10,800; social security, $702.00; Medicare, $162.00; income tax, $1,020; and net pay, $8,916. The excess withholdings corrected an error made in withholdings in September.
	29	Recorded the employer's payroll taxes, which were calculated by the payroll service: social security, $702; Medicare, $162; federal unemployment tax, $118; and state unemployment tax, $584. This, too, reflects an understatement of taxes recorded in September and corrected in this month.
	30	Purchased merchandise for $4,020 from Today's Woman, Invoice 5821, dated October 26; the terms are 1/10, n/30.
	31	Issued Checks 616 through 619, totaling $8,916.00, to employees to pay October payroll. For the sake of simplicity, enter the total of the checks on single line in the cash payments journal.
	31	Issued Check 620 for $475 to Handy Janitors for October janitorial services.
	31	Had cash sales of $1,700 plus sales tax of $85 for October 29–31.

The Fashion Rack
Postclosing Trial Balance
September 30, 2016

ACCOUNT NAME	DEBIT	CREDIT
Cash	59 800 00	
Accounts Receivable	6 210 00	
Allowance for Doubtful Accounts		4 20 00
Merchandise Inventory	88 996 00	
Supplies	4 100 00	
Prepaid Insurance	8 400 00	
Equipment	83 000 00	
Accumulated Depreciation—Equipment		7 050 00
Accounts Payable		18 300 00
Social Security Tax Payable		7 02 00
Medicare Tax Payable		1 62 00
Employee Income Tax Payable		1 020 00
Federal Unemployment Tax Payable		5 12 00
State Unemployment Tax Payable		1 268 00
Sales Tax Payable		17 820 00
Teresa Lojay, Capital		203 252 00
Totals	250 506 00	250 506 00

The Fashion Rack
Schedule of Accounts Payable
September 30, 2016

A Fashion Statement	7	8	3	0	00
Classy Threads	1	7	0	0	00
Today's Woman	8	7	7	0	00
Total	18	3	0	0	00

The Fashion Rack
Schedule of Accounts Receivable
September 30, 2016

Jennifer Brown		7	9	5	00
Megan Greening		5	2	0	00
James Helmer		8	3	2	00
Emma Maldonado		2	3	2	00
Jim Price	1	6	2	1	00
Dimitri Sayegh		5	1	0	00
Emily Tran	1	7	0	0	00
Total	6	2	1	0	00

Accounting Principles and Reporting Standards

GREEN MOUNTAIN COFFEE ROASTERS, INC.
www.gmcr.com

Green Mountain Coffee Roasters began in 1981 as a small café in rural Vermont. Today, the company is a leader in specialty coffee and coffee makers. Green Mountain Coffee Roasters, Inc. (NASDAQ: GMCR), is recognized for its award-winning coffees, innovative Keurig® Single Cup brewing technology, and socially responsible business practices.

GMCR routinely posts information that may be of importance to investors in the Investor Relations section of its website, including news releases and its complete financial statements, as filed with the SEC. In 2012, the company reported in its annual report the following:

> On the basis of generally accepted accounting principles (GAAP), we generated earnings of $2.28 per fully diluted share in fiscal year 2012 as compared to $1.11 in 2011.

Even with the outstanding growth seen by Green Mountain, accounting issues related to its revenue recognition practices have plagued the company. In 2010, GMCR saw its stock price drop by over 20 percent when the Securities & Exchange Commission requested documents related to revenue recognition practices. The company has since rebounded but the inquiry is still not over. So far, Green Mountain has not been charged with any regulatory violations and continues to cooperate fully with the investigation, but like a dark cloud, costly legal expenses and the risks of penalty continue to hang over the company and its investors.

The SEC inquiry highlighted the fact that accounting for revenue can be a challenge to organizations, but it is vital that generally accepted accounting principles be used in recording and reporting financial transactions. As in Green Mountain's case, this reliance provides assurance to all financial statement users that the company's reported results are accurate.

thinking critically

If Green Mountain Coffee Roasters were to change its revenue recognition policy, why would it be important to report this change in the financial notes of the company's annual report?

LEARNING OBJECTIVES

14-1. Understand the process used to develop generally accepted accounting principles.

14-2. Identify the major accounting standards-setting bodies and their roles in the standards-setting process.

14-3. Describe the users and uses of financial reports.

14-4. Identify and explain the qualitative characteristics of accounting information.

14-5. Describe and explain the basic assumptions about accounting reports.

14-6. Explain and apply the basic principles of accounting.

14-7. Describe and apply the modifying constraints on accounting principles.

14-8. Define the accounting terms new to this chapter.

NEW TERMS

conceptual framework
conservatism
cost-benefit test
full disclosure principle
going concern assumption
historical cost basis principle
industry practice constraint
matching principle
materiality constraint

monetary unit assumption
neutrality concept
periodicity of income assumption
private sector
public sector
qualitative characteristics
realization
revenue recognition principle
transparency

SECTION OBJECTIVES

>> **14-1.** Understand the process used to develop generally accepted accounting principles.

WHY IT'S IMPORTANT

Knowing how accounting principles are developed helps in understanding the logic underlying accounting and therefore helps learn rules.

>> **14-2.** Identify the major accounting standards-setting bodies and their roles in the standards-setting process.

WHY IT'S IMPORTANT

Documents relating to accounting principles and standards are filled with references to organizations involved in standards setting. To understand standards, it is necessary to understand the roles of these organizations.

>> **14-3.** Describe the users and uses of financial reports.

WHY IT'S IMPORTANT

Principles and standards of accounting can be developed in a logical way only if it is known who the users of the statements are and what uses they make of the statements.

TERMS TO LEARN

conceptual framework
private sector
public sector

Generally Accepted Accounting Principles

In previous chapters, you learned how to record business transactions and summarize them in financial statements. Financial statements are prepared using generally accepted accounting principles and rules. In the first section of this chapter, you will learn how these principles and rules are developed. In the second section, you will learn about the conceptual framework of accounting underlying all financial reporting for business enterprises.

The Need for Generally Accepted Accounting Principles

In order to ensure that they are meaningful and useful, financial statements are prepared using generally accepting accounting principles (GAAP). GAAP is used whether the business is a sole proprietorship managed by the owner or is a large company such as Macy's. GAAP allows the financial statements of different companies to be compared and meaningful conclusions drawn from the comparison. It also allows a company to compare its own statements from period to period.

>> **14-1. OBJECTIVE**

Understand the process used to develop generally accepted accounting principles.

The Development of Generally Accepted Accounting Principles

Accepted accounting principles are developed in several ways in the United States. In the past, unique accounting procedures and practices became widely used over time by specific industries or in accounting for specific transactions. These industry practices have sometimes become accepted as GAAP even though they may not be entirely consistent with the general requirements. In some cases, accounting rules result from a decision by the authoritative rule-making organization to permit more than one method because of industry practice. This is true, for example, in the oil and gas industries in which two methods of accounting for certain activities are allowed by the Securities and Exchange Commission (SEC). The use of two methods may yield widely differing results.

For the past half-century, however, accounting principles in the United States have been developed through a cooperative effort between the **private sector** (business) and the **public sector** (government). The Securities and Exchange Commission is the legal rule-making body from the public sector and the Financial Accounting Standards Board (FASB) is the primary representative of the private sector. Most official pronouncements of accounting principles and rules today represent a joint effort of these two organizations.

>> 14-2. OBJECTIVE

Identify the major accounting standards-setting bodies and their roles in the standards-setting process.

THE SECURITIES AND EXCHANGE COMMISSION

In 1934, the Congress of the United States established the Securities and Exchange Commission (SEC) to administer the Securities Act of 1933 and the Securities Exchange Act of 1934. Among its powers, the SEC has authority to define accounting terms and to prescribe accounting principles for companies under its jurisdiction. The SEC also determines the form and content of accounting reports that are required to be filed with the SEC. The SEC regulates the financial reporting of publicly held corporations (basically, companies whose stocks are traded in the securities exchanges and over-the-counter markets). The SEC is a dominant force in accounting because its rules must be followed by publicly held companies. Historically, however, the SEC has used its powers sparingly, preferring to let the accounting profession develop accounting principles and financial reporting standards, which are then usually adopted by the SEC as official rules. The Sarbanes-Oxley Act, passed by the U.S. Congress in 2002 in reaction to the "accounting scandals" of public companies in the early 2000s, reaffirms the SEC's role as the authoritative accounting rule-making body. The Act goes further to permit the SEC to accept the accounting and reporting rules developed by "a private-sector organization," provided certain requirements are met. Sec. 108 of the Act states: ". . . the Commission may recognize as 'generally accepted' for purposes of the securities laws, any accounting principles established by a standard setting body" (meeting certain tests). In April 2003, the SEC officially recognized the FASB as the accounting standard setter under Sarbanes-Oxley.

ABOUT **ACCOUNTING**

Authority of the SEC
The SEC is given statutory power to establish accounting and reporting rules for publicly held companies. Thus, it has the "final voice" in accounting principles for those companies.

PUBLIC COMPANY ACCOUNTING OVERSIGHT BOARD

The Sarbanes-Oxley Act also created the Public Company Accounting Oversight Board (PCAOB). The PCAOB is a private-sector, nonprofit corporation whose purpose is to oversee the CPA firms auditing publicly held companies. The PCAOB has five members, who are appointed by the SEC. Two members of the PCAOB (and only two) must be CPAs.

The PCAOB has the power to, among other things, set auditing, quality control, ethics, independence, and other standards for CPA firms engaged in auditing publicly held companies. This includes regulating the nonaudit services CPA firms provide to their audit clients, such as tax and consulting services. This authority was given to the PCAOB as a reaction to audit failures at several publicly held companies including WorldCom and Enron. Many people felt the auditors' independence from their clients had been impaired because of the large amount of fees they earned from consulting and tax services.

THE FINANCIAL ACCOUNTING STANDARDS BOARD

From its inception in 1973 until 2013, the authoritative pronouncements of the FASB were known as *Statements of Financial Accounting Standards,* or simply Standards. More than 160 such standards were issued. In mid-2010, the FASB introduced the *Financial Accounting Standards Board Accounting Standards Codification.* The Codification organized GAAP into a structure that is much easier for a professional to study and define the generally accepted accounting principle relating to a particular account or accounting issue. The Codification is now the source of all authoritative nongovernmental GAAP. All GAAP related to Assets is now found in the section of the Codification for Assets (ASC300 Assets)—likewise for all other areas of accounting. Subject areas are referred to as a Topic. All previous level U.S. GAAP is superseded by the Codification.

The FASB's work is based on a fundamental framework of accounting, developed under its ==conceptual framework== project. The goal of the project is to provide a cohesive set of closely related objectives and concepts to be used in developing accounting and reporting standards. The FASB has issued eight *Statements of Financial Accounting Concepts* that provide the guidelines on which the official *Statements of Financial Accounting Standards* are to be based. The process used by the FASB in developing the conceptual framework statements reflects deductive reasoning and involves essentially the following steps:

1. Define the goals and objectives of accounting.

2. Identify users of financial reports and the uses made of the reports.

3. Examine the qualitative characteristics that make accounting information useful.

4. Identify and define the financial elements such as assets, liabilities, revenues, and expenses, whose inclusion and classification make financial statements meaningful and useful.

5. Establish the form and content of financial statements.

6. Set forth fundamental recognition criteria.

7. Develop measurement standards for financial elements that appear in the financial statements.

Sec. 108 of the 2002 Sarbanes-Oxley Act requires the SEC to "conduct a study on the adoption by the United States financial reporting system of a principles-based accounting system." The FASB itself conducted a study and issued a report in October 2002. In July 2003, the SEC completed its study and made its report to Congress. The result is an intention for the FASB to issue "objectives-oriented standards" and to "address deficiencies in the conceptual framework." The goal is to arrive at an "internally consistent" and "complete" framework. The Codification helps achieve this desired result.

THE AMERICAN INSTITUTE OF CERTIFIED PUBLIC ACCOUNTANTS

The American Institute of Certified Public Accountants (AICPA) is the national organization of certified public accountants. Prior to formation of the FASB, the AICPA's Accounting Principles Board was recognized by the SEC as the preeminent private-sector group in developing accounting rules. Although the AICPA has much less authority and a less active role in the development of accounting standards than it held before its APB was superseded by the FASB in 1973, it continues to play an important role through its Accounting Standards Executive Committee (AcSEC). AcSEC issues three important types of documents:

1. **Accounting and auditing guides.** These releases provide guidance on accounting matters not addressed directly by the FASB and summarize the accounting and auditing practices in specific industries—for example casinos, airlines, insurance companies, and oil- and gas-producing companies.

2. **Statements of position (SOP).** SOPs provide guidance on a financial accounting question that has been raised until the FASB issues an official pronouncement on the topic.

3. **Practice bulletins.** Practice bulletins express the AICPA's position on narrow accounting issues that have not been considered by the FASB or SEC.

In addition to its work through AcSEC, the AICPA regulates auditing practices and takes the lead role in developing and enforcing ethical standards for auditors. In this role, the AICPA gives the statements of the FASB additional support by requiring that AICPA members make sure the companies being audited follow the accounting and reporting standards specified in the FASB Statements.

FEDERAL AND STATE AGENCIES OTHER THAN THE SEC

Historically, many other federal and state agencies have strongly influenced accounting and reporting standards. Regulatory agencies have had the power to prescribe detailed systems of accounting for public utilities, including the railroad and electric power industries. These agencies are concerned with regulation of price and competition more than with the development of accounting principles. As a result, the accounting and reporting requirements imposed on regulated industries frequently have not reflected GAAP.

Similarly, federal income tax requirements have had an impact on financial accounting. Businesses are not required to use the same financial accounting and tax accounting practices. However, some taxpayers adopt tax accounting rules where possible to avoid keeping two sets of records. This is possible if the tax requirements do not conflict with authoritative financial accounting principles. There almost inevitably are differences between required tax treatment and required GAAP. These differences often give rise to a unique accounting problem—the requirement that the current financial income statement should reflect the tax expense applicable to the income reported in the financial statements even though the actual tax paid is different because it is not levied on the income reported in the financial statement.

OTHER ORGANIZATIONS IN THE UNITED STATES

Other organizations and groups have over several decades been instrumental in the development and evolution of accounting principles and rules. The American Accounting Association (AAA) is one such organization. About half its members teach accounting. Many of them have written textbooks and articles dealing with accounting principles and concepts and often are involved in other accounting organizations, including the FASB. In a variety of ways, the AAA has been able to stimulate acceptance of the principles it has helped develop and perfect over the years.

As early as 1930, the New York Stock Exchange (NYSE) required corporations whose securities were traded on a public stock exchange to publish annual reports. Later, quarterly reports were required. Since 1933, the NYSE has insisted upon independent audits for all corporations that applied to have their securities (stocks and bonds) listed on the exchange.

ABOUT
ACCOUNTING
The AICPA has many resources on its website to help you learn about IFRS. www.aicpa.org.

THE INTERNATIONAL ACCOUNTING STANDARDS BOARD

Accounting principles vary from country to country. The International Accounting Standards Board (IASB) was formed to develop accounting standards that can be adopted throughout the world for publicly traded companies. The organization has issued about 40 "International Accounting Standards." The International Financial Reporting Standards Foundation is an independent, nonprofit foundation that was created in 2000 to oversee the IASB. Accounting professionals have begun using the terminology of International Financial Reporting Standards (IFRS) in reference to all internationally accepted accounting principles. In an important move, in 2002 the European Union voted to require companies whose securities are traded on exchanges in member countries to prepare financial reports on the basis of IASB Standards.

Accounting rule-making bodies in the United States historically have been reluctant to recognize as "authoritative" the standards issued by the IASB or its predecessor, the International Accounting Standards Committee (IASC). Presently, however, the SEC, the FASB, the International Accounting Standards Board, and accounting rule-making bodies from many countries are working toward the convergence of the standards issued by each organization. Because of this, new rules developed by the FASB and by the IASB have become more consistent with one another. The two organizations and accounting rule-setting bodies from other countries have worked closely in developing almost identical standards on new issues.

Section 108 of the Sarbanes-Oxley Act, in describing the attributes of a private-sector organization that might be accepted as the accounting standards setter, included: ". . . considers, in adopting accounting principles, . . . the extent to which international convergence on high quality accounting standards is necessary or appropriate in the public interest and for the protection of investors."

It can be reasonably expected that the gap between accounting statements in countries around the world will decrease dramatically in the next decade as more countries adopt IFRS for financial statements.

ABOUT

ACCOUNTING

Accounting Is Designed for Users

In order to develop accounting principles and reporting standards, it is necessary to know for whom reports are being prepared and to what uses they are put.

Users and Uses of Financial Reports

In its conceptual framework, the FASB concluded that financial reporting rules should concentrate on providing information that is helpful to current and potential investors and creditors in making investment and credit decisions. The focus is not on providing information to management, tax authorities, or regulatory agencies, because they have access to specific information from the firm's records not available to the public and often the information they need is not the same as that needed by investors and creditors.

In its conceptual framework project, the FASB also concluded that the information needed by investors and creditors should help them assess the likelihood of receiving a future cash flow, the amount of such a cash flow, and the time when the cash flow may be received. This conclusion is based on the idea that investors and creditors expect to receive a cash flow directly or indirectly from the business entity:

- *directly* from the distribution of the company's earnings, or
- *indirectly* through the disposition of their interests for cash.

Thus, financial report users need information about:

- profits
- economic resources (assets)
- claims against the assets (liabilities and owner's equity)
- changes in assets and in the claims against the assets

Information about profits appears in the income statement. Information about assets, liabilities, and owner's equity is provided primarily in the balance sheet.

The statement of cash flows provides information about the cash received from major sources during the period and the uses made of that cash. The statement of cash flows is discussed in Chapter 24.

Certain analyses of the financial statements also supply meaningful information about the results of operations and the financial condition of a business. The analysis of financial statements is discussed in Chapter 23.

It is clear from the actions of the SEC and the FASB that they interpret the Sarbanes-Oxley Act to require a stronger conceptual framework of accounting. It is equally clear that the two organizations also agree that accounting standards must be based on the conceptual framework. The SEC's 2006 report to the Congress on "principles-based" accounting observed that the first characteristic of objectives-based standards, dictated by the Sarbanes-Oxley Act, is that any standard must "be based on an improved and consistently applied framework." It is essential that accounting students understand the framework.

Section Self Review

QUESTIONS

1. What is the FASB's conceptual framework project? Why is an understanding of the conceptual framework important to those who make accounting and reporting rules?

2. Identify the governmental entity that has oversight of the development of accounting principles and explain its role in the development process.

3. Xavier Corporation is a corporation with only two shareholders (owners). Is the corporation required to file financial statements with the SEC?

4. Give two major reasons why the pronouncements of the Financial Accounting Standards Board have had a major influence on accounting in this country.

EXERCISE

5. Four organizations that play important roles in the development of accounting principles, standards, and reporting practices are the Securities and Exchange Commission (SEC), the Financial Accounting Standards Board (FASB), the Public Company Accounting Oversight Board (PCAOB), and the International Accounting Standards Board (IASB). Indicate which organization is best described by each of the following statements:

a. This organization has legal responsibility for setting accounting requirements for publicly held corporations.

b. This organization actually develops and issues most of the accounting standards today.

c. This organization is an independent, private-sector body that develops and approves International Financial Reporting Standards (IFRS).

d. This organization has the power to limit nonaudit services by CPA firms to their audit clients.

ANALYSIS

6. The financial statements for Automotive Repair Services have an auditor's notation that the statements are "not prepared in conformity with GAAP." What does this mean to you as an investor?

(Answers to Section 1 Self Review are on page 516.)

SECTION OBJECTIVES

>> **14-4.** Identify and explain the qualitative characteristics of accounting information.

WHY IT'S IMPORTANT
The qualitative characteristics provide the users a basis for relying on the statements.

>> **14-5.** Describe and explain the basic assumptions about accounting reports.

WHY IT'S IMPORTANT
The accountant bases financial reports on standard assumptions, so understanding of these assumptions is essential to understanding reports.

>> **14-6.** Explain and apply the basic principles of accounting.

WHY IT'S IMPORTANT
All accounting reports rest on the basic principles. Knowledge of the principles is essential to prepare statements and to understand statements.

>> **14-7.** Describe and apply the modifying constraints on accounting principles.

WHY IT'S IMPORTANT
Modifying conventions may justify or require the modification of basic accounting principles.

TERMS TO LEARN

conservatism
cost-benefit test
full disclosure principle
going concern assumption
historical cost basis principle
industry practice constraint
matching principle
materiality constraint
monetary unit assumption
neutrality concept
periodicity of income assumption
qualitative characteristics
realization
revenue recognition principle
transparency

The FASB's Conceptual Framework of Accounting

The rules of accounting that you are learning in this textbook are all based on the FASB's conceptual framework, so it is important that you understand the basic elements of the framework. The conceptual framework of the FASB is focused on four levels of concepts: (1) qualitative characteristics of financial reports, (2) basic assumptions underlying financial reports, (3) basic accounting principles, and (4) modifying constraints. An understanding of these elements will be of great benefit in this course as you learn how to account for and report various transactions affecting the financial statements.

Qualitative Characteristics of Financial Reports

The **qualitative characteristics** are the qualities that make accounting information useful for decision making by investors, creditors, and other users. The meanings of most of these characteristics are self-evident from their names.

Qualitative Characteristics	
Decision Usefulness	
Relevance	Faithful Representation
Confirmatory Value	Completeness
Predictive Value	Neutrality
Materiality Value	Freedom from Error

FUNDAMENTAL QUALITATIVE CHARACTERISTICS

Decision usefulness and faithful representation are the two qualitative characteristics of financial reports. These two characteristics are closely related and interdependent. First, the information should be relevant to decision makers. Further, the information should be a faithful representation of business activities. However, the framework assumes that financial statement users will have a basic knowledge of business and economics and they will devote an appropriate amount of time to studying and analyzing the statements. Published financial reports are not designed for individuals who do not possess such knowledge.

>> 14-4. OBJECTIVE

Identify and explain the qualitative characteristics of accounting information.

RELEVANCE

Relevance means that accounting information is capable of making a difference in a decision by the report user. Conversely, if information is not capable of being useful to the user in making a decision, it is not relevant. In order for accounting information to be relevant in making a difference in decision making, it must have confirmatory value, predictive value, or both. Generally, relevant information will possess both of these components. Both of these elements must have materiality value in order to be relevant.

Confirmatory Value Information that helps the statement user verify fulfillment or nonfulfillment of prior expectations or decisions is said to have confirmatory value. For example, a quarterly income statement may provide evidence that prior expectations have been met. In this context, confirmatory value deals with verifying past expectations. However, information providing confirmatory value may also be useful in predicting future results.

Predictive Value If information is relevant, it will help statement users in making predictions or forecasts about the meaning and ultimate outcome of events giving rise to the information.

Materiality Value If information is relevant, it must be significant in amount or nature that is sufficient to affect a decision. If information is not material, it need not be reported in accordance with GAAP. Materiality is an entity-specific aspect of relevance based on the nature or magnitude of items to which the information relates.

FAITHFUL REPRESENTATION

To be a faithful representation of business activities, accounting information must be complete, neutral, and free from error. Faithful representation is the concept that data shown in the financial reports reflect what really happened. If an entity reports sales of $544,000, that figure should reflect the true sales for the period. In order for financial information to be a faithful representation of business activities, the information must be complete, neutral, and free from error.

Completeness Information is complete when it includes everything necessary to reflect what happened for all of the business activities for which the firm is reporting.

Neutrality Information is neutral if the financial statements are objectively prepared and are free from bias (that is, they do not favor one group of users over the other). The information should be prepared in such a way that it is helpful and seen in the same manner by all groups.

Freedom from Error Information is free from error if the information is the best available. The conceptual framework acknowledges limitations in achieving a faithful representation due to inherent uncertainties, estimates, and assumptions. Accordingly, financial information may not always be entirely free from errors but they are expected to reflect unbiased judgments and due diligence in applying appropriate accounting principles.

ENHANCING QUALITATIVE CHARACTERISTICS

Comparability, timeliness, verifiability, and understandability are attributes that enhance the relevance and faithful representation of financial information. These attributes should be maximized individually and together.

Comparability Comparability means that the financial data is presented in such a manner that it can be meaningfully compared with the same data for other companies. Comparability enables users to identify similarities and differences among items, both between different accounting periods within a set of financial statements and across different reporting entities. Uniform and consistent accounting principles provide support for achieving this goal.

Timeliness Firms must disclose accounting information in a timely manner. Timeliness refers to information being made available to users early enough to use it in the decision process.

Verifiability Verifiability is indicated when independent measures obtain similar results. If persons outside the entity arrive at different conclusions about measurements, then the financial information cannot be said to be verifiable.

Understanding Understanding means that users of the accounting information must be able to comprehend the information within the context of the decisions that they are making. This is a user-specific quality because users will differ in their ability to comprehend any set of information.

>> 14-5. OBJECTIVE
Describe and explain the basic assumptions about accounting reports.

Underlying Assumptions

The FASB's conceptual framework lists four assumptions financial statement users should be able to assume that preparers of the statements have made in preparing the statements.

Underlying Assumptions
Separate Economic Entity
Going Concern
Monetary Unit
Periodicity of Income

ABOUT ACCOUNTING

The Business and Its Owners as Separate Entities
If the business entity is a sole proprietorship, it may be difficult to think in terms of the owner and the business as separate entities.

SEPARATE ECONOMIC ENTITY ASSUMPTION

Accounting records are kept for a specific business or activity. The separate economic entity assumption assumes that the business is separate from its owners. Transactions in the records of a business and the resulting financial statements reflect the affairs of the business—not the affairs of the owners.

It is easy to understand the separate assumption for a corporation such as Microsoft because Microsoft is legally separate from its owners. However, the separate entity concept applies equally to sole proprietorships and partnerships, even though the owners may be legally liable for all debts of the business and for actions carried out on behalf of the business.

GOING CONCERN ASSUMPTION

When transactions are recorded and financial statements are prepared, it is assumed that the business is a **going concern**—that is, it will continue to operate indefinitely. This assumption permits businesses to record property and equipment as assets at their cost without having to be concerned about what they are worth in case of liquidation in the near future.

MONETARY UNIT ASSUMPTION

There are two aspects to the **monetary unit assumption.** First is the idea that expressing financial facts and events is meaningful only when they can be expressed in monetary terms. The entity may possess many assets, usually intangible—such as goodwill it has created among customers—that cannot be specifically identified and their values determined. If these assets cannot be expressed in meaningful monetary amounts, an attempt to include them in the financial statements would result in the violation of one or more of the qualitative characteristics or basic assumptions. Similarly, there may be potential liabilities, such as a lawsuit that appears to have little validity, which have been filed against the entity. However, it may be appropriate or even necessary to discuss such potential assets or liabilities in disclosures accompanying the statements in order to give a full presentation, even though they do not possess the characteristics necessary to assign a monetary value to them.

The second aspect of the monetary unit assumption is that the value of money is stable. The assumption that the value of the monetary unit is stable allows the cost of assets purchased many years ago to be added to the costs of recently purchased assets of the same kind and the total dollar amount reported on the financial statements. This means that it is deemed to be unnecessary for accountants to convert dollars spent in different years, when the purchasing power might be quite different, to a common unit of purchasing power. This assumption has been criticized because the value of money does not, in fact, remain stable. Its purchasing power changes substantially over the years. Proposals have been made for abandoning the stable monetary concept, but the practical problems involved and the objectivity and reliability of historical cost figures have prevailed to this time.

PERIODICITY OF INCOME ASSUMPTION

The income statement covers a certain time period and the balance sheet is prepared as of the end of that time period. It is assumed that the activities of the business can be separated into time periods with revenues and expenses being assigned on a logical basis to those periods. This assumption is called the **periodicity of income assumption.** In reality, the final results of a business are known only when the business ceases to exist. When all assets are sold and all liabilities paid, the owners can determine the amount of the overall profit or loss. However, owners, creditors, and other interested parties cannot wait until a business is dissolved to make decisions. Operating and financing decisions must be made constantly throughout the life of the business. Many of these decisions are based on profit or loss for a specified period of time. Others are based on assets and liabilities as of the end of the period. Accountants have developed techniques, including the accrual basis of accounting, to prepare financial statements at regular intervals to meet the goals implied by this assumption. Many, if not most, of the concepts you learn in accounting result from the periodicity assumption.

Although the fiscal year is generally perceived as the standard accounting period, the SEC and FASB require that the same accounting rules be applied in measuring income for each quarter. Many businesses assume that the periodicity assumption can be extended even further to monthly financial statements. Obviously the assumption of periodicity has more validity for some type of business. For example, a merchandising business can measure assets, liabilities, revenues, and expenses easily each quarter, or even each month. However, an enterprise growing timber may find it much more difficult to get an accurate measure of financial results each quarter.

General Principles

Four basic principles to serve as guides to preparing financial statements are presented in the FASB's basic concepts:

Basic Principles
Historical Cost Basis
Revenue Recognition
Matching
Full Disclosure

HISTORICAL COST BASIS PRINCIPLE

Business transactions are, with few exceptions, recorded on a **historical cost basis,** which is the amount of consideration, expressed in monetary terms, involved in a transaction through dealings in the market between the business and outsiders. Assets are generally carried at historical cost, adjusted for depreciation, until they are removed from use and disposed of. Historical cost is the cost when an asset is acquired. Historical cost is preferred to some possible alternatives to cost

>> **14-6. OBJECTIVE**
Explain and apply the basic principles of accounting.

recall

Recording Assets and Depreciation
Property, plant, and equipment assets are recorded at historical, or original, cost. Depreciation is recorded in a separate accumulated depreciation account.

important!

Criteria for Revenue Recognition

Two tests must be met before revenue can be recognized: (1) the revenue must have been earned and (2) the revenue must have been realized.

important!

When Is Revenue Earned?

Revenue is earned when the entity has done all that it has to do to be entitled to all benefits to be received from the sale or service.

important!

When Is Revenue Realized?

Revenue is realized when cash, financial claims, or other assets have been received as a result of the income-earning activity.

because cost, when determined in an "arm's length" transaction with independent outsiders, is an objective, verifiable measure of initial economic value. The alternatives to using cost involve some measure or estimate of value, which is generally neither an objective nor verifiable quantity. As a result of this principle, generally an asset is recorded and remains in the account at its original cost even though its value may increase to an amount materially in excess of cost.

There are, however, important exceptions to the general rule that historical cost remains the basic carrying amount in the financial reports. For example, certain current assets—those that will be converted into cash within the next year—are carried at "the lower of cost or market" because market value is a reasonable measure of the amount that can be expected to be received for the asset within the next 12 months. Investments in securities that are expected to be sold within the next year would be shown at their market value rather than cost. *Accounts Receivable* is usually shown at the amount expected to be collected from customers, through the use of an *Allowance for Doubtful Accounts.* In addition, an asset included in plant and equipment is shown at its "impaired value" (a complex calculation) if it is apparent that future net cash flows from its future use will be less than its present book value. Nevertheless, the cost principle remains a fundamental concept in financial reporting.

REVENUE RECOGNITION PRINCIPLE

One of the greatest challenges an accountant faces is determining the period in which to record revenue and report it on the income statement. Revenue represents the inflow of new assets resulting from the sale of goods or services to an outsider. Under the **revenue recognition principle,** revenue is recognized when it is both earned and realized. The earning process is completed when the product or service has been delivered and related costs have been incurred. Usually **realization** is deemed to occur at the point at which a sale is made or a service is rendered to an outsider and delivery has been made. This is the point at which new assets are created in the form of money or in claims against others (usually taking the form of accounts receivable). The realization principle requires objective, verifiable evidence of both the earning and realization of revenue in order for income to be recorded.

However, the realization principle is the subject of much criticism. For example, if a company owns stock in another publicly traded corporation, some accountants believe that an increase in the market value of the stock should be recognized as income. This practice would, in most cases, violate the realization principle, which suggests that gain should not be recognized until the stock is sold. Accountants who support the realization principle are concerned that the "gain" might be eliminated by a decrease in stock price before the stock is sold.

There are some exceptions to the realization principle for reporting revenue. For example, contractors who build long-term projects often report income on a "percentage-of-completion" basis. If a bridge takes three years to complete, a portion of the estimated profit can be recognized by the contractor each year under the percentage-of-completion method.

In contrast, some businesses, especially service providers such as physicians, architects, and accountants, frequently recognize income only when cash is received, not when it is earned, because the rate of losses from uncollectible accounts is very high in these businesses.

The revenue recognition principle has been the subject of many SEC complaints and legal actions against registrants in recent years. Frequently, these actions result in large penalties and fines against registrants. On December 18, 2012, the Securities and Exchange Commission charged a digital company and three executives for their role in an accounting fraud that artificially inflated company revenues and misstated operating income to investors.

The SEC alleges that TheStreet Inc., which operates the website TheStreet.com, filed false financial reports throughout 2008 by reporting revenue from fraudulent transactions at a subsidiary it had acquired the previous year. The co-presidents of the subsidiary entered into sham transactions with friendly counterparties that had little or no economic substance. They also fabricated and backdated contracts and other documents to facilitate the fraudulent accounting. One co-president is additionally charged with misleading TheStreet's auditor to believe that the subsidiary had performed services to earn revenue on a specific transaction when in fact it did not perform the services. The SEC also alleges that TheStreet's former chief financial officer caused the company to report revenue before it had been earned.

The three executives agreed to pay financial penalties and accept officer-and-director bars to settle the SEC's charges.

According to the SEC's complaints filed in federal court in Manhattan, the subsidiary acquired by TheStreet specialized in online promotions such as sweepstakes. After the acquisition, TheStreet failed to implement a system of internal controls at the subsidiary, which enabled the accounting fraud.

The SEC alleges that TheStreet:

- Improperly recognized revenue based on sham transactions.
- Used the percentage-of-completion method of revenue recognition without meeting fundamental prerequisites to do so, including reliably estimating and documenting progress toward the completion of relevant contracts.
- Prematurely recognized revenue when the subsidiary had not performed actual work and therefore had not really earned the revenue.

According to the SEC's complaint, when the subsidiary's financial results were consolidated with TheStreet's financial results for financial reporting purposes, the improper revenue on the subsidiary's books resulted in material misstatements in the company's quarterly and annual reports for fiscal year 2008. On February 8, 2010, TheStreet restated its 2008 Form 10-K and disclosed a number of improprieties related to revenue recognition at its subsidiary, including transactions that lacked economic substance, internal control deficiencies, and improper accounting for certain contracts.

TheStreet's chief financial officer agreed to pay a $125,000 penalty and reimburse TheStreet $34,240.40 under the clawback provision (Section 304) of the Sarbanes-Oxley Act, and will be barred from acting as a director or officer of a public company for three years. The co-presidents agreed to pay penalties of $130,000 and $120,000, respectively, and to be barred from serving as officers or directors of a public company for 10 years. Without admitting or denying the allegations, the three executives and TheStreet agreed to be permanently enjoined from future violations of the federal securities laws.

MATCHING PRINCIPLE

To properly measure income, revenue must be matched against expired costs incurred in earning the revenue. This concept is called the **matching principle.** Many of the controversial questions in accounting involve determining when a cost should be charged as an expense. Accountants seek systematic, rational approaches for determining when to recognize revenue and when costs should be charged against revenue.

There are numerous ways to match revenue and expenses. Here are some examples:

- Manufacturing costs are identified with specific products and are charged to cost of goods sold when the products are sold.
- The cost of a building is recorded as an asset. Depreciation expense is recognized over the periods in which the asset is expected to help earn revenues for the business.
- Insurance premiums cover specific periods and are charged to expense over those periods.
- General office salaries do not clearly benefit future periods and are charged to expense when they are incurred.

The matching principle has given rise to a process referred to as the accrual basis of accounting, which you learned about in Chapter 12. The accrual basis calls for recognizing revenues or expenses in the period to which they apply, rather than in some later period when the cash is received or paid. The adjustments for prepaid rent, expired insurance, unearned income, and salaries payable that you learned in Chapter 12 were made under the accrual method of accounting to conform to the matching principle.

FULL DISCLOSURE PRINCIPLE

The **full disclosure principle** requires that all information that might affect the user's interpretation of the profitability and financial position of a business must be disclosed in the financial statements or in notes to the statements.

recall

Why Adjustments Are Made
End-of-period adjustments are made to record income and expenses in the appropriate accounting period. The goal of adjustments is to match revenues and expenses.

The accountant and company management are constantly faced with the question: "How much information is enough and how much is too much?" In recent years, there have been numerous lawsuits charging that the financial statements did not disclose facts that would have influenced investor or creditor decisions. As a result, accountants must be careful to include sufficient information so that an informed reader can obtain a complete understanding of the financial position of the business.

A primary emphasis of the SEC in financial reporting is "full disclosure." The SEC's full-disclosure policy is essentially that any information that would be likely, if disclosed, to change the user's interpretation of the statement should be disclosed. As a result, the basic financial statements may occupy only two or three pages in a corporation's annual report, but the "notes to the financial statements" explaining the items in the statements may occupy 10 or 12 pages. Because of federal regulatory legislation enacted in recent years, there is even more pressure to increase disclosures in order to help statement users better understand and evaluate the company's financial affairs.

In recent years, much attention has been given in the news media to the idea of ==transparency== in financial reporting. Both the SEC and FASB have focused recently on the topic of transparency in their public comments and in their authoritative pronouncements. Essentially, this notion is that the financial statements and the related disclosures taken together should permit interested users to receive a clear and concise understanding of the activities of the enterprise and its financial affairs.

Modifying Constraints

The accounting principles and their underlying assumptions provide a framework for analyzing business transactions in determining the accounting treatment they should be given in the financial reports. However, a number of practical considerations are recognized as constraining or modifying the application of the general principles. Here are the most important of these constraints:

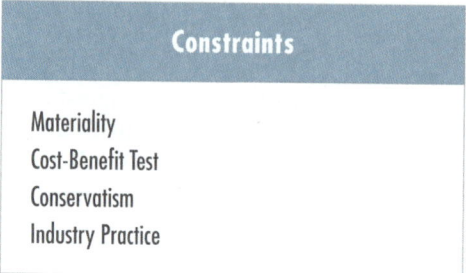

Constraints
Materiality
Cost-Benefit Test
Conservatism
Industry Practice

MATERIALITY

==Materiality== refers to the significance of an item of financial data in relation to other financial data. The rigid application of the recommended accounting treatment of an item may depend on whether or not the item is considered material in light of other items in the financial reports. Suppose that during the year a small business purchases small items of equipment, each costing $200, but with a total cost of $1,800. If the company's usual net income is only $15,000, the $1,800 cost would likely be considered material. As a result, the concept of matching would require that the assets be capitalized and depreciated. However, if Walmart purchased items of equipment costing only $1,800, the amount would be insignificant and the company likely would simply charge the costs to expense when purchased. The difference in either net income or in total assets as a result of deciding to charge the cost to expense instead of capitalizing it would be insignificant. This example suggests that the materiality constraint goes hand-in-hand with the cost-benefit test.

COST-BENEFIT TEST

Sometimes it is difficult and expensive to gather information to fully comply with an accounting principle or rule that should theoretically be applied in preparing financial statements. As a result, the conceptual framework suggests that it may be necessary to use the ==cost-benefit test==

MANAGERIAL IMPLICATIONS   <<

FINANCIAL STATEMENTS

- Management relies on the information in financial statements to make decisions.
- Management needs to understand the underlying principles used to prepare financial statements.
- Managers of large businesses compare their financial statements with those of their competitors. The universal application of accounting assumptions, principles, and modifying conventions allows financial statements to be compared.

- Proper accounting using generally accepted accounting principles can help prevent lawsuits by financial statement users.
- Full disclosure of pertinent information in financial statements and accompanying notes can reduce the possibility of lawsuits.

THINKING CRITICALLY

What are some income statement and balance sheet items that could mislead investors?

---

to determine whether the increased cost of complying with an accounting principle or standard is justified by the benefit (increased usefulness of the statements) that would result if the preferred treatment is followed.

For example, a large business may purchase thousands of inexpensive small tools with useful lives ranging from six months to two years. In theory, those tools lasting more than one year should be capitalized and their costs depreciated. However, the entity might have to incur large costs to simply keep records and identify the individual tools. The difference that might result in annual income from using the theoretically correct accounting treatment, compared to that resulting from simply charging the tools to expense when they are purchased, may be very small. As a result the tools would likely be charged to expense when purchased.

As suggested earlier, the cost-benefit constraint goes hand-in-hand with the materiality constraint. In some instances, an improvement in financial reporting resulting from applying a theoretically superior treatment to a transaction may be so small when compared to income that almost any cost of implementing the theoretically correct approach might warrant ignoring the conceptual rule. Conversely, even though an item might appear to be immaterial, that is no justification for applying the materiality constraint and arbitrarily applying a treatment that does not correspond with GAAP without applying the cost-benefit test.

CONSERVATISM

Accountants have long followed a doctrine of conservatism. **Conservatism** in accounting is the idea that "when in doubt, take the conservative action." Thus, if there is no clear evidence of how a transaction or situation should be accounted for or if there are two or more equally acceptable treatments of the transaction, the accountant should choose the conservative approach. The conservative approach is the one that would result in the least possible reported income or largest reported loss. In accounting, the conservatism notion comes into play when there is little evidence, or there is conflicting evidence, about the facts or their interpretation.

For example, Carpet Company purchased a new machine designed specifically to produce a single product and with a useful physical life of 10 years. However, there is a strong likelihood that the product will be replaced in about five years by newer products and that the machine will be of no further use to the company when that occurs. In this circumstance, conservatism dictates that the machine be depreciated over five years.

On the other hand, if there is no reason to think that the machine will not be used to manufacture the product for 10 years, but the owner feels that "you just can't ever be sure how long it might last, so we should be conservative and depreciate it over five years," it would be inappropriate to use the five-year life for depreciation. The conservatism constraint does not override other accounting concepts and principles that are clearly appropriate in the circumstances. Conservatism is not a constraint to be applied without considering other factors.

ABOUT
ACCOUNTING

The Cost-Benefit Test
In many cases, the cost-benefit relationship is very difficult to determine. Both costs and, especially, benefits are hard to measure. Benefits are often difficult to quantify and verify.

ABOUT
ACCOUNTING

What "Conservatism" Does Not Mean in Accounting
In the past, accountants have been accused of being overly conservative, to the point that they were encouraged to understate assets. This is not a proper understanding of the constraint of conservatism.

INDUSTRY PRACTICE

Historically, existing accounting practices in certain industries have sometimes become acceptable as GAAP. Typically this situation exists in an industry where there are unusual tax laws or regulatory requirements, an industry that has unusually high risks, or one that has activities or transactions to which it is difficult to apply GAAP. One example where GAAP has evolved to conform to **industry practice** is the public utility industry. For many decades, public utilities treated interest incurred on money borrowed to build a power plant as a cost of the plant, just like the cost of cement or steel. Public utility regulatory agencies required or permitted interest to be included in the cost of the plant, rather than charged to an interest expense account. This accounting practice has come to be required under GAAP for all construction projects, regardless of the industry.

The Impact of Generally Accepted Accounting Principles

This book contains many references to accounting principles, assumptions, and modifying constraints. Being familiar with these concepts will help you understand how individual transactions are accounted for and why they are handled in a specific way. Often businesses encounter new or unusual transactions that give rise to accounting questions that do not appear to have simple solutions. Almost invariably, the solutions to these questions will fall back on the concepts discussed in this chapter. Thus, an understanding of these concepts is essential to your understanding of complex accounting issues.

Section 2   Self Review

QUESTIONS

1. How is the constraint of materiality applied in accounting? List some factors that might be considered in deciding whether an item is material.

2. What are the four basic assumptions underlying financial accounting?

3. How are the qualitative characteristics of consistency and comparability similar? How are they different?

4. Why is historical cost used to initially record transactions?

EXERCISE

5. Which of the four underlying assumptions (separate entity, materiality, stable monetary unit, and periodicity of income) is most important in each situation below?

    a. Fredrick Haynes purchased a building for his business in 1996 for $300,000. In 2016, the building is still being used and has a remaining expected life of 25 years. Haynes points out that cumulative inflation has been about 100 percent since 1996, so he proposes changing the asset account from $300,000 to $600,000.

    b. Nelson Company issues each month a check to Leon Nelson, the sole proprietor, for $10,000 because he deems this a reasonable payment for the time he spends in the business. The amount paid is not charged to **Salary Expense** but to his **Drawing** account.

    c. Cantu Company immediately charges to expense any asset costing less than $200.

    d. Wilson Company prepares financial statements for each quarter of the year.

ANALYSIS

6. One week ago, Trayton Dear was appointed manager of the company for which you work. He has looked at the draft of the annual report for last year, scheduled to be issued in a few days. He states that the company needs to "take no chances" and should be conservative in its reporting. He has asked that two things be done.

    a. The company is engaged in several lawsuits, some of which are very material. The company's lawyer and its former manager think the suits are almost certain to be decided in favor of your employer and, therefore, they plan to ignore them in the financial reports. The new manager wants to either show a potential loss as an expense or to disclose the lawsuits in notes to the statements.

    b. Because losses from bad debts have been running at a fairly high rate (5 percent of net sales), he proposes that revenue should not be recognized from credit sales until the money is actually collected from customers.

Give your recommendations on his suggestions, stating the conceptual bases for your conclusions.

(Answers to Section 2 Self Review are on page 516.)

REVIEW   Chapter Summary

The increasing interest of a large and diverse group—government, owners, analysts, creditors, and economists—in financial reports ensures continuing progress in the search for accounting principles that will make the reports more meaningful, useful, and reliable. In this chapter, you have learned how accounting principles are developed and the roles of various organizations and groups in that development. In addition, you have learned fundamental facts about the Financial Accounting Standards Board's conceptual framework underlying modern-day financial reports. The importance of underlying qualitative characteristics, underlying assumptions, and basic principles in this framework has been stressed.

Learning Objectives

14-1   Understand the process used to develop generally accepted accounting principles.

In the United States, GAAP are developed cooperatively by the public and private sectors. Although the SEC has power to establish accounting rules for publicly held companies, it usually delegates the job to the private sector through the FASB.

14-2   Identify the major accounting standards-setting bodies and explain their roles in the standards-setting process.

The SEC has legislative responsibility for developing accounting and reporting rules for publicly held companies, but has authority to accept standards set by the FASB. The AICPA, the AAA, and governmental regulatory bodies also have played a role in developing GAAP. The PCAOB regulates CPA firms that audit publicly traded companies.

14-3   Describe the users and uses of financial reports.

The users of statements are the present and potential investors and creditors who use the statements in making credit and investment decisions. The focus is on information to help users assess future cash flows.

14-4   Identify and explain the qualitative characteristics of accounting information.

The basic characteristics are:

- Usefulness
- Timeliness
- Understandability
- Neutrality
- Relevance
- Reliability
- Consistency
- Comparability

14-5   Describe and explain the basic assumptions about accounting reports.

Major assumptions that preparers of financial reports should generally make:

- The business is an economic entity separate and apart from its owner(s).
- The entity will remain a going concern.
- Monetary terms is the significant feature of economic data.
- The statements are objective and not biased to benefit any involved party.
- Income is periodic, so that income can be meaningfully measured for each period and compared with other periods.

14-6   Explain and apply the basic principles of accounting.

- Transactions are recorded on a cost basis.
- Revenues are recognized when earned and realized.
- Revenues and costs should be matched in the financial reports for appropriate periods.
- Full disclosure means that all information that might affect the reader's interpretation of the statements should be disclosed.

14-7   Describe and apply the modifying constraints on accounting principles.

The modifying constraints are factors that may in some cases overrule the necessity to apply GAAP.

These constraints are:

- Materiality
- Cost-benefits test
- Conservatism
- Industry practice

14-8   Define the accounting terms new to this chapter.

Glossary

Conceptual framework (p. 488) A basic framework developed by the FASB to provide conceptual guidelines for financial accounting and statements; the most important topics are explanations of qualitative features of financial statements, basic assumptions underlying statements, basic accounting principles, and modifying constraints

Conservatism (p. 499) If alternative treatments of items are of equal validity, the conservatism constraint suggests that the alternative resulting in lowest profit should be used

Cost-benefit test (p. 498) If accounting concepts suggest a particular accounting treatment for an item but it appears that the theoretically correct treatment would require an unreasonable amount of work, the accountant may analyze the benefits and costs of the preferred treatment to see if the benefit gained from its adoption is justified by the cost

Full disclosure principle (p. 497) All information that might affect the user's interpretation of the profitability and financial condition of a business should be disclosed

Going concern assumption (p. 494) The assumption that a business will continue to operate indefinitely

Historical cost basis principle (p. 495) The principle that requires assets and services to be recorded at their cost at the time they are acquired and that, generally, long-term assets remain at historical costs in the asset accounts

Industry practice constraint (p. 500) In a few limited cases, the unusual operating characteristics of an industry, usually based on risk, special accounting principles, and procedures, have been developed; these may not conform completely with GAAP for other industries

Matching principle (p. 497) The concept that revenues and the costs incurred in earning those revenues should be matched in the appropriate accounting periods

Materiality constraint (p. 498). In some cases where an accounting item is deemed too small to affect a user's decisions, the "required" accounting may be ignored

Monetary unit assumption (p. 494) It is assumed that only those items and events that can be measured in monetary terms are included in the financial statements. An inherent part of this assumption is that the monetary unit is stable. Thus, assets purchased one year may be combined in the accounts with those purchased in other years even though the dollars used in each year actually may have different purchasing power

Neutrality concept (p. 493) Neutrality is the concept that information in financial statements cannot be selected or presented in a way to favor one set of interested parties over another

Periodicity of income assumption (p. 495) Periodicity is the idea that economic activities of an entity can be divided logically and identified with specific time periods, such as the year or quarter

Private sector (p. 487) This is the nongovernmental sector of society; in an accounting context, it is the business sector, represented in the accounting rule-making process by the Financial Accounting Standards Board

Public sector (p. 487) This is the governmental sector, represented in the accounting rule-making process by the Securities and Exchange Commission

Qualitative characteristics (p. 492) These are necessary characteristics that must be present in financial statements if they are to be credible

Realization (p. 496) Realization of revenue takes place only when cash, a financial claim, or other consideration is received for the sale of goods or services

Revenue recognition principle (p. 496) Revenue is recognized when it has been earned and realized

Transparency (p. 498) The transparency notion is that information provided in the financial statements and the notes accompanying them should provide a clear and accurate picture of the financial affairs of the company. The key to this idea is that of disclosure

Comprehensive **Self Review**

1. Why should one become familiar with IFRS?
2. If the "stable monetary assumption" were not made, what impact would this likely have on record keeping and financial statements?
3. Explain the matching principle. What impact does this principle have on end-of-period adjustments?
4. What is the full disclosure principle? How are disclosures made in financial reports?
5. How does the AICPA still have an influence on the development of accounting principles and standards?
6. In what circumstances is industry practice likely to be a factor in "generally accepted accounting principles"?

(Answers to Comprehensive Self Review are on pages 516–517.)

Discussion Questions

1. How does the materiality convention affect day-to-day accounting?
2. How are the concepts of materiality and cost-benefit related?
3. What is the periodicity of income concept?
4. In recent years, there have been many charges, some of them substantiated, that large companies have manipulated business transactions and accounting records to move income from one year to another in order to change the income reported in different years. Suggest three concepts, assumptions, principles, or conventions that such manipulation would violate.
5. Many current assets are not shown at historic cost in the financial statements. For example, inventories are usually shown at the "lower of cost or market." What concepts or conventions warrant this practice?
6. What is meant by full disclosure?
7. Why is a conceptual framework necessary in developing accounting standards and rules?
8. What two tests must be met in order for revenues to be recognized?
9. What are the two most important bodies or organizations involved in developing generally accepted accounting principles in the United States?
10. Why is it desirable to have a set of fundamental concepts to be used in developing accounting standards and rules?
11. How will U.S. companies be affected by IFRS?
12. What is meant by the concept of neutrality in accounting?
13. Explain the qualitative characteristic of comparability.
14. How is the matching concept related to the accrual basis of accounting?
15. It can be argued that the cost principle is dependent on the going concern assumption. Why?

APPLICATIONS

Exercises

Exercise 14.1

Objectives 14-5, 14-6

▶ **Applying accounting principles and concepts.**

For each of the following cases, respond to the question and indicate the accounting principle or concept that applies.

1. Mike Beasley buys and sells real estate. On December 31, 2016, his inventory of property included a tract of undeveloped land for which he had paid $800,000. The fair market value of the land was $900,000 at that date. How much income should Beasley report for 2016 in connection with this land? Why?

2. Hubbard Building Company signed a contract with a customer on November 1, 2016. The contract called for construction of a building to begin by December 31, 2016, and to be completed by December 31, 2017. The contract price was $8.0 million. Hubbard estimated that the building would cost $5 million. On November 15, 2016, the customer was required to make an advance payment of $1,000,000. No work was done on the project until January 2017. How much income from the project should Hubbard report in 2016? Why?

3. Martinez, LLC, paid insurance premiums of $7,200 on December 1, 2016. These premiums covered a two-year period beginning on that date. What amount, from this payment, should the corporation show as insurance expense for the year 2016? What accounting principles, conventions, or assumptions support your answer?

Exercise 14.2

Objectives 14-5, 14-6, 14-7

▶ **Applying accounting principles and concepts.**

For each of the following cases, respond to the question asked and indicate the accounting principle or concept that applies.

1. Richard Perez is the sole proprietor of In and Out Mini Market. Perez's accountant insists that he keep a detailed record of money and merchandise that he takes out of the business for personal use. Why?

2. At the end of each fiscal period, the accountant for Florida Company requires that a careful inventory be made of the office supplies and that the amount on hand be reported as an asset and the amount used during the period be reported as an expense. Why?

3. Haden Co. purchased many small tools during 2016 at a total cost of $8,000. Some tools were expected to last for a few weeks, some for several months, and some for several years. Haden's income for 2016 will be about $4.5 million. How should Haden account for the small tools in order to be theoretically correct? As a practical matter, how should Haden account for these tools? Why?

Exercise 14.3

Objectives 14-5, 14-6

▶ **Applying accounting principles and concepts.**

For each of the following cases, respond to the question asked and indicate the accounting principle or concept that applies.

1. On March 15 of last year, Guice Inc. purchased land for $190,000, on which it planned to construct an office building. At the end of the year, the land had increased in value to $240,000. Nevertheless, Guice recognized no income as a result of the increase in value. Is this correct or incorrect accounting? Why?

2. Three years ago, Knott Company purchased a machine for $400,000. The machine is expected to have no salvage value. Nevertheless, Knott continues to keep the asset's cost in its accounting records and to depreciate the asset over its eight-year useful life. Is this correct or incorrect accounting? Why?

3. Rutland Company has decided to charge off as a loss the portion of its accounts receivable that it estimates will be uncollectible. The accounts involved resulted from the current year's sales. Is this correct or incorrect accounting? Why?

Applying accounting principles and concepts.

◀ **Exercise 14.4**
Objectives 14-6, 14-7

For each of the following cases, respond to the question asked and indicate the accounting principle or concept that applies.

1. Arrington Company's net income is about $2.0 million a year. Arrington charges to expense all property insurance premiums when paid. Last year approximately $3,500 of these premiums represented amounts applicable to future years. Is this proper? Why or why not?

2. Lopez Products Corporation charges all of its marketing costs to expense when incurred. Why?

3. Busby Company charges off the cost of all magazine advertising in the year it is incurred even though the advertising probably results in some sales in later years. Why?

Applying accounting principles and concepts.

◀ **Exercise 14.5**
Objective 14-6

Campbell & Campbell sells copy equipment. It grants all customers a 12-month warranty, agreeing to make necessary repairs within the following 12-month after-sale period free of charge. At the end of each year, the company estimates the total cost to be incurred during the next period under the warranties for equipment sold during the current period and charges that amount to expense, crediting a liability account. Is this appropriate accounting? Why or why not?

Applying accounting principles and concepts.

◀ **Exercise 14.6**
Objective 14-6

Family Jewelers has never borrowed money. Because of rapid growth, on July 25, 2016, Saul Metcalf, the owner, applied for a loan of $150,000 from his bank. The banker asked Metcalf for copies of financial reports of Family Jewelers for 2015 and quarterly statements for 2016. Metcalf had never prepared formal financial statements for the business. He and the company's bookkeeper obtained some information from his 2015 income tax return and estimated other items for which information was not readily available. He took the statements to the banker on August 2. The banker expressed his concern over the statements. What are the most important fundamental financial reporting concepts that seem to have been violated?

PROBLEMS

Problem Set A

Understanding how and why accounting and auditing principles and standards are developed.

◀ **Problem 14.1A**
Objectives 14-1, 14-2, 14-3

Read each of the following statements carefully and indicate whether each is true or false.

1. Many nonpublic companies are not required to follow GAAP.

2. The American Institute of CPAs has, in the past, had a strong influence on the development of auditing principles.

3. The FASB is a division of the Internal Revenue Service.

4. The PCAOB regulates CPA firms that audit nonpublic companies.

5. Accounting principles and standards are based on the assumption that the statements will be read by individuals who have little understanding of accounting and financial reporting.

6. The IASB has authority to accept or reject financial accounting principles and standards developed by the FASB.

7. The FASB Standards are designed primarily for the use of the IRS.

8. Because of the Sarbanes-Oxley Act, it is probable that the FASB's conceptual framework will become less important in developing accounting principles and standards.

9. It is likely that in the future there will be a convergence of U.S. financial reporting standards and those of the International Accounting Standards Board.

10. The Sarbanes-Oxley Act places great emphasis on internal controls and fraud prevention.

Problem 14.2A

Objectives 14-4, 14-5, 14-6

▶ **Applying accounting principles and concepts.**

The accounting treatment or statement presentation of various items is discussed below. The items pertain to unrelated businesses.

INSTRUCTIONS

Indicate in each case whether the item has been handled in accordance with generally accepted accounting principles. If so, indicate the key basic concept that has been followed. If not, indicate which concept has been violated and tell how the item should have been recorded or presented.

1. The assets listed in the accounting records of Adams' Pharmacy include a money market account of Robert Adams, owner of the business. Adams has established the savings account so that if he needs to invest more cash in the pharmacy, it will be readily available.

2. On December 31, 2016, an account receivable of $1,800 due from Tollie Pettis, who is in the county jail on charges of passing bad checks, is not included in the balance sheet. The owner of the business has written off the amount because he feels certain that the debt will not be paid, even though Pettis insists that she will pay after she gets out of jail and finds a job.

3. The equipment of Sadler Plastics Company has a book value (cost less accumulated depreciation) of $180,000. However, the equipment could not be sold for more than $40,000 today. The company's owner thinks that the machinery should nevertheless be reported on the balance sheet at $180,000 and depreciated over its useful life, because the equipment is being used regularly in the business and it is expected to be used profitably for the next five years—the remaining useful life that is being used for depreciation purposes.

4. Ohio Company manufactured machinery for its own use at a cost of $600,000. The lowest bid from an outsider was $650,000. Nevertheless, the company recorded the machinery at $600,000.

5. On December 31, 2016, the balance sheet of Transit Depot reported prepaid insurance at $4,000. The prepaid insurance reflects the refund value of a three-year fire insurance policy that originally cost $6,000 on January 1, 2015.

6. At the beginning of 2016, Jamison Company bought a building for $3,000,000. At the end of 2016, the building's value was appraised at $3,300,000. Since there was an increase in value, the company did not record depreciation on the building and also did not increase the $3,000,000 recorded in the building account at time of purchase.

Analyze: If Jamison Company uses the accounting treatment described in Item 6, is net income overstated or understated for 2016?

Problem 14.3A

Objectives 14-5, 14-6

▶ **Reconstructing an income statement to reflect proper accounting principles.**

Samuel Cox, owner of Cox Video Center, sent the income statement shown on the next page to several of his creditors who had asked for financial statements. The business is a sole proprietorship that sells audio and other electronic equipment. One of the creditors looked over the income statement and reported that it did not conform to generally accepted accounting principles.

INSTRUCTIONS

Prepare an income statement in accordance with generally accepted accounting principles.

Cox Video Center
Income Statement
December 31, 2016

Cash Collected from Customers		$699,000
Cost of Goods Sold		
Merchandise Inventory, Jan. 1	$ 77,000	
Payments to Suppliers	440,000	
	517,000	
Less Merchandise Inventory, Dec. 31	87,000	
Cost of Goods Sold		430,000
Gross Profit on Sales		269,000
Operating Expenses		
Salaries of Employees	$ 81,500	
Salary of Owner	31,200	
Office Expense	32,000	
Depreciation Expense	21,520	
Income Tax of Owner	9,000	
Payroll Taxes Expense	10,000	
Advertising and Other Selling Expenses	23,900	
Repairs Expense	13,000	
Insurance Expense	5,400	
Interest Expense	13,000	
Utility and Telephone Expense	19,500	
Legal and Audit Expense	4,500	
Miscellaneous Expense	29,500	
Total Expenses		294,020
Net Loss from Operations		(25,020)
Increase in Appraised Value of Land during Year		28,000
Net Income		$ 2,980

The following additional information was made available by Cox:

a. On January 1, 2016, accounts receivable from customers totaled $27,700. On December 31, 2016, the receivables totaled $34,000.

b. No effort has been made to charge off worthless accounts. An analysis shows that $1,800 of the accounts receivable on December 31, 2016, will never be collected.

c. The beginning and ending merchandise inventories were valued at their estimated selling price. The cost of the ending inventory is determined to be $49,500, and the cost of the beginning inventory is determined at $45,800.

d. On January 1, 2016, suppliers of merchandise were owed $40,200, while on December 31, 2016, these debts were $46,425.

e. The owner paid himself a salary of $2,600 per month from the funds of the business and charged this amount to an account called *Salary of Owner.*

f. The owner also withdrew cash from the firm's bank account to pay himself $4,900 interest on his capital investment. This amount was charged to *Interest Expense.*

g. A check for $9,000 to cover the owner's personal income tax for the previous year was issued from the firm's bank account. This was charged to *Income Tax of Owner.*

h. Depreciation on assets was computed at 8 percent of the gross profit. An analysis of assets showed that the original cost of the equipment and fixtures was $67,500. Their estimated useful life is 12 years with no salvage value. The building cost $152,750. Its useful life is expected to be 25 years with no salvage value.

i. Included in *Repairs Expense* was $6,600 paid on December 22 for a new parking lot completed that day.

j. The increase in land value was based on an appraisal by a qualified real estate appraiser.

Analyze: What is the gross profit percentage based on the income statement you prepared?

Problem 14.4A
Objectives 14-5,
14-6

▶ **Reconstructing a balance sheet to reflect proper accounting principles.**

Clark Allen owns The Clark Haven, a small arts supply store. He recently approached the local bank for a loan to finance a planned expansion of his store. Allen prepared the balance sheet shown below and submitted it to one of the bank's loan officers in support of his loan application.

INSTRUCTIONS

1. Identify any errors in the balance sheet, and explain why they should be considered errors.
2. Prepare a corrected balance sheet in accordance with generally accepted accounting principles.

The Clark Haven
Balance Sheet
December 31, 2016

Assets

Cash	$ 14,400
Accounts Receivable	17,000
Inventory	41,000
Equipment (cost)	35,000
Personal Residence	208,000
Supplies	2,160
Family Auto	40,000
Total Assets	$357,560

Liabilities and Owner's Equity

Accounts Payable	$ 17,450
Note Payable on Family Car	13,000
Mortgage on House	112,000
Clark Allen, Capital	215,110
Total Liabilities and Owner's Equity	$357,560

The following additional information was made available by Allen:

a. The inventory has an original cost of $32,900. It is listed on the balance sheet at the estimated selling price.

b. The cash listed on the balance sheet includes $3,700 in Clark Allen's personal account. The remainder of the cash is in the store's account.

c. The store recently purchased a delivery truck for $39,000, financed through a bank loan. The bank has legal title to the truck. To date, the store has paid $11,000 on the loan. Of the remaining $28,000 liability, $10,600 is current and the remainder long-term. Allen did not include the truck or the liability on the balance sheet because neither he nor the business owns it.

d. Depreciation allowable to date is $7,000 on the equipment and $5,000 on the truck.

Analyze: If Allen knew that $900 of accounts receivable was not collectible, what should be done to reflect this fact on the records of the business? On the balance sheet?

Applying accounting principles and concepts.

◄ **Problem 14.5A**
Objectives 14-5,
14-6, 14-7

For each of the unrelated situations below, identify the accounting principle or concept violated (if a violation exists) and explain the nature of the violation. If you believe that the treatment is in accordance with GAAP, state the major principle or concept in support.

1. Each year Technology Support Company has a large number of uncollectible accounts. Technology charges uncollectible accounts to expense when they are written off. On the average, this is about 18 months after the due date of the account.

2. Wu Builders Company uses a large quantity of small tools. The annual purchases of the tools, which have a life of about two years, are approximately 2 percent of the company's net income for the year. Wu has followed the practice of capitalizing the cost of the tools and depreciating the cost over two years. The owner asks why the accountant spends so much time on "bookkeeping" and tells her to simply charge the tools to expense when they are purchased.

3. John Johnson owns a travel tour service. Customers must make a deposit of one-half the tour price at the time they book reservations. The balance is due 60 days prior to departure. Partial refunds are provided, depending on the date of cancellation. At the time deposits are received, Johnson records them as revenue. Refunds are treated as expenses at the time they are made.

4. Internet Sales and Exchanges Company sells such items as discontinued products and merchandise purchased from bankrupt companies. Freight costs on goods purchased are quite high. The company adds the freight costs to the purchase price and treats the total as cost of inventory.

5. Smiley Company manufactures paving equipment. It pays its salespeople a commission of 15 percent of the sales price as their remuneration. During 2016, its sales were $20,000,000 and commissions were $3,000,000. In the income statement, sales are shown as $17,000,000.

Analyze: What is the effect on sales of the procedure used by Smiley Company in question 5, above?

Problem Set B

Understanding how and why accounting and auditing principles and standards are developed.

◄ **Problem 14.1B**
Objectives 14-1,
14-2, 14-3

Read each of the following statements carefully and indicate whether each is true or false.

1. Because tax rules and financial accounting are the same, federal income tax requirements have had little impact on financial accounting in the United States.

2. The PCAOB has the power to set independence standards for CPA firms that audit publicly traded companies.

3. The Sarbanes-Oxley Act suggests a principles approach to establishing accounting standards.

4. Providing useful information to investors is one of the major considerations of the FASB in developing financial reporting standards.

5. The FASB has placed little emphasis on cash flows in its conceptual framework.

6. The balance sheet is the statement user's primary source of information about cash flows in a business.

7. The requirements of state and federal regulatory bodies, such as commissions regulating public utilities, have had little impact on accounting standards in this country.

8. Although accounting rule-making organizations in the United States have been reluctant to embrace international accounting standards, there is now a move toward developing congruence between U.S. and international standards.

9. The FASB Accounting Standards Codification is now the single source of authoritative U.S. GAAP for nongovernmental entities.

10. The SEC is the private sector's voice in the accounting rule-making process.

Problem 14.2B

Objectives 14-5, 14-6

▶ ### Applying accounting principles and concepts.

The accounting treatment or statement presentation of various items is discussed below. The items pertain to unrelated businesses.

INSTRUCTIONS

Indicate in each case whether the item has been handled in accordance with generally accepted accounting principles. If so, indicate which of the basic concepts has been followed. If not, indicate which concept has been violated and tell how the item should have been recorded or presented.

1. On December 31, 2015, Williamson Corporation valued its inventory according to an acceptable accounting method. On December 31, 2016, the inventory was valued by a different but also acceptable method, and on December 31, 2017, the inventory was valued by the method that was used in 2015.

2. Polk Manufacturing Company makes air cleaning units. The cost of manufacturing a particular unit is $640. However, when the inventory amounts are computed for the balance sheet, the amount used for this unit is $900, the normal selling price.

3. In 2016, Delight Bakeries had sales of $44 million, all on credit. Statistics of the company for prior years show that losses from uncollectible accounts are equal to about 1.5 percent of sales each year. However, Delight Bakeries charges off a loss from uncollectible accounts only when a specific account is found to be uncollectible.

4. On October 1, 2016, Young Manufacturing Company purchased some highly specialized, custom-made equipment for $950,000. Since the equipment is of no use to anyone else and has no salvage value, it was recorded in the asset account at $1. The equipment is projected to be used regularly in the business until the equipment wears out, approximately six years from the date of its purchase.

5. Each year The Land Development Company values its investments in land at the current market price.

6. Included on the balance sheet of Soothing Massage Center is the personal automobile of Mary Smith, the owner.

Analyze: If the equipment described in item 4 is depreciated using the straight-line method and has no salvage value, what amount should be charged to expense for the year ended December 31, 2016?

Problem 14.3B

Objectives 14-4, 14-5, 14-6

▶ ### Reconstructing an income statement to reflect proper accounting principles.

The income statement shown on the next page was prepared by Barbara Merino, owner of Merino's Beauty Supplies. The business is a sole proprietorship that sells skin and hair care products. An accountant who looked at the income statement told Merino that the statement does not conform to generally accepted accounting principles.

INSTRUCTIONS

Prepare an income statement for Merino's Beauty Supplies in accordance with generally accepted accounting principles.

Merino's Beauty Supplies
Income Statement
Year Ended December 31, 2016

Cash Receipts from Customers		$510,000
Cost of Goods Sold		
Merchandise Inventory, Jan. 1	$ 38,000	
Payments to Creditors	352,000	
	390,000	
Less Merchandise Inventory, Dec. 31	50,000	
Cost of Goods Sold		340,000
Gross Profit on Sales		170,000
Expenses		
Salaries Expense	$ 65,000	
Insurance Expense	3,200	
Payroll Taxes Expense	5,600	
Repairs Expense	3,700	
Supplies and Other Office Expenses	7,500	
Advertising and Other Selling Expenses	12,800	
Utilities Expense	6,400	
Interest Expense	6,700	
Total Expenses		110,900
Net Income from Operations		59,100
Increase in Market Value of Store Equipment		7,500
Net Income for Year		$ 66,600

The following additional information was made available by Merino:

a. On January 1, 2016, accounts receivable from customers totaled $35,000. On December 31, 2016, receivables totaled $30,250.

b. On December 31, 2016, accounts receivable amounting to $2,200 were expected to be uncollectible.

c. On January 1, 2016, accounts payable owed to merchandise suppliers were $22,000. On December 31, 2016, the outstanding accounts payable were $35,710.

d. Included in *Salaries Expense* is $18,000 that Merino was "paid" for her personal work in the business.

e. Included in *Interest Expense* is $3,400 that Merino withdrew as interest on her capital investment.

f. Miscellaneous repairs of $1,500 were charged to *Store Equipment* during the year. No new equipment was purchased.

g. Merino explains that since the estimated value of her store equipment has increased by $7,500 during the year, no depreciation expense was recorded. The store equipment cost $56,000 and had an estimated useful life of 10 years with estimated salvage value of $4,000.

Analyze: The entries required to correct situations a.–g. would affect several permanent accounts for Merino's Beauty Supplies. List the permanent accounts affected.

Problem 14.4B

Objectives 14-4,
14-5, 14-6

▶ **Reconstructing a balance sheet to reflect proper accounting principles.**

Country Cooking Prepared Meals is a retail shop owned by Beatrice Wilson. She wants to expand her business and has submitted the following balance sheet to her bank as part of the business loan application.

INSTRUCTIONS

1. Identify any errors in the balance sheet and explain why they should be considered errors.

2. Prepare a corrected balance sheet in accordance with generally accepted accounting principles.

Country Cooking Prepared Meals
Balance Sheet
December 31, 2016

Assets

Cash	$ 36,000
Accounts Receivable	8,500
Inventory	38,550
Store Fixtures	28,000
Store Equipment	16,000
Personal Residence	340,000
Personal Automobile	33,250
Total Assets	$500,300

Liabilities and Owner's Equity

Accounts Payable	$ 28,000
Note Payable on Personal Automobile	16,550
Mortgage Payable on Personal Residence	110,500
Beatrice Wilson, Capital	345,250
Total Liabilities and Owner's Equity	$500,300

The following additional information is provided by Wilson:

a. The inventory has an original cost of $35,000. Wilson has valued it on the balance sheet at what it would cost today.

b. Wilson has counted $8,000 in her personal savings account in the business cash account.

c. The store fixtures, shown at original cost, were purchased two years ago. No depreciation has been taken on them. Depreciation for the two years, based on their estimated life of 10 years, would be $5,600.

d. The store equipment cost $19,200. No depreciation has been computed on the equipment, but it has been written down to its estimated replacement cost by a charge to expense. Depreciation on the equipment's original cost for the 24 months since its purchase would be $3,800.

e. Both the personal residence and personal automobile are only occasionally used for business purposes.

Analyze: Based on the new balance sheet that you have prepared, what are the total current assets for Country Cooking Prepared Meals?

Applying accounting principles and concepts.

◄ **Problem 14.5B**
**Objectives 14-5,
14-6, 14-7**

For each of the unrelated situations below, identify the accounting principle or concept violated (if a violation exists) and explain the nature of the violation. If you believe that the treatment is in accordance with GAAP, state this as your position and defend it.

1. A building repair company opened for business in late 2016. On December 31 the *Services Revenue* account contained a balance of $252,000. Of that amount, $68,500 represents deposits received on contracts for services to be performed in January and February 2017.

2. In recent years, InteriorDesigns.com has enjoyed rapid growth in profits because of customer loyalty and its reputation of putting the needs of customers first. The company recently debited an account called *Goodwill,* in the amount of $150,000. The owner says this reflects the company's success in the business and the true worth of the business. The offsetting credit was to the *Owner's Equity* account.

3. Lacey Company manufactures a product requiring several parts. The company manufactures the parts, even though almost all competitors purchase the parts from outside sources, because Lacey can manufacture the parts for about 15 percent less than it would have to pay for the parts. Lacey thinks that comparability is very important in financial reporting, so when the parts are manufactured they are recorded at what the purchase price would have been. At the same time, income is recorded equal to the difference between actual cost and the hypothetical purchase price. The *Inventory of Parts* account reflects this outside purchase price and the *Finished Products Inventory* also reflects the hypothetical purchase price of the part used in manufacturing the products.

4. Downing Company sold for $550,000 land that was purchased 10 years ago for $435,000. Even though the general price level had doubled during this period, Downing reported a profit of $115,000 on the sale.

5. J. T. Winfield owns Winfield Computer Services. His annual net income is $1,500,000 and his owner's equity is $2,700,000. In December 2016, an irate customer sued Winfield for $4,000,000, alleging that an error made by Winfield had resulted in damages of that amount. Winfield's attorney thinks there may be substantial liability. Winfield does not disclose the suit in the financial statements sent to the firm's banker and to providers of equipment and services.

Analyze: Refer to situation 2, above. Assume that in item 2, Taylor Company bought all of the assets of InteriorDesigns.com, paying an amount equal to book value for all assets, including $150,000 for goodwill. Also assume that the actual values of all the other assets purchased were equal to the purchase price. Do you think that it would be appropriate for Taylor Company to record the purchase price of the goodwill at the $150,000 paid for it?

Critical Thinking Problem 14.1

Judgment Call

Logistics Distribution Center receives a number of different products in its warehouse. Logistics distributes these products by truck to customers within a radius of 150 miles. The company is located near the Jackson Regional Airport, which is owned and operated by the city of Jackson. Most of the products are received by rail or truck, but some are received by air.

The city and the local Chamber of Commerce have announced a joint undertaking to build a new divided highway to connect the airport with the interstate highway approximately three miles away. The Chamber of Commerce is attempting to raise $4,000,000 as its contribution to the new highway's cost. The Chamber has asked the 10 largest enterprises in the city to make substantial contributions. Logistics has been asked to contribute $1,000,000 of the total amount.

At a meeting of Logistics' board of directors, the request was considered. It was pointed out that although Logistics is not located on the route of the proposed new road, the road's construction would speed up access of trucks to the warehouse and should substantially increase the value of Logistics' property. It is difficult to measure the benefits of either of these factors. The company's president suggested that a major reason for making the contribution was to get good publicity and to improve the company's image in the community. "It is good advertising," he said.

The company's controller is asked how the contribution would be accounted for in the company's accounts. A major question is whether the $1,000,000 should be:

■ charged to expense when the contribution is made (thus reducing income of that period),

■ capitalized as part of the cost of the land owned by the company in the area (increasing assets and not affecting income),

■ recorded as an asset and charged to expense over a period of 10 years (thus increasing assets in the short run and spreading out the effects of the contribution on income).

What answer would you give if you were the controller? In your answer, consider the principles, assumptions, and concepts that you have studied in this chapter.

Critical Thinking Problem 14.2

Applying GAAP

Assume that you are an independent CPA performing audits of financial statements. In the course of your work, you encounter the following independent situations. Review each of the situations. If you consider the treatment to be in conformity with generally accepted accounting principles and concepts, explain why. If you do not, explain which principle or concept has been violated and how the situation should have been reported.

1. In its regional office, Southeastern Stores purchases at least 140 storage bins each year. These baskets cost approximately $20 each and have useful lives ranging from two to six years. They are depreciated over a period of four years, the estimated average life. One of the company's accountants has suggested that the costs of the baskets should be charged to expense at the time they are purchased.

2. Yondell Company prepares financial statements four times each year. For convenience, these statements are prepared when business is slow and the accounting staff is less busy with other matters. Last year "quarterly" financial statements were prepared for the five-month period ended May 31, the two-month period ended July 31, the three-month period ended October 31, and the two-month period ended December 31.

3. Equipment Supply Company has constructed special-purpose equipment designed to manufacture other equipment that will be sold to computer chip manufacturers. Due to the special nature of this equipment, it has virtually no resale value to any other company. Therefore, Equipment Supply has charged the entire cost to construct the equipment, $90 million, to expense in the current period.

4. The Discount Store spends a large sum on advertising for various sales promotions during the year. The advertising includes "institutional" ads designed to bring in customers in future years. The owner is sure that the advertising will generate revenue in future periods, but she has no idea of how much revenue will be produced or over what period of time it will be earned. In the current year, $700,000 was paid for advertising, and all of this amount was charged as an expense in the current period.

5. Get Away Vacation Resort recognizes room rental revenue on the date that a reservation is made. For the summer season, many guests make reservations as far as a year in advance of their intended visit.

6. Waynesboro Oil and Gas Company produces oil and gas from the ground. It drills wells to attempt to find the oil and gas and to produce any minerals found. On average, about one out of four wells that the company drills produces oil and gas. Drilling costs range from $700,000 to $3,000,000 for each well. The company has adopted a rule that if the well results in finding oil and gas that can be produced profitably, the drilling costs will be recorded as an asset. If a dry hole results, the drilling costs are charged to expense.

Analyze: If item 5 were recorded as described, what possible implications would this have for stockholders in the company?

BUSINESS CONNECTIONS

Judgment and Objectivity

1. A new manager of a retail company suggests that the company should prepare its income statement on the basis of cash receipts and cash expenditures (except for the acquisition of fixed assets, such as plant and equipment). He argues that managers, investors, creditors, and others are more interested in cash receipts and disbursements than in accrual-based accounting. Do you think he is correct? Explain.

2. In what situations would the going concern assumption *not* be useful to management?

3. What arguments can be given that the historical cost framework should be abandoned?

4. How can the element of personal judgment, which is involved in such matters as estimates of salvage value and useful life, be minimized to preserve the objectivity of an accounting system?

Going Concern

Computer Gaming Industries has just started business as a computer-based gaming company. Knowing that small computer businesses rarely remain in business longer than five years, Computer Gaming depreciates all of its assets for five years. The assets include a building, integrated circuit shaper, and vehicles. Is this ethical? What impact will of its action have on net income? What if any is the correct action?

Notes to Financial Statements

Refer to The Home Depot, Inc., 2012 Financial Statements (for the fiscal year ended February 3, 2013) in Appendix A.

1. Discuss the qualitative characteristics of comparability and understandability in relation to the financial statements presented. In your opinion, do the statements satisfy these two criteria required by the FASB for financial reporting?

2. "Notes to Consolidated Financial Statements" are published along with the financial statements of a fiscal period, offering detailed information on significant accounting policies and financial data. Review the consolidated balance sheets and excerpts from "Notes to Consolidated Financial Statements." Are the company's Merchandise Inventories represented on the balance sheet? Describe the discussion found in Note 1 and the principle addressed by it.

Accounting Conventions

Every business manager should know and implement the accounting conventions. Put the accounting conventions on 3x5 cards. Divide into groups of three to five students. Each student in the group will pick a 3x5 card and give an example of a violation of and compliance with the convention listed on the card.

AICPA and IMA

Certified Public Accountant (CPA) and Certified Management Accountant (CMA) are two major certifications recognized by the accounting industry. Go to the aicpa.org website and find the requirements to become a CPA. Go to the imanet.org website and find the requirements to become a CMA. The American Accounting Association serves accounting professors. Go to the AAA website at aaahq.org, and select "Placement." Determine the requirements to teach at a university.

Answers to **Self Reviews**

Answers to Section 1 Self Review

1. The conceptual framework project is designed to develop basic concepts, assumptions, and principles to be followed in developing accounting rules. It is necessary for rule makers to use a framework of concepts so that standards and rules are consistent with one another.

2. The SEC has oversight. It has the authority to develop accounting and reporting standards, but has stated that it will accept the standards of the FASB if the SEC is satisfied that those standards meet the SEC's requirements.

3. No. It would not be a publicly held corporation.

4. **a.** The SEC traditionally relies on the FASB as the provider of accounting standards.

   b. The AICPA requires its members to follow the FASB standards.

5. **a.** SEC

   b. FASB

   c. IASB

   d. PCAOB

6. If statements are not prepared in conformity with GAAP, they may be unreliable and they do not present financial affairs in accordance with established accounting principles.

Answers to Section 2 Self Review

1. Materiality is whether the omission of an item or not following GAAP for an item is likely to change the user's interpretations of statements. Factors that might be considered in determining materiality are total assets, net income, total liabilities, and owner's equity.

2. **a.** Separate entity

   b. Going concern

   c. Monetary unit of measure

   d. Periodicity of income

3. Both contain an element of comparability. Consistency means using the same principles and applications each accounting period (comparability from period to period). Comparability refers to the ability to compare one company's statements with another company's statements.

4. Historical costs are objective and verifiable.

5. **a.** Stable monetary unit

   b. Separate entity

   c. Materiality

   d. Periodicity of income

6. **a.** Since the lawsuits involve material amounts and are uncertain, it would be appropriate to disclose their existence in a note. Given the conclusion of the attorney and former manager, along with the uncertainty about any amount of loss, it would probably not be appropriate to record a loss.

   b. Reporting revenues only when credit sales are collected would violate the matching principle (matching revenues with costs incurred). However, management should make certain that the allowance for uncollectible accounts is adequate.

Answers to Comprehensive Self Review

1. The FASB and the SEC have made commitments to work with the International Accounting Standards Board on having U.S. GAAP align or converge more closely with international accounting standards.

2. The result would be that record keeping would be much more complicated, probably involving separate accounts for transactions (such as machinery purchases) made in each year. Another approach might be to attempt to keep all records in terms of "value" at the statement date.

3. Applicable costs should be matched with revenues in the income statement the same year—generally in the year of sale. This requires adjustments for prepaid and accrued expenses and for unearned and accrued income items, as well as such items as depreciation and uncollectible accounts.

4. The full disclosure principle is that all events and factors that are likely to impact the interpretation of the statements should be disclosed. Disclosures can be made in parenthetical notes to the statements or by "notes to the statements" (deemed to be an integral part of the statements). In addition, "supplemental notes" which may not be directly related to amounts shown in the statements may be included.

5. The AICPA influence is primarily through its committees that examine current issues arising in practice for which there is no clear guidance from the FASB. The Sarbanes-Oxley Act gives express power to the SEC to accept rules developed by (one) private-sector organization, so it is possible that the direct impact of AICPA pronouncements will be limited in the future.

6. Industry practice is likely to be an important consideration where there are unique operating circumstances or unique contracts involved in that industry and there is no clearly preferable application of the conceptual framework.

Accounts Receivable and Uncollectible Accounts

Federal Express
www.fedex.com

Making a sale does not always mean collecting cash. Companies who extend credit to their customers understand the benefits and drawbacks of lines of credit. While credit allows customers to purchase goods and services more efficiently, every day a company does not receive payment for a delivered product is a day that company loses opportunities to invest that money and grow its business.

FedEx is a $42.9 billion network of companies offering transportation, e-commerce, and business solutions to its loyal customers. They ship just about everything from ordinary business documents to one of grandma's special-recipe German chocolate cakes.

Converting accounts receivable into cash is critical for a service-based organization like FedEx. Most companies realize that they will never collect 100 percent of their receivables so an allowance, or estimate, for uncollectible amounts is established.

Remaining strong in this economy by delivering an outstanding FedEx experience to their worldwide customers is a commitment the company calls the *Purple Promise*. Providing this outstanding service does not insulate the company from customers that don't pay. As of May 31, 2012, using past experience as a guide, FedEx corporate accountants estimated that $178 million of their total $4.7 billion accounts receivable balance would prove uncollectible in the future. This seems like an enormous amount, but historically, FedEx, like other companies, has accepted this expense as a cost of doing business.

thinking critically
What do you think FedEx can do to minimize their uncollectible accounts?

LEARNING OBJECTIVES

15-1. Record the estimated expense from uncollectible accounts receivable using the allowance method.

15-2. Charge off uncollectible accounts using the allowance method.

15-3. Record the collection of accounts previously written off using the allowance method.

15-4. Record losses from uncollectible accounts using the direct charge-off method.

15-5. Record the collection of accounts previously written off using the direct charge-off method.

15-6. Recognize common internal controls for accounts receivable.

15-7. Define the accounting terms new to this chapter.

NEW TERMS

aging the accounts receivable
allowance method
direct charge-off method
valuation account

>> **15-1.** Record the estimated expense from uncollectible accounts receivable using the allowance method.

WHY IT'S IMPORTANT

Assets should not be overstated. In accordance with the matching principle, bad debt losses are matched with the related sales revenue.

>> **15-2.** Charge off uncollectible accounts using the allowance method.

WHY IT'S IMPORTANT

When an account is uncollectible, it should be charged off. The accounts receivable ledger should contain complete and accurate information so that future credit decisions are sound.

>> **15-3.** Record the collection of accounts previously written off using the allowance method.

WHY IT'S IMPORTANT

Customers' accounts should reflect actual payment histories.

aging the accounts receivable
allowance method
direct charge-off method
valuation account

The Allowance Method of Accounting for Uncollectible Accounts

important!

The Credit Manager
The credit manager plays a very important role in improving profitability of the business.

Most businesses extend credit to their customers because it increases sales revenues. Manufacturing enterprises, wholesale distributors, and organizations providing services to other businesses typically sell an overwhelming portion of their goods and services on credit. Service businesses such as medical providers, attorneys, auto repair garages, and others offering services to individuals also frequently extend credit. Almost invariably, when a business extends credit, some customers will not pay their bills. A firm's credit department and its management try to reduce the losses from uncollectible accounts. Typically, a customer seeking credit privileges must complete a credit application form. The applicant must provide financial information requested. In most cases, the applicant's credit record is checked through a credit report obtained from a credit agency. A credit report shows the payment record of a customer and some reports include historical or other information concerning the business or person about whom inquiry is being made.

No matter what tools are used, however, it is almost impossible to forecast with certainty whether a specific customer will prove to be a good risk. If a company has no credit losses, the business may be losing substantial sales by having an ultrastrict credit policy. Management must constantly balance the risk of higher credit losses resulting from giving credit to more applicants or from setting higher limits on the amount of credit extended individual customers (both of which may lead to increased losses) against the possibility of losing sales volume as a result of giving credit to fewer customers or setting lower limits on each customer. However, losses resulting from failure of customers to pay the amounts owed, called "uncollectible accounts expense," "losses from uncollectible accounts," or sometimes referred to as "bad debts expense," are a normal cost of doing business.

A basic question faced in accounting for uncollectible accounts is determining when they should be charged to expense. A corollary question is how to determine the amount to be charged to expense during each accounting period. Related issues for the accountant are how to make the resulting accounting entries and how to show the information in the financial statements.

Methods of Accounting for Uncollectible Accounts

Two methods are used to account for uncollectible accounts. These are the "allowance method" and the "direct charge-off method." The latter is sometimes called the "specific charge-off method."

THE ALLOWANCE METHOD

Under the **allowance method,** an estimate is made and recorded each year of the bad debt losses applicable to sales of that year, even though it may be a year or more before it is known which specific accounts are uncollectible. At the end of the accounting period, the estimated loss for the period is debited to *Uncollectible Accounts Expense* and credited to *Allowance for Doubtful Accounts.* This approach matches the estimated expense from uncollectible accounts to the revenue in the period the revenue is recognized. *Allowance for Doubtful Accounts* is subtracted from *Accounts Receivable* on the balance sheet. The net accounts receivable reflects the amount that the business thinks will be collected. For this reason, the allowance account is called a **valuation account.** The allowance method meets two of the basic concepts in the FASB's Conceptual Framework. The principle of matching revenues and related costs is applied. In addition, current assets that will be converted into cash should not be shown at more than the amount expected to be realized when they are converted. Because of these characteristics, the allowance method is required under generally accepted accounting principles.

THE DIRECT CHARGE-OFF METHOD

Under the **direct charge-off method** losses from uncollectible accounts are recorded only when specific customers' accounts become uncollectible. When that occurs, the balance due is removed from *Accounts Receivable* and the customer's account in the subsidiary ledger and is charged to *Uncollectible Accounts Expense.* The direct charge-off method is used primarily by small businesses, many of whom do not have external audits. It may also be used by large businesses that have relatively insignificant accounts receivable, in keeping with the concept of materiality. The direct charge-off method does not reflect generally accepted accounting principles because a loss from sales on account in one year frequently will not be charged to expense until a subsequent year (a violation of the matching principle) if the direct charge-off method is followed. In addition, the accounts receivable are shown at an amount greater than will ultimately be realized in cash from them. Federal income tax laws now require that the direct charge-off method be used in preparing the federal tax return. The allowance method is not acceptable for tax purposes. Using the direct charge-off method for financial reporting as well as income tax purposes, reduces the amount of time spent in accounting for uncollectible accounts. As a result, the tax requirement leads some businesses to also use the direct charge-off method for financial reporting purposes.

Because the allowance method is the generally accepted procedure and is therefore much more widely used, details of that method are discussed before the direct charge-off method is examined in detail.

Applying the Allowance Method

You will learn how to use the allowance method to account for losses from uncollectible accounts by studying Kathy's Kitchens, a retail store selling kitchen appliances, gadgets, and kitchen remodeling services. Kathy's Kitchens is owned by Kathy Kaymark, and has been in business several years. The store offers charge accounts to customers who meet its credit standards. Kathy sends customers statements of their accounts on the last day of each month,

important!

When Uncollectible Accounts Expense Is Recorded Under the Allowance Method
Under the allowance method, uncollectible accounts expense is recorded at the end of the period as an adjusting entry.

important!

Matching Uncollectible Accounts with Sales
The allowance method matches the uncollectible accounts expense with sales in the period the sales are recorded.

important!

Recording Uncollectible Accounts Expense Under the Direct Charge-Off Method
Under the direct charge-off method, bad debt expense is recorded when a customer's account becomes uncollectible.

important!

Uncollectible Accounts
Only the direct charge-off method is allowed for federal income tax purposes. The use of the allowance method is required under generally accepted accounting principles.

and the balance owed is due to be paid by the 20th day of the following month. Kathy understands that the allowance method is preferred to the direct charge-off method, so she has adopted the allowance method.

>> 15-1. OBJECTIVE

Record the estimated expense from uncollectible accounts receivable using the allowance method.

RECORDING THE ESTIMATED EXPENSE FROM UNCOLLECTIBLE ACCOUNTS WHEN THE ALLOWANCE METHOD IS USED

At the end of 2015, Kathy analyzed the bad debts record in prior years and also the amounts owed currently by each customer. On the basis of this analysis, along with information from her trade association about typical bad debt losses in that type business and from talks with other merchants in similar businesses in the community, Kathy estimated the provision for uncollectible accounts necessary at year-end 2015 to be $1,900. (Do not be concerned with the details of how this amount was determined. Three methods, to be examined later in this chapter, are commonly used as a basis for the estimate. At this point, we are interested only in the basic concepts of the recording procedure.)

When adjusting entries were made at the end of the year 2015, the estimated loss ($1,900) was recorded as a debit to the expense account, **Uncollectible Accounts Expense,** sometimes called **Bad Debts Expense** or **Losses from Uncollectible Accounts.** This account is shown in the income statement as a general expense or as a selling expense, depending on which department in the business has responsibility for making credit decisions. Good internal controls generally suggest that the credit function should not be in the sales department, a department very interested in increasing sales. As a result, **Uncollectible Accounts Expense** is usually shown under General Expenses.

important!

Uncollectible Accounts Expense on the Income Statement
Usually, *Uncollectible Accounts Expense* is shown as a general expense.

The credit part of the adjusting entry was to **Allowance for Doubtful Accounts.** Sometimes the allowance account is called **Allowance for Bad Debts** or **Allowance for Uncollectible Accounts.** Here is the journal entry made at the end of 2015 in the records of Kathy's Kitchens:

	GENERAL JOURNAL			PAGE ___1___
DATE	DESCRIPTION	POST. REF.	DEBIT	CREDIT
	Adjusting Entries			
2015				
Dec. 31	Uncollectible Accounts Expense		1 9 0 0 00	
	Allowance for Doubtful Accounts			1 9 0 0 00

THE BOTTOM LINE

Uncollectible Accounts
Adjustment

Income Statement

Expense	↑ 1,900
Net Income	↓ 1,900

Balance Sheet

Assets	↓ 1,900
Equity	↓ 1,900

recall

Contra Asset Account
Allowance for Doubtful Accounts is a contra asset account. Its normal balance is a credit. It is reported in the balance sheet as a deduction from *Accounts Receivable* to provide an estimate of collectible receivables. For this reason, it is called a valuation account.

Remember that **Allowance for Doubtful Accounts,** which reflects the estimate of losses to be incurred on sales already made, is shown on the balance sheet as a deduction from **Accounts Receivable.** Assuming that there was a zero balance in **Allowance for Doubtful Accounts** prior to the adjusting entry, that account will have a credit balance of $1,900 on December 31, 2015, after the above adjusting entry. The allowance account is a *contra* account because it is subtracted from an asset account (**Accounts Receivable**) in the balance sheet. It reduces the carrying value of the asset and is referred to as a valuation account. Here is how the accounts receivable information appeared on the balance sheet for Kathy's Kitchens on December 31, 2015:

Kathy's Kitchens Balance Sheet (partial) December 31, 2015		
Current Assets		
Cash		$ 9,320
Accounts Receivable	$46,400	
Less Allowance for Doubtful Accounts	1,900	44,500

The $44,500 balance is often called the net realizable value of accounts receivable.

Alternatively, the balance sheet may show only the net amount of *Accounts Receivable,* after subtracting out the allowance, with the amount of the allowance shown in a parenthetical note.

> At December 31, 2012, The Coca-Cola Company reported *trade accounts receivable, less allowances* of approximately $4.8 billion. This amount was net of allowances totaling $53 million.

Note again that under the allowance method the financial statements reflect the matching principle. The estimated expense for losses on sales made in 2015 is deducted in the 2015 income statement—the same year that the related revenues from sales were reported. Also, the net *Accounts Receivable* on the balance sheet reflects the amount expected to be received in cash from the debtors.

FACTORS USED TO COMPUTE THE YEAR-END PROVISION FOR UNCOLLECTIBLE ACCOUNTS

In the discussion of Kathy's Kitchens provision for uncollectible accounts at the end of 2015, you were not told how the $1,900 provision was determined. The end-of-year estimate of the amount to be charged to *Uncollectible Accounts Expense* and credited to the *Allowance for Doubtful Accounts* is usually based on one of three factors:

- net credit sales for the year
- total accounts receivable on December 31
- aging of accounts receivable on December 31

When the amount of net credit sales for the year is the basis for the provision, it is often said that the preparer is using the "income statement approach." Using sales as the estimation base emphasizes the importance of matching uncollectible accounts expense with the net credit sales generated in the same year. In this approach, the key factor is the matching principle. When the provision is based on total accounts receivable or the aging of accounts receivable, the emphasis is on the balance sheet, so it is often called the "balance sheet approach." It emphasizes the appropriate valuation of receivables—not showing the net receivables at an amount greater than the cash expected to be received from their collection.

The calculations of the uncollectible accounts adjustment for Kathy's Kitchens on December 31, 2016, under each of these three approaches illustrate how they are determined. During 2016, Kathy's Kitchens had net credit sales of $600,000. Accounts receivable at the end of the year totaled $49,000. There was a credit balance of $1,900 in the allowance account on January 1, 2016. Assume that accounts totaling $1,792 were charged off in 2016, so that there is a credit balance of $108 in *Allowance for Doubtful Accounts* prior to adjusting entries on December 31. Here is how the three approaches would be applied by Kathy's Kitchens.

PERCENTAGE OF NET CREDIT SALES

One way to estimate to uncollectible accounts expense is to multiply the net credit sales by a percentage. The percentage is based on the company's previous experience with losses from uncollectible accounts. New businesses often base the percentage on the experience of other businesses in the same industry. The percentage is calculated as follows:

$$\frac{\text{Losses from uncollectible accounts}}{\text{Net credit sales}}$$

Net credit sales is calculated as total credit sales minus the sales return and allowances on credit sales.

Kathy's Kitchens estimates that three-quarters of 1 percent (0.0075) of the net credit sales will be uncollectible. If net credit sales in 2016 are $600,000, the estimated loss from uncollectible accounts is $4,500 (0.0075 × $600,000). This is the amount to be charged to *Uncollectible Accounts Expense* and credited to *Allowance for Doubtful Accounts* in the

recall

Basing Bad Debts on Sales Provides Matching

If the estimate of uncollectible accounts is based on sales, emphasis is being placed on the matching of revenues and expenses in the income statement.

adjusting entry. It is entered on the worksheet and is later recorded in the general journal, along with other adjusting entries.

	DATE	DESCRIPTION	POST. REF.	DEBIT	CREDIT	
		GENERAL JOURNAL PAGE ___1___				
1	2016	*Adjusting Entries*				1
22	Dec. 31	Uncollectible Accounts Expense	561	4 5 0 0 00		22
23		Allowance for Doubtful Accounts	112		4 5 0 0 00	23
24		To record estimated bad debt losses				24
25		for the year, based on 0.75 percent of				25
26		net credit sales of $600,000				26

Note again that the expense charge is the focal point when sales is used as the basis for the estimate. The balance in the allowance account before the adjustment is ignored in determining how much will be charged to expense and credited to the allowance account. This is why the method is referred to as an "income statement approach."

important!

Ignore the Balance in the Valuation Account in Making the Adjustment

If the uncollectible account provision is based on sales, the existing debit or credit balance in the allowance account is ignored in making the provision.

PERCENTAGE OF TOTAL ACCOUNTS RECEIVABLE

Some accountants think that it is more important to focus on the balance in the allowance account than on the amount charged to expense. Under their approach, it is necessary to first determine the amount in the accounts estimated to be uncollectible and to adjust the *Allowance for Doubtful Accounts* to that amount. The offsetting debit to expense is the result of focusing on the balance sheet accounts.

A simple approach to determining the appropriate balance for *Allowance for Doubtful Accounts* is to apply a single percentage to the balance of the *Accounts Receivable* account. This percentage is typically based on the experience of the company during the last three or four years. The average of accounts that became uncollectible during each year of the base period is calculated. Similarly the average of accounts receivable at the end of each base period year is determined. Then the ratio of the average uncollectible accounts to the average ending balance of accounts receivable is computed. The ratio is applied to the *Accounts Receivable* balance at the date of the computation to arrive at the estimated worthless accounts. Kathy's Kitchens decides to use the ratio of average uncollectible accounts for the last three years to the ending balance in *Accounts Receivable* for the three years. The records of Kathy's Kitchens show the following:

important!

Focus on Uncollectible Amount

Many accountants think that basing the allowance on accounts receivable focuses more sharply on the critical question of the amount in the accounts that is uncollectible than does a charge off based on sales.

Date	Accounts Receivable	Uncollectible Accounts
12/31/13	$ 39,600	$2,083
12/31/14	44,360	2,145
12/31/15	46,400	2,240
Total	$130,360	$6,468
Average	$ 43,453	$2,156

The average loss over the three-year period is 4.962 percent of accounts receivable.

$$\frac{\text{Average Uncollectible Accounts}}{\text{Average Accounts Receivable}} = \frac{\$2,156}{\$43,453} = 0.04962$$

recall

Emphasis on the Balance Sheet

If the adjusting entry for uncollectible account expense is based on receivables, the emphasis is being placed on the balance sheet.

It is customary to round the percentage of loss to the nearest one-tenth of one percent. Under this convention, Kathy's rate would be rounded to 5.0 percent.

If the balance of *Accounts Receivable* on December 31, 2016, is $49,000, estimated uncollectible accounts will be $2,450 (0.05 × $49,000). Under the balance sheet approach, *Allowance for Uncollectible Accounts* is adjusted to the amount estimated to be *uncollectible*.

Assuming that the *Allowance for Doubtful Accounts* has a credit balance of $108 on December 31, before the adjusting entry has been made, it will be necessary to add $2,342 to the account to bring it to the desired balance ($2,450 − $108 = $2,342). Here is the necessary entry:

	DATE		DESCRIPTION	POST. REF.	DEBIT	CREDIT	
	GENERAL JOURNAL					PAGE _12_	
1	2016						1
2	Dec.	31	Uncollectible Accounts Expense		2 3 4 2 00		2
3			Allowance for Doubtful Accounts			2 3 4 2 00	3

After the entry has been posted, the *Allowance for Doubtful Accounts* has a credit balance of $2,450. If *Allowance for Uncollectible Accounts* had a *debit* balance of $240 prior to the adjusting entry, it would be necessary to credit the allowance account for $2,690 ($2,450 + $240 = $2,690) to arrive at the required balance of $2,450.

AGING THE ACCOUNTS RECEIVABLE

Another way to estimate uncollectible accounts is a procedure called **aging the accounts receivable.** This procedure involves classifying receivables according to how long they have been outstanding. The first step is to prepare an aging schedule. Figure 15.1 shows the aging schedule for Kathy's Kitchens. Each account is listed by name and balance. Each invoice is classified as current (within the credit period), 1–30 days past due, 31–60 days past due, or over 60 days past due. Notice that Robert Brown owes $400. Of this amount, $80 is over 60 days past due and $320 is between 31 and 60 days past due.

The longer an account is past due, the less likely it is to be collected. Following are estimated uncollectible percentages for each age group shown in the analysis of Kathy's receivables:

Category	Percentage Uncollectible
Current Accounts	0.5%
1–30 days past due	6.0%
31–60 days past due	20.0%
Over 60 days past due	60.0%

important!

Collect Accounts as Quickly as Possible
Experience has shown that the older an account receivable becomes, the less likely it is to be collected.

FIGURE 15.1

Kathy's Kitchens Aged Accounts Receivable Schedule

Kathy's Kitchens
Schedule of Accounts Receivable by Age
December 31, 2016

Customer	Balance	Current	Past Due—Days		
			1–30	31–60	Over 60
Anderson, Nick	$ 820		$ 820		
Anh, Susie	1,200	$ 1,200			
Benson, Samuel	257	37		$ 200	$ 20
Brown, Robert	400			320	80
All other accounts	46,323	36,763	6,180	1,080	2,300
Totals	$49,000	$38,000	$7,000	$1,600	$2,400

Based on these percentages, the estimated uncollectible accounts on December 31 total $2,370:

Current	0.005	×	$38,000	=	$ 190
1–30 days past due	0.06	×	7,000	=	420
31–60 days past due	0.20	×	1,600	=	320
Over 60 days past due	0.60	×	2,400	=	1,440
Totals			$49,000		$2,370

Allowance for Doubtful Accounts should then be adjusted so that its ending balance is a $2,370 credit. On December 31, before adjustments have been made, ***Allowance for Doubtful Accounts*** has a credit balance of $108. A credit adjustment of $2,262 ($2,370 − $108) will bring the account balance to the desired amount.

Allowance for Doubtful Accounts	
−	+
	Bal. 108.00
	Adj. 2,262.00
	Bal. 2,370.00

The adjustment is recorded in the general journal as follows:

GENERAL JOURNAL   PAGE ___1___

	DATE		DESCRIPTION	POST. REF.	DEBIT	CREDIT	
1	2016		Adjusting Entries				1
22	Dec.	31	Uncollectible Accounts Expense	561	2 2 6 2 00		22
23			Allowance for Doubtful Accounts	112		2 2 6 2 00	23
24			To adjust allowance account to $2,370,				24
25			based on aging of accounts receivable				25

WRITING OFF A CUSTOMER'S ACCOUNT DETERMINED TO BE UNCOLLECTIBLE WHEN THE ALLOWANCE METHOD IS USED

A basic rule is that the longer past due an account becomes, the less likely it is to be collectible. When it is concluded that a specific account is not collectible, it should be "charged off" or "written off." For example, on January 24, 2016, Kathy's Kitchens concluded that the account of James McDonald should be charged off. Kathy's had sent him numerous letters, made several telephone calls, and sent a number of e-mails. The account had a balance of $224, resulting from a sale on August 22, 2015.

The general journal entry required to charge off a customer's account when the allowance method is used is a simple one. ***Accounts Receivable*** and McDonald's account in the subsidiary ledger are credited to remove the amount due. The debit is to ***Allowance for Doubtful Accounts.*** When the allowance was credited previously by an adjusting entry, it was not known which specific accounts would be uncollectible. It is now assumed that the provision included McDonald's account, so there is no longer a need to include in ***Allowance for Uncollectible Accounts*** an amount to cover a future loss from McDonald's failure to pay this debt. Here is the journal entry to write off McDonald's account:

GENERAL JOURNAL   PAGE ___12___

DATE		DESCRIPTION	POST. REF.	DEBIT	CREDIT
2016					
Jan.	24	Allowance for Doubtful Accounts		2 2 4 00	
		Accounts Receivable/James McDonald			2 2 4 00

The debit to *Allowance for Doubtful Accounts* reduces the credit balance in that account. The total amount of accounts receivable charged off in 2016 may be more than, or less than, the balance in *Allowance for Uncollectible Accounts* at the start of the year. What happens if the amount debited to *Allowance for Doubtful Accounts* exceeds the beginning amount in the account? For example, what happens if during 2016 Kathy's Kitchens removes from *Accounts Receivable* and charges to *Allowance for Doubtful Accounts* a total of $2,018? Remember that the balance in the allowance account was only $1,900 at the start of the year. Thus, at the end of 2016 *Allowance for Doubtful Accounts* would contain a debit balance of $118 ($2,018 debit − $1,900 credit = $118 debit). On the other hand, if the amount of uncollectible accounts charged off in 2016 is only $1,700, there would have been a credit balance of $200 ($1,900 credit − $1,700 debit = $200 credit) in the allowance account before adjustments at the end of 2016. The existence of a debit balance or a credit balance in the allowance account before adjustments at the end of the year is not generally a cause for concern. When the adjusting entries have been made, that situation will be corrected. We will see later how this situation is handled in the adjustments at the end of 2016. Obviously, management will need to keep close watch every year to make sure that the estimation process being used is reasonable and the allowance balance is adequate, but not excessive.

It is important to remember that the charge-off of a specific account receivable has no impact on total assets if the allowance method is used. The credit to the asset account *Accounts Receivable* is exactly the same amount as the debit to the contra account, *Allowance for Doubtful Accounts,* so there is no change in the net amount of *Accounts Receivable.*

important!

Balance in the Allowance Account
Allowance for Doubtful Accounts
may have either a debit or credit balance before adjusting entries are posted.

important!

Is the Provision Reasonable?
It is very important for management to analyze the estimation process each year to assure that the provision for uncollectible accounts is reasonable.

At its fiscal year ending June 30, 2012, Microsoft Corporation's balance sheet showed "Accounts Receivable, Net" of approximately $15.8 billion. A note to the financial statements described activity in the allowance account for the year as follows:

> The allowance for doubtful accounts reflects our best estimate of probable losses inherent in the accounts receivable balance. We determine the allowance based on known troubled accounts, historical experience, and other currently available evidence.

The note goes further to analyze the allowance for doubtful accounts for 2012, which includes the following information in $millions.

Beginning balance (July 1, 2011)	$333
Charges to costs and expenses	+ 115
Write-offs and other	− 59
Balance at end of period (June 30, 2012)	+$389

COLLECTING AN ACCOUNT THAT HAS BEEN PREVIOUSLY WRITTEN OFF

Occasionally, an account that was written off is later collected, in whole or in part. When a firm uses the allowance method to provide for losses, the recovery of an account previously charged off as uncollectible requires two entries to record the transaction. The first entry reinstates the account receivable, and the second entry records the receipt of cash. For example, the recovery on February 9, 2017, of the $160 account of Richard Strong, charged off on July 13, 2016, is recorded in the general journal as follows:

>> 15-3. OBJECTIVE
Record the collection of accounts previously written off using the allowance method.

	DATE		DESCRIPTION	POST. REF.	DEBIT	CREDIT	
1	2017						1
20	Feb.	09	Accounts Receivable/Richard Strong	111/✓	160 00		20
21			*Allowance for Doubtful Accounts*	112		160 00	21
22			*To reverse entry dated July 13, 2013,*				22
23			*writing off this account, collected in*				23
24			*full today.*				24

GENERAL JOURNAL   PAGE _____

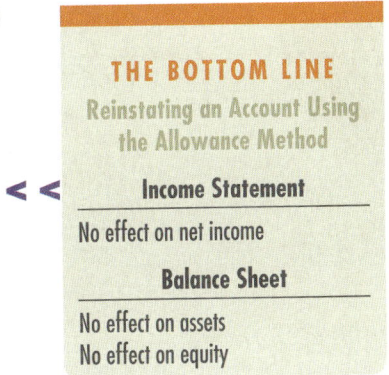

THE BOTTOM LINE
Reinstating an Account Using the Allowance Method

Income Statement

No effect on net income

Balance Sheet

No effect on assets
No effect on equity

An entry in the cash receipts journal is then made in the usual way to record the collection—by a debit to *Cash* and a credit to *Accounts Receivable.*

If the amount recovered is only part of the balance written off, an entry is made to restore *only the amount actually collected* unless the firm is almost certain that the remainder will be paid. For example, if Richard Strong pays only $60, that is the amount that will be reinstated unless Kathy's is reasonably sure the additional $100 Strong owes will be paid. After the proper reinstatement is made, an entry in the cash receipts journal is then made in the usual way to record the collection of the account receivable.

Section 1   Self Review

QUESTIONS

1. What major accounting principle supports the allowance method for reporting uncollectible accounts?

2. Johnson Industries determines its provision for uncollectible accounts by applying an estimated loss percentage of 1 percent to net credit sales. In 2016, net credit sales were $5,700,000. Prior to the adjusting entry, **Allowance for Uncollectible Accounts** contained a credit balance of $4,000. How much will be charged to **Uncollectible Accounts Expense** in 2016?

3. Martin Company determines its allowance for uncollectible accounts by applying an expected loss percentage of 1.8 percent to the total of accounts receivable, $1,200,000. Prior to the adjusting entry the allowance account has a debit balance of $800. How much will be charged to expense in the adjusting entry?

EXERCISES

4. Salazar Company uses the allowance method to record uncollectible accounts. In January 2016, it charged off the $450 account balance of Barrington as uncollectible. In June 2016, Barrington paid the entire amount charged off. What journal entries are made at the time of receipt of payment? (Give accounts and amounts.)

5. Assume the same facts as in 4, above, except that Barrington made the repayment in 2017. What journal entries would be made on receipt of payment?

ANALYSIS

6. Ace Company bases its provision for uncollectible accounts on sales. At the end of each of the past four years, the ratio of **Allowance for Uncollectible Accounts** to **Accounts Receivable** at the end of the year has been greater than it was for the prior year. What does this suggest? Explain.

7. The credit manager at Premium Office Supply has learned that a former customer who did not pay his debt, and whose account Premium had charged off as uncollectible, has just won the state lottery and the customer may now pay the debt. Should the customer's account be reinstated?

(Answers to Section 1 Self Review are on page 545.)

SECTION OBJECTIVES

>> 15-4. **Record losses from uncollectible accounts using the direct charge-off method.**

WHY IT'S IMPORTANT
Some small businesses and larger businesses with immaterial amounts of accounts receivable use this method, even though it does not comply with GAAP. Also, the direct charge-off method is required for federal income tax reporting.

>> 15-5. **Record the collection of accounts previously written off using the direct charge-off method.**

WHY IT'S IMPORTANT
Customers' accounts should reflect actual payment histories.

>> 15-6. **Recognize common internal controls for accounts receivable.**

WHY IT'S IMPORTANT
There are many activities involving accounts receivable and uncollectible accounts that provide opportunities for mishandling of funds. The accountant should be aware of steps to be taken to provide protection.

Applying the Direct Charge-Off Method; Internal Control of Accounts Receivable

The direct charge-off method for recording uncollectible account expense is simple to apply, but does not comply with generally accepted accounting principles. As discussed earlier in this chapter, however, the method is often used by small businesses and by some larger enterprises when the impact on financial statements would be immaterial. In addition, because it is required for federal income tax purposes, an understanding of the system is essential.

Recording Uncollectible Accounts When the Direct Charge-Off Method Is Used

>> **15-4. OBJECTIVE**
Record losses from uncollectible accounts using the direct charge-off method.

Earlier in this chapter it was pointed out that the direct charge-off method records uncollectible accounts expense at the time a specific customer's account is deemed to be uncollectible. Certain transactions of Romano's Auto Repair Shop will be used to demonstrate the accounting entries made when the direct charge-off method is used.

On December 22, 2015, Romano made repairs to Mike Miller's RV, charging $520 to *Accounts Receivable* and to Miller's account in the accounts receivable subsidiary ledger. On July 10, 2016, after several weeks of trying to collect the account, Romano discovered that Miller had left his job and moved to another state. Romano concludes that the account must be written off. The loss is debited to *Uncollectible Accounts Expense.* The credit is to *Accounts Receivable* and to Miller's account in the accounts receivable subsidiary ledger.

	GENERAL JOURNAL				PAGE _____	
DATE	DESCRIPTION	POST. REF.		DEBIT		CREDIT
2016						
July 10	Uncollectible Account Expense			5 2 0 00		
	Accounts Receivable/Mike Miller					5 2 0 00
	To write off uncollectible account					

There are several important points to remember about the direct charge-off method:

- It does not always match revenue and expenses. Revenue for the work done on Miller's vehicle was recognized in 2015. The bad debt expense, however, is recorded in 2016.

- It can overstate accounts receivable. Under this method, the **Accounts Receivable** balance reflects all outstanding unpaid accounts that have not been written off. No estimate is made for the accounts that might be uncollectible in the future.

- It is the only method acceptable for federal income tax purposes.

Collecting an Account Previously Written Off When the Direct Charge-Off Method Is Used

>> 15-5. OBJECTIVE

Record the collection of accounts previously written off using the direct charge-off method.

Under the direct charge-off method, the appropriate entries to record the collection of an account after it has been charged off depends on whether the collection is made in the same accounting period that the account was written off or occurs in a subsequent period.

PAYMENT RECEIVED IN PERIOD IN WHICH ACCOUNT IS CHARGED OFF

In the above example, Miller's account of $520 was written off on July 10, 2016, under the direct charge-off method. The entry was a debit to **Uncollectible Accounts Expense** and a credit to **Accounts Receivable.** Suppose that on October 29, 2016, Romano's Auto Repair Shop received $520 from Miller in full payment of his account. It takes two entries to record the transaction. The first entry is to reinstate in **Accounts Receivable** the amount being paid. This entry, which simply reverses the entry made to charge off the account as uncollectible, is made so that the customer's account will show the full history of the customer's payment record. The credit is made to **Uncollectible Accounts Expense** so that the expense account for the period will not be overstated. To the extent that there is payment in the same year, there was no net expense for the year.

THE BOTTOM LINE

Reinstating an Account Using the Direct Charge-Off Method

Income Statement

Expense	↓ 520
Net Income	↑ 520

Balance Sheet

Assets	↑ 520
Equity	↑ 520

	GENERAL JOURNAL				PAGE _____	
DATE	DESCRIPTION	POST. REF.		DEBIT		CREDIT
2016						
Oct. 2 9	Accounts Receivable/Mike Miller			5 2 0 00		
	Uncollectible Account Expense					5 2 0 00
	To reinstate Miller's account receivable					
	that was written off on July 10 and					
	collected in full today.					

The second entry records the customer's payment in the cash receipts journal in the usual way, as a debit to **Cash** and a credit to **Accounts Receivable** (and to Miller's account).

PAYMENT RECEIVED IN PERIOD SUBSEQUENT TO THAT IN WHICH ACCOUNT WAS CHARGED OFF

Suppose that the collection of Miller's account is made in January 2017, a period subsequent to that of the charge-off. In that event, the entry to reinstate the account is a debit to **Accounts Receivable** and a credit to **Uncollectible Accounts Recovered.**

	GENERAL JOURNAL		PAGE _____	
DATE	DESCRIPTION	POST. REF.	DEBIT	CREDIT
2017				
Jan. 09	Accounts Receivable/Mike Miller		520 00	
	Uncollectible Accounts Recovered			520 00
	To reinstate Miller's account receivable			
	that was written off on July 10, 2016,			
	and collected in full today.			

If the amount recovered in a period subsequent to the write-off is credited to **Uncollectible Accounts Expense,** the expense for the period of recovery will be understated.

The balance in **Uncollectible Accounts Recovered** is shown on the income statement as Other Income.

Accounting for Other Receivables and Bad Debt Losses

As with accounts receivable, notes receivable and other receivables can prove uncollectible. Losses from uncollectible notes receivable and other receivables can be handled by the direct charge-off method or the allowance method. **Uncollectible Accounts Expense** and **Allowance for Doubtful Accounts** can be used for losses from all types of receivables.

MANAGERIAL IMPLICATIONS <<

MANAGING CREDIT

- It is essential that managers establish formal procedures for granting credit to customers, for tracking accounts receivable, for ensuring that customers are paying promptly, and for collecting past-due accounts.
- Management needs to be informed about the losses from uncollectible accounts so they can:
  - establish effective credit policies,
  - weigh the cost of uncollectible account losses against the reduced sales volume caused by tight credit policies.

- Managers should use the allowance method for uncollectible accounts in order to match revenue and expenses.
- Managers are responsible for developing procedures to handle payments from customers whose accounts have been written off.

THINKING CRITICALLY

What reports would provide information to managers about how well the accounts receivable function is being managed?

>> 15-6. OBJECTIVE

Recognize common internal controls for accounts receivable.

Internal Control of Accounts Receivable

Internal control of the accounts receivable process is very important because accounts receivable represents one of the largest assets on the balance sheet for many companies. Common internal controls for accounts receivable include the following:

- Authorizing all credit sales.
- Developing procedures that ensure that all credit sales are recorded and customers' accounts are debited.
- Separating the following duties:
  - authorizing credit sales,
  - recording the accounts receivable transactions,
  - preparing bills or statements for customers,
  - mailing the bills or statements,
  - processing payments received from customers.
- Sending invoices and monthly statements.
- Authorizing charge-off of accounts.
- Aging the accounts receivable to allow management to identify and monitor slow-paying accounts.
- Investigating and taking appropriate action on past due accounts.
- Approving the write-off of accounts by authorized individuals only, and making the approvals in writing.
- Trying to collect past due accounts even if they have been written off.

Section 2   Self Review

QUESTIONS

1. What basic accounting assumptions, principles, or constraints may be used as the basis for criticizing the direct charge-off method for recording uncollectible accounts?

2. Under the direct charge-off method, when a specific account receivable is written off, what account is debited? What is the effect of the write-off on net income and on assets?

3. If an account receivable of $800 charged off in 2016 under the direct charge-off method is recovered in 2017, in what way does accounting for the recovery differ from that used if the recovery had been made in 2016?

EXERCISES

4. March 31, 2016, Barone Company wrote off the $60 account of Vic Diamond as uncollectible. The company uses the direct charge-off method. What account is debited and what account is credited to record the write-off?

5. Assume the same facts as in Exercise 4, except that Barone Company uses the allowance method. What account is debited and what account is credited to record the write-off?

ANALYSIS

6. The sales manager in your company insists that the sales department should have the authority to make final decisions in all questions that arise about credit and accounts receivable. What is your opinion? What are the reasons for your answer?

7. Barry Klein started business in March 2016. His sales for the year were $875,000 and his credit sales were $130,000. His accounts receivable on December 31 total $10,500. Kline plans to charge off uncollectible accounts only when specific accounts are deemed to be uncollectible. His accountant argues that in order to match the uncollectible accounts that may result in the future against the sales revenue in the year of sale, Klein should estimate future losses and record them in 2016. What arguments can Klein make to justify his own position?

(Answers to Section 2 Self Review are on page 545.)

REVIEW   Chapter Summary

When credit is extended, uncollectible accounts inevitably occur. Before receivables can be accurately presented in the balance sheet and net income can be properly measured, the accounts must be studied for possible adjustment to reflect such losses. In this chapter, you have learned how to adjust the value of receivables to account for uncollectible accounts.

Learning Objectives

15-1 **Record the estimated expense from uncollectible accounts receivable using the allowance method.**

The allowance method matches bad debt losses for a period against revenue received in the same period. It is consistent with generally accepted accounting principles and is the preferred method for recognizing uncollectible accounts.

- The estimate of losses from uncollectible accounts can be based on a percentage (determined by experience) of credit sales. The estimated amount is debited to *Uncollectible Accounts Expense* and credited to *Allowance for Doubtful Accounts.*

- The estimate can be based on a single rate of expected noncollectibility of all accounts receivable. On the basis of past experience, the rate is applied to the balance of *Accounts Receivable* to determine the anticipated losses from the accounts. The balance in *Allowance for Doubtful Accounts* is adjusted to this estimated loss amount.

- The estimate of uncollectible accounts can also be based on the age of accounts receivable. A different percentage for credit losses is applied to each age group, and the resulting amounts are added together. Then *Allowance for Doubtful Accounts* is adjusted to the proper balance and the same amount is charged to *Allowance for Doubtful Accounts.*

15-2 **Charge off uncollectible accounts using the allowance method.**

Under the allowance method, an account that proves uncollectible is written off by a debit to *Allowance for Uncollectible Accounts* and a credit to both *Accounts Receivable* and the customer's account in the subsidiary ledger.

15-3 **Record the collection of accounts previously written off using the allowance method.**

Under the allowance method, if all or part of an account previously written off as uncollectible is subsequently paid, the amount being paid is reinstated by a debit to *Accounts Receivable* and a credit to *Allowance for Doubtful Accounts* and

to the customer's account in the subsidiary ledger. Any cash paid at that time is recorded by debiting *Cash* and crediting *Accounts Receivable* and the customer's account in the subsidiary ledger.

15-4 **Record losses from uncollectible accounts using the direct charge-off method.**

Under the direct charge-off method of recording uncollectible accounts, *Uncollectible Accounts Expense* is debited at the time specific accounts receivable are deemed to be uncollectible. Because the expense resulting from uncollectible accounts may not be matched in the same accounting period with the revenue that gave rise to the receivable, this method is not generally acceptable. It does not conform to the matching principle. However, many small businesses, and even some larger ones with relatively small amounts of receivables, use the method. It is required to be used for federal income tax purposes.

15-5 **Record the collection of accounts previously written off using the direct charge-off method.**

Under the direct charge-off method, if an account previously charged off as uncollectible is subsequently collected in the same accounting period, the original entry to charge off the account (to the extent it is collected) is reversed. The reversing entry is a debit to *Accounts Receivable* and the customer's account in the subsidiary ledger, and a credit to *Uncollectible Accounts Expense.* At the same time, an entry is made in the cash receipts journal debiting *Cash* and crediting *Accounts Receivable* and the customer's subsidiary ledger account. If the collection is made in a year subsequent to the year in which the write-off was recorded, the entry to record the reinstatement is a debit to *Accounts Receivable* and the customer's subsidiary account and a credit to *Uncollectible Accounts Recovered.*

15-6 **Recognize common internal controls for accounts receivable.**

It is very important that management establish formal procedures for approving and granting credit, for keeping close watch on customers' accounts to assure they are paid promptly, and for properly assigning duties related to accounts receivable. A key element in internal control is to avoid giving any one person responsibility for a large number of the functions related to receivables. These functions include granting credit, recording accounts receivable transactions,

preparing bills for customers, mailing the bills and statements, processing payments from customers, approving write-offs, and trying to collect past-due accounts.

15-7 Define the accounting terms new to this chapter.

Glossary

Aging the accounts receivable (p. 525) Classifying accounts receivable balances according to how long they have been outstanding

Allowance method (p. 521) A method of recording uncollectible accounts that estimates losses from uncollectible accounts and charges them to expense in the period when the sales are recorded

Direct charge-off method (p. 521) A method of recording uncollectible account losses as they occur

Valuation account (p. 521) An account, such as *Allowance for Doubtful Accounts,* whose balance is revalued or reappraised in light of reasonable expectations

Comprehensive **Self Review**

1. If the allowance method is used, what account is debited when an account is determined uncollectible?
2. Which method of accounting for uncollectible accounts, the direct charge-off method or the allowance method, is considered generally acceptable?
3. Which method of accounting for uncollectible accounts, the direct charge-off or the allowance method, must be used for tax purposes?
4. A business using the direct charge-off method charged off the account of Samuel Adams in 2016. Adams made full payment in 2017. What account is credited when the account is reinstated?
5. In Blevins Company, the accounts receivable clerk prepares and mails statements to customers, opens mail, and makes a list of receipts, then deposits the cash and approves the write-off of delinquent accounts. Comment on this arrangement of duties.
6. When a specific account is written off under the allowance method, does the net accounts receivable balance increase or decrease? Why?

(Answers to Comprehensive Self Review are on page 546.)

Discussion Questions

1. Explain the purpose of the allowance method of accounting for losses from uncollectible accounts.
2. Name three approaches to estimating losses from uncollectible accounts when the allowance method is used.
3. Suppose that the estimate of uncollectible accounts is based on credit sales and that *Allowance for Doubtful Accounts* has a debit balance before the adjustment is made. Explain how this situation is handled.
4. If a company is interested primarily in matching expenses and revenues each period, would it base its estimate of uncollectible accounts on sales or on accounts receivable? Explain.

5. What is meant by aging the accounts receivable?

6. Under the allowance method, what account is credited in the adjusting entry to record estimated uncollectible accounts?

7. Under the allowance method, what entry is made when a specific customer's account is deemed to be uncollectible?

8. What basic accounting concepts, assumptions, principles, or constraints support the allowance method?

9. Explain how to record the collection of an account receivable in the same year in which it was previously written off if the allowance method of recording estimated doubtful accounts is used.

10. Suppose that the estimate of uncollectible accounts is based on the aging of accounts receivable and that the *Allowance for Uncollectible Accounts* has a credit balance before the adjustment is made. Explain how this situation is handled.

11. How is *Uncollectible Accounts Expense* shown on the income statement?

12. How is *Allowance for Uncollectible Accounts* shown in the balance sheet?

13. Explain the direct charge-off method for recording uncollectible accounts expense.

14. What are the major weaknesses of the direct charge-off method?

15. Under what conditions would the direct charge-off method be appropriate?

16. What entry is made to record an uncollectible account under the direct charge-off method?

17. Under the direct charge-off method, what entry is made when a firm collects an account that was charged off in a prior year?

18. List some duties that should routinely be separated as part of the internal control procedures for accounts receivable.

19. List some common internal controls for accounts receivable.

20. At December 31, 2016, Gaetano Company had accounts receivable of $1,000,000 and an allowance for uncollectible accounts of $5,500. On January 1, 2017, Gaetano Company wrote off a $500 bad debt against the allowance for uncollectible accounts. There were no other accounts receivable transactions on January 1. What is the net realizable value of accounts receivable (a) before the bad debt write-off and (b) after the bad debt write-off?

APPLICATIONS

Exercises

Estimating and recording uncollectible accounts on the basis of net credit sales.

◀ **Exercise 15.1**

Objective 15-1

On December 31, 2016, certain account balances at Galliano Company were as follows before year-end adjustments:

Accounts Receivable	$ 1,873,000
Allowance for Uncollectible Accounts (credit)	3,721
Sales	18,411,000
Sales Returns and Allowances	77,300

A further examination of the records showed that the "Sales" included $1,912,400 million of cash sales during the year. Of the sales returns and allowances, $66,600 came from credit sales. Assume that Galliano Company estimates its losses from uncollectible accounts to be 0.2 percent of net credit sales. Compute the estimated amount of *Uncollectible Accounts Expense* for 2016 and prepare the journal entry to record the provision for uncollectible accounts.

Exercise 15.2
Objective 15-1

▶ **Estimating and recording uncollectible accounts on the basis of accounts receivable when there is a credit balance in *Allowance for Doubtful Accounts*.**

Assume that Galliano Company (Exercise 15.1) makes its estimate of uncollectible accounts on December 31 as 3.2 percent of total accounts receivable. Compute the estimated amount of uncollectible accounts and give the general journal entry to record the provision for uncollectible accounts. (Obtain any information you need from Exercise 15.1.)

Exercise 15.3
Objective 15-1

▶ **Estimating and recording uncollectible accounts on the basis of accounts receivable when there is a debit balance in *Allowance for Doubtful Accounts*.**

On December 31, 2016, before adjusting entries, the balances of selected accounts of the Bayfront Equipment Company were as follows:

Accounts Receivable	930,000
Allowance for Uncollectible Accounts (debit balance)	3,000 dr.

The company has determined that historically about 3.4 percent of accounts receivable are never collected and uses this basis to determine its bad debts provision. Give the journal entry to record the company's estimated loss from uncollectible accounts on December 31.

Exercise 15.4
Objective 15-2

▶ **Recording actual uncollectible amounts under the allowance method.**

On April 30, 2016, Jackson Plumbing, which uses the allowance method, decided that the $3,700 account of Michele Waters was worthless and should be written off. Give the general journal entry to record the write-off.

Exercise 15.5
Objective 15-3

▶ **Recording the collection of an account written off in the same year under the allowance method.**

On December 8, 2016, after a threatened lawsuit by Jackson Plumbing, Waters paid the $3,700 account charged off on April 30, 2016 (Exercise 15.4). Give the entries in general journal form to reinstate Waters's account and to record the receipt of her check.

Exercise 15.6
Objective 15-3

▶ **Recording the collection of an account written off in a prior year under the allowance method.**

Assume the same facts as in Exercise 15.5, except that the recovery of the $3,700 from Waters was received on February 28, 2017. Give the entry in general journal form to record the reinstatement of Waters's account and to record the receipt of her check.

Exercise 15.7
Objective 15-4

▶ **Recording uncollectible accounts using the direct charge-off method.**

Solares Electric Services Company uses the direct charge-off method to record uncollectible accounts. On September 10, 2016, the company learned that Chris Freyer, a customer who owed $840, had moved and left no forwarding address. Solares concluded that no part of the debt was collectible. Prepare the general journal entry to write off the account.

Exercise 15.8
Objective 15-5

▶ **Recording collection of an account previously written off using the direct charge-off method.**

On December 8, 2016, Solares Electric Services Company received a check for $420 from Chris Freyer, whose $840 account was written off on September 10 (Exercise 15.7). In the accompanying letter, Freyer apologized and said he probably would be unable to pay any of the remaining balance. Give the general journal entry necessary (the entry in the cash receipts journal has been made).

Recording collection of an account written off in a prior period under the direct charge-off method.

Exercise 15.9
Objective 15-5

Use the information given in Exercise 15.8, except assume that Solares received the check for $420 on January 28, 2017 (instead of on December 8, 2016). Give the general journal entry necessary. The cash receipt has already been entered in the cash receipts journal.

PROBLEMS

Problem Set A

Estimating and recording uncollectible accounts transactions on the basis of sales.

Problem 15.1A
Objectives 15-1,
15-2, 15-3, 15-4

Montana Leather Products sells leather clothing at both wholesale and retail. The company has found that there is a higher rate of uncollectible accounts from retail credit sales than from wholesale credit sales. Montana computes its estimated loss from uncollectible accounts at the end of each year. The amount is based on the rates of loss that the firm has developed from experience for each division. A separate computation is made for each of the two types of sales. The firm uses the percentage of net credit sales method.

As of December 31, 2016, *Accounts Receivable* has a balance of $402,000, and *Allowance for Doubtful Accounts* has a debit balance of $426. The following table provides a breakdown of the credit sales for the year 2016 and the estimated rates of loss:

Category	Amount	Estimated Rate of Loss
Wholesale	$2,140,000	0.6%
Retail	599,000	1.1

INSTRUCTIONS

1. Compute the estimated amount of uncollectible accounts expense for each of the two categories of net credit sales for the year.

2. Prepare an adjusting entry in general journal form to provide for the estimated uncollectible accounts on December 31, 2016. Use *Uncollectible Accounts Expense.*

3. Show how *Accounts Receivable* and *Allowance for Doubtful Accounts* should appear on the balance sheet of Montana Leather Products as of December 31, 2016.

4. On January 20, 2017, the account receivable of Delphi Clothiers, amounting to $930, is determined to be uncollectible and is to be written off. Record this transaction in the general journal.

5. On November 26, 2017, the attorneys for Montana turned over a check for $930 that they obtained from Delphi Clothiers in settlement of its account, which had been written off on January 20. The money has already been recorded in the cash receipts journal. Give the general journal entry to reverse the original write-off.

Analyze: When the financial statements are prepared for the year ended December 31, 2016, what net accounts receivable should be reported?

Estimating and recording uncollectible account transactions on the basis of accounts receivable.

Problem 15.2A
Objectives 15-1,
15-2, 15-3

The schedule of accounts receivable by age shown on the following page was prepared for the Lucero Company at the end of the firm's fiscal year on December 31, 2016:

LUCERO COMPANY
Schedule of Accounts Receivable by Age
December 31, 2016

Account	Balance	Current	Past Due—Days		
			1–30	31–60	Over 60
Adson, Paul	$ 850.00	$ 850.00			
Allen, Alfred	1,000.00		$ 700.00	$ 300.00	
Ash, John	516.00				$ 516.00
Bae, John	260.00	260.00			
Barker, Kelsie	144.00	94.00	50.00		
Bentley, Maggie	560.00	220.00	250.00	90.00	
Blair, Herman	116.00			74.00	42.00
(All other accts.)	47,054.00	39,576.00	5,000.00	1,536.00	942.00
Totals	$50,500.00	$41,000.00	$6,000.00	$2,000.00	$1,500.00

INSTRUCTIONS

1. Compute the estimated uncollectible accounts at the end of the year using the following rates:

Current	2%
1–30 days past due	4%
31–60 days past due	10%
Over 60 days past due	30%

2. As of December 31, 2016, there is a credit balance of $308 in *Allowance for Doubtful Accounts.* Compute the amount of the adjustment for uncollectible accounts expense that must be made as part of the adjusting entries.

3. In general journal form, record the adjustment for the estimated losses. Use *Uncollectible Accounts Expense* and *Allowance for Doubtful Accounts.*

4. On May 10, 2017 the $516 account receivable of John Ash was recognized as uncollectible. Record this entry.

5. On June 12, 2017, a check for $300 was received from Zeke Martin to apply to his account, which had been written off on November 8, 2016, as uncollectible. Record the reversal of the previous write-off in the general journal. The cash obtained has already been entered in the cash receipts journal.

6. Suppose that instead of aging the accounts receivable, the company estimated the uncollectible accounts to be 2 percent of the total accounts receivable on December 31, 2016. Give the general journal entry to record the adjustment for estimated losses from uncollectible accounts. Assume that *Allowance for Doubtful Accounts* has a credit balance of $308 before the adjusting entry.

Analyze: What impact would the change in estimation method described in Instruction 6 have on the net income for fiscal 2016?

Problem 15.3A ▶ **Using different methods to estimate uncollectible accounts.**

Objective 15-1

The balances of selected accounts of the Simon Company on December 31, 2016, are given below:

Accounts Receivable	$ 950,000
Allowance for Doubtful Accounts (credit)	4,000
Total Sales	10,050,000
Sales Returns and Allowances (total)	250,000

(Credit sales were $8,600,000. Returns and allowances on these sales were $210,000.)

INSTRUCTIONS

1. Compute the amount to be charged to *Uncollectible Accounts Expense* under each of the following different assumptions:

   a. Uncollectible accounts are estimated to be 0.2 percent of net credit sales.

   b. Experience has shown that about 3.2 percent of the accounts receivable will prove worthless.

2. Suppose *Allowance for Doubtful Accounts* has a debit balance of $3,500 instead of a credit balance of $4,000, but all other account balances remain the same. Compute the amount to be charged to *Uncollectible Accounts Expense* under each assumption in item 1.

Analyze: If you were the owner of Simon Company and wished to maximize profits reported for 2016, which method would you prefer to use?

Recording uncollectible account transactions under the direct charge-off method.

◀ **Problem 15.4A**

Objectives 15-1, 15-2, 15-3

Pullman Company records uncollectible accounts expense as they occur. Selected transactions for 2016 and 2017 are described below. The accounts involved in these transactions are *Notes Receivable, Accounts Receivable,* and *Uncollectible Accounts Expense.* Record each transaction in general journal form.

DATE		TRANSACTIONS
2016		
Feb.	7	The $700 account receivable of Anne Baker is determined to be uncollectible and is to be written off.
May	16	Because of the death of Martha Falls, her account receivable of $1,100 is considered uncollectible and is to be written off.
July	2	Received $350 from Anne Baker in partial payment of her account, which had been written off on February 7. The cash obtained has already been recorded in the cash receipts journal. There is doubt that the balance of Baker's account will be collected.
July	29	Received $350 from Anne Baker to complete payment of her account, which had been written off on February 7. The cash obtained has already been recorded in the cash receipts journal.
Aug.	18	The $424 account receivable of David Nye is determined to be uncollectible and is to be written off.
2017		
Sept.	28	Received $550 from the estate of Martha Falls as part of the settlement of affairs. This amount is applicable to the account receivable written off on May 16, 2016. The cash obtained has already been recorded in the cash receipts journal.

Analyze: Based on these transactions, what net uncollectible accounts expense was recorded for the year 2016?

Problem Set B

Estimating and recording uncollectible account transactions on the basis of sales.

◀ **Problem 15.1B**

Objectives 15-1, 15-2, 15-3

The Ideal Plumbing Company provides plumbing installation for both business and individual customers. The company records sales for the two types of customers in separate *Sales* accounts. The company's experience has been that each type of sales has a different rate of losses from uncollectible accounts. Thus, the total that the company charges off for these losses at the end of each accounting period is based on two computations (one computation for each sales account). The firm uses the percentage of net credit sales method.

As of December 31, 2016, *Accounts Receivable* has a balance of $281,500, and *Allowance for Doubtful Accounts* has a credit balance of $600. The following table provides a breakdown of the credit sales by division for the year 2016 and the estimated rates of loss:

Division	Amount	Rate of Loss
Business	$1,800,000	0.4%
Individual	1,200,000	0.9%

INSTRUCTIONS

1. Compute the estimated amount of losses in uncollectible accounts expense for each of the two types of sales for the year.

2. Prepare an adjusting entry in general journal form to provide for the estimated losses from uncollectible accounts. Use *Uncollectible Accounts Expense* and *Allowance for Doubtful Accounts.*

3. Show how *Accounts Receivable* and *Allowance for Doubtful Accounts* should appear on the balance sheet of Ideal Plumbing Company as of December 31, 2016.

4. On January 28, 2017, the account receivable of Fain Enterprises, amounting to $788, is determined to be uncollectible and is to be written off. Record the transaction in general journal form.

5. On June 15, 2017, the attorneys for Ideal Plumbing Company turned over a check for $400 that they obtained from Fain Enterprises in settlement of their account, which had been written off on January 28, 2017. The money has already been entered in the cash receipts journal. Record the general journal entry to reinstate the proper amount of Fain's account.

Analyze: Assume that Ideal Plumbing Company uses a predetermined 7.0 percent rate on total accounts receivable to compute the estimated amount of uncollectible accounts receivable. What would be the amount charged to *Uncollectible Accounts Expense* on December 31, 2016?

Problem 15.2B
Objectives 15-1, 15-2, 15-3

▶ **Estimating and recording uncollectible account transactions on the basis of accounts receivable.**

The schedule of accounts receivable by age shown below was prepared for the Custom Windows Shop at the end of the firm's fiscal year on July 31, 2016:

CUSTOM WINDOWS SHOP **Schedule of Accounts Receivable by Age** **July 31, 2016**					
			Past Due — Days		
Account	**Balance**	**Current**	**1–30**	**31–60**	**Over 60**
Alvarado, Steve	$ 300.00	$ 175.00	$ 125.00		
Brass, Dennis	608.00	120.00	400.00	$ 88.00	
Chang, Charles	196.00	196.00			
Cook, Elaine	38.00	38.00			
Edwards, Brad	632.00			416.00	$ 216.00
Kieffer, Carl	264.00		264.00		
(All other accts.)	14,610.00	8,286.00	3,600.00	1,894.00	830.00
Totals	$16,648.00	$8,815.00	$4,389.00	$2,398.00	$1,046.00

INSTRUCTIONS

1. Compute the estimated uncollectible accounts at the end of the year using these rates:

Current	1%
1–30 days past due	4%
31–60 days past due	14%
Over 60 days past due	40%

2. As of July 31, 2016, there is a debit balance of $310.00 in *Allowance for Doubtful Accounts*. Compute the amount of the adjustment for uncollectible accounts expense that must be made as part of the adjusting entries.

3. In general journal form, record the adjustment for the estimated losses. Use *Uncollectible Accounts Expense* and *Allowance for Doubtful Accounts.*

4. On August 28, 2016, the account receivable of Jorge Urbina, amounting to $182, was recognized as uncollectible. Record this write-off in the general journal.

5. On September 21, 2016, a check for $250 was received from Barry King to apply on his $250 account, which had been written off as uncollectible on December 19, 2015. Record the reversal of the previous write-off in the general journal. The cash obtained has already been entered in the cash receipts journal.

6. Suppose that instead of aging the accounts receivable, the company estimated the uncollectible accounts to be 8 percent of the total accounts receivable on July 31. Assume also that *Allowance for Doubtful Accounts* has a credit balance of $125.00 before the adjusting entry. Give the general journal entry to record the adjustment for estimated losses from uncollectible accounts.

Analyze: Based on the percentages presented in Item 1, what is the average uncollectible rate for all accounts receivable?

Using different methods to estimate uncollectible accounts.

◀ **Problem 15.3B**
**Objectives 15-1,
15-2, 15-3**

The balances of selected accounts of Spartan Sportswear Company on December 31, 2016, are given below. Credit sales totaled $38,480,000. The returns and allowances on these sales were $220,000.

Accounts Receivable	$ 3,620,000
Allowance for Doubtful Accounts	6,120 (credit)
Total Sales	41,400,000
Total Sales Returns and Allowances	282,000

INSTRUCTIONS

1. Compute the amount to be charged to *Uncollectible Accounts Expense* under each of the following different sets of assumptions. Round computations to nearest dollar.

   a. Bad debt losses are estimated to be 0.32 percent of net credit sales.

   b. Experience has shown that about 3.2 percent of the accounts receivable are uncollectible.

2. Suppose that *Allowance for Doubtful Accounts* has a *debit* balance of $6,120 instead of a credit balance of that amount before adjustments, but all other account balances remain the same. Compute the amount to be charged to *Uncollectible Accounts Expense* under each of the assumptions listed in the first instruction.

Analyze: Which method results in the highest uncollectible expense for the period?

Recording transactions related to uncollectible accounts using the direct charge-off method.

◀ **Problem 15.4B**
**Objectives 15-4,
15-5**

Extreme Gamer Software uses the direct charge-off method to account for uncollectible accounts expenses as they occur. Selected transactions for 2016 and 2017 follow. The accounts involved are

Accounts Receivable, Notes Receivable, and *Uncollectible Accounts Expense.* Record each transaction in general journal form.

DATE	TRANSACTIONS
2016	
March 15	Tony Salazar, a credit customer, dies owing the firm $3,000. The account is written off.
April 22	Jared Green, a credit customer who owes the firm $2,000, declares bankruptcy. The amount is considered uncollectible and written off.
June 16	The executor of the estate of Tony Salazar sends the firm $800 in partial settlement of the account written off on March 15. The cash obtained has already been recorded.
July 13	The bankruptcy court sends the firm $1,200 in settlement of the account receivable of Jared Green which was written off on April 22. The cash obtained has already been recorded in the cash receipts journal.
Oct. 8	The account owed by a customer, May Homes, in the amount of $1,350 is determined worthless and is written off.
2017	
Feb. 12	Jared Green pays the remainder of the account that had previously been written off. (See transactions of April 22 and July 13). The cash obtained has already been recorded in the cash receipts journal.

Analyze: When the worksheet is prepared at the end of 2016, what balance should be listed for *Uncollectible Accounts Expense?* Assume that the transactions given are the only transactions that affected the account.

Critical Thinking Problem 15.1

Managing Uncollectible Accounts

The Dream Kitchen is a small chain of kitchen remodeling stores. The company's year-end trial balance on December 31, 2016, included the information shown below:

Accounts Receivable	$990,440
Allowance for Doubtful Accounts (credit)	28,200

Net credit sales for 2016, were $8,900,000. *Allowance for Doubtful Accounts* has not yet been adjusted.

INSTRUCTIONS

1. At the end of 2016, the following additional accounts receivable are deemed uncollectible:

Bob Anderson	$10,800
Suzanne Bennett	2,180
James O'Brian	4,200
Omar Tirado	5,230
Casey Wilk	3,100
Total	$25,510

Prepare the December 31, 2016, journal entry to write off the above accounts. Of the accounts to be charged off, $17,200 are more than 60 days past due, and $8,310 are from 31 to 60 days past due. Post this transaction to the T-accounts for **Accounts Receivable** and **Allowance for Doubtful Accounts.**

2. Assume that the company uses the percentage of sales method to estimate uncollectible accounts expense. After analyzing the prior year's activities, management determined that losses from uncollectible accounts for 2016 should be 0.32 percent of net credit sales. Prepare the necessary adjusting journal entry. Round calculation to nearest dollar.

3. Assume that the company uses the aging of accounts receivable method. The following information was furnished by the credit manager for use in calculating the estimated loss from uncollectible accounts. The balances of accounts were computed prior to the charge-offs in Instruction 1.

Receivable Category	Estimated Loss Rate	Balances of Accounts (before charge-offs)
Current	1%	$810,000
1–30 days past due	5%	90,000
31–60 days past due	10%	49,400
Over 60 days past due	40%	41,040
Total		$990,440

Compute the estimated uncollectible accounts as of December 31, 2016, rounded to the nearest dollar.

4. Prepare the necessary adjusting journal entry to record the estimated uncollectible accounts expense on December 31, using the aging method. Post this entry to the T-accounts for **Accounts Receivable** and **Allowance for Doubtful Accounts.**

Analyze: If a company has used three different methods for estimating uncollectible accounts for the past three years, which basic accounting principle may have been violated? Why?

Critical Thinking Problem 15.2

Credit Decisions and Consequences

Bette Springer is president of Springer Company, a manufacturer of toys for children. For the past 10 years, the company has sold its product both to wholesale and to retail dealers of toys in the northeast United States. Over the years the company has come to know its customers well. While all sales are made on credit, few credit losses have occurred. The company's experience has shown that an annual provision for uncollectible accounts of 0.3 of 1 percent of sales is adequate.

Early in 2016, Springer Company decided to expand and develop a new sales base in the southeastern United States. Springer was pleased when credit sales of $200,000 were achieved in the new territory during the year. To achieve this level of sales and get a foothold in the new territory, though, credit was granted to some customers with lower credit ratings than had been granted in the past. Springer estimated that during the initial period of development, losses from uncollectible accounts would be 3 percent of sales in the new territory.

The credit losses connected with sales in the southeast became apparent by the end of 2016. The following losses from new territory customers had been identified before year-end:

1. On September 30, it was determined that nothing could be collected from Portsmouth Toy Outlets which owed Springer $22,000. The account was written off.

2. On December 10, another new customer, Youth Fun Shops, which owed Springer $50,000, entered receivership. On that date Springer was offered, and accepted, a check for $27,500 in final settlement of the debt. The balance was charged off.

3. On December 18, Magic Toys went out of business and no collection of the $6,700 owed Springer is anticipated. The account was charged off.

The following additional information about the old territory became available on December 31:

■ Sales in the old territory totaled $6,280,000 in 2016.

■ Accounts receivable of $22,600 attributed to customers in the old sales territory were determined to be uncollectible and were written off.

INSTRUCTIONS

1. Record in general journal entries the transactions described above for Springer Company. All sales are on account. Use date of December 31 to make the entry to summarize sales for the year and to record uncollectible accounts in the old territory.

2. Give the entry on December 31 to record uncollectible accounts expense for 2016, for both territories. Make the calculation using the percentages developed by Springer.

3. Assume that the *Allowance for Uncollectible Accounts* had a credit balance of $6,200 on September 30 before any of the above entries were made. Calculate the balance in the allowance account after all of the above entries have been posted.

Analyze: Was Springer's provision for losses from uncollectible accounts adequate? Explain.

BUSINESS CONNECTIONS

Managerial FOCUS

Uncollectible Accounts

1. Why would managers use the allowance method for recording uncollectible accounts instead of the direct charge-off method?

2. Should the sales department be given final authority for approving credit applications? Why?

3. Why is an account receivable that was written off as uncollectible reinstated if it is later collected?

4. Why does management separate the authority to charge off uncollectible accounts from the authority to receive customers' cash?

Ethical DILEMMA

Percent Uncollectible

Historical data should be used to determine the percentage for uncollectible account expense. The higher the percentage, the lower the net income and the lower the income tax. Jitters Corporation, a coffee distributor, has historical data that indicate 5 percent of its sales will become uncollectible. This has been a great year for Jitters. Jitters would like to record additional uncollectible account expenses to provide a "cushion" in the Allowance for Uncollectible Accounts in case next year's results are not as good as the current year. Jitters has decided to increase the percentage for uncollectibles to 9 percent because of the high sales volume. This will increase the uncollectible account expense and thus reduce the uncollectible account expense next year. Is this ethical? If not, what would be a preferred action?

Financial Statement ANALYSIS

Balance Sheet

McCormick and Company, Incorporated reported the following in its *2012 Annual Report:*

Consolidated Balance Sheets at November 30, 2012 (millions)		
	2012	*2011*
Trade accounts receivable, less allowances of $4.0 for 2012 and $4.5 for 2011	$465.9	$427.0
Total current assets	$1,285.4	$1,222.9

Analyze:

1. What were total trade accounts receivable at November 30, 2012, before the allowance was deducted?

2. Compute the percentage increase in trade accounts receivable, less allowance, from 2011 to 2012 reported on the consolidated balance sheet.

3. What percentage of total current assets on November 30, 2012, are made up of trade accounts receivable, less allowance?

Life of an Invoice

In small groups, create a scenario for the life of an invoice. How does a sale become an uncollectible? Start at the sale of a product, when it became uncollectible, and then finally paid. Present each account receivable scenario to the class. Be sure to include all the journal entries.

Commercial Credit

The ability to buy products and services for your business on credit is important to its cash flow. Go to the Dun and Bradstreet website at www.dnb.com. Select *Business Credit, My Business Credit,* then *Credit Resource Center.* Find out the importance of commercial credit.

Answers to **Self Reviews**

Answers to Section 1 Self Review

1. Matching principle
2. $57,000 (1% $\times$ $5,700,000)
3. $22,400 ($21,600 + $800)
4. (a) Debit *Accounts Receivable* and Barrington's account in the *Accounts Receivable* ledger, $450; credit *Allowance for Doubtful Accounts,* $450. (b) Debit *Cash* and credit *Accounts Receivable* (and Barrington's account in the subsidiary ledger), $450.
5. Same as in answer 4.
6. The increasing ratio of allowance to accounts receivable suggests that the rate being used is greater than needed and should be reduced.
7. No. Nothing has happened to validate such an entry. However, every effort should be made to collect the account. The customer has the money and should be able to pay.

Answers to Section 2 Self Review

1. The method does not match revenues and expenses. It does not provide a realistic valuation of receivables and it does not comply with GAAP.
2. *Uncollectible Accounts Expense* is debited. The write-off decreases net income and assets.
3. Under the direct method, reinstatement of a charge-off in the same year as the charge-off is credited to *Uncollectible Accounts Expense.* If recovery is in later years, *Uncollectible Accounts Recovered* is credited.
4. *Uncollectible Accounts Expense* is debited for $600. *Accounts Receivable* and Diamond's subsidiary ledger account are credited for $600.
5. *Allowance for Doubtful Accounts* is debited and *Accounts Receivable* and Diamond's subsidiary ledger account are credited.
6. Generally, the sales department should not have final authority on granting credit because there is a conflict of interest. In order to increase sales, the sales department may be inclined to grant credit to less qualified applicants.
7. It appears that the uncollectible accounts are not material. The present method is much simpler and less time-consuming, and is required for federal income tax purposes.

Answers to Comprehensive Self Review

1. *Allowance for Doubtful Accounts*
2. Allowance method is generally accepted.
3. The direct charge-off method
4. *Uncollectible Accounts Recovered*
5. This is an unsatisfactory arrangement because it places in the hands of one person the opportunity to misappropriate funds and cover it up in the accounting records without detection by others.
6. Remains the same. The debit to *Allowance for Doubtful Accounts* offsets the credit to *Accounts Receivable.*

Notes Payable and Notes Receivable

Bank of America
www.bankofamerica.com

When a business wants to buy something, but doesn't have the immediate cash necessary to make the purchase, it may need to borrow money in order to accomplish its goals. That is where companies like Bank of America get involved.

Bank of America is one of the world's largest financial institutions, serving more than 59 million retail customers, individual investors, and large corporate clients. Bank of America is the largest overall Small Business Administration (SBA) lender in the United States. The corporation provides a diversified range of banking and nonbanking financial services and products domestically and internationally. Customers are connecting everyday with Bank of America's expertise so that they can get more of the solutions they need to be successful.

As the largest lender in the United States during the worst recession in 70 years, Bank of America has faced numerous challenges. Looking across every customer group they serve—whether a retail customer, a small business, or a large corporate client—the company works to maintain and build strong relationships, and this strategy is driving results. Their financial results for 2012 show the clear progress made by the company as they continue to put the nationwide mortgage issues behind them. The company earned $4.2 billion in 2012 compared to earnings of $1.4 billion in 2011 and their prospects for future improvements are great.

thinking critically
If a small business needs to borrow money, what considerations do they need to think about before they borrow the money?

LEARNING OBJECTIVES

16-1. Determine whether an instrument meets all the requirements of negotiability.

16-2. Calculate the interest on a note.

16-3. Determine the maturity date of a note.

16-4. Record routine notes payable transactions.

16-5. Record discounted notes payable transactions.

16-6. Record routine notes receivable transactions.

16-7. Compute the proceeds from a discounted note receivable, and record transactions related to discounting of notes receivable.

16-8. Understand how to use bank drafts and trade acceptances and how to record transactions related to those instruments.

16-9. Define the accounting terms new to this chapter.

NEW TERMS

bank draft
banker's year
bill of lading
cashier's check
commercial draft
contingent liability
discounting
draft
face value

interest
maturity value
negotiable instrument
note payable
note receivable
principal
sight draft
time draft
trade acceptance

Accounting for Notes Payable

In this chapter, you will learn about negotiable instruments, in particular, promissory notes.

>> **16-1. OBJECTIVE**
Determine whether an instrument meets all the requirements of negotiability.

Negotiable Instruments

The law covering negotiable instruments is a part of the Uniform Commercial Code (UCC). The UCC has been adopted by all of the states. A **negotiable instrument** is a financial document, containing a promise or order to pay, that meets all the requirements of the UCC in order to be transferable to another party. The UCC requirements specify that to be negotiable an instrument must:

- be in writing and must be signed by the maker or drawer,
- contain an unconditional promise or order to pay a definite amount of money,
- be payable either on demand or at a future time that is fixed or that can be determined,
- be payable to the order of a specific person or to the bearer,
- clearly name or identify the drawee if addressed to a drawee.

Checks are negotiable instruments. Another important negotiable instrument is the promissory note. Promissory notes may be either notes payable or notes receivable.

FIGURE 16.1   Promissory Note

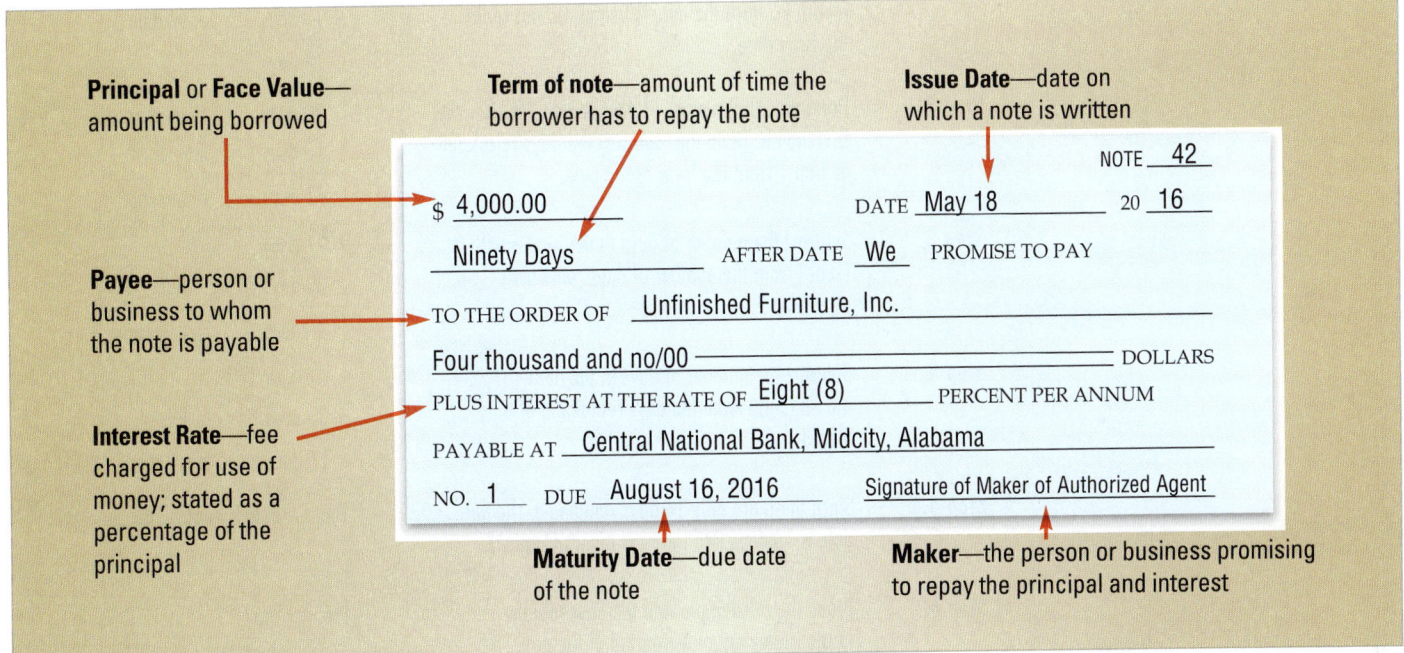

Notes Payable

On May 18, 2016, Kathy's Kitchens purchased store equipment for $4,000 from Unfinished Furniture, Inc. The supplier agreed to accept payment in 90 days if Kathy Kaymark, the owner, signed the promissory note shown in Figure 16.1. A promissory note is a written promise to pay a certain amount of money at a specific future time. For Unfinished Furniture, Inc., the promissory note provides more legal protection than an account payable.

The promissory note is a negotiable instrument. It is in writing and signed by Kathy Kaymark, owner of Kathy's Kitchens. It is an unconditional promise to pay a definite sum, $4,000. It is payable on a date that can be determined exactly, 90 days after May 18. It is payable to a specific party, Unfinished Furniture, Inc. Although not necessary for negotiability, the note specifies a rate of interest, 8 percent. The maturity value of this note is $4,080.

CALCULATING THE INTEREST ON A NOTE

>> **16-2. OBJECTIVE**
Calculate the interest on a note.

Interest is the fee charged for the use of money. Interest is calculated using the following formula:

$$\text{Interest} = \text{Principal} \times \text{Rate} \times \text{Time}$$

The time period is indicated in fractions of a year. A 360-day period, called a **banker's year,** is used for simplicity to calculate interest on a note. Interest on the note in Figure 16.1 is $80 ($4,000 × 0.08 × 90/360). The note in Figure 16.1 shows a $4,000 amount, called the **principal, face value,** or *face amount.* The **maturity value** is the total amount (principal plus interest) that must be paid when a note comes due. For the note in Figure 16.1, the maturity value is $4,080 ($4,000 + $80).

CALCULATING THE MATURITY DATE OF A NOTE

>> **16-3. OBJECTIVE**
Determine the maturity date of a note.

A note's maturity date is the number of days from the date of issue until it is due. The issue date itself is not counted. For example, a 30-day note issued on January 1 matures on January 31, 30 days after January 1. Let's find the maturity date for the note in Figure 16.1.

Step 1.	Determine the number of days remaining in the month in which the note is issued. Do not count the issue date.	31 days in May −18 days issue date ――― 13 days
Step 2.	Determine the number of days remaining after the first month. To do this, subtract the days calculated in Step 1 from the term of the note.	90 days term of note −13 days May days ――― 77 days remaining
Step 3.	Subtract the number of days in the next month (June) from the number of days remaining after Step 2.	77 days −30 days in June ――― 47 days remaining
Step 4.	Subtract the number of days in the next month (July) from the days remaining after Step 3.	47 days −31 days in July ――― 16 days remaining
Step 5.	Since there are only 16 days remaining, the due date is 16 days into the next month (August).	The due date is August 16.
Step 6.	Prove the calculation. Add the days together to see if they equal the period of the note.	Proof: May 13 days June 30 days July 31 days August 16 days ――― Total 90 days

Sometimes the term of a note is described in months instead of days. In this case, the maturity date is determined by counting ahead to the same date of the following month or months. For example, a three-month note issued on May 18 is due on August 18, regardless of the number of days in the period. If a note is issued at the end of a month, and there is no corresponding date in the month due, then the note is due on the first day of the following month. For example, a six-month note issued on August 30 should mature on February 30. Since there is no February 30, the note matures on March 1.

>> 16-4. OBJECTIVE

Record routine notes payable transactions.

RECORDING THE ISSUANCE OF A NOTE PAYABLE

A **note payable** is a liability that represents a written promise by the maker of the note (the debtor) to pay another party (the creditor) a specified amount at a specified future date. The following shows how Kathy's Kitchens records the May 18 transaction to issue a 90-day, $4,000 note payable at 8 percent annual interest to purchase store equipment:

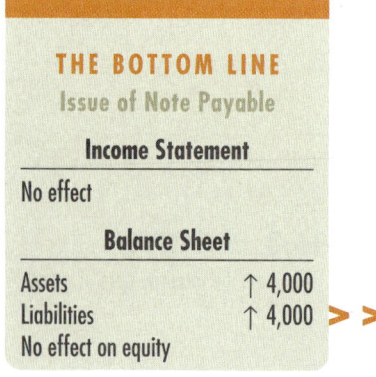

THE BOTTOM LINE

Issue of Note Payable

Income Statement

No effect

Balance Sheet

Assets   ↑ 4,000
Liabilities   ↑ 4,000
No effect on equity

>>

	GENERAL JOURNAL		PAGE ___3___		
DATE	DESCRIPTION	POST. REF.	DEBIT	CREDIT	
2016					1
May 18	Store Equipment		4 0 0 0 00		6
	Notes Payable—Trade			4 0 0 0 00	7
	Issued note payable to Unfinished				8
	Furniture, Inc., for purchase of store				9
	equipment				10

RECORDING PAYMENT OF A NOTE AND INTEREST

On the maturity date, August 16, Kathy's Kitchens pays the $4,000 principal plus the $80 in interest. This transaction is recorded as follows:

					GENERAL JOURNAL					PAGE ___6___		

	DATE		DESCRIPTION	POST. REF.	DEBIT	CREDIT	
1	2016						1
11	Aug	16	Notes Payable—Trade		4 000 00		11
12			Interest Expense		80 00		12
13			Cash			4 080 00	13
14			Payment of May 18 note to				14
15			Unfinished Furniture, Inc.,				15

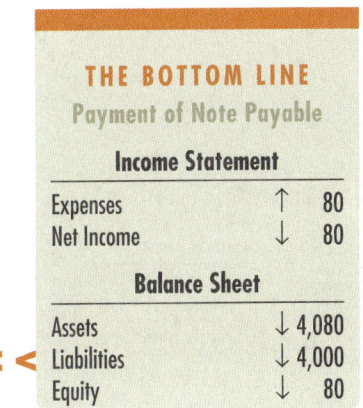

THE BOTTOM LINE
Payment of Note Payable

Income Statement

Expenses	↑	80
Net Income	↓	80

Balance Sheet

Assets	↓	4,080
Liabilities	↓	4,000
Equity	↓	80

RENEWING OR MAKING A PARTIAL PAYMENT ON A NOTE

If the issuer of a note asks and receives an extension to the maturity date, no additional accounting entries are required. On the extended maturity date, an entry is made to record payment of the note and interest for the entire period of the debt.

Sometimes at the maturity date only part of the note is paid. The partial payment is shown on the existing note, or the existing note is canceled and a new note is issued for the balance.

RECORDING THE ISSUANCE OF A DISCOUNTED NOTE PAYABLE

>> **16-5. OBJECTIVE**
Record discounted notes payable transactions.

Businesses often borrow money from banks and sign notes payable as evidence of the debts. Banks always charge interest on loans. For some promissory notes, such as the one to Unfinished Furniture, Inc., in Figure 16.1, interest is paid on the maturity date. The interest on a bank loan is usually paid at maturity. Often, however, the bank deducts the interest in advance, and the borrower receives only the difference between the face amount of the note and the interest on it to maturity. This practice of deducting the interest in advance from the principal on a note payable is called **discounting.**

On June 1, Kathy's Kitchens signed a $10,000, 6 percent, 60-day note payable with the bank. The note was issued at a discount. The interest is $100.

$$\text{Interest} = \text{Principal} \times \text{Rate} \times \text{Time}$$
$$\$100 = \$10,000 \times 0.06 \times (60/360)$$

The bank deducted the $100 interest from the face amount of the note, and Kathy's Kitchens received $9,900 ($10,000 − $100).

Kathy's Kitchens uses two note payable accounts—one for notes to vendors and the other for notes to the bank. The transaction is recorded as follows:

					GENERAL JOURNAL					PAGE ___5___		

	DATE		DESCRIPTION	POST. REF.	DEBIT	CREDIT	
1	2016						1
2	June	1	Cash		9 900 00		2
3			Interest Expense		100 00		3
4			Notes Payable—Bank			10 000 00	4
5			To record note payable issued at				5
6			a discount				6
7							7

THE BOTTOM LINE
Issue of Discounted Note Payable

Income Statement

Expenses	↑	100
Net Income	↓	100

Balance Sheet

Assets	↑	9,900
Liabilities	↑	10,000
Equity	↓	100

RECORDING THE PAYMENT OF A DISCOUNTED NOTE PAYABLE

At maturity, July 31, Kathy's Kitchens prepares a check for $10,000 to pay the note. There is no entry for interest expense because interest was paid and recorded when the note was issued. The entry is recorded as follows:

GENERAL JOURNAL   PAGE ___6___

	DATE		DESCRIPTION	POST. REF.	DEBIT	CREDIT	
1	2016						1
33	July	31	Notes Payable—Bank		10 000 00		33
34			Cash			10 000 00	34
35			Record payment of note				35
36							36

>>

USING A NOTES PAYABLE REGISTER

If a business issues many notes payable, it is convenient to maintain a notes payable register. The notes payable register shows the important information about each note payable on a single line.

At the end of each accounting period, a schedule of notes payable is prepared from the information in the notes payable register. The schedule of notes payable must agree with the *Notes Payable* account in the general ledger.

For each note payable, the notes payable register shows the following information:

- the issue date,
- the payee,
- where the note is payable,
- the term of the note,
- the maturity date,
- the face amount,
- the interest rate, if any,
- the interest amount, if any.

REPORTING NOTES PAYABLE AND INTEREST EXPENSE

Notes payable represent financial obligations of the business. They appear on the balance sheet as liabilities.

- Notes due within one year are classified as current liabilities.
- Notes due in more than one year are classified as long-term liabilities.

The notes presented in this chapter are current liabilities. Long-term liabilities are discussed in Chapter 22.

Interest expense appears on the income statement as a nonoperating expense. It is listed in the Other Income and Expenses section and is deducted from Income from Operations as follows:

Sales	$550,000
Cost of Goods Sold	(320,000)
Gross Profit on Sales	230,000
Operating Expenses	(164,000)
Income from Operations	66,000
Other Income and Expenses	
Interest Expense	(1,800)
Net Income	$ 64,200

Section 1   Self Review

QUESTIONS

1. What is the maturity date of a 120-day note issued on April 10?

2. What is the interest due on a note for $12,000 at 8 percent for 75 days?

3. How much cash will the borrower receive for a $12,000, 75 day, noninterest-bearing note discounted at 8 percent?

EXERCISES

4. Which of the following is not required for an instrument to be negotiable?

   a. It must be payable on demand or at a fixed or determinable date.

   b. It must contain an unconditional promise or order to pay a definite amount.

   c. It must be in writing.

   d. All of the above are required.

5. The total to be received when a note receivable is due is known as the:

   a. principal

   b. maturity value

   c. interest

   d. face value

ANALYSIS

6. Refer to Questions 1 and 2. Is the effective interest rate in each of these two situations identical? Explain.

(Answers to Section 1 Self Review are on pages 570–571.)

>> **16-6.** Record routine notes receivable transactions.

WHY IT'S IMPORTANT

Many businesses accept notes receivable from customers to purchase goods or to replace existing accounts receivable.

>> **16-7.** Compute the proceeds from a discounted note receivable, and record transactions related to discounting of notes receivable.

WHY IT'S IMPORTANT

Businesses can raise cash by discounting notes receivable at the bank.

>> **16-8.** Understand how to use bank drafts and trade acceptances and how to record transactions related to those instruments.

WHY IT'S IMPORTANT

Various financial instruments are used because they provide flexibility in cash management.

bank draft
bill of lading
cashier's check
commercial draft
contingent liability
draft
note receivable
sight draft
time draft
trade acceptance

Accounting for Notes Receivable

Section 1 discussed promissory notes from the debtor's perspective. This section considers the creditor's perspective.

Notes Receivable

Some businesses allow customers to issue a promissory note to finance the purchase of goods. Sometimes a business requires a customer with an overdue account to sign a promissory note for the account balance. In these cases, the promissory note is classified as a **note receivable,** which is an asset that represents a creditor's written promise to pay a specified amount at a specified future date. There are many similarities between notes payable and notes receivable. Of course, the journal entries are different.

NONINTEREST-BEARING NOTES RECEIVABLE

Customer Isabel Huang owes $1,500 to Kathy's Kitchens. The account is overdue, and Huang needs more time to pay. On September 18, Huang signs a 30-day, noninterest-bearing note for $1,500. In the event legal action becomes necessary, the note provides additional protection to Kathy's Kitchens.

1	2016					1
2	Sept.	18	Notes Receivable	1 5 0 0 00		2
3			Accounts Receivable/Isabel Huang		1 5 0 0 00	3
4			To record 30-day note receivable to			4
5			replace an overdue account receivable			5

The maturity date of the note is October 18.

Days note is issued in September (30 − 18)	12 days
Days in October	18 days
Duration of note (proof)	30 days

At maturity when Huang pays the note, the entry in the cash receipts journal is a debit to *Cash* and a credit to *Notes Receivable.* Huang's note is marked "Paid" and returned to her.

INTEREST-BEARING NOTES RECEIVABLE

>> 16-6. OBJECTIVE
Record routine notes receivable transactions.

Customers who do not pay their bills when due are expected to pay interest. Normally, promissory notes issued to replace overdue accounts are interest bearing. Interest on notes is generally paid at the maturity date. On June 12, Kathy's Kitchens accepted a 60-day, 10 percent note for $1,200 from John Woods to replace his past-due account. The transaction is recorded as follows:

1	2016				1
2	June	12	Notes Receivable	1 200 00	2
3			Accounts Receivable/John Woods	1 200 00	3
4			To record 60-day note receivable to		4
5			replace an overdue account receivable		5

The maturity date of the note is August 11.

Days note is issued in June (30 − 12)	18 days
Days in July	31 days
Total days to the end of July	49 days
Days in August to maturity (60 − 49 = 11)	11 days
Duration of note (proof)	60 days

The interest on $1,200 for 60 days at 10 percent is $20 ($1,200 × 0.10 × 60/360). Woods's payment of the note on the maturity date will include the $1,200 face amount of the note plus $20 interest. The payment would be recorded as follows:

1	2016					1
2	Aug.	11	Cash	1 220 00		2
3			Notes Receivable		1 200 00	3
4			Interest Income		20 00	4
5			Collection of John Woods's note			5
6			receivable			6

NOTES RECEIVABLE—SPECIAL SITUATIONS

Accountants must know how to record notes receivable for special situations.

Accounting for Partial Collection of a Note On August 11, Kathy's Kitchens learned that John Woods could pay only half the $1,200 note receivable. Kathy's Kitchens agreed to extend the due date for another 30 days for half the principal, $600. Kathy's Kitchens accepted payment of $20 interest and $600 principal. Partial payments are applied first to interest and then to principal. The journal entry to record the transaction is as follows:

1	2016					1
2	Aug.	11	Cash	620 00		2
3			Notes Receivable		600 00	3
4			Interest Income		20 00	4
5			Collection of interest and one-half			5
6			of John Woods's note; balance renewed			6
7			for 30 days			7

The original note can be endorsed to reflect the partial payment and the new maturity date, or Kathy's Kitchens can cancel the original note and ask John Woods to sign a new interest-bearing note for $600.

Note Receivable Not Collected at Maturity

If a note is not paid at maturity and there are no arrangements for renewal, the note is said to be "dishonored." Dishonored notes do not belong in the *Notes Receivable* account. If John Woods dishonored the original $1,200 note, the entry to transfer the balance out of *Notes Receivable* and back to *Accounts Receivable* would be as follows:

1	2016				1
2	Aug.	11	Accounts Receivable/John Woods	1 2 2 0 00	2
3			Notes Receivable	1 2 0 0 00	3
4			Interest Income	2 0 00	4
5			To charge back Woods's dishonored		5
6			note plus interest to maturity		6

Note that Woods now owes the original balance of $1,200 plus $20 interest on the note. After a note is dishonored, interest continues to accrue on the note. The interest rate is usually specified by law. In most cases, it is higher than the rate shown on the note, although the parties may agree on a rate different from the statutory rate. Promissory notes usually require the maker to pay attorney's fees and all other costs incurred by the holder for efforts to collect the note.

Notes Received at the Time of a Sale

Sometimes Kathy's Kitchens asks a customer to sign a promissory note at the time of sale. The transaction is recorded in the general journal as follows:

1	2016				1
2	Aug.	15	Notes Receivable	3 0 0 0 00	2
3			Sales	3 0 0 0 00	3
4			Received 60-day, 9% note from		4
5			Sylvia Montes on sale of goods		5

If a business routinely receives notes from customers at the time of sale, the transactions are recorded in a special Notes Receivable column of the sales journal.

DISCOUNTING A NOTE RECEIVABLE

A note receivable is an asset. At maturity date, the holder will receive cash for the note receivable. If the holder wants cash before the maturity date, the note can be discounted (sold) at the bank. The bank pays the holder the maturity value (principal plus any interest) minus the discount charge.

Noninterest-Bearing Note Receivable Discounted

On September 18, Kathy's Kitchens needed cash to pay some bills. Kathy Kaymark decided to discount a 90-day, noninterest-bearing note receivable for $3,000 that the business received from John Nguyen on July 20. The maturity date of the note is October 18.

Days note is issued in July (31 − 20)	11 days
Days in August	31 days
Days in September	30 days
Total days to the end of September	72 days
Days in October to maturity (90 − 72)	18 days
Duration of note (proof)	90 days

On September 18, Kathy's Kitchens discounts the note at Central National Bank. The bank's discount rate is 10 percent.

Calculating the Discount and the Proceeds The steps to determine the discount and the proceeds on notes receivable follow:

>> 16-7. OBJECTIVE
Compute the proceeds from a discounted note receivable, and record transactions related to discounting of notes receivable.

Step 1. *Determine the maturity value of the note.* Since the note from Nguyen is noninterest-bearing, its maturity value and face amount are the same, $3,000.

Step 2. *Calculate the number of days in the discount period.* The discount period is the number of days from the discount date to the maturity date. The discount period is 30 days.

Days note is discounted in September (30 − 18)	12 days
Days in October until maturity	18 days
Total days in discount period	30 days

Step 3. *Compute the discount charged by the bank.* The discount formula is similar to the interest formula. The time is the number of days in the discount period. The discount is $20.

$$\text{Discount} = \text{Maturity Value} \times \text{Discount Rate} \times \text{Discount Period}$$
$$\$25 \quad = \quad \$3,000 \quad \times \quad 0.10 \quad \times \quad (30/360)$$

Step 4. *Calculate the proceeds,* the amount received from the bank. This is the maturity value of the note less the discount, $2,975 ($3,000 − $25).

Kathy's Kitchens received cash for the note 30 days before the note matured in exchange for a discount fee of $25.

The discount is debited to *Interest Expense.* The credit is to *Notes Receivable—Discounted,* a contra asset account. The following is the journal entry to record the discounting of the note receivable:

1	2016					1
2	Sept.	18	Cash	2 9 7 5 00		2
3			Interest Expense	2 5 00		3
4			Notes Receivable—Discounted		3 0 0 0 00	4
5			To record discounting of			5
6			John Nguyen note			6

Contingent Liability for a Discounted Note When a note receivable is discounted, the party discounting the note endorses it. If the maker (Nguyen) does not pay the note at maturity, the bank can obtain payment from the endorser (Kathy's Kitchens). Hence Kathy's Kitchens has a contingent liability of $3,000. A **contingent liability** can become a liability if certain things happen. Contingent liabilities are shown on the financial statements so that the users are aware that the business might have a liability in the future. The contingent liability for discounted notes receivable appears on the balance sheet as follows:

Notes Receivable	$7,400
Notes Receivable — Discounted	(3,000)
Net Notes Receivable	$4,400

Another common way to show contingent liabilities is to present the net notes receivable on the balance sheet and to include a note with the information about the discounted notes receivable.

Discounted Noninterest-Bearing Note Receivable at Maturity If on October 18, the maturity date, Nguyen pays the note, Kathy's Kitchens is no longer contingently liable for the note. The following journal entry removes the asset and the contingent liability:

1	2016				1
2	Oct.	18	Notes Receivable—Discounted	3 0 0 0 00	2
3			Notes Receivable	3 0 0 0 00	3
4			Record payment of discounted note		4
5			of John Nguyen		5

Suppose on October 18 Nguyen dishonored the note by not paying it. The bank filed a formal protest. Kathy's Kitchens became liable to the bank for the maturity value of the note plus a protest fee. Central National Bank deducted the note ($3,000) and the protest fee ($30) from the checking account for Kathy's Kitchens. The bank sent a debit memorandum with the dishonored note and the protest form to Kathy's Kitchens. The journal entries to record this transaction are as follows:

■ Record the amount owed by Nguyen including the protest fee. Debit *Accounts Receivable/ John Nguyen* for $3,030 and credit *Cash* for $3,030.

■ Debit *Notes Receivable—Discounted* for $3,000 and credit *Notes Receivable* for $3,000.

Kathy's Kitchens contacted Nguyen and asked for payment of the note. Payment was not received, so Kathy's Kitchens turned the note over to an attorney for collection.

Interest-Bearing Note Receivable Discounted

Kathy Kaymark discounted another note receivable in order to meet cash needs. The $1,800, 90-day, 6 percent note was received from Kim Myers on September 29. The maturity date of the note is December 28.

Calculating the Discount and the Proceeds

On November 28, Kathy's Kitchens discounted Myers's note at the bank at 10 percent. The steps to compute the discount and the proceeds on the note receivable follow:

Step 1. *Determine the maturity value of the note.* The interest is $27 ($1,800 × 0.06 × 90/360). The maturity value is the principal and interest, $1,827 ($1,800 + $27).

Step 2. *Calculate the number of days in the discount period.* The discount period is 30 days.

Days note is discounted in November (30 − 28)	2 days
Days in December until maturity	28 days
Total days in discount period	30 days

Step 3. *Compute the discount charged by the bank.* The bank charges $15.23, 10 percent of the maturity value for the discount period ($1,827 × 0.10 × 30/360).

Step 4. *Calculate the proceeds.* The proceeds are $1,811.77, the maturity value minus the discount ($1,827.00 − $15.23).

Interest income of $11.77 will be recorded. This represents the total interest used to compute the maturity value, minus the discount charged by the bank ($27.00 − $15.23 = $11.77). It also reflects the amount by which the proceeds from discounting the note exceeds the principal of the note ($1,811.77 − $1,800.00 = $11.77).

GENERAL JOURNAL   PAGE ___10___

	DATE		DESCRIPTION	POST. REF.	DEBIT	CREDIT	
1	2016						1
32	Nov.	28	Cash		1 8 1 1 77		32
33			Notes Receivable—Discounted			1 8 0 0 00	33
34			Interest Income			1 1 77	34
35			To record discounting of Kim				35
36			Myers's note				36

The amount received from discounting an interest-bearing note may be less than the face value of the note. In that event, **Interest Expense** would be debited for the difference. For example, if the discount rate charged by the bank when the Myers note, above, was discounted on November 28 is 20 percent, the discount would be $30.45 ($1,827 × .20 × 30/360), and the proceeds would have been $1,796.55 ($1,827.00 − $30.45). Here is the necessary entry:

1	2016			
2	Nov. 28	Cash	1 796 55	
3		Interest Expense	3 45	
4		Notes Receivable—Discounted		1 800 00
5		To record discounting of Myers's note		
6				

Maturity of Discounted Interest-Bearing Note Receivable If the maker of a note receivable that has been discounted pays the holder of the note at maturity, the contingent liability of the endorser is ended. The endorser completely removes the note from the accounts. For example, if on the maturity date, December 28, Myers pays the Central National Bank, the entry below would be made:

1	2016			
2	Dec. 28	Notes Receivable—Discounted	1 800 00	
3		Notes Receivable		1 800 00
4		To record payment by Myers of discounted		
5		note receivable		

If Myers dishonors the discounted note on December 28, the bank will deduct from Kathy's account the maturity value of the note, plus a small service fee—$25 in this example. Kathy's Kitchens would again remove the note from the accounts by debiting **Notes Receivable—Discounted** and crediting **Notes Receivable.** In addition, the entire amount that the bank deducted from Kathy's account would be charged back to **Accounts Receivable** and to Myers's account ($1,827 maturity value + $25 fee).

1	2016			
2	Dec. 28	Notes Receivable—Discounted	1 800 00	
3		Accounts Receivable/Kim Myers	1 852 00	
4		Notes Receivable		1 800 00
5		Cash		1 852 00
6		To record dishonor of note by Myers		

THE NOTES RECEIVABLE REGISTER

If a firm has many notes receivable, it is convenient to maintain a notes receivable register. For each note, the notes receivable register shows the date of the note, the maker, where the note is payable, the duration, the maturity date, the face amount, the rate of interest, and the amount of interest. For each discounted note, the register also shows the discount date and the bank holding the note.

REPORTING NOTES RECEIVABLE AND INTEREST INCOME

Notes receivable appear on the balance sheet as assets.

- Notes that mature within one year are classified as current assets.
- Notes that mature in more than one year are classified as long-term assets.

The contra asset account **Notes Receivable—Discounted** appears as a deduction from **Notes Receivable.**

> Presentation of information in the balance sheet about notes payable and other liabilities varies widely from company to company. For example, a balance sheet prepared for SEC filing by Caterpillar, Inc., for December 31, 2012, showed total current liabilities of $29.7 billion. This number included $11.4 billion of "Short-Term Borrowings." Presumably this number includes notes payable and other forms of short-term obligations.

Interest income is classified as nonoperating income. It is listed in the Other Income and Expenses section of the income statement and is added to income from operations. The discount charged for discounting notes is shown as interest expense in the Other Income and Expenses section and is deducted from income from operations. The income statement for a business that received and paid interest follows:

Sales		$550,000
Cost of Goods Sold		(320,000)
Gross Profit on Sales		230,000
Operating Expenses		(164,000)
Income from Operations		66,000
Other Income and Expenses		
Interest Income	$1,800	
Interest Expense	(2,350)	(550)
Net Income		$ 65,450

Drafts and Acceptances

Negotiable instruments include drafts and acceptances.

DRAFTS

>> 16-8. OBJECTIVE
Understand how to use bank drafts and trade acceptances and how to record transactions related to those instruments.

A **draft** is a written order that requires one party (a person or business) to pay a stated sum of money to another party. A check is one type of draft. Other types are bank drafts and commercial drafts.

Bank Drafts A **bank draft** is a check written by a bank that orders another bank to pay the stated amount to a specific party. A bank draft is more readily accepted than a personal or business check. Bank drafts are used to pay debts to suppliers with whom credit has not been established.

A **cashier's check** is a draft on the issuing bank's own funds. Cashier's checks are sometimes used to pay bills. For the creditor, a cashier's check offers more protection than a business or personal check.

The business pays for the bank draft or cashier's check by issuing a business check to cover the amount of the draft or cashier's check plus the service charge.

On May 18, Kathy's Kitchens purchased a $1,412 bank draft and sent it to Home Supplies, Inc., to pay an overdue account payable to that company. The service charge for the bank draft was $12. The journal entry to record the transaction is as follows:

1	2016				1
2	May	18	Accounts Payable/Home Supplies, Inc.	1 4 0 0 00	2
3			Miscellaneous Bank Expense	1 2 00	3
4			Cash	1 4 1 2 00	4
5			To record payment of past-due		5
6			account and bank charge with draft		6

MANAGERIAL IMPLICATIONS <<

NEGOTIABLE INSTRUMENTS

- Because notes payable and notes receivable are negotiable instruments, they fall under the rules and regulations of the Uniform Commercial Code. Management needs to understand the rights, responsibilities, and obligations of the business for negotiable instruments.

- Management should carefully control and limit borrowing to minimize the interest charged for the use of funds.

- In a well-run business, managers ensure the prompt payment of debts to minimize interest expense and to maintain the company's credit rating.

- Management authorizes specific individuals to approve the use of debt.

- When cash is needed for current operations, managers need to know that notes receivable can be discounted.

- Good managers ensure that past due accounts receivable are converted into notes receivable because notes provide more legal protection and are more likely to be collected.

- Because notes and drafts are negotiable, management ensures that internal control procedures are in place.

THINKING CRITICALLY

Why might managers use outside sources of funds for their business operations? How do they acquire these funds?

Commercial Drafts A **commercial draft** is a note issued by one party that orders another party to pay a specified amount on a specified date. Commercial drafts are used for special shipment and collection situations. Commercial drafts may be either sight drafts or time drafts.

A **sight draft** is a commercial draft that is payable on presentation. When a sight draft is issued, no journal entry is made. When a sight draft is honored, the transaction is recorded as a cash receipt.

Sight drafts are used to collect past-due accounts receivable. Customers are more likely to honor a sight draft than a collection letter. The sight draft is sent to the customer's bank. If the customer does not honor the draft, the customer's credit reputation at the bank can be damaged.

Sight drafts are also used to obtain cash on delivery when shipments are made to customers with poor credit or to new customers with no credit established. The sight draft is attached to a **bill of lading,** which is a business document that lists the goods accepted for transportation by a carrier. The bill of lading is sent to a bank near the customer. The customer pays the draft in order to get the bill of lading. The customer needs the bill of lading in order to obtain the goods. The collecting bank sends the money, less a collection fee, to the business issuing the draft. When the funds arrive, the business records the transaction as a cash sale and debits an expense account for the collection fee.

A **time draft** is a commercial draft that is payable during a period of time. The time period may be a specific date, or a specific number of days either after the date of the draft or after acceptance of the draft.

No journal entry is made when a time draft is issued. If the business honors (pays) the draft, the word "Accepted" is written on the draft and it is signed and dated. The business records the acceptance of a draft as a note payable. It is returned to the drawer, who records it as a note receivable.

TRADE ACCEPTANCES

A **trade acceptance** is a form of commercial time draft used in transactions involving the sale of goods. The original transaction is recorded as a sale on credit. When the draft is accepted, it is accounted for as a promissory note. Merchants have fewer credit losses on trade acceptances than on accounts receivable. Trade acceptances can be discounted.

Internal Control of Notes Payable, Notes Receivable, and Drafts

internal CONTROL

The following are internal controls for notes payable, notes receivable, and drafts:

- Limit the number of people who can sign notes for the firm.
- Record all notes payable immediately.

- Identify a specific person or department to be responsible for prompt payment of interest and principal for notes payable.
- When paid, mark the note payable "Canceled" or "Paid" and file the note.
- Handle drafts as carefully as checks.
- Authorize only certain persons to accept notes.
- Record all notes receivable in the accounting records.
- Store notes receivable securely in a safe or fireproof vault to which access is limited.
- Verify and compare the actual notes receivable to the notes receivable register.
- Near the maturity date, inform the issuer of the approaching due date and the amount owed.
- If payment is not received on the due date, contact the issuer immediately.
- Review all past-due notes promptly and take necessary steps, including legal action, to ensure payment.

Section 2   Self Review

QUESTIONS

1. Why do businesses sometimes accept notes receivable from customers?

2. What does it mean to dishonor a note?

3. A note receivable with a maturity value of $6,200 is discounted at 10 percent with 90 days remaining until the maturity date. What are the proceeds from discounting the note?

EXERCISES

4. A company that discounts an interest-bearing note receivable:

   a. always recognizes interest income when the note is discounted.

   b. never recognizes interest income when the note is discounted.

   c. recognizes interest income only if the proceeds from discounting exceed the maturity value of the note discounted.

   d. recognizes interest income if the proceeds exceed the face value of the note discounted.

5. The *Notes Receivable—Discounted* account:

   a. contains a debit balance.

   b. reflects the amounts due on dishonored notes receivable.

   c. is shown as a liability on the balance sheet.

   d. is deducted from *Notes Receivable* on the balance sheet.

ANALYSIS

6. When an interest-bearing note receivable is accepted, instead of cash at the time of sale, does the interest on the note increase the amount reported as sales? Explain.

(Answers to Section 2 Self Review are on page 571.)

REVIEW   Chapter Summary

In this chapter, you have learned how businesses use promissory notes, drafts, or trade acceptances to pay large amounts over a period of time. You have learned about negotiable instruments and how to record common notes payable and notes receivable.

Learning Objectives

16-1   Determine whether an instrument meets all the requirements of negotiability.

A negotiable instrument is a financial document that:

- contains an order or promise to pay,
- meets all the requirements of the Uniform Commercial Code (UCC) to be transferable to another party.

The UCC requirements are as follows:

- It must be in writing.
- It must be signed by the maker.
- It must define the amount due and payment terms.
- It must list the payee.
- If addressed to a drawee, it must clearly name the person.

16-2   Calculate the interest on a note.

The borrower who signs a note payable usually pays interest on the amount borrowed. To determine the interest amount for any time period, use the formula Interest = Principal × Interest Rate × Time.

16-3   Determine the maturity date of a note.

The note's maturity date is determined at the time the note is issued, excluding the issue date itself.

16-4   Record routine notes payable transactions.

When purchasing an asset with a note, debit the asset account and credit *Notes Payable.* When paying the note payable, debit *Notes Payable* for the face of the note, debit *Interest Expense* for the interest, and credit *Cash* for the total paid (principal plus interest). *Interest Expense* appears on the income statement below Net Income from Operations in Other Income/Other Expense.

16-5   Record discounted notes payable transactions.

When money is borrowed on a note payable, the bank can deduct its interest charge immediately, called *discounting.* The borrower discounting a note payable receives the difference between the discount and the principal.

16-6   Record routine notes receivable transactions.

Notes receivable can be noninterest- or interest-bearing. Most firms charge interest.

- If the note receivable is issued at the time of a sale, record the transaction by debiting *Notes Receivable* and crediting *Sales.*
- If the note receivable results from a customer's failure to pay an accounts receivable, debit *Notes Receivable,* and credit *Accounts Receivable.*
- The recipient credits *Interest Income* for interest received when the note is paid.

16-7   Compute the proceeds from a discounted note receivable, and record transactions related to discounting of notes receivable.

A firm with an immediate need for cash can discount a note receivable. Debit *Cash* for the proceeds, credit *Notes Receivable—Discounted* for the face value, and either debit *Interest Expense* (if the proceeds are less than the principal) or credit *Interest Income* (if the proceeds exceed the principal). *Notes Receivable—Discounted* represent a contingent liability. If the note's maker fails to pay at maturity, the business must pay the bank.

16-8   Understand how to use bank drafts and trade acceptances and how to record transactions related to those instruments.

Bank drafts, commercial drafts, and trade acceptances are negotiable instruments used in business.

- Bank drafts are checks written by a bank ordering another bank in which it has funds to pay the indicated amount to a specific person or business.
- Businesses issue commercial drafts to order a person or firm to pay a sum of money at a specific time.
- Trade acceptances arise from the sale of goods. The original transaction is recorded in the same way as a sale on credit. When the draft has been accepted, it is accounted for as a promissory note.

16-9   Define the accounting terms new to this chapter.

Glossary

Bank draft (p. 560) A check written by a bank that orders another bank to pay the stated amount to a specific party

Banker's year (p. 549) A 360-day period used to calculate interest on a note

Bill of lading (p. 561) A business document that lists goods accepted for transportation

Cashier's check (p. 560) A draft on the issuing bank's own funds

Commercial draft (p. 561) A note issued by one party that orders another party to pay a specified sum on a specified date

Contingent liability (p. 557) An item that can become a liability if certain things happen

Discounting (p. 551) Deducting the interest from the principal on a note payable or receivable in advance

Draft (p. 560) A written order that requires one party (a person or business) to pay a stated sum of money to another party

Face value (p. 549) An amount of money indicated to be paid, exclusive of interest or discounts

Interest (p. 549) The fee charged for the use of money

Maturity value (p. 549) The total amount (principal plus interest) payable when a note comes due

Negotiable instrument (p. 548) A financial document containing a promise or order to pay that meets all requirements of the Uniform Commercial Code in order to be transferable to another party

Note payable (p. 550) A liability representing a written promise by the maker of the note (the debtor) to pay another party (the creditor) a specified amount at a specified future date

Note receivable (p. 554) An asset representing a written promise by another party (the debtor) to pay the note holder (the creditor) a specified amount at a specified future date

Principal (p. 549) The amount shown on the face of a note

Sight draft (p. 561) A commercial draft that is payable on presentation

Time draft (p. 561) A commercial draft that is payable during a specified period of time

Trade acceptance (p. 561) A form of commercial time draft used in transactions involving the sale of goods

Comprehensive **Self Review**

1. List the elements of a negotiable instrument.
2. How is maturity value of a note computed?
3. When is *Interest Expense* debited if an interest-bearing note payable is issued? If a note payable is discounted?
4. Which account(s) will be debited and which will be credited when an interest-bearing note receivable that has been discounted is dishonored at the time of maturity?
5. What type of account is *Notes Receivable—Discounted?* How should the *Notes Receivable—Discounted* account be shown on the balance sheet?

(Answers to Comprehensive Self Review are on page 571.)

Discussion Questions

1. How does a note receivable differ from an account receivable?

2. What is the face amount of a note? The maturity value?

3. What are the requirements that must be met in order for a document to be negotiable?

4. Explain a sight draft.

5. Explain a cashier's check.

6. When is a discounted note receivable considered a contingent liability?

7. Explain how to compute the proceeds from discounting a note receivable.

8. What is meant by "discounting a note receivable"?

9. What is a dishonored note receivable?

10. How, if at all, does computation of the maturity value of an interest-bearing note receivable differ from that for an interest-bearing note payable?

11. Explain why records must be kept of the due dates of all notes payable.

12. Are notes payable likely to be given in borrowing money? The purchase of merchandise? The purchase of equipment? Why?

13. How are notes payable maturing less than one year from the balance sheet date shown on the balance sheet?

14. What is meant by "discounting a note payable"?

15. What is the maturity value of an $8,000 note, bearing interest at 9 percent, and due 105 days after date of issue of the note?

16. If a note dated February 28 has a three-month term, on what date must the note be paid?

APPLICATIONS

Exercises

Determining the due dates of notes.

Find the due date of each of the following notes:

1. A note dated June 12, 2016, due in 120 days.

2. A note dated November 1, 2016, due two years from that date.

3. A note dated April 10, 2016, due six months from that date.

◀ **Exercise 16.1**
Objective 16-3

Determining the maturity value of notes.

Compute the maturity value for each of the following notes:

1. A note payable with a face amount of $24,000, dated June 15, 2016, due in three months, bearing interest at 7 percent.

2. A note payable with a face amount of $18,000, dated May 5, 2016, due in 45 days, bearing interest at 8 percent.

◀ **Exercise 16.2**
Objectives 16-2, 16-3

Computing the maturity value of notes payable.

Find the maturity value of each of the following notes payable:

1. A 60-day note, dated February 15, 2016, with a face value of $24,000, bearing interest at 8 percent.

2. A six-month note, dated March 10, 2016, with a face value of $9,200, bearing interest at 11 percent.

◀ **Exercise 16.3**
Objective 16-3

Exercise 16.4

Objectives 16-4, 16-5

▶ **Recording the issuance of notes payable to borrow money.**

During 2016, Jackson Company borrowed money at State Bank and Trust on two occasions. On June 8, the company borrowed $27,000, giving a 120-day, 7 percent note, and on September 8, the company discounted at 7 percent a $30,000, 90-day note payable.

1. Give entries in general journal form to record issuance of each of these notes.
2. Record in general journal form issuance of a check to pay each note.

Exercise 16.5

Objective 16-4

▶ **Recording a note given for a purchase of equipment.**

On August 1, 2016, the Castillo Company purchased a truck (delivery equipment) for $48,500, signing a 90-day, 8 percent note for the entire purchase price. Give the entry in general journal form to record this transaction.

Exercise 16.6

Objective 16-7

▶ **Recording receipt of a note receivable and subsequent discounting of the note.**

On June 3, 2016, Fidelity State Company received a $4,800, 45-day, 10 percent note from Horace Coe, a customer whose account was past due.

1. Record in the general journal receipt of the note.
2. Give the entry in general journal form to record the discounting of this note receivable on June 18 at the Second State Bank and Trust. The bank charged a discount rate of 12 percent.

Exercise 16.7

Objective 16-7

▶ **Recording payment of a discounted note receivable.**

In general journal form, give the entry required by Fidelity State when Coe paid the note discounted in Exercise 16.6 on the maturity date.

Exercise 16.8

Objective 16-7

▶ **Recording a dishonored note receivable.**

Give the entries in general journal form that Fidelity State Company would make if Horace Coe dishonored the note receivable discounted by Fidelity State in Exercise 16.6, assuming the bank deducted the maturity value of the dishonored note plus a $40 service charge from Fidelity State's bank account on the due date of the note.

PROBLEMS

Problem Set A

Problem 16.1A

Objective 16-2

▶ **Computing interest on notes payable.**

Costos Company issued the following notes during 2016. Find the interest due on each of the notes, using the interest formula method. Show all calculations.

1. A $30,000 note at 9 percent for 180 days, issued February 15.
2. A $7,000 note at 12 percent for four months. issued October 3.
3. A $35,000 note at 10 percent for 180 days, issued October 18.

Analyze: What is the balance in *Notes Payable* on December 31, 2016, assuming that all notes were paid when due?

Problem 16.2A

Objectives 16-2, 16-3, 16-4, 16-5

▶ **Recording transactions involving notes payable.**

Give the general journal entry to record each of the following transactions for Dennis Company:

1. Issued a 6-month, 9 percent note for $85,000 to purchase two forklifts on May 14, 2016 (debit *Warehouse Equipment*).
2. Discounted its own 180-day, noninterest-bearing note with a principal amount of $39,000 at the Nelson Bank and Trust on May 28, 2016. The bank charged a discount rate of 10 percent.

3. Paid the May 14 note on its due date.

4. Paid the note discounted on May 28 on its due date.

Analyze: What is the total interest expense for the year as a result of these transactions?

Computing interest and maturity value.

The following notes were received by Davis Company during 2016:

Note No.	Date	Face Amount	Period	Interest Rate
21	Jan. 5	$50,000	3 months	8%
22	June 3	14,000	90 days	10%
23	Sept. 28	8,000	3 months	9%

Compute the maturity value of each note.

Analyze: What is the total interest expense on these notes for the year?

◀ **Problem 16.3A**

Objectives 16-2, 16-3

Computing the proceeds from discounted notes receivable.

The notes receivable held by the Tolleson Company on August 3, 2016, are summarized below. On August 4, 2016, Tolleson discounted all of these notes at Neighborhood Bank and Trust at a discount rate of 10 percent. Compute the net proceeds received from discounting each note.

Note No.	Date	Face Amount	Period	Interest Rate
31	Apr. 4, 2016	$50,000	6 months	8%
32	June 11, 2016	15,000	120 days	6
33	July 31, 2016	12,000	60 days	10

Analyze: What is the net interest income or expense to be reported from these transactions assuming all notes are paid when due?

◀ **Problem 16.4A**

Objectives 16-3, 16-7

Recording the receipt, discounting, and payment of notes receivable.

On May 16, 2016, Reliable Company received a 90-day, 8 percent, $9,800 interest-bearing note from White Company in settlement of White's past-due account. On June 30, Reliable discounted this note at Fargo Bank and Trust. The bank charged a discount rate of 13 percent. On August 15, Reliable received a notice that White had paid the note and the interest on the due date. Give entries in general journal form to record these transactions.

Analyze: If the company prepared a balance sheet on July 31, 2016, how should *Notes Receivable—Discounted* be presented on the statement?

◀ **Problem 16.5A**

Objectives 16-3, 16-4, 16-6 16-7

Problem Set B

Computing interest on notes payable.

The notes listed below were issued by Keller Company during 2016:

1. A $9,500 note at 10 percent for 90 days, issued on June 15.

2. A $20,000 note at 6 percent for 30 days, issued on August 21.

3. A $30,000 note at 7.5 percent for 6 months, issued on September 28.

Compute the interest due on each of the notes at maturity, using the interest formula method. Show all calculations.

Analyze: What would be the accrued interest payable on December 31 as a result of these transactions?

◀ **Problem 16.1B**

Objective 16-2

Recording transactions involving notes payable.

Give the general journal entry to record each of the following transactions:

◀ **Problem 16.2B**

Objectives 16-2, 16-3, 16-4, 16-5

1. On June 3, 2016, Wallace Company issued a 120-day, 9 percent note for $17,500 to purchase new office equipment.

2. Wallace Company paid the June 3 note when it became due.

3. On September 18, 2016, Wallace Company borrowed money from the South Park National Bank by discounting its own 90-day noninterest-bearing $30,000 note payable at a discount rate of 10 percent.

4. Wallace Company paid the September 18 note when it became due.

Analyze: If Wallace had borrowed $30,000 from the bank on September 18, signing a 90-day note, bearing interest of 10 percent, would these be more favorable or less favorable terms for Wallace than discounting the $30,000 note at 10 percent? Why?

Problem 16.3B
Objectives 16-2, 16-3

▶ **Computing interest and maturity value.**

Kent Company received the notes listed below in 2016. Compute the interest to be paid and the maturity value of each note. Show all computations.

Note No.	Date	Face Amount	Period	Interest Rate
30	May 4	$24,000	60 days	10.5%
31	July 8	16,000	90 days	8.5
32	Aug. 20	20,000	4 months	9.0

Analyze: Assuming all notes are paid when due, what would be the balance in *Notes Receivable* on July 31?

Problem 16.4B
Objective 16-7

▶ **Computing the proceeds from discounted notes receivable.**

The following notes receivable are held by the Vasquez Company on January 1, 2016. On January 2, 2016, Vasquez discounted all of these notes at First National Bank at a discount rate of 10 percent. Compute the net proceeds the firm received from discounting each note (2016 was a leap year).

Note No.	Date	Face Amount	Period	Interest Rate
20	Sept. 20, 2015	$10,000	120 days	8%
21	Sept. 10, 2015	18,000	6 months	9
22	Dec. 1, 2015	16,000	120 days	12

Analyze: How would *Notes Receivable* be shown on a balance sheet prepared on January 2, 2016, after the transactions above have been entered?

Problem 16.5B
Objectives 16-2, 16-3, 16-4, 16-6, 16-7

▶ **Recording the receipt, discounting, and payment of notes receivable.**

On April 2, 2016, Wang Company received a 6-month, 8 percent interest-bearing note from Paula Jackson in settlement of a past-due account receivable of $12,000. On May 3, Wang discounted this note at Mercantile State Bank. The bank charged a discount rate of 10 percent. On October 2, Wang received word that the note and interest had been paid in full.

1. Give all entries, in general journal form, to record these events.

2. Assume that Jackson had failed to pay the note and that the bank charged Wang's account with the note and a $50 protest fee. Give the journal entry(ies) necessary to record these facts.

Analyze: What amount of interest income or interest expense will Wang report in 2016 as a result of these transactions assuming Jackson paid the note when due?

Critical Thinking Problem 16.1

Notes Receivable Discounted

Contemporary Furniture, a wholesale distributor of modern casual furniture, frequently accepts promissory notes from its customers at the time of sale. Since Contemporary Furniture regularly needs cash to meet its own obligations, it frequently discounts these notes at the bank.

Contemporary Furniture's accountant tells you that she does not bother to credit discounted notes to a *Notes Receivable—Discounted* account. Instead, she makes an entry debiting *Cash* and *Interest Expense* and crediting *Notes Receivable* (and *Interest Income* when appropriate). She says that using a *Notes Receivable—Discounted* account "just makes extra work, and, anyway, once the note is discounted, it becomes the bank's problem."

What is your reaction to the bookkeeper's comments?

Critical Thinking Problem 16.2

Notes Payable and Notes Receivable

Larry Sims owns Sims Auto Sales. He periodically borrows money from Biloxi State Bank. He permits some customers to sign short-term notes for their purchases. He usually discounts these notes at the bank. Following are selected transactions that occurred in March 2016. (2016 is a leap year.)

INSTRUCTIONS

1. Record each of the March transactions in the general journal. (Omit explanations.)
2. Record the additional data related to these notes for months other than March in the general journal using the appropriate dates.

DATE	TRANSACTIONS
2016	
Mar. 4	Mr. Sims borrows $20,000 from the bank on a note payable for the business. Terms of the note are 8 percent interest for 45 days.
11	A 90-day $18,000 note payable to the bank is discounted at a rate of 10 percent.
22	Sold a car to Bridgett Wilson for $13,000 on a 75-day note receivable, bearing interest at 10 percent.
23	Discounted the Wilson note with the bank. The bank charges a discount rate of 12 percent.
25	Sold a car for $15,000 to Derrick Wells. Wells paid $2,000 cash and signed a 30-day note, bearing interest at 10 percent, for the balance.
28	Terry Owens's account receivable is overdue. Sims requires him to sign a 12 percent, 30-day note for the balance of $5,500.

Additional Data

a. Sims pays all the company's notes payable on time.
b. Bridgett Wilson defaults on her $13,000 note and the bank charges the company's checking account for the maturity value of the note and a service fee of $30.
c. Derrick Wells pays his note on time.
d. Terry Owens pays his note on time.

Analyze: What is the *Notes Payable* account balance on March 25?

BUSINESS CONNECTIONS

Cash Management

Managerial FOCUS

1. You are a member of Arrow Company's internal audit staff. A review of office practices indicates that an accounting assistant routinely makes arrangements with the bank for short-term notes payable and signs the notes. Evaluate this practice. Would you recommend any changes?
2. How can management use notes receivable as a way to acquire cash?

3. Under what circumstances would management insist on having a notes receivable register and/or a notes payable register?

4. As a manager, why would you insist that dishonored notes receivable be charged back to the *Accounts Receivable* control account and the maker's subsidiary ledger account?

Contingent Liability

Ethical | DILEMMA

Dallas Corporation has a practice of discounting the notes receivable to the bank to increase its cash flow. Since the maker of the notes receivable has always paid the bank, Dallas Corporation does not list the notes receivable as a contingent liability. Is this an ethical practice? What would be compromised if the liability did not appear in the notes of the annual report?

Balance Sheet

Financial Statement ANALYSIS

The following excerpt was taken from The Home Depot, Inc. *2012 Annual Report (for the fiscal year ended February 3, 2013)*. The Balance Sheet to the Consolidated Financial Statements contained the following details on the company's current and long-term debt.

(in millions)	2013	2012
Total current liabilities	$11,462	$9,376
Long-term debt, excluding current installments	9,475	10,758
Other long-term liabilities	2,051	2,146
Deferred income taxes	319	340
Total liabilities	23,307	22,620

Analyze:

1. What percentage of total debt is represented by the current portion in 2013? In 2012?

2. What percentage of total debt is represented by the long-term portion in 2013? In 2012?

3. If interest payments totaled $632 in 2013, what average rate was paid on total debt? Use the end of year balance of liabilities for this computation.

Analyze Online: Find The Home Depot, Inc., website (www.homedepot.com). Recent financial reports are found within the *investor* link.

4. What is the fiscal period for the most recent annual report presented?

5. What long-term debt amount is reported on the balance sheet?

6. What amount of long-term debt matured in this fiscal period?

Negotiating Terms

TEAMWORK

A business manager should know how one company's transaction will affect another company. In teams of two students, assign one student to be the notes receivable clerk of Heavenly Bathes and another to be Relax Haven, the borrowing company's notes payable clerk. Relax Haven cannot make the payment on a $20,000 invoice. Negotiate the necessary arrangements between the two parties.

Uniform Commercial Code

Internet | CONNECTION

Each state develops a Uniform Commercial Code that regulates commercial transactions. Select the secretary of state for your state and locate your state's commercial code on the website. Define the Uniform Commercial Code and its purpose.

Answers to **Self Reviews**

Answers to Section 1 Self Review

1. August 8

2. Interest = $12,000 \times .08 \times 75/360 = $200

3. Proceeds = Face amount − Discount

   Discount = $12,000 × .08 × 75/360 = $200

   Proceeds = $12,000 − $200 = $11,800

4. **d.** All of the above are required.

5. **b.** maturity value

6. No. The effective rate for a discounted note is higher. In both cases, the interest paid was $200. However, in Question 2, the borrower would have the use of $12,000 for 75 days, whereas in Question 3 the borrower would have the use of only $11,800 for 75 days.

Answers to Section 2 Self Review

1. If a customer is unable to pay a currently due account receivable, it is wise to have a note receivable signed. The note receivable provides greater legal protection to its holder than does an account receivable claim.

2. Dishonor of a note means that the maker of the note does not pay it when it is due.

3. Proceeds = Maturity value − Discount

   Discount = $6,200 × .10 × 90/360 = $155

   Proceeds = $6,200 − $155 = $6,045

4. **d.** recognizes interest income if the proceeds exceed the face value of the note discounted.

5. **d.** is deducted from *Notes Receivable* on the balance sheet.

6. No. Sales are recorded at the principal amount of the note. The interest is reported as *Interest Income.*

Answers to Comprehensive Self Review

1. (a) must be in writing and signed by the maker, (b) contains an unconditional promise or order to pay a definite amount of money, (c) is payable on demand or at a time that can be determined, (d) is payable to the order of the bearer, and (e) if addressed to a drawee, the drawee must be clearly identified.

2. Maturity value of the note is the sum of (a) the principal amount of the note and (b) interest on the principal amount at the rate specified, computed from the date the note is dated until the maturity date.

3. For an interest-bearing note issued, *Interest Expense* is debited when the note matures. The interest on a note payable discounted is recorded at the date of the discounting.

4. Accounts debited and credited: *Notes Receivable—Discounted* will be debited and *Notes Receivable* will be credited. Also, *Accounts Receivable* and the customer's account in the subsidiary ledger will be debited and *Cash* will be credited.

5. *Notes Receivable—Discounted* is a contra asset account. This means that it is deducted from *Notes Receivable* on the balance sheet.

Merchandise Inventory

Chapter 17

Best Buy
www.bestbuy.com

Sixty years ago the highest-tech appliance in most homes was the radio. In 1966, Richard M. Schulze established Sound of Music, Inc., a home and car stereo store. In 1981, a tornado tore through its flagship store and the company responded with a "tornado sale" (promoted as a "best buy") to liquidate the store's merchandise and cover the costs of repairs. The overwhelming success of the sale not only made it an annual event; it also prompted the company to change its name to Best Buy.

Under the Best Buy name, the company has grown to almost $50 billion in annual revenue. The products have changed too, evolving from car stereos and VCRs to computers, DVD players, and giant HDTVs.

Best Buy has made it a priority to help customers find the products they want when they want them. The company's website allows customers to check inventories in stores in real time. Not only do customers get superior service, Best Buy can measure product demand in real time and most effectively manage inventory levels. Managing inventory levels is important to a store that has about 1 billion visitors shopping online and 600 million shoppers visiting their stores annually.

Assigning an appropriate value to merchandise inventory is important because the Merchandise Inventory account appears on both the balance sheet and the income statement. As inventory is sold, Best Buy restocks its shelves with more units purchased from suppliers. Although identical inventory is on the shelf, units are purchased at different times and thus may have a different cost to Best Buy. Best Buy must keep track of the original cost of each unit sold not only to determine the profit made on sales, but also so the ending value of inventory can be calculated.

thinking critically

If Best Buy had two identical computers in its store but because they were purchased at different times and had different costs to Best Buy, how would the sale of the lower-cost unit affect the company's financial statements vs. the sale of the higher-cost unit?

LEARNING OBJECTIVES

17-1. Compute inventory cost by applying four commonly used costing methods.

17-2. Compare the effects of different methods of inventory costing.

17-3. Compute inventory value under the lower of cost or market rule.

17-4. Estimate inventory cost using the gross profit method.

17-5. Estimate inventory cost using the retail method.

17-6. Define the accounting terms new to this chapter.

NEW TERMS

average cost method
first in, first out (FIFO) method
gross profit method
last in, first out (LIFO) method
lower of cost or market rule
markdown
market price
markon

markup
periodic inventory
perpetual inventory
physical inventory
replacement cost
retail method
specific identification method
weighted average method

SECTION OBJECTIVES	TERMS TO LEARN
>> 17-1. Compute inventory cost by applying four commonly used costing methods. **WHY IT'S IMPORTANT** Factors such as industry practices, merchandise types, and business operations affect how a business assigns costs to inventories. >> 17-2. Compare the effects of different methods of inventory costing. **WHY IT'S IMPORTANT** Inventory valuation affects the net income or net loss of a business.	average cost method first in, first out (FIFO) method last in, first out (LIFO) method periodic inventory perpetual inventory physical inventory specific identification method weighted average method

Inventory Costing Methods

Businesses report information about merchandise inventory on the financial statements. This section covers four methods used to compute the value of merchandise inventory based on original cost.

Importance of Inventory Valuation

Assigning an appropriate value to merchandise inventory is important because the *Merchandise Inventory* account appears on both the balance sheet and the income statement. Often inventory represents the largest current asset on the balance sheet. Inventory valuation also affects the net income or net loss reported on the income statement.

A higher ending inventory value results in a lower cost of goods sold, which results in higher income from operations. On the other hand, a lower ending inventory value results in a higher cost of goods sold, which results in a lower income from operations.

> On its 2012 consolidated balance sheet for fiscal year 2013, ended February 3, 2013, The Home Depot reported inventories of $10.7 billion. Inventory represents about 26 percent of the company's total assets of $41.1 billion.

We learned in Chapter 12 that many firms value merchandise inventory at the original cost of the items on hand. Merchandise inventory is counted at the end of the accounting period. The inventory value is calculated by multiplying the number of units on hand by the cost per item. Taking an actual count of the number of units of each type of good on hand is known as taking a **physical inventory.** An inventory system in which the amount of goods on hand is determined by periodic counts is called a **periodic inventory** system. It is the method that we use in this chapter.

Some businesses need to know the number of units and the unit cost for the inventory on hand at all times. These businesses use a **perpetual inventory** system, in which inventory is based on a running total number of units. Electronic equipment, such as point-of-sale cash registers and scanners, helps track all of the items as they are purchased and sold. Perpetual inventory records are discussed in a later chapter.

Assigning Costs to Inventory

>> **17-1. OBJECTIVE**
Compute inventory cost by applying four commonly used costing methods.

The cost of sold merchandise is transferred from the balance sheet (current assets) to the income statement (cost of goods sold). The amount of cost that is transferred depends on the method used to value inventory. Four methods are commonly used to value inventory. Accountants choose the method that works best for the industry and the company.

SPECIFIC IDENTIFICATION METHOD

The specific identification method of inventory valuation is based on the actual cost of each item of merchandise. Cost of goods sold is the exact cost of the specific merchandise sold, and the ending inventory balance is the exact cost of the specific inventory items on hand. Businesses that sell high-priced or one-of-a-kind items, such as art and automobile dealers, use the specific identification method. However, this method is not practical for a business where hundreds of similar items of relatively small unit value are carried in inventory.

AVERAGE COST METHOD

The average cost method uses the average cost of units of an item available for sale during the period to arrive at the value of ending inventory. It is advantageous to use the average cost method when a company's inventory is composed of many similar items that are not subject to significant price and style changes. Table 17.1, which provides an example of the average cost method, contains the following information:

important!

Physical Inventory
Whether a perpetual or periodic inventory system is used, a physical inventory should be taken at least once a year.

- There were 200 units in beginning inventory valued at $18 each.
- There were three purchases during the year, at different costs.
- The beginning inventory and purchases are added together to determine that during the year 1,000 units were available for sale at a total cost of $20,600.
- The average cost per unit is $20.60 ($20,600 ÷ 1,000).
- A physical inventory count showed 206 units on hand on December 31.
- During the year, 794 units were sold (1,000 − 206).
- Under the average cost method, the total cost of units available for sale ($20,600) is divided between the financial statements as follows:
  - Balance sheet—ending inventory is $4,243.60 (206 units × $20.60).
  - Income statement—cost of goods sold is $16,356.40 (794 units × $20.60).

recall

Cost of Goods Sold
The formula for cost of goods sold is
   Beginning inventory
+ Purchases
− Ending inventory
= Cost of goods sold

TABLE 17.1

Average Cost Method of Inventory Valuation

Explanation	Number of Units	Unit Cost	Total Cost
Beginning inventory, January 1, 2016	200	$18.00	$ 3,600.00
Purchases:			
February 19	400	20.00	8,000.00
May 12	300	22.00	6,600.00
October 3	100	24.00	2,400.00
Total merchandise available for sale	1,000		$20,600.00
Average cost ($20,600 ÷ 1,000 = $20.60)			
Ending inventory, December 31, 2016	206	20.60	$ 4,243.60
Cost of goods sold ($20,600 − $4,243.60)	794	20.60	$16,356.40

This method is sometimes referred to as the **weighted average method** because it considers the number of units in each purchase and the unit purchase price to compute a "weighted average" cost per unit.

The average cost method of inventory valuation is relatively simple to use, but it reflects the limitations of any procedure that involves average figures. The average unit cost is not related to any specific unit, and it does not clearly reveal price changes. In highly competitive businesses that are subject to considerable model or style upgrades and price fluctuations, it is desirable to have a more specific and revealing method of cost determination.

> The Coca-Cola Company's inventories are shown in the company's *2012 Annual Report* as $3.264 billion, which is approximately 10.8 percent of its current assets. A note to the financial statements comments: "We determine cost on the basis of average cost or first-in, first-out methods."

recall

Disclosure

The method of inventory valuation must be disclosed in the financial reports.

FIRST IN, FIRST OUT METHOD

For most businesses, the physical flow of inventory is "the first item purchased is the first item sold." This certainly makes sense for perishable items. Some businesses assign inventory costs using this flow. The **first in, first out method** of inventory valuation, usually referred to as **FIFO,** assumes that the oldest merchandise is sold first.

Let's calculate ending inventory under FIFO using the information in Table 17.1. During the period, 794 units were sold. Under FIFO the "first cost in is the first cost transferred out" to cost of goods sold. This matches the earliest costs with the revenue from the units sold. So the cost of the ending inventory is computed by using the cost of the most recent purchases.

Table 17.2 shows that the cost assigned to the 206 units in ending inventory is $4,732.00: 100 units purchased in October at $24 and 106 units purchased in May at $22, for a total of 206 units. During the period, there was $20,600.00 of inventory available for sale. Under the FIFO method, the cost is divided between the financial statements as follows:

- Balance sheet—ending inventory is $4,732.00.

- Income statement—cost of goods sold is $15,868 ($20,600 − $4,732.00).

TABLE 17.2

FIFO Method of Inventory Costing

Explanation	Number of Units	Unit Cost	Total Cost
From purchase of October 3, 2016	100	$24.00	$2,400.00
From purchase of May 12, 2016	106	22.00	2,332.00
Ending inventory	206		$4,732.00

> A company can use several inventory valuation methods. Most inventory costs for Dole Food Company, Inc., are determined principally on a first in, first out basis. However, specific identification and average cost methods are used for certain packing material and operating inventories.

important!

Inventory Costing and Net Income

Gross profit on sales and net income are affected by the inventory costing method.

LAST IN, FIRST OUT METHOD

The **last in, first out (LIFO) method** assumes that the most recently purchased merchandise is sold first, and thus assigns the most recent costs to cost of goods sold. The "last cost in is the first cost transferred out" to cost of goods sold. Thus, the cost of ending inventory is computed using the cost of the oldest merchandise on hand during the period.

Using the figures from Table 17.1 but applying the LIFO method, Table 17.3 shows that the cost assigned to the 206 units in ending inventory is 200 at $18 from the beginning inventory and 6 at $20 from the February 19 purchase. During the period, there was $20,600 of inventory available for sale. Under the LIFO method, the cost is divided between the financial statements as follows:

- Balance sheet—ending inventory is $3,720.00.
- Income statement—cost of goods sold is $16,880 ($20,600 − $3,720).

Under the LIFO method, the balance sheet reflects the earliest costs. The cost of goods sold reflects the costs applicable to the most recent purchases.

TABLE 17.3

LIFO Method of Inventory Valuation

Explanation	Number of Units	Unit Cost	Total Cost
Beginning inventory, Jan. 1, 2016	200	$18.00	$3,600.00
From purchase of February 19	6	20.00	120.00
Ending inventory, Dec. 31, 2016	206		$3,720.00

Comparing Results of Inventory Costing Methods

Table 17.4 shows the results obtained for the average cost, FIFO, and LIFO inventory methods. The ending inventory is highest under FIFO and lowest under LIFO. The cost of goods sold is highest under LIFO and lowest under FIFO. This is true because costs have risen during the year.

Remember the following important points about inventory valuation methods:

- Except for specific identification, the physical flow of inventory and the costs assigned to inventory are not specifically matched. Average, FIFO, and LIFO cost methods *assign* costs to inventory but do not track the cost to the specific inventory item.

>> 17-2. OBJECTIVE

Compare the effects of different methods of inventory costing.

TABLE 17.4

Comparison of Results of Inventory Costing Methods

Explanation	Units	Unit Cost	Total Cost	Ending Inventory Valuation	Cost of Goods Sold
Beginning inventory, January 1, 2016	200	$18.00	$ 3,600.00		
Purchases:					
February 19	400	20.00	8,000.00		
May 12	300	22.00	6,600.00		
October 3	100	24.00	2,400.00		
Total merchandise available for sale	1,000		$20,600.00		
1. Average cost method	206	$20.60		$4,243.60	$16,356.40
2. FIFO	100	24.00	$ 2,400.00		
	106	22.00	2,332.00		
	206		$ 4,732.00	$4,732.00	$15,868.00
3. LIFO	200	18.00	$ 3,600.00	$3,720.00	$16,880.00
	6	20.00	120.00		
	206		$ 3,720.00		

- Businesses can use separate inventory valuation methods for different classes of inventory.
- Following the consistency principle, once a business adopts an inventory valuation method, it uses that method consistently from one period to the next. A business cannot change its inventory valuation method at will, although a one-time change is acceptable.
- A business can use one inventory costing method for financial accounting purposes and another for federal income tax, with the exception of LIFO costing. A taxpayer who adopts LIFO for federal tax purposes must also adopt it for financial accounting purposes.
- FIFO focuses on the balance sheet. The most current costs are in ending inventory.
- LIFO focuses on the income statement and the matching principle. The most recent costs are matched with revenue. LIFO is considered the most conservative costing method in a period of rising prices.

A major argument supporting the LIFO method is that when sales are made, the goods sold must be replaced at current costs. It is logical that current costs incurred for replaced goods should be charged against the revenue leading to the replacement.

Since price trends represent a vital element in any inventory valuation, remember these basic rules:

- When prices are rising, cost of goods sold is highest and net income is lowest under LIFO. Therefore, in periods of inflation, LIFO results in the lowest income tax expense.
- When prices are falling, cost of goods sold is lower and net income is higher under LIFO.
- Whatever direction prices take, the average cost method almost always results in net income between the amounts obtained with FIFO and LIFO.

LIFO Use Internationally

Most of the major industrialized countries use the methods of accounting for inventories discussed in this chapter. In some countries, however, LIFO is not generally accepted.

Section 1 Self Review

QUESTIONS

1. In a period of rising prices, which inventory method (LIFO, FIFO, average cost) results in the lowest reported net income?

2. Is a company permitted to change its inventory valuation method each year? What accounting principle is involved in your answer?

3. Is it possible to apply the LIFO inventory method if items in the inventory cannot be identified as having been received as parts of specific purchases? Explain.

EXERCISES

4. Under FIFO costing, which costs are assigned to the goods sold during the period?

5. Before recommending an inventory valuation method, what questions would you ask the manager about the business and its inventory?

ANALYSIS

6. What does LIFO mean, and what is the LIFO cost flow method?

(Answers to Section 1 Self Review are on pages 596–597.)

Inventory Valuation and Control

According to the historical cost principle, assets are reported on the balance sheet at their historical cost. The conservatism convention, however, states that assets should not be overstated. This section discusses how to report the value of inventory when the cost is above the market price.

Lower of Cost or Market Rule

Market price or **replacement cost** is the price the business would have to pay to buy an item of inventory through usual channels in usual quantities. To determine market price, businesses contact their suppliers, read trade publications, or review recent purchases. If the current market price is lower than the original cost, the business uses the **lower of cost or market rule.** That is, inventory is reported at its original cost or its replacement cost, whichever is lower. There are three ways to apply the lower of cost or market rule: by item, in total, or by group.

LOWER OF COST OR MARKET RULE BY ITEM

Table 17.5 illustrates the lower of cost or market rule by item. Inventory consists of two groups of two stock items each. The report shows the quantity, cost, and market price of each item. Cost is determined using one of the acceptable methods—specific identification, average cost, FIFO, or LIFO. Each item's valuation basis (cost or market, whichever is lower) is determined; for item 2810, it is cost, $1.80, and for item 2870 it is market, $2.05. The quantity is multiplied by valuation basis and the amounts are totaled. The inventory balance reported on the balance sheet is $1,461.25.

>> **17-3. OBJECTIVE**
Compute inventory value under the lower of cost or market rule.

TABLE 17.5

Establishing Lower of Cost or Market Valuation by Item

Description	Quantity	Unit Price Cost	Unit Price Market	Valuation Basis	Amount
Group 1					
Stock 2810	150	1.80	1.95	Cost	$ 270.00
Stock 2870	225	2.10	2.05	Market	461.25
Total, Group 1					$ 731.25
Group 2					
Stock 4625	100	3.10	3.05	Market	$ 305.00
Stock 4633	250	1.70	1.80	Cost	425.00
Total, Group 2					$ 730.00
Inventory valuation (lower of cost or market by item)					$1,461.25

LOWER OF TOTAL COST OR TOTAL MARKET

Table 17.6 illustrates the lower of cost or market rule applied to total inventory, not to individual items. The cost of inventory is computed using both cost and market and then the results are compared. Inventory is valued in the balance sheet at the lower amount, $1,477.50.

> The inventories of Pier 1 Imports, Inc., are stated at the lower of average cost or market. Cost is determined using the weighted average method.

LOWER OF COST OR MARKET RULE BY GROUPS

Another way to apply the lower of cost or market rule is by groups. The lower figure (cost or market) for each group is added to the lower figures for the other groups to obtain the total

TABLE 17.6

Establishing Lower of Total Cost or Total Market Valuation

Description	Quantity	Unit Price Unit Cost	Unit Price Unit Market	Total Cost	Total Market
Group 1					
Stock 2810	150	1.80	1.95	$ 270.00	$ 292.50
Stock 2870	225	2.10	2.05	472.50	461.25
Total, Group 1				$ 742.50	$ 753.75
Group 2					
Stock 4625	100	3.10	3.05	$ 310.00	$ 305.00
Stock 4633	250	1.70	1.80	425.00	450.00
Total, Group 2				$ 735.00	$ 755.00
Total Inventory				$1,477.50	$1,508.75
Inventory valuation (lower of total cost or total market)					$1,477.50

TABLE 17.7

Establishing the Lower of Total Cost or Total Market by Groups

Lower of cost or market valuation by group (as shown in Table 17.6)	
Group 1 Cost	$ 742.50
Group 2 Cost	735.00
Total inventory valuation	$1,477.50

inventory valuation. As shown in Table 17.7, the valuation basis of both Group 1 and Group 2 is cost. Inventory is valued on the balance sheet at $1,477.50

Depending on the method used, inventory could appear on the balance sheet as one of the following amounts:

Lower of Cost or Market	
By Item	$1,461.25
By Total	1,477.50
By Group	1,477.50

Accountants select the method based on the size and variety of inventory, the margin of profit, industry practices, and plans for expansion.

■ Some accountants believe that the total method should be used. They think that the lower of cost or market rule should apply to the total inventory, not item by item. If market value of the inventory as a whole has not declined below cost, they believe inventory should be presented at historical cost.

■ Other accountants prefer the group method because it does not reflect individual fluctuations as does the item method, and it does not lump together all types of items as does the total method.

■ Some accountants choose the item method because it is the most conservative method. Almost without exception the item method results in the lowest inventory amount.

Inventory Estimation Procedures

Occasionally, managers need to know the inventory cost and cannot or do not want to take a physical count. For example, after a fire the business cannot count the items destroyed. However, for insurance and income tax purposes, the business must determine the cost of the goods destroyed. Two common techniques to estimate the cost of inventory are the gross profit method and the retail method.

GROSS PROFIT METHOD OF INVENTORY VALUATION

The **gross profit method** assumes that the rate of gross profit on sales and the ratio of cost of goods sold to net sales are relatively constant from period to period. Applying these ratios to information that may be gleaned from the records on any date of the year permits an estimate to be made of the cost of inventory at the end of a period ending on that date. This process is illustrated for the Posey Corporation, whose inventory was destroyed by fire on June 30, 2016. However, accounting records were not destroyed.

The averages of sales and data related to cost of goods sold in the years 2014 and 2015 for Posey Corporation, along with the computation of the gross profit and the cost of goods sold ratios, are determined:

Net sales	$850,000	
Cost of goods sold	493,000	
Gross profit on sales	$357,000	
Gross profit rate		$357,000/$850,000 = 42%
Cost of goods sold to net sales ratio		$493,000/$850,000 = 58%

recall

Conservatism
According to the modifying convention of conservatism, if GAAP allows alternatives, assets in the balance sheet should be understated rather than overstated.

important!

Lower of Cost or Market Rule
If the replacement cost is less than the historical cost, the inventory is reported at replacement cost.

>> 17-4. OBJECTIVE
Estimate inventory cost using the gross profit method.

These rates have been typical of those in prior years for the business. The accounting records for the period January 1 through June 30, date of the fire, show:

Inventory (at cost), January 1	$210,000
Net purchases, January 1 through June 30	315,000
Net sales, January 1 through June 30	450,000

The following steps are used to estimate the cost of inventory on hand at the time of the fire:

Step 1: *Estimate the cost of goods sold.* Sales were $450,000 for January 1 through June 30. Using the 58 percent ratio for cost of goods sold to net sales, based on averages for the prior two years, the estimated cost of goods sold is $261,000 ($450,000 × 0.58).

Step 2: *Determine the cost of goods available for sale.* Include in the computation freight-in charges and purchases returns.

Beginning inventory	$210,000
Net purchases	315,000
Cost of goods available for sale	$525,000

Step 3: *Compute the ending (destroyed) inventory.* Subtract the estimated cost of goods sold from the cost of goods available for sale.

Cost of goods available for sale (Step 2)	$525,000
Estimated cost of goods sold (Step 1)	(261,000)
Estimated cost of ending inventory	$264,000

The cost of inventory destroyed in the fire is estimated to be $264,000.

RETAIL METHOD OF INVENTORY VALUATION

>> **17-5. OBJECTIVE**

Estimate inventory cost using the retail method.

The **retail method** estimates inventory cost by applying the ratio of cost to selling price in the current accounting period to the retail price of the inventory. This widely used method permits businesses to determine the approximate cost of ending inventory from the financial records. It makes it possible for the business to prepare financial statements easily and often without taking a physical inventory count.

Using the retail method, inventory is classified into groups of items that have about the same rate of markon. **Markon** is the difference between the cost and the initial retail price of merchandise. The following steps use assumed figures to estimate the cost of inventory using the retail method:

MANAGERIAL IMPLICATIONS <<

INVENTORY

- Good managers carefully control inventory because it may represent a large part of the assets of the business.
- Management should help select an inventory costing method that is practical, reliable, and as simple as possible to apply.
- Management needs to understand how the inventory valuation method affects net income and income taxes.
- Based on the gross profit method of estimating inventory, managers can prepare budgets and financial statements when a physical inventory count is not practical or possible.

- Retail managers use the retail method of inventory valuation to estimate the cost of goods on hand. Department managers, who are not permitted to exceed their inventory budgets, use this method as often as every week.

THINKING CRITICALLY

Should the gross profit method or the retail method of calculating inventory replace the physical count of inventory?

Step 1: List the beginning inventory at both cost ($95,400) and retail ($138,700).

Step 2: When merchandise is purchased, record it at cost ($526,800 including $2,400 freight) and determine its retail value ($819,500).

Step 3: Compute merchandise available for sale at cost ($622,200) and at retail ($958,200).

Step 4: Determine net sales at retail ($815,300).

Step 5: Subtract retail sales from the retail merchandise available for sale. The difference is the ending inventory at retail ($958,200 − $815,300 = $142,900).

Step 6: Compute the cost ratio.

$$\frac{\text{Merchandise Available for Sale at Cost}}{\text{Merchandise Available for Sale at Retail}} = \frac{\$622,200}{\$958,200} = 65 \text{ percent}$$

Step 7: Multiply the ending inventory at retail by the cost ratio. The result is an estimate of the ending inventory cost, $92,885 ($142,900 × 0.65).

Step 8: Estimate the cost of goods sold by subtracting the ending inventory at cost from the merchandise available for sale at cost, $529,315 ($622,200 − $92,885).

The calculations for each step are shown below:

	Cost	Retail
Step 1: Beginning inventory	$ 95,400	$138,700
Step 2: Purchases	526,800	819,500
Step 3: Total merchandise available for sale	$622,200	$958,200
Step 4: Less sales		815,300
Step 5: Ending inventory priced at retail		$142,900

Step 6: Cost ratio = ($622,200 ÷ $958,200) = 65%

Step 7: Conversion to approximate cost:

     Ending inventory at retail × Cost ratio = $142,900 × 0.65

     Ending inventory at cost = $92,885

Step 8: Cost of goods sold = $622,200 − $92,885 = $529,315

The benefit of the retail method is that without counting inventory the business is able to estimate the ending inventory balance at cost.

The retail method is not as simple as this example suggests. Adjustments must be made for **markups,** price increases above the original markons, and markup cancellations. Adjustments are also made for **markdowns,** price reductions below the original markon, and for markdown cancellations. These details are not covered in this text.

A more accurate application of the retail method involves taking a physical inventory, which is facilitated by using scanning devices to capture the sales price marked on the merchandise. The physical inventory at retail is converted to cost by applying the cost ratio. For example, if the physical inventory count shows retail cost of $60,000 and the cost ratio is 66.67 percent, the cost of the inventory is estimated to be $40,000 ($60,000 × 0.667).

The retail method for determining cost is used by many large retailers. For example, in notes to its financial statements for the fiscal year ending January 31, 2013, The Home Depot, Inc., states:

> The majority of the Company's Merchandise Inventories are stated at the lower of cost (first-in first-out) or market, as determined by the retail inventory method.

Internal Control of Inventories

The internal controls over inventory depend on the nature of the inventory. For example, controls for expensive jewelry are more elaborate than controls over lumber. Typical inventory controls are as follows:

- Limit access to inventory of small valuable items.
- Require documents, such as approved shipping orders, before allowing items to leave the warehouse.
- Take a physical inventory count at least annually to verify that the goods on hand match the amounts in the accounting records. Use spot checks to verify the counting techniques and the item costs. Have an independent auditor observe the count.

The notes to the financial statements in The Home Depot's *2012 Annual Report (for the fiscal year ended February 3, 2013)* stress the importance of periodic inventories when a perpetual inventory system is used.

> Independent physical inventory counts or cycle counts are taken on a regular basis in each store and distribution center to ensure that amounts reflected in the accompanying Consolidated Financial Statements for Merchandise Inventories are properly stated. During the period between physical inventory counts, the Company accrues for estimated losses related to shrink on a store-by-store basis based on historical shrink results and current trends in the business. Shrink is the difference between the recorded amount of inventory and the physical inventory. Shrink (or in the case of excess inventory, "swell") may occur due to theft, loss, improper records for the receipt of inventory or deterioration of goods, among other things.

New Technology in Inventory Control

One of the problems with the use of "bar scanners" in checking inventories is that the methodology requires "line of sight" contact between the scanner and the bar code on the merchandise. This often requires physical movement of goods in the warehouse in order to obtain the line of sight. This is true not only at time of inventory taking, but in searching for goods that have been "recalled" by the manufacturer and in finding goods to move from the warehouse to the salesroom. This may be labor intensive and slow.

In the summer of 2003, Walmart launched an RFID (radio frequency identification) initiative. It asked its largest 100 suppliers to apply a "passive" electronic tag to all pallets and cases of merchandise shipped to three of its distribution centers. The system will enable the company to determine quickly whether merchandise is on hand in the warehouse or has been moved to the floor of the store. It is obvious that the technique could be very valuable, especially in the control of warehouse stocks.

The U.S. Department of Defense has announced a similar program using RFID, which means that two of the world's largest purchasers of goods plan to install the program. Other major retailers, such as Best Buy, Target, and The Home Depot, Inc., are also considering installing the technology. The system also promises to aid suppliers of merchandise in planning and controlling inventory sales to buyers using the program.

Up-to-date information about RFID can be obtained by accessing the website of the American Production and Inventory Control Society (www.apics.org).

ABOUT
ACCOUNTING

Inventory Financing

Many businesses obtain credit based on their merchandise inventory. Inventory financing uses the inventory on hand as collateral for the credit line.

Section 2   Self Review

QUESTIONS

1. Which accounting principles, concepts, or modifying conventions underlie the valuation of inventories at the lower of cost or market?

2. What does "the lower of cost or market" mean?

3. Name three ways by which the lower of cost or market rule might be applied. Which will give the lowest ending inventory valuation?

EXERCISES

4. When would a business use the gross profit method instead of the retail method to estimate the cost of ending inventory?

5. Under what circumstances would the gross profit method of estimating inventory be used?

ANALYSIS

6. Which of these inventory costing procedures does not require a physical count of the inventory items?

   a. Retail method

   b. Specific identification method

   c. Lower of cost or market method

   d. Average cost method

(Answers to Section 2 Self Review are on page 597.)

17 Chapter REVIEW Chapter Summary

It is important to account for merchandise inventory because the information appears on both the balance sheet and the income statement. Industry practices, merchandise unit costs, and merchandise price fluctuations affect how costs are assigned to inventory.

Learning Objectives

17-1 Compute inventory cost by applying four commonly used costing methods.

There are four common inventory cost flow assumptions.

- The specific identification method uses the actual purchase price of the specific items in inventory.
- The average cost method averages the cost of all like items for sale during the period to value the ending inventory unit cost.
- The FIFO method develops the cost of the ending inventory from the cost of latest purchases.
- The LIFO method develops the cost of the ending inventory from the cost of beginning inventory and earlier purchases.

17-2 Compare the effects of different methods of inventory costing.

The method used affects the net income reported.

- With rising prices, LIFO gives a lower reported net income than FIFO, as well as lower income taxes payable.
- With falling prices, LIFO gives a higher reported net income than FIFO.
- The average cost method almost always gives a result between these.

17-3 Compute inventory value under the lower of cost or market rule.

- Assets are reported on financial statements at their historical cost. However, assets should not be overstated.
- If the replacement cost of an inventory item is below its original purchase cost, it is necessary to value the inventory at the lower current value in the firm's financial records.

- Consequently, inventory is valued at either its original cost, or its replacement cost, whichever is lower. This is called the lower of cost or market.
- Cost refers to the historical cost.
- Market refers to the replacement cost.
- The lower of cost or market can be applied to individual items in the inventory, to groups of items, or to the inventory as a whole.

17-4 Estimate inventory cost using the gross profit method.

The gross profit method of estimating inventory assumes that the rate of gross profit on sales and the ratio of cost of goods sold to net sales are relatively constant from period to period. Ending inventory can be estimated using three steps:

1. Estimate the cost of goods sold by multiplying net sales by the normal ratio of cost of goods sold to net sales.
2. Determine goods available for sale by adding beginning inventory and net purchases.
3. Compute ending inventory by subtracting the estimated cost of goods sold (in step 1) from goods available for sale (in step 2).

17-5 Estimate inventory cost using the retail method.

The retail method uses the retail selling price of items remaining. The retail value is multiplied by the cost ratio of the current period to determine the approximate cost. This method entails a full consideration of markups, markup cancellations, markdowns, and markdown cancellations.

17-6 Define the accounting terms new to this chapter.

Glossary

Average cost method (p. 575) A method of inventory costing using the average cost of units of an item available for sale during the period to arrive at cost of the ending inventory

First in, first out (FIFO) method (p. 576) A method of inventory costing that assumes the oldest merchandise is sold first

Gross profit method (p. 581) A method of estimating inventory cost based on the assumption that the rate of gross profit on sales and the ratio of cost of goods sold to net sales are relatively constant from period to period

Last in, first out (LIFO) method (p. 576) A method of inventory costing that assumes the most recently purchased merchandise is sold first

Lower of cost or market rule (p. 579) The principle by which inventory is reported at either its original cost or its replacement cost, whichever is lower

Markdown (p. 583) Price reduction below the original markon

Market price (p. 579) The price the business would pay to buy an item of inventory through usual channels in usual quantities

Markon (p. 582) The difference between the cost and the initial retail price of merchandise

Markup (p. 583) A price increase above the original markon

Periodic inventory (p. 574) Inventory based on a periodic count of goods on hand

Perpetual inventory (p. 574) Inventory based on a running total of number of units

Physical inventory (p. 574) An actual count of the number of units of each type of good on hand

Replacement cost (p. 579) See Market price

Retail method (p. 582) A method of estimating inventory cost by applying the ratio of cost to selling price in the current accounting period to the retail price of the inventory

Specific identification method (p. 575) A method of inventory costing based on the actual cost of each item of merchandise

Weighted average method (p. 576) See Average cost method

Comprehensive **Self Review**

1. Suggest two situations in which it might be desirable (or necessary) to estimate inventories without a physical count.

2. How do the gross profit method and the retail method used to estimate inventory differ, if at all?

3. What is the formula for the cost ratio used in the retail method of estimating inventory?

4. How often should a physical inventory be taken?

5. Under what circumstances would it be logical to use specific identification in determining the ending inventory?

6. Name four commonly used methods or assumptions for determining the cost of an inventory.

(Answers to Comprehensive Self Review are on page 597.)

Discussion Questions

1. What accounting principle or constraint underlies the lower of cost or market rule for inventory valuation?

2. What impact does the ending inventory have on net income for the period covered by the financial statements?

3. Does the maintenance of a perpetual inventory eliminate the need for taking physical inventory? Explain.

4. Why is a perpetual inventory easier to maintain today than it would have been 50 years ago?

5. Under what circumstances is the specific identification method for determining cost of inventory items logical?

6. Explain briefly the average cost method.

7. What is meant by the *first in, first out* assumption?

8. What is meant by the term *market* as it is used in the lower of cost or market rule?

9. Explain how the lower of cost or market method is applied on a group basis.

10. Is the value of inventory likely to be lower if the cost or market rule is applied on an item-by-item basis, on a group basis, or to the inventory as a whole?

11. In a period of rising prices, is the *LIFO* method or the *FIFO* method likely to yield the larger inventory cost?

12. A company uses the *LIFO* inventory method to determine cost. One of the managers complains that this is improper. He states: "We always sell our oldest products first. So we should be using *first in, first out* inventory costing." What would you say in response to his comment?

13. Explain the retail method of inventory estimation.

14. Suggest two situations where it may be necessary or desirable to estimate the inventory without a physical count.

15. Suggest some specific controls that management must provide over inventory in a business that sells diamonds.

APPLICATIONS

Exercises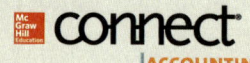

Exercise 17.1
Objective 17-1

Using the various costing methods of inventory valuation.

Information about Thompson Company's inventory of one item follows. Compute the cost of the ending inventory under (1) the average cost method (round unit cost to nearest cent), (2) the FIFO method, and (3) the LIFO method.

Explanation	Number of Units	Unit Cost
Beginning inventory, January 1	230	$365
Purchases:		
April	270	370
August	290	375
October	240	377
Ending inventory, December 31	230	

Exercise 17.2
Objective 17-3

Using the lower of cost or market method.

The following information concerns four items that 21st Century Clothiers has in its ending inventory on December 31. Two of these items are in the accessories department, and two are in the men's jackets department.

	Quantity	Unit Cost	Market Value
Accessories			
Item 620	250	$29	$ 32
Item 621	160	55	52
Men's jackets			
Item 726	110	95	102
Item 727	140	46	45

1. What is the valuation of ending inventory if the firm uses the lower of cost or market method and applies it on an item-by-item basis?

2. If the company applies the lower of cost or market method on the basis of total cost or total market, what is the value of ending inventory?

3. If the company elects to apply the lower of cost or market method to inventory groups, what is the value of the ending inventory?

Determining the effect on income of different costing assumptions.

◀ **Exercise 17.3**
Objective 17-2

Given the choice between average cost, FIFO, and LIFO, which method will give the lowest net income and which will give the highest net income in a period of rising prices?

Estimating inventory cost under the gross profit method.

◀ **Exercise 17.4**
Objective 17-4

Use the following data to compute the estimated inventory cost for Strathe Company under the gross profit method:

Average gross profit rate: 30% of sales
Inventory on January 1 (at cost): $230,000
Purchases from January 1 to date of inventory estimate: $1,040,000
Net sales for period: $1,300,000

Estimating inventory cost under the retail method.

◀ **Exercise 17.5**
Objective 17-5

Based on the following data, compute the estimated cost of the ending inventory at Crowley Company. Use the retail method.

	Cost	Retail
Beginning inventory	$215,000	$339,000
Purchases	325,000	490,000
Freight in	2,100	
Sales		507,000

PROBLEMS

Problem Set A  |ACCOUNTING

Computing inventory costs under different valuation methods.

◀ **Problem 17.1A**
Objective 17-1

The following data concerns inventory and purchases at Drake Company:

Inventory, January 1	100 units at $113
Purchases:	
January 6	70 units at $112
January 15	54 units at $112
January 22	44 units at $106
Inventory, January 31	100 units

INSTRUCTIONS

Determine the cost of the ending inventory on January 31 under each of the following methods: (a) average cost method; (b) first in, first out (FIFO) method; and (c) last in, first out (LIFO) method. When using the average cost method, compute the unit cost to two decimal places.

Analyze: Which inventory valuation method resulted in the highest dollar amount for ending inventory?

Problem 17.2A
Objectives 17-1, 17-3

▶ **Computing inventory costs under different valuation methods and applying the lower of cost or market rule.**

The following data pertains to On-Target Investment Accounting software packages in the inventory of Computer Program On-Target Outlets:

Inventory, January 1	220 units at $117
Purchases:	
May 10	160 units at $115
August 18	230 units at $114
October 1	220 units at $115
Inventory, December 31	228 units

INSTRUCTIONS

1. Determine the cost of the inventory on December 31 and the cost of goods sold for the year ending on that date under each of the following valuation methods: (a) FIFO, (b) LIFO, and (c) average cost. When using the average cost method, compute the unit cost to the nearest cent.

2. Assume that the replacement cost of each unit on December 31 is $115.25. Using the lower of cost or market rule, find the inventory amount under each of the methods given in instruction 1.

Analyze: What is the difference between the cost and market value of the inventory using the LIFO method?

Problem 17.3A
Objective 17-3

▶ **Applying the lower of cost or market rule by different methods.**

This data is for selected inventory items at Office Supply Company:

	Quantity	Unit Cost	Market Value
Printer Cartridges			
Item 119	70	$ 36.00	$ 36.50
Item 120	80	29.75	26.50
Item 121	110	33.00	28.50
Fax Machines			
Item 210	25	96.00	99.00
Item 211	20	202.00	196.00
Item 212	19	235.00	220.00

INSTRUCTIONS

Determine the amount to be reported as the inventory valuation at cost or market, whichever is lower, under each of these methods:

1. Lower of cost or market for each item separately.

2. Lower of total cost or total market.

3. Lower of total cost or total market by group.

Analyze: Which valuation method will yield the highest net income?

Estimating inventory by the gross profit method.

◀ Problem 17.4A
Objective 17-4

Over the past several years, Sullivan Electronics Company has had an average gross profit of 30 percent. At the end of 2016, the income statement of the company included the following information:

Sales		$1,759,000
Cost of Goods		
Inventory, January 1, 2016	$ 122,000	
Purchases	1,220,000	
Total Merchandise Available for Sale	1,342,000	
Less Inventory, December 31, 2016	146,875	
Cost of Goods Sold		1,195,125
Gross Profit on Sales		$ 563,875

Investigation revealed that employees of the company had not taken an actual physical count of the inventory on December 31. Instead, they had merely estimated the inventory.

INSTRUCTIONS

Using the gross profit method of inventory estimation, verify the reasonableness (or lack of reasonableness) of the ending inventory shown on the income statement.

Analyze: If a physical inventory count on December 31, 2016, revealed an ending inventory of $145,563, calculate the gross profit percentage to the nearest one-tenth of 1 percent.

Estimating inventory by the retail method.

◀ Problem 17.5A
Objective 17-5

The August 1 inventory of Haggett Company had a cost of $90,000 and a retail value of $125,000. During August, merchandise was purchased for $101,130 and marked to sell for $152,000. August sales totaled $136,000.

INSTRUCTIONS

1. Compute the retail value of the ending inventory as of August 31.
2. Compute the approximate cost of the ending inventory.
3. Compute the cost of goods sold during August.

Analyze: What is the amount of estimated gross profit on sales for the month ending August 31?

Applying the correct method of evaluating inventory.

◀ Problem 17.6A
Objectives 17-1,
17-2

Reasoner Sailing Company sells boats as a supplement to its boat storage operations. Data for its boat sales for August 2016 are given below. The beginning inventory on August 1 was composed of the following items:

	Cost	Retail
28' Starfish	$45,000	$57,000
30' Perch	65,000	85,000
24' Sea King	26,000	30,000
30' Holiday	46,000	60,000
20' Lake King	28,000	34,500

INSTRUCTIONS

Sales during the month were the 30' Holiday and the 20' Lake King, sold at the retail values shown on August 1.

1. What is the best method of valuing the ending inventory?

2. Determine the value of Reasoner Sailing Company's ending inventory of items that were brought over from the beginning inventory using this method. Assume that the company's retail values had not changed.

3. Determine the cost of goods sold during August.

Analyze: What is the estimated gross profit on sales for August?

Problem Set B

Problem 17.1B
Objective 17-1

▶ **Computing inventory costs under different valuation methods.**

The following data relates to the inventory and purchases of item 125 for Sanders Company during May:

Inventory, May 1	260 units at $21.00
Purchases:	
May 10	190 units at $20.75
May 19	140 units at $20.35
May 25	160 units at $20.40
Inventory, May 31	230 units

INSTRUCTIONS

Determine the cost of the ending inventory on May 31 under each of the following methods: (a) average cost method; (b) first in, first out (FIFO) method; and, (c) last in, first out (LIFO) method. When using the average cost method, compute the unit cost to two decimal places.

Analyze: Which inventory amount will result in the highest income for the period?

Problem 17.2B
Objectives 17-1, 17-3

▶ **Computing inventory costs under different valuation methods and applying the lower of cost or market rule.**

The following data pertain to Model Q two-wheeled trailers in the inventory of Travel Trailers Equipment Company during the year 2016:

Inventory, January 1	25 units at $2,620
Purchases:	
February 27	19 units at $2,330
August 16	23 units at $2,325
November 19	17 units at $2,435
Inventory, December 31	18 units

INSTRUCTIONS

1. Determine the cost of the inventory on December 31 and the cost of goods sold for the year ending on that date under each of the following valuation methods: (a) FIFO, (b) LIFO, and (c) average cost. When using the average cost method, compute the unit cost to the nearest cent.

2. Assume that the replacement cost of each unit on December 31 is $2,425. Using the lower of cost or market rule, find the inventory amount under each of the methods given in instruction 1.

Analyze: Using the lower of cost or market rule, which inventory amount will result in the highest net income for the period?

Applying the lower of cost or market rule by different methods.   ◀   Problem 17.3B
Objective 17-3

The following data concerns inventory at Mike's Boat & Bike Shop:

	Quantity	Unit Cost	Market Value
Motor Bike Department			
Model 705	16	$ 9,810	$ 9,775
Model 766	26	10,275	11,375
Model 815	13	12,500	12,850
Boat Department			
Model BX12	9	5,300	5,400
Model BX14	8	7,150	7,010
Model BX16	7	5,110	5,350

INSTRUCTIONS

Determine the amount that the company should report as the inventory valuation at cost or market, whichever is lower. Use each of the following three valuation methods:

1. Lower of cost or market for each item separately.
2. Lower of total cost or total market.
3. Lower of total cost or total market by group.

Analyze: Which valuation method will yield the highest net income?

Estimating inventory by the gross profit method.   ◀   Problem 17.4B
Objective 17-4

Over the last two years, McBride Company has averaged 35 percent gross profit. At the end of 2016, the auditor found the following data in the records of the company:

Sales		$6,150,000
Cost of goods sold:		
Inventory, January 1, 2016	$ 420,000	
Purchases	4,180,000	
Total merchandise available for sale	4,600,000	
Less inventory, December 31, 2016	604,000	
Cost of goods sold		3,996,000
Gross profit on sales		$2,154,000

Inquiry by the auditor revealed that employees of McBride Company had estimated the inventory on December 31, 2016, instead of taking a complete physical count.

INSTRUCTIONS

Using the gross profit method of inventory estimation, verify the reasonableness (or lack of reasonableness) of the inventory estimate made by the company's employees.

Analyze: If a physical inventory count on December 31, 2016, revealed an ending inventory of $520,000, calculate the gross profit percentage.

Estimating inventory by the retail method.   ◀   Problem 17.5B
Objective 17-5

The April 1 inventory of Alexis Stores had a cost of $918,000 and a retail value of $1,340,000. During April, merchandise was purchased for $1,069,000 and marked to sell for $1,676,000. Freight in was $18,000. April sales totaled $2,150,000.

INSTRUCTIONS

1. Compute the retail value of the ending inventory as of April 30.

2. Compute the approximate cost of the ending inventory.

3. Compute the cost of goods sold during April.

Analyze: What is the gross profit on sales for the period ending April 30?

Problem 17.6B
Objectives 17-1, 17-2

▶ **Using the correct inventory valuation method.**

Buxton Realty Group had two completed unsold buildings on hand on January 1, 2016.

Unit 06-92: Cost, $790,000; retail price, $964,000
Unit 06-94: Cost, $873,000; retail price, $1,008,000

During the period January 1 through March 31, the company completed the following construction jobs:

	Cost	Sales Price
Unit 06-95	$1,900,000	$2,290,000
Unit 07-01	919,000	1,178,000
Unit 07-03	836,000	1,115,000
Unit 07-05	1,120,000	1,450,500

All the units except 06-92 and 07-05 were sold in the quarter ending March 31.

INSTRUCTIONS

1. Determine the appropriate costing method for inventory in this construction business.

2. What value should be reported in the balance sheet for the company for the unsold units on March 31? Assume that it is firmly believed that the two houses will be sold for the retail price shown.

3. Determine the cost of goods sold in the first quarter, assuming that all houses sold were sold for the retail prices listed.

Analyze: What is gross profit on sales for the quarter ending March 31?

Critical Thinking Problem 17.1

Inventory Estimation

Wilson Computer Supply Company has just been destroyed by fire. Fortunately, however, the computerized accounting records had been "backed up" and were in a remote computer location so that the records were not destroyed. The company does not use the retail method of accounting, so although beginning inventory at cost, purchases at cost, purchases returns and allowances, freight in, sales, sales returns and allowances, and other accounting information is available, the retail method of estimating inventory destroyed cannot be used.

What suggestion can you give for determining the estimated cost of the inventory destroyed? What information is needed, and where would this information be found?

Critical Thinking Problem 17.2

Inventory Estimation

One of Pickens Company's retail outlets was destroyed by fire on March 18. All merchandise was burned. The company has fire insurance on its merchandise inventory. It will therefore file a claim for recovery of cost of the lost inventory. Clearly, a physical inventory cannot be taken because the inventory has been destroyed. The branch's records were kept by the home office, and you have been asked to examine the records to determine an estimate of the cost of the lost merchandise. As of March 18, the firm's records disclosed the following data about the beginning inventory for the year, the merchandise purchases made during the period, and total sales during the period:

	Actual Cost	Retail Sales Price
Beginning inventory, January 1	$ 90,000	$117,600
Merchandise purchases, January 1–March 18	250,000	330,500
Freight on purchases	9,300	
Total sales, January 1–March 18		360,000

INSTRUCTIONS

Determine the approximate cost of the inventory destroyed on March 18.

Analyze: Based on the cost you have computed for merchandise inventory, calculate the cost of goods sold for the period.

BUSINESS CONNECTIONS

Inventory Methods

Managerial FOCUS

1. In what special situations are inventory estimation procedures extremely useful?

2. The manager of a retail store has become concerned about the time taken to count the merchandise on hand each quarter. She argues that too much time is spent on this activity with a resulting high cost of labor. She suggests that the company need not take a physical inventory at all but could rely on the retail inventory estimation procedure to arrive at the cost of the inventory. Respond to this argument.

3. What are two specific managerial reasons for using the LIFO method of inventory valuation during a period of rising prices?

4. In order to achieve better control over its investment in inventory, the management of a retail store wishes to get an estimate of the cost of inventory at the close of business each week. Outline a procedure to obtain this estimate without actually taking a physical count.

5. Explain briefly how computers and other electronic devices, such as scanners, have made perpetual inventories more practical.

6. The purchasing manager of a retail store has suggested that the company should maintain a perpetual inventory. The controller opposes this suggestion. In your opinion, on what basis does the controller probably oppose the idea?

Missing Inventory

Ethical DILEMMA

Erica has a baby clothing shop called The Baby Store. Erica has worked in her shop for several months. Her sales have doubled each month. Erica has decided to hire Wendy, a sales associate, since she needs to be away from the shop on a regular basis. After several months, Erica noticed that her purchases increased but sales did not go up in the same proportion and inventory is low. She is finding her net income is lower than previous months. State the cause of her decreased income and determine the actions that should be taken.

Balance Sheet

The following excerpt was taken from The Home Depot, Inc. *2012 Annual Report (for the fiscal year ended February 3, 2013)*:

Consolidated Balance Sheets		
(Dollars in millions)	February 3, 2013	January 29, 2012
Assets		
Current Assets:		
Cash and cash equivalents	$ 2,494	$ 1,987
Receivables, net	1,395	1,245
Merchandise inventories	10,710	10,325
Other current assets	773	963
Total Current Assets	$15,372	$14,520

Analyze:

1. By what amount has merchandise inventory increased or decreased from January 29, 2012 to February 3, 2013?

2. What percentage of current assets is attributable to inventories at February 3, 2013?

Analyze Online: Locate The Home Depot, Inc. website (www.homedepot.com) and click on the *About Home Depot link*, then click on *Home Depot Investor Information*.

3. Find the most recent annual report. What method is used to assign cost to the merchandise inventory? (Hint: See the Notes to Consolidated Financial Statements).

4. What is the stated value of the most recent year's merchandise inventory?

Inventory Controls

Inventory control measures vary depending on the type of product to be sold. As a team, choose a type of product to be sold. Develop inventory control measures for your particular product. Determine control measures that would be the same for each business and one that would be unique for the chosen product.

Inventory Costing Methods

A corporation must disclose in the annual report how inventory is valued and costed. Go to the Balance Sheet of five retail stores, e.g., The Home Depot, American Outfitter (ae.com), Krugers, or others. Make a comparison chart showing the inventory dollars listed in the balance sheet for the current and previous years. Go to the notes included in the annual report. The notes are listed in the same order as the accounts in the balance sheet. Find the note about inventory. List the valuation and costing method for each corporation. Is the inventory the same for each type of corporation? Has the inventory decreased, remained the same, or increased? Is there a dollar difference between the LIFO and FIFO methods?

Answers to **Self Reviews**

Answers to Section 1 Self Review

1. LIFO pricing will produce the highest cost of goods sold and the lowest net income in a period of rising prices.

2. The principle of consistency requires that the same method of pricing inventory should be used each year.

3. LIFO (or FIFO) may be used regardless of actual physical flow of merchandise.

4. FIFO assumes that merchandise is sold in the order it is received. In this way, the oldest costs identified with merchandise are charged to cost of goods sold.

5. You will want to know the current and future economic outlook for the industry—how the cost of merchandise and the demands for products are likely to change.

6. LIFO stands for last in, first out. This method computes the cost of the inventory on hand as though the last merchandise received is the first to be sold. This is done so that the most current costs are matched with revenue.

Answers to Section 2 Self Review

1. The conservatism constraint is the primary underlying concept that supports the lower of cost or market rule.

2. This means the lower amount of (a) the net cost of merchandise, including freight in, or (b) the amount that it would cost to replace the merchandise today if it were bought in normal quantities and under normal operating conditions.

3. It may be applied: (a) item by item, (b) by groups of items, or (c) by total cost and total market for the entire inventory. Application on an item-by-item basis will yield the lowest inventory value.

4. The retail method assumes that perpetual records are kept of the sales price of inventory items. The gross profit method does not require that the selling price of items on hand be known.

5. The gross profit method would be used if the inventory has been destroyed by fire, theft, or other means. It may also be used to quickly estimate the cost of inventory on hand without taking a physical inventory when cost estimates are needed for managerial or operational purposes.

6. **a.** The retail method does not require a physical count of inventory items.

Answers to Comprehensive Self Review

1. The most obvious cases are when a fire or theft has occurred. Any other situation where the inventory has been physically removed or when a quick estimate is needed may call for an estimate.

2. The retail method assumes that records have been kept of all inventory transactions at sales price (including price adjustments of merchandise), as well as cost, so that the inventory value at sales price of the merchandise is always known and readily convertible to a cost basis. The gross profit method is used when retail price of inventory is unknown and has to be computed. The gross profit method uses a historical percentage rate whereas the retail method calculates the percentage using current amounts. Therefore, the retail method results in a more current gross profit percentage.

3. Cost ratio = Cost of merchandise available for sale/Retail sales price of merchandise available for sale.

4. Generally, inventory is taken once a year. If there is a history of thefts, breakage, overstocking or understocking, or other operational problems, it may be necessary to make physical counts more often.

5. When there are relatively few items and each has a high cost.

6. Specific identification, average costing, FIFO, and LIFO.

Property, Plant, and Equipment

Chapter 18

The Coca-Cola Company
www.cocacola.com

In the early 1800s, if you wanted an icy cold Coke, you had to head to your local soda fountain and sit at the counter to enjoy your Coke. It wasn't until 1899 that two attorneys from Tennessee paid The Coca-Cola Company $1 for the exclusive rights to bottle and sell Coca-Cola across the United States.

When the idea of bottling was conceived by these two entrepreneurs, they knew that they would have to invest in a bottling company that could create the packaging material—both the bottle and the label (or purchase them from suppliers)—and then bottle the finished drink. To get their Coca-Cola beverage into the hands of buyers, they invested in transportation equipment to distribute their drinks. Since those early years, the business has grown into a multibillion dollar company that sells its products in more than 200 countries. In 2012, Coca-Cola's reported investments in property, plant, and equipment, net of depreciation, amounted to over $14 billion!

If we step into a Coca-Cola bottling plant today, we might see thousands of bottles on conveyors working their way around to the syrup/soda station or getting ready to be sealed. Old equipment is replaced with new, more efficient equipment if the change can save the company production costs. Coca-Cola has become the world's largest beverage distribution system by maintaining the highest quality standards for its products and using the most cost effective production techniques. Their mission—*to refresh the world*—has become a reality.

thinking critically

When The Coca-Cola Company contemplates replacing older equipment with newer equipment, what factors would go into making the final decision?

LEARNING OBJECTIVES

18-1. Determine the amount to record as an asset's cost.

18-2. Compute and record depreciation of property, plant, and equipment by commonly used methods.

18-3. Apply the Modified Accelerated Cost Recovery System (MACRS) for federal income tax purposes.

18-4. Record sales of plant and equipment.

18-5. Record asset trade-ins using financial accounting rules and income tax requirements.

18-6. Compute and record depletion of natural resources.

18-7. Recognize asset impairment and understand the general concepts of accounting for impairment.

18-8. Compute and record amortization and impairment of intangible assets.

18-9. Define the accounting terms new to this chapter.

NEW TERMS

accelerated method of depreciation
amortization
brand name
capitalized costs
computer software
copyright
declining-balance method
depletion
double-declining-balance method
franchise
gain
goodwill
impairment
income tax method
intangible assets

loss
net book value
net salvage value
patent
real property
recoverability test
residual value
scrap value
sum-of-the-years'-digits method
tangible personal property
trade name
trademark
units-of-output method
units-of-production method

Acquisition and Depreciation

Setting up and maintaining a business often requires a large investment in property, plant, and equipment—assets often referred to as *fixed assets* or *capital assets*. In this section, two aspects of accounting for property, plant, and equipment are discussed:

- The costs of acquiring the assets.
- The transfer of the costs of these assets to expense through depreciation.

>> **18-1. OBJECTIVE**

Determine the amount to record as an asset's cost.

Property, Plant, and Equipment Classifications

As discussed in Chapter 12, *property, plant, and equipment* includes real property and tangible personal property purchased for use in the business and having a life of more than one year. **Real property** consists of land, land improvements (such as sidewalks and parking lots), buildings, and other structures attached to the land. **Tangible personal property** includes machinery, equipment, furniture, and fixtures that can be removed and used elsewhere.

The property, plant, and equipment classification does not include assets purchased for investment reasons. For example, land purchased for investment purposes is classified as other assets or investments.

Acquisition of Property, Plant, and Equipment

An important issue in accounting for property, plant, and equipment is determining which costs should be capitalized. **Capitalized costs** are all costs recorded as part of the asset's cost.

COSTS OF EQUIPMENT AND OTHER TANGIBLE PERSONAL PROPERTY

The total cost of an asset can consist of several elements. Each element is debited to the account for that asset. The acquisition cost of an asset includes:

- gross purchase price less discounts, including cash discounts for prompt payment;
- transportation costs;

- installation costs;
- costs of adjustments or modifications needed to prepare the asset for use.

On January 2, 2016, Hazlenut Company purchased store equipment for $18,000 and paid state and local sales taxes of $1,400. Transportation costs were $680. When the equipment arrived, extra features were installed at a cost of $800. The **Store Equipment** account is debited for $20,880, as summarized below:

Purchase price	$18,000
Sales taxes	1,400
Transportation costs	680
Modification and installation costs	800
Total acquisition cost of machine	$20,880

COST OF LAND AND BUILDING

The cost of land includes its purchase price, legal costs in connection with the acquisition, abstracts, title insurance, recording fees, and any other costs paid by the purchaser that are related to the acquisition.

The acquisition cost of land purchased for a building site should include the net costs (less salvage) of removing unwanted buildings and grading and draining the land. Remember that land is not depreciated.

Land improvements include the cost of installing permanent walks or roadways, curbing, gutters, and drainage facilities. These costs are debited to the asset account **Land Improvements.** Land improvements are depreciated.

If land and a building are purchased together for a single price, the purchase price is allocated between the **Land** and **Building** accounts. The amount allocated to the building is depreciated. The amount allocated to land is not depreciated.

ASSETS CONSTRUCTED BY OR FOR THE BUSINESS

When a building or other property, plant, and equipment is constructed and used by the business, the capitalized costs include all costs of labor, materials, permits and fees, insurance, measurable direct overhead, and other reasonable and necessary costs of construction. Interest costs incurred on borrowed funds during the construction period are capitalized as part of the asset.

Depreciation of Property, Plant, and Equipment

Buildings, machinery, equipment, furniture, and fixtures are depreciated because they have a limited life and will get used up or deteriorate over time. Depreciation is the allocation of the cost of the asset over the asset's useful life. Depreciation does not refer to a decrease in the market value of the asset.

RECORDING DEPRECIATION

Assets that are used for more than one year are capitalized. Asset account names are descriptive, for example, **Office Equipment, Store Equipment, Vehicles,** or **Buildings.** At the end of each accounting period, depreciation for the period is debited to **Depreciation Expense** and credited to a contra asset account, **Accumulated Depreciation. Accumulated Depreciation** shows all depreciation that has been taken during the asset's life.

For example, a business purchased a building for $500,000 on January 2, 2016. At the end of the first year, annual depreciation expense of $12,500 was entered on the worksheet as an adjustment. It was recorded as an adjusting entry in the general journal as follows:

important!

Tangible Personal Property
The term "personal" means that the property has a physical substance and is something other than real estate. Personal property is owned by the business, not by the individual owners.

ABOUT
ACCOUNTING

Fixed Assets
According to Asset Advisors, a Florida consulting firm, fixed assets represent 35 to 50 percent of the typical Fortune 500 company's assets.

recall

Land
Land is not depreciated. Land has an indefinite life. Land does not deteriorate or get used up.

>> **18-2. OBJECTIVE**
Compute and record depreciation of property, plant, and equipment by commonly used methods.

11	Dec.	31	Depreciation Expense—Buildings	12 5 0 0 00		11
12			Accumulated Depreciation—Buildings		12 5 0 0 00	12
13			To record depreciation for the year			13

The balance sheet shows a long-term asset's cost minus its accumulated depreciation. The difference is its book value, also known as its **net book value.** Book value is rarely the same as fair market value, which is the asset's price on the open market. After two years of depreciation, the balance sheet presentation for the building is as follows:

Property, Plant, and Equipment

Building	$500,000.00
Less Accumulated Depreciation	25,000.00
	$475,000.00

> In fiscal 2012, Coca-Cola recorded **Depreciation and Amortization Expense** of $1,982 billion. On December 31, 2012, the cost of its property, plant, and equipment was shown in the balance sheet at a net book value of $14,476 billion.

Depreciation information shown on the financial statements or in notes accompanying the financial statements includes:

- depreciation expense for the period;
- balances in the depreciable asset accounts, classified according to their nature or their function;
- accumulated depreciation;
- description of the method(s) used to compute depreciation.

DEPRECIATION METHODS

Several methods are used to compute depreciation. Some of them use salvage value in the calculation. Under these methods, assets are not depreciated below salvage value. *Salvage value,* **residual value,** or **scrap value** is an estimate of the amount that could be obtained from an asset's sale or disposition at the end of its useful life. The **net salvage value** is the salvage value of the asset less any costs to remove or sell it.

Straight-Line Method   The straight-line method introduced in Chapter 5 is the most widely used method of computing depreciation expense for financial statement purposes. Under the straight-line method, an equal amount of depreciation is recorded for each period over the useful life of the asset. Figure 18.1 shows straight-line depreciation of $432 per year.

FIGURE 18.1

Straight-Line Depreciation

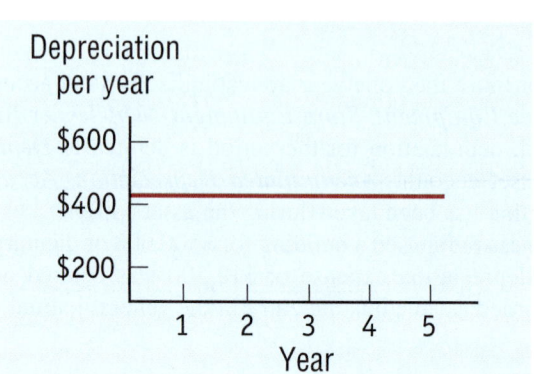

The formula for straight-line depreciation is as follows:

$$\text{Depreciation} = \frac{\text{Cost} - \text{Salvage value}}{\text{Estimated useful life}}$$

On January 2, 2016, Hazlenut Company purchased office equipment for $2,400. The equipment has an estimated useful life of five years, with a net salvage value of $240. Using the straight-line method, the annual depreciation is $432 [($2,400 − $240)/5]. ***Depreciation Expense—Office Equipment*** will be debited for $432 and ***Accumulated Depreciation—Office Equipment*** will be credited for $432 each year.

When an asset is acquired during the year, depreciation is typically calculated to the nearest month. If the asset is acquired during the first 15 days of the month, depreciation is taken for the full month. If the asset is acquired after the 15th, depreciation starts in the following month. Suppose that Hazlenut Company purchased the office equipment on September 5. The monthly depreciation is $36 ($432 ÷ 12). Depreciation for the first year is $144 (4 months × $36). The journal entry is as follows:

11	Dec.	31	Depreciation Expense—Office Equip.	1 4 4 00	11
12			Accumulated Depreciation—Office Equip.	1 4 4 00	12
13			To record depreciation for four		13
14			months on equipment acquired		14
15			September 5		15

Declining-Balance Method Under the **declining-balance method** of depreciation, the book value of an asset at the beginning of the year is multiplied by a percentage to determine depreciation for the year. The declining-balance method is an **accelerated method of depreciation,** which allocates greater amounts of depreciation to an asset's early years of useful life. The declining-balance computation ignores salvage value until the year in which the book value is reduced to estimated salvage value. Figure 18.2 illustrates the declining-balance method in graphical form.

One of the most common rates used is the **double-declining-balance (DDB).** DDB uses a rate equal to twice the straight-line rate and applies that rate to the book value of the asset at the beginning of the year. Follow these steps to calculate double-declining-balance depreciation on the office equipment for which straight-line depreciation was illustrated above:

Step 1. *Calculate the straight-line rate.*

$$\frac{100 \text{ percent}}{\text{Useful life}} = \frac{100 \text{ percent}}{5 \text{ years}} = 20 \text{ percent}$$

Step 2. *Calculate the double-declining rate.* The double-declining rate is the straight-line rate multiplied by 2, or 40 percent (20 percent × 2).

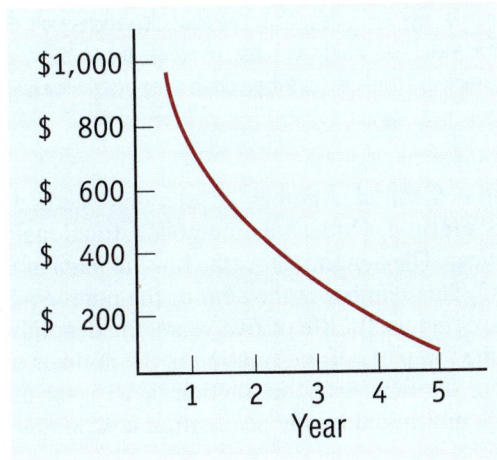

FIGURE 18.2

Declining-Balance Depreciation

TABLE 18.1

Depreciation Under Double-
Declining-Balance Method

Year	Beginning Book Value	Rate, %	Depreciation for Year	Depreciation to Date
1	$2,400.00	40	$960.00	$ 960.00
2	1,440.00	40	576.00	1,536.00
3	864.00	40	345.60	1,881.60
4	518.40	40	207.36	2,088.96
5	311.04	Limited	71.04	2,160.00

Book value at the end of five years = $240.00 ($2,400.00 − $2,160.00)

Step 3. *Compute depreciation for the period by multiplying the book value by the double-declining rate.* Repeat this step each year during the asset's useful life until the year in which the net book value would be less than salvage value.

Step 4. In the final year of depreciation, take only the amount of depreciation that will reduce the asset's net book value to its salvage value.

Here is how the double-declining-balance method would be applied to the asset purchased by Hazlenut Company:

- In the first year, the depreciation is $960 ($2,400 × 40%). *Note that salvage value is ignored in this computation.*

- At the start of the second year, the book value is $1,440 ($2,400 − $960). Depreciation for the second year is $576 ($1,440 × 40%). Note that the salvage value is again ignored in the computation.

- Similar computations are made in the third and fourth years and result in depreciation of $345.60 and $207.36 for the two years, respectively, as shown in Table 18.1. That table shows that the cumulative depreciation at the end of four years is $2,088.96. As a result, at the start of the fifth year, the asset's net book value is $311.04 ($2,400 cost − $2,088.96 depreciation taken = $311.04) This is only $71.04 greater than the estimated salvage ($311.04 − $240.00 = $71.04).

- *Remember that an asset should not be depreciated to a point that the net book value is less than the salvage value.* As a result, the depreciation for the fifth year is limited to $71.04 (unless there has been a change in the salvage value). Table 18.1 therefore shows depreciation for the fifth year is only $71.04. As a result, at the end of the fifth year the accumulated depreciation will be $2,160 and the net book value at the end of the fifth year will be $240 ($2,400 cost − $2,160 accumulated depreciation), an amount equal to estimated salvage value.

> Hasbro, the maker of games, toys, and entertainment products, depreciates tools, dies, and molds over a three-year period or their useful lives, whichever is less. An accelerated method is used. Land improvements, buildings, equipment, and machinery are depreciated using straight-line methods.

Sum-of-the-Years'-Digits Method Another accelerated method of depreciation is the **sum-of-the-years'-digits method.** Under this method, a fractional part of the asset cost is charged to expense each year. The denominator (the bottom part) of the fraction is always the "sum of the years' digits." This number is the sum of the numbers in the asset's useful life. For a machine with an expected useful life of five years, the denominator is 15 (1 + 2 + 3 + 4 + 5). The numerator (the top part) of the fraction is the number of years remaining in the useful life of the asset. For the first year, the fraction is 5/15, for the second year it is 4/15, and so on. This fraction is multiplied by the acquisition cost minus the net salvage value of the asset.

TABLE 18.2

Comparison of Depreciation Methods

	Sum-of-the-Years'-Digits Method			Other Methods	
Year	Fraction	Cost Minus Salvage	Depreciation for Year	Declining-Balance	Straight-Line
1	5/15	$2,160.00	$ 720.00	$ 960.00	$ 432.00
2	4/15	2,160.00	576.00	576.00	432.00
3	3/15	2,160.00	432.00	345.60	432.00
4	2/15	2,160.00	288.00	207.36	432.00
5	1/15	2,160.00	144.00	71.04	432.00
Total depreciation, 5 years			$2,160.00	$2,160.00	$2,160.00

The first four columns of Table 18.2 show the sum-of-the-years'-digits method for the office equipment purchased by Hazlenut Company. Depreciation for the first year of the asset's life is $720 ($2,160 × 5/15) and for the second year of life depreciation is $576 ($2,160 × 4/15). Table 18.2 compares this method with the other two commonly used methods.

Suppose that the equipment was purchased on September 5, 2016. Depreciation for the four months in 2016 would be a proportionate part of the depreciation for the first year of the asset's life, or $240 ($2,160 × 5/15 × 4/12).

For 2017, depreciation consists of the total of two parts: the depreciation for the remaining eight months of the first year (12 months) of life and depreciation for four months of the second year of life.

$2,160 × 8/12 (8 months) × 5/15 (1st year fraction)	$480
$2,160 × 4/12 (4 months) × 4/15 (2nd year fraction)	192
Depreciation for 2017	$672

Comparison of Depreciation Methods When choosing a depreciation method, much consideration is given to the matching principle. The goal is to match the cost of the asset to the periods when the asset provides benefits to the business. Review Table 18.2, which compares the three widely used methods. Notice that during the early years, the sum-of-the-years'-digits and declining-balance methods result in a larger depreciation expense than the straight-line method.

Accountants who favor the straight-line method believe that the asset provides equal benefits over its useful life. Many, however, suggest that accelerated depreciation is more logical than straight-line depreciation. They argue that typically assets are more productive in the early years of their lives, so greater benefit is gained from their use in those years. Additionally, repair costs and other maintenance costs are almost invariably higher when an asset gets older. The facts may suggest that straight-line depreciation results in a lower total cost per unit in the early years than in later years. Under the double-declining-balance and the sum-of-the-years'-digits methods, the higher depreciation costs in early years are partially offset by lower operating costs, so that there is a more nearly uniform total cost per unit of use.

Units-of-Output Method Under the straight-line and accelerated methods, depreciation is computed as a function of time. For some assets, depreciation is more directly related to the units of work produced. The **units-of-output method,** also known as the **units-of-production method,** calculates depreciation at the same rate for each unit produced. The unit of production may be measured in terms of the:

- physical quantities of production,
- number of hours the asset is used,
- other measures.

This method is often used to depreciate the cost of cars, trucks, and other motor vehicles, using miles as a measure of production.

Suppose that a business purchased a delivery truck for $64,000 in February 2016. It is expected to be driven for 112,000 miles before being traded in and its expected salvage value at that time is $8,000. During 2016, the truck was driven 17,400 miles.

Follow these steps to calculate depreciation under the units-of-production method:

Step 1. *Determine the depreciation per unit (per mile).* Divide the depreciable cost (the cost, minus estimated net salvage value) by the total miles expected to be driven during the truck's life.

$$\frac{\$64,000 - \$8,000}{112,000 \text{ miles}} = \$0.50 \text{ per mile driven}$$

Step 2. *Compute depreciation.* Multiply the number of units produced (miles driven) by the rate for each unit.

$$17,400 \text{ miles} \times \$0.50 \text{ per mile} = \$8,700$$

In its first year of operation, the truck would have depreciation expense of $8,700.

>> 18-3. OBJECTIVE

Apply the Modified Accelerated Cost Recovery System (MACRS) for federal income tax purposes.

Federal Income Tax Requirements for "Cost Recovery" (Depreciation) of Property, Plant, and Equipment

The beginning accounting course focuses on financial accounting and reporting, so generally accepted accounting principles (GAAP) are of paramount importance. However, accountants commonly are involved in maintaining tax records and in preparing federal and state income tax returns. The treatments of many items of revenue and expense for income tax purposes differ greatly from those required under generally accepted accounting principles. It is therefore important that the accountant have a basic understanding of some of the major income tax rules that differ from financial accounting.

In addition, some small businesses that do not have audits by certified public accountants may adopt some tax requirements as part of their financial accounting in order to avoid confusion and duplication of work. One of those important differences is in the area of depreciation.

Federal income tax rules basically replace the depreciation rules of generally accepted accounting principles with the Modified Accelerated Cost Recovery System (MACRS), which applies to all assets purchased after December 31, 1986. (If appropriate, however, the taxpayer can use the units-of-production depreciation method instead of MACRS.)

MACRS was designed to encourage taxpayers to invest in business property and to simplify depreciation computations. Under MACRS, the portion of asset costs charged to expense is higher in the early years of an asset's life and lower in the later years. In that sense, it is akin to accelerated depreciation methods. This results in lower taxable income and tax savings in the early years with higher taxable income and taxes in later years.

Under MACRS, property is separated into defined classes. For tangible personal property, there are six classes of property. However, almost all personal property falls in three of those classes. Those three are:

- 5-year class—automobiles, lightweight trucks, computers, and certain special-purpose property.
- 7-year class—office furniture and fixtures and most manufacturing equipment.
- 10-year class—special purpose property, such as equipment used in the manufacture of food and tobacco products.

Under MACRS, the recovery periods for real property are:

- residential rental buildings—27.5 years,
- nonresidential buildings (office buildings) placed in service after May 12, 1993—39 years,
- nonresidential buildings placed in service on or before May 12, 1993—31.5 years.

Each MACRS class has a table of percentages. To determine the cost recovery (depreciation) under MACRS, multiply the asset's cost by the MACRS percentage. Salvage value is ignored. The following table shows the MACRS cost recovery for a $20,000 five-year asset, using the percentages required each year. Almost all businesses have assets in this rate class.

Year	Percent	Original Cost	Cost Recovery
1	20.00%	$20,000	$ 4,000
2	32.00	20,000	6,400
3	19.20	20,000	3,840
4	11.52	20,000	2,304
5	11.52	20,000	2,304
6	5.76	20,000	1,152
Totals	100.00%		$20,000

Note that it takes six years to recover the entire cost of five-year properties. That is because MACRS uses the *half-year convention*. Regardless of purchase date, MACRS calculates depreciation for six months in the first year of the asset's life. The remaining six months of cost recovery is taken in the year after the end of the class life (in the sixth year for five-year property). (There are complex exceptions to the half-year convention.)

It is important that you know the basic concept of MACRS as demonstrated in the above example. It is also important to keep in mind that MACRS is not acceptable under GAAP.

important!

Different Depreciation Methods Used

Most businesses use straight-line depreciation when preparing financial statements and MACRS when preparing tax returns.

Section 1   Self Review

QUESTIONS

1. Name two methods of accelerated depreciation.

2. What account is debited and what account is credited in the journal entry to record depreciation for the year?

3. What is depreciation?

EXERCISES

4. Assuming a five-year life, a cost of $20,000, and an estimated net salvage value of $4,000, what would be the depreciation for the second year of the life of an asset if the double-declining-balance method is used?

5. An asset acquired on May 22, 2016, cost $25,000, has an estimated useful life of five years, and a net salvage value of $5,000. What is the amount of depreciation expense for 2016 if the straight-line method is used?

6. What is the numerator and what is the denominator to be used in computing depreciation for the third year of use of an asset with a life of seven years if the sum-of-the-years'-digits method is used?

ANALYSIS

7. Which method of depreciation, straight-line, or double-declining balance, will result in a higher net income during the first year the asset is in use? Why?

(Answers to Section 1 Self Review are on page 639.)

SECTION OBJECTIVES	TERMS TO LEARN
>> 18-4. Record sales of plant and equipment.	gain
WHY IT'S IMPORTANT	income tax method
Businesses routinely sell or dispose of plant assets that are no longer useful to the business.	loss
>> 18-5. Record asset trade-ins using financial accounting rules and income tax requirements.	
WHY IT'S IMPORTANT	
Both methods are important to businesses.	

Disposition of Assets

The disposition of assets involves removing the asset's cost and its accumulated depreciation from the firm's accounting records. This section discusses the accounting treatment for three asset disposal methods: scrapping, sale, and trade-in.

Method of Disposition

Most business assets are eventually disposed of. They are either scrapped because they are worn out and have no value, sold because they are no longer needed by the business, or traded in on the purchase of new assets.

When assets are disposed of, the business often incurs a gain or a loss. A **gain** is the disposition of an asset for more than its book value. A **loss** is the disposition of an asset for less than its book value. The formula is:

$$\text{Proceeds} - \text{Book value} = \text{Gain or loss}$$

There is a gain when proceeds are higher than book value. There is a loss when proceeds are lower than book value.

A gain results from a peripheral activity of the business. In contrast, revenue involves the routine activities of the business such as selling goods and rendering services. A loss also results from a peripheral activity of the business. In contrast, expenses involve the day-to-day activities of the business.

The rules of debit and credit for gain accounts are the same as for revenue accounts. Similarly, expense accounts and loss accounts follow the same rules of debit and credit.

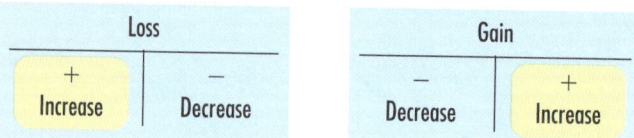

DISPOSAL BY SCRAPPING OR DISCARDING

When an asset is worn out, often it is simply discarded. For example, the computer used by Sam's Discount Stores cost $5,250 and is fully depreciated. On June 30, the computer crashed and could not be repaired for a reasonable fee. It was worthless and was discarded. There were no proceeds from the disposal and no costs were incurred in the disposal. There is no gain or loss from the disposition:

Proceeds	$0		
(Book value)	(0)		
Gain or loss	$0		

The following journal entry records the asset's disposal:

11	June	30	Accum. Depreciation—Office Equipment	5 2 5 0 00		11
12			Office Equipment		5 2 5 0 00	12
13			Discarded computer			13

If the discarded asset is not fully depreciated, depreciation is recorded up to the date of disposal. Suppose that the computer used by Sam's Discount Stores cost $5,250. Accumulated depreciation through December 31, 2015, was $4,200. On June 30, 2016, the computer crashed. The depreciation for the period January 1 through June 30 is $525. The depreciation is recorded through June 30 as follows: debit **Depreciation Expense** for $525 and credit **Accumulated Depreciation** for $525. After this entry, **Accumulated Depreciation** account balance is $4,725 ($4,200 + 525). The book value of the computer is $525 ($5,250 − 4,725). There are no proceeds and no costs incurred for the disposal. There is a loss of $525 on the disposition.

Proceeds	$ 0
(Book value)	(525)
Gain or loss	$(525)

The entry to record the disposal of the computer removes the cost of the asset and its accumulated depreciation from the accounting records. The difference, book value, is recorded as a loss.

June	30	Accum. Depreciation—Office Equipment	4 7 2 5 00		
		Loss on Disposal of Fixed Assets	5 2 5 00		
		Office Equipment		5 2 5 0 00	
		Discarded computer			

DISPOSAL BY SALE

>> **18-4. OBJECTIVE**
Record sales of plant and equipment.

Sometimes useful assets are sold so the company can purchase better assets or because the assets are no longer needed. When an asset is sold, follow these steps to record the transaction:

Step 1. *Record depreciation to the date of disposition.*

Step 2. *Remove the cost of the asset.*

Step 3. *Remove the accumulated depreciation.*

Step 4. *Record the proceeds.*

Step 5. *Determine and record the gain or loss, if any.*

Several years ago, Hunter Laboratories purchased laboratory equipment for $12,000. The balance in **Accumulated Depreciation** was $6,480 on July 1, 2016, the date the equipment is sold. This balance reflects depreciation through December 31 of the prior year. The first step is to record the depreciation expense since depreciation was last recorded. Annual depreciation is $1,080. Depreciation for the period January 1 through June 30 is therefore $540 ($1,080 ÷ 2). The entry is a debit to **Depreciation Expense—Laboratory Equipment** and a credit to **Accumulated Depreciation—Laboratory Equipment** for $540. After this entry, the accumulated depreciation account has a balance of $7,020 ($6,480 + 540) and the book value of the laboratory equipment is $4,980 ($12,000 − 7,020).

Sale for an Amount Equal to Book Value Suppose that the equipment was sold on account for book value, $4,980. Step 1, record depreciation to the date of disposition, has been illustrated. Steps 2–5 are as follows:

Step 2. *Remove the cost of the asset.* Credit **Laboratory Equipment** for $12,000.

Step 3. *Remove the accumulated depreciation.* Debit **Accumulated Depreciation—Laboratory Equipment** for $7,020.

Step 4. *Record the proceeds.* Debit **Accounts Receivable** for $4,980.

Step 5. *Determine and record the gain or loss, if any.*

Proceeds	$4,980
(Book value)	(4,980)
Gain or loss	$ 0

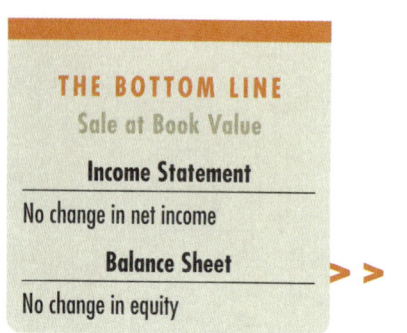

THE BOTTOM LINE
Sale at Book Value

Income Statement

No change in net income

Balance Sheet

No change in equity

>>

GENERAL JOURNAL					PAGE 7
DATE	DESCRIPTION	POST. REF.	DEBIT	CREDIT	
1	2016					1
22	July 1 Accounts Receivable		4 9 8 0 00		22
23	Accum. Depreciation—Laboratory Equipment		7 0 2 0 00		23
24	Laboratory Equipment			1 2 0 0 0 00	24
25	Sold laboratory equipment at				25
26	book value				26

Sale for More Than Book Value Suppose the equipment was sold on account for $5,520. The equipment was sold at a gain of $540.

Proceeds	$5,520
(Book value)	(4,980)
Gain	$ 540

The gain is recorded in the **Gain on Sale of Equipment** account. The gain is shown on the income statement in the Other Income section.

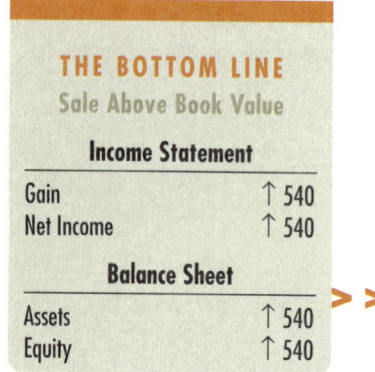

THE BOTTOM LINE
Sale Above Book Value

Income Statement

Gain	↑ 540
Net Income	↑ 540

Balance Sheet

Assets	↑ 540
Equity	↑ 540

>>

GENERAL JOURNAL					PAGE 7
DATE	DESCRIPTION	POST. REF.	DEBIT	CREDIT	
1	2016					1
22	July 1 Accounts Receivable		5 5 2 0 00		22
23	Accum. Depreciation—Laboratory Equipment		7 0 2 0 00		23
24	Laboratory Equipment			1 2 0 0 0 00	24
25	Gain on Sale of Equipment			5 4 0 00	25
26	Sale of laboratory equipment				26
27	at a gain				27

Sale for Less Than Book Value Suppose the equipment was sold on account for $4,520. The equipment was sold at a loss of $460.

Proceeds	$4,520
(Book value)	(4,980)
Loss	$ 460

The loss is recorded in the **Loss on Sale of Equipment** account. The loss appears on the income statement in the Other Expenses section.

GENERAL JOURNAL				PAGE ___7___		
DATE	DESCRIPTION	POST. REF.	DEBIT	CREDIT		
1	2016					1
22	July 1	Accounts Receivable		4 5 2 0 00		22
23		Accum. Depreciation—Laboratory Equipment		7 0 2 0 00		23
24		Loss on Sale of Equipment		4 6 0 00		24
25		Laboratory Equipment			1 2 0 0 0 00	25
26		Sale of laboratory equipment				26
27		at a loss				27

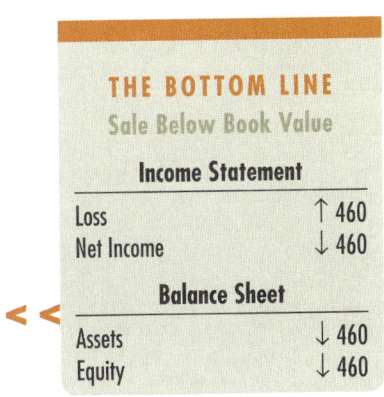

Some companies use a single account to record both gains and losses on sales of assets. The account is called *Gains and Losses on Sales of Assets.* It appears on the income statement in the Other Income section (if net gain) or Other Expenses section (if net loss).

DISPOSAL BY TRADE-IN

Businesses often trade in old equipment when they purchase new equipment. Trade-in transactions are recorded in two steps:

Step 1.   *Record the depreciation up to the date of trade-in.*

Step 2.   *Record the trade-in of the old asset and the purchase of the new asset.*

Step 1 presents no new problem. Bringing the depreciation up to date involves precisely the same calculations that would be made if an asset were sold. Depreciation is recorded for the period beginning when the date of depreciation was last recorded and ending at the end of the month nearest the date of the trade-in.

Step 2 is somewhat more complicated.

a.   *Under financial accounting rules, gains and losses are recorded as though the asset were sold.*

b.   *For federal income tax purposes, neither gains nor losses are recognized on trade-ins.*

To illustrate the financial accounting rules and the income tax rules, we will examine a typical situation. Assume that on October 1, 2016, Howard Company traded in an old truck acquired several years ago for $40,000, on a new truck. After bringing depreciation up to date, the total accumulated depreciation was $33,000, so that the book value was $7,000. The difference between the trade-in allowed and the agreed-on price of the truck is to be paid in cash

APPLYING THE FINANCIAL ACCOUNTING RULES FOR TRADE-INS

Actual gain or loss is the difference between the amount of allowance received on the trade-in and the book value of the old asset. The allowance is the difference between the fair value of the new asset and the amount of cash paid. For example, if Howard received a trade-in allowance of $7,800 on the old asset with a book value of $7,000, there is an implicit gain of $800. On the other hand, if the trade-in allowance is only $6,700 on an asset with a book value of $7,000, there is an implicit loss of $300.

Financial Accounting for Trade-In if Gain Is Realized on the Transaction   Suppose that the new truck Howard acquired has an agreed-on price of $42,000, which is also its fair value. The dealer granted Howard a trade-in allowance of $7,800 and Howard paid cash of $34,200. As a result, Howard is deemed to have received $7,800 for the old truck. The implicit gain on the trade-in is $800 ($7,800 trade-in allowance, minus $7,000 book value of the old truck.)

In this situation, the cost of the new asset is recorded at its fair market value and the difference between the trade-in allowance and book value of $800 is recorded as a gain.

Here are the steps to record the trade-in if there is a gain on the transaction:

Step 1. *Remove the cost of the old asset ($40,000).*

Step 2. *Remove the accumulated depreciation for the old asset ($33,000).*

Step 3. *Record the payment ($34,200).*

Step 4. *Record the new asset at its fair market value ($42,000).*

Step 5. *Determine and record the gain ($800).*

The journal entry to record the transaction would be:

GENERAL JOURNAL PAGE ___7___

	DATE		DESCRIPTION	POST. REF.	DEBIT	CREDIT	
1	2016						1
2	Oct.	1	Truck (new)		41 2 0 0 00		2
3			Accum. Depreciation (old truck)		33 0 0 0 00		3
4			Truck (old)			40 0 0 0 00	4
5			Gain on Trade-in of Truck			800 00	5
6			Cash			34 2 0 0 00	6
7			Trade-in of truck				7

Financial Accounting for Trade-In if Loss Is Realized on Transaction The above journal entry illustrates the financial accounting treatment for gains. For financial accounting purposes, losses are also recognized on trade-ins.

Suppose the amount allowed Howard as a trade-in value of the old asset had been $6,700, instead of $7,800 and Howard paid cash of $35,300 ($42,000 − $6,700). As a result, there would be a realized loss of $300 on the trade-in ($7,000 book value, minus $6,700 received as trade-in allowance). Remember that for financial accounting purposes, losses *are* recognized. To record a trade-in under the financial accounting rules when there is a loss on the transaction, follow these steps:

Step 1. *Remove the cost of the old asset ($40,000).*

Step 2. *Remove the accumulated depreciation for the old asset ($33,000).*

Step 3. *Record the payment ($35,300).*

Step 4. *Record the new asset at its fair market value ($42,000).*

Step 5. *Determine and record the loss ($300).*

Here is the entry required to record the trade-in of the truck by Howard:

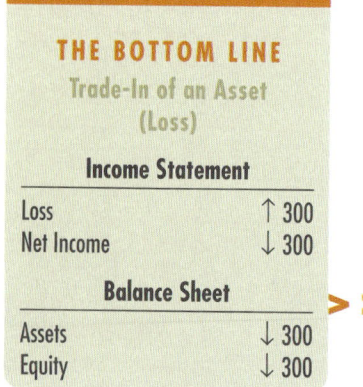

THE BOTTOM LINE

Trade-In of an Asset
(Loss)

Income Statement

Loss	↑ 300
Net Income	↓ 300

Balance Sheet

Assets	↓ 300
Equity	↓ 300

GENERAL JOURNAL PAGE ___7___

	DATE		DESCRIPTION	POST. REF.	DEBIT	CREDIT	
1	2016						1
2	Oct.	1	Truck (new)		42 0 0 0 00		2
3			Accum. Depreciation (old truck)		33 0 0 0 00		3
4			Loss on Trade-in of Truck		3 0 0 00		4
5			Truck (old)			40 0 0 0 00	5
6			Cash			35 3 0 0 00	6
7			Trade-in of truck at a loss				7

Some smaller businesses follow the income tax rules discussed below in recording trade-in transactions because it may eliminate keeping two sets of records for the same transaction. It should be noted, however, that this is not always feasible because the cost and depreciation amounts may differ for financial accounting and tax purposes.

APPLYING THE INCOME TAX RULES FOR TRADE-INS

The federal **income tax method** for trade-in transactions is easier than that for financial accounting because neither gain nor loss is recognized for tax purposes. The steps in applying the tax rules are:

Step 1.   *Remove the cost of the old asset.*

Step 2.   *Remove the accumulated depreciation for the old asset.*

Step 3.   *Record the cash payment.*

Step 4.   *Record the new asset at the sum of the book value of the old asset and the cash paid.*

Applying this basic rule to the two situations discussed above: (1) cash of $34,200 was paid on the trade-in and (2) cash of $35,300 was paid on the trade-in, no gain or loss would be recorded in either case for tax purposes. Assuming the same book value for both tax and financial reporting purposes (which is not the normal case because of the differences between depreciation calculations and MACRS cost recovery), in the first situation, the new truck would be recorded at $41,200 ($34,200 cash plus $7,000 book value of the old truck). In the second situation, the new truck would be recorded at $42,300 ($35,300 cash plus $7,000 book value of the old truck).

Section 2   Self Review

QUESTIONS

1. For financial reporting purposes, in what circumstances is a loss on the sale of a long-term asset recognized?

2. If an item of equipment is retired and scrapped or sold, how should the retirement be accounted for?

3. Explain the difference, if any, between federal income tax rules and financial accounting principles in recognizing gain or loss on the trade-in of plant and equipment assets.

EXERCISES

4. An asset that cost $40,000 and on which depreciation of $30,000 has been recorded is traded in on a new replacement asset. The sales price, also the fair value, of the new asset is $54,000. The owner of the old asset was given an allowance of $14,000 for the old asset and paid $40,000 in cash. The amount of gain or loss recorded is:

    a.   a gain of $4,000.

    b.   no gain or loss.

    c.   a loss of $4,000.

    d.   a gain of $14,000.

5. An asset that cost $50,000 was retired and sold for $32,000 cash. Accumulated depreciation on the asset was $28,000. The entry to record this retirement and sale calls for recognizing:

    a.   no gain or loss.

    b.   a gain of $8,000.

    c.   a loss of $18,000.

    d.   a gain of $10,000.

ANALYSIS

6. If a company's fully depreciated asset was scrapped but not removed from the accounting records, what would be the effect on the company's financial statements? Assume the asset has no net salvage value.

(Answers to Section 2 Self Review are on page 640.)

SECTION OBJECTIVES	TERMS TO LEARN
>> 18-6. Compute and record depletion of natural resources. **WHY IT'S IMPORTANT** Depletion matches an asset's costs with the benefits derived from its use. **>> 18-7.** Recognize asset impairment and understand the general concepts of accounting for impairment. **WHY IT'S IMPORTANT** Sometimes assets do not retain their ability to generate expected revenues. In these cases, the asset cost is adjusted in the accounting records. **>> 18-8.** Compute and record amortization and impairment of intangible assets. **WHY IT'S IMPORTANT** An intangible asset's cost is charged to expense over its assumed life.	amortization brand name computer software copyright depletion franchise goodwill impairment intangible assets patent recoverability test trade name trademark

Special Topics in Long-Term Assets

In the first two sections of this chapter, you have learned how to account for costs incurred in connection with the acquisition, operation, and disposition of property, plant, and equipment. These are very common transactions arising in almost every business. In the final section of the chapter, you will learn how to handle three less commonly encountered transactions related to assets of this type:

1. Depletion of costs of natural resources.
2. Impairment of property, plant, and equipment.
3. Costs incurred to acquire intangible assets.

In addition, you will learn some of the basic internal controls used to safeguard property, plant, and equipment—the asset category representing the largest investment of funds for most types of business.

Depletion

Natural resources, such as iron ore, oil, gold, and coal are physically removed from the land in the production process. Businesses must know how to allocate the cost of natural resources as they are taken from their source. As the resources are extracted, part of their cost is charged to expense. **Depletion** is the term used to describe allocating the cost of the natural resource to expense over the period in which the resource produces revenue.

DEPLETION FOR FINANCIAL STATEMENT PURPOSES

Depletion of the cost of natural resources for financial statement preparation is called *cost depletion.* It is similar to the units-of-output method of depreciation. The formula is:

$$\frac{\text{Cost of natural resource}}{\text{Estimated units of the resource}} = \text{Depletion per unit}$$

A business purchased a clay pit for $80,000. The clay pit is estimated to contain 500,000 tons of extractable clay suitable for making bricks. The depletion cost for each ton of clay is $0.16 ($80,000 ÷ 500,000 tons). During the first year, the business extracted 30,000 tons of clay. The depletion is $4,800 (30,000 × $0.16). The adjusting entry to record depletion follows:

11	Dec.	31	Depletion Expense	4 80 0 00		11
12			Accumulated Depletion		4 80 0 00	12
13			To record the extraction of			13
14			30,000 tons of clay			14

After the first year, the natural resource appears on the balance sheet as follows. The net book value of the natural resource is $75,200.

Property, Plant, and Equipment
Clay Deposits $80,000
Less Accumulated Depletion   4,800
Net Clay Deposits $75,200

Oil and gas production and mining operations use long-lived assets such as oil pumps and mining equipment. These assets are depreciated, usually using the units-of-output method.

DEPLETION FOR FEDERAL INCOME TAX PURPOSES

>> 18-6. OBJECTIVE
Compute and record depletion of natural resources.

Depletion for federal income tax purposes is the larger of cost depletion or percentage depletion. Cost depletion for tax purposes is computed in the same way as it is for financial statement preparation. However, the amount of cost depletion may be different because the cost (the numerator) for financial purposes may be different than the cost for tax purposes. If percentage depletion is taken on the tax return, the amount taken in any year will reduce the cost on which cost depletion is based in future years.

Percentage depletion for a property is calculated by multiplying the gross income from the sale of the natural resource by a percentage. The percentage depends on the specific natural resource.

In 2016, a mining company has sales of $1,800,000 for ore produced from a mine. For tax purposes, the book value (capitalized costs, less depletion taken in prior years) of the minerals at the beginning of the year was $16,000. The allowable percentage depletion rate for the minerals produced is 15 percent. The company will deduct $270,000 on its federal income tax return ($1,800,000 × 0.15 = $270,000). In future years, there will be no allowable *cost depletion,* but *percentage depletion* may continue to be taken even though the book value for tax purposes is zero.

Impairment of Property, Plant, and Equipment

>> 18-7. OBJECTIVE
Recognize asset impairment and understand the general concepts of accounting for impairment.

Relying on the historical cost concept and the going concern assumption, many accountants have assumed that if a long-term asset continues to be used in income production the asset will generate future cash revenues and the value of those revenues will exceed the book value of the asset. However, in the late 1980s and early 1990s, many businesses recorded "write-offs" of assets when their values declined substantially.

Because of concern over situations in which doubt exists as to whether the asset's use will generate adequate cash flows to recover the book value of assets, the Financial Accounting Standards Board issued *Accounting Standards Codification 144,* "Accounting for Impairment of Long-Lived Assets." This Statement lays out guidelines for recording impairment of property, plant, and equipment when it appears that the carrying amount of the assets may not be recoverable. Stated simply, **impairment** exists when book value exceeds the "fair value" of the asset.

The procedures and measurement techniques for recording impairment are quite complex and are beyond the scope of this textbook, but a brief summary of measuring and recording impairment will provide you with a basic understanding when you encounter circumstances suggesting that impairment may exist.

The three steps in the process of determining an impairment loss are:

Step 1. *Review circumstances that suggest impairment may have occurred.* FASB Statement 121 gives examples of events and changes in circumstance that suggest impairment *may have* occurred:

a. A significant decrease in the market value of an asset.

b. A significant change in the extent of use or way in which the asset is used.

c. A significant adverse change in the legal environment or in the manner in which an asset is used.

d. A forecast suggesting continuing losses associated with the asset. There are, however, many other economic and technical factors that may suggest assets should be analyzed for possible impairment, for example, increased competition, new technical developments, a forecast of decreased demand for the products, and so forth.

Turner Disposal Company has operated a facility to separate liquids and gaseous products from a stream of crude oil from wells. Present book value of the facility is $792,000. Revenues from the facility have decreased by approximately 14 percent during each of the last two years. *This suggests that impairment may have occurred.*

Step 2. *Apply the recoverability test.* If circumstances suggest that impairment may have occurred, the recoverability test should be applied to determine whether impairment does exist. The recoverability test is a comparison of the asset's carrying value (net book value) with the estimated net cash flows from future use of the asset, including eventual disposition of the asset. If the estimated net future cash flows are less than the asset's book value, impairment has occurred.

Obviously, in most cases it is not possible to estimate future net cash flows that are expected to be generated by a single item of equipment, such as a computer used in the office, a display rack used in a retail store, or a piece of machinery in a factory. FASB *Statement 121* states that in making impairment calculations, the unit of measurement is not a single asset, but the smallest unit of the business for which net cash flows can be determined from the assets used.

Turner made a projection of future cash inflows from services and cash outflows from expenses over the expected remaining life of the facilities and estimates that future net cash

MANAGERIAL IMPLICATIONS <<

PROPERTY, PLANT, AND EQUIPMENT

■ Property, plant, and equipment often represent the largest cash investment by the owners of a business.

■ Managers are responsible for establishing strong internal controls over property, plant, and equipment.

■ Managers should understand the different depreciation methods and how they impact the financial statements and income tax returns of the business.

■ Management should ensure that procedures are in place to monitor repairs, power consumed, and other operating costs to make sure that assets are functioning efficiently.

■ Managers must understand the methods used to record asset sales and trade-ins because the different methods have different results that impact the financial statements of the business.

THINKING CRITICALLY

How does the choice of depreciation method impact the financial statements?

flows from its operations will total $690,000. These future cash flows are less than the asset's $792,000 book value, so impairment does exist.

Step 3. *Compute the amount of the impairment.* The amount of impairment is the amount by which the asset's book value exceeds its market value. There may be instances in which the market value of an asset can be determined by quoted prices in the markets. However, these quotations may be scarce for many assets, so market value must be determined by other means. The usual methodology is to compute the "discounted value" (present value) of the stream of future net cash flows from use of the assets, calculated in step 2. Essentially, the present value of the estimated future cash flows is the amount that it would be necessary to invest today in order to earn a specific rate of return on the investment, considering the cash flows expected to be received each year during the future life of the asset. If the market value, or present value, is less than the net book value of the asset, impairment exists and should be recorded in the amount of the excess of book value over market value.

In step 2, above, Turner estimated that future cash flows were only $690,000 from an asset with a book value of $792,000. Turner then applied to the future cash stream a discount factor based on its expected rate of return on an asset of this type. In applying the discount rate, Turner estimated that the company would be willing to pay $540,000 for the asset today. That is its market value to the firm. Turner records impairment by debiting ***Loss from Impairment of Separation Equipment*** for $252,000 and crediting ***Separation Equipment*** for that amount.

> Once an impairment write-down of an asset has been made, the amount charged off is not reinstated even if the market value subsequently increases—the conservatism constraint and the realization principle in effect.

In the year following Turner's write-down of the separation equipment in the preceding example, the price of oil and gas increased dramatically, and as a result the value of the processing facility increased to $858,000. However, this increase in value is not recognized in the accounts.

Intangible Assets

In addition to property, plant, and equipment, many businesses have intangible assets. Intangible assets are assets that lack a physical substance. The major types of intangible assets are patents, copyrights, franchises, trademarks, brand names, organizational costs, computer software, and goodwill. With the exception of computer software, intangible assets usually do not have any physical attributes.

CLASSIFYING INTANGIBLE ASSETS

A patent is an exclusive right given by the U.S. Patent Office to manufacture and sell an invention for a period of 20 years from the date the patent is granted. A patent may not be renewed; however, a new patent may be obtained if significant improvements in the original idea can be demonstrated. The right to the patent may be sold, assigned, or otherwise controlled by the owner.

A copyright is the exclusive right granted by the federal government to produce, publish, and sell a literary or artistic work for a period equal to the creator's life plus 70 years.

There are two types of franchises. The first type is a right granted by a governmental unit for the business to provide a service to the governmental unit (such as cable television). The second type is an exclusive dealership or an exclusive arrangement between a manufacturer and a dealer or distributor.

Trademarks, trade names, and brand names are used to build consumer confidence and loyalty. They can be registered with the U.S. Patent Office. They can be sold, traded, or otherwise controlled by the owner.

Organizational costs are the costs incurred when organizing a business. Organizational costs include attorneys' fees, accountants' fees, legal filing fees, and other costs of beginning a business.

Computer software consists of written programs that instruct a computer's hardware to do certain tasks. Software can be developed by the company's employees or purchased outside the company. For some firms, computer software is the most important (and most costly) asset owned.

Goodwill represents the value of a business in excess of the value of its identifiable assets. Goodwill is recorded only at the time of the purchase of a business. It usually occurs when a business being purchased has extraordinary earnings or earnings potential.

> For many companies, intangible assets are a very important part of the total assets. For example, in its balance sheet at the end of 2012, Johnson & Johnson reported total assets of $121,347 billion. This total included *Goodwill,* $22,424 billion and other intangibles of $28,752 billion.

ACQUIRING INTANGIBLE ASSETS

There are two ways to acquire intangible assets: (1) produce or develop them or (2) purchase them. The general rule is that an intangible asset is recorded in the books of the firm only if it is purchased from another party. Costs to develop intangible assets internally are expensed in the year incurred to the *Research and Development Expense* account. Similarly, costs related to software development by a company are expensed in the year incurred. However, there are special rules if the software is to be sold, leased, or otherwise marketed:

1. Costs are expensed as incurred when creating the software product until technological feasibility is established for the product. *Technological feasibility* is deemed to occur when a detailed program design or a working model of the product has been developed.

2. Costs are capitalized to an asset account once a product is deemed to be technologically feasible.

>> 18-8. OBJECTIVE

Compute and record amortization and impairment of intangible assets.

DISPOSITION OF CAPITALIZED ACQUISITION COSTS OF INTANGIBLE ASSETS

For accounting purposes, costs of intangibles that have been acquired for a cost and are identified as being appropriately capitalized are classified into two groups:

1. Those that are determined to have lives that are definite or can be reasonably estimated. The most common of these are patents, copyrights, most franchises, and purchased computer software.

2. Those that do not have definite or reasonably estimable useful lives. These include organization costs, purchased goodwill, trademarks, brand names, and trade names.

Amortization of Cost of Intangibles with Estimable Useful Lives

The accounting treatment of costs of intangibles in this category is very similar to depreciation of property, plant, and equipment. The periodic transfer of intangibles' cost to expense is known as **amortization.** The costs are typically amortized on a straight-line basis or on a units-of-production basis.

In January 2016, Marcus Company purchased for $200,000 a patent which had a remaining life of 10 years. Based on straight-line amortization, Marcus recorded the following entry for amortization at the end of 2016:

11	Dec.	31	Amortization of Patent	20 000 00		11
12			Patent		20 000 00	12
13			To record annual amortization			13
14			of patent			14

An identical entry will be made at the end of 2017 so that the balance remaining in the *Patent* account on January 1, 2018, will be $160,000. Suppose in 2018 it is estimated that the patent will be of benefit only through the year 2021. Based on this estimate, the patent amortization for each year 2018 to 2021 will be $40,000 ($160,000 ÷ 4 years).

Impairment of Cost of Intangibles with Indefinite Useful Lives

When intangibles that do not have estimable lives have been purchased, an assessment must be made each year to estimate the value of the intangible. If the estimate is less than the existing book value, impairment must be recorded in the same way that impairment of property, plant, and equipment is recorded. Here, the concept of conservatism comes into play.

In 2001, Marcus Company purchased from another business a "brand name" for $400,000 and charged it to the intangible asset account *Brand Names.* Because of declining sales of the products covered by the brand and the decrease in profits on sales of the products, Marcus concluded in 2016 that the brand name was no longer worth $400,000 and that a conservative estimate of its value was $100,000. Based on that, the following entry was made by Marcus:

11	Dec.	31	Loss from Impairment of Brand Name	300 000 00	11
12			Brand Names		300 000 00	12
13			To record impairment of brand name		13
14					14

A similar assessment should be made each year to see if further impairment should be recorded. However, if the value of the intangible asset increases in years subsequent to recording impairment, the carrying value of the asset *is not increased.*

The annual report for The Coca-Cola Company and Subsidiaries for 2012 contained the following as part of its note explaining its accounting for "Goodwill, Trademarks and Other Intangible Assets."

Goodwill, Trademarks, and Other Intangible Assets

We classify intangible assets into three categories: (1) intangible assets with definite lives subject to amortization, (2) intangible assets with indefinite lives not subject to amortization and (3) goodwill. We determine the useful lives of our identifiable intangible assets after considering the specific facts and circumstances related to each intangible asset. Factors we consider when determining useful lives include the contractual term of any agreement related to the asset, the historical performance of the asset, the Company's long-term strategy for using the asset, any laws or other local regulations which could impact the useful life of the asset, and other economic factors, including competition and specific market conditions. Intangible assets that are deemed to have definite lives are amortized, primarily on a straight-line basis, over their useful lives, generally ranging from 1 to 20 years. Refer to Note 8.

When facts and circumstances indicate that the carrying value of definite-lived intangible assets may not be recoverable, management assesses the recoverability of the carrying value by preparing estimates of sales volume and the resulting gross profit and cash flows. These estimated future cash flows are consistent with those we use in our internal planning. If the sum of the expected future cash flows (undiscounted and without interest charges) is less than the carrying amount, we recognize an impairment loss. The impairment loss recognized is the amount by which the carrying amount exceeds the fair value. We use a variety of methodologies to determine the fair value of these assets, including discounted cash flow models, which are consistent with the assumptions we believe hypothetical marketplace participants would use.

We test intangible assets determined to have indefinite useful lives, including trademarks, franchise rights and goodwill, for impairment annually, or more frequently if events or circumstances indicate that assets might be impaired. Our Company performs these annual impairment reviews as of the first day of our third fiscal quarter. We use a variety of methodologies in conducting impairment assessments of indefinite-lived intangible assets, including, but not limited to, discounted cash flow models, which are based on the assumptions we believe hypothetical

(continued)

(concluded)

marketplace participants would use. For indefinite-lived intangible assets, other than goodwill, if the carrying amount exceeds the fair value, an impairment charge is recognized in an amount equal to that excess.

We perform impairment tests of goodwill at our reporting unit level, which is one level below our operating segments. Our operating segments are primarily based on geographic responsibility, which is consistent with the way management runs our business. Our operating segments are subdivided into smaller geographic regions or territories that we sometimes refer to as business units. These business units are also our reporting units. The Bottling Investments operating segments includes all Company-owned or consolidated bottling operations, regardless of geographic location. Generally, each Company-owned or consolidated bottling operation within our Bottling Investments operating segment is its own reporting unit. Goodwill is assigned to the reporting unit or units that benefit from the synergies arising from each business combination.

The goodwill impairment test consists of a two-step process, if necessary. The first step is to compare the fair value of a reporting unit to its carrying value, including goodwill. We typically use discounted cash flow models to determine the fair value of a reporting unit. The assumptions used in these models are consistent with those we believe hypothetical marketplace participants would use. If the fair value of the reporting unit is less than its carrying value, the second step of the impairment test must be performed in order to determine the amount of impairment loss, if any. The second step compares the implied fair value of the reporting unit goodwill with the carrying amount of that goodwill. If the carrying amount of the reporting unit's goodwill exceeds its implied fair value, an impairment charge is recognized in an amount equal to that excess. The loss recognized cannot exceed the carrying amount of goodwill.

Impairment charges related to intangible assets are generally recorded in the line item other operating charges or, to the extent they relate to equity method investees, in the line item equity income (loss)—net in the consolidated statements of income.

Internal Control of Property, Plant, and Equipment

The internal control of property, plant, and equipment involves physical safeguards to prevent theft or misuse. The following are standard internal control procedures for fixed assets:

- Authorize and justify the purchase of all long-lived assets.
- Assign and, if possible, engrave an identification number on each asset.
- Maintain an asset register listing all capital assets, their costs, acquisition dates, location, and any other useful information.
- Assign responsibility for safekeeping, maintaining, and operating each asset to a specific person.
- Take a physical inventory periodically. Compare the physical inventory with the asset register and investigate any differences.
- Establish procedures to authorize asset retirement, sale, or other disposition.

The internal control of intangible assets consists primarily of the safe storage of documents and protection of the storage location. Businesses need to be alert to copyright and trademark infringements. Legal action is required when an infringement of an intangible asset occurs.

Section 3   Self Review

QUESTIONS

1. Explain the test used to determine whether an asset is impaired.

2. If it is determined that an asset is impaired, how is the amount of impairment to be charged to expense computed?

3. Strategic Innovations Company spent $80 million in 2016 on research and development costs (R&D). Some work was general research seeking basic knowledge about products. Other work was getting several projects started to look into ways to develop and improve a line of drugs manufactured by the company. Other costs were incurred in the final stages of perfecting new products. How should these costs be accounted for by Strategic Innovations?

EXERCISES

4. Over a period of 50 years, Good Taste Company developed a great reputation for its soft drinks.

In 2016, Happy Times Company purchased Good Taste for $400 million. The purchase price included about $300 million as the actual value of identifiable assets and $100 million for the ownership of the trade name "Good Taste." Should the cost assigned to Good Taste be depreciated (or amortized)? If so, on what basis?

5. (Refer to Exercise 4.) Suppose that in 2018, two years after Happy Times acquired Good Taste, the sales of Good Taste soft drinks decreased drastically. Assume that Happy Times had not recorded any amortization of the $100 million assigned to the trade name. What course of action should the management of Happy Times take?

6. An oil company paid a landowner $30,000 for the mineral rights underlying his property. The well was drilled and equipped at a cost of $900,000. It is estimated that 300,000 barrels of oil will be produced from the property. Describe the method that should be used to measure and record depletion of the cost of the mineral rights as the oil is produced. How should depreciation of the costs of drilling and equipping the well be measured and recorded?

ANALYSIS

7. How are depreciation, depletion and amortization different? How are they similar?

(Answers to Section 3 Self Review are on page 640.)

18 Chapter   **REVIEW**   **Chapter Summary**

Property, plant, and equipment are those tangible assets used in carrying out the company's business operations. In this chapter, you have learned how to record transactions for the purchase, use, and disposition of these assets. You have also studied the accounting methods required to record the acquisition of intangible assets such as copyrights and patents, as well as the costs of amortization.

Learning Objectives

18-1   Determine the amount to record as an asset's cost.

The cost of an asset is its net purchase price, plus costs of transportation, installation, and all other costs necessary to put the asset into normal operation.

18-2   Compute and record depreciation of property, plant, and equipment by commonly used methods.

Costs of a tangible asset should be charged to expense over its useful life through systematic depreciation charges. Depreciation is recorded by a debit to *Depreciation Expense* and a credit to *Accumulated Depreciation.* Four widely used methods of computing depreciation for financial accounting purposes are the:

- straight-line method,
- declining-balance method,
- sum-of-the-years'-digits method,
- units-of-production method.

18-3   Apply the Modified Accelerated Cost Recovery System (MACRS) for federal income tax purposes.

Under the federal income tax laws, new assets must be depreciated under the Modified Accelerated Cost Recovery System (MACRS), with minor exceptions. Under MACRS, each type of asset is assigned to a MACRS class. Each class is assigned a different depreciable life.

18-4   Record sales of plant and equipment.

Property, plant, and equipment are disposed of in various ways; most commonly, they are sold or scrapped. At an asset's sale, its depreciation is brought up to date. Gain or loss at the time of disposal is computed by comparing the asset's net book value with the proceeds, if any, received on its disposal. For financial accounting purposes, a gain or loss may be recorded from the sale, retirement, or scrapping of an asset.

18-5   Record asset trade-ins using financial accounting rules and income tax requirements.

If a business trades old equipment when purchasing new equipment, two transactions must be recorded. The depreciation on the used equipment must be brought up to date. Then, the trade and purchase are recorded. Both gains and losses are recognized under financial accounting rules. Using the income tax method, no gain or loss is recorded on the trade-in of an asset on a new similar asset.

18-6   Compute and record depletion of natural resources.

The costs of natural resources such as mineral deposits are charged to expense on a per-unit-of-production basis for financial accounting and reporting purposes. Special rules apply for income tax purposes.

18-7   Recognize asset impairment and understand the general concepts of accounting for impairment.

If an asset's expected future net cash flows are less than the asset's book value, impairment may need to be recognized. The amount of impairment is the amount by which the book value exceeds the asset's fair value—usually defined as the discounted value of the future net cash flows from its use.

18-8   Compute and record amortization and impairment of intangible assets.

Except for software, intangibles have no physical characteristics. If they are bought from outside parties, intangibles are recorded at cost. Costs incurred by firms who produce their own intangible assets are not capitalized but are charged to *Research and Development Expense* in the year incurred. Costs of intangibles with identifiable lives are amortized. Costs of those with indefinite lives are charged to expense through impairment tests.

18-9   Define the accounting terms new to this chapter.

Glossary

Accelerated method of depreciation (p. 603) A method of depreciating asset cost that allocates greater amounts of depreciation to an asset's early years of useful life

Amortization (p. 618) The process of periodically transferring the acquisition cost of intangible assets with estimated useful lives to an expense account

Brand name (p. 617) See Trade name

Capitalized costs (p. 600) All costs recorded as part of an asset's costs

Computer software (p. 618) An intangible asset; written programs that instruct a computer's hardware to do certain tasks

Copyright (p. 617) An intangible asset; an exclusive right granted by the federal government to produce, publish, and sell a literary or artistic work for a period equal to the creator's life plus 70 years

Declining-balance method (p. 603) An accelerated method of depreciation in which an asset's book value at the beginning of a year is multiplied by a constant percentage (such as 125%, 150%, or 200%) to determine depreciation for the year

Depletion (p. 614) Allocating the cost of a natural resource to expense over the period in which the resource produces revenue

Double-declining-balance method (p. 603) A method of depreciation that uses a rate equal to twice the straight-line rate and applies that rate to the book value of the asset at the beginning of the year

Franchise (p. 617) An intangible asset; a right to exclusive dealership granted by a governmental unit or a business entity

Gain (p. 608) The disposition of an asset for more than its book value

Goodwill (p. 618) An intangible asset; the value of a business in excess of the net value of its identifiable assets

Impairment (p. 615) A situation that occurs when the asset is determined to have a fair market value less than its book value

Income tax method (p. 613) A method of recording the trade-in of an asset for income tax purposes. It does not permit a gain or loss to be recognized on the transaction

Intangible assets (p. 617) Assets that lack a physical substance, such as goodwill, patents, copyrights, and computer software, although software has, in a sense, a physical attribute

Loss (p. 608) The disposition of an asset for less than its book value

Net book value (p. 602) The cost of an asset minus its accumulated depreciation, depletion, or amortization, also known as book value

Net salvage value (p. 602) The salvage value of an asset less any costs to remove or sell the asset

Patent (p. 617) An intangible asset; an exclusive right given by the U.S. Patent Office to manufacture and sell an invention for a period of 20 years from the date the patent is granted

Real property (p. 600) Assets such as land, land improvements, buildings, and other structures attached to the land

Recoverability test (p. 616) Test for possible impairment that compares the asset's net book value with the estimated net cash flows from future use of the asset

Residual value (p. 602) The estimate of the amount that could be obtained from the sale or disposition of an asset at the end of its useful life; also called salvage or scrap value

Scrap value (p. 602) See Residual value

Sum-of-the-years'-digits method (p. 604) A method of depreciating asset costs by allocating as expense each year a fractional part of the asset's depreciable cost, based on the sum of the digits of the number of years in the asset's useful life

Tangible personal property (p. 600) Assets such as machinery, equipment, furniture, and fixtures that can be removed and used elsewhere

Trade name (p. 617) An intangible asset; an exclusive business name registered with the U.S. Patent Office; also called brand name

Trademark (p. 617) An intangible asset; an exclusive business symbol registered with the U.S. Patent Office

Units-of-output method (p. 605) See Units-of-production method

Units-of-production method (p. 605) A method of depreciating asset cost at the same rate for each unit produced during each period

---

Comprehensive **Self Review**

1. An asset with a cost of $30,000 and accumulated depreciation of $27,300 is retired and sold as junk for $800. How much gain or loss is recorded on the retirement?

2. Distinguish between the legal life and the economic life of an intangible asset. Which is used in computing amortization if amortization is appropriate?

3. How does real property differ from personal property?

4. What is the denominator of the fraction used in the calculation of annual depreciation using the sum-of-the-years'-digits method of depreciation for an asset with a useful life of ten years?

5. What generally accepted accounting principle or convention supports the writing down of impaired assets to their fair market values?

6. Under what circumstances would the unit-of-production depreciation method be the logical choice from the different methods available?

(Answers to Comprehensive Self Review are on page 640.)

Discussion Questions

1. How is the amount of impairment to be recorded determined?

2. What is the name of the process by which costs of a natural resource deposit are removed from the asset account as the resources are produced?

3. Explain how to measure the gain or loss when an old asset is traded in on a new one.

4. What are the requirements for recording an intangible asset such as goodwill?

5. Are gains and losses on trade-in transactions recognized and recorded under GAAP?

6. What accounting treatment is given to most research costs?

7. What are the two categories of intangible assets for the purposes of disposing of their capitalized costs?

8. What are the rules for determining the amount of cost in each category of intangibles in question 7 to be removed from the asset account during each accounting period?

9. Explain how double-declining-balance depreciation is computed on an asset with a life of six years.

10. What account is debited and what account is credited to record depreciation on trucks?

11. Explain how the sum-of-the-years'-digits method would be applied to an asset with a life of six years.

12. Is MACRS used for federal income tax rules acceptable under GAAP?

13. Which method will give you a higher amount of depreciation expense in the later years of an asset's life, straight-line or declining-balance? Explain.

14. What is the basic test for determining whether impairment does, in fact, exist?

15. Under what circumstances is the units-of-production method of depreciation especially desirable?

16. What information related to the company's property, plant, and equipment must be presented in the financial statements and in the notes to the financial statements?

17. Name three or more events, developments, or situations that indicate impairment of property, plant, and equipment may exist.

18. Which of these, if any, is not "real property"?

   a. Land

   b. A building

   c. A motor home being used as an office

   d. Pavement for a parking lot

19. What is meant by "capitalized costs"?

20. A company purchased some land on which an old building is located. The building has to be torn down to enable construction of a new building. Which, if any, of the following costs related to the old building should be capitalized as part of the land cost?

   a. Purchase price of the property.

   b. Permit fee for tearing down the old building

   c. Cost of tearing down the building in excess of salvage proceeds

   d. Costs of hauling off debris of old building

21. Explain how straight-line depreciation is computed.

22. What is meant by the term "personal property"?

23. Name two accelerated depreciation methods.

24. Which, if any, of the depreciation methods discussed in this chapter ignore salvage value?

APPLICATIONS

Exercises

Determining the elements that make up the cost of an asset.   ◄   **Exercise 18.1**
Objective 18-1

The following costs were incurred by Foreign Auto Parts in connection with the construction of a retail store building:

Cost of land, including $19,000 of legal costs	$400,000
Cost to demolish old building	18,750
Costs of grading land for building site	11,200
Costs related to building construction	950,000
Legal costs relating to building permits	16,975
Costs of paving parking lot	100,000

1. What is the capitalized cost of the land?

2. What is the capitalized cost of the new building?

Determining the elements that make up the cost of an asset.   ◄   **Exercise 18.2**
Objective 18-1

The Shipping Express Company incurred the costs below related to a new packing machine:

Invoice price of packing machine	$190,000
Cash discount for prompt payment	7,400
Transportation costs	4,920
Installation costs	2,625

What is the capitalized cost of the new packing machine?

Exercise 18.3
Objective 18-2

▶ **Recording depreciation.**

For the year ending December 31, 2016, Carter Manufacturing Company had depreciation totaling $76,000 on its office equipment. Give the general journal entry to record the adjusting entry.

Exercise 18.4
Objective 18-2

▶ **Computing depreciation under various methods.**

Zero Company acquired an asset on January 2, 2016, at a cost of $266,000. The asset's useful life is four years and its salvage value is $76,000. Compute the depreciation expense for each of the first two years, using the straight-line method, the double-declining-balance method, and the sum-of-the-years'-digits method.

Exercise 18.5
Objective 18-2

▶ **Computing depreciation under the units-of-production method.**

On January 10, 2016, Dallas Company purchased a machine to mold components for one of its products. Total cost of the machine was $860,000. It is expected to produce 900,000 units and to have a salvage value of $50,000. The company used the units-of-production method of depreciation.

a. In 2016, it produced 90,000 units. Compute the depreciation expense for 2016.

b. During 2017, 120,000 units were produced. Compute the depreciation expense for 2017.

Exercise 18.6
Objective 18-3

▶ **Applying Modified Accelerated Cost Recovery (MACRS) under federal income tax rules.**

On January 20, 2016, Vicksburg Transportation Company purchased a new lightweight truck for $50,000.

1. Into which MACRS "class" is this asset classified?

2. What would be the amount of cost recovery on the truck in 2016 and in 2017?

Exercise 18.7
Objective 18-4

▶ **Recording the sale of plant and equipment.**

Carter Company owns a truck that cost $51,000. Depreciation totaling $35,000 had been taken on the truck up to January 8, 2016, when it was sold for $14,150.

1. Give the journal entry to record the sale.

2. Assume, instead, that the truck is sold for $17,100. Give the journal entry to record the sale.

Exercise 18.8
Objective 18-5

▶ **Recording asset trade-ins using financial accounting rules.**

On January 5, 2012, Mountain View Company purchased construction equipment for $710,500, with a useful life of six years and estimated salvage value of $100,000. The company uses the straight-line method of depreciation. On July 3, 2016, this equipment was traded for new similar construction equipment that has a value of $800,000. The company paid $582,000 cash and was given a trade-in allowance of $218,000 for the old equipment.

1. Give the general journal entry needed on July 3, 2016, to record the trade-in. (Assume that the entry to bring depreciation up to date has been made.)

2. Assume the same facts as stated above, except that Mountain View paid cash of $514,750 on the trade-in and was given an allowance of $285,250 for the old equipment. Give the journal entry to record the trade-in.

Exercise 18.9
Objective 18-5

▶ **Reporting asset trade-ins using federal income tax requirements.**

(Refer to the truck purchased by Vicksburg Transportation Company, Exercise 18.6.)

At the beginning of the year, it became obvious that the truck purchased the year before was too small to handle many of Vicksburg's jobs. On January 4, 2017, Vicksburg traded in the old truck on a new, larger lightweight truck. Its sale price (and fair market value) was $60,000. The dealer gave Vicksburg a trade-in allowance of $7,400 for the old truck and Vicksburg paid the balance ($52,600) in cash.

1. For tax purposes, how much gain or loss is recognized on the trade-in?

2. For tax purposes, what is the basis (the cost) to be recorded for the new truck?

Computing depletion of mineral property cost.

◀ **Exercise 18.10**
Objective 18-6

Heath Mining Company acquired a mine in 2016. Capitalized costs of the minerals were $5,460,000. The company mined 200,000 tons of ore in 2016 and on December 31, 2016, it is estimated that 2,200,000 tons of ore remained in the ground.

Compute the amount of depletion expense for 2016.

Recognize asset impairment and understand the general concepts of accounting for impairment.

◀ **Exercise 18.11**
Objective 18-7

a. Orison Milling Company operates, on a contract basis, equipment that grinds and mixes grains used as animal feed. In September 2016, the book value of the equipment was $144,000. Because of declining processing fees, the company's chief financial officer became concerned that the asset might be impaired. An analysis of expected future cash flows from use of the asset resulted in an estimate of $143,000 of future cash flows. Further study led to the company's finding several almost identical processors that ranged in price from $99,000 to $101,000. The CFO decided that the asset was impaired and should be "written down" to $99,000. Do you agree?

b. What account would be debited and what account would be credited to record impairment? What would be the amount of the impairment recorded?

Computing and recording amortization and impairment of intangible assets.

◀ **Exercise 18.12**
Objective 18-8

On December 31, 2016, Warren Company's *Intangible Assets* account reflects two assets:

1. *Goodwill,* $145,000. This amount was recorded in December 2015 as part of the cost of acquiring an existing business. It represents the excess of the total purchase price, over the value of net identifiable assets. Warren has studied carefully the operations and concluded that the fair value of goodwill on December 31, 2016, is $110,000 and that benefits should exist for at least another 10 years.

2. *Patent,* $299,000. The patent was purchased on January 2015 for $322,000, when it had a remaining legal life of 14 years. On December 31, 2015, $23,000 of cost was amortized. On December 31, 2016, Warren estimates that the patent will be useful for only another 9 years (through December 31, 2025). However, it is estimated that the patent still has a value to the company of over $310,000.

For each of the intangibles—goodwill and patent—explain what entry, if any, is necessary at the end of 2016 to adjust the accounts.

PROBLEMS

Problem Set A

Determining the cost to be capitalized for acquisition of assets.

◀ **Problem 18.1A**
Objective 18-1

On January 6, 2016, Hazleton Company purchased a site for a new manufacturing plant for $3,400,000. At a cost of $21,000, it razed an existing facility (fair market value $300,000) and received $14,000 from its salvage. The company also paid $7,400 in attorney fees, $2,350 in inspection fees, and $1,650 for a permit to raze the facility. After the facility was torn down, the following costs were incurred: $60,400 for fill dirt for the site, $42,000 for leveling the site, $135,000 for paving sidewalks and curbs, and $5,200,000 for building costs of the new facility. The parking area was paved at a cost of $135,700.

INSTRUCTIONS

Compute the capitalized costs of (1) the manufacturing plant, (2) the land, and (3) the land improvements.

Analyze: Unfortunately, Hazleton's new building was not completed on schedule, but the company had to vacate the old building. As a result the business was shut down for two months. During this period, the company reported a net loss of $350,000. The president suggests that the loss should be capitalized as part of the cost of the new building. What is your recommendation?

Problem 18.2A
Objective 18-2

▶ **Using different depreciation methods and comparing the results.**

On January 4, 2016, Chicago Company purchased new equipment for $600,000 that had a useful life of four years and a salvage value of $60,000.

INSTRUCTIONS

Prepare a schedule showing the annual depreciation and end-of-year accumulated depreciation for the first three years of the asset's life under (1) the straight-line method, (2) the sum-of-the-years'-digits method, and (3) the double-declining-balance method.

Analyze: If the sum-of-the-years'-digits method is used to compute depreciation, what would be the book value of the asset at the end of 2017?

Problem 18.3A
Objective 18-2

▶ **Using the straight-line and units-of-output methods of depreciation.**

On January 5, 2016, Hill Company purchased equipment for $620,000, having an estimated useful life of five years or 295,000 units of product. The estimated salvage value was $30,000. Actual production data for the first three years were: 2016—50,000 units; 2017—66,000 units; and 2018—56,000 units.

INSTRUCTIONS

Compute each year's depreciation and the end-of-year accumulated depreciation under (1) the straight-line method and (2) the units-of-output method.

Analyze: Would the total depreciation taken over the five-year life depend on which of the two methods is used? Why?

Problem 18.4A
Objectives 18-2, 18-3

▶ **Computing depreciation and MACRS on assets.**

On January 12, 2016, Washington Company purchased a computer (cost, $13,000; expected life five years; estimated salvage value, $1,500) and a lightweight van for delivery purposes (cost, $65,500; estimated life, seven years; estimated salvage value, $6,000). For financial accounting purposes, the company uses straight-line depreciation on all assets.

INSTRUCTIONS

1. Compute depreciation of the computer cost for financial accounting purposes for 2016 and 2017.

2. Compute cost recovery of the computer cost for income tax purposes for 2016 and 2017.

3. Compute depreciation of the van cost for financial accounting purposes for 2016 and 2017.

4. Compute cost recovery of the van cost for income tax purposes for 2016 and 2017.

Analyze: What objectives or principles account for the differences between the financial accounting depreciation rules and the income tax cost recovery rules?

Problem 18.5A
Objectives 18-2, 18-4, 18-5

▶ **Recording asset trade-ins and sales.**

The transactions listed below occurred at Murphy Company during 2016:

DATE	TRANSACTIONS
Mar. 25	Exchanged a printer (Office Equipment) that had an original cost of $6,800 when purchased on January 4, 2014. The useful life of the old asset was originally estimated at five years and the salvage value at $300. The new printer had a price and market value of $11,200. Murphy gave up the old machine and paid $5,600 cash. The new printer is estimated to have a useful life of five years and a salvage value of $700.
July 19	Exchanged a truck (Vehicles) for a new one that had a sales price, and fair value, of $44,800. Received a trade-in allowance of $11,500 on the old truck and paid cash of $33,300. The old truck had been purchased for $37,760 on May 27, 2013, three years earlier. The life of the old truck was originally estimated at four years and the salvage value at $6,800. The life of the new truck is estimated to be five years and it is estimated to have a salvage value of $9,800.
Aug. 18	Sold a truck that was purchased on January 5, 2014, for an original purchase price of $45,920. It had an estimated life of four years and an estimated salvage value of $8,000. Sales price is as indicated in Instructions, below.

INSTRUCTIONS

Note: In following these instructions, assume that straight-line depreciation is used and that depreciation was last recorded on December 31, 2015. Compute depreciation to the nearest whole dollar.

1. Give the entries in general journal form to record the two exchange transactions.
2. Give the entries in general journal form to record the sale of the truck, assuming:
   a. The sales price was $22,000.
   b. The sales price was $17,000.

Analyze: What was the book value of the truck sold on August 18?

Recording asset sales and trade-ins.

◀ **Problem 18.6A**
Objectives 18-4, 18-5

Dear Company purchased four identical machines on January 10, 2016, paying $5,500 for each. The useful life of each machine is expected to be five years, with a salvage value of $700 each. The company uses the straight-line method of depreciation. Selected transactions involving the machines follow. The accounts for recording these transactions are also given.

INSTRUCTIONS

1. Record the transactions in general journal form. Round all calculations to the nearest whole dollar.

ACCOUNTS

101	Cash
141	Machinery
142	Accumulated Depreciation—Machinery
495	Gain on Sale of Machinery
541	Depreciation Expense—Machinery
595	Loss on Sale of Machinery
597	Loss on Stolen Machinery

DATE	TRANSACTIONS FOR 2016
Jan. 10	Paid $5,500, in cash, for each of four machines.
Dec. 31	Recorded depreciation for the year on the four machines.

DATE	TRANSACTIONS FOR 2017
Apr. 3	Machine 1 was stolen; no insurance was carried.
Dec. 31	Recorded depreciation for the year for the three remaining machines.

DATE	TRANSACTIONS FOR 2018
Sept. 18	Sold machine 2 for $3,200 cash.
Dec. 31	Recorded depreciation for the year on the two remaining machines.

DATE	TRANSACTIONS FOR 2019
June 4	Machine 3 was traded in for a similar machine (no. 5) with a $6,580 list price and fair market value. A trade-in allowance of $2,510 was received. The balance was paid in cash. The new machine has an estimated life of five years and salvage value of $700.
Aug. 29	Machine 4 was traded in for a similar machine (no. 6) with a $8,200 list price and fair market value. A trade-in allowance of $1,390 was received. The balance was paid in cash. The new machine has an estimated life of five years, with salvage value of $700.
Dec. 31	Record depreciation on the two new machines.

Analyze: What is the balance of the *Accumulated Depreciation* account on December 31, 2019?

Problem 18.7A ▶ **Compute and record depletion of natural resources.**

Objective 18-6

Keystone Mining Company had total depletable capitalized costs of $828,000 for a mine acquired in early 2016. It was estimated that the mine contained 920,000 tons of recoverable ore when production began. During 2016, 46,000 tons were mined, and 174,800 tons were mined in 2017.

INSTRUCTIONS

1. Compute the depletion expense in 2016 and 2017 for financial accounting purposes. What accounts will be debited and credited to record the depletion?

2. **a.** In 2016, 46,500 tons of ore were sold for $4,600,000. For tax purposes, operating expenses of the mine were $600,000. The taxpayer may deduct either cost depletion or percentage depletion, which for the type ore produced is 8 percent of production sold from the mine. (Assume, however, that percentage depletion is limited to the amount of net income from the property.) What would be the amount of percentage depletion allowable in 2016?

   b. What would be the amount of cost depletion allowable for tax purposes in 2016, assuming that capitalized mineral costs are the same for tax purposes as for financial accounting purposes?

c. What will be the amount of depletion based on cost that the company could deduct on its tax return in 2017 if it deducts percentage depletion in 2016?

d. Suppose that in the first three years of the mine's life, the company took percentage depletion totaling $820,000. In the fifth year of the mine's life, production proceeds were $5,300,000. How much percentage depletion could the company deduct in the fifth year?

Analyze: What explanation do you think might be given for the deviation of income tax rules from basic accounting principles in the determination of depletion of costs of minerals?

Recording impairment of property, plant, and equipment.

◄ **Problem 18.8A**
Objective 18-7

Galloway Realty Company owns a number of large office buildings in several cities in the United States. One of the buildings is 16 years old and has had a large number of vacant office suites for several years. The building's book value is $13.2 million. The company has examined carefully its future cash flows and has determined that it is highly unlikely that the company can recover the building's book value from future cash flows. Further study in November 2016 has resulted in three estimates of the market value of the building. All of the estimates of value are approximately $8.3 million.

INSTRUCTIONS

1. Should Galloway record impairment of the building? Why?

2. If impairment should be recorded, what is the amount of impairment?

3. What accounting entry would be necessary based on the above facts?

4. If impairment is recorded in 2016 and subsequently the value of the building increases in 2017 so that the market value exceeds the book value, should the book value of the building be increased at that time?

Analyze: How could the company use its estimates of cash flows to arrive at a "market value" of the building?

Recording intangible asset acquisition, amortization, and impairment.

◄ **Problem 18.9A**
Objective 18-8

Selected accounts of the Zena Company are listed below. On January 1, 2016, the only intangible asset in the company's accounts was *Goodwill*. This was recorded in 2009 when the company acquired another company and paid $300,000 more than the fair market value of the net identifiable tangible assets acquired. For two years, the company amortized the costs on the basis of a 40-year life, charging a total of $15,000 ($7,500 each year) to an account called *Amortization Expense— Goodwill*. However, no amortization of goodwill has been recorded since 2010. Transactions and events that took place at the company during 2016 are given below.

INSTRUCTIONS

1. Record the transactions for 2016 in general journal form.

2. Record amortization of the intangible assets, where appropriate, for the year ended December 31, 2016.

3. Record impairment of assets, where appropriate, on December 31, 2016.

ACCOUNTS

Cash
Computer Software
Patents
Product Formulas
Goodwill
Amortization Expense—Patents
Amortization Expense—Computer Software
Amortization Expense—Product Formulas
Impairment of Intangibles

TRANSACTIONS AND OTHER INFORMATION

1. On May 10, 2016, the company paid $189,000 to purchase a product formula. The formula is expected to have a useful life of seven years.

2. On July 5, the company paid $666,000 for a patent having a useful life of 9 years.

3. On September 22, the company purchased a unique computer program for $208,000. This program has an estimated useful life of four years.

4. During the year, the company recorded various cash expenditures of $220,000 for labor and supplies used in its research department. (Date entry December 31.)

5. At the end of 2016, the company reviewed the goodwill shown in the accounts. Based on the profitability of activities acquired in purchasing the other business, the owners of the business think the goodwill has a value of $230,000 and should be of benefit for many more years.

Analyze: Based on the transactions above, what is the total net book value of Zena Company's intangible assets on December 31, 2016?

Problem Set B

Problem 18.1B
Objective 18-1

▶ **Determining the costs to be capitalized for acquisition of an asset.**

On July 5, 2016, the Hilltop Company purchased a site for its new headquarters for $425,000. At a cost of $40,000, it razed two existing houses, with a total appraised value of $95,000, and received $23,000 from salvage. The firm also paid $12,000 in attorney's fees, $2,000 in inspection fees, and $700 for a permit to raze the houses. After the houses were razed, the firm incurred these costs:

$40,000 for fill dirt for the site
$30,000 for leveling the site
$80,000 for paving sidewalks and curbs
$105,500 for paving a parking lot
$3,975,000 for construction costs of new building

INSTRUCTIONS

Compute the capitalized costs of (1) the land, (2) the building, and (3) the land improvements.

Analyze: What net effect did these transactions have on the total owner's equity?

Problem 18.2B
Objective 18-2

▶ **Using different depreciation methods and comparing the results.**

On January 5, 2016, Parker Company purchased a new $650,000 machine with five-year useful life and an estimated salvage value of $50,000.

INSTRUCTIONS

Prepare a schedule showing the annual depreciation and accumulated depreciation for each of the first three years of the asset's life under (1) the straight-line method, (2) the sum-of-the-years'-digits method, and (3) the double-declining-balance method.

Analyze: If the double-declining-balance method is used, what would be the book value of the machine at the end of 2017?

Problem 18.3B
Objective 18-2

▶ **Using various methods to compute depreciation.**

Zentex Company purchased a carton fabrication unit for $990,000 on January 8, 2016. The machine's useful life is estimated as 3,000,000 units of product or eight years and its salvage value is estimated at $90,000. The number of cartons fabricated in each year, 2016 to 2018, is as follows:

Year	Cartons Fabricated
2016	320,000
2017	336,800
2018	472,000

INSTRUCTIONS

Compute the depreciation expense and accumulated depreciation at year-end for each of the three years under (1) the straight-line method and (2) the units-of-production method.

Analyze: If the units-of-output method were used, what would be the book value of the machine at the end of 2017?

Computing depreciation and MACRS on assets.

◄   **Problem 18.4B**

Objectives 18-2, 18-3

On January 6, 2016, Mayfield Company purchased a computer (cost, $20,000; expected life, four years; estimated salvage value, $4,000) and an eight-passenger van (cost, $38,000; estimated life, eight years; estimated salvage value, $8,000). For financial accounting purposes, the company has always used straight-line depreciation on all assets.

INSTRUCTIONS

1. Compute depreciation of the computer's cost for financial accounting purposes for 2016 and 2017.
2. Compute MACRS cost recovery of the computer's cost for income tax purposes for 2016 and 2017.
3. Compute depreciation of the van's cost for financial accounting purpose for 2016 and 2017.
4. Compute MACRS cost recovery of the van's cost for income tax purposes for 2016 and 2017.

Analyze: The owner suggests that to avoid duplication of work, the company should use the amount of cost recovery taken on the tax return for each asset as the amount to be used for depreciation in financial statements. Do you agree? Why?

Recording asset trade-ins and sales.

◄   **Problem 18.5B**

Objectives 18-2, 18-4, 18-5

The following transactions occurred at Wade Company during 2016:

DATE	TRANSACTIONS
Apr. 2	Traded in a copy machine (Office Equipment) that had been purchased for $5,200 on December 29, 2012. Straight-line depreciation of the old copier has been based on an estimated useful life of five years, with salvage value of $800. The new copier had a purchase price and value of $12,000. Wade received a trade-in allowance of $3,500 on the old machine and paid cash of $8,500. The new copier has a useful life of five years and an estimated salvage value of $600.
July 8	Exchanged a delivery truck (Vehicles) for a new one with a list price of $44,000, estimated useful life of five years and salvage value of $8,400. A trade-in allowance of $10,000 was received on the old truck, which had been purchased on July 1, 2013, for $33,000. Depreciation on the old truck has been based on an estimated $5,000 salvage value and a five-year life.
Sept. 23	Sold a refrigeration unit (Store Equipment) for cash (see Instruction 2). The unit was purchased on January 3, 2013, for $32,000 and was depreciated on the straight-line basis, using an estimated life of six years and a salvage value of $2,000.

INSTRUCTIONS

Note: In each case, assume that straight-line depreciation is used and that depreciation was last recorded on December 31, 2015. Compute depreciation to the nearest whole dollar.

1. Record in general journal form the two trade-in transactions on April 2 and July 8.
2. Record the sale of the refrigeration unit, assuming:
   a. the sales price was $13,500.
   b. the sales price was $10,200.

Analyze: What accounting concepts underlie the accounting treatments for the transactions of April 2 and July 8?

Problem 18.6B
Objectives 18-2, 18-4, 18-5

▶ **Recording asset sales and trade-ins.**

Liberty Company purchased four identical machines on January 4, 2016, paying $9,000 for each machine. The useful life of each machine is expected to be five years, with no salvage value expected. The company uses the straight-line method of depreciation. Selected transactions involving the machines are listed below. The necessary accounts for recording these transactions are also given.

INSTRUCTIONS

Record the transactions in general journal form. Use the following accounts, as necessary.

ACCOUNTS

101	Cash	541	Depreciation Expense—Machinery
141	Machinery	595	Loss on Sale of Machinery
142	Accumulated Depreciation—Machinery	596	Loss on Trade-In of Machinery
495	Gain on Sale of Machinery	597	Fire Loss on Machinery

DATE	TRANSACTIONS FOR 2016
Jan. 4	Paid $9,000 each for four machines.
Dec. 31	Recorded depreciation for the year on the four machines.

DATE	TRANSACTIONS FOR 2017
Mar. 31	Machine 1 was destroyed by fire; no insurance was carried.
Dec. 31	Recorded depreciation for the year for the three remaining machines.

DATE	TRANSACTIONS FOR 2018
Oct. 2	Sold machine 2 for $4,400 cash.
Dec. 31	Recorded depreciation for the year on the two remaining machines.

DATE	TRANSACTIONS FOR 2019
May 28	Traded machine 3 for a similar machine (no. 5) with an $8,800 price and fair market value. A trade-in allowance of $2,800 was received. The balance of $6,000 was paid in cash.
Sept. 3	Traded in machine 4 for a similar machine (no. 6) with a $9,200 list price and fair value. A trade-in allowance of $2,000 was received. The balance was paid in cash.
Sept. 3	Assume that the company somehow has adopted a policy of recording trade-in transactions using the rules required for federal income tax purposes—even though the cost of assets and the depreciation are determined under financial accounting rules as you have computed them previously in this problem. Give the entry that would be recorded on September 3 to record the trade-in of machine 4 on machine 6, using the facts given.

Analyze: What is the difference between the financial accounting entries and tax entries for the trade-in of machine 4?

Compute and record depletion of natural resources.

◀ **Problem 18.7B**
Objective 18-6

Perez Company acquired a mineral property and drilled an oil well in 2016. Capitalized costs subject to depletion totaled $800,000. When the well began producing in late 2016, it was estimated that one million barrels of oil could ultimately be produced from the property. In 2016, 5,000 barrels were produced and sold for $180,000. Operating costs for the property were $160,800. Sixty thousand barrels were produced and sold for $2,600,000 in 2017 and operating costs that year were $330,000.

INSTRUCTIONS

1. Compute the depletion expense in 2016 and 2017 for financial accounting purposes. What accounts will be debited and credited to record the depletion?

2. Assume that capitalized costs and operating expenses were the same for financial accounting and tax purposes. The taxpayer may deduct either cost depletion or percentage depletion. The percentage depletion for oil and gas production is 15 percent of gross income from the property, but limited to 100 percent of net income from the property. Assume that all of the oil produced is eligible for percentage depletion.

   a. What would be the amount of cost depletion allowable for tax purposes in 2016?

   b. What will be the amount of depletion that the company could deduct on its tax return in 2016?

   c. What amount of cost depletion could the company deduct on its tax return in 2017?

   d. What would be the amount, if any, of percentage depletion deductible in 2017?

   e. Suppose that in the first four years of the property's life, the company deducted depletion totaling $798,800 on the tax returns. No additional depletable costs were capitalized. In the fifth year of the property's life, proceeds of $4,800,000 were received from the oil produced, and operating expenses of $900,000 were incurred. What amount, if any, of percentage depletion may be deducted on the company's tax return in that year?

Analyze: Would the company be entitled to percentage depletion in the sixth and future years in which there was gross income that exceeded the operating expenses?

Recognize and record impairment of property, plant, and equipment.

◀ **Problem 18.8B**
Objective 18-7

Freedom Airlines is a small commercial airline operating in the United States. Because of poor economic conditions in the airline industry in 2016, Freedom has eliminated some routes and reduced the frequency of flights on all other routes. As a result, the airline has indefinitely stored 8 of its 20 aircraft. The company continues to lose money and sees no time in the foreseeable future that the parked aircraft will be operated again. The company's public accountant has told the airline officials that it must assess whether the parked planes (and perhaps some of those flying routes) should be assessed for impairment. The parked planes have a combined book value of $48 million.

Company officials have researched the problem and found that there is an abundance of identical or similar planes that could be purchased for approximately $4.5 million each. Several of these similar planes have been recently sold and the $4.5 million value for each has been accepted by company officials as being a good estimate of the going sales price and of their fair value. It has been impossible for company officials to estimate future cash flows, or if there will be any future cash flows from those planes.

INSTRUCTIONS

Answer the following questions:

1. Should Freedom Airlines record impairment of the parked planes? Why or why not?

2. If impairment should be recorded, what is the amount of impairment?

3. What accounting entry would be necessary based on the above facts?

4. If impairment is recorded in 2016 and subsequently the value of the planes increases before they are sold, with the result that market value exceeds the book value, should the value of the planes be increased at that time?

Analyze: What steps can you suggest the company take in considering whether the planes that are still flying also may be impaired?

Problem 18.9B ▶
Objective 18-8

Recording intangible asset acquisition, amortization, and impairment.

Selected accounts of the Harvard Medical Labs are listed below. Also given are some transactions and events that took place at the company during 2016.

INSTRUCTIONS

1. Record in general journal form the transactions for 2016 described.

2. Record amortization of the intangible assets for the year ended December 31, 2016.

3. Indicate what steps should be taken, if any, to properly account for the balance of $1,200,000 in the *Goodwill* account on December 31. The following accounts related to intangible assets are found in Harvard's general ledger:

ACCOUNTS

Cash	Research and Development Expense
Patents	Amortization of Patents
Computer Software	Amortization of Computer Software
Goodwill	Impairment of Intangibles

DATE	TRANSACTIONS AND INFORMATION
April 10	Purchased for cash of $420,000 a patent related to a chemical compound. It has a legal life of 12 years remaining, but is expected to be used for only 8 years because of new patents for similar products being developed.
Sept. 1	Purchased a computer software program for $36,000 in cash from a computer software supply firm. The software program is to be used in the company's inventory control system and has an estimated useful life of seven years.
Dec. 31	(Date of journal entry, reflecting summary for year.) During year, made cash expenditures of $4,000,000 for research and development costs related to a new electronic medical procedure being developed. Researchers have worked on the project for 10 months of the year and think the project will result in a valuable patent.
Dec. 31	The company examined the balance of $1,900,000 in the *Goodwill* account. This balance arose from purchase of another business two years earlier and represents the amount paid for the acquired business in excess of the value of the net identifiable assets acquired. The examination concluded that the activities acquired have continued to be very profitable and that there is no reason to record impairment on the $1,900,000 balance.

Analyze: Suppose that the examination of goodwill had revealed that the benefits (future profits) resulting from the acquisition two years ago are decreasing. Based on the estimated value of the excess of the future profits over the value of the net assets acquired, the value of goodwill is estimated to be currently only $1,300,000. What accounting entry, if any, should be made to record this fact?

Critical Thinking Problem 18.1

Depreciation Expense Company Practices

In a review of the annual reports of Pierce Wholesale Company and International Distributors, you note that Pierce Wholesale uses straight-line depreciation and International Distributors uses the declining-balance method.

1. Are these companies violating the generally accepted accounting principle of consistency by using different depreciation methods?

2. If you examined the federal income tax returns of these companies, would you expect the deductions, similar to depreciation taken on their income tax returns, to be the same as the depreciation expenses shown on their financial statements? Why or why not?

3. Assume that these companies are similar in all respects except for their difference in computing depreciation. Which company would you expect to report the lower net income for the year?

4. Who is responsible for determining the depreciation method used by the company for financial accounting purposes?

Critical Thinking Problem 18.2

Cost Capitalization, Depreciation, MACRS, Impairment

Virginia Company operates a real estate abstract, title, and insurance company. Below are selected transactions and events that occurred during the years 2016 to 2019. Using those transactions and events, follow the instructions given.

INSTRUCTIONS

1. Give the adjusting entries on December 31, 2017, to record depreciation expense for the year on all assets.

2. a. Compute the amount of MACRS cost recovery for tax purposes on the furniture and fixtures in (1) 2017 and (2) 2018.

   b. What is the MACRS recovery period for the building?

3. Should Virginia's management be concerned with the possibility of asset impairment at the end of 2019? Explain.

4. Do you agree with the company's financial manager that depreciation should be reduced in 2019 because of the decline in business? Explain your answer.

TRANSACTIONS AND EVENTS 2016 AND 2017

The company purchased a building site for $450,000 on August 2, 2016. Preparation for construction began in October. Costs, other than land costs, incurred in 2016 and 2017 were:

a. grading and preparing the site, $40,000.

b. paving the sidewalks and parking lot, $75,000 (estimated life 25 years, no salvage value; straight-line depreciation to be used).

c. fencing back of the property, $16,000, erected in same week building was completed (estimated life, 15 years; no salvage value; straight-line depreciation to be used).

d. building construction contract costs $720,000, completed June 25, 2017 (estimated life, 35 years; salvage value, $20,000; straight-line depreciation to be used).

e.   telephone system installed in the last week of June 2017, $40,000 (estimated life, six years; estimated salvage value $4,000; sum-of-the-years' digits depreciation method to be used).

f.   furniture and fixtures purchased in late June 2017, $90,000 (estimated life, 10 years; estimated salvage value, $6,000; double-declining-balance method to be used).

The company opened for business in the new building on July 5, 2017. During the remainder of 2017, the business grew at about the pace anticipated by the company's management when the project was planned.

2018 AND 2019

1.   The business continued to grow at the anticipated pace in 2018.

2.   In June 2019, a rumor was circulated that a hazardous waste deposit existed on the company's property, but no evidence was presented to support the allegation. In November 2019, an investigative team from local, state, and federal health services arrived on the scene to conduct a detailed investigation of the property. In the third week of December, they reported having found what had once been a dump site. The investigators took many samples and sent these to laboratories, then left, stating they would return in the second week of January. They hope to have tentative laboratory reports at the time of their return. The company's attorneys are concerned about the investigation because the company's insurance does not cover losses from this problem and the state law places responsibility on the current owner to clean up the property. Because of the rumors, customers were reluctant to come to the building and business declined dramatically in November and December 2019.

3.   In late December, the company's executive manager suggested that because of the decline in business the company should reduce its current depreciation charge, resulting in lower depreciation in the next few years, with greater depreciation in subsequent years. The manager thinks his plan is akin to units-of-production depreciation and he expects future business to be greater, resulting in higher depreciation at that time.

BUSINESS CONNECTIONS

Plant Asset Procedures

Managerial FOCUS

1.   Suggest three key procedures involving internal control of property, plant, and equipment that do not relate specifically to accounting records.

2.   Suggest three key procedures involving internal control of property, plant, and equipment that relate to accounting records.

3.   Generally accepted accounting principles require that all research and development costs be expensed in the year they are incurred. An officer of the company wants to amortize these costs. What can you say to explain why this accounting requirement exists?

4.   Assume that you are the accountant at a fabricating plant. One of the vice presidents has asked you why one of the pieces of equipment used in the plant is shown at its original cost in the asset accounts. Respond to the question.

5.   Suppose you are on the controller's staff at a large company. You have suggested assigning responsibility for the company's equipment to specific individuals. One supervisor has objected, saying it is a waste of time. Defend your suggestion to the controller and to the supervisor.

Goodwill

Hernandez's Auto Repair Service has been in business for five years. He has developed a great reputation of doing a good job at reasonable prices. His reputation has given him a large, loyal clientele. During those years, Mr. Hernandez has purchased net assets of $160,000 on which he owes $50,000. Hernandez has decided to sell his business and open another one 10 miles away. Rudy Rodriguez has agreed to purchase the business for $210,000. Is it ethical for Mr. Hernandez to accept a larger amount for this business than its value? If so, how would Mr. Rodriguez record this transaction? Is it ethical for Mr. Hernandez to open a new business so close to the old business?

Depreciation Amounts and Method

Refer to The Home Depot, Inc., *2012 Annual Report (for the fiscal year ended February 3, 2013)* in Appendix A.

1. Locate the Notes to Consolidated Financial Statements. Review Note 1, Summary of Significant Accounting Policies. What methods are used to depreciate the company's furniture, fixtures, and equipment? What estimated useful life is assigned to buildings?

2. Find the Consolidated Balance Sheet. What amount was charged to accumulated depreciation and amortization for the year ended February 3, 2013? What net value is reported for Property and Equipment?

Asset's Salvage Value

Property, plant, and equipment can be depreciated in various methods. As a team, select an asset to acquire and depreciate; for example, a large stamping machine. Determine the asset's cost, salvage value, life, depreciation method, and annual depreciation. Double the salvage value of the asset and explain the effect it would have on depreciation expense. Is it favorable or unfavorable, and why? Present your finding to the class.

MACRS

Depreciation is calculated differently for financial records than depreciation (cost recovery) for income tax reporting. The Internal Revenue Service recognizes only the MACRS method. *Publication 17, Your Federal Income Tax,* is an important reference for income tax preparation. Go to the www.irs.gov website and *Publication 17.* From *Publication 17*'s Table of Contents, select MACRS under GDS (General Depreciation System). Find the MACRS Table of Percentages. How does it compare to the table listed in the textbook? Go back to search and enter Topic 704. What are the five tests that must be met for an asset to be depreciable?

Answers to **Self Reviews**

Answers to Section 1 Self Review

1. Sum-of-the-years'-digits and double-declining methods.
2. Debit *Depreciation Expense,* credit *Accumulated Depreciation.*
3. Depreciation is the allocation of the cost of a long-term asset to expense during its useful life.
4. $4,800.
5. $2,333.33.
6. Numerator = 5; denominator = 28.
7. Under double-declining-balance depreciation, salvage is initially ignored and the rate is twice the straight-line rate. Straight-line depreciation yields higher income in early years and lower income in later years.

Answers to Section 2 Self Review

1. When the net book value exceeds the sales price.

2. The asset account and accumulated depreciation account are removed, and the sales proceeds are recorded. The difference between the proceeds and net book value (cost minus accumulated depreciation) is recorded as gain or loss.

3. Under tax rules, neither gain nor loss is recorded on the trade-in of an asset on a like-kind asset. Under financial accounting rules, both gains and losses are recognized.

4. **b.** a gain of $4,000.

5. **d.** a gain of $10,000.

6. The asset account and the accumulated depreciation would be overstated by the same amount. There would be no effect on net asset book value.

Answers to Section 3 Self Review

1. If the expected future cash flows from the asset are less than its book value, the asset is impaired.

2. By comparing its fair value to its book value. There may be no ready indication, such as a ready market price, of an asset's fair value. A common approach is to estimate the future cash flows from the asset's use on a year-by-year basis and to discount these future cash flows to their current value.

3. GAAP requires that "research and development costs" must be charged to expense when incurred. There are a few specified exceptions to this rule, but the costs incurred by Strategic Innovations do not fall within these exceptions.

4. The trade name is an intangible asset that does not have a legal or other definable life, so its cost is not amortized. Therefore, its cost would be subject to the impairment rules in the same way as the cost of goodwill.

5. The company should assess operations to determine that profits are adequately above what they would be without the trade name in order to assure that its carrying value is not impaired.

6. All of these costs should be transferred to expense (depletion for the mineral rights and depreciation for drilling equipment) on the unit-of-production basis as the oil is produced.

7. Depreciation is the allocation of cost of personal and real tangible property to expense over the property's useful life. Depletion is the allocation of cost of mineral rights. Amortization is the allocation costs of intangibles with estimated useful lives. All refer to the charging of the costs of assets to expense over their useful lives, but apply to different types of long-term assets.

Answers to Comprehensive Self Review

1. $1,900 loss ($2,700 book value − $800 sales price)

2. Legal life is the time period that the business or individual has legal rights to utilize whatever rights can be derived from the intangible asset. Intangibles such as copyrights, patents, and most franchises may be used exclusively only for a limited period. The economic life is the period that the intangible will provide economic benefits to the holder of the right. For example, a patent owned by a business may provide exclusive right to produce a product for another 15 years. This is the legal life. However, new processes being developed may make the existing patent obsolete within three years. Three years is the economic life. Economic life is used in computing amortization.

3. Real property comprises land and other assets that are affixed permanently to the land. It includes land, land improvements, buildings, and other structures attached to the land. Personal property comprises those assets that are not affixed to the land and are relatively moveable—such as furniture, equipment, and vehicles.

4. 55 $(10 + 9 + 8 + 7 + 6 + 5 + 4 + 3 + 2 + 1)$.

5. The matching principle of matching costs with revenues. The constraint of conservatism plays an important role in applying the matching principle.

6. When the life of the asset is limited to an estimable number of units of production.

Accounting for Partnerships

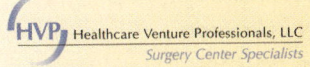

www.hvpros.com

Healthcare Venture Professionals, LLC (HVP), is a full-service management company that provides professional leadership and consultative resources to hospitals and physicians. The company is designated as an LLC, or limited liability company. It functions very similarly to a partnership where the partner-owners divide the profits of the business based on their LLC agreement. HVP's agreement, created by its members, is similar to the agreements of other LLCs. It governs the affairs of HVP and provides the procedures for admitting new members, outlines the status of the company upon a member's withdrawal, and outlines the procedures for dissolution of the business.

The founders of HVP, John Smalley and Chuck Owen, seasoned healthcare executives with 60+ years of combined healthcare leadership experience, chose to personally fund the company to eliminate undue influences from outside investors. In this way, the company is free to act in the best interest of its clients. All senior-level employees enjoy a degree of ownership and share in the success of HVP not only through higher salaries but also through profit sharing.

The company has been successful working with their clients to develop joint-ventured outpatient centers. More than 200 hospitals or healthcare systems and thousands of physicians have used their expertise.

thinking critically

Before a partnership agreement is signed by its partners, what are some possible questions that should be answered in the agreement?

LEARNING OBJECTIVES	NEW TERMS	
19-1. Explain the major advantages and disadvantages of a partnership.	articles of partnership	memorandum entry
19-2. State the important provisions that should be included in every partnership agreement.	dissolution	mutual agency
	distributive share	partnership
19-3. Account for the formation of a partnership.	general partner	partnership agreement
19-4. Compute and record the division of net income or net loss between partners in accordance with the partnership agreement.	limited partner	statement of partners' equities
	limited partnership	
	liquidation	unlimited liability
19-5. Prepare a statement of partners' equities.		
19-6. Account for the revaluation of assets and liabilities prior to the dissolution of a partnership.		
19-7. Account for the sale of a partnership interest.		
19-8. Account for the investment of a new partner in an existing partnership.		
19-9. Account for the withdrawal of a partner from a partnership.		
19-10. Define the accounting terms new to this chapter.		

SECTION OBJECTIVES

>> **19-1.** Explain the major advantages and disadvantages of a partnership.

WHY IT'S IMPORTANT

Selecting the most advantageous form of business organization contributes to the overall success of a company.

>> **19-2.** State the important provisions that should be included in every partnership agreement.

WHY IT'S IMPORTANT

A partnership agreement is a legal document that dictates the operating structure and terms of the business entity.

>> **19-3.** Account for the formation of a partnership.

WHY IT'S IMPORTANT

Assets, liabilities, and owners' capital must all be correctly stated from the partnership's start.

TERMS TO LEARN

articles of partnership
general partner
limited partner
limited partnership
memorandum entry
mutual agency
partnership
partnership agreement
unlimited liability

Forming a Partnership

Accounting procedures for a sole proprietorship have been covered in previous chapters. This chapter discusses accounting for partnerships.

The Characteristics of a Partnership

The *Uniform Partnership Act,* adopted by all 50 states, defines a **partnership** as "an association of two or more persons who carry on, as co-owners, a business for profit." The partnership form of organization is widely used in small service, merchandising, and manufacturing businesses. Historically, professionals such as accountants, lawyers, and physicians have formed partnerships to pool their talents and abilities.

> Woolpert LLP began operations in 1911. Charlton Putnam, a surveyor and landscape engineer, joined forces with Edward Deeds and Charles Kettering, inventors of the self-starting automobile ignition system. In 1916, Ralph L. Woolpert, a civil engineer, joined the company as a partner. Throughout the years, the company extended partner status to others who contributed their expertise.

>> **19-1. OBJECTIVE**

Explain the major advantages and disadvantages of a partnership.

ADVANTAGES OF THE PARTNERSHIP

A partnership has three important advantages. It pools the skills, abilities, and financial resources of two or more individuals. It is easy and inexpensive to form, especially when compared with a corporation. A partnership does not pay income tax. The partners report their shares of the partnership's income or loss on their individual income tax returns.

DISADVANTAGES OF THE PARTNERSHIP

Certain characteristics of partnerships are clearly disadvantages. Each partner has **unlimited liability** for the partnership's debts. Thus, a partner's personal assets as well as the partnership's assets can be required in payment of the firm's debts. This characteristic enhances the credit standing of the business, but it can be a danger to the individual partners.

In most states, it is possible for some partners to have limited liability. A **limited partnership** is a partnership with one or more limited partners. **Limited partners** are liable only for their investment in the partnership. State laws generally require that limited partnerships have at least one **general partner,** a partner who has unlimited liability. Limited partners are prohibited from taking an active management role and from having their names in the partnership's name.

The partnership is a **mutual agency;** each partner is empowered to act as an agent for the partnership, binding the firm by those acts so long as they are within the normal scope of the partnership's activities.

A partnership lacks continuity; it has a limited life. When a partner dies or is incapacitated, the partnership is dissolved.

Partnership interest is not freely transferable; other partners must approve the sale of a partner's interest to a new partner. Upon a transfer of interest, the existing partnership is dissolved and a new partnership must be formed.

PARTNERSHIP AGREEMENTS

>> **19-2. OBJECTIVE**
State the important provisions that should be included in every partnership agreement.

It is easy to form a partnership. Two or more partners agree to form the business entity by entering into an oral or written contract. A partnership may be deemed to have been formed without an explicit agreement if the behavior of the parties implies that a partnership exists. An oral agreement is binding on the partners, but a written contract is preferred. To avoid any future misunderstandings, an attorney prepares a legal contract forming a partnership and specifying certain details of the operation, called a **partnership agreement.** This is legally known as the **articles of partnership.** The partnership agreement can be simple, or complex and detailed. Every partnership agreement should contain the:

- names of the partners;
- name, location, and nature of the business;
- starting date of the agreement;
- life of the partnership;
- rights and duties of each partner;
- amount of capital to be contributed by each partner;
- drawings by the partners;
- fiscal year and accounting method;
- method of allocating income or loss to the partners;
- procedures to be followed if the partnership is dissolved or the business is liquidated.

Partnerships dissolve upon a partner's death, incapacity, or withdrawal.

Accounting for the Formation of a Partnership

>> **19-3. OBJECTIVE**
Account for the formation of a partnership.

Partnerships and sole proprietorships use the same types of journals and ledgers as well as asset, liability, revenue, and expense accounts. The only difference is that in a partnership, each partner has a capital account and a drawing account.

There are many ways to form a partnership. Partnerships are often formed when a sole proprietorship "takes in" a partner or partners to continue an existing business. Usually the new partners invest cash, and the sole proprietor contributes noncash assets and liabilities of the existing business. Sometimes two sole proprietors combine their operations into a partnership. Often partners start a completely new business with initial investments of cash.

When noncash assets are transferred to a partnership, they are recorded at their fair market value, as agreed to by the partners, on the transfer date. Liabilities are stated at their correct balances on the transfer date.

> Sometimes two existing companies form a partnership with a new objective or mission in mind. In February 2005, America Online, Inc., and Time Warner Cable established a partnership designed to connect computer users to the Internet. The two companies joined together to provide high-speed Internet service in New York and other areas. The cable company furnishes physical connections to the Internet, while AOL provides e-mail services and other online content.

Let's look at a partnership formed by Ellen Barret and Jerry Reed. Barret operates Old Army, a small clothing store that sells T-shirts, jeans, and other casual clothing. Reed works in another store selling athletic shoes. To get additional capital and to obtain Reed's talents, Barret offered to make Reed a partner in the business. Barret agreed to transfer the assets (except cash) and the liabilities of Old Army to the new partnership. Reed agreed to invest cash of $28,000 in the business. Figure 19.1, below, shows the balance sheet of Old Army on December 31, 2015.

After examining Old Army's assets, Barret and Reed agreed that:

■ Net accounts receivable is $19,300.

recall

Allowance Method
Under the allowance method for uncollectible accounts, an estimate is made before actual losses occur.

Accounts receivable on balance sheet	$22,300
Definitely uncollectible	(1,800)
Accounts receivable, adjusted	$20,500
Likely to be uncollectible	(1,200)
Net accounts receivable	$19,300

■ The value of merchandise inventory is $105,200.
■ The store equipment's value is $3,000 based on an appraisal.

FIGURE 19.1

Balance Sheet for a Sole Proprietor

Old Army				
Balance Sheet				
December 31, 2015				
Assets				
Cash			2 6 0 0 00	
Accounts Receivable	22 3 0 0 00			
Less Allowance for Doubtful Accounts	7 5 0 00		21 5 5 0 00	
Merchandise Inventory			115 0 0 0 00	
Store Equipment	10 4 5 0 00			
Less Accumulated Depreciation	8 0 0 0 00		2 4 5 0 00	
Total Assets			141 6 0 0 00	
Liabilities and Owner's Equity				
Liabilities				
Notes Payable—Bank	39 1 0 0 00			
Accounts Payable	36 0 0 0 00			
Total Liabilities			75 1 0 0 00	
Owner's Equity				
Ellen Barret			66 5 0 0 00	
Total Liabilities and Owner's Equity			141 6 0 0 00	

- Accrued interest payable on the note payable is $500. This liability was not recorded as of December 31.
- Accounts payable total is $34,700 as the result of settling a dispute with a creditor after the balance sheet was prepared.

Thus, Barret and Reed have agreed that the net assets Barret transferred are $53,200:

Accounts receivable	$ 19,300
Merchandise inventory	105,200
Store equipment	3,000
Notes payable	(39,100)
Interest payable	(500)
Accounts payable	(34,700)
Total	$ 53,200

MEMORANDUM ENTRY TO RECORD FORMATION OF PARTNERSHIP

The first entry in the general journal of the new partnership is a **memorandum entry,** which is an informational entry. It indicates the name of the business, the partners' names, and other pertinent information. Note that the memorandum entry references the partnership agreement, which provides information about the capital contributed by each partner and the division of income:

1	2016				
2	Jan.	1	On this date, a partnership was formed		
3			between Ellen Barret and Jerry Reed to		
4			carry on a retail clothing business under		
5			the name of Old Army, according to the		
6			terms of the partnership agreement effective		
7			this date.		
8					

INVESTMENT OF ASSETS AND LIABILITIES BY SOLE PROPRIETOR

The first journal entry records the transfer of Barret's assets and liabilities to the partnership:

9	Jan.	1	Accounts Receivable	111	20 500 00	
10			Merchandise Inventory	121	105 200 00	
11			Store Equipment	131	3 000 00	
12			Allowance for Doubtful Accounts	112		1 200 00
13			Notes Payable—Bank	201		39 100 00
14			Accounts Payable	205		34 700 00
15			Interest Payable	215		500 00
16			Ellen Barret, Capital	301		53 200 00
17			Investment of Barret			
18						

Note that the entry includes *Accounts Receivable* of $20,500 and *Allowance for Doubtful Accounts* of $1,200. All individual customers' balances, except for those that were definitely uncollectible, were transferred to the partnership. Consequently, the *Accounts Receivable* control account agrees with the total of the accounts receivable subsidiary ledger. Note that *Store Equipment* is transferred at fair market value. No accumulated depreciation is transferred. Depreciation on plant and equipment that was recorded by the

ABOUT ACCOUNTING

Family Partnerships
Family partnerships are frequently designed to facilitate transfers of property, business interests, and investments between family members in a tax-efficient manner. These partnerships permit family members to pool funds for investment purposes.

previous owner is irrelevant. Depreciation will be recorded by the partnership based on the asset's value at the date of transfer.

INVESTMENT OF CASH BY PARTNER

The next journal entry records the investment of cash by Reed:

19	Jan.	1	Cash	101	28 00 0 00		19
20			Jerry Reed, Capital	311		28 00 0 00	20
21			Investment of cash by Reed				21
22							22

SUBSEQUENT INVESTMENTS AND PERMANENT WITHDRAWALS

During the life of the partnership, additional investments are recorded in the same manner as the initial investments. When partners make cash withdrawals that are intended to be permanent reductions of capital, the withdrawals are recorded as debits to the partners' capital accounts.

DRAWING ACCOUNTS

Separate Entity

The separate entity assumption states that the business is separate from its owners. This explains why personal expenses paid by the business are charged to the partner's drawing account rather than to a business expense account.

Partners need funds with which to pay their living expenses. Partners can obtain funds by making withdrawals against anticipated income. Each partner has a drawing account to record withdrawals.

The partnership agreement of Old Army specifies that Barret can withdraw up to $2,500 each month and that Reed can withdraw up to $1,900 each month. The withdrawals are recorded in the cash payments journal. The entry is a debit to the partners' drawing accounts and a credit to cash. At the end of 12 months, on December 31, Barret's drawing account has a debit balance of $30,000 ($2,500 × 12), and Reed's drawing account has a debit balance of $22,800 ($1,900 × 12).

Partners sometimes pay their personal bills with partnership funds. This practice is not sound because it leads to confusion between business and personal transactions. If the business pays a partner's personal expense, however, the debit in the cash payments journal is to the partner's drawing account, not an expense account.

It is common for partners to take merchandise from the business for their personal use. The cost of merchandise is debited to the partner's drawing account. The credit is to the *Purchases* account if the periodic inventory method is used and to the *Merchandise Inventory* account if the perpetual inventory method is used. Note that the inventory account is not involved—if the periodic inventory method is used as illustrated in the journal entry below. The beginning inventory in the current period's cost of goods sold should agree with ending inventory of the prior period. Barret withdrew merchandise that cost $180 and had a retail sales price of $230. The transaction is recorded as follows:

1	2016						1
2	June	14	Ellen Barret, Drawing	302	1 80 00		2
3			Purchases	501		1 80 00	3
4			Cost of merchandise withdrawn				4
5			by Barret				5
6							6
7							7
8							8

Section 1   Self Review

QUESTIONS

1. What are the major disadvantages of the partnership form of business?

2. A business owner has agreed to transfer the assets and liabilities of her business to a new partnership. The new partner will invest cash in the new business in return for one-half interest. At what values should assets and liabilities of the old business be recorded in the accounts of the partnership?

3. Jackson and Jones, partners in the JJ Grocery Group, frequently withdraw cash for personal living expenses. How should these cash withdrawals be recorded in the records of the partnership?

EXERCISES

4. If the periodic inventory method is used, a withdrawal of merchandise from the business by one of the partners should be recorded as:

a. a debit to the partner's drawing account and a credit to **Merchandise Inventory** for the sales price of the merchandise.

b. a debit to the partner's drawing account and a credit to **Merchandise Inventory** for the cost of the merchandise.

c. a debit to the partner's drawing account and a credit to **Purchases** for the cost of the merchandise.

d. Some other entry.

5. An investment of cash in the partnership by Carl Smith, a partner in Smith-Kelly Web Services, should be recorded by:

a. a debit to **Cash** and a credit to **Smith-Kelly, Capital.**

b. a debit to **Smith-Kelly, Capital** and a credit to **Cash.**

c. a debit to **Cash** and a credit to **Carl Smith, Capital.**

d. a debit to **Carl Smith, Capital** and a credit to **Cash.**

ANALYSIS

6. John Monroe and Sam Hill are combining their businesses to form a new partnership. Monroe invests merchandise inventory valued at $55,500, store equipment with a book value of $600 but appraised at $4,100, and accounts receivable of $12,000, of which $800 is assumed to be uncollectible. In addition, he is transferring liabilities of $6,000 owed to creditors. After the entry to record his investment is posted, what is the balance in Monroe's partnership capital account?

(Answers to Section 1 Self Review are on page 684.)

SECTION OBJECTIVES	TERMS TO LEARN
>> **19-4.** Compute and record the division of net income or net loss between partners in accordance with the partnership agreement. **WHY IT'S IMPORTANT** The records must reflect the partnership agreement's allocation of profit and loss. >> **19-5.** Prepare a statement of partners' equities. **WHY IT'S IMPORTANT** The statement of partners' equities summarizes the changes that have occurred in each partner's equity account. The ending balance appears on the balance sheet.	distributive share statement of partners' equities

Allocating Income or Loss

Recall that a partnership does not pay income tax. The net income or net loss "flows through" to the partners, who report their share of the partnership income on their individual tax returns.

Allocating Partnership Income or Loss

At the end of a period, the closing procedures for a partnership are similar to those used for a sole proprietorship:

Step 1: *Close revenue to **Income Summary**.*

Step 2: *Close expenses to **Income Summary**.*

Step 3: *Close **Income Summary** to the partners' capital accounts.*

Step 4: *Close each partner's drawing account to the partner's capital account.*

In step 3, the business needs to determine the **distributive share,** which is the amount of net income or net loss allocated to each partner. Distributive share refers solely to the division of net income or net loss among partners, not to cash distributions.

Partners may agree to divide or allocate the income in any manner they desire. Typical considerations for each partner include the:

- amount of time spent in the business,
- skills, expertise, and experience,
- amount of capital invested.

The partnership agreement should clearly and carefully spell out the basis for allocation so that there will be no misunderstanding among the partners. *In the absence of an agreement to the contrary, partners share income and losses equally.* Typical allocations are based on a fixed ratio or on capital account balances. Some agreements call for salary allowances and interest allowances.

Let's examine the end-of-year procedures for the partnership of Barret and Reed. The following T accounts show the capital and drawing accounts for Barret and Reed at the end of the first year of business before the accounts have been closed for the year. Note that the capital accounts reflect the amounts of original investment at this point.

important!

Distribution of Income

Income allocation or division is frequently referred to as the distribution of income. This does not mean that cash is distributed to the partners.

important!

Income Allocation

Unless the partnership agreement provides otherwise, net income or net loss is allocated equally to the partners.

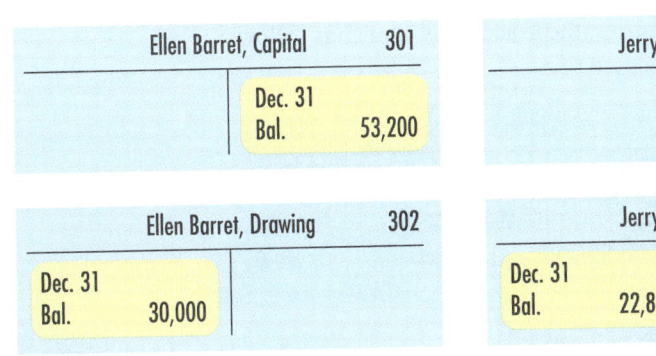

To illustrate the most common allocation methods, the allocation of income or loss is shown under four different arrangements.

AGREED UPON RATIO

Assume that Barret and Reed agreed that net income will be split in the ratio of 3:2 (3 to 2) to Barret and Reed, respectively. Follow these steps to convert the ratios to decimals:

Step 1: *Add the figures given in the ratio.*

Barret	3
Reed	2
Total	5

Step 2: *Express each figure as a fraction of the total.*

Barret's share	3/5
Reed's share	2/5

Step 3: *Convert each fraction into a percentage by dividing the numerator by the denominator.*

Barret's share	3/5 = 0.60 or 60 percent
Reed's share	2/5 = 0.40 or 40 percent

Allocating Net Income Assume that *Income Summary* has a credit balance of $100,000 (net income) after closing the revenue and expense accounts. Net income is allocated as follows:

Barret	$100,000 × 0.60 = $60,000
Reed	$100,000 × 0.40 = $40,000

Step 3 of the closing process is to close *Income Summary* to the partners' capital accounts as follows:

1	2016					1
2	Dec.	31	Income Summary	399	100 000 00	2
3			Ellen Barret, Capital	301	60 000 00	3
4			Jerry Reed, Capital	311	40 000 00	4
5			To record allocation of net income in			5
6			ratio of 3:2			6

The partners' drawing accounts are then closed to their capital accounts:

1	2016					1
8	Dec.	31	Ellen Barret, Capital	301	30 000 00	8
9			Ellen Barret, Drawing	302	30 000 00	9
10						10
11		31	Jerry Reed, Capital	311	22 800 00	11
12			Jerry Reed, Drawing	312	22 800 00	12

>> 19-4. OBJECTIVE

Compute and record the division of net income or net loss between partners in accordance with the partnership agreement.

After posting the closing entries, the T accounts appear as follows:

Income Summary			399
Dec. 31		Dec. 31	
Clos.	100,000	Net Inc.	100,000
		Bal.	0

Ellen Barret, Capital			301
Dec. 31		Dec. 31	
Draw.	30,000	Bal.	53,200
		Dec. 31	
		Net Inc.	60,000
		Bal.	83,200

Jerry Reed, Capital			311
Dec. 31		Dec. 31	
Draw.	22,800	Bal.	28,000
		Dec. 31	
		Net Inc.	40,000
		Bal.	45,200

Ellen Barret, Drawing			302
Dec. 31		Dec. 31	
Bal.	30,000	Clos.	30,000
Bal.	0		

Jerry Reed, Drawing			312
Dec. 31		Dec. 31	
Bal.	22,800	Clos.	22,800
Bal.	0		

Allocating Net Loss Assume that *Income Summary* has a debit balance of $30,000 (net loss) after closing revenue and expense accounts. This represents a net loss for the year. The loss is allocated as follows, using their allocation ratio of 3:2:

Barret	$30,000 × 0.60 = $18,000
Reed	$30,000 × 0.40 = $12,000

Steps 3 and 4 of the closing process are recorded as follows:

1	2016						1
14	Dec.	31	Ellen Barret, Capital	301	18 000 00		14
15			Jerry Reed, Capital	311	12 000 00		15
16			Income Summary	399		30 000 00	16
17							17
18		31	Ellen Barret, Capital	301	30 000 00		18
19			Ellen Barret, Drawing	302		30 000 00	19
20							20
21		31	Jerry Reed, Capital	311	22 800 00		21
22			Jerry Reed, Drawing	312		22 800 00	22

CAPITAL ACCOUNT BALANCES

Allocating net income or net loss on the basis of capital account balances is quite logical when capital is extremely important in the income-earning process. For example, partnerships that own and rent real estate often allocate income or loss based on capital account balances.

Barret and Reed agreed that net income or net loss will be allocated based on the ratio of capital account balances at the beginning of the year. The beginning balances for Barret and

Reed were $53,200 and $28,000, respectively. Follow the steps below to convert the capital account ratio to decimals:

Step 1: *Add the capital account balances.*

Barret	$53,200
Reed	28,000
Total	$81,200

Step 2: *Express each balance as a fraction and convert it to a decimal.*

Barret	$53,200/$81,200 = 0.65517 or 65.517 percent
Reed	$28,000/$81,200 = 0.34483 or 34.483 percent

Using these percentages, net income of $100,000 would be allocated as follows:

Barret	$100,000 × 0.65517 = $65,517
Reed	$100,000 × 0.34483 = $34,483

Assuming a profit of $100,000 and withdrawals of $30,000 for Barret and $22,800 for Reed, the steps 3 and 4 closing entries are as follows:

1	2016					1
2	Dec.	31	Income Summary	399	100 000 00		2
3			Ellen Barret, Capital	301		65 517 00	3
4			Jerry Reed, Capital	311		34 483 00	4
5							5
6		31	Ellen Barret, Capital	301	30 000 00		6
7			Ellen Barret, Drawing	302		30 000 00	7
8							8
9		31	Jerry Reed, Capital	311	22 800 00		9
10			Jerry Reed, Drawing	312		22 800 00	10

A net loss would be allocated in the same ratio as net income. ***Income Summary*** would be credited to close the debit balance to the capital accounts.

SALARY ALLOWANCES

Salary allowances are intended to reward the partners for the time they spend in the business and for the expertise and talents they bring to it. Barret and Reed agreed that each would work full-time in the business. Both partners recognize Barret's long experience in retail trade, her superior skill and ability, and her good reputation and established clientele.

Barret and Reed agreed that each will receive a salary allowance equal to the monthly withdrawals permitted in the partnership agreement. After considering the salary allowance, the balance of net income or net loss will be divided between Barret and Reed in the ratio of 3:2.

Salary allowances are allocations of income. Salary allowances paid in cash to partners are withdrawals. They do not represent salary expense. They do not appear in the expense section of the income statement. Salary allowances are not subject to payroll taxes or withholdings.

When salary allowances are included in the income or loss distribution formula, step 3 of the closing process has two parts:

a. *Record the salary allowances; debit **Income Summary** and credit the partners' capital accounts.*

b. *Close **Income Summary** to the partners' capital accounts based on the partnership agreement.*

important!

Salary Withdrawals
A salary withdrawal is a cash payment to a partner and is debited to the partner's drawing account. It does not represent an expense of the partnership.

important!

important!

Partnership Income

Partnership income is not taxed. Instead, partners include their share of the net income or net loss on their individual income tax returns.

Allocating Net Income Assume that the net income of Old Army was $112,800.

Step 3a: Record the salary allowances of $30,000 to Barret and $22,800 to Reed as follows:

1	2016					1
2	Dec.	31 Income Summary	399	52 800 00		2
3		Ellen Barret, Capital	301		30 000 00	3
4		Jerry Reed, Capital	311		22 800 00	4

After recording the salary allowances, **Income Summary** has a credit balance of $60,000:

	Income Summary		399
Dec. 31		Dec. 31	
Sal. All.	52,800	Net Inc.	112,800
		Bal.	60,000

The balance of **Income Summary** is allocated as follows:

Barret $60,000 × 0.60 = $36,000

Reed $60,000 × 0.40 = $24,000

Step 3b: Record the entry to close the credit balance of **Income Summary** as follows:

1	2016					1
6	Dec.	31 Income Summary	399	60 000 00		6
7		Ellen Barret, Capital	301		36 000 00	7
8		Jerry Reed, Capital	311		24 000 00	8

The partners' drawing accounts are closed to the capital accounts in the usual manner. Remember that the fact that a partner has or has not withdrawn cash as a salary allowance does not affect the profit or loss allocation.

Allocating Net Loss Assume net loss for Old Army is $30,000. Entries to record the loss distribution follow.

Step 3a: Record the salary allowances of $30,000 to Barret and $22,800 to Reed:

1	2016					1
2	Dec.	31 Income Summary	399	52 800 00		2
3		Ellen Barret, Capital	301		30 000 00	3
4		Jerry Reed, Capital	311		22 800 00	4

important!

Withdrawals Do Not Affect Profit Allocation

Even though cash withdrawn from the business by a partner may be called "salary allowance," it is debited to the partner's drawing account. The fact that the salary allowance has, or has not, been withdrawn is irrelevant in allocating net income for the period.

After this entry is posted, **Income Summary** has a debit balance of $82,800:

	Income Summary		399
Dec. 31			
Net Loss	30,000		
Dec. 31			
Sal. All.	52,800		
Bal.	82,800		

The balance of **Income Summary** is allocated as follows:

Barret $82,800 × 0.60 = $49,680
Reed $82,800 × 0.40 = $33,120

Step 3b: Record the entry to close **Income Summary** as follows:

1	2016						1
6	Dec.	31	Ellen Barret, Capital	301	49 680 00		6
7			Jerry Reed, Capital	311	33 120 00		7
8			Income Summary	399		82 800 00	8

The partners' drawing accounts are closed to the capital accounts in the usual way:

1	2016						1
10	Dec.	31	Ellen Barret, Capital	301	30 000 00		10
11			Ellen Barret, Drawing	302		30 000 00	11
12							12
13		31	Jerry Reed, Capital	311	22 800 00		13
14			Jerry Reed, Drawing	312		22 800 00	14

After the closing entries are posted, the T accounts appear as follows:

```
              Income Summary            399
  Dec. 31                    Dec. 31
  Net Loss      30,000       Clos.        82,800
  Dec. 31
  Sal. All.     52,800
                82,800
                              Bal.             0
```

```
      Ellen Barret, Capital      301              Jerry Reed, Capital       311
Dec. 31                 Dec. 31              Dec. 31                 Dec. 31
Net Loss    49,680      Bal.       53,200    Net Loss    33,120      Bal.       28,000
Dec. 31                 Dec. 31              Dec. 31                 Dec. 31
Draw.       30,000      Sal. All.  30,000    Draw.       22,800      Sal. All.  22,800
            79,680                 83,200                55,920                 50,800
                        Bal.        3,520    Bal.         5,120
```

```
      Ellen Barret, Drawing      302              Jerry Reed, Drawing       312
Dec. 31                 Dec. 31              Dec. 31                 Dec. 31
Bal.        30,000      Clos.      30,000    Bal.        22,800      Clos.      22,800
Bal.             0                           Bal.             0
```

SALARY AND INTEREST ALLOWANCES

Assume that Barret and Reed want to reward themselves for their time and skills through salary allowances of $30,000 to Barret and $22,800 to Reed. They also wish to recognize their capital investments by allowing each partner 8 percent interest on his or her capital balance at the start of the period.

The partnership agreement does not specify how the remaining income or loss is to be allocated. Remember that if the partnership agreement is silent on this matter, the remaining net income or net loss is divided equally.

Step 3 of the closing process has three parts:

a. Record the salary allowances.

b. Record the interest allowances. Credit each partner's capital account for the interest allowed, and debit *Income Summary* for the total interest.

c. Close *Income Summary* to the partners' capital accounts. Again, remember that the fact that cash has or has not been paid to the partner for this allowance does not affect these entries.

Allocation When Net Income Is Adequate to Cover Allowances Assume net income of $100,000.

Step 3a: Record the salary allowances of $30,000 to Barret and $22,800 to Reed as follows:

1	2016				1
2	Dec.	31 Income Summary	399	52 800 00	2
3		Ellen Barret, Capital	301	30 000 00	3
4		Jerry Reed, Capital	311	22 800 00	4

Step 3b: Record the interest allowances. The interest allowed is 8 percent of the beginning capital balance.

Barret	$53,200 × 0.08 × 1 year = $4,256
Reed	$28,000 × 0.08 × 1 year = $2,240

The journal entry to record the interest allowances is as follows:

1	2016				1
6	Dec.	31 Income Summary	399	6 496 00	6
7		Ellen Barret, Capital	301	4 256 00	7
8		Jerry Reed, Capital	311	2 240 00	8
9		To record 8% interest allowance on			9
10		beginning investments			10

After recording the salary and interest allowances, *Income Summary* has a credit balance of $40,704:

Income Summary		399	
Dec. 31		Dec. 31	
Sal. All.	52,800	Net Inc.	100,000
Dec. 31			
Int. All.	6,496		
	59,296		
		Bal.	40,704

Step 3c: Close *Income Summary* to the partners' capital accounts. The balance is divided equally between Barret and Reed. The entry to close the credit balance of *Income Summary* is as follows:

	2016						
11	Dec.	31	Income Summary	399	40 70 4 00		11
12			Ellen Barret, Capital	301		20 35 2 00	12
13			Jerry Reed, Capital	311		20 35 2 00	13

Allocation of Net Loss Assume that Old Army had a $40,000 net loss for the year.

Step 3a: Record the salary allowances of $30,000 to Barret and $22,800 to Reed.

Step 3b: Record the interest allowances of $4,256 to Barret and $2,240 to Reed.

After these steps, *Income Summary* has a debit balance of $99,296:

```
          Income Summary        399
Net Loss        40,000 |
Dec. 31                |
Sal. All.       52,800 |
Dec. 31                |
Int. All.        6,496 |
Bal.            99,296 |
```

The debit balance of $99,296 is divided equally between Barret and Reed.

Step 3c: Record the entry to close *Income Summary.* Debit each partner's capital account $49,648; credit *Income Summary;* $99,296.

After the closing entries are posted, the T accounts appear as follows:

```
          Income Summary              399
Net Loss      40,000 | Dec. 31
                     | Closing     99,296
Dec. 31              |
Sal. All.     52,800 |
Dec. 31              |
Int. All.      6,496 |
              99,296 |
                     | Bal.             0
```

```
     Ellen Barret, Capital    301          Jerry Reed, Capital    311
                   | Bal.        53,200               | Bal.        28,000
Dec. 31            | Dec. 31             Dec. 31       | Dec. 31
Net Loss   49,648  | Sal. All.   30,000  Net Loss 49,648| Sal. All.   22,800
                   | Dec. 31                           | Dec. 31
                   | Int. All.    4,256               | Int. All.    2,240
                   |             87,456               |             53,040
                   | Bal.        37,808               | Bal.         3,392
```

The partners' drawing accounts are closed to the capital accounts in the usual manner.

Income Less Than Difference between Partners' Allocations
Assume that Old Army had net income of $3,400.

Step 3a: Record the salary allowances of $30,000 to Barret and $22,800 to Reed.

Step 3b: Record the interest allowances of $4,256 to Barret and $2,240 to Reed.

After recording the salary and interest allowances, ***Income Summary*** has a debit balance of $55,896. The balance of ***Income Summary*** is divided equally between Barret and Reed.

Step 3c: Record the entry to close ***Income Summary.***

After the closing entries are posted, the T accounts appear as follows:

		Income Summary		399
Dec. 31 Sal. All.	52,800	Dec. 31 Net Inc.	3,400	
Dec. 31 Int. All.	6,496	Dec. 31 Closing	55,896	
	59,296		59,296	
		Bal.	0	

		Ellen Barret, Capital		301
Dec. 31 Loss	27,948	Dec. 31 Bal.	53,200	
		Dec. 31 Sal. All.	30,000	
		Dec. 31 Int. All.	4,256	
			87,456	
		Bal.	59,508	

		Jerry Reed, Capital		311
Dec. 31 Loss	27,948	Dec. 31 Bal.	28,000	
		Dec. 31 Sal. All.	22,800	
		Dec. 31 Int. All.	2,240	
			53,040	
		Bal.	25,092	

Notice that at this point, prior to closing the drawing accounts, the capital account balance for Barret increased by $6,308 and for Reed decreased by $2,908. This is due to the relationships between the income-sharing agreements and the amount of net income reported.

	Barret	Reed
Beginning capital balance	$53,200	$28,000
Ending capital balance	59,508	25,092
Difference	$ 6,308	($2,908)

Partnership Financial Statements

Once the net income or net loss distribution is complete, the financial statements are prepared.

INCOME STATEMENT PRESENTATION

With one exception, the income statements for a partnership and a sole proprietorship are identical. On a partnership's income statement, it is customary to show on the bottom of the statement the division of net income or net loss among partners. The salary allowances, interest allowances, and other allocation factors are shown.

Old Army's income statement for the most recent example follows. Revenue and expense details are omitted.

Net Income for Year			$ 3,400
Allocation of Net Income	Barret	Reed	Total
Salary Allowance	$30,000	$22,800	$52,800
Interest Allowance	4,256	2,240	6,496
Balance Equally	(27,948)	(27,948)	(55,896)
Totals	$ 6,308	($ 2,908)	$ 3,400

BALANCE SHEET PRESENTATION

The balance sheet of a partnership is identical to that of a sole proprietorship, except that the partnership's balance sheet shows the balance of each partner's capital account. The capital account partnership balance sheet appears in the Partners' Equity section.

The **statement of partners' equities** summarizes the changes in the partners' capital accounts during an accounting period. It includes the following:

- beginning capital,
- additional investments,
- share of net income or net loss,
- withdrawals,
- ending capital.

Figure 19.2 shows the statement of partners' equities for Old Army.

>> 19-5. OBJECTIVE
Prepare a statement of partners' equities.

FIGURE 19.2
Statement of Partners' Equities

Old Army
Statement of Partners' Equities
Year Ended December 31, 2016

	Barret Capital	Reed Capital	Total Capital
Capital Balances, Jan. 1, 2016	0 00	0 00	0 00
Investment During Year	53 2 0 0 00	28 0 0 0 00	81 2 0 0 00
Net Income (Loss) for Year	6 3 0 8 00	(2 9 0 8 00)	3 4 0 0 00
Totals	59 5 0 8 00	25 0 9 2 00	84 6 0 0 00
Less Withdrawals During Year	30 0 0 0 00	22 8 0 0 00	52 8 0 0 00
Capital Balances, Dec. 31, 2016	29 5 0 8 00	2 2 9 2 00	31 8 0 0 00

Section 2 Self Review

QUESTIONS

1. In the absence of an agreement to the contrary, how are partnership income and losses allocated among the partners?

2. What two allowances are commonly used in allocating net income or net loss to partners?

3. If both salary and interest allowances are made to the partners, what are the three steps in closing the *Income Summary* account to the partners' capital accounts?

EXERCISES

4. The entry to record the equal distribution of net income between two partners consists of a:

   a. debit to *Income Summary* and a credit to each partner's capital account.

   b. debit to each partner's capital account and a credit to *Cash.*

   c. debit to *Income Summary* and a credit to each partner's drawing account.

   d. debit to *Income Summary* and a credit to *Cash.*

5. The amount that each partner withdraws from a partnership:

   a. should be specified in the partnership agreement.

   b. is the base on which federal income taxes are levied on the partnership income.

   c. cannot exceed the net income reported by the partnership.

   d. is always divided evenly among the partners.

ANALYSIS

6. Clark Davis and Preston Nelson formed a partnership. Davis invested $60,000. Nelson invested $40,000. Net income for the year is $50,000. If net income is allocated based on the capital account balances at the beginning of the year, what is the income allocation for Davis and Nelson?

(Answers to Section 2 Self Review are on page 684.)

Section 3

Partnership Changes

The partners in an existing business can change. Former partners might withdraw, sell their interests, or die. New partners may be admitted.

Changes in Partners

A partnership has a limited life. Whenever a partner dies or withdraws, or when a new partner is admitted, a dissolution of the old partnership occurs. If the surviving partners continue the business, a new partnership legally exists. **Dissolution** is the legal term for termination of a partnership. It has little impact on the business activities of the partnership. On the other hand, when the business is completely terminated, it is called a **liquidation.** The business ceases to exist, and the partnership agreement is void.

When a partnership is dissolved, two steps are taken:

Step 1: *The accounting records are closed and the net income or net loss on the date of dissolution is recorded and transferred to the partners' capital accounts.*

Step 2: *Assets and liabilities are revalued at fair market value. The partners, including any newly admitted partners, agree on the amounts.*

RECORDING REVALUATION OF ASSETS

>> 19-6. OBJECTIVE

Account for the revaluation of assets and liabilities prior to the dissolution of a partnership.

The partnership agreement usually provides that when a partnership is dissolved and the business is to be continued as a new partnership, the assets and liabilities are revalued. The revaluation may require the services of a professional appraiser. The revaluation is made because the difference between the fair market value and the book value is a gain or loss resulting from events that occurred during the old partnership. The new partner does not share the gain or loss.

Based on the revaluation, the assets and liabilities are written up or down, and the difference between the book and fair market values is allocated to the original partners' capital accounts. The allocation of gains and losses is made in accordance with the formula used for sharing net income or net loss.

The partners of Key Notes Music Store agreed to admit a new partner, effective April 1. The assets and liabilities will be revalued following the close of business on March 31. Figure 19.3 shows the balance sheet of Key Notes after the closing entries are made on March 31 and net income or net loss is transferred to the partners' capital accounts.

The partners agree that:

- *Allowance for Doubtful Accounts* should be increased to $4,300,
- *Value of Merchandise Inventory* is $79,000,
- *Land* is worth $22,000 according to an appraisal,
- Liabilities are properly stated.

The result is a $6,700 net increase in assets:

Merchandise inventory	$9,000
Accounts receivable/Allowance for doubtful accounts	(2,300)
Net increase in assets	$6,700

Assume that the partners share income and losses as follows:

Lee	40 percent
Wilner	40 percent
Flores	20 percent

FIGURE 19.3
Partnership Balance Sheet

important!

Asset Revaluation

When transferred from one partnership to another, assets are revalued to their fair market value. The new value will not necessarily agree with the book value carried by the old firm.

Key Notes Music Store			
Balance Sheet			
March 31, 2016			
Assets			
Cash			60 000 00
Accounts Receivable	40 000 00		
Less Allowance for Doubtful Accounts	2 000 00	38 000 00	
Merchandise Inventory		70 000 00	
Land		22 000 00	
Total Assets		190 000 00	
Liabilities and Partners' Equity			
Liabilities			
Notes Payable—Bank	19 000 00		
Accounts Payable	23 200 00		
Total Liabilities		42 200 00	
Partners' Equity			
Tom Lee, Capital	38 300 00		
Joan Wilner, Capital	58 500 00		
Nau Flores, Capital	51 000 00		
Total Partners' Equity		147 800 00	
Total Liabilities and Partners' Equity		190 000 00	

The gain on revaluation of the assets is allocated as follows:

Lee $6,700 × 0.40 = $2,680
Wilner $6,700 × 0.40 = $2,680
Flores $6,700 × 0.20 = $1,340

Revaluation of the assets is recorded as follows:

	DATE		DESCRIPTION	POST. REF.	DEBIT	CREDIT	
			GENERAL JOURNAL	PAGE	4		
1	2016						1
2	April	1	Merchandise Inventory	121	9 0 0 0 00		2
3			Allowance for Doubtful Accounts	112		2 3 0 0 00	3
4			Tom Lee, Capital	301		2 6 8 0 00	4
5			Joan Wilner, Capital	311		2 6 8 0 00	5
6			Nau Flores, Capital	321		1 3 4 0 00	6
7			To record revaluation of assets and				7
8			allocations of gain to partners.				8
9							9

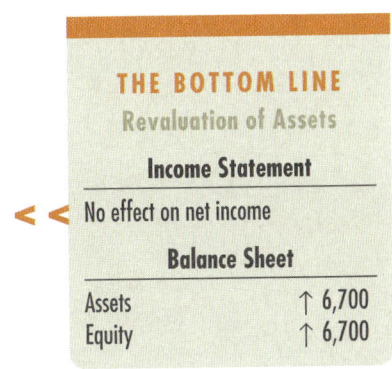

THE BOTTOM LINE
Revaluation of Assets

Income Statement
No effect on net income

Balance Sheet
Assets   ↑ 6,700
Equity   ↑ 6,700

After the entry is posted, the capital accounts contain the following balances:

Lee	($38,300 + $2,680)	$ 40,980
Wilner	($58,500 + $2,680)	61,180
Flores	($51,000 + $1,340)	52,340
Total		$154,500

ADMISSION OF A NEW PARTNER

There are two ways to admit a new partner:

1. The new partner may purchase all or part of the interest of an existing partner, making payment directly to the selling partner. In this case, no cash or other asset is transferred to the partnership.

2. The new partner may invest cash or other assets directly in the existing partnership.

Purchase of an Interest One way to join an existing partnership is to buy a portion of a partner's share of capital. The prospective partner must have the approval of the existing partners. The money or other consideration passes directly from the new partner to the selling partner and does not appear in the accounting records of the partnership.

>>**19-7. OBJECTIVE**
Account for the sale of a partnership interest.

Suppose Key Notes' books are closed and the assets revalued as described. Lee sells half his interest in the business to Beth Rivera for $32,000. Rivera pays $32,000 directly to Lee. The partnership's records do not reflect this cash transaction. In the partnership's accounting records, the transfer is recorded by a debit to **Tom Lee, Capital** for $20,490 and a credit to **Beth Rivera, Capital** for $20,490. The $20,490 is one-half of Lee's capital account balance after revaluation (0.50 × $40,980). (The other partners would have to agree to this transfer of interest to Rivera.)

Frequently the amount paid by the new partner is not the same as the amount credited to the new partner's capital account. The value of the partner's interest is a matter for bargaining between the two parties. Rivera paid $32,000 in order to obtain a capital account of $20,490. The difference between the two amounts does not affect the partnership's accounting records.

With the admission of the new partner, the current partnership comes to an end and a new partnership is established. The partners should draw up a new partnership agreement.

>> 19-8. OBJECTIVE

Account for the investment of a new partner in an existing partnership.

Investment of Assets by a New Partner A new partner may invest money or other property to obtain admission to the partnership while the existing partners remain as partners in the business. The new partner's investment, share of ownership in capital, and share of the net income or net loss are agreed upon among the partners and specified in the partnership agreement for the new partnership. The new partner may receive credit for the amount invested or for a higher or lower amount.

New Partner Given Credit for Amount Invested Suppose the four parties involved in Key Notes Music agree that Rivera will receive a one-fourth interest in the capital of the business for cash equal to one-fourth of the total capital in the new partnership. After revaluation, the capital accounts of the three existing partners total $154,500. The investment for Rivera to own one-fourth of the capital of the new partnership is $51,500:

■ The three existing partners, whose capital accounts total $154,500 after the revaluation, will own three-fourths of the business. The $154,500 is three-fourths (or 75 percent) of the new partnership capital. Each quarter interest is therefore $51,500.

■ The new partnership capital is $206,000 ($51,500 × 4).

■ Rivera is purchasing one-fourth (or 25 percent) of the new partnership capital, $51,500.

The entry to record Rivera's investment is as follows:

	2016					
10	April	1	Cash	101	51 500 00	
11			Beth Rivera, Capital	331		51 500 00
12			To record investment of Rivera for			
13			one-fourth interest in partnership			

New Partner Given Credit for More Than Amount Invested The new partner can be given credit for more capital than the amount invested. This is often done if the new partner brings to the business skills that the existing partners are eager to have. Suppose Rivera agreed to invest $45,500 for a one-fourth interest in the partnership. It takes two steps to record the investment: record the cash investment and adjust the capital account balances.

The cash investment is recorded as a debit to **Cash** for $45,500 and a credit to **Beth Rivera, Capital** for $45,500. After this entry is posted, the capital account balances are $200,000:

Lee	$ 40,980
Wilner	61,180
Flores	52,340
Rivera	45,500
Total	$200,000

According to the capital account balances, Rivera owns 22.75 percent of the partnership ($45,500/$200,000). However, Rivera paid $45,500 to purchase a one-fourth interest in the partnership. Rivera's capital account balance should be $50,000 ($200,000 × 1/4). The $4,500 ($50,000 − $45,500) increase necessary to bring Rivera's account to $50,000 is referred to as a "bonus to the new partner." The $4,500 is credited to Rivera's capital account. The debit is deducted from the original partners' capital accounts on the basis of the former partnership income and loss ratio. The amounts deducted from the original partners' accounts are as follows:

Lee	$4,500 × 0.40 = $1,800
Wilner	$4,500 × 0.40 = $1,800
Flores	$4,500 × 0.20 = $900

The general journal entry to record the bonus is as follows:

	2016						
1	2016						1
10	April 1	Tom Lee, Capital	301	1 8 0 0 00			10
11		Joan Wilner, Capital	311	1 8 0 0 00			11
12		Nau Flores, Capital	321	9 0 0 00			12
13		Beth Rivera, Capital	331		4 5 0 0 00		13
14		To record bonus allowed new partner					14

The partners' capital accounts after posting the entry for the bonus appear as follows:

Tom Lee, Capital		301	
April 1		April 1	
Rivera bonus	1,800	Bal.	40,980
		Bal.	39,180

Joan Wilner, Capital		311	
April 1		April 1	
Rivera bonus	1,800	Bal.	61,180
		Bal.	59,380

Nau Flores, Capital		321	
April 1		April 1	
Rivera bonus	900	Bal.	52,340
		Bal.	51,440

Beth Rivera, Capital		331	
		April 1	
		Invest.	45,500
		April 1	
		Bonus	4,500
		Bal.	50,000

New Partner Given Credit for Less Than Amount Invested Suppose that Rivera agreed to invest $45,500 for a one-fifth interest in the capital of the partnership. The $45,500 investment is recorded as a debit to **Cash** for $45,500 and a credit to **Beth Rivera, Capital** for $45,500.

After this entry is posted, the capital account balances are $200,000:

Lee	$ 40,980
Wilner	61,180
Flores	52,340
Rivera	45,500
Total	$200,000

According to the capital account balances at this point, Rivera owns 22.75 percent of the partnership ($45,500/$200,000). However, she paid $45,500 for a one-fifth (or 20 percent) interest in the partnership. Rivera's capital account balance should be $40,000 ($200,000 × 0.20). The $5,500 ($40,000 − $45,500) decrease necessary to bring Rivera's capital account to $40,000 is referred to as "bonus allowed the original partners." The $5,500 is debited to Rivera's capital account and credited to the original partners' capital accounts on the basis of the former partnership income and loss ratio. The amounts credited to the original partners' capital accounts are as follows:

Lee	$5,500 × 0.40 = $2,200
Wilner	$5,500 × 0.40 = $2,200
Flores	$5,500 × 0.20 = $1,100

	2016																	
1	2016																	1
10	April	1	Beth Rivera, Capital		331	5	5	0	0	00								10
11			Tom Lee, Capital		301						2	2	0	0	00			11
12			Joan Wilner, Capital		311						2	2	0	0	00			12
13			Nau Flores, Capital		321						1	1	0	0	00			13
14			To record bonus to original partners															14
15																		15

After this entry is posted, Rivera's capital account balance will be $40,000, or one-fifth of the total partnership capital of $200,000.

>> 19-9. OBJECTIVE

Account for the withdrawal of a partner from a partnership.

WITHDRAWAL OF A PARTNER

The partnership agreement should contain provisions specifying the procedures to be followed for the withdrawal of a partner. The partnership agreement for Key Notes provides that, upon withdrawal of a partner, the assets are to be revalued and the retiring partner is to be paid an amount equal to that partner's capital account after revaluation. Suppose that the partners of Key Notes agree that Nau Flores is to withdraw from the partnership after the close of business on March 31. He is to receive cash in an amount equal to the balance of his capital account after revaluation of the assets.

The revalued assets result in the following capital account balances:

Lee	$ 40,980
Wilner	61,180
Flores	52,340
Total	$154,500

The entry to record the withdrawal of Flores from the partnership is as follows:

	2016																
1	2016																1
2	Mar.	31	Nau Flores, Capital		321	52	3	4	0	00							2
3			Cash		101						52	3	4	0	00		3
4			To record cash payment made to Flores														4
5			on withdrawal from partnership														5
6																	6
7																	7

MANAGERIAL IMPLICATIONS <<

PARTNERSHIP CONSIDERATIONS

■ Management and owners need to understand the advantages the partnership form of business offers to sole proprietors who need more capital, managerial assistance, or technical help.

■ The partnership does not pay taxes. The partnership's taxable income "flows through" to the individual partners.

■ It is essential that individuals who enter into a partnership have a clear understanding of the duties, obligations, rights, and responsibilities of each partner.

■ There should be a written partnership agreement drafted by a lawyer and reviewed by the partners' accountants.

■ The partnership agreement should be very specific about the income and loss allocation formula.

■ Upon dissolution, the partnership assets and liabilities should be revalued.

THINKING CRITICALLY

What are the essential elements of a partnership agreement?

The parties might agree that the withdrawing partner is to receive either more or less than the balance of that partner's capital account at the time of withdrawal. In this event, the withdrawing partner's capital account is debited for the balance of the account:

- If the amount paid is higher than the withdrawing partner's capital account balance, the excess is debited to the capital accounts of the remaining partners according to their income and loss ratio.

- If the amount paid is less than the withdrawing partner's capital account balance, the difference is credited to the remaining partners' capital accounts based on their income and loss ratio.

After the assets of Key Notes are revalued, Flores's capital account balance is $52,340. Flores wishes to withdraw, and the partners agree to pay him $61,340 from partnership funds. The $9,000 ($61,340 – $52,340) bonus paid to the withdrawing partner is divided between the remaining partners according to their income and loss ratio of 40:40 (equally). The general journal entry to record the withdrawal of Flores is as follows:

1	2016				1
2	Mar. 31	Nau Flores, Capital	321	52 3 4 0 00	2
3		Tom Lee, Capital	301	4 5 0 0 00	3
4		Joan Wilner, Capital	311	4 5 0 0 00	4
5		Cash	101	61 3 4 0 00	5
6		To record cash payment made to Flores			6
7		on withdrawal from partnership			7
8					8
9					9

Section 3   Self Review

QUESTIONS

1. If a withdrawing partner is paid less than his capital account balance, how is the excess accounted for?

2. An existing partner sells one-half of his capital interest to a new partner. What is the accounting entry to record this transaction?

3. A new partner invests cash greater than the fractional share of the total capital being purchased. What are the accounting entries to record this transaction?

EXERCISES

4. The profit sharing percentages of partners Jones, Jackson, and Jolly are 40 percent, 40 percent, and 20 percent, respectively. Their capital account balances are $40,000, $30,000, and $20,000, respectively. Jones withdraws from the partnership and receives $36,000 from the partnership in settlement of his withdrawal. As a result of this transaction:

   a. the capital account of Jackson is not affected.

   b. the capital account of Jackson is credited for $1,000.

   c. the capital account of Jackson is debited for $1,000.

   d. the capital account of Jackson is credited for $2,667.

5. When a partner withdraws from the partnership and receives cash in excess of the balance in his capital account, the excess is:

   a. debited to the capital accounts of the remaining partners, allocated to those partners on the basis of the ratio of their capital account balances.

   b. credited to the capital accounts of the remaining partners, allocated to those partners in proportion to their profit and loss percentages.

   c. debited to the capital accounts of the remaining partners, allocated to those partners in proportion to their profit and loss percentages.

   d. debited to the capital accounts of the remaining partners, allocated equally to those partners.

ANALYSIS

6. James Miller paid $28,000 to Pete Mason for one-half of his interest in the partnership of Lane and Mason. Mason's capital account balance prior to the purchase was $50,000. What is the entry required in the partnership's accounts to record this transaction?

(Answers to Section 3 Self Review are on page 684.)

Review and Applications

19 Chapter   REVIEW   Chapter Summary

A partnership is the joining together of two or more persons under a written or oral contract as co-owners of a business. You have learned about the advantages and disadvantages of the partnership form of business. In addition, you have studied the accounting methods and procedures unique to partnerships.

Learning Objectives

19-1 Explain the major advantages and disadvantages of a partnership.

There are advantages to a partnership:

- It is relatively easy and inexpensive to form.
- It permits pooling of skills and resources.
- No income tax is paid on its profits, although partners report their share of income or loss on their tax returns.

There are disadvantages to a partnership:

- Partners have unlimited liability.
- Any partner can bind the other partners.
- The business lacks continuity.
- Ownership rights are not freely transferable.

19-2 State the important provisions that should be included in every partnership agreement.

A written agreement should detail the partnership specifics: amount of initial investment, partners' duties, fiscal year, accounting method, division of gains or losses (including any allowances for salaries and interest), policy for withdrawals, and length of partnership life.

19-3 Account for the formation of a partnership.

Assets and liabilities may be exchanged for a partnership interest:

- Assets are appraised and recorded at the agreed-upon fair market value at the transfer date.
- Each partner's capital account is credited for the amount of the investment.

19-4 Compute and record the division of net income or net loss between partners in accordance with the partnership agreement.

Division of partnership income and losses can be made in any manner. If no agreement has been made, income and losses are divided equally.

19-5 Prepare a statement of partners' equities.

A statement of partners' equities summarizes the changes in the capital accounts during the period.

19-6 Account for the revaluation of assets and liabilities prior to the dissolution of a partnership.

Before a partnership is dissolved, the business assets are revalued and the income or loss allocated according to the original agreement.

19-7 Account for the sale of a partnership interest.

A new partner may purchase a partnership interest from a current partner. The portion of ownership sold is transferred from the existing partner's capital account to the new partner's capital account.

19-8 Account for the investment of a new partner in an existing partnership.

A new partner may invest more or less than the proportionate part of total capital that the new partner will own after the investment:

- If more is invested, a bonus is recorded to the current partners (the new partner's capital account is debited and the current partners' capital accounts are credited).
- If less is invested, a bonus is recorded to the new partner (the new partner's capital account is credited and the current partners' capital accounts are debited).

19-9 Account for the withdrawal of a partner from a partnership.

When a partner withdraws, the assets and liabilities are revalued and the income or loss allocated according to the original agreement. If the amount the retiring partner is paid is different from the capital account balance, the difference is allocated to the remaining partners in accordance with their profit and loss ratios.

19-10 Define the accounting terms new to this chapter.

Glossary

Articles of partnership (p. 645) See Partnership agreement

Dissolution (p. 661) The legal term for termination of a partnership

Distributive share (p. 650) The amount of net income or net loss allocated to each partner

General partner (p. 645) A member of a partnership who has unlimited liability

Limited partner (p. 645) A member of a partnership whose liability is limited to his or her investment in the partnership

Limited partnership (p. 645) A partnership having one or more limited partners

Liquidation (p. 661) Termination of a business by distributing all assets and discontinuing the business

Memorandum entry (p. 647) An informational entry in the general journal

Mutual agency (p. 645) The characteristic of a partnership by which each partner is empowered to act as an agent for the partnership, binding the firm by his or her acts

Partnership (p. 644) An association of two or more persons who carry on, as co-owners, a business for profit

Partnership agreement (p. 645) A legal contract forming a partnership and specifying certain details of operation

Statement of partners' equities (p. 659) A financial statement prepared to summarize the changes in partners' capital accounts during an accounting period

Unlimited liability (p. 645) The implication that a creditor can look to all partners' personal assets as well as the assets of the partnership for payment of the firm's debts

Comprehensive Self Review

1. Why are the assets and liabilities revalued prior to a dissolution?
2. Explain the difference between the accounting treatment of "salary withdrawals" and "salary allowances" in allocating income or loss.
3. Explain how one partner might receive a profit allocation even though the partnership has a loss for the period.
4. What are the major disadvantages of the partnership form of business enterprise?
5. What nonfinancial information should be considered in forming a partnership?

(Answers to Comprehensive Self Review are on pages 684–685.)

Discussion Questions

1. Why should the assets and liabilities of an existing partnership be revalued when a new partner is to be admitted by the investment of cash in the organization?
2. Explain what the term "mutual agency" means in regard to a partnership.
3. Explain how the net income of a partnership is allocated if it is less than the salary and interest allowances.
4. Are partners' salaries considered to be expenses of the partnership? Explain.
5. What is the advantage of a limited partnership?
6. How does the balance sheet of a partnership differ from that of a sole proprietorship?
7. Is *Allowance for Doubtful Accounts* brought forward from the general ledger of a sole proprietorship when the firm's assets and liabilities are being transferred to the partnership? Why?

8. Why are assets of an existing sole proprietorship revalued when they are transferred to a partnership?

9. Does a partnership pay federal income tax? Explain.

10. Does a partnership continue to exist after the death of a partner? Explain.

11. What are the major disadvantages of the partnership form of business entity?

12. List the major advantages of the partnership form of business over a corporation.

13. What information appears on a statement of partners' equities?

14. The two partners in a business often pay personal bills by writing checks on the business bank account. Is this a good business practice? Explain. How should such payments be recorded?

15. Explain how the partnership accounts for the sale by a partner of a portion of his partnership interest to another individual.

16. What is the difference between a dissolution and liquidation?

17. What are typical considerations that affect the way income is allocated among partners?

18. List the steps required to dissolve a partnership.

19. Explain the use of a drawing account in a partnership.

APPLICATIONS

Exercises

Exercise 19.1
Objective 19-3

▶ **Recording cash investment in a partnership.**

In 2016, Selena Lopez invests cash of $220,000 in a newly formed partnership that will operate The Tennis Shop. In return, Lopez receives a one-third interest in the capital of the partnership. In general journal form, record Lopez's investment in the partnership.

Exercise 19.2
Objective 19-3

▶ **Recording investment of assets and liabilities in a partnership.**

Sadie Palmer operates a sole proprietorship business that sells golf equipment. In 2016, Palmer agrees to transfer her assets and liabilities to a partnership that will operate The Golf Shop. Palmer will own a two-thirds interest in the capital of the partnership. The agreed upon values of assets and liabilities to be transferred follow:

> Total Accounts receivable of $130,000 will be transferred and approximately $5,000 of these accounts may be uncollectible
>
> Merchandise inventory, $106,000
>
> Furniture and fixtures, $48,000
>
> Accounts payable, $18,500

Record the receipt of the assets and liabilities by the partnership in the general journal.

Exercise 19.3
Objective 19-3

▶ **Preparing a balance sheet for a partnership.**

On May 1, 2016, Stanley Carpenter and Fred Kenamond formed The Wine Shop. The two partners invested cash and other assets and liabilities with the following agreed upon values:

Carpenter: Cash, $13,000; Merchandise inventory, $25,000; Equipment, $77,000; Accounts payable, $12,000.

Kenamond: Furniture, $25,000; Cash, $37,000.

Carpenter is to own two-thirds of the capital, and Kenamond is to own one-third of the capital, but they will split profits and losses equally. Prepare a balance sheet for the partnership just after the assets and liabilities have been transferred to it.

Computing and recording allocation of net income with salaries and interest allowed.

◄ **Exercise 19.4**
Objective 19-4

Carla Landry and Linda Carter are partners who share profits and losses in the following manner. Landry receives a salary of $106,000, and Carter receives a salary of $150,000. These amounts were paid to the partners and charged to their drawing accounts. Both partners also receive 10 percent interest on their capital balances at the beginning of the year. The balance of any remaining profits or losses is divided equally. The beginning capital accounts for 2016 were Landry, $418,000, and Carter, $518,000. At the end of the year, the partnership had a net income of $298,000.

Compute the amount of net income or loss to be allocated to each partner.

Computing and recording allocation of net income with interest allowed.

◄ **Exercise 19.5**
Objective 19-4

Reed and Carson are partners. Their partnership agreement provides that, in dividing profits, each is to be allocated interest at 10 percent of her beginning capital balance. The balance of net income or loss after the interest allowances is to be split in the ratio of 70:30 to Reed and Carson, respectively. The beginning capital balances were Reed, $130,000 and Carson, $34,000. Net income for the year was $250,000. Compute the amount of net income to be allocated to each partner.

Computing and recording division of net income, with salaries allowed.

◄ **Exercise 19.6**
Objective 19-4

Alfred Hurley and Thomas Estes are partners who share profits and losses in the ratio of 70 and 30 percent, respectively. Their partnership agreement provides that each will be paid a yearly salary of $94,000. The salaries were paid to the partners during 2016 and were charged to the partners' drawing accounts. The *Income Summary* account has a credit balance of $340,800 after revenue and expense accounts are closed at the end of the year. What amount of net income or net loss will be allocated to each?

Computing and recording division of net loss, with no partnership agreement on method of allocation.

◄ **Exercise 19.7**
Objective 19-4

After revenue and expense accounts of The Quick Stop were closed on December 31, 2016, *Income Summary* contained a credit balance of $106,000. The drawing accounts of the two partners, Dan Eddy and Robert Jones, showed debit balances of $80,000 and $184,000, respectively. The partnership agreement is silent on the division of profits and losses. Record the general journal entries to close the *Income Summary* account and the partners' drawing accounts.

Computing and recording division of net income based on fixed ratio.

◄ **Exercise 19.8**
Objective 19-4

The net income for the new partnership known as The Convenience Place for the year ended December 31, 2016, was $34,000. The partners, Donald Jones and Amelda Loper, share profits in the ratio of 40 and 60 percent, respectively. Record the general journal entry (or entries) to close the *Income Summary* account.

Exercise 19.9

Objective 19-4

▶ **Computing the division of net income of a partnership.**

The partnership agreement of Nancy Steele and Jeffrey Wells does not indicate how the profits and losses will be shared. Before dividing the net income, Steele's capital account balance was $320,000, and Wells's capital balance was $80,000. The net income of their firm for the year that just ended was $188,000. How much income will be allocated to Steele and how much to Wells?

Exercise 19.10

Objective 19-6

▶ **Recording revaluation of assets prior to dissolution of a partnership.**

Thomas Richey and Donald Vick are partners who share profits and losses in the ratio of 40:60, respectively. On December 31, 2016, they decide that Vick will sell one-half of his interest to James Walker. At that time, the balances of the capital accounts are $260,000 for Richey and $360,000 for Vick. The partners agree that before the new partner is admitted, certain assets should be revalued. These assets include merchandise inventory carried at $206,600 revalued at $203,800, and a building with a book value of $140,000 revalued at $240,000.

1. Record the revaluations in the general journal.
2. What will the capital balances of the two existing partners be after the revaluation is made?

Exercise 19.11

Objective 19-7

▶ **Recording sale of a part interest.**

Noah Elm and Herman Totten are partners who share profits and losses in the ratio of 40 and 60 percent, respectively. The balances of their capital accounts on December 31, 2015, are Elm, $210,000 and Totten, $230,000. With Totten's agreement, Elm sells one-half of his interest in the partnership to Kaethryn Carter for $160,000 on January 1, 2016. What will the capital account balances for each of the three partners be after this sale?

Exercise 19.12

Objective 19-9

▶ **Recording withdrawal of a partner.**

Wilson, Harold, and Meeks are partners, sharing profits and losses in the ratio of 40, 30, and 30 percent, respectively. Their partnership agreement provides that if one of them withdraws from the partnership, the assets and liabilities are to be revalued, the gain or loss allocated to the partners, and the retiring partner paid the balance of his account. Meeks withdraws from the partnership on December 31, 2016. The capital account balances before recording revaluation are Wilson, $125,000; Harold, $135,000; and Meeks, $120,000. The effect of the revaluation is to increase *Merchandise Inventory* by $26,000 and the *Building* account balance by $15,000. How much cash will be paid to Meeks?

PROBLEMS

Problem Set A 

Problem 19.1A

Objective 19-3

▶ **Accounting for formation of a partnership.**

Jason Taylor operates a store that sells computer software. Taylor has agreed to enter into a partnership with Omar Poole, effective January 1, 2016. The new firm will be called Global Computing. Taylor is to transfer all assets and liabilities of his firm to the partnership at the values agreed on. Poole will invest cash that is equal to 75 percent of Taylor's investment after revaluation. The accounts shown on Taylor's books and the agreed-on value of assets and liabilities are shown below.

INSTRUCTIONS

1. Prepare the general journal entries to record the following transactions in the books of the partnership on January 1, 2016:

	Balances Shown in Taylor's Records	Value Agreed to by Partners
Assets Transferred		
Cash	$ 50,000	$ 50,000
Accounts Receivable $ 131,000		
Allowance for Doubtful Accounts 5,000	126,000	119,000
Merchandise Inventory	360,000	375,000
Furniture and Equipment 140,000		85,000
Accumulated Depreciation 60,000	80,000	
Total Assets	$616,000	$629,000
Liabilities and Owner's Equity Transferred		
Accounts Payable	70,000	70,000
Jason Taylor, Capital	$546,000	$559,000

a. Receipt of Taylor's investment of assets and liabilities.

b. Receipt of Poole's investment of cash.

2. Prepare a balance sheet for the partnership as of the beginning of its operations on January 1, 2016.

Analyze: Based on the balance sheet you have prepared, what percentage (to the nearest 1/10 of 1%) of total equity is owned by Jason Taylor?

Accounting for formation of a partnership.

◀ **Problem 19.2A**
Objective 19-3

Terry Oatis operates a small shop that sells fishing equipment. His postclosing trial balance on December 31, 2016, is shown below.

Oatis plans to enter into a partnership with Carmen Thomas, effective January 1, 2017. Profits and losses will be shared equally. Oatis is to transfer all assets and liabilities of his store to the partnership after revaluation as agreed. Thomas will invest cash equal to Oatis's investment after revaluation. The agreed values are *Accounts Receivable* (net) $14,500; *Merchandise Inventory,* $49,900; and *Furniture and Equipment,* $12,300. The partnership will operate as Oatis and Thomas Angler's Outpost.

Oatis Tackle Center
Postclosing Trial Balance
December 31, 2016

ACCOUNT NAME	DEBIT	CREDIT
Cash	4 7 5 0 00	
Accounts Receivable	16 4 0 0 00	
Allowance for Doubtful Accounts		2 5 0 0 00
Merchandise Inventory	45 0 0 0 00	
Furniture and Equipment	29 1 0 0 00	
Accumulated Depreciation		23 0 0 0 00
Accounts Payable		4 0 0 0 00
Capital		65 7 5 0 00
Totals	95 2 5 0 00	95 2 5 0 00

INSTRUCTIONS

1. In general journal form, prepare the entries to record:

    a. The receipt of Oatis's investment of assets and liabilities by the partnership.

    b. The receipt of Thomas's investment of cash.

2. Prepare a balance sheet for Oatis and Thomas Angler's Outpost just after the investments.

Analyze: By what net amount were the net assets of Oatis's Tackle Center adjusted before they were transferred to the partnership?

Problem 19.3A
Objective 19-4

► **Computing and recording the division of net income or loss between partners.**

Rosie Wilsman and Rosa Escobedo own The Spring Flower Shop. The partnership agreement provides that Wilsman can withdraw $5,000 a month and Escobedo $4,500 a month in anticipation of profits. The withdrawals, which are not considered to be salaries, were made each month. Net income and net losses are to be allocated 40 percent to Wilsman and 60 percent to Escobedo. For the year ended December 31, 2016, the partnership earned a net income of $150,000.

INSTRUCTIONS

1. Prepare general journal entries to:

    a. Close the *Income Summary* account.

    b. Close the partners' drawing accounts.

2. Assume that there was a net loss of $50,000 for the year instead of a profit of $150,000. Give the general journal entries to:

    a. Close the *Income Summary* account.

    b. Close the partners' drawing accounts.

Analyze: Assume the business earned net income of $150,000. If 2016 was the first year of operation, what balance should be reflected for the ***Rosie Wilsman, Capital*** account at the end of the year if Wilsman's beginning capital was $110,000?

Problem 19.4A
Objectives 19-4, 19-5

► **Computing and recording the division of net income or loss between partners; preparing a statement of partners' equities.**

Larry Watson and Larry Lewis own Larry's Antiques. Their partnership agreement provides for annual salary allowances of $100,000 for Watson and $90,000 for Lewis, and interest of 10 percent on each partner's invested capital at the beginning of the year. The remainder of the net income or loss is to be distributed 50 percent to Watson and 50 percent to Lewis. The partners withdraw their salary allowances monthly. On January 1, 2016, the capital account balances were Watson, $500,000, and Lewis, $460,000. On December 15, 2016, Lewis made a permanent withdrawal of $110,000. The net income for 2016 was $420,000.

INSTRUCTIONS

1. Prepare the general journal entry on December 15, 2016, to record the permanent withdrawal by Lewis.

2. Prepare the general journal entries on December 31, 2016, to:

    a. Record the salary allowances for the year.

    b. Record the interest allowances for the year.

    c. Record the division of the balance of net income.

    d. Close the drawing accounts into the capital accounts, assuming that Watson and Lewis have withdrawn their full salary allowances.

3. Prepare a schedule showing the division of net income to the partners as it would appear on the income statement for 2016.

4. Prepare a statement of partners' equities showing the changes that took place in the partners' capital accounts during 2016.

Analyze: By what percentage did Watson's capital account increase in the fiscal year 2016?

Accounting for revaluation of assets and liabilities of a partnership, investment of a new partner, and withdrawal of a partner.

◄ **Problem 19.5A**
Objectives 19-6, 19-8, 19-9

The balance sheet of Adams Pharmacy after the revenue, expense, and partners' drawing accounts have been closed on December 31, 2016, follows:

QB

Adams Pharmacy			
Balance Sheet			
December 31, 2016			
Assets			
Cash			83 4 0 0 00
Accounts Receivable			17 0 0 0 00
Merchandise Inventory			4 3 5 0 0 0 00
Equipment	174 0 0 0 00		
Accumulated Depreciation—Equipment	101 0 0 0 00		73 0 0 0 00
Building	420 0 0 0 00		
Accumulated Depreciation—Building	330 0 0 0 00		90 0 0 0 00
Land			50 0 0 0 00
Total Assets			748 4 0 0 00
Liabilities and Partners' Equity			
Liabilities			
Accounts Payable			415 2 0 0 00
Taxes Payable			23 2 0 0 00
Total Liabilities			438 4 0 0 00
Partners' Equity			
Larry Adams, Capital	170 0 0 0 00		
Hazel Adams, Capital	70 0 0 0 00		
Isiah Adams, Capital	70 0 0 0 00		
Total Partners' Equity			310 0 0 0 00
Total Liabilities and Partners' Equity			748 4 0 0 00

On that date, Larry Adams, Hazel Adams, and Isiah Adams agree to admit Vickie Neal to the partnership. The partnership agreement provides that, in case of dissolution of the partnership, all assets and liabilities should be revalued. Profits and losses are shared in the ratio of 50:25:25, to Larry, Hazel, and Isiah, respectively. The agreed upon values of the assets are as follows:

Accounts receivable	$ 15,000	Building	$139,000
Merchandise inventory	408,400	Land	103,000
Equipment	73,000		

All liabilities are properly recorded.

INSTRUCTIONS

1. Prepare the general journal entries to record revaluation of the assets.

2. Prepare the general journal entry (or entries) to record Vickie Neal's investment of $120,000, assuming that she is to receive capital equal to the amount invested.

3. Prepare the general journal entry (or entries) to record Vickie Neal's investment of $120,000, assuming that she is to receive one-fifth of the capital of the partnership.

4. Prepare the general journal entry (or entries) to record Vickie Neal's investment of $120,000, assuming that she is to receive one-third of the capital of the partnership.

5. Assume that after the revaluation had been recorded, the existing partners and Vickie Neal decided that their previous agreement should be canceled and that Vickie Neal should not become a partner. Instead, the partners agreed that Hazel Adams would withdraw from the partnership and be paid cash by the partnership.

   a. Prepare the general journal entry to record the payment to Hazel Adams if she is paid an amount equal to her capital account balance after the revaluation.

   b. Prepare the general journal entry to record the payment to Hazel Adams if she is paid an amount equal to $15,000 less than her capital account balance after revaluation.

   c. Prepare the general journal entry to record the payment to Hazel Adams if she is paid an amount equal to $12,600 more than her capital account balance after revaluation.

Analyze: Assume that only items 1 and 3 have been recorded in the records of the partnership. What is the balance of Isiah Adams's capital account at January 1, 2017?

Problem 19.6A
Objectives 19-7, 19-8

▶ **Accounting for sale of a partnership interest and investment of a new partner.**

Darren Tolliver and Henry Watson, attorneys, operate a law practice. They would like to expand the expertise of their firm. In anticipation of this, they have agreed to admit June Azua to the partnership on January 1, 2016. The capital account balances on January 1, 2016, after revaluation of assets, are Tolliver, $170,000, and Watson, $150,000. Net income or net loss is shared equally.

INSTRUCTIONS

Prepare the entries in general journal form to record the admission of Azua to the partnership on January 1, 2016, under each of the following independent conditions:

1. Tolliver sells one-half of his interest in the partnership to Azua for $138,000 cash.
2. Tolliver sells one-half of his interest in the partnership to Azua for $94,000 cash.
3. Azua invests $130,000 in the business for a 25 percent interest in the partnership.
4. Azua invests $134,000 in the business for a 30 percent interest in the partnership.

Analyze: Based only on item 3, what percentage of total equity does each partner own?

Problem Set B

Problem 19.1B
Objective 19-3

▶ **Accounting for the formation of a partnership.**

William Giese operates the Giese Broadcast Company. His postclosing trial balance on December 31, 2016, is as follows:

Giese Broadcast Company
Postclosing Trial Balance
December 31, 2016

ACCOUNT NAME	DEBIT	CREDIT
Cash	24 800 00	
Accounts Receivable	24 000 00	
Allowance for Doubtful Accounts		4 800 00
Merchandise Inventory	180 000 00	
Fixtures and Store Equipment	240 000 00	
Accumulated Depreciation		160 000 00
Accounts Payable		8 000 00
William Giese, Capital		296 000 00
Totals	468 800 00	468 800 00

Giese agrees to enter into a partnership with Hazel Borris, effective January 1, 2017. Profits and losses will be shared equally. Giese is to transfer the assets and liabilities of his store to the partnership after revaluation as agreed. Borris will invest cash equal to one-half of Giese's investment after revaluation. The agreed upon values are **Accounts Receivable** (net), $9,600; **Merchandise Inventory,** $184,000; and **Fixtures and Store Equipment** (net), $176,000. The partnership will operate as the Giese-Borris Broadcast Company.

INSTRUCTIONS

1. In general journal form, prepare the entries to record the following on the books of the partnership:

   a. The receipt of Giese's investment of assets and liabilities in the partnership.

   b. The receipt of Borris's investment of cash.

2. Prepare a balance sheet for Giese-Borris Broadcast Company for January 1, 2017.

Analyze: By what net amount was Giese's equity adjusted before the partnership was formed?

Accounting for formation of a partnership.

◀ **Problem 19.2B**
Objective 19-3

Edward Vinzant operates a store that sells paintings and portraits by local artists. Vinzant has agreed to enter into a partnership with Shirley Cosby, effective January 1, 2016. The new firm will be called The Artist's Supply. Vinzant is to transfer the assets and liabilities of his business to the partnership at the values agreed on. Cosby will invest cash that is equal to Vinzant's investment after revaluation. The accounts shown on Vinzant's books and the agreed-on value of assets and liabilities follow:

		Balances Shown in Vinzant's Records	Value Agreed to by Partners
Assets Transferred			
Cash		$ 18,000	$ 18,000
Accounts Receivable	$ 18,000		
Allowance for Doubtful Accounts	2,000	16,000	13,600
Merchandise Inventory		192,000	172,000
Furniture and Equipment	108,000		47,600
Accumulated Depreciation	82,000	26,000	
Total Assets		$252,000	$251,200
Liabilities and Owner's Equity Transferred			
Accounts Payable		0	16,000
Edward Vinzant, Capital		$252,000	$235,200

INSTRUCTIONS

1. Prepare the general journal entries to record the following transactions on the books of the partnership on January 1, 2016:

   a. Receipt of Vinzant's investment of assets and liabilities.

   b. Receipt of Cosby's investment of cash.

2. Prepare a balance sheet for the partnership as of the beginning of its operations on January 1, 2016.

Analyze: If Shirley Cosby agreed to a cash investment equal to 80 percent of the value of Edward Vinzant's investment, what would the balance of Shirley Cosby's capital account be after the formation of the partnership?

Problem 19.3B

Objective 19-4

▶ ## Computing and recording the division of net income or loss between partners.

Wayne Beasley and Barney Coda operate a retail furniture store. Under the terms of the partnership agreement, Beasley is authorized to withdraw $8,000 a month and Coda $6,000 a month. The withdrawals, which are not considered to be salaries, were made each month and charged to the drawing accounts. The partners have agreed that net income or loss is to be allocated 35 percent to Beasley and 65 percent to Coda. For the year ended December 31, 2016, the partnership earned a net income of $420,000.

INSTRUCTIONS

1. Prepare general journal entries to:
   a. Close the *Income Summary* account.
   b. Close the partners' drawing accounts.
2. Assume that there had been a net loss of $220,000 instead of net income of $420,000. Prepare the general journal entries to:
   a. Close the *Income Summary* account.
   b. Close the partners' drawing accounts.

Analyze: Barney Coda's capital account on January 1, 2016, was $300,000. What is the balance in that account as the end of 2016, assuming the profit for the year was $420,000?

Problem 19.4B

Objectives 19-4, 19-5

▶ ## Computing and recording the division of net income or loss between partners; preparing a statement of partners' equities.

Alika Myers and Cliff Hanson operate Downtown Apartments. Their partnership agreement provides for salaries of $60,000 a year for Myers and $48,000 for Hanson and for an interest allowance of 10 percent on each partner's invested capital at the beginning of the year. The remainder of the net income or loss is to be distributed equally to the two partners. On January 1, 2016, the capital account balances were $104,000 for Myers and $224,000 for Hanson. On July 15, 2016, Hanson made a permanent withdrawal of capital of $80,000 for a down payment on a yacht. The net income for 2016 was $192,800.

INSTRUCTIONS

1. Prepare the general journal entry on July 15, 2016, to record the permanent withdrawal by Hanson.
2. Prepare the general journal entries on December 31, 2016, to:
   a. Record the salary allowances for the year.
   b. Record the interest allowances for the year.
   c. Record the division of the balance of net income.
   d. Close the drawing accounts into the capital accounts, assuming that the partners had withdrawn only the full amount of their salary allowances.
3. Prepare a schedule showing the division of net income to the partners as it would appear on the income statement for 2016.
4. Prepare a statement of partners' equities showing the changes that took place in the partners' capital accounts during the year 2016.

Analyze: Do the facts stated in the problem suggest changes that probably should be made in the provision for interest in allocating income? Explain.

Accounting for revaluation of assets and liabilities of a partnership, investment of a new partner, and withdrawal of a partner.

◄ **Problem 19.5B**
Objectives 19-6, 19-8, 19-9

The balance sheet of The Office Equipment and Supply Shop after the revenue, expense, and partners' drawing accounts have been closed on December 31, 2016, is provided below.

On that date, Rush, Hatten, and Booker agree to admit Rosie Hinojosa to the partnership. The partnership agreement among Rush, Hatten, and Booker provides that in case of dissolution of the partnership, all assets and liabilities should be revalued. Profits and losses are shared in the ratio of 50:20:30 to Rush, Hatten, and Booker, respectively. The agreed upon values of the assets are given below:

Accounts receivable	$ 10,040
Merchandise inventory	202,000
Equipment	36,000
Building	58,000
Land	46,200

All liabilities are properly recorded.

The Office Equipment and Supply Shop
Balance Sheet
December 31, 2016

Assets		
Cash		45 000 00
Accounts Receivable		12 000 00
Merchandise Inventory		210 000 00
Equipment	85 000 00	
Accumulated Depreciation—Equipment	48 000 00	37 000 00
Building	210 000 00	
Accumulated Depreciation—Building	160 000 00	50 000 00
Land		22 000 00
Total Assets		376 000 00
Liabilities and Partners' Equity		
Liabilities		
Accounts Payable		215 000 00
Taxes Payable		16 000 00
Total Liabilities		231 000 00
Partners' Equity		
Helen Rush, Capital	70 000 00	
Billy Hatten, Capital	30 000 00	
Quinton Booker, Capital	45 000 00	
Total Partners' Equity		145 000 00
Total Liabilities and Partners' Equity		376 000 00

INSTRUCTIONS

1. Prepare the general journal entries to record revaluation of the partnership's assets.
2. Prepare the general journal entry (or entries) to record Hinojosa's investment of $66,000, assuming that she is to receive credit for the amount invested.
3. Prepare the general journal entry (or entries) to record Hinojosa's investment of $66,000, assuming that she is to receive one-fifth of the capital of the entity.
4. Prepare the general journal entry (or entries) to record Hinojosa's investment of $66,000, assuming that she is to receive 45 percent of the capital of the entity.
5. Assume that after the revaluation had been recorded, the existing partners and Hinojosa decided that their previous agreement should be canceled and that Hinojosa should not become a partner. Instead, the partners agreed that Booker would withdraw from the partnership.

a. Prepare the general journal entry to record the payment to Booker if he is paid an amount equal to his capital account balance after the revaluation.

b. Prepare the general journal entry to record the payment to Booker if he is paid an amount equal to $6,500 less than his capital account balance after the revaluation.

c. Prepare the general journal entry to record the payment to Booker if he is paid an amount equal to $9,000 more than his capital account balance after the revaluation.

Analyze: Assume only items 1 and 5(b) occurred. What is the balance of the *Billy Hatten, Capital* account at December 31, 2016?

Problem 19.6B

Objectives 19-7, 19-8

▶ **Accounting for sale of partnership interest and investment of a new partner.**

Fred Wu and Hunter Thompson are partners in Technology Applications. The balances of their capital accounts on January 2, 2016, after revaluation of assets were Wu, $480,000, and Thompson, $640,000. Profits and losses are shared in the ratio of 55:45 between Wu and Thompson. The partners agree to admit William Monroe to the partnership, effective January 3, 2016.

INSTRUCTIONS

Give the entries in general journal form to record the admission of Monroe under each of the following independent conditions:

1. Wu sells one-half of his interest in the partnership to Monroe for $352,000 in cash.
2. Thompson sells one-half of his interest in the partnership to Monroe for $256,000 in cash.
3. Monroe invests $480,000 in the business for a one-fourth interest in the partnership.
4. Monroe invests $480,000 in the business for a 35 percent interest in the partnership.

Analyze: What percentage of partnership equity is owned by Wu and by Thompson after transaction 4?

Critical Thinking Problem 19.1

New Partnership

Ellis Taylor has operated a successful motorcycle repair business for the past several years. Taylor thinks his business is almost too successful because he has very little time for himself. Taylor and Jane Ruby, who is also a motorcycle enthusiast, have had a number of discussions about her joining him in the business. Finally, they agree to form a partnership that will operate under the name TR Motorcycle Repair Shop. They have asked you to provide assistance, particularly with help in establishing terms for dividing partnership profits and losses.

The partners give you the following information about their plans for the business:

a. Taylor plans to contribute to the partnership the assets of his sole proprietorship. They have been appraised to have a fair market value of $750,000.

b. Ruby will invest $1,000,000 in cash.

c. Taylor will work full-time in the business while Ruby will work part-time and continue to attend the class she is taking in pursuit of a college degree.

Assume that TR Motorcycle Repair earned a net income of $490,000 during its first year of operation.

INSTRUCTIONS

1. What division of profits and losses would you suggest for Taylor and Ruby?
2. Using your proposed plan of profit sharing, prepare a schedule showing the distribution of the first year's net income to the partners.

Critical Thinking Problem 19.2

From Sole Proprietor to Partner

For several years, Herschel Anderson had operated Management Consulting Company as its sole proprietor. On January 1, 2016, he formed a partnership with Richard Harris to operate the company under the name Harris-Anderson Professional Management Consultants. Pertinent terms of the partnership agreement are as follows:

1. Anderson was to transfer to the partnership the accounts receivable, merchandise inventory, furniture and equipment, and all liabilities of the sole proprietorship in return for a partnership interest of 60 percent of the partnership capital. Assets were appraised and transferred to the partnership at the appraised values.

   Balances in the relevant accounts of Anderson's sole proprietorship at the close of business on December 31, 2015, are shown below:

Accounts Receivable	$268,000 Dr.
Allowance for Doubtful Accounts	16,000 Cr.
Merchandise Inventory	380,000 Dr.
Furniture and Equipment	239,200 Dr.
Allowance for Depreciation—Furniture & Equipment	152,000 Cr.
Accounts Payable	52,000 Cr.

   The two parties agreed to the following:
   - There were unrecorded accounts payable of $8,000.
   - Accounts receivable of $12,000 were definitely uncollectible and should not be transferred to the partnership.
   - The value of **Allowance for Doubtful Accounts** should be $16,800.
   - The appraised value of **Merchandise Inventory** was $350,000.
   - The appraised value of **Furniture and Equipment** was $70,000.

2. In return for a 40 percent interest in partnership capital, Harris invested cash in an amount equal to two-thirds of Anderson's net investment in the business.

3. Each partner was allowed a salary payable on the 15th day of each month. Anderson's salary was to be $18,000 per month, and Harris's salary was to be $16,000 per month.

4. The partners were to be allowed interest of 10 percent of their beginning capital balances.

5. No provision was made for profit division except for the salaries and interest previously discussed.

6. The partnership's revenues for the year 2016 were $4,500,000, and expenses were $3,600,000. Payments for salary allowances were charged to the partners' drawing accounts.

INSTRUCTIONS

1. Record the following information in general journal form in the partnership's records:
   a. Receipt of assets and liabilities from Anderson.
   b. Investment of cash by Harris.
   c. Summary of cash withdrawals for salaries by the two partners during the year.
   d. Profit or loss division including salary and interest allowances and the closing balance of the **Income Summary** account determined on an appropriate basis.

2. Record the journal entry to close the partners' drawing accounts into the capital accounts. No other cash was withdrawn.

3. Open general ledger accounts for the partners' capital accounts. The account numbers are: *Herschel Anderson, Capital* 301, and *Richard Harris, Capital* 311. Post the journal entries from instructions 1 and 2 to the capital accounts.

4. Prepare a schedule showing the division of net income to the partners as it would appear on the income statement for 2016.

5. Prepare a statement of partners' equities for the year.

6. On January 1, 2017, the partners agreed to admit John Amos as a partner. Amos is to invest cash of $240,000 for a one-fourth interest in the capital of the partnership. The three parties agree that the book value of assets and liabilities properly reflects their values. Give the general journal entry to record Amos' investment.

Analyze: What percentage of the total partnership capital after the admission of Amos on January 1, 2017, is owned by Anderson?

BUSINESS CONNECTIONS

Forming a Partnership

Managerial FOCUS

1. The owner of an accounting practice is considering establishing a partnership with two other persons to carry on the business. What are the major disadvantages of the partnership form of organization that she should consider in making her decision?

2. Your employer is planning to form a partnership with one of his close friends. He explains to you that because he is well acquainted with the prospective partner, there is no need to have a written partnership agreement. He asks your advice. Give him your recommendation and the reasons for it.

3. Your employer is considering investing $50,000 in a partnership. In discussing the advantages and disadvantages of the arrangement, the employer informs you that a friend has told him that his potential loss is limited to the amount invested, $50,000. Is his information regarding this arrangement correct?

4. Two individuals who are forming a partnership ask you how they should divide the income and losses of the business. What factors should you consider in making a recommendation?

5. You work for a partnership. The partnership agreement between the two partners specifies that one partner is allowed a monthly draw of $3,000 and the other a monthly draw of $2,000. The agreement does not mention salary allowances for the partners. At the end of the year, one partner maintains that a drawing is the same as a salary allowance. They ask your opinion. What do you tell them?

6. One of the partners in a partnership that employs you is retiring from the business. Her capital account has a balance of $256,000. She tells you that she expects to receive a check for $256,000 from the partnership. Explain to her the proper procedure for determining the amount she will be paid.

Know Thy Partner

Ethical DILEMMA

Perry Woodson has a great deal of experience with respiratory therapy. Lewis Mitchell has the business connection and knowledge. They have decided to start a partnership that sells respiratory equipment, employing several sales representatives. They have decided to share equally in the net income and net losses. After two years, the business is thriving having sold more than 1,000 units this year. One day, Perry receives a call from the Internal Revenue Service (IRS). Unknown to Perry, Lewis has not paid the payroll taxes for last year and is behind on the payroll taxes in the current quarter. Perry learns that Lewis has a gambling problem and there is insufficient money to pay the IRS. Lewis has no personal assets that can be confiscated. What are Perry's options for the resolution of the IRS problem? What is Perry's liability? What actions should Perry have taken prior to the partnership agreement?

Partners' Equity

The following excerpts were taken from the 10-K Annual Report filed by Kinder Morgan Energy Partners, L.P., for the year ended December 31, 2012.

Financial Statement ANALYSIS

Balance Sheets

December 31 (in millions)	2012	2011
Partners' equity:		
General partner	$ 255,000	$ 96,000
Limited partners and other	$11,324,000	$7,508,000
Total partners' equity	$11,579,000	$7,604,000

Consolidated Statements of Income

Year Ended December 31 (Unaudited)	2012	2011
Net income	$1,356,000	$1,268,000
Net income attributable to general partner	$ 17,000	$ 10,000
Net income attributable to limited partners	$1,339,000	$1,258,000

Analyze:

1. On December 31, 2012, what percentage of total equity belongs to the general partner of Kinder Morgan Energy Partners, L.P.?

2. By what amount has the equity of the limited partners increased from December 31, 2011, to December 31, 2012?

3. Based on the net earnings allocation reflected on the 2012 income statement, what percentage of earnings is allocated to the general partner? To the limited partners?

Analyze Online: Locate Kinder Morgan's website (www.kindermorgan.com). Click on *investors,* then *KMP,* and find the most recent 10-K SEC filing for Kinder Morgan Energy Partners, L.P.

4. What is the year covered by the 10-K filing?

5. What partners' equity is reported for the general partner?

6. What was the earnings allocation to the general partner? To the limited partners?

Partnership Agreements

TEAMWORK

Each partner brings certain personal skills and assets into a partnership. One partner could have the technical knowledge while the other partner has the business knowledge. This partnership agreement would easily be 50/50. However, when there are multiple partners and one brings in time, one talent, and the other physical assets, the partnership agreement becomes complicated.

In groups of three or four, decide on a partnership business. Determine what the partnership business will provide, how the partnership will allocate income and loss, and any salary arrangements. Decide when and how the partnership is dissolved should it become necessary.

Small Business Administration

Internet | CONNECTION

The Small Business Administration (SBA) website at www.sba.gov provides information for potential businesses. Find out what the SBA considers the advantages and disadvantages of partnerships. What other information does this website contain about partnerships?

Answers to **Self Reviews**

Answers to Section 1 Self Review

1. Unlimited liability of partners for partnership debts, binding obligation of partnerships for most acts of partners in business, lack of continuity, partnership equity not freely transferable.

2. At their current values as of the date of the partnership formation.

3. As debits to their drawing accounts and credits to *Cash.*

4. **c.** a debit to the partner's drawing account and a credit to *Purchases* for the cost of the merchandise withdrawn.

5. **c.** a debit to *Cash* and a credit to *Carl Smith, Capital.*

6. $64,800.

Answers to Section 2 Self Review

1. Equally between the partners.

2. Salary and interest.

3. (a) Record salary allowances.

   (b) Record interest allowances.

   (c) Close balance of *Income Summary* to partner's capital accounts.

   [**Note:** Steps (a) and (b) may be reversed.]

4. **a.** debit to *Income Summary* and a credit to each partner's capital account.

5. **a.** should be specified in the partnership agreement.

6. Davis: $30,000 [($60,000 ÷ $100,000) × $50,000].
   Nelson: $20,000 [($40,000 ÷ $100,000) × $50,000].

Answers to Section 3 Self Review

1. The excess is debited to the retiring partner's capital account and credited to the capital accounts of the remaining partners. It is allocated to them in proportion to their old relative profit and loss allocation percentages.

2. Debit the old partner's capital account for one-half of the balance of that account and credit the new partner's capital account for the same amount.

3. The first entry is to debit *Cash* and credit the new partner's capital account for the amount invested. The second entry is to debit the new partner's capital account for an amount that will reduce the new owner's capital account balance to the new owner's fractional interest multiplied by the total capital after recording the cash invested by the new owner. The reduction in the new partner's capital account is credited to the accounts of old partners in proportion to the income or loss distribution ratio of the old partners.

4. **d.** the capital account of Jackson is credited for $2,667.

5. **c.** debited to the capital accounts of the remaining partners, allocated to those partners in proportion to their profit and loss percentages.

6. Debit *Pete Mason, Capital* for $25,000 and credit *James Miller, Capital* for $25,000.

Answers to Comprehensive Self Review

1. The value changes represent income or loss that should be shared by the existing partners, not by the new partner.

2. Salary withdrawals are cash payments to be charged to the partners' drawing accounts. Salary allowances are part of the income or loss allocation and are charged to *Income Summary* and credited to the partners' capital accounts.

3. One partner may receive an interest and/or salary allowance considerably larger than the other partner receives. Allowances must be recorded, even if there is a loss.

4. The disadvantages of a partnership stem from its inherent characteristics; that is, it brings unlimited liability, mutual agency, lack of continuity, and lack of transferability.

5. Answers may vary but could include:

   - Future plans for the partnership.
   - Potential personality conflicts.
   - Differences in ethical codes of conduct.

Chapter 20

Corporations: Formation and Capital Stock Transactions

ConAgra Foods
www.conagra.com

In 1919, four Nebraska flour mills consolidated and formed the Nebraska Consolidated Mills, and eventually ConAgra. Today, ConAgra Foods is a leading food company. Its brands and products fill the pantries of 97 percent of America's households and provided over $13 billion in sales in 2012.

As of June 24, 2012, ConAgra had approximately 22,600 shareholders of record. Although these shareholders elect the company's board of directors, they probably don't discuss the day-to-day operations of the company with upper management. Nevertheless, they are the owners that profit from the success of the company through higher stock prices and dividends. ConAgra's stock was selling for $25.25 at the end of 2012 and the company paid out an annualized common stock dividend of $.96/per share to each of its shareholders.

Through strategic mergers and acquisitions, ConAgra has expanded beyond simple flour to become the market leader it is today.

thinking critically
What issues do you think ConAgra common stockholders have the right to vote on?

LEARNING OBJECTIVES

20-1. Explain the characteristics of a corporation.

20-2. Describe special "hybrid" organizations that have some characteristics of partnerships and some characteristics of corporations.

20-3. Describe the different types of stock.

20-4. Compute the number of shares of common stock to be issued on the conversion of convertible preferred stock.

20-5. Compute dividends payable on stock.

20-6. Record the issuance of capital stock at par value.

20-7. Prepare a balance sheet for a corporation.

20-8. Record organization costs.

20-9. Record stock issued at a premium and stock with no par value.

20-10. Record transactions for stock subscriptions.

20-11. Describe the capital stock records for a corporation.

20-12. Define the accounting terms new to this chapter.

NEW TERMS

authorized capital stock
bylaws
callable preferred stock
capital stock ledger
capital stock transfer journal
common stock
convertible preferred stock
corporate charter
cumulative preferred stock
dividends
limited liability company (LLC)
limited liability partnership (LLP)
liquidation value
market value
minute book
noncumulative preferred stock

nonparticipating preferred stock
no-par-value stock
organization costs
par value
participating preferred stock
preemptive right
preference dividend
preferred stock
registrar
shareholder
stated value
stock certificate
stockholders' equity
stockholders' ledger
subchapter S corporation (S Corporation)
subscribers' ledger
subscription book
transfer agent

SECTION OBJECTIVES	TERMS TO LEARN
>> **20-1.** Explain the characteristics of a corporation. **WHY IT'S IMPORTANT** The corporate form of business is widely used in the national and international marketplace. >> **20-2.** Describe special "hybrid" organizations that have some characteristics of partnerships and some characteristics of corporations. **WHY IT'S IMPORTANT** "Hybrid" organizations are becoming increasingly popular for the tax advantages and limited liability features they offer.	bylaws corporate charter limited liability company (LLC) limited liability partnership (LLP) shareholder stockholders' equity subchapter S corporation (S corporation)

Forming a Corporation

Previous chapters focused on sole proprietorships and partnerships. Now we consider the third form of business organization, the corporation.

Characteristics of a Corporation

Corporate enterprises account for a majority of business transactions, even though there are more sole proprietorships and partnerships than corporations. Most large national and international businesses use the corporate business form.

In 1818, Chief Justice John Marshall of the U.S. Supreme Court defined the *corporation* as "an artificial being, invisible, intangible, and existing only in contemplation of the law." The corporation is a legal entity, completely separate and apart from its owners. It is created by a **corporate charter** issued by a state government. Since it is a legal entity, a corporation can enter into contracts, can own property, and has almost all of the rights and privileges of a sole proprietorship or a partnership.

Corporations can have few or many owners. A *privately held* corporation is one that is owned by one or more persons and whose stock is not traded on an organized stock exchange. A *publicly held* corporation has many owners and its stock is traded on an organized stock exchange.

A **shareholder** or *stockholder* is a person who owns shares of stock in a corporation and is, thus, one of the owners of the corporation.

>> **20-1. OBJECTIVE**

Explain the characteristics of a corporation.

ADVANTAGES OF THE CORPORATE FORM

The corporate form offers some major advantages:

■ *Limited Liability.* Sole proprietors and general partners have unlimited liability; they are personally liable for all debts of the business. Shareholders have no personal liability for the corporation's debts. The corporation's creditors must look to the assets of the business to satisfy their claims, not to the owners' personal property, even in the event of liquidation. It is not unusual, however, for major shareholders of small corporations to give personal guarantees to repay its loans.

■ *Restricted Agency.* A shareholder has no right to act on behalf of the business. Instead, the board of directors controls the corporation, and the corporate officers are in direct charge of operations. For example, a person who owns 10,000 shares of Microsoft Corporation has no greater power to act on behalf of Microsoft than a person who has no ownership interest at all.

- *Continuous Existence.* The death, disability, or withdrawal of a shareholder has no effect on the life of a corporation.

- *Transferability of Ownership Rights.* Generally, shareholders can sell their stock without consulting or obtaining the consent of the other owners. Shareholders are free to shift their investments at any time, provided they can find buyers for their stock. Organized stock markets, such as the New York Stock Exchange, make it easy to sell or buy interests in corporations whose stocks are traded.

  Small companies often sell shares of stock with a contract that gives the corporation or the existing shareholders "the right of first refusal" to repurchase the shares when the shareholder wishes to sell them.

- *Ease of Raising Capital.* A corporation can have an unlimited number of shareholders. Some corporations have more than a million shareholders, making available a vast pool of capital.

DISADVANTAGES OF THE CORPORATE FORM

Although the advantages are impressive, the corporate form of operation also has certain disadvantages:

- *Corporate Income Tax.* Corporate profits are subject to federal income tax. Profits distributed to shareholders in the form of dividends are taxed a second time as part of the personal income of the stockholder. The taxation of profits at the corporate level and at the shareholder level is known as *double taxation.*

  State and local governments can also levy income taxes on corporations. In addition, most states require corporations to pay an annual franchise tax for the privilege of carrying on business in the state. In some states, especially those that have no corporate income tax, the franchise tax can be quite burdensome.

- *Governmental Regulation.* Corporations are subject to laws and regulations imposed by the state. In general, the state regulatory bodies exercise closer supervision and control over corporations than they do over sole proprietorships or partnerships. State laws may prohibit corporations from entering into particular types of transactions or from owning specific types of property. Special reports are frequently required of corporations.

ENTITIES HAVING ATTRIBUTES OF BOTH PARTNERSHIPS AND CORPORATIONS

Some business entities have characteristics of partnerships and of corporations. Three of these special entities are Subchapter S corporations, limited liability partnerships, and limited liability companies.

Subchapter S Corporations
Subchapter S corporations, also known as *S corporations,* are entities formed as corporations which meet the requirements of Subchapter S of the Internal Revenue Code to be treated essentially as a partnership so the corporation pays no income tax. Instead, shareholders include their share of corporate profits, and any items that require special tax treatment, on their individual income tax returns. Otherwise, S corporations have all the characteristics of regular corporations. The advantage of S corporations is that the owners have limited liability and avoid double taxation.

Limited Liability Partnerships
The **limited liability partnership (LLP)** is a general partnership that provides some limited liability for all partners. LLP partners are responsible and have liability for their own actions and the actions of those under their control or supervision. They are not liable for the actions or malfeasance of another partner. LLPs must have more than one owner, so a sole proprietorship cannot be treated as one. In some states, LLPs are for the service professions only, such as law, accounting, medicine, and engineering.

Except for the limited liability aspect, LLPs generally have the same characteristics, advantages, and disadvantages as any other partnership.

Limited Liability Companies
Limited liability companies (LLCs) provide limited liability to the owners, who can elect to have the profits taxed at the LLC level or on their individual

>> **20-2. OBJECTIVE**
Describe special "hybrid" organizations that have some characteristics of partnerships and some characteristics of corporations.

690 CHAPTER 20 *Corporations: Formation and Capital Stock Transactions*

income tax returns. The profits and losses can be allocated to the owners other than in proportion to the ownership interests. In most states, one individual can form an LLC. Its ownership interests are not freely transferable; other owners must approve a transfer of ownership interest. When transferring ownership, the existing LLC is terminated and a new one formed. Unlike the limited partners discussed in Chapter 19, LLC owners can take part in policy and operating decisions.

Formation of a Corporation

To understand why and how a corporation is formed, place yourself in the shoes of Jack Marvin. Marvin is the sole proprietor of Marvin's Camping Supply Store, a retail business selling camping equipment. Marvin wants to expand the variety of equipment he sells and add guidebooks.

To expand his operations, Marvin needs more money to remodel the store and buy new fixtures, to acquire more inventory, and to extend more credit to customers. Several of Marvin's friends are willing to invest as partners in his business, but he has some doubts about this. Although he needs the extra funds, he does not want to share operating control with people who know nothing about the business. Also, he does not wish to go further in debt.

Marvin's prospective backers have some doubts, too. They do not mind risking the money they invest, but they do not want to be responsible for the debts of the business. Although they do not mind letting Marvin run the business, they do want to have some voice in general policy. They would also like to be assured of a reasonable and regular return on their money.

Marvin and his friends consulted an attorney who specializes in business law and taxation. The lawyer suggested that a corporation offers the best solution to their needs. She explained the necessary steps to form a corporation. Requirements differ from state to state, but typically the process is as follows.

One or more persons, the "organizers" or "promoters," apply to a state officer, usually the secretary of state, for a charter permitting the proposed corporation to do business. The state charges a fee for the charter.

When issued, the charter specifies the exact name, length of life (usually unlimited), rights and duties, and scope of operations of the corporation. Most corporate charters grant the corporation a broad sphere of operation. The charter also sets forth the classes of stock and number of shares in each class that can be issued in exchange for money, property, or services.

Shortly after the charter is issued, the organizers meet to elect an acting board of directors. The corporation proceeds to issue shares of stock to individuals who have paid the full purchase price of the stock. The shareholders then elect permanent directors, usually the same individuals as the acting directors. The directors or shareholders approve the corporation's **bylaws,** which are the guidelines for conducting the corporation's business affairs. The board then selects officers, who hire employees and begin operating the business.

The amount received for the capital stock issued by the corporation appears on the balance sheet. The corporate equivalent of owner's equity is called **stockholders' equity** or shareholders' equity.

Structure of a Corporation

Stockholders can participate in stockholders' meetings, elect a board of directors, and vote on basic corporate policy.

The board of directors formulates general operating policies and is responsible for seeing that the corporation's activities are conducted. The board selects officers and other top management personnel to direct everyday operations. The officers hire managers who hire other employees. Officers and managers make the day-to-day decisions necessary to operate the business.

A corporation's officers include the president, one or more vice presidents, a corporate secretary, and a treasurer. The top accounting official is called the *controller* or *chief financial officer.* Large firms might have several layers of management, including division managers, department heads, and supervisors. The levels depend on the nature and complexity of the operations.

Table 20.1 shows the flow of authority and responsibility in a corporate entity.

Stockholders	• Elect directors
Directors	• Make policies
	• Appoint officers
Officers	• Carry out policies
	• Hire managers
Managers	• Oversee and supervise operations
Other employees	• Perform assigned tasks

TABLE 20.1

Flow of Corporate Authority and Responsibility

Section Self Review

QUESTIONS

1. Which level of government is responsible for issuing charters for most corporations?

2. What are the primary advantages of the corporate form of business?

3. What is the role of stockholders in running the business of a corporation?

EXERCISES

In each exercise, choose the correct option(s).

4. The stockholders of a corporation:

   a. have power to act for the business unless specifically prohibited by the corporate charter.

   b. are generally liable for the debts of the corporation.

   c. can sell their shares of stock without permission from other stockholders.

   d. are forbidden to be employees of the corporation.

5. In a corporate organization, the stockholders:

   a. must pay federal income tax on their proportional shares of profits reported by the corporation.

   b. have the right to surrender preferred stock to the corporation at any time for a payment equal to the par value of the stock.

   c. elect the directors of the corporation.

   d. are entitled to a proportionate share of dividends declared on their classes of stock.

ANALYSIS

6. Lucia Toscas and her husband, Jorje, are sole shareholders in a corporation they formed to operate their existing chain of five restaurants. Their corporation earned net income of approximately $150,000 in their first year of operations. One of Lucia's friends suggested to her that she and Jorje had made a mistake in incorporating and should operate as a sole proprietorship or partnership. What reasons may Lucia use to support their decision to incorporate?

(Answers to Section 1 Self Review are on page 724.)

Types of Capital Stock

Decisions about the classes of stock to be offered and the number of shares of each class must be made before the charter application is filed.

Capital Stock

The **authorized capital stock** is the number of shares authorized for issue by the corporate charter. Usually the authorized stock is more than the number of shares the corporation plans to issue in the foreseeable future. This gives the corporation flexibility to issue stock in the future without having to amend the corporate charter.

When a corporation *issues* stock, the stock is sold (transferred to stockholders). *Outstanding* stock is stock that has been issued and is still in circulation, meaning it is still in the hands of stockholders.

CAPITAL STOCK VALUES

There are three terms commonly used to describe stock values.

Par Value. **Par value** is an amount assigned by the corporate charter to each share of stock for accounting purposes. It is usually $100 or less; it can be $25, $5, or even less than $1 per share. Stock can be issued for more than par value. State laws prohibit the issuance of par-value stock for less than the par value.

Stated Value. State laws permit stock to be issued without par value. This type of stock is called *no-par-value stock.* The value that can be assigned to no-par-value stock by a board of directors for accounting purposes is called the **stated value.**

Market Value. **Market value** is the price per share at which stock is bought and sold. After the corporation issues stock, it can be resold for any price that can be agreed on between the shareholder and purchaser. Usually a stock's market value has little relation to its par or stated value.

CLASSES OF CAPITAL STOCK

>> 20-3. OBJECTIVE
Describe the different types of stock.

Each type, or class, of stock has different rights and privileges.

Common Stock If there is only one class of stock, the stock is called **common stock.** Each share of common stock conveys to the owner the same rights and privileges as every other share including the right to:

- attend stockholders' meetings,
- vote in the election of directors and on other matters (each share entitles the owner to one vote),
- receive dividends as declared by the board of directors,
- purchase a proportionate amount of any new stock issued at a later date, referred to as the **preemptive right.**

If a corporation has two or more classes of stock, one class is common. The other class or classes of stock have certain preferences over the common shares.

> Some corporations have more than one class of preferred stock issued. Typically these shares are issued to help finance specific activities and bear different dividend rates reflecting the differences in economic factors, interest rates prevailing, and relative risks at the time of issuance. For example, Citigroup Corporation has at least seven classes of preferred stock traded on the New York Stock Exchange.

Preferred Stock **Preferred stock** has special claims on the corporate profits or, in case of liquidation, on corporate assets. In receiving special preferences, the owners of preferred stock might lose some of their general rights, such as the right to vote. Unless the charter specifies otherwise, however, preferred stock has voting rights.

Liquidation Preferences on Preferred Stock In case of liquidation, preferred stockholders have a claim on assets before that of common stockholders. A **liquidation value** (usually par value or an amount higher than par value) is assigned to the preferred stock. After the creditors are paid, the preferred stockholders are paid the liquidation value for each share of preferred stock before any assets are distributed to common stockholders. The liquidation value of preferred stock includes any cumulative dividends that have not been paid. (Cumulative dividends are explained later in this chapter.) The liquidation preference on preferred stock is disclosed in the Stockholders' Equity section of the balance sheet.

Assume that a corporation is going out of business. It has paid all of its liabilities. There remains $1,700,000 to distribute to the shareholders. The company has outstanding 25,000 shares of $50 preferred stock, with a liquidation value of $52 per share, and 50,000 shares of $20 par-value common stock. The preferred stockholders will receive $1,300,000 (25,000 shares × $52 per share). The common stockholders will receive what's left, $400,000 ($1,700,000 − $1,300,000).

>> 20-4. OBJECTIVE
Compute the number of shares of common stock to be issued on the conversion of convertible preferred stock.

Convertible Preferred Stock **Convertible preferred stock** is preferred stock that conveys the right to convert that stock to common stock after a specified date or during a period of time. The conversion ratio is the number of shares of common stock that will be issued for each share of preferred stock surrendered. The conversion ratio is indicated on the preferred stock certificate.

Some investors are reluctant to purchase preferred stock because its market price does not increase significantly even if the corporation is quite profitable. The ability to convert preferred stock to common stock can make the preferred stock more attractive to investors. The decision to convert the preferred stock to common stock depends on the market prices, the relative dividends paid on the common and the preferred stock, and the degree of risk involved.

Assume that a corporation has outstanding 100,000 shares of 12 percent, $25 par-value preferred stock that can be converted into common stock. (The term "12 percent" refers to the dividend rate and is discussed on the next page.) The conversion ratio is two shares of common stock for each share of preferred stock surrendered. The conversion privilege is exercisable on or after January 1, 2016. A stockholder can convert 400 shares of preferred stock into 800 (400 × 2) shares of common stock.

Callable Preferred Stock   **Callable preferred stock** gives the issuing corporation the right to repurchase the preferred shares from the stockholders at a specific price. The call price is usually substantially greater than the original issue price. The rights are effective after some specified date. Callable stock gives the corporation flexibility in controlling its capital structure.

The following example illustrates the call feature. Assume a corporation issued 50,000 shares of 10 percent, $40 par-value preferred stock at $40 per share. The corporation has the right to call any part of the preferred stock any time after December 31, 2016, for $53 per share. If the corporation has funds available, or if money can be borrowed at substantially less than 10 percent, the corporation may call the preferred stock and retire it.

>> 20-5. OBJECTIVE

Compute dividends payable on stock.

Dividends on Stock

Dividends are distributions of the profits of a corporation to its shareholders. The right to receive a dividend is one of the major incentives for buying stock. The board of directors declares dividends. The board of directors has complete discretion, subject to certain legal restrictions or contractual restrictions, in deciding whether to declare a dividend and the amount of the dividend. The amount of the dividend depends on the corporation's earnings and on the need to keep profits for use in the business. Dividends are usually paid on a quarterly basis.

DIVIDENDS ON PREFERRED STOCK

Preferred stock has a priority with respect to dividends. The priority is specified in the corporate charter. Preferred stock bears a basic or stated dividend rate, called the **preference dividend,** that must be paid before dividends can be paid on common stock. The *dividend rate* is expressed in dollars-per-share per year or as a percentage. When the dividend is expressed as a percentage, the dividend amount is par value of the stock multiplied by the percentage. For example, the annual dividend on 8 percent preferred stock with a par value of $50 is $4 per share ($50 × 0.08).

Special dividend rights can improve the market demand for preferred shares of stock:

- **Cumulative preferred stock** conveys to its owners the right to receive the preference dividend for the current year and any prior years in which the preference dividend was not paid before common stockholders receive any dividends.

- **Noncumulative preferred stock** conveys to its owners the stated preference dividend for the current year, but stockholders have no rights to dividends for years in which none were declared.

- **Nonparticipating preferred stock** conveys to its owners the right to only the preference dividend amount specified on the stock certificate.

- **Participating preferred stock** conveys the right not only to the preference dividend amount but also to a share of other dividends paid.

DIVIDENDS ON COMMON STOCK

Common stock dividends are paid only after preferred dividend requirements have been met. The fewer the dividend privileges enjoyed by preferred stockholders, the higher the dividends that common stockholders can receive, especially in prosperous years.

The amount of dividends paid each year reflects such factors as the company's trend of profits and cash flows, tax laws, availability of cash, plans for future expansion, and so on. Typically, a company avoids decreases in dividend payouts because a decrease often leads to loss of investor confidence and reduced prices for the stock.

COMPARISON OF DIVIDEND PROVISIONS

Let's analyze several dividend plans.

Only Common Stock Issued Suppose that a corporation has only one class of stock—common stock. Assume that 15,000 shares of $50 par-value common stock are authorized, issued, and outstanding:

■ *Situation 1.* The board of directors declared a 5 percent dividend for the year. Total dividends are $37,500 (15,000 shares × $50 par × 0.05). (The dividend is usually announced as $2.50 per share.)

■ *Situation 2.* The board of directors decides to *pass* the dividend (not declare or pay it).

There is no guarantee that the corporation will pay dividends. The uncertainty of dividends is a risk of owning common stock.

Common and Noncumulative Nonparticipating Preferred Stock Issued Preferred stock reduces the uncertainty of dividends. Assume that a corporation has issued preferred stock and common stock as follows:

Preferred stock, 10% noncumulative, nonparticipating, ($50 par value, 1,000 shares)	$ 50,000
Common stock ($20 par value, 10,000 shares)	200,000
Total capital stock	$250,000

■ *Situation 1.* The board of directors declares dividends of $20,000. The preferred stockholders get first consideration. They receive the preference dividend of $5,000 (1,000 shares × $50 par × 0.10). There is $15,000 ($20,000 − $5,000) to distribute to the common stockholders. The dividend per share for common stock is $1.50 ($15,000 ÷ 10,000 shares).

■ *Situation 2.* The board of directors declares dividends of $10,000. The preferred stockholders receive the preference dividend of $5,000. There is $5,000 ($10,000 − $5,000) to distribute to the common stockholders. The dividend per share of common stock is $0.50 ($5,000 ÷ 10,000 shares).

■ *Situation 3.* The board of directors declares dividends of $4,000. The preferred stockholders receive all of it. The portion of the preference dividend not paid this year ($1,000) will never be paid since the stock is noncumulative. The common stockholders receive no dividends.

Common and Cumulative Nonparticipating Preferred Stock Issued When business conditions are poor, preferred stockholders have a better chance of receiving a dividend than do common stockholders. In turn, cumulative preferred stockholders have a better chance of receiving a dividend than do noncumulative preferred stockholders. The dividends not paid on cumulative preferred stock are carried forward as a continuing claim into future periods. Cumulative preferred dividends not previously paid are shown on the balance sheet or in the footnotes to the financial statements.

When dividends are paid, they are paid in the following order:

1. To holders of cumulative preferred stock for prior year dividends not paid.
2. To preferred stockholders for the preference dividend for the current year.
3. To common stockholders.

Assume that a corporation has issued preferred and common stock as follows:

Preferred stock, 10% cumulative, nonparticipating, ($50 par value, 1,000 shares)	$ 50,000
Common stock ($20 par value, 10,000 shares)	200,000
Total capital stock	$250,000

- *Situation 1.* Last year, $2,000 of preferred dividends were not paid. This year the board of directors declared dividends of $9,000. The dividends are distributed as follows:

  1. To cumulative preferred stockholders for prior year dividends $2,000
  2. To preferred stockholders for this year's preference dividend
     (1,000 shares × $50 par value × 0.10) $5,000
  3. To common stockholders ($9,000 − $2,000 − $5,000) $2,000

- *Situation 2.* The board of directors declares dividends of $45,000. In previous years, all preferred dividends were paid. The cumulative preferred stockholders will receive the preference dividend of $5,000. There is $40,000 ($45,000 − $5,000) to distribute to common shareholders. The dividend per share of common stock is $4 ($40,000 ÷ 10,000 shares).

Common and Cumulative Participating Preferred Stock Issued

When cumulative participating preferred stock is issued, dividend distributions are allocated to preferred and common stock as follows:

1. Preferred stockholders receive any prior year dividends not paid plus the preference dividend for the current year.

2. A specific rate of dividend is paid to common stockholders, equal to the same percentage rate paid to preferred.

3. The dividends that remain are shared between preferred and common stockholders. The participation terms determine how the dividends are shared. Typically, equal rates are paid on common stock and preferred stock.

Since almost all preferred stock is nonparticipating, this textbook provides examples of nonparticipating preferred stock only.

Table 20.2 summarizes the dividend rights of the different classes of stock.

CAPITAL STOCK ON THE BALANCE SHEET

Owner's equity for a corporation is known as stockholders' equity. The Stockholders' Equity section of the balance sheet includes the following information for each class of stock: the number of shares authorized and issued, the par value, and any special privileges carried by the stock. The following illustrates a typical balance sheet presentation for a corporation:

Stockholders' Equity

Preferred Stock (10% noncumulative, $50 par value, 5,000 shares authorized)	$ 50,000
At Par Value (1,000 shares issued)	
Common Stock ($20 par value, 15,000 shares authorized)	
At Par Value (10,000 shares issued)	200,000
Total Stockholders' Equity	$250,000

TABLE 20.2   **Dividend Rights of Different Classes of Stock**

Type of Stock	Dividend Rights
Noncumulative, nonparticipating preferred stock	• Has right to receive preference dividend each year before any dividend can be paid on common stock • If dividend is passed (not paid) in one year, the amount not paid is not cumulative and does not affect dividend payments in future years
Cumulative preferred stock	• Has right to receive preference dividend each year before any dividend can be paid on common stock • If dividend is passed in one year, the amount not paid carries over and must be paid in subsequent year before any dividend can be paid on common stock
Participating preferred stock	• Has right to receive preference dividend each year before any dividend can be paid on common stock • After preference dividend is paid, any additional dividend up to specified rate or amount is paid to common stockholders • After common shareholders have received the specified dividend, preferred and common stock share in remaining dividends
Common stock	• Receives dividends after preferred stock dividends are paid in accordance with contractual obligation

Section 2   Self Review

QUESTIONS

1. Why is preferred stock called "preferred"?

2. How does "participating" preferred stock differ from "cumulative" preferred stock?

3. In what ways, if any, may common stock be preferable to preferred stock?

EXERCISES

4. Carla Company has outstanding 10,000 shares of 10 percent, $50 par-value, cumulative, nonparticipating preferred stock and 25,000 shares of $20 par-value common stock. No dividends were declared in 2016. In 2017, the directors voted to distribute dividends of $48,000.

   a. What amount of dividends, if any, will be distributed to holders of preferred stock?

   b. What amount, if any, will be distributed to holders of common stock?

5. If the preferred shareholders are entitled to receive the preference rate, and in addition to share in any further dividends declared in a year, the stock is known as:

   a. cumulative.

   b. participating.

   c. nonparticipating.

   d. quasi-common.

ANALYSIS

6. Strawboys Company has outstanding 10,000 shares of 8 percent, $50 par-value, cumulative, preferred stock and 20,000 shares of $25 par-value common stock. There are no dividends in arrears on the preferred stock. In 2016, the corporation distributed dividends of $100,000. How much will be distributed to common stockholders and to preferred stockholders?

(Answers to Section 2 Self Review are on page 724.)

Recording Capital Stock Transactions

In this section, you will learn about the entries necessary to record the issuance of capital stock and the records needed to manage capital stock.

Recording the Issuance of Stock

>> 20-6. OBJECTIVE

Record the issuance of capital stock at par value.

Stock is issued after the purchaser has paid for it in full with one of the following:

- cash
- noncash assets
- services rendered

STOCK ISSUED AT PAR VALUE

Assume that Jack Marvin and his associates determine that their new corporation, Camping Supply Center, Inc., will ultimately have capital requirements of $1,800,000. The incorporators decide to issue two classes of stock, preferred and common:

Preferred stock (10%, $100 par value, noncumulative and nonparticipating, 8,000 shares)	$ 800,000
Common stock ($25 par value, 40,000 shares)	1,000,000
Total capital stock	$1,800,000

Marvin transferred the noncash assets and the liabilities of his existing business to the new corporation at the close of business on December 31, 2015. Marvin also invested cash for shares of common stock in the new corporation. Marvin's friends invested cash for common and preferred stock.

When the corporate charter was received, the accounting records were established. The following memorandum entry provides the details of the authorized capital stock:

1	2015			1
2	Dec.	31	Camping Supply Center, Inc., was formed to	2
3			sell camping equipment and supplies and to	3
4			carry on all necessary and related activities.	4
5			It is authorized to issue 40,000 shares of	5
6			$25 par-value common stock and 8,000	6
7			shares of $100 par-value, 10% preferred	7
8			stock that is noncumulative	8
9			and nonparticipating.	9

Data relating to each class of stock are entered on ledger sheets:

ACCOUNT _Common Stock ($25 Par Value; 40,000 Shares Authorized)_   ACCOUNT NO. _301_

					BALANCE	
DATE	DESCRIPTION	POST. REF.	DEBIT	CREDIT	DEBIT	CREDIT

ACCOUNT _$100 Par Value; 8,000 Shares Authorized)_   Preferred Stock (10% Noncumulative, Nonparticipating;   ACCOUNT NO. _311_

					BALANCE	
DATE	DESCRIPTION	POST. REF.	DEBIT	CREDIT	DEBIT	CREDIT

Stock Issued at Par Value for Cash   When stock is issued for cash equal to the par value of the shares, cash proceeds are credited to the capital stock account. Marvin and his colleagues purchased the following number of shares at par value for cash:

	Common Stock Shares	Preferred Stock Shares
Jack Marvin	528	
Karen Wilcox	600	400
Wibb Kamp	400	400
Jill Carrell	200	
Ramon Hill	700	

The receipt of cash was recorded in the cash receipts journal. To simplify the illustration, the entry is shown for Karen Wilcox only in general journal form. Similar entries would be made for other cash purchases of stock.

1	2015					1
11	Dec.	31	Cash ($15,000 + $40,000)	55 00 0 00		11
12			Common Stock (600 x $25)		15 00 0 00	12
13			Preferred Stock (400 x $100)		40 00 0 00	13
14			Issuance of stock to Karen Wilcox:			14
15			600 shares of common at par ($25 per			15
16			share) and 400 shares of preferred at			16
17			par ($100 per share)			17

important!

Capital Stock Account
The amount credited to the capital stock account is the par value of the stock issued.

Stock Issued at Par Value for Noncash Assets The following are the assets and liabilities transferred by Marvin to the corporation:

Assets

Accounts receivable	$ 22,500
Allowance for doubtful accounts	(1,500)
Merchandise inventory	40,000
Land	30,000
Building	72,000
Equipment and fixtures	8,000
Total assets	$171,000

Liabilities

Accounts payable	19,200
Net value of assets transferred	$151,800

Marvin and the other shareholders agreed that Marvin would be issued 800 shares of the $100 par value preferred stock, to be recorded at par value ($80,000). In addition, shares of the $25 par-value common stock are to be issued to Marvin for the difference between the net value of the noncash assets received by the corporation and the par value of the 800 shares of preferred stock. Thus, 2,872 shares of common stock are also issued:

Net value of assets transferred	$151,800
Par value of preferred stock issued (800 shares × $100 per share)	80,000
Par value of common stock to be issued	$ 71,800

Number of common shares to be issued:
  $71,800 ÷ $25 per share = 2,872 shares

The transaction is recorded as follows:

	2015							
1								1
18	Dec.	31	Accounts Receivable	22 5 0 0 00				18
19			Merchandise Inventory	40 0 0 0 00				19
20			Land	30 0 0 0 00				20
21			Building	72 0 0 0 00				21
22			Equipment and Fixtures	8 0 0 0 00				22
23			Allowance for Doubtful Accounts		1 5 0 0 00			23
24			Accounts Payable		19 2 0 0 00			24
25			Common Stock (2,872 x $25)		71 8 0 0 00			25
26			Preferred Stock (800 x $100)		80 0 0 0 00			26
27			Issuance of stock in payment for net					27
28			noncash assets of Camping Supply					28
29			Store, 2,872 shares of $25 par					29
30			common stock at $25 per share and					30
31			800 shares of $100 par preferred					31
32			stock at $100 per share					32

The assets and liability are recorded at fair market value. ***Accounts Receivable*** and ***Allowance for Doubtful Accounts*** are recorded separately. The $22,500 balance in the ***Accounts Receivable*** control account agrees with the total of the accounts receivable subsidiary ledger.

Preparing a Balance Sheet for a Corporation Figure 20.1 shows the balance sheet for Camping Supply Center, Inc., immediately following the organization of the corporation. The balance sheet reflects the acquisition of the assets and liabilities of Marvin's Camping Supply Store by the issuance of stock and the issuance of stock for cash.

recall

Owner's Investment
Common and preferred stock are owners' (stockholders') equity accounts. Increases to owners' equity accounts are recorded as credits.

>> **20-7. OBJECTIVE**
Prepare a balance sheet for a corporation.

FIGURE 20.1

Corporate Balance Sheet Prepared After Organization

Camping Supply Center, Inc.
Balance Sheet
December 31, 2015

Assets				
Current Assets				
Cash			140 7 0 0 00	
Accounts Receivable	22 5 0 0 00			
Less Allowance for Doubtful Accounts	1 5 0 0 00		21 0 0 0 00	
Merchandise Inventory			40 0 0 0 00	
Total Current Assets			201 7 0 0 00	
Property, Plant, and Equipment				
Land	30 0 0 0 00			
Building	72 0 0 0 00			
Equipment and Fixtures	8 0 0 0 00			
Total Property, Plant, and Equipment			110 0 0 0 00	
Total Assets			311 7 0 0 00	
Liabilities and Stockholders' Equity				
Current Liabilities				
Accounts Payable			19 2 0 0 00	
Stockholders' Equity				
Preferred Stock (10%, $100 par value,				
8,000 shares authorized)				
At Par Value (1,600 shares issued)	160 0 0 0 00			
Common Stock ($25 par value, 40,000				
shares authorized)				
At Par Value (5,300 shares issued)	132 5 0 0 00			
Total Stockholders' Equity			292 5 0 0 00	
Total Liabilities and Stockholders' Equity			311 7 0 0 00	

Recording Organization Costs A variety of costs are incurred when a business is incorporated, including legal fees, attorneys' fees, charter fees paid to the state, and the cost of the organizational meeting of the directors.

Organization costs are incurred to provide benefit over the entire life of the corporation because they are necessary in order for the entity to exist and carry on business. For this reason, organization costs in the past have been capitalized and amortized over an arbitrary period. A common amortization period was five years. That practice resulted from federal income tax requirements that the costs be capitalized and subsequently amortized over a period of not less than 60 months. Some corporations, however, simply recorded the costs as an intangible asset and did not amortize the costs for financial accounting purposes.

In Chapter 18, the accounting requirements for intangible assets that do not have an identifiable economic or legal life were discussed. You will recall that intangibles such as purchased "goodwill," which has an indefinite life, must be examined each year to see whether there have been developments suggesting impairment. If such developments have occurred, further tests must be made to see if there is impairment and, if so, how much. Since organization costs have no fixed legal life, these costs would, if capitalized, be an intangible that would have to be tested for impairment. But it is even more difficult to estimate the value of organization

>> **20-8. OBJECTIVE**

Record organization costs.

costs than to estimate the value of goodwill. Because of this fact, and the additional fact that the amount spent for organization costs is typically immaterial, the usual practice today is to charge organization costs to expense during the first financial reporting period after the corporation begins activities.

Some smaller companies whose shares are not publicly traded and who do not have audits by CPAs attesting that the corporation follows generally accepted accounting principles continue to capitalize organization costs and typically amortize the costs over the same period used for income tax purposes.

On January 18, Camping Supply Center, Inc., paid $2,000 of organization costs to its attorney. The amount includes legal fees, reimbursement for the charter fee, and the cost of drafting and printing the stock certificates. This reimbursement is recorded by a debit to *Organization Expense* and a credit to *Cash.*

>> **20-9. OBJECTIVE**

Record stock issued at a premium and stock with no par value.

STOCK ISSUED AT A PREMIUM

If the corporation has the potential for earning very attractive profits, investors are willing to pay more than par value to become stockholders. Likewise, if the preferred stock dividend is more attractive than other investments with similar risk, investors are willing to pay more than par value. The amount received by a corporation that is in excess of the par value is called a *premium*. A premium on preferred stock is credited to an account called *Paid-in Capital in Excess of Par Value—Preferred Stock.*

Suppose that Mai Nguyen, a new shareholder, agreed to pay $105 per share for 400 shares of preferred stock of Camping Supply Center, Inc. She paid a premium of $5 per share ($105 price−$100 par). The general journal entry for this transaction is:

THE BOTTOM LINE

Purchase of Preferred Stock
at a Premium

Income Statement

No effect on net income

Balance Sheet

| Assets | ↑ 42,000 |
| Equity | ↑ 42,000 |

>>

	2016					1
1	2016					1
2	Mar.	2	Cash	42 00 00		2
3			Preferred Stock		40 00 00	3
4			Paid-in Capital in Excess of Par			4
5			Value—Preferred Stock		2 00 00	5
6			Issuance of 400 shares for $105			6
7			per share			7

In the Stockholders' Equity section of the balance sheet shown below, the amount of the new account, *Paid-in Capital in Excess of Par Value—Preferred Stock,* is added to the par value of the shares issued to show the total paid in by that class of stockholder. (The account title might also be *Premium on Preferred Stock* or a similar name.)

important!

In Excess of Par

The amount credited to the *Paid-In Capital in Excess of Par Value* account is the price paid by the stockholder minus the par value of the stock multiplied by the number of shares issued.

Stockholders' Equity

Preferred Stock (10%, $100 par value, 8,000 shares authorized)

At Par Value (2,000 shares issued)	$200,000
Paid-in Capital in Excess of Par Value	2,000
	$202,000

At the end of its fiscal year ending January 31, 2013, Walmart had authorized 100 million shares of preferred stock with 10 cents par value, of which none had been issued. The company's authorized common stock was 11 billion shares, with par value of $0.10. The company had issued 3.5 billion shares of common stock. As a result, its Common Stock account had a balance of $332 million. At the same time, the balance sheet reflected "Capital In Excess of Par Value" of $3.620 billion and Retained Earnings of $72.978 billion.

ISSUANCE OF NO-PAR-VALUE STOCK

No-par-value stock is not assigned a par value in the corporate charter. No-par-value stock has theoretical advantages over par-value stock:

- No-par-value stock can be issued at any price. Par-value stock cannot be issued for less than its par value.

- If there is no par value, investors cannot confuse par value and market value.

No-Par-Value Stock without Stated Value Some states require no-par-value stock to be assigned a stated value. Even if it is not required, the board of directors can assign a stated value. If no-par-value stock does not have a stated value, the proceeds from the issue of shares are credited to the *Common Stock* account. For example, suppose that Nature's Best Snacks Corporation is authorized to issue no-par-value common stock. A stated value has not been assigned the shares. On March 4, the corporation issued 1,000 shares for $20 per share, and on March 15, it issued 600 shares for $22 per share. The two stock issues are recorded as follows:

1	2016				1
2	Mar.	4	Cash	20 000 00	2
3			Common Stock	20 000 00	3
4			Issue of 1,000 shares of no-par-value		4
5			common stock at $20 per share		5
6					6
7		15	Cash	13 200 00	7
8			Common Stock	13 200 00	8
9			Issue of 600 shares of no-par-value		9
10			common stock at $22 per share		10

No-Par-Value Stock with Stated Value Most no-par-value stock is assigned a stated value by the board of directors. The stated value is treated like par value. If no-par-value common stock with a stated value is issued at a price higher than the stated value, the stated value is credited to the *Common Stock* account. Any excess received over stated value is treated as a premium and credited to *Paid-in Capital in Excess of Stated Value.*

For example, Midland Music Corporation is authorized to issue no-par-value common stock. The board of directors assigned $25 as the stated value of the stock. On April 1, the corporation issued 2,400 shares at $26 per share. The stock issuance is recorded as shown:

1	2016				1
2	Apr.	1	Cash	62 400 00	2
3			Common Stock	60 000 00	3
4			Paid-in Capital in Excess of Stated		4
5			Value	2 400 00	5
6			Issue of 2,400 shares of common		6
7			stock at $26 per share		7

The credit to the *Paid-in Capital in Excess of Stated Value* account is $2,400 [($26 price − $25 stated value) × 2,400 shares]. On the balance sheet, the premium is shown as an addition to the stated value to show the total paid by common stockholders.

SUMMARY OF RECORDING RULES FOR PAR-VALUE AND NO-PAR-VALUE STOCK

Table 20.3 on the next page summarizes the effects on the capital accounts of issuing stock with and without a par value.

MANAGERIAL IMPLICATIONS <<

CORPORATION CONSIDERATIONS

- New business owners should have a clear idea of the nature of a corporation, its rights and limitations, and how the corporation differs from other forms of business organization.
- Management and stockholders need to realize that the corporation is a separate legal entity apart from its owners and that regardless of changes in ownership, the corporation continues to exist.
- New business owners need to understand the disadvantages of the corporate form of business including double taxation and government regulation.
- In order to select the most beneficial capital structure, management needs to be familiar with the various classes of stock. Management is responsible for ensuring the following:
  - Assets acquired through the issue of stock are recorded at fair market value so that the corporation's profitability can be properly computed and evaluated.
  - Capital stock issues are properly recorded and tracked.
  - Stock subscriptions are in conformity with state laws and the accounting records fully reflect all information relating to stock subscriptions.

- The corporation has adequate records to comply with legal requirements and to track stockholder transactions.
- Officers act within the limitations set by the board of directors and the shareholders.
- The bylaws and charter provisions of the corporation are carefully followed, and minutes are kept of all meetings of directors and stockholders.
- Management needs to be aware that state laws prohibit the issuance of stock at less than par value.
- Management must be aware that actions of the board of directors, as reported in the corporate minutes, often have accounting effects.

THINKING CRITICALLY

Why must the management and directors of a corporation be fully informed about laws and regulations affecting corporations? How can they find out what they need to know?

TABLE 20.3

Comparison of Rules for Par-Value and No-Par-Value Stock

Par-Value Stock	No-Par-Value Stock	
	Stated Value	No Stated Value
Par value is specified in corporate charter.	Stated value is assigned by directors. Corporate charter indicates that stock is no-par-value stock.	Corporate charter indicates that stock is no-par-value stock.
Stock certificate indicates par value.	Stock certificate generally does not show stated value.	Stock certificate shows that stock is no-par-value stock.
Change in par value requires revision of charter.	Stated value can be changed by directors.	
On issue of stock, par value is credited to capital stock account.	On issue of stock, stated value is credited to capital stock account.	On issue of stock, entire proceeds are credited to capital stock account.

Subscriptions for Capital Stock

Some prospective stockholders want to buy stock and pay for it later. They sign a subscription contract that states the stock price and describes the payment plan. They receive the stock when payment is made. A stock subscription is recorded as a receivable from the subscriber. The corporation must have stock available to issue when the subscription is paid in full.

>> **20-10. OBJECTIVE**

Record transactions for stock subscriptions.

RECEIPT OF SUBSCRIPTIONS

On May 1, Camping Supply Center, Inc., received a subscription from Tyrone Coles to purchase 400 shares of common stock at $25 per share. Coles is to pay for the stock in full on June 1. The corporation also received a subscription from Remu Patel to purchase 400 shares of preferred stock at $105 per share. Patel is to pay for the stock in two equal installments, on June 1 and July 1. These subscriptions are recorded as follows:

	2016					
1						1
2	May	1	Subscriptions Receivable—Common	10 000 00		2
3			Common Stock Subscribed		10 000 00	3
4			Subscription from Tyrone Coles to buy			4
5			400 shares of common stock at par			5
6			value of $25 per share			6
7						7
8		1	Subscriptions Receivable—Preferred	42 000 00		8
9			Preferred Stock Subscribed		40 000 00	9
10			Paid-in Capital in Excess of Par Value—			10
11			Preferred Stock		2 000 00	11
12			Subscription from Remu Patel to buy			12
13			400 shares of $100 par preferred stock			13
14			at $105 per share			14

A separate **Subscriptions Receivable** account is used for each class of stock. There are also separate **Stock Subscribed** accounts. When the subscriptions are paid in full, the stock is issued. Until then, the **Stock Subscribed** accounts appear in the Stockholders' Equity section of the balance sheet as additions to the class of stock issued.

For example, immediately after the receipt of Patel's stock subscription, the preferred stock in the Stockholders' Equity section of the balance sheet appears as follows:

Stockholders' Equity

Preferred Stock (10%, $100 par value, 8,000 shares authorized)

At Par Value (2,000 shares issued)	$200,000
Subscribed (400 shares)	40,000
Paid-in Capital in Excess of Par Value	4,000
	$244,000

COLLECTION OF SUBSCRIPTIONS AND ISSUANCE OF STOCK

When Coles pays his $10,000 subscription in full on June 1, the corporation issues 400 shares of common stock to him. The $10,000 is recorded in the cash receipts journal. To simplify the illustration, the transaction is shown in general journal form, followed by an entry to record the issuance of the stock:

	2016					
1						1
2	June	1	Cash	10 000 00		2
3			Subscriptions Receivable—Common		10 000 00	3
4			Received Tyrone Coles's subscription			4
5			in full			5
6						6
7		1	Common Stock Subscribed	10 000 00		7
8			Common Stock		10 000 00	8
9			Issued 400 shares of common stock to			9
10			Tyrone Coles			10

important!

Stock Subscriptions

Subscriptions receivable accounts are presented in the asset section. Stock subscribed accounts are presented in the Stockholders' Equity section of the balance sheet.

When these entries are posted, the *Subscriptions Receivable—Common* and *Common Stock Subscribed* accounts are closed. Both *Cash* and *Common Stock* are increased by $10,000:

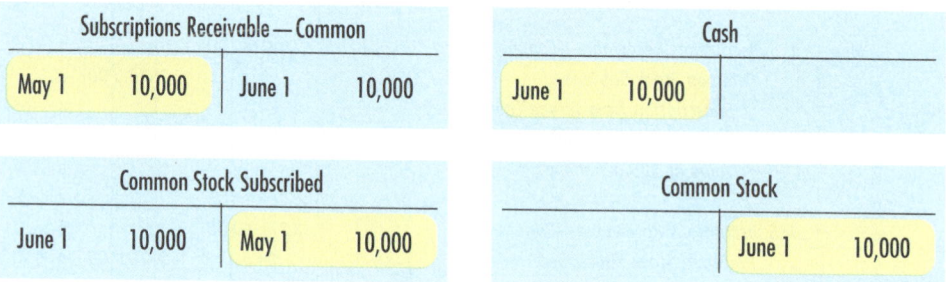

Patel paid his preferred stock subscription in two monthly installments of $21,000 each. The company debits each payment to *Cash* and credits *Subscriptions Receivable—Preferred.*

After Patel makes the second payment, the corporation issues the stock to him. The collection of the final installment and the issuance of the stock are recorded in the general journal as shown:

1	2016				1
2	July	1	Cash	21 000 00		2
3			Subscriptions Receivable—Preferred		21 000 00	3
4			Receipt of final installment from			4
5			Remu Patel on his stock subscription			5
6						6
7		1	Preferred Stock Subscribed	40 000 00		7
8			Preferred Stock		40 000 00	8
9			Issuance of 400 shares of preferred			9
10			stock to Remu Patel			10

This stock subscription transaction resulted in a $42,000 increase in *Cash,* a $40,000 increase in *Preferred Stock,* and a $2,000 increase in *Paid-in Capital in Excess of Par Value—Preferred Stock:*

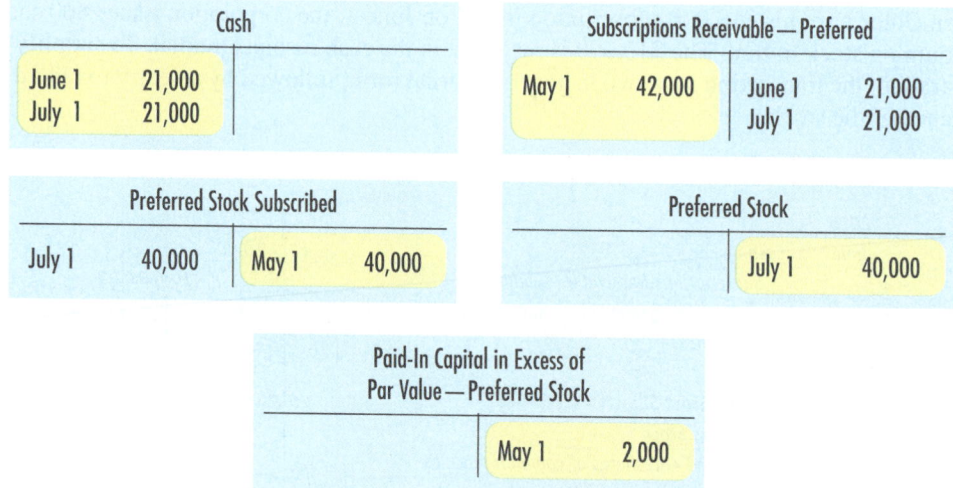

Special Corporation Records and Agents

Corporations keep detailed records of stockholders' equity. They maintain special corporate records such as:

- minutes of meetings of stockholders and directors,
- corporate bylaws,
- stock certificate books,
- stock ledgers,
- stock transfer records.

>> 20-11. OBJECTIVE
Describe the capital stock records for a corporation.

MINUTE BOOK

A **minute book** keeps accurate and complete records of all meetings of stockholders and directors. The minute book formally reports actions taken, directives issued, directors elected, officers elected, and other matters.

STOCK CERTIFICATE BOOKS

Capital stock is usually issued by a corporation in the form of a **stock certificate.** A separate series of stock certificates is prepared for each class of stock. A corporation that expects to issue few stock certificates can have them prepared in books. Each certificate is numbered consecutively and attached to a stub from which it is separated at the time of issuance. The certificate indicates the:

- name of the corporation,
- name of the stockholder to whom the certificate was issued,
- class of stock,
- number of shares.

Certificates are valid when they are properly signed by corporate officers and have the corporate seal affixed to them.

Figure 20.2 on the next page shows a common stock certificate for The McGraw-Hill Companies, Inc. Certificates for preferred stock are similar to those for common stock and include the details of the preferred stock.

Capital Stock Ledger It is essential for corporations to keep accurate records of the shares of stock issued and the names and addresses of the stockholders. This information is needed to mail dividend checks and official notices about stockholders' meetings and votes.

To keep the required information, corporations set up a **capital stock ledger,** or **stockholders' ledger,** for each class of stock issued. There is a sheet for each stockholder with the following information:

- stockholder's name and address,
- dates of transactions affecting stock holdings,
- certificate numbers,
- number of shares for each transaction.

The balance shows the number of shares held. The ledger sheets can also include a record of dividends. For each class of stock, the stockholders' ledger is a subsidiary to the capital stock account. The total shares shown in the stockholders' ledger must agree with the number of shares in the capital stock account for that class.

After the corporation issues stock, new stockholders purchase shares from existing stockholders. The process is as follows:

- The buyer pays the seller.
- The seller surrenders the stock certificate to the corporation.
- The corporation issues a new certificate to the buyer.

FIGURE 20.2

Stock Certificate

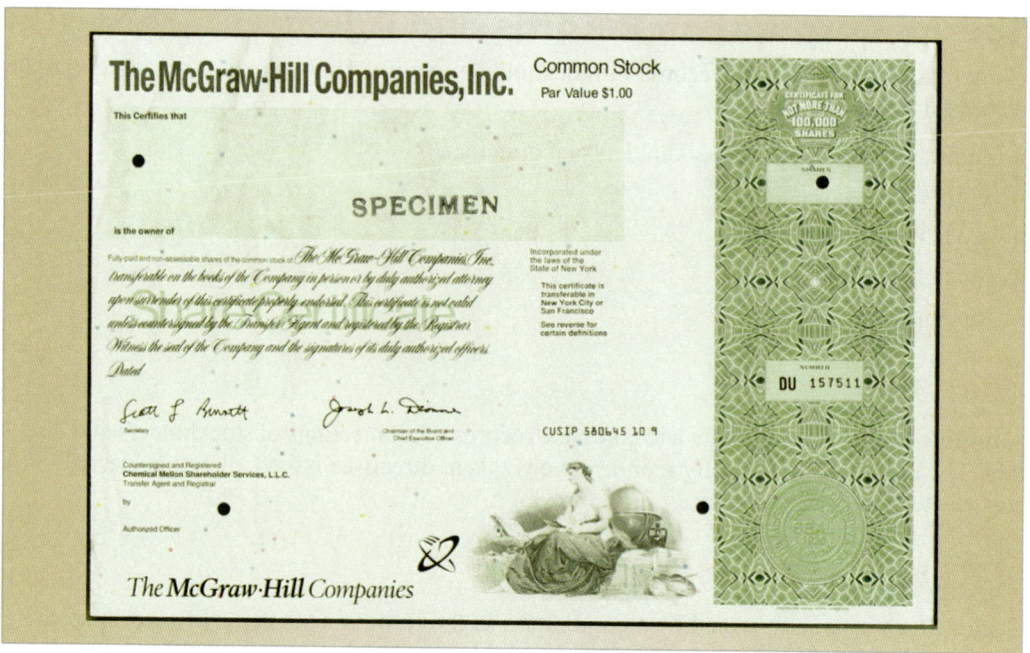

The **capital stock transfer journal** is a record of stock transfers used for posting to the stockholders' ledger. There is a capital stock transfer journal for each class of stock issued by the corporation.

RECORDS OF STOCK SUBSCRIPTIONS

The corporation tracks stock subscriptions using the subscription book and the subscribers' ledger. The **subscription book**:

■ is a listing of the stock subscriptions received,

■ shows the names and addresses of the subscribers,

■ shows the number of shares subscribed,

■ contains the amounts and times of payment.

A subscription book can contain the actual stock subscription contracts.

The **subscribers' ledger** contains an account receivable for each stock subscriber. The account is debited for the total subscription and credited when the subscriber makes payments. The subscribers' ledger is a subsidiary ledger. The balances of the individual subscriber accounts must agree with the *Subscriptions Receivable* control account in the general ledger.

SUMMARY OF STOCK CONTROL ACCOUNTS AND SUBSIDIARY LEDGERS

Table 20.4 shows the relationship between control accounts and subsidiary ledgers for corporate stock recordkeeping.

SPECIAL AGENTS

Corporations whose stock is widely held and actively traded do not keep their own stockholder records. Instead, they turn the responsibility over to a transfer agent and a registrar. The **transfer agent** receives the stock certificates surrendered. A bank that serves as a transfer agent is often chosen for its proximity to the stock exchange or market where the corporation's stock is expected to trade. The same bank may also be appointed registrar.

Control Account	Subsidiary Ledger
Common Stock	Common Stockholders' Ledger
	Contains an account for each owner of common stock and shows shares bought or transferred and the balance of shares owned
Preferred Stock	Preferred Stockholders' Ledger
	Contains an account for each owner of preferred stock and shows shares bought or transferred and the balance of shares owned
Subscriptions Receivable — Common Stock	Subscribers' Ledger — Common
	Contains the account receivable for each subscriber to common stock
Subscriptions Receivable — Preferred Stock	Subscribers' Ledger — Preferred
	Contains an account receivable for each subscriber to preferred stock

TABLE 20.4

Relationship between Control Accounts and Subsidiary Stock Ledgers

recall

Subsidiary Ledgers
The total of the individual accounts must agree with the control account in the general ledger.

An assignment form on the certificate indicates to whom a new certificate should be issued. The agent:

- cancels the old certificates,
- issues the new ones,
- makes the necessary entries in the capital stock ledger,
- prepares lists of stockholders who should receive dividend payments and notices.

The agent might also prepare and mail the dividend checks.

The **registrar** accounts for all the stock issued by the corporation and makes sure that the corporation does not issue more shares than are authorized. The registrar receives from the transfer agent all the canceled certificates and all the new certificates issued. The registrar must countersign the new certificates before they are valid.

Section 3   Self Review

QUESTIONS

1. How do stated value and par value of stock differ?

2. What are the advantages of issuing no-par-value stock?

3. What are organization costs? How are they accounted for?

EXERCISES

4. Duck Company receives a subscription to 2,000 shares of its $25 par value common stock for $31 per share. What accounts are debited and credited, and for what amounts? If a balance sheet was prepared on the following day, how would the accounts debited and credited be shown on the balance sheet?

5. Which, if any, of the following statements are generally true? The stated value of no-par common stock is:

   a. specified in the corporate charter.

   b. shown on the stock certificate.

   c. can be changed by the board of directors.

   d. credited to the **Common Stock** account when issued and any excess of issue price over stated value is credited to **Paid-in Capital in Excess of Stated Value**.

ANALYSIS

6. James McKee was one of the founders of PTM Corporation. Each of the founders, the only three shareholders, owns 10,000 shares of common stock. McKee has had disagreements with the other two owners, who have told McKee that the two of them plan to purchase another 5,000 shares each and to sell 15,000 to a new shareholder. McKee comes to you and asks you whether he should go to his lawyer with the idea of bringing a lawsuit to prevent what they plan to do. Ignoring the legal question of whether he will succeed in his lawsuit, what is the "shareholder right" that McKee is pursuing? Briefly explain that right.

(Answers to Section 3 Self Review are on pages 724 and 725.)

20 Chapter REVIEW Chapter Summary

In this chapter, you have learned about the basic characteristics of a corporation and the accounting procedures unique to its formation and operation. You have learned about capital stock transactions, dividend declarations, and reporting of stockholders' equity on the balance sheet.

Learning Objectives

20-1 Explain the characteristics of a corporation.

A corporation is organized under state law to carry on activities permitted by its charter:

- Ownership is indicated by shares of stock.
- Stockholders owning voting stock elect a board of directors.
- The board selects officers to run the business.
- The corporate charter specifies the types and amounts of capital stock authorized.
- The bylaws guide the firm's general operation, which must be consistent with charter provisions.
- The corporation is subject to federal income tax.

20-2 Describe special "hybrid" organizations that have some characteristics of partnerships and some characteristics of corporations.

A corporation formed as an S corporation is taxed as a partnership. The limited liability partnership and limited liability company avoid federal corporate income tax and also provide limited liability.

20-3 Describe the different types of stock.

If a corporation issues only one type of stock, it is called *common stock*. Common stockholders vote on corporate matters and receive dividends as declared by the board of directors.

Corporations can issue a second class of stock that carries special preferences, called *preferred stock*. Preferred stockholders are often given priority in the distribution of dividends. Liquidation value is often assigned to preferred stock; this stock class may be convertible to common stock.

20-4 Compute the number of shares of common stock to be issued on the conversion of convertible preferred stock.

Convertible preferred stock gives its owners the right to convert their shares into common stock after a specified date by using the stated conversion ratio.

20-5 Compute dividends payable on stock.

The board of directors declares dividends based on corporate earnings. Dividends are first allocated to preferred stockholders, then to common stockholders.

20-6 Record the issuance of capital stock at par value.

The entire amount of stock issued in return for a cash investment is credited to the appropriate capital stock account. Noncash assets traded for capital stock are recorded at their fair market value.

20-7 Prepare a balance sheet for a corporation.

The Stockholders' Equity section identifies the classes, values, and number of stock authorized and issued.

20-8 Record organization costs.

Organization costs are charged to expense when incurred. For income tax purposes, they are capitalized and amortized over a period of not less than 60 months.

20-9 Record stock issued at a premium and stock with no par value.

A premium on stock is recorded in a *Paid-in Capital in Excess of Par Value* account. Stock without a par value is called *no-par-value stock*. A few states require it to be assigned a stated value, similar to par value for accounting purposes.

20-10 Record transactions for stock subscriptions.

Stock can be subscribed, then paid for and issued later. It is recorded in a subsidiary ledger with a separate account receivable for each subscriber. Individual accounts receivable are controlled by a *Subscriptions Receivable* account in the general ledger.

20-11 Describe the capital stock records for a corporation.

Corporate records must include minute books, stockholders' ledgers, stock certificate books, and stock transfer records.

20-12 Define the accounting terms new to this chapter.

Glossary

Authorized capital stock (p. 692) The number of shares authorized for issue by the corporate charter

Bylaws (p. 690) The guidelines for conducting a corporation's business affairs

Callable preferred stock (p. 694) Stock that gives the issuing corporation the right to repurchase the preferred shares from the stockholders at a specific price

Capital stock ledger (p. 707) A subsidiary ledger that contains a record of each stockholder's purchases, transfers, and current balance of shares owned; also called stockholders' ledger

Capital stock transfer journal (p. 708) A record of stock transfers used for posting to the stockholders' ledger

Common stock (p. 693) The general class of stock issued when no other class of stock is authorized; each share carries the same rights and privileges as every other share. Even if preferred stock is issued, common stock will also be issued

Convertible preferred stock (p. 693) Preferred stock that conveys the right to convert that stock to common stock after a specified date or during a period of time

Corporate charter (p. 688) A document issued by a state government that establishes a corporation

Cumulative preferred stock (p. 694) Stock that conveys to its owners the right to receive the preference dividend for the current year and any prior years in which the preference dividend was not paid before common stockholders receive any dividends

Dividends (p. 694) Distributions of the profits of a corporation to its shareholders

Limited liability company (LLC) (p. 689) Provides limited liability to the owners, who can elect to have the profits taxed at the LLC level or on their individual tax returns

Limited liability partnership (LLP) (p. 689) A partnership that provides limited liability for all partners

Liquidation value (p. 693) Value of assets to be applied to preferred stock, usually par value or an amount in excess of par value, if the corporation is liquidated

Market value (p. 692) The price per share at which stock is bought and sold

Minute book (p. 707) A book in which accurate and complete records of all meetings of stockholders and directors are kept

Noncumulative preferred stock (p. 694) Stock that conveys to its owners the stated preference dividend for the current year but no rights to dividends for years in which none were declared

Nonparticipating preferred stock (p. 694) Stock that conveys to its owners the right to only the preference dividend amount specified on the stock certificate

No-par-value stock (p. 703) Stock that is not assigned a par value in the corporate charter

Organization costs (p. 701) The costs associated with establishing a corporation

Par value (p. 692) An amount assigned by the corporate charter to each share of stock for accounting purposes

Participating preferred stock (p. 694) Stock that conveys the right not only to the preference dividend amount but also to a share of other dividends paid

Preemptive right (p. 693) A shareholder's right to purchase a proportionate amount of any new stock issued at a later date

Preference dividend (p. 694) A basic or stated dividend rate for preferred stock that must be paid before dividends can be paid on common stock

Preferred stock (p. 693) A class of stock that has special claims on the corporate profits or, in case of liquidation, on corporate assets

Registrar (p. 709) A person or institution in charge of the issuance and transfer of a corporation's stock

Shareholder (p. 688) A person who owns shares of stock in a corporation; also called a stockholder

Stated value (p. 692) The value that can be assigned to no-par-value stock by a board of directors for accounting purposes

Stock certificate (p. 707) The form by which capital stock is issued; the certificate indicates the name of the corporation, the name of the stockholder to whom the certificate was issued, the class of stock, and the number of shares

Stockholders' equity (p. 690) The corporate equivalent of owners' equity; also called shareholders' equity

Stockholders' ledger (p. 707) See Capital stock ledger

Subchapter S corporation (S corporation) (p. 689) An entity formed as a corporation that meets the requirements of Subchapter S of the Internal Revenue Code to be treated essentially as a partnership, so that the corporation pays no income tax

Subscribers' ledger (p. 708) A subsidiary ledger that contains an account receivable for each stock subscriber

Subscription book (p. 708) A list of the stock subscriptions received

Transfer agent (p. 708) A person or institution that handles all stock transfers and transfer records for a corporation

---

Comprehensive **Self Review**

1. How are the *Stock Subscribed* accounts reported in the financial statements?
2. What does market value of a stock mean?
3. What information is found in the subscribers' ledger?
4. What are the duties of the corporation's registrar?
5. What is the special right conveyed to holders of convertible preferred stock?
6. What is callable preferred stock?
7. What is the special benefit of a limited liability partnership?
8. What is the "preemptive right" of a shareholder?

(Answers to Comprehensive Self Review are on page 725.)

Discussion Questions

1. Why would a new corporation issue no-par stock with a stated value, rather than par-value stock?
2. Selling stock on a subscription basis involves considerable record keeping. Why does a corporation sell its shares in this way?
3. How are the members of a corporation's board of directors selected?
4. What is the purpose of the minute book?
5. What is the role of the transfer agent?
6. What is meant by the "par-value of stock"?
7. What does the term "restricted agency" mean?
8. Who makes the day-to-day decisions necessary for a corporation to operate?
9. Describe the flow of authority and responsibility in a corporate entity.
10. What is a stock subscription?
11. What are organization costs?
12. What role does the registrar of a corporation serve?
13. How are organization costs accounted for?
14. What is the control account for the individual shareholder accounts in the common stockholders' ledger?

15. What is participating preferred stock?

16. What is cumulative preferred stock?

17. When common stock without a par value or a stated value is issued, what amount is credited to the capital stock account when the stock is issued?

18. What is convertible preferred stock?

19. What is the difference between the *Common Stock Subscribed* account and the *Subscriptions Receivable—Common Stock* account?

20. Where is the usual place for organizers of a new corporation to acquire a corporate charter?

21. What are the corporation's bylaws?

22. If there is only one class of stock, what is it called?

23. What are some benefits of a Subchapter S corporation?

24. How does par value differ from stated value?

APPLICATIONS

Exercises

Computing dividends payable.

◀ **Exercise 20.1**
Objective 20-5

Mayflower Corporation has only one class of stock. There are 90,000 shares outstanding. During 2016, the corporation's net income after taxes was $990,000. The policy of the corporation is to declare dividends equal to 20 percent of its net income. Sherrye White owns 350 shares of the stock. How much will White receive as a dividend on her shares?

Computing dividends payable.

◀ **Exercise 20.2**
Objective 20-5

International Grocer Corporation has outstanding 50,000 shares of noncumulative, 8 percent, $100 par-value preferred stock and 80,000 shares of no-par-value common stock.

1. During 2016, the corporation paid dividends of $360,000. What amount will be paid on each share of preferred stock? What amount will be paid on each share of common stock?

2. During 2017, the corporation paid dividends of $880,000. How much will be paid on each share of preferred stock? How much will be paid on each share of common stock?

Computing dividends payable.

◀ **Exercise 20.3**
Objective 20-5

Zale Corporation has outstanding 110,000 shares of 12 percent, $80 par-value cumulative preferred stock and 500,000 shares of no-par-value common stock.

1. During 2016, the corporation paid dividends of $792,000. What amount will be paid on each share of preferred stock? What amount will be paid on each share of common stock?

2. During 2017, the corporation distributed dividends of $1,720,000. What amount will be paid on each share of preferred stock? What amount will be paid on each share of common stock?

Converting preferred stock.

◀ **Exercise 20.4**
Objective 20-4

Palmer Corporation has outstanding 85,000 shares of $30 par-value preferred stock, issued at an average price of $37 a share. The preferred stock is convertible into common stock at the rate of three shares of common stock for each share of preferred stock. Sadic Judge owns 570 shares of the preferred stock. During the current year, she decides to convert 340 shares into common stock. How many shares of common stock will she receive?

Issuing stock for assets.

◀ **Exercise 20.5**
Objective 20-6

Roy Anderson, the owner of a sole proprietorship, is planning to incorporate his business. His capital account has a balance of $350,000 after revaluation of the assets. His cash account totals

$104,000. He will receive 8 percent, $40 par-value preferred stock with a total par value equal to the cash transferred. The balance of his capital is to be exchanged for shares of $40 par-value common stock with a total par value equal to the remaining capital. How many shares of preferred stock should be issued to Anderson? How many shares of common stock should be issued to Anderson?

Exercise 20.6
Objective 20-8

▶ **Accounting for organization costs.**

Zemor Company, a newly organized corporation, received a bill from its lawyers for $12,000 for time spent in organizing the company.

1. How should these costs be treated in the financial reports?
2. How should they be treated for federal income tax purposes?

Exercise 20.7
Objective 20-6

▶ **Issuing stock at par value for cash.**

On January 2, 2016, Cotton Corporation issued 35,000 shares of $10 par-value common stock and 5,000 shares of 8 percent, $50 par-value preferred stock for cash at par value. Prepare the entry in general journal form to record the issuance of the stock.

Exercise 20.8
Objective 20-9

▶ **Issuing par-value stock at a premium.**

On January 2, 2016, Better Corporation issued 3,000 shares of its $15 par-value common stock for cash at $36 a share. Prepare the entry in general journal form to record the issuance of the stock.

Exercise 20.9
Objective 20-9

▶ **Issuing no-par stock for cash.**

On January 2, 2016, Williams Corporation issued 6,200 shares of its no-par-value common stock (stated value, $45 for cash at $51 a share. Give the entry in general journal form to record the issuance of the stock.

Exercise 20.10
Objective 20-10

▶ **Transactions for stock subscriptions.**

On May 1, 2016, Antonelli Corporation received a subscription from Angelina Paz for 700 shares of its $1 par-value common stock at a price of $28 a share.

Paz made a payment of $14.00 per share on the stock at the time of the subscription. Give the entries in general journal form to record receipt of the subscription and the cash payment.

Prepare entries on June 1, 2016, to record payment of the balance of Paz' subscription and issuance of the stock.

PROBLEMS

Problem Set A

Problem 20.1A
Objective 20-5

▶ **Computing dividends payable.**

Wilson Corporation issued and has outstanding 114,000 shares of $10 par-value common stock and 3,000 shares of $50 par-value 25 percent preferred stock. The board of directors votes to distribute $7,500 as dividends in 2016, $10,500 in 2017, and $254,100 in 2018.

INSTRUCTIONS

Compute the total dividend and the dividend for each share paid to preferred stockholders and common stockholders each year under the following assumed situations:

Case A: The preferred stock is nonparticipating and noncumulative.
Case B: The preferred stock is cumulative and nonparticipating.

Analyze: If a stockholder purchased 350 shares of cumulative preferred stock in 2016, what total dividends should be paid to this stockholder in the fiscal year 2018, assuming Case B?

Computing dividends payable.

◀   **Problem 20.2A**
Objective 20-5

This problem consists of two parts.

Part I

A portion of the Stockholders' Equity section of Hatten Corporation's balance sheet as of December 31, 2016, appears below. Dividends have not been paid for the years 2014 and 2015. There has been no change in the number of shares of stock issued and outstanding during these years. Assume that the board of directors of Hatten Corporation declares a dividend of $26,250 after completing operations for the year 2016.

Stockholders' Equity

Preferred Stock (9% cumulative, $50 par value,
   2,000 shares authorized)

   At Par Value (1,600 shares issued) $ 80,000

Common Stock (no-par value, with stated value of $25,
   20,000 shares authorized)

   At Stated Value (15,000 shares issued)   375,000

INSTRUCTIONS (Calculate 2016 amounts)

1. Compute the total amount of the dividend to be distributed to preferred stockholders.
2. Compute the amount of the dividend to be paid on each share of preferred stock.
3. Compute the total amount of the dividend available to be distributed to common stockholders.
4. Compute the amount of the dividend to be paid on each share of common stock.
5. Compute the amount of dividends in arrears (if any) that preferred stockholders may expect from future declarations of dividends.

Part II

Use the information given in Part I to solve this part of the problem. Assume that the board of directors of Hatten Corporation has declared a dividend of $114,600 instead of $26,250 after operations for 2016 are completed.

INSTRUCTIONS (Calculate 2016 amounts)

1. Compute the total amount of the dividend to be distributed to preferred stockholders.
2. Compute the amount of the dividend to be paid on each share of preferred stock.
3. Compute the total amount of the dividend available to be distributed to common stockholders.
4. Compute the amount of the dividend to be paid on each share of common stock.
5. Compute the amount of dividends in arrears (if any) that preferred stockholders may expect from future declarations of dividends.

Analyze: Assume only Part 1 has transpired. If, in 2015, the board of directors declared a dividend of $60,000, what amount would be paid to preferred stockholders?

Issuing stock for cash and noncash assets at par.

◀   **Problem 20.3A**
Objective 20-6

Jone Nelson and Helen Giddings are equal partners in N&G Appliance Center, which sells appliances and operates an appliance repair service. Nelson and Giddings have decided to incorporate the business. The new corporation will be known as N&G Appliance Center, Inc.

The corporation is authorized to issue 4,000 shares of $100 par-value, 10 percent preferred stock that is noncumulative and nonparticipating, and 100,000 shares of no-par-value common stock with a stated value of $20 per share. It is mutually agreed that the accounting records of N&G Appliance Center will be closed on December 31, 2016, and that certain assets will be revalued. N&G Appliance Center, Inc., will then take over all assets and assume all liabilities of the partnership. In payment for the business, the corporation will issue 400 shares of preferred stock to Nelson and 400 shares of preferred stock to Giddings, plus a sufficient number of shares of common stock to each partner to equal the balance of the partners' capital accounts.

After the partners have recorded the revaluation of their assets immediately prior to the dissolution of their partnership and withdrawn the amounts of cash agreed on, the trial balance of N&G Appliance Center as of December 31, 2016, appears below.

INSTRUCTIONS

1. In the corporation's general journal, record a memorandum entry describing the corporation's formation on December 31, 2016.

2. Record general journal entries as of December 31 to show the takeover of the assets and liabilities of the partnership and the issuance of stock in payment to Nelson and Giddings. Use the same account titles that the partnership used for assets and liabilities. Also use two new accounts: **Common Stock** and **Preferred Stock**.

N & G Appliance
Trial Balance
December 31, 2016

ACCOUNT NAME	DEBIT	CREDIT
Cash	13 2 4 0 00	
Accounts Receivable	55 4 0 0 00	
Allowance for Doubtful Accounts		3 7 4 0 00
Merchandise Inventory	460 6 0 0 00	
Parts Inventory	40 2 0 0 00	
Land	90 0 0 0 00	
Building	553 2 8 0 00	
Accumulated Depreciation—Building		74 4 8 0 00
Furniture and Equipment	98 4 0 0 00	
Accumulated Depreciation—Furn. and Equip.		7 9 0 0 00
Accounts Payable		55 0 0 0 00
Jone Nelson, Capital		585 0 0 0 00
Helen Giddings, Capital		585 0 0 0 00
Totals	1,311 1 2 0 00	1,311 1 2 0 00

Analyze: What percentage of authorized common stock has been issued as of January 1, 2017?

Problem 20.4A
Objectives 20-6, 20-7, 20-8, 20-10

▶ ## Issuing stock at par and no-par value, recording organization costs, and preparing a balance sheet.

Denzel Corporation, a new corporation, took over the assets and liabilities of Delta Art on January 2, 2016. The assets and liabilities, after appropriate revaluation by Denzel, are as follows:

Cash	$ 51,500
Accounts Receivable	372,000
Allowance for Doubtful Accounts	(13,600)
Merchandise Inventory	700,000
Accounts Payable	(385,000)
Accrued Expenses Payable	(21,800)

The corporation is authorized to issue 600,000 shares of $15 par-value common stock and 400,000 shares of $10 par-value preferred stock. The preferred stock bears a stated yearly dividend rate of $1 per share. The transactions that follow were entered into at the time the corporation was formed.

INSTRUCTIONS

1. Make general journal entries to record the transactions.

2. Prepare the opening balance sheet as of January 2, 2016, for Denzel Corporation.

DATE		TRANSACTIONS
Jan.	2	The corporation issued 46,000 shares of common stock to James Denzel for his equity in the sole proprietorship business, and the corporation took over Denzel's assets and liabilities.
	2	Issued 3,000 shares of preferred stock at par to Harriet Denzel, James's wife, for cash.
	2	Issued 9,000 shares of common stock to Carol Kennedy. She paid $135,000 in cash for the stock.
	2	Issued 5,000 shares of preferred stock to James Walker. He paid $50,000 in cash for the stock.

Analyze: What is the current ratio for the corporation at January 2, 2016?

Issuing stock at par and at a premium, preparing Stockholders' Equity section of balance sheet, and recording stock subscriptions.

◄ **Problem 20.5A**
Objectives 20-6,
20-7, 20-9, 20-11

Jaguar Corporation was organized on March 1, 2016, to operate a delivery service. The firm is authorized to issue 75,000 shares of no-par-value common stock with a stated value of $100 per share and 30,000 shares of $100 par-value, 8 percent preferred stock that is nonparticipating and noncumulative. Selected transactions that took place during March 2016 follow.

INSTRUCTIONS

1. Set up the following general ledger accounts:

101	Cash	305	Paid-in Capital in Excess of Stated Value—Common
114	Subscriptions Receivable—Common Stock		
115	Subscriptions Receivable—Preferred Stock	311	Preferred Stock
		312	Preferred Stock Subscribed
301	Common Stock	315	Paid-in Capital in Excess of Par Value—Preferred
302	Common Stock Subscribed		

Record in general journal form the transactions listed below, and post them to the general ledger accounts.

2. Prepare the Stockholders' Equity section of a balance sheet for Jaguar Corporation, as of March 31, 2016.

DATE		TRANSACTIONS
March	1	The corporation received its charter. (Make a memorandum entry.)
	1	Issued 650 shares of common stock for cash at $100 per share to Jerri Harris.
	3	Issued 400 shares of preferred stock for cash at par value to Gloria Amos.
	5	Issued 400 shares of common stock for cash at $107 to Carolyn Reed.
	5	Received a subscription for 450 shares of common stock at $106 per share from Joan Patterson, payable in two installments due in 10 and 20 days.
	14	Received a subscription for 300 shares of preferred stock at $109 per share from Robert Tolliver, payable in two installments due in 15 and 30 days.
	20	Received payment of a stock subscription installment due from Joan Patterson (one-half of the purchase price—see March 5 transaction).
	29	Received payment of a stock subscription installment due from Robert Tolliver (one-half the purchase price—see March 14 transaction).
	30	Received the balance due on the stock subscription of March 5 from Joan Patterson; issued the stock.

Analyze: What percentage of total stockholders' equity is held by common stockholders?

Problem Set B

Problem 20.1B
Objective 20-5

▶ **Computing dividends payable.**

Sanchez Corporation issued and has outstanding 20,000 shares of $5 par-value common stock and 30,000 shares of $60 par-value, 5 percent preferred stock. The board of directors votes to distribute $60,000 as dividends in 2016, $90,000 in 2017, and $120,000 in 2018.

INSTRUCTIONS

Compute the total dividend and the dividend for each share to be paid to preferred stockholders and common stockholders each year under the following assumed situations:

Case A: The preferred stock is nonparticipating and noncumulative.
Case B: The preferred stock is cumulative and nonparticipating.

Analyze: If a stockholder owned 1,600 shares of preferred stock throughout 2016–2018, what total dividends did he receive for Case B?

Problem 20.2B
Objective 20-5

▶ **Computing dividends payable for 2016.**

This problem consists of two parts.

Part I

A portion of the Stockholders' Equity section of Harris Corporation's balance sheet as of December 31, 2016, appears below. Dividends have not been paid for the year 2015. There has been no change in the number of shares of stock issued and outstanding during 2015 or 2016. Assume that the board of directors of the corporation declared a dividend of $175,000 after completing operations for the year 2016.

Stockholders' Equity	
Preferred Stock (5% cumulative, $100 par value, 40,000 shares authorized)	
At Par Value (20,000 shares issued)	$2,400,000
Common Stock ($20 par value, 150,000 shares authorized)	
At Par Value (150,000 shares issued)	3,000,000

INSTRUCTIONS (Calculate 2016 amounts)

1. Compute the total amount of the dividend to be distributed to preferred stockholders.
2. Compute the amount of the dividend to be paid on each share of preferred stock.
3. Compute the total amount of the dividend available to be distributed to common stockholders.
4. Compute the amount of the dividend to be paid on each share of common stock.
5. Compute the amount of dividends in arrears (if any) that preferred stockholders can expect from future declarations of dividends.

Part II

Assume that after operations for 2016 were completed, the board of directors declares a dividend of $300,000 instead of $175,000. Use the information given in Part I to answer questions 1 through 5 above under these new assumptions.

Analyze: In regard to Part I, if dividends of $360,000 were declared in 2017, what per-share amount would be paid to preferred stockholders?

Problem 20.3B
Objective 20-6

▶ **Issuing stock at par for cash and noncash assets.**

Laura Cisneros and Kay Osborn are equal partners in Creative Toys Nook. Cisneros and Osborn have decided to form Toy Chest Corporation to take over the operation of Creative Toys Nook on December 31, 2016. The corporation is authorized to issue 8,000 shares of no-par-value common stock with a stated value of $25 per share and 2,000 shares of $50 par-value, 12 percent preferred stock that is noncumulative and nonparticipating. Certain assets are revalued so that the accounts will reflect current values. Cisneros and Osborn will each receive 250 shares of Toy Chest Corporation preferred stock at par value ($50) and sufficient no-par-value shares of common stock at stated value ($25) to cover the partners' adjusted net investment in the partnership.

The trial balance shown below was prepared after the firm's accounting records were closed at the end of its fiscal year on December 31, 2016, and the assets were revalued as agreed on.

INSTRUCTIONS

1. In the corporation's general journal, record a memorandum entry describing its formation on December 31, 2016.

Creative Toys Nook									
Adjusted Trial Balance									
December 31, 2016									
ACCOUNT NAME	DEBIT					CREDIT			
Cash	6	9 6 0	00						
Accounts Receivable	26	5 4 0	00						
Allowance for Doubtful Accounts							6 5 0	00	
Merchandise Inventory	102	0 0 0	00						
Furniture and Equipment	45	8 0 0	00						
Accumulated Depreciation—Equipment						2	2 0 0	00	
Accounts Payable						30	4 5 0	00	
Laura Cisneros, Capital						74	0 0 0	00	
Kay Osborn, Capital						74	0 0 0	00	
Totals	181	3 0 0	00			181	3 0 0	00	

2. Make general journal entries as of December 31 to show the takeover of the assets and liabilities of the partnership and the issuance of stock in payment to Laura Cisneros and Kay Osborn. Use the same account names that the partnership used for assets and liabilities. Also use the following new account titles: *Common Stock* and *Preferred Stock*.

Analyze: After the corporation's formation, what is the fundamental accounting equation for Toy Chest Corporation?

Issuing stock at par for cash and noncash assets, issuing stock at a premium, recording organization costs, and preparing corporate balance sheet.

◄ **Problem 20.4B**
Objectives 20-6, 20-7, 20-8, 20-9

Delta Travel Agency, a new corporation, took over the assets and liabilities of Worldwide Travel Agency, owned by Rosa Davis, on June 5, 2016. The assets and liabilities assumed, after appropriate revaluation by Worldwide Travel Agency, are as follows:

Cash	$ 58,400
Accounts Receivable	112,000
Allowance for Doubtful Accounts	(4,000)
Merchandise Inventory	248,000
Accounts Payable	(20,000)
Accrued Expenses Payable	(22,400)

The corporation is authorized to issue 300,000 shares of no-par-value common stock with a stated value of $10 per share and 20,000 shares of $25 par-value preferred stock. The preferred stock bears a dividend of $2 per share per year. The transactions entered into at the time the corporation was formed follow.

INSTRUCTIONS

1. Prepare the general journal entries to record the transactions.
2. Prepare the opening balance sheet as of June 5, 2016, for Delta Travel Agency.

DATE	TRANSACTIONS
June 5	The corporation issued to Rosa Davis common stock with a stated value equal to her net equity in the sole proprietorship business, and the corporation took over Davis's assets and liabilities.
5	Issued 4,000 shares of common stock to Ned Turner for $40,000 cash.
5	Issued 1,200 shares of preferred stock to Selena Cantu. She paid $30,000 in cash for the stock.

Analyze: What is the amount of total stockholders' equity as of June 5, 2016?

Problem 20.5B

Objectives 20-6, 20-7, 20-9, 20-11

▶ **Issuing stock at par, issuing stock at a premium, preparing Stockholders' Equity section of balance sheet, and recording stock subscriptions.**

Pet Palace Corporation was organized on January 2, 2016, to operate a chain of pet supply stores. The firm is authorized to issue 50,000 shares of $10 par-value common stock and 18,000 shares of $50 par-value, 8 percent preferred stock. The preferred stock is noncumulative and nonparticipating. Selected transactions that took place during January 2016 are given below.

INSTRUCTIONS

1. Set up the following general ledger accounts:

101	Cash	305	Paid-in Capital in Excess of Par Value— Common
114	Subscriptions Receivable—Common Stock		
115	Subscriptions Receivable—Preferred Stock	311	Preferred Stock
		312	Preferred Stock Subscribed
301	Common Stock	315	Paid-in Capital in Excess of Par Value— Preferred
302	Common Stock Subscribed		

Record the transactions listed below in general journal form and post them to the general ledger accounts.

2. Prepare the Stockholders' Equity section of a balance sheet for Pet Palace Corporation as of January 31, 2016.

DATE	TRANSACTIONS
Jan. 2	The corporation received its corporate charter. (Make a memorandum entry.)
3	Issued 3,000 shares of common stock for cash at $10 per share to Alice Young.
3	Issued 1,500 shares of preferred stock for cash at $50 per share to Marcia Greene.
10	Issued 200 shares of common stock for cash at $14 per share to Mark Merki.
12	Received a subscription for 500 shares of common stock at $12 per share from Nora Barnett, payable in two installments due in 5 and 15 days.
14	Received a subscription for 500 shares of preferred stock at $54 per share from Sun Wu, payable in two installments due in 10 and 20 days.
17	Received payment of a stock subscription installment due from Nora Barnett (one-half of purchase price—see January 12 transaction).
24	Received payment of a stock subscription installment due from Sun Wu (one-half of purchase price—see January 14 transaction).
27	Received the balance due from Nora Barnett; issued the stock.

Analyze: What percentage of authorized common stock has been issued at January 27, 2016?

Critical Thinking Problem 20.1

Understanding Stockholders' Equity

Just after its formation on September 1, 2016, the ledger accounts of the Supplies Unlimited, Inc., contained the following balances:

Accrued Expenses Payable	$ 10,000
Accounts Payable	80,000
Accounts Receivable	45,000
Allowance for Doubtful Accounts	4,000
Building	200,000
Cash	21,600
Common Stock ($20 par)	240,000
Common Stock Subscribed	60,000
Furniture and Fixtures	50,000
Merchandise Inventory	145,000
Notes Payable — Short Term	50,000
Paid-in Capital in Excess of Par Value — Common	27,600
Paid-in Capital in Excess of Par Value — Preferred	6,000
Preferred Stock (10%, $50 par)	50,000
Preferred Stock Subscribed (10%, $50 par)	20,000
Subscriptions Receivable — Common Stock	66,000
Subscriptions Receivable — Preferred Stock	20,000

The corporation is authorized to issue 100,000 shares of $20 par-value common stock and 20,000 shares of 10 percent, $50 par-value preferred stock (noncumulative and nonparticipating).

INSTRUCTIONS

1. Answer the following questions:
   a. How many shares of common stock are outstanding?
   b. How many shares of common stock are subscribed?
   c. How many shares of preferred stock are outstanding?
   d. How many shares of preferred stock are subscribed?
   e. At what average price has common stock been subscribed or issued?
   f. Assume that no dividends are paid in the first year of the corporation's existence. What are the rights of the preferred stockholders?
   g. Assuming that all of the *Paid-in Capital in Excess of Par Value—Common* was applicable to the shares of common stock that have been subscribed but not yet issued, what was the subscription price per share of the common stock subscribed?

2. Prepare a classified balance sheet for the corporation just after its formation on September 1, 2016.

Analyze: What is the current ratio for the corporation at September 1, 2016?

Critical Thinking Problem 20.2

Interpreting the Balance Sheet

The Stockholders' Equity section of Foreign Tours Corporation's balance sheet at the close of the current year follows:

Stockholders' Equity	
Preferred stock (8%, $75 par value, 100,000 shares authorized)	
At Par Value (80,000 shares issued)	$ 6,000,000
Paid-in Capital in Excess of Par Value	320,000
Common Stock (no-par value, stated value of $5, 1,800,000 shares authorized)	
At Stated Value	9,000,000
Paid-in Capital in Excess of Stated Value	12,600,000
Retained Earnings	5,600,000
Total Stockholders' Equity	$33,520,000

1. What is the amount of the annual dividend on the preferred stock? Per share? In total?
2. How many shares of common stock have been issued?
3. What was the average price paid by the stockholders for the preferred stock?
4. What was the average price paid by the stockholders for the common stock?
5. How many shares of common stock are currently outstanding (held by stockholders)?
6. If total dividends of $2,550,000 were paid to stockholders in the current year, how much was paid to the common stockholders in total? Per share? Assume that no preferred dividends are in arrears.

BUSINESS CONNECTIONS

Forming a Corporation

Managerial | FOCUS

1. Leland and Baker are establishing a new restaurant and discussing whether to organize as a partnership or a corporation. What are some of the most important characteristics of these two types of organizations that they should weigh in making the decision?
2. Leland and Baker are considering organizing as a Subchapter S corporation. What are the advantages and disadvantages they should consider?
3. Leland and Baker decide to form a regular corporation for conducting their restaurant business. They are considering whether to issue preferred stock or to borrow funds on a long-term basis. Suggest some factors they should consider. How can they make the preferred stock more attractive to investors?
4. A group of individuals is planning to form a corporation. Explain in general terms the usual steps necessary to do this.
5. Why should the management of a corporation be concerned about the realistic valuation of assets transferred to the firm?

Stock Option

Vice president Sammy Lee consults the board of directors in regard to the issuance of stock and negotiates initial public offering price per share. As a bonus at the end of each fiscal year he receives stock options. Within weeks of negotiating the highest price possible, Lee sells his stock. Is this an ethical action?

Ethical DILEMMA

Balance Sheet

The information below was compiled from The Home Depot, Inc., balance sheet and footnotes in the *2012 Annual Report (for the fiscal year ended February 3, 2013).* Use it to answer the following questions:

Financial Statement ANALYSIS

	February 3	January 29
(in millions except share data)	**2013**	**2012**
Stockholders' Equity		
Common Stock, par value $0.05; authorized: 10 billion	88	87
shares; issued: 1.754 billion shares at February 3,		
2013 and 1.733 billion shares at January 29, 2012;		
outstanding: 1.484 billion shares at February 3, 2013		
and 1.537 billion shares at January 29, 2012		

Analyze:

1. What percentage of common stock authorized has been issued at January 31, 2013?

2. What journal entry was made on the books of The Home Depot, Inc., when the company authorized the 10 billion shares?

3. If all of the common stock that The Home Depot, Inc., authorized was issued at par, how much additional capital would be raised?

Analyze Online: Log on to The Home Depot, Inc., website at www.homedepot.com. Locate the most recent annual report.

4. How many shares of common stock have been issued?

5. Have any shares of preferred stock been authorized? If so, how many?

6. What is the current market price for a share of The Home Depot, Inc. stock?

Corporation Details

Divide into teams of three or four students to decide on a new corporation. Determine a name and a product or service this corporation will provide. Develop a stock certificate for your corporation. How many shares will you ask to be authorized by the state? What will be the par value? Will these shares be preferred, common, or both? How much will you accept as a price per share for the initial public offering (IPO)?

TEAMWORK

Stock Characteristics

Go to the websites of three corporations. At the corporations' home pages, find the investor's relations (see *Customer Service* and corporate link). What is the par value of the shares of stock? How many shares are authorized, issued, and outstanding? In the last year, what changes have occurred in their stock prices? Is the stock market value at its peak or still rising? How many months is the market value listed for each share? Can you buy stock for the companies from these websites?

Internet CONNECTION

Answers to **Self Reviews**

Answers to Section 1 Self Review

1. State governments issue a vast majority of corporate charters.

2. The primary advantages of the corporate form is that owners generally have no legal liability for the debts of the corporation. Additional benefits are the ease of transferring ownership interests and the fact that the death of a shareholder does not terminate the business.

3. The major role of the stockholders is to choose the directors of the company. Stockholders have no inherent right to represent the corporation or take part in its management.

4. **c.** can sell their shares of stock without permission from other stockholders.

5. **c.** elect the directors of the corporation.

   d. are entitled to a proportionate share of dividends on their classes of stock.

6. They have escaped the legal liability associated with a partnership or sole proprietorship. In addition, they can sell the corporation or part of it without any legal problems of continuity of the business. In addition, it is much easier to find persons to purchase an ownership interest (stock) in a corporation than undivided interests in a partnership.

Answers to Section 2 Self Review

1. Preferred stock is entitled to a dividend before a dividend is paid on common stock. It may also have certain preferences over distribution of assets in the case of liquidation. In addition, there is a reasonable assurance of a constant and predictable income from dividends.

2. Participating preferred stock shares with common stock a part of increased dividends in excess of the preferred stock's rate of return. The degree of participation depends on the terms of the stock issue and is beyond the scope of this text.

3. If things go well, and large dividends are paid, common shares usually benefit from the large distribution while preferred shares do not. Participating preferred stock may be issued which provides that preferred shares participate in the higher dividends.

4. **a.** Preferred shareholders will receive the entire $48,000 in 2017. There is a carryover of $52,000 that preferred must receive in addition to future preferred dividend requirements before any dividends can be paid to common stockholders.

   b. Common shareholders will receive nothing in 2017.

5. **b.** participating.

6. Allocation is $40,000 to preferred and $60,000 to common, computed in following order:

   Step 1: To preferred: 10,000 shares × $4 per share dividend; $40,000.

   Step 2: To common: All dividend distributions remaining after preferred dividends ($100,000 − $40,000) = $60,000.

Answers to Section 3 Self Review

1. Par value is established in the articles of incorporation. Stated value is set by the directors of the corporation.

2. No-par stock makes financing more flexible. State laws prevent or discourage stock from being issued for less than par value. Having no-par stock eliminates this problem.

3. Organization costs are costs in getting the corporation into existence. They include such things as fees charged by the state, legal fees related to the incorporation, and costs of printing stock certificates. Organizations costs are generally charged to expense in the year the corporation commences business.

4. *Subscriptions Receivable* is debited for $62,000; *Common Stock Subscribed* is credited for $50,000, and *Paid-in Capital in Excess of Par* (or *Premium on Common Stock*) is credited for $12,000. On the balance sheet, *Subscriptions Receivable* is shown as a current asset, and the other two accounts are shown in the stockholders' equity section.

5. Statements **c** and **d** are true.
6. McKee wishes to pursue his "preemptive right." This gives the stockholder the right to purchase a proportionate part of any new shares issued.

Answers to Comprehensive Self Review

1. As Stockholders' Equity.
2. What stock is being sold at in the market. Sometimes market value is defined as what buyers are willing to pay for the shares.
3. It is a control account for stock subscribed, containing an account receivable from each subscriber. The balance of this account agrees with *Subscriptions Receivable* on the balance sheet.
4. The registrar accounts for all stock issued by the corporation, for transfers of shares, for cancellation of shares, and for handling certificates or other records of stock issued.
5. To convert the preferred shares into common shares under predetermined conditions and exchange rates.
6. Callable preferred stock is preferred stock that can be called and retired at the option of the corporation within specified terms, including price and time.
7. As the name suggests, it frees the partners from some of the liability of a partner. Primarily, it provides relief from liability for actions of other partners, but holds the partner liable for his or her own actions and those employees supervised by that partner.
8. The preemptive right of the shareholder is to be able to purchase a proportionate part of new shares issued by the corporation.

Corporate Earnings and Capital Transactions

McDonald's
www.mcdonalds.com

Almost 70 million people around the world visit McDonald's every day. With 34,000 restaurants in 100 countries, McDonald's is the world's leading food service retailer.

In 1965, McDonald's went public with the company's first offering on the stock exchange and sold these shares for $22.50 per share. If an investor purchased a hundred shares of stock in 1965, it would have cost $2,250. Since that time, stockholders have seen 12 stock splits—the 100 shares purchased in 1965 have turned into 74,360 shares today. The $2,250 investment is worth $7.4 million today—not a bad return! Along with the increase in shares, dividends have given stockholders something to smile about, too. Quarterly dividends have increased substantially, from $.025 per share in 1976 to $.77 in 2012. In 2012 alone, the company returned $5.5 billion to shareholders through dividends and share repurchases.

Preparing financial statements for McDonald's is similar to preparing ones for other companies with the following highlights: Their biggest expense will be *Food and Paper Products*—in fact, in 2012, over $6.3 billion of these expenses were reported on the company's income statement. And of course, on every McDonalds' balance sheet, their biggest asset will be *Property and Equipment*. After all, an *Oreo McFlurry* just wouldn't be possible without an ice cream machine and a *Double Quarter Pounder* with cheese tastes a lot better—grilled!

thinking critically

What financial and nonfinancial factors would be important in deciding whether to purchase stock in a company that is going public?

LEARNING OBJECTIVES

21-1. Estimate the federal corporate income tax and prepare related journal entries.

21-2. Complete a worksheet for a corporation.

21-3. Record corporate adjusting and closing entries.

21-4. Prepare an income statement for a corporation.

21-5. Record the declaration and payment of cash dividends.

21-6. Record the declaration and issuance of stock dividends.

21-7. Record stock splits.

21-8. Record appropriations of retained earnings.

21-9. Record a corporation's receipt of donated assets.

21-10. Record treasury stock transactions.

21-11. Prepare financial statements for a corporation.

21-12. Define the accounting terms new to this chapter.

NEW TERMS

appropriation of retained earnings
book value (stock)
Common Stock Dividend Distributable account
declaration date
deferred income taxes
donated capital
Extraordinary, nonrecurring items
paid-in capital
payment date
record date
retained earnings
statement of retained earnings
statement of stockholders' equity
stock dividend
stock split
stockholders of record
treasury stock

Accounting for Corporate Earnings

Chapter 21 will continue Chapter 20's focus on transactions that are unique to the corporate form. We will look at transactions that affect the statement of retained earnings and the Stockholders' Equity section of the balance sheet.

Corporate Income Tax

One of the disadvantages of the corporate form of business is that corporations must pay income taxes on their profits. Taxable income can be calculated differently for federal, state, and local purposes; however, the procedures to record these taxes are identical. For the sake of simplicity, we will cover federal taxes only and assume that taxable income and financial reporting income are identical. In reality, the two are often different because of special tax provisions.

>> 21-1. OBJECTIVE

Estimate the federal corporate income tax and prepare related journal entries.

FEDERAL INCOME TAX RATES

Periodically, Congress changes corporate income tax rates. As of this writing, the federal rates are:

Taxable Income		Tax Rate
First	$ 50,000	15%
Next	25,000	25%
Next	25,000	34%
Next	235,000	39%
Over	335,000*	

*See Internal Revenue Service publications for taxable incomes of more than $335,000.

QUARTERLY TAX ESTIMATES

Corporations estimate their income taxes for the year and make estimated tax payments four times during the year. To avoid a penalty, the tax deposits at the end of the year must be equal to or higher than the tax liability for the year. For calendar year corporations, the estimated tax payments are due on April 15, June 15, September 15, and December 15. To record an estimated tax payment, debit **Income Tax Expense** and credit **Cash.**

Mountain Supplies, Inc., estimated its tax liability for 2016 to be $20,000. During the year, it made four tax deposits of $5,000 ($20,000 ÷ 4). The journal entry to record the first deposit (April 15) is as follows:

1	2016				1
2	Apr.	15 Income Tax Expense	5 000 00		2
3		Cash		5 000 00	3
4		Quarterly income tax deposit			4

At the end of the year, the **Income Tax Expense** account has a balance of $20,000.

YEAR-END ADJUSTMENT OF TAX LIABILITY

At the end of the year, the tentative tax expense for the year is computed. Usually there is a difference between the tentative tax expense and the tax deposits made during the year. An adjustment is recorded to reconcile the difference.

At the end of 2016, Mountain Supplies, Inc., computed its tentative tax expense as $26,150. The corporation had underpaid its taxes by $6,150:

Tax liability for the year	$26,150
Quarterly payments	20,000
Additional tax due	$ 6,150

The amount owed is recorded in the **Income Tax Payable** account, a liability:

1	2016	*Adjusting Entries*			1
10	Dec.	31 Income Tax Expense	6 150 00		10
11		Income Tax Payable		6 150 00	11
12		Estimate of additional tax due			12

Now suppose that Mountain Supplies, Inc., computed its tentative tax expense as $19,600. In this case, the corporation would have overpaid its taxes by $400:

Tax liability for the year	$19,600
Quarterly payments	20,000
Overpaid tax	$ (400)

The overpayment would be recorded in a receivable account as follows:

1	2016				1
10	Dec.	31 Income Tax Refund Receivable	400 00		10
11		Income Tax Expense		400 00	11
12		Estimate of tax overpayment			12

recall

S Corporations

S corporations do not pay federal taxes on corporate profits. Instead, corporate income is taxed on the shareholders' individual tax returns.

Note that the adjustment is made at the time the worksheet is completed and the financial statements are prepared. Because the tax return is complex and differences exist between *taxable income* and *financial income,* this computation can also be described as an estimate. The tentative tax expense computed at the end of the year usually differs from the actual tax expense shown on the tax return. The difference is recorded in the *Income Tax Expense* account.

When the tax return was prepared, the actual tax for the year was $27,000. Mountain Supplies, Inc., sent a check for $7,000 to the Internal Revenue Service for the difference between the tax for the year and the tax deposits ($27,000 − $20,000):

1	2017					1
2	Mar.	15	Income Tax Payable	6 1 5 0 00		2
3			Income Tax Expense	8 5 0 00		3
4			Cash		7 0 0 0 00	4
5			Pay balance of federal income tax			5

This entry reduces to zero the *Income Tax Payable* account. It debits *Income Tax Expense* and records the check sent to the Internal Revenue Service. Notice that the difference between the tentative tax expense and the actual tax expense, $850, is recorded in the year following the tax year. This violates the matching principle. It does not match income tax expense to taxable income. However, these differences are usually minor and do not result in a material misstatement of income.

REPORTING INCOME TAX EXPENSE ON THE INCOME STATEMENT

There are two ways to show income tax expense on the income statement:

1. As a deduction at the bottom of the income statement, after Net Income Before Income Tax. To see this presentation, refer to Figure 21.3 on page 736.

2. As an operating expense, to emphasize that taxes represent a cost of doing business.

DEFERRED INCOME TAXES

Usually net income reported on the financial statements does not match taxable income reported on the tax return because tax laws do not always follow generally accepted accounting principles.

- Income can be included in taxable income this year and appear on the financial statements in later years, or vice versa.
- Income can be included on the financial statements but never appear in taxable income.
- Expenses can be included in taxable income this year and appear on the financial statements in later years, or vice versa.
- Expenses can be included on the financial statements and never be deducted from taxable income.

Accountants use the concept of deferred income taxes to match income tax on the financial statements to the related net income.

Deferred income taxes represent the amount of taxes that will be payable (or beneficial) in the future as a result of the difference between taxable income and income for financial statement purposes in the current and past years. Let's use depreciation to illustrate the concept.

Suppose that this year tax depreciation (MACRS) is higher than depreciation on the financial statements (straight-line). In the future, then, tax depreciation should be less than depreciation on the financial statements. As a result, in the future, when taxable income is higher because depreciation is lower, the company will owe more taxes than would be paid on the net income reported for financial accounting purposes. Those future taxes really apply to the income reported on the financial statement in prior years.

Each year, the accountant estimates the amount of future taxes that will be paid as a result of the MACRS depreciation taken in this and prior years. An adjustment for the future taxes is made to **Tax Expense** and to the liability account, **Deferred Income Tax Liability.**

Sometimes the cumulative taxable income is higher than that reported on the financial statements. This gives rise to a *deferred tax asset* because some of the taxes that have been paid apply to future financial statement income. Deferred taxes are complex and are not covered in this text. This book assumes that income on the income statement and on the tax return are the same. Therefore, the deferred tax adjustment is not necessary.

Completing the Corporate Worksheet

The worksheets for a corporation and a sole proprietorship are almost identical. The major difference is the income tax adjustment. Figure 21.1 on pages 732 and 733 shows the worksheet for Mountain Supplies, Inc., for 2016. This worksheet omits the Adjusted Trial Balance columns. It is common for the experienced accountant to enter the adjusted amounts directly in the Income Statement and Balance Sheet sections. However, when the Adjusted Trial Balance section is omitted, errors in adding and subtracting adjustments are more difficult to detect.

>> **21-2. OBJECTIVE**
Complete a worksheet for a corporation.

Study the worksheet carefully as you follow the steps to complete the worksheet for Mountain Supplies, Inc.:

Step 1: *Enter the trial balance in the Trial Balance section.* To simplify the example, control accounts for general expenses and selling expenses are used instead of individual expense accounts. There are a few unfamiliar accounts on the worksheet; they will be explained later.

Step 2: *Enter the adjustments (except the adjustment to income tax expense) in the Adjustments section of the worksheet.*

Step 3: *Extend the balances of all income and expense amounts (except income tax expense) to the Income Statement section of the worksheet.* Total the Debit and Credit columns of the Income Statement section. Write the totals on a separate paper. The difference between the totals represents the income or loss before income taxes. At this point, the Income Statement columns of the worksheet contain the following information:

	Income Statement	
	Debit	Credit
Sales		1,300,000
Purchases	850,000	
Selling Expenses	200,000	
General and Administrative Expenses	190,000	
Income Summary	200,000	250,000
Totals	1,440,000	1,550,000

The difference between the Credit and Debit column totals is $110,000 ($1,550,000 − $1,440,000). This is income before income tax.

FIGURE 21.1 A Completed, Eight-Column Worksheet

Mountain Supplies, Inc.
Worksheet
Year Ended December 31, 2016

	ACCOUNT NAME	TRIAL BALANCE DEBIT	TRIAL BALANCE CREDIT	ADJUSTMENTS DEBIT	ADJUSTMENTS CREDIT
1	Cash	70 7 5 0 00			
2	Accounts Receivable	60 0 0 0 00			
3	Allowance for Doubtful Accounts		2 5 0 0 00		(c) 9 0 0 00
4	Merchandise Inventory	200 0 0 0 00		(b) 250 0 0 0 00	(a) 200 0 0 0 00
5	Prepaid Insurance	5 0 0 0 00			(d) 2 5 0 0 00
6	Land	92 0 0 0 00			
7	Buildings	120 0 0 0 00			
8	Accumulated Depreciation—Building		4 0 0 0 00		(e) 4 0 0 0 00
9	Equipment and Fixtures	72 0 0 0 00			
10	Accumulated Depreciation—Equipment and Fixtures		6 0 0 0 00		(f) 6 0 0 0 00
11	Accounts Payable		37 2 0 0 00		
12	Dividends Payable—Preferred		10 0 0 0 00		
13	Dividends Payable—Common		16 0 0 0 00		
14	Accrued Expenses Payable				(g) 3 5 0 0 00
15	Income Tax Payable				(h) 6 1 5 0 00
16	Preferred Stock—10%, $100 Par		200 0 0 0 00		
17	Paid-in Cap. in Excess of Par—Preferred		12 0 0 0 00		
18	Common Stock, $50 Par		200 0 0 0 00		
19	Paid-in Cap. in Excess of Par—Common		4 4 0 0 00		
20	Common Stock Dividend Distributable		20 0 0 0 00		
21	Retained Earnings		50 7 5 0 00		
22	Sales		1,300 0 0 0 00		
23	Purchases	850 0 0 0 00			
24	Selling Expenses (control)	195 6 0 0 00		(c) 9 0 0 00	
25				(d) 5 0 0 00	
26				(e) 1 0 0 0 00	
27				(f) 2 0 0 0 00	
28	General and Admin. Expenses (control)	177 5 0 0 00		(d) 2 0 0 0 00	
29				(e) 3 0 0 0 00	
30				(f) 4 0 0 0 00	
31				(g) 3 5 0 0 00	
32	Income Tax Expense	20 0 0 0 00		(h) 6 1 5 0 00	
33	Income Summary			(a) 200 0 0 0 00	(b) 250 0 0 0 00
34	Totals	1,862 8 5 0 00	1,862 8 5 0 00	473 0 5 0 00	473 0 5 0 00
35	Net Income after Income Tax Expense				

	INCOME STATEMENT		BALANCE SHEET		
	DEBIT	CREDIT	DEBIT	CREDIT	
1			70 7 5 0 00		
2			60 0 0 0 00		
3				3 4 0 0 00	
4			250 0 0 0 00		
5			2 5 0 0 00		
6			92 0 0 0 00		
7			120 0 0 0 00		
8				8 0 0 0 00	
9			72 0 0 0 00		
10				12 0 0 0 00	
11				37 2 0 0 00	
12				10 0 0 0 00	
13				16 0 0 0 00	
14				3 5 0 0 00	
15				6 1 5 0 00	
16				200 0 0 0 00	
17				12 0 0 0 00	
18				200 0 0 0 00	
19				4 4 0 0 00	
20				20 0 0 0 00	
21				50 7 5 0 00	
22		1,300 0 0 0 00			
23	850 0 0 0 00				
24	200 0 0 0 00				
25					
26					
27					
28	190 0 0 0 00				
29					
30					
31					
32	26 1 5 0 00				
33	200 0 0 0 00	250 0 0 0 00			
34	1,466 1 5 0 00	1,550 0 0 0 00		583 4 0 0 00	
35	83 8 5 0 00			83 8 5 0 00	
36	1,550 0 0 0 00	1,550 0 0 0 00	667 2 5 0 00	667 2 5 0 00	

recall

Worksheet

Asset, liability, and equity accounts are extended to the Balance Sheet columns. Revenue and expense accounts are extended to the Income Statement columns.

Step 4: *Compute income tax based on income before tax.* Assume there is no difference between financial and taxable income:

First $50,000 × 15%	$ 7,500
Next $25,000 × 25%	6,250
Next $25,000 × 34%	8,500
Last $10,000 × 39% (rounded)	3,900
Total tax on $110,000	$26,150

Mountain Supplies, Inc., made tax deposits of $20,000. The difference between the tax deposits and the total tax is $6,150 ($26,150 − $20,000). An adjustment is made to debit **Income Tax Expense** for $6,150 and to credit **Income Tax Payable** for $6,150.

Step 5: *Total the columns in the Adjustments section.* Extend the balance of **Income Tax Expense** to the Debit column of the Income Statement section of the worksheet.

Step 6: *Total the Debit and Credit columns of the Income Statement section.* The difference between the totals is net income after tax.

Step 7: *Extend the adjusted balances of the asset, liability, and stockholders' equity accounts to the Balance Sheet columns.* Enter net income after income tax to the Credit column of the Balance Sheet section. Complete the worksheet in the usual manner.

>> **21-3. OBJECTIVE**

Record corporate adjusting and closing entries.

Adjusting and Closing Entries

The closing process for a corporation is similar to that of a sole proprietorship. First close revenue to **Income Summary**. Then close expenses to **Income Summary**. Finally, close **Income Summary** (net income or net loss) to **Retained Earnings**. The **Retained Earnings** account accumulates the profits and losses of the business.

Figure 21.2 shows the adjusting and closing entries for Mountain Supplies, Inc. Compare the journal entries to the worksheet to see how the journal entries are prepared.

>> **21-4. OBJECTIVE**

Prepare an income statement for a corporation.

The Corporate Income Statement

After the worksheet is complete, the financial statements are prepared. The income statement of a sole proprietorship and a corporation are similar. The major difference is income taxes. The corporate income statement contains a deduction for income tax expense.

Figure 21.3 shows the income statement for Mountain Supplies, Inc., for 2016. It is prepared from the information on the worksheet in Figure 21.1. Note that income tax expense is deducted from the Net Income Before Income Tax line to arrive at net income after income tax.

VARIATIONS IN INCOME STATEMENT PRESENTATION

Corporations use a variety of formats for the income statement. Some common variations are summarized as follows:

- Some corporations include cost of goods sold with the operating expenses. They do not show gross profit on sales. This text uses the traditional income statement with a separate Gross Profit section.

- Some corporations show income tax expense as an operating expense rather than as a deduction from net income before income tax. This presentation can be used to emphasize that income taxes are a cost of doing business like any other expense.

- If a gain or loss results from a transaction that is highly unusual, is clearly unrelated to routine operations, and is not expected to occur again in the near future, the gain or loss is shown in a separate section called **Extraordinary, Nonrecurring Items.**

Extraordinary items include gains or losses from fires, floods, and other casualties.

Figure 21.4 shows an income statement containing extraordinary items. The tax effect of each extraordinary item is offset against each gain or loss to show the gain or loss "net of taxes."

FIGURE 21.2

Adjusting and Closing Entries

GENERAL JOURNAL

PAGE ___38___

	DATE	DESCRIPTION	POST. REF.	DEBIT	CREDIT	
1	2016					1
2		*Adjusting Entries*				2
3		*(Entry a)*				3
4	Dec. 31	Income Summary		200 000 00		4
5		Merchandise Inventory			200 000 00	5
6						6
7		*(Entry b)*				7
8	31	Merchandise Inventory		250 000 00		8
9		Income Summary			250 000 00	9
10						10
11		*(Entry c)*				11
12	31	Selling Expense (control)		900 00		12
13		Allowance for Doubtful Accounts			900 00	13
14						14
15		*(Entry d)*				15
16	31	Selling Expenses (control)		500 00		16
17		General and Admin. Expenses (control)		2 000 00		17
18		Prepaid Insurance			2 500 00	18
19						19
20		*(Entry e)*				20
21	31	Selling Expenses (control)		1 000 00		21
22		General and Admin. Expenses (control)		3 000 00		22
23		Accumulated Depreciation—Buildings			4 000 00	23
24						24
25		*(Entry f)*				25
26	31	Selling Expenses (control)		2 000 00		26
27		General and Admin. Expenses (control)		4 000 00		27
28		Accum. Depr.—Equip. and Fixtures			6 000 00	28
29						29
30		*(Entry g)*				30
31	31	General and Admin. Expenses (control)		3 500 00		31
32		Accrued Expenses Payable			3 500 00	32
33						33
34		*(Entry h)*				34
35	31	Income Tax Expense		6 150 00		35
36		Income Tax Payable			6 150 00	36
37						37

GENERAL JOURNAL

PAGE ___39___

	DATE	DESCRIPTION	POST. REF.	DEBIT	CREDIT	
1	2016					1
2		*Closing Entries*				2
3	Dec. 31	Sales		1,300 000 00		3
4		Income Summary			1,300 000 00	4
5						5
6	31	Income Summary		1,266 150 00		6
7		Purchases			850 000 00	7
8		Selling Expenses (control)			200 000 00	8
9		Gen. and Admin. Expenses (control)			190 000 00	9
10		Income Tax Expense			26 150 00	10
11						11
12	31	Income Summary		83 850 00		12
13		Retained Earnings			83 850 00	13
14		Close Income Summary				14

FIGURE 21.3

Corporate Income Statement

Mountain Supplies, Inc.
Income Statement
Year Ended December 31, 2016

Sales			1,300 0 0 0 00
Cost of Goods Sold			
Inventory, January 1, 2013	200 0 0 0 00		
Purchases	850 0 0 0 00		
Goods Available for Sale	1,050 0 0 0 00		
Less Inventory, December 31, 2013	250 0 0 0 00		
Costs of Goods Sold		800 0 0 0 00	
Gross Profit on Sales		500 0 0 0 00	
Expenses			
Selling Expenses	200 0 0 0 00		
General and Administrative Expenses	190 0 0 0 00	390 0 0 0 00	
Net Income before Income Tax		110 0 0 0 00	
Income Tax Expense		26 1 5 0 00	
Net Income after Income Tax		83 8 5 0 00	

FIGURE 21.4

Income Statement Showing
Extraordinary Items

Morgan Corporation
Partial Income Statement
Year Ended December 31, 2016

Income from Operations			
Before Income Taxes			499 5 0 0 00
Income Taxes Applicable to Operating Income			169 8 3 0 00
Net Income from Operations, After			
Income Taxes			329 6 7 0 00
Extraordinary Gains and Losses			
Add Gain on Condemnation of Land by City	28 2 0 0 00		
Less Federal Taxes on Gain	7 8 0 0 00	20 4 0 0 00	
Deduct Tornado Loss on Building	16 0 0 0 00		
Less Federal Tax Reduction	6 2 4 0 00	9 7 6 0 00	
Excess of Extraordinary Gains over Losses			10 6 4 0 00
Net Income for Year			340 3 1 0 00

Section 1   Self Review

QUESTIONS

1. Where does the corporate income tax appear in the income statement?

2. At what point in preparing the corporate end-of-year worksheet does the accountant enter the adjustment for income taxes?

3. What does the account *Retained Earnings* represent?

EXERCISES

4. How do the adjusting entries for the beginning and ending inventories for a corporation differ, if at all, from those for a sole proprietorship?

5. Name some reasons why the taxable income of a corporation is likely not to be the same as its financial statement net income.

6. A corporation's taxable income for 2016 was $250,000. Using the corporate tax rates on page 728, compute the total federal income tax expense for the year.

ANALYSIS

7. On the worksheet, column totals in the Income Statement section are debit, $192,000, and credit, $242,000. Assuming income and deductions for tax purposes are the same as those for

financial accounting purposes and that the corporation had paid estimated taxes of $8,000, what is the adjusting entry for income taxes based on the income tax rates presented on page 728?

(Answers to Section 1 Self Review are on page 764.)

Accounting for Retained Earnings

The fundamental accounting equation for corporations can be restated as Assets = Liabilities + (Paid-in Capital + Retained Earnings).

Paid-in capital (or contributed capital) represents the amount of capital acquired from capital stock transactions.

Retained earnings represents the cumulative profits and losses of the corporation not distributed as dividends. Dividends reduce retained earnings.

Retained Earnings

There are legal and financial distinctions between paid-in capital and retained earnings. This is why profits and losses are accumulated in retained earnings, separate from the capital paid in by the stockholders.

It is important to remember that retained earnings does not represent a cash fund. Retained earnings are reinvested in inventory, plant and equipment, and various other types of assets. A corporation can have a large cash balance but no retained earnings. Conversely, it can have a large balance in the *Retained Earnings* account but no cash.

CASH DIVIDENDS

Stockholders receive a share of the profits of the corporation through cash dividends. Most corporations pay dividends quarterly. In some corporations, the board of directors establishes a policy of making regular cash dividends at the same or an increasing amount. A regular dividend policy tends to make a stock more attractive to investors and may help avoid sharp fluctuations in the stock's market price. Many corporations, however, retain their earnings to finance growth and do not pay cash dividends. This is especially true in the first several years of a corporation's existence.

Dividend Policy Before declaring a dividend, the board of directors considers two issues: legality and financial feasibility.

1. *Legality.* State laws differ, but in general the corporation must have retained earnings in order to declare dividends. These laws are intended to protect the corporation's creditors. The restriction prevents an *impairment of capital.* Capital is impaired when dividends are paid that reduce total stockholders' equity to less than the paid-in capital accounts, which may result from paying excessive dividends.

2. *Financial Feasibility.* The corporation must have the cash to pay the dividend. The board of directors does not declare dividends that lead to a cash shortage or other financial difficulties, even though there may be a large balance in Retained Earnings.

Dates Relevant to Dividends Three dates are involved in declaring and paying dividends:

■ The **declaration date** is the date on which the board of directors declares the dividend. The dividend declaration is recorded in the corporation's minute book. Once a dividend is declared, the firm has a liability to the stockholders for the amount of the declared dividend.

■ The **record date** is the date used to determine who will receive the dividend. The capital stock ledger is used to prepare a list of the **stockholders of record,** that is, the stockholders who will receive the declared dividend. This does not require a journal entry.

■ The **payment date** is the date on which the dividend is paid.

Declaration of a Cash Dividend Mountain Supplies, Inc.'s board of directors met on November 28, 2016, and declared cash dividends of $5 per share on preferred stock and $4 per share on common stock. The dividends are payable on January 15 to stockholders of record on December 31. On the declaration date, the firm had outstanding 2,000 shares of preferred stock and 4,000 shares of common stock. The dividend declaration is recorded as shown below:

>> **21-5. OBJECTIVE**
Record the declaration and payment of cash dividends.

important!

Journal Entries for Dividends
A journal entry is recorded on the date of declaration and the date of payment. A journal entry is not made on the date of record.

2016				
Nov.	28	Retained Earnings	10 000 00	
		Dividends Payable—Preferred		10 000 00
		Dividend declaration of $5		
		per share on 2,000 shares,		
		payable Jan. 15 to holders		
		of record Dec. 31		
	28	Retained Earnings	16 000 00	
		Dividends Payable—Common		16 000 00
		Dividend declaration of $4		
		per share on 4,000 shares,		
		payable on Jan. 15 to		
		holders of record Dec. 31		

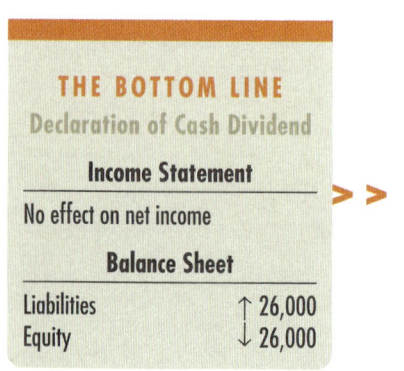

THE BOTTOM LINE
Declaration of Cash Dividend

Income Statement

No effect on net income

Balance Sheet

Liabilities   ↑ 26,000
Equity   ↓ 26,000

Dividends payable appears on the balance sheet as a current liability. An example is shown in the balance sheet presented later in this chapter (Figure 21.6, page 747).

Payment of a Cash Dividend The capital stock ledger is used to prepare a list of the stockholders and the number of shares owned on the record date. The list is used to determine the dividend due each shareholder. On January 15, 2017, the payment date, the dividend checks are issued to the stockholders on the list. The payment is recorded as follows:

	2017				
1	2017				1
2	Jan.	15	Dividends Payable—Preferred	10 000 00	2
3			Dividends Payable—Common	16 000 00	3
4			Cash		26 000 00	4
5			Payment of cash dividends			5

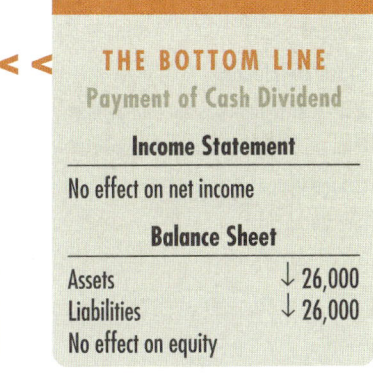

STOCK DIVIDENDS

A corporation may have retained earnings but be short of cash and unable to pay a cash dividend. Or the board of directors may want to transfer part of retained earnings to a paid-in capital account. In these cases, the board of directors may declare a stock dividend. A **stock dividend** is a distribution of the corporation's own stock on a pro rata basis that results in conversion of a portion of the firm's retained earnings to permanent capital.

>> **21-6. OBJECTIVE**

Record the declaration and issuance of stock dividends.

Suppose that, on November 30, 2016, the board of directors of Mountain Supplies, Inc., declared a stock dividend payable the following January 20 to common stockholders of record on December 28. The stock dividend is for one new share of common stock for each 10 shares held. On the declaration date, there were 4,000 shares outstanding, so 400 (4,000 ÷ 10) additional shares will be issued.

When a stock dividend is declared, the total amount charged to the *Retained Earnings* account is the estimated fair value of the shares to be issued. Assume that each share of Mountain Supplies, Inc.'s stock is expected to have a fair value of $57. A total of $22,800 (400 shares × $57 expected fair value) is debited to *Retained Earnings.* The par value of the shares, $20,000 (400 shares × $50 par), is credited to *Common Stock Dividend Distributable,* an equity account used to record par or stated value of shares to be issued as the result of the declaration of a stock dividend. The excess of the fair value over the par value, $2,800 ($22,800 − $20,000), is credited to *Paid-in Capital in Excess of Par Value—Common Stock* or to *Paid-in Capital from Common Stock Dividends.* Let's see how the declaration of a stock dividend is recorded:

	2016				
1	2016				1
2	Nov.	30	Retained Earnings	22 800 00	2
3			Common Stock Dividend Distributable		20 000 00	3
4			Paid-in Capital in Excess of Par			4
5			Value—Common Stock		2 800 00	5
6			Declaration of 10% stock dividend,			6
7			distributable on Jan. 20 to holders			7
8			of record on Dec. 28			8

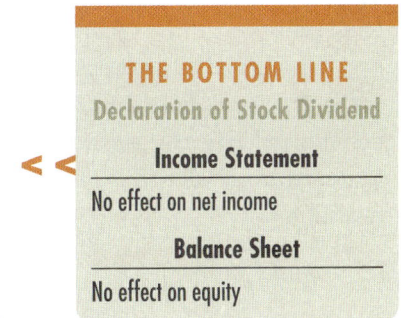

The *Common Stock Dividend Distributable* account appears on the balance sheet in the Stockholders' Equity section as a part of paid-in capital. One possible balance sheet presentation follows:

Common Stock ($50 par value, 10,000 shares authorized)	
Issued and outstanding, 4,000 shares	$200,000
Distributable as stock dividend, 400 shares	20,000
Paid-in Capital in Excess of Par	2,800
	$222,800

important!

Fair value is a concept addressed under GAAP that calls for a process to be followed in determining what the fair value of an equity (or other item) may actually be. This discussion is most appropriate in an auditing or advanced accounting text.

On December 28, a list is made of the stockholders' names, number of shares owned, and number of new shares to issue. For example, Sandra Fee owns 400 shares of common stock. She will receive 40 (400 ÷ 10) new shares as a stock dividend. On January 20, the 400 shares are distributed. This issuance of stock is recorded as follows:

	2017				
1	2017				1
2	Jan.	20	Common Stock Dividend Distributable	20 000 00	2
3			Common Stock		20 000 00	3
4			Distribution of stock dividend			4

Book value for each share of stock is the total equity applicable to the class of stock divided by the number of shares outstanding. The total book value is the same before and after a stock dividend, but each shareholder owns more shares of stock with a proportionately smaller book value per share.

Before the stock dividend, Fee owned 400 shares, or 10 percent (400 ÷ 4,000 shares), of the stock of the corporation. After the stock dividend, Fee still owned 10 percent (440 ÷ 4,400 shares) of the corporation's stock:

	Fee	Total
Shares before	400	4,000
Stock dividend	40	400
Shares after	440	4,400

In theory, a stock dividend should result in a proportionate reduction in each share's value. Sometimes the market price declines less than it should in theory because a lower price per share can result in a wider market for the shares and because investors associate stock dividends with successful corporations. Thus, after a stock dividend, the total market value of a stockholder's shares can increase slightly.

STOCK SPLITS

A **stock split** occurs when a corporation issues two or more shares of new stock to replace each share outstanding without making any changes in the capital accounts. Stock splits are often declared when the stock is relatively difficult to sell because the market price is too high. If par-value stock is split, the corporation's charter is amended to reduce the par value.

Lamp Corporation is authorized to issue 500,000 shares of no-par-value stock, with a stated value of $75 per share. There are 40,000 shares issued and outstanding. On November 2, the market price of the stock is $300 per share. The board of directors believes that if the price of the stock were lower, the shares would have a wider market. Accordingly, the board declared a 3-for-1 split and reduced the stated value to $25 ($75 ÷ 3) per share. Two additional shares will be issued for each share outstanding. The shares will be issued on November 30 to holders of record on November 15. A stockholder who owned one share of stock with a stated value of $75 before the split will own three shares of stock with a stated value of $25 per share after the split. Stockholders realize no income from the stock split, and the corporation's capital balances are not affected.

Theoretically, the market price will decrease to one-third of the original market value, or to $100 per share ($300 × 1/3). If the price per share does not decrease to its theoretical level, the total market value of a stockholder's shares will be higher.

On the date of declaration of the stock split, a memorandum notation is made in the general journal of Lamp Corporation:

1	2016							1
2	Nov.	2	On this date the board of directors declared a					2
3			3-for-1 stock split and reduced the stated value					3
4			of common stock from $75 to $25 per share.					4
5			Total outstanding shares will be 120,000					5

On November 30, a similar memorandum entry is made in the general journal to note issuance of the new shares.

An entry is made in the **Common Stock** account in the general ledger to indicate that the stated value is now $25 per share, and 120,000 shares are outstanding. The stockholders' records are changed to reflect the number of shares now held by each stockholder.

APPROPRIATIONS OF RETAINED EARNINGS

Most corporations pay out only a portion of retained earnings as dividends. They restrict dividend payments in order to reinvest in plant assets or working capital. Sometimes dividends are restricted by contract, such as the requirements of a bond issue. A footnote to the financial statements can be used to indicate how management's plans or contractual obligations will affect (restrict) the dividends. A more formal way for the board of directors to show an intention to restrict dividends is to make an **appropriation of retained earnings** by resolution. Dividends cannot be declared from appropriated retained earnings.

Mountain Supplies, Inc.'s directors foresee the need to build a $200,000 retail center within the next five years. They want to notify the stockholders that the new retail facility will be built and that dividends will be restricted. A resolution is passed at a board meeting on October 5, 2017, to transfer $50,000 from *Retained Earnings* to a *Retained Earnings Appropriated for Retail Center Construction* account. The resolution is recorded in the minutes and the general journal entry is recorded. Similar appropriations and entries are made in each of the next three years.

The balance sheet presentation shows appropriated and unappropriated retained earnings. Assume that *Retained Earnings* had a balance of $154,600 before the first appropriation. The following is the balance sheet presentation immediately after the appropriation. Notice that total retained earnings stays the same, but it now has two parts:

Retained Earnings	
Appropriated	
Appropriated for Retail Center Construction	$ 50,000
Unappropriated	104,600
Total Retained Earnings	$154,600

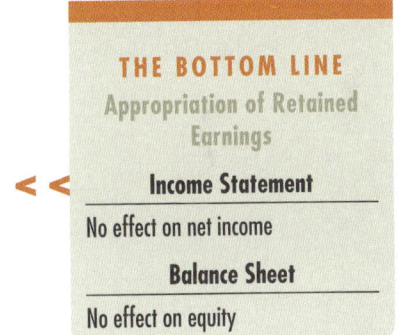

	2017				
2	Oct.	5	Retained Earnings	50 000 00	
3			Retained Earnings Appropriated for		
4			Retail Center Construction		50 000 00
5			Appropriation made by board of		
6			directors on Oct. 5		

THE BOTTOM LINE
Appropriation of Retained Earnings

Income Statement
No effect on net income

Balance Sheet
No effect on equity

Remember that retained earnings does not represent cash, nor does appropriating retained earnings provide cash. The appropriation simply restricts the amount of retained earnings available for dividends, thus making it more likely that cash will be available to build the retail center.

Assume that in six years cash was available and the retail center construction project was completed at a cost of $252,000, which is $52,000 more than appropriated. The accounting records reflect an increase to *Building* of $252,000 and a decrease to *Cash* of $252,000. The balance of the *Retained Earnings Appropriated for Retail Center Construction* account ($200,000 at this point in time) has not been affected. When the purpose for which retained earnings was appropriated has been attained, the board can direct that the balance be transferred back to *Retained Earnings*, as follows:

	2023				
2	Feb.	7	Retained Earnings Appropriated for		
3			Retail Center Construction	200 000 00	
4			Retained Earnings		200 000 00

Section 2   Self Review

QUESTIONS

1. Explain each of the three dates related to a stock dividend declaration and issue.

2. How does the general journal entry for a stock split differ from one for a stock dividend?

3. Does an appropriation of retained earnings include a transfer of cash to a restricted account? Explain.

EXERCISES

4. Which of the following will decrease total stock-holders' equity?

   a. stock dividend

   b. stock split

   c. cash dividend

   d. appropriation of retained earnings

5. The balance of an appropriated retained earnings account is reduced:

   a. as expenses are accrued.

   b. as payments are made.

   c. when the board of directors passes a resolution to return the amount to unappropriated retained earnings.

   d. when the board declares the appropriation's purpose is completed.

ANALYSIS

6. On April 20, the board of directors of Auto Corporation declared a 15 percent stock dividend payable on June 1 to stockholders of record on May 15. The stock is expected to trade at $35 per share. On the declaration date, there are 4,000 shares outstanding. The par value of the shares is $30. What amount is credited to the *Paid-in Capital in Excess of Par Value—Common Stock* account?

(Answers to Section 2 Self Review are on page 764.)

>> 21-9. OBJECTIVE
Record a corporation's receipt of donated assets.

SECTION OBJECTIVES	TERMS TO LEARN
>> **21-9.** Record a corporation's receipt of donated assets. **WHY IT'S IMPORTANT** Corporations may receive donated property as an incentive to locate in a community.	donated capital statement of retained earnings statement of stockholders' equity treasury stock
>> **21-10.** Record treasury stock transactions. **WHY IT'S IMPORTANT** The impact of treasury stock purchases must be made clear to statement users.	
>> **21-11.** Prepare financial statements for a corporation. **WHY IT'S IMPORTANT** Shareholders, analysts, and management use financial statements issued by corporations.	

Other Capital Transactions and Financial Statements

Many other transactions affect the stockholders' equity. Two types of transactions that occur often are donations of capital and purchase of treasury stock.

Other Capital Transactions

Transactions that affect stockholders' equity include the donation of assets to a corporation and a corporation's purchase of its own stock.

DONATIONS OF CAPITAL

Property can be given to a corporation. This often occurs when a community that wishes to attract new industry gives a corporation land or a building for a plant site. **Donated capital** is capital resulting from the receipt of gifts by a corporation. An asset received as a gift is recorded in the accounting records at the asset's appraised value or fair value based on similar properties. The credit is to *Donated Capital,* a paid-in capital account. This account may also be labeled *Paid-in Capital from Donations*. The following general journal entry indicates how a gift of a plant site valued at $150,000 is recorded:

1	2016				1
2	Jan.	2	Land	150 000 00		2
3			Donated Capital		150 000 00	3
4			Appraised value of plant site donated			4
5			by city			5

On the balance sheet, the *Donated Capital* account is shown as a new category under paid-in capital, following the preferred and common stock accounts.

TREASURY STOCK

Treasury stock is a corporation's own capital stock that has been issued and reacquired. To be considered treasury stock, the stock must have been previously paid for in full and issued to a stockholder. Any class or type of stock can be reacquired as treasury stock. No dividends, voting rights, or liquidation preferences apply to treasury stock.

Stockholders may benefit when the corporation repurchases common stock because there are fewer shares of outstanding stock to share the profits and dividends. If preferred stock is reacquired, the dividends on the stock are no longer payable, thus increasing the dividends available to owners of common stock.

Corporations purchase their own stock for many reasons:

■ The corporation has extra cash, and the board of directors thinks that the corporation's own stock is a better investment than other potential investments.

■ The corporation wishes to transfer treasury stock to officers and key employees in connection with incentive plans. If unissued shares instead of treasury stock were used, it would be necessary to ask stockholders to give up their preemptive rights. However, preemptive rights do not apply to treasury stock.

■ The corporation wants to create a demand for the stock and thus increase its market value.

■ In privately held corporations with few owners, the board of directors can vote to purchase the shares of a stockholder who needs cash or wishes to retire.

> In May 2012, Yahoo! (YHOO) announced a $5 billion stock buyback program. Yahoo! is authorized to repurchase up to $5 billion of its outstanding shares of common stock over the next three years.

Recording the Purchase of Treasury Stock   When treasury stock is purchased, the *Treasury Stock* account is debited for the entire amount paid. There is a separate treasury stock account for each class of stock. For example, assume that in 2018, Mountain Supplies, Inc., repurchased 500 shares of $50 par preferred stock for $52 per share. The transaction is recorded as follows:

1	2018				1
7	Jan.	10	Treasury Stock—Preferred	26 000 00	7
8			Cash	26 000 00	8
9			Purchased 500 shares of treasury stock		9

Appropriation of Retained Earnings for Treasury Stock   The purchase of treasury stock reflects a payment to a shareholder and thus reduces capital. Stockholder withdrawals could be disguised as treasury stock purchases. In order to protect creditors, some states require that retained earnings be appropriated in an amount equal to the cost of treasury stock. If a corporation does not have retained earnings with a value higher than the purchase price, it cannot purchase treasury stock. If Mountain Supplies, Inc., is required to appropriate retained earnings equal to the cost of treasury stock, the following entry would be made:

1	2018				1
11	Jan.	10	Retained Earnings	26 000 00	11
12			Retained Earnings Appropriated—		12
13			Treasury Stock	26 000 00	13
14			To appropriate retained earnings equal		14
15			to purchase price of preferred treasury		15
16			stock		16

On the balance sheet, treasury stock is deducted from the sum of all items in the Stockholders' Equity section. To see how treasury stock and retained earnings appropriated for treasury stock appear on the balance sheet, refer to Figure 21.6 on page 747.

MANAGERIAL IMPLICATIONS <<

CAPITAL TRANSACTIONS

- In order to make prudent decisions, managers need to understand how net income is calculated.
- The board of directors needs to develop a dividend policy that gives appropriate consideration to legal restrictions and to financial feasibility.
- Stock dividends offer an opportunity to make distributions to shareholders while limiting the distribution of cash.
- Stock dividends provide a means for transforming a part of retained earnings into paid-in capital.
- Both stock dividends and stock splits reduce the price per share of the company's stock, which may make the stock more marketable.

- Prudent managers inform stockholders about restrictions on dividends by appropriating retained earnings.
- Treasury stock purchases can enhance the value of the stock held by other shareholders.
- Treasury stock can be used to offer stock incentives to officers and key employees and to obtain stock for employee stock-purchase plans.

THINKING CRITICALLY

What factors should be considered before a company declares a cash dividend?

Financial Statements for a Corporation

Four financial statements are usually prepared for a corporation:

- income statement,
- statement of retained earnings,
- balance sheet,
- statement of cash flows.

Figure 21.3 on page 736 shows the income statement for 2016 of Mountain Supplies, Inc. Let's move ahead a couple of years to 2018 and examine the statement of retained earnings and the balance sheet. These statements will reflect some of the transactions that you have studied in this chapter. The statement of cash flows is explained in Chapter 24.

THE STATEMENT OF RETAINED EARNINGS

The **statement of retained earnings** shows all changes that have occurred in retained earnings during the period. The statement shows the beginning balance, the changes, and the ending balance for the unappropriated and appropriated *Retained Earnings* accounts. Because of the importance of retained earnings to the corporation and the stockholders, a statement of retained earnings should be presented as part of the financial statements.

Figure 21.5 shows the 2018 statement of retained earnings of Mountain Supplies, Inc. The unappropriated retained earnings are:

- increased by net income,
- decreased by dividends and appropriations.

Mountain Supplies, Inc., has two appropriation accounts—one for retail center construction and another for treasury stock.

Some corporations combine the statement of retained earnings with the income statement. In the combined statement of income and retained earnings, the beginning balance of *Retained Earnings* is added to the net income after taxes for the period. All other amounts are shown in the same way they are shown on the separate statement of retained earnings.

The Securities and Exchange Commission requires publicly held corporations to disclose the reasons for major changes in equity. Corporations find that the most convenient way to make the required disclosures is to prepare a **statement of stockholders' equity** (often referred to as an *analysis of changes in stockholders' equity*). It provides an analysis reconciling the beginning and ending balance of each of the stockholders' equity accounts. There is, however, no specified form for the statement, and various types of schedules are used.

>> 21-11. OBJECTIVE
Prepare financial statements for a corporation.

FIGURE 21.5   **Statement of Retained Earnings**

Mountain Supplies, Inc.
Statement of Retained Earnings
December 31, 2018

Unappropriated Retained Earnings			
Balance, January 1, 2018	254 042 00		
Add Net Income after Taxes for 2018	72 600 00	326 642 00	
Deductions			
Dividends on Preferred Stock	15 000 00		
Dividends on Common Stock	17 600 00		
Transfer to Appropriation for Retail Center Construction	50 000 00		
Transfer to Appropriation for Treasury Stock	26 000 00	108 600 00	
Total Unappropriated Retained Earnings, December 31, 2018			218 042 00
Appropriated Retained Earnings			
Appropriated for Retail Center Construction			
Balance, January 1, 2018	50 000 00		
Add Appropriation for the Year	50 000 00		
Balance, December 31, 2018		100 000 00	
Appropriated for Treasury Stock			
Balance, January 1, 2018	—0—		
Add Appropriation for the Year	26 000 00		
Balance, December 31, 2018		26 000 00	
Total Appropriated Retained Earnings, December 31, 2018			126 000 00
Total Retained Earnings, December 31, 2018			344 042 00

THE CORPORATE BALANCE SHEET

Figure 21.6 shows the balance sheet of Mountain Supplies, Inc. Since the statement of retained earnings shows changes in each account, only the ending balances of each appropriated retained earnings account and of the unappropriated retained earnings account are shown on the balance sheet. Note that:

- income tax payable and dividends payable appear in the Current Liabilities section,
- treasury stock is subtracted from the Stockholders' Equity section.

FIGURE 21.6   An End-of-Year Balance Sheet

Mountain Supplies, Inc.
Balance Sheet
December 31, 2018

Assets				
Current Assets				
Cash			168 0 8 4 00	
Accounts Receivable	245 0 0 0 00			
Allowance for Doubtful Accounts	8 6 0 0 00		236 4 0 0 00	
Merchandise Inventory			169 4 5 8 00	
Prepaid Insurance			12 0 0 0 00	
Total Current Assets				585 9 4 2 00
Property, Plant, and Equipment				
Land			92 0 0 0 00	
Buildings	120 0 0 0 00			
Accumulated Depreciation—Building	12 0 0 0 00		108 0 0 0 00	
Equipment and Fixtures	72 0 0 0 00			
Accumulated Depreciation—Equipment and Fixtures	18 0 0 0 00		54 0 0 0 00	
Total Property, Plant, and Equipment				254 0 0 0 00
Total Assets				839 9 4 2 00
Liabilities and Stockholders' Equity				
Current Liabilities				
Accounts Payable			68 0 0 0 00	
Dividends Payable—Preferred			7 5 0 0 00	
Dividends Payable—Common			4 4 0 0 00	
Accrued Expenses Payable			3 2 0 0 00	
Income Tax Payable			2 4 0 0 00	
Total Current Liabilities				85 5 0 0 00
Stockholders' Equity				
Paid-in Capital				
Preferred Stock (10%, $100 par value, 10,000 shares authorized)				
Issued 2,000 shares (of which 500 shares are held as treasury stock)	200 0 0 0 00			
Paid-in Capital in Excess of Par Value—Preferred Stock	12 0 0 0 00		212 0 0 0 00	
Common Stock ($50 par value, 20,000 shares authorized)				
Issued and Outstanding, 4,400 shares	220 0 0 0 00			
Paid-in Capital in Excess of Par Value—Common Stock	4 4 0 0 00		224 4 0 0 00	
Total Paid-in Capital			436 4 0 0 00	
Retained Earnings				
Appropriated				
For Treasury Stock Purchase	26 0 0 0 00			
For Retail Center Construction	100 0 0 0 00			
Total Appropriated			126 0 0 0 00	
Unappropriated			218 0 4 2 00	
Total Retained Earnings			344 0 4 2 00	
Less Treasury Stock, Preferred (500 shares at cost)			26 0 0 0 00	
Total Stockholders' Equity				754 4 4 2 00
Total Liabilities and Stockholders' Equity				839 9 4 2 00

Section 3 Self Review

QUESTIONS

1. How does donated capital arise?

2. Why would a corporation purchase its own stock as treasury stock?

3. Should treasury stock be shown as an asset of the corporation? Explain.

EXERCISES

4. Treasury stock is shown on the balance sheet as:

   a. a deduction from the sum of all other items in the Stockholders' Equity section.

   b. an asset.

   c. an addition to common stock in the Stockholders' Equity section.

   d. an addition to the total of all other Stockholders' Equity accounts.

5. Which of the following would not be found on the statement of retained earnings?

   a. Dividends on preferred stock.

   b. Appropriation for treasury stock.

   c. Appropriation for construction of an office building.

   d. The cash payment made when the corporation completes construction of a building for which an appropriation of retained earnings had been made.

ANALYSIS

6. The balance of the **Retained Earnings** on December 1 is $300,000. During December, dividends of $15,000 on common stock and $10,000 on preferred stock were declared. Neither dividend was paid in December. An **Appropriation for** **Building Expansion** account with a balance of $100,000 was closed and the balance transferred back to **Retained Earnings.** Net income after taxes is $90,000. What is the balance of unappropriated retained earnings on December 31?

(Answers to Section 3 Self Review are on page 765.)

REVIEW   Chapter Summary

A corporation has two major classifications of corporate capital: paid-in capital from capital stock transactions and retained earnings from its profits and losses. In this chapter, you learned also to account for corporate income taxes and to record capital transactions affecting stockholders' equity: dividends, stock splits, appropriation of retained earnings, and treasury stock.

Learning Objectives

21-1   Estimate the federal corporate income tax and prepare related journal entries.

Debit *Income Tax Expense,* and credit *Cash.* Amounts owed or overpaid are recorded as adjustments.

21-2   Complete a worksheet for a corporation.

Enter the trial balance in the Trial Balance section and the adjustments, except income tax expense, in the Adjustments section. Extend balances of all income and expense amounts except income tax expense to the Income Statement section; total its Debit and Credit columns. The difference is the income or loss before income taxes; compute income tax based on it. After entering the income tax adjustment, total the columns in the Adjustments section. Extend Income Tax Expense to the Debit column of the Income Statement section. Total the Debit and Credit columns of the Income Statement section; the difference is net income after tax. Extend the adjusted balances of the asset, liability, and stockholders' equity accounts to the Balance Sheet columns. Enter net income after income tax to the Credit column of the Balance Sheet section. Complete the worksheet in the usual manner.

21-3   Record corporate adjusting and closing entries.

Close revenues and expenses to the *Income Summary* account; close *Income Summary* to *Retained Earnings.*

21-4   Prepare an income statement for a corporation.

The corporation income statement is similar to that of a sole proprietorship, except for the inclusion of an income tax expense deduction. Extraordinary or Nonrecurring Items are shown in a separate section.

21-5   Record the declaration and payment of cash dividends.

Recording cash dividends involves the following: on the declaration date, debit *Retained Earnings* and credit *Dividends Payable.* No journal entry is made on the record date. On the payment date, record the outgoing cash and the reduction of the *Dividends Payable* liability established on the declaration date.

21-6   Record the declaration and issuance of stock dividends.

Issuance of stock dividends above par value price involves a debit to *Retained Earnings,* a credit to *Common Stock Dividend Distributable,* and a credit to *Paid-in Capital in Excess of Par Value.* Upon distribution, *Common Stock Dividend Distributable* is debited, and *Common Stock* is credited.

21-7   Record stock splits.

A memorandum entry records it on the date of declaration, and another is made on the date of issuance.

21-8   Record appropriations of retained earnings.

Debit *Retained Earnings;* credit the *Appropriated Retained Earnings* account for the appropriation amount.

21-9   Record a corporation's receipt of donated assets.

Property given to a corporation is recorded at appraised or fair value and is credited to *Donated Capital.*

21-10   Record treasury stock transactions.

Treasury stock purchase is recorded as a debit to *Treasury Stock* and a credit to *Cash.*

21-11   Prepare financial statements for a corporation.

The major corporation financial statements discussed in this chapter are the income statement, statement of retained earnings, and balance sheet.

21-12   Define the accounting terms new to this chapter.

Glossary

Appropriation of retained earnings (p. 741) A formal declaration of an intention to restrict dividends

Book value (p. 740) The total equity applicable to a class of stock divided by the number of shares outstanding

***Common Stock Dividend Distributable* account** (p. 739) Equity account used to record par, or stated, value of shares to be issued as the result of the declaration of a stock dividend

Declaration date (p. 738) The date on which the board of directors declares a dividend

Deferred income taxes (p. 730) The amount of taxes that will be payable in the future as a result of the difference between taxable income and income for financial statement purposes in the current year and in past years

Donated capital (p. 743) Capital resulting from the receipt of gifts by a corporation

Extraordinary, nonrecurring items (p. 734) Transactions that are highly unusual, clearly unrelated to routine operations, and that do not frequently occur

Paid-in capital (p. 737) Capital acquired from capital stock transactions (also known as contributed capital)

Payment date (p. 738) The date that dividends are paid

Record date (p. 738) The date on which the specific stockholders to receive a dividend are determined

Retained earnings (p. 737) The cumulative profits and losses of the corporation not distributed as dividends

Statement of retained earnings (p. 745) A financial statement that shows all changes that have occurred in retained earnings during the period

Statement of stockholders' equity (p. 745) A financial statement that provides an analysis reconciling the beginning and ending balance of each of the stockholders' equity accounts

Stock dividend (p. 739) Distribution of the corporation's own stock on a pro rata basis that results in conversion of a portion of the firm's retained earnings to permanent capital

Stock split (p. 740) When a corporation issues two or more shares of new stock to replace each share outstanding without making any changes in the capital accounts

Stockholders of record (p. 738) Stockholders in whose name shares are held on date of record and who will receive a declared dividend

Treasury stock (p. 743) A corporation's own capital stock that has been issued and reacquired; the stock must have been previously paid in full and issued to a stockholder

Comprehensive **Self Review**

1. What effect does a common stock dividend have on an individual shareholder's share of ownership in a corporation?
2. What is the difference between treasury stock and unissued stock?
3. Does an appropriation of retained earnings assure a cash balance? Explain.
4. How is treasury stock shown on the balance sheet?
5. What is the purpose of the statement of retained earnings of a corporation?
6. What is meant by "donated capital"?

(Answers to Comprehensive Self Review are on page 765.)

Discussion Questions

1. How is income tax expense classified in the corporation's income statement?

2. What causes "deferred income taxes" to arise? How are balances in "deferred income taxes" accounts disposed of?

3. Explain the three dates related to declaration and payment of a cash dividend. On which of these dates must journal entries be made?

4. Compare the effects on stockholders' equity of a cash dividend and a stock dividend.

5. When a stock dividend is declared, what journal entry is made? How is the amount of the dividend determined or measured?

6. How is the *Common Stock Dividend Distributable* account classified in the financial statements?

7. What are "extraordinary gains and losses"?

8. Where are extraordinary gains and losses shown in the income statement?

9. What effect does a stock split have on retained earnings? Explain.

10. What effect does an appropriation have on total retained earnings?

11. Several years ago a corporation made an appropriation of retained earnings because of a building project. The building project was completed in the current year. What accounting entry will probably be made with respect to the appropriation?

12. As an inducement for Paul Company to locate in Townville, the local chamber of commerce gave the corporation a tract of land with an appraised value of $250,000. How should the gift be accounted for by Paul?

13. At what amount is treasury stock shown on the balance sheet? How is it classified on the balance sheet?

14. What information is shown on the statement of retained earnings?

15. What is the purpose of the statement of stockholders' equity?

APPLICATIONS

Exercises

Estimating corporation income tax.

After all revenue and expense accounts, other than *Income Tax Expense,* have been extended to the Income Statement section of the worksheet of SueB7 Corporation, the net income is determined to be $295,000. Using the tax rates given in this chapter, compute the corporation's federal income taxes payable. (Assume that the firm's taxable income is the same as its income for financial accounting purposes.)

◄ Exercise 21.1
Objective 21-1

Recording journal entries related to taxes.

A corporation has paid estimated income taxes of $41,000 during the year 2016. At the end of the year, the corporation's tax bill is computed to be $47,500. Give the general journal entry to adjust the *Income Tax Expense* account.

◄ Exercise 21.2
Objective 21-1

Exercise 21.3
Objective 21-3

▶ **Recording closing of Income Summary**

In each of the following situations, what is the amount of profit or loss? In each situation, what account will be debited and credited, and for what amount, in the journal entry to close the *Income Summary* account?

a. The total of the Debit column in the Income Statement section of the worksheet was $759,000 and the total of the Credit column in that section was $718,000.

b. The total in the Debit column of the Income Statement section was $704,000 and the total of the Credit column was $741,000.

c. The total of the Debit column in the Balance Sheet section was $400,000 and the total of the Credit column in that section was $391,825.

Exercise 21.4
Objective 21-3

▶ **Recording closing of Income Summary.**

After the revenue and expense accounts were closed into *Income Summary* on December 31, 2016, the *Income Summary* account showed a net loss for the year of $49,000. Prepare the general journal entry to close the *Income Summary* account.

Exercise 21.5
Objective 21-5

▶ **Recording cash dividends.**

On October 15, 2016, the board of directors of Winks Corporation declared a cash dividend of $3 per share on its 85,000 outstanding shares of common stock. The dividend is payable on November 15 to stockholders of record on October 30. Give any general journal entries necessary on October 15, October 30, and November 15, 2016.

Exercise 21.6
Objective 21-6

▶ **Recording a stock dividend.**

Chek Corporation had outstanding 200,000 shares of $5 par-value common stock on August 13, 2016. On that date, it declared a 15 percent common stock dividend distributable on September 15 to stockholders of record on September 1. The estimated fair value of the shares at the time of their issue was $30 per share. Give any general journal entries necessary on August 13, September 1, and September 15, 2016.

Exercise 21.7
Objective 21-7

▶ **Recording a stock split.**

Nevada Corporation had outstanding 200,000 shares of no-par-value common stock, with a stated value of $12, on December 1, 2016. The directors voted to split the stock on a 2-for-1 basis, issuing one new share to stockholders for each share presently owned. The estimated fair value of the new share will be $7. Give any general journal entry required on December 1.

Exercise 21.8
Objective 21-8

▶ **Recording appropriation of retained earnings.**

On December 31, 2016, the board of directors of Indiana Corporation voted to appropriate $100,000 of retained earnings each year for five years to establish a reserve for contingencies. Give the general journal entry on December 31, 2016, to record the appropriation.

Exercise 21.9
Objective 21-8

▶ **Closing appropriation of retained earnings.**

Because of fears about the outcome of several lawsuits in progress during the years 2010 through 2015, Titan Corporation had appropriated retained earnings of $178,000, and transferred that amount from the *Retained Earnings* account to *Retained Earnings Appropriated for Contingencies.* In October 2016, the lawsuits were settled, and Titan Corporation paid $150,000 to settle them. The board of directors breathed a sigh of relief and on November 1, 2016, passed a resolution that the appropriation was no longer needed. Prepare the necessary journal entry on November 1 to close the appropriation account.

Exercise 21.10
Objective 21-9

▶ **Recording receipt of property as gift.**

The city of Orlando contributed to Orange Corporation a tract of land on which to build a plant. When the contribution was made on May 10, 2016, the land's appraised value was $250,000. Give the general journal entry, if any, necessary to record the receipt of the contribution.

Purchasing treasury stock.

On March 31, 2016, Carolina Corporation had outstanding 200,000 shares of 8 percent preferred stock with a par value of $10. The stock was originally issued for $13.50 per share. On that date, the corporation repurchased 15,000 shares of the preferred stock, paying cash of $13.30 per share for the stock. Give the general journal entry to record repurchase of the treasury stock.

◀ **Exercise 21.11**
Objective 21-10

Preparing Stockholders' Equity section of balance sheet.

The following are selected accounts from the general ledger of the First Company on December 31, 2016. Show how the corporation's Stockholders' Equity section would appear on the December 31, 2016, balance sheet.

◀ **Exercise 21.12**
Objective 21-11

Common Stock, $20 par, authorized 14,000 shares, issued and outstanding 10,000 shares	$200,000
Paid-in Capital in Excess of Par Value — Common	18,000
Retained Earnings (debit balance)	(34,000)

PROBLEMS

Problem Set A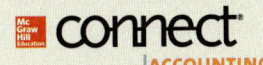

Recording federal income tax transactions and cash dividend transactions.

Selected transactions of Divad Corporation during 2016 follow. Record them in the general journal.

Analyze: What annual per share dividend was paid to common stockholders in 2016?

◀ **Problem 21.1A**
Objectives 21-1, 21-5

DATE		TRANSACTIONS
Mar.	15	Filed the federal income tax return for 2015. The total tax for the year was $136,750. During 2015, quarterly deposits of estimated tax totaling $130,000 had been made. The additional tax of $6,750 was paid with the return. On December 31, 2015, the accountant had estimated the total tax for 2015 to be $134,600 and had recorded a liability of $4,600 for federal income tax payable.
Apr.	15	Paid first quarterly installment of $42,000 on 2016 estimated federal income tax.
May	3	Declared dividend of $0.20 per share on the 50,000 shares of common stock outstanding. The dividend is payable on June 2 to stockholders of record as of May 20, 2016.
June	2	Paid dividend declared on May 3.
	15	Paid second quarterly installment of $42,000 on 2016 estimated federal income tax.
Sept.	15	Paid third quarterly installment of $42,000 on 2016 estimated federal income tax.
Nov.	2	Declared dividend of $0.20 per share on 50,000 shares of common stock outstanding. The dividend is payable on December 2 to holders of record on November 20.
Dec.	2	Paid dividend declared on November 2.
	15	Paid fourth quarterly installment of $42,000 on 2016 estimated income tax.
	31	Total income tax for 2016 was $169,040. Record as an adjustment the difference between this amount and the total quarterly deposits.

Problem 21.2A ▶
Objectives 21-2, 21-3, 21-4, 21-11

Completing a corporate worksheet, recording adjusting and closing entries, preparing an income statement and balance sheet.

Bruin Corporation has been authorized to issue 5,000 shares of 12 percent noncumulative, nonparticipating preferred stock with a par value of $100 per share and 200,000 shares of common stock with a par value of $10 per share. As of December 31, 2016, 2,600 shares of preferred stock and 19,000 shares of common stock had been issued. A condensed trial balance as of December 31, 2016, is provided below.

INSTRUCTIONS

1. Enter the December 31, 2016, trial balance on an eight-column worksheet. Provide three lines for the **Selling Expenses** control account and three lines for the **General Expenses** control account. Total and rule the Trial Balance columns.

2. Record the following transactions in general journal form, using page number 6:

   a. Ending merchandise inventory is $115,000. Close the beginning inventory and set up the ending inventory.

   b. Depreciation of buildings is $14,500 ($11,000 is selling expense; $3,500 is general expense).

   c. Depreciation of equipment is $27,000 ($18,000 is selling expense; $9,000 is general expense).

   d. Accrued expenses are $10,000 ($7,000 is selling expense; $3,000 is general expense).

   e. The balance in **Allowance for Doubtful Accounts** is adequate.

   f. The $49,300 balance in **Income Tax Expense** represents the quarterly tax deposits. Adjust the **Income Tax Expense** account using the following procedure:

   (1) Extend the adjusted income and expense items to the Income Statement columns and compute the net income before taxes.

Bruin Corporation
Trial Balance (Condensed)
December 31, 2016

ACCOUNT NAME	DEBIT	CREDIT
Cash	48 4 7 0 00	
Accounts Receivable	150 8 0 0 00	
Allowance for Doubtful Accounts		3 0 0 0 00
Income Tax Refund Receivable		
Inventory	101 0 0 0 00	
Land	110 0 0 0 00	
Buildings	348 0 0 0 00	
Accumulated Depreciation—Buildings		43 5 0 0 00
Equipment	270 0 0 0 00	
Accumulated Depreciation—Equipment		27 0 0 0 00
Accounts Payable		149 7 2 0 00
Dividends Payable—Preferred		31 2 0 0 00
Dividends Payable—Common		17 1 0 0 00
Accrued Expenses Payable		
Income Tax Payable		
Preferred Stock, 12%		260 0 0 0 00
Paid-in Capital in Excess of Par Value—Preferred		26 0 0 0 00
Common Stock		190 0 0 0 00
Retained Earnings		123 0 0 0 00
Sales (Net)		1,150 5 5 0 00
Purchases	700 0 0 0 00	
Selling Expenses Control	164 8 0 0 00	
General Expenses Control	78 7 0 0 00	
Amortization of Organization Costs		
Income Tax Expense	49 3 0 0 00	
Income Summary		
Totals	2,021 0 7 0 00	2,021 0 7 0 00

(2) Assuming that taxable income is the same as net income before income taxes, use the tax rates given in this chapter to compute the federal income tax. Round the computed tax to the nearest whole dollar. Ignore state and local income taxes.

3. Complete the worksheet as shown in the text.

4. Prepare a condensed income statement for the year.

5. Prepare a balance sheet as of December 31, 2016. The balance of *Retained Earnings* on January 1, 2016, was $171,300. All dividends for the year were declared on December 5, 2016, and are payable January 4, 2017.

6. Journalize the adjusting and closing entries on December 31. Explanations are not required.

Analyze: Assume that dividends were declared in equal amounts over the four quarters of 2016. What percentage of Bruin Corporation's annual income before tax was spent on dividends to stockholders?

Recording cash dividends, stock dividends, and appropriation of retained earnings; preparing statement of retained earnings.

◀ **Problem 21.3A**
Objectives 21-5, 21-6, 21-8, 21-11

The stockholders' equity accounts of Solomon Corporation on January 1, 2016, contained the following balances:

Preferred Stock (10%, $50 par value, 4,000 shares authorized)		
Issued and Outstanding, 1,700 Shares	$85,000	
Paid-in Capital in Excess of Par Value — Preferred	1,700	$ 86,700
Common Stock ($20 par value, 30,000 shares authorized)		
Issued and Outstanding, 15,000 Shares		300,000
Retained Earnings		207,200
Total Stockholders' Equity		$593,900

Transactions affecting stockholders' equity during 2016 follow.

INSTRUCTIONS

1. Set up a ledger account (381) for *Retained Earnings* and record the January 1, 2016, balance.

2. Record the transactions in general journal form and post them to the *Retained Earnings* account only. Use the account titles in the chapter.

3. Prepare a statement of retained earnings for the year 2016.

DATE		TRANSACTIONS
June	15	Declared a semiannual dividend of 5 percent on preferred stock, payable on July 15 to stockholders of record on June 30.
July	15	Paid the dividend on preferred stock.
Dec.	15	Declared a semiannual dividend of 5 percent on preferred stock, payable on January 15, 2017, to stockholders of record on December 31, 2016, and a cash dividend of $4 per share on common stock, payable on January 15, 2017, to stockholders of record on December 31, 2016. Make separate entries.
	15	Declared a 10 percent common stock dividend to common stockholders of record on December 31, 2016. The new shares are to be issued on January 15, 2017. A fair value price of $25 per share is expected for the new shares of common stock.
Dec.	31	Created an "appropriation of retained earnings for contingencies" of $60,000 because of the poor economic outlook.
	31	The *Income Summary* account contained a debit balance of $20,000. The board had anticipated a net loss for the year and no quarterly deposits of estimated income taxes were made, so income taxes may be ignored.

Analyze: If Solomon Corporation had not declared cash or stock dividends for common stockholders, what balance would be found in the unappropriated *Retained Earnings* account at December 31, 2016?

Problem 21.4A ▶

Objectives 21-5, 21-7, 21-8, 21-9, 21-11

Recording cash dividends, stock splits, appropriations of retained earnings, and donated assets; preparing the Stockholders' Equity section of the balance sheet.

The Stockholders' Equity section of the balance sheet of Willy Corporation on January 1, 2016, is shown below; selected transactions for the year follow:

Stockholders' Equity			
Preferred Stock (10% cumulative, $10 par value,			
200,000 shares authorized)			
Issued and Outstanding, 9,000 Shares		$ 90,000	
Paid-in Capital in Excess of Par Value		9,000	$ 99,000
Common Stock (no-par value, $50 stated value,			
300,000 shares authorized)			
Issued and Outstanding, 3,000 Shares		150,000	
Paid-in Capital in Excess of Stated Value		6,000	156,000
Total Paid-in Capital			$255,000
Retained Earnings			140,000
Total Stockholders' Equity			$395,000

INSTRUCTIONS

1. Open the stockholders' equity accounts in the general ledger, and enter the beginning balances. In addition to the accounts listed, open the following accounts:

   Donated Capital

   Treasury Stock — Preferred

   Retained Earnings — Appropriated for Treasury Stock

2. Record the transactions in general journal form.
3. Post the transactions to the stockholders' equity accounts.
4. Prepare the Stockholders' Equity section of the balance sheet.

DATE	TRANSACTIONS
Feb. 15	Repurchased 4,100 shares of the outstanding preferred stock for $45,100 in cash. The stock is to be held as treasury stock. State law requires that an amount of retained earnings equal to the cost of treasury stock held must be appropriated. Record the purchase and the appropriation of retained earnings.
Mar. 4	Declared a 2-for-1 stock split of common stock. Each shareholder will own twice as many shares as originally owned. Stated value is reduced to $25 per share. Date of record is March 15. Date of issue of new shares is April 1.
April 1	Issued new shares called for by split.
June 17	Declared semiannual dividend of 5 percent on preferred stock, to be paid on July 12 to holders of record on June 30.
July 12	Paid cash dividend on preferred stock.
Sept. 25	Purchased 600 shares of outstanding preferred stock at $10 per share to be held as treasury stock. Record appropriated retained earnings equal to cost of the treasury stock.

DATE	TRANSACTIONS
Dec. 15	Declared semiannual cash dividend of 5 percent on preferred stock to be paid on January 12 to holders of record on December 30.
15	Declared cash dividend of $1.40 per share on common stock to be paid on January 12 to holders of record on December 30.
15	Accepted title to a tract of land with an appraised value of $160,000 from the City of Greenville. The tract is to be used as a building site for the corporation's new factory.
31	Had net income after taxes for the year of $80,000. Give the entry to close the *Income Summary* account.

Analyze: If Willy Corporation had not repurchased preferred stock to place in treasury, what total stockholders' equity would be reported on December 31, 2016?

Problem Set B

Recording federal income tax and cash dividend transactions.

Selected transactions of Dallas Corporation during 2016 are given below. Record them in the general journal.

◄ **Problem 21.1B**
Objectives 21-1, 21-5

Analyze: If the dividends declared on October 30 were to be paid on January 15, what balance would be reflected in the *Dividends Payable* account on December 31, 2016?

DATE	TRANSACTIONS
Mar. 15	Filed the federal tax return for 2015. The total tax for the year was $180,000. Estimated tax deposits of $175,000 had been made during 2015, and on December 31, 2015, the accountant had accrued an additional liability of $4,000. Paid the tax due of $5,000.
Apr. 15	Paid first quarterly installment of $45,000 on 2016 estimated federal income tax.
May 30	Declared dividend of $0.10 per share on the 50,000 shares of common stock outstanding. The dividend is payable on June 30 to holders of record on June 15.
June 15	Paid second quarterly installment of $45,000 on 2016 estimated federal income tax.
30	Paid the dividend declared on May 30.
Sept. 15	Paid third quarterly installment of $45,000 on 2016 estimated federal income tax.
Oct. 30	Declared cash dividend of $0.10 per share on the 50,000 shares of common stock outstanding. The dividend is payable on December 1 to holders of record on November 15.
Dec. 1	Paid dividend declared on October 30.
15	Paid fourth quarterly installment of $45,000 on 2016 estimated federal income tax.
31	In completing the worksheet at the end of the year, the accountant estimated that the total income tax for 2016 was $175,000. The difference between this amount and the quarterly deposits is to be recorded as an adjustment.

Problem 21.2B ▶
Objectives 21-2, 21-3, 21-4, 21-11

Completing a corporate worksheet; recording adjusting and closing entries; preparing an income statement and balance sheet.

Pacific Corporation has been authorized to issue 10,000 shares of 10 percent noncumulative, nonparticipating preferred stock with a par value of $100 per share and 10,000 shares of common stock with a stated value of $100 per share. As of December 31, 2016, 800 shares of preferred stock and 800 shares of common stock have been issued and are outstanding. Dividends are paid quarterly on the preferred stock. A condensed trial balance as of December 31, 2016, is shown below.

INSTRUCTIONS

1. Enter the December 31 trial balance on an eight-column worksheet. Provide four lines for the *Selling Expenses* control account and three lines for the *General Expenses* control account. Total and rule the Trial Balance columns.

2. Enter the necessary adjustments on the worksheet, based on the following data for December 31:

   a. Ending merchandise inventory is $78,000. Close the beginning inventory, and set up the ending inventory.

   b. *Allowance for Doubtful Accounts* should be adjusted to a balance of $1,300 (debit *Selling Expenses*).

   c. Depreciation of buildings is $4,000 ($3,600 is selling expense; $400 is general expense).

   d. Depreciation of equipment is $6,000 ($2,000 is selling expense; $4,000 is general expense).

   e. Accrued expenses are $3,800 ($1,200 is selling expense; $2,600 is general expense).

Pacific Corporation
Trial Balance (Condensed)
December 31, 2016

ACCOUNT NAME	DEBIT	CREDIT
Cash	40 0 0 0 00	
Accounts Receivable	52 8 0 0 00	
Allowance for Doubtful Accounts		7 0 0 00
Merchandise Inventory	74 9 2 0 00	
Land	60 0 0 0 00	
Buildings	88 0 0 0 00	
Accumulated Depreciation—Buildings		8 0 0 0 00
Equipment	78 0 0 0 00	
Accumulated Depreciation—Equipment		12 0 0 0 00
Accounts Payable		31 4 5 0 00
Dividends Payable—Preferred		2 4 0 0 00
Accrued Expenses Payable		
Income Tax Payable		
Preferred Stock, 10%		80 0 0 0 00
Paid-in Capital in Excess of Par Value—Preferred		6 0 0 0 00
Common Stock		80 0 0 0 00
Retained Earnings		89 1 7 0 00
Sales (Net)		445 0 0 0 00
Purchases	220 0 0 0 00	
Selling Expenses Control	85 0 0 0 00	
General Expenses Control	40 0 0 0 00	
Income Tax Expense	16 0 0 0 00	
Income Summary		
Totals	754 7 2 0 00	754 7 2 0 00

f. The $16,000 balance in *Income Tax Expense* represents the quarterly tax deposits. Adjust the *Income Tax Expense* account using the following procedure:

    (1) Extend the adjusted income and expense items to the Income Statement columns. Using this data, compute the net income before income taxes.

    (2) Assuming that taxable income is the same as net income before income taxes, use the tax rates given in this chapter to compute the federal income tax. Round the computed tax to the nearest whole dollar. Ignore state and local income taxes.

3. Complete the worksheet as shown in the text.

4. Prepare a condensed income statement for the year.

5. Prepare a balance sheet as of December 31, 2016. The balance of *Retained Earnings* on January 1, 2016, was $89,170. The only dividends declared during the year were dividends on preferred stock.

6. Journalize the adjusting and closing entries on December 31, 2016. Descriptions are not required.

Analyze: Assume that dividends were declared in equal amounts over the four quarters of fiscal 2016. What percentage of Pacific Corporation's annual income before tax was spent on dividends to stockholders?

Recording cash dividends, stock dividends, appropriations of retained earnings; preparing statement of retained earnings.

◄ **Problem 21.3B**
Objectives 21-5, 21-6, 21-8, 21-11

The stockholders' equity accounts of Toy Town Corporation on January 1, 2016, contained the following balances:

Preferred Stock (8%, $50 par value, 2,000 shares authorized)		
Issued and Outstanding, 600 shares		$ 30,000
Common Stock (no-par, $25 stated value, 10,000 shares authorized)		
Issued and Outstanding, 5,000 shares	$125,000	
Paid-in Capital in Excess of Stated Value	25,000	150,000
Retained Earnings		150,000
Total Stockholders' Equity		$330,000

The transactions affecting stockholders' equity during 2016 are given below. The worksheet at the end of 2016 showed a net loss of $5,000.

INSTRUCTIONS

1. Set up a ledger account (381) for *Retained Earnings,* and record the January 1, 2016, balance.

2. Record the following transactions in general journal form using page 6. Use the account titles used in the text. No descriptions are required. Post these entries to the *Retained Earnings* account only.

3. Prepare a statement of retained earnings for the year 2016.

DATE	TRANSACTIONS
June 15	Declared a semiannual 4 percent cash dividend on preferred stock and a cash dividend of $1.00 per share on common stock. Both are payable July 15 to stockholders of record on July 1. (Make a compound entry.)
July 15	Paid the cash dividends.
Sept. 15	Declared a 5 percent common stock dividend to be distributed on October 12 to common stockholders of record on October 1. The stock is expected to have an expected fair trading value of $30 per share when issued.
Oct. 12	Distributed the common stock dividend.
Dec. 15	Declared a semiannual 4 percent cash dividend on preferred stock and a cash dividend of $0.50 per share on common stock. Both dividends are payable January 15 to stockholders of record on December 31. (Make a compound entry.)
15	Directed that retained earnings of $5,000 be appropriated each year for the next four years to purchase a new computer system. Title the account *Retained Earnings Appropriated for Equipment Acquisition.* Record the appropriation for 2016.
31	Close the debit balance of $5,000 in *Income Summary.*

Analyze: What balances should be reflected in the *Dividends Payable—Preferred* account on December 31, 2016?

Problem 21.4B
Objectives 21-5, 21-7, 21-8, 21-9, 21-11

▶ **Recording cash dividends, stock splits, appropriation of retained earnings, and donated assets; preparing the Stockholders' Equity section of the balance sheet.**

The Stockholders' Equity section of Dallas Corporation's balance sheet on January 1, 2016, follows, along with selected transactions for the year:

Stockholders' Equity

Preferred Stock (6%, $50 par value, 10,000 shares authorized)		
Issued and Outstanding, 1,000 Shares	$50,000	
Paid-in Capital in Excess of Par Value	3,500	$ 53,500
Common Stock (no-par value, $20 stated value, 20,000 shares authorized)		
Issued and Outstanding, 4,000 Shares	$80,000	
Paid-in Capital in Excess of Stated Value	3,000	83,000
Retained Earnings		165,500
Total Stockholders' Equity		$ 302,000

INSTRUCTIONS

1. Set up general ledger accounts for the stockholders' equity items and enter the given balances. In addition to the accounts listed, open the accounts *Donated Capital, Treasury Stock—Preferred,* and *Retained Earnings Appropriated for Treasury Stock.*
2. Record the transactions listed below in general journal form.
3. Post general journal entries only to the stockholders' equity accounts.
4. Prepare the Stockholders' Equity section of the balance sheet as of December 31, 2016.

DATE	TRANSACTIONS
Feb. 1	Reacquired 100 shares of preferred stock at $52 per share, and set up an appropriation of retained earnings equal to cost of treasury stock purchased, as required by law.
Mar. 1	Declared a 2-for-1 split of common stock and reduced the stated value to $10.00 per share. Date of record is March 20. Date of issue is April 1.
Apr. 1	Issued new shares of common stock called for by split.
June 20	Declared a cash dividend of 3 percent on preferred stock outstanding, payable July 10 to holders of record on July 1.
July 10	Paid cash dividends on preferred stock.
Nov. 10	Purchased 200 shares of the corporation's own preferred stock to be held as treasury stock, paying $53 per share. Appropriated retained earnings equal to cost of the shares.
Dec. 17	Declared the semiannual cash dividends of 3 percent on preferred stock and a $1 per share on common stock. Both are payable to stockholders of record on December 28 and are payable on January 8. Make separate entries.
24	Received land valued at $100,000 as a gift from a neighboring city agreeing to build a new factory.
31	The *Income Summary* account had a credit balance of $50,000 after income tax. Give the entry to close the account.

Analyze: As of December 31, what percent of total authorized preferred stock is held in treasury?

Critical Thinking Problem 21.1

Stockholders' Equity

The Stockholders' Equity section of the balance sheets for Klee Corporation on December 31, 2015, and December 31, 2016, along with other selected account balances on the two dates is provided on page 762. (Certain information is missing from the statements.)

In 2016, the following transactions affecting equity occurred:

a. Additional shares of common stock were issued in April. No other common stock was issued during the year.

b. A cash dividend of $2 per share was declared and paid on common stock in December.

c. The Treasury Stock—Preferred was purchased at par in January.

d. Additional preferred stock was issued for cash in July.

e. The yearly cash dividend of $2.00 per share was declared and paid on preferred stock outstanding as of December 3, 2016.

INSTRUCTIONS

Answer the following questions about transactions in 2016:

1. How many shares of preferred stock were outstanding at year-end?

2. How many common stock shares were outstanding at year-end?

3. How many shares of preferred stock were purchased as treasury stock?

4. How many shares of preferred stock were issued for cash?

5. What was the sales price per share of the preferred stock issued?

6. What was the total cash dividend on preferred stock?

7. What was the total cash dividend on common stock?

	2016	2015
Stockholders' Equity		
Paid-in Capital		
Preferred Stock (10 percent, $20 par, authorized 20,000 shares)		
Issued	$ 90,000	$ 65,000
Paid-in Capital in Excess of Par		
Value — Preferred	500	–0–
Common Stock ($10 par value, 200,000 shares authorized)		
Issued	750,000	500,000
Paid-in Capital in Excess of Par		
Value — Common	10,000	
Total Paid-in Capital	$ 850,500	$ 565,000
Retained Earnings		
Appropriated for Plant Expansion	$ 250,000	$ 250,000
Appropriated for Treasury Stock	40,000	–0–
Unappropriated	640,000	604,000
Total Retained Earnings	$ 930,000	$ 854,000
	$1,780,500	$1,419,000
Less Treasury Stock — Preferred	15,000	–0–
Total Stockholders' Equity	$1,765,500	$1,419,000

Analyze: What is the yearly dividend reduction because of the treasury stock purchase?

Critical Thinking Problem 21.2

Individual Investor

Lowe Tech Inc. has the following stockholders' equity on June 30, 2016:

Common Stock, $15 par (200,000 shares issued)	$3,000,000
Paid-in Capital in Excess of Par	2,000,000
Retained Earnings	4,000,000
Total Stockholders' Equity	$9,000,000

For the past three years, Lowe Tech Inc. has paid dividends of $1.60 per share. On July 1, 2016, the board declared a 20 percent stock dividend instead of the $1.60 cash dividend. Before the end of the year and after the stock dividend distribution, however, the board declared a cash dividend of $1.33 per share.

In June 2016, before the stock dividend was declared, Rosa Dodd purchased 12,000 shares of Lowe Tech Inc. stock for $60 per share. Now she is concerned because she purchased the stock expecting a $1.60 per-share dividend, only to learn that the dividend has been reduced to $1.33 per share.

Answer the following questions concerning this investment:

1. What could have caused Lowe Tech's board of directors to declare a stock dividend rather than a cash dividend in July?

2. How did the book value of Rosa's stock prior to the stock dividend compare with its book value after the stock dividend?

3. Why does the market value of the stock ($60) when Rosa purchased her shares differ from its book value at that time?

4. How does the total amount of cash dividends on Rosa's stock differ between the $1.60 per share on Rosa's original holdings and the $1.33 per share on her holdings after the stock dividend?

5. Assume the market price of the stock fell to $50 after the stock dividend was distributed. Does this drop represent a loss to Rosa?

6. What do you think would have happened to the market price of the stock if the board had not reduced the amount of the cash dividend per share of stock?

BUSINESS CONNECTIONS

Shareholder's Equity

Managerial | FOCUS

1. Three individuals are planning to form a new business. What are the five major types of entities that they can use to operate their business?

2. Assume that you are the controller of a corporation. Some members of the board of directors have asked you how the firm can have a large balance in the *Retained Earnings* account but no cash with which to pay dividends. Explain.

3. A corporation's balance sheet shows *Retained Earnings Appropriated for Plant Expansion* with a balance of $4,000,000. Does this mean that the corporation has set aside $4,000,000 in cash to expand its plant? Why would management want to establish such an account?

4. O'Neil Corporation's $50 par-value stock has a market price of $250 per share. As a result of the high price per share, finding buyers for stock that existing shareholders wish to sell has become difficult. Suggest a way for management to resolve this problem.

5. Why would the management of a corporation consider using corporate funds to purchase the firms' own outstanding stock?

6. The president of a corporation suggests to the controller that one way to convert retained earnings into permanent capital is to have a stock split. What explanation should the controller give the president?

Corporate Incentives

Ethical | DILEMMA

A small community called Center needs to increase jobs in the community. Center has some public land that could be developed. The city could sell this land to a private individual for $200,000. The city council decided, however, to make arrangements with a national chain "superstore" to receive the land free if they would build a store in their community. The superstore must first hire from the people that live in Center to receive this free land. Is it ethical for the Center City Council to propose this gift? How would the superstore record this transaction?

Statement of Shareholders' Equity

Financial Statement | ANALYSIS

Refer to the *2012 Annual Report (for the fiscal year ended February 3, 2013)* for The Home Depot, Inc., in Appendix A.

1. Based on the data presented in the consolidated statements of earnings, answer the following:

   a. What approximate income tax rate does the company pay?

   b. Did the company record an accrual for current income tax payable for the year ended February 3, 2013? If so, on which statement did you locate this information?

Dividends to Declare

The board of directors has the responsibility to determine the dollar amount of dividends to be given to investors. As a group of three or four students acting as the board of directors, determine the amount of dividends to declare for your investors given the following information: (1) 100,000 shares outstanding, (2) $249,000 in net income, (3) $1,500,000 proposed future expansion, (4) $900,000 balance in *Retained Earnings.* Should the board approve a dividend in stock, cash, or a combination of both? Justify your answer.

Earnings and Dividends per Share

From the websites of several corporations that pay dividends, find the ratio between the earnings per share and the dividends paid per share. How much of the earnings does each corporation return to its stockholders? Does the amount of retained earnings determine the amount of dividends?

Answers to **Self Reviews**

Answers to Section 1 Self Review

1. Income tax expense is usually shown as a deduction at the bottom of the income statement, after Net Income Before Tax, but is sometimes shown as an Operating Expense to emphasize that taxes are a cost of doing business.

2. After the balances of income and expense accounts—other than income taxes—have been extended to the Income Statement of the worksheet, the debit column and credit column are totaled. The difference is the income before taxes. The taxes are computed on that income and entered as an adjustment and carried forward to the debit column of the income statement section.

3. Retained earnings represent the cumulative profits and losses of the corporation that have not been distributed as dividends or transferred to Paid-in Capital through cash dividends, stock dividends, or stock splits.

4. These adjustments are the same for sole proprietorships and corporations.

5. There are many special rules—for example, depreciation calculations—for tax purposes that are not acceptable under GAAP requirements.

6. $80,750

7. Dr. *Income Tax Refund Receivable* (or a similar account), $500. Credit *Federal Income Tax Expense,* $500. ($8,000 estimate paid, minus $7,500 actual tax for the year.)

Answers to Section 2 Self Review

1. The date of declaration—the date the board of directors formally announces the dividend. The date of record—date on which owners of stock are determined and to whom dividends will be paid. The date of payment is the date on which payment is to be made.

2. A general journal entry is made to reflect a reduction of Retained Earnings for the value of a stock dividend. No entry is made in the accounts to record a stock split, except memorandum entries to note the board's action when the split is authorized and again on the date the additional shares are issued.

3. No cash is involved in an appropriation of retained earnings. Cash is involved only if a separate fund is established to pay for the object of the appropriation.

4. Of these actions, only a cash dividend (**c**) will result in a decrease in stockholder equity.

5. **c.** A board resolution is necessary to reduce appropriated retained earnings.

6. $3,000 (600 shares $\times$ $5)

Answers to Section 3 Self Review

1. Donated capital arises when assets are contributed or donated to the corporation or when the debt of the corporation is forgiven. A common transaction giving rise to donated capital is the gift of land to the corporation as an incentive to locate a new facility on the land. Similarly, cash may be given the corporation to entice it to open a business in a city.

2. A common reason is that the corporation's board decides the corporation has excess cash and concludes that its own stock represents the best available investment. Sometimes stock is repurchased to reduce the number of shares outstanding with the expectation of increasing net income per share and/or dividends per share for remaining shareholders.

3. The cost of treasury stock should not be shown as an asset on the balance sheet of the issuing corporation. It represents a deduction from the total of the corporation's other stockholders' equity accounts.

4. **a.** a deduction from the sum of all other items in the Stockholders' Equity section.

5. **d.** the cash payment made to build a building for which an appropriation of retained earnings had previously been made.

6. $465,000

Answers to Comprehensive Self Review

1. The shareholder's ownership percentage is unaffected by a common stock dividend.

2. Treasury stock is stock that has been issued, paid for, and reacquired. Unissued stock meets none of those requirements for treasury stock.

3. The appropriation account merely restricts the payment of dividends to the amount of retained earnings in excess of the appropriations. Retained earnings—and the appropriation—have nothing to do with cash.

4. On the balance sheet, treasury stock is deducted from the total of all other stockholders' equity.

5. The statement of retained earnings is to show all changes in retained earnings that have occurred during the period.

6. Donated capital represents the value of assets that have been donated to, or contributed to, the corporation. Usually such contributions are to be used for some specified purpose.

www.heinz.com

Although ketchup is the most famous Heinz product today, when Henry Heinz started the Company in 1869, his first product was bottled horseradish made from his mother's own recipe. Heinz® Ketchup came along seven years later. Today, H. J. Heinz is a $10 billion global company that employs over 32,000 people and sells about 650 million bottles of ketchup each year across six continents.

Like many large corporations, H. J. Heinz has employed various strategies to finance its operations. During 2012, the company issued $1.91 billion of notes that had various maturity dates ranging from three, five, seven, and ten years. These notes had interest rates promised by the company ranging from 1.5 to 3.4 percent.

When a company like Heinz, decides to borrow to finance its operations, it needs to consider many issues including but not limited to: can it repay the debt? What interest should it pay the holder of the debt and, of course, what will it do with the money raised? Henry John Heinz, founder of H. J. Heinz, said, "To do a common thing uncommonly well brings success." And for a company that makes approximately two single-serve packets of ketchup for every man, woman, and child on the planet, it wants its customers to continue to believe, "If it isn't Heinz, it isn't ketchup."

thinking critically

What are some other sources of long-term financing that could be used by a firm if selling bonds is not a possibility?

LEARNING OBJECTIVES	NEW TERMS	
22-1. Name and define the various types of bonds.	bond indenture	discount on bonds payable
22-2. Explain the advantages and disadvantages of using bonds as a method of financing.	bond issue costs	face interest rate
22-3. Record the issuance of bonds.	bond retirement	leveraging
22-4. Record the payment of interest on bonds.	bond sinking fund investment	market interest rate
22-5. Record the accrual of interest on bonds.	bonds payable	mortgage loan
22-6. Compute and record the periodic amortization of a bond premium.	call price	premium on bonds payable
22-7. Compute and record the periodic amortization of a bond discount.	callable bonds	registered bonds
	carrying value of bonds	secured bonds
22-8. Record the transactions of a bond sinking fund investment.	collateral trust bonds	serial bonds
	convertible bonds	straight-line amortization
22-9. Record an increase or decrease in retained earnings appropriated for bond retirement.	coupon bonds	trading on the equity
	debentures	
22-10. Record retirement of bonds payable.		
22-11. Define the accounting terms new to this chapter.		

>> 22-1. **Name and define the various types of bonds.**

WHY IT'S IMPORTANT

Corporations frequently issue bonds to raise capital.

>> 22-2. **Explain the advantages and disadvantages of using bonds as a method of financing.**

WHY IT'S IMPORTANT

The use of bonds as a method of financing carries certain financial obligations and tax implications.

TERMS TO LEARN

bond indenture
bonds payable
call price
callable bonds
collateral trust bonds
convertible bonds
coupon bonds
debentures
face interest rate
leveraging
market interest rate
mortgage loan
registered bonds
secured bonds
serial bonds
trading on the equity

Financing Through Bonds

There are many ways for corporations to raise funds. They may sell stock, or they may sign a note payable.

A long-term note may be secured by a mortgage on specific assets such as land, buildings, or equipment. A **mortgage loan** is a long-term debt created when a note is given as part of the purchase price of land or buildings.

Corporations that need long-term funds often obtain those funds by issuing bonds payable. **Bonds payable** are long-term debt instruments that are written promises to repay the principal at a future date. Interest is due at a fixed rate that is payable annually, semiannually, or quarterly over the life of the bond. Bonds are similar to notes payable, but the contract is more formal. Bonds are easily transferred from one owner (or bondholder) to another.

>> **22-1. OBJECTIVE**

Name and define the various types of bonds.

Types of Bonds

Bonds are classified by the following characteristics:

■ Bonds can be secured by collateral, or they can be unsecured.

■ Bonds can be registered or unregistered.

■ Bonds can all mature on the same date, or portions can mature over a period of several years. *Mature* means to fall due or to become payable.

SECURED AND UNSECURED BONDS

Secured bonds have property pledged to secure the claims of the bondholders. **Collateral trust bonds** involve the pledge of securities, such as stocks or bonds of other companies. A bond contract, known as a **bond indenture,** is prepared. A trustee, frequently an investment banker, is named to protect the bondholders' interests. If the bonds are not paid when due, the trustee takes legal steps to sell the pledged property and pay off the bonds.

Bonds are identified according to the nature of the property pledged and the year of maturity. Examples are as follows:

- First Mortgage 7 percent Real Estate Bonds Payable, 2023
- Collateral Trust 5 percent Bonds Payable, 2019

Unsecured bonds backed only by a corporation's general credit are called **debentures.** They involve no pledge of specific property. However, the bondholders do have some protection in case of liquidation. The claims of creditors, including bondholders, rank above those of stockholders. Creditors must be paid in full before stockholders can receive anything.

REGISTERED AND UNREGISTERED BONDS

Registered bonds are bonds issued to a party whose name is listed in the corporation's records. Ownership is transferred by completing an assignment form and having the change of ownership entered in the corporation's records. Interest is paid by check to each registered bondholder. The corporation maintains a detailed subsidiary ledger, similar to the stockholders' ledger, for registered bonds. At all times, the corporation knows who owns the bonds and who is entitled to receive interest payments.

Some bonds do not require that the names of the owners be registered. These bonds are known as **coupon bonds.** The bonds have coupons attached for each interest payment. The coupons are, in effect, checks payable to the bearer. No record of the owner's identity is kept by the corporation. On or after each interest date, the bondholder detaches the coupon from the bond and presents it to a bank for payment. Coupon bonds are often referred to as *bearer bonds* because the bearer is assumed to be the owner. Coupon bonds are rarely issued because the IRS requires corporations to report the name, tax identification number, and interest received by each bondholder. State and local governments continue to issue coupon bonds because the interest is not subject to federal income tax.

SINGLE-MATURITY AND SERIAL-MATURITY BONDS

Most bonds in an issue mature on the same day. However, **serial bonds** are payable over a period of years. For example, a corporation might issue serial bonds totaling $10 million, dated January 1, 2016, with $2,000,000 maturing each year for five years, beginning on January 1, 2026. The corporation might find it easier to retire bonds on a serial basis rather than to have all $10 million due on the same date.

OTHER CHARACTERISTICS OF BONDS PAYABLE

Bonds are issued in various denominations. The denomination specified on the contract is called the *face value.* The typical face value is $1,000 or $10,000.

Convertible bonds give the owner the right to convert the bonds into common stock under specified conditions. For example, an indenture can give the holder of a 20-year, $1,000 bond the right to convert the bond into 50 shares of the corporation's common stock at any time. When the price of the stock reaches $20 or more ($1,000 bond ÷ 50 shares of stock), the bondholder is likely to convert it into stock.

Bonds are frequently callable. **Callable bonds** allow the issuing corporation to require the holders to surrender the bonds for payment before their maturity date. Call provisions are clearly stated on the bond. The **call price** is the amount the corporation must pay for the bond when it is called. Usually the call price is slightly above the face value. If the market interest rate declines below the face interest rate on the bonds, or if the corporation has excess cash, it might call all or part of the bonds and retire them.

Market interest rate refers to the interest rate a corporation is willing to pay and investors are willing to accept at the current time. **Face interest rate** refers to the contractual interest rate specified on the bond. Market interest rate changes constantly. Face interest rate of a bond does not change.

For example, assume that on October 1, 2016, CAH Incorporated issues 20-year bonds with a face value of $100,000. The bonds mature on October 1, 2036. Under the terms of the indenture,

recall

Face Value
The term *face value* also applies to notes payable and notes receivable. It is sometimes known as *face amount.*

CAH can call the bonds at any time after October 1, 2026, at a call price of 103 (103 percent of face value). The bonds are called by CAH on October 1, 2027. Johanson, an owner of bonds with a face value of $30,000, must surrender the bonds and will be paid $30,900 ($30,000 × 1.03).

>> 22-2. OBJECTIVE

Explain the advantages and disadvantages of using bonds as a method of financing.

Stock versus Bonds as a Financing Method

Corporations raise funds through various combinations of common stock, preferred stock, and bonds. Management considers several factors when deciding whether to issue stock or bonds. Table 22.1 shows some factors to consider when comparing capital stock and bonds.

When deciding whether to issue bonds, a company needs to determine whether the rate of return on the assets acquired with the bond proceeds is higher than the interest rate paid on the bonds. Suppose that a newly formed corporation issued both common stock and bonds payable to provide total capital of $500,000. The owners invest $300,000 for common stock and borrow $200,000 by issuing bonds. The bonds pay 10 percent interest per year. The corporation's income before interest and taxes is $70,000. Assume a corporate income tax rate of 20 percent. Let's compute the rate of profit on the stockholders' investment.

Amount available to stockholders:

Net income before bond interest expense	$70,000
Bond interest expense ($200,000 × 0.10)	(20,000)
Net income before income taxes	$50,000
Income tax expense ($50,000 × 0.20)	(10,000)
Net income after taxes	$40,000

The stockholders invested $300,000 in the business, and the net income is $40,000. The stockholders earned 13.3 percent ($40,000 ÷ $300,000) profit on their equity. Let's see what happens if the owners invest $500,000 in common stock. Since there is no bond payable, there is no interest expense:

Net income before taxes	$70,000
Income tax expense ($70,000 × 0.20)	(14,000)
Net income after income taxes	$56,000

The stockholders invested $500,000, and net income is $56,000. The stockholders earned 11.2 percent ($56,000 ÷ $500,000) on their equity. With financing coming 100 percent from capital stock, the net income available to the stockholders is higher ($56,000 versus $40,000), but the rate of profit on equity is lower (11.2 percent versus 13.3 percent).

TABLE 22.1

Stock and Bonds Compared

Capital Stock	Bonds Payable
Capital stock is permanent capital. There is no debt to be repaid.	Bonds payable are debt. When the bonds fall due, the debt must be repaid.
Because the stock is permanent capital, it is classified as stockholders' equity.	Because the bonds represent debt, they are classified as long-term liabilities.
Dividends are not legally required on common stock. The requirements on preferred stock depend on the contract.	Interest must be paid on the bonds.
Dividends are not deductible for income tax purposes.	Interest is deducted in arriving at the taxable income.
Preference dividends on preferred stock are usually slightly higher than interest rates on bonds because there is more risk associated with preferred stock.	Interest rates on bonds are slightly lower than dividends on preferred stock.

The increase in the rate of profit on stockholders' equity when bonds are used is due to the fact that the company's profits are higher than the face rate of interest (10 percent) on the bonds. Using borrowed funds to earn a profit higher than the interest that must be paid on the borrowing is called **trading on the equity,** or **leveraging.** In lean years, such financing can be dangerous from the stockholders' standpoint. The bond interest expense might leave little or nothing for dividends to the stockholders. Moreover, even when the firm operates at a loss, the interest must be paid in full to the bondholders. In addition, the principal amount of the debt must also be paid when the bonds mature.

For example, if the income before interest and taxes had been only $12,000, the use of bonds payable would result in the corporation having a net loss:

Net income before bond interest expense	$12,000
Bond interest expense ($200,000 × 0.10)	(20,000)
Net loss	$(8,000)

Section 1   Self Review

QUESTIONS

1. What is a convertible bond?
2. What is the difference between registered bonds and coupon bonds?
3. Why would a corporation issue callable bonds?

EXERCISES

4. Bonds that are payable over a period of years are called:
   a. callable bonds.
   b. serial bonds.
   c. bearer bonds.
   d. coupon bonds.

5. Bonds backed only by the general credit of the corporation are called:
   a. secured bonds.
   b. collateral trust bonds.
   c. registered bonds.
   d. debentures.

ANALYSIS

6. A small corporation is considering a bond issue. The amount of stockholders' equity is $250,000. The corporation projects income before bond interest and taxes of $60,000. The corporate income tax rate is 20 percent. If $125,000 of bonds is issued at 10 percent, what is the rate of profit on stockholders' equity?

(Answers to Section 1 Self Review are on page 795.)

>> 22-3. Record the issuance of bonds.

WHY IT'S IMPORTANT
The issuance of bonds creates a long-term liability that needs to be reflected in the accounting records of the issuer.

>> 22-4. Record the payment of interest on bonds.

WHY IT'S IMPORTANT
Bondholders receive interest from the bond issuer as stated in the debt instrument.

>> 22-5. Record the accrual of interest on bonds.

WHY IT'S IMPORTANT
At year-end, expenses that have not been recorded are accrued to conform to the matching principle.

>> 22-6. Compute and record the periodic amortization of a bond premium.

WHY IT'S IMPORTANT
Bond premiums reduce the overall interest expense.

>> 22-7. Compute and record the periodic amortization of a bond discount.

WHY IT'S IMPORTANT
Issuing a bond at less than face value increases total interest expense.

SECTION OBJECTIVES

TERMS TO LEARN

bond issue costs
carrying value of bonds
discount on bonds payable
premium on bonds payable
straight-line amortization

Bond Issue and Interest

The board of directors of Technx Corporation authorized the issue of 300 registered, unsecured bonds that will mature in 10 years. The face value of each bond is $1,000. The face interest rate is 10 percent. Interest will be paid on April 1 and October 1 of each year. Interest on each bond is $100 per year ($1,000 × 0.10). Because interest is paid semiannually, each interest payment is $50 ($100 ÷ 2). Some of the authorized bonds will be sold immediately. The remainder will be held for future needs.

>> **22-3. OBJECTIVE**
Record the issuance of bonds.

Bonds Issued at Face Value

On April 1, 2016, the issue date, Technx sells 50 bonds at face value for $50,000 ($1,000 × 50). The journal entry follows:

	DATE		DESCRIPTION	POST. REF.	DEBIT	CREDIT	
			GENERAL JOURNAL			PAGE _____	
1	2016						1
2	Apr.	1	Cash		50 0 0 0 00		2
3			10% Bonds Payable, 2026			50 0 0 0 00	3
4			Issued bonds at face value				4
5							5

After the entry is posted, the ledger account for the bonds appears as follows:

ACCOUNT	10% Bonds Payable, 2026				ACCOUNT NO.	261		
	(Authorized $300,000; Interest April 1, October 1)							

						BALANCE		
DATE	DESCRIPTION	POST. REF.	DEBIT	CREDIT		DEBIT	CREDIT	
2016								
Apr. 1		J4		50 000 00			50 000 00	

important!

A buyer of bonds that are purchased on dates other than interest payment dates must include in the purchase transaction for the bonds, the amount of interest due from the last payment through the date of the bond purchase.

Notice that the amount of bonds authorized is recorded as a memorandum on the ledger account form. On the balance sheet, the bonds payable appear as long-term liabilities. (Bonds that mature within one year from the balance sheet date appear as current liabilities.) There are three ways to report bonds on the balance sheet.

1. Show the face value of the bonds authorized, unissued, and issued:

Long-Term Liabilities
10% Bonds Payable, Due April 1, 2026
Authorized $300,000
Less Unissued   250,000
Issued $ 50,000

2. Show the face value of the bonds authorized as a parenthetical note:

Long-Term Liabilities
10% Bonds Payable, Due April 1, 2026 $50,000
(Bonds with a face value of $300,000 are
authorized, of which $250,000 are unissued)

3. Show the face value of the bonds issued. Provide details about the bonds in a note to the financial statements.

PAYMENT OF INTEREST

On October 1, 2016, the first interest payment is due: 10 percent interest on $50,000 for six months. The interest is $2,500 ($50,000 × 0.10 × 1/2). The journal entry to record the payment is as follows:

>> **22-4. OBJECTIVE**
Record the payment of interest on bonds.

	DATE		DESCRIPTION	POST. REF.	DEBIT	CREDIT	
1	2016						1
2	Oct.	1	Bond Interest Expense		2 500 00		2
3			Cash			2 500 00	3
4			Paid semiannual bond				4
5			interest				5
6							6

Corporations with many bondholders open a separate checking account for bond interest payments. A separate account makes it easier to reconcile the bank account and to keep records of interest checks that have not yet been presented for payment.

recall

Interest Formula
$I = Prt$

ACCRUAL OF INTEREST

On December 31, 2016, at the end of the fiscal year, three months (October, November, and December) of bond interest is owed but will not be paid until April 1, 2017. The accrued interest is $1,250 ($50,000 × 0.10 × 3/12). The adjusting entry is as follows:

>> **22-5. OBJECTIVE**
Record the accrual of interest on bonds.

1	2016		*Adjusting Entries*				1
26	Dec.	31	Bond Interest Expense	1 2 5 0 00			26
27			Bond Interest Payable		1 2 5 0 00		27
28			*Accrued interest for three months*				28
29							29

When the adjusting entry has been posted, the ***Bond Interest Expense*** account has a balance of $3,750, the correct amount of interest for the nine months the bonds have been outstanding. ***Bond Interest Expense*** usually appears in the Other Expenses (nonoperating expenses) section of the income statement:

ACCOUNT   *Bond Interest Expense*   ACCOUNT NO. <u>692</u>

DATE		DESCRIPTION	POST. REF.	DEBIT	CREDIT	BALANCE	
						DEBIT	CREDIT
2016							
Oct.	1		J10	2 5 0 0 00		2 5 0 0 00	
Dec.	31	Adjusting	J12	1 2 5 0 00		3 7 5 0 00	

ENTRIES FOR SECOND-YEAR INTEREST

Assuming that the same bonds remain outstanding during all of the second year, 2017, the following entries would be required. Technx utilizes reversing entries:

- January 1: Reverse the accrued interest payable entry for $1,250 made on December 31:

  Debit ***Bond Interest Payable*** for $1,250.
      Credit ***Bond Interest Expense*** for $1,250.

- April 1: Record the payment of interest for six months:

  Debit ***Bond Interest Expense*** for $2,500.
      Credit ***Cash*** for $2,500.

- October 1: Record the payment of interest for six months:

  Debit ***Bond Interest Expense*** for $2,500.
      Credit ***Cash*** for $2,500.

- December 31: Record accrued interest for three months:

  Debit ***Bond Interest Expense*** for $1,250.
      Credit ***Bond Interest Payable*** for $1,250.

After these entries have been posted, the ***Bond Interest Expense*** account appears as below. Notice that on December 31, 2017, the balance in the ***Bond Interest Expense*** account is $5,000. This is the annual interest on the bonds ($50,000 × 0.10):

ACCOUNT   *Bond Interest Expense*   ACCOUNT NO. <u>692</u>

DATE		DESCRIPTION	POST. REF.	DEBIT	CREDIT	BALANCE	
						DEBIT	CREDIT
2017							
Jan.	1	Reversing	J1		1 2 5 0 00		1 2 5 0 00
Apr.	1		J4	2 5 0 0 00		1 2 5 0 00	
Oct.	1		J10	2 5 0 0 00		3 7 5 0 00	
Dec.	31	Adjusting	J12	1 2 5 0 00		5 0 0 0 00	

Bonds Issued at a Premium

Two years after the first bonds were sold, Technx issues another 50 bonds. The market interest rate is about 9.5 percent. The face interest rate on the bonds remains at 10 percent. Bondholders will be attracted by the bond interest rate, which is higher than the market rate. They will be willing to pay more than the face value ($1,000) for each bond in order to earn 10 percent interest.

On April 1, 2018, $50,000 of bonds are sold at 104.8. Bond prices are quoted in terms of percent of face value. Each bond was issued for $1,048 ($1,000 × 1.048), yielding cash of $52,400 ($1,048 × 50). The issue price in excess of face value is $2,400 ($52,400 − $50,000). The excess of the price paid over the face value of a bond is called a **premium on bonds payable.** Investors are willing to pay a premium because the face interest rate is higher than the market interest at the time the bonds are issued. This transaction is recorded in general journal form as follows:

	2018				
1					1
2	Apr.	1	Cash	52 400 00	2
3			10% Bonds payable, 2026	50 000 00	3
4			Premium on Bonds Payable	2 400 00	4
5			Issued bonds at 104.8		5
6					6

> **THE BOTTOM LINE**
> Issue Bonds at Premium
>
> **Income Statement**
> No effect on net income
>
> **Balance Sheet**
> Assets   ↑ 52,400
> Liabilities   ↑ 52,400
> No effect on equity

AMORTIZATION OF BOND PREMIUM

The issuing corporation writes off, or amortizes, the premium paid by the bond purchasers over the period from the issue date to the maturity date. Amortizing the premium reduces bond interest expense shown on the income statement. In this case, the bonds are 10-year bonds sold two years after their authorization date. That leaves eight years over which to amortize the premium.

There are two ways to compute the amortization: straight-line amortization and effective interest method. The effective interest method is covered in intermediate accounting courses. This text uses the **straight-line amortization** method, which amortizes an equal amount of the premium each interest payment date. The amortization for Technx is $300 per year ($2,400 ÷ 8 years) or $150 each bond interest payment date.

On October 1, 2018, Technx records the semiannual interest on the $100,000 of bonds outstanding. The bond interest paid is $5,000 ($100,000 × 0.10 × 6/12). Technx also records amortization of the premium received on $50,000 of the bonds. The amortization is $150 each payment date. Notice how the amortization of the *Premium on Bonds Payable* reduces the amount of *Bond Interest Expense:*

>> 22-6. OBJECTIVE
Compute and record the periodic amortization of a bond premium.

	2018				
1					1
2	Oct.	1	Bond Interest Expense	5 000 00	2
3			Cash	5 000 00	3
4			Payment of semiannual interest		4
5			on $100,000 of bonds		5
6					6
7		1	Premium on Bonds Payable	1 50 00	7
8			Bond Interest Expense	1 50 00	8
9			Amortization on $50,000 of		9
10			bonds sold at premium		10

ADJUSTING AND REVERSING ENTRIES

On December 31, 2018, an adjusting entry is made for three months of accrued interest on the entire $100,000 of bonds outstanding. The accrued interest is $2,500 ($100,000 × 0.10 × 3/12). An adjustment is also made for the amortization of bond premium at $75 for three months (3/12 × $300 annual amortization). Bond interest expense is $2,425, the interest accrued less the amount of the bond premium ($2,500 − $75). The adjustment is recorded as shown and is reversed on January 1, 2019:

	2018	Adjusting Entries			
1					1
30	Dec.	31	Bond Interest Expense	2 425 00	30
31			Premium on Bonds Payable	75 00	31
32			Bond Interest Payable	2 500 00	32
33			Accrue interest and amortize		33
34			premium for three months		34

important!

Bond Prices
If the face interest rate on bonds is lower than the market interest rate, the bonds will sell at a discount.

Bonds Issued at a Discount

Technx issues another 50 bonds on April 1, 2019. The market interest rate is 11 percent. The bonds' interest rate remains fixed at 10 percent. Investors will pay less than face value for a bond that pays interest at a lower rate than the market rate. The **discount on bonds payable** is the excess of the face value over the price received for a bond.

Technx Corporation sells 50 bonds at 97.76. Each bond is issued for $977.60 ($1,000 × 0.9776), yielding cash of $48,880 ($50,000 × 0.9776). The excess of the face value over the issue price is $1,120 ($50,000 − $48,880). The $1,120 is the discount. The entry to record issuance of the bond is shown in general journal form as follows:

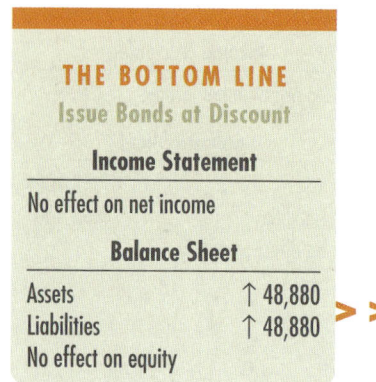

THE BOTTOM LINE

Issue Bonds at Discount

Income Statement

No effect on net income

Balance Sheet

| Assets | ↑ 48,880 |
| Liabilities | ↑ 48,880 |

No effect on equity

	2019					1
2	Apr.	1	Cash	48 880 00		2
3			Discount on Bonds Payable	1 120 00		3
4			10% Bonds payable, 2026		50 000 00	4
5			Issued bonds at 97.76			5
6						6

>> 22-7. OBJECTIVE

Compute and record the periodic amortization of a bond discount.

AMORTIZATION OF BOND DISCOUNT

The issuing corporation amortizes the discount over the period from the issue date to the maturity date. Amortizing the discount increases the bond interest expense shown on the income statement. The bonds are 10-year bonds sold three years after the authorization date. That leaves seven years over which to amortize the discount. On a straight-line basis, the amortization is $160 per year or $80 per interest payment date.

On October 1, 2019, Technx Corporation records the semiannual interest on the $150,000 of bonds outstanding. The bond interest paid is $7,500 ($150,000 × 0.10 × 6/12). The company records the amortization of the premium for six months ($150). It records the amortization of the discount for six months ($80). The bond interest expense is $7,430, the interest paid ($7,500) less the amortized premium ($150) plus the amortized discount ($80). Notice how the discount increases the actual cost of borrowing. The journal entry to record the interest payment and the amortization of the premium and the discount follows:

	2019					1
2	Oct.	1	Bond Interest Expense	7 430 00		2
3			Premium on Bonds Payable	1 50 00		3
4			Discount on Bonds Payable		80 00	4
5			Cash		7 500 00	5
6			Interest payment and amortization			6
7			of premium and discount for			7
8			six months			8

ADJUSTING AND REVERSING ENTRIES

On December 31, 2019, an adjusting entry is made to accrue interest on the bonds for the three-month period. The accrued interest is $3,750 ($150,000 × 0.10 × 3/12). An adjustment is made for the bond discount for three months ($40) and for the bond premium for three months ($75). Bond interest expense is $3,715, the interest accrued plus the discount less the premium ($3,750 + $40 − $75). The adjusting entry is recorded as follows. It is reversed on January 1, 2020:

	2019		Adjusting Entries						1
26	Dec.	31	Bond Interest Expense	3 7 1 5 00					26
27			Premium on Bonds Payable	7 5 00					27
28			Discount on Bonds Payable			4 0 00			28
29			Bond Interest Payable			3 7 5 0 00			29
30			Accrue interest on $150,000 of bonds,						30
31			amortize premium on $50,000 of						31
32			bonds, and amortize discount on						32
33			$50,000 of bonds for three months						33

Balance Sheet Presentation of Bond Premium and Discount

The ***Premium on Bonds Payable*** account has a normal credit balance. It is shown as an addition to the face value of bonds payable on the balance sheet. The ***Discount on Bonds Payable*** account has a normal debit balance; it is subtracted from the face value of bonds payable on the balance sheet. When there are both a discount and a premium on a bond issue, the two are combined and shown on the balance sheet as a single figure. For example, on December 31, 2019, Technx has a net premium on bonds payable of $875 as follows:

Discount	$ 1,120	
Amortization taken	(120)	
Unamortized discount		$1,000
Premium	$ 2,400	
Amortization taken	(525)	
Unamortized premium		(1,875)
Net unamortized premium		$ 875

On December 31, 2019, Technx reports bonds payable on the balance sheet as follows:

Long-Term Liabilities

10% Bonds Payable, Due April 1, 2026 (authorized $200,000 face value, less $50,000 face value unissued)	$150,000
Net Premium on Bonds Payable	875
Net Liability	$150,875

The book value, or the **carrying value of bonds,** is the balance of the ***Bonds Payable*** account plus the ***Premium on Bonds Payable*** account minus the ***Discount on Bonds Payable*** account:

Bonds payable
+ Premium on bonds
− Discount on bonds
Carrying value or book value

recall

Book Value

The term *book value* (or net book value) can apply to assets or liabilities. The book value of property, plant, and equipment is the original cost minus the accumulated depreciation.

Accounting for Bond Issue Costs

Bond issue costs are costs incurred in issuing bonds, including items such as legal and accounting fees and printing costs. Bond issue costs reduce the proceeds of borrowing. Bond issue cost should be shown as a deferred charge in the long-term asset category of the balance sheet. That cost would be allocated over the life of the bonds.

Section 2   Self Review

QUESTIONS

1. How are bond discounts shown on the balance sheet?

2. What is the straight-line method for amortizing bond discount or premium?

3. Why is amortization of a bond premium offset against interest expense?

EXERCISES

4. The entry to record the issuance of bonds includes a:

   a. debit to *Bonds Payable.*

   b. credit to *Bonds Payable.*

   c. credit to *Bond Interest Payable.*

   d. debit to *Bond Interest Payable.*

5. If bonds are issued for a price below their face value, the bond discount is:

   a. debited to expense on the date the bonds are issued.

   b. amortized over the life of the bond issue.

   c. shown as an addition to bonds payable in the Long-Term Liabilities section of the balance sheet.

   d. shown as a deduction to bonds payable in the Current Liabilities section of the balance sheet.

ANALYSIS

6. Ten-year bonds, dated January 1, 2016, with a face value of $100,000 are issued at 101 on January 1, 2016. How much premium will be amortized on the interest payment date, July 1, 2016?

(Answers to Section 2 Self Review are on page 795.)

>> **22-8.** Record the transactions of a bond sinking fund investment.

WHY IT'S IMPORTANT

Companies make plans to ensure that the required funds are available to pay off bonds on their maturity date.

>> **22-9.** Record an increase or decrease in retained earnings appropriated for bond retirement.

WHY IT'S IMPORTANT

Retained earnings are often restricted for specific expenditures.

>> **22-10.** Record retirement of bonds payable.

WHY IT'S IMPORTANT

Upon retirement of a bond, total long-term debt is adjusted to reflect the payment of the liability.

TERMS TO LEARN

bond retirement
bond sinking fund
investment

Bond Retirement

Bond retirement occurs when a bond is paid and the liability is removed from the company's balance sheet. When Technx's bond issue matures, the corporation has to pay bondholders the face amount of their outstanding bonds, a total of $150,000, in cash.

Accumulating Funds to Retire Bonds

In order to ensure that the cash is available, the corporation established a bond sinking fund investment account. A **bond sinking fund investment** is a fund established to accumulate assets to pay off bonds when they mature. Some bond contracts require bond sinking funds.

BOND SINKING FUND INVESTMENT

Technx Corporation decides to accumulate $30,000 per year in the bond sinking fund for each of the last five years that the bonds are outstanding. The net earnings of the fund will reduce the amount that the corporation has to add each year. Suppose that the bond sinking fund investment account is started on April 1, 2021, by making a $30,000 cash deposit. The $30,000 is immediately invested. During the year, $1,800 is earned on the sinking fund investments. Expenses of $40 are incurred in operating the bond sinking fund. Net earnings for the year are $1,760. The following year only $28,240 ($30,000 − $1,760) needs to be added to the fund. This procedure is repeated each year, so that at the end of the fifth year the fund will have the $150,000 needed to retire the bonds.

   The following journal entries are for the first transfer of cash to the fund, net earnings for the first year, second transfer of cash to the fund, and retirement of the bonds at the end of the fifth year:

>> **22-8. OBJECTIVE**

Record the transactions of a bond sinking fund investment.

1	2021						1
2	Apr.	1	Bond Sinking Fund Investment	30 0 0 0 00			2
3			Cash		30 0 0 0 00		3
4			First annual installment in bond				4
5			sinking fund				5

1	2022						1
2	Apr.	1	Bond Sinking Fund Investment	1 7 6 0 00			2
3			Income from Sinking Fund Investment		1 7 6 0 00		3
4			Net income earned by bond sinking				4
5			fund for year				5

1	2022						1
7	Apr.	1	Bond Sinking Fund Investment	28 2 4 0 00			7
8			Cash		28 2 4 0 00		8
9			Second annual installment in bond				9
10			sinking fund ($30,000 less $1,760				10
11			income earned for year)				11

1	2026						1
2	Apr.	1	10% Bonds Payable, 2026	150 0 0 0 00			2
3			Bond Sinking Fund Investment		150 0 0 0 00		3
4			Retirement of bonds				4

This illustration assumes that an outside trustee managed the sinking fund investment account and made the necessary entries to record the fund transactions. If the corporation handled the bond sinking fund itself, additional entries would be required to show the investment of the fund's cash, the receipt of earnings, and the payment of fund expenses.

Other procedures may be used to finance the sinking fund investment. For example, an assumption may be made about the rate of earnings of the fund. A constant amount would be contributed each period, which when added to the earnings would equal the required balance. If earnings differ from the rate assumed, the contributions would be adjusted.

The bond sinking fund is reported under the heading "Investments" in the Assets section of the balance sheet. Investments are usually shown before property, plant, and equipment.

>> 22-9. OBJECTIVE

Record an increase or decrease in retained earnings appropriated for bond retirement.

RETAINED EARNINGS APPROPRIATED FOR BOND RETIREMENT

To protect bondholders and to restrict dividends, the bond contract might require that retained earnings are appropriated while the bonds are outstanding. Even if the bond contract does not require an appropriation, retained earnings may be appropriated by order of the board of directors.

MANAGERIAL IMPLICATIONS   <<

RAISING CASH

- A critical management task is to ensure that cash is available to the company when it is needed.
- Managers need to know the advantages and disadvantages of raising cash through the sale of bonds and stock.
- Managers need to have a thorough understanding of bond characteristics, including the differences between registered versus bearer bonds and secured versus debenture bonds. They also need to understand convertible bonds and callable bonds.

- Bond sinking fund investments and the appropriation of retained earnings are tools that management can use to ensure that the funds are available to retire the bonds.
- Call provisions and early retirement of bonds allow for flexible financing and can reduce financing costs.

THINKING CRITICALLY

What factors would you consider in choosing between stock financing and bond financing?

Suppose that the board of directors of Technx Corporation decided to appropriate $30,000 of retained earnings during each of the last five years the bonds are outstanding. When the bonds are retired, the balance in the appropriated retained earnings account is returned to the **Retained Earnings** account. The **Retained Earnings Appropriated for Bond Retirement** account appears on the balance sheet under the heading "Appropriated Retained Earnings." The following entry shows an annual appropriation of retained earnings. Five such entries would be made. The next entry shows the appropriation being returned to retained earnings after the bonds are retired:

2021						
Apr.	1	Retained Earnings	30 0 0 0 00			
		Retained Earnings Appropriated for				
		Bond Retirement			30 0 0 0 00	
		Annual appropriation				

2026						
Apr.	1	Retained Earnings Appropriated for				
		Bond Retirement	150 0 0 0 00			
		Retained Earnings			150 0 0 0 00	
		Close appropriation account				
		upon retirement of bonds				

Retirement of Bonds

Bonds payable are usually retired at the maturity date, but some or all of the bonds can be retired prior to that date.

RETIREMENT ON DUE DATE

If there had been no bond sinking fund, Technx Corporation would have recorded the retirement on the maturity date by debiting **10% Bonds Payable, 2026,** and crediting **Cash.**

EARLY RETIREMENT

A corporation may retire bonds early because it has surplus cash, or interest rates have decreased or are expected to decrease. The corporation may purchase the bonds on the open market or, if they are callable, it may require the holders to surrender their bonds for cash.

When bonds are retired prior to maturity, the bondholders are paid the agreed-upon price for the bonds plus the accrued interest to the date of purchase. There are two steps to record the retirement of bonds:

Step 1. *Amortize the discount or premium on the bonds up to the date of retirement.*

Step 2. *Remove the book value, and record the gain or loss.*

  a. Remove the book value of the bonds.
  b. Record interest up to the date of retirement.
  c. Record the cash payment for the repurchase price and interest.
  d. Record the gain or loss (book value minus the repurchase price).

Assume that Technx Corporation decides to retire (call) the April 1, 2019, issue of $50,000 of bonds that were sold at a discount. Remember that these bonds were sold at 97.76 resulting in a debit to **Discount on Bonds Payable** for $1,120 with seven years remaining before the bonds' due date. The amortization of the discount was taken at $160 per year or $80 each time the bond interest was paid. The company has decided to retire these bonds on April 1, 2020.

> **important!**
>
> **Bond Retirement**
> The fact that retained earnings are appropriated for bond retirement does not mean that a bond retirement fund has been funded with cash.

>> **22-10. OBJECTIVE**
Record retirement of bonds payable.

> **important!**
>
> **Gain or Loss**
> The gain or loss on the retirement of bonds is the book value of the bonds minus the repurchase price.

On December 31, 2019, after adjusting entries, the related account balances of this bond issue are:

Bonds Payable		$50,000
Discount on Bonds Payable	$1,120	
Amortization of Discount on Bonds Payable through December 31, 2019	120	1,000
Net Carrying Value of Bonds		$49,000

Please remember that Technx has three bond issues and is retiring only those bonds that were issued at a discount. In this early retirement illustration, let's assume that Technx does not use reversing entries.

On April 1, 2020, the corporation repurchases and retires the $50,000 of bonds. They are purchased at 101:

Step 1. *Amortize the premium or discount on the bonds up to the date of retirement.* Remember that you previously calculated the amount of amortization of the discount would be $80 each interest payment date. Also recall that on December 31 you made an adjusting entry recording the interest expense and amortization of the discount for three months (or one-half an interest payment period).

GENERAL JOURNAL PAGE _____

	DATE		DESCRIPTION	POST. REF.	DEBIT	CREDIT	
1	2020						1
2	Apr.	1	Bond Interest Expense		40 00		2
3			Discount on Bonds Payable			40 00	3
4			Amortization of discount for three months				4
5			on bonds to be retired				5

Step 2. *Remove the book value of the bonds, and record the gain or loss on the repurchase of the bonds:*

a. Remove the book value of the bonds:

Bonds being retired	$50,000
Discount on retired bonds ($1,000 − $40)	960
Net book value of bonds	$49,040

b. Record bond interest expense up to the date of bond retirement.

$50,000 × 0.10 × 3/12 = $1,250

Recall that you already recorded three months of interest when you made the adjusting entry on December 31, 2019.

c. Record the cash payment for the repurchase of the bonds.

$50,000 × 1.01 = $50,500

d. Record the gain or loss (net book value of bonds minus repurchase price).

($50,000 − $960) − $50,500 = ($1,460) loss

	DATE		DESCRIPTION	POST. REF.	DEBIT	CREDIT	
	GENERAL JOURNAL			PAGE _____			
1	2020						1
2	Apr.	1	Bond Interest Expense		1 250 00		2
3			Bond Interest Payable		1 250 00		3
4			Cash			2 500 00	4
5							5
6	Apr.	1	Bonds Payable		50 000 00		6
7			Loss on Early Retirement of Bonds		1 460 00		7
8			Discount on Bonds Payable			960 00	8
			Cash			50 500 00	

A gain or loss on early retirement of bonds may appear on the income statement as an extraordinary gain or loss if the gain or loss is unusual and infrequent.

Section 3　Self Review

QUESTIONS

1. What is a bond sinking fund investment?

2. Why would a corporation purchase its own bonds and retire them?

3. How is gain or loss on early retirement of bonds shown on the income statement?

EXERCISES

4. The entry to record income earned by a bond sinking fund investment includes a credit to:

   a. **Bonds Payable.**

   b. **Bond Sinking Fund Investment.**

   c. **Income from Sinking Fund Investment.**

   d. **Interest Income.**

5. The entry to record retirement of a bond includes a debit to:

   a. **Discount on Bonds Payable.**

   b. **Retained Earnings.**

   c. **Bonds Payable.**

   d. **Retained Earnings Appropriated for Bond Retirement.**

ANALYSIS

6. What is the entry to record $300,000 of bonds that were retired at maturity? Retained earnings were appropriated for $300,000 for bond retirement. There was no bond sinking fund.

(Answers to Section 3 Self Review are on page 795.)

22 Chapter **REVIEW** Chapter Summary

Corporations often use bonds to acquire funds. In this chapter, you have reviewed the types of bonds frequently issued by corporations and have learned how to record a variety of bond transactions.

Learning Objectives

22-1 Name and define the various types of bonds.

- Bonds may be secured by the pledge of specific assets as security, or they may be unsecured.
- Some bonds are registered; owners are listed in corporation records. Other bonds are bearer bonds with interest coupons attached.
- Convertible bonds can be converted into common stock by the bondholder.
- Callable bonds may be recalled before their maturity date.

22-2 Explain the advantages and disadvantages of using bonds as a method of financing.

- Businesses that choose to raise capital using bonds may deduct bond interest charges when computing taxable income.
- Bonds payable are debts. The face amount of the bond must be repaid at maturity. Interest must also be paid on the bonds.

22-3 Record the issuance of bonds.

Bonds may be issued at face value, at a premium, or at a discount.

- If the bond's face interest rate exceeds the market interest rate when the bonds are issued, the bonds are issued at a premium.
- If the market interest rate exceeds the face interest rate on the bonds, the bonds are issued at a discount.

22-4 Record the payment of interest on bonds.

A bond bears interest that is usually payable annually or semiannually at a specified rate. The amount of interest is calculated and recorded as a debit to *Bond Interest Expense* and a credit to *Cash.*

22-5 Record the accrual of interest on bonds.

When bond interest dates do not coincide with the fiscal year-end, an adjustment is made for accrued bond interest at the end of the year. The adjustment may be reversed at the beginning of the next year.

22-6 Compute and record the periodic amortization of a bond premium.

The corporation writes off, or amortizes, a bond premium over the period from the issue date through the maturity date. The amortization is treated as a reduction of interest expense for that period.

22-7 Compute and record the periodic amortization of a bond discount.

A bond discount is amortized over the period that begins on the date the bonds are issued and ends on the date of maturity. The amortization is treated as an increase to interest expense for that period.

22-8 Record the transactions of a bond sinking fund investment.

A bond sinking fund accumulates cash to pay the bonds at maturity. The cash in the sinking fund is invested, earning interest to reduce the amount that the corporation will have to add in subsequent years. The establishment of the fund is recorded with a debit to *Bond Sinking Fund Investment* and a credit to *Cash.*

22-9 Record an increase or decrease in retained earnings appropriated for bond retirement.

An appropriation of retained earnings for bond retirement may be established and increased by debits to *Retained Earnings* and credits to *Retained Earnings Appropriated for Bond Retirement.* An appropriation shows that some retained earnings are not available for dividends; they are needed to pay off the bonds.

22-10 Record retirement of bonds payable.

Bonds are retired at maturity or, under certain circumstances, retired prior to maturity. The difference between the book value and the repurchase price is a gain or loss on retirement of bonds.

22-11 Define the accounting terms new to this chapter.

Glossary

Bond indenture (p. 768) A bond contract

Bond issue costs (p. 778) Costs incurred in issuing bonds, such as legal and accounting fees and printing costs

Bond retirement (p. 779) When a bond is paid and the liability is removed from the company's balance sheet

Bond sinking fund investment (p. 779) A fund established to accumulate assets to pay off bonds when they mature

Bonds payable (p. 768) Long-term debt instruments that are written promises to repay the principal at a future date; interest is due at a fixed rate payable over the life of the bond

Call price (p. 769) The amount the corporation must pay for the bond when it is called

Callable bonds (p. 769) Bonds that allow the issuing corporation to require the holder to surrender the bonds for payment before their maturity date

Carrying value of bonds (p. 777) The balance of the *Bonds Payable* account plus the *Premium on Bonds Payable* account minus the *Discount on Bonds Payable* account; also called *book value of bonds*

Collateral trust bonds (p. 768) Bonds secured by the pledge of securities, such as stocks or bonds of other companies

Convertible bonds (p. 769) Bonds that give the owner the right to convert the bonds into common stock under specified conditions

Coupon bonds (p. 769) Unregistered bonds that have coupons attached for each interest payment; also called *bearer bonds*

Debentures (p. 769) Unsecured bonds backed only by a corporation's general credit

Discount on bonds payable (p. 776) The excess of the face value over the price received by the corporation for a bond

Face interest rate (p. 769) The contractual interest specified on the bond

Leveraging (p. 771) Using borrowed funds to earn a profit greater than the interest that must be paid on the borrowing

Market interest rate (p. 769) The interest rate a corporation is willing to pay and investors are willing to accept at the current time

Mortgage loan (p. 768) A long-term debt created when a note is given as part of the purchase price for land or buildings

Premium on bonds payable (p. 775) The excess of the price paid over the face value of a bond

Registered bonds (p. 769) Bonds issued to a party whose name is listed in the corporation's records

Secured bonds (p. 768) Bonds for which property is pledged to secure the claims of bondholders

Serial bonds (p. 769) Bonds issued at one time but payable over a period of years

Straight-line amortization (p. 775) Amortizing the premium or discount on bonds payable in equal amounts over the life of the bond

Trading on the equity (p. 771) See Leveraging

Comprehensive **Self Review**

1. Generally, would an investor want secured bonds or debenture bonds? Why?
2. Name two disadvantages of raising capital through the issue of bonds payable rather than through the issue of preferred stock.
3. What factor would cause bonds to be sold at a premium?

4. Why does a corporation use an account such as *Appropriation of Retained Earnings* for bond retirement?

5. What entry, or entries, will be made when bonds are retired at maturity?

(Answers to Comprehensive Self Review are on pages 795–796.)

Discussion Questions

1. What is a collateral trust bond?
2. What is a bond indenture?
3. How is the *Bonds Payable* account classified on the balance sheet?
4. Are authorized, unissued bonds shown on the balance sheet? If so, where?
5. Why might a company use a special bank account for paying bond interest?
6. In a bond indenture dated January 1, 2016 Pink Corporation authorized the issuance of $500,000 face value, 10 percent, 20-year bonds payable. No bonds were issued until July 1, 2017, when bonds with a face value of $200,000 were issued. At that time, the market rate of interest on similar debt was 9 percent. Would the issue price of the bonds be more than or less than face value? Explain.
7. Why is a bond premium or discount amortized as part of the adjustment process at the end of the year?
8. Why is the year-end adjusting entry for amortization of a bond premium or discount reversed at the start of the new year?
9. How are the legal costs and other costs related to issuing bonds accounted for?
10. What is a bond sinking fund?
11. What is the relationship between a bond sinking fund and an appropriation of retained earnings for bond retirement? Explain.
12. Explain the accounting treatment necessary when bonds are retired before maturity.

APPLICATIONS

Exercises

Exercises 22.1 through 22.3. Third Corporation issued $600,000 of its 7 percent bonds payable on April 1, 2016. The bonds were issued at face value. Interest is payable semiannually on October 1 and April 1.

Exercise 22.1
Objective 22-3

▶ **Issuing bonds.**

Give the general journal entry to record the April 1, 2016, bond issue.

Exercise 22.2
Objective 22-4

▶ **Paying interest on bonds payable.**

Give the entry in general journal form to record the interest payment on October 1, 2016.

Exercise 22.3
Objective 22-5

▶ **Accruing interest on bonds.**

Give the entry to accrue bond interest on Third's bonds payable on December 31, 2016.

Exercises 22.4 through 22.6. Star Inc. was authorized to issue $1,000,000 of 12 percent bonds. On April 1, 2016, the corporation issued bonds with a face value of $200,000 at a price of 102.0. The bonds mature 10 years from the date of issue. Interest is payable semiannually on October 1 and April 1.

Recording issuance of bonds.

Give the general journal entry to record the April 1, 2016, bond issue.

◀ **Exercise 22.4**
Objective 22-3

Computing amortization of premium on bonds.

Using the data given above, what amount of premium will be amortized by Star Inc. on October 1, 2016, using straight-line amortization? Give the general journal entry to record this amortization.

◀ **Exercise 22.5**
Objective 22-6

Recording adjusting entry for bond interest and premium.

Using the data given above, give the adjusting entry that would be made by Star Inc. on December 31, 2016, to record accrued interest and to amortize the premium.

◀ **Exercise 22.6**
Objectives 22-5, 22-6

Recording transactions of a bond sinking fund investment.

Give the general journal entries to record the following transactions:

◀ **Exercise 22.7**
Objective 22-8

a. On December 31, 2015, Blue Bird Company established a bond sinking fund investment by depositing $25,000 with the fund trustee.

b. On December 31, 2016, Blue Bird Company recorded $2,000 net income from its bond sinking fund investment for the year.

c. On December 31, 2016, Blue Bird Company made a deposit of $23,000 into the bond sinking fund investment.

Appropriating retained earnings for bond retirement.

Record the appropriation of $75,000 of retained earnings on December 31, 2016, by Jack Inc. to establish an appropriation for bond retirement.

◀ **Exercise 22.8**
Objective 22-9

Retiring bonds before maturity.

On April 1, 2016, Chuck's Deli issued $70,000 of its 9 percent bonds, maturing 10 years later. Interest is payable semiannually on April 1 and October 1. The issue price was 94.0. Chuck's has decided to retire the bonds on August 1, 2019, three years and four months after the bonds were initially issued. The bonds were repurchased at 99. After recording the accrued interest expense payable through August 1, 2019, the balance in the **Discount on Bonds Payable** account is $2,800. Give the general journal entry to record the repurchase and retirement of the bonds.

◀ **Exercise 22.9**
Objective 22-10

PROBLEMS

Problem Set A

Issuing bonds; bond interest transactions.

The board of directors of Carlie Services Inc. authorized the issuance of $400,000 face value, 20-year, 7 percent bonds dated April 1, 2016, and maturing on April 1, 2036. Interest is payable semiannually on April 1 and October 1. Carlie uses the calendar year as its fiscal year. The bond transactions that occurred in 2016 and 2017 follow.

◀ **Problem 22.1A**
Objectives 22-3, 22-4, 22-5

DATE		TRANSACTIONS FOR 2016
Apr.	1	Issued $300,000 of bonds at face value.
Oct.	1	Paid the semiannual interest on the bonds issued.
Dec.	31	Recorded the adjusting entry for the accrued bond interest.
	31	Closed the **Bond Interest Expense** account to the **Income Summary** account.

DATE		TRANSACTIONS FOR 2017
Jan.	1	Reversed the adjusting entry made on December 31, 2016.
Apr.	1	Issued $100,000 of bonds at face value.
	1	Paid the interest for six months on the bonds previously issued.
Oct.	1	Paid the interest for six months on the outstanding bonds.
Dec.	31	Recorded the adjusting entry for the accrued bond interest.
	31	Closed the **Bond Interest Expense** account to the **Income Summary** account.

INSTRUCTIONS

Record the transactions in general journal form. Use the account names given in the chapter. Round to nearest dollar.

Analyze: Based on the transactions given, what is the balance in the **Bonds Payable** account on December 31, 2016?

Problem 22.2A
Objectives 22-3,
22-4, 22-5, 22-7

▶ ### Issuing bonds; bond interest transactions and amortization of discount.

The board of directors of Belmont, LLC, authorized the issuance of $600,000 face value, 20-year, 6 percent bonds, dated March 1, 2016, and maturing on March 1, 2036. Interest is payable semiannually on September 1 and March 1.

INSTRUCTIONS

1. Record the following transactions in general journal form. Use the account names given in the chapter. (Round to nearest dollar.)

2. Prepare the Long-Term Liabilities section of the corporation's balance sheet on December 31, 2016.

DATE		TRANSACTIONS FOR 2016
Jun.	1	Issued bonds with a face value of $500,000 at 97.63 plus accrued interest from March 1. (When bonds are issued between interest payment dates, the accrued interest is paid to the corporation by the purchaser. Credit **Bond Interest Expense.**)
Sept.	1	Paid the semiannual bond interest and amortized the discount for three months. (Make two entries. Use the straight-line method to compute the amortization.)
Dec.	31	Recorded an adjusting entry to accrue the interest and to amortize the discount. (Make one entry.)
	31	Closed the **Bond Interest Expense** account to the **Income Summary** account.

DATE		TRANSACTIONS FOR 2017
Jan.	1	Reversed the adjusting entry made on December 31, 2016.
Mar.	1	Paid the semiannual bond interest and amortized the discount on the outstanding bonds.

Analyze: What is the balance of the **Discount on Bonds Payable** account on December 31, 2016?

Issuing bonds; recording interest transactions and amortization of premium.

◀ **Problem 22.3A**
Objectives 22-3,
22-4, 22-5, 22-6

The board of directors of Arizona Motor Shops, Inc., authorized the issuance of $1,000,000 face value, 10-year, 8 percent bonds dated April 1, 2016, and maturing on April 1, 2026. Interest is payable semiannually on April 1 and October 1.

INSTRUCTIONS

1. Record the transactions below in general journal form. Use the account names given in the chapter.
2. Prepare the Long-Term Liabilities section of the corporation's balance sheet on December 31, 2016.

DATE		TRANSACTIONS FOR 2016
Apr.	1	Issued $500,000 face value bonds at 101.6.
Oct.	1	Paid the semiannual interest on the outstanding bonds and amortized the bond premium. (Make two entries. Use the straight-line method to compute the amortization.)
Dec.	31	Recorded the adjusting entry for accrued interest and amortization of the bond premium for three months. (Make one entry.)
	31	Closed the **Bond Interest Expense** account to the **Income Summary** account.

DATE		TRANSACTIONS FOR 2017
Jan.	1	Reversed the adjusting entry made on December 31, 2016.

Analyze: If the reversing entry was not recorded, what entry would be required when the interest expense is paid in April 2017?

Recording bond sinking fund transactions, retained earnings appropriated for bond retirement, and retirement of bonds.

◀ **Problem 22.4A**
Objectives 22-8,
22-9, 22-10

QB

New Computer Technology, Inc., has outstanding $600,000 of its 10 percent bonds payable, dated January 1, 2016, and maturing on January 1, 2036, 20 years later. The corporation is required under the bond contract to transfer $30,000 to a sinking fund each year. The directors have also voted to restrict retained earnings by transferring $30,000 each year on January 1 over the life of the bond issue to a **Retained Earnings Appropriated for Bond Retirement** account.

INSTRUCTIONS

1. Prepare entries in general journal form to record the January 1, 2016, issuance of bonds at face value, the establishment of the **Bond Sinking Fund Investment** account, and the appropriation of retained earnings.
2. Show how the **Bond Sinking Fund Investment** account and the **Retained Earnings Appropriated for Bond Retirement** account would be presented on the balance sheet as of December 31, 2020. (Assume that the ending balance of the **Bond Sinking Fund Investment** was $150,000 and the **Retained Earnings—Unappropriated** account was $320,210.)
3. Assuming that the **Bond Sinking Fund Investment** account had a balance of $600,000 on January 1, 2036, give the entry in general journal form to record the retirement of the bonds and remove the appropriation for retained earnings.

Analyze: What percentage of total retained earnings has been appropriated for bond retirement on December 31, 2020?

Problem 22.5A

Objective 22-10

▶ **Retiring bonds payable prior to maturity.**

On May 1, 2016, Big Star Corporation issued $600,000 face value, 10 percent bonds at 98.6. The bonds are dated May 1, 2016, and mature 10 years later. The discount is amortized on each interest payment date. The interest is payable semiannually on May 1 and November 1. On May 1, 2018, after paying the semiannual interest, the corporation purchased the outstanding bonds from the bondholders and retired them. The purchase price was 98.9.

INSTRUCTION

Give the entry in general journal form to record the repurchase and retirement of the bonds. (Use the *Loss on Early Retirement of Bonds* account.)

Analyze: If Big Star Corporation did not purchase the outstanding bonds, what total bond interest expense would have been incurred over the life of the bond?

Problem Set B

Problem 22.1B

Objectives 22-3, 22-4, 22-5

▶ **Issuing bonds; bond interest transactions.**

The board of directors of Nolen Products, Inc., authorized the issuance of $1,000,000 face value, 8 percent bonds dated April 1, 2016. The bonds will mature on April 1, 2026. The interest is payable semiannually on April 1 and October 1. The bond transactions that occurred in 2016 and 2017 are shown below.

INSTRUCTIONS

Record the transactions below in general journal form. Use the account names given in the chapter.

DATE		TRANSACTIONS FOR 2016
April	1	Issued $600,000 of bonds at face value.
Oct.	1	Paid the semiannual bond interest on the outstanding bonds.
Dec.	31	Recorded the adjusting entry to accrue the interest on the bonds issued.
	31	Closed the *Bond Interest Expense* account to the *Income Summary* account.

DATE		TRANSACTIONS FOR 2017
Jan.	1	Reversed the adjusting entry of December 31, 2016.
April	1	Paid the semiannual bond interest.
Oct.	1	Paid the semiannual bond interest.
	1	Issued $400,000 of bonds at face value.
Dec.	31	Recorded the adjusting entry to accrue the interest on all bonds issued.
	31	Closed the *Bond Interest Expense* account to the *Income Summary* account.

Analyze: What total bond interest would have been reported on the income statement for the year ended December 31, 2016?

Problem 22.2B

Objectives 22-3, 22-4, 22-5, 22-7

▶ **Issuing bonds; bond interest transactions and amortization of discount.**

The board of directors of GEH Corporation authorized the issuance of $1,000,000 face value, 6 percent bonds. The bonds mature 10 years from their issue date of March 1, 2016. The interest is payable semiannually on March 1 and September 1. Because the funds were not immediately needed, no bonds were issued until July 1, 2016. Round to nearest dollar.

INSTRUCTIONS

1. Record the following transactions in general journal form. Use the account names given in the chapter.

2. Prepare the Long-Term Liabilities section of the corporation's balance sheet on December 31, 2016.

DATE		TRANSACTIONS FOR 2016
July	1	Issued $500,000 of bonds at 97.68 plus accrued interest from March 1. (When bonds are issued between interest payment dates, the accrued interest is paid to the corporation by the purchaser. Credit **Bond Interest Expense.**)
Sept.	1	Paid the semiannual bond interest.
	1	Amortized the discount on the bonds issued.
Dec.	31	Recorded the adjusting entry to accrue the interest on the bonds issued and to amortize the discount for four months. (Make one entry.)
	31	Closed the **Bond Interest Expense** account.

DATE		TRANSACTIONS FOR 2017
Jan.	1	Reversed the adjusting entry of December 31, 2016.
Mar.	1	Paid the semiannual bond interest and amortized the discount on the bonds issued.

Analyze: What is the balance of the **Bond Interest Expense** account at December 31, 2016, prior to closing?

Issuing bonds; recording interest transactions and amortization of premium.

◀ **Problem 22.3B**
Objectives 22-3, 22-4, 22-5

The board of directors of Amora Company authorized issuance of $1,000,000 of 6 percent bonds. Each bond has a face value of $10,000. The interest is payable semiannually on February 1 and August 1. The bonds are dated February 1, 2016, and mature 10 years later.

INSTRUCTIONS

1. Record the transactions below in general journal form. Use the account names given in the chapter. (Round your numbers to the nearest whole dollar.)

2. Prepare the Long-Term Liabilities section of the corporation's balance sheet on December 31, 2016.

DATE		TRANSACTIONS FOR 2016
Feb.	1	Issued $500,000 of bonds at 104.
Aug.	1	Paid the semiannual interest on the bonds issued and recorded the amortization of the premium.
Dec.	31	Recorded the adjusting entry to accrue interest on the bonds issued and to amortize the premium for five months. Round to nearest whole dollar.
	31	Recorded the closing entry for **Bond Interest Expense.**

DATE	TRANSACTIONS FOR 2017
Jan. 1	Reversed the adjusting entry of December 31, 2016.

Analyze: If the reversing entry had not been recorded in January 2017, how would the payment of bond interest be recorded in February 2017?

Problem 22.4B

Objectives 22-8, 22-9, 22-10

▶ **Recording bond sinking fund transactions, retained earnings appropriated for bond retirement, and retirement of bonds.**

Mine Research, Inc., has outstanding $200,000 face value, 10 percent bonds payable dated January 1, 2016, and maturing 10 years later. The corporation is required under the bond contract to transfer $18,000 each year to a sinking fund. The directors have also voted to restrict retained earnings by transferring $20,000 each year to a *Retained Earnings Appropriated for Bond Retirement* account.

INSTRUCTIONS

1. Prepare entries in general journal form to record the 2016 transactions.

2. Prepare the partial balance sheet for December 31, 2025, showing the presentation of the *Bond Sinking Fund Investment* and the *Retained Earnings Appropriated for Bond Retirement* (assume *Retained Earnings—Unappropriated* has a balance of $325,000).

3. Prepare the journal entries to retire the bonds and remove the appropriation of retained earnings on January 1, 2026.

DATE	TRANSACTIONS FOR 2016
Jan. 1	Sold the bonds at 100.
1	Made the annual bond sinking fund investment deposit.
31	Recorded the annual appropriation of retained earnings.
Dec. 31	The bond sinking fund trustee reported a net income of $1,200 on the sinking fund investments for the year.

On December 31, 2025, the balance in the *Bond Sinking Fund Investment* account is $200,000. The balance in the *Retained Earnings Appropriated for Bond Retirement* account is also $200,000.

Analyze: What percentage of total retained earnings had been allocated for bond retirement at December 31, 2025?

Problem 22.5B

Objective 22-10

▶ **Retiring bonds payable prior to maturity.**

On April 1, 2016, Big Spring Corporation issued $400,000 face value, 10 percent bonds at 99.16. The bonds were dated April 1, 2016, and will mature in 10 years. The discount is to be amortized on each interest payment date. The interest is payable semiannually on April 1 and October 1. On October 1, 2019, after paying the semiannual bond interest, the corporation decided to retire the bonds. The bondholders were paid 98.5.

INSTRUCTION

Give the entry in general journal form to record the repurchase and retirement of the bonds. (Use the *Gain on Early Retirement of Bonds* account.)

Analyze: If the bond had been retired on the original due date, what credit would have been made to the *Cash* account?

Critical Thinking Problem 22.1

Financing Decision

On December 31, 2016, the equity accounts of Financial Solutions, Inc., contained the following balances:

Common stock ($10 par, 100,000 shares authorized) 50,000 shares issued and outstanding	500,000
Retained earnings	500,000

For the year 2016, the corporation had net income before income taxes of $200,000, income taxes of $70,000, and net income after taxes of $130,000. The corporation's tax rate is 35 percent.

An expansion of the existing plant at a cost of $500,000 is planned. The corporation's president, who owns 60 percent of the corporation's common stock, estimates that the expansion would result in an increased net income of approximately $200,000 before interest and taxes. The financial vice president forecasts that the increase would be only $100,000. Round all calculations to nearest dollar.

Management is considering two possibilities for financing:

a. Issuance of 40,000 additional shares of common stock for $15 per share

b. Issuance of $500,000 face amount, 10-year, 6 percent bonds payable, secured by a mortgage lien on the plant

Assume that profits from existing operations will remain the same.

INSTRUCTIONS

1. Assume that the president's estimate of net income from the new plant is correct. Prepare a two-column table for each of the proposed financing plans. Show the following items: (a) total net income before interest and tax; (b) total bond interest; (c) total income tax; (d) total income after tax; (e) present income after tax; (f) increase or decrease in total income after bond interest and tax; (g) present earnings per share of common stock (compute earnings per share by dividing the net income after taxes by the number of shares of common stock outstanding); (h) estimated earnings per share of common stock.

2. Construct a similar table, assuming the financial vice president's estimate of earnings is correct.

3. Write a brief comment on the results of your analysis.

Analyze: Assume the company issued 40,000 shares of common stock and net income before taxes was $350,000. Would shareholders have realized an increase or decrease in earnings per share over fiscal 2016?

Critical Thinking Problem 22.2

Early Retirement

On December 31, 2016, TNT Express, Inc., has $1,000,000 of 8 percent, 10-year bonds outstanding. These bonds were issued on January 1, 2010, at par value. Interest rates have dropped to 5 percent, and the president of the company is considering buying back the outstanding 8 percent bonds and issuing new 10-year bonds with an 5 percent interest rate.

1. How much money would TNT Express save in interest payments if new, 5 percent bonds were issued?

2. Under what circumstances would this action be advantageous for TNT Express?

BUSINESS CONNECTIONS

Managerial FOCUS

Financing Through Bonds

1. What would cause corporate management to obtain cash by issuing bonds instead of selling stock?

2. Which type of bonds would give management greater flexibility in formulating and controlling a corporation's financial affairs?

3. In what situations would management be wise to issue additional common stock rather than bonds to meet long-term capital needs?

4. Why would management repurchase and retire a corporation's bonds prior to their maturity?

5. Cook Corporation's board of directors is considering authorization of a new bond issue. The controller notes that the bonds are callable at 101.6 at any time beginning five years after the date of the bond contract. What does this mean? What is the advantage of such a provision?

Ethical DILEMMA

Conflict of Interest

Lawrence Smith is the president of the Smith Water Filter Company. As president, he is in control of the issuance of stocks and bonds. Three years ago when the company needed cash, Lawrence purchased from the company a $100,000, 4 percent, 10-year unsecured bond. The interest rate has begun to increase. Lawrence suggests that the company refinance the bonds to extend the life of the bonds, even though the interest rate has increased to 7 percent. Is this a conflict of interest? Why or why not?

Financial Statement ANALYSIS

Bond Financing Agreements

Refer to the *2012 Annual Report (for the fiscal year ended February 3, 2013)* for The Home Depot, Inc., in Appendix A.

Analyze:

1. Locate the Notes to Consolidated Financial Statements. The 10-Year Summary of Financial and Operating Results presents a detailed list of earnings, selected balance sheet items, cash flow data, and financial ratios. What is the long-term debt to equity ratio for 2012?

2. Over the past three years, is The Home Depot, Inc., in a better or worse financial situation in regard to the long-term debt?

TEAMWORK

Sell Stocks or Bonds

Nowhere Man Corporation is a corporate dance studio. It is a popular investment with investors between the ages of 20 and 30. Nowhere Man has a dilemma. It needs money to expand its business to cash in on its popularity. However, management is not sure whether to sell stock in the company or to sell corporate bonds. Nowhere Man has $100,000 in liabilities and 1,000,000 authorized shares of common stock of which 100,000 shares are issued. It has a bid of $1,000,000 to build the additional location. Each group of students represents the board of directors. Discuss whether the company should sell stock or bonds. What price would it need to get for each share? How much should it sell in bonds? What bond characteristics would be the best for the company?

Internet CONNECTION

Know Thy Bonds!

Educating yourself in the various bonds is important before investing in bonds. Use your favorite search engine to find websites that have tutorials about bonds. Find the bond in which you are interested. It could be convertible bonds, junk bonds, Treasury notes (STRIPS), or zero coupon bonds. Define your favorite type and find the current market value.

Answers to **Self Reviews**

Answers to Section 1 Self Review

1. A convertible bond is one that may be converted into common stock, under specified conditions, at the option of the owner.

2. Registered bonds are bonds whose owners are registered in the records of the corporation. Interest is paid each payment date to the registered owner. Coupon bonds are not registered. The corporation does not know the names of owners of the bonds. To collect interest, the bondholder clips a coupon from the bond and presents it to the bank.

3. In the event of a decrease in the market interest rate, or if the corporation has extra cash, the corporation can redeem the bonds if they are callable.

4. **b.** serial bonds.

5. **d.** debentures.

6. 15.2% ($38,000 ÷ $250,000)

Answers to Section 2 Self Review

1. Discount on bonds payable is shown on the balance sheet as a deduction from the face value of the bonds.

2. An equal amount of discount or premium is amortized each month from the issue date to the maturity date.

3. Bond premium is a device to adjust the face amount of interest to the market interest rate at the date of issuance. Thus, the premium is directly related to interest expense.

4. **b.** credit to *Bonds Payable.*

5. **b.** amortized over the life of the bond issue.

6. 50 ($1,000/10 yrs. = $100/yr. or $50/payment date)

Answers to Section 3 Self Review

1. A fund used to accumulate assets to pay off bonds when they mature.

2. Bonds may be retired prior to maturity because management has surplus cash, it wants to save interest costs, or it expects interest costs to decrease.

3. Gain or loss on bond retirement may be shown as an extraordinary item if the transaction is unusual and infrequent. Otherwise, it is shown as *Other Income* or *Other Expense.*

4. **c.** *Income from Sinking Fund Investment.*

5. **c.** *Bonds Payable.*

6. Debit *Retained Earnings Appropriated for Bond Retirement* for $300,000; credit *Retained Earnings* for $300,000. Debit *Bonds Payable* for $300,000 and credit *Cash* for $300,000.

Answers to Comprehensive Self Review

1. Secured bonds are bonds that have specific assets pledged as security. If the corporation does not pay the principal and interest, the bondholders may take possession of the assets. Debenture bonds have no specific assets pledged to secure payment. So, the secured bond is a more attractive investment.

2. Two disadvantages are (a) interest must be paid and (b) the face amount must be repaid at maturity.

3. Bonds sell at a premium when the face interest rate is greater than the market rate of interest on similar investments on the date of the sale.

4. The appropriation is intended to protect the bondholders. It clearly indicates that dividends are being restricted because of a future need to pay off the bonds.

5. When bonds are retired at maturity, **Bonds Payable** is debited and **Cash** (or **Bond Sinking Fund Investment**) is credited. If the company has **Retained Earnings Appropriated** for the bonds, that account should be closed and returned to **Retained Earnings Unappropriated.**

Mini-Practice Set 3

Corporation Accounting Cycle

The Texas Company

This project will give you an opportunity to apply your knowledge of accounting principles and pro-cedures to a corporation. You will handle the accounting work of The Texas Company for 2016.

The chart of accounts and account balances of The Texas Company on January 1, 2016, are shown on the next page. Texas *does not* use reversing entries.

INTRODUCTION

Round all computations to the nearest whole dollar.

INSTRUCTIONS

1. Open the general ledger accounts and enter the balances for January 1, 2016. Obtain the necessary figures from the trial balance.

2. Analyze the transactions on the pages that follow, and record them in the general journal. Use 1 as the number of the first journal page.

3. Post the journal entries to the general ledger accounts.

4. Prepare a worksheet for the year ended December 31, 2016.

5. Prepare a summary income statement for the year ended December 31, 2016.

6. Prepare a statement of retained earnings for the year ended December 31, 2016.

7. Prepare a balance sheet as of December 31, 2016.

8. Journalize and post the adjusting entries as of December 31, 2016.

9. Journalize and post the closing entries as of December 31, 2016.

Analyze: Assume that the firm declared and issued a 3:1 stock split of common stock in 2016. What is the effect on total par value?

	The Texas Company		
	Chart of Accounts/Account Balances on January 1, 2016		
Account Number	Account Name	Debit	Credit
101	Cash	$176,000	
103	Accounts Receivable	170,000	
104	Allowance for Doubtful Accounts		$5,000
105	Subscriptions Receivable — Common Stock		
121	Interest Receivable		
131	Merchandise Inventory	150,000	
141	Land	85,000	
151	Buildings	225,000	
152	Accumulated Depreciation — Buildings		22,500
161	Furniture and Equipment	70,000	
162	Accumulated Depreciation — Furniture and Equipment		14,000
181	Organization Costs	6,000	
202	Accounts Payable		75,000
203	Interest Payable		2,500
205	Estimated Income Taxes Payable		17,000
206	Dividends Payable — Preferred Stock		
207	Dividends Payable — Common Stock		
211	10-year, 10% Bonds Payable		100,000
212	Premium on Bonds Payable		2,625
301	5% Preferred Stock ($100 par, 10,000 shares authorized)		100,000
302	Paid-In Capital in Excess of Par — Preferred Stock		10,000
303	Common Stock ($10 par, 100,000 shares authorized)		200,000
304	Paid in Capital in Excess of Par — Common Stock		25,000
305	Common Stock Subscribed		
306	Common Stock Dividend Distributable		
311	Retained Earnings Appropriated		100,000
312	Retained Earnings Unappropriated		208,375
343	Treasury Stock — Preferred		
399	Income Summary		
401	Sales		
501	Purchases		
601	Operating Expenses		
701	Interest Income		
711	Gain on Early Retirement of Bonds Payable		
751	Interest Expense		
753	Amortization of Organization Costs		
801	Income Tax Expense		
	Totals	$882,000	$882,000

DATE	TRANSACTIONS FOR 2016
Jan. 5	Issued 1,000 shares of 5 percent $100 par preferred stock for $101 per share. (The corporation has been authorized to issue 10,000 shares of preferred stock.)
15	Paid estimated income taxes of $17,000 accrued at the end of 2015.
Apr. 1	Paid semiannual bond interest on the 10-year, 10 percent bonds payable and amortized the premium for the period since December 31, 2015. (The interest and premium were recorded as of December 31, 2015; the entry was not reversed.) The bonds were issued on October 1, 2014, at a price of 103, and they mature on October 1, 2024. Use straight-line amortization.
July 1	The Texas Company's board of directors declared a cash dividend of $0.10 per share on the common stock. The dividend is payable on July 26 to stockholders of record as of July 15.
26	Paid the cash dividend on the common stock.
Aug. 12	A purchaser of 600 shares of preferred stock issued on January 5 asked the corporation to repurchase the shares. The corporation repurchased the stock for $102 per share. The stock is to be held by the corporation until it can be resold to another purchaser.
Oct. 1	Paid the semiannual bond interest and recorded amortization of the bond premium.
Dec. 1	Because of its good cash position and current bond prices, The Texas Company repurchased and retired $20,000 par value of the 10 percent bonds that it has outstanding. The repurchase price was 98, plus accrued interest.
15	The company's board of directors declared a cash dividend of $5 per share on the outstanding preferred stock. This dividend is payable on January 10 to stockholders of record as of December 31.
15	The board of directors also declared a 10 percent stock dividend on the outstanding common stock. The new shares are to be distributed on January 10 to stockholders of record as of December 31. At the time the dividend was declared, the common stock had a fair market value of $15 per share.
30	Received a subscription for 500 shares of The Texas Company's common stock at $12 per share from the company's president. Received cash equal to one-half the purchase price on the date of subscription. The balance of the purchase price is to be paid on January 15, 2017. (The subscriber will not be entitled to the stock dividend previously declared on the outstanding shares of common stock.)
Dec. 30	Because the management of Texas foresees the need to expand a warehouse the firm owns, the board of directors has restricted future dividend payments. Record the appropriation of $100,000 of retained earnings for plant expansion.

Journalize the following summary transactions using December 31, 2016, as the record date:

	SUMMARY OPERATING TRANSACTIONS FOR 2016
1.	Total sales of merchandise for the year were $2,800,000. All sales were on credit.
2.	Total collections on accounts receivable during the year were $2,810,000.
3.	Total purchases of merchandise for the year were $1,880,000. All purchases were on credit.
4.	Total operating expenses incurred during the year were $650,000. (Debit *Operating Expenses* and credit *Accounts Payable*.)
5.	Total cash payments on accounts payable during the year were $2,335,000.
6.	Total accounts receivable charged off as uncollectible during the year were $10,000. (The Texas Company uses the allowance method to record uncollectible accounts.)

Data for Year-End Adjustments

1. The balance of ***Allowance for Doubtful Accounts*** should be adjusted to equal 3 percent of the balance of ***Accounts Receivable.*** (Debit ***Operating Expenses.***)

2. Depreciation on the buildings should be recorded. (Debit ***Operating Expenses.***) The firm uses the straight-line method and an estimated life of 20 years to compute this adjustment.

3. Depreciation on furniture and equipment should be recorded. The firm uses the straight-line method and an estimated life of 10 years to compute this adjustment. (Debit ***Operating Expenses.***)

4. Accrued interest on the outstanding bonds payable of The Texas Company should be recorded and the premium amortized.

5. The amortization of organization costs for the year should be recorded. The Texas Company was formed on January 1, 2014. Organization costs of $10,000 were incurred at the time and are being amortized over a 60-month period.

6. The ending merchandise inventory is $130,000.

Other Data

Estimated federal income taxes are to be recorded using the tax rates given on page 728.

Financial Statement Analysis

Teva Pharmaceutical
www.tevapharm.com

If looking at a company like Teva Pharmaceutical, a Jerusalem-based business that began in 1901, a potential investor would probably not be concerned with how the business began, but would tend to focus more on *current* financial statement data. Reported net income as well as changes in a company's total assets or total debts tend to be a focal point for many investors. A potential investor may also be interested in the amount of dividends that the company paid.

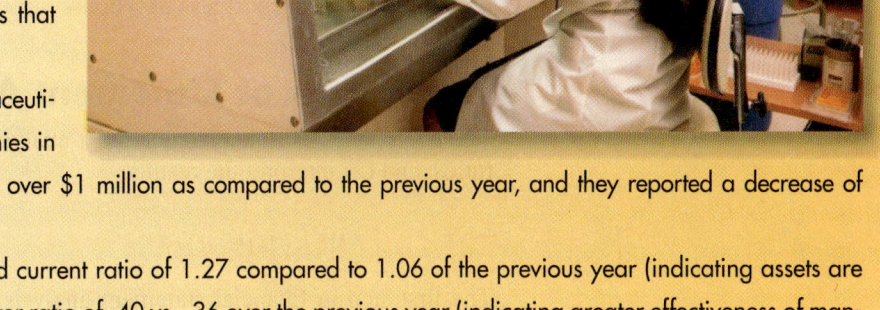

Today, Teva is the world leader in generic pharmaceuticals and among the top 15 pharmaceutical companies in the world. Its reported gross profit in 2012 was up over $1 million as compared to the previous year, and they reported a decrease of $1.2 million in their current debt.

In 2012, Teva's statements reflected an improved current ratio of 1.27 compared to 1.06 of the previous year (indicating assets are higher than liabilities) and an improved asset turnover ratio of .40 vs. .36 over the previous year (indicating greater effectiveness of management in utilizing assets to generate sales).

thinking critically

How can studying and comparing how a company performed from one year to the next help shareholders decide whether to invest in a company?

LEARNING OBJECTIVES

23-1. Use vertical analysis techniques to analyze a comparative income statement and balance sheet.

23-2. Use horizontal analysis techniques to analyze a comparative income statement and balance sheet.

23-3. Use trend analysis to evaluate financial statements.

23-4. Interpret the results of the statement analyses by comparison with industry averages.

23-5. Compute and interpret financial ratios that measure profitability, operating results, and efficiency.

23-6. Compute and interpret financial ratios that measure financial strength.

23-7. Compute and interpret financial ratios that measure liquidity.

23-8. Recognize shortcomings in financial statement analysis.

23-9. Define the accounting terms new to this chapter.

NEW TERMS

accounts receivable turnover
acid-test ratio
asset turnover
average collection period
common-size statements
comparative statements
horizontal analysis
industry averages

leveraged buyout
price-earnings ratio
quick assets
ratio analysis
return on common stockholders' equity
total equities
trend analysis
vertical analysis

Vertical Analysis

Owners, managers, creditors, and other parties use financial statements to gather the information needed to make business decisions.

The Phases of Statement Analysis

The two phases of financial statement analysis are (1) compute differences, percentages, and ratios; and (2) interpret the results.

THE COMPUTATION PHASE

The first step in financial statement analysis is the *computation phase*. Three basic types of calculations are used:

- **Vertical analysis** is the relationship of each item on a financial statement to some base amount on the statement. On the income statement, each item is expressed as a percentage of net sales. On the balance sheet, each item is expressed as a percentage of total assets or total liabilities and stockholders' equity.

- **Horizontal analysis** is the percentage change for individual items in the financial statements from year to year.

- **Ratio analysis** is the relationship between various items in the financial statements. Ratio analysis can involve items on the same statement or items on different statements. Ratio analysis is a form of analytical review.

THE INTERPRETATION PHASE

The second step in statement analysis, the *interpretation phase,* is the more difficult and important step. Financial statement interpretation requires an understanding of financial statements and knowledge of the operations of the business and the industry. In the interpretation phase, the analyst develops an understanding of the significance of the percentages and ratios computed. Analysts compare the ratios for the current year to prior years' ratios, budgeted ratios, and industry averages.

>> **23-1. OBJECTIVE**

Use vertical analysis techniques to analyze a comparative income statement and balance sheet.

Vertical Analysis of Financial Statements

Let's learn the techniques of vertical analysis of financial statements using comparative financial statements. **Comparative statements** are financial statements presented side by side for two or more years. Figure 23.1 shows the comparative income statement of Unique Products, Inc., for the years 2015 and 2016.

FIGURE 23.1   Comparative Income Statement—Vertical Analysis

	Amounts		Percent of Net Sales*	
	2016	2015	2016	2015
Revenue				
Sales	3 1 0 4 4 5 0	2 8 2 5 6 2 5	104.6	104.7
Less Sales Returns and Allowances	1 3 5 4 5 0	1 2 5 6 2 5	4.6	4.7
Net Sales	2 9 6 9 0 0 0	2 7 0 0 0 0 0	100.0	100.0
Cost of Goods Sold				
Merchandise Inventory, January 1	2 2 5 0 0 0	2 1 5 0 0 0	7.6	8.0
Purchases (Net)	1 7 0 6 5 0 0	1 5 6 5 7 2 1	57.5	58.0
Freight In	2 6 0 0 0	1 9 0 0 0	0.9	0.7
Total Merchandise Available for Sale	1 9 5 7 5 0 0	1 7 9 9 7 2 1	65.9	66.7
Less Merchandise Inventory, December 31	2 0 5 0 0 0	2 2 5 0 0 0	6.9	8.3
Cost of Goods Sold	1 7 5 2 5 0 0	1 5 7 4 7 2 1	59.0	58.3
Gross Profit	1 2 1 6 5 0 0	1 1 2 5 2 7 9	41.0	41.7
Operating Expenses				
Selling Expenses	5 2 6 4 2 5	4 9 6 7 5 0	17.7	18.4
General and Administrative Expenses	6 0 5 0 0 0	5 9 9 3 0 0	20.4	22.2
Total Operating Expenses	1 1 3 1 4 2 5	1 0 9 6 0 5 0	38.1	40.6
Net Income from Operations	8 5 0 7 5	2 9 2 2 9	2.9	1.1
Other Income				
Gain on Sale of Equipment	4 0 0 0	1 5 0 0 0	0.1	0.6
Interest Income	1 8 0 0	1 7 0 0	0.1	0.1
Total Other Income	5 8 0 0	1 6 7 0 0	0.2	0.6
Other Expenses				
Bond Interest Expense	9 5 0 0	9 5 0 0	0.3	0.4
Other Interest Expense	2 0 0 0	2 5 0 0	0.1	0.1
Total Other Expenses	1 1 5 0 0	1 2 0 0 0	0.4	0.4
Income before Income Taxes	7 9 3 7 5	3 3 9 2 9	2.7	1.3
Income Tax Expense	2 3 8 1 2	1 0 1 7 9	0.8	0.4
Net Income after Income Taxes	5 5 5 6 3	2 3 7 5 0	1.9	0.9

Rounded, percentages may not add up as expected.

VERTICAL ANALYSIS OF THE INCOME STATEMENT

Notice the income statement heading. The third line indicates the periods covered by the statement. The more recent year, 2016, is in the left column. The income statement is in condensed form. In actual practice, separate schedules of the detailed Selling Expenses and General and Administrative Expenses are provided with the financial statements.

Vertical analysis of the income statement expresses each item as a percentage of the *net sales* figure. In each column, the net sales figure is used as the base, or 100 percent. Every amount in the column is expressed as a percentage of net sales. To compute an item's percentage of net sales, divide the amount of that item by the amount of net sales. For example, in 2016 the cost of goods sold is 59.0 percent of net sales:

$$\frac{\text{Cost of goods sold}}{\text{Net sales}} = \frac{\$1,752,500}{\$2,969,000} = 0.5903 = 59.03 \text{ percent (rounded to 59.0 percent)}$$

important!

Rounding

In statement analysis, it is customary to compute percentages to the nearest one-tenth of a percent. This procedure is followed in this chapter.

important!

Percentages

In common-size statements, percentages (of net sales on the income statement and of total assets on the balance sheet) are shown instead of dollar amounts.

In making these types of computations, it is customary to carry the division one place further than needed and then round off. The usual practice is to round percentages to the nearest one-tenth of a percent. The computation in the example is made to the fourth decimal (0.5903). That decimal fraction is converted to a percentage by moving the decimal point two places to the right (59.03 percent). The percentage is then rounded to the nearest one-tenth of a percent; hence, 59.03 is rounded to 59.0.

In Figure 23.1, note that gross sales are more than 100 percent ($3,104,450 ÷ $2,969,000 = 104.6 percent in 2016). That is because of **Sales Returns and Allowances,** which are 4.6 percent of net sales.

The percentages are added and subtracted, giving informative subtotals and totals. Because of rounding, the individual percentages may not add up to 100 percent. In this case, one or more percentages is adjusted slightly until the total equals 100 percent. If the difference is more than a small amount, it is probable that an error has been made, and all the computations should be checked before adjusting any of the amounts.

Financial statements with items expressed as percentages of a base amount are called **common-size statements.** The last two columns in the comparative income statement are referred to as a *comparative common-size statement.*

Percentages obtained by vertical analysis of the income statement are useful when compared with the company's percentages for prior years. It is helpful to make comparisons with several years to detect trends, but even year-to-year comparisons are useful. For example, the comparative income statement of Unique Products, Inc., shows gross profit on sales of 41.7 percent in 2015 and 41.0 percent in 2016. A comparison with the industry average might be helpful. For example, suppose that trade association publications reveal that the average gross profit for the industry is 51.7 percent. Unique Products, Inc.'s gross profit on sales compares unfavorably to the industry average. This could be attributed to peculiarities of its operations, local competition, or other factors. However, it indicates the need for further examination.

VERTICAL ANALYSIS OF THE BALANCE SHEET

Vertical analysis of the balance sheet expresses each item as either a percentage of total assets or of total liabilities and stockholders' equity.

Figure 23.2 shows a comparative balance sheet for Unique Products, Inc., with the vertical analysis results. The pair of columns on the right shows each item as a percentage of total assets for each year. The more recent year is on the left. On December 31, 2016, the cash balance was $115,231 and the total assets were $555,711. Thus, the cash balance is 20.7 percent of total assets in 2016:

$$\frac{Cash}{Total\ assets} = \frac{\$115,231}{\$555,711} = 0.2074 = 20.7\ percent$$

In rounding off, it might be necessary to adjust one or more of the figures to obtain an even 100 percent for each total.

Vertical analysis percentages of the balance sheet are very useful when they are compared with the percentages of the same company for previous years and with those of other companies in the same industry. Changes in the percentages might reveal situations that need investigation. For example, the comparative balance sheet of Unique Products, Inc., shows that cash has increased from 15.5 percent of total assets in 2015 to 20.7 percent of total assets in 2016. The accountant may suggest that this increase be studied.

FIGURE 23.2   Comparative Balance Sheet—Vertical Analysis

Unique Products, Inc.
Comparative Balance Sheet (Vertical Analysis)
December 31, 2016 and 2015

	Amounts on December 31		Percent of Total Assets	
	2016	2015	2016	2015
Assets				
Current Assets				
Cash	1 1 5 2 3 1	8 0 7 7 3	20.7	15.5
Accounts Receivable	1 0 2 0 0 0	7 3 5 0 0	18.4	14.1
Merchandise Inventory	2 0 5 0 0 0	2 2 5 0 0 0	36.9	43.3
Prepaid Expenses	1 2 0 0	1 5 0 0	0.2	0.3
Supplies	5 0 0	2 5 0	0.1	0.0
Total Current Assets	4 2 3 9 3 1	3 8 1 0 2 3	76.3	73.3
Property, Plant, and Equipment				
Land	8 0 0 0 0	8 0 0 0 0	14.4	15.4
Building and Store Equipment	7 1 8 0 0	7 7 8 0 0	12.9	15.0
Less Accumulated Depreciation—Building and Store Equipment	2 8 5 2 0	2 3 3 4 0	5.1	4.5
Net Book Value—Building and Store Equipment	4 3 2 8 0	5 4 4 6 0	7.8	10.5
Office Equipment	1 0 5 0 0	6 0 0 0	1.9	1.2
Less Accumulated Depreciation—Office Equipment	2 0 0 0	1 5 0 0	0.4	0.3
Net Book Value—Office Equipment	8 5 0 0	4 5 0 0	1.5	0.9
Total Property, Plant, and Equipment	1 3 1 7 8 0	1 3 8 9 6 0	23.7	26.7
Total Assets	5 5 5 7 1 1	5 1 9 9 8 3	100.0	100.0
Liabilities and Stockholders' Equity				
Current Liabilities				
Accounts Payable	7 1 0 0 0	8 4 5 0 0	12.8	16.3
Sales Tax Payable	2 9 0 0	2 5 0 0	0.5	0.5
Payroll Taxes Payable	1 1 4 5	1 0 2 5	0.2	0.2
Interest Payable	8 6 0	2 1 5	0.2	0.0
Total Current Liabilities	7 5 9 0 5	8 8 2 4 0	13.7	17.0
Long-Term Liabilities				
10% Bonds Payable, 2025	1 0 0 0 0 0	1 0 0 0 0 0	18.0	19.2
Premium on Bonds Payable	3 5 0 0	4 0 0 0	0.6	0.8
Mortgage Payable	6 0 0 0 0	6 5 0 0 0	10.8	12.5
Total Long-Term Liabilities	1 6 3 5 0 0	1 6 9 0 0 0	29.4	32.5
Total Liabilities	2 3 9 4 0 5	2 5 7 2 4 0	43.1	49.5
Stockholders' Equity				
Preferred Stock ($100 par, 8%, 500 shares authorized, issued and outstanding)	5 0 0 0 0	5 0 0 0 0	9.0	9.6
Common Stock ($1 par, 25,000 shares authorized)				
Issued and outstanding: 7,000 shares in 2015; 8,000 shares in 2016	8 0 0 0	7 0 0 0	1.4	1.3
Paid-in Capital—Common Stock	4 5 0 0	3 5 0 0	0.8	0.7
Retained Earnings				
Retained Earnings—Unappropriated	2 5 3 8 0 6	2 0 2 2 4 3	45.7	38.9
Total Retained Earnings	2 5 3 8 0 6	2 0 2 2 4 3	45.7	38.9
Total Stockholders' Equity	3 1 6 3 0 6	2 6 2 7 4 3	56.9	50.5
Total Liabilities and Stockholders' Equity	5 5 5 7 1 1	5 1 9 9 8 3	100.0	100.0

Section 1 Self Review

QUESTIONS

1. How does the computation phase of statement analysis differ from the interpretation phase?

2. What is a common-size statement?

3. What item serves as the base for the percentage calculations in a vertical analysis of the income statement?

EXERCISES

4. Which of the following is true of vertical analysis?

   a. Each item on the balance sheet is expressed as a percentage of total liabilities.

   b. Each item in the income statement is divided by net sales.

   c. Each item in the income statement is expressed as a percentage of net income.

   d. The amount of increase or decrease for each item in the income statement is divided by net sales.

5. In a vertical analysis of a balance sheet, each item is expressed as a percentage of:

   a. total assets or total liabilities.

   b. total assets or total stockholders' equity.

   c. total assets or total liabilities and stockholders' equity.

   d. total liabilities or total stockholders' equity.

ANALYSIS

6. Net sales for 2015 and 2016 are $1,200,000 and $1,000,000. Net income after income taxes for 2015 and 2016 are $60,000 and $30,000. Compute the percentage of net income after taxes (based on net sales) for 2015 and 2016.

(Answers to Section 1 Self Review are on pages 841–842.)

>> **23-2.** Use horizontal analysis techniques to analyze a comparative income statement and balance sheet.

industry averages
trend analysis

WHY IT'S IMPORTANT

Analysis techniques help managers pinpoint operational or procedural problems that require investigation.

>> **23-3.** Use trend analysis to evaluate financial statements.

WHY IT'S IMPORTANT

Review of several years of financial data can reveal performance trends.

>> **23-4.** Interpret the results of the statement analyses by comparison with industry averages.

WHY IT'S IMPORTANT

Global competition requires businesses to remain in touch with industry trends and financial conditions.

Horizontal Analysis

In this section, you will learn the second type of basic calculation, horizontal analysis.

Horizontal Analysis of Financial Statements

Financial statements for two or more periods may be evaluated by means of horizontal analysis. Horizontal analysis compares the items on each line to determine the change in dollar amounts. A percentage change can be shown by using the earlier figure as the base.

HORIZONTAL ANALYSIS OF THE INCOME STATEMENT

>> **23-2. OBJECTIVE**

Use horizontal analysis techniques to analyze a comparative income statement and balance sheet.

Let's learn the techniques of horizontal analysis using the comparative income statement. Figure 23.3 on page 808 shows the comparative income statement of Unique Products, Inc., for 2015 and 2016.

Each amount for 2016 is compared to the corresponding amount for 2015. The increase or decrease of the change and the percentage of change are shown in the right two columns. Look at the sales figures. The gross sales for 2016 are higher than those for 2015. The increase is $278,825:

Sales for 2016	$3,104,450
Sales for 2015	−2,825,625
Increase	$ 278,825

To find the percentage of increase, divide the increase by the amount for the base year. The base year is always the earlier year. The percentage of increase for gross sales is 9.9 percent:

$$\frac{\text{Increase in sales}}{\text{Sales for base year}} = \frac{\$278,825}{\$2,825,625} = 9.9 \text{ percent}$$

If the amount for the most recent year is less than that for the base year, the percentage decrease is calculated in the same manner. For example, ending merchandise inventory decreased by $20,000 for 2016. Divide the decrease by the base year amount:

$$\frac{\text{Amount of decrease}}{\text{Amount in base year}} = \frac{(\$20,000)}{\$225,000} = (8.9) \text{ percent}$$

FIGURE 23.3   Comparative Income Statement—Horizontal Analysis

	Amounts		Increase or (Decrease)	
	2016	**2015**	**Amount**	**Percent***
Unique Products, Inc.				
Comparative Income Statement (Horizontal Analysis)				
Years Ended December 31, 2016 and 2015				
Revenue				
Sales	3 104 450	2 825 625	278 825	9.9
Less Sales Returns and Allowances	135 450	125 625	9 825	7.8
Net Sales	2 969 000	2 700 000	269 000	10.0
Cost of Goods Sold				
Merchandise Inventory, January 1	225 000	215 000	10 000	4.7
Purchases (Net)	1 706 500	1 565 721	140 779	9.0
Freight In	26 000	19 000	7 000	36.8
Total Merchandise Available for Sale	1 957 500	1 799 721	157 779	8.8
Less Merchandise Inventory, December 31	205 000	225 000	(20 000)	(8.9)
Cost of Goods Sold	1 752 500	1 574 721	177 779	11.3
Gross Profit	1 216 500	1 125 279	91 221	8.1
Operating Expenses				
Selling Expenses	526 425	496 750	29 675	6.0
General and Administrative Expenses	605 000	599 300	5 700	1.0
Total Operating Expenses	1 131 425	1 096 050	35 375	3.2
Net Income from Operations	85 075	29 229	55 846	191.1
Other Income				
Gain on Sale of Equipment	4 000	15 000	(11 000)	(73.3)
Interest Income	1 800	1 700	100	5.9
Total Other Income	5 800	16 700	(10 900)	(65.3)
Other Expenses				
Bond Interest Expense	9 500	9 500	0	0.0
Other Interest Expense	2 000	2 500	(500)	(20.0)
Total Other Expenses	11 500	12 000	(500)	(4.2)
Net Income before Income Taxes	79 375	33 929	45 446	133.9
Income Tax Expense	23 812	10 179	13 633	133.9
Net Income after Income Taxes	55 563	23 750	31 813	133.9
* Rounded				

A decrease can be expressed by using a negative sign before the number, italics, or parentheses.

All the amounts in the right two columns on the comparative statement are computed in the same manner. If the amount of change is zero, there is no percentage of change. When there is no amount for the base period, no percentage change is computed.

Interpretation of the Percentages   The amounts of increase or decrease can be added or subtracted in the column and will give correct subtotals at each point. However, the percentages cannot be added or subtracted. Each percentage relates only to the line on which it appears.

Some important changes shown in the comparative income statement for Unique Products, Inc., include the following:

■ Gross sales increased 9.9 percent.

■ Cost of goods sold increased 11.3 percent.

- Gross profit on sales increased 8.1 percent.
- Total operating expenses increased 3.2 percent.
- Income from operations increased 191.1 percent.
- Income tax expense increased 133.9 percent.
- Net income after income taxes increased 133.9 percent.

Horizontal analysis is especially useful in identifying items that need further investigation. For example, the increase in net sales was 10.0 percent, but the increase in cost of goods sold was 11.3 percent. An alert manager would want to determine the reasons for the increase in cost of goods sold.

Management would also be interested in learning why freight increased 36.8 percent during 2016 while purchases increased only 9.0 percent.

Keep in mind that percentages of increase or decrease can be misleading when small amounts are involved. For example, total other income decreased 65.3 percent. However, in terms of actual dollars, the amount is relatively small, from $16,700 to $5,800. On the other hand, a small percentage change is important for items involving large dollar amounts.

The process of interpretation is easier if some basis of comparison is available, such as a company budget or industry averages. Significant changes need to be investigated in detail and the reasons evaluated.

HORIZONTAL ANALYSIS OF THE BALANCE SHEET

A firm's balance sheets for two or more periods can be presented in comparative form to permit a detailed horizontal analysis. Figure 23.4 on the next page shows a comparative balance sheet for Unique Products, Inc., for December 31 of 2015 and 2016.

The calculations are the same as those for a horizontal analysis of income statements. The amounts are compared line by line. For example, for accounts receivable the difference is an increase of $28,500 ($102,000 − $73,500). The percentage of change is 38.8 percent. It is determined by dividing the amount of the change by the base year (2015) amount: $28,500 ÷ $73,500 = 38.78, or 38.8 percent.

Trend Analysis of Financial Statements

Comparing ratio and percentage relationships of the current year with those of the immediately preceding year is a normal and helpful procedure. However, comparisons between only two years could be misleading and might not be adequate to indicate long-term trends. A better technique is **trend analysis,** which compares selected ratios and percentages over a period of time. Often the time period is five years.

Let's look at one trend. The percentage of gross profit to net sales decreased from 41.7 percent in 2015 to 41.0 percent in 2016 (Figure 23.1). A higher gross profit percentage is desirable, so the decrease is unfavorable. A comparison with the several prior years follows:

	2012	2013	2014	2015	2016
Net sales	$2,055,600	$2,223,240	$2,587,500	$2,700,000	$2,969,000
Cost of goods sold	1,059,900	1,234,560	1,495,642	1,574,721	1,752,500
Gross profit on sales	$ 995,700	$ 988,680	$1,091,858	$1,125,279	$1,216,500
Percentage of gross profit to net sales	48.4	44.5	42.2	41.7	41.0

In looking at the data over five years, it is clear that the decrease in percentage from 2012 to 2016 is significant. It calls for the attention of management. Management must obtain other facts, talk with employees, and observe other trends before arriving at a solution to the problem.

important!

Base Year

In preparing horizontal percentage analyses, the earlier year is used as the base for computing the percentage of change.

inte-nal **CONTROL**

important!

Adding It Up

In horizontal analysis, the amounts in the Increase or Decrease columns can be added or subtracted vertically, but the percentages cannot be.

>> 23-3. OBJECTIVE

Use trend analysis to evaluate financial statements.

FIGURE 23.4   Comparative Balance Sheet—Horizontal Analysis

Unique Products, Inc.
Comparative Balance Sheet (Horizontal Analysis)
December 31, 2016 and 2015

	Amounts		Increase or (Decrease)	
	2016	2015	Amount	Percent*
Assets				
Current Assets				
Cash	115 231	80 773	34 458	42.7
Accounts Receivable	102 000	73 500	28 500	38.8
Merchandise Inventory	205 000	225 000	(20 000)	(8.9)
Prepaid Expenses	1 200	1 500	(300)	(20.0)
Supplies	500	250	250	100.0
Total Current Assets	423 931	381 023	42 908	11.3
Property, Plant, and Equipment				
Land	80 000	80 000	0	0.0
Building and Store Equipment	71 800	77 800	(6 000)	(7.7)
Less Accumulated Depreciation—Building and Store				
Equipment	28 520	23 340	5 180	22.2
Net Book Value—Building and Store Equipment	43 280	54 460	(11 180)	(20.5)
Office Equipment	10 500	6 000	4 500	75.0
Less Accumulated Depreciation—Office Equipment	2 000	1 500	500	33.3
Net Book Value—Office Equipment	8 500	4 500	4 000	88.9
Total Property, Plant, and Equipment	131 780	138 960	(7 180)	(5.2)
Total Assets	555 711	519 983	35 728	6.9
Liabilities and Stockholders' Equity				
Current Liabilities				
Accounts Payable	71 000	84 500	(13 500)	(16.0)
Sales Tax Payable	2 900	2 500	400	16.0
Payroll Taxes Payable	1 145	1 025	120	11.7
Interest Payable	860	215	645	300.0
Total Current Liabilities	75 905	88 240	(12 335)	(14.0)
Long-Term Liabilities				
10% Bonds Payable, 2025	100 000	100 000	0	0.0
Premium on Bonds Payable	3 500	4 000	(500)	(12.5)
Mortgage Payable	60 000	65 000	(5 000)	(7.7)
Total Long-Term Liabilities	163 500	169 000	(5 500)	(3.3)
Total Liabilities	239 405	257 240	(17 835)	(6.9)
Stockholders' Equity				
Preferred Stock ($100 par, 8%, 500 shares				
authorized, issued and outstanding)	50 000	50 000	0	0.0
Common Stock ($1 par 25,000 shares authorized)				
Issued and outstanding: 7,000 shares in 2015;				
8,000 shares in 2016	8 000	7 000	1 000	14.3
Paid-in Capital—Common Stock	4 500	3 500	1 000	28.6
Retained Earnings				
Retained Earnings—Unappropriated	253 806	202 243	51 563	25.5
Total Retained Earnings	253 806	202 243	51 563	25.5
Total Stockholders' Equity	316 306	262 743	53 563	20.4
Total Liabilities and Stockholders' Equity	555 711	519 983	35 728	6.9

*Rounded

MANAGERIAL IMPLICATIONS <<

COMPARATIVE STATEMENTS

■ Statement analysis is extremely important to managers in detecting areas of strength and weakness in a business.

■ Comparison of current data with the data of prior years indicates favorable and unfavorable trends.

■ Managers compare percentages from year to year and with industry averages in order to detect variations that require prompt investigation.

■ Management must consider certain factors when using industry averages.

THINKING CRITICALLY
What type of financial statement analysis would you use to assess profitability of a company for the last five years?

Trend analysis makes it possible to ask questions about all aspects of operations of the company. The accountant makes the most valuable contribution to the success of the business when analyzing operating data.

Comparison with Industry Averages

Trade associations survey their members to obtain financial and other data. The financial ratios and percentages that reflect averages for similar companies are called industry averages. These data are converted to a uniform presentation, usually in common-size statements arranged by company size (based on sales volume or total assets). Income statement items are expressed as a percentage of net sales and balance sheet items as a percentage of total assets. Common-size statements can be presented for one year or for several years. Individual companies compare their results to industry averages.

Let's look at an example of how the management of Unique Products, Inc., might evaluate the corporation in comparison with others in the same industry. Table 23.1 on page 812 shows highly condensed data from its income statement as well as the data provided by the trade association for companies with the same general sales level. Note that income tax expense has been omitted. Because companies included in the trade averages are sole proprietorships, partnerships, and corporations, it is not appropriate to compare net income after income taxes with entities that do not pay taxes.

You can see why the comparison to industry averages would be of interest to management, owners, and others. The operations of Unique Products, Inc., are not as efficient or as profitable as those of its competitors. Its rate of gross profit is lower (and on a downward trend) than the industry averages. Its ratio of operating expenses to net sales is higher than that of others in the industry. The end result is that Unique Products, Inc.'s ratio of income before income tax to sales is much lower than that of its competitors. Based on this comparison, management needs to immediately determine the causes of its poor results.

In comparing to industry averages, keep in mind the following:

■ Different businesses keep different types of accounts and do not classify items in the same manner.

■ No two businesses are exactly alike. There are differences in the merchandise sold, the type of customers, and the method of financing (owners' equity versus borrowed funds). Some businesses buy fixed assets while others lease all or some of the fixed assets.

■ The industry figures could include data from corporations, partnerships, and sole proprietorships. The different business entities might report salary allowances, benefits for owners, and other items in very different ways.

Despite these problems, common-size statements provided by trade associations or commercial financial service companies are important to managers in comparing their operations to other firms. They are of special value when comparing data not affected by the factors listed above.

recall

Consistency Principle
The consistency principle permits comparisons between years. Using the same methods allows meaningful comparisons.

>> **23-4. OBJECTIVE**
Interpret the results of the statement analyses by comparison with industry averages.

TABLE 23.1

Comparison of Trade Data

| | Percentage of Net Sales* | | | |
| | Unique Products, Inc. | | Industry Average | |
	2016	2015	2016	2015
Revenue				
Sales	104.6	104.7	104.0	103.5
Returns and Allowances	4.6	4.7	4.0	3.5
Net Sales	100.0	100.0	100.0	100.0
Cost of Goods Sold	59.0	58.3	50.5	47.0
Gross Profit on Sales	41.0	41.7	49.5	53.0
Operating Expenses				
Selling Expenses	17.7	18.4	18.2	20.1
General Expenses	20.4	22.2	19.5	22.0
Total Operating Expenses	38.1	40.6*	37.7	42.1
Operating Income	2.9	1.1	11.8	10.9
Other Income and Expenses				
Other Income	0.2	0.6	0.9	1.2
Other Expenses	(0.4)	(0.4)	(0.5)	(0.1)
Net Other Income or (Exp.)	(0.2)	0.2	0.4	1.1
Income before Income Tax	2.7	1.3	12.2	12.0

*Rounded

Section 2   Self Review

QUESTIONS

1. In horizontal analysis of the balance sheet, how is the percentage of change determined?

2. In the same industry, when comparing an established company and a newer one, which company would have a higher percentage of property, plant, and equipment to total assets? Why?

3. Why is comparison with industry averages helpful when analyzing financial statements?

EXERCISES

4. If a comparative balance sheet shows the amount and percentage of decrease in merchandise inventory from one year to the next, the firm used:
   a. horizontal analysis.
   b. vertical analysis.
   c. common-size analysis.
   d. trend analysis.

5. If current assets are $200,000 and total assets are $500,000, the percentage of current assets to total assets is:
   a. 15 percent.
   b. 5 percent.
   c. 40 percent.
   d. 3 percent.

ANALYSIS

6. Total selling expenses for 2015 and 2016 were $725,000 and $875,000, respectively. Net sales for 2015 and 2016 were $3,300,000 and $3,700,000, respectively. For each year, what are total selling expenses as a percentage of net sales? What is the percentage of increase or decrease of total selling expenses?

(Answers to Section 2 Self Review are on page 842.)

SECTION OBJECTIVES	TERMS TO LEARN

>> **23-5.** Compute and interpret financial ratios that measure profitability, operating results, and efficiency.

WHY IT'S IMPORTANT

Various factors, in combination with the measurement of net income, contribute to the overall prosperity of a company.

>> **23-6.** Compute and interpret financial ratios that measure financial strength.

WHY IT'S IMPORTANT

The long-term viability of a business depends on effective use of equity and earnings.

>> **23-7.** Compute and interpret financial ratios that measure liquidity.

WHY IT'S IMPORTANT

To establish financial credibility, a business needs to demonstrate its ability to pay its debts when due.

>> **23-8.** Recognize shortcomings in financial statement analysis.

WHY IT'S IMPORTANT

The analysis of financial statements, without considering different accounting processes or operational procedures, could lead to improper conclusions.

TERMS TO LEARN

accounts receivable turnover
acid-test ratio
asset turnover
average collection period
leveraged buyout
price-earnings ratio
quick assets
return on common stockholders' equity
total equities

Ratios

Ratio analysis is used to assess a company's profitability, financial strength, and liquidity. Ratio analysis investigates a relationship between two items either as a ratio (2 to 1 or 2:1) or as a rate (percentage).

Financial ratios have three classifications:

1. Profitability, operating results, and efficiency
2. Financial strength
3. Liquidity

The financial statements of Unique Products, Inc., will be used to illustrate ratio analysis. You will need to refer to Figures 23.3 on page 808 and 23.4 on page 810 while studying this section.

Profitability is measured by net income. However, a dollar amount of net income is not a sufficient yardstick. Net income of $150,000 might be excellent for a small firm but unsatisfactory for a large corporation. A number of ratios are used to determine the adequacy of a company's profit.

Profitability Ratios

RATE OF RETURN ON SALES

The rate of return on sales is a measure of managerial efficiency and profitability. It is computed as follows:

$$\frac{\text{Net income after taxes}}{\text{Net sales}} = \text{Rate of return on net sales}$$

>> **23-5. OBJECTIVE**

Compute and interpret financial ratios that measure profitability, operating results, and efficiency.

important!

Rate of Return on Sales

The rate of return on sales measures what part of each sales dollar remains as net income. It measures operating efficiency and profitability.

Some companies use income before taxes to calculate the percentage because income taxes depend on factors not related to sales. Unique Products, Inc., uses net income after income taxes to calculate the rate.

The rate of return on net sales at Unique Products, Inc., was 1.9 percent for 2016 compared to 0.9 percent in 2015 as sales increased significantly in 2016:

2016	2015
$\dfrac{\$55,563}{\$2,969,000} = 1.9\%$	$\dfrac{\$23,750}{\$2,700,000} = 0.9\%$

The higher the rate of return on net sales, the more satisfactory are the business operations. Management should look for and investigate unfavorable trends.

RATE OF RETURN ON COMMON STOCKHOLDERS' EQUITY

Corporations are expected to earn a profit for their shareholders. Preferred shareholders are entitled to the dividends provided for in the preferred stock contract. The remainder of the earnings is available to common shareholders. **Return on common stockholders' equity** is a key measure of how well the corporation is making a profit for its shareholders. It is computed as follows:

$$\frac{\text{Income available to common stockholders}}{\text{Common stockholders' equity}} = \frac{\text{Return on common}}{\text{stockholders' equity}}$$

ABOUT
ACCOUNTING

Stock Sales

From the creation of the NYSE in 1783 until 1997, stock prices were offered in increments of one-eighth of one dollar, or 12.5 cents. This changed in 1997 to one-sixteenth of a dollar, or 6.25 cents. In 2004, stock and option markets switched to the decimal system.

Step 1. *Compute income available to common stockholders.* Income available to common stockholders is net income after taxes reduced by any preferred dividend requirements. Unique Products, Inc., has a $4,000 dividend requirement for preferred stock (500 shares at $100 par value at 8 percent). Subtract $4,000 from net income after taxes to determine the income available for common stockholders:

	2016	2015
Net income after income taxes	$55,563	$23,750
Less dividend requirements on preferred stock	4,000	4,000
Income available to common stockholders	$51,563	$19,750

Step 2. *Compute the common stockholders' equity.* There are many ways to compute common stockholders' equity: end-of-year balance, average of the beginning and ending balances, average based on quarterly balances, or average based on monthly balances. Unique Products, Inc., uses the end-of-year balance of total common stockholders' equity:

	2016	2015
Total stockholders' equity	$316,306	$262,743
Less preferred stock equity	50,000	50,000
Common stockholders' equity	$266,306	$212,743

Step 3. *Divide the income available to common stockholders by the common stockholders' equity:*

2016	2015
$\dfrac{\$51,563}{\$266,306} = 19.4\%$	$\dfrac{\$19,750}{\$212,743} = 9.3\%$

The increase in the 2016 rate of return on common stockholders' equity is caused primarily by the increase in net income. As net income increases, you should expect this ratio to improve. As a common stock shareholder, you would want to monitor this ratio yearly.

EARNINGS PER SHARE OF COMMON STOCK

Earnings per share of common stock measures the profit accruing to each share of common stock owned. It is computed as follows:

$$\frac{\text{Income available to common stockholders}}{\text{Average number of shares of common stock outstanding during year}} = \text{Earnings per share}$$

Step 1. *Compute income available to common stockholders.* Subtract the dividend requirements on preferred stock from the income after income tax:

	2016	2015
Net income after income taxes	$55,563	$23,750
Less dividend requirements on preferred stock	4,000	4,000
Income available to common stockholders	$51,563	$19,750

Step 2. *Determine the average number of shares of common stock outstanding during the year.* An analysis of the common stock account reveals that 7,000 shares were outstanding throughout 2015 and most of 2016. On October 2, 2016, 1,000 additional shares were issued. *The weighted average number of shares outstanding* for 2016 was 7,250, calculated as follows:

$$7{,}000 \text{ shares} \times \frac{12 \text{ months}}{12 \text{ months}} = 7{,}000 \text{ shares}$$

$$1{,}000 \text{ shares} \times \frac{3 \text{ months}}{12 \text{ months}} = \underline{250} \text{ shares}$$

$$\text{Weighted average number of shares} = 7{,}250 \text{ shares}$$

Step 3. *Divide the income available to common stockholders by the average number of shares of common stock outstanding:*

2016	2015
$\dfrac{\$51{,}563}{7{,}250 \text{ shares}} = \$7.11$	$\dfrac{\$19{,}750}{7{,}000 \text{ shares}} = \$2.82$

Earnings per share were $7.11 in 2016 and $2.82 in 2015. The large increase in net income caused earnings per share to increase significantly even though there were more shares of stock outstanding in 2016.

Analysts, stockholders, and creditors watch the earnings per share measurement very closely. Comparing earnings per share for the same company for several years could show a trend.

PRICE-EARNINGS RATIO

The **price-earnings ratio** compares the market value of common stock with the earnings per share of that stock. It is computed as follows:

$$\frac{\text{Market price per share of common stock}}{\text{Earnings per share of common stock}} = \text{Price-earnings ratio}$$

If a corporation's common stock sells for $144 per share and its earnings are $12 per share, the price-earnings ratio is 12 to 1 ($144 ÷ $12).

The price-earnings ratio is an indicator of the attractiveness of the stock as an investment at its present market value. The amount investors are willing to pay for stock is based on expectations

important!

Price-Earnings Ratio
The price-earnings ratio depends in large part on expectations of future profitability, which cause stock prices to increase or decrease.

for the future. The price-earnings ratio is not computed for privately held companies because there is no readily available market value for the shares.

YIELD ON COMMON STOCK

For a publicly held corporation, the relationship between the dividends received by the stockholders and the market value of each share is important. The yield on common stock is computed as follows:

$$\frac{\text{Cash dividend per share}}{\text{Market price per share}} = \text{Yield on common stock}$$

For example, if the price of a share of common stock is $60 and the corporation is paying an annual dividend of $6, the yield is 10 percent ($6 ÷ $60).

RATE OF RETURN ON TOTAL ASSETS

The rate of return on total assets measures the rate of return on the assets used by a company. This rate helps the analyst to judge managerial performance, measure the effectiveness of the assets used, and evaluate proposed capital expenditures. The rate is computed as follows:

$$\frac{\text{Income before interest expense and income taxes}}{\text{Total assets}} = \frac{\text{Rate of return on}}{\text{total assets}}$$

Income before interest and taxes is used to measure how effectively management utilized the assets, regardless of how the assets were financed. If nonoperating revenue amounts (such as dividend and interest income) are large, they should not be included in income. This ensures that only income from normal business operations is considered. For Unique Products, Inc., income is computed by adding interest expense to income before income taxes.

	2016	2015
Income before income taxes	$79,375	$33,929
Interest expense	11,500	12,000
Income before interest and taxes	$90,875	$45,929

Analysts might average the assets at the beginning and end of the year, average the assets monthly, use the beginning assets, or use the ending assets. Unique Products, Inc., uses year-end total assets.

The rate of return on total assets for Unique Products, Inc., is as follows:

2015	2016
$\dfrac{\$90,875}{\$555,711} = 16.4\%$	$\dfrac{\$45,929}{\$519,983} = 8.8\%$

The results are meaningful only if compared with rates of prior years and with the industry average.

ASSET TURNOVER

important!

Asset Turnover

A low asset turnover compared to the industry average shows that the business uses more assets to generate the same sales volume as its competitors.

The ratio of net sales to total assets measures the effective use of assets in making sales. This ratio is usually called asset turnover. It is computed as follows:

$$\frac{\text{Net sales}}{\text{Total assets}} = \text{Asset turnover}$$

Assets that are not used in producing sales, primarily investments, are excluded. Assets may be measured as end-of-year totals, average of beginning and ending totals, or average of monthly totals. Unique Products, Inc., uses net sales and total assets at the end of the year.

2016	2015
$\dfrac{\$2,969,000}{\$555,711} = 5.3$ to 1	$\dfrac{\$2,700,000}{\$519,983} = 5.2$ to 1

The higher the asset turnover, the more effectively the assets of the company are being used. The trend of this ratio is important because it indicates whether asset growth is accompanied by corresponding sales growth. If sales increase proportionately more than total assets, the ratio increases, which is a favorable indicator.

Financial Strength Ratios

NUMBER OF TIMES BOND INTEREST EARNED

A corporation's bondholders and stockholders want to know if net income is sufficient to cover the required bond interest payments. Times bond interest earned measures this. It is computed as follows:

$$\frac{\text{Income before bond interest and income taxes}}{\text{Bond interest cash requirement}} = \text{Times bond interest earned}$$

Step 1. *Compute the income before bond interest and income taxes.* To compute the income amount, add the bond interest expense to income before income taxes. For Unique Products, Inc., bond interest expense was $9,500 in 2015 and $9,500 in 2016 (interest paid on the bonds minus the amortization of bond premium). Unique Products, Inc., uses the straight-line method to amortize the premium on bonds payable. The amount is computed as follows:

	2016	2015
Income before income tax	$79,375	$33,929
Add bond interest expense	9,500	9,500
Available for bond interest	$88,875	$43,429

Step 2. *Compute the cash required to pay bond interest.* The cash interest for bonds outstanding at the end of each year is computed as follows:

$$2016: \$100,000 \times 0.10 = \$10,000$$

$$2015: \$100,000 \times 0.10 = \$10,000$$

Step 3. *Compute the ratio.*

2016	2015
$\dfrac{\$88,875}{\$10,000} = 8.9$ times	$\dfrac{\$43,429}{\$10,000} = 4.3$ times

Unique Products, Inc.'s income easily covers required bond payments.

RATIO OF STOCKHOLDERS' EQUITY TO TOTAL EQUITIES

The sum of a corporation's liabilities and stockholders' equity is referred to as its **total equities.** The ratio of stockholders' equity to total equities measures the portion of total capital provided by the stockholders. It indicates the protection afforded creditors against possible losses. The more capital provided by the stockholders, the greater the protection to creditors. The ratio of stockholders' equity to total equities is computed as follows:

$$\frac{\text{Stockholders' equity}}{\text{Total equities}} = \text{Ratio of stockholders' equities to total equities}$$

>>23-6. OBJECTIVE
Compute and interpret financial ratios that measure financial strength.

recall

Bond Premium
The excess of the price paid over the face value of a bond is known as bond premium.

The ratios for Unique Products, Inc., follow:

2016	2015
$\dfrac{\$316{,}306}{\$555{,}711} = 0.57 \text{ to } 1$	$\dfrac{\$262{,}743}{\$519{,}983} = 0.51 \text{ to } 1$

In 2016, the stockholders of Unique Products, Inc., provided 57 cents of each dollar of total equities compared to 51 cents in 2015. This ratio varies widely from industry to industry. A comparison with the industry average is important in determining a desirable ratio for a particular business.

RATIO OF STOCKHOLDERS' EQUITY TO TOTAL LIABILITIES

The ratio of stockholders' equity to total liabilities is known as the *ratio of owned capital to borrowed capital*. It is computed as follows:

$$\frac{\text{Stockholders' equity}}{\text{Total liabilities}} = \text{Ratio of stockholders' equity to total liabilities}$$

The ratios for Unique Products, Inc., follow:

2016	2015
$\dfrac{\$316{,}306}{\$239{,}405} = 1.32 \text{ to } 1$	$\dfrac{\$262{,}743}{\$257{,}240} = 1.02 \text{ to } 1$

This ratio reveals a significant improvement in 2016. In 2015, stockholders provided slightly more than $1 of equity for each dollar of liability. In 2016, they provided $1.32 of equity for each dollar of debt.

In a **leveraged buyout,** the purchasers of a business buy the stock, having the corporation agree to pay the sellers. The result is that the debt created by the purchase is a debt of the corporation. In many cases, the debt, usually with a high interest rate, makes up a large part of the total equities of the corporation. In the mid-1980s to early 1990s, many corporations went bankrupt because they could not meet the interest and principal payments on the debts. The balance sheets of these corporations would reflect a very low ratio of stockholders' equity to total liabilities.

BOOK VALUE PER SHARE OF STOCK

Book value per share measures the financial strength underlying each share of stock. It is frequently reported in financial publications. It represents the amount that each share would receive in case of liquidation if the assets were sold for book value.

When there is one class of stock outstanding, the book value of each share is total stockholders' equity divided by the number of shares outstanding. If more than one class of stock is outstanding, the rights of the various classes of stock are considered. The book value of preferred stock is computed first. Then the remaining balance of stockholders' equity is divided by the number of common shares. Special treatment is given to dividends in arrears on cumulative preferred stock. In case of liquidation, the owner of a share of preferred stock will receive its par value.

$$\frac{\text{Common stockholders' equity}}{\text{Number of common shares outstanding}} = \text{Book value per share of common stock}$$

Follow these steps to compute the book value per share of stock for Unique Products, Inc.:

Step 1. *Compute the claims of preferred stockholders.* There are no cumulative dividends or special liquidation provisions for the preferred stock of Unique Products, Inc. Therefore, the book value is the same as the par value, $100 per share. There were 500

---

important!

Stockholders' Equity

A low ratio of stockholders' equity to total liabilities can be risky. The corporation might not be able to make interest and principal payments on its debts.

important!

Book Value per Share

Book value and fair market value often are quite different. Book value per share does not indicate how much the stockholder would receive if the assets were sold and the corporation liquidated.

shares of preferred stock outstanding during 2015 and 2016, so the claims of the preferred stockholders for both years are $50,000 (500 shares at $100 par value).

Step 2. *Deduct the claims of preferred stockholders from total stockholders' equity to compute the claims of common stockholders.* The common stockholders are entitled to the difference between the total stockholders' equity and the portion assigned to the preferred stock.

	2016	2015
Stockholders' equity	$316,306	$262,743
Less preferred stock equity	50,000	50,000
To common stockholders	$266,306	$212,743

Step 3. *Divide the total claims of common stockholders by the number of shares of common stock outstanding.* Unique Products, Inc., had 8,000 shares of common stock outstanding on December 31, 2016, and 7,000 shares outstanding on December 31, 2015. The book value of each share is computed as follows:

$$\text{2016} \qquad\qquad \text{2015}$$

$$\frac{\$266,306}{8,000 \text{ shares}} = \$33.29 \qquad \frac{\$212,743}{7,000 \text{ shares}} = \$30.39$$

The book value of Unique Products, Inc.'s common stock increased from $30.39 to $33.29 per share.

Liquidity Ratios

WORKING CAPITAL

Liquidity measures the ability of a business to pay its debts when due. Many businesses fail because they cannot pay their debts, even though they are profitable and have long-term financial strength. Working capital is a measure of the ability of a company to meet its current obligations. It represents the margin of security afforded short-term creditors. Working capital, sometimes called *net working capital,* is computed as follows:

$$\text{Current assets} - \text{Current liabilities} = \text{Working capital}$$

In 2016, Unique Products, Inc.'s working capital increased by $55,243. This is a significant change that needs to be investigated.

	2016	2015	Increase or (Decrease)
Current assets	$423,931	$381,023	$42,908
Current liabilities	75,905	88,240	(12,335)
Working capital	$348,026	$292,783	$55,243

CURRENT RATIO

Working capital is a very important measure of liquidity. The current ratio is another way to evaluate liquidity. The current ratio measures the ability of a business to pay its current debts using current assets. The current ratio is computed as follows:

$$\frac{\text{Current assets}}{\text{Current liabilities}} = \text{Current ratio}$$

important!

Whenever a business has long-term debt, please remember that the current year's payments (12 months) represent a current liability. For simplicity, we have not included a Current Portion of Long Term Debt liability within the Current Liabilities section of Liabilities.

>>23-7. OBJECTIVE

Compute and interpret financial ratios that measure liquidity.

recall

Current Assets

Assets are considered current if they will be converted to cash or used within one year.

In 2016, Unique Products, Inc., had $5.59 of current assets for each dollar of current liabilities.

2016	2015
$\dfrac{\$423,931}{\$75,905} = 5.59{:}1$	$\dfrac{\$381,023}{\$88,240} = 4.32{:}1$

The current ratio varies widely among industries and even from company to company within an industry. A popular guideline is that a current ratio of at least 2 to 1 is desirable in retail and manufacturing businesses. This guideline is not applicable, however, to all businesses.

From the viewpoint of a short-term creditor, the higher the current ratio, the greater the amount of protection afforded. However, the current ratio can be too high. A very high current ratio indicates that excess current assets are on hand and are not earning income. A high current ratio could be caused by large sums of money tied up in accounts receivable that might be uncollectible. A high current ratio could also be caused by obsolete inventory or an inventory level higher than required to conduct normal operations.

ACID-TEST RATIO

Although the current ratio measures a company's ability to cover current liabilities using current assets, it is not a measure of immediate liquidity. A considerable period of time might be necessary to sell the inventory and convert it into cash in the normal course of business. The **acid-test ratio** measures immediate liquidity. This ratio uses **quick assets,** which are cash, receivables, and marketable securities.

$$\frac{\text{Cash} + \text{Receivables} + \text{Marketable securities}}{\text{Current liabilities}} = \text{Acid-test ratio}$$

Unique Products, Inc.'s acid-test ratios follow:

2016	2015
$\dfrac{\$115,231 + \$102,000}{\$75,905} = 2.86{:}1$	$\dfrac{\$80,773 + \$73,500}{\$88,240} = 1.75{:}1$

The acid-test ratio shows that in 2016, Unique Products, Inc., had $2.86 of quick assets for each dollar of current liabilities. In 2015, the acid-test ratio was 1.75. This dramatic increase should be investigated.

Acid-test ratios vary widely from industry to industry. A general guideline is that the acid-test ratio should be at least 1 to 1. The due dates of current liabilities, composition of quick assets, and various operating factors are considered when evaluating the adequacy of the ratio. Comparisons with the industry average and with the company's ratio in prior years can be helpful.

INVENTORY TURNOVER

It is important that a business sell its inventory rapidly so that excess working capital is not tied up in merchandise. Inventory turnover measures the number of times the inventory is replaced during the period. The higher the turnover, the shorter the time between the purchase and sale of the inventory. Inventory turnover is computed as follows:

$$\frac{\text{Cost of goods sold}}{\text{Average merchandise inventory}} = \text{Inventory turnover}$$

Ideally, average inventory is computed using month-end balances. However, these amounts are not available to analysts outside the business. Therefore, year-end balances are often used, but they might not be typical of the inventory levels during the year. Inventory is often at its lowest level at year-end.

To compute the inventory turnover for Unique Products, Inc., follow these steps:

Step 1. *Compute the average inventory.*

	2016	2015
Inventory, Jan. 1	$225,000	$215,000
Inventory, Dec. 31	205,000	225,000
Totals	$430,000	$440,000
	÷ 2	÷ 2
Average inventory	$215,000	$220,000

Step 2. *Divide the cost of goods sold by the average inventory.*

2016

$$\frac{\$1,752,500}{\$215,000} = 8.15 \text{ times}$$

2015

$$\frac{\$1,574,721}{\$220,000} = 7.16 \text{ times}$$

The inventory turnover ratio varies widely by industry. Inventory turnover for a bakery is almost daily. A vendor of construction equipment might turn inventory just twice a year. A business must compare its inventory turnover with prior years and with the industry average.

ACCOUNTS RECEIVABLE TURNOVER

A company should collect accounts and notes receivable promptly. This minimizes the amount of working capital tied up in receivables and reduces the likelihood that accounts will become uncollectible. The **accounts receivable turnover** is a measure of the reasonableness of the accounts outstanding. This measurement uses net credit sales, which includes notes receivable from sales transactions. The accounts receivable turnover is computed as follows:

$$\frac{\text{Net credit sales}}{\text{Average receivables}} = \text{Accounts receivable turnover}$$

It is desirable to use monthly balances to compute the average receivables. However, since these amounts are not available to analysts outside the business, year-end balances are often used. Outside analysts normally use net sales since they cannot determine net credit sales. For Unique Products, Inc., accounts receivable on January 1, 2015, were $71,500. Net credit sales were $2,969,000 in 2016 and $2,700,000 in 2015.

Step 1. *Compute average accounts receivable.*

	2016	2015
Accounts receivable, Jan. 1	$ 73,500	$ 71,500
Accounts receivable, Dec. 31	102,000	73,500
Totals	$175,500	$145,000
	÷ 2	÷ 2
Average accounts receivable	$ 87,750	$ 72,500

Step 2. *Divide net credit sales by average accounts receivable.*

2016

$$\frac{\$2,969,000}{\$87,750} = 33.8 \text{ times}$$

2015

$$\frac{\$2,700,000}{\$72,500} = 37.2 \text{ times}$$

The accounts receivable turnover can be used to determine the **average collection period** of accounts receivable, or *number of days' sales in receivables*. The average collection period is computed as follows:

$$\frac{365 \text{ days}}{\text{Accounts receivable turnover}}$$

2016

$$\frac{365}{33.8} = 10.8 \text{ days}$$

2015

$$\frac{365}{37.2} = 9.8 \text{ days}$$

MANAGERIAL IMPLICATIONS <<

INTERPRETING FINANCIAL STATEMENTS

- It is important that managers understand the relationships among the items on the financial statements. Understanding these relationships will help management run the business effectively.

- Managers use statement analysis to identify areas of operations that are weak and need attention.

- It is essential that management know how to compute and interpret financial ratios. For example, a low inventory turnover compared with the industry average might reflect obsolete goods, excess merchandise, poor purchasing procedures, or other operating inefficiencies.

- Effective managers recognize the key role the accountant plays in financial statement analysis and interpretation. Accountants understand what each line on the financial statements represents and can assist management in analyzing and understanding accounting reports.

THINKING CRITICALLY
Which ratios will best measure the company's ability to meet current obligations?

Unique Products, Inc., collected accounts receivable in 2016 in about 12 days and about 11 days in 2015. As a general rule, the average collection period should not exceed the net credit period plus one-third. The credit terms for customers of Unique Products, Inc., are net 15 days. The collection period should be 20 days or less [15 + (1/3 × 15)]. For both years, the collection period for Unique Products, Inc., is much less than the guideline.

OTHER RATIOS

The number of ratios that could be developed from financial statements is almost limitless. Analysts use their preferred ratios. Financial analysts use many more ratios than those presented in this chapter. Depending on the industry, some ratios are more important than others. The ratios in this chapter are those most often used by accountants.

> > **23-8. OBJECTIVE**
> Recognize shortcomings in financial statement analysis.

SOME PRECAUTIONARY NOTES ON STATEMENT ANALYSIS

There are limits to the benefits of financial statement analysis. Financial statements use book values. Book value depends on accounting procedures and policies. Different accounting policies and procedures make it difficult to compare financial results across companies. One firm, for example, might record a purchase as an asset and another firm could record it as an expense. Businesses also have many choices regarding depreciation methods, useful lives, and salvage value.

Another limitation of financial statement analysis is that financial statements are prepared assuming that the dollar is a stable monetary unit; this is far from correct. The amounts reported do not necessarily represent dollars with today's purchasing power.

Finally, it is difficult to compare financial results of businesses that use different financing methods, classify expenses differently, have different policies for paying owner-employees, and operate as different types of business entities. Financial statement analysis is useful only if these limitations are clearly understood.

recall

Cost Basis Principle
Accounts reflect historical costs, not current market values. This must be considered when analyzing financial statements. Book value rarely reflects fair market value.

Summary of Ratios

This chapter examined many ratios that are commonly used by analysts to evaluate a business. A summary of the ratios is shown in Table 23.2.

TABLE 23.2   Summary of Ratios Used in Statement Analysis

Ratio	Equation	Performance Measured
Ratios That Measure Profitability, Operating Results, and Efficiency		
Rate of return on net sales	$$\frac{\text{Net income after taxes}}{\text{Net sales}}$$	Percentage of each sales dollar that reflects net income
Rate of return on common stockholders' equity	$$\frac{\text{Income available to common stockholders}}{\text{Common stockholders' equity}}$$	Rate of return on book value of common stock
Earnings per share of common stock	$$\frac{\text{Income available to common stockholders}}{\text{Average number of shares of common stock outstanding during year}}$$	Income accruing on each share of common stock
Price-earnings ratio	$$\frac{\text{Market price per share of common stock}}{\text{Earnings per share of common stock}}$$	Value of a share of common stock compared with income accruing to that share
Yield on common stock	$$\frac{\text{Cash dividend per share}}{\text{Market price per share}}$$	Cash income (dividend) from a share of common stock as a percentage of the market value of the share
Rate of return on total assets	$$\frac{\text{Income before interest expense and income taxes}}{\text{Total assets}}$$	Effectiveness of management in utilizing assets, regardless of how they were financed
Asset turnover	$$\frac{\text{Net sales}}{\text{Total assets}}$$	Effectiveness of management in using assets to generate sales
Ratios That Measure Financial Strength		
Number of times bond interest earned	$$\frac{\text{Income before bond interest and income taxes}}{\text{Bond interest cash requirement}}$$	Security afforded bondholders
Ratio of stockholders' equity to total equities	$$\frac{\text{Stockholders' equity}}{\text{Total equities}}$$	Portion of assets provided by stockholders and therefore security afforded creditors
Ratio of stockholders' equity to total liabilities	$$\frac{\text{Stockholders' equity}}{\text{Total liabilities}}$$	Owners' capital compared with liabilities; measures security afforded creditors
Book value per share of common stock	$$\frac{\text{Common stockholders' equity}}{\text{Number of common shares outstanding}}$$	Amount owner of each share would receive if assets were sold for their book value and the corporation was liquidated

TABLE 23.2 [continued]   Summary of Ratios Used in Statement Analysis

Ratios That Measure Liquidity		
Working capital	Current assets − Current liabilities	Dollar amount of security provided short-term creditors
Current ratio	$\dfrac{\text{Current assets}}{\text{Current liabilities}}$	Ability of business to pay current debts using current assets
Acid-test ratio	$\dfrac{\text{Cash + receivables + marketable securities}}{\text{Current liabilities}}$	Immediate liquidity or short-run debt-paying ability
Inventory turnover	$\dfrac{\text{Cost of goods sold}}{\text{Average merchandise inventory}}$	Effectiveness of control of inventory for sales volume
Accounts receivable turnover	$\dfrac{\text{Net credit sales}}{\text{Average receivables}}$	Efficiency with which sales on account are collected
Average collection period	$\dfrac{\text{365 days}}{\text{Accounts receivable turnover}}$	Average number of days required to collect sales on account

Section 3   Self Review

QUESTIONS

1. What does book value per share measure?

2. Name three measurements often used in evaluating profitability.

3. Why is it useful to know the inventory turnover for a company?

EXERCISES

4. The price-earnings ratio for common stock is computed using:
   a. par value.
   b. market value.
   c. book value.
   d. stated value.

5. The average collection period is determined by dividing:
   a. 365 days by the accounts receivable turnover.
   b. net credit sales by 365 days.
   c. net credit sales by average receivables.
   d. beginning accounts receivable by ending accountings receivable.

ANALYSIS

6. A corporation's stock is selling at $40 per share, and its earnings are $8 per share. The corporation is paying an annual dividend of $4.00. What is the price-earnings ratio? What is the yield on common stock?

(Answers to Section 3 Self Review are on page 842.)

REVIEW   Chapter Summary

Financial statement analysis involves computation and interpretation. Computation includes the calculation of percentages and ratios. Interpretation means comparing one set of figures with another (prior statements, budgets, or industrial averages) and determining the financial implications of those comparisons. The comparative statement is a convenient form for the presentation of figures for analysis and appraisal.

Learning Objectives

23-1 Use vertical analysis techniques to analyze a comparative income statement and balance sheet.

Vertical analysis expresses each item as a percentage of a base amount on the statement.

- Net sales are the base for all income statement items. To compute an item's percentage of net sales, divide the amount of that item by the amount of net sales.

Example: $\dfrac{\text{Total operating expenses}}{\text{Net sales}}$

- Total assets (or total liabilities plus owner's equity) are the base for vertical analysis items on a balance sheet. Each figure is expressed as a percentage of the base.

Example: $\dfrac{\text{Cash}}{\text{Total assets}}$

It is customary to carry the percentage computed to one decimal place further than needed and then to round it off. The usual practice is to round percentages to the nearest one-tenth of a percent.

23-2 Use horizontal analysis techniques to analyze a comparative income statement and balance sheet.

Horizontal analysis compares items from one year to the next. The amount of change and the percentage change is computed.

- Changes to items such as gross sales, cost of goods sold, operating expenses, and net income can be studied on the income statement.

Example: $\dfrac{\text{Increase in total operating expenses}}{\text{Total operating expenses for base year}}$

- A firm's balance sheets for two or more periods can be presented in comparative form to permit a comparison of items from year to year.

Example: $\dfrac{\text{Increase in cash}}{\text{Cash in base year}}$

23-3 Use trend analysis to evaluate financial statements.

Comparing ratio and percentage relationships of the current year with only those of the previous year can be misleading and are not adequate to indicate long-term trends.

Using data from five or more years, trend analysis compares selected ratios and percentages to analyze operations.

Trend analysis often omits income tax expense because the companies' forms of business could be different (that is, sole proprietorships, partnerships, corporations).

23-4 Interpret the results of the statement analyses by comparison with industry averages.

Companies often compare financial statements with industry averages to determine how the company's operations stack up against other businesses in the industry. In order to make these comparisons, similar classification structures must be in place.

Varied operational procedures and accounting treatments can create inconsistency in data presentation:

- Different businesses keep different types of accounts and do not classify items in a consistent manner.
- No two businesses are exactly alike in terms of merchandise, customers, financing, asset acquisition, and other areas.
- Industry averages might include data from sole proprietorships, partnerships, and corporations. This creates inconsistency in presentation of financial information.

23-5 Compute and interpret financial ratios that measure profitability, operating results, and efficiency.

Net income and other factors are used to evaluate profitability, operating results, and business efficiencies. Analysts review the sales of the company in relation to net income, the nature of operations, how assets are used to earn income for

Learning Objectives (continued)

the business, and how successful the company has been in rewarding its stockholders.

Measures of profitability, operating results, and efficiency include:

- rate of return on net sales,
- rate of return on common stockholders' equity,
- earnings per share of common stock,
- price-earnings ratio,
- yield on common stock,
- rate of return on total assets,
- asset turnover.

23-6 **Compute and interpret financial ratios that measure financial strength.**

The ability to satisfy long-term debt obligations and to deliver adequate dividend returns to stockholders offers key indications of a company's overall financial strength. Comparison of a company's long-term liabilities to the book value of its property, plant, and equipment can reveal the level of security afforded to long-term creditors. In addition, measurements of book value indicate the financial strength underlying each share of stock.

Measures of financial strength include:

- number of times bond interest earned,
- ratio of stockholders' equity to total equities,
- ratio of stockholders' equity to total liabilities,
- book value per share of common stock.

23-7 **Compute and interpret financial ratios that measure liquidity.**

A company's ability to pay its currently maturing debts is of critical importance to short-term creditors, long-term creditors, and stockholders. Current assets such as cash, inventories, and accounts receivable are measured against items such as current liabilities and credit sales to establish the liquidity of the business.

Measures of liquidity include:

- working capital,
- current ratio,
- acid-test ratio,
- inventory turnover,
- accounts receivable turnover,
- days' sales in receivables.

23-8 **Recognize shortcomings in financial statement analysis.**

The benefits of analysis are limited by a number of significant issues:

- Different companies use different accounting methods. No two companies are exactly the same: there are different mixes of products sold, different organizational structures, and different types of entities.
- Financial statements reflect historical costs, rather than current market values.
- Financial statements are prepared assuming that the dollar is a stable monetary unit.

23-9 **Define the accounting terms new to this chapter.**

Glossary

Accounts receivable turnover (p. 821) A measure of the speed with which sales on account are collected; the ratio of net credit sales to average receivables

Acid-test ratio (p. 820) A measure of immediate liquidity; the ratio of quick assets to current liabilities

Asset turnover (p. 816) A measure of the effective use of assets in making sales; the ratio of net sales to total assets

Average collection period (p. 821) The ratio of 365 days to the accounts receivable turnover; also called the *number of days' sales in receivables*

Common-size statements (p. 804) Financial statements with items expressed as percentages of a base amount

Comparative statements (p. 802) Financial statements presented side by side for two or more years

Horizontal analysis (p. 802) Computing the percentage change for individual items in the financial statements from year to year

Industry averages (p. 811) Financial ratios and percentages reflecting averages for similar companies

Leveraged buyout (p. 818) Purchasing a business by acquiring the stock and obligating the business to pay the debt incurred

Price-earnings ratio (p. 815) The ratio of the current market value of common stock to earnings per share of that stock

Quick assets (p. 820) Cash, receivables, and marketable securities

Ratio analysis (p. 802) Computing the relationship between various items in the financial statements

Return on common stockholders' equity (p. 816) A measure of how well the corporation is making a profit for its shareholders; the ratio of net income available for common stockholders to common stockholders' equity

Total equities (p. 817) The sum of a corporation's liabilities and stockholders' equity

Trend analysis (p. 809) Comparing selected ratios and percentages over a period of time

Vertical analysis (p. 804) Computing the relationship between each item on a financial statement to some base amount on the statement

Comprehensive **Self Review**

1. What is the difference between vertical analysis and horizontal analysis?

2. What does the current ratio tell you?

3. In general, would it be preferable in a retail store to have a higher or lower inventory turnover? Explain.

4. Name several factors that may cause misleading results when comparing percentage figures of a specific company to industry averages.

5. Explain how to compute book value per share of common stock.

(Answers to Comprehensive Self Review are on pages 842–843.)

Discussion Questions

1. What are common-size statements?

2. Why would a short-term creditor be interested in the analysis of a company's income statement?

3. If a company's net sales and its cost of goods sold both increase by 12 percent from 2015 to 2016, would gross profit on sales also increase by 12 percent?

4. What is meant by vertical analysis of the income statement?

5. In a vertical analysis of the balance sheet, what is the base for comparing each item on the statement?

6. Which is more important: a larger change in percentage or a large change in dollar amount?

7. What does the rate of net income on stockholders' equity tell stockholders?

8. What is the procedure for measuring earnings per share of common stock?

9. How does the acid-test ratio differ from the current ratio?

10. How is inventory turnover computed?

11. What does the accounts receivable turnover measure?

12. As a rule of thumb, what is the minimum desired current ratio?

APPLICATIONS

Exercises

Use the comparative income statement and the comparative balance sheet for Austin, Inc., to solve Exercises 23.1 through 23.12.

Austin, Inc.
Comparative Income Statement
Years Ended December 31, 2016 and 2015

	Amounts	
	2016	2015
Sales	1 6 7 1 0 7 5	1 5 1 9 6 6 5
Less Sales Returns and Allowances	9 6 0 7 5	8 4 6 6 5
Net Sales	1 5 7 5 0 0 0	1 4 3 5 0 0 0
Cost of Goods Sold	1 0 4 2 6 5 0	9 4 7 1 0 0
Gross Profit on Sales	5 3 2 3 5 0	4 8 7 9 0 0
Selling Expenses	2 1 5 0 0 0	2 0 5 0 0 0
General Expenses	2 1 0 0 0 0	1 9 0 0 0 0
Total Expenses	4 2 5 0 0 0	3 9 5 0 0 0
Net Income before Income Taxes	1 0 7 3 5 0	9 2 9 0 0
Income Tax Expense	3 2 2 0 5	2 7 8 7 0
Net Income after Income Taxes	7 5 1 4 5	6 5 0 3 0

Exercise 23.1
Objective 23-1

▶ **Vertical analysis of income statement.**

Using the comparative income statement, prepare a vertical analysis of all items from sales through gross profit on sales for the years 2015 and 2016.

Exercise 23.2
Objective 23-1

▶ **Vertical analysis of balance sheet.**

Prepare a vertical analysis of all asset items on the comparative balance sheet for the years 2016 and 2015.

Exercise 23.3
Objective 23-2

▶ **Horizontal analysis of income statement.**

Using the comparative income statement, prepare a horizontal analysis of all items on the income statement for 2016 and 2015.

Exercise 23.4
Objective 23-2

▶ **Horizontal analysis of balance sheet.**

Prepare a horizontal analysis of all items on the comparative balance sheet for the years 2016 and 2015.

Exercise 23.5
Objective 23-1

▶ **Rate of return on sales.**

Calculate the rate of net income on sales for 2016 and 2015.

Exercise 23.6
Objective 23-1

▶ **Rate of return on stockholders' equity.**

Compute the rate of net income on stockholders' equity for 2016 and 2015. Retained earnings on January 1, 2015, was $300,000.

Exercise 23.7
Objective 23-1

▶ **Rate of return on assets.**

Compute the rate of net income before income taxes on total assets for 2016 and 2015. Base your calculation on total ending assets each year.

Exercise 23.8
Objective 23-1

▶ **Earnings per share.**

Calculate the earnings per share of common stock for 2016 and 2015.

Austin, Inc.
Comparative Balance Sheet
December 31, 2016 and 2015

	2016	2015
Assets		
Current Assets		
Cash	135325	122816
Accounts Receivable (Net)	128000	129504
Inventory	55705	60800
Total Current Assets	319030	313120
Property, Plant, and Equipment		
Buildings (Net)	185895	175104
Equipment (Net)	69984	63840
Land	61236	55936
Total Property, Plant, and Equipment	317115	294880
Total Assets	636145	608000
Liabilities and Stockholders' Equity		
Current Liabilities		
Accounts Payable	150000	180000
Other Current Liabilities	40000	57000
Total Current Liabilities	190000	237000
Long-Term Liabilities		
Bonds Payable	110000	110000
Total Long-Term Liabilities	110000	110000
Total Liabilities	300000	347000
Stockholders' Equity		
Common Stock ($1 par)	300000	300000
Retained Earnings	36145	−39000
Total Stockholders' Equity	336145	261000
Total Liabilities and Stockholders' Equity	636145	608000

Price-earnings ratio.

Calculate the price-earnings ratio for 2016 and 2015. The common stock selling price at year-end 2016 was $2.00 and for 2015 was $1.60.

◄ **Exercise 23.9**
Objective 23-5

Current ratio.

Calculate the current ratio for 2016 and 2015.

◄ **Exercise 23.10**
Objective 23-7

Inventory turnover.

Using the data for 2016 and 2015, calculate the inventory turnover for each year. The beginning inventory for year 2015 was $98,000.

◄ **Exercise 23.11**
Objective 23-3

Accounts receivable turnover.

Compute the accounts receivable turnover on December 31, 2016, for Austin, Inc. Assume that all sales were credit sales.

◄ **Exercise 23.12**
Objective 23-3

PROBLEMS

Problem Set A

Problem 23.1A ▶

Objectives 23-1, 23-2

Horizontal and vertical analysis of income statement and balance sheet.

The EastTN Company sells computer parts through a retail store that it operates. The firm's comparative income statement and balance sheet for the years 2016 and 2015 follow:

The EastTN Company
Comparative Income Statement
For Years Ended December 31, 2016 and 2015

	Amounts	
	2016	2015
Revenue		
Sales	9 0 5 0 0 0	7 6 5 0 0 0
Less Sales Returns and Allowances	1 5 0 0 0	9 0 0 0
Net Sales	8 9 0 0 0 0	7 5 6 0 0 0
Cost of Goods Sold		
Merchandise Inventory, January 1	8 4 0 0 0	8 0 0 0 0
Net Purchases	3 0 6 0 0 0	2 6 2 0 0 0
Total Merchandise Available for Sale	3 9 0 0 0 0	3 4 2 0 0 0
Less Merchandise Inventory, December 31	8 6 0 0 0	8 4 0 0 0
Cost of Goods Sold	3 0 4 0 0 0	2 5 8 0 0 0
Gross Profit on Sales	5 8 6 0 0 0	4 9 8 0 0 0
Operating Expenses		
Selling Expenses		
Sales Salaries Expenses	8 7 0 0 0	8 0 0 0 0
Payroll Tax Expense—Selling	8 7 0 0	8 0 0 0
Other Selling Expenses	2 5 2 0 0	1 5 2 0 0
Total Selling Expenses	1 2 0 9 0 0	1 0 3 2 0 0
General and Administrative Expenses		
Officers' Salaries Expense	1 3 0 0 0 0	1 1 0 0 0 0
Payroll Tax Expense—Administrative	1 3 0 0 0	1 1 0 0 0
Depreciation Expense	8 2 5 0	8 2 5 0
Other General and Administrative Expenses	9 4 5 0	7 0 0 0
Total General and Administrative Expenses	1 6 0 7 0 0	1 3 6 2 5 0
Total Operating Expenses	2 8 1 6 0 0	2 3 9 4 5 0
Net Income before Income Taxes	3 0 4 4 0 0	2 5 8 5 5 0
Income Tax Expense	9 1 3 2 0	7 7 5 6 5
Net Income after Income Taxes	2 1 3 0 8 0	1 8 0 9 8 5

The EastTN Company
Comparative Balance Sheet
December 31, 2016 and 2015

	Amounts	
	2016	2015
Assets		
Current Assets		
Cash	1 1 1 0 2 2	4 6 2 7 5
Accounts Receivable	9 5 0 0 0	8 7 5 0 0
Merchandise Inventory	8 6 0 0 0	8 4 0 0 0
Prepaid Expenses	9 5 0 0	5 0 0 0
Supplies	1 2 0 0	5 0 0
Total Current Assets	3 0 2 7 2 2	2 2 3 2 7 5
Property, Plant, and Equipment		
Land	7 5 0 0 0	7 5 0 0 0
Building and Equipment	8 2 5 0 0	8 2 5 0 0
Less Accumulated Depreciation	(3 3 0 0 0)	(2 4 7 5 0)
Net Book Value—Building and Equipment	4 9 5 0 0	5 7 7 5 0
Total Property, Plant, and Equipment	1 2 4 5 0 0	1 3 2 7 5 0
Total Assets	4 2 7 2 2 2	3 5 6 0 2 5
Liabilities and Stockholders' Equity		
Current Liabilities		
Accounts Payable	2 7 0 0 0	5 7 0 0 0
Sales Tax Payable	1 0 0 0	3 0 0 0
Payroll Taxes Payable	1 1 4 2	1 0 2 5
Income Taxes Payable	1 0 0 0	5 0 0 0
Total Current Liabilities	3 0 1 4 2	6 6 0 2 5
Long-Term Liabilities		
Mortgage Payable	3 9 0 0 0	4 5 0 0 0
Total Long-Term Liabilities	3 9 0 0 0	4 5 0 0 0
Total Liabilities	6 9 1 4 2	1 1 1 0 2 5
Stockholders' Equity		
Common Stock ($1 par, 10,000 shares authorized;		
10,000 shares issued and outstanding)	1 0 0 0 0	1 0 0 0 0
Paid-in Capital—Common Stock	1 0 0 0 0	1 0 0 0 0
Retained Earnings	3 3 8 0 8 0	2 2 5 0 0 0
Total Stockholders' Equity	3 5 8 0 8 0	2 4 5 0 0 0
Total Liabilities and Stockholders' Equity	4 2 7 2 2 2	3 5 6 0 2 5

INSTRUCTIONS

1. Prepare both a horizontal and a vertical analysis of the statements. Carry all calculations to two decimal places, and then round to one decimal place. (Leave all vertical analysis percentages unadjusted in this problem.)

2. Make written comments about any of the results that seem worthy of investigation.

Analyze: Based on your analysis, which expense category experienced the greatest percentage change?

Problem 23.2A

Objectives 23-5, 23-6, 23-7

CONTINUING >>>
Problem

▶ **Computing financial ratios.**

Part I Using the financial statements for The EastTN Company from Problem 23.1A, calculate the following financial ratios for 2015 and 2016. Comment on any ratio that merits additional consideration.

1. Current ratio

2. Acid-test ratio

3. Inventory turnover

4. Return on sales

5. Earnings per share of common stock

6. Book value per share of common stock

7. Return on total assets

8. Ratio of stockholders' equity to total equities

9. Rate of return on stockholders' equity

10. Asset turnover

Assume all sales are credit sales.

Part II Selected ratios for other common-size companies in the same industry as The EastTN Company follow. Using these data and the ratios you computed in Part I, write brief comments on areas you feel are strengths, weaknesses, or require further observation for The EastTN Company.

1. Rate of return on stockholders' equity, 45.0 percent

2. Stockholders' equity to total equities, 0.6 to 1 (or 60%)

3. Asset turnover, 2.5 to 1

4. Merchandise inventory turnover, 4.5 times

Analyze: The EastTN Company experienced a 17.7 percent increase in net income after taxes from 2015 to 2016. What return on sales can be anticipated if net sales and net income after taxes increase by 5 percent in 2017?

Problem 23.3A

Objectives 23-5, 23-6, 23-7

▶ **Compute and interpret ratios.**

On the following page, you will find the condensed financial statements for High Inc. and Low Inc. for 2016.

INSTRUCTIONS

1. Compute the following ratios for each company:
   a. Rate of return on net sales
   b. Rate of return on total assets at year-end
   c. Rate of return on stockholders' equity at year-end
   d. Earnings per share of common stock
   e. Ratio of stockholders' equity to total equities
   f. Current ratio
   g. Asset turnover
   h. Book value per share of common stock

2. Comment on any similarities or differences in the two companies' ratios. When possible, comment on the cause for these differences.

3. From the investor's point of view, is one company more at risk than the other?

4. Would you grant a five-year loan to either company? Explain.

Income Statements
Year Ended December 31, 2016

	High Inc.	Low Inc.
Sales (Net)	8 1 5 0 0 0	6 7 0 0 0 0
Cost of Goods Sold	5 1 5 0 0 0	3 6 0 0 0 0
Gross Profit	3 0 0 0 0 0	3 1 0 0 0 0
Operating Expenses	1 7 4 5 0 0	1 3 0 0 0 0
Net Income from Operations	1 2 5 5 0 0	1 8 0 0 0 0
Interest Expense	1 0 0 0 0	0
Net Income before Income Tax	1 1 5 5 0 0	1 8 0 0 0 0
Income Tax Expense	2 8 8 7 5	4 5 0 0 0
Net Income after Income Tax	8 6 6 2 5	1 3 5 0 0 0

Balance Sheets
December 31, 2016

	High Inc.	Low Inc.
Assets		
Current Assets	1 3 5 0 0 0	1 1 4 9 0 0
Property, Plant, and Equipment (Net)	2 3 5 0 0 0	2 0 6 0 0 0
Total Assets	3 7 0 0 0 0	3 2 0 9 0 0
Liabilities and Stockholders' Equity		
Liabilities		
Current Liabilities	1 0 8 5 0 0	8 9 8 0 0
Long-Term Liabilities (Bonds Payable)	1 1 0 0 0 0	0
Total Liabilities	2 1 8 5 0 0	8 9 8 0 0
Stockholders' Equity		
Common Stock ($10 Par Value)	3 0 0 0 0	3 0 0 0 0
Retained Earnings	1 2 1 5 0 0	2 0 1 1 0 0
Total Stockholders' Equity	1 5 1 5 0 0	2 3 1 1 0 0
Total Liabilities and Stockholders' Equity	3 7 0 0 0 0	3 2 0 9 0 0

Analyze: Assume that Low Inc. believes that it can cut the cost of goods sold by 5 percent in 2017 while keeping net sales and operating expenses at 2016 levels. If the company met this goal, discuss the potential implications to the rate of return on sales and earnings per share. Assume a tax rate of 25 percent.

Problem Set B

▶ **Horizontal and vertical analysis of income statement and balance sheet.**

Jenny's Art Shop, Inc., sells vintage books. The firm's comparative income statement and balance sheet for the years 2015 and 2016 follow:

Jenny's Art Shop, Inc.
Comparative Income Statement
For Years Ended December 31, 2016 and 2015

	Amounts	
	2016	2015
Revenue		
Sales	276500	225500
Less Sales Returns and Allowances	1500	1500
Net Sales	275000	224000
Cost of Goods Sold		
Merchandise Inventory, January 1	15000	20000
Net Purchases	155000	100000
Total Merchandise Available for Sale	170000	120000
Less Merchandise Inventory, December 31	20000	15000
Cost of Goods Sold	150000	105000
Gross Profit on Sales	125000	119000
Operating Expenses		
Selling Expenses		
Sales Salaries Expenses	60000	50000
Payroll Tax Expense—Selling	6000	5000
Other Selling Expenses	2000	2500
Total Selling Expenses	68000	57500
General and Administrative Expenses		
Officers' Salaries Expense	45000	40000
Payroll Tax Expense—Administrative	4500	4000
Depreciation Expense	5000	5000
Other General and Administrative Expenses	1200	1000
Total General and Administrative Expenses	55700	50000
Total Operating Expenses	123700	107500
Net Income Before Income Taxes	1300	11500
Income Tax Expense	195	1725
Net Income After Income Taxes	1105	9775

Jenny's Art Shop, Inc.
Comparative Balance Sheet
December 31, 2016 and 2015

	Amounts	
	2016	2015
Assets		
Current Assets		
Cash	2 8 1 3 0	3 0 5 1 5
Accounts Receivable	2 7 0 0 0	2 5 0 0 0
Merchandise Inventory	2 0 0 0 0	1 5 0 0 0
Prepaid Expenses	6 5 0	5 0 0
Supplies	3 9 5	2 5 0
Total Current Assets	7 6 1 7 5	7 1 2 6 5
Property, Plant, and Equipment		
Land	3 5 0 0 0	3 5 0 0 0
Building and Store Equipment	5 0 0 0 0	5 0 0 0 0
Less Accumulated Depreciation-Bldg & Store E	(1 5 0 0 0)	(1 0 0 0 0)
Net Book Value—Building and Store Equipment	3 5 0 0 0	4 0 0 0 0
Total Property, Plant, and Equipment	7 0 0 0 0	7 5 0 0 0
Total Assets	1 4 6 1 7 5	1 4 6 2 6 5
Liabilities and Stockholders' Equity		
Current Liabilities		
Accounts Payable	7 5 0 0	8 5 0 0
Sales Tax Payable	1 2 1 5	9 7 0
Payroll Taxes Payable	9 1 0	3 5 0
Interest Taxes Payable	6 0 0	6 0 0
Total Current Liabilities	1 0 2 2 5	1 0 4 2 0
Long-Term Liabilities		
Mortgage Payable	6 9 0 0 0	7 0 0 0 0
Total Long-Term Liabilities	6 9 0 0 0	7 0 0 0 0
Total Liabilities	7 9 2 2 5	8 0 4 2 0
Stockholders' Equity		
Common Stock ($1 par, 20,000 shares authorized;		
20,000 shares issued and outstanding)	2 0 0 0	2 0 0 0
Paid-in Capital—Common Stock	5 0 0	5 0 0
Retained Earnings	6 4 4 5 0	6 3 3 4 5
Total Stockholders' Equity	6 6 9 5 0	6 5 8 4 5
Total Liabilities and Stockholders' Equity	1 4 6 1 7 5	1 4 6 2 6 5

INSTRUCTIONS

1. Prepare both a horizontal and a vertical analysis of the two statements. Carry all calculations to two decimal places, and then round to one place. (Leave all vertical analysis percentages unadjusted in this problem.)

2. Make written comments about any of the results that seem worthy of investigation.

Analyze: If Jenny's Art Shop experiences the same growth in net sales in 2017 as was reported in 2016, what net sales can be projected?

Problem 23.2B ▶

Objectives 23-1, 23-2, 23-3

Computing financial ratios.

Using the data from Problem 23.1B, Jenny's Art Shop, Inc., calculate the following financial ratios. Comment on any ratio that merits further consideration. Inventory on December 31, 2014, was $20,000.

Part I

1. Current ratio

2. Acid-test ratio

3. Inventory turnover

4. Return on sales

5. Earnings per share of common stock

6. Book value per share of common stock

7. Return on total assets

8. Ratio of stockholders' equity to total equities

9. Ratio of stockholders' equity to total liabilities

10. Rate of return on ending stockholders' equity

11. The dividend yield per share of common stock. Assume a dividend of $1.00 per share was paid in 2016 and $0.50 per share was paid in 2015. The market value per share of common stock in 2016 was $2.50 and in 2015 was $1.50.

Part II

Selected industry ratios are given below. Compare the ratios of Jenny's Art Shop, Inc., with these ratios.

1. Rate of return on sales, 8 percent

2. Return on total assets, 10 percent

3. Merchandise inventory turnover, 6 times

4. Current ratio, 2.5 to 1

Analyze: Based on the analysis you have performed, do you see a trend that could affect the company's stock in the next fiscal year?

Compute and interpret various ratios.

◀   **Problem 23.3B**

Condensed financial statements for ABC Corp. and XYZ Corp. for 2016 follow:

Objectives 23-1, 23-2, 23-3

Income Statements
Year Ended December 31, 2016

	ABC Corp.	XYZ Corp.
Sales (Net)	2 500 000	2 350 000
Costs of Goods Sold	1 475 000	1 222 000
Gross Profit on Sales	1 025 000	1 128 000
Operating Expenses	776 400	859 550
Net Income from Operations	248 600	268 450
Interest Expense	25 000	25 000
Net Income before Income Tax	223 600	243 450
Income Tax Expense	76 024	82 773
Net Income after Income Tax	147 576	160 677

INSTRUCTIONS

1. Compute the following ratios for each company:

   a. Rate of return on net sales

   b. Rate of return on total assets at end of year

   c. Rate of return on stockholders' equity at end of year

   d. Earnings per share of common stock

   e. Ratio of stockholders' equity to total equities

   f. Current ratio

   g. Asset turnover

   h. Book value per share of common stock

2. Comment on the similarities and differences in the ratios computed for the two companies, pointing out the major factor that causes differences.

3. In which corporation would stock ownership be riskier? Explain.

Balance Sheets
December 31, 2016

	ABC Corp.	XYZ Corp.
Assets		
Current Assets	558 630	526 600
Property, Plant, and Equipment (Net)	817 000	750 000
Total Assets	1 375 630	1 276 600
Liabilities and Stockholders' Equity		
Liabilities		
Current Liabilities	315 000	205 500
Long-Term Liabilities (Bonds Payable)	250 000	150 000
Total Liabilities	565 000	355 500
Stockholders' Equity		
Common Stock ($10 Par Value)	500 000	500 000
Retained Earnings	310 630	421 100
Total Stockholders' Equity	810 630	921 100
Total Liabilities and Stockholders' Equity	1 375 630	1 276 600

4. Would you consider the extension of short-term credit to ABC Corp. or XYZ Corp. riskier? Explain.

Analyze: What percentage of net sales was expended for operating expenses by ABC Corp.? By XYZ Corp.?

Critical Thinking Problem 23.1

Company Improvements

Teacher Needs Inc.'s condensed income statement and balance sheet for the years 2016 and 2015 follow.

INSTRUCTIONS

Using the following additional information, fill in the missing values:

1. Accounts Receivable increased 50 percent from 2015 to 2016.

2. There were no new purchases of land, property, or equipment in 2016.

3. Accounts Payable decreased 40 percent from 2015 to 2016.

4. No new shares of common stock were issued in 2016.

5. The company paid out cash dividends of $43,048 in 2016.

6. The inventory turnover ratio for 2016 was 6 times.

7. The asset turnover ratio in 2016 was 2.1 times and in 2015 was 2.0 times.

8. The earnings per share in 2016 was $44.624 and in 2015 was $26.00.

9. The effective income tax rate in both years was 20 percent.

Analyze: Assume that the management of Teacher Needs Inc. had been given a directive by the board of directors to improve the company's current ratio in 2016. Did the company improve its standing in this regard from 2015?

	Teacher Needs, Inc.	
	Condensed Comparative Income Statement	
	For Years Ending December 31, 2016 and 2015	
	Amounts	
	2016	**2015**
Sales	?	?
Less Cost of Goods Sold	?	120,000
Gross Profit	?	?
Operating Expenses	115,000	100,000
Net Income before Income Tax	?	?
Income Tax Expense	?	?
Net Income after Income Tax	?	?

Teacher Needs, Inc.
Comparative Balance Sheet
December 31, 2016 and 2015

	Amounts	
	2016	2015
Assets		
Current Assets		
Cash	54,600	35,500
Accounts Receivable	?	22,000
Merchandise Inventory	26,000	20,000
Total Current Assets	?	77,500
Property, Plant, and Equipment		
Land	20,000	?
Equipment	50,000	?
Less Accumulated Depreciation	(10,000)	?
Total Property, Plant, and Equipment	?	65,000
Total Assets	?	142,500
Liabilities and Stockholders' Equity		
Current Liabilities		
Accounts Payable	21,000	?
Accrued Expenses	?	?
Total Current Liabilities	24,900	40,000
Stockholders' Equity		
Common Stock ($1 par, 10,000 shares authorized)	2,000	?
Paid in Capital in Excess of Par — Common Stock	500	?
Retained Earnings	?	100,000
Total Stockholders' Equity	?	?
Total Liabilities and Stockholders' Equity	?	?

Critical Thinking Problem 23.2

Filling in the Blanks

Dave Brandon, the accountant for Street Incorporated, was asked to make a presentation to the board of directors concerning the corporation's year-end financial position. While flying to the meeting on Saturday morning, Brandon checked the papers in his briefcase and realized he had left the income statement on his desk back at the office. Since he knew there would not be enough time for anyone to get to the office and fax or e-mail him a copy of the statement, he examined the rest of the material in his briefcase to see what information was available.

A review of the statement of retained earnings revealed that net income after income taxes for the year was $108,000. From some notes he had made for the presentation, he knew that the corporation's gross profit on sales was 40 percent and net income as a percentage of net sales was 8 percent. The income tax rate for the corporation is 28 percent. Brandon also remembered that the selling and administrative expenses were the same amount. With this information, he was able to reconstruct the income statement for the corporation before the plane reached its destination.

INSTRUCTIONS

Using the same information given above, prepare an income statement for Street Incorporated for the current year. To get started, first list the major headings for a condensed income statement. Then, starting with the net income figure, work to fill in the dollar amounts based on the percentage relationships given.

BUSINESS CONNECTIONS

Statement Analysis

1. Suppose that a vertical analysis of the income statement shows an item to be 18 percent of net sales. How would this information be used in order to make it meaningful? With what would it be compared?

2. In 2016, the cost of goods sold was 66 percent of net sales. For 2015, the same item was 63 percent, and for 2014 it was 60 percent. What recommendations would you make about items or activities that should be investigated further?

3. In deciding whether an increase in accounts receivable during the current year is desirable or undesirable, what factors should management consider?

4. Management is concerned that over a three-year period a company's balance sheets show that the total stockholders' equity has changed from 56 percent to 51 percent to 43 percent of total equities. What factors might explain this trend?

5. A company's income statements reveal that its net income after taxes has been 4.3 percent of net sales for each of the past three years. During that time, the industry average has been about 7 percent. What types of questions would management want answered in seeking an explanation for this difference?

6. A company's net sales increased by 35 percent from one year to the next year. During that period, selling expenses increased by 41 percent. Is this desirable? Explain.

Timing of Adjusting Entry

The timing of adjusting entries can alter the analysis of a company. As the full-charge bookkeeper, it is your job to ensure that the adjusting entries are entered on a timely basis. You have noticed that the adjusting entry to transfer the current year's portion from mortgage payable—long term to mortgage payable—current has not been entered. You mention it to your controller and are told not to record this adjusting entry. The company is applying for a loan from the bank and the controller found out that the loan officer looks only at the current assets and current liabilities. You are further told that, if anyone questions the lack of the adjusting entry, apologize for the error and record it immediately. Is this ethical for you and the company's controller? Provide justification for your decision.

Performance Analysis

Refer to the *2012 Annual Report (for the fiscal year ended February 3, 2013)* for The Home Depot, Inc., in Appendix A.

1. Locate the consolidated statements of earnings. Using vertical analysis, what is the cost of goods sold expressed as a percentage of net sales for the year ended January 31, 2013? If the industry average for this percentage is 70 percent, is The Home Depot, Inc. performing better than the industry average or worse? Why?

2. Locate the consolidated balance sheets. Using horizontal analysis, by what dollar amount and percentage have total assets increased from fiscal year 2011 to 2012?

Vertical Analysis

Vertical analysis of comparative financial statements can indicate the success or failure of a business. As a loan officer for a bank, you must choose the company that will receive a $50,000 loan. To help make the decision, perform a vertical analysis of the two companies shown in the table below. In groups of two, decide who should receive the loan. Explain why you consider your company better able to repay the loan. Defend your decision to the class.

	Julia's Junk Store	Laura's Lost Loot
Cash	$ 30,000	$ 30,000
Accounts Receivable	2,000	3,500
Total Current Assets	40,000	50,000
Total Assets	100,000	100,000
Current Liabilities	20,000	50,000
Total Liabilities	50,000	70,000
Common Stock	20,000	20,000
Retained Earnings	30,000	10,000
Total Stockholders' Equity	50,000	30,000
Net Sales	10,000	7,000
Cost of Sales	7,000	3,500
Operating Expenses	2,000	1,500
Net Income	1,000	2,000

Trend Analysis

A wise decision is to investigate the company in which you plan to invest time or money. Go to the website of a company you have an interest in investing in or accepting employment from. Look for the trend analysis over 5 to 10 years. Is the trend declining, increasing, or remaining constant? What does this trend tell you about any investment or employment in this company? Would your investment be safe over the next five years? Do you see an opportunity for advancement if you accepted employment with this company?

Answers to **Self Reviews**

Answers to Section 1 Self Review

1. The computation phase involves simple mathematical computations. The interpretation phase considers what caused relationships or changes and what can be done to improve the relationships or changes.

2. It is a financial statement with items expressed as a percentage of a base rather than in dollar amounts.

3. Vertical analysis of the income statement is based on net sales.

4. **b.** Each item in the income statement is divided by net sales.

5. **c.** total assets or total liabilities and stockholders' equity.

6. In 2015, the percentage of net income after taxes was 5 percent. In 2016, the percentage was 3 percent.

Answers to Section 2 Self Review

1. It is determined by first subtracting an amount from the base year amount and then dividing the difference by the base year amount.

2. The newer company would probably have a higher ratio because its book value is likely to be higher (less depreciation that has been charged off), and its assets are likely to be newer, which means they were acquired at higher price levels than those acquired in earlier years by the older company.

3. Such comparisons point out areas in which the business is performing either better or worse than average. The areas showing poorer performance can be investigated to determine the reason and then to address it.

4. **a.** horizontal analysis.

5. **c.** 40 percent.

6. ■ 2015: 22.0 percent
   ■ 2016: 23.6 percent
   ■ $150,000 increase; 20.7 percent

Answers to Section 3 Self Review

1. Measures the amount each common stockholder would receive if assets were sold for their book value and the corporation liquidated.

2. Rate of return on net sales, rate of return on total assets, and earnings per share of common stock are all common measures of profitability.

3. If inventory turnover is too low, compared to industry standards, it suggests that the amounts tied up in the inventory are excessive for the sales volume being generated.

4. **b.** market value

5. **a.** 365 days by the accounts receivable turnover

6. The price-earnings ratio is $40/$8 or 5.0. The yield on common stock is $4/$40 or 10 percent.

Answers to Comprehensive Self Review

1. Vertical analysis refers to a comparison of items on an individual financial statement, using one number as the base. The income statement uses net sales as 100 percent, while the balance sheet uses total assets or total liabilities and stockholders' equity as 100 percent. Each item on the statement is compared to the base. Horizontal analysis refers to a comparison of data for the current period with data of a prior period for the financial statement.

2. It tells you the general ability of a business to pay its short-term debts on time. It is computed by dividing current assets by current liabilities.

3. A higher inventory turnover number would probably indicate that assets are being used more effectively in generating sales in a retail business.

4. Different accounting methods, different types of entities, different ages of assets, and different financing methods can impair comparability.

5. The value is determined by dividing the common stockholders' equity (total stockholders' equity minus the book value of preferred stock) by the number of shares of common stock outstanding.

The Statement of Cash Flows

Apple Inc.
www.apple.com

Apple Inc. is committed to bringing the best personal computing, portable digital music, and mobile communication experiences to consumers. It recorded over $156 billion in sales revenue in 2012 and this number is climbing, but the cash needed to pay its highly skilled and eclectic employees as well as suppliers of its many components requires that the company collect these sales on a timely basis. And they do just that! In fiscal 2012, the company generated over $50 billion in operating cash flow.

The company's unique approach to design coupled with hip advertising campaigns have generated a distinctive identity and significant brand loyalty for the Apple line of products. As of 2013, Apple had sold over 275 million iPods®, making it the best-selling digital audio player in history. Since their App Store opened in 2008, the company's incredible developer community has created an app for doing almost everything imaginable from accounting homework apps to a zombie survival guide app. In 2013, the company reported that its customers download more than 800 apps per second at a rate of over two billion apps per month!

As the company continues to evolve, it uses its surplus of cash to generously reward its shareholders. In fact, Apple is among the largest dividend payers in the world, with annual payments of about $11 billion. The company is confident about its future and this is reflected in a 2013 statement by Peter Oppenheimer, Apple's CFO: "We continue to generate cash in excess of our needs to operate the business, invest in our future, and maintain flexibility to take advantage of strategic opportunities."

thinking critically

If a company is low on cash, how does this affect the business?

LEARNING OBJECTIVES

24-1. Distinguish between operating, investing, and financing activities.

24-2. Compute cash flows from operating activities.

24-3. Compute cash flows from investing activities.

24-4. Compute cash flows from financing activities.

24-5. Prepare a statement of cash flows.

24-6. Define the accounting terms new to this chapter.

NEW TERMS

cash equivalents
direct method
financing activities
indirect method
investing activities
operating activities
operating assets and liabilities
schedule of operating expenses
statement of cash flows

SECTION OBJECTIVE

>> **24-1.** Distinguish between operating, investing, and financing activities.

WHY IT'S IMPORTANT

When forecasting the cash needs of a business, accountants need to understand how cash and cash equivalents are generated, as well as how the business uses its cash.

TERMS TO LEARN

cash equivalents
financing activities
investing activities
operating activities
statement of cash flows

Sources and Uses of Cash

Corporations issue four financial statements: income statement, balance sheet, statement of retained earnings or stockholders' equity, and statement of cash flows.

The Importance of a Statement of Cash Flows

The statement of cash flows provides information about the cash receipts and cash payments of a business. Creditors, including bondholders, noteholders, and suppliers of goods and services, review the statement of cash flows to determine how the firm will pay interest and principal on debts. Investors examine the statement of cash flows to determine if the corporation will have the cash to pay dividends. Management is also interested in cash flows. The firm needs cash to pay employees, suppliers, and to meet other obligations. Analyzing past cash flows is helpful because they indicate the sources and uses of cash in the future.

The Meaning of Cash

On the statement of cash flows, the term *cash* includes cash and cash equivalents. As you know, cash consists of coin, currency, and bank accounts. Cash equivalents are easily convertible into known amounts of cash. They include certificates of deposit (CDs), U.S. Treasury bills, and money market funds. A short-term investment is a cash equivalent if it matures within three months from the date the business acquired it. Suppose a certificate of deposit acquired by a corporation on September 1, 2015, matures on March 1, 2016. The CD is not classified as a cash equivalent on the December 31, 2015, balance sheet because the maturity date is more than three months from the date the certificate was acquired.

>> **24-1. OBJECTIVE**

Distinguish between operating, investing, and financing activities.

Sources and Uses of Cash

Cash inflows are called *sources of cash*. *Cash outflows* are called *uses of cash*. Sources and uses of cash are classified under three headings on the statement of cash flows:

- **Cash Flows from Operating Activities.** Operating activities are routine business operations. Cash inflows from operating activities include the sale of merchandise or services for cash, collection of accounts receivable created by the sale of merchandise or services, and miscellaneous sources, such as interest income. Cash outflows from operations commonly result from paying operating expenses when they are incurred, paying accounts payable for merchandise purchased on account, and paying accounts payable for operating expenses incurred but not immediately paid.

- **Cash Flows from Investing Activities.** Investing activities involve the acquisition (cash outflow) or disposal (cash inflow) of long-term assets, including land, buildings, equipment, and investments in bonds and other securities.

TABLE 24.1   Sources and Uses of Cash in a Corporation

	Sources of Cash	Uses of Cash
Operating Activities	Sale of merchandise Sale of services Interest income Dividend income Miscellaneous income	Pay for merchandise Pay taxes Pay salaries and wages Pay interest expense Pay for other expenses
Investing Activities	Sale of land, buildings, or equipment Principal payments collected on receivable for long-term assets Sale of investment in bonds or other securities	Pay for purchase of land, buildings, or equipment Pay for the purchase of investments in bonds or other securities
Financing Activities	Issuance of common stock Issuance of preferred stock Issuance of bonds payable Borrowing through signing a note payable Resale of treasury stock	Pay cash dividends on common stock Pay cash dividends on preferred stock Repay bond indebtedness Repay notes payable or other borrowing Purchase treasury stock

■ **Cash Flows from Financing Activities.** **Financing activities** involve transactions that provide cash to the business to carry on its activities. Cash inflows from financing activities include issuing bonds and capital stock for cash, borrowing cash by signing notes payable, and reselling treasury stock. Cash outflows from financing activities include paying notes or bonds payable, purchasing treasury stock, and paying cash dividends.

Table 24.1 summarizes sources (inflows) and uses (outflows) of cash.

Section 1   Self Review

QUESTIONS

1. What are cash equivalents?
2. What are investing activities?
3. Is short-term borrowing by signing a note payable a financing or investing activity? Explain.

EXERCISES

4. Investing activities include:
   a. purchases of merchandise for cash.
   b. purchases of plant and equipment for cash.
   c. purchases of prepaid expense items such as supplies and insurance for cash.
   d. issuance of common stock.

5. An example of a financing activity is the:
   a. sale of merchandise for cash.
   b. issuance of stock for cash.
   c. sale of used equipment for cash.
   d. collection of debts acquired from the sale of long-term assets.
   d. interest income
   e. resale of treasury stock

ANALYSIS

6. Indicate whether each account or transaction is a source of cash or use of cash:
   a. issuance of preferred stock
   b. interest expense
   c. taxes expense

(Answers to Section 1 Self Review are on page 876.)

SECTION OBJECTIVE	TERMS TO LEARN
>> 24-2. Compute cash flows from operating activities.	operating assets and liabilities
WHY IT'S IMPORTANT	schedule of operating expenses
The income statement reports net income on an accrual basis. It does not report actual cash flows. To identify cash flows from operating activities, the financial statement reader needs to review the statement of cash flows.	

Cash Flows from Operating Activities

To prepare the statement of cash flows, you need the income statement, schedule of operating expenses, the statement of retained earnings, and a comparative balance sheet. The **schedule of operating expenses** is a supplemental schedule showing the selling and general and administrative expenses in greater detail.

Let's use the financial statements for Unique Products, Inc., to explain the statement of cash flows. These statements appear in Figures 24.1 through 24.4.

FIGURE 24.1

Income Statement

Unique Products, Inc.
Income Statement
Year Ended December 31, 2016

Revenue			
Sales	3 1 0 4 4 5 0		
Less Sales Returns and Allowances	1 3 5 4 5 0		
Net Sales		2 9 6 9 0 0 0	
Cost of Goods Sold			
Merchandise Inventory, January 1	2 2 5 0 0 0		
Purchases (Net)	1 7 0 6 5 0 0		
Freight In	2 6 0 0 0		
Total Merchandise Available for Sale	1 9 5 7 5 0 0		
Less Merchandise Inventory, December 31	2 0 5 0 0 0		
Cost of Goods Sold		1 7 5 2 5 0 0	
Gross Profit		1 2 1 6 5 0 0	
Operating Expenses			
Selling Expenses	5 2 6 4 2 5		
General and Administrative Expenses	6 0 5 0 0 0		
Total Operating Expenses		1 1 3 1 4 2 5	
Net Income from Operations		8 5 0 7 5	
Other Income			
Gain on Sale of Equipment	4 0 0 0		
Interest Income	1 8 0 0		
Total Other Income		5 8 0 0	
Other Expenses			
Bond Interest Expense	9 5 0 0		
Other Interest Expense	2 0 0 0		
Total Other Expenses		1 1 5 0 0	
Net Income Before Income Taxes		7 9 3 7 5	
Income Tax Expense		2 3 8 1 2	
Net Income After Income Taxes		5 5 5 6 3	

FIGURE 24.2

Schedule of Operating Expenses

Unique Products, Inc.
Schedule of Operating Expenses
Year Ended December 31, 2016

Selling Expenses		
Advertising	2 2 8 0 0 0 0	
Depreciation	7 1 8 0 0 0	
Employee Fringe Benefits	3 0 0 0 0 0 0	
Freight Out and Deliveries	1 6 0 0 0 0 0	
Insurance	3 0 0 0 0 0	
Miscellaneous	2 0 7 0 0 0	
Other Taxes	3 0 0 0 0 0	
Payroll Taxes—Sales Staff	3 0 0 0 0 0 0	
Rent	1 2 0 0 0 0 0	
Repairs and Maintenance	5 0 0 0 0 0	
Sales Commissions	1 6 4 5 0 0 0 0	
Sales Salaries	1 7 5 0 0 0 0 0	
Sales Supplies	2 2 5 0 0 0 0	
Travel and Entertainment	2 6 8 7 5 0 0	
Utilities	6 5 0 0 0 0	
Total Selling Expenses		5 2 6 4 2 5 0 0
General and Administrative Expenses		
Officers' Salaries	3 5 0 0 0 0 0 0	
Office Employees' Salaries	1 5 0 0 0 0 0 0	
Payroll Taxes—Administrative Staff	3 5 0 0 0 0 0	
Office Supplies	6 5 0 0 0 0	
Postage, Copying, and Miscellaneous	7 0 0 0 0 0	
Uncollectible Accounts Expense	1 6 5 0 0 0 0	
Rent or Lease Expense	8 7 5 0 0 0	
Depreciation	5 0 0 0 0 0	
Other Taxes	1 6 5 0 0 0 0	
Utilities	1 4 2 5 0 0 0	
Total General and Administrative Expenses		6 0 5 0 0 0 0 0
Total Operating Expenses		1 1 3 1 4 2 5 0 0

FIGURE 24.3   Comparative Statement of Retained Earnings

Unique Products, Inc.
Comparative Statement of Retained Earnings
Years Ended December 31, 2016 and 2015

	Amounts		Increase or Decrease
	2016	2015	
Balance, January 1	2 0 2 2 4 3	1 6 4 9 9 3	3 7 2 5 0
Additions			
Net Income After Taxes	5 5 5 6 3	4 1 2 5 0	1 4 3 1 3
Total	2 5 7 8 0 6	2 0 6 2 4 3	5 1 5 6 3
Deductions			
Dividends, Preferred	4 0 0 0	4 0 0 0	0
Total Deductions	4 0 0 0	4 0 0 0	0
Balance, December 31	2 5 3 8 0 6	2 0 2 2 4 3	5 1 5 6 3

FIGURE 24.4   **Comparative Balance Sheet**

Unique Products, Inc.
Comparative Balance Sheet
December 31, 2016 and 2015

	Amounts 2016	Amounts 2015	Increase or (Decrease) Amount
Assets			
Current Assets			
Cash	1 1 5 2 3 1	8 0 7 7 3	3 4 4 5 8
Accounts Receivable	1 0 2 0 0 0	7 3 5 0 0	2 8 5 0 0
Merchandise Inventory	2 0 5 0 0 0	2 2 5 0 0 0	(2 0 0 0 0)
Prepaid Expenses	1 2 0 0	1 5 0 0	(3 0 0)
Supplies	5 0 0	2 5 0	2 5 0
Total Current Assets	4 2 3 9 3 1	3 8 1 0 2 3	4 2 9 0 8
Property, Plant, and Equipment			
Land	8 0 0 0 0	8 0 0 0 0	0
Building and Store Equipment	7 1 8 0 0	7 7 8 0 0	(6 0 0 0)
Less Accumulated Depreciation—Building and Store Equipment	2 8 5 2 0	2 3 3 4 0	5 1 8 0
Net Book Value—Building and Store Equipment	4 3 2 8 0	5 4 4 6 0	(1 1 1 8 0)
Office Equipment	1 0 5 0 0	6 0 0 0	4 5 0 0
Less Accumulated Depreciation—Office Equipment	2 0 0 0	1 5 0 0	5 0 0
Net Book Value—Office Equipment	8 5 0 0	4 5 0 0	4 0 0 0
Total Property, Plant, and Equipment	1 3 1 7 8 0	1 3 8 9 6 0	(7 1 8 0)
Total Assets	5 5 5 7 1 1	5 1 9 9 8 3	3 5 7 2 8
Liabilities and Stockholders' Equity			
Current Liabilities			
Accounts Payable	7 1 0 0 0	8 4 5 0 0	(1 3 5 0 0)
Sales Tax Payable	2 9 0 0	2 5 0 0	4 0 0
Payroll Taxes Payable	1 1 4 5	1 0 2 5	1 2 0
Interest Payable	8 6 0	2 1 5	6 4 5
Total Current Liabilities	7 5 9 0 5	8 8 2 4 0	(1 2 3 3 5)
Long-Term Liabilities			
10% Bonds Payable, 2025	1 0 0 0 0 0	1 0 0 0 0 0	0
Premium on Bonds Payable	3 5 0 0	4 0 0 0	(5 0 0)
Mortgage Payable	6 0 0 0 0	6 5 0 0 0	(5 0 0 0)
Total Long-Term Liabilities	1 6 3 5 0 0	1 6 9 0 0 0	(5 5 0 0)
Total Liabilities	2 3 9 4 0 5	2 5 7 2 4 0	(1 7 8 3 5)
Stockholders' Equity			
Preferred Stock ($100 par, 8%, 500 shares authorized, issued and outstanding)	5 0 0 0 0	5 0 0 0 0	0
Common Stock ($1 par, 25,000 shares authorized			
Issued and outstanding: 7,000 shares in 2015; 8,000 shares in 2016)	8 0 0 0	7 0 0 0	1 0 0 0
Paid-in Capital—Common Stock	4 5 0 0	3 5 0 0	1 0 0 0
Retained Earnings			
Retained Earnings—Unappropriated	2 5 3 8 0 6	2 0 2 2 4 3	5 1 5 6 3
Total Retained Earnings	2 5 3 8 0 6	2 0 2 2 4 3	5 1 5 6 3
Total Stockholders' Equity	3 1 6 3 0 6	2 6 2 7 4 3	5 3 5 6 3
Total Liabilities and Stockholders' Equity	5 5 5 7 1 1	5 1 9 9 8 3	3 5 7 2 8

Statement of Cash Flows

The statement of cash flows reconciles the beginning and ending cash balances. It ties together the income statement and the changes in the noncash items on the balance sheet and on the statement of retained earnings.

Figure 24.4 shows the comparative balance sheet for Unique Products, Inc. There are no cash equivalents on the balance sheet. In 2016, the beginning cash balance was $80,773; the ending cash balance was $115,231. Cash increased by $34,458. The statement of cash flows shows the factors that caused the increase in cash.

There are two ways to prepare the statement of cash flows: the direct method and the indirect method. Unique Products, Inc., uses the indirect method. The direct method will be described later in this chapter. The indirect method treats net income as the primary source of cash from operating activities and adjusts net income for changes in noncash items.

The accrual basis of accounting is used when recording transactions and preparing the balance sheet and the income statement. Net income shown on the income statement includes both cash and noncash transactions. On the statement of cash flows, net income is adjusted for the noncash items.

Figure 24.5 on the next page shows the statement of cash flows for Unique Products, Inc. Let's examine it and learn how to prepare the statement of cash flows. Throughout this chapter, you will need to refer to the financial statements and reports for Unique Products, Inc.

Cash Flows from Operating Activities

The first section of the statement of cash flows shows net cash provided by operating activities. For Unique Products, Inc., $37,958 was provided by operating activities. Since cash flows from operating activities are closely related to net income, the starting point for the analysis of the cash flows from operating activities is the net income after income taxes, taken from the income statement in Figure 24.1. The Cash Flows from Operating Activities section of the cash flows statement explains why the net cash flows from operations differs from the net income after taxes, which is $55,563, in this period. There were several income and expense items reported on the income statement that did not involve cash inflows or outflows during that period. Let's analyze those items.

EXPENSE AND INCOME ITEMS INVOLVING LONG-TERM ASSETS AND LIABILITIES

Some items on the income statement result from adjustments related to long-term assets or long-term liabilities. They do not involve cash inflows or outflows in the current year. These adjustments are added to or subtracted from net income.

Depreciation Expense The acquisition of property, plant, and equipment is reported in the Cash Flows from Investing Activities section of the statement of cash flows in the year acquired. Depreciation, depletion, and amortization of assets do not involve a cash outlay in the year the expense is recorded. Instead, these expenses represent a reduction in the net asset value. Figure 24.2 shows depreciation expense of $7,680 (sum of $7,180 recorded as selling expenses and $500 recorded as general and administrative expenses). The depreciation expense was recorded as follows:

1	2016				1
2	Dec.	31	Depreciation Expense (Selling)	7 1 8 0 00	2
3			Depreciation Expense (General)	5 0 0 00	3
4			Accumulated Depreciation	7 6 8 0 00	4

Note that the depreciation expense did not involve a cash outflow. Net income was reduced by a noncash expense. To obtain cash flows from operating activities, the depreciation expense is added back to net income.

recall

Accrual Basis
Under the accrual basis of accounting, revenues are recorded when earned and expenses are recorded when owed, not necessarily when the cash is received or paid.

>> **24-2. OBJECTIVE**
Compute cash flows from operating activities.

important!

Depreciation Expense
The depreciation expense on the income statement is not a cash outflow; therefore, it is added back to net income on the statement of cash flows.

FIGURE 24.5

Statement of Cash Flows

Unique Products, Inc. Statement of Cash Flows Year Ended December 31, 2016			
Cash Flows from Operating Activities			
Net income after taxes (per income statement)			5 5 5 6 3
Adjustments to reconcile net income to net cash			
provided by operating activities			
Depreciation Expense	7 6 8 0		
Amortization of premium on bonds payable	(5 0 0)		
Gain on sale of equipment	(4 0 0 0)		
Changes in noncash current assets and current			
liabilities			
Increase in Accounts Receivable	(2 8 5 0 0)		
Decrease in Merchandise Inventory	2 0 0 0 0		
Decrease in Prepaid Expenses	3 0 0		
Increase in Supplies	(2 5 0)		
Decrease in Accounts Payable	(1 3 5 0 0)		
Increase in Sales Tax Payable	4 0 0		
Increase in Payroll Taxes Payable	1 2 0		
Increase in Interest Payable	6 4 5		
Total Adjustments		(1 7 6 0 5)	
Net Cash Provided by Operating Activities			3 7 9 5 8
Cash Flows from Investing Activities			
Proceeds from sale of equipment	8 0 0 0		
Purchase of Office Equipment	(4 5 0 0)		
Net Cash Provided by Investing Activities			3 5 0 0
Cash Flows from Financing Activities			
Payment of Mortgage Payable principal	(5 0 0 0)		
Proceeds from issue of Common Stock	2 0 0 0		
Payment of dividends on Preferred Stock	(4 0 0 0)		
Net Cash used in Financing Activities			(7 0 0 0)
Net Increase in Cash and Cash Equivalents			3 4 4 5 8
Cash and Cash Equivalents, January 1, 2016			8 0 7 7 3
Cash and Cash Equivalents, December 31, 2016			1 1 5 2 3 1

Note: During the year, payments for income taxes were $23,813 and payments for interest expense were $11,355.

important!

Bond Interest Expense

The bond interest expense on the income statement is less than the actual cash outflow; therefore, on the statement of cash flows, the difference is subtracted from net income.

Amortization of Premium on Bonds Payable The income statement shows bond interest expense of $9,500. This is not the actual cash outflow for interest. It reflects the cash paid minus $500 of bond premium amortization. The bond interest expense was recorded as follows:

11	Bond Interest Expense	9 5 0 0 0 0		11
12	Premium on Bonds Payable	5 0 0 0 0		12
13	Cash		1 0 0 0 0 0 0	13

The amount of bond interest expense reported on the income statement understates the actual cash outflow by $500. To obtain cash flows from operating activities, the amortization of the bond premium is deducted from net income.

Gain or Loss on Sale of Equipment The income statement shows a gain of $4,000 on the sale of equipment. The equipment was sold for $8,000 cash. Thus, the proceeds from the sale of the equipment was shown as a cash inflow from investing activities. At the time of sale, the following entry was made:

21	Cash	8 000 00				21
22	Accumulated Depreciation—Equipment	2 000 00				22
23	Equipment			6 000 00		23
24	Gain on Sale of Equipment			4 000 00		24

The sale of the equipment is not a part of the routine operating activities of the business. The gain of $4,000 is a part of the $8,000 in cash received from the asset sale. As we see, the entire $8,000 was included in cash inflows from investing activities. It is therefore necessary to remove (deduct) the $4,000 of gain on sale of equipment from the net income figure in arriving at the net cash inflow provided by operations. A loss on sale of long-term assets would be added to net income.

INCOME AND EXPENSE ITEMS INVOLVING CHANGES IN CURRENT ASSETS AND CURRENT LIABILITIES

Current assets and current liabilities are often referred to as **operating assets and liabilities.** Usually, changes in current assets and current liabilities are related to routine business operations and are reflected in net income. Assume that all the changes in the current assets and current liabilities of Unique Products, Inc., resulted from routine operating activities.

Increases in Current Assets Current assets include accounts receivable, merchandise inventory, and prepaid expenses. Increases in current assets are deducted from net income to arrive at cash flows from operating activities. Look at the following examples. The comparative balance sheet for Unique Products, Inc., Figure 24.4, shows that several current assets increased during the year.

Increase in Accounts Receivable Figure 24.4 shows that *Accounts Receivable* increased by $28,500. This means that more sales on account were recorded than collected. The sales were included in net income, but the cash has not been received. To obtain cash flows from operating activities, the increase in accounts receivable is subtracted from net income.

> Amazon.com reported net loss during 2012 of approximately $39 million. During the same period, cash provided by operating activities was $4.2 billion and the balance sheet reported cash and cash equivalents of over $8.0 billion. Net sales during the same period were approximately $61.1 billion, an increase of $13 billion over 2011.

Increase in Supplies Figure 24.4 shows that *Supplies* increased by $250. This means that more supplies were paid for than were used. Net income does not reflect all cash paid for supplies. To obtain cash flows from operating activities, the increase in supplies is subtracted from net income.

Decreases in Current Assets Decreases in noncash current assets are added to net income to arrive at cash flows from operating activities. The following example will illustrate why this rule applies.

Decrease in Prepaid Expenses Figure 24.4 shows that *Prepaid Expenses* decreased by $300. This means that more was charged to expenses than was paid for prepaid expenses in arriving at net income for the year. In other words, net income reflects the use of prepaid expenses. To obtain cash flows from operating activities, the decrease in prepaid expenses is added to net income.

Decrease in Merchandise Inventory Figure 24.4 shows that *Merchandise Inventory* decreased by $20,000. This means that more inventory was sold than was purchased. The sale of the inventory was reflected in net income as cost of goods sold, but cash was not paid to replace the inventory. Net income reflects higher costs than actual cash outflows. To obtain cash flows from operating activities, a decrease in inventory is added to net income.

Increases in Current Liabilities   Current liabilities include accounts payable, sales tax payable, payroll taxes payable, and interest payable. Increases in current liabilities are added to net income to obtain the cash flows from operating activities. Look over the following situations:

Increase in Sales Tax Payable   Figure 24.4 shows that *Sales Tax Payable* increased by $400. This means that more sales tax was owed than was paid during the year. To obtain cash flows from operating activities, the increase in sales tax payable is added to net income.

Increase in Payroll Taxes Payable   Figure 24.4 shows that *Payroll Taxes Payable* increased by $120. This means that more payroll taxes were owed than were paid. To obtain cash flow from operating activities, the increase in payroll taxes payable is added to net income.

Increase in Interest Payable   Figure 24.4 shows that *Interest Payable* increased by $645. This means that more interest was recorded as expense than was paid in cash. To obtain cash flows from operating activities, the increase in interest payable is added to net income.

Decreases in Current Liabilities   Decreases in current liabilities are subtracted from net income. An illustration using *Accounts Payable* will show why this rule exists.

Decrease in Accounts Payable   Figure 24.4 shows that *Accounts Payable* decreased $13,500. This means more cash was paid on account than purchases were recorded on account. The cash was paid out but was not reflected in net income. To obtain cash flows from operating activities, the decrease in accounts payable is subtracted from net income.

Summary of Effects of Changes in Current Assets and Current Liabilities   Let's summarize how net income is adjusted for changes in current assets and current liabilities when computing cash flows from operating activities.

	Add to Net Income	Deduct from Net Income
Increase in current asset		X
Decrease in current asset	X	
Increase in current liability	X	
Decrease in current liability		X

Figure 24.5 shows all items considered when computing net cash provided by operating activities. During the year, operating activities for Unique Products, Inc., provided $37,958 of cash.

EFFECT OF NET LOSS ON CASH FLOWS FROM OPERATIONS

If the income statement reflects a net loss, the first line of the statement of cash flows is the net loss. All adjustments for changes in current assets and current liabilities are made to the net loss figure.

Section 2   Self Review

QUESTIONS

1. The income statement shows a loss of $60,000 on the sale of a building. How is the loss handled when computing net cash provided by operating activities?

2. The income statement shows depreciation expense of $25,000. How is the expense handled when computing net cash provided by operating activities?

3. During the year, the notes payable account increased from $45,000 to $50,000. How, if at all, is this reflected when computing net income from operations?

EXERCISES

4. The net cash provided by operating activities is affected by:
   a. the issue of bonds payable for cash.
   b. a purchase of land for cash.
   c. the sale of stock for cash.
   d. a change in merchandise inventory.

5. To determine the net cash provided by operating activities, an increase in prepaid assets should be:
   a. not included in the calculation.
   b. deducted from net income.
   c. added to net cash flow.
   d. added to net income.

ANALYSIS

6. The net loss for the year was $15,000. Depreciation expense was $4,000. *Merchandise Inventory* decreased by $3,000. *Accounts Receivable* decreased by $5,000. *Accounts Payable* decreased by $2,500. *Income Tax Payable* decreased by $5,000. Calculate the net cash provided or used by operating activities for the year.

(Answers to Section 2 Self Review are on page 876.)

SECTION OBJECTIVES	TERMS TO LEARN
>> 24-3. Compute cash flows from investing activities.	direct method
WHY IT'S IMPORTANT	indirect method
Cash flows from the acquisition or disposal of assets are reported separately from cash flows from operating activities.	
>> 24-4. Compute cash flows from financing activities.	
WHY IT'S IMPORTANT	
Transactions such as stock sales, securing loans, or repaying notes impact the cash balance of a business.	
>> 24-5. Prepare a statement of cash flows.	
WHY IT'S IMPORTANT	
Investors, managers, and creditors want to know the reasons for changes in a company's cash position.	

Cash Flows from Investing and Financing Activities

Investing and financing activities can produce both cash outflows and cash inflows.

Cash Flows from Investing Activities

Investing activities are transactions involving the acquisition or disposal of assets that are not consumed in routine operations within one year.

CASH OUTFLOWS FROM INVESTING ACTIVITIES

The most common cash outflows from investing activities are cash payments for purchases of property, plant, and equipment and for purchases of the stocks and bonds of other corporations.

Figure 24.4 shows that the ***Office Equipment*** account increased by $4,500 during 2016. The increase resulted from the purchase of office equipment for $4,500 in cash. This is a cash outflow from investing activities. It is reported on the statement of cash flows in Figure 24.5.

>> 24-3. OBJECTIVE

Compute cash flows from investing activities.

CASH INFLOWS FROM INVESTING ACTIVITIES

Most cash inflows from investing activities reflect the sale of land, buildings, equipment, or investments in securities of other corporations. Payments of principal received on mortgages or notes held by the company in connection with the sale of plant and equipment are classified as cash inflows from investing activities.

In 2016, Unique Products, Inc., had one cash inflow from investing activities. The corporation sold store equipment for $8,000 in cash.

Sales price (cash inflow)		$8,000
Asset cost	$6,000	
Accumulated depreciation	(2,000)	(4,000)
Gain on sale		$4,000

The statement of cash flows shows the $8,000 received from the sale of the store equipment as a cash inflow from investing activities. Recall that the gain was subtracted from net income in the Cash Flows from Operating Activities section.

At this point, it is possible to reconcile the changes in the long-term asset accounts. The net change of $6,000 (decrease) in the **Building and Store Equipment** account is reconciled as follows:

Building and store equipment, Dec. 31, 2015	$77,800
Add Purchases during 2016	–0–
Less Cost of equipment sold during 2016	6,000
Building and store equipment, Dec. 31, 2016	$71,800

The increase in accumulated depreciation can be reconciled to the depreciation expense for the year as follows:

	Accumulated Depreciation					
	Building & Store Equip.		Office Equip.		Total
2016	$28,520	+	$2,000	=	$30,520
2015	(23,340)	+	(1,500)	=	(24,840)
Increase	$ 5,180	+	$ 500	=	$ 5,680
Accumulated depreciation on equipment sold					2,000
Depreciation expense for 2016					$ 7,680

The Cash Flows from Investing Activities section of the statement of cash flows for Unique Products, Inc., shows that $3,500 cash was provided by investing activities during 2016.

Cash Flows from Financing Activities

Financing activities include debt and equity transactions.

CASH INFLOWS FROM FINANCING ACTIVITIES

Cash inflows from financing activities include amounts received from the original issue of preferred stock or common stock, the resale of treasury stock, and the issue of bonds and notes payable.

Proceeds of Cash Investments by Stockholders Figure 24.4 shows that the **Common Stock** account increased by $1,000 and the **Paid-in Capital—Common Stock** account increased by $1,000. During 2016, Unique Products, Inc., issued 1,000 shares of common stock for $2.00 per share. This resulted in a cash inflow of $2,000 (1,000 × $2.00) as reported on the statement of cash flows.

Proceeds of Short-Term and Long-Term Borrowing Figure 24.4 shows that Unique Products, Inc., did not seek additional cash from short-term or long-term note payable during 2016. If the company had obtained cash from borrowing, it would have been reported in the financing activities section of the cash flow statement as noted in Table 24.1.

During 2016, bond premium of $500 was amortized. Remember that the amortized premium was included in the Cash Flows from Operating Activities section. The change of $500 in **Premium on Bonds Payable** is reconciled as follows:

Premium on bonds payable, Dec. 31, 2015	$4,000
Add Premium on bonds sold in 2016	0
Less Premium amortized in 2016	(500)
Premium on bonds payable, Dec. 31, 2016	$3,500

important!

Investing Activities
Investing activities are transactions that involve the acquisition or disposal of assets that will not be used up or consumed in routine operations in a short time.

ABOUT
ACCOUNTING

Managing Cash
Large companies actively manage their own corporate cash. Smaller businesses often place their cash in money market funds or "sweep accounts" by their banker, due to the limited time and resources available for cash management.

>> **24-4. OBJECTIVE**
Compute cash flows from financing activities.

recall

Treasury Stock
Treasury stock is a corporation's own capital stock that has been issued, fully paid for, and reacquired by the corporation.

recall

Bonds Issued at a Premium
On the day that bonds are issued, if the market rate of interest is lower than the face rate of interest, the bonds will sell at a premium.

CASH OUTFLOWS FROM FINANCING ACTIVITIES

Cash outflows from financing activities result from the repayment of debt obligations such as bonds payable, notes payable, and mortgages; the purchase of treasury stock; and the retirement of preferred stock. The payment of cash dividends is classified as a cash outflow from financing activities. Interest expense, however, is classified as an outflow of cash from operating activities.

Payment of Mortgage Payable Figure 24.4 shows a decrease of $5,000 in the *Mortgage Payable* account during 2016. This decrease is a result of $5,000 of principal payments. These payments are shown on the statement of cash flows as a cash outflow from financing activities.

   During 2016, Unique Products, Inc., did not acquire cash through short-term borrowing, nor did it repay any short-term loans. However, if it had, these short-term transactions might not appear on the balance sheet. For example, the corporation could have borrowed $10,000 by signing a three-month note payable on March 1, 2016, and repaid the note on June 1, 2016. The note would not appear on the December 31, 2016, balance sheet. However, the note would represent both an inflow and an outflow of cash. The note would be reported in the Cash Flows from Financing Activities section of the statement of cash flows.

Payment of Cash Dividends Figure 24.3 indicates that during the year Unique Products, Inc., paid cash dividends of $4,000 on preferred stock. This amount is included as a part of cash flows from financing activities.

   The statement of cash flows shows that in 2016 cash of $7,000 was used by the financing activities of Unique Products, Inc.

>> **24-5. OBJECTIVE**

Prepare a statement of cash flows.

ABOUT
ACCOUNTING

While the FASB prefers the direct method, most businesses continue to use the indirect method for preparing the statement of cash flows.

Preparing a Statement of Cash Flows

The cash flows from the three types of business activities—operating, investing, and financing—are combined to arrive at the net change in cash and cash equivalents for the year. The net change is then combined with the beginning balance of cash and cash equivalents to reconcile to the ending balance of cash and cash equivalents. Figure 24.5 shows that the net change in the cash and cash equivalents was an increase of $34,458. The cash balance was $80,773 on January 1, 2016, and $115,231 on December 31, 2016. These are the same amounts reported on the comparative balance sheet in Figure 24.4.

DIRECT AND INDIRECT METHODS OF PREPARING THE STATEMENT OF CASH FLOWS

There are two methods of preparing the statement of cash flows: the indirect and direct methods. Figure 24.5 was prepared using the **indirect method.** Under this method, in the Cash Flows from Operating Activities section, net income is treated as the primary source of cash and is adjusted for changes in current assets and liabilities associated with net income, non-cash transactions, and other items. Most corporations use the indirect method.

   The Financial Accounting Standards Board allows the indirect or direct method. Under the **direct method,** all revenue and expenses reported on the income statement appear in the operating section of the statement of cash flows and show the cash received or paid out for each type of transaction. Under the direct method, a corporation reports cash flows from operating activities in two major classes: gross cash receipts and gross cash payments. The FASB suggests the following classifications for reporting cash inflows and outflows:

- cash collected from customers
- interest and dividends received
- cash paid to employees and other suppliers of goods or services, including suppliers of insurance and advertising
- interest paid
- income taxes paid

MANAGERIAL IMPLICATIONS <<

CASH FLOW

- Management needs to ensure that cash is available to meet operating expenses and to pay debts promptly.

- Management analyzes the statement of cash flows to evaluate the operations of the company, plan future operations, forecast cash needs, arrange proper financing, and plan dividend payments.

- Management uses the statement of cash flows to determine how well the company will be able to meet its maturing obligations.

- Management analyzes past cash flows in order to make plans that will keep the company solvent and profitable.

THINKING CRITICALLY

If the only financial statement available to you is the cash flow statement, could you evaluate the business as a potential investment?

The cash flows from investing activities and cash flows from financing activities are the same in both direct and indirect methods.

Corporations that use the direct method are encouraged to provide additional meaningful information about operating cash receipts and cash payments if feasible. The direct method is not commonly used because of the many additional disclosures and schedules that must accompany the direct method.

When the statement of cash flows is based on the direct method, it must be accompanied by a reconciliation of net income to the net cash provided by operating activities. This reconciliation shows the same information as the Cash Flows from Operating Activities section of the statement of cash flows prepared using the indirect method. The additional work is another reason that many corporations avoid the direct method of preparing the statement of cash flows. Intermediate accounting textbooks provide detailed information about the direct method.

DISCLOSURES REQUIRED IN THE STATEMENT OF CASH FLOWS

Various disclosures are added to the statement of cash flows. If the indirect method of presentation is used, the amount of interest and income taxes paid during the period are reported in notes accompanying the statement. The note at the bottom of Figure 24.5 shows that cash payments were $23,813 for income taxes and $11,355 for interest.

In order to provide complete information to statement readers, information about noncash investing and financing activities are disclosed on the statement of cash flows. Examples of financing and investing activities not affecting cash flows include issuing bonds payable for land or converting bonds payable into common stock.

important!

Disclosures
If the indirect method is used, the interest and income taxes paid during the period are separately disclosed.

The Hasbro, Inc., consolidated statements of cash flows for the fiscal year ended December 31, 2012, reported net cash provided by operating activities of $534.8 million. Net income during the same period was approximately $336 million!

Section 3 Self Review

QUESTIONS

1. During the year, equipment was sold for $50,000, and a $5,000 gain was recorded. How is this transaction reported on the statement of cash flows?

2. During the year, a corporation issued $100,000 of bonds payable in return for land with a fair market value of $100,000. How is this reported on the statement of cash flows?

3. On the statement of cash flows, how is the payment of a cash dividend reported?

EXERCISES

4. Most corporations prepare the statement of cash flows using the:

   a. accrual method.

   b. indirect method.

   c. direct method.

   d. equivalent method.

5. The purchase of equipment for cash is shown on the statement of cash flows as a(n):

   a. increase in Cash Flows from Financing Activities.

   b. decrease in Cash Flows from Investing Activities.

   c. decrease in Cash Flows from Financing Activities.

   d. increase in Cash Flows from Investing Activities.

ANALYSIS

6. A truck that originally cost $40,000 was sold for $10,000 cash. Accumulated depreciation up to the date of the sale was $36,000. A $6,000 gain was reported on the income statement. What is the effect on the statement of cash flows?

(Answers to Section 3 Self Review are on page 876.)

REVIEW   Chapter Summary

In previous chapters, you learned about the three major financial statements prepared for corporations—the income statement, the balance sheet, and the statement of retained earnings. In addition, some corporations prepare a statement of stockholders' equity. The annually published financial statements should also include a statement of cash flows showing the sources and uses of cash.

Learning Objectives

24-1 Distinguish between operating, investing, and financing activities.

The corporation's activities are divided into three categories on the statement of cash flows: operating, investing, and financing. Cash inflows and outflows from transactions for each type of activity are shown, along with the net cash inflow or outflow:

- Cash flows from operating activities involve routine business operations: selling merchandise for cash, collecting accounts receivable, paying expenses when incurred, and paying accounts payable.

- Investing activities are transactions that involve the acquisition of assets or disposal of assets such as land, equipment, or buildings.

- Financing activities involve transactions such as issuing stocks or bonds, paying a note or bond payable, or paying cash dividends.

24-2 Compute cash flows from operating activities.

The first section of the statement of cash flows involves operating activities—buying, selling, and administrative activities. This section begins with the net income amount from the income statement:

- To arrive at the net cash flow provided by operating activities, the net income amount is adjusted for noncash items used to calculate net income.

- The most common items added to net income are (1) depreciation, (2) losses on sales of assets, (3) amortization of bond discount, (4) decreases in current assets, and (5) increases in current liabilities.

- The most common items deducted from net income are (1) gains on sales of assets, (2) amortization of bond premium, (3) increases in current assets, and (4) decreases in current liabilities.

24-3 Compute cash flows from investing activities.

The second section of the statement discloses investing activities:

- Cash inflows from investing often result from cash sales of property, plant, and equipment and cash sales of the stocks and bonds of other corporations held as investments.

- Cash outflows come from cash purchases of plant and equipment and cash purchases of the stocks and bonds of other corporations.

24-4 Compute cash flows from financing activities.

The third section of the statement concerns financing activities. These activities may reflect transactions between a corporation and its stockholders:

- Cash inflows often result from the issuing of common or preferred stock or selling treasury stock.

- Typical cash outflows are dividend payments and the purchase of treasury stock.

- Cash inflows result from issuing bonds payable for cash and from borrowing money by issuing or discounting notes payable. Cash outflows result when notes payable or bonds payable are repaid. However, interest paid on debt is seen as resulting from an operating activity.

24-5 Prepare a statement of cash flows.

There are two statement preparation methods—direct and indirect:

- Most corporations use the indirect method because the statement is easier to prepare when this method is used.

- The Financial Accounting Standards Board allows either method.

- Some major transactions that do not involve cash should be disclosed in notes to the statement of cash flows.

24-6 Define the accounting terms new to this chapter.

Glossary

Cash equivalents (p. 846) Assets that are easily convertible into known amounts of cash

Direct method (p. 858) A means of reporting sources and uses of cash under which all revenue and expenses reported on the income statement appear in the operating section of the statement of cash flows and show the cash received or paid out for each type of transaction

Financing activities (p. 847) Transactions with those who provide cash to the business to carry on its activities

Indirect method (p. 858) A means of reporting cash generated from operating activities by treating net income as the primary source of cash in the operating section of the statement of cash flows and adjusting that amount for changes in current assets and liabilities associated with net income, noncash transactions, and other items

Investing activities (p. 846) Transactions that involve the acquisition or disposal of long-term assets

Operating activities (p. 846) Routine business transactions—selling goods or services and incurring expenses

Operating assets and liabilities (p. 853) Current assets and current liabilities

Schedule of operating expenses (p. 848) A schedule that supplements the income statement, showing the selling and general and administrative expenses in greater detail

Statement of cash flows (p. 846) A financial statement that provides information about the cash receipts and cash payments of a business

Comprehensive **Self Review**

1. What are the three types of activities for which cash flows must be shown in a statement of cash flows?
2. Name some financing activities?
3. During the year, accounts payable increased from $35,000 to $50,000. How, if at all, would this change be reflected in computing net income from operations?
4. Where on the statement of cash flows should a payment of interest expense be shown?
5. Where on the statement of cash flows should a loss on the sale of equipment be shown?

(Answers to Comprehensive Self Review are on page 877.)

Discussion Questions

1. What is the purpose of the statement of cash flows?
2. Where is information obtained for preparing the statement of cash flows?
3. Give two examples of cash inflows from investing activities.
4. Give two examples of cash outflows from investing activities.
5. Give two examples of cash outflows from financing activities.
6. Give two examples of cash inflows from financing activities.
7. What are cash and cash equivalents?
8. Is an investment in a corporate bond maturing 180 days after the purchase date a cash equivalent? Explain.
9. A corporation's income statement shows a gain of $8,000 on the sale of plant and equipment. In computing the net cash provided by operating activities, how would this $8,000 be treated?

10. A corporation's income statement shows bond interest expense of $16,500. Amortization of the discount on the bonds during the year was $1,500. What is the amount of cash outflow for bond interest expense?

11. Explain the difference between the direct method and the indirect method of preparing the statement of cash flows.

12. On January 1, 2016, the balance of the **Accounts Payable** account was $31,000. On December 31, 2016, the balance was $41,000. How, if at all, would this change be reflected in the statement of cash flows?

13. Why are cash equivalents included on the statement of cash flows?

14. Why must noncash investing and financing activities be disclosed on the statement of cash flows?

15. Identify in which of the three types of activities on the statement of cash flows the following transactions appear. Indicate whether each is a cash inflow or outflow:

   a. Cash dividends paid.

   b. Cash interest payment received.

   c. Cash on notes receivable collected.

   d. Cash interest paid.

   e. Cash received from customers.

   f. Cash proceeds from issuing stock.

APPLICATIONS

Exercises

Effects of transactions on cash flows.

What effect would each of the following transactions have on the statement of cash flows?

1. The sum of $5,000 in cash was received from the sale of used office equipment that originally cost $15,000. Depreciation of $12,000 had been taken on the asset up to the date of the sale. The resulting $2,000 gain was shown on the income statement.

2. The sum of $77,000 in cash was received from the sale of investments in the stock of another corporation. The stock had a book value of $90,000. The $13,000 loss on the sale was shown on the income statement.

Cash flows from operating activities.

The following data are summarized from the income statement of Paul, Inc., for the year ended December 31, 2016. Using these data and ignoring changes in current assets, current liabilities, and income taxes, prepare a schedule of cash flows from operating activities for the year. (Use Figure 24.5 as a model for this schedule.)

◄ **Exercise 24.1**
Objective 24-1

◄ **Exercise 24.2**
Objective 24-2

Paul, Inc.					
Income Statement					
Year Ended December 31, 2016					
Sales				700 0 0 0 00	
Cost of Goods Sold				330 0 0 0 00	
Gross Profit on Sales				370 0 0 0 00	

(continued)

(continued from previous page)

Operating Expenses			
Depreciation	20 5 0 0 00		
Other Selling Expenses	160 0 0 0 00		
Other Administrative Expenses	92 5 0 0 00	273 0 0 0 00	
Net Income from Operations		97 0 0 0 00	
Bond Interest Expense			
Cash Interest	20 0 0 0 00		
Amortization of Discount on Bonds Payable	3 0 0 0 00	23 0 0 0 00	
Net Income for Year		74 0 0 0 00	

Exercise 24.3
Objective 24-2

▶ **Cash flows from operating activities.**

The current assets and current liabilities of Diego Company on December 31, 2016 and 2015, are as follows. The corporation's net income for 2016 was $60,000. Included in its expenses was depreciation of $13,000. Prepare a schedule of the cash flows from operating activities for 2016. (Use Figure 24.5 as a model for this schedule.)

	Dec. 31, 2016	Dec. 31, 2015
Cash	$ 88,000	$75,000
Accounts Receivable	104,000	93,300
Prepaid Expenses	14,000	16,100
Merchandise Inventory	79,000	90,000
Accounts Payable	60,400	51,000
Notes Payable (Borrowing)	45,000	53,000

Exercise 24.4
Objective 24-2

▶ **Cash flows from operating activities.**

The income statement of Applebrook, Inc., showed net income of $70,000 for 2016. The firm's beginning inventory was $49,000, and its ending inventory was $54,000. Accounts payable were $44,000 on January 1 and $39,500 on December 31. Compute the net cash provided by the firm's operating activities during the year.

Exercise 24.5
Objective 24-2

▶ **Cash flows from operating activities.**

The following information is taken from the income statement of Purple Inc. for 2016:

Sales		$950,000
Cost of Goods Sold		600,000
Gross Profit on Sales		$350,000
Operating Expenses		
Depreciation	$ 20,000	
Other Operating Expenses	180,000	200,000
Net Income from Operations		$150,000

Additional information relating to account balances at the beginning and end of the year appears below:

	Jan. 1, 2016	Dec. 31, 2016
Accounts Receivable	$56,000	$50,000
Merchandise Inventory	74,000	78,000
Accrued Liabilities	5,000	2,500
Accounts Payable	38,000	29,000

Determine the cash flows from operations for 2016.

Cash flows from investing activities.

The following transactions occurred at Lookout Corporation in 2016. Use this information to compute the company's net cash flow from investing activities.

1. The company issued 10,000 shares of its own $5 par-value common stock for land with a fair market value of $50,000.

2. The company gave its president a loan of $85,000 and obtained a 10 percent note receivable, dated December 22, 2016, and maturing two years later.

3. The company sold a used truck for $9,000 in cash. The original cost of the truck was $34,000. Depreciation of $24,000 had been deducted.

◄ **Exercise 24.6**
Objective 24-3

Cash flows from investing activities.

The following transactions occurred at Craft Company in 2016. Use this information to compute the company's net cash flow from investing activities.

1. The company purchased a new building for $360,000. A down payment of $60,000 was made. The balance is due in four equal annual installments (plus interest) beginning July 1, 2017.

2. The company bought 1,000 shares of its own common stock for $30,000.

3. The company purchased as an investment $61,000 par value of Ridge Way Company's 10 percent bonds, maturing in five years. The purchase price was $59,000.

◄ **Exercise 24.7**
Objective 24-3

Cash flows from financing activities.

The following transactions occurred at the Indiana Company in 2016. Use this information to compute the company's net cash flow from financing activities for the year.

1. Holders of $200,000 par-value 7 percent bonds surrendered the bonds for redemption and were paid $206,000 in cash. The unamortized discount on these bonds as of the date of redemption was $1,600.

2. Cash interest of $33,700 was paid on bonds during the year. The bond discount amortized was $400.

3. Cash dividends of $50,000 were paid on common stock during the year.

◄ **Exercise 24.8**
Objective 24-4

Cash flows from financing activities.

The following transactions occurred at Peter Company in 2016. Use this information to compute the company's net cash flow from financing activities for the year.

1. The company reacquired as treasury stock 30,000 shares of its outstanding common stock, paying a total of $90,000 for the shares.

2. On November 30, the company borrowed $200,000 from the bank, signing a 90-day, 10 percent note payable.

◄ **Exercise 24.9**
Objective 24-4

PROBLEMS

Problem Set A

Prepare a statement of cash flows.

A comparative balance sheet for Cate, Inc., on December 31, 2016 and 2015, follows. Additional information about the firm's financial activities during 2016 is also given below.

INSTRUCTIONS

Prepare a statement of cash flows for 2016. Additional information for the year follows:

a. Had net income of $90,000.

b. Recorded $19,000 in depreciation.

◄ **Problem 24.1A**
**Objectives 24-1,
24-2, 24-3, 24-4,
24-5**

c. Issued bonds payable with a par value of $60,000 at par and received cash.

d. Received $20,000 in cash for the issue of an additional 2,000 shares of $10 par value common stock.

e. Purchased equipment for $60,000 in cash.

Cate, Inc.		
Comparative Balance Sheet		
December 31, 2016 and 2015		

Assets	2016	2015
Cash	1 2 5 9 0 0	7 3 5 0 0
Accounts Receivable (Net)	1 3 1 6 0 0	8 0 6 0 0
Merchandise Inventory	4 7 6 0 0	4 4 0 0 0
Property, Plant, and Equipment	2 6 0 0 0 0	2 0 0 0 0 0
Less Accumulated Depreciation	(3 9 0 0 0)	(2 0 0 0 0)
Total Assets	5 2 6 1 0 0	3 7 8 1 0 0
Liabilities and Stockholders' Equity		
Liabilities		
Accounts Payable	5 5 0 0 0	7 7 0 0 0
Bonds Payable	1 7 0 0 0 0	1 1 0 0 0 0
Total Liabilities	2 2 5 0 0 0	1 8 7 0 0 0
Stockholders' Equity		
Common Stock, ($1 par, 50,000 shares authorized, 6,000 shares issued in 2015 and 8,000 shares issued in 2016)	8 0 0 0 0	6 0 0 0 0
Retained Earnings	2 2 1 1 0 0	1 3 1 1 0 0
Total Stockholders' Equity	3 0 1 1 0 0	1 9 1 1 0 0
Total Liabilities and Stockholders' Equity	5 2 6 1 0 0	3 7 8 1 0 0

Analyze: Explain why an increase in accounts payable is considered an adjustment to cash flows from operating activities.

Problem 24.2A

Objectives 24-1, 24-2, 24-3, 24-4, 24-5

▶ **Prepare a statement of cash flows.**

Postclosing trial balance data and other financial data for The Candy Company as of December 31, 2016 and 2015, follow.

INSTRUCTIONS

Prepare a statement of cash flows for 2016. Additional information for the year follows:

a. Sold common stock for $20,000 in cash.

b. Had net income of $76,000 after income taxes.

c. Sold bonds payable for $50,000 cash at par value.

d. Completed a major addition to the building for $70,000 in cash.

e. Bought additional land for $35,000 in cash.

f. Paid common stock dividends of $25,000 in cash.

g. Amortized intangible assets for $700.

h. The short-term note payable resulted from operating activities, not borrowing or financing activities.

The Candy Company
Postclosing Trial Balance
December 31, 2016 and 2015

Account Name	2016 Debit	2016 Credit	2015 Debit	2015 Credit
Cash	8 9 4 0 0 0 0		8 5 4 0 0 0 0	
Accounts Receivable (Net)	9 1 5 0 0 0 0		8 6 0 0 0 0 0	
Merchandise Inventory	6 2 7 5 0 0 0		6 6 4 5 0 0 0	
Prepaid Expenses	2 7 0 0 0 0		2 1 0 0 0 0	
Land	7 5 0 0 0 0 0		4 0 0 0 0 0 0	
Plant and Equipment	1 8 5 0 0 0 0 0		1 1 5 0 0 0 0 0	
Accumulated Depreciation—Plant and Equipment		1 8 5 0 0 0 0		1 1 5 0 0 0 0
Intangible Assets	5 4 0 0 0 0		6 1 0 0 0 0	
Notes Payable—Short Term		6 0 0 0 0 0		1 0 0 0 0 0 0
Accounts Payable		2 5 7 5 0 0 0		3 1 7 5 0 0 0
Payroll Taxes Payable		2 7 0 0 0 0		2 5 0 0 0 0
Income Taxes Payable		1 5 0 0 0 0		3 0 0 0 0 0
Mortgage Payable, 2023		1 2 9 0 0 0 0 0		1 3 5 0 0 0 0 0
7% Bonds Payable, 2018		5 0 0 0 0 0 0		0
Common Stock $1 par		7 0 0 0 0 0 0		5 0 0 0 0 0 0
Retained Earnings		2 0 8 3 0 0 0 0		1 5 7 3 0 0 0 0
Totals	5 1 1 7 5 0 0 0	5 1 1 7 5 0 0 0	4 0 1 0 5 0 0 0	4 0 1 0 5 0 0 0

Analyze: Were activities related to operations, investing, or financing responsible for the largest net inflow of cash?

Preparing a statement of cash flows.

◄ **Problem 24.3A**
**Objectives 24-1,
24-2, 24-3, 24-4,
24-5**

The condensed income statement and comparative balance sheet of Jackson Corporation as of December 31, 2016 and 2015, are provided below. Other financial data is also given.

INSTRUCTIONS

Prepare a statement of cash flows for Jackson Corporation for 2016. Additional information for the year that is pertinent to its preparation follows:

a. No items of property, plant, and equipment were disposed of during the year.

b. Paid cash for the additions to property, plant, and equipment during the year.

c. Paid $11,000 dividends on the common stock in cash during the year.

d. Issued common stock at par value for cash.

e. Paid cash to retire the long-term note payable.

Jackson Corporation
Condensed Income Statement
Year Ended December 31, 2016

Revenues		6 8 5 5 0 0
Costs and Expenses		
Cost of Goods Sold	4 3 0 0 0 0	
Salaries Expense	1 2 6 0 0 0	
Depreciation Expense	1 6 0 0 0	
Advertising Expense	1 5 9 0 0	
Utilities Expense	1 9 0 0 0	
Total Costs and Expenses		6 0 6 9 0 0
Net Income Before Income Taxes		7 8 6 0 0
Income Taxes Expense		1 9 6 5 0
Net Income After Income Taxes		5 8 9 5 0

Jackson Corporation
Comparative Balance Sheet
December 31, 2016 and 2015

Assets	2016	2015
Cash	9 2 2 5 0	8 2 0 0 0
Accounts Receivable (Net)	5 7 1 5 0	5 3 0 0 0
Merchandise Inventory	5 0 0 0 0	5 5 5 0 0
Prepaid Advertising	9 0 0 0	1 1 5 0 0
Property, Plant, and Equipment	1 3 5 0 0 0	1 1 0 0 0 0
Less Accumulated Depreciation	(2 7 0 0 0)	(1 1 0 0 0)
Total Assets	3 1 6 4 0 0	3 0 1 0 0 0
Liabilities and Stockholders' Equity		
Liabilities		
Accounts Payable	5 1 4 5 0	8 0 5 0 0
Salaries Payable	5 5 0 0	4 0 0 0
Unearned Revenues	4 5 0 0	6 0 0 0
Income Taxes Payable	7 5 0 0	6 0 0 0
Note Payable—2018	0	4 0 0 0 0
Total Liabilities	6 8 9 5 0	1 3 6 5 0 0
Stockholders' Equity		
Common Stock ($2 par)	9 5 0 0 0	6 0 0 0 0
Retained Earnings	1 5 2 4 5 0	1 0 4 5 0 0
Total Stockholders' Equity	2 4 7 4 5 0	1 6 4 5 0 0
Total Liabilities and Stockholders' Equity	3 1 6 4 0 0	3 0 1 0 0 0

Analyze: If Jackson Corporation had written off an uncollectible account receivable of $5,500 during this fiscal period, what adjustment, if any, would be required on the statement of cash flows?

Problem 24.4A ▶ **Prepare a statement of cash flows.**

Objectives 24-1, 24-2, 24-3, 24-4, 24-5

The comparative balance sheet for Short Company as of December 31, 2016 and 2015, is shown below, followed by the condensed income statement.

INSTRUCTIONS

Prepare a statement of cash flows for 2016. Additional information for the year follows:

a. Acquired land at a cost of $90,000; paid one-half of the purchase price in cash and issued common stock for the balance.

b. Sold used equipment for $30,000 in cash. The original cost was $50,000; depreciation of $15,000 had been taken. The remaining change in the *Property, Plant, and Equipment* account represents a purchase of equipment for cash. Total depreciation expense for the year was $10,000.

c. Issued bonds payable at par value for cash.

d. Sold bond investments costing $30,000 at no gain or loss during the year.

e. Paid $25,000 cash dividends on the common stock.

Analyze: By what percentage did *Cash* increase from January 1 to December 31?

Short Company
Comparative Balance Sheet
December 31, 2016 and 2015

Assets	2016	2015
Cash	127 875	59 750
Accounts Receivable (Net)	87 000	67 750
Merchandise Inventory	84 150	75 000
Prepaid Rent	6 500	5 000
Land	120 000	30 000
Property, Plant, and Equipment	194 000	229 000
Less Accumulated Depreciation—PPE	(17 900)	(22 900)
Investment in TVA Bonds	30 000	60 000
Total Assets	631 625	503 600
Liabilities and Stockholders' Equity		
Liabilities		
Accounts Payable	67 300	88 100
Income Taxes Payable	9 750	10 500
Bonds Payable	160 000	110 000
Total Liabilities	237 050	208 600
Stockholders' Equity		
Common Stock	130 000	85 000
Retained Earnings	264 575	210 000
Total Stockholders' Equity	394 575	295 000
Total Liabilities and Stockholders' Equity	631 625	503 600

Short Company
Condensed Income Statement
Year Ended December 31, 2016

Revenues		819 000
Costs and Expenses		
Cost of Goods Sold	478 250	
Depreciation Expense	10 000	
Selling and Administrative Expenses	200 150	
Interest Expense	19 500	
Loss on Sale of Equipment	5 000	
Income Taxes Expense	26 525	
Total Costs and Expenses		739 425
Net Income After Income Taxes		79 575

Problem Set B

Prepare a statement of cash flows.

A comparative balance sheet for Cort Corporation as of December 31, 2016 and 2015, is given on the next page.

INSTRUCTIONS

Use these data to prepare a statement of cash flows for 2016. Additional information for the year follows:

◄ **Problem 24.1B**
**Objectives 24-1,
24-2, 24-3, 24-4,
24-5**

Cort Corporation
Comparative Balance Sheet
December 31, 2016 and 2015

Assets	2016	2015
Cash	5 3 6 0 0	4 9 5 0 0
Accounts Receivable (Net)	8 4 0 0 0	6 0 0 0 0
Merchandise Inventory	4 6 0 0 0	3 4 0 0 0
Property, Plant, and Equipment	1 4 0 0 0 0	1 5 0 0 0 0
Less Accumulated Depreciation	(3 6 0 0 0)	(4 5 0 0 0)
Total Assets	2 8 7 6 0 0	2 4 8 5 0 0
Liabilities and Stockholders' Equity		
Liabilities		
Accounts Payable	5 0 0 0 0	4 6 0 0 0
Total Liabilities	5 0 0 0 0	4 6 0 0 0
Stockholders' Equity		
Common Stock, ($1 par, 50,000 shares authorized:		
50,000 shares issued in 2015 and 75,000 shares issued in 2016)	7 5 0 0 0	5 0 0 0 0
Retained Earnings	1 6 2 6 0 0	1 5 2 5 0 0
Total Stockholders' Equity	2 3 7 6 0 0	2 0 2 5 0 0
Total Liabilities and Stockholders' Equity	2 3 7 6 0 0	2 4 8 5 0 0

a. Had net income of $15,100.

b. Paid $20,000 cash for new store equipment.

c. Sold used machinery for $8,000 cash. The original cost was $30,000, and the accumulated depreciation was $24,000; included the gain of $2,000 in net income.

d. Paid cash dividends of $5,000.

e. Recorded $15,000 in depreciation.

Analyze: List the transactions that required the greatest outlay of cash during fiscal 2016.

Problem 24.2B ▶ Prepare a statement of cash flows.

Objectives 24-1,
24-2, 24-3, 24-4,
24-5

Postclosing trial balance data and other financial data for Treble, Inc., as of December 31, 2016 and 2015, follow.

INSTRUCTIONS

Prepare a statement of cash flows for 2016. Additional information for the year follows:

a. Sold an unused lot for $20,000 in cash; it originally cost $10,000.

b. Constructed a new building for $150,000, of which $20,000 was paid in cash and $130,000 is a long-term mortgage payable.

c. Issued $20,000 of 10 percent bonds payable, maturing in 2021, for cash at par.

d. Sold common stock at par $25,000 in cash.

e. Had net income of $50,000 after income taxes.

f. Paid common stock dividends of $20,000 in cash.

g. Amortized organization costs of $1,000.

h. The short-term note payable resulted from operating activities, not financing.

Analyze: Did operating, investing, or financing activities generate the greatest net inflow of cash?

Treble, Inc.
Postclosing Trial Balance
December 31, 2016 and 2015

Account Name	2016 Debit	2016 Credit	2015 Debit	2015 Credit
Cash	9 4 3 5 0		5 2 5 0 0	
Accounts Receivable (Net)	6 0 7 5 0		4 5 7 5 0	
Merchandise Inventory	6 5 0 0 0		5 5 0 0 0	
Prepaid Expenses	2 5 0 0		1 0 0 0	
Land	3 9 0 0 0		4 9 0 0 0	
Plant and Equipment	2 7 5 0 0 0		1 2 5 0 0 0	
Accumulated Depreciation—Plant and Equipment		2 4 7 5 0		1 0 0 0 0
Organization Costs	4 0 0 0		5 0 0 0	
Notes Payable—Short Term		0		7 5 0 0
Accounts Payable		3 2 2 5 0		3 6 2 5 0
Payroll Taxes Payable		2 6 0 0		2 5 0 0
Income Taxes Payable		1 0 0 0		2 0 0 0
Mortgage Payable, 2020		2 0 5 0 0 0		7 5 0 0 0
7% Bonds Payable, 2018		2 0 0 0 0		0
Common Stock, $1 par		7 5 0 0 0		5 0 0 0 0
Retained Earnings		1 8 0 0 0 0		1 5 0 0 0 0
Totals	5 4 0 6 0 0	5 4 0 6 0 0	3 3 3 2 5 0	3 3 3 2 5 0

Prepare a statement of cash flows.

Pacific Corporation's comparative balance sheet as of December 31, 2016 and 2015, and 2016 condensed income statement appear below.

◀ **Problem 24.3B**
**Objectives 24-1,
24-2, 24-3, 24-4,
24-5**

INSTRUCTIONS

Prepare a statement of cash flows for 2016. Additional information for the year follows:

a. Depreciation totaling $9,000 is included in expenses.

b. Sold land for $35,000 in cash; the land, which is included in plant and equipment, had a cost of $35,000.

c. Acquired a building with a fair market value of $100,000 by issuing common stock.

d. Purchased equipment for $25,000 in cash.

e. Paid dividends of $50,000.

Pacific Corporation
Comparative Balance Sheet
December 31, 2016 and 2015

Assets	2016	2015
Cash	1 0 9 2 0 0	9 0 0 0 0
Accounts Receivable (Net)	6 5 6 5 0	7 0 0 0 0
Merchandise Inventory	5 0 0 0 0	6 4 0 0 0
Prepaid Advertising	8 0 0 0	1 0 0 0 0
Property, Plant, and Equipment	2 9 0 0 0 0	2 0 0 0 0 0
Less Accumulated Depreciation	(1 9 0 0 0)	(1 0 0 0 0)
Total Assets	5 0 3 8 5 0	4 2 4 0 0 0

(continued)

(continued)

Liabilities and Stockholders' Equity		
Liabilities		
Accounts Payable	6 4 5 0 0	9 5 0 0 0
Income Taxes Payable	6 0 0 0	2 5 0 0 0
Notes Payable—2018	2 5 0 0 0	4 0 0 0 0
Total Liabilities	9 5 5 0 0	1 6 0 0 0 0
Stockholders' Equity		
Common Stock ($1 par)	2 0 0 0 0 0	1 0 0 0 0 0
Retained Earnings	2 0 8 3 5 0	1 6 4 0 0 0
Total Stockholders' Equity	4 0 8 3 5 0	2 6 4 0 0 0
Total Liabilities and Stockholders' Equity	5 0 3 8 5 0	4 2 4 0 0 0

Pacific Corporation
Condensed Income Statement
Year Ended December 31, 2016

Revenues	7 7 5 0 0 0
Costs and Expenses	
Cost of Goods Sold	3 8 5 0 0 0
Expenses	2 9 5 6 5 0
Net Income	9 4 3 5 0

Analyze: If the company had purchased equipment on credit instead of using cash, what would the cash balance have been at year-end?

Problem 24.4B ▶ **Prepare a statement of cash flows.**

Objectives 24-1,
24-2, 24-3, 24-4,
24-5

The comparative balance sheet for Sand Products, Inc., as of December 31, 2016 and 2015, is shown below, followed by the condensed income statement and other financial data for 2016.

INSTRUCTIONS

Prepare a statement of cash flows for 2016.

a. Sold used equipment for $27,000 in cash that originally cost $32,000; accumulated depreciation was $8,000. The remainder of the change in *Equipment* represents equipment purchased for cash.

b. Issued short-term notes payable with a par value of $20,000. Retired bonds payable at maturity.

c. Paid cash dividends of $30,000.

d. Issued common stock at par value for cash.

Sand Products, Inc.
Comparative Balance Sheet
December 31, 2016 and 2015

Assets	2016	2015
Cash	1 1 8 4 1 0	1 0 1 5 0
Accounts Receivable (Net)	8 8 6 5 0	6 6 2 5 0
Merchandise Inventory	8 9 0 0 0	7 5 0 0 0
Prepaid Advertising	5 5 0 0	3 5 0 0
Land	7 5 0 0 0	7 5 0 0 0
Property, Plant, and Equipment	2 0 7 0 0 0	2 1 9 0 0 0
Less Accumulated Depreciation—Property, Plant, and Equipment	(3 4 6 0 0)	(2 1 9 0 0)
Total Assets	5 4 8 9 6 0	4 2 7 0 0 0

Liabilities and Stockholders' Equity					
Liabilities					
Accounts Payable		6 1 3 0 0		6 8 5 0 0	
Notes Payable—Short Term		2 0 0 0 0			0
Income Taxes Payable		1 0 2 5 0		8 5 0 0	
Bonds Payable			0	5 0 0 0 0	
Total Liabilities		9 1 5 5 0		1 2 7 0 0 0	
Stockholders' Equity					
Common Stock		1 5 0 0 0 0		1 0 0 0 0 0	
Retained Earnings		3 0 7 4 1 0		2 0 0 0 0 0	
Total Stockholders' Equity		4 5 7 4 1 0		3 0 0 0 0 0	
Total Liabilities and Stockholders' Equity		5 4 8 9 6 0		4 2 7 0 0 0	

Sand Products, Inc.
Condensed Income Statement
Year Ended December 31, 2016

Revenues (including gain on sale of equipment)	9 2 5 6 0 0
Costs and Expenses	
Cost of Goods Sold	5 0 1 6 0 0
Depreciation Expense	2 0 7 0 0
Selling and Administrative Expenses	1 9 5 0 0 0
Interest Expense	1 2 0 0 0
Income Taxes Expense	5 8 8 9 0
Total Costs and Expenses	7 8 8 1 9 0
Net Income After Income Taxes	1 3 7 4 1 0

Analyze: Was the amount of net cash provided by operating activities sufficient to cover the cash that the company required for financing activities? Explain.

Critical Thinking Problem 24.1

Adjustments

Street Company was formed and began business on January 1, 2016, when R. B. Street transferred merchandise inventory with a value of $60,000, cash of $55,000, accounts receivable of $60,000, and accounts payable of $35,000. Common stock with a par value of $5 per share was issued to Mr. Street. The company's common stock was recorded at par.

Street Company's statement of cash flows for 2016 is shown below and on the next page:

Street Company
Statement of Cash Flows
Year Ended December 31, 2016

Cash Flow from Operations		
Net Income		5 0 0 0 0
Adjustments		
Depreciation of building	5 0 0 0	
Depreciation of equipment	6 0 0 0	
Increase in accounts receivable	(1 5 0 0 0)	

(continued)

Increase in inventory		(8 0 0 0)	
Increase in prepaid insurance		(8 0 0)	
Increase in accounts payable		1 7 0 0 0	
Increase in income tax payable		2 5 0 0	6 7 0 0
Net cash flow provided by operations			5 6 7 0 0
Cash Flow from Investing Activities			
Purchase of land		(3 0 0 0 0)	
Purchase of building		(2 5 0 0 0)	
Purchase of equipment		(6 0 0 0 0)	
Net cash used in investing activities			(1 1 5 0 0 0)
Cash Flow from Financing Activities			
Issuance of common stock at $5/share		5 0 0 0	
Borrowing at bank by issuance of note payable		4 0 0 0 0	
Net cash provided by financing activities			4 5 0 0 0
Net decrease in cash balance			(1 3 3 0 0)
Cash balance, January 1, 2016			5 5 0 0 0
Cash balance, December 31, 2016			4 1 7 0 0

Note: A building was acquired at a cost of $250,000. Cash of $25,000 was paid, and a mortgage of $225,000 was given for the balance.

INSTRUCTIONS

Based on the data supplied, prepare the December 31, 2016, balance sheet for the corporation.

Analyze: Describe four adjusting entries that were made by Street Company in fiscal 2016.

Critical Thinking Problem 24.2

Transactions

Grace Jones, the bookkeeper for Tenn Valley Company, asks for your help in identifying whether the following transactions should be reported on the corporation's statement of cash flows. Prepare a list for Jones indicating whether or not each transaction should be reported on the statement. If the transaction should appear on the statement, indicate whether it should be classified as a financing activity, an investing activity, or an operating activity. If the transaction should not be part of the statement of cash flows, explain why not.

1. Prepaid three months of rent on warehouse storage facilities at the end of the year.
2. Paid suppliers amounts due on accounts payable.
3. Issued common stock for cash.
4. Collected an accounts receivable from a customer.
5. Paid cash dividends on common stock.
6. Purchased common stock of Apple as investment for cash.
7. Borrowed cash, signing a short-term note that was repaid before the end of the year.
8. Paid federal income taxes due.
9. Issued long-term bonds for cash.
10. Used proceeds from bond issue to purchase new equipment for plant.

11. Received principal payments on note receivable held in connection with sale of building last year.

12. Distributed a stock dividend on common stock.

BUSINESS CONNECTIONS

Using All Statements

Managerial FOCUS

1. How can the statement of cash flows help management arrange for proper financing?

2. A corporation's income statement shows a net income of $10,000 after income taxes for the year. Its statement of cash flows shows that its cash balance increased by $150,000: net cash outflow from operating activities, $100,000; net cash inflow from financing activities, $50,000; and net cash inflow from investing activities, $200,000. The president of the corporation has commented, "Even though the company's profit is small, it is clear, based on our positive cash flow, that we are doing quite well." Do you agree with this comment? Why or why not?

3. A member of a corporation's board of directors commented that because the statement of cash flows and the income statement are so similar, there is no need to prepare the income statement. Respond.

4. Assume that you are an accountant preparing the statement of cash flows for the year. Should the cash proceeds of $100,000 from a short-term note payable discounted in May of this year be included in the statement? The note was repaid in October. Would it be preferable to simply ignore both the loan and the repayment because it might confuse management to show both? Explain.

5. A potential customer has applied for an open-account credit line with a manufacturing firm. Explain how the potential customer's statement of cash flows would help to evaluate its short-term debt-paying ability.

Delay Payment of Bonds

Ethical DILEMMA

Cailey Corporation has a cash flow problem. They have bonds due before the end of the fiscal year. They will need to sell more bonds to pay the bonds due. Ida, the controller, understands that many investors consider the cash flow statement to be the key statement that indicates the company's future value. She has decided to delay the payment of the bonds until after the end of the fiscal year. This will show a higher balance in cash since the bonds will not be paid. There will be no indication in the financial statements that she has defaulted on the bonds. It is Ida's plan to issue additional bonds after the close of the fiscal year to pay off the current bonds. However, she will need to record the interest paid in the current fiscal year. Are Ida's actions acceptable accounting practices?

Statement of Cash Flows

Financial Statement ANALYSIS

Refer to the *2012 Annual Report (for the fiscal year ended February 3, 2013)* for The Home Depot, Inc., in Appendix A.

1. Locate the consolidated statements of cash flows for the year ended January 31, 2013. What net cash was (1) provided by operations? (2) used in investing activities? (3) used by financing activities?

2. Is the most significant source of cash generated from the company's operating, investing, or financing activities?

Cash Flow Information

As a team of four students, obtain the cash flow statements from two companies. Each group of two students should explain their company's cash flow statements to the other two students. The explanation should include the following: (1) Has cash increased or decreased? (2) What is the main source of cash? (3) What are the principle uses of cash? (4) Is the company's business expanding or contracting? (5) Has more common stock been sold? (6) Is the company paying down debt or getting further into debt? (7) Has treasury stock been purchased?

Different Business, Different Cash Flow?

Go to the website for Macy's (macysinc.com), IBM (ibm.com), and Microsoft (Microsoft.com). Compare the cash flow from operating, investing, and financing of the three companies for three years. Is there a difference in the cash flow for the type of business (compare Microsoft to Macy's)? Does a company that has been in business for a long time like IBM have a higher cash balance than Microsoft?

Answers to **Self Reviews**

Answers to Section 1 Self Review

1. Short-term liquid investments that are easily convertible into cash.
2. Transactions that involve the acquisition or disposal of long-term assets.
3. This transaction is one of financing the business, not an investing activity.
4. **b.** purchases of plant and equipment for cash.
5. **b.** issuance of stock for cash.
6. **(a)** source, **(b)** use, **(c)** use, **(d)** source, **(e)** source

Answers to Section 2 Self Review

1. The loss does not relate to operating activities and must be added back to net income.
2. Depreciation expense does not reflect a cash outlay, so it must be added back to net income.
3. An increase in notes payable does not affect cash flow from operations, unless the notes were credited when merchandise inventory or other operating assets were purchased.
4. **d.** a change in merchandise inventory.
5. **b.** deducted from net income.
6. $10,500 used

Answers to Section 3 Self Review

1. $50,000—included as inflow from investing activities. $5,000 gain—deducted from net income.
2. Disclosed in footnotes to the statement.
3. As cash used in financing activities.
4. **b.** indirect method.
5. **b.** decrease in Cash Flows from Investing Activities.
6. $6,000 gain—subtracted from net income. $10,000—included as cash inflow from investing activities.

Answers to Comprehensive Self Review

1. Operating, investing, and financing activities are shown in a statement of cash flows.

2. Financing activities are transactions that provide or use cash through selling stock, issuing bonds, or paying cash dividends.

3. The increase in accounts payable must be added to net income to arrive at cash flow from operations.

4. In a note to the statement of cash flows.

5. In the operating activities section as an addition to net income.

Mini-Practice Set 4

Financial Analysis and Decision Making

C&C Supplies, Inc.

This project will give you an opportunity to evaluate financial statements and to make decisions based on the information presented in the financial statements of C&C Supplies, Inc.

C&C Supplies, Inc., sells a variety of consumer products. The firm is organized as a corporation. The fiscal year-end is the same as the calendar year-end, December 31.

The *Study Guide & Working Papers, Chapters 14–24*, contain the following financial statements for C&C Supplies, Inc.:

- Comparative Income Statement (Years Ended December 31, 2016 and 2015)
- Comparative Balance Sheet (December 31, 2016 and 2015)

The instructions for completing Mini-Practice Set 4 are in the *Study Guide & Working Papers, Chapters 14–24*. Retained Earnings on January 1, 2015, was $188,442.

APPENDIXES

Appendix A

The Home Depot 2012 Financial Statements (for the fiscal year ended February 3, 2013)

Item 8. Financial Statements and Supplementary Data.

Management's Responsibility for Financial Statements

The financial statements presented in this Annual Report have been prepared with integrity and objectivity and are the responsibility of the management of The Home Depot, Inc. These financial statements have been prepared in conformity with U.S. generally accepted accounting principles and properly reflect certain estimates and judgments based upon the best available information.

The financial statements of the Company have been audited by KPMG LLP, an independent registered public accounting firm. Their accompanying report is based upon an audit conducted in accordance with the standards of the Public Company Accounting Oversight Board (United States).

The Audit Committee of the Board of Directors, consisting solely of independent directors, meets five times a year with the independent registered public accounting firm, the internal auditors and representatives of management to discuss auditing and financial reporting matters. In addition, a telephonic meeting is held prior to each quarterly earnings release. The Audit Committee retains the independent registered public accounting firm and regularly reviews the internal accounting controls, the activities of the independent registered public accounting firm and internal auditors and the financial condition of the Company. Both the Company's independent registered public accounting firm and the internal auditors have free access to the Audit Committee.

Management's Report on Internal Control Over Financial Reporting

Our management is responsible for establishing and maintaining adequate internal control over financial reporting, as such term is defined in Rule 13a-15(f) promulgated under the Securities Exchange Act of 1934, as amended (the "Exchange Act"). Under the supervision and with the participation of our management, including our Chief Executive Officer and Chief Financial Officer, we conducted an evaluation of the effectiveness of our internal control over financial reporting as of February 3, 2013 based on the framework in *Internal Control – Integrated Framework* issued by the Committee of Sponsoring Organizations of the Treadway Commission (COSO). Based on our evaluation, our management concluded that our internal control over financial reporting was effective as of February 3, 2013 in providing reasonable assurance regarding the reliability of financial reporting and the preparation of financial statements for external purposes in accordance with U.S. generally accepted accounting principles. The effectiveness of our internal control over financial reporting as of February 3, 2013 has been audited by KPMG LLP, an independent registered public accounting firm, as stated in their report which is included on page 28 in this Form 10-K.

/s/ FRANCIS S. BLAKE

Francis S. Blake
Chairman &
Chief Executive Officer

/s/ CAROL B. TOMÉ

Carol B. Tomé
Chief Financial Officer &
Executive Vice President – Corporate Services

Report of Independent Registered Public Accounting Firm

The Board of Directors and Stockholders
The Home Depot, Inc.:

We have audited The Home Depot, Inc.'s internal control over financial reporting as of February 3, 2013, based on criteria established in *Internal Control – Integrated Framework* issued by the Committee of Sponsoring Organizations of the Treadway Commission (COSO). The Home Depot, Inc.'s management is responsible for maintaining effective internal control over financial reporting and for its assessment of the effectiveness of internal control over financial reporting, included in the accompanying Management's Report on Internal Control Over Financial Reporting. Our responsibility is to express an opinion on the Company's internal control over financial reporting based on our audit.

We conducted our audit in accordance with the standards of the Public Company Accounting Oversight Board (United States). Those standards require that we plan and perform the audit to obtain reasonable assurance about whether effective internal control over financial reporting was maintained in all material respects. Our audit included obtaining an understanding of internal control over financial reporting, assessing the risk that a material weakness exists, and testing and evaluating the design and operating effectiveness of internal control based on the assessed risk. Our audit also included performing such other procedures as we considered necessary in the circumstances. We believe that our audit provides a reasonable basis for our opinion.

A company's internal control over financial reporting is a process designed to provide reasonable assurance regarding the reliability of financial reporting and the preparation of financial statements for external purposes in accordance with generally accepted accounting principles. A company's internal control over financial reporting includes those policies and procedures that (1) pertain to the maintenance of records that, in reasonable detail, accurately and fairly reflect the transactions and dispositions of the assets of the company; (2) provide reasonable assurance that transactions are recorded as necessary to permit preparation of financial statements in accordance with generally accepted accounting principles, and that receipts and expenditures of the company are being made only in accordance with authorizations of management and directors of the company; and (3) provide reasonable assurance regarding prevention or timely detection of unauthorized acquisition, use, or disposition of the company's assets that could have a material effect on the financial statements.

Because of its inherent limitations, internal control over financial reporting may not prevent or detect misstatements. Also, projections of any evaluation of effectiveness to future periods are subject to the risk that controls may become inadequate because of changes in conditions, or that the degree of compliance with the policies or procedures may deteriorate.

In our opinion, The Home Depot, Inc. maintained, in all material respects, effective internal control over financial reporting as of February 3, 2013, based on criteria established in *Internal Control – Integrated Framework* issued by the Committee of Sponsoring Organizations of the Treadway Commission.

We also have audited, in accordance with the standards of the Public Company Accounting Oversight Board (United States), the Consolidated Balance Sheets of The Home Depot, Inc. and subsidiaries as of February 3, 2013 and January 29, 2012, and the related Consolidated Statements of Earnings, Comprehensive Income, Stockholders' Equity, and Cash Flows for each of the fiscal years in the three-year period ended February 3, 2013, and our report dated March 28, 2013 expressed an unqualified opinion on those consolidated financial statements.

/s/ KPMG LLP

Atlanta, Georgia
March 28, 2013

Report of Independent Registered Public Accounting Firm

The Board of Directors and Stockholders
The Home Depot, Inc.:

We have audited the accompanying Consolidated Balance Sheets of The Home Depot, Inc. and subsidiaries as of February 3, 2013 and January 29, 2012, and the related Consolidated Statements of Earnings, Comprehensive Income, Stockholders' Equity, and Cash Flows for each of the fiscal years in the three-year period ended February 3, 2013. These Consolidated Financial Statements are the responsibility of the Company's management. Our responsibility is to express an opinion on these Consolidated Financial Statements based on our audits.

We conducted our audits in accordance with the standards of the Public Company Accounting Oversight Board (United States). Those standards require that we plan and perform the audit to obtain reasonable assurance about whether the financial statements are free of material misstatement. An audit includes examining, on a test basis, evidence supporting the amounts and disclosures in the financial statements. An audit also includes assessing the accounting principles used and significant estimates made by management, as well as evaluating the overall financial statement presentation. We believe that our audits provide a reasonable basis for our opinion.

In our opinion, the Consolidated Financial Statements referred to above present fairly, in all material respects, the financial position of The Home Depot, Inc. and subsidiaries as of February 3, 2013 and January 29, 2012, and the results of their operations and their cash flows for each of the fiscal years in the three-year period ended February 3, 2013, in conformity with U.S. generally accepted accounting principles.

We also have audited, in accordance with the standards of the Public Company Accounting Oversight Board (United States), The Home Depot, Inc.'s internal control over financial reporting as of February 3, 2013, based on criteria established in *Internal Control – Integrated Framework* issued by the Committee of Sponsoring Organizations of the Treadway Commission (COSO), and our report dated March 28, 2013 expressed an unqualified opinion on the effectiveness of the Company's internal control over financial reporting.

/s/ KPMG LLP

Atlanta, Georgia
March 28, 2013

THE HOME DEPOT, INC. AND SUBSIDIARIES
CONSOLIDATED BALANCE SHEETS

amounts in millions, except share and per share data	February 3, 2013	January 29, 2012
ASSETS		
Current Assets:		
Cash and Cash Equivalents	$ 2,494	$ 1,987
Receivables, net	1,395	1,245
Merchandise Inventories	10,710	10,325
Other Current Assets	773	963
Total Current Assets	15,372	14,520
Property and Equipment, at cost	38,491	38,975
Less Accumulated Depreciation and Amortization	14,422	14,527
Net Property and Equipment	24,069	24,448
Notes Receivable	140	135
Goodwill	1,170	1,120
Other Assets	333	295
Total Assets	$ 41,084	$ 40,518
LIABILITIES AND STOCKHOLDERS' EQUITY		
Current Liabilities:		
Accounts Payable	$ 5,376	$ 4,856
Accrued Salaries and Related Expenses	1,414	1,372
Sales Taxes Payable	472	391
Deferred Revenue	1,270	1,147
Income Taxes Payable	22	23
Current Installments of Long-Term Debt	1,321	30
Other Accrued Expenses	1,587	1,557
Total Current Liabilities	11,462	9,376
Long-Term Debt, excluding current installments	9,475	10,758
Other Long-Term Liabilities	2,051	2,146
Deferred Income Taxes	319	340
Total Liabilities	23,307	22,620
STOCKHOLDERS' EQUITY		
Common Stock, par value $0.05; authorized: 10 billion shares; issued: 1.754 billion shares at February 3, 2013 and 1.733 billion shares at January 29, 2012; outstanding: 1.484 billion shares at February 3, 2013 and 1.537 billion shares at January 29, 2012	88	87
Paid-In Capital	7,948	6,966
Retained Earnings	20,038	17,246
Accumulated Other Comprehensive Income	397	293
Treasury Stock, at cost, 270 million shares at February 3, 2013 and 196 million shares at January 29, 2012	(10,694)	(6,694)
Total Stockholders' Equity	17,777	17,898
Total Liabilities and Stockholders' Equity	$ 41,084	$ 40,518

See accompanying Notes to Consolidated Financial Statements.

THE HOME DEPOT, INC. AND SUBSIDIARIES
CONSOLIDATED STATEMENTS OF EARNINGS

	Fiscal Year Ended[1]		
amounts in millions, except per share data	February 3, 2013	January 29, 2012	January 30, 2011
NET SALES	$ 74,754	$ 70,395	$ 67,997
Cost of Sales	48,912	46,133	44,693
GROSS PROFIT	25,842	24,262	23,304
Operating Expenses:			
Selling, General and Administrative	16,508	16,028	15,849
Depreciation and Amortization	1,568	1,573	1,616
Total Operating Expenses	18,076	17,601	17,465
OPERATING INCOME	7,766	6,661	5,839
Interest and Other (Income) Expense:			
Interest and Investment Income	(20)	(13)	(15)
Interest Expense	632	606	530
Other	(67)	—	51
Interest and Other, net	545	593	566
EARNINGS BEFORE PROVISION FOR INCOME TAXES	7,221	6,068	5,273
Provision for Income Taxes	2,686	2,185	1,935
NET EARNINGS	$ 4,535	$ 3,883	$ 3,338
Weighted Average Common Shares	1,499	1,562	1,648
BASIC EARNINGS PER SHARE	$ 3.03	$ 2.49	$ 2.03
Diluted Weighted Average Common Shares	1,511	1,570	1,658
DILUTED EARNINGS PER SHARE	$ 3.00	$ 2.47	$ 2.01

(1) Fiscal year ended February 3, 2013 includes 53 weeks. Fiscal years ended January 29, 2012 and January 30, 2011 include 52 weeks.

See accompanying Notes to Consolidated Financial Statements.

THE HOME DEPOT, INC. AND SUBSIDIARIES
CONSOLIDATED STATEMENTS OF COMPREHENSIVE INCOME

amounts in millions	Fiscal Year Ended[1]		
	February 3, 2013	January 29, 2012	January 30, 2011
Net Earnings	$ 4,535	$ 3,883	$ 3,338
Other Comprehensive Income (Loss):			
Foreign Currency Translation Adjustments	100	(143)	206
Cash Flow Hedges, net of tax	5	5	(116)
Other	(1)	(14)	(7)
Total Other Comprehensive Income (Loss)	104	(152)	83
COMPREHENSIVE INCOME	$ 4,639	$ 3,731	$ 3,421

(1) *Fiscal year ended February 3, 2013 includes 53 weeks. Fiscal years ended January 29, 2012 and January 30, 2011 include 52 weeks.*

See accompanying Notes to Consolidated Financial Statements.

THE HOME DEPOT, INC. AND SUBSIDIARIES
CONSOLIDATED STATEMENTS OF STOCKHOLDERS' EQUITY

amounts in millions, except per share data	Common Stock		Paid-In Capital	Retained Earnings	Accumulated Other Comprehensive Income (Loss)	Treasury Stock		Stockholders' Equity
	Shares	Amount				Shares	Amount	
Balance, January 31, 2010	**1,716**	**$ 86**	**$ 6,304**	**$ 13,226**	**$ 362**	**(18)**	**$ (585)**	**$ 19,393**
Net Earnings	—	—	—	3,338	—	—	—	3,338
Shares Issued Under Employee Stock Plans	6	—	42	—	—	—	—	42
Tax Effect of Stock-Based Compensation	—	—	2	—	—	—	—	2
Foreign Currency Translation Adjustments	—	—	—	—	206	—	—	206
Cash Flow Hedges, net of tax	—	—	—	—	(116)	—	—	(116)
Stock Options, Awards and Amortization of Restricted Stock	—	—	214	—	—	—	—	214
Repurchases of Common Stock	—	—	—	—	—	(81)	(2,608)	(2,608)
Cash Dividends ($0.945 per share)	—	—	—	(1,569)	—	—	—	(1,569)
Other	—	—	(6)	—	(7)	—	—	(13)
Balance, January 30, 2011	**1,722**	**$ 86**	**$ 6,556**	**$ 14,995**	**$ 445**	**(99)**	**$ (3,193)**	**$ 18,889**
Net Earnings	—	—	—	3,883	—	—	—	3,883
Shares Issued Under Employee Stock Plans	11	1	196	—	—	—	—	197
Tax Effect of Stock-Based Compensation	—	—	(2)	—	—	—	—	(2)
Foreign Currency Translation Adjustments	—	—	—	—	(143)	—	—	(143)
Cash Flow Hedges, net of tax	—	—	—	—	5	—	—	5
Stock Options, Awards and Amortization of Restricted Stock	—	—	215	—	—	—	—	215
Repurchases of Common Stock	—	—	—	—	—	(97)	(3,501)	(3,501)
Cash Dividends ($1.04 per share)	—	—	—	(1,632)	—	—	—	(1,632)
Other	—	—	1	—	(14)	—	—	(13)
Balance, January 29, 2012	**1,733**	**$ 87**	**$ 6,966**	**$ 17,246**	**$ 293**	**(196)**	**$ (6,694)**	**$ 17,898**
Net Earnings	—	—	—	4,535	—	—	—	4,535
Shares Issued Under Employee Stock Plans	21	1	678	—	—	—	—	679
Tax Effect of Stock-Based Compensation	—	—	82	—	—	—	—	82
Foreign Currency Translation Adjustments	—	—	—	—	100	—	—	100
Cash Flow Hedges, net of tax	—	—	—	—	5	—	—	5
Stock Options, Awards and Amortization of Restricted Stock	—	—	218	—	—	—	—	218
Repurchases of Common Stock	—	—	—	—	—	(74)	(4,000)	(4,000)
Cash Dividends ($1.16 per share)	—	—	—	(1,743)	—	—	—	(1,743)
Other	—	—	4	—	(1)	—	—	3
Balance, February 3, 2013	**1,754**	**$ 88**	**$ 7,948**	**$ 20,038**	**$ 397**	**(270)**	**$ (10,694)**	**$ 17,777**

See accompanying Notes to Consolidated Financial Statements.

THE HOME DEPOT, INC. AND SUBSIDIARIES
CONSOLIDATED STATEMENTS OF CASH FLOWS

	Fiscal Year Ended[1]		
amounts in millions	February 3, 2013	January 29, 2012	January 30, 2011
CASH FLOWS FROM OPERATING ACTIVITIES:			
Net Earnings	$ 4,535	$ 3,883	$ 3,338
Reconciliation of Net Earnings to Net Cash Provided by Operating Activities:			
Depreciation and Amortization	1,684	1,682	1,718
Stock-Based Compensation Expense	218	215	214
Goodwill Impairment	97	—	—
Changes in Assets and Liabilities, net of the effects of acquisitions and disposition:			
Receivables, net	(143)	(170)	(102)
Merchandise Inventories	(350)	256	(355)
Other Current Assets	93	159	12
Accounts Payable and Accrued Expenses	698	422	(133)
Deferred Revenue	121	(29)	10
Income Taxes Payable	87	14	(85)
Deferred Income Taxes	107	170	104
Other Long-Term Liabilities	(180)	(2)	(61)
Other	8	51	(75)
Net Cash Provided by Operating Activities	6,975	6,651	4,585
CASH FLOWS FROM INVESTING ACTIVITIES:			
Capital Expenditures, net of $98, $25 and $62 of non-cash capital expenditures in fiscal 2012, 2011 and 2010, respectively	(1,312)	(1,221)	(1,096)
Proceeds from Sale of Business, net	—	101	—
Payments for Businesses Acquired, net	(170)	(65)	—
Proceeds from Sales of Property and Equipment	50	56	84
Net Cash Used in Investing Activities	(1,432)	(1,129)	(1,012)
CASH FLOWS FROM FINANCING ACTIVITIES:			
Proceeds from Long-Term Borrowings, net of discount	—	1,994	998
Repayments of Long-Term Debt	(32)	(1,028)	(1,029)
Repurchases of Common Stock	(3,984)	(3,470)	(2,608)
Proceeds from Sales of Common Stock	784	306	104
Cash Dividends Paid to Stockholders	(1,743)	(1,632)	(1,569)
Other Financing Activities	(59)	(218)	(347)
Net Cash Used in Financing Activities	(5,034)	(4,048)	(4,451)
Change in Cash and Cash Equivalents	509	1,474	(878)
Effect of Exchange Rate Changes on Cash and Cash Equivalents	(2)	(32)	2
Cash and Cash Equivalents at Beginning of Year	1,987	545	1,421
Cash and Cash Equivalents at End of Year	$ 2,494	$ 1,987	$ 545
SUPPLEMENTAL DISCLOSURE OF CASH PAYMENTS MADE FOR:			
Interest, net of interest capitalized	$ 617	$ 580	$ 579
Income Taxes	$ 2,482	$ 1,865	$ 2,067

(1) *Fiscal year ended February 3, 2013 includes 53 weeks. Fiscal years ended January 29, 2012 and January 30, 2011 include 52 weeks.*

See accompanying Notes to Consolidated Financial Statements.

NOTES TO CONSOLIDATED FINANCIAL STATEMENTS

1. SUMMARY OF SIGNIFICANT ACCOUNTING POLICIES

Business, Consolidation and Presentation

The Home Depot, Inc. and its subsidiaries (the "Company") operate The Home Depot stores, which are full-service, warehouse-style stores averaging approximately 104,000 square feet of enclosed space, with approximately 24,000 additional square feet of outside garden area. The stores stock approximately 30,000 to 40,000 different kinds of building materials, home improvement supplies and lawn and garden products that are sold to do-it-yourself customers, do-it-for-me customers and professional customers. The Company also offers over 600,000 products through its Home Depot and Home Decorators Collection websites. At the end of fiscal 2012, the Company was operating 2,256 The Home Depot stores, which included 1,976 stores in the United States, including the Commonwealth of Puerto Rico and the territories of the U.S. Virgin Islands and Guam ("U.S."), 180 stores in Canada and 100 stores in Mexico. The Consolidated Financial Statements include the accounts of the Company and its wholly-owned subsidiaries. All significant intercompany transactions have been eliminated in consolidation.

Fiscal Year

The Company's fiscal year is a 52- or 53-week period ending on the Sunday nearest to January 31. The fiscal year ended February 3, 2013 ("fiscal 2012") includes 53 weeks and fiscal years ended January 29, 2012 ("fiscal 2011") and January 30, 2011 ("fiscal 2010") include 52 weeks.

Use of Estimates

Management of the Company has made a number of estimates and assumptions relating to the reporting of assets and liabilities, the disclosure of contingent assets and liabilities, and reported amounts of revenues and expenses in preparing these financial statements in conformity with U.S. generally accepted accounting principles. Actual results could differ from these estimates.

Fair Value of Financial Instruments

The carrying amounts of Cash and Cash Equivalents, Receivables and Accounts Payable approximate fair value due to the short-term maturities of these financial instruments. The fair value of the Company's Long-Term Debt is discussed in Note 11.

Cash Equivalents

The Company considers all highly liquid investments purchased with original maturities of three months or less to be cash equivalents. The Company's cash equivalents are carried at fair market value and consist primarily of money market funds.

Accounts Receivable

The Company has an agreement with a third-party service provider who directly extends credit to customers, manages the Company's private label credit card program and owns the related receivables. The Company evaluated the third-party entities holding the receivables under the program and concluded that they should not be consolidated by the Company. The agreement with the third-party service provider expires in 2018, with the Company having the option, but no obligation, to purchase the receivables at the end of the agreement. The deferred interest charges incurred by the Company for its deferred financing programs offered to its customers are included in Cost of Sales. The interchange fees charged to the Company for the customers' use of the cards and any profit sharing with the third-party service provider are included in Selling, General and Administrative expenses ("SG&A"). The sum of the three is referred to by the Company as "the cost of credit" of the private label credit card program.

In addition, certain subsidiaries of the Company extend credit directly to customers in the ordinary course of business. The receivables due from customers were $42 million and $45 million as of February 3, 2013 and January 29, 2012, respectively. The Company's valuation reserve related to accounts receivable was not material to the Consolidated Financial Statements of the Company as of the end of fiscal 2012 or 2011.

Merchandise Inventories

The majority of the Company's Merchandise Inventories are stated at the lower of cost (first-in, first-out) or market, as determined by the retail inventory method. As the inventory retail value is adjusted regularly to reflect market conditions, the inventory valued using the retail method approximates the lower of cost or market. Certain subsidiaries, including retail operations in Canada and Mexico, and distribution centers, record Merchandise Inventories at the lower of cost or market, as determined by a cost method. These Merchandise Inventories represent approximately 24% of the total Merchandise Inventories balance. The Company evaluates the inventory valued using a cost method at the end of each quarter to ensure that it is carried at the lower of cost or market. The valuation allowance for Merchandise Inventories valued under a cost method was not material to the Consolidated Financial Statements of the Company as of the end of fiscal 2012 or 2011.

Independent physical inventory counts or cycle counts are taken on a regular basis in each store and distribution center to ensure that amounts reflected in the accompanying Consolidated Financial Statements for Merchandise Inventories are properly stated. During the period between physical inventory counts in stores, the Company accrues for estimated losses related to shrink on a store-by-store basis based on historical shrink results and current trends in the business. Shrink (or in the case of excess inventory, "swell") is the difference between the recorded amount of inventory and the physical inventory. Shrink may occur due to theft, loss, inaccurate records for the receipt of inventory or deterioration of goods, among other things.

Income Taxes

Income taxes are accounted for under the asset and liability method. The Company provides for federal, state and foreign income taxes currently payable, as well as for those deferred due to timing differences between reporting income and expenses for financial statement purposes versus tax purposes. Deferred tax assets and liabilities are recognized for the future tax consequences attributable to temporary differences between the financial statement carrying amounts of existing assets and liabilities and their respective tax bases. Deferred tax assets and liabilities are measured using enacted income tax rates expected to apply to taxable income in the years in which those temporary differences are expected to be recovered or settled. The effect of a change in income tax rates is recognized as income or expense in the period that includes the enactment date.

The Company recognizes the effect of income tax positions only if those positions are more likely than not of being sustained. Recognized income tax positions are measured at the largest amount that is greater than 50% likely of being realized. Changes in recognition or measurement are reflected in the period in which the change in judgment occurs.

The Company and its eligible subsidiaries file a consolidated U.S. federal income tax return. Non-U.S. subsidiaries and certain U.S. subsidiaries, which are consolidated for financial reporting purposes, are not eligible to be included in the Company's consolidated U.S. federal income tax return. Separate provisions for income taxes have been determined for these entities. The Company intends to reinvest substantially all of the unremitted earnings of its non-U.S. subsidiaries and postpone their remittance indefinitely. Accordingly, no provision for U.S. income taxes for these non-U.S. subsidiaries was recorded in the accompanying Consolidated Statements of Earnings.

Depreciation and Amortization

The Company's Buildings, Furniture, Fixtures and Equipment are recorded at cost and depreciated using the straight-line method over the estimated useful lives of the assets. Leasehold Improvements are amortized using the straight-line method over the original term of the lease or the useful life of the improvement, whichever is shorter. The Company's Property and Equipment is depreciated using the following estimated useful lives:

	Life
Buildings	5 – 45 years
Furniture, Fixtures and Equipment	2 – 20 years
Leasehold Improvements	5 – 45 years

Capitalized Software Costs

The Company capitalizes certain costs related to the acquisition and development of software and amortizes these costs using the straight-line method over the estimated useful life of the software, which is three to six years. These costs are included in Furniture, Fixtures and Equipment as discussed further in Note 4. Certain development costs not meeting the criteria for capitalization are expensed as incurred.

Revenues

The Company recognizes revenue, net of estimated returns and sales tax, at the time the customer takes possession of merchandise or receives services. The liability for sales returns is estimated based on historical return levels. When the Company receives payment from customers before the customer has taken possession of the merchandise or the service has been performed, the amount received is recorded as Deferred Revenue in the accompanying Consolidated Balance Sheets until the sale or service is complete. The Company also records Deferred Revenue for the sale of gift cards and recognizes this revenue upon the redemption of gift cards in Net Sales. Gift card breakage income is recognized based upon historical redemption patterns and represents the balance of gift cards for which the Company believes the likelihood of redemption by the customer is remote. During fiscal 2012, 2011 and 2010, the Company recognized $33 million, $42 million and $46 million, respectively, of gift card breakage income. This income is included in the accompanying Consolidated Statements of Earnings as a reduction in SG&A.

Services Revenue

Net Sales include services revenue generated through a variety of installation, home maintenance and professional service programs. In these programs, the customer selects and purchases material for a project, and the Company provides or arranges professional installation. These programs are offered through the Company's stores and in-home sales programs. Under certain programs, when the Company provides or arranges the installation of a project and the subcontractor provides material as part of the installation, both the material and labor are included in services revenue. The Company recognizes this revenue when the service for the customer is complete.

All payments received prior to the completion of services are recorded in Deferred Revenue in the accompanying Consolidated Balance Sheets. Services revenue was $3.2 billion, $2.9 billion and $2.7 billion for fiscal 2012, 2011 and 2010, respectively.

Self-Insurance

The Company is self-insured for certain losses related to general liability (including products liability), workers' compensation, employee group medical and automobile claims. The expected ultimate cost for claims incurred as of the balance sheet date is not discounted and is recognized as a liability. The expected ultimate cost of claims is estimated based upon analysis of historical data and actuarial estimates.

Prepaid Advertising

Television and radio advertising production costs, along with media placement costs, are expensed when the advertisement first appears. Amounts included in Other Current Assets in the accompanying Consolidated Balance Sheets relating to prepayments of production costs for print and broadcast advertising as well as sponsorship promotions were not material at the end of fiscal 2012 and 2011.

Vendor Allowances

Vendor allowances primarily consist of volume rebates that are earned as a result of attaining certain purchase levels and advertising co-op allowances for the promotion of vendors' products that are typically based on guaranteed minimum amounts with additional amounts being earned for attaining certain purchase levels. These vendor allowances are accrued as earned, with those allowances received as a result of attaining certain purchase levels accrued over the incentive period based on estimates of purchases.

Volume rebates and certain advertising co-op allowances earned are initially recorded as a reduction in Merchandise Inventories and a subsequent reduction in Cost of Sales when the related product is sold. Certain advertising co-op allowances that are reimbursements of specific, incremental and identifiable costs incurred to promote vendors' products are recorded as an offset against advertising expense. In fiscal 2012, 2011 and 2010, gross advertising expense was $831 million, $846 million and $864 million, respectively, and is included in SG&A. Specific, incremental and identifiable advertising co-op allowances were $85 million, $94 million and $90 million for fiscal 2012, 2011 and 2010, respectively, and are recorded as an offset to advertising expense in SG&A.

Cost of Sales

Cost of Sales includes the actual cost of merchandise sold and services performed, the cost of transportation of merchandise from vendors to the Company's stores, locations or customers, the operating cost of the Company's sourcing and distribution network and the cost of deferred interest programs offered through the Company's private label credit card program.

The cost of handling and shipping merchandise from the Company's stores, locations or distribution centers to the customer is classified as SG&A. The cost of shipping and handling, including internal costs and payments to third parties, classified as SG&A was $435 million, $430 million and $410 million in fiscal 2012, 2011 and 2010, respectively.

Impairment of Long-Lived Assets

The Company evaluates its long-lived assets each quarter for indicators of potential impairment. Indicators of impairment include current period losses combined with a history of losses, management's decision to relocate or close a store or other location before the end of its previously estimated useful life or when changes in other circumstances indicate the carrying amount of an asset may not be recoverable. The evaluation for long-lived assets is performed at the lowest level of identifiable cash flows, which is generally the individual store level.

The assets of a store with indicators of impairment are evaluated by comparing its undiscounted cash flows with its carrying value. The estimate of cash flows includes management's assumptions of cash inflows and outflows directly resulting from the use of those assets in operations, including gross margin on Net Sales, payroll and related items, occupancy costs, insurance allocations and other costs to operate a store. If the carrying value is greater than the undiscounted cash flows, an impairment loss is recognized for the difference between the carrying value and the estimated fair market value. Impairment losses are recorded as a component of SG&A in the accompanying Consolidated Statements of Earnings. When a leased location closes, the Company also recognizes in SG&A the net present value of future lease obligations less estimated sublease income. The Company recorded impairments and lease obligation costs on closings and relocations in the ordinary course of business, as well as for the closing of seven stores in China in fiscal 2012, which were not material to the Consolidated Financial Statements in fiscal 2012, 2011 or 2010.

Goodwill and Other Intangible Assets

Goodwill represents the excess of purchase price over the fair value of net assets acquired. The Company does not amortize goodwill but does assess the recoverability of goodwill in the third quarter of each fiscal year, or more often if indicators warrant, by determining whether the fair value of each reporting unit supports its carrying value. The Company assesses qualitative factors to determine whether it is more likely than not that the fair value of each reporting unit is less than its carrying amount as a basis for determining whether it is necessary to complete quantitative impairment assessments. During fiscal 2012, for all reporting units other than the China reporting unit, the Company used qualitative factors to determine that its goodwill balances for each reporting unit were not impaired. For the China reporting unit, the Company recorded a charge of $97 million to impair all of the goodwill associated with that reporting unit in fiscal 2012. Impairment charges related to the remaining goodwill were not material for fiscal 2012, 2011 or 2010.

The Company amortizes the cost of other intangible assets over their estimated useful lives, which range up to ten years, unless such lives are deemed indefinite. Intangible assets with indefinite lives are tested in the third quarter of each fiscal year for impairment, or more often if indicators warrant. Impairment charges related to other intangible assets were not material for fiscal 2012, 2011 or 2010.

Stock-Based Compensation

The per share weighted average fair value of stock options granted during fiscal 2012, 2011 and 2010 was $9.86, $7.42 and $6.70, respectively. The fair value of these options was determined at the date of grant using the Black-Scholes option-pricing model with the following assumptions:

	Fiscal Year Ended		
	February 3, 2013	January 29, 2012	January 30, 2011
Risk-free interest rate	**1.2%**	2.0%	3.1%
Assumed volatility	**27.0%**	27.3%	26.4%
Assumed dividend yield	**2.3%**	2.7%	2.9%
Assumed lives of options	**5 years**	5 years	5 years

Derivatives

The Company uses derivative financial instruments from time to time in the management of its interest rate exposure on long-term debt and its exposure on foreign currency fluctuations. The Company accounts for its derivative financial instruments in accordance with the Financial Accounting Standards Board Accounting Standards Codification ("FASB ASC") Subtopic 815-10. The fair value of the Company's derivative financial instruments is discussed in Note 11.

Comprehensive Income

Comprehensive Income includes Net Earnings adjusted for certain gains and losses that are excluded from Net Earnings under U.S. generally accepted accounting principles. Adjustments to Net Earnings and Accumulated Other Comprehensive Income consist primarily of foreign currency translation adjustments.

Foreign Currency Translation

Assets and liabilities denominated in a foreign currency are translated into U.S. dollars at the current rate of exchange on the last day of the reporting period. Revenues and expenses are generally translated using average exchange rates for the period and equity transactions are translated using the actual rate on the day of the transaction.

Segment Information

The Company operates within a single reportable segment primarily within North America. Net Sales for the Company outside the U.S. were $8.4 billion, $8.0 billion and $7.5 billion for fiscal 2012, 2011 and 2010, respectively. Long-lived assets outside the U.S. totaled $3.1 billion and $3.1 billion as of February 3, 2013 and January 29, 2012, respectively.

Reclassifications

Certain amounts in prior fiscal years have been reclassified to conform with the presentation adopted in the current fiscal year.

Five-Year Summary of Financial and Operating Results
The Home Depot, Inc. and Subsidiaries

amounts in millions, except where noted	2012[1]	2011	2010	2009	2008
STATEMENT OF EARNINGS DATA[2]					
Net sales	$ 74,754	$ 70,395	$ 67,997	$ 66,176	$ 71,288
Net sales increase (decrease) (%)	6.2	3.5	2.8	(7.2)	(7.8)
Earnings before provision for income taxes	7,221	6,068	5,273	3,982	3,590
Net earnings	4,535	3,883	3,338	2,620	2,312
Net earnings increase (decrease) (%)	16.8	16.3	27.4	13.3	(45.1)
Diluted earnings per share ($)	3.00	2.47	2.01	1.55	1.37
Diluted earnings per share increase (decrease) (%)	21.5	22.9	29.7	13.1	(39.6)
Diluted weighted average number of common shares	1,511	1,570	1,658	1,692	1,686
Gross margin – % of sales	34.6	34.5	34.3	33.9	33.7
Total operating expenses – % of sales	24.2	25.0	25.7	26.6	27.5
Interest and other, net – % of sales	0.7	0.8	0.8	1.2	1.1
Earnings before provision for income taxes – % of sales	9.7	8.6	7.8	6.0	5.0
Net earnings – % of sales	6.1	5.5	4.9	4.0	3.2
BALANCE SHEET DATA AND FINANCIAL RATIOS[2]					
Total assets	$ 41,084	$ 40,518	$ 40,125	$ 40,877	$ 41,164
Working capital	3,910	5,144	3,357	3,537	2,209
Merchandise inventories	10,710	10,325	10,625	10,188	10,673
Net property and equipment	24,069	24,448	25,060	25,550	26,234
Long-term debt	9,475	10,758	8,707	8,662	9,667
Stockholders' equity	17,777	17,898	18,889	19,393	17,777
Book value per share ($)	11.97	11.64	11.64	11.42	10.48
Long-term debt-to-equity (%)	53.3	60.1	46.1	44.7	54.4
Total debt-to-equity (%)	60.7	60.3	51.6	49.9	64.3
Current ratio	1.34:1	1.55:1	1.33:1	1.34:1	1.20:1
Inventory turnover	4.5x	4.3x	4.1x	4.1x	4.0x
Return on invested capital (%)	17.0	14.9	12.8	10.7	9.5
STATEMENT OF CASH FLOWS DATA					
Depreciation and amortization	$ 1,684	$ 1,682	$ 1,718	$ 1,806	$ 1,902
Capital expenditures	1,312	1,221	1,096	966	1,847
Cash dividends per share ($)	1.160	1.040	0.945	0.900	0.900
STORE DATA					
Number of stores	2,256	2,252	2,248	2,244	2,274
Square footage at fiscal year-end	235	235	235	235	238
Increase (decrease) in square footage (%)	—	—	—	(1.3)	1.3
Average square footage per store (in thousands)	104	104	105	105	105
STORE SALES AND OTHER DATA					
Comparable store sales increase (decrease) (%)[3]	4.6	3.4	2.9	(6.6)	(8.7)
Weighted average weekly sales per operating store (in thousands)	$ 627	$ 601	$ 581	$ 563	$ 601
Weighted average sales per square foot ($)	319	299	289	279	298
Number of customer transactions	1,364	1,318	1,306	1,274	1,272
Average ticket ($)	54.89	53.28	51.93	51.76	55.61
Number of associates at fiscal year-end (in thousands)[2]	340	331	321	317	322

(1) Fiscal year 2012 includes 53 weeks; all other fiscal years reported include 52 weeks.

(2) Continuing operations only.

(3) Includes Net Sales at locations open greater than 12 months, including relocated and remodeled stores and excluding closed stores. Retail stores become comparable on the Monday following their 365th day of operation. Comparable store sales is intended only as supplemental information and is not a substitute for Net Sales or Net Earnings presented in accordance with generally accepted accounting principles. Net Sales for the 53rd week of fiscal 2012 are not included in comparable store sales results for fiscal 2012.

Appendix B

Combined Journal

Most small businesses have just a few employees and can devote only a limited amount of time to the preparation of accounting records. To serve the needs of these businesses, accountants have developed certain types of record systems that have special time-saving and labor-saving features but still produce all the necessary financial information for management. One example of such a system is the combined journal discussed in this appendix.

Small firms play an important role in our economy today. In fact, almost one-half of the businesses in the United States are classified as small entities. Despite their limited size, these businesses need good accounting systems that can produce accurate and timely information.

Systems Involving the Combined Journal

The **combined journal,** also called the *combination journal*, provides the cornerstone for a simple yet effective accounting system in many small firms. As its name indicates, this journal combines features of the general journal and the special journals in a single record.

If a small business has enough transactions to make the general journal difficult to use but too few transactions to make it worthwhile to set up special journals, the combined journal offers a solution. It has many of the advantages of special journals but provides the simplicity of a single journal. Like the special journals, the combined journal contains separate money columns for the accounts used most often to record a firm's transactions. This speeds up the initial entry of transactions and permits summary postings at the end of the month. Most transactions can be recorded on a single line, and the need to write account names is minimized.

Other Accounts columns allow the recording of transactions that do not fit into any of the special columns. These columns are also used for entries that would normally appear in the general journal, such as adjusting and closing entries.

Some small firms just use a combined journal and a general ledger in their accounting systems. Others need one or more subsidiary ledgers in addition to the general ledger.

DESIGNING A COMBINED JOURNAL

To function effectively, a combined journal must be designed to meet the specific needs of a firm. For a new business, the accountant first studies the proposed operations and develops an appropriate chart of accounts. Then the accountant decides which accounts are likely to be used often enough in recording daily transactions to justify special columns in the combined journal.

Consider the combined journal on the next page, which belongs to Quality Lawn Care and Landscaping Services, a small business that provides lawn and landscaping services. In designing this journal before the firm opened, the accountant established a Cash section with Debit and Credit columns because it was known that the business would constantly be receiving cash from customers and paying out cash for expenses and other obligations. Debit and Credit columns were also set up in Accounts Receivable and Accounts Payable sections because the firm planned to offer credit to qualified customers and would make credit purchases of supplies and other items.

After further analysis it was realized that the business would have numerous entries for the sale of services, the payment of employee salaries, and the purchase of supplies. Therefore, columns were established for recording credits to *Sales*, debits to *Salaries Expense*, and debits to *Supplies*. Finally, a column was set up for an Other Accounts section to take care of transactions that cannot be entered in the special columns.

FIGURE B.1   Combined Journal

COMBINED JOURNAL

	DATE	CK. NO.	DESCRIPTION	POST. REF.	CASH DEBIT	CASH CREDIT	ACCOUNTS RECEIVABLE DEBIT	ACCOUNTS RECEIVABLE CREDIT
1	2016							
2	Jan. 3	711	Rent for month			1 0 5 0 00		
3	5		Treschell Seymore	✓			2 5 0 00	
4	6		C & M Garden Supply	✓				
5	7		Cash sales		2 3 0 0 00			
6	7	712	Payroll			7 8 0 00		
7	10		Annie McGowan	✓	1 5 0 00			1 5 0 00
8	12		The Greenery	✓				
9	13		Allen Clark	✓	4 4 0 00			4 4 0 00
10	14		Cash sales		2 7 7 0 00			
11	14	713	Payroll			7 8 0 00		
12	17		Jessica Savage	✓			1 7 5 00	
13	18		Lawn and Garden Supply	✓				
14	19	714	Telephone service			2 0 1 00		
15	20		Ned Jones	✓	1 2 5 00			1 2 5 00
16	20		Starlene Neal	✓			1 1 0 00	
17	21		Cash sales		2 5 4 0 00			
18	21	715	Payroll	✓		7 8 0 00		
19	24		Lawn and Garden Supply	✓				
20	25		Jeraldine Wells	✓			2 2 5 00	
21	26	716	Ace Garden Supply			4 6 0 00		
22	28		Cash sales		2 2 0 0 00			
23	28	717	Payroll			7 8 0 00		
24	30		Note issued for purchase					
25			of landscape equipment					
26	31		Juanda Fischer	✓			9 8 00	
27	31		Totals		10 5 2 5 00	4 8 3 1 00	8 5 8 00	7 1 5 00
28					(101)	(101)	(111)	(111)

RECORDING TRANSACTIONS IN THE COMBINED JOURNAL

The combined journal shown in Figure B.1 contains the January 2016 transactions of Quality Lawn Care and Landscaping Services. Notice that most of these transactions require only a single line and involve the use of just the special columns. The entries for major types of transactions are explained in the following paragraphs.

Payment of Expenses   During January, Quality Lawn Care and Landscaping Services issued checks to pay three kinds of expenses: rent, telephone service, and employee salaries. Notice how the payment of the monthly rent on January 3 was recorded in the combined journal. Since there is no special column for rent expense, the debit part of this entry appears in the Other Accounts section. The offsetting credit appears in the Cash Credit column. The payment of the monthly telephone bill on January 19 was recorded in a similar manner. However, when employee salaries were paid on January 7, 14, 21, and 28, both parts of the entries could be made in special columns. Because the firm has a weekly payroll period, a separate column in the combined journal was set up for debits to Salaries Expense.

PAGE ___1___

ACCOUNTS PAYABLE DEBIT	ACCOUNTS PAYABLE CREDIT	SALES CREDIT	SUPPLIES DEBIT	SALARIES EXPENSE DEBIT	OTHER ACCOUNTS ACCOUNT TITLE	POST REF.	DEBIT	CREDIT	
									1
					Rent Expense	511	1 0 5 0 00		2
		2 5 0 00							3
	4 5 0 00		4 5 0 00						4
		2 3 0 0 00							5
				7 8 0 00					6
									7
	2 2 5 00		2 2 5 00						8
									9
		2 7 7 0 00							10
				7 8 0 00					11
		1 7 5 00							12
	1 2 0 0 00				Equipment	131	1 2 0 0 00		13
					Telephone Exp.	514	2 0 1 00		14
									15
		1 1 0 00							16
		2 5 4 0 00							17
				7 8 0 00					18
	2 9 0 00		2 9 0 00						19
		2 2 5 00							20
4 6 0 00									21
		2 2 0 0 00							22
				7 8 0 00					23
					Equipment	131	8 5 0 0 00		24
					Notes Payable	201		8 5 0 0 00	25
		9 8 00							26
4 6 0 00	2 1 6 5 00	10 6 6 8 00	9 6 5 00	3 1 2 0 00			10 9 5 1 00	8 5 0 0 00	27
(202)	(202)	(401)	(121)	(517)			(X)	(X)	28

Sales on Credit   On January 5, 17, 20, 25, and 31, Quality Lawn Care and Landscaping Services sold services on credit. The necessary entries were made in two special columns of the combined journal—the Accounts Receivable Debit column and the Sales Credit column.

Cash Sales   Entries for the firm's weekly cash sales were recorded on January 7, 14, 21, and 28. Again, special columns were used—the Cash Debit column and the Sales Credit column.

Cash Received on Account   When Quality Lawn Care and Landscaping Services collected cash on account from credit customers on January 10, 13, and 20, the transactions were entered in the Cash Debit column and the Accounts Receivable Credit column.

Purchases of Supplies on Credit   Because the firm's combined journal includes a Supplies Debit column and an Accounts Payable Credit column, all purchases of supplies on credit can be recorded in special columns. Refer to the entries made on January 6, 12, and 24.

Purchases of Equipment on Credit   On January 18, Quality Lawn Care and Landscaping Services bought some store equipment on credit. Since there is no special column for equipment, the debit part of the entry was made in the Other Accounts section. The offsetting credit appears in the Accounts Payable Credit column.

Payments on Account   Any payments made on account to creditors are recorded in two special columns—Accounts Payable Debit and Cash Credit, as shown in the entry of January 26.

Issuance of a Promissory Note   On January 30, the business purchased new cleaning equipment and issued a promissory note to the seller. Notice that both the debit to *Equipment* and the credit to *Notes Payable* had to be recorded in the Other Accounts section.

POSTING FROM THE COMBINED JOURNAL

One of the advantages of the combined journal is that it simplifies the posting process. All amounts in the special columns can be posted to the general ledger on a summary basis at the end of the month. Only the figures that appear in the Other Accounts section require individual postings to the general ledger during the month. Of course, if the firm has subsidiary ledgers, individual postings must also be made to these ledgers.

Daily Postings   The procedures followed at Quality Lawn Care and Landscaping Services will illustrate the techniques used to post from the combined journal. Each day any entries appearing in the Other Accounts section are posted to the proper accounts in the general ledger. For example, refer to the combined journal shown on pages B-2 and B-3. The five amounts listed in the Other Accounts Debit and Credit columns were posted individually during the month. The account numbers recorded in the Posting Reference column of the Other Accounts section show that the postings have been made.

Because Quality Lawn Care and Landscaping Services has subsidiary ledgers for accounts receivable and accounts payable, individual postings were also made on a daily basis to these ledgers. As each amount was posted, a check mark was placed in the Posting Reference column of the combined journal.

End-of-Month Postings   At the end of the month, the combined journal is totaled, proved, and ruled. Then the totals of the special columns are posted to the general ledger. Proving the combined journal involves a comparison of the column totals to make sure that the debits and credits are equal. The following procedure is used:

Proof of Combined Journal	
	Debits
Cash Debit Column	10,525
Accounts Receivable Debit Column	858
Accounts Payable Debit Column	460
Supplies Debit Column	965
Salaries Expense Debit Column	3,120
Other Accounts Debit Column	10,951
	26,879
	Credits
Cash Credit Column	4,831
Accounts Receivable Credit Column	715
Accounts Payable Credit Column	2,165
Sales Credit Column	10,668
Other Accounts Credit Column	8,500
	26,879

After the combined journal is proved, all column totals except those in the Other Accounts section are posted to the appropriate general ledger accounts. As each total is posted, the account number is entered beneath the column in the journal. Notice that an X is used to indicate that the column totals in the Other Accounts section are not posted, since the individual amounts were posted on a daily basis.

TYPICAL USES OF THE COMBINED JOURNAL

The combined journal is used most often in small professional offices and small service businesses. It is less suitable for merchandising businesses but is sometimes used in firms of this type if they are very small and have only a limited number of transactions.

Professional Offices   The combined journal can be ideal to record the transactions that occur in a professional office, such as the office of a doctor, lawyer, accountant, or architect. However, special journals are more efficient if transactions become very numerous or are too varied.

Service Businesses   The use of the combined journal to record the transactions of Quality Lawn Care and Landscaping Services has already been illustrated. The combined journal may be advantageous for a small service business, provided that the volume of transactions does not become excessive and the nature of the transactions does not become too complex.

Merchandising Businesses   The combined journal can be used by a merchandising business, but only if the firm is quite small and has a limited number and variety of transactions involving few accounts. However, even for a small merchandising business, the use of special journals might prove more advantageous.

Disadvantages of the Combined Journal

If the variety of transactions is so great that many different accounts are required, the combined journal will not work well. Either the business will have to set up so many columns that the journal will become unwieldy, or it will be necessary to record so many transactions in the Other Accounts columns that little efficiency will result. As a general rule, if the transactions of a business are numerous enough to merit the use of special journals, any attempt to substitute the combined journal is a mistake. Remember that each special journal can be designed for maximum efficiency in recording transactions.

Glossary

Absorption costing The accounting procedure whereby all manufacturing costs, including fixed costs, are included in the cost of goods manufactured

Accelerated method of depreciation A method of depreciating asset cost that allocates greater amounts of depreciation to an asset's early years of useful life

Account balance The difference between the amounts recorded on the two sides of an account

Account form balance sheet A balance sheet that lists assets on the left and liabilities and owner's equity on the right (*see also* Report form balance sheet)

Accounting The process by which financial information about a business is recorded, classified, summarized, interpreted, and communicated to owners, managers, and other interested parties

Accounting cycle A series of steps performed during each accounting period to classify, record, and summarize data for a business and to produce needed financial information

Accounting Standards Codification The source of authoritative U.S. GAAP

Accounting Standards Update Changes to Accounting Standards Codification are communicated through Accounting Standards Update covering approximately 90 topics

Accounting system A process designed to accumulate, classify, and summarize financial data

Accounts Written records of the assets, liabilities, and owner's equity of a business

Accounts payable Amounts a business must pay in the future

Accounts payable ledger A subsidiary ledger that contains a separate account for each creditor

Accounts receivable Claims for future collection from customers

Accounts receivable ledger A subsidiary ledger that contains credit customer accounts

Accounts receivable turnover A measure of the speed with which sales on account are collected; the ratio of net credit sales to average receivables

Accrual basis A system of accounting by which all revenues and expenses are matched and reported on financial statements for the applicable period, regardless of when the cash related to the transaction is received or paid

Accrued expenses Expense items that relate to the current period but have not yet been paid and do not yet appear in the accounting records

Accrued income Income that has been earned but not yet received and recorded

Acid-test ratio A measure of immediate liquidity; the ratio of quick assets to current liabilities

Adjusting entries Journal entries made to update accounts for items that were not recorded during the accounting period

Adjustments *See* Adjusting entries

Aging the accounts receivable Classifying accounts receivable balances according to how long they have been outstanding

Allowance method A method of recording uncollectible accounts that estimates losses from uncollectible accounts and charges them to expense in the period when the sales are recorded

Amortization The process of periodically transferring the acquisition cost of intangible assets with estimated useful lives to an expense account

Appropriation of retained earnings A formal declaration of an intention to restrict dividends

Articles of partnership *See* Partnership agreement

Asset turnover A measure of the effective use of assets in making sales; the ratio of net sales to total assets

Assets Property owned by a business

Audit trail A chain of references that makes it possible to trace information, locate errors, and prevent fraud

Auditing The review of financial statements to assess their fairness and adherence to generally accepted accounting principles

Auditor's report An independent accountant's review of a firm's financial statements

Authorized capital stock The number of shares authorized for issue by the corporate charter

Average collection period The ratio of 365 days to the accounts receivable turnover; also called the number of days' sales in receivables

Average cost method A method of inventory costing using the average cost of units of an item available for sale during the period to arrive at cost of the ending inventory

Average method of process costing A method of costing that combines the cost of beginning inventory for each cost element with the costs during the current period

Balance ledger form A ledger account form that shows the balance of the account after each entry is posted

Balance sheet A formal report of a business's financial condition on a certain date; reports the assets, liabilities, and owner's equity of the business

Bank draft A check written by a bank that orders another bank to pay the stated amount to a specific party

Bank reconciliation statement A statement that accounts for all differences between the balance on the bank statement and the book balance of cash

Banker's year A 360-day period used to calculate interest on a note

Bill of lading A business document that lists goods accepted for transportation

Blank endorsement A signature of the payee written on the back of the check that transfers ownership of the check without specifying to whom or for what purpose

Bond indenture A bond contract

Bond issue costs Costs incurred in issuing bonds, such as legal and accounting fees and printing costs

Bond retirement When a bond is paid and the liability is removed from the company's balance sheet

Bond sinking fund investment A fund established to accumulate assets to pay off bonds when they mature

Bonding The process by which employees are investigated by an insurance company that will insure the business against losses through employee theft or mishandling of funds

Bonds payable Long-term debt instruments that are written promises to repay the principal at a future date; interest is due at a fixed rate payable over the life of the bond

Book value That portion of an asset's original cost that has not yet been depreciated

Book value per share The total equity applicable to a class of stock divided by the number of shares outstanding

Brand name *See* Trade name

Break even A point at which revenue equals expenses

Break-even point (BEP) The sales volume when total revenue equals total expenses

Budget An operating plan expressed in monetary units

Budget performance report A comparison of actual costs and budgeted costs

Business transaction A financial event that changes the resources of a firm

Bylaws The guidelines for conducting a corporation's business affairs

Call price The amount the corporation must pay for the bond when it is called

Callable bonds Bonds that allow the issuing corporation to require the holder to surrender the bonds for payment before their maturity date

Callable preferred stock Stock that gives the issuing corporation the right to repurchase the preferred shares from the stockholders at a specific price

Canceled check A check paid by the bank on which it was drawn

Capacity A facility's ability to produce or use

Capital Financial investment in a business; equity

Capital stock ledger A subsidiary ledger that contains a record of each stockholder's purchases, transfers, and current balance of shares owned; also called stockholders' ledger

Capital stock transfer journal A record of stock transfers used for posting to the stockholders' ledger

Capitalized costs All costs recorded as part of an asset's costs

Carrying value of bonds The balance of the *Bonds Payable* account plus the *Premium on Bonds Payable* account minus the *Discount on Bonds Payable* account; also called *book value of bonds*

Cash In accounting, currency, coins, checks, money orders, and funds on deposit in a bank

Cash discount A discount offered by suppliers for payment received within a specified period of time

Cash equivalents Assets that are easily convertible into known amounts of cash

Cash payments journal A special journal used to record transactions involving the payment of cash

Cash receipts journal A special journal used to record and post transactions involving the receipt of cash

Cash register proof A verification that the amount of currency and coins in a cash register agrees with the amount shown on the cash register audit tape

***Cash Short or Over* account** An account used to record any discrepancies between the amount of currency and coins in the cash register and the amount shown on the audit tape

Cashier's check A draft on the issuing bank's own funds

Certified public accountant (CPA) An independent accountant who provides accounting services to the public for a fee

Charge-account sales Sales made through the use of open-account credit or one of various types of credit cards

Chart of accounts A list of the accounts used by a business to record its financial transactions

Check A written order signed by an authorized person instructing a bank to pay a specific sum of money to a designated person or business

Chronological order Organized in the order in which the events occur

Classification A means of identifying each account as an asset, liability, or owner's equity

Classified financial statement A format by which revenues and expenses on the income statement, and assets and liabilities on the balance sheet, are divided into groups of similar accounts and a subtotal is given for each group

Closing entries Journal entries that transfer the results of operations (net income or net loss) to owner's equity and reduce the revenue, expense, and drawing account balances to zero

Collateral trust bonds Bonds secured by the pledge of securities, such as stocks or bonds of other companies

Combined journal A journal that combines features of the general journal and the special journals in a single record

Commercial draft A note issued by one party that orders another party to pay a specified sum on a specified date

Commission basis A method of paying employees according to a percentage of net sales

Common costs Costs not directly traceable to a specific segment of a business

Common-size statements Financial statements with items expressed as percentages of a base amount

Common stock The general class of stock issued when no other class of stock is authorized; each share carries the same rights and privileges as every other share. Even if preferred stock is issued, common stock will also be issued

***Common Stock Dividend Distributable* account** Equity account used to record par, or stated, value of shares to be issued as the result of the declaration of a stock dividend

Comparative statements Financial statements presented side by side for two or more years

Compensation record *See* Individual earnings record

Compound entry A journal entry with more than one debit or credit

Computer software An intangible asset; written programs that instruct a computer's hardware to do certain tasks

Conceptual framework A basic framework developed by the FASB to provide conceptual guidelines for financial statements. The most important features are statements of qualitative features of statements, basic assumptions underlying statements, basic accounting principles, and modifying constraints

Conservatism The concept that revenue and assets should be understated rather than overstated if GAAP allows alternatives. Similarly, expenses and liabilities should be overstated rather than understated

Contingent liability An item that can become a liability if certain things happen

Contra account An account with a normal balance that is opposite that of a related account

Contra asset account An asset account with a credit balance, which is contrary to the normal balance of an asset account

Contra revenue account An account with a debit balance, which is contrary to the normal balance for a revenue account

Contribution margin Gross profit on sales minus direct expenses; revenues minus variable costs

Control account An account that links a subsidiary ledger and the general ledger since its balance summarizes the balances of the accounts in the subsidiary ledger

Controllable fixed costs Costs that the segment manager can control

Convertible bonds Bonds that give the owner the right to convert the bonds into common stock under specified conditions

Convertible preferred stock Preferred stock that conveys the right to convert that stock to common stock after a specified date or during a period of time

Copyright An intangible asset; an exclusive right granted by the federal government to produce, publish, and sell a literary or artistic work for a period equal to the creator's life plus 70 years

Corporate charter A document issued by a state government that establishes a corporation

Corporation A publicly or privately owned business entity that is separate from its owners and has a legal right to own property and do business in its own name; stockholders are not responsible for the debts or taxes of the business

Correcting entry A journal entry made to correct an erroneous entry

Cost basis principle The principle that requires assets to be recorded at their cost at the time they are acquired

Cost-benefit test If accounting concepts suggest a particular accounting treatment for an item but it appears that the theoretically correct treatment would require an unreasonable amount of work, the accountant may analyze the benefits and costs of the preferred treatment to see if the benefit gained from its adoption is justified by the cost

Cost center A business segment that incurs costs but does not produce revenue

Cost of goods sold The actual cost to the business of the merchandise sold to customers

Cost of production report Summarizes all costs charged to each department and shows the costs assigned to the goods transferred out of the department and to the goods still in process

Cost variance The difference between the total standard cost and the total actual cost

Coupon bonds Unregistered bonds that have coupons attached for each interest payment; also called *bearer bonds*

Credit An entry on the right side of an account

Credit memorandum (accounts receivable) A note verifying that a customer's account is being reduced by the amount of a sales return or sales allowance plus any sales tax that may have been involved

Credit memorandum (banking) A form that explains any addition, other than a deposit, to a checking account

Credit terms Terms for payment on credit by buyer to seller

Creditor One to whom money is owed

Cumulative preferred stock Stock that conveys to its owners the right to receive the preference dividend for the current year and any prior years in which the preference dividend was not paid before common stockholders receive any dividends

Current assets Assets consisting of cash, items that normally will be converted into cash within one year, or items that will be used up within one year

Current liabilities Debts that must be paid within one year

Current ratio A relationship between current assets and current liabilities that provides a measure of a firm's ability to pay its current debts (current ratio = current assets ÷ current liabilities)

Debentures Unsecured bonds backed only by a corporation's general credit

Debit An entry on the left side of an account

Debit memorandum A form that explains any deduction, other than a check, from a checking account

Declaration date The date on which the board of directors declares a dividend

Declining-balance method An accelerated method of depreciation in which an asset's book value at the beginning of a year is multiplied by a percentage to determine depreciation for the year

Deferred expenses *See* Prepaid expenses

Deferred income *See* Unearned income

Deferred income taxes The amount of taxes that will be payable in the future as a result of the difference between taxable income and income for financial statement purposes in the current year and in past years

Departmental income statement Income statement that shows each department's contribution margin and net income from operations after all expenses are allocated

Depletion Allocating the cost of a natural resource to expense over the period in which the resource produces revenue

Deposit in transit A deposit that is recorded in the cash receipts journal but that reaches the bank too late to be shown on the monthly bank statement

Deposit slip A form prepared to record the deposit of cash or checks to a bank account

Depreciation Allocation of the cost of a long-term asset to operations during its expected useful life

Differential cost The difference in cost between one alternative and another

Direct charge-off method A method of recording uncollectible account losses as they occur

Direct costing The accounting procedure whereby only variable costs are included in the cost of goods manufactured, and fixed manufacturing costs are written off as expenses in the period in which they are incurred

Direct expenses Operating expenses that are identified directly with a department and are recorded by department

Direct labor The costs attributable to personnel who work directly on the product being manufactured

Direct materials All items that go into a product and become a part of it

Direct method A means of reporting sources and uses of cash under which all revenue and expenses reported on the income statement appear in the operating section of the statement of cash flows and show the cash received or paid out for each type of transaction

Discount on bonds payable The excess of the face value over the price received by the corporation for a bond

Discounting Deducting the interest from the principal on a note payable or receivable in advance

Discussion memorandum An explanation of a topic under consideration by the Financial Accounting Standards Board

Dishonored check A check returned to the depositor unpaid because of insufficient funds in the drawer's account; also called an *NSF check*

Dissolution The legal term for termination of a partnership

Distributive share The amount of net income or net loss allocated to each partner

Dividends Distributions of the profits of a corporation to its shareholders

Donated capital Capital resulting from the receipt of gifts by a corporation

Double-declining-balance method A method of depreciation that uses a rate equal to twice the straight-line rate and applies that rate to the book value of the asset at the beginning of the year

Double-entry system An accounting system that involves recording the effects of each transaction as debits and credits

Draft A written order that requires one party (a person or business) to pay a stated sum of money to another party

Drawee The bank on which a check is written

Drawer The person or firm issuing a check

Drawing account A special type of owner's equity account set up to record the owner's withdrawal of cash from the business

Economic entity A business or organization whose major purpose is to produce a profit for its owners

Electronic funds transfer (EFT) An electronic transfer of money from one account to another

Employee A person who is hired by and works under the control and direction of the employer

Employee's Withholding Allowance Certificate, Form W-4 A form used to claim exemption (withholding) allowances

Employer's Annual Federal Unemployment Tax Return, Form 940 Preprinted government form used by the employer to report unemployment taxes for the calendar year

Employer's Quarterly Federal Tax Return, Form 941 Preprinted government form used by the employer to report payroll tax information relating to social security, Medicare, and employee income tax withholding to the Internal Revenue Service

Endorsement A written authorization that transfers ownership of a check

Entity Anything having its own separate identity, such as an individual, a town, a university, or a business

Equity An owner's financial interest in a business

Equivalent production The estimated number of units that could have been started and completed with the same effort and costs incurred in the department during the same time period

Exempt employees Salaried employees who hold supervisory or managerial positions who are not subject to the maximum hour and overtime pay provisions of the Wage and Hour Law

Expense An outflow of cash, use of other assets, or incurring of a liability

Experience rating system A system that rewards an employer for maintaining steady employment conditions by reducing the firm's state unemployment tax rate

Exposure draft A proposed solution to a problem being considered by the Financial Accounting Standards Board

Extraordinary, Nonrecurring Items Transactions that are highly unusual, clearly unrelated to routine operations, and that do not frequently occur

Face interest rate The contractual interest specified on the bond

Face value An amount of money indicated to be paid, exclusive of interest or discounts

Fair market value The current worth of an asset or the price the asset would bring if sold on the open market

Federal unemployment taxes (FUTA) Taxes levied by the federal government against employers to benefit unemployed workers

Financial statements Periodic reports of a firm's financial position or operating results

Financing activities Transactions with those who provide cash to the business to carry on its activities

Finished goods inventory The cost of completed products ready for sale; corresponds to the *Merchandise Inventory* account of a merchandising business

Finished goods subsidiary ledger A ledger containing a record for each of the different types of finished products

First in, first out (FIFO) method A method of inventory costing that assumes the oldest merchandise is sold first

Fixed budget A budget representing only one level of activity

Fixed costs Costs that do not change in total as the level of activity changes

Flexible budget A budget that shows the budgeted costs at various levels of activity

Footing A small pencil figure written at the base of an amount column showing the sum of the entries in the column

Franchise An intangible asset; a right to exclusive dealership granted by a governmental unit or a business entity

***Freight In* account** An account showing transportation charges for items purchased

Full disclosure principle The requirement that all information that might affect the user's interpretation of the profitability and financial position of a business be disclosed in the financial statements or in notes to the statements

Full endorsement A signature transferring a check to a specific person, firm, or bank

Fundamental accounting equation The relationship between assets and liabilities plus owner's equity

Gain The disposition of an asset for more than its book value

General journal A financial record for entering all types of business transactions; a record of original entry

General ledger A permanent, classified record of all accounts used in a firm's operation; a record of final entry

General partner A member of a partnership who has unlimited liability

Generally accepted accounting principles (GAAP) Accounting standards developed and applied by professional accountants

Going concern assumption The assumption that a firm will continue to operate indefinitely

Goodwill An intangible asset; the value of a business in excess of the net value of its identifiable assets

Governmental accounting Accounting work performed for a federal, state, or local governmental unit

Gross profit The difference between net sales and the cost of goods sold

Gross profit method A method of estimating inventory cost based on the assumption that the rate of gross profit on sales and the ratio of cost of goods sold to net sales are relatively constant from period to period

Gross profit percentage The amount of gross profit from each dollar of sales (gross profit percentage = gross profit ÷ net sales)

High-low point method A method to determine the fixed and variable components of a semivariable cost

Historical cost basis principle *See* Cost basis principle

Horizontal analysis Computing the percentage change for individual items in the financial statements from year to year

Hourly rate basis A method of paying employees according to a stated rate per hour

Impairment A situation that occurs when the asset is determined to have a fair market value less than its book value

Income statement A formal report of business operations covering a specific period of time; also called a profit and loss statement or a statement of income and expenses

Income Summary **account** A special owner's equity account that is used only in the closing process to summarize the results of operations

Income tax method A method of recording the trade-in of an asset for income tax purposes. It does not permit a gain or loss to be recognized on the transaction.

Independent contractor One who is paid by a company to carry out a specific task or job but is not under the direct supervision or control of the company

Indirect expenses Operating expenses that cannot be readily identified and are not closely related to activity within a department

Indirect labor Costs attributable to personnel who support production but are not directly involved in the manufacture of a product; for example, supervisory, repair and maintenance, and janitorial staff

Indirect materials and supplies Materials used in manufacturing a product that may not become a part of the product

Indirect method A means of reporting cash generated from operating activities by treating net income as the primary source of cash in the operating section of the statement of cash flows and adjusting that amount for changes in current assets and liabilities associated with net income, noncash transactions, and other items

Individual earnings record An employee record that contains information needed to compute earnings and complete tax reports

Industry averages Financial ratios and percentages reflecting averages for similar companies

Industry practice constraint In a few limited cases unusual operating characteristics of an industry, usually based on risk, for which special accounting principles and procedures have been developed. These may not conform completely with GAAP for other industries

Intangible assets Assets that lack a physical substance, such as goodwill, patents, copyrights, and computer software, although software has, in a sense, a physical attribute

Interest The fee charged for the use of money

International accounting The study of accounting principles used by different countries

Interpret To understand and explain the meaning and importance of something (such as financial statements)

Inventory sheet A form used to list the volume and type of goods a firm has in stock

Inventory turnover The number of times inventory is purchased and sold during the accounting period (inventory turnover cost of goods sold average inventory)

Investing activities Transactions that involve the acquisition or disposal of long-term assets

Invoice A customer billing for merchandise bought on credit

Job order A specific order for a specific batch of manufactured items

Job order cost accounting A cost accounting system that determines the unit cost of manufactured items for each separate production order

Job order cost sheet A record of all manufacturing costs charged to a specific job

Journal The record of original entry

Journalizing Recording transactions in a journal

Just-in-time system An inventory system in which raw materials are ordered so they arrive just in time to be placed into production

Labor efficiency variance *See* Labor time variance

Labor rate variance The difference between the actual labor rate per hour and the standard labor rate per hour multiplied by the actual number of hours worked on the job

Labor time variance The difference between the actual hours worked and the standard labor hours allowed for the job multiplied by the standard cost per hour

Last in, first out (LIFO) method A method of inventory costing that assumes that the most recently purchased merchandise is sold first

Ledger The record of final entry

Leveraged buyout Purchasing a business by acquiring the stock and obligating the business to pay the debt incurred

Leveraging Using borrowed funds to earn a profit greater than the interest that must be paid on the borrowing

Liabilities Debts or obligations of a business

Limited liability company (LLC) Provides limited liability to the owners, who can elect to have the profits taxed at the LLC level or on their individual tax returns

Limited liability partnership (LLP) A partnership that provides some limited liability for all partners

Limited partner A member of a partnership whose liability is limited to his or her investment in the partnership

Limited partnership A partnership having one or more limited partners

Liquidation Termination of a business by distributing all assets and discontinuing the business

Liquidation value Value of assets to be applied to preferred stock, usually par value or an amount in excess of par value, if the corporation is liquidated

Liquidity The ease with which an item can be converted into cash; the ability of a business to pay its debts when due

List price An established retail price

Long-term liabilities Debts of a business that are due more than one year in the future

Loss The disposition of an asset for less than its book value

Lower of cost or market rule The principle by which inventory is reported at either its original cost or its replacement cost, whichever is lower

Management advisory services Services designed to help clients improve their information systems or their business performance

Managerial accounting Accounting work carried on by an accountant employed by a single business in industry; the branch of accounting that provides financial information about business segments, activities, or products

Manufacturing business A business that sells goods that it has produced

Manufacturing cost budget A budget made for each manufacturing cost

Manufacturing margin Sales minus the variable cost of goods sold

Manufacturing overhead All manufacturing costs that are not classified as direct materials or direct labor

Manufacturing overhead ledger A subsidiary ledger that contains a record for each overhead item

Manufacturing Summary account The account to which all items on the statement of cost of goods manufactured are closed; similar to the *Income Summary* account

Marginal income The manufacturing margin minus variable operating expenses

Markdown Price reduction below the original markon

Market interest rate The interest rate a corporation is willing to pay and investors are willing to accept at the current time

Market price The price the business would pay to buy an item of inventory through usual channels in usual quantities

Market value The price per share at which stock is bought and sold

Markon The difference between the cost and the initial retail price of merchandise

Markup A price increase above the original markon

Matching principle The concept that revenue and the costs incurred in earning the revenue should be matched in the appropriate accounting periods

Materiality constraint The significance of an item in relation to a particular situation or set of facts

Materials price variance The difference between the actual price and the standard cost for materials multiplied by the actual quantity of materials used

Materials quantity variance The difference between the actual quantity used and the quantity of materials allowed multiplied by the standard cost of the materials

Materials requisition A form that describes the item and quantity needed and shows the job or purpose

Materials usage variance See Materials quantity variance

Maturity value The total amount (principal plus interest) that must be paid when a note comes due

Medicare tax A tax levied on employees and employers to provide medical care for the employee and the employee's spouse after each has reached age 65

Memorandum entry An informational entry in the general journal

Merchandise inventory The stock of goods a merchandising business keeps on hand

Merchandising business A business that sells goods purchased for resale

Merit rating system See Experience rating system

Minute book A book in which accurate and complete records of all meetings of stockholders and directors are kept

Monetary unit assumption It is assumed that only those items and events that can be measured in monetary terms are included in the financial statements. An inherent part of this assumption is that the monetary unit is stable

Mortgage loan A long-term debt created when a note is given as part of the purchase price for land or buildings

Multiple-step income statement A type of income statement on which several subtotals are computed before the net income is calculated

Mutual agency The characteristic of a partnership by which each partner is empowered to act as an agent for the partnership, binding the firm by his or her acts

Negotiable A financial instrument whose ownership can be transferred to another person or business

Negotiable instrument A financial document containing a promise or order to pay that meets all requirements of the Uniform Commercial Code in order to be transferable to another party

Net book value The cost of an asset minus its accumulated depreciation, depletion, or amortization, also known as book value

Net income The result of an excess of revenue over expenses

Net income line The worksheet line immediately following the column totals on which net income (or net loss) is recorded in two places: the Income Statement section and the Balance Sheet section

Net loss The result of an excess of expenses over revenue

Net price The list price less all trade discounts

Net sales The difference between the balance in the *Sales* account and the balance in the *Sales Returns and Allowances* account

Net salvage value The salvage value of an asset less any costs to remove or sell the asset

Neutrality concept The concept that information in financial statements cannot be selected or presented in a way to favor one set of interested parties over another

Noncumulative preferred stock Stock that conveys to its owners the stated preference dividend for the current year but no rights to dividends for years in which none were declared

Nonparticipating preferred stock Stock that conveys to its owners the right to only the preference dividend amount specified on the stock certificate

No-par-value stock Stock that is not assigned a par value in the corporate charter

Normal balance The increase side of an account

Note payable A liability representing a written promise by the maker of the note (the debtor) to pay another party (the creditor) a specified amount at a specified future date

Note receivable An asset representing a written promise by another party (the debtor) to pay the note holder (the creditor) a specified amount at a specified future date

On account An arrangement to allow payment at a later date; also called a charge account or open-account credit

Open-account credit A system that allows the sale of services or goods with the understanding that payment will be made at a later date

Operating activities Routine business transactions—selling goods or services and incurring expenses

Operating assets and liabilities Current assets and current liabilities

Opportunity cost Potential earnings or benefits that are given up because a certain course of action is taken

Organization costs The costs associated with establishing a corporation; an intangible asset account

Outstanding checks Checks that have been recorded in the cash payments journal but have not yet been paid by the bank

Overapplied overhead The result of applied overhead exceeding the actual overhead costs

Overhead application rate The rate at which the estimated cost of overhead is charged to each job

Owner's equity The financial interest of the owner of a business; also called proprietorship or net worth

Paid-in capital Capital acquired from capital stock transactions

Par value An amount assigned by the corporate charter to each share of stock for accounting purposes

Participating preferred stock Stock that conveys the right not only to the preference dividend amount but also to a share of other dividends paid

Partnership A business entity owned by two or more people who carry on a business for profit and who are legally responsible for the debts and taxes of the business

Partnership agreement A legal contract forming a partnership and specifying certain details of operation

Patent An intangible asset; an exclusive right given by the U.S. Patent Office to manufacture and sell an invention for a period of 20 years from the date the patent is granted

Payee The person or firm to whom a check is payable

Payment date The date that dividends are paid

Payroll register A record of payroll information for each employee for the pay period

Periodic inventory Inventory based on a periodic count of goods on hand

Periodic inventory system An inventory system in which the merchandise inventory balance is only updated when a physical inventory is taken

Periodicity of income assumption The concept that economic activities of an entity can be divided logically and identified with specific time periods, such as the year or quarter

Permanent account An account that is kept open from one accounting period to the next

Perpetual inventory Inventory based on a running total of number of units

Perpetual inventory system An inventory system that tracks the inventories on hand at all times

Petty cash analysis sheet A form used to record transactions involving petty cash

Petty cash fund A special-purpose fund used to handle payments involving small amounts of money

Petty cash voucher A form used to record the payments made from a petty cash fund

Physical inventory An actual count of the number of units of each type of good on hand

Piece-rate basis A method of paying employees according to the number of units produced

Plant and equipment Property that will be used in the business for longer than one year

Postclosing trial balance A statement that is prepared to prove the equality of total debits and credits after the closing process is completed

Postdated check A check dated some time in the future

Posting Transferring data from a journal to a ledger

Preemptive right A shareholder's right to purchase a proportionate amount of any new stock issued at a later date

Preference dividend A basic or stated dividend rate for preferred stock that must be paid before dividends can be paid on common stock

Preferred stock A class of stock that has special claims on the corporate profits or, in case of liquidation, on corporate assets

Premium on bonds payable The excess of the price paid over the face value of a bond

Prepaid expenses Expense items acquired, recorded, and paid for in advance of their use

Price-earnings ratio The ratio of the current market value of common stock to earnings per share of that stock

Principal The amount shown on the face of a note

Private sector The business sector, which is represented in developing accounting principles by the Financial Accounting Standards Board (FASB)

Process cost accounting A cost accounting system whereby unit costs of manufactured items are determined by totaling unit costs in each production department

Process cost accounting system A method of accounting in which costs are accumulated for each process or department and then transferred on to the next process or department

Production order *See* Job order

Profit center A business segment that produces revenue

Promissory note A written promise to pay a specified amount of money on a specific date

Property, plant, and equipment Long-term assets that are used in the operation of a business and that are subject to depreciation (except for land, which is not depreciated)

Public accountants Members of firms that perform accounting services for other companies

Public sector The government sector, which is represented in developing accounting principles by the Securities and Exchange Commission (SEC)

Purchase allowance A price reduction from the amount originally billed

Purchase invoice A bill received for goods purchased

Purchase order An order to the supplier of goods specifying items needed, quantity, price, and credit terms

Purchase requisition A list sent to the purchasing department showing the items to be ordered

Purchase return Return of unsatisfactory goods

Purchases **account** An account used to record cost of goods bought for resale during a period

Purchases discount A cash discount offered to customers for payment within a specified period

Purchases journal A special journal used to record the purchase of goods on credit

Qualitative characteristics Traits necessary for credible financial statements: usefulness, relevance, reliability, verifiability, neutrality, understandability, timeliness, comparability, and completeness

Quick assets Cash, receivables, and marketable securities

Ratio analysis Computing the relationship between various items in the financial statements

Raw materials The materials placed into production

Raw materials ledger card A record showing details of receipts and issues for a type of raw material

Raw materials subsidiary ledger A ledger containing the raw materials ledger cards

Real property Assets such as land, land improvements, buildings, and other structures attached to the land

Realization The concept that revenue occurs when goods or services, merchandise, or other assets are exchanged for cash or claims to cash

Receiving report A form showing quantity and condition of goods received

Record date The date on which the specific stockholders to receive a dividend are determined

Recoverability test Test for possible impairment that compares the asset's net book value with the estimated net cash flows from future use of the asset

Registered bonds Bonds issued to a party whose name is listed in the corporation's records

Registrar A person or institution in charge of the issuance and transfer of a corporation's stock

Reinstate To put back or restore an accounts receivable amount that was previously written off

Relevant range of activity The different levels of activity at which a factory is expected to operate

Replacement cost *See* Market price

Report form balance sheet A balance sheet that lists the asset accounts first, followed by liabilities and owner's equity

Residual value The estimate of the amount that could be obtained from the sale or disposition of an asset at the end of its useful life; also called salvage or scrap value

Responsibility accounting The process that allows management to evaluate the performance of each segment of the business and assign responsibility for its financial results

Restrictive endorsement A signature that transfers a check to a specific party for a stated purpose

Retail business A business that sells directly to individual consumers

Retail method A method of estimating inventory cost by applying the ratio of cost to selling price in the current accounting period to the retail price of the inventory

Retained earnings The cumulative profits and losses of the corporation not distributed as dividends

Return on common stockholders' equity A measure of how well the corporation is making a profit for its shareholders; the ratio of net income available for common stockholders to common stockholders' equity

Revenue An inflow of money or other assets that results from the sales of goods or services or from the use of money or property; also called income

Revenue recognition principle Revenue is recognized when it has been earned and realized

Reversing entries Journal entries made to reverse the effect of certain adjusting entries involving accrued income or accrued expenses to avoid problems in recording future payments or receipts of cash in a new accounting period

Salary basis A method of paying employees according to an agreed-upon amount for each week or month

Sales allowance A reduction in the price originally charged to customers for goods or services

Sales discount A cash discount offered by the supplier for payment within a specified period

Sales invoice A supplier's billing document

Sales journal A special journal used to record sales of merchandise on credit

Sales return A firm's acceptance of a return of goods from a customer

Sales Returns and Allowances A contra revenue account where sales returns and sales allowances are recorded; sales returns and allowances are subtracted from sales to determine net sales

Salvage value An estimate of the amount that could be received by selling or disposing of an asset at the end of its useful life

Schedule of accounts payable A list of all balances owed to creditors

Schedule of accounts receivable A listing of all balances of the accounts in the accounts receivable subsidiary ledger

Schedule of operating expenses A schedule that supplements the income statement, showing the selling and general and administrative expenses in greater detail

Scrap value *See* Residual value

Secured bonds Bonds for which property is pledged to secure the claims of bondholders

Semidirect expenses Operating expenses that cannot be directly assigned to a department but are closely related to departmental activities

Semivariable costs Costs that vary with, but not in direct proportion to, the volume of activity

Separate entity assumption The concept that a business is separate from its owners; the concept of keeping a firm's financial records separate from the owner's personal financial records

Serial bonds Bonds issued at one time but payable over a period of years

Service business A business that sells services

Service charge A fee charged by a bank to cover the costs of maintaining accounts and providing services

Shareholder A person who owns shares of stock in a corporation; also called a stockholder

Sight draft A commercial draft that is payable on presentation

Single-step income statement A type of income statement where only one computation is needed to determine the net income (total revenue − total expenses = net income)

Slide An accounting error involving a misplaced decimal point

Social entity A nonprofit organization, such as a city, public school, or public hospital

Social Security Act A federal act providing certain benefits for employees and their families; officially the Federal Insurance Contributions Act

Social security (FICA or OASDI) tax A tax imposed by the Federal Insurance Contributions Act and collected on employee earnings to provide retirement and disability benefits

Sole proprietorship A business entity owned by one person who is legally responsible for the debts and taxes of the business

Special journal A journal used to record only one type of transaction

Specific identification method A method of inventory costing based on the actual cost of each item of merchandise

Standard cost card A form that shows the per-unit standard costs for materials, labor, and overhead

Standard costs A measure of what costs should be in an efficient operation

State unemployment (SUTA) taxes Taxes levied by a state government against employers to benefit unemployed workers

Stated value The value that can be assigned to no-par-value stock by a board of directors for accounting purposes

Statement of account A form sent to a firm's customers showing transactions during the month and the balance owed

Statement of cash flows A financial statement that provides information about the cash receipts and cash payments of a business

Statement of cost of goods manufactured A financial report showing details of the cost of goods completed for a manufacturing business

Statement of owner's equity A formal report of changes that occurred in the owner's financial interest during a reporting period

Statement of partners' equities A financial statement prepared to summarize the changes in the partners' capital accounts during an accounting period

Statement of retained earnings A financial statement that shows all changes that have occurred in retained earnings during the period

Statement of stockholders' equity A financial statement that provides an analysis reconciling the beginning and ending balance of each of the stockholders' equity accounts

Statements of Financial Accounting Standards Accounting principles established by the Financial Accounting Standards Board

Stock Certificates that represent ownership of a corporation

Stock certificate The form by which capital stock is issued; the certificate indicates the name of the corporation, the name of the stockholder to whom the certificate was issued, the class of stock, and the number of shares

Stock dividend Distribution of the corporation's own stock on a pro rata basis that results in conversion of a portion of the firm's retained earnings to permanent capital

Stock split When a corporation issues two or more shares of new stock to replace each share outstanding without making any changes in the capital accounts

Stockholders The owners of a corporation; also called shareholders

Stockholders of record Stockholders in whose name shares are held on date of record and who will receive a declared dividend

Stockholders' equity The corporate equivalent of owners' equity; also called shareholders' equity

Stockholders' ledger See Capital stock ledger

Straight-line amortization Amortizing the premium or discount on bonds payable in equal amounts each month over the life of the bond

Straight-line depreciation Allocation of an asset's cost in equal amounts to each accounting period of the asset's useful life

Subchapter S corporation (S corporation) An entity formed as a corporation that meets the requirements of Subchapter S of the Internal Revenue Code to be treated essentially as a partnership, so that the corporation pays no income tax

Subscribers' ledger A subsidiary ledger that contains an account receivable for each stock subscriber

Subscription book A list of the stock subscriptions received

Subsidiary ledger A ledger dedicated to accounts of a single type and showing details to support a general ledger account

Sum-of-the-years'-digits method A method of depreciating asset costs by allocating as expense each year a fractional part of the asset's depreciable cost, based on the sum of the digits of the number of years in the asset's useful life

Sunk cost A cost that has been incurred and will not change as a result of a decision

T account A type of account, resembling a T, used to analyze the effects of a business transaction

Tangible personal property Assets such as machinery, equipment, furniture, and fixtures that can be removed and used elsewhere

Tax accounting A service that involves tax compliance and tax planning

Tax-exempt wages Earnings in excess of the base amount set by the Social Security Act

Temporary account An account whose balance is transferred to another account at the end of an accounting period

Time and a half Rate of pay for an employee's work in excess of 40 hours a week

Time draft A commercial draft that is payable during a specified period of time

Time ticket Form used to record hours worked and jobs performed

Total equities The sum of a corporation's liabilities and stockholders' equity

Trade acceptance A form of commercial time draft used in transactions involving the sale of goods

Trade discount A reduction from list price

Trade name An intangible asset; an exclusive business name registered with the U.S. Patent Office; also called brand name

Trademark An intangible asset; an exclusive business symbol registered with the U.S. Patent Office

Trading on the equity See Leveraging

Transfer agent A person or institution that handles all stock transfers and transfer records for a corporation

Transfer price The price at which one segment's goods are transferred to another segment of the company

Transmittal of Wage and Tax Statements, Form W-3 Preprinted government form submitted with Forms W-2 to the Social Security Administration

Transparency Information provided in the financial statements and notes accompanying them should provide a clear and accurate picture of the financial affairs of the company

Transportation In account See Freight In account

Transposition An accounting error involving misplaced digits in a number

Treasury stock A corporation's own capital stock that has been issued and reacquired; the stock must have been previously paid in full and issued to a stockholder

Trend analysis Comparing selected ratios and percentages over a period of time

Trial balance A statement to test the accuracy of total debits and credits after transactions have been recorded

Underapplied overhead The result of actual overhead costs exceeding applied overhead

Unearned income Income received before it is earned

Unemployment insurance program A program that provides unemployment compensation through a tax levied on employers

Units-of-output method *See* Units-of-production method

Units-of-production method A method of depreciating asset cost at the same rate for each unit produced during each period

Unlimited liability The implication that a creditor can look to all partners' personal assets as well as the assets of the partnership for payment of the firm's debts

Updated account balances The amounts entered in the Adjusted Trial Balance section of the worksheet

Valuation account An account, such as *Allowance for Doubtful Accounts,* whose balance is revalued or reappraised in light of reasonable expectations

Variable costing *See* Direct costing

Variable costs Costs that vary in total in direct proportion to changes in the level of activity

Variance analysis Explains the difference between standard cost and actual cost

Vertical analysis Computing the relationship between each item on a financial statement to some base amount on the statement

Wage and Tax Statement, Form W-2 Preprinted government form that contains information about an employee's earnings and tax withholdings for the year

Wage-bracket table method A simple method to determine the amount of federal income tax to be withheld using a table provided by the government

Weighted average method *See* Average cost method

Wholesale business A business that manufactures or distributes goods to retail businesses or large consumers such as hotels and hospitals

Withdrawals Funds taken from the business by the owner for personal use

Withholding statement *See* Wage and Tax Statement, Form W-2

Work in process Partially completed units in the production process

Work in process subsidiary ledger A ledger containing the job order cost sheets

Workers' compensation insurance Insurance that protects employees against losses from job-related injuries or illnesses, or compensates their families if death occurs in the course of the employment

Working capital The measure of the ability of a company to meet its current obligations; the excess of current assets over current liabilities

Worksheet A form used to gather all data needed at the end of an accounting period to prepare financial statements

Credits

Chapter 12
Page 397   Steve Mack/FilmMagic

Chapter 13
Page 437   The McGraw-Hill Companies/Lars A. Nikki, photographer

Chapter 14
Page 485   The GREEN MOUNTAIN COFFEE® trademarks and advertisements are used with permission from Green Mountain Coffee
Roasters, Inc
Page 485   AP Photo/Toby Talbot
Page 515   THE HOME DEPOT and the Home Depot logo are trademarks of Licensor TLC, Inc., used under license

Chapter 15
Page 519   The McGraw-Hill Companies, Inc./Jill Braaten, photographer

Chapter 16
Page 547   AFP/Getty Images
Page 570   THE HOME DEPOT and the Home Depot logo are trademarks of Licensor TLC, Inc., used under license

Chapter 17
Page 573   The McGraw-Hill Companies, Inc./Andrew Resek, photographer
Page 596   THE HOME DEPOT and the Home Depot logo are trademarks of Licensor TLC, Inc., used under license

Chapter 18
Page 599   Dave Becker/Stringer/2013 Getty Images
Page 639   THE HOME DEPOT and the Home Depot logo are trademarks of Licensor TLC, Inc., used under license

Chapter 19
Page 643   Healthcare Venture Professionals logo used with permission of Healthcare Ventures Professionals, LLC
Page 643   Photodisc Collection/Getty Images

Chapter 20
Page 687   Bloomberg via Getty Images
Page 723   THE HOME DEPOT and the Home Depot logo are trademarks of Licensor TLC, Inc., used under license

Chapter 21
Page 727   The McGraw-Hill Companies, Inc./John Flournoy, photographer
Page 763   THE HOME DEPOT and the Home Depot logo are trademarks of Licensor TLC, Inc., used under license

Chapter 22
Page 767   Heinz logo used with permission of H.J. Heinz Company
Page 767   AP Photo/Don Ryan
Page 794   THE HOME DEPOT and the Home Depot logo are trademarks of Licensor TLC, Inc., used under license

Chapter 23
Page 801   Royalty-Free/Corbis
Page 840   THE HOME DEPOT and the Home Depot logo are trademarks of Licensor TLC, Inc., used under license

Chapter 24
Page 845   AFP/Getty Images
Page 875   THE HOME DEPOT and the Home Depot logo are trademarks of Licensor TLC, Inc., used under license

Index

Key terms and page numbers where defined in the text are in **bold.**

SAMPLE GENERAL LEDGER ACCOUNTS

Account Name	Classification	Permanent or Temporary	Normal Balance
INCOME STATEMENT			
Fees Income	Revenue	Temporary	Credit
Sales	Revenue	Temporary	Credit
Sales Discounts	Contra Revenue	Temporary	Debit
Sales Returns and Allowances	Contra Revenue	Temporary	Debit
Purchases	Cost of Goods Sold	Temporary	Debit
Freight In	Cost of Goods Sold	Temporary	Debit
Purchases Discounts	Contra Cost of Goods Sold	Temporary	Credit
Purchases Returns and Allowances	Contra Cost of Goods Sold	Temporary	Credit
Direct Labor	Cost of Goods Manufactured	Temporary	Debit
Indirect Labor	Cost of Goods Manufactured	Temporary	Debit
Indirect Materials and Supplies	Cost of Goods Manufactured	Temporary	Debit
Payroll Taxes—Factory	Cost of Goods Manufactured	Temporary	Debit
Repairs and Maintenance—Factory	Cost of Goods Manufactured	Temporary	Debit
Depreciation—Factory	Cost of Goods Manufactured	Temporary	Debit
Insurance—Factory	Cost of Goods Manufactured	Temporary	Debit
Property Taxes—Factory	Cost of Goods Manufactured	Temporary	Debit
Advertising Expense	Operating Expense	Temporary	Debit
Amortization Expense	Operating Expense	Temporary	Debit
Bank Fees Expense	Operating Expense	Temporary	Debit
Cash Short or Over	Operating Expense	Temporary	Debit
Delivery Expense	Operating Expense	Temporary	Debit
Depreciation Expense	Operating Expense	Temporary	Debit
Insurance Expense	Operating Expense	Temporary	Debit
Payroll Taxes Expense	Operating Expense	Temporary	Debit
Property Tax Expense	Operating Expense	Temporary	Debit
Rent Expense	Operating Expense	Temporary	Debit
Research and Development Expense	Operating Expense	Temporary	Debit
Salaries Expense	Operating Expense	Temporary	Debit
Supplies Expense	Operating Expense	Temporary	Debit
Telephone Expense	Operating Expense	Temporary	Debit
Uncollectible Accounts Expense	Operating Expense	Temporary	Debit
Utilities Expense	Operating Expense	Temporary	Debit
Workers' Compensation Insurance Expense	Operating Expense	Temporary	Debit
Gain/Loss on Sale of Assets	Other Income/Expense	Temporary	—
Interest Income/Expense	Other Income/Expense	Temporary	—
Miscellaneous Income/Expense	Other Income/Expense	Temporary	—
Income Tax Expense	Other Expense	Temporary	Debit
STATEMENT OF OWNER'S EQUITY			
*(Owner's Name), Capital	Owner's Equity	Permanent	Credit
(Owner's Name), Drawing	Owner's Equity	Temporary	Debit
STATEMENT OF PARTNERS' EQUITY			
*(Partner's Name), Capital	Partners' Equity	Permanent	Credit
(Partner's Name), Drawing	Partners' Equity	Temporary	Debit
STATEMENT OF RETAINED EARNINGS			
*Retained Earnings—Appropriated	Stockholders' Equity	Permanent	Credit
*Retained Earnings	Stockholders' Equity	Permanent	Credit

*Account also appears on the balance sheet.